Rarely, if ever in history, have many millions of Christians experienced a more radical change from severe restrictions and persecution to a transformation toward liberty and altered mission opportunities in such a short time as the one that is the context of this remarkable book. Amazingly comprehensive and varied it includes authors from nearly all confessional backgrounds and theological perspectives. Read some articles or read all – you will be rewarded by the deep insight into the past, present, and future of Christian mission in this turbulent part of Europe.

Prof. Dr. Paul Mojzes, Editor-in-Chief of *Occasional Papers on Religion in Eastern Europe,* Co-Editor of the *Journal of Ecumenical Studies*

This is a wonderfully comprehensive and informative book on a subject about which little has been written or is known. It provides a veritable encyclopaedia that will be a useful addition to any mission scholar's library.

Prof. Dr. Allan H. Anderson, Professor of Mission and Pentecostal Studies, University of Birmingham, UK

Among the burgeoning areas of research and investigation under the general rubric of 'Studies in World Christianity' is the whole thematic area of the missional church in central and Eastern Europe. In the last decades there has been a remarkable growth in rigorous study of the Christian movement in cultures so long profoundly shaped by the Russian Empire. The dynamism and energy of emerging Christian witness in a great diversity of shapes and approaches calls for disciplined analysis and reflection. This volume of essays is an important and comprehensive expansion of the missional literature on this crucial part of the world church, both inviting and enabling critical and constructive interaction across cultural boundaries.

Prof. Dr. Darrell Guder, Henry Winters Luce Professor of Missional and Ecumenical Theology, Princeton Theological Seminary

REGNUM EDINBURGH CENTENARY SERIES
Volume 34

Mission in Central and Eastern Europe: Realities, Perspectives, Trends

REGNUM EDINBURGH CENTENARY SERIES

The centenary of the World Missionary Conference of 1910, held in Edinburgh, was a suggestive moment for many people seeking direction for Christian mission in the 21st century. Several different constituencies within world Christianity held significant events around 2010. From 2005, an international group worked collaboratively to develop an intercontinental and multi-denominational project, known as Edinburgh 2010, based at New College, University of Edinburgh. This initiative brought together representatives of twenty different global Christian bodies, representing all major Christian denominations and confessions, and many different strands of mission and church life, to mark the centenary.

Essential to the work of the Edinburgh 1910 Conference, and of abiding value, were the findings of the eight think-tanks or 'commissions'. These inspired the idea of a new round of collaborative reflection on Christian mission – but now focused on nine themes identified as being key to mission in the 21st century. The study process was polycentric, open-ended, and as inclusive as possible of the different genders, regions of the world, and theological and confessional perspectives in today's church. It was overseen by the Study Process Monitoring Group: Miss Maria Aranzazu Aguado (Spain, The Vatican), Dr Daryl Balia (South Africa, Edinburgh 2010), Mrs Rosemary Dowsett (UK, World Evangelical Alliance), Dr Knud Jørgensen (Norway, Areopagos), Rev John Kafwanka (Zambia, Anglican Communion), Rev Dr Jooseop Keum (Korea, World Council of Churches), Dr Wonsuk Ma (Korea, Oxford Centre for Mission Studies), Rev Dr Kenneth R. Ross (UK, Church of Scotland), Dr Petros Vassiliadis (Greece, Aristotle University of Thessalonikki), and co-ordinated by Dr Kirsteen Kim (UK, Edinburgh 2010).

These publications reflect the ethos of Edinburgh 2010 and will make a significant contribution to ongoing studies in mission. It should be clear that material published in this series will inevitably reflect a diverse range of views and positions. These will not necessarily represent those of the series' editors or of the Edinburgh 2010 General Council, but in publishing them the leadership of Edinburgh 2010 hopes to encourage conversation between Christians and collaboration in mission. All the series' volumes are commended for study and reflection in both church and academy.

Series Editors

REGNUM EDINBURGH CENTENARY SERIES
Volume 34

Mission in Central and Eastern Europe: Realities, Perspectives, Trends

Edited by
Corneliu Constantineanu, Marcel V. Măcelaru,
Anne-Marie Kool and Mihai Himcinschi

First published 2016 by Regnum Books International
Regnum is an imprint of the Oxford Centre for Mission Studies
St Philip and St James Church
Woodstock Road
Oxford OX2 6HR, UK
www.ocms.ac.uk/regnum

09 08 07 06 05 04 03 7 6 5 4 3 2 1

British Library Cataloguing in Publication Data
A catalogue record for this book is available from the British Library

ISBN: 978-1-506476-14-8

Typeset by Words by Design

Front cover photo shows Victory Square, Timisoara, Romania.

Academic Referees:
Prof. Dr. Paul Mojzes (Rosemont College, USA)
Prof. Dr. Allan H. Anderson (University of Birmingham, UK).
Prof. Dr. Darrell Guder (Princeton Theological Seminary, USA)

Distributed by Fortress Press in the US and Canada

CONTENTS

PREFACE

The Edinburgh 2010 Common Call emerged from the Edinburgh 2010 study process and conference marking the centenary of the World Missionary Conference, Edinburgh 1910. The Common Call, cited below, was affirmed in the Church of Scotland Assembly Hall in Edinburgh on 6 June 2010, by representatives of world Christianity, including Catholic, Orthodox, Evangelical, Pentecostal, and other major Protestant churches.

As we gather for the centenary of the World Missionary Conference of Edinburgh 1910, we believe the church, as a sign and symbol of the reign of God, is called to witness to Christ today by sharing in God's mission of love through the transforming power of the Holy Spirit.

1. Trusting in the Triune God and with a renewed sense of urgency, we are called to incarnate and proclaim the good news of salvation, of forgiveness of sin, of life in abundance, and of liberation for all poor and oppressed. We are challenged to witness and evangelism in such a way that we are a living demonstration of the love, righteousness and justice that God intends for the whole world.

2. Remembering Christ's sacrifice on the Cross and his resurrection for the world's salvation, and empowered by the Holy Spirit, we are called to authentic dialogue, respectful engagement and humble witness among people of other faiths – and no faith – to the uniqueness of Christ. Our approach is marked with bold confidence in the gospel message; it builds friendship, seeks reconciliation and practises hospitality.

3. Knowing the Holy Spirit who blows over the world at will, reconnecting creation and bringing authentic life, we are called to become communities of compassion and healing, where young people are actively participating in mission, and women and men share power and responsibilities fairly, where there is a new zeal for justice, peace and the protection of the environment, and renewed liturgy reflecting the beauties of the Creator and creation.

4. Disturbed by the asymmetries and imbalances of power that divide and trouble us in church and world, we are called to repentance, to critical reflection on systems of power, and to accountable use of power structures. We are called to find practical ways to live as members of One Body in full awareness that God resists the proud, Christ welcomes and empowers the poor and afflicted, and the power of the Holy Spirit is manifested in our vulnerability.

5. Affirming the importance of the biblical foundations of our missional engagement and valuing the witness of the Apostles and martyrs, we are called to rejoice in the expressions of the gospel in many nations all over the world. We celebrate the renewal experienced through movements of migration and mission in all directions, the way all are equipped for mission by the gifts of the Holy Spirit, and God's continual calling of children and young people to further the gospel.

6. Recognising the need to shape a new generation of leaders with authenticity for mission in a world of diversities in the twenty-first century, we are called to work together in new forms of theological education. Because we are all made in the image of God, these will draw on one another's unique charisms, challenge each other to grow in faith and understanding, share resources equitably worldwide, involve the entire human being and the whole family of God, and respect the wisdom of our elders while also fostering the participation of children.

7. Hearing the call of Jesus to make disciples of all people – poor, wealthy, marginalised, ignored, powerful, living with disability, young, and old – we are called as communities of faith to mission from everywhere to everywhere. In joy we hear the call to receive from one another in our witness by word and action, in streets, fields, offices, homes, and schools, offering reconciliation, showing love, demonstrating grace and speaking out truth.

8. Recalling Christ, the host at the banquet, and committed to that unity for which he lived and prayed, we are called to ongoing co-operation, to deal with controversial issues and to work towards a common vision. We are challenged to welcome one another in our diversity, affirm our membership through baptism in the One Body of Christ, and recognise our need for mutuality, partnership, collaboration and networking in mission, so that the world might believe.

9. Remembering Jesus' way of witness and service, we believe we are called by God to follow this way joyfully, inspired, anointed, sent and empowered by the Holy Spirit, and nurtured by Christian disciplines in community. As we look to Christ's coming in glory and judgment, we experience his presence with us in the Holy Spirit, and we invite all to join with us as we participate in God's transforming and reconciling mission of love to the whole creation.

Themes Explored

The 2010 conference was shaped around the following nine study themes:

1. Foundations for mission
2. Christian mission among other faiths
3. Mission and post-modernities
4. Mission and power
5. Forms of missionary engagement
6. Theological education and formation
7. Christian communities in contemporary contexts
8. Mission and unity – ecclesiology and mission
9. Mission spirituality and authentic discipleship

The Regnum Edinburgh Centenary Series to Date

Against this background a series of books was commissioned, with the intention of making a significant contribution to ongoing studies of mission. This series currently includes:[1]

Edinburgh 2010: Mission Then and Now, David A. Kerr and Kenneth R. Ross (eds).

Edinburgh 2010 Volume II: Witnessing to Christ Today, Daryl Balia and Kirsteen Kim (eds).

Mission Continues: Global Impulses for the 21st Century, Claudia Wahrisch-Oblau and Fidon Mwombeki (eds).

Holistic Mission: God's Plan for God's People, Brian Woolnough and Wonsuk Ma (eds).

Mission Today and Tomorrow, Kirsteen Kim and Andrew Anderson (eds).

The Church Going Local: Mission and Globalization, Tormod Engelsviken, Erling Lundeby and Dagfinn Solheim (eds).

Evangelical and Frontier Mission: Perspectives on the Global Progress of the Gospel, A. Scott Moreau and Beth Snodderly (eds).

Interfaith Relations after One Hundred Years: Christian Mission among Other Faiths, Marina Ngursangzeli Behera (ed).

Witnessing to Christ in a Pluralistic Age: Christian Mission among Other Faiths, Lalsangkima Pachuau and Knud Jørgensen (eds).

Mission and Post Modernities, Rolv Olsen (ed).

A Learning Missional Church: Reflections from Young Missiologists, Beate Fagerli, Knud Jørgensen, Rolv Olsen, Kari Storstein Haug and Knut Tveitereid (eds).

Life-Widening Mission: Global Anglican Perspectives, Cathy Ross (ed).

Foundations for Mission, Emma Wild-Wood and Peniel Rajkumar (eds).

Mission Spirituality and Authentic Discipleship, Wonsuk Ma and Kenneth R. Ross (eds).

A Century of Catholic Missions, Stephen Bevans (ed).

Mission as Ministry of Reconciliation, Robert Schreiter and Knud Jørgensen (eds).

Orthodox Perspectives on Mission, Petros Vassiliadis (ed).

Bible in Mission, Pauline Hoggarth, Fergus Macdonald, Knud Jørgensen and Bill Mitchell (eds).

Pentecostal Mission and Global Christianity, Wonsuk Ma, Veli-Matti Karkkainen and J. Kwabena Asamoah-Gyadu (eds).

Engaging the World: Christian Communities in Contemporary Global Society, Afe Adogame, Janice McLean and Anderson Jeremiah (eds).

Mission At and From the Margins: Patterns, Protagonists and Perspectives, Peniel Rajkumar, Joseph Dayam, I.P. Asheervadham (eds).

The Lausanne Movement: A Range of Perspectives, Margunn Serigstad Dahle, Lars Dahle and Knud Jørgensen (eds).

---

[1] For an up-to-date list and full publication details, see www.ocms.ac.uk/regnum/

Global Diasporas and Mission, Chandler H Im & Amos Yong (eds).
Theology, Mission and Child: Global Perspectives, B Prevette, K White, CR Velloso Ewell & DJ Konz (eds).
Called to Unity for the Sake of Mission, John Gibaut and Knud Jørgensen (eds).
Freedom of Belief and Christian Mission, Hans Aage Gravaas, Christof Sauer, Tormod Engelsviken, Maqsood Kamil and Knud Jørgensen (eds).
Korean Church, God's Mission, Global Christianity, Wonsuk Ma and Kyo Seong Ahn (eds).

FOREWORD

This 34th volume in the Regnum Edinburgh Centenary Series makes a truly significant contribution to ecumenical missiological reflection. It highlights the challenges and opportunities facing Christian mission in post-Communist Central and Eastern Europe, thereby setting a clear agenda for missiologists in that context. At the same time, it invites and enables missiologists from other parts of the globe to enter into meaningful dialogue with them, to explore the similarities between their respective contexts, and to learn from the creative initiatives being undertaken there.

I wish to commend the editors and contributors for four specific features of the volume. Firstly, for the underlying theological method that gives it coherence. The sub-title (Realities, Perspectives, Trends) outlines the key dimensions of contextual theologising: Realities (context analysis = See), Perspectives (theological reflection = Judge) and Trends (ministry activities = Act). Due to the wide range of themes, not all the contributions emphasise these three these dimensions equally, but the overall effect of the volume is to expose the reader to the energy and passion evident in contextual missiological reflection in the region. The reader gets a clear view of the realities "on the ground" in post-Communist Central and Eastern Europe, she is intellectually stimulated and enriched by creative theological proposals, and encouraged by the courageous witness and service of Christian communities amidst challenging circumstances.

Secondly, I wish to commend the editors for the broad inclusiveness of their project. The confessional and geographical spread of the more than thirty participants is truly impressive, allowing readers from other parts of the world to appreciate both the richness and the complexity of the church situation in Central and Eastern Europe. In its almost 700 pages, the volume is a veritable mine of information and inspiration.

Thirdly, I particularly appreciated the theological depth evident in the contributions. As with other theologies emerging out of places of suffering and deprivation on earth, recovering from legacies of sustained totalitarian rule and state propaganda, these contributions do not exude cheap triumphalism or superficial optimism; instead, a humble, grateful and grounded hope permeates the volume. It is "with gentleness and reverence" that I hear them giving an account of the hope that is in them – a hope nurtured by a persistent faith in the resurrection of the Man of Nazareth.

Fourthly, the detailed case studies from numerous countries provide an insightful picture of the historical backgrounds and the contours of the present challenges facing churches in their witness and service in Central and Eastern Europe. The volume avoided the temptation of trading in vague and nice-sounding generalities or abstract theological ideas. In the best tradition of missiological research and reflection, the contributors are rooted in concrete communities of faith, grounded in particular political, cultural and economic realities, discerning where God is at work and how to participate in God's mission of love, freedom, joy and justice.

I sincerely hope, with the editors, that this volume will be used widely and productively as a textbook in theological education across Central and Eastern Europe (and further afield), so that it may stimulate ongoing reflection and action for the coming of the Reign of God. The contributors have rendered a sterling service to worldwide missiological literature by producing this book.

The remark in the Editorial Introduction that the demise of Communism brought not only religious freedom but also political instability, nationalism, ethnic prejudice, bureaucratic tyranny, and a litany of other woes, reminded me of the parable in Matthew 12:43-45 of the demon who left a person and later returned to its "empty house" with seven other spirits "more wicked than itself." The church of Jesus Christ faces enormous challenges emerging from the emptiness created by totalitarian regimes and the snowballing of evil resulting from their demise. May this volume inspire and empower us all to bring the humanising and liberating gospel of Jesus Christ into this broken world so deeply loved by God.

JNJ (Klippies) Kritzinger
Emeritus Professor of Missiology
University of South Africa, Pretoria

MISSION IN CENTRAL AND EASTERN EUROPE: EDITORIAL INTRODUCTION

The Context

Central and Eastern Europe is one of the areas of the world that has undergone profound transformations during the 100 years delimited by the two Edinburgh gatherings that inspired the *Regnum Edinburgh Centenary Series*. It is the place in which Marxist ideology gave birth to the communist hegemony that has affected the European arena for over half a century. It is the place from where there came wars, violence and genocides that have affected countless people in Europe and beyond. It is also a place where the demise of ideologically driven totalitarian regimes in 1989 has not only brought the religious freedom many had hoped for, but resulted also in further social and political instability characterized by nationalism, ethnic prejudice, bureaucratic tyranny, economic paralysis, religious fragmentation and increasingly widening economic gaps leading to poverty and despair, work migration and widespread corruption.

Nonetheless, Central and Eastern Europe is also a context that presents us with unique opportunities for mission and therefore an interesting field to look at from the perspective of mission studies. It is the place where eastern and western culture and expressions of Christianity alternately meet, clash and/or converge. It is also a place where Christianity and Islam have co-existed for centuries. And most importantly, it is a unique place, for in spite of oppressive political regimes and a lack of religious freedom, the historical churches in the region have – albeit to various degrees – preserved a strong sense of Christian identity, often closely related to national identity, and Evangelical Christianity, in some quarters, has flourished as church membership has grown notably.

Moreover, after 1989, the new-found freedom which Eastern Europe experienced, has allowed communities in the region to interact with the previously limitedly accessible western world, which, in connection with the noted growth of the Evangelical communities, has resulted in a number of developments we consider as missiologically significant: (1) The opportunity to do intentional cross-cultural mission, something which has indeed come strongly into focus in some circles; and (2) The less intentional but probably even more effective cross-cultural ministry taking place due to the phenomenon of economically motivated migration – in some places in Western Europe, the large diaspora Christian communities coming from Eastern Europe have surpassed in number the indigenous groups.

In addition to these, we ought to point out other changes, gradually taking root in the region, all of which are reflected in one way or another in the papers included in this volume: (1) The emergence of a sense of missional responsibility within local churches, which emboldens them to break out of the ghetto-like existence to which Christian communities were reduced during decades of communist restrictions, and urges them to become witnesses in their own contexts; (2) The increased preoccupation with finding contextually appropriate expressions of Christian faith and holistic mission within the region; (3) The novel awareness churches have that there is much need for innovative partnerships and ecumenical co-operation among Christian traditions that previously were strongly opposed to each other; (4) A dawning of the reality that the incarnation of Christ has implications for the public arena, including social reconciliation and transformation; (5) The strengthening of a vision for reaching out to the marginalized and often despised Roma, often in surprising realization of what God is already doing among them; (6) The establishing of new forms of missional learning and of missiological research to strengthen the process of writing indigenous theological textbooks.

The Book

In the light of all the above, the present book, *Mission in Central and Eastern Europe: Realities, Perspectives, Trends*, attempts to accomplish a threefold aim: to celebrate a faithful, persevering church under communism, while also acknowledging the shortcomings, within and outside the church, that characterized mission in Central and Eastern Europe during the communist decades prior to 1989; to offer a complex analysis and evaluation of missionary endeavours in the region since the fall of communism and an assessment of current mission theory and practice; and to project new directions in and for mission, spelling out lessons to be learned as we identify both the challenges and opportunities lying ahead, and considering the missiological implications related to the specific experience of the church in Central and Eastern Europe.

The book brings together over forty significant contributions from theologians, missiologists and practitioners from Central and Eastern Europe, coming from thirteen different countries, and representing different Christian traditions and confessions. Contributions therefore reflect the various forms of Christianity and the geographical regions under scrutiny.

Part One

The volume is structured in three parts. The first section begins with a general overview on mission understanding and practice in Central and Eastern Europe before and after 1989 in three chapters. Here we have, in the opening chapter by Peter Kuzmič, a brief history of Christianity in the region under scrutiny, and a description of Christian witness in this part of the world as a complex story of pain, glory, persecution and freedom. In the second chapter, looking more specifically at the numerous mission initiatives, Anne-Marie Kool explores carefully the question of what has been achieved in 25 years of East European mission. She identifies four distinct periods in mission, which moved from underground mission, to euphoria, to disillusionment, to an innovative new paradigm. Similarly, through an interview analysis about the mission of the church in the same period, Alex Vlasin reveals a slow but steady shift in various initiatives in missions and calls for further co-operation and partnerships.

Chapters Four and Five in the first section bring the Bible to the fore as the foundation for, and the message of, mission. Marcel Măcelaru argues that reading the Bible as a theological narrative, which tells the Story of God in, with and for the world, is a missiological imperative. Such a hermeneutic provides for an understanding of Christian existence as participation in God's Story. Ciprian Terinte examines the *kerygmatic* speeches found in the book of Acts, pinpointing the major Christological ideas available in the apostolic preaching recorded in this New Testament writing. The hope is that the apostolic example will help the reader formulate a relevant, theologically sound, evangelistic discourse for Central and Eastern Europe.

The last chapter in the first section introduces the imperative of ecumenism for mission in the context of a diverse European Christianity. In an increasingly secularized Europe, argues Ovidiu Druhora, an authentic Christian witness can only be manifested through a radically new, effective and action-oriented ecumenical dialogue, and through a rediscovery of the Spirit of life.

Part Two

In the second part of the book, which is also the largest, the readers will discover a richness of case studies of ongoing missiological endeavours and concrete manifestations of the embodiment of the gospel in various and specific contexts in Central and Eastern Europe. This part provides a unique insight into the complex experiences and situations of Christian churches and their roots, taking into account denominational variations and different missiological emphases. The section begins with Mihai Himcinschi's argument for an Orthodox foundation for mission – the Holy Trinity, and with Gheorghe Petraru's presentation of the essentials of Orthodox mission in Christian history and of principles of Orthodox missiology – *missio Dei* or *missio Trinitatis* – as theological science.

Continuing the discussion from an Orthodox perspective, we then have Gelu Călina's reflection on the intersections of the Kingdom of God with the kingdoms of this world, illustrated by the difficult and complex church-state relationship in the totalitarian regime of Romania; Dana Bates' case study on Orthodox youth mission, specifically the New Horizons Foundation and the IMPACT programme, which illustrates the way in which the contextualization of the gospel in an Orthodox setting has enabled both a more profound theological vision of youth ministry and the development of practical partnerships with the Orthodox Church for serving the younger generation, and Zorica Kuburić's Serbian perspective on 'The Future of Orthodox Christianity in the Context of a Theology of Integrity'.

Dănuţ Mănăstireanu's personal account of the remarkable Lausanne-Orthodox Initiative, which brings together for dialogue on mission the evangelical Lausanne Movement for World Evangelism and the Orthodox churches, is the last of the batch of studies presented in the second part of the volume that make reference to Orthodox Christianity in the region. Mănăstireanu outlines the history of the initiative, the plans of the leadership group for future similar encounters, the opportunities and obstacles, and pinpoints various prospects for the development of co-operation in holistic mission between Orthodox and Evangelical communities round the world.

The second part of the volume continues with a study by Anton Rus that introduces the reader to the Greek-Catholic Church in Romania and presents the fundamentals of mission from the perspective of this unique Byzantine church. Following this prelude, the section focuses on Roman Catholic expressions of Christianity and perspectives on mission. We have first a study by Jan Górski, who offers a comprehensive take on mission in Poland, and Jarosław M. Lipniak's study, which looks at the same geographical context but with a more specific focus on Roman Catholic mission after the political transformation of the early 1990s. Following then is a study by Mato Zovkić, a Roman Catholic theologian located in Sarajevo, who has worked to promote dialogue with Muslims in the spirit of Vatican II and the post-conciliar guidelines of the Catholic magisterium. Given this expertise, his is the only study in the volume that gives a comprehensive perspective on the encounter between Christianity and Islam in Bosnia and Herzegovina.

Another shift in focus is introduced in the study authored by Pavol Bargár, which explores the topic of Christian mission in the Czech Republic from an ecumenical (evangelical) perspective. He argues that, in order for Christian churches and communities to pursue their missional calling in the Czech context, they ought to take specific contextual identifiers seriously, as many aspects of such identifiers – post-rationalistic, post-ideological, post-optimistic, post-traditional, post-individualistic and post-materialistic – have significant potential for establishing and pursuing authentic and relevant Christian presence, witness and mission. Writing from within the same context, we also have Zuzana Jurechová and Viktória Šoltésová, who report on two significant mission conferences held in Prague and Bratislava in 2011.

The next five studies focus on the Romanian context from an evangelical perspective. Vasile Marchiş evaluates the broad spectrum of views on evangelism within Romanian Pentecostalism, and points to the need for further theological reflection on how the relationship between the gospel, Christian community and Christian witness is understood. Only in this way, he argues, can the churches formulate a missionary task that will make Christian communities relevant as social and cultural witnesses today. Marcel Măcelaru offers a case study on practices of evangelization and church growth by looking at the example of the Elim Pentecostal Church from Timişoara, Romania. The study covers the period 1990-1997, a time during which membership in this local Pentecostal community more than tripled in number, thus making this denomination one of the largest Pentecostal churches in Europe. Gheorghe Riţişan and Corneliu Constantineanu present a remarkable case study on cross-cultural mission originating from Eastern Europe through an analysis of the ecclesiological and missiological context that led to the establishment of the Romanian Pentecostal Agency for Foreign Mission (APME) – one of the youngest yet very dynamic missionary structures currently operating in Europe. In another paper, Ligia Măcelaru and Marcel Măcelaru report on ACAS (Association for Capacitating People with Special Abilities), a ministry focusing primarily on children and adults with disabilities. The authors hope to raise awareness regarding the urgency of such missiological endeavours in this part of the world. Along similar lines, the study by Bill Prevette and Corneliu Constantineanu that concludes this section on mission in the Romanian context from an evangelical perspective, addresses the issue of children at risk in Romania. The authors offer a historical analysis, pinpointing the factors that caused the serious child crisis in this country, and argue for serious biblical, theological and missiological reflection, leading to engagement on behalf of these children in need.

Two articles that bring to fore the Hungarian context come next. First, Ábrahám Kovács explores the nineteenth-century roots of the rather debated question, especially after the Holocaust, of mission to the Jews. He investigates and assesses the way in which Jewish mission took place in Hungary via Scottish Evangelicalism, transplanted by the Calvinism of the Free Church of Scotland into Central Europe's largest country, the Hungarian Kingdom, of the late nineteenth and early twentieth centuries. Second, Dorottya Nagy uses the example of Chinese Christian migrants in Hungary, seen within the global framework of Christian interconnectedness, to advance a proposal for interdisciplinarity in mission studies. Of particular interest is the attention she gives to 'migration', as an analytical category and social reality, showing its importance for religious studies from a theological-missiological perspective. She argues that research must move beyond the so-called church-sect typology and the new religious movements framework, on the one hand, and beyond secularization theories and market theories of religion and methodological nationalism/ethnicity, on the other.

Kostake Milkov's study sifts the focus to the Macedonian context and advocates 'dialogue as mission'. The study illustrates a holistic and integrative understanding of Christian mission in relationship to contemporary culture by pointing to the Balkan Institute for Faith and Culture, in Skopje, Macedonia.

The next set of studies, offered in the second part of the book, have theological education as their common theme. Parush R. Parushev addresses the challenges of contextualization, credibility and relevance of evangelical theological education from a convictional theological perspective. He argues that such education should be guided by a bi-focal vision: a) to aim at strengthening the convictional identity of the faith community which it addresses (through practices of informal and formal learning); b) to participate in the mission of the public university to educate the whole person (through practices and teleological aims of academic theological education). Julijana Mladenovska-Tešija, focusing on the Croatian context, examines Protestant theological institutions of higher education and reflects upon the relationship between their academic roles and the churches these serve. The three-axial framework within which the discussion is placed includes: the local context (transitional, minority), the European educational agenda ('the Bologna paradigm'), and a global perspective on education (educational trends in a globalized world). The article also offers proposals and recommendations for the future of Protestant higher education in Croatia on the basis of the Edinburgh 2010 Pointers on Theological Education. Eric J. Titus offers a personal reflection on the transformational experience he had being engaged in cross-cultural mission in Croatia, where he, as a US citizen, served for several years as a lecturer in a seminary. Using Caesar's crossing of the Rubicon as a metaphor, the author reflects on the 'inability' to truly return home – that is, to become again what one was before answering Christ's call to mission. Wojciech Szczerba reports on the evolution and activity of the Evangelical School of Theology (EST) from Wrocław, Poland since 1990. He shows how changes within the Polish context (historical, social, cultural and religious), have prompted changes within the nature and activity of EST, from a basic Biblical theological seminary serving the Evangelical community in Poland, to the current EST Educational Centre, which offers versatile programmes and projects for a much larger Christian community in Poland and abroad. This particular case study illustrates the way in which the mission, vision and values of an institution can remain relevant and find new applicability, even when faced with changing cultural and social environments. Finally, the article by Peter Penner, although not on theological education *per se*, is included here because it provides a good example of the kind of work awaiting theologians and theological institutions in Eastern and Central Europe. Penner reports on the completion of the Slavic Bible Commentary, a one-volume collaborative work, in which specific interpretative keys were used, focusing on contextualization, missional relevance, and community hermeneutics. The purpose of the commentary is to help church and mission leaders, preachers and teachers of the church, to understand and apply the word of God within their local contexts as involvement in the mission of God.

The final batch of articles in the second part deal with Roma Christianity in Eastern and Central Europe. First, Anne-Marie Kool looks at the way in which East European churches have responded to the Roma people since the fall of the Berlin Wall. She first offers a bird's-eye view on the issue, especially with respect to the Conference of European Churches (CEE), the European Baptist Federation, Gypsy Pentecostalism, and the Roman Catholic Church. The chapter then gives a critical analysis of the underlying 'models' or paradigms used by churches, seeking to uncover the motivation behind these responses. Finally, a way forward is proposed, aiming to overcome the limitations of the current paradigms and ending with some practical suggestions. It is argued that a key question for the East European 'majority' churches is how they could facilitate moving from 'mission to the Roma', to 'Roma churches', to a 'church for all'! This is an important chapter, which draws lessons from how churches and mission organizations are responding to the Roma people, and subsequently initiates a process of reflection on the issue, from a missiological perspective, hoping to stimulate further research at grassroots level. Second, Melody J. Wachsmuth shows that currently, despite vast international attention and allocated financial resources from the European Union, NGOs and religious entities – as well as Romani politicians, intellectuals, and grassroots organizations – steps to minimize Romani social isolation and poverty continue to make small, non-existent, or even retroactive progress in the CEE. Historically, the church's relationship with the Roma largely mirrored, and still continues to mirror, societal attitudes. Juxtaposed with these realities is the continued growth of Roma Christianity, particularly in Pentecostal and charismatic forms in the CEE. With an eye to the historical and current context, this chapter draws from secondary and primary sources to present a general introduction to Roma Christianity in south-eastern Europe, Bulgaria and Romania, and draws out certain themes, questions and challenges that appear across multiple contexts. These challenges and themes highlight further areas of study as well as pinpoint the Roma church's important role within its respective society and the global church at large. Finally, Aleksandar Apostolovski offers a detailed case study of a Roma community in Macedonia. He provides a theological evaluation of the use of education – the operation and effects of the after-school programme and literacy classes – in the missionary activities of the Evangelical Church Saraj, located on the western outskirts of Skopje, Macedonia. It is suggested that greater appreciation of the world as God's restored temple, and of reading and writing as means of practising *imitatio Dei* may be of use for any missionary activities among Roma children.

Part Three

The third part of the book looks at challenges and opportunities for Christian mission in Central and Eastern Europe. In a few programmatic articles, several missiological implications are drawn and directions for further missiological reflection and activity are given. The section begins with two articles reflecting on aspects of mission theory and practice in the light of new contextual realities European churches face. Bogdan Dolenc looks at the role of ecumenical dialogue in a new Europe and indicates specific steps towards a purification of historical memories in the Balkans. Pavel Černý advances a relevant mission theology for the post-secular environment, with a focus on the situation in the Czech Republic. He addresses relevant missiological questions arising in the context of contemporary multi-faith society, envisions new ecclesiological forms, and summarizes both the holistic and the kenotic dimension of the church. He shows that churches and theological institutions must put more emphasis on changing their missional paradigm so as to respond to the spiritual hunger evident in the contemporary population, which is longing for spiritual experiences.

The third section of the book also includes a batch of articles that focuses on themes and activities we consider relevant for the future of mission in the region. Branimir Dukić, a marketing specialist, offers an interesting perspective on the possibilities of marketing for religious organizations in the digital age. Eugen Jugaru underlies the important contribution Christian business people can bring to societal progress. Reference is made to two important documents, the *Lausanne Document on Business as Mission* and the *Oxford Declaration on Christian Faith and Economics*, both of which identify business activity as an important instrument for mission. Also in this section, Corneliu Constantineanu and Marcel V. Măcelaru report on an event whose strong future outlook justifies its mention here. The report summarizes the findings of the September 2013 *Reimagining the Seminary* conference, which took place in Bucharest, Romania. The purpose of the meeting was to offer theological educators and church leaders a platform for interaction as they addressed topics related to the task and method of theological institutions in the context of new social, political, economic and ecclesial realities. The particularity of this event was its focus on the nature and values of the Kingdom of God, as expressed by Jesus' symbolic gesture of placing a child in the midst of a theological argument on leadership in the Kingdom (Matthew 18), as its central theological motif and primary missiological motivator.

Another topic of interest addressed in this part of the book pertains to the public face of Christian faith and consequently Christian mission. First, Mihai Himcinschi makes an argument for nation-building as an important missiological contribution by the church in contemporary society, and to that end he explores the implications of Trinitarian monotheism. Second,

Corneliu Constantineanu reflects on public theology as a missiological endeavour of the church in our post-totalitarian, ever-in-transition, context. Learning from, and in interaction with, those who have reflected on these issues before us, he points out several significant features of public theology, and highlights some of the most relevant issues of public engagement in the context of Central and Eastern Europe.

We found it only appropriate that the book should conclude with Anne-Marie Kool's 'A Missiologist's Look at the Future: A Missiological Manifesto for the 21st Century', an article in which the author seeks to contribute to, and encourage, the ongoing conversation on the future of the church in mission in Europe, with a special focus on Central and Eastern Europe. The article is based on the author's personal experience of living and working as a missionary and missiologist in the eastern part of Europe, while also keeping in touch with missiological developments in her own country of birth, the Netherlands, elsewhere in Europe, and in North-America. The result is a missiological manifesto for Europe, a statement of vision and values, reflecting on future perspectives and challenges in key areas for mission as a starting-point for further discussion.

As evident from the final chapter, which reflects well the final purpose of the whole volume, we hope that the collection of papers offered will serve as a tool for further reflection on mission in Central and Eastern Europe in the lifelong learning of pastors, church leaders, missionaries and leaders of mission organizations, as well as a foundation for further academic reflection on mission. We also hope that this volume will be used as a textbook in missiological and theological education, as it contains contributions to be used as missiological dimensions of the various disciplines of Biblical Studies, Church History, Systematic Theology and Practical Theology.

Acknowledgments

Finally, a few words of gratitude are in place. The 'making' of this volume, evidently a complex undertaking, would not have been possible without the support of people and organizations that have contributed, in a way or another, to this project. We are grateful for all the help we have received and hopeful that the feeling of satisfaction that we, authors and editors, have as this volume 'comes to life', will be the experience of our supporters as well. A special thank you goes to the editors of the *Regnum Edinburgh Centenary Series* for their favourable reply to our proposal to include a volume on Eastern and Central Europe in the series, and to the publisher for all the assistance provided. Last, but not least, we are deeply indebted to the authors, who have co-operated with such generosity of their time and forbearance in waiting. Any praise this volume deserves belongs to them.

Part One

CHRISTIANITY IN EASTERN EUROPE: A STORY OF PAIN, GLORY, PERSECUTION AND FREEDOM

Peter Kuzmič

East and West: Definitions and Boundaries

Europe is a complex and not easily definable continent. Geographically, it is the western peninsula, a part of the much larger land mass stretching between the Atlantic and Pacific Oceans (Eurasia). When it is conventionally defined as the continent running 'from the Atlantic to the Urals', Russia, east of the Ural Mountains, is actually assigned to the continent of Asia. The present definition of Europe is based upon particular cultural, religious, economic and political factors and developments that gradually led to the well-known equation of Europe with Christendom. A contemporary of Martin Luther, the geographer Wachelus, published in 1537 a woodcut map of Europe as 'The Queen Virgin' that was to illustrate the unity and integrity of 'Christian Europe' as conceived by medieval Catholic ideology related to the concept of the 'Holy Roman Empire'. Wachelus' map shows Spain as the head of the virgin, Italy as its right arm, and Denmark the left; Germany, France and Switzerland are the breast; Poland, Hungary, 'Illyricum', Albania, Greece, Lithuania, Romania, Bulgaria and others are all identified on the (continental) virgin's illustrious gown.[1]

For the purposes of this chapter, the pertinent question is: what is 'Eastern Europe?' There is no standard definition because Europe's political and geographic boundaries do not always match and have been subject to frequent fluctuation and multiple overlaps. The dilemmas and ambiguities of boundaries between Eastern and Western Europe can be illustrated at the very point of the arrival of the Christian message. Following the Jerusalem Council c. 48 CE, St Paul, the Apostle to the Nations, and his missionary team crossed over from Asia to Europe with the gospel of Jesus Christ, in response to an unusual vision of the 'Macedonian call' (Acts 16:93). Thus began the early church's evangelization of the continent of Europe and the long process of the

* This paper was originally published in Charles E. Farhadian (ed), *Introducing World Christianity* (Oxford: Blackwell, 2012), 77-90. Republished here with permission.

[1] See Peter Kuzmič, 'Europe', in James M. Phillips and Robert T. Coote (eds), *Toward the 21st Century in Christian Mission* (Grand Rapids, MI: Eerdmans, 1993), 148-63.

universalization of Christianity. At this point, however, it might be appropriate to ask whether this mission began in Western or Eastern Europe? Greek Macedonia is geographically and culturally considered to be part of 'Southern/Eastern Europe' and yet, as the working definition of this chapter will show, modem Greece, though Eastern Orthodox by religion, is by the very reconfiguration of European geo-political realities considered a western country.

The division of Europe into 'Western' and 'Eastern' is traceable back to the division between the western and eastern parts of the Roman Empire. Following the Middle Ages, the Ottoman line of division was imposed with the Turkish Muslim advance on Europe and its centuries-long subjugation of the Balkans. The East-West division is thus marked by several important and fluctuating boundary lines on the map of the diverse continent that is historically marked by numerous ethnic frontiers and cultural divides, along with traditional and modern political divisions.

Historically speaking, the most durable division of the continent is the thousand-years long religious 'fault line' separating Western Catholic (Latin-based, after sixteenth-century, including Protestant) Christianity, and Eastern Orthodox (Greek-based and later Slavonic) Christianity. Geographically, this line begins in the very north with the border between Finland and Russia and then moving south, separating the Baltic states (Estonia, Latvia and Lithuania) from its recent ruler Russia, proceeding to draw the religious line of distinction along the border between Poland and its eastern neighbours, Belorussia and Ukraine. It continues south, separating Hungary and, somewhat less precisely, Transylvania from its larger modern home state of Romania, dividing Catholic Croatia from Orthodox Serbia within the former Yugoslav federation, to touch the Adriatic coast south of the religiously more complex Bosnia and Albania, assigning Montenegro and (the former Yugoslav Republic) Macedonia to the larger Slavic Orthodox world. To the east of the continent, there is no real or religiously definable boundary, but simply, geographically, the Ural Mountains and the Caspian Sea.

The term 'Eastern Europe', as it is generally used today, is actually a political concept based on the realities of the post-World War II division of the continent. Although there are considerable shared ethnic (Slavic nations) and religious (Orthodox-dominated lands) commonalities, the concept in no way indicates geographic or cultural unity. For our purposes here, 'Eastern Europe' denotes primarily that geographical area from the Elba River to the Ural Mountains that was until recently named the 'Eastern Bloc', which stood for the political entity consisting of the communist countries in Central, East Central and south-eastern Europe. This bloc of countries was until 1990 represented by its powerful political patron, the Soviet Union (USSR), and included Bulgaria, (former) Czechoslovakia, (former) German Democratic Republic (GDR), Hungary, Poland, Romania and, to some extent, Albania and (former) Yugoslavia.

Under Soviet control and direction, they constituted a new entity in world politics as expressed by their economic and military unifying bodies (Comecon, Warsaw Pact). During the dangerous Cold War era of the twentieth century, this communist-dominated 'Eastern Europe' was considered the arch-enemy of the free western world and its brutally imposed 'Iron Curtain' division of Europe was powerfully symbolized by its physical expression in the Berlin Wall.

The countries of formerly communist-dominated Eastern Europe represent diverse cultural landscapes, which often had very little or nothing in common. It includes the homeland of the Reformation – Germany's eastern part, which enjoyed Soviet-controlled 'independent' existence as the German Democratic Republic (GDR) from 1949 to 1990, as well as Catholic-dominated Poland and Czechoslovakia (now Czech Republic and Slovakia), while Hungary, Slovenia and Croatia were and continue to be regularly counted as 'East' European, even though as lands of 'Mitteleuropa' they despise that designation for cultural and religious reasons, considering themselves to be more western than eastern. Several of these also took pride in their history of the Habsburg tradition. Finally, there are the Balkan states of Albania, the ethnically related youngest and most vulnerable independent nation of Kosovo (2008), Montenegro (2005), Serbia, Romania and Bulgaria – the latter four largely Orthodox in religion, and all with shared experiences of centuries of Ottoman Turkish rule.

Consequently, Eastern Europe's history and religious topography are characterized by an unusual variety conditioned by the intersections of competing historical forces and their attendant civilizations, cultures and faiths. The limited length of this chapter calls for only a broad sweep in our panoramic overview, as we contextually define 'Eastern Europe' using the modern political concept developed in the aftermath of World War II and problematized by the events of the 'Great Transformation' (1989).[2] Older Christian confessional divisions of Europe, the role of Islam, and their implications for and impact upon 'new Europe' – a continent currently undergoing comprehensive and intensive integrative processes prior to full membership in the European Union – will be explored.

Introducing and Assessing Eastern Christianity

With the collapse of communist totalitarian regimes and the opening of Eastern Europe and the former Soviet Union, Orthodox churches of the East, especially the Russian Orthodox Church, once again became major players in the religious theatre of world communions. And yet they are still the least-known of the three major branches of world Christianity (i.e.

[2] 'Great Transformation' in this context applies to the dramatic change related to the collapse of communism as most vividly and symbolically expressed in tearing down of the Berlin Wall on 9th November 1989, and the subsequent dismantling of single-party regimes and socialist federations under their control.

Roman Catholic, Eastern Orthodox, Protestant). While not completely neglecting the better-known Catholic Church and various expressions of Protestant Christianity in Eastern Europe, this introduction will (especially for the benefit of western readers) pay more attention to the disproportionately neglected Eastern Orthodoxy. Due to the broader focus of this chapter, I will forgo any pretensions of being comprehensive in historical treatment, doctrinal expositions and contextual particularities. It is a picture painted with rather broad brush strokes, pointing out only those developments and features that help us understand the less familiar and yet crucial ecclesial characteristics, cultural habits and socio-political dimensions of the Orthodox churches of Eastern Europe today.[3]

Eastern Orthodoxy is the generally accepted designation referring to the majority of the self-governing (autocephalous) national Orthodox churches that are theologically defined as Chalcedonian (from the Council of Chalcedon, 451) so as to distinguish them from the (non-Chalcedonian) Oriental Orthodox churches (Coptic, Syrian, Armenian, Ethiopian, and other less numerous bodies). All Orthodox churches in Eastern Europe are Chalcedonian in their creed, and confess fidelity to the seven ecumenical councils beginning with Nicaea (325) as their norm. They became Eastern as a result of a long and complex process of estrangement from Rome-based western Christianity. The Eastern Orthodox, in a similar way and yet in competition with the Roman Catholic Church, claim a direct and unbroken continuity with the faith and authority of the apostles, and appeal to the tradition of the 'undivided church' which preceded the final break ('Great Schism') between Rome and Constantinople ('New Rome') in 1054.

The theological and cultural divide was reinforced when in 1204 western crusaders went on the rampage to slaughter, rape and mutilate the inhabitants, and then destroy and pillage the beautiful and wealthy city of Constantinople,[4] the centre of Byzantium. The atrocities committed against Eastern Christians deepened the distrust, increased the enmity, and widened the chasm between the Western and Eastern Christendom. These painful historic memories have become germane again in the discussions about the present erosion of confidence between Orthodoxy and Catholicism, as well as in the context of current debates about increased animosity and perceived threats to Christian civilization due to the growth of Islam in Europe. I agree with one of the most learned and ecumenically open Orthodox bishops that 'the crusades brought a result that was just the opposite of what they intended. These wars created for centuries a fear and a suspicion between Christians and Muslims. In the end, they mutilated and

[3] The most helpful general resource work on Orthodoxy written by insiders is Ken Parry, David J. Meffing, Dimitri Brady, Sidney H. Griffith and John F. Healey (eds), *The Blackwell Dictionary of Eastern Christianity* (Oxford: Blackwell, 1999).

[4] See Jonathan Phillips, *The Fourth Crusade and the Sack of Constantinople* (New York: Penguin Group, 2005).

mortally wounded not Islam, but one of the most vital and flourishing cultures, the Christian Byzantine'.[5] Attempts at reconciliation and reunion between Rome and Byzantium (prompted by renewed threats of Islamic expansionism) at the Councils of Lyons (1274) and Florence (1439) failed because of opposition from the Russian Orthodox and Greek monastic communities. Relations between the 'First Rome' and 'Second Rome' (Constantinople, the seat of the Ecumenical Patriarch) have improved considerably since 1965 when mutual excommunications of 1054 were solemnly lifted during a remarkable meeting of the Ecumenical Patriarch Athenagoras (otherwise known as a reconciler of churches) and Pope Paul VI. Relations with theologically and culturally even more estranged Protestant Christianity have improved in the twentieth century through their common membership and intensive co-operation in ecumenical bodies, particularly the World Council of Churches (WCC), which most of the national Orthodox churches joined in the 1960s, and the Conference of European Churches (CEC), which the Protestants and Orthodox jointly established in 1959.

The Orthodox Church is one and many at the same time, as it is a family of churches that share the same ancient faith, being in communion with each other while remaining independent in their administration in the context of their own nations. The majority of the countries of Eastern Europe are religiously shaped and dominated by Eastern Orthodox Christianity. The Slavic nations were first evangelized in the ninth century by Byzantine missionaries Cyril and Methodius (and their disciples) who, in both bridge-building and competitive ways, are venerated and claimed by both the Orthodox and Catholic churches.[6] The most numerous attendants of the Eastern churches today are those of the Russian Orthodox Church (76 million). The following are approximate statistics of nominally declared Orthodox in other nations: Ukraine (28 million), Romania (19 million), Serbia (7 million), Bulgaria (6 million), and Greece (9 million). The Georgian Orthodox Church (2.5 million) is the oldest in the territory of the former Soviet Union (Georgia is now an independent nation in conflict with Russia), and was founded in the fifth century through missionary work by St Nina, a slave woman who is counted as 'equal to the apostles' in the Orthodox register of saints, a noteworthy curiosum for a church adamantly opposed to the ordination of women. It is not as well known that the Orthodox tradition represents strong religious minorities (recognized as autonomous churches) in the predominantly Roman Catholic nations of Eastern Europe, such as former Czechoslovakia and Poland (850,000 Orthodox), in mainly Lutheran Finland, and in Albania. One should add that Orthodox churches in the Ukraine and Bulgaria are sadly divided, and

[5] Anastasios Yannoulatos, 'Culture and Gospel: Some Observations from the Orthodox Traditions and Experience', in *International Review of Mission,* 74.294 (1985), 195.

[6] Peter Kuzmič, 'Slavorum Apostoli, The Enduring Legacy of Cyril and Methodius', in Tim Perry (ed), *The Legacy of John Paul II* (Downers Grove, IL: IVP Academic, 2007), 267-89.

that the Macedonian and fledgling Montenegro Orthodox churches are (due to Serbian opposition) not recognized by other autocephalous Orthodox churches. Divisions and the lack of recognition have since had ramifications on political and other levels:

> Church autocephaly has usually been valued both as an authentication of Christian culture/national identity and as an assurance of the exclusion of foreign clerical or even political influence. It is something more as well, namely, a definition of the arena in which church-state issues will be resolved and of the status and prerogatives to be enjoyed by the ecclesiastical organization in this relationship.[7]

In the Ukraine, Belorussia and Romania, there are large numbers of Christians who worship like the Orthodox but recognize the authority of the Roman Pope. They are properly named Eastern-rite Catholics, but are frequently also called 'Greek Catholics' or (in a somewhat derogatory way) 'Uniates'.[8] Their clergy may marry and they were able to retain Eastern Orthodox liturgy, spirituality, ecclesiastical customs and rites when they re-entered into full communion with the Roman Catholic Church. These hybrid churches are a result of religious compromises, created under political pressure from the Rome-favouring local rulers in 'fault line' areas of shifting borders. Over the centuries, however, these Eastern-rite Catholic Churches acquired a distinctive cultural and ecclesial character and a genuine identity. In regions under Soviet control, they were forced by Stalin to join the more easily subdued Russian Orthodox Church. In terms of relationships between East and West, they have remained an open wound and a serious bone of contention, a cause of constant tensions and periodic conflicts. These conflicts have intensified following recent political changes, especially as Eastern-rite Catholics (Uniates) regained their religious freedom and came once again under the jurisdiction of papal authority. Violent clashes ensued, especially in western Ukraine, over the (re)claiming of properties and places of worship. Although the Vatican ideally sees these churches as ecumenical bridge-builders, pointing to the desired full reunion of the Catholics and Orthodox,[9] the Orthodox interpret their very existence and territorial corollaries as an explicit Roman negation of their own (Orthodox) ecclesial character and as an instrument of western proselytism.

---

[7] Pedro Ramet, 'Autocephaly and National Identity in Church-State Relations in Eastern Christianity: An Introduction', in Pedro Ramet (ed), *Eastern Christianity and Politics in the Twentieth Century* (Durham, NC: Duke University Press, 1988), 19.

[8] 'Uniates' and 'uniatism' are widely used pejorative terms to label the thorny ecumenical and political problem of the status and relationships of the Eastern Christians who are under Roman Catholic jurisdiction.

[9] See R.G. Robertson, *The Eastern Christian Churches* (3rd edn; Rome: Pont. Institutum Studiorum Orientalium, 1990); and the 'Decree on Eastern Catholic Churches', in *Orientalium Ecclesiarium*, Vatican II, 21st November 1964.

Safeguarding Spirituality

The majestic city of Constantinople, the historical centre of Eastern Orthodoxy, was named after its founder, the Roman Emperor Constantine the Great (285-337). He is considered a saint in the Eastern Church, not only for making Christianity the privileged religion of empire and convening the first Ecumenical Council in Nicaea (though he was not even baptized at the time), but also for laying the foundations of Christian Byzantium. In order to break with the republican and pagan traditions of Rome, he moved the capital to the new city, and so, from the fourth to the eighth centuries, the Roman Empire, now centred in Constantinople, intentionally developed into a 'Christian Empire'. This process was made easier by the splintering of the West into numerous barbarian kingdoms, while the East remained strong and united under the powerful Byzantine emperor who reigned over a large empire, legally Christian and viewed theologically as an earthly expression of the heavenly reign of Christ. The emperor was seen as head of both the church and the state, or at least in control of the head of the church. This strengthened the link between the two and shaped the background for what modern Orthodoxy came to understand as the desirable 'symphony' between the temporal (state) and spiritual (church) rulers. There were, viewed from a modern perspective, numerous abuses by emperors claiming absolute power over both realms who frequently took advantage of the church's spiritual authority to support and extend their political and earthly ambitions. Some of the emperors, however, sincerely sought (as both 'priest' and 'king') to make their earthly empire a replica of the Kingdom of heaven and allowed the church to share the state's judicial authority. This led to some beneficial results in the area of public welfare and in the provision of imperial funds to support ecclesial causes, such as the construction of magnificent church buildings, among which, as the most outstanding example, the world-famous Hagia Sophia Cathedral still stands (though transformed into a mosque after the fall of Constantinople to Turkey in 1453).

Byzantine theocratic totalitarianism, frequently referred to in a derogatory sense as 'caesaropapism', was curbed in the ninth century when the rights and lines of authority of the emperor, and those of the patriarch as head of the church, were more clearly delineated, thus reducing the power of the emperors to impose their absolute will on the Byzantine Church. It took considerable time and obvious abuses of power, with consequential damages for both church and the state, before the lesson was learned that an earthly empire cannot be transformed into a 'Christian society' and that God's Kingdom will only be fully realized in the eschatological future. Today's search for the modern equivalent of a 'symphony' between secular and spiritual authorities in Orthodox-dominated Russia, Serbia, and to lesser extent in other post-communist nations, should also be politically and theologically questioned, as it is based on anti-democratic ethno-religious homogenization of their nations and leads to marginalization, as well as occasionally to the legally induced discrimination of religious minorities, including well-established Protestant churches.

In the Byzantine imperially patronized church, which additionally became stained by growing moral laxity through the centuries, we must notice three significant developments that served as protective and redemptive responses to these and other spiritually disparaging forces. First was the search to safeguard the heart of the gospel through monasticism. In the previously persecuted church, it had been the martyrs, as the community of the committed followers of Christ, who clearly marked the line of radical separation between the pagan state and the church. In the imperially privileged church there was no need for martyrs, and committed Christians who became monks now replaced them as 'white martyrs' who through ascetic lives of self-denial died daily to the vainglory and luxury offered by the earthly powers. In addition to spiritual disciplines, some early monastic communes also developed work disciplines that made them prosperous economic co-operatives. The spiritual and social influence of the monks (the Byzantine Church's 'democratic front') was important in balancing and moderating the power of both emperor and bishop by pointing to the primacy of the transcendent and by acting as reminders of the eschatological dimensions of divine reign. Monks play a similar role within the contemporary Orthodox world, with spiritual and theological influence beyond measure. The largest and most influential monastic centre in the Orthodox world today is Mount Athos in Greece, with about twenty semi-independent monasteries, including Russian, Serbian and Bulgarian communities.

The second response to the secularizing threat of an increasingly shallow and officially favoured Christian religion was a move to preserve the purity of Orthodoxy by protecting its very heart – namely, the sacred liturgy. Georges Florovsky (1893-1997), a universally recognized spokesman for Orthodoxy and a formative theological figure in guiding its participation in the wider ecumenical search for Christian unity, summarized the nature of their faith most aptly: 'Christianity is a liturgical religion and the Church is first of all a worshiping community.'[10] The roots of this commitment go back to the times when ancient sanctuaries were filled with superficially baptized masses and the spiritual centre of the liturgy had to be safeguarded by its withdrawal behind an iconostasis (a wall covered with icons), where the laity were (and still are) forbidden to enter. The consequences of spiritually motivated withdrawal from the world into monastic communities, with the safeguarding withdrawal of the heart of liturgy into a sanctuary separating its most sacred functions from the less spiritual laity, can be questioned at several levels. This dual move within a superficially 'Christian empire' did, however, help preserve Orthodoxy through the centuries of persecution under both the onslaught of Islam and the

[10] Georges Florovsky, *Christianity and Culture* (Belmont, MA: Nordland, 1974), 132.

antagonistic communist attempts to destroy religion. A third structural safeguard at the level of church leadership came the early rule mandating that a bishop had to be chosen from a monastic community.

Later centuries were not kind to Christianity in many lands of Eastern Europe when their nations and churches faced major political, military and religious threats to their very survival. It was the spirituality and the learning of the monastic communities that preserved the sense of nationhood, language and culture under the Islamic Ottoman-Turkish imposition for nearly half a millennium. They also, in an uncompromised way, kept alive certain endangered national and spiritual values under communism, to which we now turn.

Religion under Pressure: Communism's Treatment of Christianity

Dogmatic Marxism and historic Christianity have by and large consistently viewed each other as irreconcilable enemies because of fundamental differences in their worldviews, though one could also argue that they are actually relatives – relatives historically and philosophically at odds with each other. Oswald Spengler, for example, claimed that 'Christianity is the grandmother of Bolshevism', while Nicolas Berdyaev argued that communism and Christianity were rival religions, and William Temple explained the similarity of Christian and Marxist social ideas by pronouncing the latter a Christian heresy.[11] One thing is sure: 'Generally speaking, Marxists hate all gods, including the Christian God-man Jesus Christ'.[12]

It is a well-known fact that wherever Marxist communists came to power, their long-term goal was not only a classless but also a non-religious society. Consistent with their politics, derived from the philosophy of dialectical materialism and joined with revolutionary practice, they viewed Christian faith as superstitious, obscurantist, obsolete and pre-scientific, and thus a totally irrelevant way of thinking and living. Christian institutions were treated as reactionary remnants of the old social order and a hindrance to the progress of the new society and the full human liberation of their citizens. Since the Communist Party and its members had a monopoly on both power (which they abused) and truth (which they distorted), they developed comprehensive strategies and powerful instruments for the gradual elimination of all religion. This included restrictive legislation, comprehensive programmes of systemic atheization of younger generations through educational institutions and fully controlled media, manipulation of the selection of church leadership, and effective monitoring of their activities. In contrast, for example, to the government-

[11] Cf. David Lyon, *Karl Marx: A Christian Appreciation of His Life and Thought* (Tring, UK: Lion Publishing, 1979), 11-12.

[12] Peter Kuzmič, 'How Marxists See Jesus', in Robin Keeley (ed), *Handbook of Christian Belief* (Tring, UK: Lion Publishing, 1982), 108.

sponsored educational agencies and youth organizations pursuing a comprehensive campaign of the indoctrination of children and youth in 'scientific atheism', Christian organizations for youth and children were forbidden, Sunday schools outlawed, and youth under the age of 18 years old forbidden to attend church services. As late as the 1980s, the Soviet government proudly claimed that one of the successes of its educational system was evident in the fact that about 90% of young people aged 16 to 19 adhered to atheism as their worldview.

Within communist-dominated nations, specialized legislation regulated and restricted the status and practice of religious communities. The USSR first introduced 'A Law on Religious Associations' in 1929, after Stalin had consolidated power. The law contained some sixty Articles that stated what religious organizations could or could not do, and what the rights and duties of believers were. During the Stalinist period of intense persecution, especially up to World War II, limiting Articles were vigorously applied and almost regularly over-enforced through the abuse of political power by ambitious regional and local administrators and police. The Law on Religious Associations became a model for similar legislation that was introduced in the late 1940s in other Eastern bloc and socialist countries. More instruments for the control and oppression of Christian communities were introduced, such as central government offices, administrative apparatuses at all levels of governance, and specialized police and judicial departments. Co-operative leaders of registered Christian bodies were given some incentives, and government-controlled unions were imposed on smaller Christian denominations. The best-known among these was the All-Union Council of Evangelical Christians-Baptists (AUCECB) in the former Soviet Union, composed of Evangelicals, Baptists, Pentecostals and Mennonites. Their unregistered counterparts were treated as enemies of the state, exposed to harsh treatment and periodic physical persecution. Waves of comprehensive and vigorous national anti-religious campaigns, such as during the Khrushchev era in the early 1960s, did not succeed in eliminating religious life but contributed rather paradoxically to a resurgence of spirituality and the growth of all religious communities.

It must be pointed out, however, that practical policies differed from country to country and, at different periods, even within the same nation, depending on what was considered to be politically expedient during various historical periods and in diverse regions. Generalizations are problematic, for Eastern Europe has never been totally monolithic regarding the treatment of religion, due to the complexity of the national, cultural and religious history of different nations, and at times depending on international relationships and considerations.[13] It is legitimate, however,

[13] One of the most reliably balanced studies of the topic is presented by Trevor Beeson, *Discretion and Valour* (London: Collins, 1974) revised edn, 1982.

to conclude that, at best, Christian faith was reluctantly tolerated, with its adherents socially marginalized and discriminated against as 'second-class citizens', while, at worst, practising believers were brutally persecuted, church buildings closed or destroyed, and their institutionalized religion outlawed. In Albania, for example, all visible expressions of religion were, by force of law, totally eradicated, with that small neo-Stalinist country at that time (after 1967) priding itself as being the 'first atheistic state in the world'.

Modes of Survival: Between Resistance, Resignation and Accommodation

What lessons can be drawn from the precarious existence of the church under pressure? Christians who live under repressive political (or religious, as in the case of countries with Islamic governments) systems that are antagonistic to their faith face serious trials and severe temptations. Valuable lessons have been learned in observing and comparing how Christians in their vulnerable existence responded to the challenges of a totalitarian society. I shall briefly outline the experience of the churches under communism through three different kinds of response, fully aware that there were occasional overlaps and circumstantial inconsistencies in all of them. These observations are partially based on my firsthand experience and study of the social behaviour of minority Protestant communities, their encounter with the challenges of Marxist rule in general, and communist treatment of Christian churches and believers in particular.[14]

The first impulse of many Christian communities who suddenly found themselves surrounded by an aggressive enemy and ruled over by an atheistic system was to *react by fighting back,* taking a posture of *active opposition* to the government and its policies. The simple reasoning was that the new system was ungodly and evil, inspired by the devil, and so should neither be obeyed nor tolerated, but rather actively opposed in the name of Christ. At times, it was simply the fight for church property and resistance to the revolutionary overthrow of the established order. There are obvious dangers in this posture of unrelieved hostility in any context of social change. In Eastern Europe, such opposition was constantly based on an oversimplified political and correspondingly spiritual division of the world, with the accompanying character of an eschatological struggle between the children of light and the children of darkness. 'During the times of the "Cold War" when the political antagonism between the Western and Eastern bloc countries came to a very critical and dangerous

[14] See Peter Kuzmič, 'Evangelical Witness in Eastern Europe', in Waldron Scott (ed), *Serving Our Generation: Evangelical Strategies for the Eighties* (Colorado Springs, CO: WEF, 1980), 77-86; and Ibid., 'Pentecostals Respond to Marxism', in Murray A. Dempster, Byron D. Klaus and Douglas Petersen (eds), *Called and Empowered: Global Mission in Pentecostal Perspective* (Peabody, MA: Hendrickson Publishers, 1991), 143-64.

climax, there was in fashion much over-generalized and simplistic speaking of the "Christian West" and "atheistic East" and mutual denunciation in almost mythological terms'.[15] History records that, in most countries, the first years of the communist takeover were marked by bitter and at times *violent confrontations*. In some cases, the state resorted to the most brutally repressive measures, producing countless Christian martyrs, and causing enormous devastation of church property and institutions. Christians who were trapped into the assumption that their major task was to fight communism (a modern-day Crusader mentality) handicapped themselves by becoming incapable of practising forgiveness and being a living witness to the communists.

The second, materially and physically less costly, reaction was to *withdraw from the social scene,* literally to 'flee the world'. This *posture of resignation* in order to avoid confrontation and compromise took place either by internal or external emigration. Both were caused by fear of engaging with the new system that was conceived of as evil, powerful and bent on the total destruction of those who dared to oppose it. Most of the communist countries practised a 'closed borders' foreign policy and thereby refused to allow their citizens to emigrate to other countries. Yet history records periods in which governments granted passports and encouraged 'undesirable elements' to leave their homelands on grounds of ethnic or religious differences. The best-known cases were the Jews and, among Christians, large numbers of Pentecostal emigrants from the Soviet Union in the late 1980s.[16] Those who opted for the easier *internal withdrawal* by isolating themselves from the surrounding secular society, though spiritually motivated like the monastic communities, were by and large lost for any effective social impact. They very often developed a ghetto mentality, with a passive if not reactionary lifestyle, and were conspicuous by a high degree of legalism and insularity that made them incapable of a positive 'salt and light' influence on their society. They often developed their own pietistic sub-culture with its own pattern of behaviour, language, dress code and even hymnology. By the neo-Protestant groups (Baptists, Pentecostals, Adventists, and Mennonites), such internal withdrawal was very often doctrinally undergirded by apocalyptic, escapist eschatologies that, in their general outlook on life, seemed to validate certain aspects of Marxist criticism of religion as offering only 'pie in the sky'. Extreme examples of such isolated groups of conservative Christians, both Orthodox and Protestant, have at times been highlighted in Soviet and allied anti-Christian propaganda to prove the socially and mentally harmful effects of Christian faith. This internal withdrawal universally tends to lead

---

[15] Peter Kuzmič, 'Christian-Marxist Dialogue: An Evangelical Perspective', in Vinay Samuel and Albrecht Hauser (eds), *Proclaiming Christ in Christ's Way: Studies in Integral Evangelism* (Oxford: Regnum, 1989), 161.

[16] Kent R. Hill, *The Puzzle of the Soviet Church: An Inside Look at Christianity and Glasnost* (Portland, OR: Multnomah, 1989), 292-93.

to a loss of relevance, denies the mission of the church, and undermines any Christian impact on culture, for it deals with outdated issues, answers questions that are no longer asked, and has very little to say to its contemporaries and their society.

The third model of responding to the new ideological environment was to *conform* or *compromise,* to tailor the message and the method to the new situation, thereby *accommodating to the prevailing ideology.* Some Christian leaders were denigrated by others for yielding ground theologically and otherwise establishing rapport with the new rulers and gaining some concessions, if not privileges, in the areas of limited religious freedom, social status, international travel and so on. Charges of opportunism and selfish careerism by suffering believers and religious dissidents were not uncommon. In all Christian churches, but especially within the neo-Protestant camp, different degrees of accommodation and resistance often led to splits between those denominations that registered with the government and agreed to observe the restrictions of the letter of the law, and those that rejected the legal regulations and operated in a clandestine way and thereby became known as 'underground churches'.

The compromising approach may at times appear to have been naïve and its motives questionable, though in many cases it also provided evidence of the diplomatic skills of church leaders who were able to negotiate settlements that led to a temporarily beneficial (to critics: morally and theologically dubious) *modus vivendi* between church and state. The obedient attitude to the government by some apparently sincere leaders was additionally justified by their patriotism (as it is frequently done today in China) and by appeals to the apostolic admonition to 'submit to the governing authorities, for there is no authority except that which God has established' (Rom. 13:1).

A brief concluding theological observation about the most important lesson from and for Christians under pressure: the church of Jesus Christ is a pilgrim community – *communio viatorum* – 'in the world' but not 'of the world', still on the journey to the eternal city and, therefore, never comfortably at home in any society. As Jan Milic Lochman, a Czech theologian, reminded us at that time, 'any attempt to relate the gospel too closely to an ideology is dangerous for its integrity and its identity'.[17] An uncritical identification with the world inevitably leads to a critical loss of both identity and spiritual authority and thereby discredits the preserving and transformative mission of the church in the world.

---

[17] Jan Milic Lochman, *Encountering Marx: Bonds and Barriers Between Christians and Marxists* (Philadelphia, PA: Fortress Press, 1977).

From Painful Transition to Hopeful Future

Challenges for the post-communist era Christians and their churches in Eastern Europe are many. With the rather sudden collapse of totalitarian regimes, as dramatically illustrated in November 1989 by the tearing down of the most powerful symbol of a divided Europe – the Berlin Wall – a new spirit of hope filled the widened horizons of unexpected freedom. Many Christians all across Eastern Europe interpreted those events as *The Gospel's Triumph Over Communism,* to borrow the title of Michael Bourdeaux's book,[18] describing them as the providential work of the Lord of history who has seen their suffering and longing for freedom, answered their prayers, and provided them with a special *kairos* period to call their nations back to God and to the spiritual foundations for a free and truly 'new society'.

The general euphoria of East Europeans with a newly found freedom in the early 1990s, however, was quickly replaced by a sober encounter with many grim realities that appeared to threaten the prospects of free, peaceful and prosperous societies. The lack of a developed political culture and other obstacles to the consolidation of democratic institutions are key reasons why some nations of Eastern Europe are still going through very difficult political transitions from one-party totalitarian regimes towards stable multi-party parliamentary democracies. Transition continues to be equally painful economically as several nations have moved too rapidly and in ethically dubious ways away from the centrally planned 'command' economies towards desired viable free-market economies. Large-scale corruption in the process of privatization of formerly state-owned factories and land has created new injustices, causing massive unemployment and social disparities as a result of chaotic 'wild capitalism'. Social unrest, disillusionment of the impoverished masses, and the general mentality of dependence has created environments conducive to new authoritarian rulers, as well as to manipulations by populist politicians hungry for power and personal enrichment. Unfortunately, by and large, East European churches failed to provide effective and credible ethical correctives to these dubious processes. Developing a spirituality for transformative social engagement remains one of the priority tasks of the churches if they are to be credible and effective instruments of the Kingdom of God among the broken kingdoms of the post-communist world.

One of the major problems for national churches is the temptation to return to a quasi-Constantinian model of the church-state relationship. After prolonged periods of external persecution, societal marginalization and internal weaknesses, the church is again favoured by (frequently former communist!) rulers and bestowed privileges of public treatment incompatible with modern democratic societies. For example, in 2007, the

[18] Michael Bourdeaux, *The Gospel's Triumph over Communism* (Minneapolis, MN: Bethany House Publishers, 1991).

government of Serbia passed a law that does not recognize Baptist, Pentecostal or Adventist religious communities as churches, and refuses to give them legal status. Laws in Russia, Belarus and several other countries have in recent years adopted similarly restrictive legislations. Although the intensive process of replacement of a singular communist ideology by nationalistic ideologies did lead to partially valid rediscoveries of ethno-religious identities, the discernible shifts 'from totalitarianism to tribalism' (issuing in inter-ethnic conflicts and wars) and 'from rights to roots' threatened democratic processes and diminished the liberties and human rights of vulnerable minorities. In such contexts, some national Orthodox churches seemed to still operate with the outdated view of canonical authority over a territory, which caused many tensions – for example, in Russia – where both Catholics and Protestants were accused of proselytism and illegitimate encroachment on areas supposedly under their control. A competent scholar of religion in Eastern Europe has identified and described this phenomenon as follows:

> Ecclesiastical nationalism consists in several distinct aspects of church activity: in the church's preservation and development of the cultural heritage, in the church's use of a special language for liturgy and instruction, in the advancement of specific territorial claims on putative ethnic grounds, and in the cultivation of the social idea itself, that is, the idea that a given people, united by faith and culture, constitutes a nation.[19]

Since the fall of communism, both Orthodox churches (in the republics of the former Soviet Union and Yugoslavia) and Catholic churches (in Poland, Hungary, Slovakia and Croatia) have in varying degrees reasserted their claims of monopoly on the religious life of their nations. In these countries, belonging to the national church has become less a question of doctrinal persuasion or moral conviction, and more an issue of national identity, patriotism and ethno-religious folklore.

Protestant churches are small minorities in most of these nations and are in general looked upon with suspicion as adherents of that radical movement that in the past has divided Christendom, and as a modernized, western faith, and thus a foreign intrusion that in the present, in its various fragmented forms, threatens the national and religious identity and unity of the people.[20] Democratically and ecumenically illiterate clergy, with intolerant militant fanatics among them and in their flocks, are fiercely opposed to evangelizing evangelicals and their western partners, for they view them as disruptive sectarians involved in dangerous proselytizing and unpatriotic activities. Most traditional Protestant churches are in decline,

[19] Ramet, 'Autocephaly and National Identity in Church-State Relations in Eastern Christianity', 10.

[20] See the excellent symposium: John Witte Jr. and Paul Mojzes (eds), 'Pluralism, Proselytism, and Nationalism in Eastern Europe', special issue, *Journal of Ecumenical Studies* 36.1-2 (Winter-Spring, 1999), 1-286.

while Baptist, Pentecostal and charismatic churches are attracting young people and flourishing in countries like the Ukraine and Romania.

Now that the Iron Curtain is down, most East European nations, for reasons of security and economic prosperity, aspire to membership in NATO and the European Union (EU). Although the enlargement of these transnational entities and Europe's integrating processes cause tensions with Russia and its neighbours, further unification of the continent is inevitable. In addition to political and economic reasons, it is obvious that a common Christian history and culture make it unacceptable for the continent to be divided permanently between the more advanced western part, marked by democracy, economic prosperity and general vitality, and the eastern part, as less democratic, prosperous or stable. Such a division is unsustainable and would do damage to both. The new and united Europe and its churches need each other to rediscover the full meaning and respect for life and personhood, to provide for the protection of human rights of minorities, work for social justice, practise solidarity, and to bear witness to a future that transcends the vision of a common economic and political space. Europe also needs, as frequently reminded by the late Pope John Paul II, an intensive re-evangelization and rediscovery of the gospel based on spiritual values.

Over the last twenty years, European churches' otherwise frustrated search for ways of finding greater unity and co-operation across age-long and deeply entrenched confessional divisions has made some significant advances. The Conference of European Churches (CEC), to which almost all Orthodox, Protestant, Anglican and independent churches belong, and the Council of European Bishops' Conferences (CCEE), composed of all National Catholic Bishops Conferences, have organized three significant European Ecumenical Assemblies: in Basel (1989), Graz (1997), and – the first one in an East European country – Sibiu, in Romania (2007). And in 2001, after a prolonged and careful pan-European study period, they also jointly adopted a finely balanced document, *Charta Oecumenica: Guidelines for the Growing Co-operation among Churches in Europe,* in whose preamble we read: 'Europe – from the Atlantic to the Urals, from the North Cape to the Mediterranean – is today more pluralist in culture than ever before. With the gospel, we want to stand up for the dignity of the human person created in God's image and, as churches together, contribute towards reconciling peoples and cultures.'

A search for a more hopeful future for Christian witness in a more unified and secularized Europe continues, with the full realization that it requires a renewed definition of the mission of the Christian churches. This has been programmatically expressed by the document *Churches in the Process of European Integration,* issued by CEC in 2001:

> The substantial role of Christian Churches in society – in debate about values in society, politics, culture and science, in their pastoral and diaconal roles and their ethical contribution – needs to be recognized. Christian churches are

> not only part of European history, but also a vital and integral part of the functioning social infrastructure. In spite of the fact that there is not an ecclesial unity, the voice of the Christian churches needs to be taken into consideration. The variety of church and religious traditions in Europe is to be understood not as an obstacle but as an enrichment, which could be of use in the creation of a common European structure. It is completely unsatisfactory to pursue exclusively the pattern of market values to create a common Europe. Accompanying ethical and spiritual dimensions are essential for the success of the project... There is a role for the churches and religious communities as guardians, independent of state power, of many European traditions as well as guardians of the specifically ethical dimension of this process. This role is substantial and truly irreplaceable.[21]

[21] Peter Pavlovic, 'Churches in the Process of European Integration', Conference of European Churches – Church and Society Commission: www.cec-kek.org/English/ IntegrationprocE-print.htm (accessed 15th May 2009).

Revolutions in European Mission: 'What has been achieved in 25 years of East European mission?'[1]

Anne-Marie Kool

Introduction

Thirty years ago, Václav Havel's book *The Power of the Powerless* (*Versuch, in der Wahrheit zu leben*) made a great impact on me.[2] He described life under communism as living in lying, and his alternative and courageous attitude to stand for truth made me wonder whether I would have been so courageous. It was a situation he referred to as 'the people pretended to follow the party, and the party pretended to lead'.[3] Although Havel did not write from a Christian perspective, he still teaches us very much what mission is all about: it is sharing biblical Truth as embodied in Jesus Christ, and living out that Truth in everyday life, whatever the consequences. Havel was willing to suffer for it, and as a consequence of his courageous attitude, he was imprisoned several times. Following the events of 1989, he was chosen as the first president of the Czech Republic, and three times re-elected. Early 1989, he had been sentenced to eight months of prison for 'hooliganism', but was freed early.[4]

The apostle Paul suffered for different reasons. He was not afraid to witness to Jesus Christ. When in Acts 20 he looks back on his life as a missionary, he remembers his ministry, not in terms of numbers, how many people were converted, or how many churches he planted, or how many cities he had visited. He summarized his ministry, not in terms of success but in terms of suffering as a ministry of tears. The secret of his life was God!

In this paper I will explore the question: 'What has been achieved in 25 years of East European mission?' in two parts. In the first part, I will deal with four different periods: 1) Pre-1989; 2) 1989-1998: Euphoria; 3) 1998-

---

[1] This chapter was first presented as a keynote address at a conference with the theme: 'Revolutions in European Mission', organized by the European Evangelical Mission Association held in Bucharest, 18th-21st November 2014.

[2] Václav Havel and Gabriel Laub, *Versuch, in der Wahrheit zu leben* (Reinbek bei Hamburg: Rowohlt, 1990); Václav Havel and John Keane, *The Power of the Powerless: Citizens against the State in Eastern Europe* (London: Hutchinson, 1985).

[3] 'Václav Havel 1936-2011: Living in Truth: The unassuming man who taught, through plays and politics, how tyranny may be defied and overcome', in *The Economist* (2011): www.economist.com/node/21542169

[4] 'Václav Havel 1936-2011'.

2008: Disillusionment; 4) 2009-2014: Towards an innovative new paradigm. In the second part, I will focus on the challenges as we look to the future. I will start with introducing my personal perspective and the context of mission in Eastern Europe, using the image of mission as bridge-building, inspired by the city I have called my home for almost three decades: Budapest. The mission paradigm dominant in this period was rather individualistic in character, doing mission the Frank Sinatra way – 'my way' – with a strong focus on success. It was a paradigm strongly influenced by 'the West'. In this paper, it will be argued that the paradigm for mission in this region can be better captured as mission through suffering, both before and after 1989, also taking a community perspective into consideration.[5]

'What has been achieved?'

The given title for the keynote address on which this chapter is based was 'What has been achieved in 25 years of East European mission?' The online Oxford Dictionary defines 'achieve' as 'successfully bring about or reach (a desired objective or result) by effort, skill, or courage', as in: 'He achieved his ambition to become a press photographer.'[6] It is a similar question that motivated mission leaders in 1910 and in 2010 to convene the world mission conferences in Edinburgh with the purpose of 'taking stock', sitting down, looking back and drawing lessons. The past 25 years have been marked more by activism than by reflection, so it is important to assess and evaluate what has been done in terms of mission in (Central and) Eastern Europe, and to draw lessons for the future.

The question is what criteria should be used in evaluating what is referred to by many as an 'emerging missionary movement', as if before 1989 no mission work took place.[7] The question could be understood as evaluating a business plan. Money has been invested, and now it is time to look at the revenues – whether the investment yielded enough value for money. This approach would be based on a secular worldview, focusing on numbers, and would be a peculiar way of evaluating a missionary movement with a strong evangelical stance. Such an approach would be more interested in the successes, in what has been accomplished, than in quality – like counting how many people are converted or how many missionaries are sent 'overseas' from Eastern Europe. Although such

---

[5] Recently Scott Sunquist published a new introduction to world mission informed by his experience in South East Asia, with a similar emphasis: *Understanding Christian Mission: Participation in Suffering and Glory* (Grand Rapids, MI: Baker Academic, 2013). His main thesis is: 'Mission is from the heart of God, to each context, and it is carried out in suffering in this world for God's eternal glory' (xii). Sunquist calls us to participate in the suffering and glory of Christ.

[6] www.oxforddictionaries.com/definition/english/achieve

[7] See e.g. Anne-Marie Kool, *God Moves in a Mysterious Way: The Hungarian Protestant Foreign Mission Movement (1756-1951)* (Mission: Zoetermeer: Boekencentrum, 1993).

criteria give the impression of being biblical, still the main focus is on numbers and 'output'. Another approach could be to assess and evaluate the impact of the gospel on the societies of Eastern Europe and wherever missionaries are working. How did mission in Eastern Europe result in transformed Christian lives and transformed societies, showing less corruption, less broken families, less addiction to alcohol and drugs, less exclusion of e.g. Roma, less conflict and more co-operation? In short, would it be possible to look at the fruit of the Spirit?

This chapter rather seeks to analyze what has happened in what was till recently referred to politically as 'Eastern Europe', rather than dealing with the issue of 'criteria' to assess what has been 'achieved'. Many different people have in one sense or another been part of this mission movement: as missionaries, mission agencies, churches, donors, or as those that have been praying. It is important to continue the conversation with each one of these actors in a process of mission as learning and listening. These players are all 'disciples' and learners, but also people who have something to contribute! This volume brings together some of these contributions to enrich this learning experience, showing that Eastern Europe is a laboratory for mission worldwide, and as such there are lessons to be learned for 'East' and for 'West', in how we do mission 'our way'.

My Personal Perspective

This article is semi-autobiographical, as I started out as a literature smuggler in 1978, and have since 1987 been actively participating in this 'emerging' mission movement, researching the history of the Hungarian Protestant foreign mission movement during the last two centuries. Through my research I gained insight into mission under communism and earlier times. I am greatly indebted to the Hungarian pioneers in mission, as I gained much from their writings, and from personal encounters. Their godly lives, often grown out of religious oppression and suffering have been and still are a rich source of inspiration. They have shown me God's faithfulness in difficult times.[8]

Many of those involved in this chapter of mission history in Eastern Europe have gone through difficult times as they pioneered their organizations, or were sent as one of the first missionaries to 'faraway-istan', with recently established mission organizations that were still in the process of learning by doing. For not a few people, it was not success but suffering that characterized their mission work, and still there was fruit! There is much reason for celebrating God's faithfulness as, despite our lack of experience, and despite our struggles, he has worked out far more than we dared to imagine in the early 1990s.

---

[8] See also: Anne-Marie Kool, 'Behind the Former Iron Curtain: Teaching Missiology in Central and Eastern Europe', in Grace Barnes and Gwen Dewey (eds), *Wild: Women in Leadership Development* (Woodinville, WA: Harmon Press, 2013).

This article is a work in progress. I do not pretend to have the final word, but rather consider it as a starter for discussion. Much more research needs to be done into what has been 'accomplished', by whom, where, and why. It is based on numerous conversations with friends as well as on some of my earlier publications.[9] I also owe very much to the publications and conversations with colleagues like Peter F. Penner[10] and Scott Klingsmith.[11] Also the East West Christian Ministry Report, since its beginning in 1993, edited by Mark Elliott, offers a rich source for mission in Central and Eastern Europe after 1989.[12]

Mission as Bridge-Building between East and West[13]

The churches in the 'post-communist' societies of Eastern Europe are facing complex challenges in their efforts to be witnesses for Jesus Christ in word and deed, both in local and global contexts, resulting in a need for a greater emphasis on building bridges. Not only bridges between the church and the secularized or nominal Christian world, also between generations, between denominations, between different ethnic groups, and between

---

[9] 'Leadership Issues in Central and Eastern Europe: Continuing Trends and Challenges in Mission and Missiology,' in *Acta Missiologiae* 1.1 (2008); 'Trends and Challenges in Mission and Missiology in "Post-Communist" Europe', in *Mission Studies* 25 (2008); 'The Church in Hungary and Central and Eastern Europe: Trends and Challenges', in *Princeton Theological Seminary Bulletin* 28.2 (2007); 'Die Eu – Osterweiterung – Eine Herausforderung Für Die Kirchen: Die Antwort Der Kirchen in Mittel- Und Osteuropa Auf Die Herausforderung Des Post-Kommunismus' (Frenswegen, Germany: Leuenberg Nord-West Gruppe, 2004); 'A Protestant Perspective on Mission in Eastern and Central Europe', in *Religion in Eastern Europe* 20.6 (2000).

[10] Mary Raber and Peter F. Penner (eds), *History and Mission in Europe: Continuing the Conversation* (Schwarzenfeld, Germany: Neufeld Verlag, 2011); Anne-Marie Kool and Peter Penner, 'Theological Education in Eastern and Central Europe: Major Developments and Challenges since 1910', in David Esterline, Dietrich Werner, Namsoon Kang and Joshva Raja (eds), *The Handbook of Theological Education in World Christianity* (Oxford: Regnum, 2010); Peter F. Penner, 'Western Missionaries in Central and Eastern Europe', in *Acta Missiologiae* 1.1 (2008); Peter F. Penner (ed), *Ethnic Churches in Europe: A Baptist Response*, Occasional Publications (Schwarzenfeld, Germany: Neufeld, 2006); Walter W. Sawatsky and Peter F. Penner (eds), *Mission in the Former Soviet Union* (Schwarzenfeld, Germany: Neufeld Verlag, 2005); Peter F. Penner, *Christian Presence and Witness among Muslims* (Schwarzenfeld, Germany: Neufeld Verlag, 2005); Peter F. Penner (ed), *Theological Education as Mission – Mission in Theological Education* (Schwarzenfeld, Germany: Neufeld Verlag, 2005).

[11] Scott Klingsmith, 'The Romanian International Mission: A Case Study', in *East-West Church & Ministry Report* 13.2 (2005); 'Missionary Sending Movements: A Polish Case Study', in *East-West Church & Ministry Report,* 13.1 (2005); 'Advantages Romanians Bring to Missions', in *East-West Church & Ministry Report,* 13.2 (2004); 'Missionary Sending Movements in East-Central Europe: A Romanian-Albanian Case Study', in *East-West Church & Ministry Report,* 12.4 (2004); 'Hungarian Missionary Sending Efforts: A Case Study', in *East-West Church & Ministry Report,* 12.3 (2004); *Missions beyond the Wall: Factors in the Rise of Missionary Sending Movements in East-Central Europe* (Nürnberg, Germany: VTR Verlag, 2012).

[12] www.eastwestreport.org (accessed 28th November 2014).

[13] Kool, 'The Church in Hungary and Central and Eastern Europe'.

nationals and foreign missionaries. These bridges can be compared with the many bridges that cross the River Danube, the second largest river in Europe after the Volga. Extending for 2860 km on its way from the Black Forest to the Black Sea, the Danube flows through or forms a border with nine countries.

The oldest bridge in Budapest, the Chain Bridge, named after Count István Széchényi, offers interested insights in the nature of mission in Eastern Europe.[14] Three elements could be identified: the first element has to do with the company that built the bridge. Széchényi was an ardent Anglophile and introduced several modern British inventions to Hungary. The bridge was completed with Scottish help in 1849, thus helping the flow of traffic between Buda and Pest. The bridge was a good example of nationals and foreigners working together to improve the life of the city and make mutual engagement easier. The co-operation between nationals and foreigners in missions in Central and Eastern Europe has been a learning curve, full of misunderstandings and tensions. Individualistic, self-sufficient mindsets clashed with community-oriented, 'dependent' mindsets, learning to understand each other, seeking to bridge the differences, with the ultimate goal of easing the flow of the gospel out of the ghetto into the world and improving the life of cities.

A second important element is that a bridge makes it possible for traffic to flow in both directions. The mighty Danube is a formidable obstacle for the city of Budapest, but the many bridges allow the two parts of the city to engage with each other. There seem to be unbridgeable gaps between the various ethnic groups in the post-communist world, especially between the Roma and the majority society. Church communities are deeply divided over ethnic and denominational issues, and on whether to hold more traditional or more open views. Reconciliation as a theological concept is accepted, as it relates to the good news of the Kingdom that the gap between God and men has been bridged in Jesus Christ, but there is a long way to go in translating that into social reconciliation – practice often seems to lag behind belief.

Finally, it is important that bridges link two different banks of the city. The Chain Bridge may have quickly improved the flow of traffic but it has taken a much longer period for the mindsets in the two parts of the city to change. One travel guide records that both parts of the city still retain their own distinct identity. Buda, the guide states, is old, proud, quiet and a bit dotty, like an old aunt you only visit at weekends. Pest, on the other hand, is beautiful, confusing, often loud and incomprehensible, and quite likely to keep you awake far into the night. Yet both cities work together and provide the necessary components that make this vibrant city what it is – perhaps a model for the mission of the church in the Conference of European Churches! Uniformity is not a precondition for unity, and bridge-

---

[14] I owe some of these insights to the Very Revd Dr Ivan Patterson, in a paper on 'Mission in Hungary', May 2006.

building does not mean that an individual's identity is dissolved. 'West' is not always 'best'.

In the following part, an historical overview will be given of the missionary movement in Central and Eastern Europe in three different periods, starting with a brief summary of mission under communism.

Pre-1989: Mission under Communism

This period can be characterized by a moral vacuum. Under communism, not only the social, economic and political structures of a given society were forcefully rearranged, but individuals and societies were required to undergo re-education in order to conform to a certain ideological mould. Attempts were made to ensure a collective 'value replacement' surgery in which the Judeo-Christian ethical norms of the past were 'declared obsolete and useless' in building the future of communism.[15] As it turned out, the first part of the surgery, calling for the destruction of the old values in the individual or in society, was much easier to accomplish than the second, that of implanting the new Marxist values. It left many individuals, especially young people in an unprecedented moral vacuum – in national, family and individual life – representing to this day the greatest challenge to the churches in filling such existential emptiness. Although communism did immense harm to faith communities, we can also see that, through persecution, the faith of the community was strengthened, as was apparent in the case of Catholic Poland or different Baptist communities in Russia.

Mission work under communism was characterized by many people in the 'West' praying for the 'East'. It consisted of smuggling Bibles and literature. Leaders of churches were trained – underground – by co-workers of organizations like Biblical Education by Extension, travelling under another name, who made regular trips. Churches in the East were forced to live in a ghetto, but pastors were very creative in organising youth camps and outings during which they evangelized the young people. In a remarkable book, *Holy Spy: Student Ministry in Eastern Europe*,[16] Alex Williams tells the story of what mission under communism look liked. African students were given opportunities to study in closed countries like Romania, Bulgaria and Russia. Some of them were very active missionaries.[17] So much more happened than we know of. The story needs to be written down and shared!

---

[15] László Medgyessy, 'Mission or Proselytism? Temptations, Tensions and Missiological Perspectives in Eastern European Christianity: A Case Study of Hungary', in Christine Liennemann-Perrin, H.M. Vroom and Michael Weinrich (eds), *Contextuality in Reformed Europe : The Mission of the Church in the Transformation of European Culture, Currents of Encounter* (Amsterdam and New York: Rodopi, 2004), 105.

[16] Alex Williams, *Holy Spy: Stories from Eastern Europe* (Fearn: Christian Focus/Budapest: Harmat, 2003).

[17] Williams, *Holy Spy*, 148ff.

Mission under communism was not a success story. It was a story of suffering. Many informers were active in society, but also within the churches. And many of them are still alive. The past is still with us. Recently I was told the following story. A woman, when only 16 years old, was asked by her aunt to enlist with the authorities to help register people that were considered dangerous to communism. For the next five years of her life, she became more and more involved in actively beating up people, even shooting them, including pastors and members of churches. Then 1956 came and she fled Hungary, with the burden of her youth with her. She married and lived abroad, selling bags in markets. Only her husband knew her story: no-one else. She did not want to have anything to do with religion. She lived a completely isolated life. Her conscience was still accusing her. She died recently, and I stood at her death-bed and was asked by her husband to be present at her funeral. Only a handful people were present. Afterwards he told me her story.

After what is often coined as 'the changes' in 1989, a new era started. There was euphoria all over after the Berlin Wall came down.

1989-1998: Euphoria after the Wall Came Down

In October 1994, a consultation was convened in Oradea, Romania, focusing on the issue of Theological Education and Leadership Development in Post-Communist Europe.[18] The Consultation produced a significant document: The Oradea Declaration.[19] It describes the differences and similarities with the West European context, pointing to the atmosphere of euphoria in 1994 and the 'special Kairos times' – a time of 'unprecedented opportunities for the gospel of Jesus Christ' – and to the complexities faced in equipping new leaders The new possibilities are tempered by 'the rapid secularization of our societies' and by the increase of some historic tensions between evangelicals and the Orthodox and Roman Catholic churches.[20] It states that these tensions have 'the potential of diverting the energies of all Christians from the God-given possibilities of our time, and this would be a tragedy of profound consequences'. The Oradea Declaration continues by stating that the situation is even more complicated by 'the flood of well meant, but sometimes misguided, wasteful and inappropriate efforts from foreign agencies'.[21] It also

[18] See also Kool, 'A Protestant Perspective on Mission in Eastern and Central Europe'.

[19] 'The Oradea Declaration', in John C. Bennett et al (eds), *Equipping for the Future: Consultation on Theological Education and Leadership Development in Post-Communist Europe* (Oradea, Romania: unpublished, 1994). The entire document can be found at the end of this book in the Historical Document section.

[20] One of the continuous tensions has been the issue of proselytism. The scope of this presentation does not allow for a more detailed treatment. See, for an overview of the discussion, Kool, 'A Protestant Perspective on Mission in Eastern and Central Europe', and Kool, 'The Church in Hungary and Central and Eastern Europe', 159-63.

[21] 'The Oradea Declaration'.

recognizes the often overlooked rich heritage of the historic churches in the region: 'We thank God that Christian faith came to our lands many centuries ago, resulting in the establishment of historic churches. Through these churches, many aspects of our national cultures and identities have been shaped and preserved. We pray for the renewal of these churches by the transforming power of the gospel resulting in holy living and authentic witness to Christ.'[22]

In 1993, Anita Deyneka, speaking from her experience in Russia, is concerned with how to make the expatriate involvement more useful to the churches in Eastern Europe: 'How strategic is Christian assistance from afar? And how can such assistance be made more strategic? How can the many tributaries co-operate and converge – not only with each other as Westerners – but perhaps most importantly with our brothers and sisters in the East – so that an ocean of blessing will overflow?'[23]

A first characteristic of this period was that many theological institutions were established to train pastors for Evangelical churches. During this time, the external conditions had to be created – buildings, libraries, etc. – for which funds had to be raised and programmes developed. A number of networks for theological education were developed, several in Central Europe, others in the former Soviet Union.[24] Professors, mostly from western countries, came to teach 'in the western way', with a western mindset and view of mission, 'overseas mission', because no qualified local lecturers were available.[25] At the same time, these professors from the West played a window-opening role to the countries that had been virtually cut off from developments in world Christianity for such a long time. A second characteristic was the massive 'invasion' of evangelical missionaries that took place. By far the majority came with no background knowledge in culture or language, in an attitude of 'the need to bring Jesus' to Eastern Europe.[26] But for centuries, millions of people have worshipped Jesus Christ in Central and Eastern Europe. Miroslav Volf reminds us that what was rather needed was 'to wash the face of Jesus… dirtied not only by communist propaganda, but also by so many compromises of our churches'.[27]

A third characteristic was the massive financial support from the West. In this period, salaries were still low, so costs were also relatively low. It

[22] 'The Oradea Declaration'.

[23] Anita Deyneka, 'Building Bridges for God's Kingdom: Questions to Help Western Missions Think More Strategically', in Sharon Linzey, M. Holl Russin and Mark R. Elliott, *East-West Christian Organizations: A Directory of Western Christian Organizations Working in East Central Europe and the Newly Independent States Formerly Part of the Soviet Union* (Evanston: Berry Publishing, 1993).

[24] Kool and Penner, 'Theological Education in Eastern and Central Europe'.

[25] Kool, 'Leadership Issues in Central and Eastern Europe', 135-39.

[26] Kool, 'A Protestant Perspective on Mission in Eastern and Central Europe'.

[27] Miroslav Volf, 'Fishing in the Neighbor's Pond: Mission and Proselytism in Eastern Europe', in *International Bulletin of Missionary Research,* 20 (1996), cited in Kool, 'A Protestant Perspective on Mission in Eastern and Central Europe'.

resulted in a situation where the readiness and willingness of local people and churches to donate to missions in East European countries was 'overruled' by well-meaning western organizations and churches.[28] Their self-supporting capacity was strongly diminished or disappeared completely.

A fourth characteristic was the attempt to encourage partnership among the 200 evangelical mission organizations working in the region, for which purpose the Lausanne Committee for World Evangelization convened a summit conference in Budapest in 1991 on 'Evangelization in Post-Marxist Contexts'.[29] A six-point strategy for mission groups working in Eastern Europe and the former USSR was outlined, with the purpose of discouraging 'freelance entrepreneurial approaches': 1. Enabling churches and mission organizations in eastern countries to undertake their own work of evangelizing their own people; 2. Modelling and encouraging co-operation in the work of evangelization; 3. Going where Christ is not named or known; 4. Undertaking involvement over the longer term that aims to produce fruit that will remain; 5. Working only from an adequate understanding of the people and their contexts; 6. Working with complete ethical and financial integrity.[30]

A fifth characteristic was the establishing of two different kinds of mission agencies, illustrating the dilemma of doing mission the 'western way' or the 'eastern way', out of a sense of nostalgia. The first kind is the re-establishing of former mission agencies, like in Hungary: the *Evangélikus Külmissziói Egyesület* (Hungarian Lutheran Foreign Mission Society)[31] and the Liebenzell *Misszió Molnár Mária Alapitvány*,[32] both with strong roots in the past.[33]

The second kind is the establishing of mission agencies as branches of European mission agencies. In Hungary, as the fruit of regular visits of Piet and Joke Koen from the Netherlands, Wycliffe Hungary was established in 1998. Missionaries serve in South Asia, Romania, Croatia, Great Britain, Nigeria, Cameroun, Hungary and Papua New Guinea.[34]

---

[28] Penner, 'Western Missionaries in Central and Eastern Europe'.

[29] Lausanne Committee for World Evangelization: Budapest Summit Statement to those Working in Eastern Europe and USSR, 1st-7th September 1991; as quoted by James A. Scherer, 'Revolution in the East and Its Missionary Implications for Christians in the West', in *Dialog,* 31.2 (1992), 114.

[30] www2.wheaton.edu/bgc/archives/GUIDES/046.htm#5a (accessed 17th November 2014).

[31] http://ekme.lutheran.hu (accessed 2nd December 2014).

[32] www.liebenzell.hu/index.php?option=com_content&view=frontpage&lang=hu (accessed 2nd December 2014).

[33] Cf. Kool, *God Moves in a Mysterious Way.*

[34] www.wycliffe.hu (accessed 2nd December 2014). See also Klingsmith, 'Hungarian Missionary Sending Efforts'.

The birth of BSM Poland, a partner of Wycliffe, in 1995[35] is described by Scott Klingsmith who conducted ground-breaking research into indigenous East-Central European missionary-sending efforts that began in 2000.[36] Their missionaries were trained 'the Polish way', in the train to the mission field in Central Asia. His research showed the advantages Polish missionaries enjoyed working in Central Asia. The older ones especially already spoke Russian, the standard of living was not so different, and the cultural gap not as great as for westerners. Another advantage was that the Poles did not need visas. An interesting observation was that, 'since Poles do not have money, they focus on relationships. People they serve likewise have little money and value relationships'. Finally, Poles had experience of living under Soviet domination, and therefore go to Central Asia as fellow-sufferers.[37]

Also, the start of the Romanian mission movement was researched by Klingsmith.[38] He observes that there were already leaders with a broad national platform for spreading the vision. When they began to speak about the urgency of missions, they had a ready audience. Since the 1989 Revolution, Romania had sent short- and longer-term missionaries to a wide range of countries, including Afghanistan, Albania, China, Egypt, India, Iran, Ireland, Israel, Kenya, Libya, Macedonia, Moldova, Pakistan, Russia (particularly Siberia), Spain, Turkey, Ukraine, Uzbekistan and Vietnam. In addition, several people were working cross-culturally within Romania, particularly with Turks and Gypsies. Many Romanians had also been on short-term mission trips. The number of short-termers was undoubtedly in the hundreds. Many young people had served with Operation Mobilization and Youth with a Mission in various projects, and many mission schools and seminaries were encouraging or requiring a short-term experience as part of their programme.[39] Klingsmith tells us the story of the Hobans, serving in Albania from 1994, living at the same level as the villagers, and having to face hardships of various kinds there. They hauled water by donkey and for three years did not have a car. They went as newly-weds to the village of Pinet to establish a Christian presence, and were adopted and protected by the village. 'During the violence in 1997 many foreigners were evacuated, but the Hobans decided to stay. The villagers told them: "You'll be the last to die. First, we will die; then our children will die; only then would you die".'[40] In a sense, a western mission

---

[35] Klingsmith, 'Missionary Sending Movements: A Polish Case Study'. See also: www.bsm.org.pl/en/about_us/cooperation/wycliffe_bible_translators.html (accessed 2nd December 2014).

[36] Klingsmith, *Missions beyond the Wall.*

[37] Klingsmith, 'Missionary Sending Movements: A Polish Case Study'.

[38] Klingsmith, 'The Romanian International Mission'; 'Advantages Romanians Bring to Missions'; *Missions beyond the Wall.* See also Kool, 'The Church in Hungary and Central and Eastern Europe: Trends and Challenges', 155-59.

[39] www.eastwestreport.org/articles/ew13206.html

[40] Klingsmith, 'Missionary Sending Movements in East-Central Europe'.

organization had to be a role model for the initiative of Aletheia Church, even though some Western missionaries had created problems in Romania by their attitude. But even that was taken as an example to learn from: 'If this is what a missionary is, we can do a better job than they do. We have people who are more mature, better prepared, more experienced, and able to teach.'[41]

It is remarkable that in a poor country like Romania, the churches are able to support their local missionaries, one of them the Hoban family in Albania, with US$250 per month. One respondent of Scott Klingsmith emphasizes: 'Economics is not the biggest problem. People think first you have to have money. Not True. Money is only money. Most important is vision.'[42] The Aletheia Church was one of the first churches in Romania to send out missionaries without support from an outside organization and, even though at some point that was offered, the offer was declined. The leaders felt that 'God had called them to do it, so they asked God to supply the needs'.[43]

So in this period mostly short-term missionaries were sent, by local churches, without an agency to support them, without any cross-cultural training. Others were sent through a foreign mission agency or they just went by themselves, often without even their local church's knowledge.[44]

A final characteristic of this period was that the 'flow' of partnership was mainly from west to east. A strong sense of partnership was fostered when Christian communities round the world prayed for the churches struggling in the Soviet empire. The collapse of the USSR was seen as an answer to their prayers. Peter F. Penner directs attention to the paradox that when the doors finally opened for Christian mission, these churches that had survived the persecution of the Soviet empire were neglected by the rest of the world: 'After the changes, it seemed, the same churches the West was praying for were suddenly not useful any more'.[45] Many western missionaries did not co-operate at all with the churches in the Conference of European Churches (CEE) in ways appropriate to the situation of the latter. Instead, they chose to do it in ways that reflected their own cultural mores and missionary traditions.[46] In this period, scholarships offered opportunities to study in the West: so also an east-to-west flow began, and there were also 'exposure' visits to the West. Changes were in the air.

---

[41] Klingsmith, 'Missionary Sending Movements in East-Central Europe'.
[42] Klingsmith, 'Missionary Sending Movements in East-Central Europe'.
[43] Kool, 'The Church in Hungary and Central and Eastern Europe'.
[44] Personal communication of Ghiță Rițișan to author, 17th November 2014.
[45] Penner, 'Scripture, Community, and Context in God's Mission in the FSU', 10, cited in Kool, 'Trends and Challenges in Mission and Missiology in "Post-Communist" Europe', 29.
[46] Penner, 'Scripture, Community, and Context in God's Mission in the FSU'.

1998-2008: Disillusionment

The period of euphoria was followed by a period of disillusionment. There was a great sense of uncertainty regarding the direction of mission work. Copying 'nostalgia' models did not work, and copying 'imported' models did not work either. It became clear that still many shadows of the past were alive that needed to be taken seriously. In some places, they even grew stronger.

The first characteristic of this period of disillusionment was that shadows of the past were still alive.[47] Four such 'shadows' could be detected. The first was a lack of unity among the churches. An effective policy of the communist governments of divide and conquer was expressly to create mistrust and divisions between denominations and within the Christian congregations by spreading rumours and creating fear. As a result, Christianity in Central and Eastern Europe still suffers from many divisions. It still has a long way to go towards restoring relationships in a process of reconciliation. These divisions were reinforced by the countless independent mission initiatives imported from the West following the changes. A second, closely related, shadow of the past was mistrust. Communist government policy was to foster distrust and division between, and within, congregations by spreading rumour and fear. One could never be sure who the stool-pigeon was, or who informed on the congregations to the authorities. According to a Hungarian sociologist, the greatest obstacle to the 'changes' in society was the lack of trust.[48] If trust is lacking, co-operation stagnates, not only within the church and the congregations, but in relationships between denominations and church associations. No community-disrupting force is stronger than this one.[49] Even now, in many places throughout the CEE, the Christian community is wracked by division. The third shadow of the past was that Christians were considered to be second-class citizens, with limited opportunities. That affected their attitudes and mindsets. Many had an 'inferiority complex', while 'to be recognized as a believer was something similar to living with a physical handicap'.[50] Many were afraid of being involved in outreach and preferred to spend most of their time with other Christians, preferably from the same denomination. Where many did not learn to carry responsibility, it is interesting to note that, on the other side of the coin, many pastors often adopted an attitude of over-responsibility for their parishioners, in the sense

---

[47] Kool, 'A Protestant Perspective on Mission in Eastern and Central Europe'.

[48] I. Gábor Kovács, 'A Magyarországi Református Egyház Küldetése a Szociológus Szemével' (paper presented at *A Református Értelmiségi Konferencia. A Magyarországi Református Egyház balatonszárszói Soli Deo Gloria Konferenciatelepén*, 21st-23rd August 1998), 40.

[49] D. Machajdik and Juraj Kusnierik, *The Church in Central Europe: Not Prepared for Freedom* (Sen Research Papers: Bratislava: SEN, 1999), 17, cited in Kool, 'Trends and Challenges in Mission and Missiology in "Post-Communist" Europe', 28.

[50] Juraj Kusnierik and Milan Eieel, *Shadows of the Past: The Impact of Communism on the Way People Think in Post-Communist Society* (Sen Research Papers: Bratislava: SEN, 1997), 22, cited in Kool, 'A Protestant Perspective on Mission in Eastern and Central Europe'.

of being responsible for their personal decisions, their relationships, the quality of their family lives, etc. They took on a kind of a Christian *guru* role, without whom no major life decisions could be taken.[51] A fourth shadow of the past was the dichotomy between the public and the private. During the communist period, sometimes quite rigorous pressure was exercized to keep faith and religion in the private sphere. A ghetto mentality was the result. Churches were not allowed to be 'relevant', to speak to the context, and were pictured as outmoded, only for the 'old ladies with a scarf'. This dichotomy was reinforced by a nineteenth-century pietism with its narrow view of spirituality as a personal, existential and emotional relationship with God, which had a strong influence in Eastern Europe. An ongoing consequence is that the majority of Christians still live in two separate worlds.[52] It is this same theology which is critiqued by the younger generation. A strong emphasis towards integration of the Christian faith into all areas of life can be detected, based on a larger view of God and his Kingdom. There is now a growing interest in public theology. Kosta Milkov established the 'Balkan Institute for Faith and Culture' in Macedonia, with a vision of using the theological and cultural legacy of the Balkans to engage in a dialogue and debate with the most representative aspects of society, such as the university, the arts, the media, the governing structures, and other agents that form public opinion.[53] Marcel Măcelaru and Corneliu Constantineanu recently established the 'Institute for Faith and Human Flourishing' in Timişoara, Romania, with a distinctive vision statement of 'advancing the integration of earnest theological reflection, genuine Christian spirituality and transformative public engagement for life'.[54]

A second characteristic that strengthened the disillusionment was the fact that donors started to pull out, as new challenges arose – such as China. It was enlarged by increasingly high donor expectations, as mission agencies and churches in the West made more and more use of business models. These focused on short-term projects, dominated by a value-for-money perspective and characterized by a secular worldview. These models were strongly output-oriented, focusing on success and results. They clashed with post-communist realities that were not output-focused. The western paradigm of mission clashed with the East European mindset.

A third characteristic that led to disillusionment were conflicts and divisions, and the struggle for co-operation. An ambiguous view of the role of western missionaries emerged. Although there was definitely a sense of appreciation for what they did, critical voices could also be heard. With regard to the situation in the former Soviet Union, Peter Penner was

---

[51] Marsh Moyle, 'Shadows of the Past: The Lingering Effects of the Communist Mindset in the Church and Society', in *Transformation,* 16.1 (1999).

[52] Kusnierik and Eieel, 'Shadows of the Past', 23.

[53] www.rzim.eu/meet-our-associates-kosta-milkov (accessed 17th November 2014).

[54] Corneliu Constantineanu to author, 'Notes', email, 2016.

concerned not to dismiss the past fifteen years of struggle for co-operation between East and West as unworkable by re-emphasizing that much good had come from the West.[55] Speaking from the Romanian context, Dănuţ Mănăstireanu similarly credits western missionaries for their positive contribution, although he also refers to general discontent in post-communist Europe 'with the way most Western missionary agencies handled their relationships with nationals'.[56] Concerning co-operation with local churches, Mănăstireanu agrees with Penner that 'many western missions were building their own missionary empires as if no indigenous churches existed in former communist countries'.[57] A major problem facing many missionaries was their lack of cultural and contextual formation. As one of them expressed it: 'Our team had little understanding for cultural differences or the impact and need for contextualization. We came over with the mentality that what worked in the US would also work in Eastern Europe.'[58] Another confessed openly: 'Our understanding of the local church was basically non-existent.'[59]

The question could be asked: why did missionaries start 'building their empires'? Undoubtedly one factor was the shift in mindset in supporting missionaries, and the above-mentioned commercialization of mission. When they are not planting their own flags, or building 'memorials for (their) actions',[60] but working invisibly within existing structures, donors easily get the impression that their missionaries have not done enough to prove their success. Secondly, many missionaries who came to work in the post-communist world lacked understanding of the situation of the local church, because they were supported by or worked with a para-church organization and not with a particular church. They often work independently of local churches and they do not understand their important role. Their understanding of mission tends to be more pragmatically related to enhancing numerical growth rather than reflecting a good understanding of the biblical concept of mission. The predominant mission paradigm used in post-communist Europe by western missionaries is expansionist, reflecting a nineteenth-century colonial understanding of missionary activity, or what David Bosch refers to as the Enlightenment Mission Paradigm.[61] It conceives of mission as what takes place 'overseas', in a

---

[55] Penner, 'Scripture, Community, and Context in God's Mission in the FSU', 31.

[56] Dănuţ Mănăstireanu, 'Western Assistance in Theological Training for Romanian Evangelicals to 1989', in *East-West Church & Ministry Report,* 14.4 (2006), 7; and David Novak, 'Czech Evangelicals and Evangelism', in *East-West Church & Ministry Report,* 13.1 (2005).

[57] Mănăstireanu, 'Western Assistance in Theological Training for Romanian Evangelicals to 1989', 7; Novak, 'Czech Evangelicals and Evangelism', 8-10.

[58] Mănăstireanu, 'Western Assistance in Theological Training for Romanian Evangelicals to 1989', 2.

[59] Kool, 'Trends and Challenges in Mission and Missiology in "Post-Communist" Europe', 30.

[60] Penner, 'Scripture, Community, and Context in God's Mission in the FSU', 30.

[61] David J. Bosch, *Transforming Mission: Paradigm Shifts in the Theology of Mission* (American Society of Missiology Series, 16: Maryknoll, NY: Orbis Books, 1991), 274ff.

foreign country. It conjures up the image of an individualistic, 'heroic' missionary, sent by a mission society. Though some of these missionaries do try to work with the local churches and acquire an understanding of the local language, they are more inclined to operate as a culturally homogeneous group, often led by US team leaders and US-based mission agencies, instead of working with and partnering nationals. Penner observes that 'the team decides what their philosophy of ministry is, what can be done and what should not be done, often neglecting the existing national ministries'. He wonders 'how 'effective can such a mission be when it makes decisions on an unknown context without partnership in the decision-making process or at least with a mixed, not solely Western, team?'[62]

Thus in this period, a new search for partnership and co-operation could be detected, like the Romanian International Mission (Misiunea Internațională Romană – MIR) (1999).[63] A new paradigm started to emerge.

2009-2014: Towards a New, Innovative Mission Paradigm for Central and Eastern Europe

After a period of euphoria, marked by attempts to import western mission paradigms or to reintroduce mission paradigms of the past, a period of disillusionment followed. Neither of the two attempts seemed to be satisfactory for addressing the shadows of the past in the post-communist contexts of Central and Eastern Europe.

The scope of this presentation does not allow for a full treatment of the new, innovative and creative mission paradigm that is now emerging. It will be presented as a discussion starter. The term 'innovative' is used, because this paradigm differs from the 'traditional', western mission paradigm of 'overseas' mission. It relates to the flexible and creative way in which Central and East Europeans had to learn to find a way in and adapt to the challenges of their (post-communist) contexts. Similarly, to David Bosch in his seminal book *Transforming Mission*, in which he deals with elements of an emerging post-modern or ecumenical paradigm,[64] I will present four elements of this new, innovative mission paradigm for Central and Eastern Europe.

New Perspectives in Partnership and Co-operation

The first element is the emerging of new perspectives in partnership and co-operation. Two new perspectives in partnership and co-operation could be identified. One is the birth of indigenous mission agencies, with more

---

[62] Penner, 'Critical Evaluation of Recent Developments in the CIS', 129-30.

[63] See e.g. Klingsmith, 'The Romanian International Mission'.

[64] Bosch, *Transforming Mission*.

equal partnering of 'East' and 'West', while the other is that of crossing the traditional frontiers of the evangelical and ecumenical movement.

A remarkable feature of mission in Central and Eastern Europe, following the fall of the Berlin Wall, is that missionaries from these former communist countries can now be found in countries like Iran, Iraq, Afghanistan, Turkey, China, North Africa and Mongolia, sent by emerging indigenous mission agencies like the Pentecostal Association for Foreign Mission in Romania (APME), established in 2006.[65] In 2011, it had sent out 32 missionaries to countries or regions like Asia, Macedonia, Uganda, Albania, Southeast Asia, Sudan, Middle East, Namibia, Kosovo, Spain, Central Asia, Bulgaria, Ethiopia, East Asia, Mozambique, Madagascar, Africa and Papua New Guinea. By 2014, this number has increased to 51 missionaries in twenty countries.[66] 98% of the donations came from Romanians, 60-70% of them in Romania, and 30-40% from Romanians in the diaspora. This overall percentage of 98% was still 80% in 2011. These so-called 'diaspora Romanians' play a significant role in supporting cross-cultural mission, but also as missionaries themselves. Recently two couples from the diaspora Romanian community were sent out as missionaries through APME.

Another new perspective in partnership and co-operation are initiatives which cross the traditional evangelical and ecumenical divides. One such initiative is the Lausanne Orthodox-Evangelical Dialogue that has its roots in the Lausanne III in Cape Town consultation in 2010, and has been held now twice in Albania and once in Helsinki.[67] Such initiatives are also taking place at a local level, like the dialogue with some Orthodox representatives in Kiev, initiated by the Ukrainian Evangelical Theological Seminary.[68] The Global Christian Forum also shows that the traditional 'divides' are becoming obsolete. The WCC organized a consultation on the place of evangelism in theological education in Europe in 2012, and is now planning to publish a handbook on evangelism.[69] For organizations and churches in some western countries, such initiatives may not be easy to understand, and – probably more important – difficult to 'defend' to their donor constituency.

---

[65] www.apme.ro (accessed 1st December 2014). See also the chapter by G. Riţisan on APME in this volume.

[66] Personal communication with G. Riţisan by email with author, 17th November 2014.

[67] Available at: www.loimission.net (accessed 1st December 2014).

[68] Presentation at the Missiological Conference organized by the College of Theology and Education in Chişinău, Republic of Moldova: 'Evangelical Mission in the Eastern European Orthodox Contexts: Bulgaria, Romania, Moldova and Ukraine', 22nd-23rd March 2013. See also the chapter by Dănuţ Mănăstireanu on the Lausanne Orthodox Initiative elsewhere in this volume.

[69] www.oikoumene.org/en/press-centre/news/consultation-plans-a-handbook-on-evangelism-in-europe-1 (accessed 1st December 2014).

Missionaries, Local Churches and Their Members as Agents of Mission

A second element of an emerging new, innovative paradigm for mission is the growing vision of the nature of the local church as missional church, actively participating in mission. Elsewhere I have extensively dealt with the fact that since Edinburgh 1910 significant changes have taken place in the formation for mission and in the agents of mission.[70] The 'Antioch paradigm' as proposed by Wilbert Shenk, focuses on the organic and complementary mode of mission and offers an integral connection between the various agents of mission. In Central and Eastern Europe, a shift can be observed from the 'traditional' mission paradigm with the missionaries as sole agents of mission to the local church as an agent of mission.

The characteristics of the traditional – Edinburgh 1910 – paradigm are that missionaries are sent from the 'Christian' West to the 'non-Christian' rest, with missionaries as key 'active' players and the churches fulfilling a rather 'passive' role of praying and giving. In Europe, including Central and Eastern Europe, the mainline churches are struggling with a large passive fringe as a mission challenge; an active role is often played by the mission societies, who are the 'circle of people committed to mission'.

Shenk emphasizes that, in the Antioch paradigm, the church works out its missionary existence in the world. Mission in western culture calls for a 'fundamental reorientation of the church in modern culture to mission to its culture'.[71] In Luke's twofold model, he identifies the organic mode or the witnessing of the disciple community scattered under the impact of persecution and, secondly, the complementary mode: certain individuals set apart for itinerant ministry. Thus three kinds of agents of mission can be identified. First of all, Paul and Barnabas who, as cross-cultural missionaries, are sent on an innovative mission expedition to other cultures. Secondly, the Antioch church as a missional church, that 'organically' serves as an open, welcoming and witnessing community in its own urban setting, seeking to overcome the shadows of the past, and searching for ways to come 'out of the ghetto into the world'. The third kind of agent are the members of Antioch church, who are missionaries to their own community, families and workplaces. That implies a changed role for pastors in training church members to be 'local' – cross-cultural – missionaries in the secularized context. Developing a theology of work, and

[70] Anne-Marie Kool, 'Changing Images in the Formation for Mission: Commission V in the Light of Current Challenges: A Western Perspective', in Kenn Ross (ed), *Edinburgh 1910: Mission Then and Now* (Oxford: Regnum, 2009).

[71] Wilbert R. Shenk, 'The Training of Missiologists for Western Culture', in J. Dudley Woodberry, Charles E. Van Engen, and Edgar J. Elliston (eds), *Missiological Education for the 21st Century: The Book, the Circle and the Sandals: Essays of Paul E. Pierson* (Maryknoll, NY: Orbis Books, 1996); 'Training Missiologists for Western Culture', in *Changing Frontiers of Mission* (American Society of Missiology Series, 28: Maryknoll, NY: Orbis Books, 1999), cited in Kool, 'Changing Images in the Formation for Mission, 169.

training church members to be witnesses in their professions is related to this challenge.[72]

A Holistic Understanding of Mission

A third element of the unfolding innovative paradigm is the emergence of a holistic understanding of mission. In the previous two periods, evangelism and social action were often considered as two competing, unrelated elements of mission. The scope of this presentation does not allow for more than one example: Beginning of Life (BOL) (2002) Moldova.[73] BOL's first responses to the acute problems of Moldovan society were individual consultations with women in the abortion unit of the municipal hospital, and abortion prevention education for teens in schools, as the number of aborted children in Moldova during the year exceeded 50% of the number of children who were born. In 2006, BOL was reorganized to gain an extended official status and opportunities as a public association. In 2007, BOL began to develop a new programme to combat human trafficking and sexual violence in Moldova. In February 2009, a 'House of Change' was established as a rehabilitation centre for victims of human trafficking and sexual exploitation. In subsequent years, the team and the range of BOL projects expanded greatly. By 2013, BOL were running another four centres: the Urban Centre; the Psychological Art Studio; the 'Dream House' Prevention Centre for girls at risk; and a Humanitarian Aid Centre.

Local and Global Involvement in Mission

A fourth element of the emerging new mission paradigm emphasizes a closer connection between the 'local' – like mission work by the Antioch church in the local context – and the 'global', like the innovative mission work of Paul and Barnabas in cross-cultural settings. Mission has a worldwide dimension, as the whole church is called to take the whole gospel to the whole world, but the 'world' starts at our doorstep.[74] 'Local' and 'global' are different categories from 'home' and 'foreign' mission, dominating the traditional mission paradigm. More and more churches in Central and Eastern Europe, especially in Ukraine, Romania, Moldova and Bulgaria are sending missionaries to other countries. In this way, they also allow their local churches to gain an insight into world Christianity and reduce provincialism.

In the meantime, the reality of the slogan 'Mission in Six Continents', first introduced at the Conference on World Mission and Evangelism in

[72] Kool, 'Changing Images in the Formation for Mission'.

[73] www.bol.md (accessed 1st December 2014).

[74] Anne-Marie Kool, 'Grenzenlos Berufen – Trends, Gefahren und Aufgaben in Der Weltmission Heute', in *Transparent,* 2014.4 (2014): www.annemariekool. org/2014/11/trends-gefahren-und-aufgaben-in-der.html

Mexico City (1963), is slowly breaking through, after half a century (sic!).[75] At the World Mission Conference in Edinburgh in 1910, it dawned that the whole world, including Europe, was a mission field.[76] Revisiting mission in Europe should be high on our agenda too.[77] Ulrich Parzany reminds us that Europe is a unique mission field: it is 'post-Christian', which means 'that we do not start at zero'.[78] Europe has a long Christian history. Parzany continues: 'We have to be thankful for what the Lord did in building his church of true believers. Especially, we are thankful for the Reformation Movement and the renewal of churches through Pietism and revival movements during the last 300 years up to now.'[79] Viggo Sogaard adds, that one of the negative consequences is that 'Christian tradition produced immunization of many nominal Christians against the gospel'.[80] Even after 25 years, this assessment still stands, although there are significant differences in the religious situation of Western, Northern, Southern and Eastern Europe. There are also significant differences between the various Christian traditions.

Challenges for Mission in, to and from Central and Eastern Europe

After this first, historical part, with an analysis of 25 years of East European mission, we now direct our attention to the future, briefly outlining the challenges for mission in, to and from Central and Eastern Europe. Often mission work in the eastern part of Europe, 'East European mission', has been viewed from a western, West European or North American perspective. Publications on mission in this region were also dominated by this perspective, as newsletters and websites were – understandably – written under missionary or mission agency auspices, and by western missionaries. The expression 'understandably' is deliberately chosen, because western missionaries and mission agencies were responsible for raising funds for their own mission work, and often for their 'indigenous' co-workers as well. A second reason for the dominance of this 'missionary perspective' is that relatively little research has been undertaken by local scholars, and often the research that has been undertaken is sitting in someone's computer or desk drawer, or is available at a significant cost on the ProQuest website. 'Local' research and 'indigenous' writing and publication as well as distribution is still in its

---

[75] David J. Bosch, *Witness to the World: The Christian Mission in Theological Perspective* (London: Marshall, Morgan & Scott, 1980), 189.

[76] Cf. Kool, 'Changing Images in the Formation for Mission'.

[77] See my 'A Missiologist's Look at the Future: A Missiological Manifesto for the 21st Century' in the present volume, pp. 698–712..

[78] Ulrich Parzany, 'Cooperation in World Evangelization: A Call for Help from Europe', in *World Evangelization,* XVI.60 (1989).

[79] Parzany, 'Cooperation in World Evangelization'.

[80] Viggo Sogaard, 'Re-Evangelizing Europe: Utopia or Reality?', in *World Evangelization,* XVI.60 (1989).

infancy. It is a time-consuming and costly venture that does not yield quick results and is difficult to measure in terms of output.[81]

In the following section, an attempt is made to write on the challenges for mission in, to and from Central and Eastern Europe from a local, grassroots perspective. Therefore, a different wording is chosen, marking a shift from a predominantly geographical, West-East paradigm and direction, often referred to as 'Eastern European Mission', to a cross-cultural, multi-directional character.

The relative proximity of current areas of crises in the Middle East, Russia and China – often with a large percentage of young people searching for new meaning – combined with the strength and flexibility of this "non-western" mission movement – in the so-called evangelical Bible-belt countries like Romania, Ukraine, Moldova and Bulgaria[82] – provide the context for the challenges for mission in, to and from Central and Eastern Europe. They constitute the economic and geopolitical implications for mission in Central and Eastern Europe.[83]

The following six main challenges can be identified. The scope of this article does allow only for a brief treatment.

'Mission from the Margins'

The 10-12 million Roma (Gypsy) minority is considered one of the greatest challenges Europe faces. A massive exclusion is still going on in Europe, as well as in Eastern Europe. That is now a reality.[84] Many false negative images exist. Many European churches, including the Central and East European churches seek in various ways to respond to the Roma people, often living at the margins of society. At the same time, signs of what are generally referred to as 'revivals' among the Roma.[85] In 2014, an international conference was organized by a Chinese mission organization with 200 participants, half of them Roma pastors or Roma Christian

---

[81] Cf. J. Samuel Escobar, 'Evangelical Missiology: Peering into the Future at the Turn of the Century', in William D. Taylor (ed), *Global Missiology for the 21st Century: The Iguassu Dialogue* (Globalization of Mission Series: Grand Rapids, MI: Baker Book House, 2000).

[82] See e.g. Susan Wunderink, 'Eastern Europe's Evangelical Hub: A Scholar Discusses the Development of Evangelicalism in Ukraine', in *Christianity Today* (2008): www.christianitytoday.com/ct/2008/januaryweb-only/105-22.0.html

[83] I.K. in presentation at a conference with the theme: Revolutions in European Mission, organized by the European Evangelical Mission Association held in Bucharest, 18th-21st November 2014.

[84] Klaus-Michael Bogdal, *Europa Erfindet Die Zigeuner: Eine Geschichte Von Faszination Und Verachtung* (Berlin: Suhrkamp, 2011); 'Europe Invents the Gypsies:The Dark Side of Modernity', in *Eurozine,* 24 (February, 2012): www.eurozine.com/articles/2012-02-24-bogdal-en.html

[85] See e.g. Katharine Quarmby, 'Romani Pilgrims: Europe's New Moral Force', *Newsweek Limited*: www.myilibrary.com?id=662195>; Miroslav A. Atanasov, *Gypsy Pentecostals: The Growth of the Pentecostal Movement among the Roma in Bulgaria and Its Revitalization of Their Communities* (The Study of World Christian Revitalization Movements in Pentecostal/Charismatic Studies), (Lexington, KY: Emeth Press, 2010).

workers. As a result, national and regional indigenous Roma initiatives were established to network, connect and research for the sake of sharing the gospel and seeing transformation in Roma communities throughout Europe. The aims are fivefold: '1. Share the vision (with Roma leaders, non-Roma leaders, local churches, organizations, movements, mission organizations, different denominations, EU governments…); 2. Educate / empower / equip (Roma leaders, non-Roma leaders who are working among Roma, youth, church, movements); 3. Encourage transformation (in individuals, communities, whilst encouraging reconciliation between Roma and non-Roma); 4. Attract missionaries (research mission field, attract local and global missionaries, train missionaries); and 5. Encourage (local churches, ministries, mission initiatives).'[86] Little is known about 'revivals' going on in France and Spain, as well as in Slovakia, Romania, Serbia, Bulgaria, Finland and Russia. More research is needed to map the Roma Christian communities, the nature of these revivals, and who the Roma pastors leading these communities are. These Roma Christian communities are increasingly reaching out from the 'margins' to the majority society, as in Spain where more research has been undertaken.[87]

Giving Roma Christianity a face, taking steps towards getting to know Roma church history, will not only be beneficial in teaching the Roma churches, but also in helping the majority society to break out of entrenched stereotyped images and move from image to reality. In this process, a key motto should be: 'Nothing about us without us.'[88]

Theological and Missiological Education

After 1989-1991, there has been a great need for well-equipped leaders in the churches of Eastern Europe, able to deal with the burning issues of the context we face, like the churches' response to nationalism and ethnicity, the revitalization of the churches for local and global mission, how to communicate the gospel in a relevant way to the secularized de-churched (nominal) and un-churched people of former communist countries, and how to move towards reconciliation in church and society. A common difficulty these churches and their educational institutions face, according to Jason Ferenczi, is the need to 'develop leaders who can articulate a Christian worldview in the context of extremely pluralistic societies, in a way that answers the deep spiritual questions of a highly educated population'.[89]

---

[86] http://romanetworks.com/vision-and-mission (accessed 18th February 2016).

[87] See e.g. Paloma Gay Y Blasco, 'Gypsy/Roma Diasporas. A Comparative Perspective', in *Social Anthropology,* 10.2 (2002).

[88] Anne-Marie Kool, 'Eastern European Churches' Responses to the Roma People', in *Great Commission Center International. International Roma Consultation: Roma for the Nations, Budapest 29th September-3rd October 2014* (Budapest: unpublished, 2014).

[89] Jason E. Ferenczi, 'Theological Education in the Former Soviet Union: Some Recent Developments', in *Religion in Eastern Europe,* 21.6 (2001), 1.

Peter Penner sums up some of the failures of his generation in establishing new theological institutions in the former Soviet Union: '(We) have failed to prepare adequate national leadership and to keep the needed balance between the indigenous and the expatriate influences... to invest in more quality instead of bricks and mortar, in closer links between church and theological institutions, in better co-operation between institutions, preparing these institutions to merge, if necessary, in order to become mutually stronger and more relevant, and also to invest in a stronger network with the global, and specifically European, family of theological institutions.'[90]

Wojtek Kowalewski identifies a number of major challenges for theological education.[91] The first one calls for 'the recognition of the holistic content of the gospel... which is to be relevant to all spheres of life and is not just limited to the "spiritual"'.[92] Another challenge is that of being relevant to the local context, that of '"hearing" and "understanding stories" of contemporary people... and seeking new ways of missional interaction with these stories within broadly understood Christian community life'.[93] A third challenge is to 'develop a new theology of openness to others, a theology of dialogue, a theology of reconciliation understood in spiritual and social terms'.[94] Kowalewski expresses his hope that this radical rethinking will prevent a further marginalization of evangelical Christianity, which is caused by an approach to mission as a form of a '"hit-and-run" attitude... based on individual as opposed to communal confrontation and consequently putting great emphasis on "the saving of individual souls rather than a broader healing of the land or any consideration of the social implications of obedience to the gospel"'.[95]

One of the important issues raised time and again is that of co-operation. There are a number of national and regional networks for theological education, but they operate rather independently of each other. Another challenge in theological education is that of creative educational methods, like (hybrid) distance-learning, and exposure visits, in which students are 'plunged' into new contexts to experience the diversity of our society and the power of what God can do. Increasingly, theological schools in Central and Eastern Europe are making links with schools in the 'majority world', with theological schools in, for instance, Africa and Asia, but it is still

---

[90] Penner, *Theological Education as Mission*, 344.

[91] Wojciech Kowalewski, *A Theology of Mission for Post-Communist Poland: Towards an Integrative Approach* (Cardiff: Cardiff University, 2004); 'Missiological Challenges in Polish Evangelical Theological Education', in Peter F. Penner (ed), *Theological Education as Mission* (Schwarzenfeld, Germany: Neufeld Verlag, 2005).

[92] Kowalewski, 'Missiological Challenges in Polish Evangelical Theological Education', 337.

[93] Kowalewski, 'Missiological Challenges in Polish Evangelical Theological Education', 337.

[94] Kowalewski, 'Missiological Challenges in Polish Evangelical Theological Education', 339.

[95] Kowalewski, 'Missiological Challenges in Polish Evangelical Theological Education', 339, quoting Malcolm Clegg.

incidental. In cases where it takes place, it proves to be very beneficial, as mutual issues are recognized.

In many CEE theological institutions, 'getting a degree' seems to be more important than education for transformation, of oneself, and of church and society, related to the challenge of the relevance of missiological research and education.[96] It is important to research mission practice by analyzing what has been done in mission in a particular country or denomination in CEE over the past 25 years, comparing it with developments worldwide and across denominations and countries, and drawing lessons for the future.

Another challenge is co-operation between mission practitioners and missiologists, to enable cross-fertilization to take place between mission theory and mission practice, so characteristic for the discipline of missiology.[97] In order to facilitate and promote the study of contextual mission theory on the mission practice of Central and Eastern Europe, the Central and East European Association for Mission Studies[98] was established in 2002 by a number of people interested in the study of mission in this region. We hardly knew of each other's areas of research, teaching or publications. Since this – pioneering – situation in Central and Eastern Europe differs so much from countries in Western Europe, for instance, where missiology has been well established for one and a half centuries, the need was increasingly felt to establish a special Central and East European international and interdenominational platform to serve and to co-ordinate the modest initiatives in this field, linked internationally with the International Association of Mission Studies.[99]

A related challenge in missiological education and research is nurturing integrity in mission practice and methods, to uncover secular world views

---

[96] Cf. Joshua T. Searle and Mykhailo N. Cherenkov, *A Future and a Hope: Mission, Theological Education, and the Transformation of Post-Soviet Society* (Eugene, OR: Wipf & Stock, 2014). See also Anne-Marie Kool, 'From Marginalization to Revitalization: Missiology's Contribution to the Renewal of Theological Curricula of Theological Institutions in Eastern European Contexts', in Mihai Malancea (ed), *Evangelical Mission in the Eastern Orthodox Contexts: Bulgaria, Romania, Moldova, Ukraine* (Chişinău: Universitatea Divitia Gratiae, 2013).

[97] Kool, 'Bridging the Gap between Mission Theory and Mission Practice in Mission in Central and Eastern Europe', in *Beyond the Iron Curtain: Being Church in Central and Eastern Europe Twenty Five Years after the Political Changes* (Heiligenkreuz, 2015).

[98] www.ceeams.org (accessed 1st December 2014).

[99] The aims of CEEAMS are similar to those of IAMS: to promote the scholarly study of theological, historical and practical questions relating to mission in Central and Eastern Europe; to disseminate information concerning mission among all those engaged in such studies and among the general public; to relate studies in mission to studies in theological and other disciplines; to promote fellowship, co-operation and mutual assistance in mission studies; to organize international conferences of missiologists; to encourage the creation of centres of research; and to stimulate publications in missiology.

in our missionary methods and to strengthen biblical perspectives in our mission work.[100]

Missionary Spirituality[101]

In 2004, Adrian Dorin Giorgiov analyzed sources of stress and potential burn-out among Hungarian Baptist pastors in Romania, focusing on accountability systems that might help to alleviate the problem. The study indicated that isolation and overwork took their toll in that 77.6% of the pastors indicated estrangement from their fellow pastors, and that only a few pastoral couples have close friends in church, 'because shared confidential information might be compromised'.[102] Unfortunately, not much has changed ten years later.

The related challenge is how to maintain and nurture a healthy missionary spirituality as a pastor or mission worker, when having to operate under the pressures of well-meaning donors operating with a business mindset, of getting good value for money. There is a need for a spirituality that functions as a kind of 'lifeline' in our daily mission work, supporting a healthy balance between action and reflection, and between work and rest.

Jonathan Bonk emphasizes the importance of such a missional spirituality: 'God can and does love the world, but human beings are so constituted that they cannot. When we try, our expressions of love for the multitudes inevitably degenerate into pious posturing. We are called upon to love one another, spouse, neighbour, stranger and enemy – whatever the cultural or cross-cultural context.'[103] He adds that this is a great challenge for each of us, even the most pious but, without it, our missiology is not worth much. 'Wherever the context of our missionary work, unless we fall into the ground and "die" at this personal level, our missiology means nothing. Given the ways in which we missiologists have come to envision and project the Christian task, this fact is of profound missiological import.'[104]

In order to restore and nurture relationships, with God, with each other, with ourselves, and with our community, time is needed – time to reflect, time to repent, time to seek healing and restoration by God. But the paradox is that time is just what is most lacking, as we often hear. Possibly we could speak also about a crisis in the structuring of our time. The order of time

[100] J.N.J. (Klippies) Kritzinger, 'Nurturing Missional Integrity' (paper given at the KRE-CIMS Seminar in Budapest in October 2011).

[101] Kool, 'Leadership Issues in Central and Eastern Europe', 144ff.

[102] Kool, 'Leadership Issues in Central and Eastern Europe', 144ff.

[103] Jonathan Bonk, William D. Taylor (ed), 'Engaging Escobar… and Beyond', in *Global Missiology for the 21st Century: The Iguassu Dialogue* (Globalization of Mission Series: Grand Rapids, MI: Baker Book House, 2000), 53.

[104] Bonk and Taylor, 'Engaging Escobar… and Beyond', 53; Kool, 'Leadership Issues in Central and Eastern Europe'.

established by God in creation through the periods of Sabbath – in which people were to turn not to themselves but to God alone – has been replaced by an order of time determined by their work requirements. Instead of religion, our order of time is determined by the requirements of economy and consumption, which has serious missiological repercussions.

The 'Commercialization' of Mission Organizations and Churches

An important challenge is to 'bring our missionary methods under the Word of God', as it was coined by Lesslie Newbigin in 1962.[105] Especially in North America, but increasingly also in Europe and CEE, churches and mission organizations operate on the basis of secular business principles instead of theological principles.[106] They focus more on output and results instead of fruits growing in a hidden way, on value for money instead of free grace, on success stories instead of sacrifice and commitment, on quantity instead of quality, on superficial quick results instead of long-term transformation and incarnation, on clinging to power instead of submitting oneself to humble service. Thus secular values are permeating the church, robbing it of its missionary zeal. Fortunately, it would be a grave mistake to generalize.

Otherness and Reconciliation

One of the burning challenges is that of 'otherness', especially related to the Roma (Gypsies), but also to the refugees and migrants. It calls for a theology of reconciliation.[107] It is well known that Miroslav Volf has dealt extensively with the concept of 'otherness' and ethnicity, dealing specifically with his own, Croatian, roots. He is of the opinion that otherness should be placed at the centre of theological reflection. 'The future of the whole world depends on how we deal with ethnic, religious and gender otherness'.[108] Volf's response to otherness is a 'theology of embrace'.[109] On the basis of his Central-East European experiences, he calls attention to the fact that evangelical and pietistic groups have forgotten about the importance of reconciliation between people because their faith has become a matter of an individual relationship between God and man. In other words, the doctrine of reconciliation is reduced to

---

[105] Lesslie Newbigin, 'Bringing Our Missionary Methods under the Word of God', in *Occasional Bulletin from the Missionary Research Library,* 13.11 (1962). See also Kool, 'Changing Images in the Formation for Mission'.

[106] *The Thailand Report on Secularists: Christian Witness to Secularized People,* Lausanne Occasional Paper No. 8 (Lausanne Committee for World Evangelization, 1980).

[107] See my other contribution in this volume: 'Eastern European Churches Engaging Roma People: Historical and Missiological Perspectives', pp. 522–545.

[108] As preceding.

[109] Miroslav Volf, *Exclusion and Embrace: A Theological Exploration of Identity, Otherness, and Reconciliation* (Nashville, TN: Abingdon Press, 1996).

'reconciliation of the soul with God'. People are seen as sinners before God, they are called to repent, to receive forgiveness and a new life in Christ. The problem is that this central belief is considered to have consequences only for private morality, for 'Sunday', with no consequences for 'Monday' or the other days of the week or for other areas of life. The problem of otherness is an 'anti-mission' imperative, which divides and which hinders people from crossing cultural and ethnic barriers with the gospel.

Conclusions

What has been achieved in 25 years after the fall of the Berlin Wall? A revolution has taken place in mission in Central and Eastern Europe. The new mission paradigm is not a copy-and-paste variety of the western mission paradigm, but a new innovative mission paradigm is emerging, characterized by suffering instead of by success, focusing on individual and community, instead of the sole individualistic focus of the West. This new paradigm bears contours of the Antioch paradigm with a threefold focus on the agents of mission, also focusing on the local church and its members. It is enriched by a two-way partnership model in which both partners learn from each other and are invigorated by the different perspectives they bring to the table. There is also a mutual honesty in challenging the others' fundamental presuppositions on what mission is all about.

It was a naïve presupposition of western missionaries and mission agencies to try to mould Central and East European mission to fit our western models. That did not work. Coming out of a period of four, and in some cases seven, decades of suffering, mission as suffering is a more adequate paradigm than that of success. In this emerging new paradigm focusing on God's mission, Peter Kuzmič's words written 25 years ago, are well-chosen and still valid:

> We need enablers, we need partners, we need better trained missionaries, servants, credible witnesses who help bring the whole Gospel, which... covers proclamation of truth and exhibition of love, manifestation of power and integrity of life. In the task of world evangelization, it will also require less competition and more co-operation, less self-sufficiency and more self-denial, less ambition and more willingness to serve, less of a drive to dominate and more of the desire to develop.[110]

[110] Peter Kuzmič, 'How to Teach the Truth of the Gospel', in J.D. Douglas (ed), *Proclaim Christ until He Comes* (Minneapolis, MN: World Wide Publications, 1990), 201.

Twenty-Five Years of Mission Movement in Central and Eastern Europe: An Indigenous Perspective

Alexandru Vlasin

Introduction

Since the Evangelical churches[1] located in the Central and East European countries represent only a minority of the Christian population, there is little research concerning them in regard to Christian mission. Most of the academic investigation has been developed by western missionaries.[2] Therefore, through the present paper, an indigenous view of the Christian mission movement, limited to the Evangelical churches in Central and Eastern Europe (further known as CEE), can be presented.

The present research results from a desire to analyze the last twenty-five years, after the fall of the Iron Curtain, followed by comments concerning potential future developments. Consequently, there are a few statements that need to be made. First, a distinction needs to be made between the ministry developed by international mission bodies in the CEE nations and the mission work initiated by the people from this region in order to reach other countries. To a certain degree, our research incorporates both. The first section deals with the ministry developed by western missionaries, while the second deals with the missionary work initiated by nationals. Secondly, the research cannot reveal the entire work God has developed in this part of the world. It is limited to the view of the interviewers and to the capacity of the researcher to craft their answers. Further research could analyze the perspective of western missionaries working in this part of the world to bring in the other side of the picture. Therefore, such limitations could spur a future research project.

For the purpose of this research, a qualitative methodology was used with semi-guided interview questions. The interviews were taken in a

---

[1] The Evangelical churches in CEE countries are also known as Protestant churches that incorporate three major denominations: the Pentecostal Church, the Baptist Church and the Brethren Church. These churches commonly formed local Evangelical Alliance branches and are usually the dominant evangelical churches in the country. They are distinct from the mainline churches which are either the Catholic Church or the Orthodox Church.

[2] See Scott Klingsmith, 'Factors in the Rise of Missionary Sending Movements in East-Central Europe' (PhD thesis, Trinity International University, 2002); see also the work produced and published by Anne-Marie Kool: www.annemariekool.org

direct, face-to-face discussion approach.[3] The number of participants was twelve. All participants are mission leaders representing either a local branch of an international mission organization or a specific denomination in a particular country.[4] The respondents are from eight countries in Central and Eastern Europe.[5] The themes discussed include the impact of the fall of the Iron Curtain on the churches in CEE countries, the contribution of western churches to mission development in CEE countries, and potential future ways to develop international mission work in this part of the world.

The interview guide included six major questions with some additional questions as seen below:

1. *What was the impact of the fall of the Iron Curtain with regards to mission in your country?* Additional questions were: What happened to the churches after the fall of the Iron Curtain? What was the impact of that event in your country regarding mission?
2. *What was the contribution of the missionaries coming from the West to your country?* With the help of this question, we also discussed the types of activities and practical help received by the national churches. Moreover, theological and missiological concepts were presented as understood by locals and taught by western missionaries. Furthermore, a third aspect was acknowledged in the set of the skills developed by local church leaders and missionaries with the help of foreign missionaries. Also, the question opens the discussion about what the interviewers learned to do in practice as they worked alongside western missionaries.
3. *How do you think missionaries coming from the West affected mission development in your own country?* The intention was to see how western missionaries helped develop indigenous mission in their receiving country.
4. *If there were no western missionaries in your country starting with tonight, what would you do in mission?* In other words, what mission work would you do tomorrow if no foreign missionaries were allowed to stay in your country?
5. What missionary activities have you started or initiated on your own, without being helped by westerners?
6. What do you think will happen in the next twenty-five years in mission in our part of the world?

---

[3] The interviews took place in Kiev (June 2014) and Bucharest (September 2014) on the occasion of international mission gatherings.

[4] All the participants represent mission organizations operating under the denominational groups in their countries. The denominational groups are the Pentecostal, Baptist and Brethren churches. These churches started their mission agency within their own structure or a separate mission agency under their umbrella. Half of the participants belong to the Baptist groups. The other half is equally shared between Pentecostal groups and Brethren groups.

[5] We will use regions when analysing the interviews, as follows: CIS includes Russia, Belarus and Ukraine; Central Europe (CE) includes Poland and Hungary; Eastern Europe (EE) includes Romania, Moldavia and Bulgaria.

The Interviews' Brief Transcripts

The words of the participants are more powerful than any quantitative analysis of their responses.[6] Therefore, annotated elective quotes from the interviewees will be introduced in order to better understand: a) the participants' usage of mission theory concepts phrased in their own words; b) their feelings and reflection regarding relationships with the western missionaries; c) their hopes and wishes for the future missions movement. Therefore, the interviews' transcripts were organized in the order of the questions used in the interview guide:

1. Question number one: *What was the effect of the fall of the Iron Curtain with regards to mission in your country?* The answers to the first question were divided into two categories: one demonstrating the positive impact of the fall of the Iron Curtain upon the CEE countries. The other category is the negative impact perceived by the respondents as a result of the transition to freedom.

The positive impact was supported by all the interviews who mentioned that the fall of the Iron Curtain was a release from communist bondage and that now freedom had come, bringing more opportunities to travel and more opportunities for evangelism and church planting. In essence, they said: 'We discovered there is something more beyond our region. We discovered a new world' (I.EE). 'There are no limits to preaching any more. People started to respect us as the Evangelical Church' (R.CIS). 'We started to create a new worldview for ourselves and for our churches' (D.CE). 'We started to organize events very easily, quickly. It was so easy to do them' (M.EE). 'We started to learn new languages. Then we started to do public evangelism. We got in contact with mission organizations from abroad' (V.EE).

Other respondents said that 'a lot of missionaries from abroad started to come in and eventually we were allowed to have them in the country. Then we had opportunities to evangelize and to send people abroad' (G.EE). While others talked about 'a sense of a spiritual revival, a moment when our country realized that we could again do missions as we did before communism, before 1944' (A.CE). Another mentioned that 'a lot of resources arrived, a lot of missionaries brought material things and help, and we could see stadiums full of people who heard the gospel' (P.EE). All these are answers which bring out the positive impact of the fall of the Iron Curtain.

The negative impacts were also revealed with phrases like: 'We started to have a lot of problems. We started to understand that once freedom was here, it was not easy to change our mentality. Maybe the political

---

[6] In order to protect the identity of the participants, their names will not be given in full nor will they be connected with the organizations or mission bodies they represent. Therefore, codes will be used as follow: the initial letter of the participants' name followed by the region they belong to (see also footnote 5). For example, a person named Alexandru from Romania will receive the code: A.EE.

environment had changed, but not our mentality. People didn't know how to handle freedom; they didn't know what to do with it' (A.CE). The image of the Evangelical churches was perceived as being a 'foreign entity, not of the land, not of the national people major group' (P.EE). So, as missionaries came in, a lot of activities and a lot of evangelism has been done but local people would say: 'Oh, these foreign Evangelical groups are not ours, it's not part of our own culture, they were not created in our own nation.' Thus, in some areas, some damage was done to the local Evangelical churches.

2. Question number two: *What have missionaries done to help the national church?* First, the participants talked about social work activities developed by western missionaries such as: centres for disabled people, orphanages, day and night centres, and humanitarian aid for poor families. Moreover, missionaries also got involved in teaching English, creating seminars for state schools in the area of public health or social issues, in sports activities, and camp ministries. Additionally, Christian bookstores and libraries were started. Books were translated into the vernacular languages or brought from abroad. A lot of practical help was also received in the field of community development, and even agricultural projects were initiated. All the interviewees agree that the western missionaries' contribution was immense towards the social and spiritual development of their countries.

Secondly, when theological and missionary schools were discussed, participants' answers were: 'Well, they taught us a lot of doctrine. They told us about their experience in mission. They helped us to create and organize mission work' (G.EE). One respondent mentioned that 'the missionaries actually explained the missiological understanding of organising a mission agency. We began to learn that mission was to be found in the Bible. However, for many years it looked as though we couldn't understand it. Our understanding was so limited that we did not get involved. Although we preached about mission, we did not get involved in it. This is what we started to get from those missionaries coming from abroad' (I.EE). Another participant said: 'All of a sudden we started to understand what holistic mission was. The westerners, yes, they helped us materially, but also started to develop in us a mentality, a way of thinking missiologically' (M.EE).

Nevertheless, there were people who mentioned that 'these missionaries have not taught us how to do mission' (V.EE). In fact, said another interviewee, missionaries have said nothing about mission for ten years. He continued with: 'Western missionaries only started to tell us about mission after 2000' (D.CE). When asked to explain this answer further, the respondent couldn't explain why, but continued to say that 'unfortunately, only 25% of the missionaries that were coming to our country were efficient or helpful'. Other participants commented that 'missionaries just came to learn a new language and be in another country' (P.EE).

However, when the interviews talk about the western missionaries' contribution to teaching mission, there seems to be plenty of input. One of the interviewers said: 'We caught a vision for international mission. We understood eventually that *we* needed to be missionaries as well. We understood the importance of the sacrifice' (N.CIS). Another participant said. 'We understood what the correct motivation for mission was. We understood generosity – that this was a theological concept and what we needed to teach East European people. We understood that we needed to support our own missionaries. We understood and we continue to learn how to help our churches develop mission' (I.EE). Other said: 'Eventually we acknowledged our mission potential and the need to be bold in evangelism' (D.CE). Yet another participant said: 'We learned how to take care of our own missionaries. We understood how to help other nations, that we needed to help them to develop mission in their own countries' (M.EE).

Thirdly, as the interview continued, a further question asked was: what skills have you learned from western missionaries? Participants mentioned: gospel presentation and ministry skills for planting churches; building trust and healthy relationships to promote co-operation among different churches and denominations; working with people outside the churches; organizing short mission trips; ways of mobilizing churches for mission and how to administer an office for external missions. All mentioned that these skills developed in a one-to-one encounter with the missionaries they worked with.

3. Question number three: How do you think missionaries coming from the West affected mission development in your own country? The answers below are again classified into negatives and positives.

The negatives are: 'They did not help us much. They came to our country with no strategy and we understood that' (V.EE.). Another answer was: 'You know… they had their own agenda' (M.EE). Others mentioned that some missionaries had immoral behaviour when they arrived on the field, and also said that 'basically they wanted to do their own activity, their own things; they were not really interested in us and in mission as such' (D.CE). 'A lot of them did not establish relationships with local churches. Others were more interested in building churches. They created their own mission organizations. They didn't help me because I had my own plans' (R.CIS). One interesting answer mentioned that 'missionaries did not tell us that we also needed to do mission. We were not told by them that we also needed to engage in world mission' (M.CIS).

However, the positive impact of western missionaries was obvious: 'These missionaries helped us in our churches, supporting our own missionaries, linking them with western missionaries and western mission organizations' (I.CIS). 'They worked alongside us to develop missions. They started to teach us practical work. They also helped us financially to develop offices for mission and with their example, we were encouraged by them' (V.EE). Another stated that 'when we looked to the missionaries and their sacrifice in coming over, we said, "If they can do it here, we can definitely do it somewhere else." So we were encouraged in doing mission' (D.CE). Western missionaries opened the world for local churches. They helped pastors and church members travel for short mission trips. 'We started to learn how to form teams and how to work in teams. We started to learn how to recruit workers and the process of recruiting missionaries. We understood how to interview the candidates. We understood how to start promoting missions in our churches, how to start a mission agency. There are many aspects in which missionaries had an impact in developing mission in our country' (G.EE, V.EE). Another said that 'the western missionaries' sacrifice by going into spiritually very difficult areas to plant churches in our country helped us do the same' (I.CIS).

4. Question number four: *If there were no western missionaries in your country starting with tonight, what would you do in mission?* Someone said: 'We would continue to go on as if nothing had happened. It doesn't affect us at all. It's all right' (I.CIS). Others said: 'For some of our churches and some of the projects we have, it would be a disaster' (N.CIS; M.CIS. A.CE). Another said: 'If the missionaries left, then we would eventually employ our own people; the local people should do what the missionaries are doing right now. If the missionaries left, we would mobilize the church and we would continue to do the mission work ourselves' (G.EE, V.EE). 'Our own evangelism would drop, because most of the evangelism in our country is done by missionaries,' said another participant (P.EE). Another said: 'Our foreign English schools would suffer; the number has dropped lately anyway' (D.CE). And another mentioned that: 'Without them, we would continue to work together in our country. We do not depend on their financial assistance or their money, in either the theological education or the missionary challenges we face' (G.EE; I.CIS; V.EE). Someone else said: 'Well, we would lose a lot of good human resources' (P.EE). And then one said: 'We would eventually start to do the work inside and outside the church ourselves' (I.EE).

5. Question number five: *What missionary activities have you started or initiated on your own, without being helped by the Westerners?* One participant said that '70% of the money that we are using right now in one of the social projects comes from abroad. However, the initiative, the design of the project and the human effort is entirely our own. We don't depend on the missionaries' work, but we do depend on their money' (M.CIS). Another participant said: 'Well, we started to send missionaries without the help of westerners. We want to create a framework for the new generation to be mission-minded and that is our desire, to be our local passion' (N.CIS). Another said that 'all our initiatives after the Revolution in 1990, everything we started, projects and everything, was initiated by western missionaries. However, now we want to do it on our own' (I.CIS). One of the respondents said: 'There was a missionary in my country; he

worked here for twenty years. This missionary said: When I go to a local pastor and ask him, "Would you like to start a project, to do something together?" most of the time I get the answer: "Yes, let's do it, but I'm leading it. We will do it my way"' (M.EE).

The western missionaries are generally acknowledged by people from CEE countries as being the 'experts with expertise' in the field of evangelism, church planting and other mission work. However, some respondents mentioned that missionaries might not understand the real life situation in the host countries (D.CE; R.CIS). Therefore, local people plan to use the mistakes made by missionaries to advance their work for the Kingdom (D.CE). For instance, in adapting evangelistic methods to the mindset of the nationals (A.CE). Moreover, some participants said that, in international mission, they helped western missionaries and missionary agencies (partners of East European churches) better contextualize the message in countries with similar cultural traits as theirs (N.CIS. A.CE). Moreover, mission work initiated by nationals included entering places where Westerners were not accepted or wanted to go (M.EE).

Furthermore, there are various projects started by the nationals with no western influence or support. Such work includes initiative for Roma ethnic groups, projects in hospitals, jail ministry, and other social projects started by local churches. Thus, this is proof there is now initiative among people in East European countries. The leaders of national churches now understand that they need to take the initiative and it is obvious that there is a lot of initiative visible nowadays.

6. The sixth and last question: *What do you think will happen in the next twenty-five years in mission, in our part of the world?* Somebody said: 'Hopefully, we will have stability in the church so we can send missionaries from our own churches' (P.EE). Someone else said that 'interest for mission would grow in our churches. The number of pastors and schools that would include missions would grow. God calls more people into international mission. And sending people on short-term mission trips would help us to send people on long-term mission trips' (V.EE).

It seems there is interest and growth within the area of serving cross-culturally within the borders of their own country, as with Roma and other nationalities. Nevertheless, sending missionaries to Asia or Africa is also developing as well. Some also said that 'we continue to be influenced by the West, but then we must make sure that we are working together rather then separately' (A.CE). Another said that he believed mission 'has not reached every member of the churches right now, and the passion for mission will eventually reach the entire church, everyone – the members and the leaders' (P.EE).

Someone else said that: 'I can foresee better co-operation between the churches and a great number of missionaries would be sent and supported by our nations' (A.CE). Someone even mentioned that the Catholic Church was willing to work together with them in mission projects, shaping their missiological understanding and the spirit of mission (D.CE). Another said that 'the old model of sending missionaries is kind of dying out and a new model should replace it quickly', meaning a church revival (A.CE). Someone else ventured further to suggest that a model of 'Orthodox Church' in mission could also emerge within the Evangelical Church where the support comes from the local government and not only from the traditional source – for example, local church offerings (M.EE).

'Mission-minded local churches will prevail, joined by the increased desire to do mission,' thinks another participant (P.EE). A few respondents mentioned that mission schools would be started and more missionaries would be sent in the future (G.EE; R.CIS; V.EE; I.CIS). Another respondent said: 'We are definitely going to have, in the next twenty-five years, a sending system of our own, one that would be 100% our own. And if we are able to develop that, then we will have the independence of sending missionaries without the help of others' (I.EE). Even more, one mission leader said that 'evangelism and social justice will continue to be combined, and this will help us make progress in our mission' (N.CIS).

Interpretation and Observations

In his book *Revolutions in World Mission,* Yohannan advised western missionaries and churches to pray and support the local missionaries.[7] Hence, this research revealed the help received and its impact on the targeted countries. Moreover, within the co-operation between western and eastern countries, it is important to see if mission work was limited to the western church helping East Europeans churches to do the job. Or is there more to it?

Analyzing the above answers to the research questionnaire and looking at what is actually happening in Central and East European countries, we have to admit it is very encouraging. But there is still more work to be done. The national churches in Eastern Europe are still in a learning process; however, we can see the shift from the point when western missionaries had a major role in teaching and modelling cross-cultural mission and employing social justice activities, to the point where local churches and leaders started to take the initiative. This shift is from dependency to independence. However, the process will perhaps continue to interdependence when the two parties will partner for the sake of the gospel. This is fascinating and calls for celebration, bringing hope for the future.

Below are a few general comments and an overview interpretation of the research. Later, we will venture into making some suggestions for further co-operation among Western and East European mission agencies and

[7] K.P. Yohannan, *Revolution in World Missions* (GFA Books, 2002), 42-45.

churches with the hope of seeing mission develop more in this part of the world.

The missionaries' work invested in East European countries in the past 25 years is surely bringing fruit. We can clearly see that after the fall of the Iron Curtain there was an abundance of missionaries who were active in many areas of church and social life. Without doubt, this influenced the local churches and spurred their interest in engaging in similar work. Even though some missionaries' negative example and influence was acknowledged by the local churches, they displayed maturity in dealing with it. The desire of national believers for mission and evangelism, coupled with the example and resources of international missionaries, allowed the region to experience great development, not only in the number of local congregations, but also in the expansion of vision for mission beyond the country's borders. Moreover, local churches were eventually able and willing to openly engage in social work activities, and to assist in the needs of local communities. With the resources received, they were now agents of social change for local administrations, and their communities benefited.[8] Under communism, evangelical believers were known as good neighbours, but now they were viewed as good Samaritans. Of course, this was made possible with the help of western Evangelical churches, which sent many resources – in people, goods, and money.

In many countries behind the Iron Curtain, theological education was another domain little developed before 1989. The change was obvious. Theological schools were started and many local churches initiated theological training programmes for their own needs. Mission education had been ignored for many years, but today there is an obvious development with positive prospects for further advancement. International missionaries modelled not only an understanding for mission, but also formed practical skills among local church leaders and members. It is important to mention that, due to the communist regime in CEE countries, many men were prevented from taking initiatives in any aspects of life. People were not encouraged to create or to take charge in order to do something on their own. During this time, traditional thinking was to 'stay humble' and not initiate any project or activity outside normal routine. Among the Evangelical churches such initiatives could be viewed as displaying pride and a lack of spirituality. So the interviewed leaders have been cautious when answering the last three interview questions regarding potential future developments.

The attitude of national mission leaders regarding their capacity to carry on mission work with little or no help from the international community can be compared with the attitude of a teenager dreaming of doing great

[8] Alexandru Vlasin, 'The Impact of Evangelical Denominations on Social Work Values in Romania', in Corneliu Constantineanu, Georgeta Rață and Patricia Runcan (eds), *Values of Christian Relationships* (Puterea de a fi altfel, 3: Bucharest: Editura Didactică şi Pedagogică, 2014), 121-24.

work on his own. The desire not to depend on others is good, but an attitude of total independence may not be. The intention is laudable but the reality may prove to be too difficult in practice, if not impossible. Certainly, there are churches which can continue to work on their own, but the expertise and experience of the international community is of value to any church, especially those engaged in cross-cultural mission. So a healthy growth from dependence is not actually independence but interdependence.

Today, for the research participants as leaders in a CEE country, it seems easier to look at the last 25 years and judge the actions of international missionaries and mission agencies coming into Central and Eastern Europe. However, the fact that national leaders are able now to make distinction between missionaries with strategy and those with no direction, or to have the courage to suggest negative aspects of international missionaries' work, can be viewed as an act of maturity. Nonetheless, this also reflects back on these leaders as they start to send missionaries out to other nations. They also need to evaluate their own strategy in sending workers from Eastern Europe. Moreover, missionaries from CEE nations should be adequately trained and supported. Their work requires resources, too. Are nations newly established with missionary work ready to replicate the work Western churches did for them? Self-awareness and critical observation are very important and can help develop better models for mission work, especially if there is openness and co-operation between the two parties.

It is also very important to note the optimistic views of mission leaders when it comes to the future development of mission work from and within the region. While many international mission agencies are shrinking or even ending their contributions in CEE, East European mission leaders believe mission will grow. Their position is not to be ignored due to the continuous growth of the number of Evangelical churches in the region. There is still a sense of hope among churches and their leaders. While the work is great and challenging, mission passion continues to increase among the Evangelical churches. Many young people want to undertake mission work and take over the task of spreading the word of God among other nations.

Suggestion for Further Mission Development

One of the greatest needs among mission leaders is experienced pastors that can lead churches in mission – pastors who know how to motivate pastors and church leaders to work alongside people who lead missions in East European countries, in order to shape their theology and praxis. This will help national pastors and churches develop the right worldview for mission and help them move from being merely receivers to being senders of missionaries.

Another suggestion that could be useful for East European church leaders is, as missionaries are sent out from this region, they are to tell the receiving churches and leaders that they also need to engage in mission. There is no reason to wait ten years before instructing local churches about their responsibilities in mission. Western missionaries waited until 2000 before they slowly passed the mission baton to the national churches in Central and Eastern Europe. Mission work should be the DNA of every church and of every believer.

Western missionaries are not invited to leave Central and Eastern Europe. The negative feedback in this document should not justify anyone leaving the region or not even coming to this area. Working together is the key to success. Planting churches and developing social work projects is still needed. The best way to do it is by marrying the contribution of both sides. Western missionaries and local church leaders could learn together how to develop mission in and from CEE. Each one depends on the other. There is no mission without co-operation. One of the shortcomings among East Europeans is a lack of strategic thinking. Very little research is done by local people. Local people are very good at creating new relationships, but need researched direction and empowerment to form good strategy.

Central and East European missionaries need to learn a lot from the experience and practice of international workers. Churches and pastors could be helped if these missionaries would start educating them regarding mission work. Practical aspects like writing newsletter and teaching mission in Bible study groups could really help mission develop.

One last important aspect is the celebration of mission. Central and East European people are traditionally reserved when it comes to celebration. For some Christians, the trauma of forcefully celebrating communist dictatorships against their will left deep scars, while for other believers celebrating with joy could be viewed as sin. Nevertheless, celebrating success in mission could be another way of promoting mission work among churches. It is important to celebrate God's work among the nations. The delight that comes from seeing people being saved gives glory to God and brings joy to any church. So, let's celebrate God's work in Central and Eastern Europe with the anticipation of extraordinary mission work for the future.

THE BIBLE, CHRISTIAN EXISTENCE AND MISSION

Marcel V. Măcelaru

Introduction – Setting the Stage

Growing up in a Christian Pentecostal family in Romania, I learned from an early age that the Bible is 'the word of God from cover to cover'. This inevitably earned it a special place in my life, for not only was I supposed to handle the Bible with care, always with clean hands and preferably reading it in a prayerful position, but I was also repeatedly warned to neither 'add' nor 'take away' from its words – evidently an allusion to Revelation 22:18-19, which in our ecclesial context was interpreted as a reference to the integrity and ultimate authority of the Protestant canon. It never occurred to me during those years that the Bible is, in fact, many things to different people. That is, that the Bible, itself a multifaceted body of literature, is approached, perceived and interpreted in different ways by people of various convictions and from all walks of life. This being the case, though, a discussion about the nature and use of the Bible is inevitably a complex undertaking – one actually worthy of an entire hermeneutical treatise. The reader should not, however, expect an exposé of this kind here. Given the typical limitations an assignment such as the present one has, this essay does not lend itself to such a grandiose task. The plan underlying the thoughts below is in fact more specific and the argument has been developed with the following three editorial guidelines in mind.

First, as indicated in the title of this essay, I am to talk about the Bible *in relation to* Christian existence.[1] More precisely, I focus on the function of

[1] The argument developed in this paper builds on my earlier work on hermeneutics, mission and Christian identity. See Marcel V. Măcelaru, 'Communicating the Gospel to Postmodern People: Lessons from C.S. Lewis, J.R.W. Stott and N.T. Wright', in Alexandru Neagoe and Heleen Zorgdrage (eds), *Postmodernity – Friend or Foe? Communicating the Gospel to Postmodern People: Lessons from Central and Eastern Europe* (Utrecht, Netherlands: Kerkin Actie/Timişoara: Mirton, 2009), 123-47; 'The Bible Then and Now: Prolegomena to Biblical Interpretation', in Miroslav Volf, Corneliu Constantineanu, Marcel V. Măcelaru and Krešimir Šimić (eds), *First the Kingdom of God: A Festschrift in Honor of Prof. Dr Peter Kuzmič* (Osijek, Croatia: Evanđeoski Teološki Fakultet, 2011), 107-24; 'The Role of the Bible in Shaping Cultural Identities', in Janez Juhant and Bojan Žalec (eds), *Humanity after Selfish Prometheus: Chances of Dialogue and Ethics in a Technicized World* (Berlin: LIT Verlag, 2011), 167-73; 'Burdens of Identity: On Christian Existence in a Post-Christian World', in Corneliu Constantineanu, Georgeta Raţă and Patricia Runcan (eds), *Values of Christian Relationships* (Puterea de a fi altfel, 3: Bucharest: Editura Didactică şi Pedagogică, 2014), 169-74; 'Human Flourishing – A Theological Perspective', in Georgeta Raţă and Patricia

the Bible as a foundation for Christian identity and living. I argue that reading the Bible appropriately is key to embracing a truly Christian mode of existence[2] – a claim which, evidently, obliges missiologists and biblical scholars alike: the first to place biblical interpretation at the centre of their work, and the second to employ a hermeneutic that reveals the missiological character of biblical theology. An Old Testament scholar myself, I have come to the conclusion that biblical interpretation should never be limited to parsing Hebrew verbs, studying the literary features of the various biblical writings, or even establishing what the text meant to whom. Rather, the ultimate aim of any Bible reader should be to reflect on the theological contribution the text she/he interprets makes to the overall message of the Scriptures, and thereafter highlight its implications for the life and mission of the church in the world today.

Second, this paper also follows the thrust of this volume as a whole. Concretely, I write as an East European, from within, about and for the East European context. This is important inasmuch as theological discourse, like any other discourse, is both a contextual and a contextualized activity. Therefore, the reader should bear in mind that, besides personal particulars, such as the reminiscence with which I started this essay, which are implicitly woven into the tapestry of the argument, a general East European historical, social, political, cultural and religious milieu is assumed below, even though this may not be evident, at every turn, in the text. This is not to say that the points I raise would not be valid beyond the geographical confines established here. However, I neither make such claims, nor do I plan to speak to other contexts, with which I am only tangentially familiar. As for the ways in which Eastern Europe is distinct from other European or non-European contexts, the essays collected in the present volume provide sufficient information to help the reader form an image about the region, about its unique history, distinct ethos, particular challenges and varied opportunities.

Third, the volume in which this paper appears is part of the Regnum series on mission coming out of the Edinburgh 1910-2010 tradition. This means that the missiological philosophy which first inspired the historic World Missionary Conference convened by John Mott in Edinburgh in

---

Runcan (eds), *Happiness through Education* (Puterea de a fi altfel, 1: Bucharest: Editura Didactică şi Pedagogică, 2014), 233-36.

[2] As John B. Cobb ('The Intrapsychic Structure of Christian Existence', in *JAAR,* 36 (December 1968), 328-29) explains that 'we can think of our existence in terms of five dimensions or levels: the body, the emotions, the reason, the will, and the spirit... Each of these levels has a certain independence of all the others. At the same time, it affects all the others and is affected by them. A man's selfhood may be constituted at any one of them, and he may seek to become fully human from that perspective. For all men, the body and the emotions are given, but one who identifies himself with them may participate little or not at all in some of the other levels. Wholeness can thus be found most easily from a center in these foundational levels. Christian existence, on the other hand, involves the identification of the self with the spirit. The Christian quest for full humanity is the far more difficult quest for the excellence of all five dimensions unified around this center'.

1910, and is now spelled out in the Edinburgh 2010 Common Call, the document produced at the centennial re-gathering, provides a launching pad for the 'call' below. Along similar lines, I affirm that mission, that is, God's redemptive activity that is carried out in and through God's people, in the world, is first a call to 'being', which in turn gives birth to specific 'doing' – it is unavoidably a distinct mode of existence. I affirm that a correct reading of the Bible, consisting of contextualized applications of its message, makes this mode of existence appropriately Christian. I also affirm that only when living such an existence true human flourishing, as intended by the Creator, becomes possible. Given these, it is evident that Biblical hermeneutics is a fundamental missiological task; and as such, reconsidering the nature and use of the Bible today, which is the subject of this essay, is a 'must' in a volume on mission.[3]

Biblical Hermeneutics – The Predicament

Although most people would have no problem identifying the Bible as a foundational Christian document, for many it is also a peculiar text, unusual and at times difficult to understand. This is because the Bible is a complex collection of ancient writings, which originated in, and therefore are witnessing to, socio-cultural contexts that are quite alien to the 'modern' reader. Moreover, passed on from generation to generation, over a long period of time, the Bible came to us via an intricate process of composite authorship, manuscript production and preservation, translation and interpretation. Given all these, regardless of how familiar one is with the final product, the cultural, geographic, temporal and linguistic differences that separate these ancient writings from their 21st-century audiences, as well as the convoluted journey that brought the biblical text from its authors to its readers, make reading the Bible with understanding a real interpretative predicament.

Needless to say, in response to such difficulties, over the years, a plethora of methodological tools has been developed and sizable stacks of

---

[3] The foundational role of the Bible in and for mission, reaffirmed in the *Edinburgh 2010 Common Call*, has been on the scholarly agenda on both sides of the 'fence' – Mission Studies and Biblical Studies – for quite some time. See, for instance, Donald Senior and Caroll Stuhlmueller, *The Biblical Foundations for Mission* (Maryknoll, NY: Orbis Books, 1983); Lesslie Newbigin, *The Gospel in a Pluralist Society* (Grand Rapids, MI: Eerdmans, 1989); David J. Bosch, *Transforming Mission: Paradigm Shifts in Theology of Mission* (American Society of Missiology Series, 16: Maryknoll, NY: Orbis Books, 1991); Richard Bauckham, *Bible and Mission: Christian Witness in a Postmodern World* (Carlisle, UK: Paternoster Press/Grand Rapids, MI: Baker Academic, 2003); Rollin G. Grams, I. Howard Marshall, Peter F. Penner and Robin Routledge (eds), *Bible and Mission: A Conversation Between Biblical Studies and Missiology* (Schwarzenfeld, Germany: Neufeld Verlag, 2008); Dean Flemming, *Recovering the Full Mission of God: A Biblical Perspective on Being, Doing and Telling* (Downers Grove, IL: IVP, 2013); and, of course, the volume on this topic in the Regnum Edinburgh Centenary Series: Pauline Hoggarth, Fergus Macdonald, Bill Mitchell and Knud Jørgensen (eds), *Bible in Mission* (Oxford: Regnum, 2013).

books that describe how these tools work have been written – all of these in the hope that reading the Bible according to 'this' or 'that' hermeneutical model will result in a faithful rendering of its meaning. The assumption behind this development of study materials is that the solution to uncertainty in interpretation is to educate oneself better in the 'secrets' of hermeneutics. However, the truth be told, in the study of an ancient text such as the Bible, no one can guarantee a 100% interpretative 'accuracy', inasmuch as the goals pursued by the interpreter revolve around 'discovering' the meaning this text might have had for its ancient authors and their audiences, contexts to which the contemporary Bible reader has only inferred access, if having any whatsoever. Admittedly, the use of suitable study tools at each interpretative step helps bring our readings closer to the target. That is, exegetical methodologies do provide a fair amount of certitude as to the 'correctness' of one's historical and literary interpretative conclusions. Nevertheless, when considering that, in practice, for many believers, the use of exegetical tools advocated by the 'professional' Bible interpreter is rather a 'strange new world' that does not intersect with one's devotional reading of the Scriptures – an impasse that is rarely taken into account in discussions on biblical interpretation – it is rather doubtful that the proliferation of study aids and methodological expertise will have the hoped-for missiological impact that an increased Bible presence within our communities would undoubtedly bring.

To explain, it is commonly assumed, especially among 'professional' Bible interpreters, that the quality of one's interpretation, and therefore the level of biblical understanding one has, increases in direct ratio with how one manages to make use of the methodological knowledge available. The danger of such reasoning, however, lies in the fact that it leads to the conclusion that, where lack of such methodological knowledge is the norm, the reading of the Bible being done is only of little consequence. In other words, such a perspective holds that, without the benefit of specific methodological education, there can be no appropriate reading of the Bible, and therefore no true applicability of its message in the life of the believer. However, I propose that such thinking is, at least in part, fallacious. For many East European Christians, including the present author, this conclusion does not describe the 'experience' we had reading the Bible before more 'sophisticated' tools to help our biblical interpretation became accessible in the region. Therefore, although the need for, and usefulness of, methodology is undeniable, experience also shows that lack of hermeneutical expertise does not prevent the believer from attaining genuine spiritual enrichment through Bible reading and meditation. In fact, the evidence tells a different story – for all the talk about Europe-wide secularization and the systematic 'de-Christianization' of Central and Eastern Europe during the communist era, the fact of the matter remains that the Bible has played (and can therefore continue to play) an important role in the formation of our culture and identity.[4] It seems to me, therefore, that Biblical hermeneutics, within a missiological context, should be less concerned with the proliferation of interpretative methodologies, and more with the Bible itself – that is, with what the Bible is and how it 'functions'.

The Bible – The What and the How

Probably the most obvious thing about the Bible, and strangely, also one often ignored, is the fact that it is a collection of works of literature. Indeed, at first glance, what one gets when one opens the Bible are stories, poems, songs, wisdom sayings, parables and other such literary genres. In fact, for the student of literature, the Bible can be a veritable feast, for it contains a multitude of literary genres and styles, it displays high levels of literary artistry, and it abounds with astonishing literary effects. As such, to some extent, the work of interpretation done by the Bible reader is not much different from the analysis one would undertake when reading other literature. This work requires some level of familiarity with the rules guiding different literary genres and the ability to play by those rules when reading the biblical text.

It should be stressed however that, unlike many of the literary creations familiar to us today, the Bible is literature rooted in history. It originated in concrete historical contexts, it tells of historical events, it addresses historical (real) audiences, and it makes historical claims. Still, the Bible is not a historical treatise *per se*, not in the way in which we would conceive of such a work today. The historical data available in the Bible comes to us embedded within literary frameworks. Thus, although we ought to assume the historical validity of the events it mentions, their presentation is not chronological and objective, but rather governed by the characteristics of the literary genre chosen as a vehicle for the ideas the Biblical authors intended to transmit. In fact, recognizing this particular blending of history and literature, Friedman writes:

> If it is true that the literary scholar cannot make a 'clean break' with history, one can say with at least as much certainty that the historian cannot move without literary skills, and literary concerns. One must deal with the matter of intention, with matters of narrative voice. One must be sensitive to ideological colouring of narrative. One must make judgements with regard to narrative reports: does the author report a fact in a certain manner because he believes that it happened that way, or because he seeks a certain artistic effect, e.g. a symmetry or paronomasia? Perhaps most important, and at the most basic level, one must have a sense of poetry… The book which is our

---

[4] To give but one example, in Romania, arguably the place where communist-led anti-Christian opposition was greater than anywhere else in Eastern Europe, at the 2011 census a staggering 93% of the citizens have declared themselves Christian. Admittedly, this does not prove that all of these are also regular Bible readers; however, the very fact that so many identify with Christianity speaks volumes about the influence the Bible, its foundational book, can play within society.

> primary source for a millennium of Israelite history is written *mostly* in poetry. The study of that material requires a particular combination of historical and literary skills.[5]

Of course, due to his larger objective, which is to evaluate the possibility of objective historical discourse within the Hebrew Bible, Friedman searches for an integration of historical and literary methodologies. Nonetheless, it seems to me that the very fact that what the reader encounters when opening the Bible is text and not the history behind it, the literary mindset I suggest above should be adopted, in large measure, by the student of history as well.

Having noted these, however, we have seen only part of the picture. In fact, for the believer, the most significant aspect of the Bible is its value as theology – that is, its revelatory and deontological scopes. Revelatory because it talks about God and God's relationship with those whom he chooses as his people – a content which serves the purpose of making God known to the reader inasmuch as such knowledge can be mediated through text; and deontological because it plays a prescriptive role within believing communities – a function which makes the Bible the believers' moral guide *par excellence*, an authoritative source of information regulating their doing.

Needless to say, the interpretative ideal would be to address literary, historical and theological concerns together, in much the same way in which they are inseparable as features of the Bible. However, I am not altogether sure that in the practice of the average Bible reader such balance is achieved; at least not consciously so. This is the case, I argue, because, within faith contexts, what one looks for when one reads the Bible is neither the entertainment that literature can offer nor the satisfaction of historical discovery students of ancient texts may have. Rather, the reading of the Word within Christianity is central to achieving union with Christ and communion with one another. And although not all of those who identify themselves as Christian hold such a 'high' view of the Bible – as I was gently reminded by a distinguished missiologist not long ago – the notion of Bible reading for theological and spiritual enrichment is common across all Christian traditions, regardless of how this is put into practice in the life of the individual believer and within the community to which one belongs. As such, Bible reading, whether informed hermeneutically or not, is an intrinsic part of a believer's 'social imaginary'.[6] Together with other Christian practices, such as worship, prayer, charity and discipleship, the

---

[5] Richard Elliot Friedman, 'The Prophet and the Historian: The Acquisition of Historical Information from Literary Sources', in Richard Elliot Friedman (ed), *The Poet and the Historian: Essays in Literary and Historical Biblical Criticism* (Harvard Semitic Studies, 26), (Chico, CA: Scholars Press, 1983), 5.

[6] On 'social imaginary', see Charles Taylor, *Modern Social Imaginaries* (Durham, NC: Duke University Press, 2004), 23-30; and *A Secular Age* (Harvard, MA: Harvard University Press, 2007), 171-76.

reading of the Word contributes to how one 'intuitively "understands" the world in the light of the fullness of the gospel'.[7] Consequently, the Bible becomes a lens through which believers codify and interpret their context, and make sense of their life circumstances.

The Bible as the Story of God

The function of the Bible noted above becomes evident when taking into consideration how one's 'social imaginary' is being moulded. In the words of James K.A. Smith,

> The 'social imaginary' is an affective, non-cognitive understanding of the world. It is described as an *imaginary* (rather than a *theory*) because it is fuelled by the stuff of imagination rather than the intellect: it is made up of, and embedded in, stories, narratives, myths and icons. These visions capture our hearts and imaginations by 'lining' our imagination, as it were – providing us with frameworks of 'meaning' by which we make sense of our world and our calling in it. An irreducible understanding of the world resides in our intuitive, pre-cognitive grasp of these stories.[8]

I propose that, for the believer, the Bible is such a 'framework of meaning'. It provides a Story[9] that is 'utterly true, crucially important, and often complex... grander than the grandest epic, richer in plot and more significant in its characters and descriptions than any humanly composed story ever could be'.[10] Admittedly, from a literary perspective, the Bible does not contain only prose, for only about 40% of its literature is in fact narration. However, I advance that, from a theological point of view, both narrative and non-narrative parts come together in a coherent whole that tells *the Story of God with, in and for the world.* It tells of a God who acts within human history – of the beginning of it all at creation, of the development of God's plan in the election and life of Israel, of a culmination brought about in Christ's incarnation, death and resurrection, of the continuation of God's work in and through the church, which is to be his agent in the world today, and of the eschatological conclusion of this history at the end of time, when God's purposes for creation will come to full fruition.[11]

---

[7] James K.A. Smith, *Desiring the Kingdom: Worship, Worldview and Cultural Formation* (Cultural Liturgies, 1), (Grand Rapids, MI: Baker Academic, 2009), 68.

[8] Smith, *Desiring the Kingdom*, 68.

[9] Below, whenever capitalized, the word 'Story' is used with specific reference to the biblical meta-narrative introduced in the present section. In non-capitalized occurrences, the generic sense of the word is in view.

[10] Gordon D. Fee and Douglas Stuart, *How to Read the Bible for All Its Worth: A Guide to Understanding the Bible* (Grand Rapids, MI: Zondervan, 1982), 74.

[11] On the theological significance of God's acts within human history, see Dietrich Ritschl, 'Praising God as Interpreter and Critic of History', in David S. Cunningham, Ralph Del Colle and Lucas Lamadrid (eds), *Ecumenical Theology in Worship, Doctrine, and Life: Essays Presented to Geoffrey Wainwright on His Sixtieth Birthday* (Oxford: OUP, 1999), 69-77.

One may, of course, also wonder whether the Story I advocate for here is *de facto* available – whether the thematic logic implied above is not invalidated by the post-structuralist claim that such overarching structures are merely imaginary solutions imposed upon otherwise disparate elements, and whether such coherence is even possible in the light of the fact that the Bible is a multiplex collection of writings, both in terms of its form and in terms of its formation. I argue, evidently, that it is both possible and available. The general possibility that disparate literary pieces can come together in the manner noted above finds support in Genette's observations regarding the process of emplotment inherent to any story.[12] He shows that the constitutive parts of a story (in the original French, *histoire*) are distinct from, and have a different role from, the story itself. Thus, while the literary components that are brought together represent the signifiers, the story which results from their combination is the signified – that is, a complete thematic universe – which functions according to a specific overarching ideological plan that is greater than any individual meaning each constituent part may have. Applied to the case in view, such a perspective suggests that the Bible is more than the sum-total of its constituent parts. It also allows for the possibility that the Bible is a unified construct that functions according to a specific theological logic.

Incidentally, this perspective echoes the conclusions reached by biblical scholars with regard to the genesis and formation of the biblical text. It is widely accepted that the Bible is the result of a repetitive process of editing and actualization through which initially disparate 'literary sources' were combined and came to form the 'books' one finds in the current form of the text. More importantly, the development described culminates in the 'canonization' of the collection.[13] From a literary point of view, this meant literary stabilization and (the beginning of) textual standardization, thus bringing the editorial processing of the literature to an end. From a historico-theological point of view, the canonization of the collection is even more significant. It first entailed the selection of specific writings out of a larger pool of literary works – such selection, regardless of how (un)conscious its processes might have been, carryies the implication that the writings included in the canon were deemed 'worthy' of being singled out; and since the purpose of the collection at the time of its formation was decidedly religious, the value attached to the writings included in the canon must be described along such lines as: 'revelatory significance' and 'deontological importance'. Second, it entailed the intentional arrangement

[12] See Gerard Genette, *Narrative Discourse* (Ithaca, NY: Cornell University Press, 1980), 25-26; *Narrative Discourse Revisited* (Ithaca, NY: 1988), 13-14.

[13] Regarding the process of canonization and its consequences for interpretation, see Jed Wyrick, *The Ascension of Authorship: Attribution and Canon Formation in Jewish, Hellenistic and Christian Traditions* (Cambridge, MA: Harvard University Press, 2004); and Lee Martin McDonald and James A. Sanders (eds), *The Canon Debate* (Peabody, MA: Hendrickson, 2002), 3-263.

of the works in the collection according to a specific, pre-established logic. As argued by Gillingham, this intentionality is evident in both canonical traditions – the Jewish and the Christian.[14] If so, regardless of how the logic employed functioned, the important point for this study is the possibility that such a dominant teleology was present. Its implication is that, from its very beginnings as Scripture, the Bible addresses its readership through an overarchingly coherent theological message rather than through disparate 'opinions' about its subject-matter, as some contemporary 'biblical theologies' would have us believe. As such, regardless of the position taken by the reader on its authority and revelatory value, the rationale which gave birth to the canon of Scripture – that is, the overall thematic arch that binds its parts together – is inescapably part of the process of interpretation, at all times and in all circumstances of Bible reading.

Such a perspective on the Bible resembles, in part, the notion of the 'canonical narrative' that has been advanced within the Narrative Theology movement.[15] As explained by Soulen, a 'canonical narrative' is 'an interpretative instrument that provides a framework for reading the Christian Bible as a theological and narrative unity'.[16] As such, although it arises from the biblical canon, a canonical narrative is not identical with the canon. Rather, it is a reflection of the interpreter's vision regarding the way the Bible 'hangs together' as a theological whole.

In a similar manner, I propose the notion of 'story' in order to make sense of the teleology of occurrences that constitute the Bible. However, I depart form the position advocated in the Narrative Theology camp in regard with what the biblical Story is and how it operates. To explain, taking into account the assertion I made earlier regarding the fact that the Bible is rooted in history, it is inevitable that the Story of the Bible recounts the experiences of live entities within real contexts. In other words, this is a Story which witnesses to, and impinges upon, socio-historical contexts and the human agents that are acting in them at every step and in every milieu belonging to its formation, transmission and interpretation. As such, the biblical story is not just a construct, the product of inventor-authors, nor even just an ethnography, the product of observer-authors. The connection between the story and its tellers, in this case, goes much deeper – this is a Story told by people who are, in a sense, 'inside' it, inside the Story. To borrow from D. Carr, this is a Story that is 'told in being lived, and lived in

[14] On the logic that binds together the books of the Bible, see Susan E. Gillingham, *One Bible, Many Voices: Different Approaches to Biblical Studies* (London: SPCK, 1998), 46-71.

[15] For good introductions to Narrative Theology, see Michael Goldberg, *Theology and Narrative: A Critical Introduction* (Nashville, TN: Abingdon, 1982); Gabriel Fackre, 'Narrative Theology: An Overview', in *Interpretation,* 37.4 (1983), 340-52; and George W. Stroup, *The Promise of Narrative Theology* (London: SCM Press, 1984).

[16] R. Kendall Soulen, *The God of Israel and Christian Theology* (Minneapolis, MN: Fortress Press, 1996), 13.

being told'.[17] As such, the biblical Story is the product of what one may call '*participant*-authors'.[18]

I argue that this participative nature of the Bible makes it also a Story with which its readers can identify. Consequently, for its readers, the Bible can become a Story that helps 'order' their understanding of themselves and of the world in which they live – an identity-forming Story. Of course, the 'power' of the Bible to provide such grounding becomes available only inasmuch as readers are creatively involved in reading-constructing (and not just reading-discovering) its plot. Such power exists when tellers and their audiences 'co-operate' in bringing together the elements necessary to create a meaningful telling; that is, in the case in view, when readers of the Bible harmonize their personal stories with the traditions and beliefs expressed by the authors of the Bible, thus participating in the 'production' of a Story appropriate to their circumstances and goals. *Mutatis mutandis*, the biblical Story does not address readers only, but rather what one may call *participant*-receivers.[19]

Pointing to the participative nature of identity-telling/identity-forming narratives, Paul Ricoeur explains this connection between a story and its teller-receiver suggestively:

> In this narrative we make from our lives, or from segments of our lives, many narratives or a single narrative, who are we? Are we a character in this narrative? Are we the narrator? Or are we the author?... We are capable of occupying each of these three positions, character, narrator, author, in turn. We cannot rest with any one of them. Surely we are a character, but it is we who tell the story; therefore, we are its author. But we cannot simply be the author because we are already caught up in the stories of other lives. This, I believe, is one key characteristic of a lived narrativity, of what may be called in English 'enacted narratives'.[20]

Seen in this light then, the biblical Story is no less than a form of enacted autobiography; a Story which provides participant-receivers with the means to make sense of life experiences, and to articulate individual and collective identities.

---

[17] Carr, 'Narrative and the Real World', 126.

[18] For the notion of 'participant-authors', I draw on J. Hart, 'Cracking the Code: Narrative and Political Mobilization in the Greek Resistance', in *Social Science History,* 16.4 (1992), 633-34.

[19] On the 'participation' suggested here, see further, Stanley M. Hauerwas, *Christian Existence Today: Essays on Church, World, and Living in Between* (Grand Rapids, MI: Baker Books, 1995).

[20] Paul Ricoeur, *Figuring the Sacred: Religion, Narrative, and Imagination* (Minneapolis, MN: Augsburg Fortress Press, 1995), 309-10.

The Bible and Christian Identity

Every society or culture is an enterprise in world-construction and world-maintenance.[21] This is an activity in which humans employ both cognitive and non-cognitive processes. Non-cognitive inasmuch as one's 'social imaginary' – that is, one's affective understanding – plays a crucial role in how one makes sense of the world;[22] and cognitive inasmuch as world-construction is a rational process that is influenced by people's world-views[23] – that is, by the system of assumptions they hold as true, according to which they act, and through which they interpret reality.[24]

Within this world-building activity, the telling of stories is a fundamental way of assigning meaning to experience. This is because humans naturally use a narrative style in order to mediate between their world of thought and feeling and the outer world of observable actions and states of affairs. As such, stories become the best means humans have to gain understanding about themselves in relation to others.

This perspective on stories and their function brings powerfully into play the social-constructivist evaluation of identity. According to this view, identity is a product of the mind, defined and propagated through the creative power of imagination.[25] It has a narrated character, because it consists of the 'story' we tell in response to the question 'who are you?', and it is disseminated through re-telling and further interpretative elaboration.[26] As such, both personal and collective identities are available in, and can be shaped through, story-telling. In Carr's words:

> A community… exists by virtue of a story which is articulated and accepted, which typically concerns the group's origins and its destiny, and which interprets what is happening now in the light of these two temporal poles.[27]

I suggest that the Bible is such an identity-forming story. It describes events, actions, people – that is, occurrences that resemble its readers' experiences. In this way, the Bible helps locate the reality of its readers within its story-universe, therefore making the Story of God it presents their Story as well. This is because the process of narrativization, through which real-life occurrences and characters become part of the literary universe of the Bible, also works to bring 'to life' a world that is presented by literature 'in front of itself… as the *horizon of possible experience* in

---

[21] See in this regard, Peter L. Berger and Thomas Luckmann, *The Social Construction of Reality: A Treatise in the Sociology of Knowledge* (Garden City, NY: Anchor Books, 1967).
[22] Cf. Smith, *Desiring the Kingdom*, 62-71.
[23] On 'world-view', see David Burnett, *Clash of Worlds* (Crowborough, UK: MARC, 1990).
[24] Cf. Clifford Geertz, *The Interpretation of Cultures* (New York: Basic Books, 1973).
[25] E.g. Bernard Anderson, *Imagined Communities: Reflections on the Origins and Spread of Nationalism* (London: Verso, 1991).
[26] On 'narrative identity', see Paul Ricoeur, *Time and Narrative* (three vols; Chicago, IL: University of Chicago Press, 1984, 1985, 1988).
[27] D. Carr, 'Narrative and the Real World: An Argument for Continuity', in *History and Theory*, 25.85 (1986), 128.

which the (literary) work displaces its readers'.[28] In other words, the telling of this Story is doing more than just describing; it is also *generating* something – a world that has previously existed only in rhetorical presentation.[29]

Furthermore, it is important to note in this context that the plot developed in the Bible tells more than just a familiar story; it is in fact a Story that tells of forces, ideas and events that surpass the human realm. It is a literary-theological portrayal of divine-human encounters, a 'sacred history', as it were, that tells of *God* and humans in the world. I argue that this blending of the divine and the human makes the biblical Story a uniquely powerful telling, that creates within its participant-readers a sense of belonging to a 'sacred space'[30] under the 'sacred canopy'[31] of God. This is because the narrativization of human experience in the Bible is tied to deontology, thus grounding the participative emplotment through which this Story comes into being on the authority of the revelatory claims made by the Scriptures.

Given the above, the recounting of the past provided in the biblical Story becomes a springboard for new modes of envisioning the future. The biblical Story, from this perspective, is not only descriptive but also *pre*scriptive; it not only makes sense of past events, but also shapes the future through ethical and other claims embedded in it. In this manner, the biblical Story in fact provides a compelling framework of reference, for individuals and communities alike. For the participant-reader(s) it becomes a foundational narrative – or perhaps *the* foundational narrative – that not only provides a 'model for' but also a 'model of' reality.[32] In other words, it acts to transform world-views and reshape social-imaginaries, and therefore it becomes the primary medium for self-identification and self-location.

To be compelling, of course, the Story's vision of the future must be consistent and attainable. A Story which people will find hard to understand or believe cannot motivate the struggle for its realization. However, a Story that builds coherently on the past, accurately assesses the possibilities of the present, and presents an appealing future, also enlarges people's views of their possibilities. It motivates a remaking of its readers' 'lived story' so that it resembles more closely the Story they desire. It prompts people to change lived events, by acting upon them, until these come to resemble the Story. In other words, the biblical Story, thus appropriated, serves to activate and transform reality, and therefore to

---

[28] Paul Ricoeur, 'The Text as Dynamic Identity', in M.J. Valdés and O. Miller (eds), *Identity of the Literary Text* (Toronto: University of Toronto Press, 1985), 183.

[29] Cf. Searle, 1995.

[30] Cf. Mircea Eliade, *The Sacred and the Profane: The Nature of Religion* (New York: Harcourt Brace, 1959).

[31] Cf. Peter L. Berger, *The Sacred Canopy: Elements of a Sociological Theory of Religion* (New York: Anchor Books, 1967).

[32] The 'model for/model of' language used here is borrowed from Clifford Geertz, *The Interpretation of Cultures* (New York: Basic Books, 1973), 93ff.

influence and shape one's very identity. The biblical Story, when thus appropriated, becomes the very Story readers of the Bible tell about themselves.

The Bible and Christian Existence

In an article published in 2006, Philip Jenkins has argued that, while the Bible speaks powerfully to Christians in the global South, to their brethren in the global North its message is increasingly alien.[33] This situation, he proposes, has to do with the fact that stories of pain, poverty, war and illness, as well as many of the social and religious customs and rituals recorded in the Bible, are analogous to life experiences which those in the South have and which those in the North lack. This leads to the conclusion that, to the Christians in the South, the participatory reading for which I advocate above is attainable. To Christians in the North, however, the world the Bible describes must mean very little, if it means anything at all. Consequently, to them, a mode of existence that is activated by participation in the biblical Story, is in fact inaccessible.

Of course, Jenkins wrote about a world that no longer exists. Not only that the East, in Europe, has gradually come to resemble the West, as ours is well on the way of becoming 'a society characterized by a relativized value system, supplied by a post-modern consciousness, and a confused self-image, whereby old definitions of societal homogeneity are... being replaced with the "multicultural" persona ushered in by globalization',[34] but also, the North nowadays feels more and more like the South, given the plethora of complex issues facing our communities: pronounced economic instability and a deepening division of the society between rich and poor; massive migration and the real or imagined threats that come with it, making our once safe environment a place of uncertainty; dysfunctional political systems and corrupt politicians who lack the will power to imagine and implement swift and decisive solutions; and the resurgence of age-old nationalistic and ethno-religious identities, endangering European unity. The question to ask before concluding this study, therefore, is not whether the Bible can speak relevantly to people in (Eastern) Europe today, but rather how such an impact can be realized? That is, how does one participate in the biblical Story, so that embracing a true Christian mode of existence becomes that person's reality?

I submit that such participation is made possible when the re-telling of the biblical Story is done in ways that provide people and communities with new models of action, meaning and values. Such an objective requires a mode of invocation within which the world evoked by the Bible is re-enacted in our world; for it is only through such re-enactment that the Story

---

[33] See Philip Jenkins, 'Reading the Bible in the Global South', in *International Bulletin of Missionary Research,* 30.2 (2006), 67-73.

[34] Măcelaru, 'Burdens of Identity', 169.

being told becomes the 'sacred space' within which the individual or the community exists. Only through such re-enactment can the Story being told become the Story being lived.

As for practical ways in which such re-enactment is accomplished, I suggest, together with Constantineanu, that participation in God's Story is about living in the here and now according to the principles of the world the Bible evokes:

> To live by the authority of Scripture means to allow ourselves to be permanently shaped and moulded by the story of the Bible, especially as we are constantly tempted to think and to do as the world is and does! It is only the Scriptures that can judge and redeem our own actions and lives. That is why we should allow Scripture to teach us, to guide us, to bring us back to the biblical view of the purpose and meaning of life… It is only the Bible that shows the true nature of God and his plans for the world; it is only the Bible that reveals the true authority of the cross, and challenges the world's authority and power of domination and control. It is only the Bible that reveals the true God who can redeem the world. That is why we have to read and tell the world the true story of God.[35]

Thus, participation in God's Story is about embracing a truly Christian mode of existence. And since 'Christian existence cannot flourish apart from belief in and worship of God as he is known in Jesus',[36] participation in God's Story is identification of, and involvement with, God's redemptive activity in the world today.

A Missiological Imperative – In Lieu of a Conclusion

The argument developed above brings powerfully into view an understanding of Christianity in terms of participation in the biblical Story. Admittedly, alternative definitions of Christian identity are both available and in use. Such definitions have put forward: (1) Christian institutions and structured religion; (2) Christian doctrines; and (3) Christian customs and rituals. Nevertheless, I argue that, upon closer scrutiny, none of these suffices. Regarding the first, affiliation to a certain religious organization cannot be taken as proof of one's Christian commitment. Regarding the second, not only that belief cannot be objectively measured, but anyone in the least familiar with the Christian environment knows that varying, and many times contradictory, doctrines are affirmed by different Christian groups. As for the third, identifying the practices that make one distinctively Christian is equally problematic, for the rituals performed by believers are as many as the people performing them. As such, I argue that outward characteristics and practices alone are inadequate as depictions of true Christian commitment. In fact, Europe itself is a clear case in point.

[35] Corneliu Constantineanu, 'The Authority of Scripture as the Word of God', in *Kairos,* 4.1 (2010), 20.
[36] Cobb, 'The Intrapsychic Structure of Christian Existence', 339.

With a few exceptions, a genuinely Christian ethos is hardly the norm in our communities; and this in spite of all the Christian elements (institutions and practices) that are still prominent, and the centuries-old history of Church-State symbioses which make up the unique Christian hegemony that gave our *Vieux Continent* the label of 'Christendom'.

In addition to the above, it seems to me that such definitions of Christian existence are also inadequate as models for mission. More often than not, such depictions of Christianity have proved to be too rigid to be useful in missional contexts, especially when those contexts were culturally and socially significantly different from the places whence the message bearers came. The history of Christian mission presents numerous examples of mission agencies and missionaries that have transported to new contexts, together with their message, a mixture of 'Christian' features and traditions that had more to do with 'tried' ways of doing church rather than with the essence of the gospel of Jesus Christ.[37]

I suggest, however, that the constructivist approach to Christian identity introduced above may operate better, especially in places where gospel proclamation is perceived as aggressive 'westernization', and where conversion translates as a peculiar withdrawal from society. How, for instance, would a Bosnian Muslim (whose allegiance to Islam may rather be a matter of culture than a matter of faith) respond if the invitation to embrace a Christian mode of existence would be defined as 'participation in the Story of God' rather than as an obligation to undergo an unwanted cultural re-adjustment? Or, how would an 'undecided' Romanian (whose idea of 'following Christ' pertains to acceding to burdensome behavioural restrictions – admittedly, an image Evangelical Christians in the region often project) react if understanding that Christianity is not about self-imposed social alienation but rather about assuming one's place as a protagonist in the only true Story of the world – the biblical Story?

Undoubtedly, a genuinely Christian experience demands inclusion in the body of Christ, which is outwardly expressed as communion with fellow believers. However, I argue that such inclusion must not require the shedding of one's cultural identity or the forsaking of one's social environment. If Christian existence in the world today is defined in terms of participation in the biblical Story, then the focus shifts from external, static, identity markers to self-articulations of beliefs, thoughts and attitudes – that is, to a dynamic, internalized appropriation of the gospel ethos. Unquestionably, such an embrace of the gospel ethos will always lead to outward manifestations of one's faith. Nevertheless, the manifestations in this case will pertain more to contextualized practices of Christian virtues rather than to institutionalized religion and narrowly defined church affiliations.

---

[37] On this, see further G. Lings and S. Murray, *Church Planting: Past, Present and Future* (New York: Grove Books, 2003).

It is therefore the conclusion of the present author that, if anything, the argument above points to a quite crucial missiological task: the imperative to propagate Bible reading and Bible knowledge within our troubled world. Peter Kuzmič expresses well the urgency of this mission:

> ... the church must *reclaim the historical reliability and truthfulness of the Christian gospel.* The spiritual crisis of Europe is also an intellectual crisis, a crisis of truth which is in the very centre of the 'modern eclipse of God'. In our age of relativity, atheism, agnosticism and denial of all absolutes, when the very truth of any truth is under suspicion, the validity of the gospel truth is either outrightly denied or largely ignored. All across Europe, the proclamation of the gospel has to become once again communication of knowledge of the foundational facts of Christian faith as revealed in the Holy Scriptures and centred in the life, teaching, death and resurrection of Jesus Christ: 'By this Gospel you are saved, that Christ died for our sins, according to the Scriptures, that he was buried, that he was raised on the third day according to the Scriptures, and that he appeared' (1 Cor. 15:2-5). The faithful, brave and creative proclamation of the gospel must be grounded in these foundational facts of the universally valid truth, for truth is foundational for trust... This gospel must be unashamedly proclaimed all across the lands of Europe as not only the truth about God and our own lost condition apart from Christ but also as 'the power of God for salvation for everyone who believes' (Rom. 1:16).[38]

Of course, as I suggested above, such proclamation is more than the mere *speaking* of the truth of the gospel. Effective proclamation, in the context of today's Europe, is about *living* that truth faithfully. In this way, the resulting mode of existence will also be a demonstration of the divine plan for humanity. This, I propose, is a much-needed 'counter-measure' to the emergence and persistence of modes of existence that foster exclusion and enmity, selfishness and injustice, falsehood and disbelief. It is only by promoting familiarity with the Bible within our communities that a mode of existence as participation in God's Story becomes attainable. And it is through such participation that God's purposes for the creation are activated, within us, and through us for the world. In N.T. Wright's words:

> Scripture is the book that assures us that we are the people of God when, again and again, we are tempted to doubt. Scripture is the covenant book, not just in order that we can look up our pedigree in it and see where we came from (Abraham and so on), but the book through which the Spirit assures that we are his people and through which he sends us out into the world to tell the Jesus story, that is, the Israel story which has become the Jesus story which together is God's story for the world. And as we do that in the power of the Spirit, the miracle is that it rings true and people out there in the world know, in this or that fashion, that this strange story which we are telling does in fact run deeper than the world's stories. It does in fact tell them truths which they half-knew and had rather hoped to forget. It is the story which confirms the fact that God has redeemed the world in Jesus Christ. It is the story which

[38] Peter Kuzmič, 'Christian Mission in Europe', *Themelios* 18.1 (1992), 23.

breaks open all other world-views and, by so doing, invites men and women, young and old, to see *this* story as *their* story. In other words, as we let the Bible be the Bible, God works through us – and it – to do what he intends to do in and for the church and the world.[39]

[39] N.T. Wright, 'How Can the Bible Be Authoritative?' in *Vox Evangelica,* 21 (1991), 14.

JESUS IN APOSTOLIC PREACHING ACCORDING TO THE BOOK OF ACTS

Ciprian Flavius Terinte

Introduction

In our times, much has been said about the need for a new evangelization of western society, which currently continues on the road of de-Christianising and secularization. In Eastern Europe, Christianity has been a little self-reliant seeing that, although people had lived for four decades under the atheistic, communist totalitarianism, yet they still expressed their allegiance to the church. However, we suddenly realized that the situation was about to change in our backyard too, and society was fast moving towards a matter-of-fact materialism and consumerism. Facing these political, cultural, social and religious changes, the church finds itself in a mission field in many respects similar to that of the early church. Christians need to bear witness and have their answer ready for people who ask them the reason for the hope that they have. Therefore, even though we may be situated in a more conservative religious background, we must take seriously the invitation of the *Common Call* of Edinburgh 2010, to 'mission from everywhere to everywhere' and to 'proclaim the good news of salvation'. But what should be emphasized in our discourse when we share the gospel with people so that our speech might be 'authentic dialogue, respectful engagement and humble witness… *to the uniqueness of Christ*'?

In this regard, the discourses found in the book of Acts are an ever-flowing source of inspiration for the preaching, catechetical activity and the testimony of the contemporary church. One of the characteristic features of this New Testament writing is the alternation of discursive and narrative passages, the two aspects being complementary: the discourses pointing to the significance of the narratives.

In this paper, I shall examine some of the speeches found in the book of Acts, in an attempt to emphasize those Christological ideas that appear to be of paramount importance for the evangelistic endeavours of the apostles. The sermons we shall examine are part of the unique revelation of God that forms our New Testament, and must be foundational for our own faith and understanding of the gospel. Their rhetorical method of proclamation, point for point, may not be applicable to every situation, but reflection on the theological issues they affirm will be a stimulus to effective evangelism in every age and culture, including the East European one. After all, 'preaching is always the means to conversion in Acts'.[1]

[1] James D.J. Dunn, *Unity and Diversity in the New Testament* (London: SCM Press, 2006), 11.

Due to the constraints of this paper, in what follows I shall approach only the *kerygmatic* discourses found in the book of Acts,[2] because they are the most relevant for the idea of public proclamation of the gospel. I will continue by emphasizing and finally systematizing those ideas about Jesus that occur most frequently in the *kerygmatic* sermons found in the book of Acts, ideas that form the Christological core of apostolic preaching. In pursuit of this objective, I will survey these five texts from the book of Acts, approaching exegetically especially the verses in which Christological statements are found.

As a definition of *kerygma*, I will adopt the one that Bultmann gave. *Kerygma*, he said, is 'personal address which accosts each individual, throwing the person himself into question by rendering his self-understanding problematic, and demanding a decision of him'.[3] The main reason for leaving aside the apologetic and ecclesiastical speeches is that they do not contain substantial catechetical or doctrinal material, but defend arguments and resolutions of the early church leaders (1:16-22; 15:7-11, 13-21) or some piece of advice for Christian elders (20:13-38). Consequently, they do not really fit into the 'preaching' category.

Regarding the authorship of the discourses found in Acts, most scholars agree that they are not an exact record of what the speakers said but summaries of their speeches. As for their rhetorical structure and theological content, some scholars say that they are both Luke's contribution,[4] while others argue that Luke shaped only the rhetorical structure, whereas the theology of each discourse reflects the *kerygma* of the early church.[5] This debate is not really germane to our purpose in this

---

[2] It is useful though to know that scholars – as Constantin Preda reminds us (*Propovăduirea apostolică: structuri retorice în Faptele Apostolilor* (Bucharest: IBMBOR, 2005), 12) – have divided the discourses delivered by Christian speakers in the book of Acts into three groups: *kerygmatic* discourses containing the primary message which were addressed to both Jews and pagans (2:14-41; 3:12-26; 13:16b-41; 14:8-20; 17:16-34); apologetic sermons defending unjustly accused Christians (4:8-12, 19-20; 5:29-32; 7:2-56; 22:1-21; 24:10-21; 26:1-23); and ecclesiastical discourses intended for an already Christian audience (1:16-22; 15:7-11, 13-21; 20:17-35). This author mentions a fourth category – the juridical discourse – found only in the lawyer Tertullus' plea in front of procurator Antonius Felix (24:2-8).

[3] R. Bultmann, *Theology of the New Testament*, Vol. 1 (London: SCM Press, 1952), 307.

[4] We include in this category also authors like, for example, Christopher Tucket who suggested that 'the speech in Acts 2 placed on Peter's lips may not tell us so much about Luke's own views, but more about what Luke thought were the kinds of things Peter said, or should have said, in the context in which the speech is now placed within the story' ('The Christology of Luke-Acts,' in Joseph Verheyden (ed.), *The Unity of Luke-Acts* (Leuven, Belgium: Leuven University, 1999), 141).

[5] It is worth recalling here Cadbury's remarks of nearly eighty years ago: 'Critics of the secular school would scrutinize (Luke's) speeches particularly. They were the most prized parts of the classical historians and the most carefully composed parts in contemporary historiography… Like Thucydides and the other best composers of speeches, he attempted to present what the speakers were likely to have said' (Henry J. Cadbury, 'The Speeches in Acts', in Kirsopp Lake and Henry J. Cadbury (eds), *The Beginnings of Christianity, Part I: The Acts of the Apostles: Additional Notes to the Commentary* (London: Macmillan, 1933), 425 and 426-27 respectively).

paper because, whatever the case may be, what we have in these speeches reflects the main points of the apostolic *kerygma.* It is worth mentioning though that we believe that – as Beverly Gaventa put it – 'Lukan theology is intricately and irreversibly bound up with the story he tells and cannot be separated from it'.[6]

Peter's Sermon at Pentecost (Acts 2:14-40)

The events of Pentecost (2:1-47) are cast in such a way as to show that they represent the fulfilment of the Old Testament promises of the Davidic messianic kingdom. Peter thus delivers the first recorded sermon of the Christian church. It is the first of the missionary speeches in Acts, an address delivered to Jews, *kerygmatic* and Christological in content. Luke uses Peter's sermon to establish his main point at the opening of this book: the messianic kingdom of David was now being offered again (Acts 2.36; 3.19-26).

The early apostolic preaching usually consists of four elements: (1) the announcement that the age of fulfilment has arrived; (2) an account of the ministry, death and triumph of Jesus; (3) citation of Old Testament scriptures whose fulfilment proves the identity of Jesus; (4) a call to repentance.[7] Most of the commentators see that Peter's sermon has them all in its three major sections: verses 14-21 (the time has come); verses 22-36 (Jesus – the Davidic king announced in the Old Testament) and verses 36-40 (the need to repent). The first part of the speech says that the phenomena of the day of Pentecost are a fulfilment of prophecy (v. 16-21). The gift of the Spirit at Pentecost is a fulfilment of the prediction of Joel 2:28-32 that God would one day pour out his Spirit on all people. The subordinate emphasis here is directed to the need of the Jerusalemites to repent (v. 21): 'And it shall come to pass that everyone who calls upon the name of the Lord shall be saved.'[8] In this context, 'the Lord' can only refer to Jesus (1:24; 2:36, 38).

More important for the purposes of this study is the second part of Peter's speech (vv. 22-36) which contains the *kerygmatic* proclamation of God's activity in raising Jesus from the dead and the application of David's words to Jesus. Peter's presentation of the gospel begins with a reference to the miracles of Christ as evidence that he was accredited by God (v. 22). At the beginning the proclamation centres on Jesus as an earthly being. He is not 'the Christ', but Jesus, the Nazarene. Peter calls Jesus ἀνήρ, a man, and this is the starting-point of Lukan Christology in Acts, for Luke never

---

[6] Beverly Roberts Gaventa, 'Toward a Theology of Acts: Reading and Rereading', in *Interpretation,* 42 (1988), 150.

[7] F.F. Bruce, *The Book of the Acts* (New International Commentary on the New Testament: Grand Rapids, MI: Eerdmans, 1988), 63.

[8] All Scripture quotations, unless otherwise indicated, are taken from the *Holy Bible: English Standard Version* (ESV).

mentions anything about the pre-existence or incarnation of Christ.[9] The divine accreditation is shown through 'mighty works and wonders and signs' (δυνάμεσι καὶ τέρασι καὶ σημείοις). The term δύναμις is regularly used for miracles in the Gospels (Luke 10:13; 19:37) and will be used of Paul's miracles (Acts 19:11). To this, Luke adds τέρατα καὶ σημεῖα ('wonders and signs'), a phrase derived from the Septuagint, where it often describes God's mighty acts on behalf of Israel (Ex. 7:3; Deut. 4:34; 28:46; 29:2; 34:11, Ps. 135:9; Isa. 8:18).[10]

Next, Peter presents the death of Christ as having been caused by the audience, but also as being 'according to the definite plan and foreknowledge of God' (v. 23). Luke is sometimes castigated for not having a 'theology of the cross', but here he clearly refers to the death of Jesus and relates it to God's salvific plan. The crucifixion of Jesus is not the end of the matter. Continuing the idea of God's sovereignty, Peter declares that 'God raised him up' (v. 24). The resurrection is thus depicted not as an achievement of Jesus, but the result of God's powerful action. God raised Jesus 'loosing the pangs of death'. Part of this phrase is borrowed from Psalm 18:4 and provides an image in which death is regarded as being 'in labour' and unable to hold back its child. The implication is that Jesus was raised because he already was the Messiah, not that he became Messiah through resurrection.[11] The statement that 'it was not possible for him to be held by it (death)' clearly shows that Peter is using the resurrection as a validation of Jesus' life and ministry.[12]

With the declaration of verse 24, the speech had reached its climax. It now remained only to demonstrate that the resurrection had been foretold in Scripture, that its reference was to the Messiah, and that by fulfilling prophecy, Jesus proves to be Messiah. Peter did this by reference to Psalm 16:8-11. The rabbis also interpreted Psalm 16:10 as a reference to resurrection.[13] David did not write about himself, but about another, since his tomb was proof that his body was in the ground. If David wrote of another, he did so as a prophet and in the same prophetic way he wrote Psalm 132:11, with its promise that God would raise one of his sons as king. Peter understood it of one king, the Messiah. The messianic interpretation of Psalm 132:11 was brought back to Psalm 16:10, now slightly changed to meet the case by reading 'his flesh' (Acts 2:31) in place of 'your holy one'. It was Jesus who was not abandoned to the grave and whose body did not see decay. The resurrection proves that Jesus is the

---

[9] J.A. Fitzmyer, *The Acts of the Apostles: A New Translation with Introduction and Commentary* (New Haven, CT: Yale University Press, 2008), 254.
[10] Fitzmyer, *The Acts of the Apostles*, 255.
[11] D.G. Peterson, *The Acts of the Apostles* (Pillar New Testament Commentary: Grand Rapids, MI: Eerdmans, 2009), 147.
[12] Ajith Fernando, *Acts* (NIV Application Commentary: Grand Rapids, MI: Zondervan, 1998), 103.
[13] D.J. Williams, *Acts* (New International Biblical Commentary: Peabody, MA: Hendrickson, 1990), 52.

Messiah, who fulfils a complex of Jewish hopes. He is the king and the saviour of Davidic descent, who reigns for ever over God's people, bringing the blessings of forgiveness and peace with God.

Resurrection was followed by ascension 'to the right hand of God' (Acts 2:32-33).[14] In the ancient world, the right hand was often identified with greatness, strength, goodness and divinity.[15] From Psalm 110:1 it will shortly be demonstrated that the right hand of God is the proper place for the Messiah (vv. 34-35). Meanwhile, Peter claimed that what they now saw and heard was Jesus' gift 'poured out' on his people (v. 33). Significantly, in the words of Joel, it was God who poured out his Spirit. But according to Peter, Jesus acted on God's behalf. 'He had become the divine executor',[16] sharing fully in God's heavenly rule.

The claim is now clinched by a proof from Scripture, namely Psalm 110:1: 'For David did not ascend into the heavens, but he himself says, "The Lord said to my Lord, 'Sit at my right hand, until I make your enemies your footstool'"'. In their Old Testament context, these words of the psalm commemorated the enthronement of a king, who is invited by Yahweh to assume a position of honour beside God. Jesus' discussion of this text indicates that a messianic interpretation was already known to the teachers of the law in his day (Luke 20:41-44). The victorious status acquired by the newly enthroned Davidic king is applied to the risen Christ. The exaltation of Jesus is an integral part of the primitive apostolic message, as it remains an integral part of the historic Christian creeds. In other words, resurrection and ascension belong together in Christian theology.

Peter concludes his scriptural argument by saying that, as a result of God's raising and exalting him, the crucified Jesus has become a victor, known as κύριος and χριστός.[17] The first of these two Christological titles

---

[14] The dative case of the Greek in v. 33 (τῇ δεξιᾷ οὖν τοῦ θεοῦ ὑψωθείς) could be rendered either 'with the right hand of God' (instrumental sense, as NEB), or 'at the right hand of God' (local sense, as ESV). The latter sense is preferred by the majority of commentators, but in either case the point remains that Jesus had been exalted to a position of power and authority, marked by his receiving from the Father the promised Holy Spirit to give to God's people.

[15] Peterson, *The Acts of the Apostles*, 150.

[16] Williams, *Acts*, 53.

[17] This may sound like an adoptionist claim, but Conzelmann rightly asserts that Luke makes no essential distinction between κύριος and χριστός. Luke derives the combination of the two titles from the scriptural proof, the results of which he summarizes here; he obtains the Messiah title from Psalm 16 and the κύριος title from Psalm 110. 'Luke is not reflecting on the time of installation at all but simply sets forth God's action in opposition to the behaviour of the Jews' (H. Conzelmann, *A Commentary on the Acts of the Apostles* (Hermeneia: A Critical and Historical Commentary on the Bible), (Philadelphia, PA: Fortress Press, 1987), 21). In the same line of thought, C. Kavin Rowe ('Acts 2.36 and the Continuity of Lukan Christology', in *New Testament Studies,* 53 (January 2007), 37-56) offers an argument for a reasoned rejection of the majority view in the modern period. Modern interpreters (Wrede, Bultmann, Cullmann, Ulrich Wilckens, C.K. Barrett) seem to be united in their opinion that Acts 2:36 promulgates a Christology that is recognizably different from Luke's own view – that Jesus has been made Lord and Messiah by virtue of his resurrection. According to Rowe, this tension is due to the

implies that Jesus in his risen status has been made the equal of Yahweh of the Old Testament, for 'Lord' was used by Palestinian Jews in the final pre-Christian centuries as a title for Yahweh.[18] The second title means that Jesus in his risen status has been made by God the anointed agent to bring deliverance to the people of Israel, who were expecting the coming of a Messiah. The messianic position relates back to the prior claim of Joel 2:32 that whoever calls on the name of 'the Lord' will be saved (Acts 2:21). Jesus is the Lord on whom to call since he is the Messiah. God now calls people to himself through Jesus, and offers them forgiveness and the Holy Spirit in the name of Jesus Christ. As Lord, Jesus demands repentance and baptism (2:38), which is an outward expression of allegiance to him. This is an important feature of the apostolic *kerygma* as the right way to respond to the gospel message.

Peter's Sermon after the Healing of the Lame Beggar (Acts 3:12-26)

The healing of the lame beggar became the occasion for Peter's second sermon in Jerusalem. He began by identifying Jesus as the one glorified by the God of Abraham, Isaac and Jacob. The cripple had been cured because Jesus had been glorified. From his place of exaltation, Jesus had endowed his disciples with power to act in his name and to perform mighty works such as he himself had performed in the days of his bodily presence among them. Both the description of Jesus as the Servant and the reference to his being glorified after terrible humiliation and suffering are drawn from the portrayal of the obedient and suffering Servant of the Lord in Isaiah 52:13-53:12 which begins: 'Behold, my servant… shall be high and lifted up, and shall be exalted.' Almost certainly, Peter had in mind the resurrection and ascension of Jesus which means that this prophecy had been fulfilled in those events. Jesus is the messianic figure who accomplished God's saving purposes for Israel and the nations by fulfilling the pattern set out in that prophecy.

The Jerusalemites are directly charged with repudiating Jesus. Peter stresses the gravity of this rejection by describing Jesus as 'the Holy and Righteous One'. From Acts 7:52 and 22:14, it seems that 'the Righteous One' (ὁ δίκαιος) was a messianic designation, derived from prophetic expectations (e.g. Isa. 32:1; 53:11; Jer. 23:5; Zech. 9:9; cf. 1 Enoch 38:2; 53:6; Ps. Sol. 17:35).[19] The use of 'the Holy One' here may even owe

---

collision of different interpretative contexts. The conclusion of his compelling overview of Lukan Christology is that the biblical writer 'creates a narrative Christology in which Jesus' identity as κύριος stands at the centre'. Thus, Rowe's point is that the 'making' in Acts 2.36 does not refer to an ontological transformation in the identity of Jesus or his status but to an epistemological shift in perception of it by the human community: 'In the Lukan narrative, there was not a time when Jesus was not κύριος… Acts 2:36, that is, does not contradict Lukan Christology but expresses it.'

[18] Fitzmyer, *The Acts of the Apostles*, 260.

[19] Peterson, *The Acts of the Apostles*, 175.

something to Peter's already having employed it in quoting from Psalm 16:10 ('your Holy One'). The accusation of verse 14 is repeated in more harsh terms, charging them with killing 'the author of life' (τὸν ἀρχηγὸν τῆς ζωῆς).[20] By virtue of his death and resurrection, Jesus is the originator of new life for others, as the argument in verses 16-21 goes on to suggest. His life-giving power has just powerfully worked the restoration of life to the lame man's limbs. It appears again that the apostolic preaching in Acts loves to emphasize the contrast between men's treatment of Jesus and God's. 'You killed the author of life, whom God raised from the dead.' This is what you did, but God brought him to life again, and we bear witness to the fact of his resurrection.

The death of Christ is again given as a fulfilment of prophecy: 'But what God foretold by the mouth of all the prophets, that his Christ would suffer, he thus fulfilled' (v. 18). Most obviously, prophecies of the suffering servant of God in Isaiah and passages reflecting the experience of David or some other righteous sufferer in the Psalms were applied by earliest Christian preachers to the passion of Jesus (e.g. Psalms 22, 31, 34, 69).

Peter refers again to the fulfilment of old prophecies when he tells that times of refreshment will come as a result of their repentance (3:19). This was part of Jewish eschatology. But Peter says that this will come only when God sends the Christ following their repentance (v. 20). This announces the second coming of Christ. Thus, while the messianic age has dawned, it has not yet been consummated. He remains in heaven (v. 21a) until the time of the final restoration promised by the prophets (v. 21b).

Even Moses, the first and greatest of Israel's prophets, predicted the day of Christ (Acts 3:22-23). There follow words from Deuteronomy 18:15-19: 'The Lord God will raise up for you a prophet like me from your brothers. You shall listen to him in whatever he tells you.' Moses' prophecy came to be regarded as messianic in its scope.[21] Peter describes Jesus as the

---

[20] The term ἀρχηγός in Greek literature and the papyri hovers between the two senses of 'leader, prince' and 'author, originator'. According to P.-G. Müller (*EDNT*, I, 163-4), it occurs four times in the NT (here, in 5:31, and twice in Hebrews (2:10; 12:2)), exclusively as a Christological title for the exalted Jesus. The expression occurs 35 times in the Septuagint with nine Hebrew equivalents bearing the senses of confidant, physician, family or tribal representative, head, tip, (tree-)top, supervisor, prince, and leader. The credo theme of 'led out of Egypt' is here transposed into Christological-titular usage and denotes the exalted Jesus as the eschatological leader of the new people of God on its exodus into the *doxa* of the resurrection. However, the results of lexicographical investigation of secular Greek indicate an extremely rich spectrum of meaning for the word. C.K. Barrett (*A Critical and Exegetical Commentary on the Acts of the Apostles* (Edinburgh: T&T Clark, 2004), 197) notes that its primary adjectival sense is 'beginning, originating'. Philo uses the closely related ἀρχηγέτης of God (*De Ebr.* 42), of Adam in his perfection (*De Op. Mundi* 142), and of Noah (*De Abr.* 46) as the τέλος of an old race and the ἀρχή of the new. In Acts 5:31, the sense of founder and protector (σωτήρ) is probably best, and this also fits the contrasting structure of the present verse: 'him who was bringing life into the world, and thereby establishing a new age, or reign, you put to death.'

[21] The text comes from a context in which Moses was warning against the use of divination as a means of ascertaining God's will. 'God has not permitted you to do so,' he said, but 'will

promised prophet because he brings the ultimate revelation of God's will and leads God's people to final salvation. Jesus is for Israel now what Moses was at the time of the exodus. By their response to the risen Jesus, Peter's audience will show whether they belong to the true Israel or not![22]

F.F. Bruce observes that 'in Peter's speech on the day of Pentecost, the person and work of Jesus are expounded in terms of a "Son of David" Christology. In his present speech, at least two, and possibly three, Christologies are presented side by side: a 'Servant' Christology, possibly an 'Elijah' Christology, and certainly a 'prophet' Christology'.[23] The statement that 'God, having raised up his servant, sent him to you first' (Acts 3.26) implies the sort of sequence present in Isaiah 49:5-6, where the messianic character of the text will come to 'restore the tribes of Jacob' so that they can be 'a light for the Gentiles' and bring God's salvation 'to the ends of the earth'. Thus, that significant prophetic oracle, which reveals the way in which God will ultimately fulfil his promise to Abraham, appears to lie behind the final call of Peter's sermon. In this sequence of thought, the raising up of Jesus refers to God sending him as Saviour, to fulfil the divine plan for Israel and the nations. In Peterson's view, at this point in the narrative, Peter clearly anticipates that the messianic salvation will somehow be extended to the nations.[24]

Peter's Sermon in Cornelius' House (Acts 10:34-43)

Although Martin Dibelius regarded this speech as an interpolation into the original Cornelius story,[25] modern commentators seem to follow F.F. Bruce's view that Peter's address is devoted almost entirely to a summary of the apostolic preaching.[26] Moreover, the fact that the speech is more strongly marked by Aramaisms than Peter's speeches in the earlier chapters in Acts suggests that its text is not Luke's free invention, but a rather literal reproduction of what he found in his source.

---

raise up for you a prophet.' The original sense was that he would send them a prophet from time to time as occasion demanded, but the use of the singular, *a* prophet, led to the view that one prophet in particular was intended, a second Moses, who would appear at the end of the age, either as the Messiah or as some other eschatological figure.

[22] Peterson, *The Acts of the Apostles*, 183.

[23] Bruce, *The Book of the Acts*, 87. In this author's opinion, it must not be supposed that these Christologies were kept separate at that time, each being developed independently by one group or school of thought within the early church. 'They have been interwoven throughout the course of Christian history, and such evidence as is available indicates that it was so from the beginning.'

[24] Peterson, *The Acts of the Apostles*, 185.

[25] M. Dibelius, *Studies in the Acts of the Apostles* (London: SCM Press, 1956), 110.

[26] Bruce, *The Book of the Acts*, 212. C.H. Dodd (*The Apostolic Preaching and its Developments* (London: SCM Press, 1936), 56) has rightly said before that 'the speech before Cornelius represents the form of *kerygma* used by the primitive Church in its earliest approaches to a wider preaching'.

Peter begins the fourth of his messages in Acts – one of which has not been approached in this paper – with a remarkable confession: 'Truly I understand that God shows no partiality, but in every nation anyone who fears him and does what is right is acceptable to him' (10:34-35). No longer was God only for the Jews, and no longer was Jesus only a Jewish Messiah. Here comes a new theology of remnant Christians from all nations of the world. John Polhill noticed an interesting interplay in the verse between the narrow nature of the gospel's beginnings and its unlimited scope. God sent a message to his people, 'the people of Israel'. But its content was peace through Christ, who is 'Lord of all' (v. 36). If he is truly Lord of all, then the gospel is for all peoples, not just the people of Israel.[27]

In verse 38, Peter attempts to show that Jesus' ministry was accredited by God. He begins with 'how God anointed Jesus of Nazareth with the Holy Spirit and with power', and ends with 'for God was with him'. In between, Peter sums up Jesus' healing and exorcising activity: 'He went about doing good and healing all who were oppressed by the devil.' The statement that Jesus of Nazareth was 'anointed' by God with the Holy Spirit and power is reminiscent of the words of Isaiah 61:1-2: 'The Spirit of the Lord God is upon me, because the Lord has anointed me…' The prophet who sees himself in these verses may be assuming the role of the Servant of Isaiah 42:1–53:12. The Servant is first presented in Isaiah 42:1 as God's chosen one on whom he had put his Spirit.[28]

Five times in Acts, the apostles speak of witnessing the resurrection. This risen Lord sent Peter and the other apostles to testify that Jesus is God's appointed 'judge of the living and the dead' (vv. 39-42). It seems that judgement is an essential part of the evangelistic message.

The work of the risen Christ is by no means limited to the execution of judgement; he is also the one through whom, as the prophets agreed, those who believe in him will have their sins forgiven (v. 43). Richard Pervo makes a connection between this assertion and what has been said earlier in 2:38-39 which means that the prophetic texts apply also to Gentiles.[29]

Paul's Sermon in Pisidian Antioch (Acts 13:16b-41)

The Christian missionaries cross to Asia Minor, where Paul's first recorded sermon is preached in Pisidian Antioch. This speech was addressed not only to Jews but also to Gentiles who worshipped God, who were apparently also present in the synagogue service.

The first paragraph concerns God's choice of Israel and the displacement of the nations of Canaan in favour of God's chosen people (vv. 17-19). The

[27] J.B. Polhill, *Acts* (New American Commentary: Nashville, TN: Broadman & Holman Publishers, 1992), 261.

[28] Bruce, *The Book of the Acts*, 213.

[29] R.I. Pervo, *Acts* (Hermeneia: A Critical and Historical Commentary on the Bible), (Minneapolis, MN: Fortress Press, 2009), 281.

second section is the displacement of Saul with David, the king of God's choice (vv. 20-22). A third theme is John the Baptist, introduced with reference to Jesus (vv. 23-25). John preached repentance and baptism to all the people of Israel. Jews of his day would have seen baptism as part of converting to Judaism so the speech implied that those who thought of themselves as Jews also needed conversion. Thus the 'chosen people' now had themselves to repent or perhaps be displaced.

Paul reviews Israel's history, but his purpose is to show God at work until the promises are fulfilled in Jesus the Messiah, rejected by the Jerusalem leaders, but divinely approved by the mighty act of the resurrection.[30] Like Peter (3:17), Paul explains the guilt for this crime on the grounds that the people who lived in Jerusalem, and even their leaders, did not recognize Jesus as the Saviour, nor did they understand the words of the prophets (vv. 26-27). This idea of prophetic fulfilment occurs three times in this sermon (vv. 27, 29, 32-33). As we have seen in Peter's speeches (2:23; 3:17-18; see also 4:27-28), [31] the paradox is that, acting in ignorance and trying to get rid of Jesus, the people of Jerusalem actually played a role that had been predicted, contributing to the exaltation of Jesus as Messiah. The action of God is set against the action of the people of Jerusalem and their rulers. God raised Jesus up from death, and over a period of many days he appeared to his disciples who had accompanied him from Galilee to Jerusalem, and were therefore well qualified to be public witnesses to his resurrection and messiahship (10:30-31).[32]

The good news concerned the Messiah whom God had promised to their fathers and had now sent. The central point of the good news was the resurrection of Jesus, and in this connection Paul cited the words of Psalm 2:7 where God said to the Messiah: 'You are my Son, today I have begotten you.' To what does 'today' refer? Most commentators agree that in the context Paul seems to have been implying the day of Jesus' resurrection. Jesus was indeed the Son of God from all eternity and recognized as such

---

[30] F.F. Bruce (ed), *New International Bible Commentary* (Grand Rapids, MI: Zondervan, 1979), 1290.

[31] The similarity between Peter's speech in Jerusalem on the day of Pentecost and Paul's speech in the synagogue of Pisidian Antioch has caused some readers to question the authenticity of one, if not both, of the two speeches. More common is the view that both the Petrine and Pauline speeches are Lukan compositions, a view based on the twofold ground of their common style and common interdependent exegesis. But we should bear in mind the fact that the common outline of the primitive *kerygma* may be traced throughout the New Testament, no matter who the speaker or writer may be. Even so, in C.H. Dodd's opinion (*The Apostolic Preaching and its Developments*, 30), 'if we recall the close general similarity of the *kerygma* as derived from Acts, as well as Paul's emphatic assertion of the identity of his gospel with the general Christian tradition, we shall not find it altogether incredible that the speech at Pisidian Antioch may represent in a general way one form of Paul's preaching, the form, perhaps, which he adopted in synagogues when he had the opportunity of preaching there'.

[32] Paul did not say anything of Jesus' appearance to him, perhaps because he had not followed Jesus as the others had done or seen him die. So instead of including himself among the witnesses, he presented himself as an evangelist.

throughout his earthly life. But it was through the resurrection that he was exalted to God's right hand, enthroned as Son of God, and recognized as such by believing humans.[33] In his commentary on the psalm, two further passages are adduced: Isaiah 55:3 (slightly modified) and Psalm 16:10, introduced by Paul to declare that, in raising Jesus, it was God's purpose that he should not decay (v. 35). Thus the resurrection of Jesus is the ultimate evidence that the Kingdom of God has arrived, bringing forgiveness and anticipating the restoration of all things.[34]

The preaching was regularly rounded off with a direct application to the hearers. Following the exposition of the Christ event is an offer of forgiveness (v. 38) and justification (v. 39). Verse 39 contains ideas that are typical of Paul's letters: belief, justification, and the inability to be justified by the Law of Moses. Forgiveness of sins has been regularly proclaimed at the end of similar speeches in Acts (cf. 2:38; 3:19; 5:31; 10:43), but now justification is mentioned as well.[35] According to Peterson, the expression in Acts 13:39, ἐν τούτῳ πᾶς ὁ πιστεύων δικαιοῦται, could certainly be understood in the normal Pauline sense – namely, that justification sets people free from the service of sin, so that they can offer themselves to God as 'instruments of righteousness' (Rom. 6:11-14).[36] Consequently, ESV correctly translates it: 'by him everyone who believes is freed from everything.' Such justification and renewal is now available for everyone who believes, who trusts in the promises of the gospel, and relies on the work of Christ that makes all this possible.

Paul's Sermon in the Athenian Areopagus (Acts 17:22-34)

Paul's speech on the Areopagus is a masterpiece of missionary discourse. Paul sought to establish a link with the Greek philosophers without

---

[33] Bruce, *The Book of the Acts*, 260; Polhill, *Acts*, 304; Fitzmyer, *The Acts of the Apostles*, 516; Peterson, *The Acts of the Apostles*, 391-92; Pervo, *Acts*, 339.

[34] Williams, *Acts*, 236.

[35] This verse seems to imply that within certain limits, that is, insofar as it is obeyed, the Law of Moses can provide the basis of justification, as though Christ's work were simply to justify what the Jewish law could not. That is, it could mean that the Law of Moses was capable of setting things right in some matters, but that Jesus could provide justification in all cases. This is a very different understanding both of the law and of the work of Christ from that found in Paul's epistles (cf. e.g. 2 Cor. 3:9; Gal. 2:16, 20). But, as Williams points out (*Acts*, 236-37), 'the difference between this passage and the epistles is more apparent than real. The "everyone" of verse 39 includes the Gentiles (or so it seems) without any reference to their keeping the law, and so, we conclude, this verse does affirm, with the epistles, the all-sufficiency of Christ's work'. Bruce (*Acts*, 262) also shows that 'grammatically, the words could indeed be taken to mean that Christ provides for everyone who believes justification from all those things from which Moses' law provides no justification – namely, most deliberate sins. But quite certainly they mean that believers in Christ are *completely* justified ("justified from all things") – something which Moses' law could never achieve for anyone'. In other words, Moses' law does not justify; faith in Christ does.

[36] Peterson, *The Acts of the Apostles*, 394.

compromising the gospel.[37] He began by pointing to an idol he had seen in the market-place as 'the unknown god'. The Greeks had perhaps erected it in case they might have left a god out whom they would not want to offend. In any event, the God they did not know was the only real God, and Paul now proceeded to present him. He pictured him as the God who made all things, the providential God who sets all boundaries of time and space. The philosophers could easily follow this, particularly the Stoics. They would especially agree that 'we are his offspring', where Paul actually quoted a Stoic poet. He did so not to support his message but to prove the fallacy of their idolatry (v. 29). If we are born in God's image, he said, then we are wrong when we make idols. Idolatry gets things backward; it makes God into man's image.

Such ignorance might have been overlooked in the past but the time had come for its judgement. Only one course was open – repentance, a complete turnabout from their false worship and a turning to God. The concept of repentance must have sounded strange to the Athenians. Even stranger was Paul's warning of God's coming day of judgement (v. 31). Greek thought had no room for such an eschatological judgement as the biblical revelation announces. But not only is the judgement day fixed; the agent of the judgement has also been appointed. That one who has been a man should be exalted to the role of universal judge is unheardof and needs proof. God provided this by raising him from the dead. It is evidently implied that the man had died, but nothing is said of the manner or significance of his death.[38] Just as Peter had pointed to the resurrection as proof to the Jews that Jesus is Messiah, so to the Gentiles Paul pointed to the resurrection as proof that he is the coming judge of all humanity.[39] Jesus' resurrection is the best proof of a general resurrection and makes Jesus the key figure in God's plans for humanity.

Major Christological Ideas of the Kerygmatic Discourses Found in the Book of Acts

Systematizing Christological ideas of the apostolic preaching presents us with the danger of ignoring its diversity. *Kerygma* is always situational to some degree, conditioned by the circumstances which called the proclamation forth. This makes very unlikely that the *kerygma* can be abstracted from these different contexts as a fixed formula which can be

[37] Commentators often have said that the Paul of the epistles would never have preached this sermon because its thought would have been alien to him. In John Polhill's opinion (*Acts*, 377), such is not the case. The idea of a 'natural revelation' is certainly present in Rom 1:18-32 even though the application differs. In 1 Thess. 1:9-10, Paul summarized his preaching to the Gentiles at Thessalonica. There the elements are strikingly the same as in the Areopagus speech: turning from idols to a living God, the return of the Son from heaven, the resurrection, the wrath to come. This is almost a summary of the appeal in Acts 17:29-31.

[38] Barrett, *A Critical and Exegetical Commentary on the Acts of the Apostles*, 853.

[39] Polhill, *Acts*, 377.

applied in every situation. However, we can attempt an aerial survey of the *kerygmatic* discourses found in the book of Acts, concentrating on picking out their key Christological ideas.

First of all, we should note that the sermons in Acts proclaim Jesus. Jesus has become the content of the message. The principal focus falls on the resurrection of Jesus (Acts 2:24, 32; 3:15; 10:40; 13:30, 33; 17:31). The resurrection is depicted not as Jesus' own doing but as *the result of God's powerful action* and as *a validation of Jesus' life and ministry*. By virtue of his death and resurrection, Jesus is the author of new life for others (3:16-21). The resurrection also *proves that Jesus is the Messiah*, who fulfils all Jewish hopes. He is the king of Davidic descent, who reigns over God's people, bringing the long-promised eternal blessing. In the sermons that we have just examined the apostles also suggested that Jesus' resurrection *makes possible and anticipates the general resurrection* that God will bring about.

Consequently, along with the emphasis on the resurrection, there are some roles attributed to the exalted Jesus in the *kerygmatic* discourses: the bestowal of the Spirit at Pentecost, the beginning of this new epoch of salvation history (Acts 2:33), and the role of judge at the end (10:42; 17:31). The exalted Messiah was thought to be the one empowering those who acted 'in the name of Jesus' (2:38; 3:16). According to the apostles, Jesus was acting on God's behalf – that is, he became the divine executor, sharing fully in God's rule. Yet there is nothing about the rich sense of union between believer and exalted Lord, as in the writings of Paul and those of John.

Although it is never said that Jesus died on our behalf or for our sins, the Acts sermons mention the death of Jesus as being according to the definite plan of God (2:23; 3:13-17; 10:39). Little attempt is made in the apostolic sermons to explain how the death of Jesus actually achieves our salvation. The focus in Acts is mostly on the offer of forgiveness, not on the process by which atonement for sins was accomplished.[40]

The proclamation of Jesus in the Acts sermons demands repentance and faith. With the demand is coupled the promise of forgiveness (2:38; 3:19; 10:43), salvation (2:21; 13:26) and the gift of the Spirit (2:38; 3:19; 10:44-47). Jesus, in his risen and glorified status, has been made by the Father the anointed agent to bring deliverance to God's people. Men are called by God to himself through Jesus to receive forgiveness and the Holy Spirit. But the gift of salvation is no longer for ethnic Israel only, but for believers from all nations of the world (3:25; 10:34-35).

---

[40] The vicarious sufficiency of the cross of Christ is a major theme in Paul's gospel (Rom. 3:25; 1 Cor. 15:3; 2 Cor. 5:14-21, as it is in 1 Peter, Hebrews and Mark (10:45). Whether the case of Acts is a true representation of the primitive *kerygma* or a reflection of Luke's own theology is not entirely clear. In James Dunn's view (*Unity in Diversity*, 18), the mention 'for our sins' in the tradition handed down to Paul (1 Cor. 15:3) and the fact that Luke omits Mark 10:45 suggests the latter. Dunn assumes that Luke was somewhat influenced by the diaspora Judaism of his time which also sought to play down the notion of atonement by sacrifice.

In conclusion, the most regular and basic Christological element of the *kerygmatic* discourses in Acts is *the resurrection of Jesus* always accompanied by *a call for repentance and faith* and *the promise of forgiveness and salvation* to those who so respond.

Conclusions and Implications for Christian Witness in Post-Communist Central and Eastern Europe

In Athens, Paul not only 'reasoned in the synagogue with the Jews and the devout persons', but he also went to the market-place 'every day' to speak with those who gathered there (Acts 17:17). His presence aroused the curiosity of the philosophers, and they asked him an explanation of his teaching. Under communism, the church in Central and Eastern Europe tended to become an end in itself, because it fought for its own survival. Now the time has come to think of the church as a means to an end. Christians need to move out into the battlefield of the public sphere with a compelling public discourse and a faith-at-work mind and mission. We need to make some adjustments to the way we had been thinking for a long time. When the idea arises that the children of God in the workplace are a legitimate form of the church, it proposes a significant innovation for many of them. The people of God needs to be taught that it is impossible to embrace the New Testament understanding of salvation and for it to affect only one's personal relationship with God. It must also transform one's socio-economic relationships. Thus, Christian political, civic and economic engagement must seek to transform individuals and institutions.

The removal of religion from people's conscience and the destruction of churches were important goals of the communist regimes, because these were serious obstacles in building socialism and creating the 'new man'. This 'new man' that communism wanted to create was meant to be part of a society which lacked spirituality but with right behaviour, a society without God but concerned with an angelic image of the 'new man'. Therefore, as we learn from the book of Acts, the centrality of Jesus, the incarnate God and the prototype of God's new humanity is paramount for the evangelistic endeavours in the ex-communist countries.

While communism banned religion altogether, post-modernism accepts it, but only as a diffuse, nonconformist and contesting religiosity. In the past two decades, Romanians, for example, have shown a growing interest in various spiritual quests. Generally speaking, they have been valuing esoteric movements, a fascination with Oriental mysticism and stories about the para-normal and the occult. Preaching a high Christology might be very appropriate in such conditions, because people would find out that their inclination towards mysticism – which is said to be typical for eastern societies – is in fact an expression of their inner desire after their Creator, which can be satisfied only through a personal and ineffable communion with Christ through the Holy Spirit.

But post-modern religiosity suggests that people can also have a spiritual life outside the church. They can call themselves 'believers' without integrating into a community that shares their faith in God and the risen Christ. It is true that, in their speeches as recorded in the book of Acts, the apostles did not outline an ecclesiology of the early church. However, one must not omit the fact that the immediate consequence of the apostolic preaching of Christ was the founding of numerous communities of believers as local expressions of the new and universal Israel of God. Through such warm and caring Christian communities, Eastern Europe societies can recover from social infirmities – like mistrust and division – that communism brought on them.

Communism created a system that led to absolute dependency on the regime as well, providing very few possibilities for the individual to survive alone in that environment. Thus, the consequences of the fall of the Iron Curtain include what might be called a post-communist consumerism. In their research, economists envisage the development of the present hyper-consumption society in Romania outlining the explosion of consumption credits. The financial newspaper announced in 2008 that Romania was the country of consumption credits with more than 76% of existing debts falling into this category. Under such conditions, it is the church's mission to focus people's attention on their most urgent need – the forgiveness of sins and eternal life.

But the most pernicious plague that communism caused in Eastern Europe is corruption. When more than 98% of Romanians declare themselves as holding a form of Christian faith, one would expect that such a country would reflect Christian values in all spheres of daily life, including the economy, politics and society. Unfortunately, various studies regarding corruption paint a dissonant image of how everyday life is lived in Romania. For example, in the Transparency International's report *Corruption Perceptions Index for 2015,* Romania ranks 26th in the EU with a score of 46/100, and from the European Union family it scores higher only than Greece, Bulgaria and Italy.[41] The situation raises the question: does the church make any attempt to correct the diverging direction between what Romanians say they believe and what they actually do? Let us not forget that, according to the book of Acts, the call to repentance was a pervasive ingredient of the apostolic preaching and the same call is needed in today's post-communist East European society.

---

[41] www.transparency.org.ro/index.html (accessed 27th January 2016).

Secularization, Ecumenism and Christian Witness in Europe

Ovidiu Dorin Druhora

Introduction

Europe exists by virtue of culture and language, not as land surrounded by water, but defined by the encounter between law, religion and philosophy. In this context, religion, especially Christianity, played a decisive role in shaping European identity. However, in modern times, Europe witnessed the great divorce between its historic faith and philosophy, resulting in the rise of the state with varying levels of the suppression of Christianity. A notable, but increasingly forgotten exception to this trend being the church-based 'velvet revolution' overthrow of communism. Ironically, into this spiritual vacuum, European elites are counter-attacking with a state-sponsored invasion of fanatical religionists who violently oppose the secularism of their hosts!

The Secularization of Europe

Earliest Protestantism

There is no satisfactory date to mark the beginning of European secularization, but the movement that gave it life and shaped its early course was the Protestant Reformation. According to medieval historian Brad Gregory, the Protestant Reformation was responsible for secularizing and pluralizing society.[1] In other words, Christians have secularized Europe, either indirectly or unintentionally. The Reformation aimed to create a politically and religiously whole Europe. Christianity was fundamentally called into question.

Luther's insurgency would show the people that there was a liberal middle ground between Catholicism and secularism. The cure for a totalitarian, oppressive Romanist dogma was to give voice and empowerment to the masses, elevating their authority via 'the priesthood of all believers'. This idealized Protestant democratized 'priesthood'

---

[1] See Brad Gregory, *The Unintended Reformation: How a Religious Revolution Secularized Society* (Cambridge, MA: Harvard University Press, 2012).

splintered exponentially. In the end, 'The Church' became 'the churches'.[2] Division proliferated, and today our world is host to over 30,000 denominations.[3] Pluralism grew out of these ideological personality conflicts, often egged on in part by political motivation. With its implied relativism, 'tolerance and pluralism' became the banner under which the Enlightenment promoted its programmes towards the ideal of self-actualization – the secularized template for the *ubermensch* of Nietzsche and Hitler, and 'the new communist man' of Marx and Stalin. Under the Enlightenment, then Romanticism, humankind emerged as the measure of all things. Meanwhile, constant warfare between and within 'Christian' organizations, led to the quest for a 'natural religion' reduced to a few bland tenets on which most reasonable men could agree. An active and present God was all but banished from such, at best, deistic formulations.

The secular 'doves' emerged to reveal religion's true colours. There was no agreement in Christianity; therefore, dysfunctional theological discourse would be abandoned for the noble consensus of 'settled science'. In the seventeenth century, we witnessed the redefinition of *avaritia*,[4] nurtured by widespread economic reform, industrial revolution and urbanization. In some of the most secular countries, France and England, merely talking about religion in a university setting was seen as either reactionary or nostalgic – in any case, 'offensive'. 'Dialectical materialism' became trendy, dominating academic and public discourse. The horror of world wars, and nuclear mutually assured destruction, led Europeans, by the mid-twentieth century, to realize that it was far better to go shopping than go to war. Chasing the 'good life' in lieu of 'God's Life' characterized modern consumerism and welfare capitalism.

Desacralizing and Re-Sacralizing the Public Sphere

Perhaps most critically, secularism is an attack on the traditional form of sacredness, namely, the idea of sanctity of life and its by-products: sanctity of land and of labour. In return, it attempts to 'reinvest' these secular spheres with quasi-sacred significance. Amid Karl Marx's empathy with the 'sigh of the oppressed creature', we glimpse a sense of the sacred dissociated from a religious leviathan that merely serves to perpetuate suffering – a sacred redefined as a radical commitment to liberation without reference to a divine Redeemer.

> We develop new principles for the world out of the world's own principles. We do not say to the world: Cease your struggles; they are foolish; we will give you the true slogan of struggle. We merely show the world what it is

[2] See Charles J. Chaput, 'Life in the Kingdom of Whatever': www.thepublicdiscourse.com/2012/11/6902

[3] Martin Marty (ed), *Religions of the World: The Illustrated Guide to Origins, Beliefs, Traditions and Festivals* (New York: Random House, 2009), 240.

[4] Jonathan Patterson, *Representing Avarice in late Renaissance* (Oxford: OUP, 2015), 16.

> really fighting for, and consciousness is something that it has to acquire, even if it does not want to.[5]

To be operational, modernity requires not just a mere ideological modification, or a redefinition of sanctity; it also needs to exalt the secular to the same level as the sacred. Without this exaltation, modernity cannot fully expand and has no legitimacy to redefine social life. The end-game for secularization is not just separating state and church, or simply 'privatizing' faith. Secularization has profaned the sacred, and has sacralized the profane.[6] Indeed, for Marx and his followers in Christian liberalism, the final, evolved stage of communism, populated by the ideal 'new communist man', derived from the 'Kingdom of God' of Jesus and the sharing society of Christians described in Acts 4. Similarly, the one-thousand-year millennial Kingdom (*Reich Gottes*) of Christ morphed into Hitler's National Socialist 'Reich that will last a thousand years'.

What Happened to Europe?

While it is true that Europe is only a part of the bigger global picture, it is undoubtedly a crucial part in the neo-secular cartography since it is widely perceived as the most secular continent. Europe is not founded upon anything other than traditions – there is no European self-foundation. Europe emerged from something else – an amalgam of Judeo-Christian, Greek and Roman philosophies with a façade that Adrian Pabst calls 'vestigial' Christian.

Europe as a secularized culture is a relatively recent trend. For instance, France – often cited as an ultra-secular country – pushed away its Catholic traditions only in its post-World War II reconstruction, in the 1950s during a period of rapid modernization and heavy reliance on the military-industrial complex (Italy, Spain and Greece – even Britain and the Netherlands – all saw the process of de-Christianization begin in the mid-1960s). Additionally, with the explosion of the liberal Sexual Revolution came the era of aggressive feminism that encouraged women to stop going to church. For a Europe, which had largely inherited its prayers and customs for her mothers, this was overwhelming.

As a modern invention, secularization, like modernity itself, is in a profound identity crisis. It struggles to reinvent itself with notions of sacredness, while powerful extremist forces rise to replace it. Grace Davie, in her book *Religion in Britain Since 1945*, uses the phrase 'believing without belonging', suggesting that while Europe still believes in God,

---

[5] Karl Marx, 'Letter from the Deutsch-Französische Jahrbücher to Ruge, 1843', in William Smaldone, *European Socialism: A Concise History with Documents* (Lanham, Maryland: Rowman & Littlefield, 2014), 73.

[6] Mircea Eliade, *Sacrul şi Profanul* (trans. Brânduşa Prelipceanu; Bucharest: Humanitas, 1995), 16.

she's disillusioned with the church as an institution.[7] Later, in *Religion in Modern Europe*, she introduces the notion of 'vicarious religion', where commitment to Christ or the church is almost absent in Europe and religion is performed by an active minority – *the belongers* – on behalf of a much larger number – the wider population – who implicitly not only understand, but quite clearly approve of what the minority is doing. In other words, there is a relationship between the nominal member and the active member.[8]

In Europe, historical churches are often used as public utilities, upon demand, often at birth or death. Davie illustrates that if you ask Europeans if they believe in God, and you're not specific about the God in question, you'll get about 70% saying yes. If you ask, 'Do you believe that Jesus Christ is the Son of God?' the number is significantly lower. In other words, if you turn your question into a credal statement, the affirmations decrease. The looser your definition of belief, the higher the percentage of believers. The disjunction of active and inactive, of dropping in or regular commitment, is as common in secular life as it is in religious life.[9]

The *European Values Study* from 1999 to 2000 analyzed two indicators of religious belief among younger people. One was belief in a soul, and the other was belief in a 'God in me'. In other words, a belief in an after-life, but also in the notion of a personal God, my God, as opposed to a transcendent God – the notion of immanence.[10]

Pierre Manent, the French philosopher, adds yet another layer. Manent explains that in Europe we are witnessing the re-emergence of the 'religion of humanity', a peculiar cohabitation between secular religion and institutional religion that is giving birth to a new form of humanist religion – of 'man the measure of all things', with no reference to transcendence – a passing from the revealed religion to a form of naturalism and self-made goodness. This religion of humanity marks the subtle autonomy of 'God in me' but with no connection with a transcendent God. We can save ourselves just by being good and compassionate to others. Modern western man is thus caught between this double imperative and contradiction: compassion for and competition with his fellow man. This confusion ultimately isolates man from those around him.[11] Secularization, the opiate of progress, has run its course, intellectually and socially. Most recently, secularism's blasé posture of denial in the face of radical terror has lost its major appeal. Just as the ultimate secularization of communism imposed on the Soviet Bloc produced a spiritually pent-up demand and a resulting Christian revival, will the more benign, but dying, secularization of the

[7] Grace Davie, *Religion in Britain since 1945: Believing without Belonging* (Making Contemporary Britain: New York: John Wiley & Sons, 1994).
[8] Paper presented by Grace Davie at the *Pew Forum's Biannual Faith Angle Conference* on religion, politics and public life, in Key West, Florida, December 2005.
[9] Davie, *Pew Forum's Biannual Faith Angle Conference.*
[10] Davie, *Pew Forum's Biannual Faith Angle Conference.*
[11] Pierre Manent, *Seeing Things Politically* (South Bend, IN: St Augustine's Press, 2015).

West revive a genuine Christian spirituality – in face of the ferocious shar'ia spirituality of an invading Islam?

Ecumenism in Europe

> In order to unite, we must first love one another. In order to love one another, we must first get to know one another.[12]

Dialogue was engrained in the heart of man from the very beginning of creation. Made in the image and likeness of God, with an insatiable need for communication, man has long yearned for that perfect communion (Gen. 1:26). The first question recorded in the history of humanity was: (Adam) 'Where are you?' Second to this, was a relational question that emphasized communication and communion, this time addressed to Cain: 'Where is Abel, your bother?' (Gen. 4:9). This searching line of dialogue threaded the life of the prophets. Then God went silent for the next 400 years. When he finally broke his silence, he did it in flesh and blood. 'The Word became flesh and dwelt among us' (John 1:14).

The cross is the ultimate symbol of dialogue. When asked about the biggest commandment of all, Jesus' answer came clothed in the vocabulary of relationship and dialogue, expressed in two dimensions: vertical – 'You shall love the Lord your God with all your heart and with all your soul', and horizontal – 'You shall love your neighbour as yourself' (Mark 12:30-31). James later designated this relational, dialogical language to be 'the royal law' (Jas 2:8).

Moreover, on the day of Pentecost they each spoke in their own language, no Esperanto, no Euro-speech. The miracle was not, as many theologians would like us to think, the unification of language. The miracle is the fact that they communicated and agreed with one another: 'All these with *one accord* devoting themselves to prayer' (Acts 1:14; 2:44); they were 'of one heart and soul' (Acts 4:32).

The Great Commission in Mark 16:15: 'Go into all the world and proclaim the gospel to all creation' further underscored the relational and dialogical nature of the command: 'Go therefore and make *disciples* of all nations' (Matt. 28:19).

Obviously, when applying this command, the first generation of Christians, particularly the Jews, had problems relationally and dialogically with the Gentiles: 'Now those who were scattered because of the persecution that arose over Stephen travelled as far as Phoenicia and Cyprus and Antioch, speaking the word to no one except Jews' (Acts 11:19). The barrier was finally broken and Luke reveals that: 'there were some of them, men of Cyprus and Cyrene who, on coming to Antioch, spoke to the Hellenists also, preaching the Lord Jesus' (Acts 11:20). In this

---

[12] Cardinal Joseph Suenens, *Boundless Grandeur: The Christian Vision of A.M. Allchin*, (Eugene, OR: Wipf and Stock, 2015), 23.

way, the first international missionary centre was established in Antioch, out of which the names of Paul, Barnabas and others would rise to prominence. Paul's creed for mission was: 'I have become all things to all people, that by all means I might save some' (1 Cor. 9:22).

Paul McParlan uses the 'spider web' analogy: the church has a structure and connectivity, but the focal point is always Christ.[13] This oneness and, at the same time, particularity of identity is a keystone of Christianity. 1 Corinthians 12:27: 'Now you are the body of Christ and individually members of it.' It is only after understanding and embracing this 'individual oneness' in Christ that we can move to dialogue. Before we can dialogue with atheists, leftists, Muslims and others, Christians need to learn to dialogue with each other.

The Quest for Dialogue in Europe

December 1997 marked the time when a new vocabulary emerged within the vision for a new Europe. The European parliament adopted a budget specifically designed for '*The soul of Europe*'.[14] Given that the 'soul of Europe' was not a top priority at the beginning of the European unification project, the prerequisite of a soul now became a component of the shape of this 'new Europe'. The architects in Brussels designated a budget for the soul because, as they put it: 'We find ourselves at a crossroads in this historical process when building the (new) Europe is not just a simple political and economic exercise, but has also a spiritual and ethical dimension.'[15]

John Paul II, in one of his final addresses to the members of the European Committee of Bishops, echoed this sentiment. The Pope offered that the process of European integration was not just economic and political but also religious, 'by the presence of all the values existent throughout the continent'.[16]

No matter how ground-breaking these declarations may have seemed at the time, the Pope, along with the politicians in Brussels, were merely bringing to the council a long legacy of ecumenism that birthed a lineage of standard-bearers still in existence today. It is worth mentioning some of them to see a clearer picture of how far ecumenical dialogue has come.

---

[13] Paul McPartlan, *The Eucharist Makes the Church: Henri de Lubac and John Zizioulas in Dialogue* (London: T & T Clark, 1996), 274.

[14] Alastair Hulbert, 'A Soul for Europe: Ethics and Spirituality', in *Carrefour Newsletter*, Forward Studies Unit, European Commission, April 1998, No. 8, 12.

[15] Hulbert, 'A Soul for Europe', 13.

[16] Pope John Paul II, 'L'Eglise contribute o processes integration européenne dans un esprit de cooperation', in *L'Osservatore Romano,* 10.15 (April 2001), 2.

The World Council of Churches

With antecedents as early as 1910 in the Edinburgh Missionary Conference, Europe instigated the revival of a new ecumenical movement that would soon be organized and endorsed by church and state. From the ashes of World War II, the World Council of Churches was organized on 23rd August 1948, in Amsterdam. Then, 147 churches from various confessions and countries committed themselves to dialogue. Currently, there are 345 church members.[17]

The goal of the WCC was plainly stated at its convening Assembly in August 1948:

> Our name indicates our weakness and our shame before God, for there can be and there is finally only one Church of Christ on earth. Our plurality is a deep anomaly. But our name indicates also that we are aware of that situation, that we do not accept it passively, that we would move forward towards the manifestation of the one holy church.[18]

Critics noted that simply combining a collection of stagnant and diverse organizations, some even controlled by atheist Marxists, was unlikely to produce a dynamic, or even viable, outcome.

The European Evangelical Alliance

On its official website, the EEA says that it exists 'to foster unity and evangelical identity and provide a voice and platform to evangelical Christians. Seeking empowerment by the Holy Spirit, it extends the Kingdom of God by proclamation of the gospel to all nations and by Christ-centred transformation within society.'[19]

The EEA brings together both the national Evangelical Alliances of Europe and a large number of pan-European mission agencies. It has existed as a regional group since the 1950s, but traces its roots to the 1846 conference at which the World Evangelical Alliance (WEA) was established. It is the European section of the WEA. Seeking Christ-like transformation in Europe, the European Evangelical Alliance serves as the dynamic centre for equipping and resourcing, the trusted European-wide Evangelical voice, and the connecting hub for greater strategic impact.[20]

The Lausanne Movement

The Lausanne Movement began with the evangelist Billy Graham. As he started preaching internationally, he developed a passion to 'unite all

---

[17] https://www.oikoumene.org/en/member-churches (accessed 5th December 2015).
[18] *Formation of the World Council of Churches*, 66: www.wayoflife.org/database/wcc.html (accessed 5th December 2015).
[19] www.europeanea.org/index.php/about-eea (accessed 5th December 2015).
[20] From the EEA home website: www.europeanea.org/index.php/about-eea

evangelicals in the common task of the total evangelization of the world'. In the 1970s, Billy Graham perceived the need for a global congress to re-frame Christian mission in a world of political, economic, intellectual and religious upheaval. The church, he believed, had to grasp the ideas and values behind the rapid changes in society.

The Lausanne Movement connects influencers and ideas for global mission, with a vision of the gospel for every person, an evangelical church for every people, Christ-like leaders for every church, and Kingdom impact in every sphere of society.[21]

The Conference of European Churches

Following the WCC paradigm, The Conference of European Churches (CEC) came into being as a way for the churches in Europe to support each other in a ministry of reconciliation. The first Assembly was held at Nyberg, 6th-9th January 1959.

With its radar on Europe, the CEC raised the possibility of a common mission for European churches in the context of rapid change within Europe's borders, especially the challenges brought about by the fall of communism and the rise of sharp nationalistic sentiments and religious intolerance. The CEC became, by default, the enforcer of WCC's ecumenist agenda: finding the common denominator in order to combat individualism, secularism and radicalism.[22]

For the scope of this paper, we will mention only two major CEC assemblies, both preceding a historical event – the first, in May 1989 in Basel, Switzerland (*Peace and Justice*), and the second in 1997 in Graz, Austria (*Reconciliation – Gift of God and Source of New Life)*. These two assemblies were precursors to a major event that took place in Strasbourg, France, on 22nd April 2001, when CEC issued a major document called *Charta Oecumenica* – the guideline for the growing co-operation among the churches of Europe. This document wedded Europe's fate to that of the church, affirming that 'we work towards a humane, socially conscious Europe, in which human rights and the basic values of peace, justice, freedom, tolerance, participation and solidarity prevail' (Article 7 of the Constitution).[23] The CEC no longer saw its own mission of ecumenism as different from that of Europe's unification praxis. Their fates were intertwined.

The CEC's efforts to build a dialogue among the 'churches' grew exponentially with EU integration. Led by the Roman Catholic Church,

---

[21] Lausanne Movement: https://www.lausanne.org/about-the-movement

[22] Conference of European Churches, continues the vision and strategy of the WCC, only with a focus on the European continent.

[23] Viorel Ioniță and Sarah Numico (eds), *Charta Oecumenica* (Geneva: WCC Publications, 2013).

religious leaders on all sides built dialogue bridges with the Orthodox Church and with the Protestant churches as well as with other religions.

The Conciliar decree *Ad Gentes* further extended the mission of the Catholic Church to all people in such a way that the Catholic Church itself became the universal sacrament, based on her own catholicity.[24]

The defining event occurred on 7th December 1965, with the performance of two simultaneous liturgies, one at the Vatican, the other in Constantinople, a symbolic casting out of the historical anathemas between the two churches. Fourteen years later, on 30th November 1979 – two days after Pope John Paul II's first papal visit to Turkey, and almost one and a half years before the Turk, Mehmet Ali Agca, attempted to kill him – Dimitrios I, the ecumenical patriarch made a striking announcement at Constantinople: a Catholic-Orthodox committee was established to begin an official dialogue between the two churches. Then, in May 1999, during John Paul II's visit to Romania – the first papal visit to a majority Orthodox country – Romanian Patriarch Teoctist states: 'This meeting is nothing else but the supreme will of God and the work of the Holy Spirit.'[25]

An important document regarding that dialogue is a papal pastoral letter, *Orientale Lumen,* from 1995, concentrating on the likeness of Christ as understood by both churches. In doing so, the Pope set a precedent for casting the dialogue in the very image of Christ himself.[26] Cardinal Ratzinger followed in his footsteps, writing *The Note about the Sister Church* addressed during Session 8 in the Baltimore meeting in July 2000, and sent to all Roman-Catholic episcopates worldwide.[27] Ratzinger took it a step further and extended the concept of *Sister Church* to Lutheran, Anglican, Episcopal and Evangelical churches alike.[28]

Dialogue was also developing in the 'official' relationships between Anglicans and Catholics. The Orthodox Church and the Lutheran Church followed suit. The dialogue between the Romanian Orthodox Church and the Evangelical Church of Germany is a notable example.

Finding its footing in 1979, this dialogue progressed into twelve official meetings. Father Dumitru Stăniloae, one of its main actors, saw ecumenism as the next stage in Christianity: 'A reality in which the Holy Spirit encourages all Churches to love each other. Schism was not just a simple open conflict,' said Stăniloae, 'but a lack of love.'[29] Slowly, dialogue

---

[24] Mgr. H. Teisser, *La mission de l'Eglise* (Paris: Desclée, 1985), 36; and Gheorghe Petraru, *Ortodoxie si Prozelitism* (Iaşi, Romania: Trinitas, 2000), 96.

[25] PF Părinte Patriarh Teoctist, 'O întâlnire sub semnul harului', in *Vestitorul Ortodoxiei,* XI.226-227 (1st June 1999), 1.

[26] *Orientale Lumen,* Il regna, 9/1995, 266; and Dumitru Popescu, *Ortodoxie şi Catolicism: dialog şi reconciliere* (România creştină, 1999), 125.

[27] Dumitru Abrudan, 'Dialogul teologic ortodox-catolic', in *Telegraful Român,* 148.29-32 (1st and 15th August 2000), 1-2.

[28] Ioan I. Ică, Jr., 'Dialogul Ortodoxo-Catolic', in *Renaşterea,* XI.10 (October 2000), 8-9.

[29] Lucian Leuştean, 'Interreligious Dialogue and its perspective for the European Ecumenism', *Journal for the Study of Religion and Ideologies*, RSI, Nr. 2 (2002), 39.

seeped its way down to emerging themes in theology. In Western Europe, for instance, the resurgence of Trinitarianism in recent decades, advanced by theologians like Colin Gunton, Thomas Torrance and others, was profoundly influenced by Orthodox theologians John Zizioulas, Andrew Louth and Andrew Walker.[30]

Albeit outwardly positive, these forms of dialogue are classic examples of a 'horizontal ecumenism', etched in paper and compiled in documents. Institutionalized ecumenism is, at its best, superficial; at its worst, devoid of a spiritual core.

The current Romanian Patriarch, Daniel, was one of the first major Orthodox leaders to point out this shortcoming: 'There is no crisis for the true (spiritual) ecumenism,' he said, 'only the institutional, the superficial and secularized ecumenism is in crisis.'[31]

The Need for True Ecumenism

Visser 't Hooft, a leading voice in inter-religious dialogue, also maintains that 'the true premise for a genuine dialogue is not that the partners need to completely agree, and compromise their own beliefs, but to accept each other as persons'.[32] We cannot simply have a dialogue on paper that attempts to unify abstract ideas into some *corpus callosum* of the church; one that befriends with the right hand and casts into hell with the left. The search for true ecumenism is the acceptance of the salvation of the other.

Two Case Studies

The Fellowship of St Alban and St Sergius (St Albans, UK)

Under the auspices of the Student Christian Movement, a young Russian refugee by the name of Nicolas Zernov organized a series of conferences in the English town of St Albans with the aim of bringing together young eastern and western Christian students to openly discuss their similarities and differences.[33]

The Anglo-Russian Student Conferences of 1927 and 1928 were some of the first organised opportunities for the future church leaders to network

[30] Constantin Pătuleanu, 'Dialogul teologic bilateral dintre EKD si BOR, Glosar VIII, Bucureşti, 3-8 iulie 1998', *BOR,* CXVI. 7-12 (1998), 145.

[31] I.P.S. Daniel, Mitropolitul Moldovei şi Bucovinei, 'Ideal şi criză în mişcarea ecumenică: ecumenism spiritual şi ecumenism secularizat', in *Vestitorul Ortodoxiei* XI.218-219 (31 January 1999), 1-2.

[32] *Lignes Directrices de l'Action Oecumenique de la Fédération des Eglises protestantes de la Suisse* (Fédération des Eglises Protestantes de la Suisse, 1994), 436-37.

[33] For more details about the history of the Fellowship, see: Nicolas Zernov and Militza Zernov, 'The Fellowship of St Alban and St Sergius: A Historical Memoir': www.sobornost.org/Zernov_History-of-the-Fellowship.pdf

with Christians of other traditions, namely Evangelicals, Methodists and Scottish Presbyterians.

Their chapel services were celebrated in both the Orthodox and the Anglican traditions. The ongoing fellowship currently publishes the periodical *Sobornost*. With its headquarters at Oxford, this grassroots movement has established branches elsewhere in Britain as well as in Bulgaria, Denmark, Greece, Romania, Russia and Sweden.[34]

Ecumenism Behind Bars (Communist Romania)

Friday, 12th February 2016, at the international airport in Havana, Cuba, Pope Francis met the Russian Patriarch Kirill of Moscow. Paul Gavrilyuk, in an article posted on Academia on 6th February,[35] asks an important question: why is Patriarch Kirill willing to meet with the 'Pope of surprises'?[36]

According to official sources, the declaration of Orthodox-Catholic co-operation will involve such items as support for the plight of Christians in the Middle East, the Syrian refugee crisis, secularization, and Christian teaching regarding the family. These are issues of global importance that quite rightly require Christian co-operation.

The joint declaration signed between the two heads of the churches consisted of thirty specific statements. After they had acknowledged the mutual tradition they had shared for the first millennium of Christianity, the very first concern addressed was in defence of persecuted Christians: 'Our gaze must first turn to those regions of the world where Christians are victims of persecution.'

Suffering for the cause of Christ was part of Christian witness since the foundation of the church (Acts 1:8). The Greek verb *martureo* means 'witness', and has the same root as the word *martyres* – the martyrs of the faith. The blood of the faithful was 'the seed of the new believers'.[37]

Suffering for Christ always kept alive the passionate fire of purity and commitment of the faithful. The church of the first centuries of Christianity had a peculiar view about this. Ignatius, bishop of Antioch in the second century, desired martyrdom and associated this experience with the

[34] Zernov and Zernov, 'The Fellowship of St Alban and St Sergius', 19.

[35] Paul Gavryliuk, 'Why Is Pope Meeting with Patriarch Kirill of Moscow': https://www.academia.edu/21609549/Why_Did_the_Patriarch_Kirill_of_Moscow_Agree_to_Meet_with_Pope_Francis_A_Primer_in_the_Byzantine_Politics_of_the_Russian_Orthodox_Church

[36] See 'A Pope of Surprises', in *Life Hope and Truth* (July/August 2015): http://lifehopeandtruth.com/discern/july-aug-2015/a-pope-of-surprises

[37] Tertullian, Apologia, Letter to the Roman Governor.

metaphor of a new birth: 'My birth is imminent. Forgive me, brethren. Do not prevent me from coming to life.'[38]

In the 45 years of communist repression in Romania, my country of birth, we witnessed firsthand the life of the suffering church. Over two million Christians were thrown into prison, including some 5,000 Orthodox Christian priests of the official national church. No denomination was safe. In 1948, the government abolished the Uniate Eastern-Catholic churches (the second largest religious grouping in Romania, with 1.5 million people in 1948) and forcibly integrated them into the Romanian Orthodox Church. A total of 400 priests in the Eastern Catholic churches were killed by the state. In theory, religious denominations were permitted to organize and function, but in practice the regime found many ways to suppress those who threatened 'public security'. Legislation was passed that took control of all aspects of religious life, and required all religious denominations to have central organizations that required state approval, while all religious leaders needed to be registered and approved by the government. The communists seized complete control of the church, and began persecuting its membership, while the church hierarchy turned a blind eye and, in many cases, even co-operated, using its resources to assist the state in its terror campaign against targeted members. The hierarchy, for their part, denied the existence of persecution.

Behind bars, however, where Christian prisoners were stripped of their identity, possessions and families, and were socially ostracized, authentic Christianity shined as never before. A new identity was forged. Their identity and communion with Christ and his followers, through suffering, gave them strength to endure, and even more, the privilege of rejoicing in chains – a mystery never fully understood by outsiders.

Their brand of ecumenism survives to this day. For instance, when jihadists in the Middle East behead a Christian, nobody jumps up to claim that a Coptic Orthodox or an Evangelical Ethiopian, or a Melkite Catholic Syrian has died. We simply say: a Christian brother has died.

A Page from the Journal of Happiness

As founder of The Agape Pro Humanitas Foundation, I have co-ordinated the collection of over eighty hours of audio-visual history from clerics and lay men and women imprisoned for their faith in the years that preceded the 1989 Revolution. Irrespective of religious affiliation, this audio-visual history includes testimonies from pastors, monks, priests, bishops and lay believers of all confessions. A clear thread line emerges from every testimony of those imprisoned: there was no place for denominationalism in the *gulag*. Religious arrogance and its walls came crumbling down.

[38] Ignatius of Antioch, Letter to the Romans 1.1-7.3, in Jan Willen van Henten and Friedrich Avemarie (eds), *Martyrdom and Noble Death: Selected Texts from Greco-Roman, Jewish and Christian Antiquity* (London: Routledge, 2002), 107.

Prayer meetings, Eucharistic services, baptisms and Bible study were routine and had a very ecumenical character. Miracles were nearly a daily occurrence. (There are several accounts of Jesus appearing to prisoners.) Some were miraculously saved from the firing squad, literally at the eleventh hour. Others were healed and fed mysteriously in solitary confinement. These miracle stories found their way to every church congregation regardless of denomination. Their individual narratives poured into the metanarrative – 'Christ and Him crucified' – giving the entire Christian identity of that time a true mark of authenticity.

My thesis on 'ecumenism behind bars' is that, through suffering, torture and persecution, Christians were forced to reconsider and rediscover their true faith. They were together on the path of experiencing again the love and communion of the saints from the New Testament church, where the presence of God and the power of the Holy Spirit were 'tangible'. Through the love and power of Christ in them they were united in suffering and also in witness. Divinely-revealed dreams, visions, miracles, healings, the power to forgive their torturers and lead them to Christ, were their everyday testimony. This ecumenism behind bars was the 'true spiritual ecumenism', and was in fact their pure experience of 'Authentic Christianity'.

The following examples barely scratch the surface of this entire cosmos that is ecumenism behind bars – an ecumenism one can argue in its purest form.

Nicolae Steinhardt, an atheist intellectual Jew from Bucharest, who refused to collaborate with the *Securitate* (the communist secret service) and become an informant against his own father (a scientist educated in Switzerland and a colleague of Albert Einstein). In prison, he met authentic Christianity and in just a few months after his imprisonment, he became a Christian. Steinhardt specifically requested to have an ecumenical baptism. In his prison diary, he writes: 'I entered prison blind; now I leave with my eyes wide open. I came with a false self-image, arrogant and very infatuated with myself; now I leave completely healed and restored.'[39] He later went on to publish his prison diaries as *Jurnalul Fericirii* ('The Diaries of Happiness').

Francisc Visky, a pastor in the Hungarian Reformed Church in Romania, was the leader of the Bathanist Movement (house prayer and Bible study). Pastor Visky was sentenced to 22 years in prison on trumped up sedition charges. His wife and their seven children were also sent to a concentration camp in an undisclosed part of the country. Visky was sent to Gherla, one of the most atrocious prisons, and known for executing priests. Visky always referred to Gherla as 'his own parish'. 'In prison I learned to laugh,' writes Visky. 'To laugh, and to hold on to God, wrestling with Him for a sign. The madness of the world, including that of the (then) Soviet system, can only be dispelled by the foolishness of God. The antidote to fear is

[39] Nicolae Steinhardt, *Jurnalul Fericirii* (Iași, Romania: Editura Polirom, 2008), 515-16 (translation mine).

love. There is no other way. We are free to love our enemies. We cannot fear those whom we love.'[40]

Richard Wurmbrand, a Lutheran pastor from Bucharest, was shackled and passed through some of the worst prison camps, surviving over sixteen years of torture and starvation. Eventually, he escaped to America, where he testified before the US Senate Judiciary Committee in 1966, stripping his shirt to reveal his scars. From then on, Wurmbrand would be known as the 'Voice of the Martyrs' throughout the Christian world. 'Often, after a secret service,' he told American senators, at the height of the Cold War, 'Christians were caught and sent to prison. There, Christians wore chains with the gladness with which a bride wears a precious jewel received from her beloved.'[41]

Vasile Răscol, a Pentecostal pastor, arrested for Bible smuggling, was sentenced to two years in prison. Silvia Tărniceru, a Baptist Sunday school teacher, was also imprisoned for Bible smuggling – their biographies tell stories of prayer meetings in which all Christians, regardless of their denomination, participated. Răscol and many others testify about being led by the Holy Spirit through dreams, visions and prophecies – often receiving songs by inspiration, healing and strengthening one another after torture sessions – all together, Orthodox, Catholic, Lutheran, Evangelical, speaking to each other through scriptures and hymns. Nicolae Moldoveanu and Traian Dorz were such poets and composers among them. *Secularism put them behind bars but ecumenism freed them.* A new ecumenism deeply rooted in spiritual experience surfaced within these prison cells.

A Hidden and Forgotten Treasure

These sufferings were not unique to the communist *gulag*. German theologian Dietrich Bonhoeffer is a distinctive example of suffering as a result of outspoken criticism of the Nazi regime – one of the few German Christian voices who dared to openly oppose Hitler. At a time when the established churches in Germany, both Protestant and Catholic, fell silent, Bonhoeffer and others – including Karl Barth and Martin Niemöller – founded the breakaway Confessing Church. When Lutheran tradition effectively neutralized the radical ethics of the Sermon on the Mount by reducing it to an impossible standard to convict men of sin, Bonhoeffer argued that Jesus really wished us to live the Sermon on the Mount. At first a committed pacifist, Bonhoeffer later began to regard ethics, not as a fixed set of rules but as an attempt to follow Christ in one's own unique circumstances. Those were the voices of the martyrs who followed Christ into the fiery furnace, forging a now-forgotten legacy. The voice of the twentieth-century martyrs said: 'We are called upon not to be successful,

[40] Ferencz Visky, *The Foolishness of God* (Cluj-Napoca, Romania: Koinonia Publishing, 2010).

[41] Richard Wurmbrand, *Tortured for Christ* (Bartlesville, OK: VOM Publishing, 1967).

but to be faithful.'[42] Bonhoeffer was faithful to the giving of his own life, which he did as willingly and serenely as any martyr, in Russia, Romania or today's Middle East. Their way of rediscovering and experiencing 'authentic Christianity' behind bars is the legacy of persecuted Christians throughout history, probably the most hidden and forgotten treasure of Christianity. We are all inheritors of it. For they reveal, to this day, that Christian dialogue and unity is the only real hope for a new Europe!

Conclusions

Christian Witness in Europe

What is the key for a stronger, more authentic Christian witness in Europe? If institutional ecumenism and ecumenical dialogue has been buried in encyclicals, documents and books written after each meeting or conference – what then is the way forward?

Although ecumenical dialogue is the call to tear down walls and build new bridges, true dialogue cannot be institutionalized. It is a proactive force moving in the DNA of every authentic Christian. In this Christ-centred dialogical matrix, communication always leads to community. Once there, it can strive to rise to the next level – vertical and horizontal communion.

What about pluralism, which many countries with big denominations (Orthodox and Catholic) view as a threat? The multiplicity of ethnic minorities and religious views in fact helps the ecumenical dialogue.[43] It moves people away from the centrifugal forces tearing them apart. It does so by redefining the characteristics that make them unique as citizens and believers connected with a diverse body – not against 'otherness' but for 'oneness'.

Issues, Problems and Barriers

Central and Eastern Europe rose from the ashes of communism to a grassroots ecumenism that sparked the hopes of young people. But where are we today? Are we to adopt a doomsday view and speculate that the only hope for a resurrected dialogue is the rise of secularism and militant persecution that will eventually force us to sit at the non-denominational table of suffering? An uncommunicative church will not only lose its place in the emerging geo-political framework; it will be drowned out by the rising voices of post-materialism and new social movements that galvanize the cultural sphere as a major arena for collective action in lieu of

---

[42] Mother Theresa, *Everything Starts from Prayer* (Ashland, OR: White Cloud Press, 2009), 37.

[43] Dănuţ Mănăstireanu, Society for the Ecumenical Dialogue Interview (Anaheim, CA, September, 2014).

instrumental action by the state. Marxist sociologist Claus Offe characterizes this as 'bypassing the state'. From America's 'Occupy Wall Street' and 'Black Lives Matter' to Greece's *Syriza* (a Greek adverb meaning 'from the roots' or 'radically'), these new social movements[44] have occupied the vacuum created by an increasingly uncommunicative and out-of-touch church. It is noteworthy that intrinsic to all of these uprisings was a serious need for dialogue that respective actors were unwilling or unable to have.

Without an ontic referent, these movements are mere imitators of authentic Christian dialogue with a mutilated outward expression in much the same way that neo-communism casts itself as a secular form of early authentic Christianity. Nascent, sustainable dialogue develops at the grassroots and grows from there, bypassing bureaucracy, eventually reaching the top strata of ecclesial institutions – heights which institutionalized ecumenism has reached only symbolically. Of course, direct influence from progressive leaders like Pope Francis serve as wonderful public relations. But such people are the exception, rather than the rule in the Christian world.

The ecumenical paradigm identified to be the most relevant and specific to culture and religion is a western construct, namely the paradigm of 'programmatic ecumenism'. It is based on a systematic pragmatic 'problem-solving' approach. The mechanics of which are aimed at:

1. Identifying dialogical impediments.
2. Addressing these problems in the ecumenical forum.
3. Identifying and/or suggesting solutions (via common statements).
4. Applying these solutions by trickling down decisions reached in ecumenical forums to the grassroots level of church communities.[45]

The vision of programmatic ecumenism is that, by taking these successive steps, churches will soon reach an organic agreement, a full theological communion, and an implicit structural and institutional unity. This approach, with all its pragmatism, has not been very successful. The impasse of the past two decades has ushered in a 'winter of ecumenism', and with it a general hibernation vis-à-vis ecumenical dialogue.[46] This attitude is a result of modern ecumenism's fast, logical and systematic solutions to temporary problems. The Edinburgh Missionary Conference of 1910 is an archetypal example of this.

Driven by the watchword of the Protestants at the time, 'The Evangelization of the World in This Generation', the conference's *raison d'être* has continued to call for pressing ecumenical missionary efforts well beyond the twentieth century. Defined by obligation and urgency, this 'New Reformation' as dubbed by Robert. S Bilheimer, ultimately

---

[44] Nelson A. Pichardo, 'New Social Movements: A Critical Review', in *Annual Review of Sociology*, 23 (1997), 411-30.

[45] Răzvan Porumb, Society for Ecumenical Dialogue Interview (Anaheim, CA, August 2014).

[46] Porumb, Society for Ecumenical Dialogue Interview.

compromised ecumenical endeavours by generating impatience and a rushed overly pragmatic approach to centuries-long issues. Edinburgh exposed programmatic ecumenism as a major challenge for ecumenical endeavours throughout the world.[47] Again, the main obstacles were impatience and a lack of clear focus on innate spiritual ecumenism and commitment in faith to Christian unity. Patience was the missing ingredient – something which, as George Florovsky reminds us, is the greatest ecumenical virtue.[48]

The Ecumenism of the Future

In praying for the unity of the church, Christ was modelling a spiritual dimension that ecumenism must have and without which it cannot exist. In *prayer*, Christ cast ecumenism as a spiritual enterprise. This does not confine it to a detached, reflective, philosophical sphere. Ecumenism is expected to be a fundamentally active, *spiritual praxis*. More than a programme or organization, ecumenism is something that 'happens to the soul of Christians', as stated by the British ecumenist Oliver S. Tomkins.[49] It is a mission that starts at a personal level akin to one's 'pastoral' or 'societal' mission within the church. It then expands to the outer walls to encompass the entire Christian world.

More specifically, formal ecumenism could examine and learn from informal Christian 'ecumenical' movements that are growing in biblically-normative Christian ways. Most notably, the exploding global charismatic movement unites diverse Christian groups in experiencing Jesus 'in life and power'.[50]

St Paul laid out the normative presentation of the gospel at its most authentically effective: 'I will not venture to speak of anything except what Christ has accomplished through me in leading the Gentiles to obey God in "word and deed" – by the power of signs and wonders, through the power of the Spirit of God'. The New Testament normative gospel is thus 'the *dunamis* (miracle power) of God towards healing/rescue/ salvation' (Rom. 1:16). Perhaps if the various factions of Christianity are to recover the success of the early church and of this 750 million-member movement of the 21st century, then they may need to evaluate the dynamic of the Holy Spirit who unites a wide range of Christians in the original, authentic mission and message of Jesus commissioned to his disciples in Matthew 10, Mark 6, Luke 9, Matthew 28:19-20 and Acts 1:8. If today's church(es) can agree on and practise the original, authentic gospel of Jesus in 'word

---

[47] George Florovsky, 'The Limits of the Church', in *Church Quarterly Review* (1933), 117-31.

[48] Florovsky, 'The Limits of the Church'.

[49] Matt Stefon (ed), *Christianity: History, Beliefs, and Practice* (New York: Britannica Education Publishing, 2012), 352.

[50] David Barrett, *World Christian Encyclopaedia* (Oxford: OUP, 2001), projected 811 million Pentecostals/charismatics by 2020.

and deed', then this form of ecumenism could become similarly successful in its struggle against secularism and radicalism.

Ecumenism as a Permanent Calling

Moreover, ecumenism is a *permanent calling* and an *ongoing process*. If theology has always pursued a path towards unity and countering separations, then it has an inherent ecumenical agenda. The permanent task of theology, as Yves Congar suggests, is 'to discover what unites'.[51] What unites is the presence and power of the Holy Spirit. This movement shows the way to overcome the three ecumenical vices identified by Gillian Evans: 'fear, resentment and hopelessness'.[52] This charismatic, active ecumenical movement does not follow 'a spirit of fear, but of power, love and discipline' (2 Tim. 1:7).

One of the main tasks of a dialogue participant is to negotiate a path over the 'trust/suspicion' polarity and embrace trust as the only way forward, despite all the risks it implies.[53] To embrace authentic Christian dialogue is to embrace the cross and its resultant power of the Spirit; to share in the long-neglected experience and action of the Holy Spirit, and his gifts and graces for all humankind.

[51] Gillian R. Evans, *Method in Ecumenical Theology* (Cambridge: CUP, 1996), 20.
[52] Evans, *Method in Ecumenical Theology*, 226.
[53] Lausanne-Orthodox Initiative, Conference Press Release (Anaheim, CA, August 2014).

Part Two

THE FOUNDATION FOR MISSION IN THE ORTHODOX CHURCH: THE HOLY TRINITY

Mihai Himcinschi

Introduction

The Orthodox Church has never neglected the social implementation of its soteriological and eschatological content due to the fact that it has a missionary character in its own being.

At the beginning of the third millennium of Christianity, the social, political, economic and cultural problems, to which several others are added, cannot be placed on a parallel with ecclesiastical life. The missionary purpose and the meaning of the church in the new missionary context – European, as well as worldwide – is difficult but not impossible to accomplish. The entire world, today's society, cannot acquire its Christly aspect trough itself; it can only do it to the extent to which Christ – the head of the church – extends himself through his limbs (the church) on a terrestrial level.

Thanks to its teachings about the uncreated energies that can give wisdom to the entire creation, the church did not accept the Nestorian-like separatism between its being and the created world, but neither did it promote the confused monophysitism which – in the vision of some confessions or religious beliefs – can fuse matter with God, the church with the world, the divine grace with the created energies of some laws or principles purely natural.

The preoccupation of the church... " with the following: "The preoccupation of the church with community life and social brotherhood shows that all dogmas and creeds ought to lead to and bring to the fore the meeting between God and the world. That requires an understanding of the socio-political reality from the perspective of the church's faith as well as from other ordinary perspectives (social, cultural, economic, political, etc.), for God's presence in the world is universally and perfectly meeting the human existence.

What are the implications of this universality? The moralizing Christian message is destined for all people and for each individual. In other words, the social doctrine of the church does not address only Christians but the entire human race, the church being unable to remain passive to the toils to which all human beings are subjected and which are cast upon and resolved in the restorative work of the sole Survivor: Jesus Christ.

Trinitarian Community and the Socio-Political Communion

The Divine Revelation – A Premise of the Social Implementation of the Church

In Christian theology, the word 'revelation' refers to the fact that the infinite and uncreated God freely makes himself known to the finite and created world, especially in the history of his chosen people – Israel – and in Jesus Christ's life, death, and resurrection. Revelation expresses God's love for the world whose destiny is to take part in God's glory through the ascended Christ.

Revelation is a call for the world to answer to God's love, to understand the purpose of life as communion with God and communion with the entire world.

Revelation is seen as an act through which the Triune God communicates himself, reveals himself to the finite world, an act whose implications are not fully understood by today's society. 'From this point of view, we can say that our social programme is the Holy Trinity, and in this direction we must set the mission of the church in the future' (our translation).[1]

The discovery of the Trinity from the economical point of view is a work defying description and beyond all reasoning. It cannot be defined in its fullness using abstract terms through the categories of perception and objective thinking or through its social component. When we try to transmit to others the way in which God makes himself known, the language (symbols, images, notions, facts, metaphors, etc.) we use does not portray the event in its entirety. Revelation is a condition in people's decision of believing and, accordingly, it gives them the possibility of being in communion with God. This relationship is based upon God's merciful initiative and people's honesty in receiving his gift. In his wisdom and kindness, God decided to reveal himself and share with us the hidden purpose of his will (Eph. 1:9). In accordance with his will, through Jesus, man can participate through the Holy Spirit in the Trinitarian life of God (Eph. 2:18, 2 Pet. 1:4).

It is in the act of the divine revelation that the Holy Spirit becomes active helping the human being to recognize God's love for the world: 'No one can say, "Jesus is Lord" except by the Holy Spirit' (1 Cor. 12:3). The Comforter, the Spirit of truth, was sent to guide us towards the whole truth (John 16:13) and to remind us of what Jesus said and made known to all of us about God (John 14:26). God addresses the entire world and all social classes through the Holy Spirit, but even then, only to the extent to which each person is submitted to the Spirit, can one hear and understand in one's

[1] D. Popescu, *Hristos-Biserică-Societate* (Bucureşti: Editura Institutului Biblic şi de Misiune al B.O.R., 1998), 43.

heart (John 3:8). This communion between God and the world is indirect, and it is expressed in words and deeds that show the way in which people understood and responded to the presence of God in their life in different periods of their existence. However, it can also be a direct discovery as a consequence of the unmediated intervention of the Trinity on a personal or social level.

This use of the term 'revelation' avoids the danger of minimizing the role of dogma in theology or the meaning of religious experience. The first place that is given to communion and to social brotherhood shows that all dogmas and creeds must emphasize and lead to the meeting between God and the world. Moreover, at the same time, these must also be meaningful so that the people can understand the socio-political reality from the perspective of the church's faith as a consequence of God's presence at all its levels (social, cultural, economic, political, etc.).

This personal proximity to the Holy Trinity on a social level has ecumenical meaning as well: it helps to underline the great fundamental truth of the revelation accepted by Christians – especially – and it establishes the ultimate and most purified developments of the Trinitarian doctrine at the level of society. Such a vision does not defame the fact that the interpretations of the church in regard to God's revelation could not have been formed from elements of the environment or of religious knowledge with socio-political implications. People are never completely free of the theories or the systems of creation. Nevertheless, we must insist upon the statement according to which it is only the dogmas that supply us with the correct interpretation of human knowledge socially implemented, irrespective of the position on which these are situated. The social perspective of the church helps a person to know if a doctrine from the social field is authentic and according to the criterion of true religious knowledge – the gospel – and, hence, if it had a revelation fundament.

The Economical Trinity

Why is it necessary for us to discuss the social issue in connection with Trinitarian doctrine? Can we determine how Christians should behave in the world through the reading of the gospel, of the apostolic traditions, of the history of the church and of the Holy Fathers? Certainly, this is the way that most Christians followed in the old days and are still following even today.

The social reasoning of the church is based upon two sources which confer on it originality and which must provide a fundament for the entire research of the Christian social ethics: The revelation of God as Trinity takes place on the economic level and wants to uplift man from the social level to the one of the intra-Trinitarian love, and shows that the human being as God's image is an enhancing factor of communion in the love towards other human beings and towards God. 'Through (the Son's) love, the Father also loves us; through the arrival of the Spirit we become the dwelling place of the Father and of the Son and of the Holy Spirit... The holy Trinity holds everything in place; it unites them and it connects them to Itself and, by uniting them as such, it makes them strong and unbreakable.'[2]

This life in communion is confronted with some serious obstacles. The first of these is that of the political and social issues which emerge in the context of a particular time and space, in a context which is very far from the context and the events that were suggested as a guide of authority. This difficulty in itself can be controlled by endeavour. If any biblical text represents the eternal word of God to the world, then, as a consequence, we and the European social context must certainly obey it. But is there any particular biblical text which refers to contemporary society, and is it also eternally valid in regard of God's will about the political and social order? There might not be one, even if inspired, because it is meant for the implementation of God's will in a particular situation from the past, or it can be addressed in such a subtle or very appropriate manner to the given situation from those days, events with which we would be confronted, of course, under a different form today.

There is the risk of placing the social doctrine at the same level as the revelation. This is how the social theologies with a so-claimed revelation character have appeared, especially in the Protestant world.

It is important to fundament the social thinking of the church upon the revelation but the latter will always be far superior through its content, destination and purpose. The gospel is the main source of social education, provided that the different stages of man's history can receive it at a social level too, without losing its divine character. Thus, 'refusing a social doctrine derived from the gospel means transforming the social doctrine of the Church into a simple human work'.[3]

The social aspect of the church is a specific reality – a key to God's revelation in regard to our Christian understanding of it – a process of understanding that was revealed and that developed gradually throughout history. We have a tendency to disagree with this statement because the texts of the Old Testament are, in general, considered eternal commandments for the social action or about the moral truth. It is obvious that this danger is smaller where the New Testament or the Fathers are preoccupied by the social area. Even as such, we cannot forget that the indications of the Trinity's revelation and the patristic commentaries of it find us among fallen and limited human beings. Due to their relationship with God, the disciples, the apostles and their followers were closer to the social meaning of the gospel than we are. 'The quality of our vices shapes us and, in a way, leads to the imprint of God in us through the work of

[2] Saint Symeon the New Theologian, *Cele 225 de capete teologice şi practice* (Filocalia românească VI: Bucureşti: Editura Institutului Biblic şi de Misiune al B.O.R., 1977), 18, 60.

[3] Jean-Marie Aubert, *Morale sociale pour notre temps* (Paris: Desclée, 1970), 45.

virtue. God represents a good entity in an uncreated manner, a manner improper to the being. However, we can also show ourselves as such by evolving it in our vices and our behaviour if, by our own will, we choose the desire and the fervour to achieve the things that are worthy of admiration. But, if we have a healthy mind und understanding, we will not consider that, by having God's image shining in the quality of the morals within our souls, we have a similar, unchanged being such as the one of God because that can go as far as considering ourselves to be equal to Him in all with those that pertain to His characteristics.'[4]

More importantly, the full meaning of Christ's Embodiment, Crucifixion, Resurrection and the Holy Spirit's descent has become the imprint of social thinking through time.

This brings us to the second and most crucial common difficulty of our behaviour in relationship to the gospel. What is the status of Christians who note or reflect God's revelation? What and who does the revelation discover? A Muslim would say that it is the Qur'an which represents the word of Allah, and that it is this that discovers the will of God in relationship to the human being. Many Christians would diminish the social claim for the word of the gospel and they would diminish it even more for the subject of the Revelation: the Holy Trinity – towards which it aims as being outside the social area. Some will say that the gospel is generally not God's word to the world or its problems, but that it only reveals God himself in action – in parallel with the world or above it, God who could be in relationship with human beings and with the created world. Herein, we can understand something about a certain interior thinking and especially about the radical conclusions that must be drawn in regard to the relationships between man and God and among people themselves.

If this point of view is correct, it does not mark a crucial difference between Islam and Christianity but it suggests that, for a Christian, the texts of the Scriptures are significant in relationship to the God he discovers and to his action oriented towards people and towards the world in historical context. There is, thus, the possibility that a text, whether scriptural or patristic could serve as an immediate or indubitable guide for the revealing action of the Trinity with a clear comprehension of the Revelation – of which this text is a part – and of the purpose which is distant. 'The three most ancient opinions concerning God are Anarchia, Polyarchia, and Monarchia. [...] Anarchy is a thing without order; and the Rule of Many is factious, and thus anarchical, and thus disorderly. [...] Monarchy is that which we hold in honour. It is, however, a Monarchy that is not limited to one Person, for it is possible for Unity, if at variance with it, to come into a condition of plurality.'[5]

---

[4] Saint Cyril of Alexandria, *Despre Sfânta Treime* (P.S.B. 40: București: Editura Institutului Biblic şi de Misiune al B.O.R., 1994), 20.

[5] Saint Gregory of Nazianzus, *Cele 5 cuvântări teologice* (Bucureşti: Anastasia Press, 1993), 53.

Christianity knows a Unique Principle for everything. But this Unique Principle is not a unique person, for a unique person sets itself in contradiction to its self and it comes to a standstill in the same disorder if it looks for a variation inside itself merely out of boredom. A Unique Principle, having in itself only love – love which is achieved between the persons that do not contradict, but love each other – is truly an all-loving Unique Principle. The person does not want to be alone. It wants to be with another being and it wants to be in plenary love with the other. The supreme existence is supreme love, and this is the supreme unity between people.[6]

If social doctrine is viewed in the perspective of a generally human understanding of God's revelation of himself and through his action oriented – generally – towards creation and – specifically – towards man, then we can approach the revelation's content from the perspective of the social and political directions and from the direction of power. Hence, we can speak about a facile adoption of the political, social or economic concepts that can be possible through the biblical interpretation. Theology, in its true meaning, becomes now the focus of the Christian perspective about the socio-political realities as it should be for any other ecclesial activity.

There is a third ethical line of the motivation favouring the same approach. The ones who obey the biblical texts or the rules in a verbal form or the moral laws which have been precisely formulated will see that the letter of the biblical texts will truly dominate. As far as human beings are concerned, what is unveiled as a divine order will soon become a complex lawful case with arguments. The special defence or hypocrisy will not be decreased by the instauration of the appearing. These are dangers that the Jews, the Christians and the Muslims have come to avoid – due to the monotheistic and personal faith about the divinity – to the extent to which they believe that their faith obliges them to adopt such a social vision.

If we must draw on the origin of the social and political action through God's revelation about himself and his relationship to his creation and to people, in particular, the subsequent danger is that our judgement about the social aspects can rather influence in practice our opinion about the Triune God than our understanding of the revealed social aspects. Even hermits fall short of making presuppositions about their times in regard to normative social structures and to political action. 'The world of Christians, and their way of life, and their mind, and discourse, and practice, is one thing; and that of the men of this world, another. And the difference between them is very wide. If the sight if an earthly king is something all wish to see, and everyone who passes through the city of the king desires at least to catch a glimpse of his beauty or the elegance of his garments or the splendour of his purple, the beauty of his many pearls, the comeliness of

[6] D. Stăniloae, *Note 83*: Saint Gregory of Nazianzus, *Cele 5 cuvântări teologice*, 138.

his crown, the impressive retinue that accompanies him, spiritual people, however, spurn all of these things because they have experienced another heavenly, incorporeal glory. They have tasted another ineffable beauty and have participated in other riches. They have received in the inner person another Spirit.

'The people of this world who possess the spirit of the world have a great yearning to see an earthly king, at least to feast upon his comeliness and glory. In proportion as his share of visible accessories is greater than that of others, so even to have only seen him, the king is something desired by all. Each man inwardly says to himself: "I would really like someone to give me something of that glory, comeliness and splendour." He believes that king is happy, a man as him, of the earth, having the same weakness of passions, subject to death. He makes him an object of envy because of his fleeting comeliness and desired glory.'[7]

The Triune Persons and the Social Persons

Few men have a close connection with God but fail from coming to peace with themselves in concern to the socio-evangelic doctrine. The descent of God and the revelation, in general, on an earthly level would mean the creation of an idol. In the same time, true Christians believe that man is created in the image and likeness of God and, accordingly, we expect for them to find the social elements revealed by God in the human life which lead to perfection. It will be impossible to identify which of these will be analyzed and put to work except for those which are in the direct light of the self-revelation of God. From here on, we will try to prove through a statement rather than through an argumentative approach that that revelation of God is set towards the world and that only seen through the intra-Trinitarian life can it be expressed socially so that it might shine forth a light in social and political life.

Between people, there is a *perichoresis* – a reciprocal indwelling – according to the Trinitarian model – the third is spiritually present among the two as the Spirit is among the Father and the Son – the difference between the manner in which the Spirit is indwelling with the Son compared with the one in which the Father is indwelling with the Son is that the Father makes it possible by bringing to the Son the testimony of the Spirit as an emphasized manifestation of the paternal love which intensifies in the Son his son-like feelings through this very presence of the Son in the self as witness of the paternal love. For this reason, only through the irradiance of the Spirit from the Son in human beings their accentuated son-like feelings for the Father are present. The uniqueness of the divine Persons is as big as the unity between them. These two maintain each other

---

[7] Saint Macarius of Egypt, *Omilii duhovniceşti* (Bucureşti: Editura Institutului Biblic şi de Misiune al B.O.R., 1992), 111-12.

in balance. Through them the uniqueness and communion between human beings is maintained in God.[8]

In general terms, our knowledge about God derives from his action oriented towards the people from the old Israel, in the first place, and then, towards the new one which is the church.

In relationship with the world, the revelation of God about himself is that of Creator, Supporter and Renewer of the whole world. He made time and space move. He is present in creation and yet he remains transcendently beyond it. It is through his word and will that he will support the world in its being under all aspects of the social concept. God reveals himself as redeemer of man, too, due to the weakness of the relationships between people, of the created being itself, and due to the sickness produced by the sin which altered the human dynamism of the communion between man and God, and also between men on earth. Through the law of the Old Testament given to Moses, through the prophetic mission inspired by the Holy Spirit in the ethical and aesthetic applications of the relationship between God and his world and, finally, through the mission of his Son who embodied himself for us on earth and through the overflow of the Spirit on Pentecost Day, God progressively brings humanity to an interpersonal and life-giving relationship with him.

God could forgive man for breaking the law before the embodiment. By all means, the law seen as an external word can improve life but it cannot arrive at the absolute knowledge of God or to the plentiful abiding with him through grace. The radical change comes when God as a Person – a Trinity of Persons – and not his will, becomes known and loved by humanity. The offering and the acceptance of the triune interpersonal relationship with all its implications has represented the gift of real and eternal life.

Christ's earthly life in communion to his father and the revelation over men finds its culminating point in his extended hands on the Cross – an example and a symbol, such as our ability of transforming God's creation into an instrument of pain and of its surpassing. He turns man towards himself through the acceptance of pain and in this ultimate voluntary acceptance through love, man accepts the final agony of death.

Christ's crucifixion and his resurrection in the power of the Holy Spirit shift the laws of our universe towards its commencing point. It is our natural supposition that love is a great thing in human experience which presupposes life. The divine Trinitarian life consists in the love-based relationship between the divine Persons. When God's love is portrayed in the ultimate point of the acceptance of death in our mundane terms, death is the one that must be defended because God's love remains; God's life is made of the Trinitarian love reverberated through man and the entire creation. Hence, the unity of the Trinity is unbreakable in relation to the creation.

---

[8] D. Stăniloae, *Note 64*: Saint Athanasius the Great, *Epistola I către Serapion* (P.S.B. 16: București: Editura Institutului Biblic și de Misiune al B.O.R., 1988), 50.

The creation cannot be maintained in a state of tributary communion based upon a mono-personal principle which ignores the other two personal Realities. No human being can socially appropriate the tributary love to such an extent as to be capable of sharing it with the others because the isolated being cannot represent the peak of the plenipotentiary ontological existence of human nature.

Accordingly, in this soteriological action of the Triune God which is fulfilled once but always present, we were given a model in human terms. Crowned by Christ's love in the historical experience of having offered the life, the death and the resurrection, inspired by the Holy Spirit existent in history through the act of Pentecost as divine Hypostasis, freed from the chains of historical necessity, it becomes possible for us to live in relationship with the Triune God and in relationships with the people which attempt to be based upon the relationship between the three persons of the Trinity.

The church has been centred on the same salvation experience. The Fathers have studied God's action oriented towards us in history and they saw that sometimes there is a distinction, if not a contradiction, between this and the eternal communion of the three persons of the Trinity. The last can be brought closer to the first, but how can it surpass them? First, we can underline a conceptual pattern of the understanding or we can appeal to our own experience of the revelation of love, being certain that such a relationship appears as a fundament in the self-revelation of God as a loving Lord in his action within the church throughout time. 'The Church is the indwelling of those who are in the indwelling of the Persons of the Holy Trinity, an indwelling brought in us through the embodied Christ.'[9]

Naturally, we cannot become intimate with the Triune God without using the concepts based on human language. If we grant priority to a conceptual understanding of God, we will see that some human concepts have become determined. We have enough types of social experiences different from the conceptual thinking of the church implemented at a social level: for example, those of the action based upon the instinctive answer of the isolated individual. More relevant here, we have the expression of the love about which we can speak using many concepts, but whose depths and power we cannot transmit through any other concepts than those that we can use as examples. It is a level of expression in which we know how to be ourselves even when we sacrifice ourselves or we share ourselves through love to those who love us. 'The saints have ascended far above from the material duality for the wise unity of the Trinity, this shows that surpassing these through their ascension above matter and shape… (the saints) have united themselves to God and have received the grace of being one with the pristine light (in three hypostases).'[10]

---

[9] D. Stăniloae, *Note 159a*: Saint Athanasius the Great, *Epistola I către Serapion.*

[10] Saint Maximus the Confessor, *Ambigua* (P.S.B. 80: Bucureşti: Editura Institutului Biblic şi de Misiune al B.O.R., 1983), 183.

Even where love is expressed as ecstasy, where we can find ourselves beyond the others, what gives us inner joy and the profundity of love is the mutual sharing without the addiction surged from necessity. There is, of course, the social love that surges from necessity, which has great importance in human life such as the love that connects a child with his mother. It is the human expression of the love that descends on a social level through an addiction based on the necessity which helps us appreciate the economic communion of the Trinity.

The mystery of the Trinity remains a mystery because concepts can only elucidate; they cannot uncover the secret of such a communion of life in love while an understanding based on a parallel even to the deepest human experiences will not lead us by itself to God. It is the same as when once someone reaches on a faraway ladder something on its highest step and then lets it go: the concepts will always be essential in guarding the mystery of the lack of understanding but they will never make us worthy of meeting God. Such concepts, even the greatest ones, such as the persona versus the nature or freedom and love must be seen as derived and not determined from the Father, the Son and the Spirit in their communion: the Father offers himself to the Son in a relationship that produces love and self-revelation – the Father discovers himself freely to the Spirit in a loving, self-revealing relationship – the Son and the Spirit both answer to the Father through the revelation in love of One to the Other as to the latter. From here on we must understand the experiences of our inter-human – and interpersonal – relationships as most profound, as a reflection of the eternal communion with the Triune God. 'From the communion with the Triune God that is within us and which is different from the communion that we, the people, share, we also gain power from above for the strengthening of the relationships between us and Him. If it were not for this superior community between the Son and the Spirit, there would not be anything to determine the Son to commune with us. It is not enough to have one communion between the Son and the Father to determine the Son not to confound with us and yet to strengthen his communion with us. Another communion between the two Persons – that is, between the Son and the Spirit – who come in us is necessary for these should be sufficient in their communion which is different from communion with us. This superior community should give us strength in our communion with God and among ourselves.'[11]

What are the social implications of the eternal intra-Trinitarian communion? The personal relationships in the Trinity are those of love based on freedom, and not in and by a deterministic necessity. These are truly relationships of love because they do not arise from *necessity* and are truly free because they are not constrained within the divine Persons which do not prevent them from discovering each other. The Father is the one

[11] D. Stăniloae, *Note 53*: Saint Maximus the Confessor, *Ambigua*.

who creates and makes proceed not through an eternal exercise of dominating power but through revelatory love – the path of ecstasy and sacrifice. The relationship of the Father with the Son can be seen as a model for every humanly characteristic relationship, while that of the Father and the Spirit becomes a model for every interpersonal relationship. What is certain is that the only knowledge that we may have about God is that of this free communion of the three divine Persons in love that, even if distinct, move each other. The Trinitarian Persons wanted their love to become available for the human beings, the rational beings who will begin their existence by communing with them; whatever they will share will remain unshared even within the created power; they will move towards it and the other beings in a loving relationship by showing themselves to the human beings as a model of the communion in love. 'Each Person of the Trinity is present in what is given during Baptism without being confounded with the others. All Three are present for they represent the immortal life and the perfect love. When I show love to someone else when united to the love of the other who in his turn loves as well, we do not confound each other but rejoice in this common love for the other and we give him love as a starting-point for communion.'[12] Human concepts are part of this creation. To speak about the Trinity as Persons means affirming God in the Trinity and the endless and extemporaneous love of the Three Persons in the ecstatic self-discovery of the One to the Other as primary to our knowledge of the world. In short, the Persons are placed ahead of the concepts. This is not due to the fact that the word 'person' is sometimes taken as a concept, but due to its overcoming through the experience of the love in freedom because the life of the three Persons of the Trinity is the lesson that must be given to God's actions towards us revealed in the Scriptures, and because the human experience of the loving persons in freedom is our deepest and strongest experience and it completely resembles this one.

God means Three Persons and it is only in this manner that God is Love. These are not mere fundamental statements of the Christian truth, but these are also statements that are closely related.

There will be two possibilities of approaching this truth: one is that this unique God has always been in an independent relationship of love with our world which, because it is created, was and always is the object of eternal love; such love in freedom will not be accidental or, at least, it will not be secondary to the created beings in the image of God since such a dependent-on-the-world God is absolutely free. Another possibility of approach consists in the fact that this God does not have the experience of love before the creation of the world and, thus the ability to love – even if not necessarily through the gift of freedom – will be accidentally or at least secondary to the created people by such a God.

---

[12] D. Stăniloae, *Note 160*: Saint Athanasius the Great, *Epistola I către Serapion.*

The natural reply of the contemporary man to such a Creator will either be subjected to the loving power of God, to his will and commands or to the social affirmation of the human freedom independent of the Trinity. Moreover, loving and forgiving as this God does for us, man, created in the image of God, will logically see the necessity of love and forgiveness and will promote these socially.

The ones which are tempted to travel on any of these ways will meet a serious social barrier in human experience, the experience of freedom and the experience of philanthropic love known as some of the most profound experiences of the human personality in which the conscience of the inter-human life is not abolished but can be shared in the mutuality of a common joy or of a common purpose. This is the point in which human nature created in the image of God can confirm what Trinitarian Christians believe. Faith in one God is basically subversive to the mundane socio-political condition and that of the institutions because these are able to make a non-revelatory request at any point. If one God is the ultimate judge, the ultimate value of a society that sets an evangelical model for itself cannot be attached to other atheist structures or institutions, even less to some individuals who are in a position in which they have temporary power and who do not want to consider God's intervention in their lives.

Conclusions

It is true that outside the church, Christians can easily argument political positions in terms of the self-revelation of the Trinity. At a greater or lesser extent, it is essential to use the language and the concepts that the others use but this only accentuates the importance of being capable of identifying what the characteristics are, where the common interest is and in what point the using of any language starts to distort an understanding of the human life and activity which is proper for Trinitarian Christianity.

It is not really necessary to make a full analysis of this subject in order to see that the modern western world still assures us that in its Christian faith will continue to exploit and to support its Christian heritage. The importance of the moral principle still remains, where it is in less agreement in regard to the source of morality and proclaims these high concepts about the human individual which serves to the fulfilment of life where what can be attributed to the human life and personality it is doubtful.

The fact that this should be as it is, is a tribute to our days and to the power of the Christian message. In the Christian tradition, there are words about truth and power, about the man who continues to believe in the truth even when God's revelation is questioned. It is also true that sharp minds can see through the inconsistency and the search for a morality which is consistent with its fundamental creeds. Judging by some of its previous attempts applied unsuccessfully, the results of this research can be a disaster for humanity.

In this situation, anyone who believes in God has the same duty – that of showing how his faith in God and in the other is in harmony. For a concept of the belief about man, this should be connected with this concept about God. If someone believes in the self-revelation of God as Trinity and in his implications in the human being, then he should be ready to elaborate these implications for the world with the assurance that this is possible.

We believe that the image of man finding himself by finding others in the unity of the church and the communion of the people, of man as creator of the self, and as servant and priest of God's creation, and of the man who is more enriched as he gives more, more profound as he searches the self is a viable image. It is one which brings man and God and man and man together but which can share a clearer, warmer light over other human preoccupations – even over those which usually take place in the disquieting twilight of the entangled battles and of the uncertain results as well as those from the political world.

PRINCIPLES OF ORTHODOX MISSIOLOGY

Gheorghe Petraru

Introduction

The Orthodox Church clearly distinguishes between 'mission', in the sense of fundamental apostolic vocation of the Universal Church to proclaim the Holy Gospel and 'missions', as evangelizing activities of a confession or denomination in a non-Christian space. The latter activities were often related to the colonizing process, i.e. 'cultural and political oppression'.[1]

The Christian mission for the western world is especially a title of personal glory and evokes the idea of space, territory, geography and context, hence the visible extension of the church by the establishment of new communities in countries with 'unfaithful' people; however, that necessary inner fusion between the Christian tradition and local cultural peculiarities leading to real inculturation is not always reached. For the Orthodox Church, the object of mission was rather to 'hold the people to the faith in a permanent historic continuity. The Orthodox Church has tended to condemn those who have left the church rather than to judge those who are still outside the Orthodox faith. The command to mission is based on the invocation and adoration of the name of the Lord: *Hallowed be Thy Name!* The proclamation is identified with doxological *martyria,* with *leitourgia*; hence the insistence on tradition and on the apostolic succession'.[2] Therefore, until recently, the Orthodox Church was considered to be a *non-missionary church* in the western world and by many Orthodox Christians as well; furthermore, it was deemed to be a space for mission, i.e. *terra missionis*. Despite all this, it was still necessary to clarify the fact that 'mission methodology was different in the Eastern world, as opposed to the Western one'; in fact, the missionary imperative of the Orthodox Church is more obvious, the preaching of the gospel and the Eucharist are directly related, the centre of missionary work is the liturgy, and Orthodoxy 'in its liturgical structure is a Missionary Church in itself'.[3]

Today, the Orthodox Church is present everywhere in the world due to the local churches canonically depending on a mother church, e.g.

[1] Ion Bria, *Martyria, Mission, The Witness of the Orthodox Churches Today* (Geneva: WCC Publications, 1980), 3.

[2] Bria, *Martyria, Mission*, 4.

[3] George Lemopoulos, *You Shall Be My Witnesses: Mission Stories from the Eastern and Oriental Orthodox Churches* (Tertios: Katerini, 1993), 179.

Constantinople, Moscow or Bucharest,[4] and it pretends to be the most faithful paradigm of the Church of the Apostles and of the Church Fathers of the first Christian millennium.

The Orthodox mission means the preaching of the gospel as a *doxological testimony* of the integral divine discourse in liturgy and prayer.[5] God is praised for the redemption of man in the Christian tradition as Christ's church in the communion of grace with God as Trinity. This clarifies and explains the insistence of the Orthodox Church on tradition and apostolic succession. The biblical text that reflects the essence of the Orthodox mission is the one from St John the Evangelist: 'For God so loved the world that he gave his one and only Son, that whoever believes in him shall not perish but have eternal life' (John 3:16), obviously related to the Great Missionary Commandment for the evangelization of the entire world (Matt. 28:19-20). Not involved so much in dialogue with intellectualist western theology, bringing unlimited and sometimes sterile arguments of some theologians to bear on issues of demythologization and remythologization of theology or the promotion of secularism, the Orthodox Church is faithful to realistic hermeneutics, to spiritual practice and the divine liturgy. The mission of our church is totally faithful to Christ and his church as communion to Trinity and to the saints, even in the sense of the 'new kenotic-perichoretic relational ontotheology'.[6]

The Ontology of Mission

Trinity and Mission

By 'mission', in the Orthodox sense, we understand the testimony on *God the living – the Trinity* that created and redeemed the world due to the divine eternal love that called man to God. *Trinitarian Theology* shows that God is Trinity – Father, Son and Holy Spirit – the life of perfect communion of the three divine Persons, calling humanity to share divine life as redemption in the eternal Kingdom of God preached by Christ and partly accomplished in his church in the history of humanity.

Definitely, the sense of mission is not only to pass on intellectual convictions, doctrines or knowledge and moral teachings, but also to transmit the life of communion in God to humanity redeemed by Christ. It can be said that *missio Dei* or *missio Trinitatis* is a 'programme' of the Holy Trinity for the entire creation whose purpose is to be the Kingdom of

---

[4] Gheorghe Petraru, *'Mergeți în toată lumea și propovăduiți Evanghelia la toată făptura...': O istorie a misiunilor creștine (Go in the World and Preach the Gospel to All Beings)* (Iași, Romania: Sf. Mina, 2013), 251-82.

[5] Nicholas Wolterstorff, *Divine Discourse: Philosophical Reflections on the Claim that God Speaks* (Cambridge: CUP, 1995).

[6] Kevin J. Vanhoozer, *Remythologizing Theology: Divine Action, Passion, and Authorship* (Cambridge: CUP, 2010), 139.

God. Therefore, 'the inherent internal dynamics of the structure pertaining to every human being, in particular and the universe in general, is to be the Kingdom of God. True life is life in the communion of the Holy Trinity, the source of human existence, in Christ through the Holy Spirit coming from the Father and going to Him'.[7] The 'original model of mission' is the one from the intra-Trinitarian life which is original reality, the unique reality that, in a simple and necessary way,[8] calls us all to redemption and unites all people in and as church. Trinitarian theology is essential for Orthodox mission because the church confesses God as Trinity, the truth and its life. Orthodox mission must be understood in the spirit of Orthodox theology and ecclesiology. Orthodox theology is marked by the realist understanding of divine revelation presented in the biblical text which narrates the history of human salvation from the beginning to Christ, the incarnate God, and the descent of the Holy Spirit at Pentecost. God as a living person is always present in his creation, but from Pentecost a 'new reality came into being in the world, a body more perfect than the world, the Church founded in a twofold divine economy, that means the work of Jesus Christ and the work of the Holy Spirit, the two persons of the Holy Trinity sent to the world. The two works lie at the foundation of the Church and are necessary for us in order to come to union with God'.[9] So, one must take into account the gospel and the entire Bible with the realistic and typological senses of its interpretation – that is, the conscience and the feeling of the actual presence of divine transcendence, theologically of the Trinity in the eternal uncreated energies in our life through the human face of Jesus of Nazareth in the Holy Spirit. Christian people and communities experience this spiritual communion in the history of our salvation. As A. Yannoulatos writes, beyond the spirit of the world, including our historical cultures, the church turns to the 'constants of the Gospel'[10] – that is, the divine-human person of our Lord Jesus Christ incarnated, transfigured on Tabor Mountain, crucified, resurrected, and the Spirit that came into our world, the creation of the Father, named as such in Jesus' prayer.

As a matter of fact, there is a Trinitarian principle of church mission, a divine project for the world to become the church, a way in our life in history to the heavenly Kingdom promised in the New Testament by Jesus himself. It is a historical, but also a spiritual and sacramental, continuation of biblical Israel in the communion of the Trinity fully revealed in the church, and sharing the divine love and life to humankind renewed in

---

[7] Ion Bria (ed), *Go Forth in Peace: Orthodox Perspectives on Mission* (Geneva: WCC Publications, 1986); Valer Bel, *Misiunea Bisericii în lumea contemporană (Mission of the Church in the Contemporary World)* (Cluj-Napoca, Romania: Renaşterea, 2010), 21ff.

[8] 'Apostolat', in *Dictionnaire de la vie spirituelle* (Paris: Les Editions du Cerf, 1987), 35.

[9] Vladimir Lossky, *Teologia Mistică a Bisericii de Răsărit (The Mystical Theology of the Eastern Church)* (trans. Vasile Raducă; Bucureşti: Anastasia), 187.

[10] Anastasios Yannoulatos, *Ortodoxia si problemele lumii contemporane (Facing the World: Orthodox Christian Essays on Global Concerns)* (trans. Gabriel Mândrilă; PhD, rev. Prof. Constantin Coman, Bucureşti: Bizantina, 2003), 114.

Christ and sanctified by the Spirit. In mission, the Orthodox Church stresses the importance of the gospel, the beautiful flavour of patristic texts interpreting God's revelation in human history in an intellectual way, as noted by some missiologists;[11] this is also done in a sacramental, liturgical and spiritual dimension in unity of the faith and openness to the society of the constants of our historical and contemporary Christian witnesses.

The Romanian theologian Dumitru Stăniloae stated that the Trinity was 'the structure of supreme love',[12] i.e. the logical consequence of the biblical, ontological 'God is love' (1 John 4:8), the eternal love between the Trinitarian persons revealed in the history of redemption. In the world, the church is, really, the spread of this love through the grace of the Holy Sacraments given to Christian people by the sacramental hierarchy that incorporates them into the Kingdom of God for redemption and joy in the uncreated light of the Trinity. Thus, the mission of the church is, as St Peter (2 Pet. 1:4) claims and as patristic theology understood, the ecclesial sense of the world as 'participation of the faithful to the deification in the communion of the Holy Trinity, which leads to their own deification; this is known to the ones that try to be more united in Christ by the imitation of His life as *holiness*',[13] in fact, the sense of internal mission in missiology.

Christ's Centrality

The confession of faith 'Jesus is Lord' (Rom. 10:9) or the invitation and the urge that 'every tongue acknowledge that Jesus Christ is Lord, to the glory of God the Father' (Phil. 2:11) is the foundation and the heart of theology. Therefore, sending the Son into the world, 'for God so loved the world that he gave his one and only Son, that whoever believes in him shall not perish but have eternal life' (John 3:16) is the beginning and defines Christian mission accurately. The Word of God, the Incarnated One, Saviour of the world and the Creator is the *centre* in a double sense, ontological and dynamic; actually, this is a dynamic ontology that integrates man and the cosmos, without suppressing them, but giving them their true value and consistency in themselves in divine order. As eternal Logos of the Father, he is the foundation and model, the sense of human existence. As human-divine person, as incarnated Logos, he is our partner in dialogue; by assuming human plenitude, he cures it, restores it, deifies it. Christ is the Logos of all things and the Logos is the image of the Father. The world has an ontological foundation in God, for all things are in relation with the

---

[11] David J. Bosch, *Transforming Mission: Paradigm Shifts in Theology of Mission* (Maryknoll, NY: Orbis Books, 1991), 206.

[12] Dumitru Stăniloae, *Teologie Dogmatică Ortodoxă* 1 *(Orthodox Dogmatic Theology)* (București: Editura Institutului Biblic și de Misiune al Bisericii Ortodoxe Române, 1978), 282.

[13] 'De ce suntem Ortodocși' ('Why We Are Orthodox'), excerpt from the review *Teologie și Viață* 4-8 (1991), 13; *Witness through 'Holiness' of Life,* in *Martyria/Mission,* 50; Archbishop Anastasios (Yannoulatos), 'Orthodox Mission: Past, Present, Future', in Petros Vasiliadis (ed), *Orthodox Perspective on Mission* (Oxford: Regnum, 2013), 26.

Logos, 'man being the face of Logos as the person who thinks', loves, has will and desire.[14] Christ's redemption has a cosmic dimension, in the sense revealed in the Bible, and Christ is the fulfilment of humanity's expectation to be freed from its bondage of decay (Rom. 8:19-23). But as Christ's mission took place in a world of 'decay', thus making unavoidable the passage to resurrection, the mission of the church 'takes place in a context of the spiritual fight with evil, sin, implying conversion, paschal and baptismal passing of the world to a new creation. This is not a fight that only shows itself in people's souls, but penetrates all social life and natural existence through pain, suffering and death'.[15]

Mission under the Cross, Christ's sacrifice, cannot only remain at the dimension of Calvary, for Christ's resurrection brings light, grace and the love of God into the horizon of human and cosmic existence. So, although God is powerful, he finds the path of humility, *kenosis* in Christ in order to get closer to people, respecting their freedom in choosing him and calling them to communion with the Self. God brings to date the kenotic Christic act through his church. In its humility, the church takes people to a graceful deifying state of communion with God in order know and love him. The mission of the church is, first of all, a victory over the powers of sin and selfishness, with the obvious social implications in history, not to mention cosmic nature. Above all, due to his sacrifice and the grace of the Holy Spirit, which is present and works in his church, Christ saves us from spiritual and eternal death; they are brought to us by sin with unfortunate ontological and cognitive consequences for man in the sense of losing the knowledge of God, communion with him for whom man was created from divine love by the Logos of the Father (John 1:1-3). Yet Christ remains in a permanent state of sacrifice even after the unique crucifixion on Golgotha, doing it for us and with all his church, as Orthodox theology interprets it according to Cyril of Alexandria.[16] We are set on the path of the Kingdom by his means, on the right side of the Father and the sacrifice of Eucharist by which we are united with Christ, the real one for our own deification.

Secondly, Christian mission is not controlled by historical powers; it needs to be understood from an eschatological perspective, as well, in the Kingdom of heaven when all will be truly revealed and fulfilled. Christian mission can only be understood in the light of Christ's incarnation, it is Christocentric, in a permanent internal dynamic between cross and resurrection, pain and joy, hope and fulfilment. Christ's crucified love is the reason and power of the mission of his church, of the missionary theologian engaged in mission, as Christ's witnesses in any historical context, be it in freedom, persecution or even death. Missionary testimony

---

[14] Bria, *Go Forth in Peace*, 4.

[15] Bria, *Go Forth in Peace*, 5.

[16] Dumitru Stăniloae, *Teologia Dogmatică Ortodoxă* 3 *(Orthodox Dogmatic Theology)* (București: Editura Institutului Biblic şi de Misiune al Bisericii Ortodoxe Române, 1978), 107-08.

is strong when fulfilled in weakness (2 Cor. 12:9) when Christ is with us. The purpose of the church's mission is the *anakephalosis* of humanity and the universe in Christ, for Christ to be everything in all (1 Cor. 15:28). Jesus Christ is the centre of the new humanity, of human unity restored (1 Pet. 5:1; Col. 3:4).

Evangelization implies a focus on Christ, Son of God the True, who came to restore humanity and give it the possibility of deification, which was actually the primordial purpose of man's creation by God: the saving of the world, the ontological and existential meaning of man is given by Christ, who becomes the centre of the spiritual life of man: 'I am crucified with Christ: nevertheless I live; yet not I, but Christ lives in me: and the life which I now live in the flesh I live by the faith of the Son of God, who loved me, and gave himself for me' (Gal. 2:20). The good news is that God took shape as human to save us and live in us: 'The Word became flesh and made his dwelling among us. We have seen his glory, the glory of the one and only Son, who came from the Father, full of grace and truth' (John 1:14). All people want to live for ever. But to have eternal life they need Christ: 'Now this is eternal life: that they know you, the only true God, and Jesus Christ, whom you have sent' (John 17:3). The church is the body of Christ and that is why we find redemption in Christ: the liturgical life of the church and the Holy Scriptures mirror the centrality of Christ – which is essential for the preaching of his gospel and understanding why the gates of hell cannot conquer his church.

The Pneumatological and Sacramental Dimension

The pneumatological and sacramental dimension is essential for the mission of the church because Christ is inseparable from the Person of the Holy Spirit and his work of life that spiritually refines man. The Holy Spirit continues, confirms and strengthens the work of Christ (John 15:26), making all things new and therefore his work is one of soteriological efficacy from an anthropological perspective in a broader cosmic sense. The Holy Spirit and its invocation in the first prayer of the Orthodox Church, 'O Heavenly King...' gives man grace for its sacramental integration into the structure of the church; it also turns the bread and wine at the Eucharist into the Body and Blood of Christ, who is present in the church, the new creation as in the beginning in primordial waters, thus intermediating its permanent immaculate union with Christ, the Bridegroom. The Holy Spirit is not an impersonal power, but the living Spirit of God who is also the Spirit of communion, the one who works by the sacraments of the church to make the faithful people of God holy, and redeem them through synergy, working together with God. The Holy Sacraments make up the church through the new ones that are incorporated by the grace of the Spirit.

The Holy Sacraments are received by man in the local church, his parish. The parish is, thus, the environment, the field, the horizon where redeeming union with God is truly fulfilled when the gracious Holy Sacraments, as performed by the ordained canonical priest, are received; this is done in communion and submission with the kyriarch of the place that ensures the ecclesial unity of the people of God in the universal church. As usual, most of our Christians occasionally take part in sacramental celebrations, baptism, matrimony or funeral-related hierurgies. Some do not know the really deep mystagogic significance of sacramental acts in relation with the biblical text; they are united with Christ and, as St Paul wrote, these earthly men are less shaken inside existentially and spiritually by the enlightened and redeeming divine work. Certainly, the sacramental dimension of the Christian condition in time implies the knowledge of divine truth of life and redemption; this involves a permanent use of the text of Scripture, the great text of Christianity that comprises the historical revelation of God which culminates in Christ, an act of love and divine offering for the man who experiences God's work and presence in his concrete life but particularly in the condition of prayer, meditation and liturgy. It is this dimension that confers heavenly atmosphere on Orthodoxy in the melody of hymns that reproduce biblical godly words of a poetic creativity inspired by the hagiographies taken by the Holy Spirit to the communion of saints. In this sense, rediscovering and becoming aware of the liturgical and sacramental work of the church towards her sons, Orthodox lay people, is an urgent impetuous mystagogic and missionary exigency that can only have as its starting-point the real and concrete fact that the sacrament, as Father Stăniloae claims, 'is made in the encounter in faith of two people in the ambience of the church full of the Holy Spirit, and in bodily contact between two people, along with the confession through words of this faith; of the one that performs the sacrament and the other that receives it'.[17] Mystagogic in the sense of an intense and deep experience of faith in personal and missionary interiority; of a public communitarian witness of faith, visibility with an impact on the less initiated ones in the great mystery of Christianity, as St Paul said. However, in the sacraments, as B. Sesboüé put it, Christ has a major role as the original sacrament by the founding words and sacramental gestures[18] then taken over by the church and its sacramental hierarchy. Through the Holy Spirit, and for man, it institutes the personal thought and experienced relationship with God.

The sacraments of the church institute and make permanent the relationship with God, the redeeming communion and are 'in carnal relation with God'[19] in the sense of something concrete, palpable, intensely felt as a presence, a relation, as love between two people – in the Holy

---

[17] Stăniloae, *Teologia Dogmatică Ortodoxă* 3, 8.

[18] Bernard Sesboüé, *Invitation à croire: Des sacraments crédibles et désirables* (Paris: Cerf, 2009), 31.

[19] Sesboüé, *Invitation à croire*, 38, 174.

Sacraments, but especially in the Eucharist where Christ is the 'bread of life' (John 6:48, 51) for the Christian, according to St John. Considering these aspects, and the fact that the Orthodox Christian, in general, is rather a believer of liturgical and sacramental character than of the biblical one, in the sense that in his spiritual life the reading of the Bible receives less importance than church attendance and devotion to God and his saints – reference is made here to practitioners of faith in the sociological sense, since they make a smaller segment of the larger group of believers that declare themselves Orthodox and participate in the life of the Parish – a thorough understanding of the sacramental dimension becomes available. That is, one's personal existence, within the horizon of the Orthodox community, where the Holy Sacraments are fulfilled by the priest, rendering man and church as Body of Christ. All Holy Sacraments show a normal life in Christ known from the scriptures, through which we are spoken the hypostatic Word of God and whose words are repeated in the ritual of the Sacrament, thus becoming prayer. Therefore, it can be said that the church *exists* and *makes* things happen in the sense that it fulfils the sacraments and, in their turn, they fulfil the church,[20] i.e. they permanently make up the sacramental Body of Christ, the holy and heavenly people of God in the pilgrimage to the eternal citadel to God's Kingdom. What is said in the Liturgy of the Sacrament, the words have the power to make what is said is made effective through the Holy Spirit.

Therefore, at the level of parish as integral church in the local community by the reception of the Holy Sacraments, man is on the path which makes him real in relationship, or in communion, with God. Thus, the messianic prophecy, *God is with us,* is fulfilled for man as son of God whom he names, adores and invokes as Father after the divine discovery towards deification, divine-humanization, Christification and trinitarization[21] according to Justin Popovich's text that contains so many substantial expressions full of theological sense. Sacramentality is the way of communion between God and man, the state of man's being pervaded and thus shining by Christ's glory, the uncreated eternal light of the Holy Spirit, the entire Holy Trinity.

---

[20] Sesboüé, *Invitation à croire,* 40, 52.

[21] Père Justin Popovitch, *Philosophie orthodoxe de la vérité. Dogmatique de l'Eglise Orthodoxe, Tome cinquième* (Lausanne Switzerland: L'Age d'Homme, 1997), 247; Henri Bourgeois, Bernard Sesboüé and Paul Tihon, *Histoires des Dogmes* (Bernard Sesboüé (ed); Les Signes du salut 3: Paris: Desclée, 1995), 16. The authors show that despite the absence of the term 'Sacrament' in the Bible, it has imposed itself for a few decades as a notable act of Christian inculturation founded in the tradition of the church that needed to avoid confusion with the mystery traditions of old, the exact definition and sense being that of a 'sacred engagement for God', the alliance with Jesus Christ that fulfils the old pledge of the people of Israel.

Church and Mission

The Orthodox concept of mission depends on understanding the nature of the church, starting from Christ who brings the good news, the path that necessarily takes one to his church which gives the good news. By sending the Holy Spirit, Christ wanted his work to be continued in the church, a universal sacrament of redemption by its inherent missionary nature. For the church, *to be* is to proclaim the gospel of redemption unceasingly and to spread the grace of the Holy Spirit towards sanctification and deification so that we cannot speak of the church and mission separately. Instead, we can speak of *the mission of the church*, of its members, the clergy and the faithful, confessing and living, fulfilling the commandments of the One that called them 'out of darkness into his wonderful light' (1 Pet. 2:9). The church is the prophetic, sacerdotal and royal people of God who prefigures Christ's fullness and his eschatological reign by the reconciliation of everything, thanks to him. The church needs to bring all people to her because they are all created and redeemed by God in Christ. Therefore, the church cannot be conceived of as a purely human group in history falling back on its own interests that are mundane and ephemeral. The church would then lose its character, its divine aspect, by the Trinity itself being present in its divine-human structure. In its missionary essence, the church is in itself the sense of mission. Mission is an essential act of the new divine-human reality, the church, the body of Christ that has brought fullness to the world, the cosmos, ever since the Pentecost.

The church is not a voluntary association of individuals (Congregationalist ecclesiology), a *corpus Christianorum*, the result of a historical accident, but the reality of God's economy to unite everything in Christ 'to bring unity to all things in heaven and on earth under Christ.' (Eph. 1:10, 23). It is the mystery of our life in Christ, the here and now visible manifestation of the presence of Christ through the Holy Spirit in our life.

The Orthodox mission is to be interpreted as the extension of the same holy Church in time and space with its people growing through the centuries in their own cultural, historical area, but also with its people going to new places and keeping in their mind and in their heart the Christian tradition from home, maintaining the faithful people of God in the communion of saving grace of the one and only church of the apostles, of the Fathers of the one and undivided church from the beginning until today, in the dynamics of the same biblical and dogmatic faith. Evangelization includes everyone, because all people recognize the transitory nature of the world and miss God. However, they can become sons of God by union with Christ, keeping at the same time their personal uniqueness. Orthodoxy affirms that everything that exists in man must enter the Kingdom of God. Everything that represents man must be immortalized, deified and united for ever with God. It results from here that by union with God, man does not lose his personality, in the modernist sense, because my soul and my love remain mine even after union with God.

Therefore, mission is not the proclamation of theoretical truths or ethical principles, but the assemblage of people to become members of the Christian community in a concrete visible form. To build the body of Christ is the apostolic vocation of the church itself by the work of the Holy Spirit. The church, in a missionary aspect, fulfils the mandate and Christ's will by the work of the Holy Spirit; despite the troubles of time, it remains faithful to God and the gates of Hades will not overcome it (Matt. 16:18). The church is the Kingdom of God that has paradoxically come and will come.[22] The church proclaims and anticipatively updates in time and history the Kingdom of God in the Holy Spirit which constitutes its essential vocation starting from Pentecost. Apostolicity is one of the church's fundamentals, this attribute testifying to the unceasing continuity of the ecclesial organism in unity and holiness by sacramental hierarchy that continues the apostolic work through the Holy Spirit. The sacramental act of incorporation in the church of Christ is made with the conscience that the baptized one 'builds on the foundation of the apostles and prophets', and the church is incomplete without one of the many that Christ 'won' spilling his blood. The purpose of preaching the gospel and mission is of establishing Eucharistic communities in every human settlement; by means of the liturgy and the celebration of the redeeming presence of God in grace; they are summoned to witness to Christ, to fulfil his commandments, to show love spiritually and materially by philanthropic acts. In Orthodox missiology, the term 'missional' is not used but hermeneutics shows the holistic dimension of church mission related to Trinity, its real and current communion with the people of God in redeemed history.[23]

Orthodox mission is to be understood as an apostolic task and in the creeds from Nicaea and Constantinople we thus confess the faith in the one holy, catholic and apostolic church. In this sense, mission is an act of the missionary church, not an act of human adventure. Through mission, the church is extended and new Christian communities come into being in new places, in communion with the centre sending missionaries under the blessing of the local bishop of a church. The structures of the new church and of the sending church are the same in sacramental communion, worship and charity, and in spiritual and liturgical unity, under the guidance of the local synod or of the bishop with his canonical ordained priests.

The church gives fullness to the human being that cannot achieve holiness without God. Therefore, becoming aware of the quality of church members is a maximum requirement in the present context of Orthodox

---

[22] Stăniloae, *Martyria – Mission*, 9.

[23] Craig Van Gelder, Dwight J. Zscheile, *The Missional Church in Perspective: Mapping Trends and Shaping the Conversation* (Grand Rapids, MI: Baker Academic, 2011), 44-45; James A. Scherer and Stephen B. Bevans (eds), *New Directions in Mission and Evangelisation* (Maryknoll, NY: Orbis Books, 1992), 209.

mission. By means of the sacramental integration in the Body of Christ, the Christian has the responsibility of witnessing to the grace received, of living according to the biblical commandments, the tradition of the church in a theological, confessing and ecclesial existence. Therefore, according to the ecclesial principle of *sensus fidelium*, 'the missionary and pastoral rehabilitation and reactivation of laymen are crucial problems for every local Church',[24] for every community and Orthodox parish in which it is absolutely necessary for Christian unity and holiness to be reflected. As the people of God gathered in a certain geographical place, as parish, the local missionary church,[25] the church by the clergy and the faithful is assembled to update the variety of ministry and charisma perennially shown in Christian history according to their importance in various contexts. Thus, the entire people of God had a major role in the mission of the church in history which can be illustrated by means of significant contributions regarding the identification and veneration of national and local saints in the introduction of the living language, both spoken and written in the church service and sermon, in the organization of the local church, respecting the national and cultural values. In the Romanian Orthodox Church, the aspect of missionary work is mapped out by the following statistics of priesthood taught in our faculties of theology.

The highest authority of the Romanian Orthodox Church, in all its fields of activity, is the Holy Synod. It consists of 53 hierarchs: one patriarch, eight metropolitans, eleven archbishops, nineteen bishops, two assistant bishops to the Patriarch, ten assistant bishops and two assistant hierarchs.[26] Within country borders, the Romanian Patriarchy consists of a number of 14,648 church units as follows: one Patriarchy Centre, six metropolitan sees, ten archdioceses, thirteen dioceses, one vicarage, 176 deaneries, 11,394 parishes and 2,360 branches, 493 monasteries, 184 sketes, and ten metochions.[27]

From the statistics presented by the Chancellory of the Holy Synod of the Romanian Orthodox Church, 'there are 9,321 church buildings, out of which there are 102 eparchies (87 built plus fifteen under construction), one vicarage, 174 deaneries having their own location (153 built plus 21 under construction), 8,075 parish buildings (7,486 built plus 598 under construction), 969 monasteries (847 built plus 122 under construction); and within church units, there are 12,720 church cemeteries, out of which there

[24] Ion Bria, *Destinul Ortodoxiei (Fate of Orthodoxy)* (Bucureşti, 1989), 99.

[25] Robert S. Rivers, *From Maintenance to Mission: Evangelisation and the Revitalisation of the Parish* (Mahwah, NJ: Paulist Press), 38. The American theologian stresses the aspect of an ecclesial parochial centralism which may resemble the Eucharistic vision and theology of the Church in N. Afanasiev who lays emphasis on the mission of laity in his work, *Biserica Duhului Sfânt (1)/ The Church of the Holy Spirit* (trans: Elena Derevici; Cluj-Napoca, Romania: Patmos, 2008), contrasting the thesis of the metropolitan J. Zizioulas for which the centre of ecclesial power is the bishop.

[26] www.patriarhia.ro/_layouts/images/File/ADM_2011.pdf (accessed 15th June 2013).

[27] www.patriarhia.ro/_layouts/images/File/ADM_2011.pdf (accessed 15th June 2013).

are 12,349 parochial cemeteries (861 urban plus 11,488 rural), 371 monastery cemeteries (293 monasteries plus 78 sketes)'.[28] At this level of data and figures, 'within the Romanian Patriarchy, there are 15,596 religious units, out of which there are 66 cathedrals (31 eparchy cathedrals plus 35 church cathedrals); 11,214 parochial churches, 1,992 church branches, 563 monastery churches, 357 cemetery churches, 16 sixteen foundational churches, sixty isolated churches, 322 parochial heads, 245 monastery chapels, 561 churches and chapels in state institutions (81 – army, 38 – prisons, 28 – Ministry of Internal Affairs, 3 – SPP/SRI/STS (Romanian state institutions), 225 – hospitals, 87 – educational units, 14 – social care and foster homes, 15 – state cemeteries, 70 – other institutions)'.[29] Previously, at the end of 2008, 'in the social-philanthropic mission of the church, the following were involved: 29 counsellors, 33 eparchial inspectors, 228 social assistants (155 theologians and 73 non-theologians with a degree in the field), 103 missionary priests and 121 social workers, 184 volunteers and 296 from other categories of personnel that work at the Social Work Bureau at the level of the Patriarchal Centre and the eparchial centre'.[30]

Moreover, without having access to a detailed account of military priests and churches in military units, from the Account of the Social-Philanthropic Sector of the Romanian Patriarchy for 2011, we note that 'religious and spiritual assistance in military units, hospitals and social homes was ensured by a number of 507 priests, of which 146 in military units and prisons and 361 in hospitals, social care units, cemeteries and educational units. In all of the units mentioned above, at present there are 487 churches and chapels, twenty churches being in various stages of construction and renovation'.[31]

In church units (patriarchy, eparchies, deaneries, monasteries, sketes) the following can be encountered at the level of management: '53 management personnel (hierarchs) corresponding to public staff; 1,024 clerical staff functions contributing to salaries in the state budget: one patriarchal administrative vicar, 28 patriarchal counsellors, twenty eparchial administrative vicars, seven church general inspectors/ patriarchal secretaries, 161 administrative counsellors, 141 secretaries for the Chancellory of the Holy Synod/ eparchial inspectors, 42 eparchial secretaries, 24 exarchs, 161 deans, 439 abbots and trustees.[32] The document issued by the Chancellory of the Holy Synod reads that 'in the Romanian

[28] www.patriarhia.ro/_layouts/images/File/ADM_2011.pdf (accessed 15th June 2013).

[29] www.patriarhia.ro/_layouts/images/File/ADM_2011.pdf (accessed 15th June 2013).

[30] Dorel-Nicolae Moţoc, 'Darea de seamă a sectorului social filantropic al Administraţiei Patriarhale cu privire la activitatea social-filantropică desfăşurată în cuprinsul eparhiilor Patriarhiei Române în anul 2008' ('Account of the Social Philanthropic Sector of Patriarchal Administration on Social-Philanthropic Activity in Romanian Patriarchy Eparchies in 2008'), in BOR (ROC), CXXVII.1-4 (2009), 81.

[31] www.patriarhia.ro/_layouts/images/File/ADM_2011.pdf (accessed 15th June 2013).

[32] www.patriarhia.ro/_layouts/images/File/ADM_2011.pdf (accessed 15th June 2013).

Orthodox Church (patriarchy, eparchies, deanery, parishes, branches, monasteries and sketes, budgetary institutions) there are 14,231 active priests and deans, out of which 13,765 priests and deacons in parishes, monasteries, sketes, eparchial centres and deaneries; 466 priests in state institutions. Vacant clerical positions – 1,321, out of which there are 192 management personnel and 1,129 priests and deacons'.[33]

Liturgy and Mission

An essential principle of Orthodox missiology is *the proclamation of the gospel by doxology and liturgy*, a principle according to which prayer and the liturgical representation of the gospel or revelation have a primal role in Orthodoxy. Consequently, 'the communion that confesses Christ is, at the same time, the communion that prays to Him, adores Christ as God. In history, God's adoration in the Church was the expression and guarantee of keeping the divine revelation'.[34] The redeeming events in the life of Christ are expressed and represented in the liturgy, i.e. his messianic activity and the preaching of the good news of the gospel, death and resurrection. At the same time, the liturgy, updating the redeeming events and offering us the Eucharistic Christ, anticipates the future Kingdom for Christians. By the Eucharist, Christians are 'christified', they experience the fullness of redemption because 'the Lord is good' (Ps. 34:4). Thus, between the gospel and the Eucharist, in Orthodoxy, there is a strong organic connexion: 'Therefore go and make disciples of all nations, baptizing them' (Matt. 28:19-20). True life depends on the sacramental act of consuming the Eucharistic Christ, eating and drinking the Body and the Blood of Christ (John 6:53).

Orthodox mission is divided into liturgy and the sacraments, the liturgy and the Eucharist imprinting the true rhythm of mission; first of all, *gathering* (*ek-kaleo*) and then *sending*, '*In peace we shall exit*'. The Eucharist creates communion, gathers Christians, unites them in Christ, and between them and from this peak of adoration each one becomes an apostle of Christ for the witnessing of the sublimity of the life with Christ, in Christ. Therefore, in Byzantium, the centre of mission was liturgy. By its structure and the liturgical aspect, the Orthodox Church is a missionary church.[35] Despite all these, given its function and ecclesial dimension, the liturgy of the Orthodox Church cannot be reduced to ritualism, introverted life, but it accomplishes a genuine openness towards the world and social life with its communitarian problems. If Christian mission lacked the doxological, liturgical dimension, it would be mere religious ideology, a peculiar activity of human vanity and selfishness. St John Chrysostom acknowledges these missionary aspects: 'Would you do honour to Christ's

[33] www.patriarhia.ro/_layouts/images/File/ADM_2011.pdf (accessed 15th June 2013).

[34] Bria, *Go Forth in Peace*, 17.

[35] Lemopoulos, *You Shall Be My Witnesses*, 179.

body? Neglect Him not when naked; do not while here you honour Him with silken garments, neglect Him perishing without cold and nakedness. For He that said, This is my body, and by His word confirmed the fact, This same said, You saw me an hungered, and fed me not; and, Inasmuch as you did it not to one of the least of these, you did it not to me.'[36]

In Orthodoxy, *the gospel is preached in the Liturgy, in the sacraments of the church, in other divine services, the seven praises of the daily liturgical cycles of saints.*

In the Orthodox cycle, the holy scriptures are the spring and foundation of the entire liturgical and spiritual life of the church. Orthodox liturgical ritual is characterized by impressive biblical phraseology, extended texts taken from the Old and New Testaments at each ordinance typically established by the church. The biblical message is liturgically brought to date in the prayer of the church, especially in its liturgy, when the church performs the Eucharist; it is by the Eucharist that the church fulfils itself in communion with Jesus Christ. The Bible is alive in liturgy, the liturgical acts vivify and give sense to the words of the scriptures interpreted and brought to date according to the requirements of Christians nowadays and since for ever, all called to holiness, a state of inner grace that passes beyond words, radiates for the Christian communion overall. This state is given by participation to 'the divine nature' (2 Pet. 1:4), the communion with the Holy One.

But on the other hand, the prayer itself springs from man's purest feeling, the simple thought risen to God for praise, gratitude or demand; it bears the seal of spiritual biblical experience in a continuity of invocation and fulfilment of human hope in time and eschatological perspective. Drawing on P. Florensky, D. Stăniloae presents a structure of prayer according to the following scheme:

a. Addressing God, '*God the Almighty*..., or *Jesus Christ, our Lord*..., or *God, heavenly King, Comforter, true Spirit*... that expresses the essence of public or private prayer, i.e. the invocation of the presence of God the transcendent, the mystery of the divine name invoked by the faithful man who feels God in his proximity, more in his heart, lives overwhelmed and transfigured by the divine presence.
b. The anamnetic aspect of prayer, i.e. the recall of the wonderful acts of God from the history of divine economy, the revelation, the self-communication of his eternal will and love for man and his redemption. His involvement in human history for man in order to be in communion with God and the trust that makes man open towards God and his work confirm the identity and continuity of divine redeeming acts for people since the beginning of time: 'Jesus Christ, Our Lord, you entered the garment of the tax

[36] Homily 50 on Matthew.

collector Zacchaeus and redeemed him and his household…', or 'You came to Cana in Galilee and blessed the wedding there…'.

c. The demand, thanks to which the desire of the faithful or of the celebrating community comes into force, is presented trustfully to God based on the fulfilment of the prayers by him in the history of the economy of redemption, of the church: 'Watch over those that pray to you and guard them from all evil', or 'receive the prayer of your humble subjects and with your unseen help bless this wedding…'.
d. God's praise in the Trinity, the Father, Son and Holy Spirit, this enumeration was consecrated in the Christian tradition based on the chronology of the economy of each divine person towards humanity.
e. The doxological confirmation by the word *Amen* needs to be understood from the perspective of divine truth, of the faithfulness that God has for his people.[37]

In the liturgical acts, the revelation is brought to date, 'God with us', the economy of redemption in its dynamic to the Kingdom of God who is efficiently present in the perspective of life and redemption in the community of his own, in the church, the *axis mundi* and liturgical centre of creation by the grace of the Spirit as has always been with his people.

Spirituality and Mission

The Orthodox Church has a liturgical, communitarian spirituality, but also a *personal dimension*, fruit of ascesis and love sprung from God as love's source (1 John 4:8). This is a missionary factor of an exceptional quality and the utmost value, extremely important for the mission of the church, for Christian witness. The Christian aim is holiness achieved by communion with holiness in itself, God's being. If the Orthodox Church is the holder of an exceptional legacy of liturgical spirituality, we may rightfully assess that the evening stars on the sky of the church are those of ascetic and mystical spirituality, the saints as an inexhaustible spring of spiritual growth. The saints, martyrs, known and unknown devout people, the hesychasts of the Orthodox Church, are the ones that achieved likeliness with the image of God via the holiness of their life, prayer and contemplation, love of their neighbour which effaces separation, thus creating an environment that irradiates light, joy, communion and the view of God. The holiness of life, holiness as divine gift obtained from the spiritual fight with the attempts, the passions, the devil by the classic steps of Christian spirituality, purification, illumination and above all, *unio mystica*, the suffering of deification through grace, the essential anthropological concept of

[37] Dumitru Stăniloae, *Spiritualitate şi comuniune în Liturghia Ortodoxă (Spirituality and Communion in the Orthodox Liturgy)* (Bucureşti: Institutul Biblic), 87.

Orthodox theology is the absolute human goal. The Orthodox Church gives an authentic goal to the Christian world which is viable and experienced in the love that offers itself and transfigures; this is a difficult, yet possible goal, achievable by the grace of the Holy Spirit by the charismatic diversity in the Christian East. This includes what we call a secularized world which refuses God because of its various ideologies. The holiness with its balance is the value nowadays imposed on the entire Christianity which unfortunately faces spiritual influences foreign to the genuine Christian spirit. This also holds true for the unchristian spaces of the Far East, the new gnosis, the occultism of the 'parallel tradition' with the attempt of some forces to create 'a new world', 'a new religion', illusions of the un-rooted man in the spiritual Christian tradition. As acknowledged by the Christian West that admires the ascetic-mystical, sacramental and liturgical spirituality of Orthodoxy nowadays and the Church Fathers, 'perhaps the Christian East in helping man to discover himself as a religious athlete, with a corresponding spirituality that can save him from an easy and false absorption in the divine impersonal essence of Oriental mysticism which tends towards a carnal union with Christ'.[38]

Between mission and holiness, there is a deep intimate relationship because the first effectively fulfils itself when the theological and missionary priest preaching Christ radiates the power and warmth of the Spirit by his personal life in Christ. Therefore, 'the man who has the Holy Spirit inside him is able to understand the deep sense of Scriptures and guides others on the path of holiness and fullness of life'.[39] Orthodox spirituality also has a theological foundation; it is a Trinitarian, Christological, pneumatological-sacramental one in the ecclesial community by the participation of the clerical man to the life of his neighbours, the improvement of spiritual life of the community whose member is in the freely and personally assumed anachoresis for more union and intelligible vision of God.[40]

Spiritual exercises, ascesis are a rebirth to us in the Spirit of Christ up to the state of deification – theosis which is achieved through personal endeavour and is, at the same time, a gift of God due to the state of adoration, prayer, contemplation, meditation. Holiness is the sense of Christian life; holiness, as act of purification, illumination, mysterious union with God in grace by putting on the full armour of God (Eph. 6:11-18) which is God's will and work for people, the sublime gift of the Holy Spirit.

---

[38] Frances Colte, *The Mission of Eastern Christian Education in the West* (Diaconia 4: Fordham University, 1973), 338-39.

[39] Charles André Bernard, *Traite de théologie spirituelle* (Paris: Cerf, 1986), 25.

[40] Dumitru Stăniloae, *Spiritualitatea ortodoxă: Teologia morală ortodoxă* 3 *(Orthodox Spirituality: Orthodox Moral Theology)* (Bucureşti: Editura Ştiinţifică şi Enciclopedică, 1981), 24-49.

The Christian is the person 'in the image of God' that received, by baptism, via the Sacrament of Unction, the 'mark of the Holy Spirit as gift' of God which is united with Christ himself in the Eucharist, fearfully and humbly consuming his Body and Blood as bread and wine. Therefore, the Christian is a *theophorus*, a bearer of God, by the divine grace inside him and a confessor of divine love for the redeemed world; this was achieved by means of Christ's sacrifice whose heavenly fruit are benefits for man in the church. Thus, the Christian permanently needs to prove by words and facts this quality and, in Christ, this valour of his in the intimacy of personal prayer, in the presence and communitarian service in the institutions of the state, of society, in general by practising Christian values, responsibility and love. Nowadays, it is necessary to overcome a dualism which unfortunately shows in some Christians; it is the case of a pathological halving in a spiritual and moral manner by the affirmation and practice of faith individually, privately, egotistically and the lack of Christian engagement for the world, which is even more serious for the institution of the church whose member one becomes by baptism. The stress on the mystagogic aspect of Christian life needs to fall in parallel with the visible, concrete, public witnessing of quality, of the honour of the Christian. In fact, the sense of Christian life is the acquisition of the gift of the Holy Spirit that makes man's face shine when improved by eternal divine light that shone in Christ on Tabor and that accepts people loved by God; 'I am loved that so I exist.'[41] The spiritual experience of the missionary involves the equivalence between speech and the living of Christ in prayer.

Culture and Mission

Contextualization of the scriptures, of Christian universal in national culture and local specificity is a principle and one of the personal, special qualities of Orthodoxy by which it expresses itself osmotically, naturally, ontologically; certainly, this happens after a long historical experience with its positive and negative realms, the relationship between national culture and Christian faith. In the perspective of present missiology, 'inculturation' signifies the insertion of values in the spiritual inheritance, the cultural legacy, one's own life conceptions. In the Christian vision nowadays, inculturation is the movement of local values and cultures by which they become 'basic instruments and powerful means to present, restate and live Christianism'.[42] From a missiological perspective, inculturation is the evangelization process by which the Christian message and life are assimilated by a culture so that they express themselves by means of the

[41] Ioannis Zizioulas, Metropolitan of Pergamos, *Comuniune şi alteritate: Fiinţarea personal-eclesială (Communion and Otherness)* (trans. Liviu Barbu; Bucureşti: Sophia, 2013), 145.
[42] 'Inculturation', in *Dictionary of the Ecumenical Movement* (Grand Rapids, MI: Geneva, 1991), 506.

specific elements of that culture and make up a principle of inspiration, in norm and power of unification that transfigures the respective culture. Therefore, the integration of Christianism in ethnical culture (indigenization) is the transfiguration of the richness of human culture and history of a people in existence, in its manifestation in the light of the scripture of Christ, of eternal truth. In fact, the history of Orthodox peoples overlapped, identified with Orthodoxy itself which created and shaped the profile of a national culture. The historical vocation of Orthodoxy may be expressed as follows: 'A mission to serve the Church, the Church to serve the nation.'[43] The Orthodox Church served the people in its whole, not only the ruling class, but also the ecclesial community sometimes even against authorities.

Moreover, as Ion Bria claimed, 'the local Church is the one that creates culture in the process of reception and transmission of the gospel via cult, ethos and spirituality. Culture is not an independent anonymous construct; every local church, every nation, has its own cultural configuration'.[44] A simple acknowledgement of the spiritual and cultural patrimony of an Orthodox country is suggestive in this sense. As shown by C. Nicolescu, 'the Church proposed itself to the world by culture… and first rank culture' because Christ, its Lord, is an intellectual that taught the 'academics' of the Temple as Logos of God.[45]

The current configuration of the Orthodox Church shows great cultural and geographical diversity, both in terms of national Orthodox churches and the increasing Orthodox presence in the 'diaspora'. On the one hand, local Orthodox churches have imprinted themselves on the specific culture and traditions of peoples it encountered throughout history; thus, we can now speak of Byzantine, Slavic, Latin and Arab Orthodoxy. On the other hand, the rise of Orthodoxy in new geographical areas in Asia, Africa and America, raises the problem of a transfer of authority from mother churches to the new centres.

As Ion Bria claimed, Orthodoxy is 'a factor of history of a people or nation. In the case of many countries from the Middle East, Central and Eastern Europe, the history of a nation cannot be understood without the history of a local Church. Orthodoxy always defended "the polyphonic system" in which every local Church defends its ethnic and cultural identity, its specific mission. Being autonomous and autocephalous – having limited territory and its own synod – any local Church is a prototype within a universal community'.[46]

---

[43] Stăniloae, *Martyria – Mission*, 10.

[44] Ion Bria, *Studii de Misiune şi Ecumenism (Studies of Mission and Ecumenism)* (Sibiu: Astra Museum, 2013), 176.

[45] Costion Nicolescu, 'Iarăşi despre cult şi cultură: cultura cultului şi cultul culturii' (On Cult and Culture: Culture of the Cult and Cult of Culture), in *Ortodoxia* 1 (2015), 286, 290.

[46] Ion Bria, *Tratat de Teologie Dogmatică şi Ecumenică (Treatise of Dogmatic and Ecumenic Theology)*, (Bucureşti: Editura România creştină, 1999), 276.

The Orthodox Church and Ecumenism

Finally, we cannot omit the *ecumenic* dimension of Orthodoxy which, in the ecumenical movement, is defined as 'the current, historical, seen form of Universal Church undivided as in the first centuries. It preserves the dogmatic basis, the liturgical structure and canonical order that supports the unity of Universal Church'.[47] Due to these essential elements, Orthodoxy 'is not a confessional form of faith and spirituality reserved to a restrained group, a nation, region or culture; on the contrary, it has an ecumenic dimension'.[48] The notion of ecumenism etymologically comes from the Greek word *oikoumene,* being the medium-passive form of the verb *oikein* – to live. *Oikoumene* is the inhabited world, the entire earth, the people's home. This implies ontologically the idea of the unity of humanity, a unity of being, a truth that is unique for all as they are unitary in life, and received the same unique life. In a theological sense, *oikoumene* refers to the unity of creation, the humanity in God the Creator and Redeemer of all people. In classical antiquity, by *oikoumene* we understand the civilized Greco-Roman world which was united as far as its politics, administration and cultural diversity were concerned. This also holds true for the religion of the peoples within the empire. In the Christian sense, the term 'ecumenical' may be understood from the perspective of what is universal, catholic, a reality that characterizes all people, a truth which is for all, as the truth of Christ's gospel. Therefore, for the first time, this sense of ecumenism is found in St Ignatius of Antioch, a visionary of Christian ecumenicity who gives Christological, ecclesial and sacramental connotations to the term. Thus, 'the faithful should be where the bishop is, as the Universal Church is where Christ is'.[49]

By participating in the activity of the Ecumenic Council of Churches and inter-theological dialogues, Orthodoxy makes known its legacy of spirituality and genuine Christian theologization. The ecumenic dimension is, for Orthodoxy, the confession of the whole Christian truth, hence the possession of truth; but on the other hand, we can also speak today about a geographical universality of Orthodoxy among the inner Catholicity and universality of its message.[50]

The ecumenical dialogue has opened new possibilities of common Christian testimony and shows itself both *on the theological plan* (and this is harder due to the promotion of unlimited diversity without unit exigency; the Orthodoxy actually warned the Ecumenical Council of Churches that the purpose of this Christian organism is to restore the unit of the church. However, there can be a distancing from Christian understanding biblically, revelationally and dogmatically founded and spiritually-liturgically lived

---

[47] Ion Bria, *Credinţa pe care o mărturisim (The Faith We Confess)*, (Bucureşti: Editura Institutului Biblic şi de Misiune al Bisericii Ortodoxe Române, 1987), 12.
[48] *Destinul Ortodoxiei (Fate of Orthodoxy)*, 13.
[49] St Ignatius of Antioch, *Către Smirneni, 8:1-2,* in P.S.B.1, 184.
[50] Olivier Clement, *L'Eglise Orthodoxe* (Paris: P.U.F., 1965), 32.

within the canonical-sacramental borders of the church, of essential Christian teaching: the Trinitarian God, redemption, Bible, church and others), but especially in the plan of *practical*, social life: mutual help, the week of continuous prayer, common catechesis, etc. Currently, Orthodoxy is undergoing a crisis of the ecumenical movement due to various factors: the inter-communion with the heterodox ones, language, the ordination of women, the rights of sexual minorities and religious syncretism.

These situations are not compatible with the spirit of Orthodoxy, which pertains to integrism. These are groups which refuse the Christian model proposed by ecumenists. They have developed their current structure since the first centuries and this stance is present in their theological theses. Specifically this refers to all confessions belonging to special spiritual and cultural spaces such as the Mediterranean Basin.

Orthodoxy is characterized nowadays as it has always been, in its missionary work, by *faith* in our fathers, apostles and martyrs, *hope* in our presence in this world and in every place where Providence allowed us to exist through *love* in theology and our service.

In the Orthodox sense, there is only a church, 'the ark of redemption', whose institutional and spiritual-sacramental borders coincide. The Universal Church is identical with the Orthodox Church. Criticized by ecumenists as exclusivist, this concept is shared by most Orthodox theologians, although there are also voices that accept the thesis on the charismatic limits of the church and believe there is a certain state of ecclesiality beyond Orthodoxy. Who breaks from the church, by either wrong teaching (heresy) or disobedience (schism) loses the communion of the Spirit. Man becomes son of God by his church which became one in the sacrament of baptism. The Eucharist seals the gracious sacramental union with Christ. The foundation of this ecclesiological vision consists in the ontological unity of God who gives himself to the church, the one undivided in history. As Christians, we head not only to unity, but our entire existence also derives from the inseparable space between the three persons of the Holy Trinity given to us, the people, as historical event on the day of Pentecost. Orthodoxy embraces this ecclesiological concept which is the undivided church of the first Christian millennium that follows in history the church of Pentecost by its faithfulness to Christ and his teaching dogmatically formulated and experienced in the most convincing manner and sublimely by the saints of the church. The succession of the grace and the uninterrupted continuity of sacramental priesthood are also essential in Orthodoxy which is the expression of the communion of saints and angels led by the Holy Virgin in the mystical body of the church with Christians in this world.

The Kingdom of God and the Kingdoms of the World: Church-State Relationships in the Context of the Romanian Totalitarian Political Regime

Gelu Călina

Introduction

The present paper explores the intersection of totalitarian regimes and Christianity, with particular reference to the Orthodox confession within the geographical area of Romania. It first introduces the context of totalitarian regimes in Europe during the twentieth century, focusing on communist ideology, Nazi doctrine, and Italian fascism, and then it gives an overview of the relationship between state and church in Romania after World War II, till the Romanian revolution on 22nd December 1989. A major part of the paper pertains to communist ideology, because after 1945 Romania was one of the communist countries, following World War II.[1]

Throughout the paper we will present some of the most important aspects of the encounter between the Romanian totalitarian state and the traditional churches, paying particular attention to the oppression of Christian believers by the communists. Although I write as an Orthodox, this study is not limited to Orthodox believers, who make the majority of Christian people in Romania, but rather we have in view the whole church, that is, the Church as a divine- human institution. We will consider the strategies of oppression developed by the communists, political and the arsenal of methods used by the police in order to fight and subjugate the Orthodox Church as well as other confessions.

The communist regime monitored in particular the Romanian Orthodox Church, given the national history of the church and the considerable respect and attention paid to it by most of the Romanian population. During this period, the clergy or theology professors, ordinary Christians and those who before 1945 had worked in the Romanian state administration were persecuted by the policing bodies of the communist regime (the Securitate and the Miliția). It is a period when important intellectuals persecuted by the regime were able to find a place of refuge inside Romanian Orthodox

---

[1] Dennis Deletant, *Ceaușescu and the 'Securitate': Coercion and Dissent in Romania, 1965-1989* (London: Hurst & Co. / New York: M.E. Sharpe, 1995), 6.

Church structures.[2] After 1945, a Soviet model of state governance was imposed on Romania, which endeavoured to impose complete control over church life; however, we now know that that objective was never reached.

Finally, it will be argued that the church was one of the most effective institutions that opposed the Romanian totalitarian regime.

'My kingdom is not of this world' (John 18:33, 36)

Through its members, the church is present in the society. This can be an active presence or one that makes little difference in the life of the community. An active presence is beneficial even from a state/governing body perspective in as much as rights and obligations of citizens are supported and promoted by religious institutions, which is a factor that contributes to a better functioning of the state. As time goes by, religious behaviour leads to the establishment of standards as well as to some solid benchmarks against which we daily measure ourselves. Due to the fact that God's Kingdom is not of this world, the church has a permanent prophetic calling. From this perspective, the church cannot be thought of as simply a human institution, but as a divine-human one.

Given these, from a missionary perspective, one cannot affirm that nowadays there is nothing to be done. After the first phase in the history of the church – its birth – a consolidation phase followed, a phase which will only end with the Second Coming of Jesus Christ. Considering mission from such an eschatological biblical perspective, we know that there are standards of life to which all members of the church, clergy and ordinary believers, are called; and as a guiding thread towards the Kingdom of Christ, monasticism has had and still has a special place within the life of the church – just as Israel was a guiding light for all the nations. In other words, it is more appropriate to look at the life of the contemporary church from the perspective of the *eschaton* than to try to explain in a linear manner what the church is and ought to do.[3]

Unfortunately, humanity has never escaped totalitarian dictatorship regimes[4] or other forms of restriction of freedom; the communist ideology wanted to create the new human being from the working class, a plan that was supposed to eliminate all the evil in the world. In East European countries, where communist ideology was imposed by force, the atheistic

---

[2] Mihai Ungheanu, 'Introducere', in Cristina Păiuşan and Radu Ciuceanu (eds), *Biserica Ortodoxă Română sub regimul communist, 1945-1958*, Vol. 1 (Bucharest: Institutul Naţional pentru studiul totalitarismului, 2001), 32.

[3] '... therefore the nature of the Church is never to be finally defined in static terms, but only in terms of that to which it is going. It cannot be understood rightly except in perspective which is at once missionary and eschatological.' Cf. Lesslie Newbigin, *The Household of God: Lectures on the Nature of the Church* (London: SCM Press, 1953), 18.

[4] Michael Schäfer, 'Luigi Sturzo as a Theorist of Totalitarianism', in Hans Maier (ed), *Totalitarianism and Political Religions. Volume I: Concepts for the Comparison of Dictatorships* (New York: Routledge, 2004), 23-25.

socialist society communists would establish was a constant threat to the church and its mission. Nowadays communist regimes have come to an end. However, their nightmares, that is, the destructive ideas that contradicted the noble ideals of the post-World War II world, which communism promoted, did not.

This ideology, that propagated – by undemocratic means – the profile of the so-called 'new man', was from the beginning in competition with the church. The Marxist critique of religion that was employed by communist ideologues within the totalitarian Romanian state contributed significantly to dissipating the link between religion and society, and also it reinforced the process of the privatization of religion.[5] The Romanian communist state openly displayed its opposition to the social dimension of the Christian message and thus smothered the critical voice of the church within Romanian society.

As we know, through the New Testament, we are called to embrace a new spiritual inheritance. And through baptism, we are called to choose life, to begin to respond positively to a spiritual call that man has and which has been planted within him since the time of creation. Mankind's restoration in Christ and the resulting community, the church, have been around for two thousand years. That is why the communist ideology was directed against the church, its main competitor, and the church's sacramental programme; and also why communist propaganda endeavoured to reduce the church to silence or even to destroy it.

Totalitarianism: The Extreme Left

What amazes us today is the question: how was it possible in Europe, during the twentieth century that several totalitarian ideologies – which created, in their turn, other totalitarian regimes –developed?[6] From recent research it is clear that – regardless whether they were left-wing[7] ideologies, like communism, or right-wing ones, such as fascism and Nazism – all totalitarian regimes were established to the detriment of the moral discernment of modern man.[8]

The European extreme left was founded with the *Communist Party Manifesto*[9] by Friedrich Engels and Karl Marx in 1848. Some ideas of this communist manifesto were used during the Revolution of 1848 and are based on the ideas of Utopian socialism and materialist philosophy. Socialism is based on the idea of a proletariat organized in order to build a

---

[5] Johann Baptist Metz, *Sulla teologia del mondo* (Brescia, Italy, 1969), 107-09.

[6] Marcello Flores (ed), *Nazismo, fascismo, comunismo: Totalitarismi a confronto* (Milano, Italy: Bruno Mondadori, 1998).

[7] Norberto Bobbio, *Dreapta şi stânga: Raţiuni şi semnificaţii ale unei diferenţieri politice* (Bucharest: Editura Humanitas, 1999), 101.

[8] Hannah Arendt, *Le origini del totalitarismo* (Torino, Italy: Einaudi, 2004).

[9] K. Marx and F. Engels, *Manifestul Partidului Comunist* (Bucharest: Editura Politică, 1962).

society without social classes. They oppose liberalism and capitalism in general, and seek a world without social classes, where justice is fulfilled.

Marxist socialism is based on a materialistic doctrine of history (historical materialism) and the fact that the interests of the society take precedence over the interests of the individual. Communism represents the major socialist concept that enables the transformation of society. In 1919, on Lenin's initiative, when the Russian Bolsheviks met several representatives of world socialism, Communist International (Comintern) was created for the purpose of overthrowing the global bourgeoisie and the creation of an international Soviet republic. Comintern held several global congresses and advocated the establishment of communist parties worldwide.

The matrix of the implementation of this communist ideology lies in the installation of a single party that did not allow the actions of other organizations that opposed it. This objective had been implemented in the inter-war period in three countries: Italy, Germany and the Soviet Union, though leftist ideology was used only in the case of the Russians. What the totalitarian ideologies had in common was the fact that they all required citizens to follow an ideology, left or right, while those who opposed it were considered enemies and subject to violent repression through imprisonment in camps or were condemned to death.

Through the revolution of October 1917, Vladimir Ilyich Lenin began the transformation of Czarist Russia into the Soviet Union; the civil war that followed between the 'reds' (Bolshevik) and the 'whites' (conservatives and liberals) was won by the Bolsheviks, who applied a vast programme of Marxist reforms. Lenin developed some political and economic theories that were intended to be an improvement on the Marxist theses, and wanted Marxism to be applied not only to Russia but also to the countries of Eastern Europe, where an agricultural economy was dominant.

Under the dictatorship of Stalin, Marxism-Leninism became a political theory and generated a workers' bureaucratized state which was politically maintained – but as though by criminals. Stalin elaborated several economic plans for a period of five years to modernize the Soviet Union, for it to become the first state in the industrial world to be based on communist and collectivist principles. He invested heavily in industry, infrastructure, and scientific and technological education, in order to transform traditional Russian society, but the dictatorial manner in which it was carried out was characteristic of a totalitarian regime.

This process of Stalinist modernization of state and society had dramatic consequences on the population, who suffered so that the 'new man' (*homo Sovieticus*[10]) might be built: they were deprived of freedom of thought and expression and of freedom of movement, because the state considered it had the sacrosanct right, conferred by its ideological monism, to intervene

[10] Alexander Zinoviev, *Homo Sovieticus* (New York: Atlantic Monthly Publisher, 1985).

and remove any voice that would not respect the will of the party. Due to the violent oppression enforced by the Communist Party, citizens from the Soviet Union and Eastern Europe lived with the fear of expressing themselves in public or at home, confining their utterances to whispers,[11] for every word could have been used by the informers who were encouraged by the party to come to the state authorities in order to 'unmask' any 'class enemy'.

In 1953, Stalin's successor, Nikita Khrushchev, began a process of de-Stalinization, considering that Stalin's Marxism was ineffective, and condemned Stalin's cult of personality. There were no significant changes in communist ideology until 1985, when economic reforms (*perestroika*) were initiated by the Soviet's new President Mikhail Gorbachev. The most important measure applied by Gorbachev allowed the economic restructuring of the state factories, starting in 1987, in order to establish production based on demand rather than producing merchandise only to be left unsold – enterprises became self-financing. Gorbachev's most radical economic reform occurred in 1988, when the Supreme Soviet approved Gorbachev's law that allowed the creation of some small private companies.

The Extreme Right

A European extreme right developed in two countries, Italy and Germany, based on grievances arising after World War I. On 30th October 1922, the Italian dictator Benito Mussolini received from King Victor Emanuel III the mandate to legally form the government after fascist troops (*Le camicie nere* or 'Blackshirts'[12]) had entered Rome and threatened to take power by force. The politico-military action orchestrated by Mussolini through which he managed to come to power in Italy is known in the Italian history as the 'March on Rome' and was the beginning of the dissolution of the Italian liberal state.[13] The Italian fascist era lasted nearly twenty years and every year this military event[14] was celebrated with pomp by the fascists, being considered as the beginning of the fascist revolution.

The Italian Fascists (PNF) (*i Fasci Italiani di combattimento / 1919*) are the result of the reform movement *Fascio d'azione rivoluzionaria interventista* created in Milan in 1914 by Mussolini and Alceste De Ambris. Since the late 1920s until the fall of Mussolini on 25th July 1943, the National Fascist Party was the only party of the Italian Kingdom, thus making it a fascist regime. Since 1921, within the PNF there was created

---

[11] Orlando Figes, *The Whisperers: Private Life in Stalin's Russia* (New York: Metropolitan Books, 2007).

[12] *Squadristi* were the Blackshirts who were the armed section of the National Fascist Party led by Mussolini.

[13] Renzo De Felice, *Breve storia del fascismo* (Milano, Italy: Mondadori, 2000).

[14] *Enciclopedia Universale Garzanti* (Milano, Italy: Garzanti libri, 1995), 898.

the *Avanguardia giovanile fascista*, a structure aimed at recruiting young people, students or school pupils in order to physically and patriotically reorganize the youth, and became the *I fasci giovanili di combattimento*. Between 1922 and 1925, Mussolini led coalition governments made up of nationalists, liberals and populars, and strengthened the state authority even by involving fascist party members in power structures.

It is significant that the Blackshirts,[15] who were fascist party members were transformed into a civilian police body, established on a voluntary basis and aimed at the progressive identifying of the Italian state with the fascist party. In 1936, the fascists entered into an agreement with Nazi Germany (the Rome-Berlin Axis), and in 1939, Mussolini's dictatorship issued anti-Semitic laws by which Jews were expelled from the public services. *Il Duce* was arrested by order of the king on 25th July 1943, but Italy continued the war until 1945. The fascist movement condemned liberalism and communism, and managed to obtain the support of the Italian population for a long period, but there was a big difference between what the fascist movement wanted to be and what the fascist regime installed by Mussolini really was.[16]

As regards the relationship with the Roman Catholic Church, it has to be remarked that Mussolini managed to sign a Concordat with the Vatican in 1929. This treaty has regulated many of the relationships between church and state in Italy and it is regarded as support shown by the fascist movement towards the Roman Church. The Concordat, negotiated by Mussolini, put an end to the tensions and lack of recognition between the Italian Kingdom and the Holy See. The situation lasted from 1871, when the Italian government issued the *Special Guarantees Law (La Legge delle Guarentigie)* for the Pope and the Vatican City. This law was not accepted by Pope Pius IX, who condemned in his encyclical *Ubi nos* both the fund and guarantees announced by this law, showing that the encyclical could not separate spiritual power from secular.

Through the new Concordat, the Pope agreed that bishops should swear allegiance to the Italian state before their appointment as clergy, while priests were forbidden to engage in politics and were exempted from military service. On the other hand, the state undertook to reconcile with Roman Catholic teaching laws concerning marriage and divorce. By signing this pact, Roman Catholicism became a state religion and it was also decreed that the public education system would include Roman Catholicism among the compulsory subjects of study.

In terms of economic policy, the fascist regime promoted a policy oriented towards the total economic independence and towards the creation of a social state. Fascism acted as a political religion who wanted the renovation of the ancient Rome cult and the creation of the 'new man'.

---

[15] *La milizia volontaria per la sicurezza nazionale.*

[16] Renzo de Felice, *Intervista sul Fascismo* (Milano: Mondadori, 1992), 40.

Nazism

Between 1933 and 1945, Nazi Germany (the Third Reich) became a totalitarian state under the leadership of Adolf Hitler. National Socialism was a right-wing ideology characterized by racism, populism and totalitarianism. Although it had a socialist vision, Nazism differed from the Socialist International of Marxist origins, practised at that time in the Soviet Union. Economically, Nazism campaigned to eradicate unemployment and promoted an economy based on industry and the production of goods, designed to lead to the full independence of the economy of Germany, although the German economy was geared primarily to the production of military equipment.

Hitler's political theories were based on the existence of a superior race (*Herrenvolk*), the German Aryan race, which was not to be involved with other, inferior, races. After coming to power, Hitler established a dictatorship that persecuted various social categories (Hebrews, Gypsies, Slavs and homosexuals) and religious groups (Jehovah's Witnesses) with the stated purpose of combining all the Germanophile territories in Europe into one single state.[17] According to Hitler's vision, the state could not rely on democracy, because – he declared – the state was considered an authority in the service of the Nazi party.

Nazism promoted anti-Semitism and led to the death of millions of Jews in concentration camps. NSDAP (NAZI party) propaganda mixed various pagan rituals with esoteric elements, exalting the German race and preparing for armed intervention in order to conquer those countries that did not obey the German leader. The Nazis had the aim of removing all churches in Germany, while Jesus was regarded by Hitler as an Aryan, but Nazi ideology exalted itself above traditional religions while neglecting Christian doctrine.

General Characteristics of Totalitarianism

The concept[18] of the totalitarian transformation of a state was used in Italy by Luigi Sturzo,[19] in order to describe Giovanni Gentile's and Benito Mussolini's concept of state. Sturzo attacked the totalitarian tendencies of fascist ideology, highlighting the similarities between fascism and communism. Jens Petersen[20] believes that the adjective *totalitarian*

---

[17] Domenico Fisichella, *Analisi del totalitarismo* (Messina-Firenze, Italy: D'Anna, 1976), 209.

[18] Jens Petersen, 'La nascita del concetto di "Stato totalitario" in Italia', in *Annali dell'Istituto italogermanico in Trento* 1 (1975), 143-56. 'Die Geschichte des Totalitarismusbegriffs in Italien', in Hans Maier (ed), *'Totalitarismus' und 'Politische Religionen'* (Paderborn, Germany: 1996), 15-35.

[19] Luigi Sturzo, *Popolarismo e fascismo*, in *Opera omnia*, vol. II/t.4 (Bologna, Italy: Zanichelli, 1956), 235.

[20] See Jens Petersen, 'Die Entstehung des Totalitarismusbegriffs in Italien', in Manfred Funke (ed), *Totalitarismus: Ein Studien-Reader zur Herrschaftsanalyse moderner Diktaturen* (Bonner Schriften zur Politik und Zeitgeschichte, XIV), (Dusseldorf, Germany: 1978), 105-28;

referring to the state was first used by Giovanni Amendola in 1923. The monopole of an ideology[21] is managed by the sole party in power and means the interference with any form of free thinking which is not in agreement with official ideology. The sole party is led by a charismatic leader to whom the party had organized an often exaggerated cult of personality.

Hannah Arendt believes that genuine totalitarianism took place in the Soviet Union and in Nazi Germany, but in the case of Italian Fascism, there was only one totalitarian episode. She defines totalitarianism, not by political science terminology, but as an ethical process, an auto-destructive dynamic that has its roots in the dissolution of the social classes.[22]

From what we have presented up till now it is evident that totalitarian[23] regimes use ideologies or political myths[24] for the building of a over-powerful state which maintains a continuous propaganda claiming to solve all human problems, hence the syntagm of *political religions.*[25] So, in order to replace an effective political practice with a new one, one needed such a strong political message so that the old resorts of the modern state can dislocate and the new one to impose. Although the modern state is not perfect, however, Christianity has entered into an alliance with political power, with the representatives of the sensible universe, succeeding to put the social life within a supra-rational order.

A New Kingdom on the Earth: Communism

Today we have much information about the crimes against the church after the 1917 under the Soviet regime; but the same insidious propaganda was unleashed in other countries of Eastern Europe too. They were forced to become socialist republics (Albania, Bulgaria, Czechoslovakia, Estonia, Latvia, Lithuania, Moldova, Poland, Romania, Yugoslavia and Hungary). In this vast area, from the Far East to south-eastern Europe, the church was subject to persecutions that took place behind the 'Iron Curtain', as Winston Churchill called it, on 5th March 1946.

Communist ideology[26] was not alone in building a totalitarian political system, but it must be put on the same plane as Marxism, fascism[27] or

---

Michael Schäfer, 'Luigi Sturzo as a Theorist of Totalitarianism', in Hans Maier (ed), *Totalitarianism and Political Religions. Volume I: Concepts for the Comparison of Dictatorships* (New York: Routledge, 2004), 23.

[21] Emilio Gentile, *Fascismo: Storia e interpretazione* (Roma-Bari: Laterza, 2002), 72.

[22] Arendt, *Le origini del totalitarismo.*

[23] Walter Schlangen, *Die Totalitarismustheorie: Entwicklung und Probleme* (Stuttgart, Germany: 1976), 26-37.

[24] Emilio Gentile, *Il culto del littorio: La sacralizzazione della politica nell'Italia fascista* (Roma-Bari: Laterza, 2009).

[25] Georges Balandier, 'Le sacré par le détour des sociétés de la tradition', in *Cahiers internationaux de sociologie,* 100 (1996), 5-12.

[26] Raymond Aron, *Démocratie et Totalitarisme* (Paris: Gallimard, Folio Essais, 1965).

national socialism, which, using religion or some aspects of it, manipulated the masses in establishing their totalitarian states.[28] Communism and Nazism stated from the very beginning that they did not allow religion to be active within their domains; but if we look retrospectively, we see that, through insidious propaganda, they created a pseudo-religion that subjugated the entire state, all its members, violating the right to liberty of conscience or religious freedom.

Under communism, the person is called an individual but is controlled in all the aspects of social and private life. The traditional family has also been threatened by this new ideology of the 'new man', which promised another way of being fulfilled as a human.

The concept of the 'new man' was present at the very start of communism, and from the analysis used to implement this doctrine, we find that the development of an actual religious cult was attempted. Romanians swallowed in disgust the cult of the Russian or Romanian communist leaders, among them Vladimir Lenin, Joseph Stalin, Sergei Kirov, Ana Pauker, Vasile Luca, Petru Groza, Nicolae Ceauşescu, etc. For a period, they were called 'apostles of communism'. Within state institutions such as schools, railway stations and other public places, paintings were displayed, containing the images or other artistic samples of these communists. It should be noted that communist propaganda recommended changing the names of their leaders, most of them using pseudonyms instead of their real names, and the biographies of some of the leaders were also modified.

After analyzing the public messages sent by communist leaders in the public arena, of the methods of political communication and of the structure of the communist propaganda machine, it can be concluded that we had to deal with a pseudo-religion which wanted to incarnate itself by force into all the members of the state. Although the communists asserted that religion was opium for the people, communist propaganda did, however, make use of some of the religious ways they adapted; for instance, a cult of the personalities of the communist leaders who had to replace the entire Christian calendar resulted.

Communism wanted to rewrite the old hierarchies using symbolic language; it created a new mythology and also pseudo-mysticism, where ethnicity was inferior to the quality of members of the Communist Party. Party membership conferred a special status in society and extra civic rights and privileges. Welcoming a new member to the ranks of the party organization became a performance intended to show the strength of the party and was part of a mythology of the communist hero that built the multilaterally developed socialist society.

---

[27] Luigi Sturzo, 'Italia e fascismo (1926)', in *Opera Omnia,* I/t.1, (Roma: Istituto Luigi Sturzo, 2001), 113-14. See: www.sturzo.it

[28] Vittorio Strada (ed), *Totalitarismo e totalitarismi* (Venezia, Italy: Marsilio, 2003).

The ideology of the communist hero was promoted through various ways and aimed to overtake the transcendental message of the church in the collective mentality and to impose new moral standards within society. We should note the process of submission of all the plans of Romanian society took place from the beginning under the direction and the co-ordination of the Romanian Communist Party, which was, in turn, subordinated to the Soviet Communist Party. The Romanian Communist Party forced the King of Romania, Michael I, to abdicate on 30th December 1947, then dissolved the political parties and manipulated the parliamentary elections, the basis of the totalitarian regime.

Church and State Relationships in Romania

Since 1947, communist ideology in Romania gradually seized, by force, all the strategic areas of the state. In order to legitimize some violent interventions and to legitimize the working class as a social class bearing a special message, the communists developed a propaganda that resembled a pseudo-religion[29] in the attempt to give a 'sacred' environment to communist ideology by the use of various ceremonies or rituals.

Murders and lies[30] were also used as methods to impose by force the totalitarian regime in Eastern Europe; Romanian communism was built as an appendage of the Soviet Communist Party, subordinated and led by Moscow. In 1948, many Soviet advisers arrived in the country and, from the shadows, led the Stalinization transformation of Romania in the presence of the Red Army who was still occupying the country.

The major consequences of the brutal intervention of communism in the structure of the Romanian state after 1947 can be stated as follows: the removal of the multi-party system from East European countries and the imposition of a single party – the Communist Party – and of a single ideology; the subjugation of the judiciary to the Romanian Communist Party; the establishment of a repressive system based on the political police (*Securitate*)[31] which was charged with removing all those whose opinions were different from those of the Communist Party; the total control of the media; the exclusion of religion from the public sphere as a source of knowledge; the promotion of atheism; forced collectivization; the nationalization and confiscation of people's goods and of private industry in order to control the whole economy;[32] the rewriting of the nation's history; and indifference towards public property.

---

[29] Enzo Traverso, *Il totalitarismo. Storia di un dibbatito* (Milano, Italy: Bruno Mondadori, 2002), 115.

[30] Stéphane Courtois, *The Black Book of Communism: Crimes, Terror, Repression* (Boston, MA: Harvard University Press, 1999).

[31] Cristian Troncotă, 'Din istoria aparatului de Securitate în Romania, 1948-1965', in *Arhivele totalitarismului,* 26-27.1-2 (2000), 16.

[32] Gail Klingman and Katerine Verdery, *Ţăranii sub asediu: Colectivizarea agriculturii în România, 1949-1962* (Iaşi, Romania: Polirom, 2015).

In Romania, the socialist state fought hard from 1947 till 1989 to evict the Orthodox Church from public life. The Orthodox Church was not the only church in Romania which was subject to the regime's anti-religious persecution.[33] Nowadays, after a tremendous number of documents have been studied and published, we can say that every day religion was on the communist agenda, since the Romanian socialist state was established in 1947, relying on the Soviet Communist Party's force. In this respect, any religious argument or any religious activity was treated by the new authorities with suspicion; not only Orthodox Christians, but also Roman Catholics, Protestants and other religions found themselves in the same situation.[34] Because the Orthodox Church was and continues to be the largest Christian community in Romania, the authorities' attention was focused mainly on it.

The totalitarian communist ideology limited the social status of the Orthodox Church and its sphere of influence. We can state that, from the very beginning, the church and the communist state were realities that mutually excluded each other. The communist ideology was built on a basis of scientific socialism and targeted the building of a new world and, indirectly, the 'new man', not by persuasion but by the destruction of the basis of the old world. The recent history of Romania (1947-1989) – unfortunately – is one of the areas where this 'revolutionary project' was applied.

The analysis of the passage of the Romanian Orthodox Church (ROC) through the communist period will take longer than estimated, while research of the archives of the former Romanian Secret Service[35] (*Securitate*) has published ample and serious studies about this period. These studies, as a result of the research of the *Securitate*[36] archives, led to a complex image of the Romanian Orthodox Church that immediately after the Revolution of 1989 was accused of collaboration with the communist regime, without taking into account the ecclesiological conception of the Romanian Orthodox Church, but also the religious policy imposed by the

---

[33] *Martiri pentru Hristos din România, în perioada regimului comunist,* Bucureşti (Bucharest: Ed. Institutului Biblic şi de Misiune al Bisericii Ortodoxe Române, 2007), 39-40. This paper presents 241 Christian martyrs (207 Orthodox, thirty Catholics, four Evangelical Protestants) that died in Romania during communist persecution. Most were priests, theology professors, lawyers, students, monks and even farmers.

[34] Cristina Păiuşan, Radu Ciuceanu, *Biserica Ortodoxă Română sub regimul communist, 1945-1958,* Vol. I (Bucharest: Institutul Naţional pentru studiul totalitarismului, 2001).

[35] To have some idea about the power and the way the Romanian Intelligence Service *Securitate* worked in order to maintain 'internal discipline' (Marius Oprea, *Bastionul cruzimii: O istorie a Securităţii (1948-1964)* [Bucureşti: Ed. Polirom, 2008], 10), among the Romanian citizens who opposed the new totalitarian regime, we present a few bibliographic sources: Dennis Deletant, *Ceausescu and the 'Securitate': Coercion and Dissent in Romania, 1965-1989* (London: Hurst & Co. / New York: M.E. Sharpe, 1995). *Communist Terror in Romania: Gheorghiu-Dej and the Police State, 1948-1965* (London: Hurst & Co. / New York: St Martin's Press, 1999). Marius Oprea, *Banalitatea răului: O istorie a Securităţii în documente 1949-1989* (Bucharest: Polirom, 2002).

[36] www.cnsas.ro

communists. It is very important to note the role that security officers have had in imposing this religious policy by the communist state.

The *Securitate* had the most enormous role, that of the instrument of fear, having as its purpose the monitoring and full control of the entire population;[37] it had its own mode of operation designed to protect the totalitarian regime of any enemy inside or outside the country. In 1948, along with the establishment of the *Securitate*, within the Directorate of Information 1, there was created the *Nationalities, Cults & Sects* Service, which followed the 'activity of the cults and religious sects in terms of their interference in domestic politics'.[38] Making use of the immense power that it was given by the Communist Party, this institution did everything – against human rights and liberties – to enforce any policies of the communist regime which were not accepted by the population.

Romanian society has undergone a brutal transformation through which the old political institutions were either abolished or reduced to silence; instead of them, the party-state imposed a totalitarian state of Soviet inspiration. By blackmail, betrayal, murder, terror, the confiscation of goods or properties, an entire process of Sovietization of the Romanian state developed, led by the Communist Party which, as mentioned, was subordinated to the Soviet Communist Party.[39] Within the relationship with the churches, the *Securitate* considered from the beginning that they would encourage subversive elements, and to this end, special 'attention' was paid to monks, who were considered a 'black army',[40] and therefore as an enemy to be prevented from any manifestation.

As one can see from the research of a first part of the informative reports published up till now, the Romanian Orthodox Church, since 1945, has been the target of a coherent plan initiated by the Romanian Communist Party and applied by the *Securitate*. This plan principally aimed at the annihilation of the influence of the Romanian Orthodox Church in the social arena and its transformation into a propaganda tool of the Communist Party in support of the policy of the new Stalinist state. Through oppression and blackmail, the *Securitate* recruited its informers from church members and, again, the church was subjected to incessant siege and pressure. In order to reduce the influence of the Romanian Orthodox Church among the population, the decision to reduce the number of monasteries and, indirectly, of monks, was taken by the Communist Party and the *Securitate*, while the number of faculties of theology and theological seminaries was also reduced. Decree 410/1959 was intended to produce a 'monastic reform' under state control and, without consulting the

---

[37] Deletant, *Ceaușescu and the 'Securitate'*, 1.

[38] Oprea, *Bastionul cruzimii*, 56.

[39] Oprea, *Bastionul cruzimii*, 21.

[40] The 'syntagm' was invented by the Internal Affairs Minister, Alexandru Drăghici.

Romanian Orthodox Church, it was preceded by a regulation of monastic life issued by the Department of Religious Affairs.[41]

Decree 410/1959, promulgated by the Great National Assembly (Parliament), was allegedly meant to be a reforming law regarding monastic establishments, even if it was not issued by the Synod, but it caused a lot of pain in the monasteries because it gave the communist authorities the opportunity to commit abuses against monks. Before this decree, the communist state had issued Decree 177/1948 through the Department of Cults, *organising* the religious arena on a new basis. Decree 410/1959 restricted the access of any person to the status of monk on the criterion of age: women were allowed to become nuns after reaching 50 years of age, and men after 55. Another condition for becoming a monk was giving up one's salary or pension. As a result of the abuse applied by this decree, about 3,000 people were expelled from monasteries.

The abusive interpretation of the laws of the period led to the dissolution of about ninety monasteries between 1959 and 1960, and the monks and nuns who were cast out were prohibited from wearing their frocks in public.[42] With the participation of the party activists but also with the help of the security officers, there was commissioned a series of actions through which priests and bishops were to be intimidated and punished if they opposed any form of the new communist theses. Obviously, they resisted steadfastly and this led to the creation of new laws to protect the new Romanian People's Republic from its enemies. Religion as a subject taught in schools was excluded from the curriculum in 1948, and religious services began being forbidden in hospitals and military units.[43]

Repression against these priests or bishops – belonging not only to the majoritarian Orthodox Church,[44] though it suffered the most – took various forms, specific to Soviet areas of influence,[45] many undergoing a hasty trial and being sentenced to prison.[46] Today, there are many known cases of

---

[41] Radu Ciuceanu, 'Cuvânt înainte', in Cristina Păiuşan and Radu Ciuceanu (eds), *Biserica Ortodoxă Română, 1945-1958,* Vol. I (Bucharest: Ed. Institutului Naţional pentru studiul totalitarismului, 2001), 14.

[42] Adrian Nicolae Petcu, 'Chestiunea monahală în Republica Populară Română', in *Dosarele istoriei,* VII, 10.74 (2002), 55-58. See also Constantin Aioanei and Cristian Troncotă, 'Contra armatei negre a călugărilor şi călugăriţelor', in *Magazin istoric* XXX, 1.346 (1996), 3-5. Constantin Aioanei and Cristian Troncotă, 'Desfiinţaţi mănăstirile: un ordin care nu a mai sosit', in *Magazin istoric,* XXXII, 8.337 (1996), 29-32.

[43] See: http://patriarhia.ro/v-b-biserica-ortodoxa-romana-in-perioada-dintre-1944-si-1989-151.html

[44] Păiuşan and Ciuceanu, *Biserica Ortodoxă Română sub regimul communist 1945-1958,* Vol. I, 84-88. *Martiri pentru Hristos din România, în perioada regimului comunist*, 35-39.

[45] Most often they were accused of plotting against the state, espionage or counter-revolutionary actions. There was no chance of proving one's innocence, because the prosecution and the judges were under the control of the Communist Party and were willing to put into practice any order concerning the punishment of anybody who 'threatened the communist establishment'.

[46] The Communists organized a prison system where political prisoners were subjected to a brutal process of so-called 're-education', a process that most often led to the illness of some

priests who died in communist prisons because they asserted their faith.[47] Together with them, there were many believers imprisoned for reasons not normally considered criminal offences. In recent years, many volumes – the result of research at the National Archives – have been published on members of the clergy or Christians who opposed the totalitarian state in various ways. Important information was discovered in the confessional or in family archives, all of them contributing to the elaboration of the biographies of martyrs who confessed Christ during this period and suffered various punishments – torture, imprisonment without rights, starvation, and even violent death.[48]

In socialist Romania, religion became an otherwise irrelevant private matter but the communist state did everything in its power to deprive the church of every means by which it could be a major force in society.[49] Patriarch Justinian Marina (1901-1977) was one of the targets of the Romanian Communist Party. The Party leadership ordered *Securitate* bodies through specific NKVD (Narodny komissariat vnutrennikh del" = People's Commissariat of Internal Affairs, the Soviet police and secret police force) methods to make every effort to limit the powers of the patriarch; they were aware of the fact that the Romanian Orthodox Church was a factor in the national resistance against the new totalitarianism.[50]

In practice, the church does and must pay attention to good behaviour in all areas of human activity, good behaviour which had been previously defined by the church. As the modern state becomes ever stronger, we are

---

detainees or even to their death. The most terrible prisons were at Sighet, Jilava, Aiud, Gherla, Piteşti, and Rîmnicu Sarat. Some political prisoners were deported to concentration camps all over the country (Slobozia, Craiova, Târgu Jiu, Lugoj), or to Siberia; sometimes an entire family was displaced to the other side of the country and, in this way, lost their family property.

[47] Mihai Săsăujan, 'Măsuri represive comuniste împotriva preoţilor chiaburi în anii 1950-1952', in *Arca* 10-12 (2001), 178-200. 'Preoţi ortodocşi din Episcopia Aradului deţinuţi şi arestaţi în anii 1948-1953', in *Facultatea de Teologie din Arad la 10 ani de existenţă* (Arad, 2001), 251-61. Raluca Spiridon and Adrian Nicolae Petcu, 'Represiunea statului comunist asupra Bisericii Greco-Catolice din România', in *Rost* II.12 (2004), 29-32. Dănuţ Doboş, 'Aspecte ale represiunii comuniste împotriva Bisericii Romano-Catolice, 1945-1964', in *Pro Memoria,* 4 (2005), 200.

[48] Dorin Dobrincu (ed), *Proba infernului: personalul de cult în sistemul carceral din România potrivit documentelor Securităţii, 1959-1962* (Bucharest: Scriptorium, 2004). See also Păiuşan and Ciuceanu, *Biserica Ortodoxă Română sub regimul communist 1945-1958.* Ana Maria Rădulescu, *Slujitori ai Bisericii din Olt şi Romanaţi, prigoniţi în timpul regimului communist* (Ed. Episcopiei Slatinei şi Romanaţilor, 2013). Paul Caravia and Vergiliu Constantinescu, *Biserica întemniţată: România, 1944-1989* (Bucharest: Institutul Naţional pentru studiul totalitarismului, 1998). Octavian Roske, *Mecanisme represive în România, 1945-1989. Dicţionar biografic* (Bucharest: Institutul Naţional pentru studiul totalitarismului, Bucureşti, 2004).

[49] George Enache, 'Patriarhul Justinian şi apostolatul social', in *Ortodoxie şi putere politică în România contemporană* (Bucharest: Nemira Publishing House, 2005), 90.

[50] Ungheanu, 'Introducere', 24-28. See also Adrian Nicolae Petcu, 'Ministerul Cultelor şi slujitorii altarului', in *Pro Memoria* 3 (2004), 308. See also Adrian Nicolae Petcu (ed), *Partidul Securitatea şi Cultele, 1945-1989* (Bucharest: Nemira, 2005).

dealing with two parties which claim to define and influence human behaviour. In Romania in the year 2006, Law 489 was promulgated, a Law of the Cults which regulates religious freedom and the general bases of them, making possible their structuring at various levels. The neutrality of the clergy in political matters is a process in development and needs to be consolidated, and though political parties seek the support of various Romanian Orthodox Church communities of electors, it has been shown that belonging to a certain denomination does not influence elections in a significant way.

Ever since 1990, the Romanian Orthodox Church has stated that it intends to take part in all public activity of the newly-established state, as it had before 1947, thus wishing to bridge the period of communist persecution. In this respect, the Romanian Orthodox Church asked to be acknowledged as a majority church which had an essential contribution to make to the foundation of the modern national Romanian state and nation. Even though such an acknowledgement did not happen precisely in order to maintain the equality of the cults, the involvement of the Romanian Orthodox Church in the public arena can be seen at the level of the army, police and prisons, where permanent religious assistance is offered; to this end, in 2000 a Law of the Military Clergy was promulgated. The relationship between church and state in Eastern Europe, especially in Romania, did not have the same stormy history as in the West, since the Orthodox Church did not have the tradition of being a patron to the kingdoms of this world, as in other Christian traditions.

We can say now that the churches in Eastern Europe remained one of the most important institutions able to stand against the totalitarian regimes and not to submit themselves to the political programme imposed by communism, and so helping humankind to be in communion with the person of Christ. The notion of *public* is accurately defined by its opposite to *private*, intimate, so that it includes politics, the economy, education, and structures of the state. *Private space* is conceived of as being out of the reach of public concern. Private means personal. Into its weak form of today, *private* means, in theological terms, the 'privatization' of religion. The pastoral orientation of the Orthodox Church could not ignore the actions of the political class, since the latter is the patron of education (that has come to be strictly dependent upon the state, as it has assumed the ideological grounding of its citizens) through its specific institutions, the mass media and the passing of legislation.

In regard with the Christian *desideratum* of safeguarding morality and good manners, in all spheres of human activity, the church in Eastern Europe faces the same problems as churches in the west. Today, the political structure of the state takes upon itself competencies in all domains of human life – no matter whether Christianity is recognized or ignored – including the spiritual sphere, which it thinks it could properly manage. But they are all wrong, because they retain neither the competence nor the means which are specific to the church, and what they cover are only digests of 'political religions' suitable for use when in a position of power.

Individualism or collectivism have damaged ecclesial anthropology, highlighting the idea of social emancipation for humans. What is then most intriguing is the fact that for now there is no obvious winner in the age of modernity and that to the old problems are added others, which are also very well continued by the social and political model of modern democracy. The new democracies of Eastern Europe wish to follow tried and tested western models, including the rights of minorities, especially religious ones. The relationship between the church through its confessional Christian minorities and other religions should be well balanced. Cultural and religious plurality allows religious minorities in Romania to be better protected in law than the country's main religious institution (the Romanian Orthodox Church), as stated by the principle of the religious liberty and equality.

The social impact of the Romanian Orthodox Church's message is considerable, this fact being attested by all the opinion polls in which the Romanian Church is always joined by the Army. These two traditional institutions have much in common but they are also clearly distinct from each another. By this criterion, the coherence of the evangelistic message, very efficiently disseminated by the church's hierarchic organization, stands out very clearly. Even if the church is not an institution in a secular sense, it is usually portrayed by the mass media as one of them. Under these circumstances, the encounter between modern man and the church is perceived through the use of language rich in concepts or terms with no sacred dimension. Modern culture is rarely an adequate vehicle for such dialogue, because it is tainted and has become the repository of values with little connection with Christianity.

Conclusions

As an all-inclusive political system that relied on coercion, totalitarianism in Eastern Europe has left deep marks not only on the collective mentality, but also on public behaviour, the latter being heavily affected by the demagogy of the single party. The concept of the 'class enemy' or of the 'state enemy' has not yet been removed from the collective mind, and it was a means of supporting the doctrine of the 'new man's' creation. This insidious propaganda tried to establish a new anthropology that had nothing to do with the roots of European humanity, which are deeply linked with the church, so that the Christian communities which stood against totalitarian ideologies became public enemy number one, whatever their professed confession.

Christianity with and for the Younger Generation: A Case Study in Orthodox Youth Mission

Dana Bates

Introduction

This article will discuss in 'archival' fashion and serve as a case study for the work of our organization (the New Horizons Foundation) with Orthodox youth in Romania. The case study will start by presenting a mission strategy/blueprint document created in 2003 that shows how Adventure Education and Service Learning are effective approaches for youth development and ministry in a post-communist context characterized by corruption and learned helplessness. The study will then describe how a deep awareness of, and commitment to, contextualizing the gospel in an Orthodox context has enabled both a more profound theological vision of our youth ministry itself, as well as practical partnerships with the Orthodox Church for serving the younger generation. In this context, I will offer a youth ministry proposal presented to the Orthodox Church that both highlights New Horizon's 'IMPACT' programme model itself and how this interfaces with Orthodox theology – and particularly Irenaeus' holistic vision: The Glory of God is Humanity Full Alive. Finally, instances of actual and planned collaboration with the Romanian Orthodox Church will be highlighted.

Part I: Mission Strategy 2003-2008

This section should not be construed as a complete doctrinal position or statement of faith, but rather reflects our understanding of the *missio Dei* – God's mission in the world in the *early years* of our ministry as it intersects with the particular issues facing the post-communist culture of Romania and our background in experiential education. We were influenced largely by the *shalom* view of mission[1] articulated by Nicholas Wolterstorff from the Reformed tradition. He writes:

---

[1] The second section of this paper shows how our youth ministry models were contextualized in terms of Orthodox theology. This mission strategy 2003-2008 was developed before adequate experience with, or study of, Eastern Orthodoxy. However, this *shalom* perspective that was so influential upon our approach is evident in Orthodoxy as well, as will be seen below.

> But we have seen that the church exists not for its own sake but for the sake of God's cause in the world. That cause is the overcoming of alienation from God and liberation from the oppression, deprivation and suffering in which sin works itself out, so that human beings may dwell in God's shalom, where there is harmony and delight in all dimensions of existence.[2]

The importance of this *shalom* perspective for our work will be seen in examining the potential tensions between a predominately 'proclamational' approach to mission, and a 'transformational' perspective,[3] and how this plays out in Romania.

Mission as Transformation or Proclamation?

A *proclamational* approach to mission is interested in the cluster of strategies related to personal salvation, direct evangelism and church planting. The goal here is for people to hear the story of the gospel, and accept Jesus Christ as personal Lord and Saviour. Issues such as working for justice, while not unimportant, tend to be viewed as secondary and are not part of salvation *per se*. A *transformational* approach to mission, on the other hand, while not necessarily neglecting proclamation, seeks in its very understanding of the gospel to address the cultural, structural, economic and other factors that impinge on people's well-being. The gospel in this transformational approach is not separate from questions of social action and justice. Bryant Meyers, in a seminal article in World Vision's publication 'Together', asserts that a holistic (i.e. Biblical) ministry is 'one in which compassion, social transformation and proclamation are inseparably related'.[4] While this statement might sound good in theory, matters may not be so straightforward in practice. Though there need not necessarily be a tension between these two domains – of salvation understood as proclamation, and salvation understood as holistic multi-dimensional transformation – in actual experience, there often is.[5]

This is because, in many contexts, the more proclamational the emphasis is in one's mission strategy,[6] the less transformational in terms of promoting justice and public action it can be. There are at least three reasons for this. The first is because proclamation tends to be linked with

---

[2] N. Wolterstorff, *Educating for Responsible Action* (Grand Rapids, MI: Christian Schools International and Eerdmans, 1980), 13.

[3] B.L. Myers, *Walking with the Poor: Principles and Practices of Transformational Development* (Maryknoll, NY: Orbis Books, 1999); *Working with the Poor: New Insights and Learnings from Development Practitioners* (Monrovia, CA: World Vision, 1999).

[4] T. Yamamori et al, *Serving with the Poor in Asia: Cases in Holistic Ministry* (Monrovia, CA: MARC-World Vision, 1995), 1.

[5] Noted mission scholar David Bosch argues that 'the relationship between the evangelistic [proclamational] and the societal [transformational] dimensions of the Christian mission constitutes one of the thorniest areas in the theology and practice of mission' – D.J. Bosch, *Transforming Mission* (Maryknoll, NY: Orbis Books, 1992), 401.

[6] Especially if one is a foreigner living in a context where one was brainwashed to mistrust any and all foreigners, as was the case under Communism.

specific denominations, and their respective 'cultures', theological vocabularies and symbolic universes, which are often perceived as imported and alien. This means that proclamational approaches to mission almost never get the buy-in necessary by the multiple stakeholders in a community, even if they are *also* trying to work for transformation and effect sustainable change. Secondly, broad transformational impact (or even relief work which aims at amelioration) usually involves partnering with larger organizations such as government ministries that cannot, by the nature of modern pluralistic democracies, explicitly support evangelistic or denominational activities. The third reason is that heavily weighted proclamational strategies *usually* originate from an individualistic paradigm of salvation that fails to connect the gospel and the Kingdom with larger cultural and socio-economic issues.[7] Thus, it is often the case in concrete experience that transformational and proclamational approaches are at cross purposes.

We argue that the missiological burden for Romania is weighted (but not exclusively) towards the transformational approach. The reasons for this will become clearer throughout this document, but suffice it to say that most believe this is 'best practice' for Romania. Evangelical theologian Miroslav Volf argues, in his article 'Fishing in Someone Else's Pond', that Protestant Christians should work with the Orthodox for the betterment of society and joint Christian witness.[8] World Vision as an organization is successful precisely because such transformational strategies are informed by the *shalom* perspective.[9] Silviu Rogobete, elder of one of the largest and most influential Baptist churches in Romania (and also Chair of the Political Science Department at the University of Timisoara), strongly recommends foreign missionaries to partner with the Orthodox. And in terms of firsthand experience, we have found the Orthodox to be eager partners; difficulties in partnership usually arise because of the narrow-mindedness of western missionaries who see Orthodox as objects of conversion.

Because of the peculiarities of Romania's situation – being both newly democratic and with the predominance of the Orthodox Church – we believe we have developed an effective synthesis between the proclamational and the transformational mission approaches. What has given us success in terms of cultural penetration with the transformational aspects of the gospel has been that we have been very careful with how proclamation is done. Publicly, it is always done in a way that is culturally sensitive, and can be seen as helping Romanians live up to the best in their

---

[7] J.J. Stamoolis (ed), *Three Views on Eastern Orthodoxy and Evangelicalism* (Grand Rapids, MI: Zondervan, 2004).

[8] M. Volf, 'Fishing in the Neighbor's Pond: Mission and Proselytism as Challenge to Theology and Church Life in Eastern Europe'. *Occasional Papers on Religion in Eastern Europe* 16.1 (1996), art. 5.

[9] Myers, *Walking with the Poor*, 259.

own cultural self-identity, which is closely linked with the Orthodox Christian faith. And always, we carefully select Orthodox Romanians to share about faith issues (proclamation) in a way that Baptists or Pentecostals could all agree with, but done under the open eye of the Orthodox Church, to avoid misunderstanding.

More will be said on this below, but despite their compromises with communism, partnering with the Orthodox Church provides the strongest leverage for *both* the transformational and proclamational aspects of mission in Romania. It may seem counter-intuitive, *but we are able to share more in terms of proclamation by having a predominantly transformational mission focus.* Verbal witness comes from 'earning the right to be heard', one of the key principles of our sending organization, Young Life.

Trust No One: Suspicion as Romania's National Disease

Earning the right to be heard is especially challenging in Romania. Indeed, one who has not spent many years in a post-communist context, or been a serious student of totalitarian regimes, can never fully understand the horrors of these regimes, and the degradation of culture and personality that followed in its wake. Interpersonal trust, the capacity for self-organization, and the moral values that make co-operation possible – honesty, responsibility, interpersonal respect – were *intentionally* decimated in Romania.[10] Communism sought complete domination, and used whatever means – deception, criminality, terror, genocide, concentration camps – to consolidate its power. Hannah Arendt, a leading scholar of totalitarianism, writes: 'Wherever it (communism) rose to power, it developed entirely new political institutions and destroyed all social, legal and political traditions of the country.[11]

One of the principle strategies of all communist regimes for total domination was social atomization – the *intentional* sowing of mistrust and mutual suspicion at all levels of society. The strategy which the ancient Romans applied to their external enemies – Divide and Conquer – was applied under communist regimes to their own people. Friends betrayed friends to the *Securitate* secret service agents (rumoured to have numbered one in three people), family members betrayed family members, and special incentives (holiday homes, honours and economic privileges) were given to the most egregious informants. All civic society organizations (any organization not directly controlled by, and therefore not a propaganda

---

[10] M. Klicperova et al, 'In the Search for a Post-Communist Syndrome: A Theoretical Framework and Empirical Assessment', in *Journal of Community & Applied Social Psychology* 7.1 (1997), 39-52; G. Bădescu et al, 'Civil Society Development and Democratic Values in Romania and Moldova', in *East European Politics and Societies* 18.2 (2004), 1-26.

[11] H. Arendt, *Totalitarianism: Part Three of the Origins of Totalitarianism* (San Diego, CA: Harcourt Brace Jovanovich Publishers, 1968).

agent for, the Party) were severely curtailed. The churches were either repressed (non-Orthodox) or infiltrated (Orthodox).[12] Many of our Romanian friends knew – or at least believed – that their priest/confessor was also a *Securitate* agent. Romania was a country of whispers and fear where intimate conversation might prove costly, if not deadly. From the point of view of the Communist Party whose goal was absolute loyalty, the logic for this social atomization is simple: to pit the lonely and terrified individual against the overwhelming, ultimate and arbitrary power of the state. David Kideckel, anthropologist and lifelong student of Romania, writes about the outcome of this process:

> The socialist system, though ostensibly designed to create new persons motivated by the needs of groups and society as a whole, in fact created people who were of necessity self-centered, distrustful and apathetic to the very core of their beings.[13]

Václav Havel, one of the most astute commentators of communism, wrote about his own country (and Romania suffered under a more severe form of communism):

> We live in a spoiled moral environment... We have become morally ill because we are used to saying one thing and thinking another. We have learned not to believe anything, not to care about each other, to worry only about ourselves. The concepts of love, friendship, mercy, humility or forgiveness have lost their depths and dimension, and for many of us they represent only some sort of psychological curiosity or they appear as long-lost wanderers from a faraway time.[14]

And Havel further notes: 'The former regime (communism) systematically mobilized the worst human qualities, like selfishness, envy and hatred'.[15] Finally, one historian writes:

> Transition from autocracy to democracy has been, historically, a difficult process even under the best of circumstances... The 'Golden Age' [the term used for the worst years of deprivations prior to the revolution of 1989] left Rumania bankrupt politically, economically and morally. Years of economic privation, social incarceration, intellectual abuse, and isolation from the outside world had brutalized the population. Suspicion, jealousy, and fear of institutions... could not be erased overnight.[16]

These are features of the general post-communist context. But not only were we called to work in a post-communist society, not only were we called to work in one of the most challenging post-communist countries,

---

[12] L. Stan and L. Turcescu, 'The Romanian Orthodox Church and Post-Communist Democratisation', in *Europe-Asian Studies* 52.8 (2000), 1467-88.

[13] D.A. Kideckel, *The Solitude of Collectivism: Romanian Villagers to the Revolution and Beyond* (Ithaca: Cornell University Press, 1993), xiii.

[14] W. Echikson, *Lighting the Night: Revolution in Eastern Europe* (New York: William Morrow & Co., 1990), 136.

[15] V. Havel, 'Politics, Morality, and Civility', in D.E. Eberly (ed), *The Essential Civil Society Reader* (Lanham, MD: Rowman & Littlefield, 2000), 393.

[16] S. Fischer-Galati, *20th Century Romania* (New York, Columbia University Press, 1991).

but we also ended up in perhaps the most challenging regions of Romania – the Jiu coalmining valley.[17] Just as in the USA, the decline of the coal industry devastated an already underdeveloped area known as 'Appalachia', so the Jiu Valley in the Carpathian mountains is in severe economic decline, with unemployment averaging over 50% in an area containing about 200,000 people. It is a mono-industrial region, mining low-grade brown lignite coal, that has been declared 'severely disadvantaged' by World Bank specialists. Not only this, but the miners' protests (in the late 1970s) about working conditions in the mines frightened Ceauşescu so much that he intentionally destabilized the region to break down solidarity and decimate leadership. While parts of Romania are progressing rapidly today, the Jiu Valley is called the 'forgotten' zone. Even many Romanians fear this region as miners, afraid of losing their jobs after the 1989 Revolution, marched, clubs in hand, on the capital city Bucharest and beat dozens of people showing any signs of western influence.[18] Eventually, these marauding miners were met with tanks and sent home, signalling the demise of this mono-industrial area and the miners' future. As a result of this social dislocation and economic freefall, alcoholism, domestic violence, apathy, suspicion and corruption are rampant. In 1999, when we started work in the Jiu Valley, we were the only foreign workers of any type – and this is significant as communism taught its subjects to be *especially* suspicious of westerners.

Despite these challenges, Romania is undoubtedly a religious culture – largely unaffected by the religious pessimism of the Enlightenment. After the demise of communism, Romanians returned to their churches (especially Orthodox) in droves. Most figures state that approximately 86% of the population are Orthodox, with a significant amount of Hungarian Reformed, Catholic, and what are called the 'neo-Protestants' – Baptists, Pentecostals and Seventh Day Adventists. Despite the infiltration of the Orthodox Church by the Romanian secret police (*Securitate*) under communism, the Orthodox Church remains among the most trusted institutions in Romania.[19] Religion is taught in state schools, and the Romanian self-identity is habitually expressed in openly spiritual terms. Being an Orthodox Christian and being Romanian are often seen as synonymous – it is an inalienable part of the Romanian historical and spiritual cultural heritage.

If it should be thought that the popularity of the Orthodox Church can facilitate an easy break with their communist past, much of the church (especially the older generation) reflects the prevailing culture, and does

---

[17] The reason for this was not masochistic, but because of the beautiful Retezat National Park as a context for outdoor education.

[18] T. Gallagher, *Modern Romania* (New York University Press, 2005).

[19] These figures do seem to be declining. In 2003, the rate was extremely high, up to a 90% trust rate, whereas now the figure varies, but hovers around 55% to 65%: www.agerpres.ro/english/2015/12/22/inscop-survey-presidency-gains-while-church-loses-public-trust-18-16-33

little to challenge the 'culture of corruption' that makes life miserable for so many – except for elite government 'gatekeepers' who can procure bribes. The prophetic voice of the Orthodox Church is weak, as many of the priests were compromised and perceived as left-over 'plants' from the intrusive communist era. This lack of a prophetic voice is also said to be due to the Orthodox mystical dimension which 'tends to make an individual or group withdraw from the world, devalue history, claim that one's true home is not here but in heaven, and seek communion with God without attending to one's neighbour'.[20]

Also, despite belief in Christian Orthodoxy, many Romanians have distorted views of God linked with the prevalence of fate and superstition (and this is not inherent to Orthodoxy, but is found in many developing contexts). Many Romanians are largely disconnected from a meaningful and productive relationship with their own experience – limiting *self-efficacy* – the sense that one can play a positive role in the world. A common characteristic of underdeveloped cultures is this very reliance upon fate, and the use of talismanic or superstitious practices to manipulate this fate. However, as Paulo Friere (author of the famous *Pedagogy of the Oppressed*) writes:

> When superficially analyzed, this fatalism is sometimes interpreted as a docility that is a trait of national character. Fatalism in the guise of docility [passivity] is the fruit of an historical and sociological situation, not an essential characteristic of a people's behavior. It almost always is related to the power of destiny or fate or fortune – inevitable forces – or to a distorted view of God.[21]

This reliance on fate and/or superstition diminishes strategic thinking and rational thought – the consideration of alternative ways of achieving a particular end and the selection of the optimal one based on available information. This has serious effects on vocational and leadership capacities that are linked to socio-economic development, which is important in an EU country where 40% continue to be at risk of poverty and social exclusion and 29% are seriously materially deprived.[22]

The 25th December 1989 saw the public execution of the dictator Ceausescu and his wife Elena, and through the prison bars of totalitarianism (*'where every decision is made for you'*) walked a people unused to the responsibilities and the discipline needed for the productive

---

[20] Bosch, *Transforming Mission*, 402. Again, in my PhD thesis, I take exactly the opposite point here – that Bosch fundamentally misreads Orthodox mysticism, and that this mysticism is closely linked with a transformation of Aristotle's *phronesis*, or practical reason, that has love of one's neighbour at its core. Dumitru Stăniloae makes this abundantly clear in his magnificent work, *Orthodox Spirituality* (South Canaan, PA: St Tikhon's Orthodox Theological Seminary Press, 2003).

[21] P. Freire, *Pedagogy of the Oppressed* (New York: Continuum, 1998).

[22] This is from a 2015 UN Human Rights report: http://chrgj.org/documents/end-of-mission-statement-on-romania-by-professor-philip-alston-united-nations-human-rights-council-special-rapporteur-on-extreme-poverty-and-human-rights

use of freedom. Into this vacuum were sucked the values of consumerism, immediate gratification, short-term thinking and the infectious greed (Alan Greenspan's term), unchecked by a tradition of civic virtues and discipline. This lack of civic tradition raises the spectre of what dissident Alexander Solzhenitsyn warned against – 'rampant materialism, secularism, atheism, and moral/ethical relativism'.

This precisely mirrors the situation of the Galatians when Paul wrote: 'You are free in Christ, only do not use your freedom to indulge the flesh, but rather to serve each other and the common good' (paraphrase).[23] Communism created what has been called *homo duplex* – an individual who is intimate and responsible in his private sphere, but apathetic and often corrupt in the public sphere.

These other-regarding values are not only intrinsically worthwhile for community development, and key for sustainable economic development. As Václav Havel put it so well:

> Without commonly shared and widely entrenched moral values and obligations, neither the law, nor the democratic government, nor even the market economy, will function properly.[24]

Common Ground: Social Capital, Civic Society and Sustainable Development

Given this context, our projects that will be described below, are designed to rebuild the spiritual and moral culture of Romania and develop a common ground whereby Romania's many stakeholders can agree. This is significant since a primary problem in 'Balkan' countries is precisely the inability to collaborate for the common good.

Though the language may sound strange at first, we are convinced of the ability of a social science paradigm called 'social capital' to help restore *shalom*/harmony to Romania. Social capital studies the multi-dimensional importance of values that facilitate interpersonal trust – and it is precisely interpersonal trust which communism intentionally decimated. And the bottom line is that societies with higher levels of trust perform better on all levels, not least economically. This means that, in the big picture, our standards *for* living determine our standards *of* living. And this is important for Romania where almost one out of every two children is at risk of

---

[23] Orthodoxy has a strong theology of the common good. John Chrysostom writes: 'The most perfect rule of Christianity, its exact definition, its highest summit, is this: to seek what is for the benefit of all' – T. Ware, *The Orthodox Way* (Crestwood, NY: St Vladimir's Seminary Press, 1998, 39). This quote has become central to framing our work with the Orthodox.

[24] V. Havel, 'Politics, Morality and Civility', in Don E. Eberly (ed.), *The Essential Civil Society Reader: The Classic Essays* (Lanham, Maryland: Rowman & Littlefield Publishers 2000), p. 401.

poverty, and 34% suffer from severe material deprivation.[25] Social Capital development helps realize both Kingdom values and through it, God's concern for the poor. In other words, the social capital paradigm redirects narrow self-interest to broader purposes – and helps achieve what Alexis Tocqueville called 'self-interest rightly understood'.[26]

Corrupt, dysfunctional, apathetic societies have low levels of interpersonal trust. They treat family members with respect, but predatory behaviour, Machiavellian deception and trickery are the *norms* outside the family sphere (called 'amoral familialism').[27] This 'ethic' makes any type of collaborative behaviour outside the biological family or tribe highly suspect, irrational and dangerous. Yet, as many scholars within the social capital movement have pointed out, Protestants in Northern Europe managed to take seriously the ethical implications of Jesus' teaching,[28] and saw it as a religious duty to treat with honesty and respect the 'other'. Apparently, a high enough percentage adhered to this ethic that it 'extended the radius' of trust, creating a safe zone of co-operation and exchange, and made possible many things that contributed to the prosperity and standards of living that we take for granted today – from traffic lights to more complex forms of social organization such as joint stock companies and the abstract expression of these ethical commitments to generalized 'others' in the Universal Declaration of Human Rights.[29]

We have experienced firsthand the corruption[30] generated by 'amoral familialism' – treating ethically only those within the family unit or tribe. We also believe this is why Jesus stressed several times in the gospel 'Who is my family, but he who does the will of God?' One might just as well call this social capital 'Samaritan Capital'. For social capital is not just community, but a certain kind of community that embraces all by virtue of

---

[25] http://chrgj.org/documents/end-of-mission-statement-on-romania-by-professor-phili p-alston-united-nations-human-rights-council-special-rapporteur-on-extreme-poverty-and-human-rights

[26] A. de Tocqueville, *Democracy in America* (London: Penguin Classics, 2003).

[27] E. Banfield, *The Moral Basis of a Backward Society* (New York: The Free Press, 1958).

[28] This sentence reflects a form of 'Orientialism' or, to put it crudely, 'West is the Best; East is the Least'. I no longer hold such views. This attitude is prevalent in the 'Culture Matters' literature: see L.E. Harrison and S.P. Huntington (eds.) *Culture Matters: How Values Shape Human Progress* (New York: Basic Books, 2000); L.E. Harrison, *The Central Liberal Truth: How Politics Can Change a Culture and Save It from Itself* (Oxford: OUP, 2006), of which the social capital discourse is a part. The heyday of the social capital movement is over as its claims became too grandiose, almost mystical (B. Fine, *Theories of Social Capital: Researchers Behaving Badly* (London: Pluto Press, 2010)). However, this approach remains paramount, especially for post-communist cultures where interpersonal trust is a key issue.

[29] F. Fukuyama, *Trust: The Social Virtues and the Creation of Prosperity* (New York: Free Press Paperbacks, 1996); 'Social Capital, Civil Society and Development', in *Third World Quarterly* 22.1 (2001), 7-20.

[30] In 2006, we finished a painful two-year court case against a local official on the Mayor's council who stole money in every way conceivable, even fabricating false government (IRS/Garda Financiară) documents and impersonations. Even though this person was found guilty of felony-level crimes, he never lost his public office.

their shared humanity, and is transformative for societies and the ethical basis for broadly shared economic development.

There are places in the world where basic moral norms are flouted not just by the few but by the many – and openly.[31] And it is not simply that they are flouted, but rather the benefits of co-operation, trust and ethical behaviour have been little experienced – and thus the self-discipline required is not valued. For many, their operating assumptions on how life 'works' are that people get ahead by crafty forms of deceit and theft – or at best, by luck or Fate – but rarely by hard work, co-operation and strategy. And the lack of this ethical commitment to honesty and respect degrades social and economic productivity (except for the fact that security companies are thriving). Romania, a country where everyone claims to be Christian, has a serious lack of social, moral, Samaritan capital – yet precisely because of the preponderance of Orthodoxy, there is a foundation upon which to rebuild.

Though the language of social capital may sound strange,[32] we believe this framework creates common ground where Christians and non-Christians, both wanting the best for Romania, can meet. As Nobel Economist Amartya Sen expresses it, values are like oxygen: 'You don't notice them until they are not there, and their lack can be deadly.'[33] Concentrating on developing social capital can free energies from unproductive interpersonal suspicions towards trust, collaboration and productive endeavours. Increasing social capital can pave the way for the restoration of community institutions, and recover the spirit of volunteerism and responsible citizenship, and draw Romanians together at a time of social isolation and fragmentation. But how can this be done? How to turn noble theory into relevant and operational practice? The next section will focus on two powerful and practical solutions for rebuilding social capital and especially among youth: Adventure Education and Service Learning.

Adventure Education

When we moved to Romania to start an outdoor adventure programme for character development, we had no idea how relevant it would be for the

---

[31] Even this statement must be qualified in the light of our fifteen-plus years of experience. It is not the many who are corrupt, but the political elites from the communist regime who, especially in Romania, managed to retain their positions. In 2015, winds of change were in the air; civil society was on the move and there was finally a sense of optimism that Romania was becoming a functional democracy.

[32] For those interested in learning more about social capital, two recommended titles are Francis Fukuyama's *Trust: The Social Virtues and the Creation of Prosperity,* and Robert Putnam's *Bowling Alone* (New York: Touchstone, 2000). For social capital in relation to the Romanian context, see V. Tismăneanu, *Reinvinting Politics* (New York: The Free Press, 1992); G. Bădescu et al, 'Civil Society Development and Democratic Values in Romania and Moldova', in *East European Politics and Societies* 18.2 (2004), 1-26.

[33] A.K Sen, *Development as Freedom* (Oxford: OUP, 1999).

post-communist trauma. The experiential, learn-by-doing approach to values development struck a cultural chord. Besides running a community based camp with Romania's only ropes course (built by the industry leaders Project Adventure)[34] where we take 500 youth each summer, we have developed a partnership with the University of Timisoara and are making this discipline sustainable.

Adventure Education is sweeping the world; ropes courses are popping up from the Amazon to Papua New Guinea. Why? Not just because it is fun, but because it is a powerful tool for social transformation.

> Change for society and communities is the altruistic end point sought by adventure programs. While the immediate goals and primary focus for learning may well be to change people, the ultimate impact is to make the world a better place to live in some small way.[35]

Adventure Education is a powerful and proven *transformational* mission strategy. Studies published in the American Psychological Association journal claim the ability of Adventure Education programmes to increase interpersonal trust and self-efficacy – the sense that one can make a difference in the world. Indeed, one who has studied the origin of the Outward Bound movement (the pioneers of Adventure Education) will understand that, even though it is not overtly Christian in language, the entire movement was launched as a way to instil Christian values and more specifically, Samaritan Service.[36] But while these pedagogies have become largely secularized in the West, because of Romania's unique religious context, it is culturally sensitive to frame these values in spiritual terms or, in other words, to include *proclamational* elements in these *transformational* pedagogies.[37]

Dr Bud Williams, head of the Wheaton College Adventure Education programme asks why outdoor education is so popular and meaningful. It is because:

1. Genuine community is experienced (props are taken away).

---

[34] A 'ropes course' involves a series of initiatives, often high in the air and on belay, that challenge youth to become more trusting, more empowered (self-efficacy), solving problems, etc. The literature on outdoor education as a therapeutic instrument is very strong – J.C. Miles and S. Priest (eds), *Adventure Programming* (State College, PA: Venture Publishing, 1999); B. Williams, *Five Values of Christian Camping* (CCCA Focus Series: Christian Camp and Conference Association, 2009). We also have peer reviews before and after studies on our 'Viața' Adventure Education camp (J.S. Feenstra, 'Summer Camp and Positive Youth Development: Program With Romanian Youth', in *The Physical Educator,* 72 [2015], 185-99).

[35] Miles and Priest, *Adventure Programming*, xiii.

[36] C.P. Stetson, 'An Essay on Kurt Hahn, Founder of Outward Bound (1941), 1886-1974', available online at: <http://www.kurthahn.org/wp-content/uploads/2017/02/2017-stet.pdf>, accessed on: 23 January 2017.

[37] It is important to stress again here that our strategy, when discussing anything specifically religious, was to have Orthodox leaders, namely priests, to do the proclamational aspects. This is especially important because foreigners are viewed with suspicion.

2. Ministry to the whole person takes place (through the stimulation of risk and a new environment, campers are impelled into trusting experiences).
3. Relationship building teaches social skills... mentors are visual examples of how to live when tired, how to control anger, how to discipline with love, etc.
4. Memory making: the product of heightened senses, total engagement and readiness to learn, combined with spiritual truths attached to these memory-making experiences equals life shaping memories.
5. Leadership Development: very few opportunities exist for young people to be given significant responsibility for others, especially responsibility for ministering to others. To build leadership skills, people must be given responsibility for others and be mentored in the process of ministering and mentoring.[38]

Adventure Education is important also for Romania because it reaches out to different learning styles and provides an alternative to an educational system that is extremely rigid and authoritarian; indeed, teachers often discourage students from participation in extra-curricular activities – even though there is a strong empirical synergy between formal and non-formal education.[39]

Service Learning

Outdoor Education is a wonderful short-term catalyst for community, a 'shot in the arm', but we realized it could hardly provide a permanent year-round incubator for youth transformation. Furthermore, Adventure Education is quite expensive to replicate on a national scale. We soon discovered another experiential education methodology that opened the door to a bigger strategy for a transformation mission approach, and that was *Service Learning.* We chose this strategy because it was already well developed and it would be possible to transfer this to the state school system, and to NGOs and churches.

What is Service Learning? Service Learning uses youth-led community service projects as the vehicle for achieving both social improvements and personal transformation. Service Learning fosters those 'intangibles' – empathy, personal values, beliefs, awareness and social responsibility, and helps foster a sense of caring for others. Multiple studies have demonstrated its ability to promote academic and social improvements as well.[40] Service Learning provides students with opportunities to use newly

---

[38] Williams, *Five Values of Christian Camping*, 6.

[39] J. Kielsmeier, 'Service-Learning: The Time is Now', in *The Prevention Researcher,* 18 (2011), 3-7.

[40] R.C. Wade, *Community Service Learning: A Guide to Including Service in the Public School Curriculum* (Albany, NY: State University of New York, 1997); J.C. Kielsmeier,

acquired skills and knowledge (e.g. computer, project management or other) in real-life situations. Students perform a valuable, significant and necessary service, which has real consequence for the community.

Service Learning is based on a reciprocal relationship in which the service reinforces and strengthens the learning, while the learning reinforces and strengthens the service, and more substantive solutions are reached. The follow diagram outlines the process (Linthicum 1999):[41]

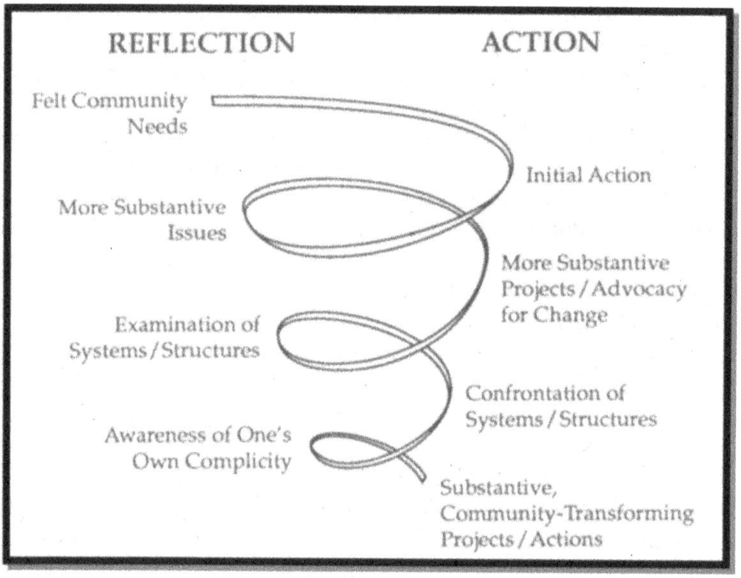

The benefits of Service Learning include:[42]

- Increases retention of learning through practical outlets.
- Increases the relevancy of education to students 'living in the real world'.
- Teaches positive values, leadership, citizenship and personal responsibility.
- Invites and trains students to become active members of their community.
- Teaches job skills and prepares students for careers.

'Recasting the Role of Youths in the 21st Century: Rebuilding Civil Society Through Service-Learning and Civic Engagement', in *Service Learning and Social Capital* (Cluj, Romania: National Youth Leadership Council, 2004); S.H. Billig, 'Why Service Learning is Such a Good Idea', in *Colleagues,* 5.1 (2010), 5-7; A. Furco, 'A Research Agenda for K-12 School-based Service-Learning: Academic Achievement and School Success', *10th Annual International Research Conference on Service-Learning and Community Engagement* (Indianapolis, IN: 2010); Kielsmeier, 'Service Learning'.

[41] R.C. Linthicum, *Empowering the Poor* (Monrovia: Marc Books [World Vision], 1999).

[42] Wade, *Community Service Learning.*

- Contributes to the much-needed 'social intelligence' and relational competencies necessary to succeed in complex organizations.
- Students experience practically the benefits of values of co-operation and trust. Values are effectively internalized.
- Other values: Problem-solving skills, self-discipline, self-knowledge, environmental awareness and appreciation, communication skills including conflict resolution.

Critical to the effectiveness of both Service Learning and Adventure Education are creative, constructive ways for developing positive social and spiritual values. Stories, 'wisdom' literature, journaling, guided discussions, a hero-bank, team-building games, community service, and ecological and religious narratives were all used as tools to help youth internalize spiritual values. As will be seen below, these methods over time coalesced into the IMPACT 'model,' which is being embraced by the Orthodox Church and has now spread to fourteen countries.

Here though are some final quotes that were important for us when we started our ministry.

Mentioned above was the *shalom* perspective, which parallels a 'Kingdom' perspective. This perspective broadens mission beyond individual conversion to include what Nobel Prize winner Amartya Sen calls the removing of 'unfreedoms' or obstacles to human flourishing.[43] Missiologist Verkuyl notes:

> Viewing our missionary task within the wider perspective of the Kingdom will lead us to still another insight: participation in the fight against every vestige of evil plaguing mankind.[44]

And:

> Salvation is as coherent, broad and deep as the needs and exigencies of human existence.[45]

This type of holistic theology inspired us to move to Romania and to discover just how transformative experiential education, especially Adventure Education and Service Learning, could be for advancing *shalom* in this post-communist context. And even though we knew almost nothing about Orthodoxy when we moved to Romania in 1999, we slowly began to discover the deep transformational theology that exists in major strains of her teaching – but which had been partly buried because of communism. This next section will now go into greater detail about the IMPACT model itself, and how the moral/spiritual aims of experiential education, but especially Service Learning, resonate so strongly with Orthodox theology.

---

[43] A. Sen and M. Nussbaum (eds), *The Quality of Life* (Oxford: Clarendon Press, 1993); Sen, *Development as Freedom*.

[44] J. Verkuyl, *Contemporary Missiology: An Introduction* (Grand Rapids, MI: Eerdmans, 1988).

[45] Bosch, *Transforming Mission*, 400.

Part 2: IMPACT Youth Model 2008 to the Present

The above section was largely based on a document that served as our initial mission strategy and was developed in 2003. Since then, we have not only kept on track, but to our great delight and even surprise, our IMPACT model (described below) grew rather quickly, first locally in our coalmining region, then up to 180 clubs (2009) in Romania – and currently 150. It is important to note that our first 'national' project was through the Orthodox Church as part of a USAID faith-based grant working with the church to reduce HIV-AIDS discrimination. Though IMPACT was a small part of the budget of this project, it had outsized results in terms of the 'success story' of the project itself. Furthermore, in large part due to our Orthodox friends (several priests) on the staff of World Vision Romania, the IMPACT model has been successfully vetted outside Romania and is spreading round the world via World Vision and others, such as the Christian Reformed Church.[46]

IMPACT was born and developed in Romania, which is critical to its success in other developing contexts. It was developed from 2002 in the challenging context of the Jiu Valley and evolved in dialogue with the local assets and challenges of the post-communist legacy: particularly low social capital and learned helplessness.[47] IMPACT as an educational and youth development model is not a western import (the three-part structure described below is unique to it), though it does borrow from various best practices such as Adventure Education and Service Learning, which are deeply linked with the concern to generate a practical expression of Christian love.[48]

Key to understanding IMPACT, both its ambitions and its structure, is in the expression: 'IMPACT is simply a youth model that takes the Second Great Commandment as seriously as the first.'[49] Most youth models focus either on love of God (proclamation, prayer, Bible study), or love of man (transformation: community service); IMPACT seeks to integrate these[50] in

---

[46] The IMPACT model is built into the global strategy for the Christian Reformed World Mission as a method for community transformation.

[47] Klicperova et al, 'In the Search for a Post-Communist Syndrome'.

[48] However, because of the strong 'faith-versus-works' dichotomy in many Protestant contexts, these originally Christian pedagogies that emphasized human action (even though they started as expressions of faith) became secularized.

[49] More technically, Maximus the Confessor asserts that the 'logos' or purpose of man 'is best comprehended in the dual duty to love God and man. The two commandments (*logoi*) correspond to the two fundamental dimensions of human existence… one Godward and one manward… that need actualization. But neither can they be actualized without each other' – L. Thunberg, *Man and the Cosmos: The Vision of St Maximus the Confessor* (Crestwood, NY: St Vladimir's Seminary Press, 1985), 24.

[50] Admittedly, we are not always able to keep the balance between the proclamational and transformational sides. Our work in the state school system sometimes means the proclamational side is not as evident. However, Service Learning is an agent for the Kingdom, even when undercover, as practices are bearers of theology and persons act their way into

an attractive format for youth, and follows the Orthodox vision of living both commands.[51] Indeed, we slowly began to see that Orthodox theology could provide a powerful theological rationale for Service Learning and the IMPACT model. As Dumitru Stăniloae argues, speaking of a love that is simultaneously fully natural and spiritual: 'The activity by which we help our neighbors and ourselves to grow crystallizes in the virtues which culminate in love.'[52] This growth in love is the essence of salvation, or what is often called 'deification' in Orthodoxy – and it is at the heart of the IMPACT model.

IMPACT is, to use the terms of Stăniloae's disciple Ion Bria, a 'liturgy after the liturgy',[53] a way to live out practical love or service in the world. Nicholas Cabasilas wrote: 'Two things, then, commend us to God, and in them lies all the salvation of men. The first is that we be initiated into the most sacred Mysteries; the second, that we train the will for virtue.'[54] IMPACT's fundamental aim is to 'train the will for virtue' through the active practice of neighbour love. IMPACT is a framework for helping youth live out what Stăniloae asserts as a need for Orthodoxy: it 'must go beyond its theoretical anthropology to become like a Saint, involved in the specific human relationship found in the complicated circumstances of our daily lives'.[55]

The profound transformational emphasis in much of Orthodox theology can be seen in this quotation from Archbishop Aram Keshishian:

> *Diakonia* [service] belongs to the very nature of the church. Being in communion with Christ is loving one's neighbor, being with the sick and afflicted. These are not just the 'moral obligations' of the church but rather its constitutive elements. The church does not 'have' a *diakonia*; it is a *diakonia*, namely a continuous and committed discipleship to Christ for the rebuilding of world community and re-creating the fallen world according to the plan of God. Through *diakonia* the church becomes one with Christ and at the same time brings Christ to the world. *Diakonia* is both the expression of the unity of the church and the implementation of the gospel message.[56]

---

believing as much as believe their way into action (D.G. Myers, *The Pursuit of Happiness* (New York: Avon Books, 1992).

[51] IMPACT emerges out of a patent frustration with Protestant models of ministry that, while having many good features that can attract youth, are simply unbiblical because they can view one being in a 'personal' relationship with God (the first Great Commandment) without recognizing what is everywhere in the Scriptures (and especially clear in 1 John) is that one cannot be in an authentic personal relationship with God without simultaneously being in personal loving relationships with one's neighbours, and especially the vulnerable.

[52] Stăniloae, *Orthodox Spirituality*, (Waymart, PA: St. Tikhon's Monastery Press, 2013), 44.

[53] I. Bria, *Liturgy after the Liturgy: Mission and Witness from an Orthodox Perspective* (Geneva: WCC Publications, 1996).

[54] N. Cabasilas, *The Life in Christ* (Crestwood, NY: St Vladimir's Seminary Press, 1974), 110.

[55] D. Stăniloae, *Theology and the Church* (Crestwood, NY: St Vladimir's Seminary Press, 1980, 19. Ideally, for an Orthodox context, IMPACT would encourage youth to participate in the liturgy in the regular sense of the term.

[56] A.A. Keshishian, *Orthodox Perspectives on Mission* (Oxford: Regnum, 1992), 100-01.

The foundational structure of the IMPACT model was designed to mirror both of the Great Commandments and to structure *diakonia* into youth ministry. There are three basic 'methods' that serve as the *foundation* for IMPACT: (a) Fun team-building activities to attract youth;[57] (b) Stories (love of God; proclamation);[58] (c) Service Learning (*diakonia*; transformation). Every club meeting incorporates each of these three elements with generous amounts of debriefing. The fun attracts the youth to healthy forms of recreation that also teach life skills and breaks down barriers and helps the group to bond. Liliana Olăraşu, a teacher who is also an IMPACT leader, notes that 'these non-formal activities that seem like games, are actually well organized, well thought out and constructive learning activities'.[59] The narrative or story dimension is the second key element and can include spiritual discussions, scripture lessons, video clips, or anything to promote healthy discussion and the internalization of spiritual values. Lastly, is what is called the 'Service Learning' component: 2-3 times a year, the youth themselves do community analysis and identify a community burden and learn the skills required to address it – more on these below. One IMPACT youth writes perceptively: 'In IMPACT we can do whatever we think necessary, and our activities coincide with the needs of society.'[60] Because the youth themselves identify the community burdens, and these burdens emerge from their own lived experience, their motivation is incredibly high. This motivational element is the key to success and internalizes an activist faith – youth experiencing themselves as capable, loving beings, experiencing themselves as agents of positive change for *shalom*.

To give a picture of what this can mean, and how powerful this process can be, here is a concrete example of love in action, of youth addressing burdens that they themselves recognize in society.

---

[57] The founder of this approach was German educator Kurt Hahn, whose whole philosophy was based on the Parable of the Good Samaritan and the need to inculcate in every human being, particularly the young, an instinctive desire to 'do unto others as one would have done unto oneself'. Because of a theology that separated Grace from Nature and works, such approaches (including Service Learning) became secularized in the West. Orthodoxy does not separate grace from human experience, and grace works through, or synergizes with, human agency. This is why Orthodoxy, or at least some expressions of it, provides the proper spiritual home for IMPACT.

[58] IMPACT was intentionally designed to work in both secular and faith-based contexts. It is our 'policy' as an organization not to dictate the 'story' dimension for a partner organization implementing IMPACT. For example, in working with the Reformed Churches, their selection of texts for the 'story' dimension might be different for an Eastern Orthodox context. And the same holds true for working in state schools where a more 'civic' framing of the virtues is appropriate. Even though the IMPACT approach is highly flexible, its most complete expression is in terms of salvation as a process of 'living out the Great commandments'.

[59] P. Teampău, *Success Stories in the IMPACT Program* (Cluj, Romania: New Horizons Foundation in partnership with The Center for Democracy Studies, 2012), 12.

[60] Teampău, *Success Stories*, 39.

Example Youth Community Service Project: Spice Shops Closed by Youth

Constanta, a busy seaside port long known for its lasciviousness, was dotted with 'spice shops'. These were set up near schools and sold drugs that, technically, were not yet illegal, but were nevertheless dangerous, and thousands of youth were addicted, and lives and families were being destroyed. The Constanta IMPACT Club decided that these 'spice shops' must be shut down. They wrote a project, and first approached the Mayor. He ignored their request. They were undaunted and then canvassed the city and collected over 1,000 signatures. They then organized a city-wide march that attracted thousands of marchers, rallying round the theme: 'Don't throw your life away for 10 lei ($3).' The Mayor was there. At the end of the march, a young teenage woman in an IMPACT club came to the microphone to speak to the crowd. She spoke of the awful things about these 'spice shops', and then divulged that she too had previously been addicted, and she begged and pleaded for help. The mayor relented, and city-wide these drug dens were closed and thousands of lives transformed!

These youth-led 'service-learning' projects form the core of IMPACT – and there are hundreds more examples of this practical or 'lived theology'. Based on the strength of these projects and the learning achieved through them, IMPACT is considered a global best practice by youth development experts:

> The New Horizons Foundation brings together the art and science of youth development in a comprehensive model that merits examination by

> development professionals world-wide. Whenever I am asked to discuss best practice in the field of Service Learning, New Horizon's IMPACT program is the example that I provide. (Cathryn L. Thorup, PhD, Senior Fellow at the International Youth Foundation).[61]

The spirituality of IMPACT consciously follows that of St Chrysostom who wrote: 'The most perfect rule of Christianity, its exact definition, its highest summit, is this: to seek what is for the benefit of all.'[62] IMPACT aims at a practical, 'problem-solving' form of love that seeks to 'Bear one another's burdens and so fulfil the law of Christ' (Gal. 6:2). It is significant that the Early Fathers called Christ not merely *Logos*, but *Logos praktikos*, and Maximus the Confessor affirms that 'the Logos of God is revealed in practical things'.[63] In Orthodoxy, loving action must come before or in conjunction with true knowledge, or genuine theological understanding. Stăniloae writes, summarizing the thought from Evagrus Ponticus to St Maximus the Confessor:

> The believer who wants to gain perfection, before he becomes a gnostikos (a knower) must be a praktikos (a doer). Someone can't see the logoi (the true purpose and meaning) in things and by them God the Word, the Logos, if he hasn't first dedicated himself to a working philosophy or a 'doing of the commandments'.[64]

The foundational aim of IMPACT is to provide an attractive and replicable structure for this working philosophy of 'doing the commandments', of incarnating a Christ-shaped love in the world.

The Wider Benefits of IMPACT: Employability, Entrepreneurship, and More

Successfully implementing a quality IMPACT community project not only activates Christ-shaped virtues such as compassion, but it enlists a diverse set of competencies related to 'project management'. Core to the IMPACT model is that it combines compassion (and other character traits[65]) with the

---

[61] http://noi-orizonturi.ro/index.php/en/about-nhf/experts-about-nhf/111-cathryn-l-thorup-expert.html – while Mario Matos, Executive Director of the Center for Transforming Mission (associated with the Christian Reformed Church) writes:

> As an organization that seeks the peace of our city, through the social and spiritual renewal of people and places, CTM Dominican Republic has found the IMPACT Program to be a very effective tool that serves not just to equip the youth to be agents for social change, but it is also a very effective instrument that brings together the whole community, as it provides opportunities to engage their parents, the public sector (schools, the city hall, and other public institutions), the private sector (as businesses sponsor the youth in their Service Learning community projects), the non-profit sector and the faith community. IMPACT has been an answer to our prayers.

[62] Ware, *The Orthodox Way*.

[63] S.S. Harakas, *Toward Transfigured Life: The Theoria of Eastern Orthodox Ethics* (Minneapolis, MN: Light and Life Publishing Company, 1983), 3.

[64] Stăniloae, *Orthodox Spirituality*, 43.

[65] The IMPACT approach is currently being operated around the Values in Action approach linked with Positive Psychology of Martin Seligman. This is a 'virtue' or strength-based approach to youth development. Interestingly, 'spirituality' is a key strength in itself, but also

development of various competencies: personal, interpersonal, technical skills such as budgeting and planning, public relations – in fact, all aspects of implementing a successful project for the common good. To drive forward the growth and learning process in IMPACT, each youth-led project should aim towards a higher level of complexity and dig deeper into community issues and thus demand the exercise of greater competencies. (The curricula we have developed over fifteen years drives this process forward.) Thus, not only do these projects incarnate neighbour love, they teach a broad set of life skills or competencies that can help youth become productive members of society, and even become better students with the increased likelihood of gaining a satisfying job in the future.[66]

Resting upon the methodological *foundation* of a) games, b) stories, and c) community projects, the IMPACT educational model is further developed upon four *pillars* that structure the curricula: active citizenship, employability, social entrepreneurship and leadership. These four 'pillars' represent a curricular progression in terms of the competencies[67] that are developed through the implementation of the community service projects. As mentioned, each project should become increasingly complex and thus demand the incorporation of more skills and deeper community involvement whilst moving towards sustainability. This drives the learning forward, keeps the youth interested, and increases the impact upon society. Furthermore, IMPACT has developed a set of performance indicators (in an attractive youth 'passport'), and comes with a complete TOT and coaching and monitoring system. It is an approved non-formal educational approach, endorsed by the Romanian ministry of education.

Father Stăniloae encourages us to 'increase the assets of love'.[68] The multi-dimensional nature of IMPACT cultivates a diverse set of assets, and

---

a strength that empowers other strengths such as creativity, integrity, etc. C. Peterson and M.E.P. Seligman, *Character Strengths and Virtues: A Handbook and Classification* (Oxford: OUP, 2004). This VIA framework allows us to employ state-of-the-art social science, but in a way that reinforces spiritual values: www.viacharacter.org/www/Character-Strengths/VIA-Classification for more information

[66] Many studies round the globe have revealed a synergistic relationship between formal and non-formal education: youth who participate in 'Service Learning' clubs do better in school and other outcomes such as civic engagement (Wade, *Community Service Learning*; Billig, 'Why Service Learning is Such a Good Idea').

[67] 'Competency' carries rich moral connotations. Competencies involve Knowledge, Values, Attitude, and Skills (KVAS). In a certain sense, character development, to be a coherent notion, must be translated into competencies if character is actually exercised in a concrete context for a concrete project/task. Without using the language of competence, virtue theorist Linda Zagzebski (*Virtues of the Mind: An Enquiry into the Nature of Virtue and the Ethical Foundations of Knowledge* (Cambridge: CUP, 1996), 136) gets at this with the notion of 'non-moral' facts:

> A kind, compassionate, generous, courageous or just person aims at making the world a certain way, and reliable success in making it that way is a condition for having the virtue in question. For this reason, virtue requires knowledge, or at least awareness, of certain non-moral facts about the world. The nature of morality involves not only wanting things, but being reliable agents for bringing those things about.

[68] Stăniloae, *Orthodox Spirituality*, 203.

means that not only ethical but effective, not only compassionate but also competent, agents of change are developed.[69] Or, as one youth put it more simply: 'In school we learn different sciences; here [in IMPACT] we learn to be better!'[70]

In Romania, both in the state education system, but also in the Orthodox Church, there is a need for a youth approach that has wide appeal from communities – from schools, teachers, priests, and especially the youth. IMPACT works successfully with a wide range of youth, urban and rural, including at-risk youth. This is because youth themselves choose community service projects appropriate to their level of challenge. Furthermore, IMPACT as a 'spiritual' model has wide appeal because it is based on a theology of working for the common good (cf. Chrysostom above) and all the projects must meet a transparent public need. IMPACT is attractive to all simply because its activities do, in fact, aim to benefit all – but especially the most vulnerable.

This practice-based spirituality of the common good that is also fun (and profitable – in terms of life and future employability skills) can draw generations of youth into the church. As an expression of the mission of the church, it will help youth, who are created in God's image, to be 'agents of their own development and of the development of others'.[71] Youth want and need to participate in meaningful ways in the development of society. IMPACT within the church can link gaining important life-skills with a vibrant spirituality, giving youth real chances to experience themselves as the 'faithful', as *living* Orthodox theology as practical service on the altar of the world.

IMPACT in the church can reach an entire generation of youth because it provides a fun and challenging way of displaying life in the church, not only as participating in the Sunday liturgy (important as this is!), but as an entire way of life (ethos) based on living out a Christ-shaped practical love.[72] As the Apostle John says, 'Dear children, let us not love with words

---

[69] J.S. Nye-Jr, *The Powers to Lead* (Oxford: OUP, 2009). Archbishop Anastasios of Albania notes that the Fathers understood Orthodoxy 'as an approach toward and account of life that embraces everything, life in its entirety, in all its dimensions and meanings', and they 'struggled for an all-encompassing change in human affairs'. The three hierarchs' teaching was that 'change for the good' is the core of our Christian heritage. A.Y. Anastasios, *Facing the World: Orthodox Christian Essays on Global Concerns* (Crestwood, NY: St Vladimir's Seminary Press, 2003), 155-56. IMPACT seeks to embrace this vision.

[70] Teampău, *Success Stories in the IMPACT Program*, 31. This quotation, and others, is from a year-long qualitative study of the effect of the IMPACT programme on both youth and teachers by the Center for Democracy at Babes-Bolyai. One important fact about this quote also for this context is that in Orthodox morality ('learning to be better') and spirituality (one's relationship with God) are not separate categories as is often the case in the West.

[71] G. Tsetsis (ed), *Orthodox Thought: Reports of Orthodox Consultations Organized by the World Council of Churches, 1975-1982* (Geneva: WCC Publications, 1983), 91.

[72] M. Volf and D.C. Bass (eds), *Practicing Theology: Beliefs and Practices in Christian Life* (Grand Rapids, MI: Eerdmans, 2002).

or speech but with actions and in truth' (1 John 3:18). Actions speak louder!

Youth everywhere long for three things: fun, learning, and ways to serve meaningfully in the building of a better society.[73] Youth are not the future of society – they are 'the now' – and they know it! IMPACT as a tool within the church can provide a replicable, scalable pathway for youth to experience Orthodoxy as 'concerned with the aspirations and the problems of mankind as a whole… a theology which is concerned to provide ever deeper foundations for human co-operation and for the service of all mankind'.[74]

Conclusion

By way of conclusion, this paper has served as a case study for our New Horizon's youth work in Romania, focusing on Adventure Education and Service Learning. More specifically, it has highlighted our ongoing attempts to contextualize experiential education both for post-communism but also within the Orthodox Church with whom we have worked since 2003. Currently (March 2016), we are preparing training with the church involving three different bishoprics, and the church is providing a generous portion of the costs. It is our hope and prayer that this experiment in youth ministry using experiential education to promote *diakonia*, framed in ever better ways through an ongoing dialogue with an Orthodox theology of reflection on lived experience, can indeed be a blessing and become ever more widely embraced by the church. Though we would love to see more progress with the church in terms of youth ministry partnership and national extension, we have every reason to remain hopeful.

---

[73] In the West, it is rather clear that the lack of social concern by the various churches is the number one reason youth abandon the institutions. D. Kinnaman, *You Lost Me: Why Young Christians Are Leaving Church… and Rethinking Faith* (Grand Rapids, MI: Baker Books, 2011); D. Kinnaman and G. Lyons, *UNchristian: What a New Generation Really Thinks About Christianity… And Why It Matters* (Grand Rapids, MI: BakerBooks, 2007).

[74] Stăniloae, *Theology and the Church*, 223.

The Future of Orthodox Christianity in the Context of a Theology of Integrity: A Perspective from Serbia

Zorica Kuburić

> In the future, the only kind of school that will last is one that finds ways and means to put to use words and concepts that it teaches children in the everyday life of the school. Only the school responsible for the content that is taught there has a chance for educating young people for the truth, for the future, for life.[1]

Introduction

Christian mission, as derived from the New Testament, refers to spreading love instead of hatred, to orientation towards life instead of death, to a vision of the future instead of the past. The Christian mission is the salvation of the world from sin and self-destruction by acceptance of Christ's sacrifice for humankind's sin of 'knowing good and evil'. The Christian mission is preaching God's goodness which leads to salvation. The method used for spreading Christian teaching has to reflect the content in order to be successful. From the Christian perspective, mission is a project for the future that has two perspectives: one that longs for and announces the future, and the other that derives from fear and exudes a threat, but also a hope for that future that is never to happen. A path to the future is paved by expectations, either positive or negative. Positive and negative expectations are equally suggestive and the expectations themselves are built into the realization of the future.

Besides these emotional factors that affect a description of a possible future, there are facts from the past upon which a vision of the future can be constructed. If we start by assuming that history is repeating, that the future has been already seen, as the wise Solomon said: 'What has been will be again, what has been done will be done again, there is nothing new under the sun' (Eccl. 1:9). However, when the past becomes a paradigm for the future, when it becomes a remedy for the uncertainty of today, this feeds

[1] Svetomir Bojanin, *Tajna škole* [Secret of School] (Novi Sad, Serbia: Šoso 'Milan Petrović', 2002).

the rise of fundamentalisms and traditionalisms which draw their identity from history.[2]

Besides generally defined starting-points for studying religion and its development, it should be emphasized that each religion took roots in the context of the society in which it came into existence. Consequently, it is impossible to observe Christianity outside the context of Judaism or the social reality of the modern world, where it is one of the leading world religions.

Đuro Šušnjić writes that 'from the fact that a faith has become large, global, universal, it can be concluded that it has succeeded first and foremost because of its ability to answer not only individual wishes and special needs but also the needs of man as man, regardless of the surroundings'.[3] Spiritual forms of integration are needed when familial and tribal relationships are weakened, but they are possible where it is preached that all people are brothers and sisters, children of one heavenly Father.

The history of opinions about religion can be reduced to an assumption that religion will falter when faced with scientific ideas and in the face of a modern and secular way of life. However, the opposite occurred at the end of the twentieth and the beginning of the 21st century. Once again, religion has become influential, reviving old forms of worship and offering new beliefs. The analysis has shown that religiosity, particularly traditional religiosity, has increased greatly in periods of conflicts, when it functions as a means of cultural defence. However, other formats of religiosity are also present. The revitalization of religion when understood in the context of the process of de-secularization that has taken place in societies where Eastern Christianity predominates, is followed by a declarative religiosity which is not accompanied by the essence of the faith, because the form it takes, the conformism it demands and the superstition which accompanies it, are obstacles to genuine conversion and internal change. Declarative religiosity emphasizes belonging rather than believing.[4] This is the perspective that we discuss in this paper – the way religious people talk about the future of Orthodox Christianity in answer to the question: *How do you see the future of the Serbian Orthodox Church*?

Integrative processes within Christian churches in Europe take place on several different levels. Political ecumenism is recognizable in a parallel process of European integration and in demonstrating a power that is formed on an institutional level. The development of the ecumenical movement since the Edinburgh Missionary Conference in 1910[5] has been possible because of political support, a support which has had its friends

---

[2] Z. Krstić, 'Pravoslavlje i modernist – teme praktične teologije', in *Službeni glasnik* (2009), 169-75.

[3] Đuro Šušnjić, *Značenje, teorije, preplitanja, susreti* (Belgrade: Čigoja štampa, 1998).

[4] Z. Kuburić, D. Gavrilović, 'Revitalizacija religije u savremnoj Sribji', in *Religija i tolerancija*, 10.18 (2012), 201-14.

[5] Kirsten Kim and Andrew Anderson (eds), *Edinburg 2010: Mission Today and Tomorrow,* in Regnum Edinburgh Centenary Series 5 (Oxford: Regnum, 2011).

and followers, its observers and critics. This type of integration is based on a religious dialogue and tolerance, as well as on dogmatic minimalism. Relations towards these processes are clearly marked by the history of their development. However, in this paper, I would like to raise a question about a dogmatic ecumenism that does not give up on religious teaching and that distances itself from politics. This type of approach is seen as a religious fundamentalism which until recently has been criticized within Orthodox Christianity, as well as within other parts of the Christian church.[6]

The Revitalization of Religious Power

In her book *The Case for God*, Karen Armstrong states that religion did not cease to exist and, in some circles, it became even more militant than ever before. The beginning of the 21st century witnessed an awakened and very vital religious power. Fundamentalists brought faith out of the shadows in which it had hidden and showed that in contemporary society it could be used to attract considerable support. Armstrong believes that fundamentalism is based on a theology of anger and hatred, and defines it as a militant form of faith which sees its survival in the fight against a hostile world.[7]

Contemporary society is frequently split into 'two nations' – the secular and the religious. Both live in the same country, but do not share the same views, because what is sacred and positive for one appears to be demonic and deviant in the eyes of the other, and they are deeply afraid of each other.[8] This atmosphere of fear pervades both the theologies of the fundamentalists and the ideologies of the secularists, and an attempt to use religious fundamentalism to achieve secular and pragmatic goals will prove counter-productive: efforts to manipulate and to establish control have thus caused oppositions, with tragic outcomes such as that witnessed in the conflict in Yugoslavia.[9] Since myth cannot be explained from a rational and logical standpoint, it can hardly be implemented as practical politics. And when a myth is transformed into practical politics, then even ethnic cleansing is justified.

Joseph Wiinikka-Lydon[10] uses qualitative analysis of two statements by a Croat of the Catholic faith and by a Serb of the Orthodox faith to illustrate his hypothesis on the connection between a religious idea of a need to convert someone other to one's own faith, and ethnic cleansing

---

[6] Krstić, 'Pravoslavlje i modernist – teme praktične teologije'.

[7] Karen Armstrong, *Bitka za Boga* (Fundamentalizam u judaizmu, kršćanstvu i islamu, Sarajevo: Šahinpašić, 2007), 397.

[8] Armstrong, *Bitka za Boga*, 451-52.

[9] Z. Kuburić, 'Pred izazovom verskih sloboda, Mogu li muslimani I hrišćani da žive pod istim krovom?', in *Diskursi*, 3.4 (2013), 121-38.

[10] Joseph Wiinikka-Lydon, 'Ethnic Cleansing as Religious Practice: Religion, Ethnicity, and Political Conflict in Bosnia during the War', *Journal of Inter-Religious Studies* 11 (2013), 18-33.

(genocide) in a situation where religion and nation are so intertwined that it is expected of all members of a certain ethic group to be members of the same religion. A conversion which occurs somewhere between the use of religion and its misuse in politics can be followed by a logic of violence and the attempt to suppress the freedom of others to choose who they want to be.

Societies become polarized, the gap grows larger between the secular and the religious sectors of populations, and the need to separate politics from religion grows stronger, promoting the notion of the complementarity of the two realms against visions of the exclusive power of one or the other.

There are different approaches to the question of secularization. Max Weber held that secularization had already taken place: 'The world is disenchanted. Secularization has yet to occur, says Karl Löwith. Secularization should never have happened, says Karl Schmidt. It has brought about a momentous change, a "translation" of devastating consequences from the theological to the political.'[11]

There are authors who begin their papers on this topic with an apology to Friedrich Nietzsche for the fact that 'God is most definitely not dead. Indeed, God is a stronger, more global force in the world today than he has been in generations'.[12] Confident predictions about the end of religion worked on an incorrect assumption. The conclusion leads these authors to predict that things are not going to be much different in lifetimes, and religion is still going to be powerful and influential.

One argument for the claim that religion will continue to grow stronger in the future starts with the fact that at the beginning of the twentieth century, half the world's population affiliated themselves with one of the five major religious traditions: after a hundred years of forced secularization and scientific advance, this number had not declined. Two thirds of the world population are now affiliated with some religion. The number of those who believe in God but do not belong to any denomination has also increased. David Barrett has dedicated his life to observing the world religious scene.[13] His own and many other sociological surveys confirm the revitalization of religion on a local scale as well.[14]

---

[11] Gil Anidžar, S*emiti, Rasa, religija, književnost* (Belgrade: Centar za medije i komunikacije, 2014), 50.

[12] *Reza Aslan,* 'Redefining Community: Religion of the Future', 6th September 2010: www.patheos.com/Resources/Additional-Resources/Redefining-Community-Religion-of-the-Future.html (accessed 5th March 2014).

[13] D.B. Barrett, G.T. Kurian and T.M. Johnson, *World Christian Encyclopedia: A comparative survey of churches and religions in the modern world*, 2nd edition, 3 Vols (New York: Oxford University Press, 2001).

[14] Dragoljub Đorđević (ed), *Povratak svetog?* (Niš, Serbia: Gradina, 1994); Andrijana Mladenović (ed), *Religioznost u Srbiji 2010.* (Istraživanje religioznosti građana Srbije i njihovog stava prema procesu evropskih integracija: Beograd: Hrišćanski kulturni centar; Centar za evrpske integracije; Konrad-Adenauer-Stiftung, 2011); Kuburić and Gavrilović, 'Revitalizacija religije u savremenoj Srbiji'.

Worldmark Encyclopedia of Religious Practices,[15] a three-volume work with over 1,800 pages, illustrates the importance of religion in 193 countries of the world. Its presentation of the origin, development and contemporary status of beliefs and practices round the globe is a significant source for theoretical reflection about the world and the place that religion has in it.[16]

The process of globalization has certainly contributed to the spread of this trend in which religious identities have gained a new level of importance throughout the world. Decreasing distances, bringing people together, communication via the Internet and the creation of virtual communities – all these have contributed to the disintegration of territorial communities and to the decreasing importance of political and national identities. In this process, religious identities have become more important. Globalization has transformed the means by which the identification of self takes place in any given social context. The apparent need for 'roots' in this new context is based on the perceived need for – and efficacy of – the kind of security offered by old and proven models of identification, and it is in large part because of this that religious identities have grown in importance.[17]

However, in addition to the predominance of the religious over the secular, and to the theistic over the atheistic viewpoint, rivalry within monotheism should also be taken into consideration. In this respect, any discussion about the future of Christianity will have to tackle the problem of ecumenism and of Christian integration within a singular socio-political context in which, on the one hand, it is emphasized that Christian disunity is shameful given the words of Christ that 'all may be one' (John 17:21) and, on the other hand, given the demand from many Christians to be detached from a society tainted by the sinfulness referred to in the words: 'Come out of her, my people, so that you will not share in her sins, so that you will not receive any of her plagues' (Rev. 18:4). Thus the processes of integration/unity and separation within Christianity have their dogmatic foundations.

---

[15] R. Thomas Riggs and G. Thomson (eds), *Worldmark Encyclopedia of Religious Practices*, 3 Vols (Thomson Galaxy): www.cengage.com/search/productOverview.do?Ntt=Worldmark+enciclopedia+of+religiou+practice||157262706652333139419875739361744975038&N=197&Ntk=APG%7C%7CP_EPI&Ntx=mode%2Bmatchallpartial (accessed 5th March 2014).

[16] Z. Kuburić, 'Religion in Serbia and Montenegro', in Riggs and Thomson, *Worldmark Encyclopedia of Religious Practices*, 307-12.

[17] Z. Kuburić, 'The Role of Religion in Identity Formation and Social Distancing in the Balkans', in *Divided God and Intercultural Dialogue* (Ljubljana: Dijački dom Ivana Cankarja: KUD Pozitiv, 2008), 153-70; Zorica Kuburić, 'Religious and National Identity in the Process of Globalization in Serbia,' in Danijela Gavrilović (ed), *Religion and Globalization* (Niš, Serbia: Yugoslav Society for the Scientific Study of Religion, 2005); Zorica Kuburić, 'Religion between Regional and Universal Identity', in G. Bašić and S. Devetak (eds), *Democracy and Religion* (Belgrade: ERC, ISÇOMET, 2003), 234-40.

From its dogmatic foundations, several crucial issues could be identified as those upon which the future of Christianity has been built. Salvation from sin and mortality is a fundamental teaching that has had diverse interpretations from the very beginning, which consequently resulted in a turbulent relational dynamic among religious communities. History, observed from the perspective of Christianity, has always been associated with God's providential salvation of man from sin. The concept of salvation has been interpreted both in terms of justification by works and justification by faith. During its entire history, this was a crucial question for Christianity, in its teachings, rituals and practice. Exaggeration has caused division and conflict. In the theology of integrity, when it comes to salvation, one does not renounce good deeds, although faith is emphasized in an attempt to combine the Law and the justice of God with God's mercy. This theological school finds its motto in the words: 'This calls for patient endurance on the part of the people of God who keep his commands and remain faithful to Jesus' (Rev. 14:12). In these words from the New Testament, besides the central words pertaining to 'the command of God and faith in Jesus', Christians have a message for their future.[18]

The term 'people of God', whether it designates a visible or invisible community, always points to the idea of collectivity – that in the future, the people referred to will rejoice in the presence of God: 'They will see his face, and his name will be on their foreheads' (Rev. 22:4).

A Theology of Integrity

One of a number of possible dogmatic perspectives on the development of Christianity lies within the 'theology of integrity'. This term designates an attempt to integrate Christian beliefs on the basis of early Christian teaching contained in the words of Jesus: 'Do not think that I have come to abolish the Law and the Prophets; I have not come to abolish them but to fulfil them' (Matt. 5:17).

One layer of the theology of integrity is related to religious teaching that represents religion as the entirety of God's revelation from its beginning, including also the reform which forms Christianity itself. In this sense, the diversification and multiplication of believing communities follows along the lines of the historical development of Christianity from a religion of belonging19 to a religion of believing, from a religion of distancing oneself and rejection to inclusive religiosity. On a practical level – the development of Christianity and inter-religious relations – those with a strong Jewish phyletism based on the Ten Commandments will be singled out by God.[20]

---

[18] Z. Kuburić, *The Self-image of Adolescents in the Protestant Family* (Lewiston, NY: Edwin Mellen Press, 2014).

[19] D. Grace, *Religija u modernoj Evropi: mutiacija sećanja* (Zagreb: Golden Marketing, Tehnička knjiga, 2005).

[20] Z. Kuburić, *Verske zajednice u Srbiji i verska distanca* (Novi Sad, Serbia: CEIR, 2010).

The development of Christianity and the formation of new communities of Christians follow a path which often branches into belonging, believing and behaving. The theology of integrity seeks to unite all three aspects into a whole which carries a moral lesson.

The second layer of the theology of integrity is related to the church as an institution which has its historical development as a communion which constitutes an unbreakable whole, which is, in the words of Paul the Apostle, 'the body of Christ' (1 Cor. 12:27) 'of which I became a minister according to the stewardship from God that was given to me from you, to make the word of God fully known' (Col. 1:25). A secret of the theology of integrity is in a paradoxical revelation of the mystery to Gentiles: 'the mystery hidden for ages and generations but now revealed to his saints' (Col. 1:26). This communion, in revealing the mystery, is the mission of the church which can be realized only in dialogue with those who do not know God. The theology of integrity seeks to create communion between 'the people of God' who know and 'the people of God' who do not know 'the mystery', making everyone perfect in Jesus Christ (Col. 1:26-28).

The third layer of the theology of integrity attempts to make a connection between humankind and the source of power. Paul the Apostle expresses this in the following words: 'For this I toil, struggling with all his energy that he powerfully works within me' (Col. 1:29). The essence of any religion is in making this connection, and one usually speaks about the vertical relationship between humankind and God, and the horizontal relationship between humans. Christianity insists here on one word – *love*. Within Christianity, the word 'love' is synonym to 'God'. John the Apostle calls upon Christians: 'Beloved, let us love one another, for love is from God, and everyone who loves is born of God and knows God. Anyone who does not love does not know God, because God is love' (1 John 4:7-8).

Two recent key documents on mission, one from the ecumenical side and one from an evangelical perspective, give us focus on the theology of life and the theology of love.[21] The mission of God flows from the love of God. Love for God and love for people constitute the commandments on which hang all the law as the fulfilment of the law. The theology of integrity starts when love becomes visible with faith and hope. The invitation is: 'Let us strive for a culture of full integrity and transparency.'

When we discuss the theology of integrity, we refer primarily to aspects of religious teachings; however, the theology of integrity is not exhausted in the teachings – teachings are only its beginning or its end; they are life condensed into words, and life itself is embodied in an individual who lives

[21] *WCC Together Towards Life: Mission and Evangelism in Changing Landscapes*, 5th September 2012: https://www.oikoumene.org/en/resources/documents/commissions/mission-and-evangelism/together-towards-life-mission-and-evangelism-in-changin g-landscapes; *Cape Town Commitment: A Confession of Faith and a Call to Action* – Third Lausanne Congress on World Evangelization (Cape Town, 16th-25th October 2010): https://www.lausanne.org/content/ctc/ctcommitment

by knowing their faith and the community to which he or she belongs. Therefore, it is possible to analyze the theology of integrity from the perspective of psychology, sociology and philosophy. The behaviour of a person who has a mature personality is seen in an ability to maintain their dignity by behaving in harmony with accepted moral values. More about phases of emotional development and maturity of personality, as well as about aspects of mature religiosity, is found elsewhere in this volume.[22]

Integrative and Disintegrative Processes within Christianity

Inter-generational transmission of Christian teachings occurs as a process of serial reproduction, building on previous interpretations, bringing new elements of understanding old truths, whilst changing and adding – but also forgetting – certain details. The diversification that took place in a historical perspective is clearly recognized by viewing a cross-section of Christian communities in the modern world. Christianity has diversified and changed from early divisions based on who follows which apostle, to the East-West Schism (1054), to Protestantization in the sixteenth and nineteenth centuries, and to the contemporary growth of independent churches based on individualism.

Writing about Orthodoxy, Bogdan Đurović comments that, for every religious community, it is of essential importance to determine the basic elements of Orthodoxy, 'both in order to eliminate heretical interpretations and deflections, and because of preaching, education and worship. Christianity, depending on denominations, formed its orthodoxy through creeds designed at (ecumenical) councils, through encyclicals, by declaring dogmas in theses and papers on confessing the faith, and through catechisms. Although all Christian communities have been continuously reconsidering and harmonizing the basic postulates of this Orthodoxy, there are still differences in their understanding'.[23]

As religious identity has been seen to be important in the context of the process of globalization, in view of the extent to which the borders of political, territorial and national identities were shaken, so too has ecumenism – as a political movement bringing people together on the grounds of the relativization of the truth – contributed to a different kind of human encounter, still conceived on the basis of religious teaching and seeking the truth. Pluralism and post-modernism, both internalizing a loss of hope in the truth, search for the thread that connects universal values and does not give up on the absolute truth, which is integrated in Christianity in

---

[22] E. Erikson, *Identitet i životni ciklusi* (Belgrade: Zavod za udžbenike, 1986); S. Hrnjica, *Zrelost ličnosti,* (Belgrade: Zavod za udžbenike, 2010); Zorica Kuburić, *The Self-Image of Adolescents in the Protestant Family: A Study of Seventh-Day Adventist Families in Predominantly Orthodox Serbia* (Lewiston, NY: Mellen Press, 2015).

[23] Bogdan Đurović, 'Pravoverje', in A. Mimica and M. Bogdanović (eds), *Sociološki rečnik,* (Belgrade: Zavod za udženike, 2007), 436-37.

the name of Christ, who spoke of himself as 'the way and the truth and the life' (John 14:6).

The Future of the Serbian Orthodox Church in the 21st Century

Writing about Orthodox Christianity, Dragoljub Đorđević suggests that it would be an unrealistic expectation from a sociological perspective to hold that there is a bright future for the Orthodox faith, and implies a possible future for a movement based on inner spirituality instead: 'Sociologists say that such confessional Orthodox Christianity, resembling Catholicism and Protestantism, cannot count on a forthcoming time of success – expecting that at one point the entire Universe will be Orthodox... In that context, contrary to earlier hopes, the odds of Orthodox Christianity are more than merely in its favour if it is not reduced exclusively to a Christianity of laws and customs, or a mass sociological religiosity of the external type, but to a persistent *liberation of the inner man in Orthodox spirituality*'.[24]

Surveys conducted in Serbia[25] indicate that the external type of religiosity is predominant and, despite the revitalization of religion, that this is essentially a ritual behaviour reducible to form and conformism only. Religiosity here has been studied on the basis of religious affiliation, belief in God and practices in everyday life that are associated with religious teaching. It is not easy to examine the level of inner peace and trust in God as well as the autonomous morality and altruism which could be indicators of inner religiosity. From these studies, we have a fairly compelling picture of the present state of religious life in Serbia. However, the question of the future presents the greatest challenge.

We discussed the future of Orthodox Christianity with students of the Faculty of Philosophy in Novi Sad, with members of the Serbian Orthodox Church in Belgrade and with religious teachers of the Eparchy of Žiča in Užice and Kraljevo. The attitudes of both clergy and laity will be presented through an analysis of their responses.[26]

We elicited the attitudes of students at the Faculty of Philosophy in Novi Sad towards the Orthodox Church, and to its development in the future, through a qualitative study. The Serbian Orthodox Church was discussed mostly by its members, but also by those who belong to other religious communities. However, we did not make the distinction between criticism and self-criticism. Content analysis singled out some responses that represent the empirical reality of the church as well as the expectations of

---

[24] Dragoljub Đorđević, 'Pravoslavlje', in Mimica and Bogdanović, *Sociološki rečnik*, 436-37.

[25] Andrijana Mladenović (ed), *Religioznost u Srbiji 2010*; Zorica Kuburić, 'Serbian Orthodox Church in Kosovo and Metohija: Between Past and Future', in *Balkan Journal of Philosophy*, 6.2 (2014), 137-46.

[26] 'Perspektive pravoslavnog hrišćanstva u 21. veku', in Dragoljub Đorđević, Predrag Stajić and Dragan Todorović (eds), *Hrišćanstvo u 21. veku* (Niš, Serbia: Prometij, Leskovački kultruni centar, JUNIR), 199-223.

the students regarding the future of the church. Jelena Stojmenković gave a sharp critique in her term paper:

> I was thinking whether I should research and speak about a popular topic – so to say *modernization* of the clergy, their incomes, their fleet of cars, their excessive involvement in politics of the State, or something else. Newspaper headlines such as: *Arrogant Driver: a Giant of the Moscow Patriarchate Parked in a Pedestrian Zone; The Limousine Assembly Begins: Fleet of Cars of the Bishops Similar to the Cannes Festival; Honourable Fathers on Dishonourable Mission*, indeed deserve further investigation and discussion whether we have a good example of temperance in the 21st century. However, it is perhaps better to start from your own back yard. The majority religion in the Republic of Serbia is Christianity, i.e. Orthodox Christianity. Of a huge number of believers, how many are true believers? How many of us are familiar with the history of our Church, with customs that exist in our religion? How many of us know how to behave like a true believer in the way it is prescribed?[27]

Besides the critique directed at the church, at priests and believers and their behaviour, there is still love for the church, which is based on the consciousness of one's own sinfulness. In that regard, Jovana Stojmenković finishes her paper with a sentence from the New Testament: 'Who is without sin, let him be the first to throw a stone.'[28]

Nataša Პršo sees the Serbian Orthodox Church as a national church that becomes stronger in times of trouble, because it is then that people turn to God in prayer. What this sociology student emphasized is faith in Orthodox Christianity that is formed in the family, carried in the heart and defended with national pride, i.e. through Serbian obstinacy:

> An economically poor situation, e.g. an increased number of the poor, turns people to God. Man achieves an equilibrium through prayer and a strength of will to carry on quietly. This is the reason why Serbian obstinacy is going to wake up and it won't give up in the face of the temptations that we face every day. Orthodox Christianity is much more accepted among Serbs today, and it is because of the religious education in elementary and secondary schools. The number of children that choose religious education grows bigger. They are very satisfied with the answers they receive there. In this way, the Serbian people will not abandon its teachings, and their identity will grow stronger – in every sense. Even if they move to another continent, every Serb carries the obstinacy of the Serbian people that will help them endure any temptations.[29]

Božana Ciganović, a sociology student, bases her opinion on the future of the church on indicators that are not in its favour. Contemporary trends of atheization through education, religiously mixed marriages and European integration are not in favour of the Serbian Orthodox Church. In her opinion:

---

[27] Jovana Stojmenković, 'Srpska pravoslavna crkva u 21. veku' (Term paper, Faculty of Philosophy, Novi Sad, Serbia, 2014), 2.

[28] Stojmenković, 'Srpska pravoslavna crkva u 21. veku', 6.

[29] Novi Sad, Serbia: 3rd December 2013.

> The number of the members of the Serbian Orthodox Church can significantly decrease because the world modernizes in the sense that the majority of people call themselves non-believers; in other words, they do not belong to any faith. Also, there are much more religiously mixed marriages, where children are left to choose their religion – whether they will belong to the religion of their mother or their father, and this is how the number of believers decreases. The concept of the European Union, such as it is today, cannot accept the Serbian Orthodox Church, because of the influence that the Church has on people. Modernization and ecumenism are methods of moulding into a Roman-Catholic-Protestant system that is contrary to what is Orthodox and what is Svetoslavlje (a Serbian form of Orthodoxy).[30]

Marija Šmit in her response indicates that modern man is conflicted between keeping the tradition and pursuing a career, and in this sense Orthodox Christianity has to make a compromise. In addition to that, religious freedom goes so far that practices incompatible with Biblical teaching are acceptable:

> Because we live in a world that moves fast forward, there are more and more people who want to advance in their professional life and to make a career, and less and less of them pay attention to traditional values. Also, religious education in schools is only elective, and this illustrates the tolerance of the Serbian Orthodox Church. I believe that every man has freedom to choose the religion he wants, no matter what kind of family he comes from. In a modern society, this is sometimes a problem: what religion will a child accept if he comes from a mixed family? There are some disagreements within the Serbian Orthodox Church (for instance, concerning the immortality of the soul). I believe that most believers wish these problems to be solved and a compromise made. For example, homosexuality is not permitted according to the Bible, but it is acceptable in the modern world.[31]

Nikolina Rakić, a journalism student, is pessimistic when it comes to the future of the Serbian Orthodox Church, and the reasons she mentions are as follows:

> The Serbian Orthodox Church, because it is a national church, will always have more believers in Serbia than other religious communities. But I believe that the number of believers will decrease for several reasons. The first is because the number of non-believers is growing. Then also, those who are Orthodox go to church less and less often. And finally, Serbians are becoming poorer, and the fees that priests charge are higher and higher, as well as the lack of humanitarian aid to people. Even people who used to be firm believers now say that priests are thieves, and they start to hate the politics of the Orthodox Church and have their own ideas about God. The only thing which I think will not disappear is the celebration of *slavas*, because it is part of tradition and familial heritage.[32]

Dejan Đolović, a journalism student, is also critical:

---

[30] Novi Sad, Serbia: 3rd December 2013.

[31] Novi Sad, Serbia: 3rd December 2013.

[32] Novi Sad, Serbia: 3rd December 2013.

> In Orthodox Christianity, modesty is one of the major virtues, but when we see patriarchs and proto-hierarchs driving bullet-proof cars, leading dissipated lives and committing every type of sin, one must wonder how bright the future of the oldest and the most important faith of our people really is. Another reason for the weakening of the Serbian Orthodox Church is the large number of sects – both those that are established and those that are newly formed. There are plenty of them, so we conclude that people, seeking some improvement in the field of religion, decide to change their faith. The future of the Serbian Orthodox church is now determined by its involvement in politics.[33]

Olja Jojkić, a journalism student, has high hopes primarily regarding *slava* celebrations, where she supports the idea that what we all honour and respect has its own future, and people gladly hold on to such customs. She also finds baptism and communion to be the very reflection of Orthodox Christianity with a future of its own, emphasizing that the marriage ceremony is the most beautiful:

> The only thing I don't see in the future is the breaking of basic rules as well as disregarding basic norms. As a devoted believer, I am of the opinion that by lighting a candle in a church and placing money on an icon at least once a week, we shall nourish this beautiful culture and further preserve Orthodox Christianity, and also pass on such values to future generations.[34]

Students gave numerous opinions to complete the picture of the of the church's future. I shall quote Saška Jeličić, a journalism student, who, among other things, says:

> In order for a church to be a real church and to survive into the future, it is important not to interfere with the affairs of the state, nor to take part in media scandals, and also to remain aloof from economic interests. The Serbian Orthodox Church can survive as a guardian of tradition only if it manages to settle internal conflicts and become more tolerant towards other religions. Thus, my vision of the future of the Serbian Orthodox Church, as well as the vision of many others, is not so great at this moment.[35]

Opinions of Religious Teachers on the Future of the Serbian Orthodox Church

A study of the opinions of religious teachers towards the future of the Serbian Orthodox Church was conducted with religious teachers of the Žiča Eparchy from 7th February 2014 to 23rd March 2014, using a questionnaire and interviews. The target group included 72 religious teachers of the Serbian Orthodox Church, 56 (78%) of whom were male, and sixteen (22%) female, teachers – along with two Protestant theologians. The educational level of the teachers were as follows: faculty degree 83%,

[33] Novi Sad, Serbia: 3rd December 2013.
[34] Novi Sad, Serbia: 3rd December 2013.
[35] Novi Sad, Serbia: 3rd December 2013.

associate degree 7%, high school degree 7%, master's degree 3%. The teachers' places of employment were: elementary schools (45: 62%), vocational high schools (17: 24%), gymnasiums (grammar schools) (10: 14%).

Based on a qualitative analysis of the replies of religious teachers regarding the future of their church, we selected the following opinions; some of them are based on reflections about theology, teaching and the future. As for the teachings that would be examined in questionnaires and interviews, we chose first the beliefs which are considered to be foundational to Christianity. Other questions were more focused on the relationship between Orthodox Christianity and the rest of society, and also between church and state. However, the majority of respondents considered the possible future in terms of a dialogue with other Christian churches and other religions.

The following opinion of one of the religious teachers shows trust in the future of Orthodox Christianity based on three key beliefs: the church was founded by the incarnated God; Christ is its essence and the Resurrection is its greatest power – based on quotations from famous writers. This teacher's optimism is based on the fact that some westerners, including some western theologians, have converted to Orthodox Christianity:

'Orthodox Christianity, in spite of all the temptations, hardships and evils of this world, provides a sure way to salvation, i.e. entering the Kingdom of God'; 'The perfection of Christianity and the imperfection of the Christians' – Berdyaev. 'If someone were to prove to me that Christ was outside the Truth, I would rather stay with Christ' – Dostoevsky. Vladeta Jerotić spoke best on this matter, stating that, unlike other religions, Christianity was founded by the incarnated God. 'When the Second coming of Christ takes place, none knows but our Father in Heaven. I wait for the resurrection of the dead and the life to come.'[36]

Another religious teacher also points to three possible paths for the development of Christianity: the first is already well known to us – the ethno-phyletistic, closed and local Christianity; the second is global and universal, based on a mission of love carried worldwide; while the third is syncretistic:

> The future of Orthodox Christianity in the 21st century could develop in two directions: 1. The first is ethno-phyletistic and restricted, which sees Orthodox Christianity as an addition to national identity, spreading an atmosphere of panic concerning the forthcoming 'day of judgement'; 2. The second way is missionary, big-hearted, a true way of living in Christ, followed by the creation of an authentic Orthodox culture with its further spread in Asia, Western Europe and North America. A small number of Orthodox Christians will give in to syncretism which says: 'All paths lead to God.'[37]

[36] Religious teacher, Užice, February 8, 2014.

[37] Religious teacher, Užice, February 8, 2014.

As for demographic trends, the religious teachers predict the number of Orthodox Christians to decrease. There are two types of believers at risk: nominal believers of no living faith, and fanatical believers, prone to a rigid understanding of faith, closed and fundamentalist in orientation. True believers are those who know precisely what and why they believe, to which religious education contributes, as is stressed in the responses of some religious teachers:

> I expect in the future a significant reduction of the number of Orthodox Christians. So-called 'nominal Christians', who only declare as Christians, will slowly fall away, since they have no thorough rootedness in liturgical life, nor sufficient knowledge of the essentials of the faith. Believers who are alert and conscious of having faith, those who know exactly what they believe and why, will stand firm. This will be greatly influenced by religious education, with its contribution to the quality of life in Church communities. Those strong, fundamentalist, xenophobic, closed groups like sects, who interpret Orthodoxy in a rigid, apocalyptic and intolerant way towards everything that is different, will also stand firm.[38]

A critical attitude and concern about the church is found in an opinion expressed by another teacher of religious studies, who emphasizes the problem of the insufficient development of Orthodox Christianity, as well as its alienation from modern issues of life, for it leaves believers without answers to many questions. This vision of the future is related to the appeal that advocates reform and revival of the church as an institution.

> Orthodox Christianity in Serbia has been mostly reduced to a habitual practice. Unless a global rebirth takes place (from clergy to laity), I find the living Church mostly likely to be lost, and therefore Orthodox Christianity as well. The Church does not give answers to the questions of modern man, so people will be forced to seek answers elsewhere.[39]

A more comprehensive opinion of another religious teacher identifies a possible future in the reinforcement of true religion. He then points to a possible spiritual dying and falling from the faith:

> *A positive attitude*: terminological familiarization of the works of the holy Fathers of the Church (in translation) for a modern man; launching of a parish life in its true sense; through 'suffering' of a man and the clergy in life and in the world, avoiding quantity and prioritizing quality to its full essence. *A negative attitude*: fear of progressive estrangement of the clergy from the people (insufficient presence and accessibility of the shepherd-priest but also the bishop who, even when among people, does not hear the voice of the people, due to the lack of direct contact, through conversation) and further spiritual withering which will eventually lead to estrangement from the faith and clergy, or to falling from faith (atheism). *Objectively*: it is very hard, but

[38] Religious teacher, Užice, February 8, 2014.
[39] Religious teacher, Užice, 8th February 2014.

> it is the cross we should carry, for the Lord never burdens us with more than we can take...[40]

A concept of Christian mission based on early stages of Christianity indicates that there was clearly no intention to form a separate religion. Pluralism permitted Jewish Christianity to exist as one group among many without severing its links with the main body. The members continued to worship in the temple and synagogues. The situation changed after the Jewish War and the destruction of Jerusalem.[41] In the Orthodox Church today there is a tendency and possibility for many alternative groups and a need for internal mission. There are also challenges for mission outside. However, in place of mission and dialogue, there is still the dominant fear of the other.[42] The importance of Christian mission is a challenge to Orthodoxy, still waiting for a response:

> Considering the impossibility of gathering a Pan-Orthodox Council, as well as the very precedence of Orthodox churches (by this I refer to the problem of leadership between Constantinople and Moscow), Orthodox Christianity is greatly challenged. One of the challenges is a possible schism within the Orthodox Church. Since the unsolved problems within the institution of Church remain, the Orthodox Church lags behind the Catholic and Protestant Church, which are more zealous in their missions. Avoiding a dialogue with the above-mentioned churches takes us further from the unity with other churches. Islam is certainly a new challenge for Orthodox Christianity, as it spreads more and more over the world. The future of Orthodox Christianity is, therefore, not so promising unless we first settle problems within our Church and then with other churches and religions. By disregarding the message of Christ 'Go and preach', Orthodox Christianity as a church loses its mission, essence, and hence the purpose of its existence.[43]

The religious teachers perceive the future exhaustively through tasks that stand before the church as an institution, starting from co-operation with the state, through media, to internal reform:

> 1. More solid co-operation with state institutions; 2. More frequent presence of the Church in social media, television and radio programmes; 3. The Church is not to be engaged in politics, but it should hold a clear opinion on every issue; 4. False teaching and radical slogans within the Church such as 'Orthodoxy or death' must be eradicated; 5. The Church is not to be conservative and must keep up with world trends; 6. Some of the canons should be reassessed, such as the Question of virginity; 7. Enhanced co-operation on an ecumenical level, e.g. solving the question of the calendar;

---

[40] Religious teacher, Užice, 8th February 2014.

[41] David Bosch, *Transforming Mission: Paradigm Shifts in Theology of Mission* (New York: Orbis Books, 1991).

[42] Dragomir Janković, 'Dvadeset i prvi vijek: Mejnstrim i pseudopravoslavlje', in Dragoljub Đorđević, Predrag Stajić and Dragan Todorović (eds), *Hrišćanstvo u 21. Veku* (Niš, Serbia: Prometij, Leskovački kultruni centar, JUNIR, 2014), 189-98.

[43] Religious teacher, Užice, 8th February 2014.

> 8. Other differences, for which there is no solution, are not to be considered as sinful; 9. Spreading love and understanding.[44]

> Just as the Slavs had the holy brothers, Cyril and Methodius, over more than a thousand years ago, the rest of the world could benefit from such missionaries nowadays. Human alienation as well as the Apocalypse would both be postponed. In the times of slavery under the Turks, the Greek people found comfort in the idea of a new Byzantine empire. If Russia was again to become an empire, Russia would play a great role in the future of mankind. Good Russian missionaries would spread the ideas of Orthodoxy worldwide, bringing about well-being, a glimpse of Heaven.[45]

The replies of the religious teachers show clearly that religious education represents an investment in the future of both the society and the church. Their influence is recognized not only in the classroom among children, but also in the assembly hall among colleagues and within the local community. Since Orthodox Christianity is taught in other classes, from the Serbian language to fine arts, obviously the future of the church is sustainable if we pass it on as a cultural heritage to future generations.

Conclusion

We have theorized about many possible futures of Christianity and the Serbian Orthodox Church, using the model of the theology of integrity, seeing the future through the eyes of believers, laity and clergy.

The past is often seen as a guarantee of the future; mappings and reflections occur independently from a single prospective of the sequences in the course of time. In this manner, Orthodox Christianity has its history of 'carrying the cross' in terms of accepting suffering and defeating it through faith and hope.

Our respondents were students, theologians and religious teachers, who best equipped to visualize the future. Their responses and opinions display a critical attitude towards the lives of those who represent the church and towards inconsistent believers. They clearly pointed to imperfections but also to possible reforms within the church. The capacity to face the future is more likely to be found in religion than in society as a whole. Two paths point to the future: one lies in the teaching of the church, which brings the hope of salvation and eternal life, and the other one lies in communion with love among believers.

---

[44] Religious teacher, Užice, 8th February 2014.

[45] Religious teacher, Kraljevo, 22nd March 2014.

THE STORY OF THE LAUSANNE-ORTHODOX INITIATIVE: A PERSONAL PERSPECTIVE

Dănuţ Mănăstireanu

Introduction

This article presents the personal perspective of the author as a core group leader of the Lausanne-Orthodox Initiative (LOI). It outlines the history of the initiative and it describes the first three LOI consultations, and some of their outcomes, as well as the plans of the leadership group for future similar encounters. The second part of the paper discusses the opportunities and the obstacles of this Evangelical-Orthodox dialogue on mission, and it explores various prospects for the development of co-operation in holistic mission between Orthodox and Evangelical communities round the world.

Early History

Sometime in 2009, in preparation for the third Lausanne Congress, held in Cape Town in 2010, I received a message from Douglas Birdsall, the executive leader of the Lausanne Movement. I had met him as a member of the Lausanne Theology working group, led by Christopher Wright. His question – which, as it became clear later, he also addressed to other Lausanne leaders – was a simple one: could we suggest the names of a few Orthodox leaders who were engaged, one way or another, in dialogue with Evangelicals, who would be willing and able to participate as external observers at the Cape Town Congress?

Because of my commitment to Evangelical-Orthodox co-operation in my own country, Romania, I was in contact with such people and I did recommend a few, as did others. As a result, three Romanian Orthodox priests participated in this event, where they met with a few other fellow Orthodox leaders, Eastern and Oriental, and they were actively involved in the plenary sessions and the small group meetings organized during the congress.

Alongside the Orthodox group, there was also present at the congress a group of Catholic leaders, from various parts of the world. I had myself the privilege of having a Catholic bishop as a member in the small group to which I was assigned during the congress, and that was a delightful experience. Canon Dr Andrew Norman, Principal of Ridley Hall, in Cambridge, UK, was the official Lausanne host for these ecumenical observers. During the congress, he hosted a number of meals and formal meetings with guests from outside the Evangelical communion.

It is not clear whether Douglas Birdsall had considered any definite follow-up of such contacts after the Cape Town Congress, but probably not in well-defined terms. Nevertheless, he surely hoped that the seeds planted in Cape Town would bear fruit in the future.

The Cape Town Lausanne Congress

Strangely, in God's providence, it was a stressful event, which took place during the congress, that played an important role in the establishment of the LOI.

In one of the plenary sessions at the Cape Town Congress, Paul Eshleman, Vice President of Campus Crusade and head of the Strategy Commission of the Lausanne Movement, did a presentation on 'unreached people groups', which created a serious stir among a number of ecumenically minded participants. The reason for this was that, in his presentation, Paul Eshleman reported as 'unreached with the gospel' the majority of Eastern and Oriental Orthodox people groups in the diaspora. A number of us, scandalized by this anti-ecumenical offence, protested formally to the Lausanne Movement leaders. Not long after this, I personally wrote to Paul Eshleman, in order to tell him about the offence caused by this insensitive reference to our ecumenical guests. To his credit, Mr Eshleman apologized for what happened and promised to correct the errors in the document and 'to send out a revised listing of the Unreached People Groups to those who made commitments to People Groups at the Lausanne Congress'.[1]

Towards the end of the congress, one of the Oriental Orthodox leaders present there, Bishop Angaelos, from the Coptic Orthodox Church in the United Kingdom, contacted Mrs Leslie Doll and one of the senior Lausanne leaders, Mrs Grace Mathews. He suggested that the Evangelicals and the Orthodox should do something together in order to bridge the gap of misunderstanding and mistrust that separated us. This idea was in perfect harmony with the hopes of Douglas Birdsall that had prompted him to invite ecumenical observers to Cape Town. The immediate outcome of all this was the establishment of the LOI. A second result was the Lausanne-Catholic Initiative, which was unfortunately later abandoned, even before it had really taken off, mostly because of the opposition to it of some less ecumenically minded Lausanne leaders.

---

[1] Quoted from Paul Eshleman's email message to the author, dated 6th December 2010.

The LOI Leadership

Bishop Angaelos and Mrs Grace Mathews became co-chairs of this initiative, having Canon Mark Oxbrow, from Faith2Share in Oxford, UK, as the facilitator. They have subsequently called a number of like-minded Evangelical and Orthodox leaders to join them on the LOI steering committee, which was going to meet, both virtually and face-to-face, a number of times a year in order to explore together mutual understanding, respect and support. They also explored the possibility of collaboration in mission between the two ecclesial communities, with a view to organizing a larger consultation, possibly in June 2012.

The steering committee currently includes up to twenty members from various Orthodox (Eastern and Oriental), and Evangelical (mainline and low church) communities from different parts of the world. The core group of this committee, made up of up to twelve members, leads current LOI activities. There is also a group of advisors, which includes a number of experts. One of the first tasks of this initial group was to define more clearly the goal of the LOI. The LOI mission statement, as found on the LOI website, is as follows:

> The goal of the Lausanne-Orthodox Initiative is to reflect constructively on the history of relationships between Orthodox and Evangelicals in order to work towards better understanding, and encourage reconciliation and healing where wounds exist. Through this process, Evangelicals and Orthodox will be mutually enriched and strengthened in the work of mission, working towards mutual respect, support and co-operation in the spirit of our Lord's prayer for His Church in John 17.[2]

The LOI Consultations

Since its inception, in 2011, until 2015, the LOI steering committee has organized three Orthodox-Evangelical consultations, with 60-70 participants in each of them, representing the most important Orthodox and Evangelical communities in Western, Central and Eastern Europe, Middle East, Africa, Asia, and the United States. The first two consultations (in 2013 and 2014) were organized at St Vlash Orthodox Academy in Durres, Albania, at the invitation of His Beatitude Metropolitan Anastasios Yannoulatos, the head of the Orthodox Church in Albania.

The communiqué of the first LOI consultation sums up well the hopes and prospects of this initiative:

> As we move forward together, the goal of the Lausanne-Orthodox Initiative is to reflect constructively on the history of relationships between Orthodox and Evangelicals in order to work towards better understanding, and encourage reconciliation and healing where wounds exist. Through this process, Evangelicals and Orthodox will be mutually enriched and strengthened in the

[2] http://loimission.net

> work of mission, working towards mutual respect, support and co-operation in the spirit of our Lord's prayer for His Church in John 17. To achieve this goal, the Lausanne-Orthodox Initiative is committed to encouraging members of its two traditions to: pray for each other and study Scripture together; encourage mutual understanding, respect and appreciation of one another's tradition and practice; promote collaboration in mission wherever this is possible; build short-term and long-term mission partnerships; and facilitate the exchange and sharing of resources for mission.[3]

The third LOI Consultation, in September 2015, was organized at the Sofia Centre in Helsinki, Finland, at the invitation of His Eminence Archbishop Leo of Karelia and All Finland. As the final communiqué says, during this event, besides the current topics, participants were invited to reflect, from their particular perspectives, on the great challenge of the refugee crisis created by the war in Syria:

> The critical realities of contemporary mission and the need for Gospel ministry were brought home to the consultation on Wednesday afternoon when an Orthodox youth worker joined the consultation, by Skype, from Aleppo, Syria, and spoke of the tragedy which continues to unfold in his country. This was also the week during which the refugee crisis in Europe escalated, forcing governments to open borders and reconsider their humanitarian responsibilities.[4]

Two successive attempts, in 2014 and 2015, to organize such a consultation in Romania were not successful because of the strong opposition to ecumenism in some ecclesial circles, mostly Orthodox, but also Evangelical, in that country.

The LOI website has been the main vehicle for disseminating the various contributions at the three LOI consultations. One may also find there an impressive list of resources related to the interface of Orthodoxy and Evangelicalism, both in terms of theology and of mission. The website is also the means for sharing constantly relevant news and prayer requests related to the interaction of Evangelicals and Orthodox, and is open for any other relevant contributions.

The most important presentations made during the plenary sessions of the first two LOI consultations have been published in 2015 by Regnum, in Oxford, UK.[5] The book deals with important topics like the Biblical roots of mission, evangelism and Christian witness versus proselytism, 'canonical territory' and other ecclesiological implications for mission, soteriology in general and conversion in particular, scripture and tradition, etc.

---

[3] www.loimission.net/st-vlash-consultation/communique

[4] www.loimission.net/2015-loi-consultation-communique

[5] Mark Oxbrow and Tim Grass (eds), *The Mission of God: Studies in Orthodox and Evangelical Mission* (Oxford: Regnum, 2015).

Previous Evangelical-Orthodox Encounters

This was certainly not the first formal Evangelical-Orthodox encounter in history. In the last half-century, a number of theological dialogues between Evangelicals and Orthodox have been organized, in which representatives of the two ecclesial communities explored together what united and what separated them. One specific incentive for these encounters was the – somewhat surprising – synergy that the Orthodox have found with Evangelical members of the World Council of Churches (WCC), in their common attempt to counteract the liberal theological agenda of some of the Protestant members of that ecumenical organization.

These dialogues have resulted in a number of publications[6] which, undoubtedly, have contributed to a better understanding of the degree of theological compatibility between the two communities. The WCC was not the only institution that initiated such ecumenical contacts: the British Evangelical Alliance, for instance, published in 2001 the results of such a dialogue between Evangelicals and the Orthodox in the UK.[7]

In addition, in Romania, Evangelical and Orthodox theologians met in 2009 and explored their current relations, at the launch of the Romanian translation[8] of the book *Three Views on Eastern Orthodoxy and Evangelicalism*,[9] which was organized at the University of Cluj-Napoca by Fr Stelian Tofană, professor at the Orthodox faculty at that university. He was joined at this meeting by the author of this paper and by Dr Bradley Nassif, one of the key contributors to the book.

The Changing Ecumenical Landscape

It is beyond any doubt that such initiatives are beneficial for both communities. However, by themselves, they will not be able to make disappear the differences between the two communities. The realization of this fact, in recent years, has led the ecumenical movement to a process of

---

[6] Among the books published, we could mention the following: Huibert van Beek and Georges Lemopoulos (eds), *Proclaiming Christ Today: Orthodox-Evangelical Consultation, Alexandria, 10th-15th July 1995* (Geneva / Białystok, Poland: WCC Publications/ Syndesmos, 1995); Huibert van Beek and Georges Lemopoulos (eds), *Turn to God, Rejoice in Hope: Orthodox-Evangelical Consultation, Hamburg, 30th March-4th April 1998* (Geneva: WCC Publications, 1998); Tim Grass et al (eds), *Building Bridges: Between the Orthodox and the Evangelical Traditions* (Geneva: WCC Publications, 2012). To these we could add a much larger number of articles in theological and ecumenical journals.

[7] Tim Grass (ed), *Evangelicalism and the Orthodox Church: A Report by the Evangelical Alliance (UK) Commission on Unity and Truth among Evangelicals (ACUTE)* (Carlisle, UK: Paternoster, 2001).

[8] *Ortodoxie și evanghelism: Trei perspective* (Iași, Romania: Adoramus, 2009). A second edition of this translation was published by Editura Casa Cărții, Oradea, Romania, in 2015. It contains new introductions to the Romanian edition, written by Dr Stelian Tofană from an Orthodox perspective, and the author of the present paper for the Evangelicals.

[9] James Stamoolis (ed), *Three Views on Eastern Orthodoxy and Evangelicalism* (Grand Rapids, MI: Zondervan, 2004).

redefinition. As Fr Ioan Sauca, WCC Associate General Secretary for Ecumenical Formation and Education, suggested during the last LOI consultation, younger ecumenical leaders are not so interested any more in theological dialogue, because of the perceived risk of these becoming attempts to alter participants' confessional identity. They are also suspicious of efforts to bring about (institutional) ecclesial unity, because of their tendency to reduce Christian identity to the lowest common denominator, ending possibly in a compromise on the essentials. Rather, they are much more ready to engage with others in common action, leading to human flourishing, expressed in justice and reconciliation in the communities where they live. It is for similar reasons that the LOI, in the spirit of the Lausanne Movement, has adopted a focus on missions rather than on doctrinal definition.

Besides the need to redefine the aims of ecumenical efforts away from a search for theological agreement, with a move towards common action, we have to admit that classic ecumenical dialogues have resulted in insignificant co-operation between various ecclesial communities. Through his work in World Vision International, the author of the present essay has been involved constantly with church leaders and church communities in this field in the past two decades. As we have observed, at least in certain parts of the world, such as Eastern Europe and the Middle East, ecumenical relations between various Christian confessions not only did not progress, but in fact became even more problematic than in the past.

Obstacles and Opportunities

After the fall of communism, which kept most majority Orthodox countries under oppressive regimes, ecumenical relations, including those between Evangelicals and the Orthodox, improved tremendously for a few years. However, this positive evolution could not be sustained and relations between the two communities are currently worse than they were before 1989 and we can barely see any signs of hope for the future. The reasons are very diverse. On the one hand, western missionary organizations started targeting the newly opened countries which they considered 'unreached' with the gospel, if not straight 'pagan'. To be fair, western missionary agencies tended to treat in the same 'imperialistic' manner Evangelicals in these countries, which they have often completely ignored, if they could not be subordinated to their expansionist purposes.

On the other hand, Orthodox communities in these countries have witnessed a growing nostalgia for, and attempts to restore, the privileged status that their community enjoyed before communism and, implicitly, a subservient status for minority religious communities, which were often severely persecuted under regimes dominated by Orthodox hierarchies.

Besides this mostly political dynamic, we have witnessed all over Eastern Europe a resurgence of *philetism* – the idea of defining a nation's identity as a blending of denominational and ethnic compositions, expressed in convictions like, 'to be Russian (or Romanian, or Serbian, etc.) means to be Orthodox', or worse, in bellicose slogans like 'Orthodoxy or death'. This is an old heresy, which was condemned at the Orthodox Synod held in Constantinople in 1872,[10] yet it is quite alive in many Orthodox contexts today, whether in majority Orthodox countries or in the Orthodox diaspora. It is true that the decision to condemn was never fully accepted by the larger Orthodox churches. Such realities could not encourage in any way the growth of trust, let alone genuine co-operation, between the two traditions.

Indeed, as the saying goes, 'there is a lot of water under the bridge' that aims to cross the divide between various Orthodox and Evangelical communities. Many Evangelicals are proselytizing Orthodox people, which they actually consider as non-Christians and idolaters, while the Orthodox majority often uses state mechanisms to restrict and persecute Evangelicals, which they describe as sectarians, schismatics and heretics. Such realities have created huge historical barriers between these two groups, which are not easy to overcome. Yet, in both the Orthodox and the Evangelical communities there are plenty of people of goodwill, who believe that these undeniable difficulties can be progressively eliminated –

- when leaders and simple members of the two communities are ready to admit their (and their own communities') faults in creating such difficulties for Christian partnership in mission;
- when they admit to their prejudices and are ready to go beyond meetings and dialogues, to actually cross the 'bridge' over the divide, and to start working together with believers from the other community, as fellow members of the Body of Christ, pursuing the *missio Dei* in a broken world in need of faith, hope and love.

This is precisely what the LOI's efforts try to accomplish, by God's grace.

Although the LOI has been the result of a meeting of minds and hearts of some Lausanne leaders and of a number of Orthodox leaders, it does not mean that it has enjoyed the constant support of the entire leadership of the Lausanne movement, or that there is a consensus about it among the Orthodox hierarchy. Unfortunately, there are Lausanne leaders who are not so happy with such ecumenical dialogue on missions. The same is true of a number of Evangelical leaders in Eastern Europe who, strangely, given their claimed gospel commitment, cannot forget, nor forgive, the persecution to which their communities were submitted under Orthodox-dominated regimes in their countries. There may or may not be a connection but, as a matter of fact, beyond the first few months, none of the LOI-related activities and meetings have been funded by Lausanne, but by

[10] Sabrina P. Ramet, *Religion and Nationalism in Soviet and East European Politics* (Durham, NC: Duke University Press, 1989) 354-55.

other Christian agencies, like the American Bible Society (ABS),[11] and a number of private donors, both Orthodox and Evangelical. Furthermore, it has been particularly difficult to get funding for the LOI from Orthodox sources, which is not unique for such ecumenical initiatives.

At the same time, there are enough Orthodox hierarchs and centres of power (like many of the leaders of the monastic communities on Mount Athos)[12] which are firmly against any ecumenical engagement of Orthodox communities, and are, as such, as sectarian in their views as some of the Evangelical leaders. This grim reality underlines not only the particular difficulties encountered by the LOI's efforts, but also its importance for common witness to the gospel of our Saviour Jesus Christ.

The LOI promises not to shy away from such 'hard places', in both Orthodoxy and Evangelicalism. As James Stamoolis says in a document addressed to the core group of the LOI steering committee, in its meeting in January 2016, what we need in order to move forward is 'a recognition of differences among those who worship the same Triune God and understand that salvation is only in Jesus and that, in the power of the Holy Spirit, we can live lives that are fulfilling, because they are lived as God wants us to live them, and *kerygmatic*, in that Jesus is proclaimed to a lost and dying world that is 'without God, therefore without hope' (Eph. 2:12).[13]

Future Prospects

One of the hopes of the LOI leaders was that our efforts would lead to initiatives for actual collaboration in mission between Orthodox and Evangelical believers. We have to admit that, even if we have seen a few such attempts, we have not yet been very successful in this direction. When we discussed our disappointment in this area during a meeting of the core group of the LOI steering committee, we realized that, in fact, such initiatives might flow more naturally from a regionalization of LOI consultations, a direction that we decided to take during the coming years, not to the detriment of, but in parallel with (possibly less frequent), global events.

---

[11] ABS is particularly interested in this initiative in the light of its co-operation with both Orthodox and Evangelicals in majority Orthodox countries, particularly in Eastern Europe.

[12] The 'holy mountain' of Athos hosts the most important Orthodox monastic community in the world, including twenty monasteries, plus other houses and hermit cells. On this, see further in G. Giacumakis, Jr., 'Mount Athos', in J.D. Douglas (ed), *The New International Dictionary of the Christian Church* (Grand Rapids, MI: Zondervan, 1978). The Synaxis (council) of Superiors of the twenty Holy Monasteries of the Holy Mountain of Athos have often made strong statements against the ecumenical engagement of various Orthodox churches – see an example of this from 1999: http://orthodoxinfo.com/ecumenism/athonite_bartholomew.aspx

[13] James Stamoolis, 'The Challenges and Promise of the Lausanne-Orthodox Initiative', unpublished paper.

A number of such regional initiatives have already been discussed during the last two LOI consultations. One of them envisioned organising an African event in October 2016, in Ethiopia, at the invitation of the head of the Ethiopian Orthodox Church. There are also plans for organising such a consultation between Evangelical and Orthodox leaders in the United States, and possibly India. The newly established Osijek Institute for Missions Studies (OSIMS) in Croatia, might also become a centre for interactions between Evangelical and Orthodox leaders in Central and Eastern Europe.

One other important direction for the LOI process is that of organising issue-based consultations, the first one being theological education, as we can read in the communiqué of the LOI Consultation in 2015: 'Late one evening almost one third of the participants attended an "optional" session on theological education and the formation of leaders within our respective communities. The aim was to learn what is being done, and could be done, to build better relationships between our respective communities and to influence a younger generation of leaders.'[14]

We have already begun to make plans for a gathering of theological educators from the two ecclesial communities, possibly in the autumn of 2017, with a view to finding ways in which Evangelical and Orthodox theological schools and educators could work together to inculcate in the next generation of church leaders a better reciprocal understanding, and more positive and fruitful co-operation between the two traditions.

In the same vein, there have been already a number of teacher exchanges between Evangelical and Orthodox schools, as well as participation of theologians from both traditions at theological research conferences. Yet, to be fair, most invitations to such interactions have been issued by Evangelical schools and we are still waiting to see more Orthodox theological schools reciprocating.

We need to underline at this point that a critical factor for the future of this initiative is the extent to which we will be able to attract to it younger Orthodox and Evangelical believers, who are passionate about seeking justice and reconciliation in their communities, together with Christians from other church traditions.

Again, the effectiveness of the LOI process, in terms of impact, depends largely on the extent to which we use the most adequate means of communication for disseminating its concrete results. In a world in which printed media, like religious books and theological journals, on the one hand, and institutions, on the other, have a decreasing impact, it is essential that we use effectively virtual media and a networking approach for promoting better understanding and co-operation between Orthodox and Evangelical Christians. As the younger generation is more media-savvy and naturally inclined towards networking as means of interaction, we hope that

[14] www.loimission.net/2015-loi-consultation-communique

they will increasingly play a more central role in taking the LOI process to a new level.

These days, God seems to be doing something new in the area of Christian unity. As we have seen above, younger ecumenists do not see their distinct confessional identities as an obstacle, but rather as an asset, for reciprocal spiritual enrichment in interdenominational co-operation. Such common missional engagement will bless the world with a more consistent effort towards building justice and reconciliation, and will bring joy to the heart of the Father of our Lord and Saviour Jesus Christ, who prayed that we all 'might be one', as the Father and the Son are one (John 17:11).

Foundations for Mission in the Greek-Catholic Church from Romania

Anton Rus

Introduction
Evangelization and the Missionary: The Characteristics of the Christian Faith

The Christian church has been a missionary community from the very beginning. Its creator sent the apostles to propagate the gospel,[1] and the institution of the church has spread and developed over centuries, thanks to the missionary activities carried on by Christians. Paul travelled all over the known world during his many missionary journeys, in which he preached and convinced many people to change their religious beliefs. Gospel preaching is not breaking the fundamental right to religious liberty. The belief that no one can be saved without believing and without being baptized inspired great missionary initiatives 'to save the unbelieving ones' soul'. St Francis Xavier was one example of the many great missionary saints.

In the present work, we shall refer to the co-ordinates of missionary activity in the Greek-Catholic Church of Romania. The Romanian Church which united with Rome or the Greek-Catholic Church was founded in 1700, when many Romanian Orthodox people from Transylvania united with the Roman Church, whilst however keeping the eastern religious tradition. The Greek-Catholic Church is a legitimate church, *sui iuris*, free-standing, but one which is in communion with the Pontiff of Rome, being one of the Eastern Catholic Churches, which means that it belongs to the great family of the Catholic Church. So, the documents to which we refer belong to either the Romanian Greek-Catholic Church or to the magisterial documents of the Catholic Church; therefore, the sources of our study come

---

[1] After the resurrection, Christ tells the apostles: 'But you will receive power when the Holy Spirit has come upon you; and you will be my witnesses in Jerusalem, in all Judea and Samaria, and to the ends of the earth.' (Acts 1:8); and before ascension, he sends them to evangelize: 'Go therefore and make disciples of all nations, baptizing them in the name of the Father and of the Son and of the Holy Spirit, and teaching them to obey everything that I have commanded you. And remember, I am with you always, to the end of the age.' (Matt. 28:19-20); 'And he said to them, "Go into all the world and proclaim the good news to the whole creation".' (Mark 16:15); '…and that repentance and forgiveness of sins is to be proclaimed in his name to all nations, beginning from Jerusalem.' (Luke 24:47); 'If I proclaim the gospel, this gives me no ground for boasting, for an obligation is laid on me, and woe to me if I do not proclaim the gospel!' (1 Cor. 9:16).

from these respective documents. It is not our purpose to draw a hermeneutics of mission, or to present the theological basis of mission, about which there is a rich bibliography.[2] The *Catholic Church Catechism* itself, published in 1992, speaks about the church's missionary aspect,[3] and the canonical law stipulates the need for each church to take responsibility for gospel preaching all over the world.[4] Within this context, our purpose is to present the theoretical principles that guide the missionary activity and the practical actions on which the Romanian Greek-Catholic Church bases its missionary activity.

A Short History of the Greek-Catholic Church in Romania

The Greek-Catholic Church from Transylvania appeared in 1700, the year representing the Union year because a great part of the Romanian Orthodox Church from Transylvania united with the Catholic Church. In this present study, dealing with its mission, we could say that the birth of this church is the result of a certain missionary activity, in the in the sense that this unification can be construed as an expansion of the Catholic Church; also, from the point of view of the medieval and post- Tridentian theology, this can be construed as an attempt to bring back to the true church the Romanian people of Transylvania, who were Orthodox and therefore 'schismatic'. Another aspect that should be considered was the counter move to the Calvinist missionary efforts that took place in Transylvania. Since receiving Calvinism meant receiving a largely unknown foreign faith that had no saints, feasts, icons, etc., the Romanian people preferred a religion, Roman Catholicism, which was more in harmony with their soul – in fact a return to the faith of their ancestors of the first millennium, who were under the authority of the Roman bishop.[5] Thus, the Greek-Catholic Romanians, or the 'united', do not consider themselves to be the result of Roman-Catholic missionary work, but that they have consciously assumed the process of union with Rome in the restoration of the church's unity, modelled on the Council of Florence. After the union, the Greek-Catholics

---

[2] H. de Lubac, *Le fondement théologique des missions* (Paris, 1946); Y. Congar, *Un peuple messianique* (Paris: Cerf, 1975); A. Shorter, *Theology of Mission* (Cork, Irish Republic: 1972); L. Rütti, *Zur Theologie der Mission: Kritische Analysen und neue Orienterungen* (München: Kaiser Grünewald, 1972); G. Colzani, *La missionarietà della chiesa* (Bologna, Italy: 1975); S. Dianich, 'Missione', in Giuseppe Barbaglio and Severino Dianich (eds), *Nuovo Dozionario di Teologia* (Milan, Italy: Ed. San Paolo, 1994), 927-40.

[3] *Catechism of the Catholic Church* (Citta del Vaticano: Libreria Editrice Vaticana, 1993), 839-56.

[4] *Codex Canonum Ecclesiarum Orientalium (Code of Canons of Eastern Churches),* Title XIV, *About the Evangelism of the Nations,* can. 584-94, trans. Iuliu Muntean (Cluj-Napoca, Romania: Cluj University Press, 2001), 321-25.

[5] Augustin Bunea, *Încercare de istoria Românilor până la 1832* (Bucureşti: Ed. Academiei Române, 1912); Zenovie Pâclişanu, *Istoria Bisericii Române Unite* (Târgu-Lăpuş, Romania: Ed. Galaxia Gutenberg, 2006); Octavian Bârlea, *Unirea Românilor (1697-1701)* (Munich, Germany: Ed. Misiunii unite româneşti din RFG, 1990).

began missionary activity themselves in order to persuade their Romanian Orthodox brethren to join the Catholic Church – using its bishops and written catechisms.

Later, the Greek-Catholic Church from Transylvania became involved in supporting missionary activity, using classical means. First of all, it kept alive in its Christians the consciousness of the church's missionary responsibility. It did this through celebrating World Mission Day, officially initiated in 1926 by Pope Pius XI at the demand of the Pontifical Mission Societies, to be celebrated throughout the Catholic world on the penultimate Sunday of October (in honour of St Therese of the Child Jesus, St Francis Xavier and the patron saints of mission).

On the 19th January 1935, at the proposal of the episcopate of the Greek-Catholic Church of Romania, the Congregation for the Oriental Churches appointed the Rev. Dr Brînzeu, canon in Lugoj, as president of the Pontifical Society for Faith Propagation in Romania. Bucharest was chosen as the headquarters of this society.[6] In 1946, Dr I. Bălan, the bishop of Lugoj, named all the vicars-parochial as principals of the Pontifical Society for Faith Propagation. In October 1946, the Members' Register of the Pontifical Society was introduced in each parish. Following Pope Pius XI's urge, which stated that 'all Catholics must be members of this society', Bishop John mentions here that all Catholic Christians from 12 years old could become members of this Society. After the liturgy, in accordance with this missionary intention, one of the following devotions was to be officiated: the Adoration Hour, the Eucharistic Blessing, Paraklesis and the Rosary. At the end of the liturgy and the devotions, this prayer is to be uttered:

> O God, who wishes all people to be saved and to find the real truth, please send workers to your harvest. Grant them to make your word known with boldness, that your gospel may be spread and all people receive the light, to know you as the only true God, you and the One you sent, Jesus Christ, your Son and our God, for ever and ever. Amen.[7]

A different method of supporting mission was the collection of funds. The Greek-Catholic Diocese of Lugoj, at a conference on 12th September 1935, sent a communication to all the parishes that, on the penultimate Sunday of October each year, Mission Day, a collection would be undertaken to support mission, the proceeds to be sent by 31st October to the cashier of the Romanian National Council of Missions.[8] In each parish it was asked that a missionary committee be initiated, and that the significance of the Mission Day is explained in sermons delivered in the week before its celebration; it urged the members of the missionary

---

[6] 'Opera pentru Propagarea Credinţii în România', in *Cuvântul Adevărului* 4-5 (April-May 1935), 216; *Cuvântul Adevărului* 6 (June 1935), 268.
[7] 'Idei practice pentru ziua misionară', in *Sionul Românesc,* 19 (1946), 43-44; *Sionul Românesc,* 21-22 (1947), 50.
[8] 'Ziua misionară', in *Sionul Românesc,* 16-17 (1935), 60.

committee to gather lists from the parish over the whole week, in order to collect subscriptions for the missionary collection. *Catholic Action* (AGRU) and the members of the women's reunion would be asked to help. There would be separate collections too in schools, from the pupils. Thus, all efforts would be made to ensure success. The spiritual aspect would not be omitted, urging Christians to confess and share their Christ on Mission Day, thus receiving indulgence.[9] After Mission Day in 1935, at the beginning of the following year, a meeting of the National Council of the Pontifical Society for Faith Promotion took place in Bucharest. An account was given of its first year of activities, observing that the Society ended its first year of activity with an excellent result for the Mission Day collection, the money being gathered from Blaj, Cluj, Oradea, Lugoj and Maramureş. The secretary of the Supreme Council of the Vatican expressed much satisfaction about this result.[10]

On 27th-29th April 1937, the Conference of the Superior Council of the Pontifical Society for Promoting the Faith took place in Rome. Romania participated also with the priest N. Brânzeu, the national chairman of the Society. Romania was placed in the first class, because it produced good results. The leadership of the Society in Rome thanked Romania and Canon Dr N. Brânzeu for the collections done in 1937-1938.[11] It can be seen that for some time the Romanian Greek-Catholic Church had become an active member of the Universal Catholic Church, experiencing not only its successes, but also its hardships and suffering. In 1936, it was said that the Greek-Catholic Church of Romania had been considered at Rome as a church that could not help itself, but that it had often needed Pontifical help, gathered from the Catholic Christians' mercy – especially those of the Latin rite – all over the world. Receiving this support was not considered to be humiliating, as the Popes used to help even western nations on certain occasions. But the fact that Greek-Catholic Romanian people received without giving was considered degrading – and this gave an unfavourable impression, especially because the Catholic Church had greater shortages in other places than Romania: the papal Rome, loving the Romanian people, overwhelmed it with kindness without noticing what the Romanian people gave. But recently the situation has changed – it is said that, in 1936, the Greek-Catholic Church from Romania expressed itself increasingly more worthy, and the Romanians gifts for the missionary purposes of the Universal Church were increasing.

Another method of involvement in mission by the Romanian Greek-Catholic Church was through the missionary press. The first periodical which the Romanian Greek-Catholic Church dedicated to foreign missions was the magazine *Misionarul*, the organ of the Pontifical Society for the

[9] N. Brînzeu, 'Dumineca misionară', in *Cuvântul Adevărului,* 10-11 (Oct-Nov 1936), 417.

[10] 'Opera Pontificală pentru Propagarea Credinţei', in *Cuvântul Adevărului,* 5 (May 1936), 217.

[11] 'Acta cooperationis Missionariae Sanctae Sedis on 28th Feb 1939', in *Unirea,* 25 (1939), 2.

Propagation of Faith in Romania, under the leadership of the president of this Society, Canon Dr N. Brânzeu, and the Franciscan monk I. Bălan, the editor. It has appeared quarterly, at Lugoj, since 1936. The first edition contains the statutes and regulations of the Pontifical Society, offering explanations and giving missionary news, in Latin and Romanian, from all over the Catholic world; it also contains an account of the collection taken in the country for the Society. This magazine has appeared as a result of the fact that a countrywide society needs a proper authority to develop in believers an understanding of membership of the great Catholic family. In order to support missionary enthusiasm, the Franciscan monk Pr I. M. Gârleanu printed a small magazine for children entitled *Micul Misionar* which appeared monthly at Oradea between 1937 and 1940, under the care of Diocesan Committee for Missions.

At the fifty-year jubilee since St Theresa de Lisieux's death (1947), a Franciscan collaborator group, led by Pr Iuliu Hirțea, the confessor of the Academy of Theology in Oradea, published the book *După cincizeci de ani: Patroana Misiunilor sărbătorită pe plaiurile românești*, a book which takes into account also the date of 19th October 1947, Mission Day. The book conveys circulars to the Greek-Catholic Church bishops on the Jubilee and Mission Day, the letter of St Pope Pius XII to the Bishop of Lisieux, a conference of Pr Dr Iuliu Hirțea about 'Missions and St Theresa', other materials and a chronicle about the Therezian Jubilee's celebration in Romania.

We also record different texts of the bishops, which advised priests and believers to promote missions,[12] articles by different authors about the missionaries' sacrifice,[13] or common meditations on Mission Day in the 1940s.[14] There were also believers or priests who left their inheritance to external missions.[15]

In 1948, the Romanian Greek-Catholic Church was declared illegal by the communist regime which had come to power, and so it entered a tough period of persecution.[16] Some Orthodox clergy considered that the destruction of the Greek-Catholic Church is a just course of action, against

---

[12] Episcop Alexandru, 'Misiunile', in *Sionul Românesc,* 19-21 (1928), 74-76; PS Dr Ioan Bălan, 'Missionary Day 1945', in *Sionul Românesc,* 19 (1945), 47-49.

[13] Dumitru Neda, 'Pământul multor lacrimi – Jertfe misionare în țara Negusului [Abisinia sau Etiopia]', in *Calendarul de la Blaj* (1936), 76-84.

[14] Pr Vasile Lupu, 'Meditații pentru opera misionară', in *Unirea,* 39 (1942), 2-8; 'Misionarism extern', in *Cultura Creștină,* 7-9 (July-Sept 1942), 525; Ioan Vesa, 'De ziua misionară', in *Cultura Creștină,* 10-12 (Oct-Dec 1942), 688-89.

[15] 'Victor Cinca', in *Cuvântul Adevărului,* 8-9-10 (Aug-Oct 1940), 397.

[16] The Association of Romanian Catholics of America, *Ten Years Ago: The Story of the Persecution of the Catholic Church of Byzantine Rite in Romania,* (Youngstown, OH, 1958); Anton Moisin, *Istoria marii prigoane contra Bisericii Române Unite cu Roma, Greco-Catolice, între anii 1948-1998* (Vol. I, Sibiu, 1998); Gabriel Catalan, 'Prigoana anticatolică în România între 1949-1953: Arestări și procese ale unor clerici și credincioși', in Romulus Rusan (ed), *Anii 1949-1953: Mecanismele terorii* (București, Fundația Academia Civică, 1999), 124.

'Catholic missionary proselytism',[17] while the communists also considered it as opposition to 'capitalistic papal imperialism'[18]. After 1948, the Romanian Greek-Catholic Church lived on only in secret, in catacombs, and could not develop its outside missionary activity. But the church's resistance and the continuation of under-cover pastoral activities during the atheist regime, could be regarded as an expression of authentic mission. Greek-Catholic bishops were arrested, some of them even died in communist prisons, while others were placed under house arrest. Their martyrdom was a sign of their fidelity to the church's mission.[19] Greek-Catholic priests continued to administer baptisms, weddings, confessions and to give Communion to believers 'illegally', celebrating the Holy Eucharist in clandestine makeshift chapels in private homes, in order to maintain its missionary activity.[20] During the communist regime, Romania was a true land of mission. In December 1989, after the fall of the communist regime in Bucharest, the Greek-Catholic Church was rehabilitated, but its restoration is taking time – with churches having to be rebuilt; from those lost to the Orthodox Church in 1948 only a few were recovered – and having to develop mission further internally to recover or provide spiritual assistance to its believers, and externally in diaspora, to develop new communities there where Greek-Catholic believers travelled to work on business.

So, as we observed, the Romanian bishops, the priests and the Greek-Catholic believers were successfully involved in missionary activity in the inter-war period, celebrating Mission Day, organizing collections for missions, and in publishing different books and missionary magazines.

Missionary Principles as described by the Magisterial Documents that Guided Missionary Activity in the Greek-Catholic Church in Romania

The guidance principles of the missionary activity of the Greek-Catholic Church in Romania, are aligned to those of the common tradition of the Catholic Church that can be verified in a series of pontifical documents

---

[17] Al. Rădulescu and C. Sădeanu, *Reîntregirea Bisericii româneşti din Ardeal* (Bucureşti, 1948), 3-5.

[18] A. Bratu and I. Manea, 'Vaticanul, agenţia imperialismului american', in *Scânteia* (23rd July 1948).

[19] Anton Moisin, *Cei şapte episcopi greco-catolici români care au pierit în prigoana comunistă* (Cluj-Napoca, Romania: Ed. Viaţa Creştină, 2010). It is the ongoing process of beatification of the seven bishops who died as martyrs under the Communism between 1950 and 1970: Valeriu Traian Frenţiu; Iuliu Hossu; Alexandru Rusu, Ioan Bălan, Ioan Suciu, Vasile Aftenie and Tit Liviu Chinezu.

[20] Anton Rus, Aura Gherman, *Catacombe şi Lumini: Viaţa şi activitatea Pr Ioan Roşca în timpul persecuţiei Bisericii Greco-Catolice* (Blaj, Romania: Ed. Buna Vestire, 2003).

released at the highest level.[21] Presenting these texts, we present in fact the history of the Greek-Catholic Church in Romania regarding mission.

Chronologically, the two documents refer to Mission of the Second Council of the Vatican. The first is *Nostra aetate* (28th October 1965).[22] The Declaration is about church relations with non-Christian religions. The Declaration begins with a description of the common origin of all people, and stating the belief that all return to the same God. The external questions people asks of themselves, even from the beginning, and the way in which different religions, such as Hinduism and Buddhism, tried to answer them, all these we can find in the introduction. The wish of the Catholic Church is to accept some of the truth from other religions, but only if this reflects Catholic doctrine and they lead a human's soul to Christ. It shows what the Islamic and Jewish religions have in common with Christianity and Catholicism, such as veneration of a single and unique God, the creator of heaven and earth, who is all-powerful and merciful. As all people are created in the image of God, discrimination against any person or group because of their colour, their origin or their religion, etc. is against the doctrine of the church.[23]

The second important document of the present study is *Ad Gentes* (7th December 1965).[24] The Decree of II Vatican Council on church missionary activity, according to which the purpose of the mission is to prolong in time and space the mission of Christ (no. 3). We present the main guidelines of this document because they are extremely important in determining the boundaries of mission: the church is the universal sacrament of salvation (no. 1), the church is by nature a missionary church (no. 2); the whole nation of God is summoned to mission (no. 36); the relationship between God and the world, between the church and culture, is one of dialogue and co-operation (no. 10).

Finally we come to what is nowadays the most important document on mission within the Catholic tradition. It is about the *Redemptoris missio* (7th December 1990),[25] the Encyclical Letter of Pope John Paul II about the permanent validity of the church's missionary mandate. The document is a real missionary *summa*. The Encyclical approaches the theme of the urgency and actuality of the church's missionary activity in the contemporary world. The first problem dealt with by the Encyclical is that

---

[21] Claudia Carlen, *The Papal Encyclicals: 1740-1981* (five vols.), (Raleigh, NC: The Pierian Press, 1990). The volumes present 280 encyclicals in English from Benedict XIV to John Paul II: www.papalencyclicals.net

[22] www.vatican.va/archive/hist_councils/ii_vatican_council/documents/vat-ii_decl_19651028_nostra-aetate_en.html

[23] Augustin Cardinal Bea, 'The Church and the non-Christian Religions', in *The Way to Unity after the Council* (London: G. Chapman, 1967).

[24] www.vatican.va/archive/hist_councils/ii_vatican_council/documents/vat-ii_decree_19651207_ad-gentes_en.html

[25] http://w2.vatican.va/content/john-paul-ii/en/encyclicals/documents/hf_jp-ii_enc_07121990_redemptoris-missio.html

of terminology, asking if it is proper to use the expression *missio ad gentes* or whether this phrase should be replaced with the expression 'inter-religious dialogue' or the term 'evangelism' (no. 4). The text asks the question: 'Does respect for consciousness and liberty expel any intention of conversion?' The Encyclical's answer pleads for the legitimacy of the specific missionary activity that takes place between non-Christians and which aims at their conversion to Christ, and the organization of an indigenous church. Observing that the missionary enthusiasm of the church for non-Christians has weakened, the Pope assures non-Christians and the authorities from countries to which missionary activity is directed, that mission has only one purpose: to serve the individual by revealing God's love expressed in Jesus Christ (no. 2). The whole of Chapter I is dedicated to the theological and Christological basis of mission: 'Jesus Christ – the unique saviour'. The church always teaches that in the work of Christ's redemption lies everybody's salvation. The Bible texts that refer to these documents are Acts 4:12 and 1 Timothy 2:5-7. The Holy Spirit himself, working through *semina Verbi* (seeds of the Word) in other cultures and religions, prepares them to reach maturity in Christ (no. 28). The document acknowledges the possibility of salvation in non-Christian religions for all those who have not yet received the gospel of Christ through no fault of their own, but that this salvation could be won only by Christ's mediation, and that this was not parallel or additional to salvation through Christ (no. 5).

Chapter II, the Encyclical deals with the theme of God's Kingdom, which is inseparable from Christ. The church has no purpose in itself except to serve the Kingdom. The church is the common or ordinary means of salvation (nos. 9, 18, 55). Chapter III is dedicated to *the Holy Spirit, as the instigator of mission*. The Spirit is the one that, beginning at Whitsun, inspires the church and propagates it to the ends of the earth, beyond any geographic, ethnic or religious barrier (no. 25). Chapter IV is about the *horizons of mission*: the Encyclical Letter ascertains the complexity of the missionary situation – expressed by the facts of urbanization, mass migration, the waves of refugees, the de-Christianization of certain countries with an ancient Christian tradition, and the increasing influence of the gospel in countries with a great majority of non-Christians. Mission is addressed to people and groups who do not believe in Christ, who are far from Christ, among whom the church has not sunk its roots, whose culture has not yet been influenced by the gospel (no. 34). The *difficulties* seem insurmountable and could easily lead to discouragement if it were a merely human enterprise. In certain countries, missionaries are refused entry. In others, not only is evangelization forbidden but conversion as well, and even Christian worship. Elsewhere, the obstacles are of a cultural nature: passing on the gospel message seems irrelevant or incomprehensible, and conversion is seen as a rejection of one's own people and culture (no. 35). There are also internal difficulties – like the lack of interest and hope, the decrease of vocation, religions relativism – and even disunity between Christians (nos. 36, 50). The church respects the individual's liberty. The church proposes; it imposes nothing. It respects all people and cultures and recognises one's conscience (no. 39). Chapter V discusses 'The Paths of Mission'. The first form of evangelization is witness. Next follows proclamation. Proclamation is the unchanging priority of mission. The sole topic of the gospel, is Christ crucified, dead and risen. Propagating this gospel is not a strictly personal activity, the missionary being sent by the church (no. 45), while the missionary sometimes gives up his life for Christ's name as a martyr. Apart from other forms of mission, also to be flagged up is involvement in the world of communication (no. 37), working for peace, for the development and liberation of nations, for people's and nations' rights, for the promotion of women's and children's rights, for the protection of the created world, for scientific research, international relationships (no. 37), and also providing a response to a generation in search of significance, characterised by a return to religion (no. 38).

All mission is based on the non-negotiable principle of charity, the source and criterion of mission. Among the purposes of mission, the first is that of personal and individual conversion to Christ, while only the second is that of founding a local church, which in turn has to become a missionary one (nos. 46, 48-49). Conversion that takes place deep in the heart is evident in receiving the sacraments, the first of which is Baptism, the entrance door into the church (no. 47). 'The Ecclesial Basic Communities', meaning Christian groups which, in families or in small groups, meet for prayer, for reading the scriptures and for catechesis, are as a force for evangelization (no. 51). The church has to impress the gospel on popular culture, through inculturation, but without compromising the integrity of the Christian faith (no. 53). Such communities could express their Christian experience in original forms, according to their own cultural traditions, but they should be in harmony with the impartial requirements of the faith (no. 53). Inter-religious dialogue (55-57) may co-exist with mission. Even if the church acknowledges what is true and sacred in non-Christian religious traditions, this fact does not reduce the obligation to propagate Jesus Christ. Among the motivations and bases of mission, the first is the missionary mandate of Christ, applicable to all believers (62). The church is missionary because it was founded by Christ in order to bring salvation to all people. Another argument which the encyclical letter added is the right that all nations have to hear the Saviour's message: everyone has the right to hear God's good news as found in Jesus Christ (46).

Chapter VI talks about leaders and workers in the missionary apostolate, starting from 'Peter and the other Apostles' (Acts 2:14, 37). Those primarily responsible for missionary activity are the college of bishops, headed by the successor of Peter (no. 63). Then follow the *Missionaries* (no. 65). This requires careful reflection, especially on the part of the missionaries themselves, who may be led, as a result of changes occurring within the mission field, to no longer understand the meaning of their vocation or to know exactly what the church expects of them today. The following words of II Vatican Council are a point of reference: 'Although the task of spreading the faith falls, to the best of one's ability, to each disciple of Christ, the Lord always calls from the number of his disciples those whom he wishes, so that they might be with him and that he might send them to preach to the nations. Accordingly, through the Holy Spirit, who distributes his gifts as he wishes for the good of all, Christ stirs up a missionary vocation in the hearts of individuals, and at the same time raises up in the church those institutes which undertake the duty of evangelization, which is the responsibility of the whole church, as their special task' (*Ad Gentes,* Chapter IV, 23-27). It is about a special vocation of those who have a natural inclination, the appropriate skills and temperament, and are ready to take courageously the responsibility of their complete engagement in mission duty, far away from their homes and mother country, possibly even suffering persecution. Diocesan Priests (67) must be filled with a sense of missionary zeal and to be willing to serve for a while in mission territories, along with monks and nuns from the Institutes of Consecrated Life, and even missionary religious sisters, in self-giving love, in the total and undivided manner of the church's missionary calling (65-70). All the laymen have an important part to play in the mission activity. Based on their baptismal promises, they have the obligation and right to work individually or in association with others, in the world of social, political or economical areas in lay missionary associations, international Christian volunteer organizations, ecclesial movements, groups or in different kinds of fellowship. So does that army of *catechists*, both men and women, worthy of praise, to whom missionary work among the nations already owes so much. Imbued with the apostolic spirit, they make a singular and absolutely vital contribution to the spread of the faith and of the church by their strenuous efforts (no. 73). Besides catechists, mention must also be made of other ways of serving the church and her mission; namely, other church personnel: leaders of prayer, song and liturgy; leaders of basic ecclesial communities and Bible study groups; those in charge of charitable work; administrators of church resources; leaders in the various forms of the apostolate; teachers of religion in schools. All members of the laity ought to devote a part of their time to the church, living out their faith authentically (no. 74).

Besides human resources, there are also other structures for missionary activity. The first is *The Congregation for the Evangelization of Peoples* in Rome. It falls to the congregation responsible for missionary activity to direct and co-ordinate throughout the world the work of evangelism and of missionary co-operation. Hence, its task is to recruit missionaries and distribute them in accordance with the more urgent needs of various regions, draw up an ordered plan of action, issue norms and directives, as well as principles which are appropriate for the work of evangelization, and assist in the initial stages of their work (no. 75). An important role is played by the four pontifical missionary societies: the Pontifical Society for the Propagation of the Faith (PSPF), the Pontifical Society of Saint Peter the Apostle (PSSPA), the Pontifical Society of Missionary Childhood (MCA), and the Pontifical Missionary Union (PMU). Episcopal conferences and their various groupings have great importance in directing and co-ordinating missionary activity at national and regional levels (no. 76).

In Chapter VII, entitled 'Co-operation in Missionary Activity', certain co-operative forms of mission, such as prayer and sacrifice for missionaries (78), are specified, promoting missionary vocation in the parishes and in families, and creating favourable conditions for encouraging vocations amongst the young (79-80), supporting the material needs of the mission by collecting aid (chapels, schools, seminars, dwellings) and charity, through education and propagation, especially on World Mission Day – the last Sunday of October each year (no. 81). Among new forms of missionary co-operation, due to increased mobility, should be mentioned the following: international tourism, knowledge of the missionary life and of new Christian communities, visiting missions, the good example and evidence that Christian workers give when they work for a period of time in countries where Christianity is unknown, forbidden or persecuted, showing hospitality and Christian love to the disciples of a non-Christian religion or to refugees from non-Christian countries settled in a traditionally Christian country (82), missionary promotion and formation among the people of God, spreading information through missionary publications and audio-visual aids, the study of missiology in theological education, etc.

Chapter VIII presents 'Missionary Spirituality' and expresses living in perfect union with the Holy Spirit and Jesus Christ. The missionary must love the church and humanity as Jesus did. The missionary is urged on by a 'zeal for souls', a zeal inspired by Christ's own love, which takes the form of concern, tenderness, compassion, openness, availability and interest in people's problems. The true missionary is the saint. A missionary is really such only if he commits himself to the way of holiness. The church's missionary spirituality is a journey towards holiness. The missionary is a person living the Beatitudes. Before sending out the Twelve to evangelize, Jesus, in his 'missionary discourse' (cf. Matt. 10), teaches them the path of mission: poverty, meekness, acceptance of suffering and persecution, the desire for justice and peace, and charity – in other words, the Beatitudes, lived out in the apostolic life (cf. Matt. 5:1-12). By living the Beatitudes, the missionary experiences and shows through his way of life that the Kingdom of God has already come, and that he has accepted it. The characteristic of every authentic missionary life is the inner joy that comes from faith. In a world tormented and oppressed by so many problems, a world tempted to pessimism, the one who proclaims the good news must be a person who has found true hope in Christ (no. 91). In the end, entrusting the church to the mediation of Mary, the mother of Jesus, the Holy Father urges: 'Dear brothers and sisters: let us remember the missionary enthusiasm of the first Christian communities. Despite the limited means of travel and communication of those times, the proclamation of the gospel quickly reached the ends of the earth. And this was the religion of a man who had died on a cross, 'a stumbling block to Jews and folly to Gentiles'! (1 Cor. 1:23). Underlying this missionary dynamism was the holiness of the first Christians and that of the first Christian communities (no. 90). Summarizing, the last chapter approaches the theme of communion with Christ, which is the essentially specific note of missionary spirituality. This can be seen in love for a close one, in love for the church, and in the holiness of the missionary life.

As shown by this incursion, the texts or missionary interventions offer rich teaching about the fundamental aspects of mission, as perceived and assumed by the Greek-Catholic Church in Romania.

Mission Prospects for the Greek-Catholic Church in Romania

If, before 1948, the Greek-Catholic Church in Romania acceded enthusiastically to the different missionary initiatives (the celebration of World Mission Day, Christians applying for the pontifical missionary societies and priests for the Pontifical Missionary Association of Clergy, the publication of missionary magazines, collections for missions, etc.), as matters stand – in the words of the second sub-title of the present study – after coming out of the catacombs (1989), the church focused on its self-recovery, whilst not forgetting its missionary consciousness. Institutional and spiritual renovation itself called for missionary activity, of re-evangelization, to recover the meaning of the sacred, to gather its own believers into the newest 'legal' church structures. In spite of the present deficiencies of the missionary field (a certain reduction of the missionary spirit – while there is no document of the Romanian Greek-Catholic Episcopacy or of the Romanian Greek-Catholic Synod dedicated to mission, nor symposium or teaching or discussion about mission at a national level, while at the Greek-Catholic theological university there appeared not even a missionary vocation, but inter-religious lectures,[26] etc.), the church is capable of getting out of itself and being involved in building the Kingdom of heaven outside its territories too.[27] So after the 1990s, at the theological faculty from the episcopal centres (Blaj, Oradea, Cluj, Lugoj, Baia Mare), World Mission Day was celebrated on the penultimate Sunday

[26] The Theological Faculty in Blaj organized the lecture series, 'The Healing of Memories', in co-operation with the Reconciliatio Foundation, and involved in inter-religious mutual projects, in which Christians, Muslims and Jews took part. See Patricia Dobríková, Walter Gebhardt, Grzegorz Giemza, Vasile Grajdian and Adrian Kacian, *Trauerbegleitung in unterschiedlichen kulturellen, sozialen un religiösen Kontexten* (Dziegielów: Ed. Warto, Polonia, 2015).

[27] Ciprian Ghişa, 'The Greek-Catholic Church in Romania Facing the Challenges of the Post-Modern Society', in *Journal for the Study of Religions and Ideologies*, 38.13 (2014), 3-28.

of October every year.[28] The laity associations, together with their responsible priests, set the programme which consists of reading the Pope's Message, prayer for mission and missionaries, presenting lectures and conferences about missions, and about great Christian missionary figures (St Francis Xavier, St Therese of the Child Jesus, etc.), and on other missionary themes. Another missionary activity at episcopal level was the assignment of a person responsible for mission at that level. Every year on Mission Day, collections are organized for missions.[29] Officials have been sent to conferences organized at a national level by the Roman Catholic Church. In the religious diocesan press of the church or in other periodicals,[30] articles about mission have been published. In 2006, the Synodal Ecumenical Missionary Committee of the Greek-Catholic Church was founded; its objectives are to write documents and to co-ordinate activities regarding the missionary and ecumenical aspects of the church, under the co-ordination of the Alexandru Mesian, Bishop of Lugoj. The important aspect is that the Greek-Catholic Church in Romania has a Romanian Greek-Catholic missionary in Uganda, Pr Cristin Maria Marincean[31] who was visited by the Romanian Greek-Catholic Bishop Alexandru Mesian 3rd-11th December 2008, this visit being a first for a Romanian Greek-Catholic bishop to this African country, and having a missionary purpose.[32] Besides these initiatives, the church proposes to enlarge its interest in mission, applying other recommended actions, some of which we specify. For example, some missionary diocesan centres should be created in the dioceses (institute, office, bureau, department), which should give an impetus to missionary activity in the dioceses and belong to a missionary centre at church level. The Missionary Centre, which will be a central pastoral institution of the church synod, will have the task of promoting and co-ordinating the different missionary activities, and co-ordinating all the existing missionary influences in the diocese, including Caritas (the charity agency of the Roman Catholic Church), with the centre for processing migrants, to share with everybody different initiatives and church missionary information, to look for ways and means of expressing the missionary task of the church, to prepare each year

---

[28] www.bru.ro/blaj/ziua-mondiala-a-misiunilor-2007-la-blaj

[29] Pr Ioan Fărcaş, *Liturgical Agenda 2015* (Blaj, Romania, PH. Buna Vestire, 2014), 19. Printed with the blessing of his Beatitude Cardinal Lucian, Archbishop and Metropolitan of Alba Iulia and Făgăraş – Blaj, Major Archbishop of the Romanian Church United with Rome the Greek-Catholic PH.

[30] Cf. William Victor Alexandru Bleiziffer, 'Missio Dei – fundamentul misionar al Bisericii', in *Cultura Creştină,* 1 (2001), 199-209; Anton Rus, 'Misiunile externe ale Bisericii', in *Discobolul,* 49-50-51 (January-March 2002), 99-104.

[31] Pr Cristin, born in Zalău, is the first Romanian Greek-Catholic missionary in Africa, where he has been since 2001. He attended theological studies in Rome where he was received in the Congregation 'Servi di Maria'. In 2005, he was ordained priest by the PS Bishop Alexandru Mesian in Lugoj. Pr Cristin continues as a monks' trainer in Uganda, at Jinja, but he is also a vicar in Bugeagali.

[32] www.bru.ro/lugoj/vizita-in-uganda-a-ps-episcop-alexandru-mesian-de-lugoj

material to animate missionary life in the parishes, to organize testimonies of the lay missionaries or acknowledged people in the parochial communities, to support the organization of missionary events, to elaborate and distribute grants, meaning a base document which contains also the Message of the Holy Father for Mission Day, to be sent to parishes together with the diocesan bulletin. Parochial missionary groups or prayer groups for mission have also been established to keep alive missionary awareness and to develop different initiatives, promoting missionary vocations, organizing young missionary groups in parishes, subscriptions to different missionary magazines, organizing the collecting of funds, missionary exhibitions, fraternities between parishes from the country and the parishes from missionary areas, adopting missionaries at a distance, or of a seminarian from the theological seminars in mission countries (it could be a personal, group or parochial initiative). On Mission Day we felt we could promote an initiative called 'A Gift for Mission' which gives the opportunity to parishes, to Christians and to different associations to donate sacred and ornate liturgical objects, sanitary material, etc. for churches in missionary areas, this being a simple way of creating awareness of shared responsibility for mission; donations would be sent, through the diocesan missionary centre, to the Apostolic Society in Rome, which would distribute them to missionaries throughout the world.

We hope that our study achieved its purpose, to present the missionary involvement of the Greek Catholic Church from Romania. Research results lead to the fact that this East European Church has acknowledged its missionary responsibilities, and received the documents regarding the missionary commitment of the Catholic Church and its engagement in missionary activity. Our recommendation is to try new paths in ecumenical dialog, and maintain international relationships with other churches and related religious communities.

To sum up, although the Greek-Catholic Church from Romania has had a troubled history, which had to rise to the difficult challenges it has passed through, it did not forget its missionary calling, and in the future it will propagate a missionary consciousness and to promote different initiatives as an expression of its ecclesiological maturity.

MISSION IN POLAND: A ROMAN CATHOLIC PERSPECTIVE

Jan Górski

Introduction

The church in every time and place does its best to realize the great missionary mandate of Jesus. It belongs to its nature.[1] It proves its viability. The realization of the missionary mandate is determined in the context of historical, geographical, cultural, religious and other elements, such as transport, weather, economy. In all these activities God is visible, he who wants to lead to salvation every human being. He uses in this vision the work of man. We are at the same time witnessing and participating in God's plan for the salvation of the world.

As we are talking about 'mission in a Roman Catholic perspective', it is obligatory to analyze documents such as the II Vatican Council Decree *Ad Gentes*, and its definition of mission.[2] Another is the Encyclical of John Paul II, *Redemptoris Missio*, with its new dimension of mission.[3] Finally, an analysis of the context of mission – Poland, with its tradition, history and its actual situation.

Poland adopted Christianity at the end of the first millennium. After that, the country initially targeted for mission has increasingly become itself a missionary country. This reflects the inclusion of the church in this area in the trend of fast, active participation in mission. The Synod of Łęczyca (1285) stated that the mission in Poland had been completed and had already taken the church into other areas.[4]

Subsequent to the Christianisation of Poland, the country came under the jurisdiction of the Bishop of Rome, although the eastern territories were evangelized by the centres of Eastern Christianity (Byzantium, Kiev). The frequent change of borders and the wars limit the analysis and evaluation of the history of the church in Poland. However, knowledge of this past generally helps to better asses the current situation of Christianity in the country and its missionary commitment. The events that shaped the life of the church in Europe have also impacted Poland. The numerous wars and

---

[1] II Vatican Council, *Decree on the Mission Activity of the Church* (AG), 1965, 2.
[2] AG 6.
[3] John Paul II, *Redemptoris Missio* (RM), 1990, 33.
[4] B. Kominek, *Polski Synod* (Katowice, Poland: Księgarnia i Drukarnia Katolicka S.A. Katowice, 1939), 10; W. Góralski, 'Synody w historii Kościoła w Polsce', in *Studia Płockie* 27 (1999), 151.

the search for new trade-routes became opportunities for establishing contacts with other cultures and religions. The presence of the Jews, Tatars, Karaites and, later, the Christian religion is evidence of the mosaic, in which the Catholic Church took part.

Missionaries – Poles worked often as members of orders in international groups, as in other nations.[5]

The great impetus for the development of the missionary cause was brought to our country by our fellow countryman, Pope John Paul II (1920-2005).[6]

The purpose of this article is to attempt to show the current conditions of the mission of the Catholic Church in Poland, taking into account the historical and cultural context of the country.

The History of Christianity in Poland

The history of Christianity on Polish territory began officially with the baptism of Mieszko I in 966. The document *Dagome Iudex* is a confirmation of this fact in the international arena. The territory being described is located at the border between areas under Byzantine and Roman influence. Thus, there is some interest to explore the role in this region of the mission of the Soluns Brothers: Cyril – Constantine (826-869) and Methodius (c. 815-885). Facts in this regard include the existence in the Kraków rite of the liturgy of Cyril and Methodius and the existence of other evidences of Byzantine influence in cities of eastern Poland.[7]

The presence of Christianity sanctioned the establishment of the first metropolis in Gniezno (1000), at the tomb of St Adalbert with suffragans, Kraków, Wrocław, Kolobrzeg, thus covering the whole territory of the Piast Polish.

Therefore, there is the question of understanding the nature of mission. History shows great awareness of the missionary role of the church, since King Boleslaw Chrobry sent Bishop Adalbert of Prague (c. 956–997) to evangelise Prussia, a place where Adalbert later died as a martyr.[8]

The first areas of missionary commitment were the Baltic regions. However – and here Poland was not alone – from the north, on the territory of present-day Estonia and Latvia were influences from Scandinavian missions.

The mission conducted by the church in Poland can be described as Slavic mission, although the links and with, and the influence, of

[5] See 'Misjonarze polscy w świecie', in *Nasza Rodzina*, Numéro Spécial 1976. For current statistics of Polish missionaries in the world, see: www.misje.pl/aktualnosci/wydarzenia/235/statystyka-misyjna-co-mowia-liczby (accessed 19th February 2016).

[6] See J. Górski, *Jan Paweł II: Misjonarz świata* (Katowice, Poland: Księgarnia św. Jacka, 2006).

[7] See J. Pelikan, 'Cyril-Constantine', in Gerald H. Anderson (ed), *Biographical Dictionary of Christian Missions* [*BDCM*] (New York: Macmillan Reference, 1998), 163; 'Methodius', 456.

[8] See H.W. Genischen, 'Adalbert of Prague', in Gerald H. Anderson (ed), *BDCM*, 4-5.

Byzantium and later of Russia, should also be mentioned. Historical and linguistic studies show the importance of the meeting of these two trends of Christianity in Poland and its subsequent fruits: tolerance and dialogue.

Missionary Activity to Other Countries

The greatest missionary work of the church in Poland is evangelism and the baptism of Lithuania (1386).[9] That was of course linked with political and military domination.

Polish territory led by a communication route to Asia. In the legation of the Holy See – Rome, participated Benedict Polak from Wrocław.[10]

As such, another important aspect of the missionary work is the mission of the Polish king in Iran. In the 1640s, the Polish King Wladyslaw IV took care of the Catholic Church in the capital of Persia. Within this context, it should be mentioned that many missions were operated by Polish Catholic monks at the end of the seventeenth century in Persia: there were twelve centres of mission directed by Augustinians, Carmelites, Capuchins and Jesuits.

In the following years, the involvement of the Polish Church in missions took place in the framework of religious congregations, which belonged to the monks from this area – Franciscans, Carmelites, Jesuits – and later formed new missionary congregations. Missionary activity is also reflected in numerous articles published in Kraków (Publishing house Szembek) and Lviv.

Later, the great contribution of missionary ideas for Christian families, was made by Maria Teresa Ledóchowska (1863-1922), founder of *Echo z Afryki* and the Congregation of St Peter Claver. These works were awakened by the missionary spirit over the partitions, even in the field of missionary co-operation, especially for Africa.[11]

Florian Paucke (1719-1780) took part in Jesuit missions in South America.[12] That was also a contribution in socio-cultural experiments in Latin America. Other Jesuit missionaries with a relationship with Asian culture and authority were missionaries in China.[13]

---

[9] A. Miotk, *Aż na krańce świata* (Warszawa: Verbinum, 2005), 71.

[10] J. Górski, *Propedeutyka misjologii* (Kraków, Poland: Wydawnictwo Naukowe Papieskiej Akademii Teologicznej, 2000), 65-66.

[11] See J. Górski, 'Ledóchowska, Maria Teresa', in Gerald H. Anderson (ed), *BDCM*, 390.

[12] W. Kowalak, 'Baucke, Paucke Florian', *Encyklopedia Katolicka*, Vol. 2 (Lublin, 1976), 101.

[13] See J. Konior, *Historia polsko – chińskich kontaktów kulturalnych w XVII w.* (Kraków, Poland: WAM, 2013).

Missiology: The Chair of Missiology in Warsaw and Other Centres of Missiology in Seminaries and Universities

The beginnings of missiology in Poland can be traced to the first part of the twentieth century, before World War II. Apart from some attempts at the theological level, such as a handbook of missiology, one important feature was the development of the missionary movement.[14] This movement shaped attitudes supportive of missionaries, including various areas of the church's life, from childhood onwards, through parish groups, to the academic missionary movement. The knowledge model of missions did not differ substantially from the Catholic, which functioned in other countries and often had the character of a heroic-adventure. This can be read in the missionary literature of that period. It should be noted that many Polish missionaries worked as citizens of other countries, particularly Germany and Austria, because Poland was under occupation till 1918. When Poland regained independence, the missionary movement was very much alive. In 1927, there took place in Poznań the International Academic Missionary Congress. Many prominent missiologists gave speeches – for example, Joseph Schmidlin ('Mission ad Wissenschaft') and Pierre Charles ('Les Missiones et les Etudiants').[15] Later, World War II (1939-1945) effectively inhibited the development of the missionary movement.

Change came during the Second Vatican Council (1962-1965). One of the main issues was ecclesiological reflection. The model of a more dynamic image of the pilgrimage of God's people arose from a more stagnant one.[16] The share of Polish bishops in the Council brought the church renewal to our country. There was also a revival in ecumenical relations. The communist government gave permission for the first Polish missionaries to leave. After many years under communist rule, the first departure of missionaries from Poland was possible only in 1965. It marked the beginning of a new situation in our church and in theological education.[17]

During the revival in 1968,[18] the first chair of missiology in Poland was established at the Academy of Catholic Theology (ATK) in Warsaw.[19]

---

[14] See H. Król, *Podręcznik nauki o misjach* (Kraków, Poland: 1938).

[15] See *Księga pamiątkowa Międzynarodowego Akademickiego Kongresu Misyjnego,* (Poznań, Poland: Wydawnictwo Św. Wojciecha, 1927).

[16] J. Górski, 'New Ecclesiologies', in *Swedish Missiological Themes,* 90.4 (2002), 469.

[17] J. Górski, 'Missiological Studies and Animation in Poland', in S. Karotemprel (ed), *Promoting Mission Studies* (Shillong, India: 2000), 151-53.

[18] After Vatican II there was a revival and development in theology. In 1968, Poland published the official translation of the conciliar documents. O. Zapłata began the study of these documents, especially the Decree *Ad Gentes*, in which he sought reasons for the development of missiology in Poland. See W. Kowalak, 'Feliks Zapłata SVD – twórca misjologii w Polsce', in A. Miotk (ed), *Misjologia XXI wieku. W 20 rocznicę śmierci ojca Feliksa Zapłaty SVD – twórcy misjologii w Polsce* (Warszawa: Verbinum, 2004), 48-49.

[19] See F. Jabłoński, *Misjolodzy Polscy. Informator* (Warszawa: Missio Polonia, 2005), 18; Por. J. Górski, 'Twenty Years of Missiology in Poland', *Omnis Terra* [Engl.], No. 199 (1989), 366-67.

Prof. Feliks Zapłata SVD (1914-1982) began to lecture to commissioned missionaries the theology of communication for students' catechetics. Studies launched a new speciality missiology with ten students which in 1981 continued the work of Prof. Zapłata. Prof. Władysław Kowalak SVD was his long-time associate. Both the profile and the programme was created with missiologists from other countries.[20] The chair was for many years the only Catholic one in any faculty throughout Eastern Europe. Evidence of activity in this period included numerous diplomas and promoted doctorates and symposia in the field of missiology. The materials were published by *Zeszyty Misjologiczne ATK* and *Biuletyn misjologiczno-religioznawczy* in the journal *Collectanea Theologica.*[21] Other books and individual articles were published in a few theological journals, which appeared with the consent of the communist authorities.

The Church in Poland after 1989

The year 1989 brought major changes in Poland and throughout the Eastern bloc – changes related to the recovery of freedom in religious and intellectual life. Gradually the autonomy of universities was restored and resulted in the development of intellectual life. Political freedom facilitated the exchange of knowledge and scientific achievements in other countries, including Poland's neighbours, which were in the same or a worse situation. That was the time for missionary ideas and co-operation in Eastern Europe (Russia, Belorussia, Lithuania, Latvia and Estonia). The countries of Central and Eastern Europe began international co-operation with the rest of the world. There was now the possibility of publishing in foreign journals, participating in international conferences and symposiums, and the possibility also of belonging to international institutions and scientific organizations.

New Paradigms of Missiology

Missiology should take into account relationships with ecumenism, not only for historical reasons, but also with ecclesiological basics. The Protestants laid the foundation for the development of missiology. It is impossible not to refer to the World Missionary Conference in 1910 in Edinburgh, which was also an ecumenical conference. An important event was the initiative to establish CEEAMS (Central and Eastern European Association for Mission) within IAMS (International Association for

---

[20] See J. Różański, 'Wkład prof. dr. hab. Władysława Kowalaka SVD w rozwój misjologii w Polsce', in J. Różański (ed), *Misje i religie* (Górna Grupa: Verbinum, 2014), 11-25; J. Górski, 'Zapłata, Feliks', in Gerald H. Anderson (ed), *BDCM*, 760.

[21] See *Zeszyty Misjologiczne ATK*. The list of topics promoted at the time of doctoral and master's – See J. Różański, 'Wkład prof. dr. hab. Władysława Kowalaka SVD w rozwój misjologii w Polsce', 18-25.

Mission Studies). The event was preceded by a meeting of missiologists in both individual and group meetings at conferences worldwide. The ecumenical dimension of missiology is still a work in progress in Poland. The publication of *Transforming Mission* by David Bosch in Poland was a major step that raised hopes.[22] This publication was, however, cautiously accepted by Catholic missiology and other Christian denominations.

The past is an opportunity to evaluate. Missiology in Warsaw, which was launched at a difficult time, was a model for future centres. It prepared academics specialised on mission and developed the autonomy of mission studies as a discipline.

Whereas these academic efforts have helped missionary practice, perhaps too little attention has been paid to shaping the theology of mission in order to respond to the rapidly changing context, and consequently the paradigm of mission. Clearly, the historical and practical trends have prevailed thus far.[23] There was therefore a lack of relevant scientific studies in such subjects as ecology, the mission of immigrants and ethnic minorities, and also a lack of research in women's participation in missionary work. Today, we must look for new Areopagus-es, where the church will be able to enter into dialogue with the contemporary world.[24] A relatively large amount of research has been taken up in relation to the theme of dialogue with religions.[25]

Missiology needs to co-operate with other disciplines of theology and other fields of science. In this way, the discipline of 'missiology' will extend its area of research.

Tasks of Missiology

Missiology in Poland is taught at many theological faculties: Warsaw, Kraków, Katowice, Opole, Olsztyn, Lublin – and it is also taught in the majority of Polish seminaries. Research is also conducted more and more at the interface of missiology and other disciplines, such as ethnology, social sciences, economics. The impact of missiology on other theological disciplines is a necessity inspired recently also by Pope Francis. It is enough to take only a broader look at the programme contained in the *Evangelii Gaudium* (2013). Theology must have a missionary dimension;

[22] See David J. Bosch, *Oblicza misji chrześcijańskiej. Zmiany paradygmatu w teologii misji* (Katowice, Poland: Wydawnictwo Credo, 2010).

[23] See J. Górski, 'Missiology Today: New Dimensions and Perspectives', in *Swedish Missiological Themes* 91.4 (2003), 623-32.

[24] J. Górski, *St Paul and the New Areopaghi: The Presentation of Instrumentum laboris,* 2.

[25] About the mission and dialogue is often undertaken largely through *Redemptoris Missio,* 4: 'Is missionary work among non-Christians still relevant? Has it not been replaced by inter-religious dialogue?'

without it, it becomes passive.[26] In 2006, the initiative Association of Polish Missiologists (SMP) was born, its aim being scientific reflection on the missionary activity of the church and the promotion of missiology in ecclesiastical and academic environments.[27] SMP currently has about forty members, and its president is Prof. Dr Hab. Jan Górski. The annual publication *Studia Misjologiczne* is issued under the auspices of the Association.

Missionary Activity

The missionary activity of the church in Poland is based also on the work of Polish missionaries. 2065 Polish missionaries currently work in 97 countries. The major group are monks who work in Africa and Latin America. The second largest group are nuns, mostly in Africa. Currently there are more than 300 Polish *fideidonum* priests (mostly in Latin America), with over 60 lay missionaries (mostly in Africa). The countries where most Polish missionaries work are Brazil, Bolivia, Cameroon, Argentina and Kazakhstan. The largest number of *fideidonum* priests are coming from the dioceses of Tarnow, Katowice and Przemysl. Among the Polish missionaries there are over 20 missionary bishops (most of them in Latin America).[28]

Conclusion

Having seen some details regarding Polish mission and missiology, the two terms that come to mind are 'co-operation' and 'practice'. In theological research this has prompted the question whether we need more practical or more fundamental theology.

Another topic that seems very important is the ecumenical dimension of our missiology. Due attention needs to be paid to new Christian movements and other religions. This is a fresh task for our theological and religious studies.

The the church in Poland can be presented as a two-layered reality: the first is the layer of the hierarchical church, the official, who undertakes the recommendations of the various documents of the Magisterium. The second is the parish layer. It seems that within these

---

[26] See J. Górski, 'Wpływ posoborowej misjologii na współczesną teologię', in G. Wita (ed), *Wciąż u początków... 50-lecie Ad gentes i 90 lat zaangażowania (archi)diecezji katowickiej w misję Kościoła powszechnego* (Katowice, Poland: Wydawnictwo Św. Jacka, 2015), 65.

[27] Stowarzyszenie Misjologów Polskich, *Statut Stowarzyszenia Misjologów Polskich* (Katowice, Poland: Drukarnia Archidiecezjalna w Katowicach, 2007), ch. 5, par. 1.

[28] *Polscy misjonarze w świecie* (Górna Grupa: Verbinum, 2015), Vols I-III; Dane Komisji Episkopatu Polski ds. Misji z dn. 1st October 2014: www.misje.pl/misje-318 (accessed 21st June 2015). For more about the work of Polish missionaries, see J. Mil and J. Piotrowski (eds), *Udział Kościoła w Polsce w misji ad gentes podczas pontyfikatu Jana Pawła II* (Warszawa: Missio Polonia, 2004).

structures of the church much work and effort is still necessary if a more pastoral model of mission is to be created.

THE MISSION OF THE CHURCH IN POLAND AFTER POLITICAL TRANSFORMATION

Jarosław M. Lipniak

The Republic of Poland is one of the largest countries of Europe with respect to both territory and population. Poland is also one of the few countries that are almost culturally uniform and where religious adherence is both significant and visible. Polish Catholicism, although in general regarded as folklore and traditional, has been subject to essential transformations recently.[1] After regaining sovereignty in 1989, the Catholic Church in the 'country-upon-Vistula' faced a difficult challenge in adjusting to a pluralistic community.

A Church Getting Lost?

The role of the Catholic Church in the downfall of communism, in preserving the culture and identity of the people, is indisputable. Even so, the transformation that followed brought about a completely new reality. The primacy of the church was built first of all on moral grounds which it was very difficult to manage in a democratic situation, a consumerist community and amidst a plurality of opinions and ethical behaviour.[2]

In this new democratic arena, the Catholic Church had difficulty in defining its place in the public sphere. Its role in the face of new media, a presence in the schools, and its influence on political discourse – to mention only these examples – had to be redefined. The pre-war model had yet to be reconstructed and, in the post-war period, the communist authorities had contrived to make its natural development impossible. In these new circumstances, the church in Poland was clearly adrift.[3]

Paradoxes of the Religious Life of Poles

The religious life of modern Poles is full of paradoxes. On the one hand, the Poles consider themselves believers, while on the other hand they treat what is preached by the Catholic Church selectively and often do not accept

---

[1] P. Cywinski and M. Przeciszewski, 'L'Eglise en Pologne après 1989 face aux nouveaux défis de la democratie', in *Institut Catholique de Paris,* X (2004).

[2] J. Baniak, 'Kościół instytucjonalny w krytycznym spojrzeniu dzisiejszych katolików polskich', in *Przegląd Religioznawczy,* 2.240 (2011), 105-07.

[3] R. Rogowski, *Kościół zagubiony*, in *Katolicyzm Polski na przełomie wieków. Mity, rzeczywistość, obawy, nadzieje* (J. Baniak (ed); Poznań, Poland, 2001), 89-93.

postulated moral requirements. Sociologists distinguish four groups of believers. The first, about 15% of Poles, are deeply believing people, regularly practising and fully identified with the church and its teaching. The second group, to which 35-55% of Polish society belongs, are also regularly practising believers, connected with the church but not always accepting its moral and social message. The third group, about 20-25%, are believers but irregularly practising (attending Mass at least once a month), and more weakly linked with the church, while often critical of its social message. Finally, the fourth group (20-30% of Poles) are believers, but generally not practising.

It seems that most Poles are less and less resistant to secularization. The effect of this transformation is the fact that many people, particularly the young, have stopped seeking God. We observe in Poland more and more people who are religiously indifferent and some who are not interested in matters of faith at all. The fact of secularization, de-Christianization and living as though God did not exist are the result of many factors both in the Catholic Church and beyond. Undoubtedly, the beginnings of secularization should be sought in the Enlightenment, with its philosophy setting rationality against faith. Further catalysts were the philosophies of Nietzsche and Marx directly negating the meaning of religion. This dynamic social transformation could also be said to have started from the Industrial Revolution, continued with industrialization, urbanization, migration and the transformation of the multi-generational model of family life, and ended with globalization and the dominance of hedonism and materialism. It is also necessary to take a realistic view that the salt of the gospel has in some parts of the world lost its flavour, and the command to 'go and preach' has been reduced to an institutional expectation that petitioners will enter the church through its administrative office. What was taking place in western Europe after the Second Vatican Council occurred in Poland only after 1989. This is currently a real challenge for the Catholic Church in Poland in the 21st century.

In the history of Christianity, whenever the church found itself in the presence of new challenges and threats, there were times when it was able not only to define the situation but, more importantly, to find a way of creating opportunities for evangelism. This was the case in the sixth century, when St Benedict and Cassiodorus determined the church's intellectual and educational direction, and as a consequence its missionary activity for several centuries. It was the case in the Middle Ages, when the development of urban civilization met with the expansion of gnostic heresies, and the Dominicans and Franciscans developed new evangelization techniques both in the universities and among the increasing urban population. It was the same during the Reformation in the sixteenth century when the Jesuits emphasized development of the educational system. And today, when we look at the situation of the church both in Poland and throughout Europe, we see the increasing threat of secularization. Secularization is the biggest threat – and not only to religion but also to civilization. For these processes strike not only at the Christian identity of our continent and its position in the world but, through triggering the mechanisms that lead to the death of civilization, they hit out at the very essence of humanity.

A small decrease in the number of people going to church is offset by increasing numbers of believers who regularly receive the sacraments. Those going to communion during this period doubled – from 7.8% in 1980 to 17.1% in 2014. It can be said that the faith of the Poles became more and more mature, more often resulting from personal choice, and not only from tradition passed on in the family.

The 'Selectivity of Faith'

Experience to date has shown that the fundamental problem of modern Polish religious observance is a phenomenon defined as 'selectivity of faith', i.e. a lack of acceptance of certain aspects of the Catholic Church's teaching. Although over 92% Poles affirm to be religious, far less of them actually believe in God, and only 69% believe in eternal life. 65.8% of those interviewed believe in the resurrection. It has been stated that 72.8% of Poles believe in the existence of heaven, but only 31% are able to agree on the existence of hell. No better is the acceptance of the church's moral teaching. Standards of sexual ethics preached by the church are not accepted by most Polish Catholics. The ban on pre-marital sexual relations is recognized by one third of interviewed, but only a quarter accept the ban on artificial contraception.[4]

However, at the same time, the presence of the faith and the church in the public sphere in Poland is fully accepted: almost 90% of Poles accept the presence of crosses in public houses, 70% accept the presence of priests on television, expressing the church's opinion on moral and other topics. The degree of general acceptance of the church has also increased. At the end of the 1980s, this index was over 90%. It rapidly decreased at the beginning of the 1990s till it reached 40%. But from 1993, it was increasing to 75% where it stands now. Contrary to current opinion, studies of the Institute of Statistics of the church indicate that 87% of Polish Catholics represent attitudes of tolerance and ecumenism, and only 11% display an intolerant attitude.

It means that, to date, the practices of the younger generation were an expression of tradition rather than the practice of religion. When living conditions change, some customs and practices disappear and deep secularization takes place. Analysis of the statistical data relating to the situation, particularly in big cities, is cause for concern, because we see in

---

[4] Cywinski and Przeciszewski, 'L'Eglise en Pologne après 1989 face aux nouveaux defis de la democratie'.

Poland a clear decline in religious observance, particularly among the young educated generation in big cities, and this group that is the most dynamic and creative element in Polish society. This decline in religious observance is accompanied by the development of selective attitudes which as a consequence leads to the disintegration of a religious world-view. Unfortunately, this process of selectivity and the relativization of the faith is already quite deeply rooted.

The Mission of Religious Education

Generally, Poles welcomed the return of religious education in schools after the restoration of democracy in 1989. The participation of school pupils in religious education was quite significant. It is estimated that 95% of primary school pupils received this, and about 80% in high schools and secondary schools. Before the introduction of religious education, some people were afraid that it would create an intolerant atmosphere.[5] Sociological studies carried out regularly have shown that such fears were unjustified. Religious education in Poland is targeted exclusively at those who ask for it. Those of different Christian denominations and other religions may take part in religious classes organized by their churches and religions.

Polish experience indicates that the result of the introduction of religious education is not free of problems. On the one hand, it is observed that pupils do not pay close attention in religious classes. It has also led to a weakening of the relationship between catechists and parents, and the parents' interest in religious education was clearly reduced. The relationship between those being catechized and the parish their family belongs to were weakened. From the above data, it is clear that the church in Poland needs to think again about some reforms in the field of religious education.[6] This need is particularly evident at the level of lower secondary and secondary schools.[7]

For years, youth have been assessing the quality of religious classes. According to the Pallottine Institute of Statistics of the Catholic Church, in 1992, only 36% of those surveyed felt the classes were interesting, while about 40% felt that they did not differ from other subjects, and 25% were of the opinion that the classes were boring and nothing important was learned. A large number of young people from Warsaw (40% of those surveyed in 2013) felt the content of religious education was interesting and were happy to receive it. 28% of the pupils surveyed gave it an average

---

[5] A. Czaja, 'Teologia w perspektywie ekumenii', in *Studia Oecumenica,* 14 (2014), 126.

[6] F. Szulc, 'Doświadczenie Kościoła dziś', in A. Jarząbek (ed), *W trosce o Kościół. Tydzień Eklezjologiczny '97: Kościół tajemniczy – Kościół tajemnic. Tydzień Eklezjologiczny '98: Posługiwania w Kościele* (Lublin, 2000), 38-39.

[7] Z. Marek, *Religia: pomoc czy zagrożenie dla edukacji?* (Kraków, 2014).

grade, while 8.5% thought it was bad and 5% as very bad. Boys were more critical than girls.

Teachers of religion themselves were well evaluated by the pupils. In Warsaw, over half the pupils surveyed (57%) consider their relationship with the teachers was good or very good, 16% had minor objections, while 8% had bigger ones.

About 35,000 teachers work in Polish schools. Over half of them are lay people. A third of them are diocesan priests; the others are nuns. They must all have had higher theological education. There are enough teachers in modern Poland. The number of those wanting such work exceeds demand – this being the overall situation in the labour market.

The catechists have to match up expectations of the youth and seek new forms of content-related teaching and maintaining contact with their pupils. Some catechists keep up with these changes, others do not. The church in Poland ensures a wide range of workshops and training for catechists, if the catechists feel a need for training. It often happens that when a catechist qualifies as a teacher (the highest degree of promotion in school), there is no further motivation for improving one's training.[8]

The status of the catechist as pedagogues differs from case to case. Some of them are treated as members of the teaching staff with full rights – sharing the responsibility for educating the youth. In schools they even perform managerial functions. The others remain in the background and are not held in great esteem. Much depends on that how the catechist relates to teachers and the school's management. Through the perspective of these relationships will the church be perceived.[9]

It seems that the crisis of faith among modern youth has not been caused by the resumption of religious education though there are some who think it has; but it seems that one reason for this crisis of faith is a crisis in the family, its fabric undermined after years of communism and living in a modern neo-liberal environment, which has taken its toll of religious observance. The waywardness of the younger generation during the communist period, perceived as a form of religious observance lulled the family into a situation in which family teaching and daily prayers were superseded, Thanks to religious education, the availability of the religious classes is higher than it was before 1989, and thanks to newly devised programmes, one may say that religious knowledge was reliably transmitted.[10]

Religious education put new challenges before the parish priests however. In the mindset of many priests there is the view that 'the school will deal with the religious education' of young people. Some parish priests have forgotten that they are responsible for teaching in schools within their

---

[8] K. Misiaszek, *Koncepcja nauczania religii katolickiej w publicznej szkole polskiej: próba oceny* (Warszawa, 2010), 34.
[9] Misiaszek, *Koncepcja nauczania religii katolickiej w publicznej szkole polskiej: próba oceny.*
[10] P. Sroczyński, *Katecheza Kościoła współczesnego* (Legnica, 2015), 19.

parish. They think that, as soon as five pupils from the parish have been taught in the school, no-one need be interested in teaching. Before the church there is more than ever still the challenge of completing this teaching by ministry in the parish. In the parishes there takes place the preparation for first Communion and Confirmation, while there are marriage courses and more besides.

The Catholic Church in Poland is invariably of the opinion that the first place for the child's formation is the family. It cannot transfer this obligation to the church or the school. So, it is important that family teaching, family prayers and experiencing holidays together, all combine to provide an example of how to live. After delegating religious education to the schools, the most urgent task of the church would appear to be the formation of the parents. Without also addressing their education, it is difficult to achieve good catechetical education of children. Because the school or the church do not relieve parents of the need to bring up their children in the faith, they must have suitable intellectual and moral qualifications to be up to the task.

Vocations to the Priesthood and Foreign Missions

The Catholic Church in Poland in particular does not know the meaning of 'a crisis of vocations to the priesthood and monastic orders'. Despite Poland experiencing a demographic crisis for twenty years, with the country becoming depopulated and ageing, over the past dozen years, it still has the highest number of vocations to priesthood in Europe.[11] In 2014, were four thousand young people in seminaries. Such a large number of clergy, seminarians and neo-presbyters makes the Catholic Church in Poland is one of the youngest churches in Europe, with the average age of the ordinary priest 45-50 years old. On the whole, in Poland there are at present about 27,000 priests at work, including 22,000 diocesan and 5,000 monastic ones. Large numbers of Polish clergy are being exported as missionaries despite Poland having little tradition of this.[12]

In 2014, most Polish missionaries were working in Africa: 828 in all. The countries where most Polish missionaries have been for years are: Cameroon – 123, Zambia – 78, Madagascar – 58, Tanzania – 67, Republic of South Africa – 45, Democratic Republic of Congo – 46, and Rwanda – 41. In Africa there are 81 diocesan priests, 379 monks, 345 nuns and 23 lay people. In South and Central America there are 786 missionaries and nuns from Poland. The most Polish missionaries are found in: Brazil – 261, Argentina – 122, Bolivia – 119, Peru – 61, and Paraguay – 39. In South and Central America live 161 diocesan priests, 442 monks, 163 nuns and twenty lay people. There are 314 Polish missionaries in Asia. For many

[11] J. Baniak, *Powołania do kapłaństwa i do życia zakonnego w Polsce w latach 1900-2010: studium socjologiczne* (Poznań, Poland: 2012).

[12] M. Jagodziński, *Misje: teologia, historia, rzeczywistość* (Radom, Poland: 2013), 54.

years many Polish missionaries have worked in Kazakhstan – 106, Israel – 53, Japan – 29, Philippines – 31, Uzbekistan 17, and Taiwan – 14. In Asia there are 41 diocesan priests, 141 monks, 126 nuns and six lay people. In Oceania there are 70 missionaries, most of whom work in Papua New Guinea – 66. In Oceania, there are 13 diocesan priests, 51 monks, five nuns and one lay person. In North America, there are 17 missionaries. Most of them work in Canada – 12, plus Alaska – 5. In North America, there are six diocesan priests, ten monks and one nun.[13]

The numerical data entitle one to reasonable optimism. The church in Poland is missionary-minded and is called to continue the mission of Christ. Younger people go on missions at the age of about 30. One may believe that they might stay there longer. Physically, they are able to endure climatic difficulties or a variety of tasks. The young age of missionaries is evidence of the fact that the Polish clergy must be doing something right. The cause for anxiety can only come from the fact that fewer people will decide to go on missions. And after all often the service of secular people on missions is simply salutary. They are needed in particular to occupational formation of the nurses, teachers or other professions.

The Role of the Laity in the Church's Mission

The mission of the church is service to humanity and its salvation in Christ. A sign of the times for the modern church, particularly important in the context of the process of re-evangelization, is developing the vocation of the laity, and in renewal movements.[14] These are resources which the church in Poland has not been taking full advantage of. Up till now, the laity were often treated in the parishes as superfluous or even as a problem, rather than as living examples offering the potential of living out the gospel in daily life. However, laity goes its own path, sometimes far from council and post-council intellectual avant-garde.

All too often the minor role of lay people in the church in Poland results from a lack of mutual trust on both sides. A significant part of the clergy cling to the adage: 'Only we are the church', and many lay people cannot bring themselves to say: 'We are also the church.' It often happens that lay people complain that priests do not want to listen to them, do not ask for their opinion, or do not wish to make use of their suggestions.[15] On the other hand, a lot of priests worry that lay people are hopelessly passive, and want no responsibilities. So the priests are afraid of suggesting anything to them because they know that they will not take it up. This situation resembles a vicious circle. Then parish life gradually comes to a standstill.

---

[13] *Polscy misjonarze w świecie: 50 lat od Dekretu soborowego* (Pieniężno, Poland: 2015), 33.

[14] B. Giemza (ed), *Europa dla Chrystusa – Chrystus dla Europy: reewangelizacja cywilizacji zachodniej* (Kraków, Poland: 2009).

[15] K. Kwiatkowski, *Rola laikatu w dziele nowej ewangelizacji w świetle wybranych wypowiedzi Jana Pawła II* (Lublin, 2009), 45.

In order to escape from this vicious circle, above all else, a deep ecclesial awareness that we are all the church is necessary. Yet, in theory, this may not be possible. Lay people have to be made to feel that they are important. They have to feel that they are really co-owners of the church, and that not only declaratively but in concrete practical ways.[16]

Taking the apostolate of the laity seriously requires from Polish clergy the rejection of a negative mentality about it, and changing the mindset that only they have the obligation of preaching the gospel. There are a lot of parishes where there are no pastoral activities. Often one hears of events where groups of lay people ask for pastoral care and receive a negative answer from the priests. There are several reasons for this. Polish clergy are hard-working: priests have many duties, such as the daily office, religious education, preparation for confirmation, baptism, matrimony, etc., so they do not have enough time for other groups. As the priests are not able themselves to conduct all of them, so they should be prepared to delegate to lay people the functions of community leaders. It would justify theological faculties preparing hundreds of graduates in theology every year. Many of these would later find work in the parishes.[17]

Thus, a challenge for the church in Poland is the rejection of a certain antipathy towards lay people. A Polish cardinal at the Vatican, Zenon Grocholewski, during his speech at Synod, asked: How come that, with an increase in the number of Catholic educational institutions, at the same time a crisis in faith is increased? Is it not so that we learn about God, whereas in fact we do not know him or live in him?

This question is intensely discussed in the Polish hierarchy. Cardinal Stanisław Dziwisz spoke about the power finding its source in the mercy of God and which allows the human being to avoid entering a spiritual desert. Cardinal Kazimierz Nycz recalled that the church should not teach pastoral helpers or catechist, but rather ministers of the gospel who not only teach but live the faith. Cardinal Michalik paid attention to the fact that if we speak about weak faith and a uninspiring transmission of the gospel, so we should see ourselves as those mainly guilty of this. Archbishop Gądecki presented the dangers that lie in wait for young people, in particular the individualism found everywhere, and he appealed for an adequate answer to this issue, giving the example of an adult catechist who might witness to the faith.

The task currently before the church is an issue of how to take the gospel to people who do not go to church. There are such places and people whom the priests find it more difficult to reach but whom lay people could reach faster. Thus, a task for the clergy is the sensitizing of believers so that they

---

[16] W. Szymczak, 'Religijność – aktywność – obywatelskość. O społecznym potencjale organizacji religijnych w Polsce', in *Roczniki Nauk Społecznych,* 2 (2010), 98.

[17] G. Pyźlak, *Formacja świeckich pracowników duszpasterstwa rodzin: studium z duszpasterstwa rodzin w świetle badań doradców życia rodzinnego i absolwentów diecezjalnych studiów rodziny* (Lublin, 2013).

are aware of the fact that they are also responsible for bringing Christ to the modern world – particularly those areas where the clergy are not able to reach.

Today's society does not want to listen. The faith is becoming taboo and it does not appear to befit the 'modern' human being to talk of the Resurrected Christ. Therefore, the church – and not only in Poland – has to find a remedy for this.

The Mission of the Ecumenical Dialogue

One current feature characterizing ecumenism in Poland is the cordial exchange of preachers: during the Holy Masses, particularly during the Week of Prayer for Christian Unity, a homily is preached in Catholic churches by ministers of other religious denominations, while Catholic priests do the same the services at partner churches. This 'community of pulpit' is only what is already happening in other parts of the world. This tradition was started by Cardinal Stefan Wyszyński in 1963, so that the first chairman of Polish Ecumenical Council, the Lutheran bishop Zygmunt Michelis, was able to preach homilies at masses for Christian Unity in one of the Warsaw churches. Though such a practice is not in accordance with the guidelines of the Holy See, the Papal Council for Promoting Christian Unity agreed to continue with it. Archbishop Alfons Nossol, long-time (1984-2006) chairman, first of the Committee and later of the Council for Ecumenism emphasized that the Catholic Church in our country was often ahead of official decisions and Vatican guidelines in establishing contact with Christians of other denominations.

In many dioceses, such ecumenical services extend beyond the Week of Prayer, as for instance in the Opole diocese where even the beginning of Advent is celebrated by different denominations together in a form of ecumenical prayer vigil. In some towns there also takes place the second cycle of ecumenical prayers – before the ceremony of Pentecost – and there are services regularly celebrated every month. Joint prayers by churches have also included May Ecumenical Bible Days, organized since 1994 by the Bible Association in Poland, founded by Protestants with activities in which the Catholic Church also takes part.

The Bible plays its part in linking together Christians in Poland. In 1993, the National Committee of the Bible Association in Poland, with reference to an intention of the second Plenary Synod of the Catholic Church in Poland, decided to start work relating to the translation of the Holy Bible. We have been waiting until now for a joint translation of the New Testament.

From the theological side, ecumenical dialogue is being pursued at Catholic schools of higher education. There are three ecumenical institutes in Poland: at the Catholic University of Lublin (since 1983; administered by Leonard Górka), at the Papal Academy of Theology in Kraków (since

1995; administered by Łukasz Kamykowski), and at the University of Opole (since 2000; managed by Piotr Jaskóła), and the Department of Ecumenism and Intercultural Dialogue at the Papal Faculty of Theology in Wrocław (since 2014; administered by Jarosław Lipniak). Ecumenical issues also feature at university and papal faculties of theology and in seminaries.[18]

Ecumenical dialogue also has its practical dimension. It is expressed among other things in sharing places of worship, when another church community is deprived of theirs (as happens, for instance, in the Opole and Warmia provinces).

Ecumenical chapels exist at, among other places, the branch of the Silesian University in Cieszyn, at Warsaw and Katowice airports, in hospitals at Radom and Bielsko-Biała, and in Biała Podlaska prison, while in Kielce an ecumenical place of worship was established. For many years, Catholic-Orthodox processions have been taking place in graveyards.

A visible sign of good ecumenical relationships is the fact that church leaders have invited each other to important celebrations for their communities, while they also take part side-by-side in different state celebrations. It is difficult to enumerate today all the ecumenical initiatives, services and festivals which take place throughout the country.

The main challenge facing Christians in Poland is regulating the issue of marriage between different denominations. The solemnization of a marriage by those of different denominations does not present problems, though some years ago one person had to take the faith of their partner. After marriage, where a witness may be also be a non-Catholic, the clergy of both churches very often assist and bless the relationship.

However, according to the binding regulations of the Code of Canon Law, based on the instruction of the Conference of the Polish Episcopate from 1986, a Catholic wishing to marry someone belonging to another denomination has to gain the consent of the local bishop. Otherwise such marriages are invalid. Giving the required consent depends on three conditions being met: first, the Catholic partner must declare a desire to minimize the risk losing faith, and to make a solemn promise that the couple will do the best to see that children are baptized and brought up in the Catholic Church. The second condition is notification, in due time, of their partner that such promise was made. The third is instruction of both sides by the priest about the aims and attributes of marriage according to the Catholic faith. The Committee for Dialogue has prepared ecumenical instruction on the marriages of Christians of different denominations which is waiting to be approved by the Vatican. With an awareness of ecumenical documents regarding mixed marriages, Pope Benedict XVI spoke at a meeting on 25th May 2006. He revealed that this text would include 'joint Christian teaching on marriage and the family', 'the rules of entering into

[18] Czaja, 'Teologia w perspektywie ekumenii', 126.

interdenominational marriages accepted by everybody', and 'the concrete pastoral programme including such marriages'. The Pope said, 'I wish all the churches could approach this issue with a growing trust and co-operate fully respecting the rights and responsibilities of married couples when starting their own families and bringing up children in the faith.'

These words aroused hope in the member-churches of the Polish Ecumenical Council for a change of what had hitherto been Catholic practice on this issue. Catholics themselves do not generally require declarations on bringing up children, as such matters are for the parents to decide. They would like to abolish the requirement that a declaration in writing be made by the non-Catholic partner that no obstacles would prevent the Catholic education of the children – but instead that assurance be given that both spouses will try to bring up their children in the spirit of Christianity. The point is that nobody should be forced to bring up the children in the faith of just one parent – mostly that of the mother, as she is usually the one responsible for most religious education in the family. Therefore, we strongly emphasize the need to bring children up in a Christian manner, whilst leaving to the parents any decision on the actual denomination. The members of the Committee for Dialogue decided to follow the example of similar Italian instructions approved by the Holy See, adapting it to Polish conditions. However, it is very unlikely that full consent can be reached between churches on mixed marriages, especially if some of them do not acknowledge the sacramental character of marriage.

In Poland after 1989, a real breakthrough took place regarding the divisions between denominations with the coming of much greater mutual understanding.

The Mission of Charities Aid

This is one of the most dynamically developed sectors of the church's activity in Poland. In 1990, 'Caritas Poland', the official structure in this sector, was restored, together with 44 autonomous diocesan branches of Caritas. Very extensive charitable activities are also run by almost all monastic orders (232 treatment and care units), along with several hundred Christian foundations and numerous apostolic movements.

Caritas is known above all for its all-Polish collections such as its Christmas Eve Aid for Children and its Lent Charity. Caritas runs healing house for the poor and over 170 care homes for the sick. Nearly 60,000 volunteers co-operate with it. The organization also helps emigrants, refugees, Polish community centres and victims of disasters and wars all over the world.

The Christian churches in Poland have been running charitable activities jointly. In 2000, the Christmas Eve Aid for Children, initiated by Caritas, included the Lutheran Diaconate and Orthodox Mercy Centres called 'Eleos'. Before Christmas they distributed candles in the parishes for

Christmas Eve meal tables. Income from their sale was designated for children affected by poverty and violence and helped over half million children. About seven million candles are sold every year. Benedict XVI, at a meeting in the Lutheran Church of the Holy Trinity in Warsaw on 25th May 2006, praised Polish Christians for this ecumenical charity activity and encouraged its development.

Emigration and Family Ties

The family and traditional social ties have been the strength of the church in Poland until now. Today, young graduates look for work beyond where they live. Nearly three million people have emigrated; hence the strength of such ties is declining. Scientists predict that every third emigrant family will disintegrate. Judges, psychologists and sociologists agree that one of the most important reasons for separation arises from emigration.

Three categories of emigrants can be distinguished in Poland. The first is those who left the country for good. The second consists of those who go abroad for a shorter period. And the third consists of what are defined as 'shuttle emigrants' – seasonal workers. The most important reason for such migration is employment.[19]

More common is the emigration of whole families who decide to live abroad – something often done by stages: mostly, the father leaves first, to be followed later by the family. Typically, it has been happening for some years. Bringing up the children in e.g. the UK or Ireland can be much more beneficial than in Poland. There are many social benefits which mean that woman can stay at home and look after the children, and the husband's salary is often enough to make an honest living and even to have savings. Additionally, many of these families consider the future of their children, wanting to give them a chance to learn English which may be essential for their future. In such circumstances, emigration obviously helps the family and is particularly beneficial for the children who have a stress-free mother to themselves all the time. So emigration does not necessarily involve children becoming 'Euro-orphans'.

The second largest group are parents, either or both, who live abroad, leaving their children at home. There are many fathers in the UK or Ireland who are 45 years old who are employed in civil engineering or transport. They often emigrate, not because of a shortage of work but because of low salaries in Poland which did not give them much quality of life. The children miss out on their father, rarely seeing him, as he is physically absent. How children cope with such separation depends to a great extent not only on their age but on earlier emotional and spiritual ties forged by the father.

---

[19] J. Młyński and W. Szewczyk, *Migracje zarobkowe Polaków: badania i refleksje* (Tarnów, Poland: 2010), 23.

Emigration is not necessarily a threat to marriage and the family but can also offer opportunities. Emigrating may even provide the opportunity to enhance family relationships. There are groups of marriages and families that decided to fight for their relationships, wanting to develop dialogue and mutual understanding, to deepen such relationships. The bigger difficulty for emigrants is to mobilise and nurture family relationships than to seek a job.

Poles have to learn to live and function with the phenomenon of emigration. In this connection, institutions or organizations supporting the marriage and family placed in such contexts need to be developed. Emigration or other forms of separation caused by migration is also a challenge for the churches – to take note of this problem and react to it appropriately.[20]

The Mission of the Social Media

Social communications, defined also as the mass media, consist of television, video, radio, press and the Internet. Nobody needs to be convinced that we daily enjoy the benefits of these devices to a greater or lesser extent. They include all spheres of human life, and influence the way we view the world around us, our way of thinking and acting, and can shape new mindsets.

In such circumstances, there stands before the church the extremely important task of the skilful and responsible use of the mass media.[21] The mass media may also be used in the service of evangelization. As John Paul II said on 7th March 1996 in a speech addressed to members of the Plenary Assembly of the Pontifical Council for Social Communications: 'Evangelization in the media of social communications is accomplished not only through a truthful and compelling presentation of the message of Jesus Christ. It is also fostered by presenting news about what the church is doing in the name of Jesus, in all her many different activities in every corner of the world: in schools, in hospitals, in refugee relief programmes, in care for the poorest and most easily forgotten members of society'.

Up till now, the church in Poland has somewhat neglected this important sector of social life. It is certainly not enough to claim that television and films deprave and promote aggression! It is also not sufficient to enjoy Catholic Radio and television programmes. Also the religious press, if it wants to influence crowds of believers, cannot be limited to a narrow understanding of pastoral activity in the church. It is not only the fault of church opposers that the values of the church are rejected. It is also the sin of negligence of church members!

---

[20] K. Bielawny, *Zmiany demograficzne w wyniku emigracji w archidiecezji warmińskiej na koniec 2012 r.* (Olsztyn, Poland: 2013).

[21] M. Przybysz and T. Wielebski, *Media w duszpasterstwie* (Warszawa, 2014).

Today in Poland, the situation of the Areopagus at Athens where St Paul made a speech (Acts 17:22-31) is being repeated. For St Paul almost any occasion and any place were seen as opportunities for preaching the gospel using language suitable to the community being addressed. The Areopagus was at that time the cultural centre of educated Athenian people. The Apostle to the Nations did not hesitate at the opportunity of speaking to the Athenians. The world of the mass media is one of the most important types of a modern Areopagus in which the church needs to be present.[22] It is a special field for the apostolate of secular Catholics – in particular, journalists and Christian authors.

Summary

The previous pastoral conservatism of the Catholic Church in Poland could easily lead to a weakening of the faith of younger generation. It would be an irreparable loss for the future of Polish Christianity. Although the church is indestructible, this does not mean that local churches are not threatened by diminution or even disappearance. In many crises up till now, the church has been able to diagnose threats correctly and find the appropriate answers, and at the same time to forge suitable instruments of evangelization. The experience of the church in western Europe also shows that local churches are unfortunately not always most able to counteract the threats of de-Christianization effectively. Great help in determining the direction of pastoral strategy was given by the pontificate of Benedict XVI who pointed out areas for pastoral 'attack'. The defence of the Word's rationality is the most important intellectual challenge for the church in the 21st century. God is always able to find human beings but human beings can find God only in the rational world.

---

[22] Jan Paweł II, Encyklika *Redemptoris missio* (Vatican 1990), 37.

The Encounter Between Christianity and Islam in Bosnia and Herzegovina: A Missiological Perspective

Mato Zovkić

Being a Catholic theologian in Sarajevo, personally involved in motivating Christians and Muslims to support shared values in our multi-religious country, I rely on my experience of living among Bosnian Muslims and on recent guidelines of the Catholic magisterium regarding mission and dialogue. About three years ago I had a meeting with a Muslim theologian who teaches at the Faculty of Islamic Studies in Sarajevo and he had provided the book *Islam: Introduction and Approach. An Independent Study Textbook* by Sobhi Malek,[1] translated into Croatian. In this book, the author presents his experience of evangelization among Muslims in Africa, and sets out to introduce Islam to evangelical Christians. In his lessons he quotes letters from converts and asks Christian preachers not to treat Muslims as enemies who should be defeated but to offer their own personal experience of Jesus as the light of life. However, the Sarajevo professor characterized the Croatian translation of this book as a tool for proselytizing, which could divert Muslims from their religious and ethnic identity in our region.

Muslims of Bosnia and Herzegovina as a Relative Majority Population in this Slav and European Country

From AD 1463 to 1878 Bosnia and Herzegovina (BiH) was ruled by Ottoman invaders and during that period a large part of the Slav population accepted Islam as their faith affiliation. After the Berlin Congress in 1878, where Austria-Hungary was entrusted by the European powers with administration of this territory, Muslims were enabled to choose their religious leaders, run schools for the education of imams and shar'ia judges and ensure confessional religious instruction of their school-age students in state schools. From 1918 to 1991 BiH was part of Yugoslavia and its Muslim population was treated in the same way as other religiously affiliated groups and individuals – which meant they faced discrimination and were treated as second-class citizens in a state that was officially atheist, though they were not formally persecuted. After the disintegration

[1] Sobhi Malek, *Uvod u islam* (Osijek, Croatia: Nakladni zavod Evanđeoske Crkve, 2002).

of Yugoslavia in late 1991, the democratically elected government of BiH organized a referendum on 1st March 1992. Citizens were asked if they wanted to stay within a truncated Yugoslavia or form a new independent country. Muslims, as an ethnic and religious group, together with Croats-Catholics, opted for independence. Only 63.04% of our citizens were allowed and willing to take part in the referendum and 62.53% of those who participated voted for their country's sovereignty.[2] That political decision prompted Orthodox Serbs in the country to wage a war for ethnic territory, assisted by the Yugoslav army. In December 1995 the Dayton accords stopped the war and required the three ethnic communities – Muslim Bosniaks, Orthodox Serbs and Catholic Croats – to live in one country, which is barely viable because of the conflicting ethnic interests of a population in which ethnic and religious identity coincides.[3] Muslim citizens constitute a relative majority of the population. They belong to the Turkish Sunni tradition, moderate in practising their faith and ready to live in a secular state which was going to join the EU in the near or distant future. According to the April 1991 census, BiH, one of six republics of Yugoslavia, had 4,377.033 inhabitants. Of these, 1,630.033 or 43.5% were Muslims. According to the October 2013 census, the country's population was 3,791.622, of whom 48.5% were Muslim Bosniaks.

The war for ethnic territory from 1991 to 1995 was not an armed conflict of religions, but it had religious connotations due to an overlap of ethnicity and religious affiliation among the conflicting parties.[4] Now, the first mission task of Orthodox, Catholic and Protestant Christians regarding Muslims in this country was to address distant and recent past experience, to contribute to shared moral values and common needs, and to respect each other's religious, ethnic and cultural identities. I am writing this essay in the aftermath of 11th July 2015, the twentieth anniversary of the Srebrenica massacre or genocide, an occasion that rekindled sharp debates between Bosniaks and Serbs. Bosniaks insist that this was a genocide. Serbs acknowledge that what happened was a terrible massacre of innocent Muslim adult men and boys, but they contend that it was not a genocide, because that would mean that Serbs are a genocidal people. Similarly, Bosniaks are fond of alluding to the Ottoman period of this country's history as an ideal era of tolerance because of the Millet system regarding Jews and Christians in the empire and the 1463 Ahdnama, a document granting safe passage and relative religious freedom to the Bosnian

---

[2] See Paul Mojzes (ed), *Religion and the War in Bosnia* (Atlanta, GA: Scholars Press, 1998).

[3] See Mato Zovkić, 'Faith and National Identity of Catholics in Bosnia-Herzegovina', M. Ipgrave (ed), *Building a Better Bridge: Muslims, Christians and the Common Good. A Record of the Fourth Building Bridges Seminar Held in Sarajevo, Bosnia-Herzegovina, May 15-18, 2005* (Washington DC: Georgetown University Press, 2008), 35-39.

[4] See Mitja Velikonja, *Religious Separation and Political Intolerance in Bosnia-Herzegovina* (Texas: A & M University Press, 2003); Gorana Ognjenović and Jasna Jozelić (eds), *Politicization of Religion, the Power of Symbolism: The Case Study of Former Yugoslavia and its Successor States* (New York: Palgrave Macmillan, 2014).

Franciscans by Mehmet II the Conqueror. This was consistent with the Millet system allowing Jews and Christians to live within the empire if they paid taxes and obeyed the Sultan and his regional representative.[5] 'Bosfor', a Bosnian-Turkish friendship NGO has provided Bosnian and English translations of the Ahdnama, characterizing this document as 'the oldest human rights declaration in history, written in 1463, promulgated 326 years before the 1789 French Revolution, and 485 years before the 1948 Universal Declaration of Human Rights'.[6] Serious Bosniak scholars do know that in 1465 five Bosnian Franciscans were killed in Visoko and that hundreds of Christian churches were destroyed by Turks because implementation of the Sultan's orders depended on the goodwill of his local military representatives and judges in Bosnia. Muslims who mythologize about the Ottoman period of Bosnian history may play into the hands of Christian extremists who claim that Muslims should not be trusted.

In my experience, most Muslim religious and political leaders in BiH are proud of their ethnic and religious identity, but they are European Muslims with more than 130 years of experience of living under non-Muslim rule, ready to practise their faith in the pluralistic society of this and other European countries. I would simply cite the published texts and personal attitudes of Professors Ahmet Alibasic, Fikret Karčić, Enes Karić, Adnan Silajdzic, Dzevad Hodzićc, Tarik Haveric and others.[7] As in other Balkan countries, they eagerly strive to reconcile their faith affiliation and their nationhood as an integral part of their social and political activities in a pluralistic society.[8]

Mission and Dialogue in Bosnian Context

Individual conversions or 'defections' do take place in BiH, mostly because of mixed marriages. After the fall of the communist regime, hundreds of

[5] See Noel Malcolm, *Bosnia: A Short History* (London: Pan Macmillan, 2002), 43-50. Marko Attila Hoare, *The History of Bosnia: From Middle Ages to Present Day* (London: Saqi, 2007), 55-56. The book *Christians and Jews in the Ottoman Empire: The Functioning of a Plural Society*, Benjamin Braude and Bernard Lewis (eds) (New York, 1982) has been translated into Bosnian and published in Sarajevo in 2007 by the Centre for Advanced Studies under the leadership of Professor Ahmet Alibasic of the Faculty for Islamic Studies in Sarajevo.

[6] www.ottomansouvenir.com/General/the_ahdname_of_sultan_Mehmet (accessed 15th June 2015).

[7] See Hansjörg Schmid, *Islam im europäischen Haus: Wege zu einer interreligiösen Sozialethik* (Freiburg, Germany: Herder, 2012). In his bibliography, this author enlisted 25 titles by Fikret Karčić and three by Enes Karić. See also Armina Omerika (ed.), *Muslimische Stimmen aus Bosnien und Herzegowina: Die Entwicklung einer modernen islamischen Denktradition* (Freiburg, Germany: Herder, 2013).

[8] See Ina Merdjanova, *Rediscovering the Umma: Muslims in the Balkans between Nationalism and Transnationalism* (Oxford: OUP, 2013); Mato Zokvić, 'Muslime in Bosnien-Herzegowina zwischen inneren Dialog und Beziehungen zu Andersglaubenden', in *Religionen unterwegs* (Vienna), 21. Jg. Nr. 2 (June 2015), 4-9.

lapsed Christians and Muslims began joining their practising fellow believers at Sunday or Friday worship, and several hundred adults in Sarajevo gave their consent for prescribed baptismal instruction before they were baptized and joined other Catholics in urban parishes. In assisting such individual choices, Christian and Muslim faith ministers respect the human right of such individuals to choose their faith affiliation, but the era of mass conversions is over. None of our faith communities has a programme for mass conversion of 'the others', because we feel primarily bound to offer pastoral care to our own flock and to educate them to respect those who have been born and brought up in families of a different faith or ethnic affiliation. This depends mostly on religious leaders and teachers of religion who have a unique opportunity to influence their respective flocks at weekly prayer services and in confessional religious instruction in state schools, which was reintroduced in 1993. Believing Christians and Muslims do co-operate at the local level and through their institutions.

A modest but stable instrument of mutual encounter and co-operation is the Interreligious Council (IRC), established in June 1997 by four religious leaders who have their seats in Sarajevo: Reis Dr Mustafa Cerić, Orthodox Metropolitan Nikolaj Mrdja, Catholic Archbishop Vinko Puljic, and the President of the Jewish community in BiH, Jacob Finci. Dr Cerić signed an open letter from 38 Muslim leaders to Pope Benedict XVI dated 13th October 2006 in response to the Pope's lecture in Regensburg. The Grand Mufti of BiH was also one of 138 original signatories to the Appeal 'A Common word between you and us' addressed to Benedict XVI and other Christian leaders on 13th October 2007, which was an invitation from Muslim scholars to dialogue based on love of God and love of neighbour, as enjoined by the New Testament and the Qur'an. This letter, and enclosed documents of implementation, was translated into Bosnian and published in book form by el-Kalem, a Muslim publishing house in Sarajevo.[9] The general purpose of the IRC is to foster a faith-motivated strengthening of tolerant civic society. In view of this, the IRC implements projects acceptable to the four partners, and these projects are directed by four employees nominated by the respective religious leaders. One of these projects is a short history that presents the activities of the two churches and the two religious communities that are members of the IRC. Baptist Pastor Tomislav Dobutović has represented reformed Christian churches in BiH.[10]

---

[9] English original: *A Common Word Between You and Us* (Jordan: The Royal Ahl Al-Bayt Institute for Islamic Thought, 2009). Bosnian translation: *Zajednička riječ za nas i vas* (Sarajevo: el-Kalem and CNS, 2010).

[10] Ifet Mustafic (ed), *Religije u Bosni i Hercegovini: Monografija vjerskih zajednica i crkava – Religions in Bosnia and Herzegovina: Profile of Religious Communities and Churches* (Sarajevo: IRC, 2012). Bosnian and English text of T. Dobutović, entitled 'Reformation Heritage Churches', 220-27. Christians of reformed orientation moved to BiH c. 1860 and there are today twelve registered churches which have c. 2,500 members. The reason they

Teachers of religion in state schools are being trained and nominated by their religious superiors. School textbooks for confessional religious instruction are being prepared by education experts from the respective religions, and authors and teachers who use these textbooks strive to present the faith of 'others' in a way that the 'others' would recognize, without polemic or caricature. On one occasion, a Muslim theologian analyzed the image of Muslims in the textbooks for Orthodox and Catholic students and criticized the harsh presentation of local Ottoman rulers in BiH, which could inspire contemporary Christian students to discriminate against their Muslim peer group.[11] With the support of the IRC, the catechetical offices of Muslims, Orthodox and Catholics have since 2013 organized an annual seminar for teachers of religion where they exchange their professional experience, discussing shared values and problems.

Vatican II opened a period of dialogue with followers of non-Christian religions with its Declaration on the relationships of the church with non-Christian religions, of 28th October 1965 (*Nostra aetate*), and with the Declaration on religious liberty, of 7th December 1965 (*Dignitatis humanae*). Through the ecumenical council and through the documents adopted by vote by the participating bishops, a time of inter-religious dialogue was inaugurated and this has required a new approach to Christian evangelization in a pluralistic world.[12] I would briefly recall that the focus has shifted from religious truth *per se* to people who have the right to preserve their religious identity even if, from a Christian point of view, their religion might be perceived as in error. A new attitude towards non-Christians emerged from the efforts of Cardinal Augustin Bea to reach an acceptable reformulation of attitude towards the Jewish people. He informed the fathers that Pope John had specifically instructed the Secretariat to address the church's relationship with the Jewish people, because of the vicious outburst of anti-Semitism in the modern world that culminated with National Socialism in Germany. 'It was a German who spoke. At the end the cardinal underscored that this was not a religious text and did not touch on the difficult questions of the relationship of Arab nations to the state of Israel or to Zionism'.[13] American theologian John C. Murray built into the *Schema* on Religious Liberty the experience of the church in the US of being neither privileged nor persecuted. Cardinal Richard Cushing, Archbishop of Boston and a personal friend of the Kennedy family, defended the proposed text in the name of the US bishops: 'The declaration, while needing further work, was on the right track and

---

were not invited to join IRC is the centuries-long presence of Islam, Orthodoxy, Catholicism and Judaism in BiH with ther inherited values and problems.

[11] See Mato Zovkić, 'Govor o islamu u školskom vjeronauku', *Katehza,* 31.2 (2009), 101-11.

[12] See Michael L. Fitzgerald and John Borelli, *Interfaith Dialogue: A Catholic View* (Maryknoll, NY: Orbis Books, 2006). David L. Coppola (ed), *What Do We Want Others to Teach About Us?* (Fairfield, CT: Sacred Heart University Press, 2006).

[13] John W. O'Malley, *What Happened at Vatican II* (Cambridge, MA: The Belknap Press, 2008), 195-96.

was vitally important for the church in today's world. One aspect in particular was of highest importance: through this declaration the Catholic Church would show itself to the world as protagonist for human and civil liberty in religious matters.'[14]

The recent Catholic magisterium constantly reiterates that dialogue does not exclude mission. Indeed, it is a new form of mission. Christians are encouraged to evangelize by witnessing to the manner in which their faith in Jesus the universal Saviour makes them human and humane. Pope John Paul II, in his 1990 Encyclical *Redemptoris Missio* (RM), chapter V, entitled 'Paths of mission' (RM 41-60), points out that the first form of evangelization is the witness of the missionary, of the Christian family and of the ecclesial community.

> The evangelical witness which the world finds most appealing is that of concern for people, and of charity toward the poor, the weak and those who suffer. The complete generosity underlying this attitude and these actions stands in marked contrast to human selfishness. It raises precise questions which lead to God and to the Gospel. A commitment to peace, justice, human rights and human promotion is also a witness to the Gospel when it is a sign of concern for persons and is directed toward integral human development. Christians and Christian communities are very much a part of the life of their respective nations and can be a sign of the Gospel in their fidelity to their native land, people and national culture, while always preserving the freedom brought by Christ. Christianity is open to universal brotherhood, for all men and women are sons and daughters of the same Father and brothers and sisters in Christ (RM 42,3-43,1).[15]

In this chapter, followers of other religions are called our brothers and sisters, and the Pope stresses that proclaiming Christ to non-baptized people should not be confused with inter-religious dialogue. Dialogue should be conducted and implemented with Christian conviction that the church is the ordinary means of salvation while other religions stimulate the church 'to examine more deeply her own identity and to bear witness to the fullness of revelation which she received for the good of all' (RM 56,1).

> This gives rise to the spirit which must enliven dialogue in the context of mission. Those engaged in this dialogue must be consistent with their own religious traditions and convictions, and be open to understanding those of the other party without pretense or close-mindedness, but with truth, humility and frankness, knowing that dialogue can enrich each side. There must be no abandonment of principles nor false irenicism, but instead a witness given and received for mutual advancement on the road of religious inquiry and experience, and at the same time for the elimination of prejudice, intolerance and misunderstandings. Dialogue leads to inner purification and conversion which, if pursued with docility to the Holy Spirit, will be spiritually fruitful.
> A vast field lies open to dialogue, which can assume many forms and

---

[14] O'Malley, *What Happened at Vatican II*, 217.

[15] Quotations from English translation of *Redemptoris Missio* taken from the Vatican website, 18th July 2015.

> expressions: from exchanges between experts in religious traditions or official representatives of those traditions to cooperation for integral development and the safeguarding of religious values; and from a sharing of their respective spiritual experiences to the so-called 'dialogue of life', through which believers of different religions bear witness before each other in daily life to their own human and spiritual values, and help each other to live according to those values in order to build a more just and fraternal society (RM 56,2-57,1).

On 19th May 1991, the Pontifical Council for Interreligious Dialogue and the Congregation for Evangelization of Peoples published the joint document *Dialogue and proclamation. Reflection and Orientations on Interreligious Dialogue and the Proclamation of the Gospel of Jesus Christ.*[16] After the Introduction (nos. 1-13), these two Dicasteries of the Roman Curia in charge of moderating Catholic efforts for dialogue and mission deal in the first part with inter-religious dialogue (nos. 14-54) and in the second with proclaiming Jesus Christ to human beings in a pluralistic world (nos. 55-85).[17] The document depicts four possible forms of dialogue:

- – The dialogue of life, where believers of different faith affiliations strive to live in an open and neighbourly spirit;
- – The dialogue of action, where Christians and others collaborate for the integral development and liberation of people;
- – The dialogue of theological exchange, where specialists seek to deepen their understanding of each other's religious heritage and spiritual values; and
- – The dialogue of religious experience, where those of different faith affiliations share their spiritual riches (no. 42).

The document puts forward the characteristics of dialogue and proclamation, and then studies their mutual relationship. It points out that proclamation should be confident in the power of the Holy Spirit, faithful in transmitting the teaching received from Christ and preserved in the church, humble, respectful, dialogical and enculturated (no. 70). Among the external difficulties of evangelization may be a different concept of human rights or the identification of a particular religion with the national culture (no. 74). Here is the way this document binds inter-religious dialogue and proclamation in the mission of the church:

> Interreligious dialogue and proclamation, though not on the same level, are both authentic elements of the Church's evangelization mission. Both are legitimate and necessary. They are internally related, but not interchangeable: true interreligious dialogue on the part of the Christian supposes the desire to

[16] English translation available on the Vatican website and in the book: Francesco Gioia (ed), *Interreligious Dialogue: The Official Teaching of the Catholic Church from the Second Vatican Council to John Paul II* (Boston, MA: Pauline Books and Media, 2006), 1156-89.
[17] For a critical evaluation of these two documents by Catholic and Protestant scholars, see William R. Burrows (ed), *Redemption and Dialogue: Reading 'Redemptoris Missio' and 'Dialogue and Proclamation'* (Maryknoll, NY: Orbis Books, 1993). The book was digitalized in 2009.

> make Jesus Christ better known, recognized and loved; proclaiming Jesus Christ is to be carried out in the Gospel spirit of dialogue. The two activities remain distinct but, as experience shows, one and the same local Church, one and the same person, can be diversely engaged in both. In actual fact, the way of fulfilling the Church's mission depends upon the particular circumstances of each local Church, and of each Christian. It always implies a certain sensitivity to the social, cultural, religious and political aspects of the situation, as also attentiveness to the 'signs of times' through which the Spirit of God is speaking, teaching and guiding. Sensitivity and attentiveness are developed through a spirituality of dialogue. This requires a prayerful discernment and theological reflection on the significance in God's plan of the different religious traditions and the experience of those who find in them their spiritual nourishment (nos. 77-78).

The Catholic Church encourages and fosters inter-religious dialogue between herself and other religious traditions but also among religious traditions themselves. This is the way to become ever more active as a sign and instrument of communion with God and unity among all people. In motivating religious institutions to collaborate, the church promotes justice, love and peace for all (no. 80). In its conclusion, the documents suggest: 'It is also important that the specific studies on the relationship between dialogue and proclamation be undertaken, taking into account each religion within its geographical area and its socio-cultural context' (no. 88). Mgr Michael L. Fitzgerald, in his capacity as secretary of the Pontifical Council for Interreligious Dialogue, has creatively contributed to the outcome of this document. In his analysis of the document from the point of view of how Christians should treat Muslims, published in 2003, he concludes that Jesus, respected by Christians and Muslims, inspires us to dialogue although our beliefs about him remain significantly different.[18]

On 23rd November 2013, Pope Francis published his programmatic document, the Exhortation *Evangelii Gaudium – The Joy of the Gospel.* In it, the Pope presents his view of the mission of the Catholic Church to fellow bishops, priests, deacons, men and women of consecrated life, and to the lay faithful in the modern world. Besides the introduction (1-18), the document contains five chapters:

1. The church's missionary transformation;
2. Amid the crisis of communal commitment;
3. The proclamation of the gospel;
4. The social dimension of evangelization;
5. Spirit-filled evangelizers.

[18] Michael L. Fitzgerald, '"Dialogue and Proclamation": A Reading in the Perspective of Christian-Muslim Relations', in Daniel Kendall and Gerard O'Collins (eds), *In Many and Diverse Ways: In Honor of Jacques Dupuis* (Maryknoll, NY: Orbis Books, 2003), 181-93. Cardinal Avery Dulles in his essay 'World Religions and the New Millennium', in the same book, 3-13, concludes that in the time of intensive globalization inter-religious dialogue is not a luxury but a necessity in view of preventing disastrous conflicts among embittered groups.

In the fourth chapter, having in mind the public space of Christian pastoral activity, the Pope binds the confession of the faith and commitment to society, especially to the poor throughout the world. In this chapter he treats four fields of the church's activity:

- – Communal and societal repercussions of the *kerygma* (177-185);
- – The inclusion of the poor in society (186-216);
- – The common good and peace in society (217-237); and
- – Social dialogue and contribution to peace (238-258).

Pope Francis depicts his vision of Christian mission in a pluralistic world on the basis of his theological education and pastoral experience in South America. This is why the original of the document is in Spanish, his native language. As well as Spanish, official translations into Croatian, Dutch, French, English, German, Italian, Latin, Polish and Portuguese are available on the Vatican website. The German Jesuit priest Felix Körner is a Christian expert on religions, especially Islam, and lectures on religions at the Pontifical Gregorian University in Rome. In his presentation of this document he sees as its key concepts 'Verständnis – understanding' and 'Offenheit – openness'. He points out that the section on inter-religious dialogue, including Islam, should be viewed in the context of the whole section on social dialogue and as a contribution to peace.

In paragraphs 252 and 253 Pope Francis gives a fresh impulse to dialogue with Muslims. He expresses his admiration for Muslim believers who are deeply convinced that their life is from God and for God, and who feel the need to respond to God with an ethical commitment towards the poor and the needy. In his support for dialogue and co-operation he stresses that the partners should be fully grounded in their own identity and should therefore have special training on both sides. He urges Christians as majority inhabitants of western countries to respect and assist immigrant Muslims in their countries 'in the same way we expect and we hope and ask (for Christians) to be received and respected in countries of Islamic traditions'. This is the principle of *positive reciprocity* which was introduced by Pope John Paul II. Bosnian Muslim theologian Enes Karić, in his April 2014 interview in *Diwan*, a religious magazine for Bosnian Muslims in the diaspora, acknowledged that Muslim minorities in European countries enjoy greater religious freedom and civil protection than Christian minorities in Muslim countries. Pope Francis is convinced that the majority of Muslims are tolerant and this 'should lead us to avoid generalizations, for authentic Islam and a proper reading of the Qur'an are opposed to every form of violence'.[19]

---

[19] Enes Karić, 'Der christliche Osten und der islamische Westen', in *Diwan* (April 2014), 18-20.

From Distorting Each Other's Faith and History to Mutually Acceptable Presentations

Muslims of BiH are not a danger to other citizens or Europeans. They are fellow travellers who expect full freedom to practise their faith in a secular state and to contribute to the common good of pluralistic civic society. Full freedom of religion involves not only the right to stick to one's faith affiliation and preach it. What about religious polemic? Can we attack each other's religion, striving to strengthen our own flock in their faith? In my introduction I mentioned a Muslim professor of theology in Sarajevo who complained that the 2002 Croatian translation of the book on Islam by Sobhi Malek was an intellectual attack on today's Muslims. Before we go deeper into this question I would like to mention a historical phenomenon in the Ottoman Empire which some Muslims still defend and Christians bitterly criticize. During the sixteenth and seventeenth centuries there existed the institution of 'boys' tribute' or Devşirme, which enabled state officials to abduct boys from Christian families, take them to central state institutions, convert them to Islam and educate them as future employees, mostly military personnel. According to Noel Malcolm 'at least 200,000 children from the Balkans had passed through the system in its two centuries of operation'.[20] While some critical Muslim scholars point out that this procedure was against Muslim law, others still defend it as a unique chance for boys to be educated and to make military or political careers.

Let us now turn to polemical texts of Muslims on Christianity and vice versa. Relying on Qur'an 4:155-157, Muslims believe that Jesus did not die on the cross; he was Allah's Prophet and obedient servant without claiming any transcendental identity, but evangelists and other early Christians distorted his deeds and words.

Maurice Bucaille (1920-1998) was a French medical doctor, brought up as a Christian; in 1973 he became family physician to King Faisal of Saudi Arabia and probably that time accepted Islam; in 1976 he published his book *La Bible, le Coran et la Science*. In 1978 the book was published in English, gradually translated into the languages of large Muslim populations and sold millions of copies. This book was translated and published by el-Kalem in Sarajevo, twice – in 1978 and in 2001. The book is viewed by numerous Bosnian Muslim intellectuals as scientific evidence that the Qur'an is right and the New Testament wrong concerning the teaching and life of Jesus, the son of Mary. Bucaille is appreciated by Muslims in Europe as a western intellectual who has significantly contributed to Islamic thought in the West.[21]

---

[20] Malcolm, *Bosnia: A Short History*, 45-46.

[21] See Salah Salem Abdel Radaq, *Neo-Muslim Intellectuals in the West and Their Contributions to Islamic Thought and the Formation of Western Islam: An Explanatory Investigation of the Religious and Literary Activities of Western Neo-Muslim Intellectuals* (Leuven, Belgium: Peeters, 2008), 138-41, 473-83.

Ahmed Hussein Deedat (1918-2005) was a Muslim scholar, public speaker and missionary of Indian-South African descent. His sharp discussions with Baptist preachers before a South-African audience may have sounded attractive without being insulting, but the effect in Bosnia and elsewhere was different. Two of his books were translated and published by private publishers in Bosnia in 2009: *Qur'an or the Bible? Which is God's Word?* and *The Choice – Islam and Christianity*. Private translators and publishers of pamphlets and books against Christianity contribute towards a hostile mentality and side with extremist movements. Some Muslim intellectuals would like their leaders to pay more attention to extremist movements in protecting their own believers from such influence.[22]

As a Catholic New Testament exegete, I strive to draw the attention of my students and readers to diversities about Jesus in the Qur'an and the New Testament as a matter of faith, not of ideology or politics. In explaining to their audience how the gospel of Jesus was watered down in the four canonical gospels of early Christianity, Muslim authors in Bosnia are reluctant to read and accept Christian authors who insist on three stages of gospel material: 1. Jesus preached the word of God and enacted God's mercy towards humans, 2. The apostles and their collaborators left behind their preached material about the words and deeds of Jesus, 3. Evangelists chose from this material as real authors in shaping their gospels which the early church accepted in its canon as inspired and therefore containing God's revelation. For us Christians, diversities in the canonical gospels are not distortions of Jesus' words and deeds but progress in understanding and interpreting them in a changed social and religious environment outside Palestine. As we would like 'the others' to speak about 'us' so that we might recognize ourselves in our Christian identity, so we should treat them in the same way.

Despite the general objection that in the canonical Christian gospels the words and deeds of historical Jesus have been distorted, the saying of Jesus on the Advocate (*Parakletos*) whom he will send and who will testify (John 15:26), Muslim interpreters of the Qur'an since the thirteenth century have applied to Muhammed as the seal of God's prophets (Q 33:40). 'Seal' means the last and therefore most important. The Qur'an points out that Muhammed's coming has been announced by the gospel (7:157) and by Jesus himself (61:6). Muslim authors explain that the Greek word *parákletos* has been changed from the Aramaic *periklytos*: 'This prediction is supported by several references in the Gospel of John to the *Parákl̄etos* (usually rendered as 'Comforter') who was to come after Jesus. This

---

[22] In my presentation at the Tagung organized by Akademie der Diözese Rottenburg-Stuttgart on 22nd November 2009, I examined ten books or pamphlets against Christianity recently published by private Muslim publishers in Bosnia. See Mato Zovkić, 'Dialogische und polemische Wahrnehmungen des Christentums durch Muslime in Bosnien-Herzegowina', in *Vrhbosnensia* (Periodical of Catholic Faculty of Theology in Sarajevo), 1 (2010), 159-71.

designation is almost certainly a corruption of *Períklytos* ('the Much-Praised'), an exact Greek translation of the Aramaic term or name *Mawhamana*. (It should be borne in mind that Aramaic was the language used in Palestine in the time of, and for some centuries after, Jesus, and was thus undoubtedly the language in which the original – now lost – texts of the Gospels were composed.) In view of the phonetic closeness of *Períklytos* and *Parákl*ē*tos*, it is easy to understand how the translator – or, more probably, a later scribe – confused these two expressions. It is significant that both the Aramaic *Mawhamana* and the Greek *Períklytos* have the same meaning in the two names of the Last Prophet, *Muhammad* and *Ahmad*, both of which are derived from the verb *hamida* ('he praised') and the noun *hamd* ('praise')'.[23] Among others, such explanation of the saying on the Paraclete from John's Gospel is transferred by Dzemaludin Latic, a professor of the Faculty of Islamic Studies in Sarajevo, in his textbook on world religions for Muslim students in state high schools in BiH. Muslim interpreters here enforce an allegorical meaning of a New Testament saying without any discussion of the hermeneutical approach to Christian writings written about five hundred years before the Qur'an.

Muslims are the relative majority population in BiH. After the fall of the one-party Marxist regime in 1991, religions were admitted to the public space in our society and we should demonstrate that our respective faith makes us able to live in peace and to contribute towards building up a just civic society. In other European countries, some other denominations may be the faith of the majority but we theologians should teach and research, having in mind the multi-religious and plural situation in our multicultural societies. In the decades after Vatican II we Catholics spoke a lot about enculturation, but now some theologians prefer so-called 'enreligionization'.[24] For us Christians of all denominations, the mystery of

---

[23] *The Message of the Qur'an* (translated and explained by Muhammad Assad; Istanbul: Işaret Yayinlari, 2006), 861. This book, published for the first time in 1980 in Gibraltar, has been translated into Bosnian as *Poruka Kur'ana* (Sarajevo: El-Kalem, 2004). Abdullah Yusuf Ali, *The Meaning of the Holy Qur'an* (Beltsville, MD: Amana Publications, 2006), in explaining Q 61:6 (on page 1461) mentions John 14:16, 15:26 and 16:7 where *Parakletos* is mentioned by Jesus, and points out: 'Our doctors contend that Paracletos is a corrupt reading for Periclytos, and that in the original saying of Jesus there was a prophecy of our Prophet *Ahmad* by name. Even if we read 'Paraclete', it would apply to the Prophet, who is 'a mercy for all creatures' (21:107) and 'most kind and merciful to the Believers' (9:128).

[24] 'Risulta chiaro che è sempre l'altro colui che dovrà comprendere, giudicare e a sua volta accetare ciò che gli si offre. La 'inculturazione' indica che ciò non puo avvenire negando la propria *cultura*, ma in essa e a partire da essa. Orbene, con la *religione* accade qualcosa di rigorosamente analogo: chi ascolta è una persona religiosa che, dall'ottica della propria religione, accoglie e discrimina (o rifiuta) ciò che le viene annunciato. È ciò a cui vuole alludere la 'interreligionazione', parola probabilmente brutta, ma di anima generosa e fraterna. Chiarisce e sviluppa un autentico attegiamento fatto sia di accoglienza che di offerta'. See Andres Torres Queiruga, 'Ripensare il pluralismo: dall'inculturazione all' inreligionazione', in *Concilium*, 1 (2007), 129-40, cit. 137.

Christ remains the enduring criterion for the nearness or distance of a certain religion.[25]

Is apologetics acceptable in times of ecumenical and inter-religious dialogue? Apologetics was and still is based on 1 Pet. 3:15, where the writer asks that believers be able to give a reason (*apología*) for the faith that is in them. This is exemplified by Luke in Acts as he brings out the very first preaching of the apostles and their collaborators. If we analyze the discourses and procedures of Peter, Paul, Stephen, Jacob and others in the Acts, we see that they used Old Testament quotations apologetically. Thus an apologetic concern is deeply involved in the intention, the structure and the content of the New Testament. The word 'apologetic' in the theological context comes from the adjective *apologēticos* used substantially and from the verbal root *apologeisthai* meaning to answer, to account for, to defend, to justify. The American Jesuit Avery Dulles (1918-2008), well known for his 1974 book *Models of the Church*, published three editions of his book *A History of Apologetics* (1971, 1999 and 2005). In the final edition he points out that apologetics is 'consciously involved in dialogue, prevents faith from turning in upon itself, as though it were of concern to believers only. Besides dealing polemically with objections against Christianity from outside, it seeks to show the believers themselves why their faith is reasonable and responsible'.[26] He considered Vatican II to be 'irenic' and open to contemporary pluralism that makes it difficult to identify the adversary with whom the apologist should be in conversation. 'For some years apologetics fell into a general disrepute from which it has not entirely recovered, at least in Europe. Serious scholars in European universities, wary of apologetics, diverted their energy to the newly developing discipline of fundamental theology, practised primarily for the guild of professors and graduate students. Going somewhere beyond merely academic audiences, major theologians such as Rahner and Balthasar conducted apologetics of a sort in their efforts to describe the process by which people can come responsibly to Christian faith. A few Catholic authors as Hans Küng and Luigi Giussani wrote major popular works for non-believers and marginal Christians'.[27] He believes that adherence to the gospel must have an ecclesiastical dimension and in this way apologetics seeks to show why it is reasonable, with the help of grace, to accept God's word as it comes to us through scripture and the church. 'The Catholic Church has taught, and continues to teach, that there are sufficient signs to make the assent of faith objectively justifiable... Apologetics justifies itself, time and time again, as a distinct discipline and

---

[25] See Ugo Sartorio, 'Rendere ragione della fede cristiana oggi', in *Crescere oggi,* XVI.4 (94) (1996), 5-26. Horst Bürkle, 'Introduzione. Religione e religioni'; G. Tanzella Niti and G. Maspero, *La verità della religine: La specifità cristiana in contesto* (Rome: Pontificia Università della Santa Croce, 2007), 13-34.

[26]Cardinal Avery Dulles, *A History of Apologetics* (San Francisco, CA: Ignatius Press, 2005), 328.

[27] Dulles, *A History of Apologetics*, 365.

as a normal ingredient in authentic evangelization, catechesis, theology, ecumenism, and inter-religious dialogue.'[28] He advocates an apologetics of religious testimony which can capitalize on personalist categories of Christian philosophers. As guidelines, he proposes convergence, firmness, novelty, transformation and illuminative power.[29]

Analyzing strengths and weaknesses of some American textbooks, Richard Gaillardetz, professor of Catholic Studies at the University of Toledo in Ohio, pinpoints five recommendable qualities of the new apologetics: 1. *Passionate and positive*, 2. *Dialogical*, 3. *Ecumenical*, 4. *Historically responsible*, 5. *Culturally engaged*. He sees the need for more theologians who are informed by the best insights in contemporary theology and can present those insights with passion and enthusiasm in ways that affirm and enrich ordinary believers. 'As long as theologians are content to lecture only in university classrooms and limit their publications to scholarly pieces in academic journals, the theological community will continue to cede the stage to those who offer a narrower and more rigid appropriation of Catholic tradition but are willing to bring the Catholic theological heritage to the people and provide them with the substantive 'meat' for which they yearn'.[30]

Heinrich Fries blames traditional apologetics for over-emphasizing Catholic matters at the expense of other matters in the realm of belief and the Church.[31] In his view, fundamental theology should reach students and other people in their pluralistic context. All disciplines of theology should avoid distance from the world and a ghetto mentality. Theology cannot produce the faith and, therefore, theologians suppose that they are addressing a believing audience or readers who are already engaged. They can contribute towards the unity of ecclesiastical faith and preserve an open approach in their research and their lectures.[32]

In Catholic tradition, theology is *scientia fidei, scientia revelationis*; it assists the believer's search for an understanding of the faith, and it is indispensable for the church. Theologians research and explain the faith of the church from within, as intellectual servants of a believing community.

---

[28] Dulles, *A History of Apologetics*, 367.

[29] See Avery Dulles, 'The Rebirth of Apologetics', in Avery Dulles, *Church and Society* (New York: Fordham University Press, 2008), 430-42.

[30] Richard R. Gaillardetz, 'Do we need a new(er) Apologetics?' in *America Magazine* (2nd February 2004), 26-33.

[31] 'Apologetik verstand sich als Verteidigung des Eigenen und als Abwehr des Anderen'. Therefore, he proposed the new name of fundamental theology for this theological discipline: 'Apologetik versteht sich heute als Fundamentaltheologie. Sie markiert ihre Geschichte als Weg von der Verteidigung zur Grundlegung. Sie ist überzeugt, dass erst von diesem positiv zu verstehenden Umfassenden und Grundlegenden aus eine Antwort gegeben werden kann. Erst innerhalb dieses Ganzen und Grundlegenden kann und muss auch die legitime Funktion der Verteidigung und der Auseinandersetzung gesehen und geführt werden' – Heinrich Fries, 'Von der Apologetik zur Fundamentaltheologie', in *Concilium* 6.6/7 (1969), 442-47, cit. 442-43.

[32] See Heinrich Fries, *Funamentaltheologie* (Graz, Austria: Verlag Styria, 1985), 149-50.

In its 1990 *Instruction* ***Donum Veritatis*** *on the ecclesial vocation of the theologian,* the Congregation for the Doctrine of the Faith first deals with religious and moral truth as God's gift to his people, then outlines the ecclesiastical vocation of the theologian and the relationship of the theologian to the teaching authority within the church. Theology results from the need of God's people to understand their faith and give an account of it to people of goodwill:

> In order to exercise the prophetic function in the World, the People of God must continually reawaken or 'rekindle' its own life of faith (cf. 2 Tim. 2:6). It does this particularly by contemplating ever more deeply, under the guidance of the Holy Spirit, the contents of the faith and by dutifully presenting the reasonableness of the faith to those who ask for an account of it (cf. 1 Pet. 3:15). For the sake of this mission, the Spirit of truth distributes among the faithful of every rank special graces 'for the common good' (1 Cor. 12:7-11) (*Donum Veritatis*, 5).

Theological science helps the people of God fulfil the Apostle's command to give an account of their hope to those who ask. Theology 'offers its contribution so that the faith might be communicated. Appealing to the understanding of those who do not yet know Christ, it helps them to seek and find the faith. Obedient to the impulse of truth which seeks to be communicated, theology also arises from love and love's dynamism. In the act of faith, man knows God's goodness and begins to love him. Love, however, is ever desirous for a better knowledge of the beloved. From this double origin of theology, inscribed upon the interior life of the people of God and its missionary activity, derives the method with which it ought to be pursued in order to satisfy the requirements of its nature' (*Donum Veritatis*, 7).

Theologians research the content of revealed truth and help the Christian community to witness to it in the various cultural and life situations of their fellow humans. Theologians of different disciplines are enabled and bound to participate 'in the building up of Christ's Body in unity and truth. Their contribution is needed more than ever, for evangelization on a world scale requires the efforts of the whole people of God' (*Donum Veritatis*, 41). Theologians can essentially contribute towards formulating the faith of the church in different cultures and historical periods. In performing their task, theologians must take into consideration the double aspect of their ministry: ecclesiological and scientific. Pope John Paul II in his encyclical *Veritatis Splendor* regrets that, in certain currents of modern thought, freedom is 'exalted to such an extent that it becomes an absolute, which would then be the source of values'. This crisis of truth obscures 'the idea of universal truth about the good, knowable by human reason'. Such an outlook 'is quite congenial with an individualistic ethic, wherein each individual is faced with his own truth, different from the truth of others. Taken to its extreme consequences, this individualism leads to a denial of the very idea of human nature' (*Veritatis Splendor,* 32). Echoing the doctrine of Vatican II, he says: 'Although each individual has a right to be respected in his own journey in search of the truth, there exists a prior moral obligation, and a grave one at that, to seek the truth and to adhere to it once it is known' (*Veritatis Splendor,* 34). Followers of monotheistic religions believe that human freedom finds its authentic and complete fulfilment in accepting God's sovereignty and obeying his commandments. This is why Christian theologians, as intellectual servants of the ecclesiastical community, assist their students in finding the religious and moral truth and accepting it.

In his encyclical *Fides et Ratio*, relying on Paul's discourse at Athens (Acts 17:26-27) John Paul II develops the traditional Christian conviction that 'in the far reaches of the human heart there is a seed of desire and nostalgia for God... It is essential, therefore, that the values chosen and pursued in one's life be true, only true values can lead people to realize themselves fully, allowing them to be true in their nature. The truth of these values is to be found not only by turning in on oneself but by opening oneself to apprehend that truth even at levels which transcend the person. This is an essential condition for us to become ourselves and to grow as mature, adult persons' (*Fides et Ratio*, 24-25). Since the truth conferred by revelation is a truth to be understood in the light of reason, Christian philosophers and theologians have a magnificent ministry and mission: 'Fundamental theology should demonstrate the profound compatibility that exists between faith and its need to find expression by way of human reason fully free to give its assent. Faith will thus be able to show fully the path to reason in a sincere search for the truth. Although faith, a gift of God, is not based on reason, it can certainly not dispense with it. At the same time, it becomes apparent that reason needs to be reinforced by faith, in order to discover horizons it cannot reach on its own' (*Fides et Ratio*, 67). Here we can see the right and duty of theologians not only to explore the faith of the church but also to defend it. They have been set apart by their respective dioceses and religious orders to study the shared faith of the church and they should give back by continuous studying, explaining and defending that faith.

Among the current tasks of theology John Paul II lists 'to mediate the content of faith to different cultures in a coherent and conceptually clear way' by renewing its specific methods and by continuous enquiry of God's plan of salvation revealed in Jesus Christ (*Fides et Ratio*, 92). Theologians of all branches contribute towards an understanding of revelation and the content of faith, and the gist of it is God's *kenosis* in the death and resurrection of Jesus.

To conclude this section, Christian preachers and theologians should neither ignore polemical articles and books in which the faith of the church is being ridiculed nor waste too much time on them. In the multicultural and multi-religious context of BiH, the first duty of Christian shepherds and theologians is pastoral care of their own fellow Christians within their respective churches and parish communities. In doing this, they should not distort the faith and history of Islam but look for mutually acceptable representations of each other's faiths. As intellectual servants of the church, they should keep in mind such writings and educate their congregations and students of theology so that they may face religious criticism and persevere in their Christian identity. Theologians are entrusted and charged with explaining and defending the faith of the church but in a dialogical way. The social and religious context of BiH requires a fair presentation of Islam to Christians and of Christianity to Muslims. I know of some pamphlets and books of this kind prepared for a mixed audience in Italian, English and German but not in the languages of Bosnia and Herzegovina. The initiatives for such texts should come from religious leaders, and texts should be prepared by experts who should write in plain and simple language.

Conclusion

At this point I would like to tell the story of a Sarajevo Muslim theologian who was invited to give a presentation in Zagreb at a conference on Christian-Muslim dialogue organized by the Mufti of Croatia, by the Jesuit Faculty of Philosophy in Zagreb and by an Iranian institute. This professor told me that his Iranian colleague confided his intention to invite publicly the majority Christian audience in the conference room to convert to Islam because he felt this was his duty. The Sarajevo Muslim beseeched his Iranian partner not to do this because it would damage the good relations between Christians and Muslims in the region. The Iranian gave up and so saved the audience from insult and provocation. Muslims and Christians feel bound to *preach their faith in the public space* but they should keep in mind people's legitimate faith and cultural affiliation. We, believing citizens of former socialist countries, now have an opportunity to offer moral values to our societies and perform our mission activity within that framework. We must learn how to behave in the public space.[33]

Applied to the perspective of Christian mission in Bosnia and Herzegovina, this means that Catholic, Orthodox and Protestant Christian ministers, theologians and teachers of religion in state schools should not look at Muslims in this country and in other European countries as a danger. Faced with polemics against Christianity in Muslim theology books or school textbooks for religious instruction, they should deal with these problems in order to enable their faithful to remain practising Christians and become instructed in their own faith tradition. Christian faith ministers and missionaries should look for authentic information about Islam as the

[33] See Vernon Ruland, *Conscience Across Borders: An Ethics of Global Rights and Religious Pluralism* (San Francisco, CA: University of San Francisco, 2002); David Hollenbach, *The Global Face of Public Faith: Politics, Human Rights and Christian Ethics* (Washington, DC: Georgetown University Press, 2003); Miroslav Wolf, *A Public Faith: How Followers of Christ Should Serve the Common Good* (Grand Rapids, MI: Brazos Press, 2011).

faith tradition of their fellow citizens and help their flock to acquire sufficient basic knowledge about Muslims, because an unknown neighbour can easily be transformed into an enemy. We would expect a similar approach on the Muslim side regarding Christians.

There is no need, I think, to emphasize that Christian witnesses and preachers must be open to, and even look for, God-seekers who may be dissatisfied with their former religious tradition and may need personal assistance to resolve their spiritual dilemmas. We all believe that God wants us to be happy and to respect people's personal search for happiness. This is their religious and human right.

Mission in the Czech Republic: An Ecumenical Perspective

Pavol Bargár

Introduction

The present paper explores the topic of Christian mission in the Czech Republic. It first introduces the context of Czech society, especially with respect to the issue of religion. The paper then gives a critical overview of the mission pursued by select Czech churches. Afterwards, certain features of the current Czech context will be identified as important points of departure for Christian mission and dialogue with contemporary society and culture. Finally, a particular case study will be presented, exploring the mission of the Christian community called *Ta Cesta* (Czech for 'The Way') in relation to characteristic marks of contemporary Czech society and culture, such as post-rationalistic, post-ideological, post-optimistic, post-traditional, post-individualistic and post-materialistic, as identified in the preceding part of the paper. It will be argued that Christian churches and communities, in the pursuit of their missionary calling in the Czech context, ought to take these context identifiers seriously as many aspects of these identifiers bear significant potential for establishing and pursuing authentic and relevant Christian presence, witness and mission.

Czech Society and Religion

The Czech Republic is a Central European country which was established on 1st January 1993 as one of the successor states of former Czechoslovakia. It is commonly referred to as a post-communist country due to the fact that Czechoslovakia was part of the Soviet bloc with the Communist Party of Czechoslovakia as the ruling party for a significant part of the twentieth century (1948-1989). Even though some scholars call for a moratorium on the use of the adjective 'post-communist', maintaining that this term suggests that 'attitudes of party state times have remained with us',[1] I would still argue that it is precisely this 'political connotation',

---

[1] See János Pásztor, 'What Does It Mean to Be a Missionary Church Today?', in *The Church in Reformed Perspective: A European Reflection. Report and Papers from a European Consultation Reformed Theologians held at the International Reformed Centre John Knox from January 9 to 13, 2002* (Geneva: Centre International Réformé, 2002), 85-107, here 96. Cf. also Anne-Marie Kool, 'Trends and Challenges in Mission and Missiology in "Post-Communist" Europe', in *Mission Studies* 25 (2008), 21-36, here 24.

this shared heritage of the life 'in the shadow' of the past communist regime, which continues to exercise a major impact on and implications for the life of the societies and people in these countries up till now, including Christian churches and their mission.

The four decades of communist rule are often presented as the reason for the claim that the Czech Republic is one of the 'most atheistic countries in the world'. However, an increasing number of (especially Czech) scholars have challenged this claim.[2] The criticism can be led in at least two respects. First, it seems that the Czechs do not largely identify with atheism. In the last census (2011) only 1,075 respondents explicitly associated themselves with this worldview. This represents a negligible fraction of c. 10.5 million people in the Czech Republic. Nevertheless, it is probably fair to say that the Czech Republic is one of the most secularized countries in the world.[3] In the 2011 census, c. 3.6 million people reported they were without any religious belief.[4] In addition, 707,649 said they were believers without ties to any church or religious community. While this figure can be interpreted as evidence of the contemporary phenomenon of 'believing without belonging',[5] it is maybe even more intriguing to note that over 4.77 million respondents refused to answer the question about religious belief at all.[6] For some researchers this is an expression of what they refer to as the timid or shy spirituality of the Czech people, by which they mean the deep-rooted unwillingness of the Czechs to discuss their religiosity or spirituality in public.[7] In this regard, sociologists of religion in the Czech Republic observe parallel developments within western European countries, such as the significance of out-of-church movements, anti-clericalism, de-traditionalization, but also the rise of new spiritual outlets.[8]

---

[2] Cf. e.g. Dana Hamplová and Zdeněk R. Nešpor, 'Invisible Religion in a "Non-believing" Country: The Case of the Czech Republic', in *Social Compass* 56.4 (2009), 581-97.

[3] Cf. e.g. Olga Nešporová and Zdeněk R. Nešpor, 'Religion: An Unsolved Problem for the Modern Czech Nation', in *Sociologický časopis / Czech Sociological Review* 45.6 (2009), 1215-38: http://sreview.soc.cas.cz/uploads/e770ee18424bf0845 cbd5c6b0066bf0b4cb46fe5_NesporovaNesporSC2009-6.pdf (accessed 25th June 2015).

[4] 'Atheism' and 'no religious belief' were two separate options in the survey.

[5] Cf. Grace Davie, *Religion in Britain Since 1945: Believing Without Belonging* (Oxford: Wiley-Blackwell, 1994).

[6] For more information on the census, see: https://www.czso.cz/csu/sldb/census_information (accessed 25th June 2015).

[7] See Pavel Hošek, 'Discerning the Signs of the Times in the Post-Communist Czech Republic: A Historical, Sociological and Missiological Analysis of Contemporary Czech Culture', in Tomáš Halík and Pavel Hošek (eds), *A Czech Perspective on Faith in a Secular Age* (Washington, DC: The Council for Research in Values and Philosophy, 2015), 13-42, here 27-28: www.crvp.org/book/Series04/master-czech.pdf (accessed 25th June 2015).

[8] For a more detailed discussion see Zdeněk R. Nešpor, 'Religious Processes in Contemporary Czech Society', in *Sociologický časopis/Czech Sociological Review*, 40.3 (2004), 277-95: http://sreview.soc.cas.cz/uploads/fcf88a37d748c9fe3369b9c87d51d1d 3a7ff0ebd_525_25nespor15.pdf (accessed 25th June 2015).

The second challenge to the claim mentioned above about communist rule being the reason for the alleged atheism of the Czech people focuses on the causal relationship between Czech atheism (or, perhaps more appropriately, a special kind of religiosity) and the communist regime. It can be convincingly argued that communism cannot be the sole reason behind Czechs' stance on religion by merely comparing it with those of other post-communist countries. For example, the rate of religiosity in neighbouring Poland or Slovakia is much higher. Scholars therefore give other, additional reasons for this development. They include the course of events of the Czech national revival in the nineteenth century (i.e. the process of Czech identity formation as a process of anti-Germanism and anti-Catholicism), modernizing trends in the nineteenth century, such as liberalization, urbanization and industrialization of the Czech lands as the 'industrial heart' of the Austro-Hungarian Empire, or the expulsion of Germans of Catholic faith from the Sudetenland after 1945 which came to be resettled by a population from lower social classes with lukewarm or negative attitudes to the church.[9]

Based on sociological data, it must be clearly said the number of people who publicly declare to profess a faith, let alone ecclesiastic forms of Christianity, has been constantly decreasing over the last few decades. According to the 2011 census, only some 1.46 million out of 10.5 million claimed allegiance to a church or a faith community.[10] The largest church was the Roman Catholic Church with slightly over 1,083,000 members.[11] It was followed by the Evangelical Church of Czech Brethren and the Czechoslovak Hussite Church with c. 52,000 and 39,000 adherents respectively.[12] As for other Protestant denominations, although the numbers of their adherents have in most cases been increasing, at the same time it must be said that their membership numbers several thousands.[13]

---

[9] For a helpful discussion and references to relevant literature on these topics, see Hošek, 'Discerning the Signs of the Times', 15-20.

[10] Due to specific historical reasons but also the current immigration politics of the Czech Republic, the share of adherents of religions other than Christianity is negligible. According to the last census there were some 6,000 Buddhists, 2,000 Hindus, 3,500 Muslims and 1,500 Jews living in the Czech Republic. However, some interpreters of the data claim that these figures do not necessarily have to reflect reality as significant numbers of especially Jews and Muslims might not have identified themselves as such because of the fear of rising anti-Semitism and Islamophobia respectively. See Ivan Štampach, 'České náboženské trendy', in *Dingir*, 15.1 (2012), 4-6, especially 6.

[11] However, in 1991 it was 4,021,000 and in 2001 2,740,000 people.

[12] Both of these churches reported significant losses in membership since 1991. The Evangelical Church had 204,000 and 117,000 adherents in 1991 and 2001 respectively, while 178,000 and 99,000 people claimed adherence to the Czechoslovak Hussite Church in 1991 and 2001 respectively. For the completeness' sake, it ought to be noted that church membership among the Czech people had been dropping even before 1991. However, the data from 1991 on are given in this paper since it was the first census after the fall of the communist regime.

[13] For reference on the relevant figures from the 1991, 2001, and 2011 censuses, see Zdeňek Vojtíšek, 'Srovnání výsledků sčítání lidu v otázce náboženství v letech 1991, 2001 a 2011', in

What follows is a critical overview of the mission pursued by selected Czech churches. For space limitations, it was not possible that all Christian churches registered and/or present in the Czech Republic could be discussed. The following discussion, therefore, includes the Roman Catholic Church, the Evangelical Church of Czech Brethren and the Czechoslovak Hussite Church. In addition, the mission of the Church of Brethren is also discussed as a main representative of smaller Protestant Churches in the Czech Republic.[14] All these churches are member churches of the Ecumenical Council of Churches in the Czech Republic, the Roman Catholic Church being an associate member, while the other three are full members.[15] The topic is dealt with in the light of the themes and issues introduced and elaborated by the Edinburgh 2010 Mission Conference.[16] A particular, albeit largely implicit, attention will be paid to the nine conference themes, succinctly laid down in *A Common Call*, as well as to the transversals to which the conference constantly attended.[17] The reflection pursued in this paper draws upon the premise that these themes, together with the transversals, can establish the basis for a model of holistic mission which can be very relevant for the Czech context.

The Roman Catholic Church in the Czech Republic

The Roman Rite has been present in the territory of the present-day Czech Republic since the ninth century; it was soon to be followed by the Eastern Rite which, however, gradually vanished here.[18] Today, an overwhelming majority of Catholic believers in the Czech Republic belong to the Roman Catholic Church (Czech: *Římskokatolická církev*) of the Roman Rite.

The main aims and calling of the Roman Catholic Church are based on Jesus' Great Commission to take the gospel to the world (Matt. 28:19-20), to serve others in love (John 13:14-15; 13:34-35), to turn to God in Jesus'

Dingir, 15.1 (2012), inside back cover. The chart uses the data published by the Czech Statistical Office at www.czso.cz/csu/2008edicniplan.nsf/p/4032-08 and www.scitani.cz

[14] In the 2011 census, almost 11,000 people claimed their adherence to the Church of Brethren. With the figures growing from 2,759 people in 1991 and 9,931 people in 2001, the Church of Brethren is one of those denominations which show a growth in membership.

[15] For the official website of the Ecumenical Council of Churches in the Czech Republic, see: http://ekumenickarada.cz (accessed 26th June 2015).

[16] For detailed information on the conference as well as access to relevant resources, see the official website at: www.edinburgh2010.org (accessed 26th June 2015).

[17] The English version of *A Common Call* is available online at: www.edinburgh 2010.org/fileadmin/Edinburgh_2010_Common_Call_with_explanation.pdf (accessed 26th June 2015). For detailed information on the Edinburgh 2010 study process, see Daryl Balia and Kirsteen Kim (eds), *Witnessing to Christ Today* (Regnum Edinburgh Centenary Series 2), (Oxford: Regnum, 2010).

[18] The latter came back to the territory of the Czech Republic as the Byzantine Rite with migrant workers from the eastern part of Czechoslovakia after World War I. It is represented by a tiny part of the believers who are organized in the Greek Catholic Church (Czech: *Řeckokatolická církev*). In the 2011 census, a little fewer than 10,000 people claimed adherence to the Greek Catholic Church.

name (John 16:26) as to a loving Father (Matt. 6:9-13) under the guidance of the Holy Spirit (John 16:7-15) in the expectation of the ultimate fulfilment in the glory of God and the light of the resurrected Christ, the Lamb of God (Rev. 21:1-22:5).[19]

In its mission and service the Roman Catholic Church is closely related to international Roman Catholic organizations and structures, especially to the Magisterium. It is clear, not only from the practical work in particular areas of church life, but also from the field of theology. Behind the ministry of the Roman Catholic Church there is a well elaborated theological foundation. As a result, this church seeks to be, and is, active in many areas of life and it pursues its ministry in many different ways, including liturgy, proclamation, education, service and dialogue. A great emphasis is laid, not only on the proclamation of the gospel, but also on involvement in political, societal, cultural and environmental issues.[20]

With regard to the explicit term 'mission', however, it is – surprisingly enough – understood usually in a rather narrow and specific sense. When mission is mentioned in the Roman Catholic Church, what is in most cases meant is the ministry of the church in (until now) mainly non-Christian, usually developing, countries. It is similarly intriguing that although the proclamation of the gospel is regarded as the prime task of the church, such an understanding of mission puts an even greater emphasis on development, humanitarian and social aid – service to one's neighbour.

To complement the term 'mission', the Roman Catholic Church also employs the term 'evangelization'. As a rule, the latter refers to catechetical and pastoral ministry among those who have encountered the gospel before, and are perhaps even baptized and belong to the church. Evangelization then strives to take up these 'roots' and to revive and strengthen the faith of such people. That is the reason why the missional activity of the Roman Catholic Church in the Czech Republic is referred to as evangelization[21] and the term mission is used almost exclusively for 'foreign mission' which represents the realm of ministry of the Pontifical Mission Societies (*Missio*).[22] Therefore, it could be argued that the Roman Catholic Church still maintains the essentially outdated distinction between 'home mission' (i.e. evangelization) and 'foreign mission' (i.e. mission).

Another rather surprising observation is that in the materials of the Roman Catholic Church the term 'mission' in the sense of particular,

---

[19] The information about the Roman Catholic Church above is processed according to the official website of the Ecumenical Council of Churches in the Czech Republic: www.ekumenickarada.cz/in/316#.VYvOHPntmko (accessed 25th June 2015). Available in Czech only.

[20] These are the topics that have been usually labelled as the JPIC (i.e. justice, peace and the integrity of creation) model in both Roman Catholic and ecumenical theological circles.

[21] Evangelistic endeavours primarily intended for people in the Czech Republic are co-ordinated through the site http://evangelizace.cz (accessed 25th June 2015). Available in Czech only.

[22] See www.missio.cz (accessed 25th June 2015). Available in Czech only.

practical missional involvement of the church is consistently used in the plural, i.e. 'missions'. This term then refers to particular mission endeavours pursued in various parts of the world. It is noteworthy that in ecumenical circles worldwide the term 'missions' (plural) ceased to be used in the 1960s and the concept of 'mission' in the singular came to be intentionally preferred instead.[23] In the background of this shift there is an emphasis on the concept of *missio Dei*: God pursues God's mission in and with the world, and this mission is integrated. The church which participates in God's work should therefore see this essential unity as well. Various missional activities are but manifold expressions and components of this single mission.

Therefore, when the Roman Catholic Church repeatedly speaks about missions in the plural, it gives the impression that the theological concept of *missio Dei* is not of major importance. Indeed, as stated above, the model of proclamation of the name of Jesus Christ and his work as well as that of JPIC seem to play a more prominent role.[24]

The Roman Catholic Church collaborates with Caritas in the Czech Republic to provide social and charitable services which represent an inseparable part of its missional work.[25] It has a superb infrastructural system at its disposal for social service which is not limited to members of the church, but serves society as a whole. In spite of the fact that this ministry is rarely labelled explicitly as mission, its links with missional engagement is also underscored by the fact that both charity and mission are supervized by the same bishop. The Roman Catholic Church in the Czech Republic puts a strong emphasis on dialogue with society in various fields, including culture, politics, science, arts, ecology, reconciliation and interfaith relations. Many topics on this agenda are pursued by the Czech Christian Academy[26] and the Moravian-Silesian Christian Academy.[27]

Theological education is provided by theological faculties in Prague,[28] Olomouc[29] and České Budějovice.[30] In spite of the fact that these faculties

---

[23] A symptomatic *pars pro toto* illustration represents the change of the name of a missiological journal published by the World Council of Churches (WCC). In 1967, its name changed from *International Review of Missions* to *International Review of Mission*.

[24] This paper makes use of the categorization of models of mission as suggested by S. Bevans and R. Schroeder. These two missiologists recognize three main models of mission in the twentieth century, namely, mission as participation in *missio Dei*; mission as liberating service of the reign of God; and mission as proclamation of Jesus Christ as universal saviour. In addition, they suggest their own model, mission as prophetic dialogue, as an appropriate model of mission for the 21st century. Even though the latter is not explicitly discussed in this paper, there are significant parallels between Bevans and Schroeder's models and between what will be referred to in the final part of this paper as holistic mission. For references, see Stephen B. Bevans and Roger P. Schroeder, *Constants in Context: A Theology of Mission for Today* (Maryknoll, NY: Orbis Books, 2004), 283-395.

[25] www.charita.cz/en (accessed 25th June 2015).

[26] www.krestanskaakademie.cz/home?lang=EN (accessed 25th June 2015).

[27] www.mska.biz (accessed 25th June 2015). Available in Czech only.

[28] Catholic Theological Faculty of Charles University in Prague: www.ktf.cuni. cz/KTFENG-1.html (accessed 25th June 2015).

do not offer missiology as a study programme or even a separate course, all of them offer a considerable number of more or less missiologically relevant courses (usually as part of their programmes which focus on social work).

The Evangelical Church of Czech Brethren

The Evangelical Church of Czech Brethren (Czech: *Českobratrská církev evangelická*) is a mainline Protestant church which was established in 1918 through the unification of Lutheran and Calvinist branches of the Reformation; nevertheless, it dates its continuous identity all the way back to the Patent of Toleration by the Emperor Joseph II of Austria in 1781. The Evangelical Church of Czech Brethren is a member church of the World Communion of Reformed Churches (WCRC), the World Council of Churches (WCC), the Conference of European Churches (CEC), the Community of Protestant Churches in Europe (CPCE), the Lutheran World Federation (LWF), and the Ecumenical Council of Churches in the Czech Republic.[31]

It ought to be appreciated that the Evangelical Church of Czech Brethren does not see its missional service merely as spontaneous events organized without deeper reflection. By contrast, it gives this theme space in the church's policy statements (e.g. those by the Synodal Council, the chief executive body of the church). In addition, the church has founded the Advisory Committee for Evangelism and Mission to assist in its engagement in the field of mission. It was thanks to the efforts of this committee (at times in collaboration with the Advisory Committee for Theology) that several official statements have been published with regard to the mission of the Evangelical Church of Czech Brethren. These statements make especially visible the theological work they had been invested with. It can be therefore argued that the Evangelical Church of Czech Brethren attempts to found and reflect on its missional engagement theologically. The missiological model which it draws upon is first and foremost that of *missio Dei*; it is especially evident in the document *Misijní poslání církve* ('The missionary task of the church').[32] This is a very positive step; however, one also needs to acknowledge certain shortcomings in this regard. The document does not understand the concept of *missio Dei* as generously as it possibly could; there is virtually nothing mentioned about the struggle for justice and peace, dialogue with non-

---

[29] Sts Cyril and Methodius Faculty of Theology, Palacký University in Olomouc: www.cmtf.upol.cz/en (accessed 25th June 2015).

[30] Faculty of Theology, University of South Bohemia in České Budějovice, Czech Republic: www.tf.jcu.cz/?set_language=en (accessed 25th June 2015).

[31] According to the official website of the Ecumenical Council of Churches in the Czech Republic: www.ekumenickarada.cz/in/309#.VYleM_ntmko (accessed 23rd June 2015).

[32] Available (in Czech) from: www.e-cirkev.cz/data/att/Misijn%C3%AD%20posl%C3%A1n%C3%AD%20c%C3%ADrkve.pdf (accessed 23rd June 2015).

Christians, striving for reconciliation, inculturation or environmental issues. It is, of course, due to the date of origin of the document (1981). Having acknowledged that, it is even more regrettable that the Advisory Committee for Evangelism and Mission had not revised and updated the document before recommending it to the 32nd General Assembly (Synod) of the church in 2009.

The same can be said about another document from the 1980s, *Prax církve jako nástroj misie* ('Church praxis as an instrument of mission').[33] This document construes mission exclusively as something which goes on within church walls. The societal dimension of mission is altogether absent. Again, it is perfectly understandable, taking into account its date of origin (1983). However, it must be said that this text also requires revision.

It is interesting to note that a more recent document (2009) or, more precisely, a list of (twelve painful) points of mission is not written in the spirit of the *missio Dei* model any more.[34] Here, there is a more robust emphasis on the proclamation of the gospel in the sense of preaching the good news about Christ and his work. Again, however, a societal, extra-ecclesial, systemic impact of the gospel is downplayed; what is first and foremost underscored is mission within the framework of the church.

Such a missiological trend is, to a certain extent, in tension with the policy statement of the recent Synodal Council[35] which vehemently acknowledges the importance of mission, not only by way of proclaiming the gospel in a way that is intelligible to contemporary society (with an emphasis on contextualization and inculturation), but also by way of civic and political involvement and dialogue with as many segments of society as possible.[36]

Nevertheless, it seems that many of these missional activities take place more or less ad hoc. Furthermore, they are pursued by a limited number of particular congregations or individuals. It especially regards efforts in the area of interfaith dialogue, endeavours with respect to reconciliation and social and civic justice, help to refugees or minorities, etc. Even though such a 'non-institutional' approach is, naturally, not in itself wrong, it is nevertheless to be regretted that the whole sophisticated administrative structure (e.g. Advisory Committee for Evangelism and Mission), supported by the official documents and statements, is not able to realize its potential to an even greater degree.

On the other hand, a very powerful and well worked-out missional instrument is the Diaconia of the Evangelical Church of Czech Brethren

---

[33] Available in Czech from: www.e-cirkev.cz/data/att/Synod%201983_Praxe%20c%C3%ADrkve%20jako%20n%C3%A1stroj%20misie.pdf (accessed 23rd June 2015).

[34] The document is available (in Czech) from the Advisory Committee's website: http://poemcce.blog.cz/0911/12-neuralgickych-bodu-misie (accessed 23rd June 2015).

[35] The term of the Synodal Council in question ended in November 2015.

[36] Cf. the document *Čtyři misijní artikuly* ('Four articles on mission'): http:// www.e-cirkev.cz/data/att/%C4%8Cty%C5%99i%20misijn %C3%AD%20artikuly.pdf (accessed 23rd June 2015).

with its system of social services, having a presence in many spheres of human life and helping wide strata of society.[37]

Theological education, primarily the education of ministers, is provided by the Protestant Theological Faculty of Charles University in Prague.[38] Even though there are no study programmes in missiology, the Faculty offers an optional missiological course every semester. The education of social workers is on the agenda of both the Protestant Theological Faculty and the Evangelical Academy;[39] in addition, the latter also provides education for catechists.

The Evangelical Church of the Czech Brethren seeks to pursue mission in an ecumenical way and with a great sensitivity and understanding for contemporary society and the post-modern world.

The Czechoslovak Hussite Church

The Czechoslovak Hussite Church (Czech: *Církev československá husitská*) is a liturgical Christian church which draws from both Scripture and Christian tradition, thus combining Catholic and Protestant elements and emphases. The Czechoslovak Hussite Church was established on 8th January 1920, growing out of the Modernist movement within the Roman Catholic Church. It is a member of the WCC, the CPCE, the CEC, and the Ecumenical Council of Churches in the Czech Republic.[40]

The goal of the Czechoslovak Hussite Church is to fill all dimensions of life with the Spirit of Christ, that is, to be his effective instrument in this world. In its approach to the world, it holds a positive attitude, seeking understanding.[41]

The Czechoslovak Hussite Church understands its missional calling as composed of the proclamation of the gospel, the administration of the sacraments, and social and charitable service to people. To a certain extent, it is connected with its identity as a liturgical church; a major emphasis is laid on celebrating the liturgy and administering the sacraments.[42] It can be said that proclamation of the gospel is limited to church services; for instance, evangelization in the sense understood in evangelical churches and communities is virtually absent within the Czechoslovak Hussite Church.

---

[37] www.diakonie.cz/en (accessed 23rd June 2015).

[38] http://web.etf.cuni.cz/ETFENG-1.html (accessed 23rd June 2015).

[39] http://eapraha.cz/joomla/index.php/english (accessed 23rd June 2015).

[40] For further information in English about the Czechoslovak Hussite Church, visit: http://ccsh.cz/view.php?id=336 (accessed 23rd June 2015).

[41] This information is processed in accordance with the data available on the website of the Ecumenical Council of Churches in the Czech Republic: www.ekumenickarada.cz/in/308#.VYlSpPntmko (accessed 23rd June 2015).

[42] There are seven sacraments observed by the Czechoslovak Hussite Church, following the example of the Roman Catholic Church.

Mission as 'proclamation of the gospel in deed' is provided by the Diaconia and Mission of the Czechoslovak Hussite Church.[43] This organization is active in the field of social and charitable services which are provided not only for church members but also for society at large. Its work is focused especially at the elderly, the disabled, children, the youth and socially excluded people. The objective is to provide conditions for a dignified life, an alternative for meaningful leisure time or a chance to be integrated into society.

It is noteworthy that within the Diaconia and Mission the 'missional' dimension is curbed at the expense of the diaconal one; although the word 'mission' stands in the name of the organization, its website, for example, mostly speaks about *diakonia* or social service only. Since the two terms are not synonymous, such a practice significantly narrows down not only the theological profile of the organization, but also its practical impact. Even though social engagement is interpreted quite generously in terms of its content, many dimensions of mission are still absent (e.g. interfaith dialogue, reconciliation, inculturation, eco-justice, church planting, etc.). This trend may be for several reasons. One of them might be, for instance, the understanding of the church, mentioned earlier, which perceives the liturgical space (i.e. preaching, the sacraments) as the place *par excellence* for proclaiming the good news, while outside this sacred realm it is not appropriate to exercise anything else but charitable service interpreted in 'civic' terms. Another reason might be the effort by the Czechoslovak Hussite Church to strive for a certain kind of 'contextualization', i.e. to avoid the contested term 'mission' in the context of the secular Czech Republic and to serve the public by way of more acceptable social engagement (*diakonia*) instead.

The latter possible reason is also supported by the fact that the Czechoslovak Hussite Church seeks to be a church which speaks into the situation of contemporary human beings and society clearly and comprehensibly.[44] It is closely related with the choice of language and methods of involvement in society. The mission of the Czechoslovak Hussite Church can, therefore, be understood as a presence in the world of the church whose task is to brighten and transform the world by the power of Christ's gospel. As a rule, the world is viewed positively and with empathy; negative phenomena are criticized, yet such criticism is always to be accompanied by an effort for understanding. The Czechoslovak Hussite Church tries to keep channels of understanding open with culture (e.g. lectures, concerts, exhibits, discussions, etc.) as well as science. Its claim to allegiance to the legacy of St Cyril and St Methodius, St Wenceslas, and Jan Hus as well as the Hussite movement represents a particular effort to establish or deepen points of contact for interaction with Czech society.

---

[43] http://diakonie.ccsh.cz (accessed 23rd June 2015). Available in Czech only.

[44] Cf. the church's self-description at its official website: http://ccsh.cz/view.php?id=336 (accessed 23rd June 2015).

Several mission projects, such as those intended for helping Africa,[45] still betray signs of maintaining the somewhat artificial division between 'foreign' and 'home' mission. This contrast becomes even more apparent when one notices an interesting fact that, when referring to projects for Africa (e.g. AFA – Africa for Africa) the term 'mission' is used,[46] while in case of 'home mission' (for instance, activities of the Diaconia and Mission) the term *diakonia* is preferred.

With regard to the projects seeking to help Africa it is, however, significant that these are ideally intended to be no more than mere assistance to Africans in their efforts to help themselves (cf. '*Africa* for Africa'; emphasis added). This attempt to pursue contextualization is to be assessed positively.

Theological education is provided by the Hussite Theological Faculty of Charles University[47] and by the Hus Institute for Theological Studies in Prague.[48] In the Czech context it is significant from a missiological perspective that the Hus Institute for Theological Studies offers a study programme on missionary and social work. However, the profile of the graduate seems to indicate that the programme strives to produce 'mission managers' rather than theologians of mission.[49] This observation leads us to our final point. The theology of mission/missiology does not find any major response within the Czechoslovak Hussite Church. Therefore, it does not seem that the mission work of this church is grounded in missiological models, concepts or visions.

The Church of Brethren

The Church of Brethren (Czech: *Církev bratrská*) draws from the legacy of both the Bohemian and European Reformation; it has its place among free evangelical and Reformed churches. The Church of Brethren is a member of the International Federation of Free Evangelical Churches (IFFEC), the WCRC, the CEC, and the Ecumenical Council of Churches in the Czech Republic.

The Church of Brethren understands its main task as preaching and interpreting God's word. The proclamation has evangelizing emphases; it seeks to engender conversion to Christ and spiritual birth from the power of the Holy Spirit. Catechesis, spiritual growth and active discipleship are of prime importance.

---

[45] Cf. most notably, the initiative 'Africa for Africa' (AFA) which is a project founded in 2009 and supported by the Prague diocese of the Czechoslovak Hussite Church. For more information in English see: www.africa-for-africa.eu/project (accessed 23rd June 2015).

[46] Although understood especially in terms of humanitarian aid.

[47] www.htf.cuni.cz/HTFN-1.html (accessed 23rd June 2015).

[48] www.hitspraha.cz (accessed 23rd June 2015). Available in Czech only.

[49] The programme is offered in co-operation with St Elisabeth's College of Healthcare and Social Work, Bratislava: www.hitspraha.cz/proc-studovat-vs.html (accessed 23rd June 2015). Available in Czech only.

A significant number of laypersons are involved in church life within the Church of Brethren. They are led and trained to witness and some of them even to preach and interpret the Bible. A lot of attention is given to the education of children, youth and young families. In order to foster other ministries, congregations initiate and maintain, for example, volunteer groups, musical bands, evangelization/mission, Bible or prayer groups, etc. The church has always linked the message with diaconal service both within congregations and in church institutions.[50]

Evangelization activities within the Church of Brethren are co-ordinated by the Evangelization Committee of the Board of the Church of Brethren.[51] Mission outside the Czech Republic is on the agenda of the Foreign Mission Agency.[52] Social services and charities are provided by the Diaconia of the Church of Brethren.[53]

The missional engagement of the Church of Brethren is decisively shaped by its nature as an evangelical church. A strong emphasis is put on conversion – turning away from the old lifestyle and accepting the Lord Jesus Christ as one's personal Saviour. That is most likely also the main reason why the general discourse within the Church of Brethren tends towards evangelization rather than mission (cf. the Evangelization Committee). Proclamation of the Word, spiritual growth and discipleship are highlighted. Mission is usually mentioned with regard to so-called 'foreign mission'. It is also implied by the traditional division between 'home' and 'foreign' mission (cf. Evangelization Committee vs Foreign Mission Agency).

With regard to the latter, there is not much visible effort made to pursue indigenous mission in the sense of supporting local missionaries and church leaders from the country in question. Instead, Czech missionaries are sent to foreign countries. It is the result of a robust emphasis that Christians are to go and serve, which is biblically supported by a selection of proof-texts (cf. Matt. 9:37-38; 28:19-20; Mark 16:15; John 20:21; and Acts 1:8).

A great role in the missional engagement of the Church of Brethren is played by individual congregations. They represent the centre of gravity of missional work; denomination-level committees or agencies serve as co-ordinating bodies rather than key actors. In addition, the congregations establish various special-purpose entities or citizens' associations whose main aim is to provide the public with social and charitable services in the spirit of Christian values. It is this diaconal ministry which is inseparable from the missional work of the Church of Brethren.

---

[50] The data about the Church of Brethren has been drafted using the information available on the official website of the Ecumenical Council of Churches in the Czech Republic: www.ekumenickarada.cz/in/307#.VYlESvntmko (accessed 23rd June 2015).

[51] www.cb.cz/evangelizace (accessed 23rd June 2015). Available in Czech only.

[52] www.jdete.org/cz (accessed 23rd June 2015). Available in Czech only.

[53] www.cb.cz/diakonie (accessed 23rd June 2015). Available in Czech only.

It seems that major missiological models still prevalent today (*missio Dei*, liberation, JPIC) do not meet with much response in the Church of Brethren, with a possible exception of the proclamation model which – as stated above – represents the core of the mission work in the Church of Brethren (i.e. evangelization).

Much emphasis is placed on work with children and youth (camps, weekend retreats), the elderly (retirement homes) or the disabled (various types of disabilities, including combined disabilities). There are also efforts to participate in novel forms of evangelization – the media, technology, arts (for instance, initiatives such as TURBO 316,[54] EXIT 316, the experimental theatre 'Střep'[55]).

There is a noticeable interest in pursuing Christian apologetics as well as a dialogue with philosophy and contemporary culture. However, one needs to ask whether this interest is a result of the theological direction of the Church of Brethren, or whether it merely reflects the personal interest of David Novák, chair of the Evangelization Committee, who is the author of an overwhelming majority of the materials.[56]

A positive development represents engagement in ecological issues and a concern for God's creation which is largely thanks to the Czech branch of the A Rocha organization.[57]

Theological education for the purposes of the Church of Brethren is provided by the Evangelical Theological Seminary which also offers courses in missiology.[58] It meets the needs for the education of not only future pastors and social workers in the church, but also of all those who are interested in pursuing education in the field of theology and social work (at certificate, diploma and bachelor levels) in order to serve in their congregations more effectively.

Contemporary Czech Context: Some Essential Characteristics

In common with many other European countries, contemporary Czech society and culture can be identified as post-modern and post-Christian. While the use of the latter identifier can be justified by pointing to the fact that, increasingly, many Europeans in general and Czechs in particular do not see themselves as Christian, and Christianity has ceased to be a major societal player, the former is arguably more elusive. The post-modern has

---

[54] http://turbo316.kam.cz (accessed 23rd June 2015). Available in Czech only.
[55] https://cs-cz.facebook.com/pages/Divadlo-St%C5%99ep/169830376450036?sk=info &tab=page_info (accessed 23rd June 2015). Available in Czech only.
[56] For some materials in English see David Novák's personal website: http://cb.cz/novak/node/35 (accessed 23rd June 2015).
[57] www.arocha.cz/en (accessed 23rd June 2015).
[58] https://etspraha.cz (accessed 23rd June 2015). Available in Czech only.

become a contested term, loaded with various different meanings.[59] For the purpose of the present discussion, the current, post-modern and post-Christian context of the Czech Republic will be interpreted by way of a set of characteristics as discerned by Pavel Hošek.[60] Hošek suggests that these characteristics represent areas for a promising dialogue between Czech Christians and 'seekers', i.e. people looking for answers to the existential questions of life.[61] Let us consider these characteristics one by one in a greater detail.

First, contemporary Czech culture can be described as *post-rationalist*. In the wake of the horrors of the twentieth century, faith in reason, as one of the gods of the Enlightenment and modernity, has been shattered. In addition, people have come to acknowledge that human beings are more than merely 'rational machines', and to appreciate non-rational components of the human spirit, such as imagination, emotion, intuition and spiritual experience. Furthermore, the recent rediscovery of the significance of the body represents another major development in this regard. Christians can welcome this situation as Christianity is essentially irreconcilable with the modernist reduction of human beings to a 'ghost in a machine'.[62]

Second, contemporary Czech culture is also *post-ideological*. Arguably the most famous definition of the post-modern is 'incredulity towards metanarratives'.[63] It means, in other words, that there is suspicion of ideologies as specific sets of abstract assertions proclaimed as 'revealed truths'. In the Czech context, this distrust is even intensified by long-lasting experience with the ideology of communism. Instead of metanarratives, concrete stories of particular individuals or communities are becoming more relevant. Christians can accept this situation as an opportunity to present their faith not as a worldview, but rather as a quality of life, as 'being there for others', following the example of their Master.[64]

Third, contemporary Czech culture can also be characterized as increasingly *post-individualistic*. While it is true that recent cultural developments did not lead to the end of European individualism, still more and more people give friendship and relationships with a number of

---

[59] For a helpful analysis and discussion, see James K.A. Smith, *Who's Afraid of Postmodernism? Taking Derrida, Lyotard, and Foucault to Church* (Grand Rapids, MI: Baker Academic, 2006), especially 18-26.

[60] Cf. Hošek, 'Discerning the Signs of the Times', 31-41. Hošek also discussed this theme in an earlier study published in Czech: Pavel Hošek, *A bohové se vracejí: Proměny náboženství v postmoderní době* (Jihlava, Czech Republic: Mlýn, 2012), especially 120-32.

[61] Cf. Hošek, 'Discerning the Signs of the Times', 31-32. More on the concept of 'seekers' may be found in Tomáš Halík, 'The Church for the Seekers', in Tomáš Halík and Pavel Hošek (eds), *A Czech Perspective on Faith in a Secular Age* (Washington, DC: The Council for Research in Values and Philosophy, 2015), 125-31: www.crvp.org/book/Series04/master-czech.pdf (accessed 25th June 2015).

[62] Cf. Hošek, 'Discerning the Signs of the Times', 32-33.

[63] Jean-François Lyotard, *The Postmodern Condition: A Report on Knowledge* (Minneapolis, MN: University of Minnesota Press, 1984), xxiv.

[64] Cf. Hošek, 'Discerning the Signs of the Times', 33-34.

'significant others' as a key aspect for making up their identity, not least due to deepened feelings of isolation and loneliness. In contrast with the past, when extended family, town/village, religion, and/or nation played a major role, today a group of friends has become one of the most important factors in forming contemporary Czech people's identity, serving as a kind of 'adoptive family'. Christians can also welcome this post-individualistic tendency as it recognizes the significance of interpersonal relationships and of community which is, in fact, one of the central tenets of the biblical message.[65]

Fourth, current Czech culture is considerably *post-traditional*. For various reasons, many Czechs have a problematic, if any, relationship to the past. The loss of a link with tradition as a meaningful story of the past can be seen behind the rootlessness of many, especially young, people today. This situation leads some to 'inventing' stories of their past (for instance, neo-paganism, mythology, etc.). However, it can also represent a great opportunity for Christians to show the meaningfulness and vitality of their story and offer it as an inspiring alternative for consideration by others.[66]

Fifth, contemporary Czech culture is in many respects *post-optimistic*. The Enlightenment optimism with its belief in constant progress was ended by the horrific events of the twentieth century, such as the *shoah*, the two world wars, the ideologies of communism and Nazism, Hiroshima, and other wars and genocides. Moreover, people struggle to learn how to live under the shadow of a constant nuclear threat, with ecological crises and the scarcity of resources being an indisputable reality. In addition, the gap is increasingly widening between the 'haves' and the 'have-nots'.[67] Indeed, this reality makes prospects for a 'bright future' problematic and challenges any optimism. However, such a situation is one in which Christians can make a significant contribution, 'guided by their faith and their hope to the knowledge that all these phenomena and processes that may threaten the future of humankind on earth are not the final horizon'.[68] Far from being mere spiritual barbiturates, such faith and hope are to be a motivation to take concrete steps by implementing the values and ideals of the Kingdom of God.[69]

And finally, sixth, contemporary Czech culture is becoming more or less *post-materialistic*. It seems that years of state-imposed atheism led Czech people to realize the certain unattractiveness of a materialistic worldview. And indeed the contemporary Czech context can be described as a religious market-place with a colourful variety of spiritual 'goods' and experience

---

[65] Hošek, 'Discerning the Signs of the Times', 34-36. Cf. also David J. Bosch, *Transforming Mission: Paradigm Shifts in Theology of Mission* (Maryknoll, NY: Orbis Books, 1991), 363-67.

[66] Cf. Hošek, 'Discerning the Signs of the Times', 36-38.

[67] Cf. Bosch, *Transforming Mission*, 356-57, 361-62.

[68] Hošek, 'Discerning the Signs of the Times', 39.

[69] Hošek, 'Discerning the Signs of the Times', 38-40.

available 'for sale'.[70] Recent statistics show that the number of Czechs who explicitly say they are without a religious belief has significantly dropped in recent decades: while in the 2001 census there were over 6 million of them, in 2011 it was only 3.6 million.[71] Even though this trend brings with it many serious problems (for instance, shallow 'experience-religiosity', the commodification and commercialization of religion, etc.), it simultaneously represents a missional opportunity for Czech Christians who can present their faith as an attractive, yet authentic and profound alternative.[72]

The Ministry of *Ta Cesta* as an Example of Relevant Christian Mission in the Contemporary Czech Context

The discussion so far has shown that while the Czech people are significantly distrustful of organized forms of religion (cf. the numbers of church members have been constantly decreasing; in addition, this trend is also regularly confirmed by public opinion polls and surveys[73]), there is nonetheless a considerable demand or thirst for spirituality and/or religion in its non-institutional forms (cf. increasing numbers of believers without ties to a church or religious community, the blooming of the 'religious market', etc.). In the light of this development, it seems that the *modus operandi* of Christian mission in the Czech Republic ought to be reconsidered in several respects. While it is important that established churches continue with their ministry as part of their involvement in *missio Dei*, it is becoming increasingly clear that other forms of and approaches to missional engagement should be pursued. If the characteristics of contemporary Czech culture discussed above are correct – and it is one of the main arguments of this paper that they are – they ought to be taken into serious consideration in the process.

The rest of the present paper will introduce the ministry of one such initiative called *Ta Cesta* as an example of a possibly relevant and inspiring way to be involved in Christian mission in the contemporary context of the Czech Republic. Its ministry will be analyzed through the hermeneutic lenses of the above-mentioned six features of contemporary Czech culture. Such a hermeneutical attitude is informed by the Christian principle of discerning the signs of the times.[74]

The material for this part of the paper was gathered during fieldwork which the author has been conducting in the long term since 2011, and more intensively with a focus on this paper in the first half of 2015. The

---

[70] Cf. Hošek, 'Discerning the Signs of the Times', 28-29.

[71] Cf. Zdeňek Vojtíšek, 'Srovnání výsledků sčítání lidu', inside back cover.

[72] Cf. Hošek, 'Discerning the Signs of the Times', 40-41.

[73] Cf. Hošek, 'Discerning the Signs of the Times', 17-18.

[74] Cf. the title and the main argument of Hošek's article; see Hošek, 'Discerning the Signs of the Times', especially 13. Cf. also Bosch, *Transforming Mission*, 428-31. And cf. first and foremost, Matt. 16:2-3.

field research was ethnographic in approach and was conducted in the form of participant observation during worship services as well as an annual general meeting (22nd February 2015) and supplemented with interviews with the leadership of the case-study community. In addition, online resources (the website and Facebook page of *Ta Cesta*) were analyzed.[75]

Ta Cesta, which is the Czech expression meaning 'The Way', is a Prague evangelical community.[76] The three predicates are at the same time a key to understanding the identity of *Ta Cesta*: people belonging to *Ta Cesta* love the city (i.e. Prague) in which they live and want it 'to be healed from its wounds and to become a place where all its inhabitants can live joyfully'; they believe that the gospel (Greek: *euangelion*) 'still has the power to direct, inspire and transform human lives even today' (its evangelical basis); and they 'learn to live not only for themselves, but they seek to support one another and share their joys and sorrows' (its community-relatedness).[77] It was established in 2009 as a citizens' association (not as a registered faith community!), inspired by the words from Scripture: 'For I am with you, and no one will lay a hand on you to harm you, for there are many in this city who are my people' (Acts 18:10 NRSV). *Ta Cesta* seeks to be 'a normal church for normal people'. Even though it does not have registered membership and there are, therefore, no exact statistics about the people involved in *Ta Cesta*, there are about 150, mostly but not exclusively young, people who participate in the life of the community more or less regularly; of these, there are about 35 people who could be labelled as 'core members'. Sunday worship services, followed by conversations and fellowship over a common meal and drinks, take place on evenings in a student club affiliated with Charles University of Prague. Usually, some 50-60 people attend, very often including guests and visitors.

However, Sunday evening worship services are not the only or, arguably, even the main activity of the community. *Ta Cesta* seeks to be 'the community of communities'. Therefore, there are several smaller groups as part of *Ta Cesta* which meet together regularly during the week. The purpose of these groups or communities-within-the-community is threefold. First, they strive to strengthen their own fellowship as a group. This is done especially by way of dining together in the house of one of the members. Second, they go and do together 'something fun' in the city. This

---

[75] I am very grateful to all people who helped me accomplish this research, especially to Alexander Flek, one of the founders and the leader of *Ta Cesta*.

[76] For more information, see their official website: http://tacesta.cz (accessed 26th June 2015). Further news can be followed at the initiative's Facebook page: https://cs-cz.facebook.com/TaCesta (accessed 26th June 2015). It is surprising that the two Internet resources are in Czech only, given the fact that several English-speaking people belong to *Ta Cesta*. On the other hand, such praxis may underscore the rootedness in the local Czech context which the community emphasizes.

[77] The quotations above are translations of the self-description of *Ta Cesta* to be found at: http://tacesta.cz/jsme (accessed 26th June 2015).

would include attending concerts, theatre performances, exhibits, etc. And last but certainly not least, they pursue some kind of social service or ministry for the sake of people in Prague. This is very much in tune with *Ta Cesta*'s overall vision: to serve more people outside the community itself. It is clear that *Ta Cesta* is very much missionally focused.

After this brief introduction,[78] let us now discuss the ministry of *Ta Cesta* within the hermeneutical framework provided by the six above-mentioned features of contemporary Czech culture. It was argued, first, that contemporary Czech culture is *post-rationalist.* The ministry of *Ta Cesta* takes this insight seriously, yet there is arguably space for further elaboration in this regard. On the one hand, it is true that human beings are not perceived simply as 'ghosts in a machine', but that non-rational aspects, such as imagination, emotion and experience, as well as the dimension of the body in general, are also emphasized. One can observe this, for instance, with regard to the creative use of arts and music in ministry or to the importance attributed to dining together. On the other hand, a major part of the Sunday worship service is taken up by a more or less typical Protestant sermon. Although delivered in an informal style, and at times making creative use of gadgets and works of contemporary culture, the sermons still largely attempt to appeal to the rational element of the spirit of the listeners. Moreover, such an approach reinforces the binary opposition between the speaker and the listener, discouraging more experiential and interactive modes of participation. In spite of the fact that the communion (or Lord's Supper), which is part of each worship service, represents an important corrective to this practice, there is undoubtedly room for further exploration with respect to how non-rational dimensions could be engaged in the ministry of *Ta Cesta.*

Second, contemporary Czech culture was described as *post-ideological.* This characteristic very much applies to the ministry of *Ta Cesta,* too, particularly in two respects. Rooted in a post-communist context, first, members of the community are suspicious and critical of any ideologies. This is clearly visible in sermons which critically engage with recent events in the Czech, as well as in wider, contexts in the community's pursuit of faithful and relevant participation in *missio Dei.* The second respect, then, has to do with the fact that *Ta Cesta* apparently does not seek to be 'just another worldview' or metanarrative, but rather accentuates its story as a community, as well as the stories of its individual members[79] in order to present an alternative way of life which might be attractive to other people.

The third feature, *post-individualistic*, relates to the *modus vivendi* of *Ta Cesta* probably most strongly. It has already been noted that the emphasis

[78] Much of this information was presented at the general assembly meeting of *Ta Cesta* on 22nd February 2015.

[79] In this regard, it is important to note that each worship service includes an informal interview with somebody from the community or with a guest who shares their life-story with the others.

on a community is one of the three main thrusts of *Ta Cesta*. Moreover, there is not just one chief community that meets for Sunday worship services but, to be sure, the core lies in the above-mentioned small communities which meet, enjoy themselves and serve during the week. In addition, there are also weekly Bible studies, encouraging people to read, interpret and meditate upon the Scriptures together with others. Furthermore, people associated with *Ta Cesta* spend holidays and/or weekend retreats together which is another expression of the importance given to interpersonal relationships. Finally, the regularly held Lord's Supper is a robust symbol and practice to counter the pervasive individualism typical of our age.

Fourth, contemporary Czech culture was characterized as *post-traditional*, which is another feature that clearly plays an important role in the ministry of *Ta Cesta*. The people involved in this community come from various backgrounds, both Christian and secular. Some of them have never been affiliated with any church; others have previously experienced disappointment in organized religion; and yet others are still more or less active members of traditional/established Christian churches. In its practice, *Ta Cesta* can be characterized as 'post-traditional' because it goes beyond the usual patterns of belonging and non-belonging, and invites people not to membership in an organized religious group but rather to participation in a shared story. *Ta Cesta* is an ecumenical community which sees itself as part of the world Christian movement/church and, indeed, its practice is in many respects 'traditional' (for instance, the use of the lectionary; the usual scheme of the worship service consisting of hymns, prayers, a sermon, the Lord's Supper, and a blessing; the ministry 'portfolio' which does not differ very much from those of established churches, etc.). However, because of its ability to embrace people with no Christian background and to invite them to be 'part of the story', while respecting their right to maintain their own identities, the term 'post-traditional' seems to be appropriate to describe the ministry of *Ta Cesta*.

Fifth, *post-optimistic* is a feature which is perhaps not readily visible vis-à-vis *Ta Cesta* and its mission. However, one must clearly say that those who feel at home in this community are well aware and critical of what is going on in their city and society. Therefore, they are neither naïve nor ignorant with regard to both the present and the future. Moreover, their theology lies in the creative tension between 'already' and 'not yet' which gives their ministry a clear and strong focus on the here and now, in addition to the expectation of the *eschaton*. The ministry of *Ta Cesta* can be characterized as a witness to the hope for the coming King and his Kingdom, and as work towards its realization.

And finally, the ministry of *Ta Cesta* is surely in line with the observation on the *post-materialistic* character of contemporary Czech culture. It represents an expression of the pursuit of transcendence among both spiritual seekers, not rooted in any particular tradition, and members of established churches who are nonetheless searching for new modes of religious experience as well as for innovative ways of serving others. However, with its strong foundation in Christian tradition (which is, nevertheless, creatively accepted and transformed) and a clear emphasis on authentic witness and ministry for the sake of others, *Ta Cesta* can hardly be dismissed as a mere 'spiritual commodity'.

To be sure, there are words of caution, question marks and critical comments to be made regarding the existence and ministry of *Ta Cesta*. Let us mention three of them, in addition to those discussed above. First, one must be cautious not to view this approach to mission as one to be applied universally in the context of the Czech Republic. This is a particular type of urban mission which would not necessarily have to work in other, especially rural, settings.[80] Second, there is the issue of the financial sustainability of the whole initiative. At present, almost 80% of the budget of *Ta Cesta* consists of funds coming from US-based donors.[81] This fact represents a challenge not only to the indigenous character of its ministry, but also to its long-term sustainability after funding from the USA is discontinued. And third and finally, *Ta Cesta* might need to explore further ways of actively engaging a more people in its ministry, including leadership positions, as it still seems to be too centred on the figure of Alexander Flek who remains as its almost exclusive preacher and one of the few key leaders of the community.

In spite of these reservations, however, *Ta Cesta* undoubtedly represents one of the most fascinating and inspiring new ways of pursuing Christian mission in the Czech Republic today due to its attentiveness to contemporary culture, its creative, yet faithful relationship to the gospel, and its emphasis on the significance of community. *Ta Cesta* might possibly serve as a relevant model for Christian mission in contemporary Czech society – a society that is post-modern, post-Christian, and characterized by a deep distrust of institutions of any kind.

Conclusion

This paper has explored the topic of Christian mission in the Czech Republic from an ecumenical perspective. Having introduced the historical, sociological and political context and its peculiarities vis-à-vis religion in general and Christianity in particular, it has provided a critical overview of mission pursued by select Czech churches which are either full or associate members of the Ecumenical Council of Churches in the Czech Republic.

[80] To be fair to *Ta Cesta*, one must of course immediately say that they never stake any claims to universality in their missional approach. This comment is, therefore, not meant as a word of criticism, but rather as a warning to anybody who might possibly view the kind of ministry *Ta Cesta* pursues as a missional panacea.

[81] According to the financial report presented at the *Ta Cesta* general assembly meeting on 22nd February 2015.

Reflecting on their missional endeavours in the light of the themes and issues introduced and elaborated by the Edinburgh 2010 Mission Conference, one can make at least two basic remarks. First, there is hardly any explicit missiological reflection or discussion in Czech churches on the Edinburgh 2010 Mission conference themes. Having said that, however, one also needs to acknowledge – and this is the second remark – that there exists a certain degree of engagement with these themes nonetheless, albeit more at a level of practical ministry rather than that of theological/missiological reflection. As a result, one can therefore discern the presence of certain Edinburgh 2010 main themes (such as mission and unity; theological education and formation; forms of missionary engagement) as well as transversals (for instance, youth and mission; Bible and mission) in the ministry of the Czech churches, although the adequacy of their treatment is questionable. In addition, there are then those main themes and transversals which are treated clearly inadequately, yet are nevertheless present. Such main themes include, for instance, foundations for mission, Christian mission among other faiths, and Christian communities in contemporary contexts; in the case of the transversals, these could be healing and reconciliation, and the contextualization, inculturation and dialogue of worldviews. Finally, there are those main themes and transversals suggested by the Edinburgh conference which in the Czech context are virtually not addressed at all, including mission and post-modernity, mission and power, and mission spirituality (as the main themes) as well as women and mission, subaltern voices, and ecological perspectives on mission (as transversals). While this paper does not want to suggest that these themes and transversals represent an absolute must for authentic and faithful Christian mission, it seeks to argue that they can establish the basis for a model of holistic mission which could very well be relevant in the Czech context. Taking them into consideration intentionally and with utmost seriousness, Czech churches might be enabled to participate in *missio Dei* more fully, pertinently and genuinely.

Given the peculiarities of the contemporary Czech context, such as the low rate of church membership and the high rate of distrust of organized religion, one needs to acknowledge the role new, non-institutional mission initiatives are to play in post-modern and post-Christian Czech society. As demonstrated in the paper, these might be of major significance for Christian mission, especially if they focus on the importance of community and are able to respond creatively to some of the key issues and features of contemporary culture.

The two modes mentioned above are not intended to compete with each other, but rather to be mutually complementary. The mission of established Christian churches, such as the four discussed in this paper, pursued holistically as inspired by the insights from the 2010 Edinburgh Mission conference can be enriched and supplemented by the ministry of alternative

Christian communities, such as *Ta Cesta*, in the pursuit of participation in God's mission in the Czech Republic in the 21st century.

The Social Context of Work in Christian Churches: A Reflection of the CECMS Conference in April 2011 in Prague

Zuzana Jurechová

Each missionary attempt of the Christian church to spread the witness of the Divine Revelation to others takes place in a specific social setting. The conditions we live in influence our daily life, but since they are often quite complex, multi-layered and interrelated, we – in our practical everydayness – usually do not have enough time or energy to undertake a more profound research of this system of actions and reactions. Thus one of the main aims of missiology is to make what we usually call 'conditions' more transparent and understandable.

This short contemplation stood at the birth of the project undertaken by the CECMS named 'The church and Its Context' which climaxed in (1) publishing of the collective monograph *Crisis Situations in the Czecho-Slovak Context after 1989* in February 2011; and (2) organizing two conferences in April 2011 – in Prague (1st April) and in Bratislava (14th April). In the following lines I will try to briefly summarize and reflect on the main theses and inspiring thoughts we could hear at the Prague meeting.

Crisis as a Key to 'Context'

Why 'the church and its context', and why 'crisis situations'? We simply wanted to use the concept of 'crisis situations' as a gateway to the wide and multi-faceted topic of 'context'. The conference was meant as an experiment enabling us to make space for a discussion between human scientists and researchers and representatives of various Christian churches – a space that would be no longer bound to a single academic discipline or a single dogmatic tradition, a space that would approach closer the reality we live in, so that it could offer useful and practical insights into current events around us. We were wondering how the confrontation of the academic sphere of scholars and the world of the churches would look like. Would communication be possible? Would they be able to enrich one another's thoughts? Could the churches somehow profit from the knowledge provided by the scholarly standpoint, gain a new idea of humanity in its actual needs and, consequently, re-evaluate their missionary approach, teachings and offers?

Five researchers from the Czech and Slovak Republics accepted an invitation to the Prague conference: philosopher Václav Němec, sociologist Markéta Sedláčková, sociologist Jiřina Šiklová, theologian Pavol Bargár and sociologist Ľubomír German. In addition, four representatives of the churches accepted the invitation, but unfortunately only two of them were able to come – Roman Juriga, vice-chairman of the Eastern Orthodox Academy in Vilémov at Litovel and chief editor of monthly magazine *Hlas Pravoslaví* ('The Voice of Eastern Orthodoxy') and Karel Šimr, a pastor of the Evangelical Church of Czech Brethren in Chrást u Plzně. Papers of the researchers, dealing with the topic of miscellaneous crises which began to emerge in Czech and Slovak society after 1989, had been published in the reviewed collective monograph and sent to the church representatives in advance so that they were able to prepare their responses and reflections. Finally, seventeen people attended the conference, which made the atmosphere very pleasant and intimate – there was no need to use a microphone or amplifier, and discussion thus became more spontaneous and dynamic.

Democracy, Family, Consumerism, Corruption... and the Church

Václav Němec opened the conference with his paper which reflected on the crisis of democracy. He explained that democracy is interwoven with a complex network of human relationships and the mutual interactions of individuals. Institutions in which people work have their own patterns of regulations and orders, and it is expected that people will adopt them voluntarily. If this does not happen, the democratic system should be equipped with legal tools to enforce obedience to the institutional patterns. But when even this does not work, i.e. when legal tools are missing or fail to maintain the democratic order, and people lack the ability to fulfil their moral 'roles', we can speak about a crisis of democracy. Such a crisis can be the result of a situation when we try to apply the old patterns of behaviour in new conditions of democratic transformation. I asked myself whether this depiction does not also fit the situation of the churches. From a sociological viewpoint, the church is nothing other than an institution based on democratic principles while, at the same time, it also influences democracy as such. The church with a transparent 'network of relationships' can lead its members to act democratically even outside the church's institutional borders – and the other way round. But even churches cannot protect themselves from the repetition of negative behavioural patterns from the past, and thus its members should always reflect on the 'network of relationships' and support such behaviour that is in line with Christian values. The question is whether we – maybe because of a lack of time and space for an open discussion – do not rather tend to overlook the 'networks of relationships' in our churches and all the setbacks they bring, and whether we do not use words about 'forgiving love' to conceal and cover those maladies instead of curing them.

The reflection on democracy also continued in the paper of sociologist Markéta Sedláčková. It seems that people in general have a very vague understanding of the term 'democracy'. What most people consider 'democracy' – i.e. 'free elections' – is rather a caricature of the original concept. Dr Sedláčková builds her interpretation of democracy upon the one of its fundamental prerequisites – social trust that shapes civic society and aims towards collective civic actions and initiatives. The birth of social trust is always preceded by the process of 'socialization', i.e. conforming to the system. People born before 1989 (and were thus brought up in the communist era) show more ability at such social integration than their parents, but obviously less than those born after 2000. Democracy helps the churches in their active life. A malfunction of democracy also affects the churches. If old behavioural patterns prevail in civic society, they also prevail in the churches. While in society it is often hard to recognize and point out these patterns, the churches – at least theoretically – should be equipped to do so with better democratic tools of critical debate and self-reflection thanks to a warmer, more familiar atmosphere. Thus the churches in general have the best potential to give their members a 'practical lesson in democracy', which could then spread into the everyday life of civic society.

The life of an individual is originally and with the greatest impact shaped by his family. Jiřina Šiklová offered her reflection on contemporary family life and the crisis it faces. She suggests we should finally put an end to the search for someone to blame for the current negative situation in families and grasp the 'power of powerless': i.e. be aware of our freedom to act according to our own opinions and consciousness. Despite this freedom, the current attitude of society is characterized instead by 'rejection' and 'anger', which Šiklová considers a manifestation of self-confidence being lacking and our adoption of the 'powerless' attitude. Can the church be somehow helpful in this? What is its attitude towards mixed marriages? Certainly there is still a certain tension in the attitude of churches towards mixed marriages, since the aim of churches is to support marriages where both members are of the same confession. However, it would be better if, in compliance with the Scriptures, it protected the family as an institution *per se*, regardless of differences in the confession of its members. Pastor Karel Šimr brought an inspiring insight. In his personal experience mixed marriages can play a very important and positive role in the ecumenical life of the church. Owing to mixed marriages in his congregation, he and his congregation participated at many ecumenical events – biblical lessons, passion plays or collections, which were organized spontaneously and which would probably not otherwise have taken place.

In his paper, Protestant theologian Pavol Bargár reflected on the concept of 'consumerism', which is very often being misused by church representatives and authorities as a code-word to label a 'common danger' of any kind. On the contrary, an exaggerated demonization of 'consumerism' and 'the consumer society' prevents churches from becoming engaged with the real problems – the causes and effects of excessive consumption. Instead of an extravagant call for asceticism and self-denial, Bargár suggests the churches should admit that moderate consumption brings joy and pleasure, and we would be better to look elsewhere for the real roots of excessive consumption.

'Consumerism' as a negative concept and as an invisible power that does away with the ethical boundaries of our behaviour, was also introduced by the paper of the last speaker at the conference, sociologist Ľubomír German. He focused mainly on the analysis of 'white-collar' crime. He defined this term as a situation resulting from the conflict of two contradictory concerns of 'white-collars': (1) as workers and citizens, they are obligated to bear responsibility for public welfare (or company benefit); (2) as private subjects, they also aim at their personal profit or power, regardless of moral standards or ethical considerations. Nonetheless, the concept of 'white-collar' crime cannot be limited to the crimes of individuals, as the term also inevitably includes the crime of companies and organizations abusing their powers. There are many crafty and well-concealed varieties of such abuse and so the majority of 'white-collar' crime remains unseen and unpunished. Moreover, 'white-collar' crime is contagious and can spread throughout all social classes, and adapt according to circumstances. Therefore, anti-corruption measures must be enforceable, so that obeying the rules would simply be more profitable than breaking them.

What Can We Do to Raise Public Awareness in the Churches?

Discussion during the conference revealed an interesting fact: church workers are far better informed about public affairs than researchers are about church activities and events. It implies a question: What can we do to raise public awareness in the churches? What tools or means should we use to inform society about the wide range of the church's beneficial activities? Church activities hold a secure place in society besides the activities of other civic organizations and associations, and it is rather a pity that they have not found an appropriate way of demonstrating this.

Roman Juriga presented the activities of the Eastern Orthodox Church and Eastern Orthodox theology as an active response to current social questions, making his case with the holding of several conferences organized by the Eastern Orthodox Church in recent years. Just as his colleague Karel Šimr, Juriga highlighted the importance of biblical ethics. They agreed that biblical ethics represents the fundamental power upon which social transformation and progression can be built. An ecumenical atmosphere was spontaneously penetrating the whole conference and there was thus no need to press it further. In the encounter with the insights from the field of humanities, the ecumenical dimension seemed rather an essential necessity, which the churches can no longer avoid if they want to work not only for the benefit of Christianity but for the good of human society generally. Undoubtedly, the church must remain an unambiguous 'constant' in society but it should not forget, above all, that it is still a part of it.

The reflections of the current crises presented from various points of view generally showed many accords and convergences, these being sometimes complementary. However, they brought many insights important for shaping our critical thought and attitudes for practical living. In my opinion, the conference succeeded in avoiding both critical thought purely for its own sake and the often hasty and premature pastoral evaluation of crisis situations. Creating a diverse interdisciplinary and ecumenical environment made for a great deal of pleasure for all of us and, hopefully, it will characterize all our future projects.

To Recognize the Finger of God

Let me conclude with a few words from the opening speech of Joel Ruml, Chairman of the Ecumenical Council of Churches in the Czech Republic, which I quote without comment:

Crisis evokes fear, an image of failure, and that is why we spontaneously try to avoid the whole issue. We dream about a *status quo* of ease and well-being – but only crisis can bring fundamental changes. Even the Scripture knows the possibility of 'teaching an old dog new tricks'. God is not a motionless principle, but he has always entered and still enters our present situation. Thus the most important thing in life is to recognize the proverbial finger of God. God's people had chance to grow when they succeeded in recognizing the finger of God in the crisis situations they had to face. It is not a matter of our specializations. A dividing line is not drawn between 'specialists' and 'laypeople', but between those who are willing to see further and those who are in every situation satisfied with seeing only the surface of things, what is 'obvious' and 'logical'. Christians lift up their eyes and hopes to God and they see, in everyday struggles, a great companion in life, a companion in personal joy and a confessor in the times of crisis. With this very attitude they can contribute towards improving the life of society as a whole.

CRISIS SITUATIONS IN THE CZECHO-SLOVAK CONTEXT AFTER 1989: A REFLECTION ON THE CECMS CONFERENCE IN APRIL 2011 IN BRATISLAVA

Viktória Šoltésová

The Bible and the Church Today

Jiří Lukeš analyzes the selected defence speeches of the Apostle Paul from the book of Acts. After his rejection by the Jerusalem audience, Luke begins to present Paul also as a 'secular' person. It is known that the apostle Paul had knowledge of classical rhetoric. This biographical fact, as well as Paul's Roman citizenship, is repeatedly highlighted by Luke in the context of Paul's future witness in Rome. In his speech before Agrippa, Paul refers to Christianity as a significant social phenomenon. As Lukeš writes, a crisis situation does not lead to a change in the strategy of Paul's mission; it does not mean the abandonment of his mission. Recurring crises were perhaps the main reason why the apostle Paul reached a deeper interpretation of the 'theology' of the Cross of Christ.

An application of the New Testament text in the practice: the known efficient methods for doing mission appear to be less applicable in recent decades. The content of the message does not change, but some strategies are changing. Paul does not change his strategy – not only was it the way to proceed with mission, but it was a timeless purpose to preach Christ to the Gentiles too. If we would like to interpret the missionary situation of the church today in the light of this analysis, we could just focus on a new understanding of the nature and quality of mission. Empirical studies mostly focus on missionary experience. On the one hand, there exist a few partial researches on missionary strategies which map out the reactions of missionary workers, while on the other hand, we are entirely missing the reactions of converts, which would help us to fill in the mosaic of knowledge on the effectiveness of missionary work. If we want to concentrate our view on the situation in the Czecho-Slovak context, their voices should be also heard.

Juraj Laššuth discusses the thesis of *the end of history* famously introduced by the author Francis Fukuyama. In addition to being its open critic, Laššuth focuses on the impact that Christians might have in the world of today. He defines the fundamental problems of social and political relations. According to Kant, the author reminds us, despotism in religious thinking and policy manifests itself differently: 'Their common feature is the inability to use the intellect without the direction of someone else.' It is a government that is not based on consent and does not reflect the law of liberty. The author sees the concept of the end of world history in the context of Christianity as an establishment of the fullness of God's Kingdom on earth. He points out two main and related texts from the Old Testament as interpreted in Christianity:

– *Isaiah's tradition of the servant* (the world is empty and waits for God's good news – everyone will believe in God – eternal peace).

– *Daniel's vision of the Kingdom of the Son of Man* (duality of the two ways of the governance – the battle between divine forces and anti-divine forces – the world as a hostile place).

Jesus is committed to both traditions and the functioning of the church becomes a situation known as '*already and not yet*'. Paul's sceptical theology, focused on the suffering of Christians in the world, is balanced by the optimistic view of the book of Acts. The author discusses political theology in relation to the Roman Empire; this was an important question for the early church. In his writings, Eusebius, the bishop of Caesarea, tried to deal with the new situation in state-church relations (the year 313, with the Edict of Milan, which brought the end of Christian opposition by the Roman Empire, is considered the end of history). In this context, Laššuth suggests an association with the perception of the political situation in the Czech Republic. For example, he quotes Masaryk's notion of the conflict between theocracy and democracy during World War I. In the light of developments after the fall of the communism, he sees signs of the end of history in rhetoric of a defeat of 'the last enemy'. The concept of the end of history was evident in the rhetoric of politicians and priests in the period after the Velvet Revolution (the 1989 non-violent anti-communist upheaval in former Czechoslovakia). The use of this concept is not surprising, given the historical experience of the persecution of Christian churches. Laššuth mentioned several ways in which Christians can respond to the situation of 'the end of history'. He regards a redefinition of problems as a viable way – not the end of history, evil remains, but at the same time there is real hope for change. As an alternative to the concept of the end of history, he offers the concept of the world polytheism of values and the world political sphere, where these values meet. A reflection on the plurality of the concepts of goodness is to be found in the works of Max Weber and Hans Morgenthau, as well as in the theology of Reinhold Niebuhr. The major representatives of this theory of ethical realism are A. Lieven and J. Hulsman. Unlike Kant's optimism with regard to the end of history, Morgenthau puts forward realistic expectations in terms of political philosophy. *The evil cannot be destroyed, only limited.* Morgenthau sees the tragic situation of man in the world. Laššuth considered political realism to be a suitable alternative activity of the Christian in the world, in the tradition of Augustine and Paul. He proposed the concept of the political sphere as a space for meetings of the plurality of values and in order to avoid the disappointment of the controversial 'end of history' in the future.

Let us look at the role of Christians in the world through the eyes of another author, a theologian dealing with Christian ethics. According to I. Kišš, Christians need to seek the implementation of justice in the world by analogy with the basic ethical values of the spiritual Kingdom of God. The latter include justice, love, freedom, equality, truth, peace, kindness, community, respect for life and an ethical phenomenon of work. The spiritual values of the Kingdom of God must become ethical and human values round the world. Christian ethics has significant specificity. Its centre is not mediated by abstract and normative acts (as in Old Testament ethics), but by the particular person of Jesus Christ. According to H.U. von Balthasar, Christ is the specific categorical imperative, because he is a personal and particular standard, not just a formal universal standard of ethical behaviour. The morality of the New Testament underlines three essential aspects: the coming of the Kingdom of God, the fulfilment of the law – a call to conversion and repentance, and the supreme order to fulfil God's will. The ideal Christian life is to follow the example of Jesus Christ.

Society and Economy

Markéta Sedláčková explores democracy and trust in democracy in the context of Czech society. A functioning civic society is dependent on the quality of social relationships; the author highlights the need for a general trust in the functioning of democracy. She follows the decline of trust in democracy in the Czech Republic (for example, the legislative elecctions of 1998). Legitimacy – trust in the legitimacy of the democratic system is crucial. However, researchers are encountering different understandings of democracy in different population groups; linguists pointed out differences in the understanding of spoken language in relation to its scientific definition. The author quotes a certain research of democratic values in the Czech Republic, as well as the trust in institutions and the general trust in other people. Researchers found a lack of confidence in different areas of society; the author sees this as a possible hindrance in the development of a democratic society and of a market economy system.

Quality of life requires integrity: material and spiritual-cultural values. Values affect the relationship with self and others, but also with the environment. Today, more and more researchers speak about a crisis in value systems. Schwartz's research has confirmed that the basic problems that societies are facing are those between the individual and society: ensuring the responsible behaviour of the members of society and the relationship of humankind to nature and the global community.[1] Every person has his values and goals; for society, it is important to discern how individual values have an objective validity, since every society applies a particular system of values.[2] The importance of universal values for which there is a consensus between the theories of religious and secular values has been shown by E. Bergin and I.R. Payne.

Confidence in the democratic system is a specific problem of the research of values. In contrast to objective moral requirements (such as Kant's categorical imperative), there is a dominance of individual freedom, which can be traced, for example, in S. Kierkegaard's work. According to M. Buber, interpersonal communication is a fundamental fact of human existence. As the basis of our humanity he determined a relationship. This principle opens to him new perspectives in cultural anthropology as well as philosophical, religious and political issues. A need for social values and democracy is often denied today. A representative of *neo-pragmatism*, R. Rorty, expressed the philosophy of values as follows: 'The dichotomy of facts and values has arisen as a consequence of the dichotomy of the objective and the subjective, therefore the term "objective value" sounds to us today as mythological as a winged horse.'[3] From this perspective, the proclamation of objective values (such as democracy) as the development of the social relations is inadequate for a pragmatically oriented society. However, without accepting objective values, a society cannot be functional in practice.

A reassessment of advertising budgets in the transition between phases of the economic cycle is noted by Andrej Miklošík in his presentation. He pointed out, *inter alia*, long-term trends in the transfer of expenditure on advertising in the modern media like the Internet, mobile phones advertising, etc. Based on his research, he notes that advertisers in Slovakia are more conservative in comparison with the US.

Harold Laswell – a political scientist and one of the founders of the discipline of communication – constructed a basic model of medial communication: 'Who says to whom through what channel and for what effect?' The audience is also the producer and consumer of thinking. The consumer decodes and interprets the media in ways that are created from his social and cultural situations and the subjective examination of these effects. Researchers have started to use the term 'interpretative community'. An issue of sub-cultures and their preference to certain kinds of content in the media is an independent chapter of global research.

In the United States, 2% of the gross national product was used for advertising in 1986 (Association of National Advertisers, USA, 1988),

---

[1] S.H. Schwartz, 'A Theory of Cultural Values and Some Implications for Work', in *Applied Psychology*, 48.1 (1999), 23-47.

[2] J. Grác, *Pohľady do psychológie hodnotovej orientácie mládeže* (Bratislava: Slov. pedagogické nakladateľstvo, 1979), 36.

[3] V. Brožík, *O hodnotách a ľuďoch* (Nitra, Slovakia: FF UKF, 2006), 118.

excluding the expenses for design, marketing and production. Among the principles defined by the 'American Advertising Federation' there is also included one that says: 'Good advertising informs the consumer and helps him buy more wisely.' However, the producers of advertisements put a great emphasis on the emotional part of the personality of the consumer.[4] TV commercials usually last for 60, 30, 15 or even 10 seconds. Most of them are dramatizations of the lifestyle, enjoyment and benefit of the consumer society. TV advertising often takes the structure of *conflict-resolution* from television programmes. This raises a serious question: *Is advertising information or persuasion?*

To learn how to watch advertisements critically is an important task for experts who can help us avoid the manipulation. In order to sell certain products, corporations are inventing campaigns to associate their products with positive and desirable examples.

Advertising sells its products and an image of the world through a verbal and visual expression and a design effect calculated in a certain psychological and marketing strategy. The mass media reach a large audience; they have great political and economic influence. Their control has become a particular problem for a democratic state. Therefore, knowledge of the problems of mass culture, mass communication and the mass media are becoming a focus of those sciences which are concerned with the issues of collective behaviour. These facts lead us to recommend confronting the freedom of creative expression with the need to protect children and youth from the negative effects of the mass media. It seems to be an urgent social need, which ultimately reflects the wishes of parents and professionals.

Personality and Identity

In his paper, Alexander Plencner deals with popular culture. It includes a crisis of intimacy and communication, as well as a crisis of gender identity as its accompanying phenomenon. The crisis of communication results in remorse, self-pity, explosions of anger, manipulative forms of communication, etc. In recent modern society, man has lost confidence in knowing his own experience. Our author explores the above-mentioned factors in the case of contemporary 'lifestyle magazines' that offer insight into an imaginary ideal world. After a detailed analysis of variables, the author concludes by saying that modern man lacks the concept of *the meaning of life as a stabilizing perspective*.

The concept of the meaning of life is a relevant topic. V.E. Frankl considered the search for the meaning of life to be a basic human responsibility; he called finding an individual lifelong meaning an

[4] J. Downing, A. Mohammadi and A. Srebreny-Mohammadi, *Questioning the Media: A Critical Introduction* (London: Sage Publications, 1991), 330.

'occupation'.[5] Basic human needs also include 'the will to meaning'. Frankl puts the meaning of life to the spiritual dimension of man (not necessarily in a religious sense). He describes three categories of values: *creative values, experiential values and attitudinal values.* Individual elements of his theory are closely related to the search for one's own worldview and value system. P.T.P. Wong clarified his concept of the noetic dimension of personality; this, according to him, lies in the overlapping of psychological and spiritual dimensions.[6] As noted by Chlewinski, the central object in human consciousness controls the functioning of a human. If religiosity as an individually lived religion is the central value, then the other values are subordinate.[7] In Slovakia, P. Halama examined how values and value systems affect human behaviour. According to Halama, the development of *existential intelligence* helps an individual to interpret his life as meaningful and can offer valuable goals to live his life as meaningful.[8]

In her presentation entitled 'The Continuity and Transformation of Childhood in the Pedagogical Context', Mária Matulčíková draws attention, *inter alia*, to the influence the media have on today's children. She supports the *media education* of children, focusing on the research of the role and authority of fathers in the present-day concept of a family.

Media research, with a particular focus on issues affecting children, is a standard attempt to create insight into the long-term socialization effects of mass communication. D. Morley was interested in the role of watching TV, which he called a 'policy of the living room'. It would be interesting to look at the relationships between parents and children in the context of media behaviour. The media play an important role in ordering our daily lives and social relationships. For a child, it is extremely important to meet the needs of security, stimulation and success; for the further development of the child's personality it is of great importance to meet the needs of one's own responsibility.[9] The approach of J. Piaget, who deduced the formation of children's moral attitudes from internal sources, is inconsistent with theories that favour the impact of socialization and the socio-cultural environment. According to Muchova, the role of parenting is to create a psychological 'basis' for the adoption of the Christian message.[10] The family is the first environment where socialization as well as education of the child begins; by implication, it applies to the formation of his personality, too. The task of catechesis is to strengthen positive socializing effects of interpersonal relations, but also to build a child's relationships on biblical foundations. The willingness to forgive, help and receive is a

---

[5] V.J. Drapela, *Přehled teorií osobnosti* (Prague: Portál, 1997), 145-53.

[6] P. Halama, 'Teoretické a metodologické prístupy k problematike zmyslu života', in *Československá psychologie,* 44.3 (2000), 216-36.

[7] M. Stríženec, *Psychológia náboženstva* (Bratislava: Veda, 1996), 66.

[8] P. Halama, *Zmysel života z pohľadu psychológie* (Bratislava: SAP, 2007), 107.

[9] M. Homola, *Motivace lidského chování* (Prague: Státní pedagogické nakladatelství, 1977).

[10] L. Muchová, *Úvod do náboženské pedagogiky* (České Budějovice: Pedagogická fakulta Jihočeské univerzity, 1992).

litmus paper of the unity with God (Matt. 5:45, 48 and 6:12, 25, 40-45). The desire for value-education is one of the responses to the crisis of orientation, caused by a rapid cultural transformation of modern societies.[11]

There are many ways in which parents, teachers and religious institutions try to convey values. A direct inculcation of values shows the best results if there is a complete agreement on how desirable values are formed. The restriction of the direct inculcation of values lies in the fact that this method often leads to discrepancies between theory and practice. Another way to communicate values is to give an example. Being a role model is therefore an effective way of teaching values, because it represents a living example of the practice. Of course, everyone serves as an example, whether or not everyone is conscious of it. We note how other people behave and how to handle a serious decision. Also, we look at whether their behaviour matches their proclaimed faith. Everyone always serves as an example to others, be it a positive or negative model. Similar to inculcation, being a role model is an important and necessary method of the transmission of values; of course, it also has its limitations. The main problem is that people are surrounded by many different examples they can follow. The role of the father also consists in trying to help children to choose their life values.

Conclusion

The modernity project of human freedom assumes that everyone wants to be a mature personality who sees his life as a vocation. But it is not so. Therefore, we ask whether Czech and Slovak society as a whole in the post-communist period, as well as families and individuals, do not miss this unifying element. This conference in Bratislava, as an output of the above-mentioned interdisciplinary research, brought a constructive debate on critical social situations from the perspective of theologians, Christian workers and experts in social sciences. It is precisely these 'views inside the house from other parallel windows' which represent a new refreshing aspect that can produce good fruit in the study of missiology in our context.

---

[11] W. Brezinka, *Filozofické základy výchovy* (Prague: Zvon, 1996).

Romanian Pentecostal Missiological Praxis: Towards an Integrative Approach

Vasile Marchiş

Introduction

The religious contemporary context in Romania is a peculiarly complex one and generalizations are hardly possible since the situations and status of the churches differ and there are significant variations between different regions of the country. Doing mission in the contemporary context requires thoughtful reflection on the part of the church. Although the emerging contemporary context is a complex phenomenon, the reality of its existence is becoming clearer. Into such ferment, the church faces increasing challenges while it seeks to communicate the gospel in the contemporary Romanian context. While in some senses, it has never been harder to communicate the gospel faithfully, in other ways the doors of opportunity are wider now than they have been for a long time. To meet these challenges and maximize the opportunities, the church in the contemporary context is called to struggle with the messages and the meanings of post-modern culture until it can confidently announce that which represents the good news of Christ.

Taking all this into consideration, it is important to reflect on the role of Christian community in today's society from a missiological perspective. Christian witness in the social and cultural sphere in many ways rests upon a Christian understanding of reality and the way the Christian church responds to that reality. The Christian community draws its self-understanding from the gospel and therefore it is important to give theological attention to the gospel in relation to Christian witness in contemporary post-communist society.

When it comes to defining the various forms and expressions of Christian witness among Romanian Pentecostals, there are many strong convictions, beliefs and so-called sacred practices which are usually determined by particular ecclesial formulations and often reduced to specific emphases. In broad generalization, it may be said that Romanian Pentecostals put greater emphasis on the centrality of evangelism in mission, i.e. verbal proclamation, notwithstanding the fact that a growing number of them also point to the importance of social action.

The present paper will evaluate the broad spectrum of views on evangelism represented within Romanian Pentecostalism. It will point to the need for further theological reflection on the relationship between the gospel, Christian community and witness in order to clarify the missionary task facing the Christian community that is also relevant to the church's social and cultural witness today.

Evangelism in Contemporary Romania: The Challenge for Pentecostals

Although the term 'evangelism' is used very often in the discourse of the churches and viewed as an essential part of their outreach ministry, it is not always clear what it means, especially in terms of its relationship with ecclesiology. Different church leaders, evangelists and theologians emphasize various facets, and most discussions on this theme focus rather on various methodological approaches and their effectiveness, rather than seeking to understand and define what evangelism is. This is further complicated by the fact that, unlike western missiological language, which distinguishes 'evangelism' from 'evangelization', there is only one word in Romanian *evanghelizare*, which encompasses all sorts of meanings.[1] In the Romanian context, it is important to mention that what Pentecostals mean by 'evangelism' is admittedly not always the same as when used by the Romanian Orthodox Church. So, for example, any activities aimed at 'soul saving', which are part of the evangelistic outreach of Romanian Pentecostalism, are perceived by the national church as culturally destructive proselytism. On the other hand, the efforts of the Romanian Orthodox Church to re-evangelize are often disqualified by Pentecostals as further nominalizing a society already deeply embedded in Orthodoxy, and criticized for being tradition-based rather than biblical and therefore lacking any emphasis on repentance and Christ-centred renewal. Whilst recognising that, 'ultimately, mission remains indefinable; it should never be incarcerated in the narrow confines of our own predilections',[2] and though both 'mission' and 'evangelism' are terms that have been used with a 'wide diversity of meaning',[3] it is still necessary to attempt some integration of the relationship between evangelism and the Christian community, theology and the gospel, within the broader view of social and cultural witness.

Ronald J. Sider points to four divergent models when it comes to defining evangelism: 'Individualistic Evangelical', 'Radical Anabaptist', 'Dominant Ecumenical', and 'Secular Christian'. In order to understand these four basic types, it is essential to grasp the underlying issues that shape these four different models. There are ten such underlying issues that differ in these models on the basis of the interpretation of 'sin',

---

[1] John Clarke, *Evangelism that Really Works* (London: SPCK, 1995), 4-5.

[2] David J. Bosch, *Transforming Mission: Paradigm Shifts in the Theology of Mission* (The American Society of Missiology Series, 16), (Maryknoll, NY: Orbis Books, 1991).

[3] John M. Hitchen, 'Evangelism and Mission – What is the Gospel?', in *Scottish Bulletin of Theology*, 19.1 (2001), 21.

'anthropology', 'content of the gospel', 'meaning of salvation', 'history and eschatology', 'source of theological truth', 'object of evangelism', 'the way the gospel is shared', 'the way the society is changed', and 'locus of God's activity'.

By applying Sider's typology, Romanian Pentecostals would be classified into the 'Individualistic Evangelical' category. Thus 'evangelism' is often perceived by many as a synonym of 'mission' and thereby understood on a local level as a 'given', something that is essentially part of the church's ministry, that all its members are encouraged to participate in, not necessarily understanding what is meant by it, apart from sharing faith with others in the hope of seeing local churches growing in numbers. It is here that churches today lack clarity both in defining their missional[4] task in wider terms and in understanding their own faith.

This relates to the wider issue of needing to integrate evangelism, theology and the church rather than placing a special emphasis on fervent spiritual activism, which is characteristic of Romanian Pentecostalism. Though in some important ways evangelistic fervour has to be seen as significant for mission today, especially when perceived as an expression of one's faith in everyday life, activism alone fails to address some important aspects of mission by overemphasizing the personal/human contribution in terms of what Christians plan and do for God.

It also results in definitions of evangelism in terms of 'method' and 'style', usually relating to different types of proclamation seeking to expose individuals' sin and calling for repentance and a personal decision to follow Christ. The decades following the fall of communism were marked by discussions centred on various methods and styles of evangelism. In the beginning of 1990s, only few months after the overthrow of Ceausescu's regime, representatives from Baptist, Pentecostal, Brethren and the Lord's Army formed the Romanian Evangelical Alliance with co-operative evangelism as one of its five-pointed adopted strategy.[5] In the first decade of the 1990s, mass evangelistic campaigns were the fashion. In partnership with western missionary organizations, Romanian Evangelicals have seen such events as important steps in raising awareness for public proclamation of the gospel and hoped that through their association with gifted western evangelists their credibility would be established in the eyes of the Romanian people.

Iosif Ţon, a prominent evangelical leader, remarked in his capacity as the President of the Romanian Missionary Society, that both the local churches and western missionary agencies placed too much emphasis on evangelism. A decade later, Paul Negrut, principal of Emanuel Bible

---

[4] Ronald Sider, 'What is the Gospel?', in *Transformation,* 16.1 (1999), 26.

[5] The five-point strategy adopted by the Romanian Evangelical Alliance targets evangelism, church-planting, Christian education, the fostering of a work ethic, and the promotion of democracy. Dwight Gibson, 'Evangelical Alliances: They Make Common Cause and Common Sense', in *East-West Church & Ministry Report,* 1 (Spring 1993), 3.

Institute, Oradea, Romania, summed up the missionary efforts as attempts to strategize and co-ordinate missionary work through a focus on resources, projects, results, frustrations, misunderstandings and the like. As such, 'projects' and 'money' became the marks of missiological correctness, which was symptomatic of the fact that the church and its missionary mandate were hardly mentioned.[6] The polemic points to some of the deep problems faced not only by Romanian Pentecostals but also by other evangelical churches seeking rapid growth after the fall of communism, and hoping that various methods, plans and strategies would resolve this issue. However, Bosch warns that the definition of evangelism 'primarily in terms of method and its aim solely in personal, spiritual, and otherworldly categories is... dangerous reductionism'.[7] Unfortunately, some Pentecostals in Romania, uncritically and unintentionally, fell into such reductionism, which put a greater emphasis on continuous searches for new methods and styles reaching unbelievers but without placing this in the wider holistic framework of mission. Sometimes the results of this approach are contrary to the objectives. This concern is expressed in an article by Iosif Ţon, *Towards Reformation in Romania*, where the author points to the problem of an overemphasis on numerical church growth without an equal emphasis on qualitative church growth. Both individual western missionary and western missionary organizations seemed to be motivated towards seeing good results evangelistically, being able to report upon their return to the West many conversions in Romania as a result of their ministry. Ţon identifies this strategy as seriously flawed, especially as applied to the Romanian context where the evangelist's call to accept Jesus is gladly accepted by everyone because they do not understand what it means. No wonder, Ţon says, that in a city like Constanţa there were 26.000 conversions reported when in actuality the total evangelical population amounts to only 1,000. Mănăstireanu concludes that the mass evangelism strategy in Romania proved partly ineffective due to little appreciation shown for 'the way Romanians think or understand God'.[8] Ţon challenged a sole emphasis on evangelism (focused on numerical growth) and suggested that it needed balancing with a deeper pastoral role for people, oriented towards 'training locals to organize and pastor churches, to work with youth and other people. Otherwise, the conversions will come to nothing'.[9] The OCI Preliminary Report on 'the state of the Evangelical Church in Romania', identifies some barriers to evangelism which are classified in three groups: 'internal barriers', 'external barriers' and

[6] Paul Negrut, 'Church and Mission: An Eastern European Perspective', in *Transformation*, 16.1 (1999), 22.

[7] Bosch, *Transforming Mission*, 150.

[8] Dănuţ Mănăstireanu, 'Evangelical Denominations in Post-Communist Romania', in *East-West Church & Ministry Report* 6 (Summer 1998), 7-10.

[9] Ţon, *Reformation in Romania*, 1.

'spiritual barriers'.[10] Significantly, among the 'internal barriers' the report points to 'language barriers', 'cultural barriers' and 'philosophical barriers', which all affect evangelism. The report shows that the economic situation in Romania created new challenges in developing new attitudes toward the economic, political and social contexts: 'as the church experts show, the largest barriers to accepting the gospel are often more social than religious'.[11] There are some concrete pastorally challenging issues when it comes to defining the evangelistic task today. What it is important to note in this context is that within the individualistic evangelical model there are two sub-groups: one that, while believing that evangelism is primary, still insists that evangelism and social action are both important; the other focuses largely, if not exclusively on evangelism.[12] In other words, while the first group's mission thinking includes both evangelism and social action, the second group completely identifies mission with evangelism. There are examples of both these schools of thinking among Romanian Pentecostals, but as already noted, due to the rapidly evolving transitional context, there is a growing concern to include social responsibility within the framework of evangelism. Many Pentecostals are beginning to realize that a sole emphasis on proclamation is not enough in today's context. While a combination of individualistic orientation of evangelism with an emphasis on gaining new converts and initiating them into Christian communities is probably one of the strongest objectives among Romanian Pentecostals, it by no means follows an integrative approach to mission, and when it is emphasized at the expense of a balanced approach to missions, it can lead to a very narrow understanding of both the gospel and evangelism.

The second approach to evangelism which Sider identifies as 'radical Anabaptist' also finds its expression in the Romanian Evangelical milieu, mainly among some of the more progressive evangelical churches. The important difference between this model and the 'individualistic evangelical' one lies in an awareness of the social dimension of sin and therefore a broader view of evangelism. Unlike the first model, the understanding of the gospel is not individualistic, but it does not equate salvation with socio-political liberation either. Bill Prevette's study on 'Evangelical Faith Based Agencies and Churches Involved with Children and Youth at Risk in Romania since 1989' provides helpful background to the emergent progressive evangelical churches that are keen to stress an evangelism strategy that does not emphasize the individualistic approach.[13] His research uncovered an emerging generation of Romanian Evangelicals

[10] 'God's Heart for Romania', in *Report on the State of the Evangelical Churches in Romania* (OC International and Misiunea Mondială Unită, 2001), 38-50.
[11] 'God's Heart for Romania', 45.
[12] Sider, 'What is the Gospel?', 33.
[13] Bill Prevette, 'Evangelical Faith Based Agencies and Churches Involved with Children and Youth at Risk in Romania since 1989' (unpublished seminar paper, presented at the Oxford Centre for Mission Studies, 26th October 2005).

that adopted cultural and theological positions distinct from that of the majority conservative Evangelical churches. Called 'hybridized Evangelicals', they are adaptive, open to new ideas, consider relevance to the greater culture to be important, and want to be engaged with social concerns and broader cultural issues. They are increasingly involved with youth and children at risk and the poor, and are set to represent a new form of Romanian Evangelicalism aimed to have a sustainable impact and influence on Romanian culture. Thus, evangelism is still central in this model, but it is not limited to a verbal proclamation and implies a life of discipleship, and in this way the church as a community of the redeemed is seen as part of the gospel. Significantly, research conducted by Corneliu Constantineanu, a Romanian Pentecostal theologian, on *The Social Significance of Reconciliation in Paul's Theology, with Particular Reference to the Romanian Context,* contributes to a growing awareness of the social dimension of Paul's gospel and challenges the church in Romania to broaden her understanding of evangelism. Based on extensive biblical exegesis, Constantineanu explains that Paul's intention was to show that the gospel the believers have received has clear and concrete implications for their everyday lives.[14] Furthermore, Constantineanu uses the model of social reconciliation found in Paul as a criterion for assessing the practice of reconciliation within the Romanian Evangelical churches. Regarding Evangelical Christians in Romania, he finds that their Christian lives are shaped by significant understanding of Scripture (and Paul's teaching in particular), and that their understanding and practice of reconciliation have strong Pauline resonances. The experience of reconciliation, in Christ, is for them a social reality manifested within the community, which enables them to transcend ethnic and social barriers. While this was a positive assessment compared with Paul, 'Evangelical Christians have also fallen short of Pauline reconciliation by withdrawing from the wider world and thus limiting Paul's notion to insiders'. [15] Constantineanu urges Evangelical Christians to serve the gospel by promoting a 'spirituality that leads to the well-being and human flourishing of all in the Romanian context'. A proper eschatological understanding of reality modelled on the eschatological outlook of Paul's Christianity would not hinder their involvement or suggest a withdrawal from an active social life. By placing Christian existence in a larger framework within which everything else makes sense and is placed in its proper dimension, allows for a serious engagement of the church with the wider political life of society while at the same time relativizing the ultimate claims of politics.[16] The Pentecostal theologian

[14] Corneliu Constantineanu, 'The Social Significance of Reconciliation in Paul's Theology, with Particular Reference to the Romanian Context' (PhD dissertation, University of Leeds School of Theology and Religious Studies and the Oxford Centre for Mission Studies, 2006), 279.

[15] Constantineanu, 'The Social Significance', 271.

[16] Constantineanu, 'The Social Significance', 273.

argues that for Paul to respond to the gospel is 'to acknowledge and accept the truth it proclaims, and to live according to the logic of the gospel, the logic of the Kingdom of God, the logic of the vision of the new creation'.[17] But to live according to the logic of the gospel and in the light of the life of Christ also means 'to be community oriented; and that is a community where everyone is to nurture and embody reconciling practices, which enhance and enrich life together: harmony and solidarity, peace, love, and regard for others'.[18] By integrating the concept of reconciliation in Paul's thought with the close relationship of his theology to ethics, Constantineanu combines a very important emphasis on both word and deed instead of an exclusive proclamation of the word. In this way, the significance of 'lifestyle evangelism' gains momentum, indicating the important and much-needed shift to a broader understanding of evangelism, beyond that of verbal proclamation that effective evangelism will require, raising standards of modelling personal and social ethics in the light of the gospel.

This is a broad spectrum of views of evangelism within Romanian Evangelicalism. It becomes obvious that is not an easy task to define 'evangelism' in relation to 'mission'. There is no consensus in global missiology either about the relationship of evangelism with mission. Thus, the meaning, means and message of evangelism continue to be defined in various ways, often depending on a perception of its position in relation to mission. Some use 'mission' and 'evangelism' synonymously in different variations which range from an exclusive understanding of mission/evangelism as 'soul activity', with some balanced attempts which point to the importance of social responsibility, to complete identification of mission/evangelism with this-worldly projects aiming to transform the existing structures of society.[19] Others distinguish 'evangelism' from 'mission'. There are various approaches. Some see the difference between 'evangelism' and 'mission' in that the goal of the two are not the same, and stress that 'evangelism' has to do with communicating the gospel in a post-Christian context, while 'mission' refers to sharing the faith in the developing world. Others emphasize the importance of 'evangelism' as a broader term than mission, or the other way round.[20] The missiologist David Barrett, who studied the various developments and tensions associated with the term 'evangelism' throughout history and as used by different traditions, noted that the word 'evangelize' has come to be understood in two quite different senses. In the first sense, 'to evangelize' means 'to preach, bring, tell, proclaim, announce, declare (the gospel), whether people accepted it or not, whether they are then won or converted

[17] Constantineanu, 'The Social Significance', 251.
[18] Constantineanu, 'The Social Significance'.
[19] David Bosch, 'Evangelism: Theological Currents and Cross-Currents Today', in *International Bulletin of Missionary Research,* 11.3 (1987), 98.
[20] Bosch, 'Evangelism', 98-100.

or not, although this is the intent'; while in the second definition it is defined as 'not just to proclaim but to actually win or convert people to the Christian faith'.[21] The difference between these two descriptions is based on the premise of whether the intended results for this activity (i.e. the number of conversions) are to be included. Effectively, the first definition is preferred by biblical scholars, most of whom disagree with the perceived equation of 'evangelization' with 'conversion', while the second is often used by practitioners which categorize their ministry in terms of its results and attribute the first definition as 'mere proclamation' or 'seed sowing' which results in the people receiving 'only rudimentary exposure' to the good news.[22] Similarly, *The Evangelical Dictionary of World Missions*, which contains a definition of 'evangelism' addresses the issue of limiting the term 'evangelism' exclusively as either 'the gospel declaration' or 'seeking to rectify injustice', and contends that both are necessary.[23] It also includes other definitions related to different variations of evangelism in contemporary missiology, such as 'cross-cultural evangelism',[24] 'crusade evangelism',[25] 'presence evangelism' and 'proclamation evangelism,'[26] 'life-style evangelism',[27] 'child evangelism',[28] and also a special section on 'evangelism and social responsibility'.[29] Evangelism has been a priority among Pentecostals throughout their history; however, there have been various degrees of approach about evangelism and social ministry in Pentecostal practice. Grant McClung has listed various alternatives explaining the relationship between the two as 'social ministry is evangelism', 'social ministry or evangelism', 'social ministry for evangelism', 'social ministry and evangelism', and 'social ministry in evangelism'.[30] Clearly, there are some disagreements, misconceptions and differing perspectives when it comes to defining mission and evangelism, which are often the source of some reservations in this area of church ministry. Nevertheless, as Andrew Kirk stresses in what concerns the church today: 'There can be no authentic evangelism apart from a living testimony to the transforming power of the gospel in action.'[31]

Keeping in perspective the complexity of the relationship between mission and evangelism, it is important nonetheless to attempt some

---

[21] David Barrett, *Evangelize: A Historical View of the Concept* (New Hope: 1987), 51.

[22] Barrett, *Evangelize*, 51.

[23] Robert E. Coleman, 'Evangelism', in A. Scott Moreau and Harold A. Netland (eds), *Evangelical Dictionary of World Missions* (Grand Rapids, MI: Baker Book House, 2000), 341-44.

[24] Guthrie, in *Evangelical Dictionary of World Missions*, 244.

[25] Harber, in *Evangelical Dictionary of World Missions*, 247.

[26] Prigodich, in *Evangelical Dictionary of World Missions*, 785, 791.

[27] Beougher, in *Evangelical Dictionary of World Missions*, 578.

[28] Klaus, in *Evangelical Dictionary of World Missions*, 176.

[29] Hiebert and Cox, in *Evangelical Dictionary of World Missions*, 344.

[30] Grant McClung, *Connecting to God's Work in Your World* (Cleveland, TN: Pathway Press, 2000), 164-65.

[31] Andrew J. Kirk, *What Is Mission? Theological Explorations* (London: DLT, 1999), 57.

integration of these approaches within the Romanian context. Given the situation where mission among many Pentecostals, as already referred to, has still often and uncritically been identified with evangelism that is mainly understood in individualistic terms of proclamation, it is essential to broaden the scope between mission and evangelism. Such broadening of terms becomes theologically possible if mission is not treated synonymously with evangelism, but rather distinguished from it. Furthermore, a consideration of mission as embracing both evangelism and social action is deeply significant in the light of today's situation in Romania. However, in order to set the framework for the reconceptualization of the mission-evangelism relationship, it is first necessary to define the content of the gospel that constitutes both of them.

The Content of the Gospel – The Good News of the Kingdom

Positive steps forward in mission and evangelism require a clear understanding of the message as it is the evangel that determines evangelism. Thus, giving theological attention to the gospel will inevitably lead to a renewal in mission and more evangelism in new directions. The issue has been at centre stage in ecumenical circles culminating into how the concept of salvation is understood by different Christian traditions. With the emergence of Liberation Theology, the concept of salvation was approached from the perspective 'of liberation from the power of destructive forces of life', and the rise of South African Black Theology linked the gospel with the issue of identity and human dignity before God as well as liberation from guilt and oppression.[32] Disagreements over the meaning of salvation plagued the ecumenical dialogue of the twentieth century and is summed up by Bosch's helpful portrayal of the issue as follows: 'When the Evangelicals ask the ecumenists whether you weep for lost souls, the ecumenists ask the Evangelicals, do you weep for starving people?'[33]

Differing views are compounded by the linguistic variances used by New Testament writers to portray 'salvation' to cover everything to which mission is called. For example, Luke emphasizes salvation here and now, while Paul puts greater emphasis on the future and final dimensions of salvation.[34] Luke uses salvation language to portray a wide range of life-transforming experiences and liberation from various enslaving powers such as poverty, discrimination, illness, demon possession, sin and so

[32] Risto A. Ahonen, *Mission in the New Millennium: Theological Grounds for World Mission* (Helsinki: Finnish Evangelical Lutheran Mission, 2000), 86.
[33] Bosch, *Transforming Mission*, 393.
[34] Stan Nussbaum, *A Reader's Guide to Transforming Mission* (Maryknoll, NY: Orbis Books, 2005), 97.

forth.[35] Forgiveness of sins thus opens the door to renewal of every aspect of life, bringing healing and liberation so that a person might lead a life of human dignity.[36] Paul emphasized salvation as reconciliation with God, but as a process that had both social and political consequences. For him, new life and spiritual renewal are an essential part of the process of being saved, but everything focuses on the future and return of Christ. Paul's view of reconciliation is spelled out in Romans 5:10: 'For if while we were enemies, we were reconciled to God through the death of his Son, much more surely, having been reconciled, will we be saved by his life.' For Paul, salvation is an eschatological process, in which the future is already present.[37]

Ronald Sider points out that contemporary evangelicals fall short of defining the gospel in the way that Jesus did. Frequently, the impression is given that the core of the Christian faith, the essence in comparison with which other things are less important, is forgiveness of sins. Sider argues that forgiveness of sins is not the primary way in which Jesus spoke about the gospel.[38]

Most exegetes today agree that the ministry of Jesus, as described in the gospels, focused on 'announcing' and 'demonstrating' the Kingdom of God which formulated one of the central aspects of his teaching ministry and reflected the good news of the Kingdom. At the heart of the Jesus message in reference to the gospel, was the gospel of the Kingdom mentioned in 122 instances in Matthew, Mark and Luke.[39] Of all the gospel writers, Mark seems to vividly capture the essence of the message of Jesus as the gospel of the Kingdom of God. After John was put in prison, Jesus went into Galilee, proclaiming the good news of God: 'The time has come,' he said. 'The kingdom of God is near. Repent and believe the good news!' (Mark 1:14-15, NIV). It is noteworthy that Jesus is said to proclaim a 'gospel', a 'good word', a message of liberation, even the 'gospel of God'. This is no slip of the pen; it is the older phrase that is sometimes also used by Paul (e.g. Rom. 1:1; 1 Thess. 2:2). It denotes a wider movement in Israel's history in which Jesus came to play a crucial role.[40] Paul Hanson describes the event as the culmination of a long-awaited decisive action in addressing evil… and making way for the Kingdom of God. Jesus' message announced to those who believe the gospel that even now God was the

---

[35] Norman E. Thomas, *Classic Texts in Mission and World Christianity* (Maryknoll, NY: Orbis Books, 1995), 122-23.

[36] Ahonen, *Mission in the New Millenium*, 86.

[37] Nussbaum, *A Reader's Guide to Transforming Mission*, 97.

[38] Sider, 'What Is the Gospel?', 31.

[39] Sider, 'What Is the Gospel?', 31.

[40] Peter J. Thomson, 'Jesus and His Judaism', in Markus Bockmühl (ed), *The Cambridge Companion to Jesus* (Cambridge: CUP, 2003), 29.

compassionate Deliverer, not willing the death of the sinners, but the sinner's salvation.[41]

Furthermore, commenting on this passage in Mark 1:15, Padilla emphasizes that the good news of the Kingdom concerns 'something that can be seen and heard' and points to five characteristics of the gospel:

> (1) It is news concerning a historical fact, an event that is taking place and that affects human life in every way; (2) it is news that is of public interest, having to do with the whole of human history; (3) it is news related to the fulfilment of Old Testament prophecy (the *malkuth Yahveh* announced by the prophets and celebrated by Israel has become a present reality); (4) it is news calling for repentance and faith; and (5) it is news resulting in the formation of a new community, a community of people who are personally called.[42]

Jesus' proclamation at the beginning of his ministry spoke of the presence of God in his actions, particularly in the miracles, in the healings that he performed: the presence of the Spirit of God signifies the presence of the Kingdom. When John the Baptist sent messengers to ask Jesus whether 'he was the one who has come', he replied: 'Go back and report to John what you have seen and heard: the blind receive sight, the lame walk, those who have leprosy are cured, the deaf hear, and the good news is preached to the poor' (Luke 7:22, Matt. 11:5).[43] Thus Jesus announced and demonstrated the arrival of the reign of God among the people in various modes, not only bringing healing to the physically ill, but also offering forgiveness to sinners, fellowship to the outcast, and ministry among the poor, all of which constituted part of the 'politics of the Kingdom of God',[44] work concerned with the making of whole persons, relationships and bodies. Restoration to wholeness in the light of God's Kingdom is central to Jesus' proclamation of the gospel.

However, as Ron Sider argues, such wholeness articulated in the good news of the Kingdom, has to incorporate both a 'vertical' and a 'horizontal' component. The vertical aspect emphasizes that people can enter Jesus' Kingdom only by 'sheer divine grace', which can only be actualized by faith alone in Jesus' atoning death on the cross and his resurrection – the heart of the Christian faith. But that is 'only half of the meaning' of the gospel of the Kingdom.[45] Jesus was not a 'lone ranger' or an 'isolated prophet', and so he called a group of disciples to follow him and inspired

---

[41] Paul D. Hanson, *The People Called: The Growth of Community in the Bible* (Louisville, KY: Westminster John Knox Press, 2001), 397-98.

[42] René C. Padilla, *Mission Between the Times. Essays on The Kingdom* (Grand Rapids, MI: Eerdmans, 1985), 189.

[43] Douglas J. Moo (ed), Divine Healing in the Health and Wealth Gospel, in *The Gospel and Contemporary Perspectives, Vol. 2: Viewpoints from Trinity Journal* (Grand Rapids, MI: Kregel Publications, 1997): 62.

[44] René C. Padilla, 'The Politics of the Kingdom of God and the Political Mission of the Church', in Vinay Samuel and Chris Sugden (eds), *Mission as Transformation: a theology of the whole gospel* (Oxford: Regnum, 1999): 180-98.

[45] Sider, 'What is the Gospel?', 32.

them to live in a way that would reflect a visible expression of Jesus' teaching, new reconciled relationships and the new community which formulate the horizontal aspect of the gospel of the Kingdom.[46]

In other words, a right relationship with God, according to Jesus' teaching, cannot be separated from right relationships with others. It implies that both vertical and horizontal aspects are implicit in the gospel which is not just limited to the 'spiritual realm'. There is overwhelming agreement among scholars that the message of Jesus had political and economic implications. Politically, anyone announcing the coming of the Kingdom of God is at least by implication criticizing the present kingdom. On the economic side, in the gospel narratives, the preaching of the Kingdom of God contains socio-economic components in that justice prompted affirmative action in view of impending realities.[47] The coming reign of God brought about a reformation of life at all levels – personal, social, political and economic.[48] It is also important to note that the gospel also has an eschatological dimension that is both realized and future. Jesus spoke repeatedly about the present arrival of the Kingdom: 'For in fact the kingdom is among you' (Luke 17:21), while the final arrival of the Kingdom of God, which will take place in the future and which Jesus was anointed to proclaim and inaugurate as the promised outpouring of the Spirit, makes present the 'last days' (Acts 2:17).[49] The dynamic interplay between the 'already' and 'not yet' of the Kingdom points to it both as present and eschatological reality. In the context of the proclamation of the arrival of the Kingdom of God, the gospel is the good news as it points to 'God's act of eschatological deliverance in Christ'.[50] The intervention of God, which is the content of the gospel, establishes the entire renewal of human life and history. Therefore, the gospel points to the need for the re-ordering of human life in the light of Christ's transformative action on the cross.

There are at least two important implications of such an understanding of the gospel. First, the grace that enables the good news of the Kingdom to be demonstrated is followed by the imperative to believe and follow Jesus (Mark 1:15). Cray, commenting on a theology of the Kingdom, emphasizes that 'the kingdom invades the old age through the person and ministry of Jesus, and that this ministry consists both of the proclamation of the kingdom with the accompanying call to follow Jesus, and of the effective demonstration of the power and reality of the kingdom'.[51] As such, the

[46] Sider, 'What Is the Gospel?', 32.

[47] Jonathan J. Bonk, *Mission and Money: Affluence as a Missionary Problem... Revisited* (Maryknoll, NY: Orbis Books, 2006), 208-09.

[48] Hanson, *The People Called*, 420.

[49] Eckhard J. Schnabel, *Early Christian Mission: Jesus and the Twelve* (Vol. 1), (Downers Grove, IL: IVP, 2004), 212-13.

[50] John Webster, 'Eschatology, Anthropology and Modernity', in *International Journal of Systematic Theology*, 2.1 (2000), 13-28.

[51] Graham Cray, 'A Theology of the Kingdom', *Transformation* 5.4 (1988), pp. 24-32.

grace mediated by Jesus does not articulate 'a vague tolerance associated with principled commitment',[52] but rather points to a holistic vision of a good life in all its aspects, which is built on the values of the Kingdom. Nevertheless, even such an understanding of the Kingdom, which incorporates both 'divine initiative' and 'human response', can only partially reveal the complete scope of God's reign, and that for as long as we still live in the 'already' and 'not yet' eschatological tension.[53]

Secondly, the proclamation of the gospel is not just directed to isolated individuals, but seeks to create life-transforming communities called to bring an authentic witness to the dynamics of God's Kingdom in the world. As Ramachandra has put it, 'The gospel creates new human community and that new human community is itself part of the gospel to be proclaimed.' According to this, the gospel brings a message of faith in a communal God who cares, who is active in love and who sets people free. Castro comments on the content of the evangelistic message by referring to the theme of the Nairobi assembly, 'Jesus Christ Frees and Unites', which affirms that:

> The gospel always includes the announcement of God's kingdom and love through Jesus Christ, the offer of grace and forgiveness of sins, the invitation of repentance and faith in him, the summons to fellowship in God's church, the command to witness to God's saving words and deeds, the responsibility to participate in the struggle for justice and human dignity, the obligation to denounce all that hinders human wholeness, and a commitment to risk life itself.[54]

Such an understanding of the gospel is a call to manifest God's love through word and deed, and to integrate service with proclamation that is not triumphalist, but rooted in solidarity with the hurting world. All too often, this Kingdom dimension of the gospel is neglected in the contemporary practice of evangelism. A limited understanding of the gospel, or rather a preoccupation with only certain aspects of it, which oft times is present in churches when doing evangelism, often affects not only the practice of evangelism, but also its perception by the wider community. Therefore, it becomes necessary to reflect on evangelism in the light of the holistic content of the gospel.

Towards a Theology of Evangelism for the Whole Gospel

The *annus mirabilis* of 1989 ended for the Romanians with the overthrow of one of the harshest and most nationalistic communist dictatorships in Europe. The Romanian Pentecostals expressed great enthusiasm about the new era and recognized in this God acting as the Lord of history who

---

[52] Cray, 26.

[53] Cray, 32.

[54] Emilio Castro, 'Liberation, Development and Evangelism: Must We Choose in Mission?', *Occasional Bulletin of Missionary Research* 2.3 (1978), pp. 87-91.

answered their prayers and provided them with a special *kairos* period to call the nation back to God and to the spiritual foundations for a free and truly new society. Therefore, when commenting on 'evangelism in Romania' since 1990, not many Pentecostals link it with 'theology', but rather focus on the practical methods and programmes employed in 'soul saving' and church planting. René Padilla warns against the dangers of divorcing evangelism from theology, which can easily lead to reductionist interpretations of the gospel and an inadequate practice of evangelism. He further asks a challenging question: 'Can there be evangelism that is really biblical – that really presents the whole counsel of God – without theological reflection that seeks to understand the relevance of the gospel to the totality of human life in a given context?'[55] This is certainly a valid question when considering the theology of evangelism in post-communist contexts. Kusnierik and Moyle observe that, among evangelicals in Central and Eastern Europe, important concepts of 'creation', 'sin', and 'the Kingdom of God' have little impact for the life of the individual and society.[56] As an isolated social minority, Romanian Pentecostalism emerged from decades of communist persecution with little experience in relation to issues of social concerns, or the structures of civic society. In addition, the normative theologies of the Romanian Pentecostals had been influenced by both the cultural roots of Romanian Orthodoxy and a pietistic theology that elevated personal holiness over social concern. Cristian Romocea, an emerging Romanian leader, describes the theological understanding of the churches:

> Neo-Protestant Churches in Romania do not generally have a clearly defined social agenda, or when some of their theologians do, it is completely isolated from an adequate theological notion. Neo-Protestant churches in particular tend to reduce social reality to its vertical, individual aspect which refers to the relationship among church members and with God, with no bearing on further implications for wider society. This stance corresponds to their pietistic and socially conservative tendencies in which their relationship with God is a personal matter which does not retain a wider social implication.[57]

Pentecostal theologian Constantineanu points out that, since their inception, neo-Protestants saw themselves persecuted and pushed to the very margins, making it difficult for them to engage effectively in any way with the social or political life of the country. Marked by a weak organizational apparatus and no public platform to articulate their convictions, and backed by their own eschatology, 'Romanian neo-Protestants compensated by living in the spirit, in the heavenlies – and

---

[55] René C. Padilla, *Mission Between the Times: Essays on the Kingdom* (Grand Rapids, MI: 1985), 99-100.

[56] Juray Kusnierik and Moyle Marsh, *Trends – Ten Years On* (unpublished Sen Research Pape; Bratislava, 1999), 34.

[57] Cristian Romocea, 'A Strategy for Social Reconciliation in the Ethnic Conflict in Transylvania', in *Religion in Eastern Europe*, XXIII (5th October 2003), 26.

their sense of what is to be church was thus freed from the call to be reconciling in the world outside church. They turned the Christian faith into a private religiosity with all the drawbacks that result from that.'[58]

A 2005 study about attitudes towards the church's intervention in politics shows that Romanian neo-Protestants[59] tend to deny not just the duty but also the right of the church to interfere with political issues and intervene in social problems. They regard experiencing a 'spiritual awakening' as the only legitimate way of solving such problems.[60] In their theology, evangelization is understood as providing the fundamentals of moral reform and the subsequent transformation of Self. Thus, the neo-Protestants' identity 'transcends the strict barriers of belonging to a particular national community... inevitably leading to a certain marginalization'.[61] Because of their conservative stance on many issues, Pentecostals are criticized at times for supporting policies often associated with anti-liberal and non-democratic principles. They are frequently perceived as being more interested in their own social, economic and political interests than in supporting and encouraging renewal in society. Similarly, they show an obsession with structural expansion and the pursuit of power and property rather than committing themselves to help the poor, pursuing justice for the weak and marginalized, and empowering the powerless.[62]

Romanian sociologist of religion Rogobete notes that neo-Protestant churches practise a form of religious sectarianism – the construction of a parallel world, an alternative to the secular world. They are separated from the world, self-sustaining and self-sufficient, with well-defined boundaries and high walls, with strict rules of adherence and expulsion. It is a religion that constructs its own social world with its own alternative culture. It reflects a lack of trust in the state's institutions, and it sets up its own schools, businesses and leisure activities. They are dominated by a simplified epistemology, often linked with the literal application of Bible texts. Hermeneutics is denounced as demonized. Rogobete concludes that

---

[58] Corneliu Constantineanu, 'The Social Significance of Reconciliation', 264-65.

[59] The term 'neo-Protestants' refers to a group of churches consisting largely of Baptists, Pentecostals, Christians according to the Gospel (the Romanian designation for 'Brethren') and Seventh-day Adventists. In order to distinguish them from the mainline Protestant communities, the Romanian authorities referred to them as 'neo-Protestants' (a name adopted subsequently by these churches to identify and present themselves). Even though they arrived in Romania beginning with the eighteenth century, but mostly in the late nineteenth and early twentieth centuries, these churches grew very quickly and became among the largest communities of neo-Protestants in Europe.

[60] This point is reiterated also by theology lecturer Dănuţ Mănăstireanu, who notes amongst neo-Protestants an obsessive preoccupation with revivals as an answer to the plethora of societal problems in Romania. See 'Evangelical Denominations in Post-Communist Romania', 7-10.

[61] Gavril Flora, Georgina Szilagyi and Victor Roudometof, 'Religion and National Identity in Post-Communist Romania', in *Journal of Southern Europe and the Balkans,* 7.1 (April 2005), 44-45.

[62] Mănăstireanu, 'Evangelical Denominations in Post-Communist Romania', 10.

such an approach, rooted in self-sufficiency, runs the risk of further exacerbating social isolation and marginalization.[63]

In the light of these considerations, it is important to evaluate how these views are reflected in the changing mentality of Romanian Pentecostals today. In order to illustrate present ways of thinking about evangelism and mission, I conducted a survey during May-November 2008 which was completed by 162 respondents. Of a total of fourteen questions included in the survey, twelve were selected for the purpose of this chapter. The criterion in choosing the respondents was on the basis of their claimed Pentecostal affiliation and involvement in Christian ministry. So the survey was completed by only four groups of people: pastors, church leaders, lecturers (theologians) and theology students from the main representative Pentecostal seminaries located in the capital Bucharest, and the other from the city of Arad in western Romania. Out of the total of 162, 84 were pastors (thus representing 20% of 400 pastors), 36 were presbyters (unlike other evangelical groups, in Romanian Pentecostal churches the function of the presbyters differs from that of the pastor, in that they perform all church functions under the supervision of the pastor) and twenty were theology students. 96% of respondents were male, as women are not ordained in Romanian Pentecostal Churches.

All the participants were made aware that the questionnaire was part of a doctoral thesis on Romanian Pentecostalism under completion at the department of Pentecostal & Charismatic studies at the University of Birmingham, UK, entitled: 'A Theology of Mission for a Post-Communist Context: An Integrative Approach' by the present author, supervized by Dr Allan Anderson. The purpose of the questionnaire was stated as intended to identify key issues facing Romanian Pentecostalism today. The questionnaire states that participants and answers given were entirely confidential and anonymous.

This is a thematic survey of a selected group of people and as such, it does not claim to be a normative value for the whole of the Pentecostal movement in Romania, and can serve only as an informative indicator of certain tendencies and views among Pentecostal pastors, leaders, lecturers and theology students.

[63] Silviu Rogobete, *Religie şi schimbare socială: Câteva reflexii asupra rolului religiei în societatea contemporană* (Religion and Change: Reflections on the Role of Religion in the Contemporary Society – unpublished draft article, New Europe College, 2002), 4-8.

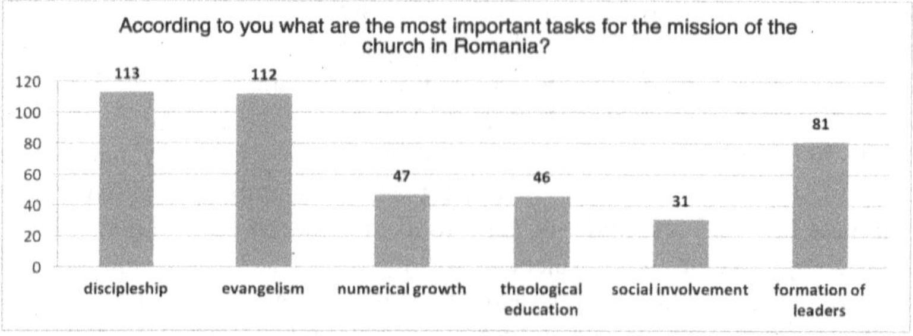

The aim of this question was to identify certain priorities in mission as perceived by various Romanian Pentecostal leaders. The result quite clearly indicates that the vast majority of respondents (70%) claimed that 'evangelism', 'discipleship' and the 'formation of leaders' were the most important priorities in mission. What is surprising is that only 29% of respondents claimed that the priority task was the 'numerical growth' of the church, while in actual practice there seemed to be a far greater emphasis on this element. While 19% claimed that 'social involvement' was very important, 43% claimed it to be important (this is the second highest total in the 'important' category). This points to a growing recognition of the social implications of the gospel.

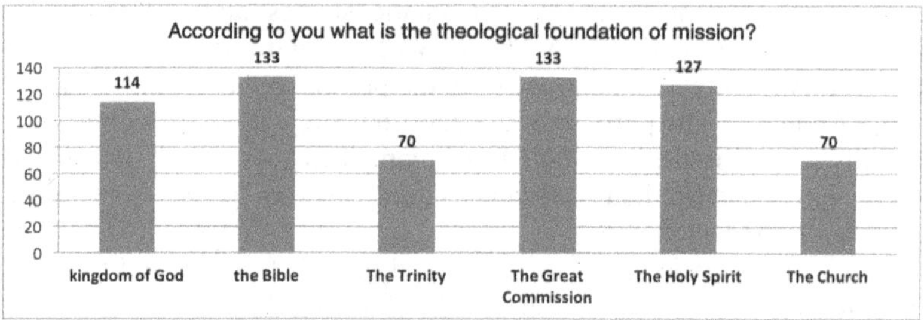

This question sought to identify the theological foundations of mission, especially in relation to the answer given to the first question on the priorities of mission. 'The Bible', 'the Great Commission' and 'the Holy Spirit' seem to stand out as the most important theological foundations of mission. The most surprising results from this question concern 'the Trinity' and 'the Church' being seen as foundational. While a considerable group named 'the Trinity' as a foundation for mission, there is still need for a greater awareness of the theological and practical implications of the doctrine of the Trinity for church and mission.

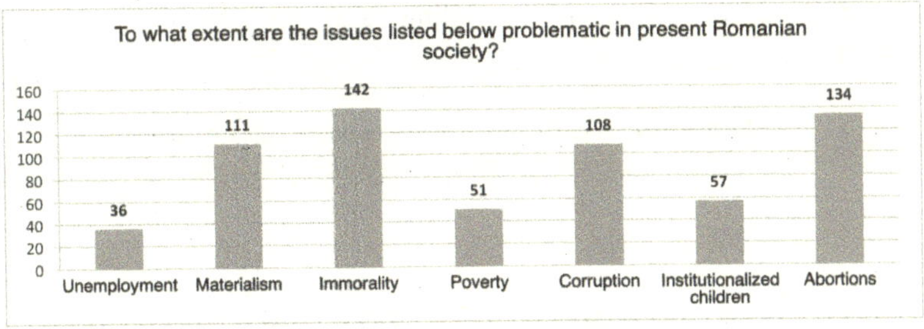

The purpose of this question was to see what social issues were deemed important. 'Immorality', 'abortion', 'materialism' and 'corruption' were named as the biggest social issues, which raises many questions about the Christian response. 'Unemployment' did not seem to be a pressing social issue since Romania has been experiencing population losses to nearly every western country. Addressing 'poverty' did not rank high, as Romania's economic boom between 2003 and 2008 led to rapid gains in poverty reduction; however, some regions of the country still rank as the poorest in the EU. What is surprising is that only 35% considered the issue of orphaned/institutionalized children as a very important social issue.

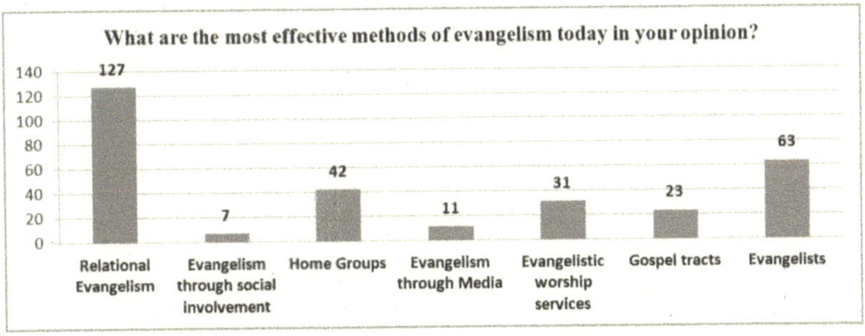

This question sought to evaluate the perception of contemporary models in comparison to 'traditional approaches'. What is quite notable is that the category of 'relational evangelism' seemed to be most effective. More traditional approaches such as 'evangelistic worship services', and the use of 'evangelists' seem to have lost their priority status in mission. Even so, the two categories were identified by 53% of respondents as effective evangelism models. This points to a broader change taking place in the church that requires more personal and participative models of evangelism. A growing number of respondents (25% 'most effective', 54% effective) saw 'home groups' as having potential to meet present needs. Significant numbers of respondents considered 'evangelism through social involvement' (45%), 'evangelism through media' (48%), 'gospel tracts' (40) and 'evangelists' (51%) as effective tools in mission. What is notable is that a great majority (38% most effective, 51% effective) saw evangelism done by someone with a special calling as a very important evangelism strategy.

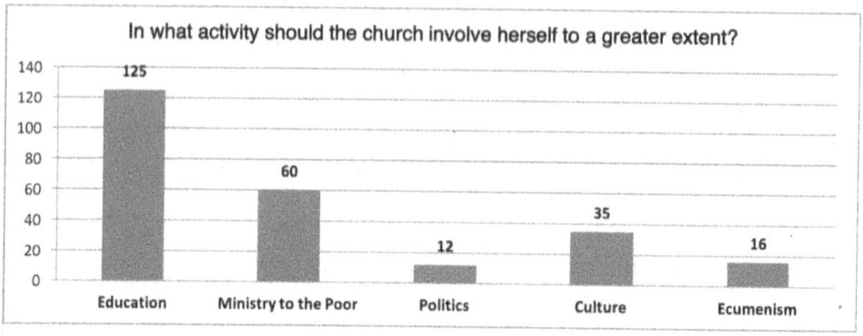

Significantly, the largest group of respondents point to 'education' as the highest priority (77%). It points to a growing need for information and understanding of the multifaceted situation that Romanians find themselves in. (This is not just limited to Christians.) 'Ministry to the poor' is seen as important by a vast majority of respondents (53%). This points to an increasing social consciousness among Romanian Pentecostal leaders. However, involvement with 'politics' (7% very significant), 'culture' (21% as very significant) and 'ecumenism' (9% very significant) does not seem to be as important as other issues.

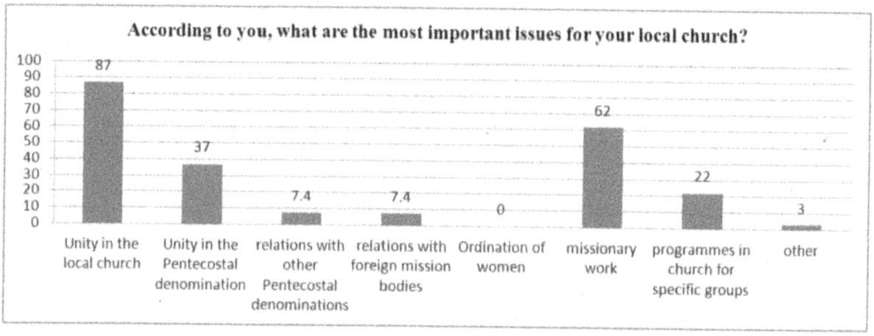

The aim of this question was to determine priorities in terms of issues confronting the local church. 87% of respondents, by far the highest percentage, were concerned with maintaining 'unity in the local church'. 62% of respondents expressed the need for the local church to be involved in 'missionary work'. 'Unity within the denomination' was seen as most important by 37% of respondents. 'Relations with other Pentecostal churches' and 'relations with foreign mission bodies' were seen as relevant only by 7.4% respondents. The most surprising issue concerns the 'ordination of women' in pastoral positions. None of the respondents regarded the issue as most important, 3.7% of respondents deeming it important, 14% as less important and the great majority of respondents 74% as unimportant.

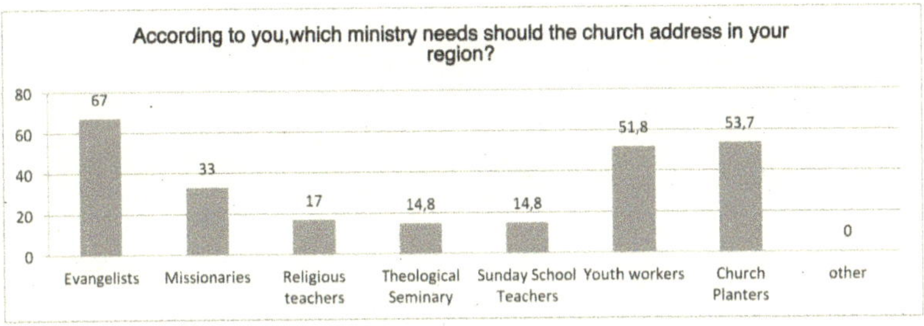

The purpose of this question was to see how each local church saw the ministry needs of the church in its regional context. 67% of respondents identified the need to train 'evangelists' as the most important priority. 'Youth workers' 51.8%, 'church planters' 51.8% and 'missionaries' 33% were identified by respondents as very important priorities for the regional needs of the local church. Religious Teachers 17% very important, 'theological seminary' and 'Sunday school teachers' 14.8% were seen by respondents as very important priorities for the church. There does not seem to be a strong bond between local churches and theological schools.

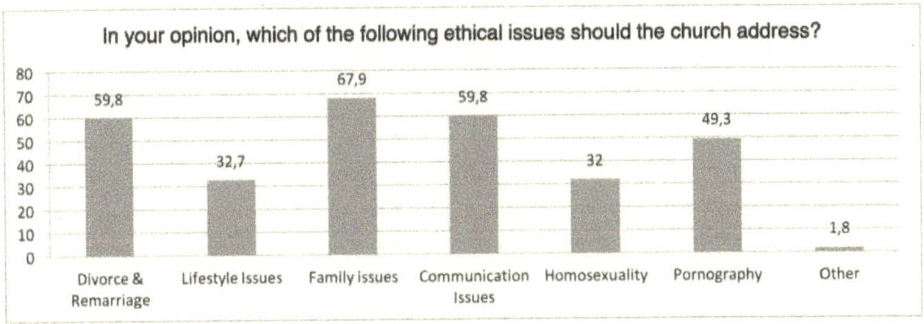

This question sought to identify what ethical issues are deemed important by the leaders of the Pentecostal churches. 'Family issues' 67.9% with an emphasis on marital issues and children's education, 'divorce & remarriage' 59.8% and 'communication issues' (within the Christian community) 59.8% were named as the most important ethical challenges for the church. The issue of 'pornography' 49.3%, 'lifestyle issues' (appearance and behaviour) 32.7%, and 'homosexuality' 32% were listed as very important by respondents as well.

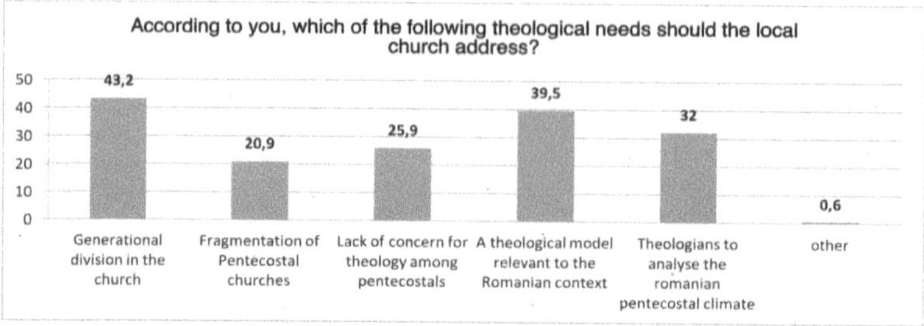

This question sought to outline which theological challenges were deemed as most challenging for the local churches. The single highest concern was identified by 43.2% of respondents as posed by the 'generational division in the church', closely identified by 39.5% of respondents as the need for a theological model relevant to the present Romanian context. There is a rapidly growing division between the younger Pentecostal leaders in Romania and their elders. This has created ongoing power struggles within the church. 39.5% of respondents pointed towards the importance of theologians able to analyze the current 'Romanian Pentecostal climate'. This is reflected also by 25.9 of respondents who drew attention to the challenge posed by the 'fragmentation of churches' taking place within the Romanian Pentecostal churches.

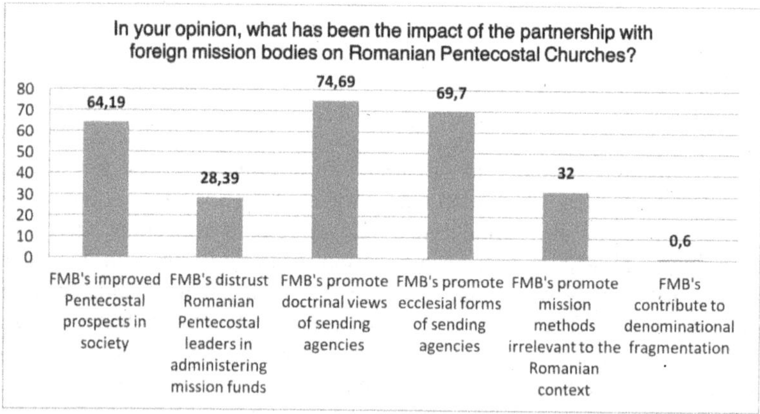

The purpose of this question was to assess the efficacy and the partnership outcome of local churches with foreign mission organizations. Overall, 64% of respondents described in positive terms the dynamic of partnership with western agencies. Nevertheless, there is agreement over certain aspects of the partnership in terms of 'doctrinal' 74.6% respondents, 'ecclesial' 69.7% respondents, and 'mission methods' 32% of respondents. What is interesting is that Romanian leaders did not seem to establish the link between the operational methods of western missionary organization and its influence on 'denominational fragmentation'. As more Romanian Pentecostal leaders worked with western FBOs after the 1989 revolution, they begun adopting some western cultural and theological positions. The primary outcome led to the creation of a new form of Romanian Pentecostalism whose leaders gave rise to emergence of hybrid churches and ministries largely dependent on western funding and assistance.

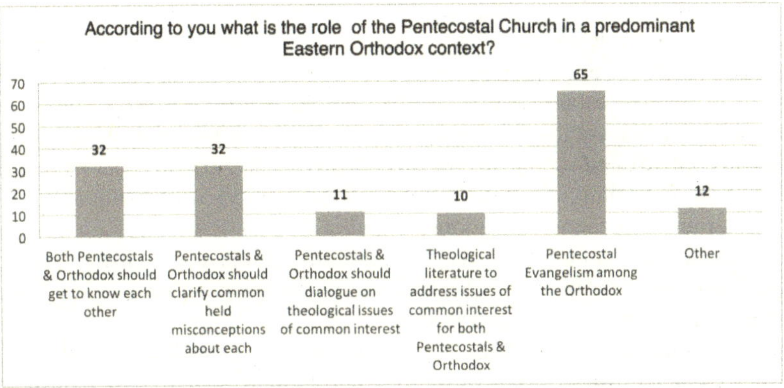

The purpose of this question was to see how the Pentecostal leaders in Romanian saw their role and responsibilities in a context predominantly shaped by Eastern Orthodoxy. Romania contains the largest population of Orthodox Christians in the world today, second only to Russia. Romanian Pentecostalism is only a marginal minority representing about 1% of the population. Historic difficulties have characterized Pentecostal attitudes towards the Orthodox Church, and difficulties remain in areas of communication and religious freedom between Orthodox and Pentecostals in Romania. 65% of respondents identified 'evangelization of the Orthodox' as the most important task of the Pentecostal Church in Romania. 32% of the respondents pointed to both the need for 'Pentecostals and Orthodox to learn more about each other' and for both 'Pentecostals and Orthodox to work towards clarifying misconceptions they have about each other'.

Summary and Conclusions

A general overview of the survey points to certain tendencies that are significant when it comes to considering a theology of evangelism for the whole gospel. First, it seems that the working practical implementation of the Kingdom of God for evangelism is one of the key issues. In other words, while many Romanian Pentecostals claim the Kingdom of God to be central to their mission, it does not seem to be applied in practice to evangelism, which is often solely concerned with 'soul saving'. Furthermore, evangelism done by people with this special calling can very easily become, for the believers in churches, a way of easing their conscience for not being involved evangelistically in the natural environment where they spend most of their lives. The Kingdom is then often interpreted in 'spiritual' terms without taking into consideration its broader social implications. Admittedly, there are signs now that Romanian Pentecostal scholars are becoming interested in serious reflection on the social dimension of their faith.

Secondly, there does not seem to be a clear connection between Church and Kingdom in Romanian Pentecostal thinking which sometimes results in limited views of ecclesial life by seeing the role of the church exclusively as a vehicle to establish God's Kingdom in people's hearts. This often results in a black-and-white vision of the world, a rejection of culture at large, while discouraging any involvement with it. Thus, another reflection has to do with thinking about the role of the Trinity. Vital elements of the Trinitarian faith cannot be ignored in today's mission thinking. Finally, the importance of seeking new ways of thinking about evangelism that will take into consideration a holistic view of the gospel that touches every aspect of life must not be overlooked.

If Romanian Pentecostals are to serve the gospel and promote a spirituality that leads to the well-being and human flourishing of all in the Romanian context, they have to enlarge the view they hold to enlarge their view of reconciliation with the social dimension that we have explored in Paul. A proper eschatological understanding of reality should not hinder in any way their involvement in the world. On the contrary, far from suggesting a withdrawal from active social life, the eschatological outlook of Paul's Christianity – by placing Christian existence in a larger framework within which everything else makes sense and is placed in its proper dimension – allows for a serious engagement of the church with the wider political life of society while at the same time relativizing the ultimate claims of politics.[64]

Romanian Pentecostals need to undergird their actions with a search for a theology of the whole gospel that addresses all aspects of culture and society, and which is not limited to the spiritual. They must integrate their praxis into a holistic vision of the Kingdom of God and proclaim the gospel for what it was, is and shall for ever remain: a public statement – about the whole of reality, about God, about human beings, about the world, about truth, about meaning, about life.

---

[64] Constantineanu, 'The Social Significance of Reconciliation', 264-65.

HOLISTIC MISSION IN POST-COMMUNIST ROMANIA: A CASE STUDY ON THE GROWTH OF THE 'ELIM' PENTECOSTAL CHURCH OF TIMIŞOARA (1990-1997)

Marcel V. Măcelaru

A Missiological Turning Point

However else it may have been interpreted, I regard the anti-communist uprising that took place in Timişoara, Romania, in the last weeks of December 1989, to be a turning point, with deep missiological implications, in the history of the region.[1] Not only did the events in Timişoara marked the 'beginning of the end' for one of the most repressive totalitarian regimes the communist Eastern Europe has known – Nicolae Ceauşescu's 24-year rule of Romania – thus making space for much-needed and long-awaited political, economic and societal reforms, but it also revealed, quite dramatically, the failure of decades of communist propaganda; the cry for freedom that somehow united the thousands of demonstrators filling the streets of Timişoara during those days had strangely turned out to be a defying 'God exists!' that challenged foundational communist notions of materialistic atheism.

To me, that was a cry of vindication. As a believer, I had been mocked and despised for my 'naïveté' by those who had had the 'benefit' of communist atheistic education. But now, the people who were once taught to deny God's existence were proclaiming something I had believed all along. Here was a testimony to the fact that longing for God is part of who we are, and that humanly devised ideologies could neither fulfil nor suppress this inherent need for transcendence. And even more than vindication, the cry of the demonstrators was reason for hope – hope that the oppressive context in which I had lived would, at last, end; hope that my country would become a society in which freedom and truth would prevail; and hope that the newly discovered religious liberty would trigger a resurgence of true Christian commitment, perhaps even a fully-fledged, revival.

Needless to say, as I am writing these thoughts now, more than 25 years after the fall of communism, the better Romania I had hoped for continues to be a 'dream' in the making. As we have had to discover, the change of

---

[1] On 'turning points' and their significance, see Romeo V. Turcan, 'The Philosophy of Turning Points: A Case of De-Internationalization', in *Advances in International Management* 26 (2013), 219-35.

political regimes did not bring about changed mentalities; therefore, much more remains to be done and many wrongs have yet to be corrected. However, one also has to recognize that vital steps towards a truly democratic, prosperous society have been taken, and more importantly, that a shift in the way Romanians perceive, and relate to, Christianity has definitely taken place; as the 2011 census showed, a staggering 93% of the citizens of Romania nowadays consider themselves Christian.

Admittedly, since the census could not measure Christian commitment, the numbers being circulated do not prove that a Christian revival is under way. They point however to the fact that the anti-communist 'revolution' (as the 1989 uprising is otherwise referred to) did create unprecedented opportunities for mission which, over the past 25 years, have been fruitful, in some places more than in others, as various missionary enterprises were undertaken in the region.

The case study below presents one such 'enterprise' – the mission strategy and praxis of the 'Elim' Pentecostal Church in Timişoara, Romania (henceforth EPC)[2] during the period 1990-1997. This is, I propose, an outstanding example of holistic mission undertaken during the confusing time of 'transition' that succeeded the fall of communism in Eastern Europe, transition for which most churches in the region were by no means prepared. The intelligence of the vision driving the praxis of this church during those years and its successful outcome justify, I propose, the inclusion of EPC's story in the present volume.[3]

EPC – The Story up to 1990

EPC represents a unique case of church growth within the Romanian, and indeed, Eastern European context. After the fall of communism, in a relatively short period of time (seven years), membership of the congregation more than doubled, over thirty new satellite churches were

---

[2] Although named 'Elim', EPC is neither a part of, nor connected with, the 'Elim' Pentecostal Movement in UK and Ireland. EPC is one of the many churches that form Cultul Creştin Penticostal – Biserica lui Dumnezeu Apostolică din România (The Pentecostal Christian Denomination – The Apostolic Church of God of Romania). The congregation adopted the name 'Elim' on 20th November 1988, at the inauguration of the worship facilities it has used ever since (see 'Inaugurarea unui lăcaş de închinăciune la Timişoara', in *Buletinul Cultului Penticostal* XXXVII.1 (January-February 1989), 4-5). For the sake of simplification, the abbreviation EPC is used in this paper to identify the congregation throughout its entire history.

[3] Most of the information regarding EPC provided below is available in *Elim*, a magazine EPC has published since 1992 on EPC's website: www.elim.ro and in *Cuvântul Adevărului*, the official bulletin of the Romanian Pentecostal Denomination: http://digitallibrary.usc.edu/cdm/search/collection/p15799coll14/searchterm/Pentecostal%20Theological%20Institute%2C%20Bucharest%2C%20Romania/field/parta/mode/exact – while data was also obtained through personal observation (during the period under scrutiny, I have been an active member of EPC), interviews with various members of the church, and from EPC's official records, to which I had access December 1999-January 2000.

planted in the region, the impact of the church within the country grew significantly due to various ministries addressing social needs that sprung out of it, and news of the 'revival' that was taking place in Timişoara began spreading in Romania[4] and beyond.[5]

No success, however, happens in a vacuum. In fact, I suggest that the seeds of EPC's missiological ethos were sown earlier in the history of the church and its 1990-1997 mission praxis was rooted in strategies that were tested and proven effective during the long years before the fall of communism. Therefore, I will prelude the discussion on the 1990-1997 period with an overview of EPC's story before 1990, aiming to identify such 'seeds' and to show the development of such strategies.

EPC – The Early Years (1928-1946)

The story of EPC,[6] up until the years in view here, covers two distinct periods of time; each of these has had its specific challenges, but also each

---

[4] Information about EPC appears in different publications (primarily Christian) in Romania. For example, see the listings in footnotes throughout this paper. For specific references to EPC's growth, see Teodor Codreanu, 'Biserica Penticostală Elim – Timişoara', in *Cuvântul Adevărului* III.8, 2nd Series (August 1992), 19; 'Semicentenarul Bisericii Penticostale Filadelfia din Timişoara', in *Cuvântul Adevărului* VII.1-2, 2nd Series (January-February 1996), 24; 'Botez nou-testamental la Biserica Penticostală "Elim", Timişoara', in *Cuvântul Adevărului*, VIII.4, 2nd Series (April 1997), 2; Ioan Bochian, 'În vizită la pastorul Teodor Codreanu - Timişoara', in *Cuvântul Adevărului* XIII.9-10, 2nd Series (September-October 2002), 18; Cornelius Merca, 'Elim-ul... la 15 ani', in *Cuvântul Adevărului* XV.1, 2nd Series (January 2004), 2; 'Teodor Codreanu, 1928-2004', in *Cuvântul Adevărului* XV.11, 2nd Series (November 2004), 23; and Pavel Riviş Tipei, 'Aniversare – 85 de ani', in *Cuvântul Adevărului* XIX.2, 2nd Series (February 2008), 6.

[5] Although references to EPC in non-Romanian literature are more recent, their very existence proves that information about EPC's unique case has spread beyond Romania's borders long enough and to the extent that it became worth mentioning even within academic contexts. See, for instance, Rodica Pandrea, 'A Historical and Theological Analysis of the Pentecostal Church in Romania', in *The Journal of the European Pentecostal Theological Association* XXI (2001), 117; Peter Kuzmič, 'Pentecostal Theology and Communist Europe: Pentecostal Power under Political Pressure', in William K. Kay and Anne E. Dyer (eds), *European Pentecostalism* (Global Pentecostal and Charismatic Studies, 7: Leiden, Netherlands: E.J. Brill, 2011), 350; Bill George, '"To All Who Are Afar Off": The Incredible International Growth of Pentecostalism', in *Evangel* 103.5 (May 2013), 15; and Bill Prevette, 'Evangelical Faith Based Agencies and Churches involved with Children and Youth at Risk in Romania since 1989', in *OCMS Seminar Paper* (26 Jan. 2015), 6: http://prevetteresearch.net/wp-content/ uploads/image/all/January%2026th%20OCMS%20Seminar%20paper.pdf (accessed 13th July 2016).

[6] For EPC's story presented here, see Codreanu, 'Biserica Penticostală Elim – Timişoara', 19; Cornelius Merca, 'Din istoricul Bisericii Apostolice Penticostale "Elim" Timişoara', in *Elim* 36-37 (1998), 14-15; Ibid. 'Elim-ul... la 15 ani', 2; and the historical overview provided on EPC's website 'Biserica "Elim" de-a lungul timpului': www.elim.ro/despre-biserica-penticostala-elim-timisoara/biserica-elim-de-a-lungul-timpului (accessed 14th April 2016). See also Mărioara Măcelaru, *Însemnări pe uşiorii casei* (Timişoara, Romania: Casa Literaturii Creştine, 2007), an autobiography that makes various references to EPC's post-1960 history. The historical data available in these publications has also been used to corroborate

one is a testimony to the congregation's unique focus on mission. The first period starts sometime in the year 1928, with a few Pentecostal believers who began gathering for prayer and Bible study in various private homes within the city of Timişoara, and concludes with the official inauguration of the church as a religious entity, within the legal framework of the time, on 3rd November 1946, under the name *Biserica Apostolică Penticostală* (The Pentecostal Apostolic Church).

Information about this period is scarce, as much of the life of the church took place 'underground'; Pentecostalism – which in its early years was regarded a dangerous 'sect' – did not become a legally recognized 'religion' within the legal framework of Romania until 1946. We know, however, that about 1928 prayer and Bible study meetings became regular events and that they continued, in various locations throughout the city of Timişoara, until 1935. These, I suggest, are the years in which the core identity of the group as a 'church' began to take shape, for in their aftermath, from 1935 onwards, the believers organized themselves into a congregation, initially of about thirty members, under the leadership of Pastor Alexandru Izbaşa, and met regularly in the house of Ioachim Ţunea.

Not much is known about the mission praxis of the group either. Unquestionably, the data available shows progress, as eleven years later, when the 'legalization' of the church took place, the congregation had allegedly grown to about 100 members. This would translate as an average growth rate of 7% per annum. However, since no membership records are available, it is unclear how many of these were adult members and how many were children, and also how many members were new converts and how many were believers coming from other congregations who had simply joined the newly-founded church.

EPC – The Communist Era (1946-1989)

The second period in EPC's history covers the years under the communist totalitarian regime (1946-1989).[7] On the one hand, these are years marked by persecution and restrictions – methods of control exercized by communist authorities who endeavoured to curb the progress of the congregation. Thus, in 1960 communist authorities withdrew EPC's 'approval' to exist as a congregation on its own and 'decreed' that believers who wanted to continue meeting should share the worship hall with Hungarian and German believers in a facility that was both small and inadequate. Also, during the 1960s, strict interdictions in terms of worship

---

information about EPC obtained from several interviews with members of the congregation (see footnotes below).

[7] Besides the sources listed in footnote 6 above, information for this part of EPC's story comes from Maria Măcelaru, interview by the author (Timişoara, Romania, 17th December 1999), and Dorel M. Măcelaru, interview by the author (Timişoara, Romania, 20th January 2000), both interviews using written notes.

practices were applied – no music, preaching, prayer or other kinds of manifestations were allowed during church meetings, nothing other than what was sanctioned beforehand by the Departamentul Cultelor (the Department of Religious Affairs – the branch of government through which communists controlled religious groups and implemented repressive anti-religious policies).[8]

This situation continued until 1973, when, in the context of Ceauşescu's bid for better trade relations with the West, some relaxation in communist policies regarding the status of religious communities in the country became necessary.[9] This created an opportunity for re-launching EPC as a congregation on its own. On 11th March 1973, a group of Romanian believers, which by now was numbering about 300 members under the leadership of Pastor Teodor Codreanu, began gathering in a new location; admittedly, in a property in need of much renovation, but one used solely by EPC. The limitations imposed by communist authorities however did not come to an end there, for it took another fifteen years of 'negotiation' with the Department for Religious Affairs and finally the demolition of the building EPC was using before the church received permission to build the adequate facilities currently in use (see an image[10] of the current facilities below).

The period 1946-1989, on the other hand, is also testimony to God's faithful protection and provision, and to the believers' steadfast commitment to God and his mission in the world. Thus, after moving into its own facilities in 1973, in spite of further restrictions and harassment, the church continued to register steady growth, records showing that by December 1989, when the communist period ended, EPC's size had surpassed the 2,000-member threshold. This translates as an average 5.83% annual growth rate over the entire period (1946-1989).

It should be noted, however, that in fact, during this period, the development of the congregation took place in three distinct stages. During 1946-1973, that is, the period of harsh communist restrictions, and their

[8] On these, see Măcelaru, *Însemnări pe uşiorii casei*, 74-75.

[9] As early as 1962, communist Romania had refused to integrate fully with the Council for Mutual Economic Assistance (COMECOM) of the Soviet bloc. Beginning in 1965, after Ceauşescu became the General Secretary of the Romanian Communist Party (and therefore the *de facto* ruler of Romania), a western-oriented foreign policy was pursued, aiming to diminish Soviet influence in the country and to increase trade and other opportunities with western nations. This indeed resulted in Romania being granted the MFN (Most Favoured Nation) trade status by the USA in 1975. Among the (cosmetic) changes Ceauşescu had to make in pursuing his goals was the granting of more freedom to religious groups in the country. Of course, this 'relaxation' of communist policies did not bring the end of the communist oppression of religious communities in Romania; changes implemented were superficial, and communist persecution continued, albeit admittedly in subtler ways. On these, see further, Juliana Geran, 'Why Romania No Longer Deserves to be a Most Favoured Nation': www.heritage.org/research/reports/1985/06/why-romania-no-longer-deserves-to-be-a-most-favored-nation (accessed 15th July 2016).

[10] For this, and other images of EPC's current facilities, see: www.elim.ro/gallery-list/ arhiva-aur-biserica-penticostala-elim

consequences (for instance, EPC's leadership during these years was changed seven times, and that not necessarily according to the wishes of the congregation, for it was a typical practice of communist authorities to impose on congregations the leaders they could control), growth was slower: an average annual rate of 4.15%.

The situation changes significantly from 1973 onwards, for by April 1987, when construction of the current worship facilities was approved, the congregation had already reached approximately 1,200 members – that is, an average annual growth rate of 10.41%. This increase in growth was undoubtedly helped by the re-launching of EPC as a congregation, in its own facilities, in 1973, and the stabilization of EPC's leadership.[11] More importantly, however, the missiologically significant turning point seems to be the appointment of Teodor Codreanu as EPC's pastor. Being mission-oriented, Pastor Codreanu developed a mission strategy tailored to work in spite of the constraints of the communist context. He taught the congregation to adopt four fundamental practices which, with hindsight, very effectively nullified the impact that the restrictions imposed by the communist authorities would have had on religious communities. As described by Pastor Codreanu, these practices were:[12]

[11] Teodor Codreanu continued as pastor of EPC until his death in September 2004. It should be noted though that during the last six years of his life he suffered a series of severe vascular accidents which gradually impaired him, thus making 1997 his last year of full-time service as EPC's pastor. As a result, from 1998, EPC entered a six-year period of transition during which a new leadership emerged and new priorities were defined. Consequently, although EPC's focus on mission has remained a constant priority, methods and emphases have shifted sufficiently to justify the marking of 1997 as the end of a distinct mission period in the life of the church. Thus, the 1997 time limit chosen for the present study. On Teodor Codreanu as EPC's pastor, see 'Noi ordinări de păstori', in *Buletinul Cultului Penticostal* 5-8 (1976), 38; 'Absolvenții cursului Biblic, Seria IV, 1975-1976', in *Buletinul Cultului Penticostal* 5-8 (1976), 38; Bochian, 'În vizită la pastorul Teodor Codreanu – Timişoara'; 'Teodor Codreanu, 1928-2004'.

[12] Teodor Codreanu, taped interview by author (Timişoara, Romania, 18th December 1999).

1. *The participation of each EPC member into an unbroken 'chain' of fasting and prayer.* This 'chain' began in 1973, when each EPC member voluntarily choose one day a week in which (s)he would fast and pray for the well-being and progress of the congregation; this continued over the years, as each new convert that became part of the congregation was invited to join in and commit to fasting and prayer as well. Specifically, explains Pastor Codreanu, people prayed that God's power would become manifest within the congregation in ways which would challenge the absurd claims of the communist atheists that no spiritual reality was really available and the Marxist charge: 'Die Religion... ist das Opium des Volkes'.[13] Such propaganda was intended to extirpate the idea of divine transcendence from society; however, manifestations of divine power attracted non-believers to turn to God, especially when they needed to see God working in similar ways in their own lives. Needless to say, the numerous stories of conversion in the aftermath of divine miraculous interventions in the life of believers and non-believers alike are proof of the effectiveness of this practice.[14]
2. *Pastor Codreanu's emphasis in his sermons of the importance of living a moral, exemplary life as a mission strategy.* Such morality helped to counteract the communist claim that Christians – 'repenters', as we were labelled – were a danger to society, a 'contagion' that had to be eradicated. Evidently, the purpose of such lies was to alienate believers from society, to isolate them and eventually eliminate any public influence they might have had. The moral quality of the believers' lives, however, contrasted powerfully with the corruption, demagogy and falsehood that characterized the communists and their propaganda, thus attracting non-believers to the church. In Codreanu's words: 'People were seeking the church because that was the only place within Romanian society where they could hear the truth.'[15]
3. EPC members were encouraged to talk one-on-one to family members, friends and neighbours about God's existence, in spite of the fact that any attempt to 'pass the faith on' was regarded by the communists as a grave political error. Also, they would extend invitations to non-believers they came in contact with to attend church meetings. Thus, although public, open proclamation of the gospel was restricted by the communists, preaching in the church itself, which was usually evangelistically oriented, provided non-

[13] Karl Marx, 'Zur Kritik der Hegel'schen Rechtsphilosophie', in Arnold Ruge and Karl Marx (eds), *Deutsch-Französische Jahrbücher* (Paris: Bureau der Jahrbücher, 1844), 71 – republished as 'Zur Kritik der Hegelschen Rechtsphilosophie', in *Marx-Engels-Werke, Bd. 1* (Berlin: Dietz Verlag, 1976), 378.

[14] E.g. Măcelaru, *Însemnări pe uşiorii casei.*

[15] Teodor Codreanu, taped interview by author (Timişoara, Romania, 18th December 1999).

believers with the opportunity to hear the good news. In addition to these sermons, evangelistic messages were also delivered on most occasions when meetings outside the church building were permitted: at wedding parties, during funerals, and even during the Christmas season when the traditional carol-singing on Christmas Eve would turn into night-long Christian musical strolls of church youth on the streets of Timişoara. Pastor Codreanu also explained that children from non-believing families who befriended children from EPC's families and began attending Sunday school classes, were encouraged to tell their parents everything they had heard in EPC. All these ensured that the message of the gospel would reach beyond the 'walls' which the communists attempted to raise around believing communities.

4. The fourth practice adopted by EPC as mission strategy during the communist years was grassroots social assistance and charity work. Since the communists denied the right of religious organizations to participate in education, charity and other community-directed activities, mission outreach and social work at the institutional level was not possible. EPC's function as a social agent was therefore severely limited, for such separation of faith from the reality of everyday practice would make any religious community socially irrelevant. However, as Pastor Codreanu explained, a large mission board was formed within EPC which was charged with the task of visiting every EPC family, with the purpose of intervening and helping in situations of illness, poverty, loneliness, disability, etc. Such visits became a testimony of true sacrificial love to non-believers in the city of Timişoara, and when faced with similar liminal situations, many of these specifically asked to be visited and helped. Needless to say, it was often the very gesture of love one would receive that would prompt him/her to enquire about God and eventually to convert.

Needless to say, these practices were crucial in shaping EPC's missiological ethos from 1973 onwards. Furthermore, as will be seen below, these provided a foundation for the mission praxis of EPC after the fall of communism as well.

Finally, the third stage of growth during the communist era refers to the period between April 1987 and January 1990. I have identified this as a distinct stage because documents show that, within only three years, the number of adult believers in EPC increased from 1,200 to 2,130.[16] This would translate as a record 21.08% annual growth rate, which effectively marks EPC as the fastest-growing Pentecostal congregation during that period in Romania, and probably in Eastern Europe. I suggest that the

[16] On these statistics, see A. Trip, 'Biserica Elim 1992 – Retrospectivă', in *Elim* 1 (1992), 11.

'secret' of such increase in growth is to be found in two specific events which enhanced, and added to, the mission practices described above.

The first of these was the September 1985 Billy Graham evangelistic campaign in Romania, which concluded in Timişoara with a meeting that gathered some 150,000 people in the central square of the city.[17] Although no altar call or other such 'follow-up' was permitted by the communist authorities, I submit that this event contributed to bringing the Christian message (and therefore EPC and other similar communities) to the fore in both talk and general awareness. Admittedly, Billy Graham's sermon itself could not have had much impact, for the Securitate (the communist Secret Police) confined the evangelistic meeting to the Timişoara Metropolitan Cathedral and did not allow the service to be broadcast to the people gathered outside, so only approximately 5,000 people actually heard the message. However, the believers who had gathered in the square hours before the meeting actually used this opportunity to speak to others about their faith and made their 'presence' widely known as they sung Christian choruses together throughout the entire time the meeting was taking place in the cathedral.[18] All in all, I suggest that this event helped non-believers realize that Christianity was neither extinct nor a phenomenon on the margins of the society – both claims made by communist ideologues. Rather, the high international profile of Billy Graham and the turn-out of tens of thousands of people in the square provided sure proof that 'there was something there worth exploring'.

The 'awakening' provided by this evangelistic campaign was followed in Timişoara, and more specifically in EPC's case, by another significant event which, I suggest, created the unique context of growth being documented. I refer to the 1987-1988 demolition of EPC's old church building and the construction of the current facilities. To be sure, the demolition programme was not an act of repression directed against EPC alone. Rather, it was part of a master 'urbanization' plan Ceauşescu began implementing in the early 1980s.[19] Paradoxically, though, the very tool of oppression – Ceauşescu's 'urbanization' plan – became, in EPC's case, an opportunity for mission. First, it provided for the creation of an emotional

---

[17] See Billy Graham, *Just As I Am: The Autobiography of Billy Graham* (HarperCollins, 1999), 942-43; John Pollock, *The Billy Graham Story* (Grand Rapids, MI: Zondervan, 2003), 223-31. For a Romanian perspective, see 'Reflections on Billy Graham's Trip to Romania', in *Religion in Communist Lands* XIV (Summer 1986), 224-27.

[18] Information about the event also comes from personal observation as I was one of the thousands who did not gain access to the cathedral and ended up spending the time singing Christian hymns in the square of Timişoara.

[19] Ceauşescu's 'urbanization' plan consisted of the demolition of tens of thousands of private properties and the construction of 'efficiency' apartment buildings instead – apartments within which families that were left without a home in the demolition process were forced to live but now, of course, paying rent to the communist government. This was, evidently, a strategy through which the communist government gained more control over people's lives. The information comes from personal observation, as the present author has experienced Ceauşescu's forced urbanization first-hand.

bond, as private citizens who had suffered similar treatment by the communist authorities began to identify and sympathize with the church.

Secondly, the subsequent construction of new facilities became a testimony in and of itself, for not only was it completed in seventeen months of intensive labour round the clock, but also it was done entirely by members of EPC and other Christian brethren who joined in as volunteers in order to help the project. Moreover, the expenses of the construction were supported by EPC from donations given by its members, who each committed to contribute the equivalent of twenty monthly incomes (salaries, pensions, and other forms of revenue), payable in instalments over a period of ten years. Even those who could not commit to financially support the project, or to work at the construction site, found ways to contribute by waiting long hours in queues to purchase the food and fuel needed by the workers (which at that time in Romania were scarce and available only in the form of strict rations). These sacrifices were not ignored, for news about what was happening started spreading throughout the city, and non-believers who had been wavering with indecision began joining in both the work and the congregation.[20] As records show, within the three short years taken by the construction project and its aftermath, over 900 new converts joined EPC,[21] bringing the number of adult believers in EPC at the beginning of the period under scrutiny (1990-1997) to 2,130.

---

[20] As a volunteer worker myself, I have personally witnessed the events described. See also Codreanu, 'Biserica Penticostală Elim – Timişoara', 19.

[21] The impact the construction project had on the growth of the church is a recurring motif in several interviews. E.g. Teodor Codreanu, taped interview by author (Timişoara, Romania, 18th December 1999; D. Tecar, interview by author (Timişoara, Romania, 19th December 1999), using written notes; V. Goagără, interview by author (Timişoara, Romania, 19th December 1999), also using written notes. According to Tecar, this impact is undeniable, for after the inauguration of the new building in 1989, an upsurge of new converts was recorded: during 1989, EPC held five water-baptism services, with the service held on 23rd April 1989 adding a record 158 new members to the community, thus making this the second highest number of candidates baptised in one baptism service in the history of EPC – the highest number being recorded at the service on 10th May 1992, with 189 candidates. This was a clear departure from a pattern of three water-baptism services per year, of an average of 100 candidates each. Published figures confirm this estimate: Codreanu, 'Biserica Penticostală Elim – Timişoara', 19 (10th May 1989 – 189 candidates); 'Botez nou-testamental cu 136 de suflete la Timişoara', in *Cuvântul Adevărului*, V.4, 2nd Series (April 1994), 20 (9th January 1994 – 136 candidates); 'Pe scurt', in *Cuvântul Adevărului,* V.12, 2nd Series (December 1994), 19 (25th September 1994 – 70 candidates); 'Botez nou-testamental la Biserica Penticostală "Elim", Timişoara', 2 (19th January 1997 – 106 candidates); A.M. Anescu, 'Legământ', in *Cuvântul Adevărului,* IX.3, 2nd Series (March 1998), 20 (11th January 1998 – 82 candidates); Ghiţă Bodrojan, 'Primul rod în anul 2000', in *Cuvântul Adevărului,* XI.2-3, 2nd Series (February-March 2000), 5 (16th January 2000 – 93 candidates); Corneliu Merca, 'Botez la Elim, Timişoara', in *Cuvântul Adevărului,* XV.5, 2nd Series (May 2004), 2, 20 (2nd April 2004 – 58 candidates).

EPC – Mission in Post-1989 Romania (1990-1997)

The decade after the fall of communism in Romania represents a time of transition, both at the macro-level, as these are the years during which the ideals of freedom that had animated anti-communist demonstrators in December 1989 were challenged at every turn by neo-communist agendas promoted by elected officials, such as Ion Iliescu (president of Romania 1990-1996 and 2000-2004) and other such figures that were clinging to the past, and at the micro-level, as these are also the years during which the stabilization of new leadership structures and a search for a genuine Pentecostal identity, untainted by the compromises of the past,[22] began taking place within the Romanian Pentecostal denomination. For EPC, however, these are years during which the mission work of the congregation resulted in unprecedented growth. These are also the years in which the mission strategy of the church, tested and sharpened during the communist era, became the foundation upon which new endeavours, that would not have been possible prior 1989, were undertaken. The result: according to available membership records, coupled with oral reports obtained via interviews, was an average annual growth rate of approximately 20%, reaching in 1997 some 7,000 adult believers and over 2,500 children and adolescents.

It should be clarified, however, that while the figures above include a fairly precise estimate of new converts that joined EPC from 1990 until 1997, they only approximate the number of converts in the over thirty satellite churches established by EPC during the same period.[23] Also, it takes into account (again, an estimate) the number of people that converted in EPC and subsequently left Romania as work-migrants, and the converts that left EPC and joined other newly established congregations in Timişoara. Since precise information on all these categories is not available in EPC's records, such estimates are the best that can be provided.[24]

There is, of course, a clearer record with regard to the growth of EPC itself. This shows that, even when considered alone, EPC's average growth rate remained impressive: 10.66% per annum, with 1992 and 1994 being the years with the highest yield (with growth rates of 14.37% and 14.87% respectively), by contrast with 1996, when there was only a 6.95% increase.[25] The highest number of converts that joined EPC over a one-year

---

[22] On the duplicitous attitude shown by some of the Pentecostal leaders during the communist period, including collaboration with communist oppressors and compromise for personal benefits, see Vasilică Croitor, *Răscumpărarea memoriei: Cultul Penticostal în perioada comunistă* (*Redeeming the Memory: The Pentecostal Denomination during the Communist Period*) (Medgidia, Romania: Succeed Publishing, 2010).

[23] E.g. 'Pe scurt', in *Cuvântul Adevărului,* VI.11, 2nd Series (November 1995), 15.

[24] On these, see further Merca, 'Elim-ul… la 15 ani', 2.

[25] Discrepancies appear at some points between the records of EPC that I had access to and figures given in various publications or stated in interviews. Where such was the case, I generally sided with the more conservative numbers. For published figures, see Trip, 'Biserica Elim 1992 – Retrospectivă', 11; Codreanu, 'Biserica Penticostală Elim – Timişoara', 19;

period was recorded in 1994, with 440 new members, while the total number of new converts over the seven-year period under scrutiny was 2,198 – that is, a total growth of 103.19%. The four charts provided below help 'paint' a clearer picture.

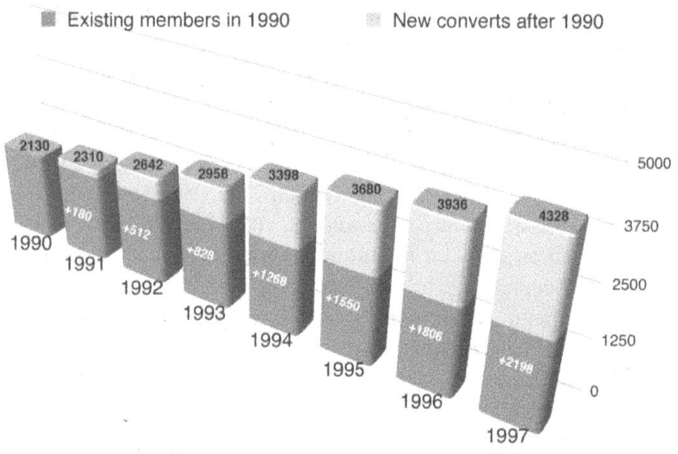

Total growth during 1990-1997 (number of new converts)

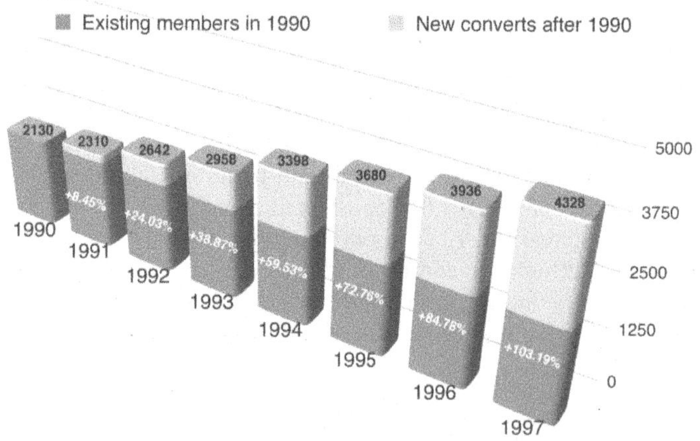

Total growth during 1990-1997 (percentages)

Merca, 'Din istoricul Bisericii Apostolice Penticostale "Elim" Timişoara', 14-15; Ibid. 'Elim-ul... la 15 ani', 2; 'Teodor Codreanu, 1928-2004', 23; and 'Biserica "Elim" de-a lungul timpului': www.elim.ro/despre-biserica-penticostala-elim-timisoara/biserica -elim-de-a-lungul-timpului (accessed 14th April 2016).

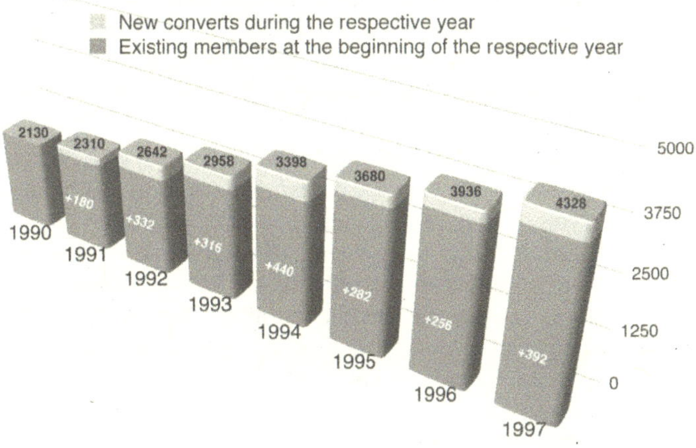

Annual growth (number of new converts)

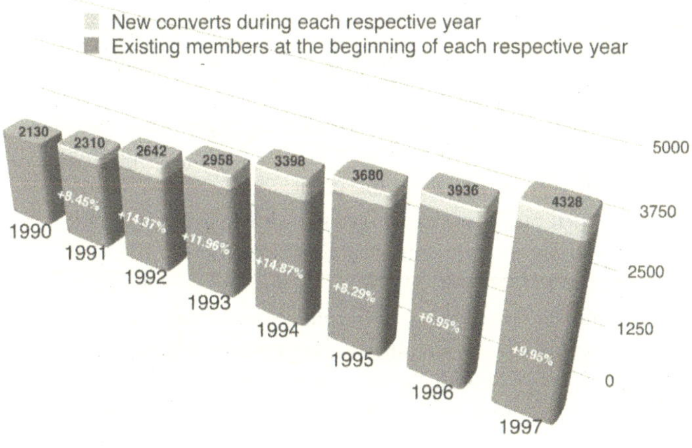

Annual growth (percentages)

In terms of mission strategies, the research undertaken has revealed that EPC's post-1989 praxis built on the four pillars described earlier (prayer and fasting; high morality; a focus on evangelism; charity and social involvement), while at the same time taking advantage of the opportunities for mission that opened up in the context of post-1989 religious freedom.

First, the 'chain' of prayer and fasting continued, both at individual and ecclesial levels. Home-based prayer groups, as well as meetings with the whole congregation, took place on a weekly basis, while the ordained ministers of EPC were available for people seeking pastoral advice and specific prayer for healing or other needs, irrespective of whether they were members of EPC or non-believers. Testimonies of divine intervention were recorded[26] and every December a special thanksgiving celebration was held during which EPC members could share with fellow believers and other participants their experiences of divine deliverance.

Second, the emphasis on holiness remained a constant of EPC's ethos as well, although, according to Pastor Codreanu, the 'enemy' to be unmasked was no longer communist propaganda, but the 'shocking' customs and unprecedented accessibility to western cultural features that had the potential to become a threat to the integrity of Romanian believers. Also, during this period, due to the cross-cultural exchanges that took place between Romanians and visitors from abroad, new concepts of worship and service to God became available. In EPC's answer to all this, one could observe a tendency to preserve the traditions of the past, although there was also much openness from EPC's leadership to enter fruitful partnerships with foreign mission agencies and missionaries for as long as these paid due attention in their approach to mission to the specifics of the Romanian Christian ethos.

Third, the new-found freedom of expression was seen by EPC as an opportunity to increase its evangelistic efforts. Thus, during the period in view, EPC was involved (as partner or as sole organizer) in several evangelistic rallies in the city of Timişoara:[27]

- June 1990, with evangelist Luis Palau (Argentina / USA) as speaker – CFR Stadium, Timişoara (EPC as partner, together with other evangelical churches from the city).
- 10-12 April 1992, with evangelist Len Linstrom (Canada) as speaker – CFR Stadium, Timişoara (EPC as organizer).
- 13-14 April 1992, with the Rev. Al Smith (USA) and Pastor Teodor Codreanu as speakers – 'Olimpia' Sports Hall, Timişoara (EPC in partnership with the Romanian Mission of Chicago).
- 20-22 July 1992, with the Rev. Al Smith (USA) and Pastor Teodor Codreanu as speakers – 'Olimpia' Sports Hall, Timişoara (EPC in partnership with the Romanian Mission of Chicago).
- 24-26 July 1992, with evangelists Lennart Charlsson and Leif Svenson (Sweden) as speakers – 'Olimpia' Sports Hall, Timişoara (EPC in partnership with the Romanian-Swedish Humanitarian Christian Centre).
- 6-8 November 1992, with evangelists Lennart Charlsson and Leif Svenson (Sweden) as speakers – 'Olimpia' Sports Hall, Timişoara (EPC in partnership with the Romanian-Swedish Humanitarian Christian Centre).

---

[26] E.g. Codreanu, 'Biserica Penticostală Elim – Timişoara', 19; Viorica Coman, 'Lanţul vindecărilor', in *Cuvântul Adevărului* VII.8-9, 2nd Series (August-September 1996), 16.

[27] On these, see 'Info Elim: 20 Noiembrie 1988-20 Noiembrie 1998', in *Elim* 36-37 (1998), 20; and

- 4-6 June 1993, with evangelists Lennart Charlsson and Leif Svenson (Sweden) as speakers – 'Olimpia' Sports Hall, Timişoara (EPC in partnership with the Romanian-Swedish Humanitarian Christian Centre).
- 7-8 May 1994, with evangelist Iohan Maasbaah (Holland) as speaker – 'Olimpia' Sports Hall, Timişoara (EPC as organizer).

In addition to these, EPC has participated every year in the so-called 'Marşul Învierii' (Resurrection March), an ecumenical event involving all Christian denominations (including the historic churches) in Timişoara. The event has taken place every Easter Monday since 1990, and it consists of a procession through the city, which is concluded with an evangelistic service in an open arena in one of the parks of Timişoara.

It should be noted in this context that 1992, the year in which EPC was involved in five evangelistic rallies, has also been identified in the charts above as one of its best years in terms of growth.

Besides the evangelistic rallies listed above, in 1991 EPC, in partnership with the Evangelical Theological Seminary of Osijek, Croatia, launched a theological educational programme (which later developed into the 'Elim' Evangelical Theological Seminary) with the purpose of training mission workers and church planters.[28] As a result, in 1992 EPC organized twelve missionary teams which were charged with planting a new church in every city and village in the Banat area (the western part of Romania) that did not have at least one Pentecostal church in it. The impact and scope of this ministry increased over time to the point that church-planting teams were sent to reach other areas of the country (Oltenia – southern Romania)[29] and Romanian ethnics living in Serbia.[30] The fruits of this ministry are evident in the over thirty satellite churches that were started during the period in view.

Finally, regarding EPC's fourth mission strategy, the charity work and social involvement of the congregation during the seven years under scrutiny was remarkably broad in its scope and diversified in its impact. Although not all the activities that could be listed under this category were recorded, research shows clearly that it is in this area that EPC's mission agenda was most obvious. Thus, records show that over 30% of EPC's budget during this period was directed at funding charitable and other social care activities.[31] Below, I describe the most representative

[28] 'Elim' Evangelical Theological Seminary is recognized as one of the denominational educational institutions: Pavel Riviş Tipei, 'Raportul Consiliului Bisericesc la Congresul al VI-lea al Bisericilor Apostolice Penticostale din România: Mandatul noiembrie 1994-noiembrie 1998', in *Cuvântul Adevărului* X.1, 2nd Series (January 1999), 8.

[29] On which, see 'Biserica "Elim" de-a lungul timpului'; see: www.elim.ro/despre-biserica-penticostala-elim-timisoara/biserica-elim-de-a-lungul-timpului

[30] On which, see G. Mozor, 'Binecuvântări pe Meleagurile Banatului Iugoslav', in *Elim* 1 (1992), 5.

[31] In most cases, charitable and social activities are not mentioned beyond expense entries in the budget of EPC. As such, the information provided in this section was obtained primarily

occurrences, many of which also represent starting-points for long-term (sometimes still ongoing) ministries:

- 1992 onwards – in the aftermath of a disastrous earthquake witch took place in the city of Voiteni and the surrounding area, EPC, in partnership with the Romanian-Swedish Humanitarian Christian Centre, provided humanitarian aid to affected families, especially families that had many children. This was the beginning of a longer-term partnership between the two institutions and the regional Romanian authorities, which later on focused on providing humanitarian aid to orphanages in the cities of Timişoara, Lugoj and Periam.[32] The ministry developed further as members of EPC began individual involvement in the lives of orphan children from these institutions, through donations as well as by welcoming them into their homes and, in some cases, by adoption.[33]
- 1992-1995 – EPC sent aid to war orphans in Osijek, Croatia.[34]
- 1992-1995 – EPC provided aid for Serbian refugees in the camps in Călacea and Buziaş.[35]
- 1993 onwards – EPC organized special church events, coupled with material aid for children with disabilities[36] and orphan children infected with HIV.[37]
- 1993 onwards – EPC organized and funded summer camps for orphan children and children coming from families without material means.[38]
- 1993 onwards – EPC began providing regular aid to elderly people in asylums or hospitals, especially those without relatives. Also,

---

from announcements of, and reports about, such activities recorded in EPC's periodical *Elim*. The periodical, published since 1992, has become one of the most respected Pentecostal publications in Romania, widely distributed in the country, and abroad among Romanian diaspora churches. For references confirming the impact of *Elim*, which appear in the official periodical of the Romanian Pentecostal Denomination, see 'Biblioteca redacţiei', in *Cuvântul Adevărului*, VII.5, 2nd Series (May 1996), 12; 'Pe scurt', in *Cuvântul Adevărului*, VIII.4, 2nd Series (April 1997), 16; 'Lumina vechilor cărări', in *Cuvântul Adevărului*, IX.5, 2nd Series (May 1998), 2; and Pavel R. Tipei, 'Raportul Consiliului Bisericesc la Congresul al VII-lea al Bisericilor Apostolice Penticostale din România pentru mandatul 1998-2002', in *Cuvântul Adevărului*, XIII.11, 2nd Series (November 2002), 7.

[32] On which, see Ion Pitic, 'Avem o colaborare bună în toate domeniile', interview by G. David, in *Elim*, 1 (1992), 5.

[33] On which, see 'Ştiaţi că…?', in *Elim*, 2 (1993), 9.

[34] On which, see E. Codreanu, 'De la inimă la inimă', in *Elim*, 8 (1994), 21; J. Paulus, interview by C. Constantineanu, in *Elim*, 10 (1994), 14; E. Codreanu, 'Un zâmbet fericit pe feţe nevinovate', in *Elim*, 17 (1995), 18.

[35] I. Moroşan, interview by author (Timişoara, Romania, 19th December 1999), using written notes.

[36] On which, see L. Măcelaru, 'Mâinile care vindecă', in *Elim*, 42-43 (1999), 8.

[37] On which, see E. Codreanu, 'Stropi de binecuvântare', in *Elim*, 4 (1993), 14.

[38] On which, see C. Constantineanu and T. Stoia, 'Tabăra de vacanţă Petroşani – 1993', in *Elim*, 6 (1993), 14.

volunteers from among EPC members started providing transport for elderly people to and from church.[39]

- Late 1993 – the EPC's Women's Association was launched. Its primary function was involvement in various types of charitable activities for the benefit of both believers and non-believers. The organization was self-funded.
- December 1993 – EPC launched a hospital ministry: teams of believers were organized and funded to visit patients in the Timiş County Hospital every Sunday. The purpose of the ministry was to identify and help people who had no family support.[40]
- December 1993 – EPC launched a prison ministry: teams of believers were organized and funded to visit and, when permitted, give aid to inmates in the 'Popa Şapcă' Prison in Timişoara. Also, when permitted, inmates were invited to visit EPC and worship together with the congregation.[41]
- June 1995 – EPC began sending aid to the leprosy colony in Tichileşti, Brăila, the last place of its kind in Europe.[42]

From the record of EPC's ministries provided above, it is evident that the most significant year from a social assistance perspective was 1993. Most ministries of this type in EPC had their beginning at some point during that period. I suggest that the effects of this emphasis were evident in the upsurge of new converts that led to the peak of EPC's growth registered in 1994.

Conclusion

EPC's unique record of growth presented above provides a telling example of how the praxis of a congregation animated by a proper vision and informed by the right strategy can have effective outcomes even if operating within unfavourable contexts. Although EPC's success story is most visible in the period after 1989, the information provided above shows that the seeds of that success were sown in the years preceding the fall of communism. This, I suggested, was due to the mission intelligence of Pastor Teodor Codreanu, whose fourfold mission strategy made EPC an efficient 'engine' of mission in both the pre- and the post-1989 Romania. Thus, in the midst of a regime that aimed to silence religious communities and to smother any desire for social engagement, the mission strategy adopted kept the outward orientation of the congregation alive and the rate of its growth high. After the fall of communism, the same mission strategy

---

[39] On which, see G. Gui, 'Sărbătoare la Azilul din Ciacova', in *Elim,* 5 (1993), 15.

[40] On which, see M. Măcelaru, 'Alege să slujeşti', in *Elim,* 7 (1993), 10.

[41] On which, see C.G. Câmpan, 'Două ore deosebite petrecute de Biserica Elim împreună cu tineri din Penitenciarul Timişoara', in *Elim,* 42-43 (1999), 27.

[42] On which, see V. Păscălin, 'Tichileşti – tabăra de leproşi din România', in *Elim,* 16 (1995), 20; Ibid., 'Noi veşti din tabăra de leproşi de la Tichileşti', in *Elim,* 23 (1996), 15.

provided a foundation for notable evangelistic efforts and broad social involvement, which together contributed to unprecedented upsurges in both EPC's membership and influence.

In the light of these, I conclude that the practices of prayer and fasting, the leading of a moral life, the focus on speaking out the message of the gospel, and charitable social involvement, all provide a model for ministry that reflects a holistic understanding of our God-given charge to be his witnesses in the world (Acts 1:8). They should not be taken as separate mission objectives but as an integrated mission plan – an 'edifice' that will stand tall for as long as its four pillars are equally developed.

APME – A Case Study in Cross-Cultural Mission Originating from Eastern Europe

Gheorghe Rițișan and Corneliu Constantineanu

Introduction

In 1997, at the European Conference of Church of God in Kirchheim, Germany,[1] when the Romanian delegation was presented, the moderator said: 'The president of *The Sleeping Giant* will greet the audience.'[2] At first, Pastor Pavel Riviş Tipei, who led the delegation, did not understand the meaning of the words. Only when the moderator reminded him that he represents the largest Pentecostal denomination in Europe and that this major church had not sent any missionaries beyond its borders did the president of the Pentecostal Christian Church in Romania[3] (CCPR) understand the reference.

The metaphor of *The Sleeping Giant* was not new, but it fitted the situation of CCPR perfectly.[4] Analyzing closely the reports presented every four years at CCPR congresses after the revolution in December 1989,[5] one can clearly see the remarkable passion that believers in the Pentecostal churches had for internal evangelism and church planting. At the same time, one cannot overlook the total lack of interest for foreign mission, at least in the first decade. In 1989 there were about 700 licensed Pentecostal churches; four years later, at the Fifth Congress in November 1994, it was reported that there were already 1,740 licences issued for churches and subsidiaries,[6] while in 2006 there were 2,476 churches and subsidiaries in the country and 248 churches in the European diaspora.[7]

Despite these extraordinary achievements in internal evangelism and church planting fifteen years after the fall of the communist regime, CCPR

---

[1] *Cuvântul Adevărului (The Word of Truth)*, December 1997, 19. (*Cuvântul Adevărului* is the magazine of the Romanian Pentecostal Christian Church).

[2] Interview with Pastor Tipei, 16th July 2015. He was the president of the Romanian Pentecostal Christian Church between 1994 and 2014.

[3] In Romanian: Cultul Creştin Penticostal – Biserica lui Dumnezeu Apostolică din România. Abbreviated to CCPR.

[4] The situation was the same in the entire Evangelical movement. See: Scott Klingsmith, *Missions Beyond the Wall: Factors in the Rise of Missionary Sending Movements in East-Central Europe* (Edition Afem Mission Academics, 2012).

[5] The revolution changed the political regime in Romania, from communist to democratic.

[6] *Cuvântul Adevărului*, December 1994, 4-5.

[7] *Cuvântul Adevărului*, November 2006, 5-6. In 1998, there were 2,142 churches and subsidiaries (*Cuvântul Adevărului*, December 1998, 10). In 2002, there were 2,443 churches and subsidiaries (*Cuvântul Adevărului*, November 2002, 5).

did not manage to send and support a single long-term missionary abroad through its own Department for Evangelism and Mission[8] (DEM). This unusual situation greatly determined the birth of the Romanian Pentecostal Agency for Foreign Mission[9] (APME) as a foreign mission structure operating within CCPR.

This paper offers a short analysis of the context that led to the establishment of APME and outlines the main steps in the process of the development of the organization in its first decade of existence, during which it became one of the youngest and most dynamic missionary structures in Europe. It begins by mentioning the factors that prevented CCPR from participating in foreign mission immediately after the fall of the communist regime, despite the fact that it was one of the largest Pentecostal movements in Europe. At this point we will also define the term 'missionary' that we are going to use in the study, and we will enumerate some of the missionary activities of CCPR in the 1990s that preceded and prepared the way for the birth of APME, but at the same time highlighted the need and demanded the existence of a well-organized sending and supporting structure for Romanian young people in foreign mission. The second part of the paper will describe the process of the birth of APME and the important role the founding team played in the existence of the agency and in articulating its mission, vision, values and work philosophy. The main section of the paper will present the components of APME's work strategy which led to implementing its vision and fulfilling its objectives. We will then show the importance of internal and foreign partnerships in the activity of APME. A final section will list a few lessons learned in the ten years of APME's existence. The case study will close with a short conclusion in which we will mention once again the elements that highlight the development of APME from its founding till the present day, and also the challenges that the organization faces over the next few years.

Because APME operates mostly in the Romanian Pentecostal churches, the study will analyze the evolution of CCPR's stance on foreign missions from 1990 till 2015 and the interaction between APME and CCPR during this period.

The Context of APME's Birth and the Propagation of Missiological Concepts in CCPR Churches

'... your faith in God has become known everywhere' (1 Thess. 1:8).

For fifteen years after 1989, CCPR did almost nothing in terms of sending and supporting Romanian missionaries, although DEM has existed since

---

[8] In Romanian: Departamentul de Evanghelizare si Misiune. Abbreviated to DEM.

[9] In Romanian: Agentia Penticostala de Misiune Externa. Abbreviated to APME.

1994.[10] A series of factors – political, economic but also theological (ecclesiological) – contributed to the fact that CCPR was not involved in foreign mission in the years immediately after 1989. Maybe the most important factor was the communist system which, for half a century, had isolated CCPR from other Pentecostal churches in the world[11] and, implicitly, from global missionary projects. Romania became a huge concentration camp behind the 'Iron Curtain' and for the majority of its citizens it was practically impossible to go beyond the borders. Even after the fall of the communist regime, it was very difficult for Romanians to travel abroad and obtain visas for certain nations, until 2007 when it became an EU member. Furthermore, the fact that Romania was isolated and unable to do foreign mission brought a severe deficiency in the church's theology – the mandate of the Great Commission (Matt. 28:18-20) did not exist in CCPR's requirements. Moreover, the influx of foreign missionaries into Romania after 1989 brought the false impression that Romania was a mission field and not a country with real sending potential. The 1995 edition of *Operation World* mentions that there were 165 foreign missionaries in Romania, sent by 38 agencies.[12] The first edition of the 21st century of the same publication shows that their number had grown to 453.[13] This aspect, along with the lack of tradition in mission, led to the formation of a certain mindset, according to which foreign mission must be done by others – by those with more experience of it, by those who were better prepared, and not by Romanians. The economic crisis (inflation reached over 100% in some years) also fuelled the development of the mentality that we were too poor to do foreign mission and support our workers. Finally, the ministry of evangelism and church planting in Romania was successful, the church was focusing on the least evangelized areas of the country, and these factors led to an unanimously accepted belief in CCPR that we were already doing mission by concentrating on our fellow countrymen.[14] This problem arose because the terms 'mission' and/or 'missionary' either did not exist for a long time in the documents of CCPR, or their definition was ambiguous.[15] For instance, during communist

[10] Valeriu Andreiescu, *Istoria Penticostalismului Românesc* (Oradea, Romania: Casa Cărții, 2012), Vol. II, 465. The first DEM co-ordinator was Pastor Iacob Berghianu.

[11] Cameron Wilson, *He Discovered His Mission* (USA, DYM Publishing, 2013), 150.

[12] Patrick Johnstone, *Operation World: A Day-to-Day Guide to Praying for the World* (Carlisle, UK: OM Publishing, 1995), 463.

[13] Patrick Johnstone and Jason Mandryk (eds), *Operation World: 21st Century Edition* (Carlisle, UK: Paternoster Lifestyle, 2001), 536. The 453 foreign missionaries from Romania were sent by 85 mission agencies.

[14] In 1998, there were reportedly 90 internal evangelists (*Cuvântul Adevărului*, December 1998, 10); in 2002, 156 evangelists (*Cuvântul Adevărului*, November 2002, 5); in 2006, there were 349 evangelists (*Cuvântul Adevărului*, November 2006, 5-6), and in 2010, 346 evangelists (*Cuvântul Adevărului*, December 4, 6).

[15] Andreiescu, *Istoria Penticostalismului Românesc*, 464. The term 'missionary' does not appear in any confession of faith of CCPR before 1989. For the first time, the term

oppression, 'mission' almost exclusively meant that a group of believers travelled from one church to another to serve by preaching, singing or reciting poems. After 1989, things went to the other extreme: almost everything that was being done outside the church walls was considered 'mission'. This led to the term 'mission' being emptied of any meaning – as Stephen Neill said: 'If everything is mission, nothing is mission.'[16]

As for the term 'missionary', article 25 of the CCPR by-laws of 1997 defines for the first time who and what missionaries are: 'Workers sent by the church in the country or abroad to establish new churches by spreading the Gospel, to strengthen smaller churches and to do social and humanitarian activities'.[17] The next CCPR official documents which define the missionary's work made only small changes regarding his status, activity or area of ministry.[18] These examples show the difficulty of finding a satisfactory and comprehensive definition of mission. They also showcase the attempts of the pastors in the Church Council of CCPR to standardize this type of ministry that was beginning to take place among other ministries that existed and were recognized by the church.

Taking into account everything mentioned above, the founders of APME[19] realized they had to state right from the beginning in the by-laws of the organization the mission and vision of APME, and also define the term 'missionary' that they were going to use in the future. These missionaries would be Romanian believers, ready to dedicate themselves to long-term ministry[20] (at least 10-15 years on the mission field) who would be involved especially in projects of planting new churches, Christian education and Bible translation.[21]

The lack of Romanian missionaries sent abroad by the DEM of CCPR does not mean that nothing happened during all these years in the Pentecostal movement concerning mission. In his grace, God started in the first few years after the Revolution to infuse the church with these new concepts (foreign mission, cross-cultural missionaries, mission agencies) and to prepare the field and the people who would later be more involved in foreign mission.

Undoubtedly, the mission conferences organized during that time had the primary role of preparing those who would later be involved in mission

---

'missionary' appears in the CCPR by-law of 1992, but it seems to be synonymous with the term 'evangelist'.

[16] Quoted in David Bosch, *Transforming Mission* (Maryknoll, NY: Orbis Books, 2011), 523.

[17] Statutul de organizare şi funcţionare al Uniunii Penticostale – Biserica lui Dumnezeu Apostolică, Bucuresti, 1997, 7-8.

[18] Andreiescu, 467.

[19] Pastors Emil Meştereagă, Dumitru Mircea Deteşan, Vasilică Croitor, Gheorghe Riţişan and Richard Bruce Cunningham Jr.

[20] Manualul Misionarului APME (APME Missionary's Manual), 7. The Missionary's Manual dictates the relationships inside APME. Manualul Misionarului was finalized and approved by the whole APME body (Board of Directors, staff, missionaries) at their retreat in 2011 in Agigea, Constanţa.

[21] Manualul Misionarului, 3.

and also in preparing future mission candidates. The most renowned conferences in CCPR were the series called *RoMisCon* that were launched by the Rev. Cameron Wilson and his wife, Marvel. The first conference took place in 1996,[22] in Betania Church in Arad. Their initiator would later declare that these conferences 'promoted a rapid growth in world missions knowledge and commitment'.[23] Furthermore, because the conferences were organized in different locations each year, the concepts of 'mission' and 'missionary' spread easily in different geographical areas of the country. In the first years, the speakers were exclusively foreign missionaries and workers. Later on, especially after the 2003 *RoMisCon* in Medgidia,[24] Romanian pastors began to be more involved both in organizing and speaking in these seminars. After the launch of APME in 2006, this organization began to be fully involved in all the organization of the *RoMisCon* conferences.

As far as bringing awareness to the leaders of CCPR about the need of a sending structure for missionaries, the conferences in Buşteni[25] (2001 and 2002) and Buziaş[26] (2003), organized by DEM, FIDA[27] and PEM[28] and co-ordinated by Pastor Ioan Bochian,[29] were of great importance. Arto Hamalainen's sessions, called 'The basic requirements for missionary work' and 'Strategies in modern missions'[30] brought an especially important contribution to the birth of APME. Some of the future founding members[31] of APME participated at and were involved in these conferences, where they became aware of the importance of organizing mission at a national level.

Apart from these missionary conferences in Romania, international conferences played an important role in forming and guiding the Romanian Pentecostal leaders when it came to mission. It is worth mentioning here that pastors Vasilică Croitor and Gheorghe Riţişan, together with George Găvruş (a missionary in Central Asia) participated at the Consultation on Muslim Evangelism in Baguio, Philippines, in February 2005.[32] The discussions that took place there with leaders of Pentecostal world mission,

---

[22] Wilson, *He Discovered His Mission*, 154. *RoMisCon* is the acronym of the Romanian Missionary Convocation.

[23] Wilson, *He Discovered His Mission*, 154.

[24] A town in Constanţa County, in the south-east of Romania.

[25] Andreiescu, *Istoria Penticostalismului Românesc*, 467.

[26] Andreiescu, *Istoria Penticostalismului Românesc*, 469.

[27] FIDA is the mission organization of the Pentecostals in Finland.

[28] PEM stands for Pentecostal European Mission – a network of over 35 European mission organizations.

[29] Andreiescu, *Istoria Penticostalismului Românesc*, 465. Pastor Ioan Bochian was the co-ordinator of DEM between 1998 and 2002.

[30] Andreiescu, *Istoria Penticostalismului Românesc*, 469. Arto Hamalainen was the President of FIDA and PEM.

[31] Andreiescu, *Istoria Penticostalismului Românesc*, 467-69. The pastors were Emil Meştereagă, Gheorghe Riţişan, Rick Cunningham and Vasilică Croitor.

[32] Andreiescu, *Istoria Penticostalismului Românesc*, 470.

especially with Brad Walz,[33] and also the examples of other Pentecostal churches that organized their own foreign mission agencies (especially in Argentina) had a decisive role in the emergence of APME.

Theological institutes and Bible schools also greatly contributed to spreading missiological concepts and preparing Romanian young people for mission. Towards the end of the 1990s, the Pentecostal Theological Institute in Bucharest, the Betania Faculty of Theology in Arad and the Romanian Bible Institute in Bucharest started to offer more and more mission courses and to organize missiological symposiums. The speakers were mostly active missionaries with wide experience in such ministry. They had a distinct role in confirming the call to mission that some students had.[34] The Eastern European Bible College in Oradea also contributed to forming and then sending many young people into mission. In partnership with the Pentecostal Mission and Charity Society in Romania (SPMCR), this school sent the first Romanian missionaries to India.[35] After 2000, the first mission schools were founded in Romania.[36] In Constanța, Pastor Gheorghe Rițișan founded *The Mission and Evangelism School in Dobrogea* (SMED)[37] with the exclusive objective of preparing career missionaries. A year later, at the initiative of Pastor Pavel Tipei and Franz Johansen, the mission school *Team-Action* Romania (SMTAR) in Arad came into being. It specializes mostly in training young people for short-term mission.

Youth camps organized in Romania after the fall of the communist regime constitute a third means of spreading the concept of mission. The youth camps and conferences organized by the *Peniel Foundation*[38] contributed by far the most in raising awareness among youth about the Great Commission, recruiting mission candidates and supporting mission financially.

Ever since the first camp organized in 1995, at each *Peniel* meeting at least one seminar is dedicated to foreign mission where career missionaries are invited to address the young people. During the *Peniel* camps the need of a mission agency was more obvious than anywhere else.[39]

Pastors and young people also participated in short-term missionary trips that contributed to bringing awareness to the churches concerning the great

---

[33] Brad Walz is the chairman of Assemblies of God World Mission Commission.

[34] David Leatherberry, a former missionary in Afghanistan, was one of the professors at the Romanian Bible Institute in Bucharest that impacted George Găvruș's ministry in Central Asia.

[35] Andreiescu, *Istoria Penticostalismului Românesc*, 350, 471-72.

[36] Andreiescu, *Istoria Penticostalismului Românesc*, 468.

[37] Since 2007, it has been called The Romanian Center for Cross-Cultural Studies (CRST).

[38] The director of the *Peniel Foundation* is Lucian Oniga.

[39] An incident that took place at a youth camp is worth mentioning: after Pastor Rick Cunningham had preached about mission and challenged young people to go to the mission fields, at the end of the seminar a young man came up and said: 'I believe God is calling me to go on the mission field. What do I have to do?' Rather embarrassed, Rick answered: 'I have no idea!'

spiritual and financial needs that exist all round the world, but were almost unknown to most people. The reports the participants presented upon returning home helped prepare the churches and pastors to answer these needs both by praying and by financially supporting those who were ready to go to the mission fields. A small part of these missionary trips are presented by Professor Andreiescu in *The History of Romanian Pentecostalism.*[40]

Finally, another element that contributed to raising foreign mission awareness in CCPR were the foreign missionaries themselves in the country. There is not a list of all the missionaries present in Romania after 1989 that were active in the Pentecostal churches, but the president's report from October 2006 mentioned the fact that sixteen Assemblies of God missionaries and two Church of God missionaries were working with CCPR.[41] Of those mentioned, the Rev. Cameron Wilson and Rick Cunningham had essential roles in the birth of APME – the latter eventually becoming one of the founding members of the agency.

Laying the Foundation for APME: The Team, the Mission, the Values, the Vision

'*Set apart for me Barnabas and Saul for the work to which I have called them*' (Acts 13:2). As was previously mentioned, there has been a DEM (Department for Evangelism and Mission) in the CCPR ever since 1994. Many pastors that were a part of DEM in the years after it was founded were remarkable people. Many of them initiated and co-ordinated vast evangelism projects in Romania, organized mission conferences or sent cross-cultural missionaries from the church they pastored. However, in 2006 there was still not a single Romanian missionary sent and supported in an organized manner through DEM. The giant was still sleeping…

In the context of this painful reality, the Holy Spirit brought together a group of pastors[42] and gave them a mission: establishing a functioning mission agency to serve the CCPR. This mission materialized on 2nd February 2006 when APME officially came into being.[43] This team of founders still forms the Board of Directors (hereafter the Board) of APME and represents the leading organism of the organization. Although it started as an organization independent of the official structures of the CCPR, APME had the approval of the leaders of that time, precisely because, from the very beginning, its founders planned for the agency to be an instrument

[40] Andreiescu, *Istoria Penticostalismului Românesc*, 468-78.

[41] *Cuvântul Adevărului*, December 2006, 11.

[42] The founding members of APME that also formed the first Board of Directors were the following pastors: Emil Meştereagă – president, Mircea Deteşan – vice-president, Vasilică Croitor – secretary, Gheorghe Riţişan and Rick Cunningham – members. Two years later, pastors Iacob Berghianu from Târgu Mureş and Florinel Cîmpeanu from Chicago (USA) were invited to join the Board of Directors of APME.

[43] Andreiescu, *Istoria Penticostalismului Românesc*, 478.

which would help CCPR in fulfilling the mandate that Jesus Christ gave his church in Matthew 28. The secret of the foundation and development of APME lies in the existence, from its outset, of a united, loyal and dedicated team of pastors, with a vision and a passion for this ministry that was absolutely essential in the CCPR: foreign mission. Two years later, to prove APME's willingness to work together with the structures of CCPR and also in order to be transparent in its ministry, the founders of APME considered it important to have a Reference Board to which they would be accountable and give reports. From the start, its president has been Pastor Moldovan Ioan, the co-ordinator of DEM in the CCPR, and most of the Reference Board members are pastors with great influence in CCPR. For the current activities of co-ordinating the missionaries' ministries, the agency has an executive team made up of the president of APME and six other employees.[44] The team grows along with the number of missionaries. The following diagram shows how APME is organized:

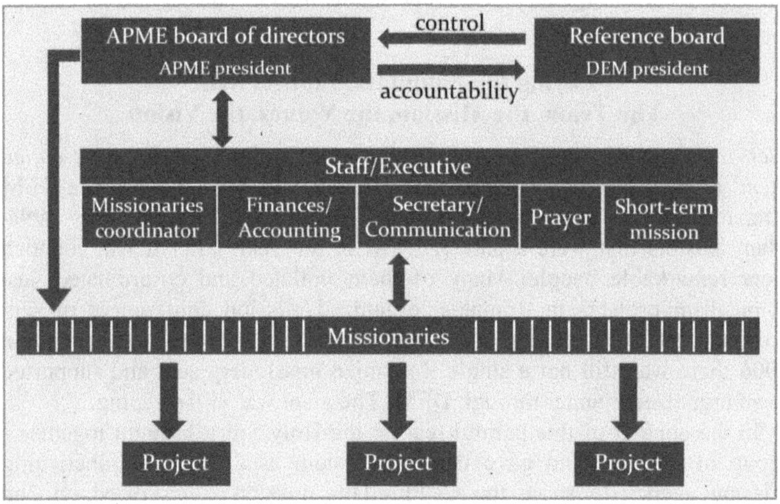

After APME was formed, one of the key roles of the Board was establishing what the mission, values and vision of APME were. After that, it was essential to articulate a work philosophy and a strategy to reach the vision. From the very beginning, the founders established that APME existed in order to mobilize Romanian churches to be involved in foreign mission and to facilitate the process of recruiting, training, sending and supporting Romanian missionaries, especially among unreached ethnic groups.

[44] Since 2008, Pastor Gheorghe Rițișan has served as president of APME. APME's executive team members are: Daniel Bujeniță, Florin Popa, Vlad Luca, Iacob Nicolae, Mircea Deteșan Jr. and Irisa-Iulia Rițișan.

Apart from its mission, APME also has a set of values that its members believe, support and share. The most important of those values are: a divine calling into ministry, being filled with the Holy Spirit, cross-cultural mission, church planting, discipleship, teamwork, accountability, modesty, and cultural sensitivity.

APME's vision, for which every member strives and prays is the following: having the Great Commission as a foundation, depending on God and partnering with local churches, sending and supporting 200 Romanian long-term missionaries by 2020, participating in this way for the fulfilment of our Saviour's commandment to make disciples of all nations.

During the stage of setting the right foundation for APME, a very important aspect was deciding what kind of administrative model the new organization would adopt, taking into account relationships with the existing structure of CCPR and with local churches. Regarding this aspect, Arto Hamalainen, a prominent European mission leader, wrote: 'The Pentecostal missionary movement is based strongly on denominational thinking. The differences are mostly in the role of the local church and the mission body. Some movements like those in the Nordic countries of Europe are strongly based in the local churches, while some others emphasize centralized governing and recruiting.'[45] Without claiming to have found the perfect model, APME's leaders considered that in Romania, the best structure would be something between the two models, which would maximize the strengths of each and minimize the weaknesses. In other words, the local church would have an important role in the process of recruiting, and especially in sending, the missionaries. No missionary could leave for the mission field without the approval of the church, expressed through the recommendation of the pastor. On the other hand, although the agency merely facilitates the process of sending the missionaries to the field, it holds the final word in the vetting process of a candidate. After the missionaries have left, APME is the instrument that co-ordinates the entire process of sending financial support, administering the funds, keeping track of their reports and keeping the missionaries accountable both concerning their ministry and the way the funds are spent. On the other hand, CCPR, through the president of APME's Reference Board, holds the position of control over all mission activity. In other words, the local church sends the missionaries and APME co-ordinates, while CCPR, through DEM, controls the ministry.

APME's Strategy in Fulfilling the Vision

'I will not venture to speak of anything except what Christ has accomplished through me in leading the Gentiles to obey God by what I

---

[45] Arto Hamalainen, *How to Start Missionary Work in New Sending Countries?* (Helsinki: Fida International, 2003), 23.

have said and done – by the power of signs and wonders, through the power of the Spirit of God. So from Jerusalem all the way to Illyricum, I have fully proclaimed the gospel of Christ' (Rom. 15:18-19). The strategy deals with the answers to a few simple questions: How? What? Which? How do we reach the goals we set for our ministry? What must be done in order for the mission of the organization not to become a simple phrase written on a piece of paper? What are the steps that must be taken for the vision to be achieved?

The following diagram sums up the structure of APME, the organizing model proposed by the founders, and also the intended strategy for fulfilling the vision (having at least 200 long-term Romanian missionaries by 2020). The elements of the strategy are placed in a natural order of progression, but currently the agency is at a stage where the team implements all these elements at the same time.

At the current stage of its development and evolution, APME considers that the following seven elements of the strategy are vital:

A. Mobilizing CCPR – involving the local church and its resources in cross-cultural mission. There are at least three main categories of resources in every local church that can and must be taken into account and mobilized: spiritual resources – fasting and praying for missionaries and missionary causes; human resources – potential mission candidates; financial resources – offering financial support for missionary causes.

APME mobilizes believers both at a national/regional level, and at a local level. Nationally, APME mobilizes especially through the annual *RoMisCon*[46] conferences. These conferences target especially pastors and key leaders from the CCPR churches and are organized entirely by APME. The strategy is that of making the pastors aware of the importance of the Great Commission and involving their churches in foreign mission. The conferences organized in the Regional Communities of CCPR[47] have the same purpose, but they last only a day and they target both pastors in that region and local church leaders, elders or deacons. These conferences are organized by APME, together with the regional department of mission. The APME team also organizes day-long conferences about foreign mission in local churches or events called *Mission Sunday*. For such an event, the executive team of APME co-operates with the local pastors. Afterwards, as a result, the local church will often decide to support the ministry financially.

An extraordinary tool of mobilizing the local church (or a group of churches) for mission that APME has been using and that has proved very successful is the *Kairos* course.[48] Pastor Mircea Deteşan is the co-ordinator of the course in the Pentecostal movement and he already has an ample team of instructors that can teach the course anywhere in the country and in the Romanian diaspora.

B. Recruiting missionaries is the next element in APME's strategy of fulfilling the vision. Recruiting is a process that sets out to identify the candidates' call to mission, their biblical and missiological training, their physical, mental and emotional health, their linguistic and natural abilities necessary for serving as missionaries, and last but not least, the recommendations of their pastor and of others who know them well. Most of the time, the candidate is the one that initiates the process of working with APME. This process is finalized by a final interview that the candidate has with the Board of APME. If the candidate is not rejected after the interview, he/she is either accepted directly as an APME missionary and begins the following necessary steps, or needs additional training and is guided towards a Bible school or mission school.

C. Training is another fundamental element in APME's strategy of forming long-term missionaries. The statistics show that most of the missionaries who failed on the mission field had a precarious missiological training or none at all. That is why APME emphasizes the importance of proper training for all mission candidates. The school that serves APME's vision the most in terms of training is the Romanian Center for Cross-

---

[46] The conferences last three days and apart from a specific theme, there are certain seminars that repeat each year, like the ones about the need of a mission agency, and its role in sending and support missionaries, how the local church can be involved in mission, etc.

[47] *Cuvântul Adevărului*, November-December 2014, 7. In the CCPR there are nine Regional Communities, one Hungarian Community and two territorial communities in diaspora (Spain and Italy).

[48] See: www.kairoscourse.org

Cultural Mission (CRST)[49] in Agigea, Constanţa. CRST has a two-year training programme with daily courses, and it has functioned in this format since 2002.[50] The first year offers basic biblical courses while the second year offers mission courses, including courses on Islam,[51] Buddhism and Hinduism. Practice is a very important part of the training – for three weekends each month the students are involved in church planting projects co-ordinated by Pentecostal leaders in Dobrogea.[52] There is a strong organic and strategic link between APME and CRST.[53]

Another part of the training process of each candidate is participating in an orientation course taught by members of the Board of APME and the executive team. The course lasts 3-5 days and it aims to teach the future missionary the vision, mission, values, practices and strategy of APME. The basic instrument for this course is the Missionary's Manual,[54] a document that dictates the missionary's status and relationships between the missionaries and the executive team (and Board) of APME.

D. Sending – a process of preparation carried out by APME and the missionaries between the moment they are vetted and when they arrive on the mission field. During this stage, the missionaries and the APME team work on finalizing a plan of placing the missionaries on a mission field and elaborate a general ministry plan for when they arrive there. If they are going to work with local partners (or in partnership with other mission agencies), a protocol is written that dictates the role of each party in supporting and mentoring the missionaries. Also, the necessary budget for the ministry is determined at this stage and the vetted candidate begins raising the necessary funds by visiting churches. When the necessary funds are raised, APME and the missionary take care of the final details – signing the work contract, getting health insurance for the country in which they will serve, obtaining a visa, getting the necessary vaccines, buying travel tickets, etc. This whole process culminates in a special 'sending' service in which a representative from APME joins the missionary in his/her home church.

E. Support on the mission field. This element of the strategy consists of continually assisting the missionary after his/her departure – emotionally, spiritually and financially. The missionaries' co-ordinator from the executive team communicates with the missionaries on a monthly basis, he

---

[49] See: http://crst-ct.ro

[50] For more information concerning the beginnings of CRST, see Andreiescu, *Istoria Penticostalismului Românesc*, 192, 469.

[51] The Islam courses (IIS) are organized in partnership with Global Initiative USA and last for six weeks.

[52] This is the south-east region of Romania, in the south-east of the country, situated between the Danube and the Black Sea, and is home for 70,000 Muslims.

[53] Pastor Gheorghe Riţişan, the president of CRST's board, is also the president of APME. Three other members of CRST's Board (Rick Cunningham, Bujeniţă Daniel and Daniel Hădărean) also serve in APME. Since 2008, the executive director of CRST has been Ileana Hrişcă.

[54] See note 21 above.

mentors them, identifies the problems, and tries to offer solutions to minor issues. Any complicated situations that demand the intervention of the Board are communicated to the President of APME and/or Board. Each member of the Board is responsible for missionaries in a defined geographical region.[55] The missionary is obliged to send a monthly Activity Report and a Financial Report. In return, every month, the financial director sends the necessary amount for the ministry in the missionary's account, according to the budget and the expenses on the mission field.

An important aspect of supporting missionaries is prayer. The spiritual warfare in which missionaries are involved (of which the apostle Paul spoke, Eph. 6:11-20) demands an increased focus on prayer. APME created a Prayer Department that has a part-time employee who is in charge of creating the Annual Prayer Calendar for APME[56] and also of sharing the updated prayer requests of missionaries with believers in CCPR. Each week, the churches can intercede for an APME missionary or for a major religious group unreached with the gospel.

F. Returning from the mission field – assisting the missionary in returning home for valid reasons. The return is done in a planned manner, after terms of 3-4 years on the mission field. The main purposes are the missionary's spiritual, physical and emotional recovery; strengthening relationships with their churches and sponsors and, in some cases, replenishing the budget for the next term on the mission field. After an evaluation of the situation, the leaders of APME may suggest a period of 6-12 months of rest in Romania. If necessary, special counselling is offered either in country, or abroad in member care centres. As an exception, missionaries can return earlier in the case of health problems for them or family members, or for visa or safety issues.

G. Lastly, in order to fulfil the vision, APME believes it is extremely important to promote the missionaries' work when and where it can be done. By promoting their work, needs on the mission field are brought to the attention of believers and churches. The purpose is that of having as many partners as possible in prayer and for supporting the missionaries.

In order to promote the ministry, APME uses a multitude of instruments, the best-known being *Noi Frontiere* magazine,[57] the APME newsletter (*APME News)* and APME's website. Each year APME publishes a brochure with basic information regarding all the missionaries, which is

---

[55] The seven areas are: Western Europe, Eastern Europe, Middle East/Central Asia, Sub-Saharan Africa, North Africa, India/Nepal and East Asia.

[56] About 5,000 copies of the Prayer Calendar are printed and distributed in Romanian churches in the country and diaspora, but also in small house prayer groups. The same prayer requests can be accessed online on APME's website either in PowerPoint format or as a video clip.

[57] *Noi Frontiere* magazine has existed since 2004, and is released six times a year with a circulation of 1,500 copies; it promotes the work philosophy and projects of APME and CRST.

distributed in churches. Each week on CREDO TV[58] APME has a programme called *To the ends of the earth* which contains interviews with missionaries or people involved in mission. Christian radio stations, especially *Radio Vocea Evangheliei*[59] also broadcast interviews with APME missionaries or make the mission of the organization known. *Cuvântul Adevărului*, the official magazine of CCPR, has a page dedicated to mission in almost every issue, where APME is able to promote projects and mission-related events.

In the current stage of the development of APME, we consider that all the elements above – mobilization, recruiting, training, supporting, returning, promoting – represent a very adequate strategic package to fulfil the vision of having at least 200 long-term Romanian missionaries by 2020.

The Importance of Partnerships in the Mission of APME

'In all my prayers for all of you, I always pray with joy because of your partnership in the gospel from the first day until now!' (Phil. 1:4-5). The concept of missio Dei is central to APME. Mission belongs to God and APME missionaries are workers together with him (1 Cor. 3:9) in his mission.[60] Beyond this fundamental partnership with God, partnership with the churches and organizations that share the same values and purposes are crucial for APME. A good definition of partnerships by Luis Bush is: 'An association of two or more autonomous bodies who have formed a trusting relationship and fulfil agreed expectations by sharing complementary strengths and resources to reach their mutual goals.'[61] In the context of the birth of new churches in the southern hemisphere that send missionaries, in the context of globalization, migration and free circulation, mission cannot be conceived and developed without this strong component – partnerships. The mission of our days is one of inter-ethnic and multicultural teams and of networks of mission organizations that share the same values. That is why the strategic package of APME is placed in a basket of multiple partnerships, both internal and foreign.

a. APME's internal partnerships. From the beginning, APME wanted to be an instrument that would facilitate the involvement of the churches with CCPR in mission, and that is why the main internal partner of the agency is the local church. In almost all the seven stages of the APME strategy, we work together with local churches, but especially in the sending and

[58] Credo TV: www.credo.tv. Their programmes are also broadcast by Alfa Omega TV: www.alfaomega.tv

[59] The Voice of the Gospel (RVE) – a national radio station supported by the Evangelical Alliance in Romania: www.rve.ro

[60] Gheorghe Rițișan, in *Noi Frontiere,* November-December 2011, 2.

[61] Luis Bush, quoted in Arto Hamalainen and Grant McClung (eds), *Together in One Mission: Pentecostal Cooperation in World Evangelization* (Cleveland, TN: Pathway Press, 2012), 244.

supporting of missionaries. Implicitly, the partnership extends to the DEM of CCPR.

In terms of training, APME has a special partnership with CRST. The Center's curriculum is created in such a manner as to serve APME's work philosophy. That is why, during the two years at CRST, the main focus is on courses of church planting, cross-cultural communication, evangelism in Islamic, Buddhist or Hindu contexts, and also on good missionary praxis.

As far as the aspect of promotion is concerned, the platforms through which APME's ministry is made known in the evangelical context of Romania are the Noi Frontiere Foundation, which publishes the magazine of the same name, Credo TV and Alfa Omega TV.

When it comes to placing missionaries on the mission field in inter-ethnic teams, out of the international organizations that have offices in Romania, APME's closest partnerships are with OM and YWAM, in mutual projects of discipleship and church planting, and with Wycliffe in projects of Bible translation.

b. APME's foreign partnerships. Being a new organization, without many contacts on different mission fields, APME realized from the beginning the importance of developing strategic quality partnerships with organizations that have a history and experience of mission, with projects and missionaries present in many countries – ones that could help APME in placing Romanian missionaries in areas where there are no APME teams or missionaries already present.

Since 2007,[62] APME has been part of PEM. From this position, APME can benefit from missiological and strategic resources available from these partnerships, and can also participate in reaching the objectives PEM has set for 2020.[63] Another valued partner of APME, WAGFMC (World Assemblies of God Fellowship Missions Commission), had an important role not only in the birth of APME but also later on in facilitating placing missionaries in different countries in AOG teams and in mentoring them. Discover Your Mission[64] – the sister organization of APME, that mobilizes and promotes mission in the Romanian diaspora in the USA and Canada – contributes substantially to the financial support of missionaries and national conferences. Apart from these important and strategic partnerships, APME has built and continues to build specific partnerships for certain mission fields, for certain missionaries or certain missionary projects with other appropriate mission organizations.[65]

---

[62] Andreiescu, *Istoria Penticostalismului Românesc*, 481-82.

[63] Arto Hamalainen, *Together in One Mission*, 309-17. PEM objectives by 2020 include sending 3,000 long-term missionaries and 7,000 short-term workers, and having 100,000 intercessors.

[64] Andreiescu, 482. Discover Your Mission (DYM) was founded by Cameron Wilson. Since 2010 the organization has been led by Pastor Florin Cîmpean.

[65] Global Initiative (in training), Shelter Now International, Ljus i Oster (Light in the East).

Lessons Learned in the First Decade of APME's Existence and Challenges for the Future

Although ten years of life represents a very short period of time for a mission organization, these few years were enough to be able to identify a few important lessons and aspects to ponder – both for mission organizations that are just starting out as well as for ones that have been functioning for a long time. We will mention a few that were fundamental for APME.

a. It was essential to form and consolidate a team of visionary ministers, sensitive to the voice of the Holy Spirit, involved in foreign mission, and who make the Great Commission a priority in their work. This aspect is especially important because APME operates in Eastern Europe. In this region, by tradition, most of the leaders are trying to keep under their influence and co-ordinate various projects at the same time, which sometimes leads to blockages or even the death of many good initiatives.

b. The founders of APME were determined not to transform the mission agency over time into a parachurch organization, independent and autonomous from the Pentecostal movement, but to model it as an instrument for the CCPR churches in fulfilling their mission. Despite certain fears or reservations that existed briefly on both sides, being transparent in administering the funds and being accountable before DEM of CCPR, led to strong relationships of trust between APME and the leaders of CCPR.

c. The agency placed great emphasis on adequate biblical and missiological training of all mission candidates. We believe that a two-year training programme is minimal for long-term results on the mission field. Almost every time there was a degree of haste and candidates tried to short-circuit this process, there were failures. Another lesson in terms of training is requiring that the missionaries speak English at a satisfactory level before they leave for the mission field, and also that they learn right from the beginning the language of the people they serve.

d. It is not as important for us to know the missionary and candidates as it is that they know the values of APME and its work philosophy. Accepting missionaries and candidates already formed in other mission organizations or those who left independently to go to the mission field led to difficulties on both sides in adjusting and, unfortunately, to painful separations.

e. Any missionary enterprise implicitly means entering a spiritual war. We understood that it is essential to organize a strong national prayer support system for missionaries, especially when they are involved in unreached people groups or when they serve in geographical areas with security issues.

f. We learned right from the beginning that we could not develop adequately and could not activate the entire potential of CCPR churches without properly mobilizing them. Identifying all the necessary instruments for mobilization was, and probably will continue to be, one of APME's greatest challenges in years to come.

g. Leaders must be in continual dependence on the Holy Spirit and must understand and correctly answer to the great problems and phenomena that affect our world and society from a missiological standpoint (migration, urbanization, Islam's revitalization, secularization, the social polarization of humankind, the crises of basic resources, pollution, etc.). But they must do this without losing sight of the fact that sin continues to be the greatest problem of humankind, and that God's solution to the problem remains the project of redeeming humankind and restoring the Creation through Jesus Christ, His Son.

Conclusion

In 2006, there were no cross-cultural Romanian missionaries sent and supported by the CCPR. At the time of this being written,[66] there are 59 long-term missionaries, vetted by APME, which serve in 21 countries across three continents. About 15-20 mission candidates, already equipped and trained, are in the advanced stages of being approved and they will reach the mission fields in less than two years. 47% of active missionaries serve in Islamic contexts, 18% in Christian-Animistic contexts, 16% in Buddhist contexts, 14% in Hindu contexts, and 5% are involved in Bible translation in partnership with Wycliffe.[67]

If in the 1990s the main motto in the Romanian churches was 'We are too poor to send missionaries', in 2015 the income for foreign mission at APME totalled US$ 928,644, over 99% of the funds coming from Romanian churches and believers in Romania and the diaspora.[68]

In 2006, when it was founded, APME had only the formal approval of the leaders of CCPR to function and at that time it was an organization independent of the structures of CCPR. Now, following the decision of the National Council of CCPR in 2014, APME is officially the agency of CCPR. In 2006, the Department for Evangelism and Mission (DEM) of CCPR was a non-functional structure of the CCPR, now, DEM is the organism that controls and evaluates APME's activities and helps promote it in the churches of Romania.

In 2006, APME was struggling to be born. Now, the growth and development of the organization is a source of inspiration and a model for other national churches that do not have a missionary sending structure. In the past few years, the president of APME and/or members of the Board of APME were invited to many national (for instance Bulgaria, Estonia, Spain, Italy) and international conferences to present the ministry of APME. Probably the most representative events were the WAGMC

[66] February 2016.

[67] APME President's report for the Reference Board, 19th February 2016, Cluj-Napoca.

[68] APME President's report for the Reference Board, 19th February 2016, Cluj-Napoca.

Congresses in Cancun (2012) and Bangkok (2015) where the president of APME and Rick Cunningham, the secretary for International Relations of APME, had sessions very well received by the participants. In November 2015, at the PEM Consultation in Torino, Italy, APME President Gheorghe Rițişan was elected Vice-Chairman of PEM.[69]

It is amazing and at the same time a cause for praise that, at the beginning of this century, God chose to call for his mission a church and a nation that basically did not exist before in the annals of modern world mission. I believe that the key element for the birth and development of APME is the fusion brought by the Holy Spirit between a team of visionary people and a passion for foreign mission. Articulating, very clearly, from the beginning, the mission, vision, values and work strategy was a vital aspect in the coherence and dynamics of APME's development. Moreover, the partnerships – both internal and foreign – gave consistency and weight to APME. It is also worth mentioning again that, because of the development of a relationship of trust and support between the Board of APME and DEM of CCPR, the centralized structure of CCPR was not an obstacle, but a factor in accelerating the concept of foreign mission in Romanian churches and their involvement and participation in mission.

Despite these accomplishments, the involvement of CCPR in world mission is still slim considering the immense potential it currently has: nearly 3,000 Romanian churches[70] in the country and the diaspora, accounting for over 360,000 Pentecostal believers.[71] That is why, in the future, one of the greatest challenges for APME lies in finding ways necessary to mobilize these resources for foreign mission. Another challenge on APME's future agenda is persuading the Romanian churches in diaspora to come out of their ethnocentric isolation, equipping them to serve in the new spiritual, political and social context of the West, especially in reaching migrants. Certainly, in order to be able to face these challenges, it must be continually rethinking the internal structure of APME, its executive staff and its partnerships.

---

[69] http://pem.pef.eu/pem-info/pem-committee

[70] In 2014, at the Xth Congress, President Pavel Riviş Tipei's report shows there were 2,996 Pentecostal churches in the country and in the diaspora, apart from the USA (*Cuvântul Adevărului*, Nov-Dec. 2014, 6-7).

[71] www.recensamantromania.ro/wp-content/uploads/2012/08/TS8.pdf

EMPOWERING PEOPLE WITH DISABILITY TO REACH THEIR FULL POTENTIAL WITHIN THE COMMUNITY: THE CASE OF ACAS

Ligia M. Măcelaru and Marcel V. Măcelaru

> In life we cannot do great things. We can only do small things with great love.
>
> Mother Teresa

Preamble

During the autumn of 2015, while participating in an educational project in Manhattan, New York, I (Marcel V. Măcelaru – henceforth, MVM) was asked to write a reflection paper on 'a flourishing urban ministry'. Needless to say, the task gave me pause at first, as questions regarding what 'flourishing' means and how it could be measured flooded my mind. Did it have something to do with 'success'? Was it about the 'prominence' of the ministry? Was I supposed to present an organization that had 'a great impact' within its context? Or was I just to focus on an example that brought to the fore such qualities as faithfulness and commitment? Although I did not think that what was being asked of me were numbers, amounts or growth rates, it soon became clear that such a discussion could not dismiss quantitative assessments altogether. Consequently, even though I decided that, within the context of the project for which I was writing, 'flourishing' had something to do with the excellence of one's praxis, I also had to ensure that the ministry I chose to present contributed in measurable ways to enhancing the quality of its beneficiaries' lives. In the end, I wrote about ACAS (Asociația pentru Capacitarea Abilităților Speciale – The Association for Capacitating Special Abilities), a charity based in the city of Timișoara, Romania, whose stated vision is to 'empower people with disabilities to reach their full potential within the community'.

To me, ACAS best embodies what I then understood by 'a flourishing ministry'. As a ministry that developed in response to specific needs within the community, the work methodology adopted by ACAS is governed by concrete quality standards which ensure that such needs are suitably addressed. Being a Christian ministry in which praxis works hand-in-hand with theological reflection, the programmes ACAS devises and implements are founded on a holistic understanding of personhood. And given the nature of the work being done, which qualifies as holistic mission, the positive impact ACAS has on the life of its beneficiaries is easily measurable and thoroughly documentable. It is these, and other similar characteristics that will become obvious below, that prompted the inclusion of ACAS' story in this volume on mission in Central and Eastern Europe. Thus, in the following pages I will come back to my New York topic, although this time in a different manner. Instead of offering my reflections on the matter, I reproduce below an interview with Ligia M. Măcelaru (henceforth LMM), the founding president of ACAS,[1] in the hope that the story of this ministry, as told by its founder, will challenge readers to reflect themselves on 'flourishing' and its implications for holistic mission work within their own contexts.

Interview

MVM: What is ACAS, and how did the idea of such a ministry take shape?
LMM: ACAS is a volunteer-based ministry addressing holistically the needs of children and adults with disabilities. It began over twenty years ago as a friendship between me and the mother of a girl with special needs (Raluca), and it grew over the years into a fully-fledged ministry. Currently, ACAS is a registered charity, consisting of seven founding members and a network of over 100 volunteers, all of which donate time and resources, as needed, to carry out the mission of the association.

The story begins in the spring of 1993 when, during a Sunday church service, I noticed for the first time a mother and her four-year-old quadriplegic daughter. They were new to the church and had only just begun attending meetings on a regular basis. During that time, I was working as the National Supervisor for International Adoptions for an NGO in Timişoara, Romania. The work was vast and overwhelming, for abandoned children filled orphanages throughout Romania. The miserable conditions in which they lived and my deep conviction that every child deserved a family gave me no time for rest – I was constantly on the road, working on this or that adoption project.

I remember that, when I was a student in a social work programme at the University of Timişoara, I was asked to work in one of the assisted-living homes for the elderly, an offer I refused because nothing seemed more urgent than finding a family for every abandoned child living in an orphanage. I even told the professor who was offering me that job that the two categories of people I would never be able to work with (due to the emotional strain this would bring) were children with special needs and old people. Little did I know that 22 years later these would be the categories I would mostly assist.

---

[1] Ligia M. Măcelaru, interview by Marcel V. Măcelaru (Timişoara, Romania, 18th October 2015), using written notes. The interview has been translated from Romanian and summarily edited by Marcel V. Măcelaru.

As the time went by, I got really close to Raluca (the four-year-old quadriplegic girl) and her mother Valentina, and thus became aware of the challenges they had to face. I began finding out how little was available in Romania in terms of support systems for children with special needs and their families; how most kindergartens would deny Raluca enrolment into their programme because of a lack of adequate facilities or trained personnel, or even a lack of understanding that the physical impairments Raluca faced did not make her a lesser person. I saw that even basic equipment, such as a wheelchair suitable for a person of Raluca's age and condition, was by no means available at the time in Romania. To sum it up, it was for the first time that I began seeing the larger picture – that is, the shortfalls in the area of services for people with disabilities and the need for a ministry that would address those shortfalls holistically. Thus, I can say that, in a way, ACAS is a response to the needs of children and adults with disabilities, and their families, within the communities in which they live.

MVM: So how did ACAS actually start?
LMM: In 1999, I began working as Executive Director for an NGO that provided medical and other relief to Romania. It was during that time that we received a donation of wheelchairs for children. I remember crying with happiness when I first saw them, for it was out of that donation that Raluca finally got her very first wheelchair. In the process of distributing these wheelchairs, I visited about forty families that had children with disabilities. It was during those visits that I was touched: touched by the needy little faces I could not erase from my mind – and, if I may say so – touched irreversibly by the tears of a God who suffered together with little ones in need. That is when this ministry began taking shape.

Starting from there, over the years, the ministry of ACAS developed gradually as we became aware of more and varied needs. My friendship with Raluca and her family made me realize the need for support groups for parents that had children with disabilities. About the same time. a network of volunteers who would supervize and care for the children with special needs during the support group meetings was initiated. And since these volunteers needed specific training to do the work that was expected of them, a volunteer summer school was also launched. Then the next target group identified that obviously needed our attention consisted of the siblings of children with disabilities. For them we organized summer camps, led by qualified personnel, running specifically designed recreational and educational programmes. Needless to say, over the years, many such initiatives have been implemented and various short- or long-term projects have been added to the activities of ACAS.

MVM: Did you work on your own or did you partner with other people and organizations?

LMM: There are many people who, over the years, have been involved in this ministry. In a way, these people are the tools God used to shape the ministry into what it is today. Sometimes I worked with whole teams of volunteers and other times it was only me and one or two other people. I have also collaborated with other organizations that address similar needs; for instance, with *Joni & Friends* and with *Life without Limbs*. There were also many times I worked alone. All in all, I believe God will use people that make themselves available to participate in God's mission in the world. As the Bible says, 'We are God's workmanship, created in Christ Jesus to do good works, which God prepared in advance for us to do' (Eph. 2:10). May God help all of us to actually do so!

MVM: Can you describe in more detail the objectives and types of programmes implemented by ACAS?

LMM: The vision of ACAS states that we are here in order to empower those with special needs to reach their full potential within the community. From this springs our mission to address the needs of children and adults with disabilities, and of their families, in the context of their communities. Our final goal is to improve the quality of their lives in their entirety.

In order to accomplish this mission, we have developed three types of programme:

- Immediate and irregular assistance, consisting of
  - Free professional evaluation of the person with mobility deficiencies in order to determine which equipment would best serve their needs.
  - Free mobility equipment supply, adjustment and maintenance.
  - Training for the best use of mobility equipment.
  - Counselling for those with special needs and their families.
- Long-term, ongoing programmes, consisting of
  - Support groups for parents and siblings of children with disabilities.
  - Summer camps for children with special needs.
  - Summer educational camps for siblings of children with special needs.
  - Volunteer networks and specific volunteer training programmes.
  - Specific educational programmes for adults with disabilities (e.g. work-skills development to help with becoming self-supporting individuals).
  - Publishing and distribution of Christian literature and other help materials for children and adults with special needs, their families and their caretakers.
  - Career advice for adults with special needs.
- Community education, consisting of

- Design and implementation of activities aiming to raise awareness in the community (church and society) in regard with the needs of children and adults with disabilities and their families.
- Design and implementation of activities aiming to create and promote a friendly, inclusive climate within families, churches and society, for those with special needs.
- Organization of public debates, conferences and other such events within which people with special needs and the average member of the community can meet, interact, get to know each other and form friendships.

MVM: Why is such a ministry needed? What does the government do to provide the necessary assistance?

LMM: From its very conception, ACAS was developed to respond to real needs that are either not addressed by Romanian legislation or not provided for by the social services in the country. It is undeniable that the situation has improved tremendously over the past 25 years. The current legal framework reflects, at least in theory, the main principles and rights of people with disabilities as defined by CRC (Convention on the Rights of the Child) and CRPD (Convention on the Rights of Persons with Disabilities). Unfortunately, the practical implementation of these principles remains problematic. There is no 'at hand' information for people with disabilities. There is little or no co-operation between state social services and other agencies and the various NGOs that provide support services for people with disabilities. There is a tremendous need for support groups, founded on Christian values, for parents and siblings of children with disabilities. There are virtually no adequate educational programmes for the community (in either church or society) that would help develop a mentality of acceptance and inclusion of people with disability. Even the most basic requirements, such as access to public services for people with disabilities, and access to mainstream education for children with special needs are not always provided.

Within this context, the need for ACAS and other such organizations is evident. For instance, an area where our role has become crucial is the distribution of free mobility equipment. In fact, this is an activity that occupies most of my time. By mobility equipment I mean wheelchairs, walkers, crutches, portable toilets, toilet raisers, shower chairs, transfer solutions, medical beds, hoists. Unfortunately, within the current legal framework in Romania, people with disability are provided by the state with only one service free of charge – such as one post-operative therapeutic intervention (rehabilitation procedure), after which the patient has to support the costs of his/her rehabilitation. Also, one is provided with only one item of mobility equipment every five years (such as a wheelchair, or crutches, or a toilet raiser, or a portable room toilet), and even then, the item is only partially compensated through one's medical insurance. And since most of the time such mobility equipment is too expensive, people that need it have to learn to live without it.

MVM: What is different about ACAS? What makes you unique?
LMM: From the very beginning, we decided to adopt a holistic approach in our practice. This, I believe, is what distinguishes us from other organizations that share our objectives. For instance, our assessment of the needs of each person with disabilities we work with is done in a holistic, integrative manner, taking into account not only the physical and intellectual, but also the emotional, social and spiritual dimensions of the client. Also, when deciding on solutions, this is done in a personalized manner – each case we encounter is treated individually, and our approach often differs from one case to another. Also, speaking of what we do differently, I think the support network ACAS provides for those with disabilities that we work with and for their families is unique in our context.

MVM: Who are the actual beneficiaries of your ministry? Can you give some examples?
LMM: According to the latest official figures published by the Romanian government on 31st March 2016, there are currently almost 770,000 people with various disabilities living in Romania. Approximately 750,000 of these are under the care of their families or living alone, while about 18,000 are institutionalized in care centres administered by the Romanian authorities. However, we should remember that Romania is still influenced by its communist past. Since, before 1989, the general attitude towards those with disability was severe marginalization, it is no wonder that in our context disability still caries a social stigma. This causes people who would probably qualify as 'disabled' to deny registering as such and therefore lose social assistance to which they would be legally entitled. So, I believe that the official numbers given by the government are inaccurate, and in fact the number of people with disability is much higher. Also, the lack of education in the area is another factor – people who may suffer from temporary impairment may not even realize that they could benefit from the assistance provided under the law for people with disabilities.

All in all, there are many people who qualify to become beneficiaries of our services. First, there are those with permanent disabilities. Under this rubric I should specify that we pay special attention to children with permanent mobility impairments, for the kind of specialized assistance they need is not always provided under the state care system or by other organizations. I refer here to the fact that the mobility equipment they use (especially wheelchairs) has to be adaptable and adapted accordingly as the child grows. Second, the other categories of people we serve would be those with acquired and temporary disabilities, those in palliative care (the terminally ill), and those in geriatric care (the elderly). All these need mobility equipment that is specifically tailored to their needs. Third, we also aim to provide counselling and education for parents, siblings and even the extended family of those with disability. And last but not least, we see ourselves as providing a positive service to the community as well, through volunteer networks and educational programmes. That is, because the empowerment of a person with disability to become a full participant in the social, political, economic and/or spiritual life of the community is undoubtedly always a gain for everyone.

MVM: So, how do these beneficiaries find ACAS? And what is the process, from beginning to end? What do you actually do? For instance, what happens from the moment a person needs an item of mobility equipment until the moment the needed item is provided?

LMM: Although we have not been preoccupied with 'advertising' our programmes, a system of spreading the news about ACAS has developed over the years that functions pretty well – in fact, so well that we are constantly flooded with more requests for mobility assistance than we can actually deal with. Some of our beneficiaries are advised to seek our help by the regional office of the Romanian Agency for the Protection of Persons with Disabilities (a governmental organization), especially in cases when no further aid is available through state-sponsored means. Others find out about ACAS while undergoing therapy – in most hospitals in Timişoara, medical personnel know our contact details and recommend our services to people in need of assistance. Other cases arrive on our doorstep via churches from Timişoara and the region. And then, of course there are people who find about us from former or current beneficiaries and their families, or even people who simply walk in and ask for help when they see mobility equipment displayed in our back yard.

As for the process, it begins when I am contacted over the phone by the person in need, the caregiver or by a family member. During that initial contact, I usually collect some information about the case (the contact details of the person in need and general information about his/her condition) and schedule a visit to the person in need. The purpose of the visit is to asses what type of mobility equipment is needed, what are the medical recommendations for such equipment, and what changes, if any, have to be made in terms of accommodation in order to maximize the mobility of the impaired person – sometimes a situation can be improved a lot by simply moving furniture about in order to create more space, by building ramps for easier accessibility, or by installing handrails. Also, during the visit I take specific measurements of the person in need. These help with the adjustment of the donated mobility equipment to fit the size of the beneficiary and his/her impairment. In subsequent visits, after the mobility equipment is delivered, I also instruct the user and the caregiver on how to best use it. I also do counselling – instructive, supportive and spiritual. All in all, the average time spent on a case is 6-8 hours, not counting travel time, which can sometimes be quite long.

MVM: How did you start the support groups and what happens there?
LMM: The idea of starting a support group came out of my conversations with Valentina, Raluca's mother. She kept telling me how much it meant to her to have someone to talk to and share with. And she would always mention that there were many more parents in need of such support. This prompted me to ask from my church's registrar a list of all the families attending our church that had children with special needs. To my astonishment, I was given a list with three names, and that while a list I had begun compiling already had 37 families on it. The ignorance and indifference church leadership was showing towards families facing disability was shocking! I realised that the situation was not an isolated case, but was probably typical of most churches in Romania. This was a powerful motivator to start the support group and to expand its scope beyond my church and the list I had compiled. Currently, after twelve years of activity, the support group is attended by 73 families, coming from different churches in Timişoara. We meet once a month and typically meetings gather about thirty people. Each meeting is devoted to a particular topic, and guest speakers (people with disability, health professionals, pastors, theologians) are invited to share with the group.

MVM: What about the summer camps for siblings of children with disabilities? What happens there?
LMM: The summer camps gather about seventy participants aged 14-24 each year. They last for five days and participants are encouraged to register for the entire educational cycle – that is, to return for four years in a row. During those four years some twenty topics of specific concern to the participants are addressed. The camp is organized with the help of volunteers and is run by a leadership team consisting of a co-ordinator, a counsellor / psychologist, a special education tutor / pedagogue, and a special activities (sports) co-ordinator. Although the primary purpose of the camp is education, we also aim to provide professional counselling in an environment that promotes emotional healing and bonding.

MVM: You also mentioned volunteer training. What does that consist of?
LMM: The educational programme we provide for volunteers lasts approximately three months and it consists of general presentations of various abilities, a practical component in which participants are given the chance to experience for 2-3 days what living with a disability is like, and intensive communication training: braille and sign language. The primary aim of the programme was to prepare volunteers to entertain children with disabilities while parents attended support-group meetings, but its scope developed as volunteers are now also involved in home visits, occasional

outdoor activities with children with special needs, and the maintenance and distribution of mobility equipment.

MVM: In conclusion, can you share about a programme or an experience which you feel most defines what ACAS is and stands for?

LMM: About four years ago, while hanging out with two of my dearest friends and collaborators, we began wondering what a rehabilitation programme based on leisure and sport activities would look like. The conclusion of that discussion was that one of the two friends I was talking to, a professional swimming trainer, begun a volunteer-run swimming programme for children with various disabilities (visual impairment, mobility impairment, Down's syndrome, etc.). This had an unexpected effect – a group of professional athletes, seeing what my friend was doing, volunteered to do a 7-km hike at a mountain resort taking 25 children with disabilities (11 with mobility impairments). The hike would then finish with a picnic and other outdoor activities. The aim was to give these children a chance to experience nature in all its beauty. One of the mothers, whose 12-year-old son was bound to a wheelchair, was telling me how her boy 'proposed' to her to go out with him, fishing. Imagine the joy of that little boy when I told him that he could spend an entire day up in the mountains! This is what ACAS is all about – about the joy of little children. About hands joined together to do good. And about love – God's love touching us, and through us touching our neighbour.

CHILDREN AT RISK IN ROMANIA: A HISTORICAL ANALYSIS

Bill Prevette and Corneliu Constantineanu

Introduction: The Plight of Children in Eastern Europe

There is no doubt that the situation of millions of children in our world today shows just how important and urgent it is to give our full missiological attention to, and act on behalf of, children. From malnourished, poor child soldiers of Africa, to the abandoned street children of Eastern Europe, to the slum children of Latin America and prostitute and child workers in Asia – in all these we discern a desperate cry of children for help and intervention. There are indeed more challenges facing our present world regarding children: the enormous *number* of children representing a large proportion of contemporary societies in several parts of the world; the tremendous *needs* of these children; a *history* of suffering under slavery, colonization and racism; the *marginalization* of children in society and in terms of education; the challenge of *globalization* and the specific concerns that this particular development brings to the life of the church.[1] The state of affairs in former communist context is similarly dramatic. According to a recent UNICEF report, there is still an annual rate of some 15,000 children being abandoned in those countries.[2] Romania is a case in point.

Just after the collapse of communism in 1989, some dramatic and disturbing images of orphan and institutionalized children in Romania made public news for the entire world.[3] There were horrible stories of pain,

---

* This study is an expanded and revised version of 'Social and Structural Factors with Outcomes for Children in Romania', a chapter from Bill Prevette, *Child, Church and Compassion: Towards Child Theology in Romania* (Oxford: Regnum, 2012). Published here with permission.

[1] See Victor Nakah and Johannes Mlherbe, 'Child Theology – A Challenge to Seminaries', in Keith J. White, et al (eds), *Now and Next: A Compendium of Papers Presented at the 'Now & Next' Theological Conference on Children, Nairobi, Kenya, March 9-12, 2011* (Penang, Malaysia: Compassion International, 2011).

[2] See the report of Sofia Marie-Pierre, the regional director of UNICEF, in 'Quinze mille enfants abandonnés chaque année dans les pays post-communistes', in *Le Monde*, on-line edition, 21st November 2012.

[3] For this description and for a theological elaboration as well as missiological implications of this state of affairs, see Corneliu Constantineanu, 'Welcome: Biblical and Theological Perspectives on Mission and Hospitality with a Child in the Midst', in Bill Prevette, Keith J. White, Rosalee Velloso Ewell and Darren J. Konz (eds), *Theology, Mission and Child: Fresh Perspectives* (Regnum Edinburgh Centenary Series, 24: Oxford: Regnum, 2014).

abandonment, violence and exclusion. Similarly, the worldwide newspapers made this their headlines for many years: 'Institutionalized children confined and abused', 'Romania's lost children: thousands of children in Romania are orphaned or abandoned by their families', 'Invisible children: Romania's orphan tragedy', 'Children in distress', 'The Nameless Children of Romania'. Twenty-five years later, there are still far too many stories of child abandonment and street children, not to mention the plight of Roma children or the tragedy of the so-called 'eurorphans' – the hundreds of thousands of children left behind by their parents who had migrated for work in Europe. There is still a perception that the state institutions are able to handle appropriately the plight of such children, and this contrary to the evidence that such institutionalization is against children's interests, and that children in such institutions are left with severe physical, psychological and cognitive disability. There is thus an absolute urgency to reflect theologically and missiologically, and act on behalf of children in Romania and elsewhere. In such circumstances the churches need to consider more seriously and without delay their task in serious theological reflection and missiological engagement for welcoming children and for creating a really hospitable space where they can develop holistically.

It is not news to say that children have been rather a neglected subject in our theological and missiological thinking and praxis. The situation seems to change, however, and it is with some sense of relief that, in recent years, we see concentrated efforts by various organizations and networks (such as the Child Theology Movement, the Global Children's forum, the 4-14 Window Global Initiative, the Global Alliance for Advancing Holistic Child Development, Viva – to name just a few) as well as by various historians and theologians dealing with the important issues of children, mission and theology. One cannot but appreciate the more recent increasing interest in children and childhood studies in different academic fields, not least in theological studies.[4] A special note should be made of the

[4] There are several solid theological books on the subject from among which I would mention the most relevant. I will begin with arguably one of the most valuable and extended endeavours called 'The Child in Religion and Ethics', a project directed by Marcia J. Bunge, and the significant books that came out of that project: Marcia Bunge (ed), *The Child in Christian Thought* (Grand Rapids, MI: Eerdmans, 2001); Marcia J. Bunge, Terence Fretheim and Beverly Roberts Gaventa (eds), *The Child in the Bible* (Grand Rapids, MI: Eerdmans, 2008); Marcia J. Bunge and Don S. Browning (eds), *Children and Childhood in World Religions: Primary Texts and Sources* (Rutgers University Press, 2009); Marcia J. Bunge (ed), *Children, Adults, and Shared Responsibilities: Jewish, Christian, and Muslim Perspectives* (Cambridge: CUP, 2012); Marcia J. Bunge (ed), *Child Theologies: Perspectives from World Christianity* (Grand Rapids, MI: Eerdmans); There are also several other significant books worth mentioning: Bonnie J. Miller-McLemore, *Let the Children Come: Reimagining Childhood from a Christian Perspective* (San Francisco, CA: Jossey-Bass, 2003); Joyce Ann Mercer, *Welcoming Children: A Practical Theology of Childhood* (St Louis, MO: Chalice Press, 2005); David H. Jensen, *Graced Vulnerability: A Theology of Childhood* (Cleveland, OH: Pilgrim Press, 2005); Kristin Herzog, *Children and Our Global Future: Theological and Social Challenges* (Cleveland, OH: Pilgrim Press, 2005); Keith J. White, et al (eds), *Now and*

significant way in which the Child Theology Movement has contributed to the subject, by highlighting the profound theological and missiological significance of Christ's action of placing the child in the centre of a theological conversation.[5] All these, including the present chapter in a particular way, are excellent efforts towards an appropriate understanding of the situation of children in our world and for the significant missiological implications resulting from this.[6]

The child-care crisis in Romania has been the subject of much discussion and academic interest over the past years. The plight of institutionalized children and the failed policies of the Romanian government have been the subjects of documentaries, dissertations, books and numerous studies on abandonment and adoption.[7] This chapter attempts to review and interact with some of this literature and discuss the factors that caused the child-care crisis in Romania. The purpose is to review the more important socio-structural causes that led to the crisis for children and describe the context encountered by the Faith Based Organizations (FBOs) that arrived in Romania in the early 1990s. It is hoped that this historical analysis will give a better understanding of the actual situation of children

---

Next: a Compendium of Papers presented at the 'Now & Next' Theological Conference on Children, Nariobi, Kenya, March 9-12, 2011 (Penang, Malaysia: Compassion International, 2011).

[5] For the most articulate theological arguments for Child Theology, see the book written by the founders of this movement: Haddon Willmer and Keith White, *Entry Point: Towards Child Theology with Matthew 18* (USA: WTL Publications Ltd, 2013). Other relevant works done by members of the child theology movement include Keith J. White and Haddon Willmer, *An Introduction to Child Theology* (London: Child Theology Movement, 2006); Haddon Willmer, *Experimenting Together: One Way of Doing Child Theology* (London: Child Theology Movement, 2007); Sunny Tan, *Child Theology for the Churches in Asia: An Invitation* (London: Child Theology Movement, 2007); John Collier (ed), *Toddling to the Kingdom* (London: Child Theology Movement, 2009); Bill Prevette, *Child, Church and Compassion: Towards Child Theology in Romania* (Oxford: Regnum, 2012).

[6] For an excellent, extended review of some major theological works on children see Jerome W. Berryman, 'Children and Christian Theology: A New/Old Genre', in *Religious Studies Review*, 33.2 (April 2007), 103-11.

[7] I reviewed several, but there are many others: V. Groza, 'US Policy Promotes Institutionalization of Children in Romania'; Case Western University School of Applied Social Science: http://msass.case.edu/faculty/vgroza/international/adoption/uspolicy.htm (accessed 20th September 2005); D. Costin-Sima and S. Cace (eds), *The Street Between Fascination and Slavery* (Bucharest: UNICEF, Echosoc, 2003); C. Zamfir (ed), *For a Child Centered Society* (Bucharest: UNICEF, 1997); M. Jigau et al, *The Participation and Education of Roma Children,* The Institute for Research in the Quality of Life (Bucharest: UNICEF, 2002); S.D. Ryan and V. Groza, 'Romanian Adoptees', in *International Social Work,* 47.1 (2004), 53-79; E.W. Ames and M. Carter, 'Development of Romanian Orphanage Children Adopted to Canada', in *Canadian Psychology,* 33.2 (1992), 503-26; J. Dickens, 'Protecting the Rights of the Child in Romania: Children's Rights Perspectives on Romania's 1997 Childcare Reforms', in *European Journal of Social Work,* 2.2 (1999), 139-50; J. Dickens and J. Watts, 'Developing Alternatives to Residential Care in Romania', in *Adoption and Fostering,* 20.3 (1996), 8-13; C. Zamfir and E. Zamfir, *Children at Risk in Romania: Problems Old and New* (Florence, Italy: UNICEF International Child Development Centre, Report, No. 56, 1996).

at risk in Romania, and will represent a good foundation for further missiological reflection and action on behalf of the children of Romania.

Socialist Policies with Long-Term Effect on Families and Children

There were a number of socialist policies that had a detrimental impact on both children and families. These policies are described as 'structural' or 'macro causes' in the literature and include economic factors, employment, the role of women in the workforce, the juxtaposition of the state to the family, the policy of increasing the size of the population, demographic policy, the ban on abortion and the institutionalization of children.

Economic Factors

After a short period of economic growth, between 1950 and 1969, the Romanian economy experienced a state of decline which became much more dramatic by the end of the 1970s. There were many structural factors that were inherent in the socialist system which eventually contributed to the child-care crisis, these were 'macro factors' as they affected not just families with children but also every aspect of Romanian life and society.[8] Zamfir refers to this as a 'structural crisis' which he identifies with the state-controlled economy, the bureaucratic apparatus and socialist ideology. The socialist system placed stress on the collective rather than on the individual. He refers to this as a type of super-industrialization.

> … with economic branches aberrantly developed, physically and morally old technologies, distorted price controls, growing unsolvable stocks of products [combined with the] irrational and arbitrary character of the political leadership, the lack of an articulate macro-economic vision, and thus the incapacity to bring the state economy out of the crisis.[9]

Initially, the state had promised benefits to all its citizens: guaranteed jobs for all, pensions for the vast majority, free education and health care services, cheap and relatively abundant housing, and highly subsidized basic goods and services, welfare benefits, including child allowances and scholarships. A prominent role was assigned to universal education and health care. These promises soon evaporated with the continued decline of the economy throughout the 1970s, largely attributable to the fiscal mismanagement of the government which became mired in corruption. Romania was exporting most of its low-priced agricultural crop and

---

[8] I acknowledge Robila's PhD dissertation, in which she located several studies concerning poverty in Romania, and dedicates the opening chapter to a discussion of poverty and its impact on the Romanian family. See Mihaela Robila, 'The Impact of Financial Strain on Adolescents' Psychological Functioning in Romania: the Role of Family Processes'. PhD dissertation, Syracuse: Syracuse University, Graduate School of Psychology, 2002.

[9] C. Zamfir; M.A. Pop and E. Zamfir, *Romania during the '89s-'93s: The Dynamics of Living Standards and of Social Protection* (Bucharest: Editura Expert, 1994), 3.

manufacturing, and paying a revenue tax to Soviet Union, while state revenues were not being reinvested in the infrastructure and the local economy. In the 1980s, Ceauşescu began spending vast sums of money on building projects in downtown Bucharest like the monolithic presidential palace. Albania apart, it became the poorest country in the communist bloc, and was looked upon by some historians as Eastern Europe's most glaring economic failure.

The Socialist Ideology of Work and Its Implications for Women

In order to build a new socialist order, all citizens were expected to contribute to the building of socialism and the state. This axiom served as a legitimate mandate to mobilize the adult population but it had consequences: 'All citizens were formally categorized as productive or non-productive members of society.'[10] This mandate for all to work redefined the role of women in society. Women were encouraged to be contributing members of the socialist society which meant that they would be contributing through their work. The government actively promoted the role of women in the workforce and Ceauşescu proclaimed they were equal to men in society:

> The socialist system has ensured full equality between men and women in all the fields of activity. Women equally participate now in the entire social and economic activity, in the leadership of all the fields of activity, in accordance with their capacities and possibilities... Women work side-by-side with men in industry, agriculture, transport, in all the sectors producing material goods, take part in scientific and cultural activity, in the formation and education of the young generation, the protection of public health, the progress of cities and villages – in a word, in the effort for ensuring the well-being, and increasing the level of civilization, of the Romanian people.[11]

The socialist system in theory promised to women an equal place in society and in the workplace, reflecting the Marxist ideology that women would help make a new order as heroes of the state:

> Woman should also occupy leading positions, according to her capacities and real possibilities. There is no difference concerning her political and intellectual capacity. There are numerous examples of heroines in our history,

---

[10] G. Kligman, *The Politics of Duplicity: Controlling Reproduction in Ceauşescu's Romania* (Berkeley, CA: University of California Press, 1998), 24. This is one of the most thorough studies I read; it details with extensive annotation the dark period especially for Romanian women between 1966 and 1995. The author's works are cited in numerous journals and books and helped me locate several important sources.

[11] N. Ceauşescu, *Creşterea rolului femeii în viaţa economică şi social-politică a României socialiste (Increasing the Role of Women in the Economic, Social and Political Life of Socialist Romania)* (Bucharest: Editura Politică, 1980), 24-25. For this and other quotes from Ceauşescu, the translation was provided by Anca Cristina Constantin.

> as well as in the history of mankind. Women's participation in difficult situations during the revolutionary fight was equal to men's.[12]

Not only were women expected to be productive in the workforce but they were also encouraged in their patriotic role of motherhood. Within this responsibility, the education of children was considered critical so that they would grow up to honour and respect the state. The state enforced the ideology that mothers had a solemn duty to ensure that their children were brought up in the true spirit of socialism:

> Women, mothers are always present with their strong personality, their peculiar enthusiasm in giving birth to children and educating the young generation... Our socialist system pays special attention to the family, to its continuous consolidation and strengthening, to rearing and education children... woman has always... accomplished the noble mission of transmitting to the young generations the virtues of our people, its supreme traditions, passionate love of the country, the sense of dignity, justice and truth. The Romanian people have always honoured the woman-mother... One of the most important duties of women as mothers and educators is to devote themselves to rearing the young generations in the spirit of ardent patriotism, respect and appreciation for the glorious past of our people, and desire to dedicate their entire lives to the development of our socialist country and communist ideals. Women are required to carefully and patiently shape the children's personality, to leaven within their consciousness the high ethical principles of our society, to develop their passion for work and study, the new man's characteristics.[13]

Since women were the natural bearers of children, the state recognized it had an obligation to help women as they worked and contributed to the economy. This was done by providing various forms of social assistance: guaranteed maternity leaves, job security, and child-care facilities. These benefits were designed to be positive incentives and to assure the state of the women's contribution to the labour pool. It was at this juncture that the state began to take upon itself the more traditional nurturing and care-giving roles normally assumed by women in the home. Despite the promise of gender equality under the socialist system and the legislation of women's rights as workers, this often conflicted with their natural role as mothers. 'This contradiction in women's roles as both workers and (re)producers helped to blur the distinctions in the public and private spheres of daily life.'[14]

The Socialist Ideology of the Family

Elevating the role of women in the workplace also had an impact on the way men understood their roles in the home as fathers and husbands. The

---

[12] Ceauşescu, *Role of Women*, 16.
[13] Ceauşescu, *Role of Women*, 26.
[14] Kligman, *The Politics of Duplicity*, 26.

traditional Romanian family structure is patriarchal; this type of family organization was usurped by the socialist state to legitimize its rule over the population.[15] The state became the father and caregiver of the people, and Ceauşescu was called the 'father of the people' in print, media, massive rallies and in all public gatherings. Heredity played an important role in the socialist state; it was important to know one's family heritage as this played an important role in determining the status of a socialist citizen.[16] The family was juxtaposed, if not subjugated, to the state under communism which resulted in a 'diminished sense of personal accountability for children'.[17]

The Socialist Plan to Increase the Population of Romania

The Demographic Policy that Led to the Increase in the Birth Rate

After World War II, live birth rates had fallen sharply, not surprising given the impact of the war and the poverty that was widespread in the country. The country was not unlike other European countries struggling to recover from years of conflict. Abortion was legalized in 1957 and offered at a small fee. Most families at this time had no more than one or two children. The situation continued in the years 1956-1966, although some groups like the gypsies and religious sects continued with higher birth rates. By 1966 Romania had one of the lowest fertility rates in the world.[18] The high cost of raising a child began to be a factor in the size of families. Those families that could afford a better standard of living, i.e. a car, clothing and housing, had smaller families, while those that had a large number of children could afford very few material options, and in most cases both parents had to work. Since wages were set by state policy, new attitudes began to emerge concerning children. Children became a source of economic stress on

---

[15] The family type was patriarchal in that the husband and his family connections determined kinship lines. However, the Romanian woman has always had a strong influence in the home and community; she is usually the one who will discipline the children and keeps 'order around the house'. These implications will be noted further when I discuss the contemporary understanding of the Romanian family and evangelical church in reference to children at risk.

[16] A myth was created about Ceausescu and his family origins; in fact, he came from a very poor family and his father was an alcoholic. Some scholars suggest that his need to project himself into the role of 'father of the nation' was engendered by his own questionable family heritage. The party made family background, *origine sănătoasă* (healthy origin), important for work, placement and service to the state. 'A healthy family history did not contain priests (especially Uniate or Greek Orthodox ones), landowners, relatives abroad, former political prisoners, or divorced members' (Kligman, *The Politics of Duplicity*, 32).

[17] M. Burke, *Child Institutionalization and Child Protection in Central and Eastern Europe* (Florence, Italy: UNICEF International Child Development Centre, 1995), 21.

[18] 'A pronounced decline in birth rate occurred: from 25.6 live births per 1,000 inhabitants in 1955, it dropped to 14.3 per 1,000 in 1966. By 1965, the birth rate had reached 1.91 per 1,000 population, the second lowest rate in Europe, higher only than Hungary, where the birth rate was 1.81.' Zamfir & Zamfir, *Children at Risk in Romania,* 16.

families – each additional child becoming a greater strain on an already low income.

Planned and managed economies depended on a stable workforce, so control of population demographics was a common socialist policy. However, the Ceauşescu regime would give new meaning to the term 'demographic policy' and introduced new laws with abysmal consequences. Kligman is right when she says that 'in Romania, the demographic policy – *politica demografică* – was explicitly politicized for the purpose of building socialism'.[19]

The Official Banning of Abortion: Decree 770/1966

In 1966, the Romanian government introduced an official ban on abortion with the infamous '770 Decree'.[20] As birth rates fell throughout Central and Eastern Europe, governments sought ways to boost the birth rate. The solution that Romania took was unique in the region. Since the government considered population growth essential, the response was to simply ban abortions and the use of all contraception available at the time. The policy was applied with no room for compromise on the part of women or families. The draconian measures included obligatory medical check-ups and punishments involving fines and imprisonment.[21] Income was taxed up to 20% if people remained childless, regardless of whether they were married or not. Kligman is again to the point: 'By legislating reproductive behaviour, the state intruded into the most intimate realm of social relationships. This radical alteration of social relationships and the organizing structures of everyday life was a primary objective of the development strategies promulgated by communist planners.'[22]

There were some steps taken to support families with children such as a small financial allocation for mothers with three or more children. Zamfir claims these support measures were generally perceived by the public to be

---

[19] Kligman, *The Politics of Duplicity*, 9.

[20] The 770 decree read in part: 'The practice of abortion is both an antinational and antisocial act, and an impediment to the normal development of our population. It is necessary to introduce the most perfect order and discipline with respect to the application of the existing laws and regulations pertaining to the interruption of pregnancy.' Quoted from 'Decision of the Political Executive Committee of the Central Committee of the Romanian Communist Party', by Kligman, 42.

[21] Women under the age of 45 were rounded up at their workplaces every one to three months and taken to clinics where they were examined for signs of pregnancy, often in the presence of government agents – dubbed the 'menstrual police' by some Romanians. A pregnant woman who failed to produce a baby at the proper time could expect to be summoned for questioning. Women who miscarried were suspected of arranging an abortion. Some doctors resorted to forging statistics. Dr Geta Stănescu of Bucharest explained that 'if a child died in our district, we lost 10-25% of our salary. But it wasn't our fault: we had no medicine or milk, and the families were poor'. K. Breslau, 'Overplanned Parenthood: Ceauşescu's Cruel Law', in *Newsweek* (22nd January 1990), 33-37.

[22] Kligman, *The Politics of Duplicity*, 22.

'token signs of the position of the government rather than serious initiatives'.[23] As expected, following the decree, birth rates began to rise steadily but studies by the state showed that rates then began to return to previous levels, due in part to illegal abortions, poverty and deteriorating health care for mother and the new-born, especially for those not privileged by the party. By 1973, the total fertility rate had dropped back to 2.4 children per woman from a high of 3.7. In 1967, the number of unwanted children had begun to steadily rise.[24]

There were some exceptions to the fall in birth rates, notably among the gypsies and the 'members of religious sects' and in some geographic regions like the north-east where there were many poor and isolated villages – it could be explained that in these groups and regions there was a strong historical tradition of supporting large families.

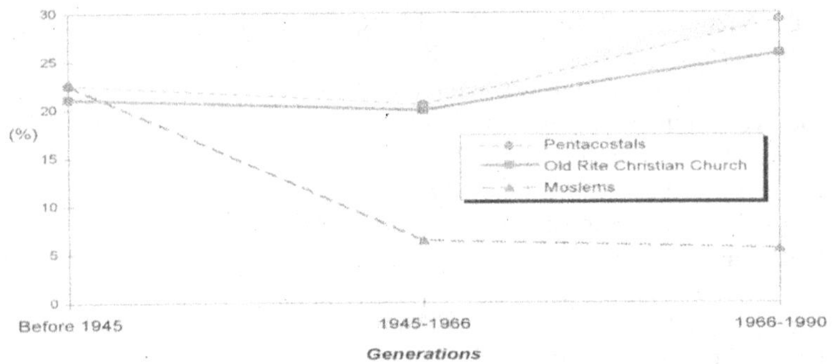

Figure 1. Selected religious sects – families with six or more children; in percentages of the relevant population group:[25]

[23] Zamfir and Zamfir, *Children at Risk in Romania,* 15. For an insight into the lives of women under the communist regime, see the documentary, *Diamonds in the Dark*, directed by Olivia Carrescia in which archival footage and interviews relate the women's struggles for survival under Ceauşescu. 'The chronic lack of heat and electricity, and the long lines for crumbs of food, were just some of the burdens borne by women. Professionals, students, factory workers and farm workers; all were obliged to take part in pro-Ceausescu demonstrations, take care of home and family, and produce more children for the regime' (excerpt from *Diamonds in the Dark*, 2000).

[24] Kligman argues that 'the poorest women were especially vulnerable to abortion-related complications and as a result were more likely to become maternal mortality statistics'. Kligman, *The Politics of Duplicity*, 8.

[25] See Zamfir and Zamfir, *Children at Risk in Romania,* 23. They labelled the sects as Pentecostals and the Old Rite Christian Church, a traditional sect which separated some centuries ago from the Russian Orthodox. I include this diagram as it confirms field observations in my research. I visited many Pentecostal families that had more than eight or nine children. Pentecostal churches in Romania regularly taught their members in the communist era that a large family was a sign of 'God's blessing'. I suspect this is an example of the sacralization of state policy, and that further demographic research into the size of Pentecostal families would indicate that birth rates have markedly declined since the mid-1990s, despite the continued teaching that 'children are a blessing from God'.

Increase in the Numbers of Unwanted Children

By 1974, the government redoubled its efforts so that planned and centralized reproduction matched expected outcomes. The intention was to increase the population from 23 million to 40 million; penalties against abortion were stiffened to include imprisonment or being put to death. The results of these measures was an even greater number of unwanted children, many being born to poor families that could not afford illegal abortions or the added burden of more children in the home. The solution put forward by the state to care for the many unwanted children were state institutions, orphanages and hospitals.

There were three distinct phases to the growth in numbers of unwanted children in Romania. The immediate post-war years where the number of orphaned or abandoned children increased; then the period in the late 1960s and early 1970s when the numbers of live births declined and the economy improved somewhat; and finally the period beginning in the late 1970s when chronic economic stagnation and decline, coupled with a higher birth rate led to a sharp rise in the number of unwanted children. The following factors have been identified by Zamfir as factors in the rise of child abandonment:[26]

1. As income declined and the cost of living escalated in a worsening economy, the result was a reduced interest in adopting children.
2. Adoption carried a social stigma; the children available for adoption were seen as bearers of negative traits of their parents.
3. Socialism had reinforced the preference for centralized organization and had created a pathological distrust of the private lives of individuals; thus the state was perceived as a solution for all problems.
4. Most of the abandoned children were born in poorer families with no other option for income and parents were encouraged to leave the children in institutions – after all, the state knew best how to care for children.
5. The number of illegal and botched abortions contributed to an increase in maternal mortality, and this contributed to abandonment. (Even after the revolution in 1989, when abortion was legalized, maternal mortality and child abandonment has remained high.)

The Institutionalization of Children under Socialism

The Romanian state began opening child-care institutions at the end of World War II and continued to build these institutions throughout the next

[26] Zamfir and Zamfir, *Children at Risk in Romania,* 29, 50. See also Zamfir et al, *Romania during the '89s-'93s,* 27.

45 years.[27] As the economy deteriorated and state enforced its birth policies and anti-abortion laws, a crisis developed for children at risk from poverty, abandonment, physical and mental disability, or ethnic origin. Thousands of children were abandoned in maternity hospitals and then placed by the authorities in orphanages. Families that could not afford to care for their existing children would simply abandon new ones at the hospitals on delivery.[28] Children were placed in institutions for other reasons, such as physical or mental disability, family dysfunction, poverty, repeated hospitalization or juvenile delinquency. However, once a child was placed in an institution, it was almost impossible to reverse the decision. Since abandoned children were not evaluated at any level, the people who ran the institutions rarely recommended that children return home.

Before the systemization policy had weakened the social fabric of the country, families had been able to turn to neighbours and extended family to help with special needs or when extra care for children was required. The years of propaganda were effective in convincing families that the benevolent state would take care of children when the family could not. When Ceauşescu was finally ousted in 1989, it was estimated that 80,000-100,000 children were living in 600-700 child-care institutions.[29] The government did not keep statistics on the annual rate of child abandonment in Romania before 1990. However, FBOs and NGOs estimate the number at 9,000 to 12,000 a year; abortion statistics from this period are also difficult to estimate but are better documented.[30]

At the beginning of the institutionalization process, significant resources had been allocated to child-care institutions as the state was obliged to provide care for children. Families were assured that they would be properly cared for but conditions deteriorated rapidly. There are a number

---

[27] Abandonment and institutionalization are not recent phenomena in Romania or elsewhere, nor are institutions to house children in need unique to Romania: this has been common practice in Europe since the late Middle Ages. In the aftermath of World War II there were homes for orphans and abandoned children that were nothing like the ones that many now associate with the 'orphanages of Romania'. However, the conditions that will be described here are unique in Romania's history.

[28] See particularly A. Johnson and V. Groza, 'The Orphaned and Institutionalised Children of Romania', in *Journal of Emotional and Behavioural Problems,* 2.4 (1993), 49-52; A.K. Johnson et al, 'Foster Care and Adoption Policy in Romania: Suggestions for International Intervention', in *Child Welfare,* 72.5 (1993), 489-506.

[29] V. Groza et al, *A Peacock or a Crow? Stories, Interviews and Commentaries on Romanian Adoptions* (Euclid, OH: Williams Custom Publishing, 1999); J. Triseliotis, 'Setting Up Foster Care Programs in Romania: Background, Possibilities and Limitations', in *Community Alternatives*, 6.1 (1994), 75-92.

[30] Kligman documents: 'In 1983, for every child born there were about 1.5 abortions. The fact that 742,000 women were registered as pregnant in 1983 invalidates certain attempts to justify reduced birth rates in terms of the state of health conditions. Unfortunately, of the 700,000 pregnant women, more than 420,000 had abortions, which represent approximately 60%. Data also shows that only 9% of these abortions, i.e. only 37,000 out of 42,000, were due to medical reasons, which demonstrates that medical causes did not determine this inadmissible number of abortions.' Kligman, *The Politics of Duplicity*, 95.

of factors that contributed to the horrific conditions that developed in the institutions and were reported so widely by the western media in the early 1990s.

The Shadow Economy and Theft of Resources Intended for Children

The chronic economic crisis in Romania was eased somewhat due to a 'non-formal' economy or shadow economy. This economic matrix involved corruption, regular theft from state institutions and many 'off the hook' enterprises. When legal resources such as wages and pensions or state services were inadequate, the illegal economy was responsible for making up the difference. Children in state institutions were at a distinct disadvantage as they depended on resources that came only through official channels.

It became widely accepted that the state's resources could be used for one's private benefit and reflected in the Romanian proverb, 'They pretend to pay us, we pretend to work.' It was very common for staff members in social institutions frequently to steal food, clothing and health care products that had been allocated to children. The economic crisis and inefficiency contributed to the siphoning of funds away from social programmes; despite the official ideology, children in the institutions were not high on the list of priorities for the state as they presented no threat and could not complain about their conditions. Budgets for the maintenance of buildings and facilities were never adequate. Staff in the institutions received very low wages, contributing to lack of morale, while theft was seen as legitimate compensation. Staff training was inadequate and there were chronic shortages of medicine.[31]

The Lack of Specialized Training and Medical Models of Child Care

All training and specialization in the social sciences was abolished in Romania in 1969, and training in the universities of sociology and psychology in 1978.[32] The theory was that a socialist state did not have social problems as the system could solve all problems; the social work profession was redundant. All human problems could be solved through administrative, bureaucratic and political mechanisms which were based on the ideology of the human system with power vested in the state. Since there were no trained social professionals, programmes such as crisis interventions, family foster care services, domestic adoption or home-based care did not exist. When the children became ill, hospitals would often refuse to treat them since they had no family identities. It was common for

[31] J. Dickens and V. Groza, 'Empowerment in Difficulty', in *International Social Work*, 47.4 (2004), 472.

[32] Zamfir and Zamfir, *Children at Risk in Romania.*

children to remain in the institutions gravely ill and receive no medical treatment. Visitors to Romania in the early 1990s reported seeing small burial grounds behind the institutions, since the children had no family to claim them and no identity, they could not be buried in 'holy ground'. Children had no advocates or adult voices to speak out on their behalf.

All the institutions for 0-to-3 year-olds operated as orphanages or *leagăne* under the authority of the Ministry of Health. The directors were medical doctors, and the only trained personnel in them were one or two underpaid nurses or nurse's aids. They frequently resembled hospitals for the terminally ill. The other women that worked in the institutions usually had only a high school degree as nursing training had been greatly reduced in 1976.[33] The average child to caregiver ratio was one aide (*infirmiere*) to every 25 children which made it impossible to give the children much in the way of personal care. Children were often forced to spend all their time in bed as there was no space allocated for play, or intellectual or developmental activities. The medical model in the institutions gave one primary obligation to the doctor and staff: 'Keep the children alive', therefore psycho-social care was not provided. Even in homes for older children, the only activity conducted by the trained staff was medical care.[34]

The Classification and Selection of Children

Once children in the orphanages reached the age of three, they were divided into two or three groups: normal children, minor disabled children, and unsalvageable children. Those classified as 'normal children' could pass an assessment by a physician. With no training in child development, the criteria used for placement was uncomplicated: if these children could walk, talk, masticate, use the toilet, and had no physical difficulty or defects, then they were 'normal'. They were sent to training schools where they lived in group home environments, were fed, clothed and sheltered and received some form of education. Few gypsy children were judged normal. Discrimination against gypsies resulted in their over-representation in the orphanage system. They were as likely as children with disabilities to be sent to dystrophic centres (institutions for 'irrecoverable' children – i.e.

---

[33] Nursing schools in Romania were never lost under communism – nursing (like social work) had been established in university education by the late nineteenth century. Nurses assigned to work with children in institutions were usually under-trained and under-paid – this was not a position a nurse would aspire to. See K. Horner, 'Building a New Framework for Romania's Throwaway Children', in *Together,* 32 (1991), 14-15.

[34] There was a tragic irony in this: 'The emphasis on a medical approach to the problems of children rather than on the creation of socially and emotionally stimulating environments was responsible to a great extent for the deterioration in the state of health of the children and significant delays in their physical and psychological development', Zamfir and Zamfir, *Children at Risk in Romania*, 31-32.

those considered to be unsalvageable) simply based on their ethnicity.[35] The 'normal' children were under the guidance of the Ministry for Education until the age of 18.

The second group was made up of those children who had minor disabilities. These were the children that were deaf, blind or had problems that were considered to some degree to be 'salvageable'. These children were sent to what were euphemistically described as 'special schools or hospitals'. These schools may have been called 'special' but they were not as well supplied as normal schools. These children were also under the Ministry of Education.

The third category were the children that were diagnosed with physical, medical or other problems that were considered too severe for a normal life and were sent to a dystrophic centre. These children 'from whom God seemingly had looked away' (to borrow a phrase from Romanian poet Mircea Dinescu) were placed under the direction of the Ministry for the Disabled. They were labelled as 'non-productive' in a society ideologically focused on production, and condemned by Darwinian notions of 'fit' and 'unfit'.[36] This category included those with legitimate mental and physical disabilities, including many children with minor conditions that could have been easily corrected, such as having large or malformed ears, cross-eyes or club feet. Because these children had been neglected in their early years, rarely picked up, held or spoken to, they experienced poor muscle development and physical co-ordination. Unfortunately, many of these children were misdiagnosed as disabled and sent to an orphanage for the irrecoverable. It is believed that the main purpose in sending children to these homes was to hide them away, reinforcing the myth that Romania did not have any social problems or disabled children.[37]

Conditions in the Institutions

To say that the institutions that served as homes to the thousands of Romanian children were poorly maintained and managed would be a gross understatement. The three-tiered system had resulted in different standards for different kinds of institutions. Some were better maintained than others,

[35] See L. Morrison, 'Ceausescu's Legacy: Family Struggles and Institutionalization of Children in Romania', in *Journal of Family History,* 29.2 (2004), 168-82.

[36] Kligman, *The Politics of Duplicity*, 322.

[37] Sadly, this situation has not been completely remedied in Romania. Even in 2006, the Mental Disability Rights International (MDRI) has found children with disabilities hidden and wasting away, near death, in Romania's adult psychiatric facilities. A report released by MDRI ('Hidden Suffering: Romania's Segregation and Abuse of Infants and Children with Disabilities'), describes teenagers weighing little more than 12 kg. Some children were tied down with bed sheets, their arms and legs twisted and left to atrophy. Despite Romanian government claims that it had ended the placement of babies in institutions, MDRI found infants languishing in a medical facility so poorly staffed that the children never left their cribs. Many of these children had no identity papers. Officially, they did not exist: www.mdri.org (accessed 13th December 2006).

but this would be a case of comparing bad with worst. I arrived in Romania in 2002 and visited some of the orphanages that had been 'renovated'; these had received significant foreign funding for infrastructure, physical improvement and staff training. Twelve years after the revolution, these facilities were still in very poor repair, walls were crumbling, heating was inadequate, and spaces for the children were overcrowded and dirty. Children were neglected and some were extremely violent with both staff and other children.[38]

When western child-care professionals, media, FBOs and NGOs arrived in Romania, they were shocked at the conditions they discovered in the hospitals, institutions and orphanages. The worst conditions were found in the homes for the 'irrecoverable' children. Images of children rocking back and forth, some chained to cribs – children who were overly active were restrained either physically with straps or chemically through tranquilizers – and others resembling survivors of concentration camps, were documented and sensationalized in documentaries such as ABC's '20/20' 'The Shame of the Nation'.[39] I interviewed a number of western and Romanian Christians that visited the institutions when they were first opened to the public in 1990, the following comment is typical:

> I had never seen anything like this: we were shocked that the children were being kept like caged animals; they were not permitted to leave their rooms, and some could not leave their beds. The smell was horrible, nothing had been properly cleaned, sheets and bed clothes were soaked with human waste. The people who were in charge stood around drinking coffee and smoking cigarettes; no one seemed to care about the children. The saddest were the babies and the very young children: they were never picked up; some would just lie and stare at the ceiling; I did not know if they were in a trance or coma (RH, Personal interview, 2003).

Groza provides a more nuanced description of an institution he visited in 1990:

> The orphanages were colourless, shockingly quiet and devoid of any of the usual visual or auditory stimulation that children usually receive from bright colours, pictures and displays. Walls were painted in dark browns to hide the dirt. The paint absorbed any light – when the lights were working – making halls and bedrooms darker. It seemed as if the entire building was sucking the souls of the children, and perhaps the staff that worked there. There were no

[38] The cases selected for study did not include the worst of the institutions that I visited. Several institutions I saw in my initial survey were being sponsored by Romanian governmental assistance and fit the description here. Most of the private institutions funded FBOs and NGOs were in much better condition with cleaner and well managed facilities.

[39] This is the ABC News Programme 20/20: interview with Barbara Walters and Hugh Downs, 19th October 1989. I was living in Thailand when I first saw this programme and had just returned from a short trip to Cambodia to assess the possibility of our organization beginning childcare work there. My first impression on seeing these images was that Romania had set up these institutions to torture children, as had occurred in the late 1970s in Cambodia under Pol Pot. I found it hard to believe that the institutions in the documentary were intended to be actual 'homes' for children.

toys. There was no exercise or exposure to the outside. Most of the time, the children did not have enough to eat or drink. Consequently, most children were below the twentieth percentile for height and weight compared with normally developing children, and grossly delayed in motor and mental development. One consequence of low height and weight is greater susceptibility to diseases. While official data were not available, some staff said that mortality rates in the winter could reach 40%. Recent information suggests that 50% died within the first 24 months.[40]

Studies in the early 1990s of the institutions found that staff ratios ranged from 8:1 to 35:1, and children received the minimum of personal interaction with adults. Crying children were ignored – a behaviour caretakers adopted both out of necessity and as a policy. Children who were left lying in cribs were not stimulated or moved for most of the day. For the children in the worst institutions, no educational or recreational programming was provided. Parents of babies in the institutions were only allowed to visit one hour a week and were not allowed to hold the child; they were only allowed to sit by the bed. As children became older, they had to entertain themselves as best they could and learn to defend themselves against the more aggressive children in the orphanages. Sexual abuse was suspected between staff and children and children with other children, but this is not well documented in the literature.[41] The institutions lacked hot water, soap, washing machines, linen for the beds; children wore and slept in constantly soiled bed linen and clothes. In addition to a lack of running water, sewer systems were either inadequate or did not exist.

The effects of institutionalization on children was first documented by Henry Dwight Chapin and the subsequent studies in child abandonment by J. Bowlby. These have provided theoretical frameworks for ongoing research into these issues in Romania.[42]

---

[40] See Groza et al, *A Peacock or a Crow*, 33-34, and particularly Chapter 3: 'Dickens, Boys Town or Purgatory: Are Institutions a Place to Call Home?' which provides a poignant firsthand description of life inside the institutions in the early 1990s.

[41] I make this observation from both interviews in Romania and from my personal experience growing up in an orphanage. There were times that staff in our home would abuse children both physically and sexually; threats were commonplace to make sure that we did not talk about this treatment to other adults.

[42] See particularly Johnson and Groza, 'The Orphaned and Institutionalised Children of Romania'; and A.K. Johnson et al, 'Foster Care and Adoption Policy in Romania: Suggestions for International Intervention', in *Child Welfare*, 72.5 (1993): 489-506. I trust that future scholars will join efforts in assessing to what degree faith-based interventions have assisted in rebuilding the lives of institutionalized and abandoned children. Romania's national crisis with children continues, many people of faith, both Evangelical and Orthodox, are engaged in providing care for thousands of children; however, little work has been done to empirically document faith-based interventions. Future work remains to be done to measure and evaluate faith-based impact and outcomes in the lives of children.

Summary – How Institutionalised Children were Understood under Socialism

Under communism, children in the institutions came to be understood as a product of the specific ways in which the discourse surrounding children was manipulated by the socialist system. Four main ideas emerge concerning 'the institutionalised child' in communist Romania:[43]

1. The institutionalised child was understood as different from the 'norm' – as a child in need of protection, devalued and strongly stigmatised.
2. Children who suffered from any kind of disability were most devalued, being seen as unproductive members of society.
3. Parents were encouraged to place all disabled children in institutions at birth and to 'forget about them'.
4. The institutionalization of children served to reinforce the construction of 'otherness' or 'abnormality', and the felt need to separate the child from wider society, a practice which in turn fortified the policy of institutionalization.

The state refused to rectify the underlying structural issues which led to the abandonment of the majority of Romania's 'unwanted' children, and therefore identified the children themselves as a 'social problem' to be removed. Because the state had taken upon itself the mandate to solve all social problems, responsibility for unwanted institutionalised children was removed from the families or parents. When families did place children in orphanages, the children became the property of the state and very few records or information were kept about the child's family, the children easily became lost in the system. Finally, the medicalization of child care meant that abandoned children were treated as a medical problem to be diagnosed and treated; children were not seen as complex human beings that needed love and attention. The Romanian medical community that took responsibility for these abandoned children knew this was not a government priority.[44]

The Situation for Children at Risk after 1989

The situation immediately following the death of Ceauşescu and his wife released a wave of renewed hope and expectation in the country. Now that

---

[43] See especially M. Burke, *Child Institutionalization and Child Protection in Central and Eastern Europe* (Florence, Italy: UNICEF International Child Development Centre, 1995); G. Lansdown, *Disabled Children in Romania: Progress in Implementing the Convention on the Rights of the Child* (London, Disability Awareness in Action, 2003); Curtis, *Under the Influence? Local NGOs and Discourse in Post-Communist Societies*. MSc thesis (London: London School of Economics and Political Science, Department of Social Policy, 2004).

[44] In 1989, the total government health care budget for 'developed' Romania's 25 million people was $7 million – or 28 cents per capita, which could be compared to 'developing' Uganda's 56 cents per capita or the United States' $2,000 per capita. See K. Horner, 'Building a New Framework for Romania's Throwaway Children', 14.

the people were rid of their despised dictator, a new government was to be formed and Romanians hoped for a total restructuring of the economy and state. The expectations and anticipation for quick change in Romania proved to be short-lived and soon gave way to disappointment and renewed cynicism towards the government. There was an immediate fiscal crisis as state enterprises and holdings were privatized in a take-over by ex-party members and the Securitate (the communist Secret Police). This was followed by a collapse of the national currency with rapid hyper-inflation. In April 1991, food prices soared 200-600% as the government faltered in creating a free economy. These developments did little to alleviate the crisis of children still languishing in the institutions scattered all over the country.

Media coverage focused the world's attention on the orphanages and abandoned children and provoked an international response from public and private foundations, governments, NGOs, FBOs, volunteers and researchers who 'poured into the country filling the reopened spaces of civil society'. By 1992, there were approximately 400 NGOs that had been registered in Romania providing humanitarian assistance, personnel, training and technical assistance. However, many agencies, both NGOs and FBOs, entered the country and did not register with the government as child protection laws that had been written in the 1970s were inadequate for monitoring or co-ordinating this activity. Analysis of NGO sector effectiveness points to a lack of co-ordination on behalf of these agencies.[45]

Poverty and Economic Decline Following 1989

In much of Central and Eastern Europe, poverty increased tenfold after 1989. Figures from both Romania and Russia indicated that the social composition of the poor was significantly skewed towards children in 1992 and 1993. In Romania, the proportion of children living in poverty in 1990 was 4.4%, and by 1994 these figures had increased to 37.5%.[46] Reductions in public services, health care, education and social provision had disproportionately serious effects on children and families, while child poverty rates increased one-and-half times more than the overall poverty rates. Romanian economic output did not increase significantly: real wages and employment lagged behind. The rapid decline in the economy affected poor families and infant mortality rates increased rapidly. In his report 'For

[45] J. Dickens and V. Groza, 'Empowerment in Difficulty', in *International Social Work*, 47.4 (2004), 469-87. The authors identify some of the problems caused by reactive, crisis-oriented international intervention, and then describe developments in child welfare policy and provision in Romania up to 2000. They identify key issues for international NGO intervention and for implementing empowerment approaches in situations where there were desperate shortages of resources, skills and experience.

[46] UNICEF, *Children at Risk in Central and Eastern Europe: Perils and Promises* (Florence, Italy: UNICEF International Child Development Centre, Regional monitoring report, No. 4, 1997).

a Child Centred Society', Zamfir stated that 50% of the total number of children living in the poorest families represented 30% of the total child population.[47] By reintroducing abortion in 1990, Romania hoped to reduce the number of abandoned children. Though the number of new-born children was reduced by 38% between 1989 and 1996, the number of abandoned children increased.[48] Immediately following the elimination of the infamous '770 abortion decree', the number of legally performed abortions for women aged 15-49 years skyrocketed: 992,265 abortions were performed in 1990; 450,000 abortions each year during 1991-1996, and 223,914 additional abortions in 2003.[49] In the period 1990-2000, 70% of Romanians indicated that their incomes were barely sufficient or insufficient to cover necessities and were dissatisfied with their earnings. By 1997, about three quarters of the child population in Romania were living in families with lower incomes, and half that number was living in poverty.[50]

Increasing Numbers of Children Institutionalised during 1989-1995

As stated above, there could have been as many as 100,000 children living in institutions in 1989. That number declined in 1993 to 73,000 largely due to international adoption. It is estimated that between January and July 1990 over 10,000 children were taken out of Romania by international adoption agencies, and in many cases this was done with dubious legality and almost no assessment of the children's needs.[51] The numbers of toddlers aged 0-3 living in institutions rapidly increased by as much as 45% over the same time period. By 1994, UNICEF estimated the overall numbers had increased to over 98,000 children.

Hundreds of children continued to be abandoned at birth by mothers that could not afford to care for their children. Some hospitals would keep these abandoned babies for up to three months and then they were placed in an institution. Throughout the 1990s, this scenario was repeated in many hospitals in large cities all over the country on a regular basis. Children that were disabled in any capacity were also regularly placed in institutions.

---

[47] C. Zamfir (ed), *For a Child Centered Society* (Bucharest: UNICEF, 1997).

[48] M. Roth, 'Children's Rights in Romania: Problems and Progress', in *Social Work in Europe,* 6 (1999), 30-37.

[49] The total number of legal abortions by women aged 15-49 years old between 1990-2003 was 6,483,177. (Anuar statistic 2004, Capitolul 14 - Sănătate (Annual Statistics, 2004, Chapter 14 - Health), 2004, 16)

[50] UNICEF, *Children at Risk,* 25.

[51] V. Groza, S.D. Ryan and S.J. Cash, 'Institutionalization, Behaviour and International Adoption: Predictors of Behaviour Problems', in *Journal of Immigrant Health,* 5.1 (2003), 5-17.

HIV/AIDS in Post-Communist Romania – Its Impact on Children

The first AIDS cases were diagnosed in 1985 but the situation was firmly and deliberately hidden by the regime. The unchecked spread of the disease affected the rising number of institutionalised children. In 1990, health officials and others encouraged parents to institutionalize their AIDS-infected children. Romania in 1990 had 54% of all paediatric HIV infections in Europe.[52] Experts are not sure how the virus entered the country but suspect it might have been introduced by foreign students and Romanians returning from work abroad in Africa as Ceauşescu had established trade channels with leaders of non-aligned African governments. The hospitals and institutions of Romania had very poor screening of blood supplies before 1990; the re-use of syringes and unsterilized medical instruments was common during 1987-1991 which led to the infection of thousands of new-borns and infants. As a result, there were 3,372 recorded cases of AIDS in December 1994. What is specific to Romania is the distribution of these cases. Of those individuals who had AIDS, 236 were adults, and 3,136 were children and teenagers, or .03% of all children and teenagers in the country. After 1994, there was an increase of HIV/AIDS incidence among young adults, resulting largely from heterosexual transmission (Evolution of the HIV/AIDS Infection in Romania, during 1985-2003, 2004:7). In 2001, the Ministry of Health declared HIV/AIDS a national health priority and developed a plan for universal access to treatment, with the purpose of extending access to medicines for people living with HIV/AIDS and increasing the quality of the treatment. In 2002 a law was passed granting free treatment and supplementary nutrition for people with the disease. A new strategy was implemented by the government in 2005 to contain the virus and focus on prevention, especially among young people and vulnerable groups.

---

[52] S. Watkins, 'Battling the Virus in Romania', in *Together,* 47 (1995), 11-13.

Street Children – Categories for a New Phenomenon in Romania[53]

Institutions and orphanages became increasingly overcrowded and the quality of care deteriorated. As explained above, the socialist system was dismantled before social and educational services and support systems were implemented to accommodate the growing numbers of children in the orphanage system. Consequently, there were thousands of 5-17 year-old children with uncertain futures due to the lack of long-term planning for their integration into the school system. Children began to run away from institutions, medical staff at orphanages did not try to dissuade them from leaving as runaway children were often the most difficult to discipline and were difficult to control. This created a new crisis for children as they had nowhere else to go and turned to the streets for survival. By 1991 there were hundreds of children living on the streets, sleeping in railway stations the parks in the summer, and in the underground system of sewers in the winter. These numbers escalated until the number in Bucharest was estimated to be over 10,000 in 1995.[54]

The most visible and marginal group are called *children in the street* or what UNICEF calls 'children with no family contact'. These children are under 18, live permanently on the streets, have no address and no connection with family or adult guardians. They live entirely by their own wits; they have no home to fall back on, each child providing his own material and psychological support. In Romania most of these children had run away from orphanages. They found their way to the cities, particularly Bucharest, conductors on trains usually letting them travel free, and they found a new home living in organized gangs or simply finding a group that would accept them. Bucharest's central station, *Gara de Nord,* became a magnet and night shelter for these children and soon FBOs and voluntary agencies began to set up halfway houses and shelters where these children could find a meal or someone who offered some concern.[55]

A second group is represented by *children of the street* or children with occasional family contact. These are children who have at least a living

---

[53] 'The term "street children" is problematic as it can be employed as a stigmatizing label – one of the greatest problems such children face is their demonization by mainstream society as a threat and source of criminal behaviour. Yet many children living or working on the streets have embraced the term, considering that it offers them a sense of identity and belonging. The umbrella description is convenient shorthand, but it should not obscure the fact that the many children who live and work on the street do so in multifarious ways and for a range of reasons – and each of them is unique, with their own, often strongly felt, point of view. The exact number of street children (globally) is impossible to quantify, but it is likely to number in the tens of millions or higher; some estimates place the figure as high as 100 million. It is likely that the numbers are increasing as the global population grows and as urbanization continues: 6 out of 10 urban dwellers are expected to be less than 18 years of age by 2007.' See 'The State of the World's Children 2006: Excluded and Invisible': www.unicef.org/sowc06 (accessed 13th February 2006).

[54] See D. Costin-Sima and S. Cace (eds), *The Street Between Fascination and Slavery.*

[55] C. Dobrisan and J. Kachelmyer, *Odyssey of a Romanian Street Child* (Lake Mary, FL: Creation House Press, 2002).

relative or parent but the children are so alienated from them that they rarely see them. These children spend a variable amount of time on the streets, maybe for a day or a week at a time. The longer these children spent time on their streets, the more they learned to fend for themselves. They often came from abusive home situations; they could go home but life on the streets was preferable to regular beatings from alcoholic fathers:

> Their initial experience is that life on the streets, though difficult, is more bearable than life with their families. They enjoy the freedom, and the lack of family tensions, and the streets generally provide them enough excitement, camaraderie and material subsistence to seem preferable to their bad family situations. Generally, their family links deteriorate as they become more involved with 'street culture'. Some of them work at legitimate jobs, but the majority drift into whatever offers some income, whether it is selling flowers or drugs, shining shoes or stealing, begging or prostitution.[56]

A third group is known as *children on the street*, or children with continuous family contact. This became the largest group in Romanian cities, consisting of children who live with at least one or both of their parents, or some other adult relative, and are simply working in the streets to help provide some family income. These children do not attend school during the day and come from extremely poor families and unstable homes. This category also best describes the many gypsy children that are working in the streets of Romania. These children could be in school but instead they join the swelling population of street children.

> The children drop out of school and are free to roam the streets. In Romania, public education up to the eighth grade is compulsory and in theory is provided free. But there were mitigating factors that cause children to opt out of the system: the costs of school supplies, teachers often demand bribes; ethnic children (e.g. Roma gypsy) face discrimination and are not given places in the schools.[57]

Children and youth that learn to live on the streets became more susceptible to drug abuse and violent crime. Throughout the 1990s, drug abuse escalated, street children could be seen carrying glue bottles and plastic bags, they would inhale the styrene fumes by placing a small amount of glue in the bag: this was known as huffing, *aurolac,* and most of the children became hooked on these substances which helped to ease hunger pains and dull emotions. UNICEF reported:

> Substance abuse rates are proportionately higher among marginalized youth, street children and children of minorities (particularly gypsy children), and the use of drugs can be a gateway for involvement in drug trafficking and other criminal activities and opens the door for many of these children into the world of organized crime and prostitution.[58]

---

[56] Jones, 'Ministering to Street Children', in *Together,* 32 (1991), 3-5.

[57] Interview with Bunaciu, 2004. Otinel Bunaciu is the president and director of Project Ruth, a large FBO working with Gypsy children in Bucharest.

[58] UNICEF, *Children at Risk,* 49.

Once children are established on the streets, they have a very low probability of ever returning to normal home life. The street child is exposed to sex, abuse and is a negative socialization process that destabilizes their personality:

> Most writing about… young people living on urban streets… assumes, even insists, that they live in disorganized, illegal misery. They are described as psychologically and irretrievably damaged, unable to form relationships as the children that they are and definitely destined for emotional, social and economic failure as the adults they will become.[59]

However, the idea of the street child as always in misery is being challenged by those investigating the attempts of children to reconstruct lost families and create self-supportive networks. One study in Bucharest by Fulbright scholars Flannigan and Nicholas interviewed 130 children living on the streets and surveyed a number of NGOs to determine what street children understood of their rights and their perceptions of the role of both the government and NGOs. The authors concluded that street children indeed have strong opinions about how these agencies should understand their situation and help them find a voice in society.[60]

The children on Romanian city streets learned to survive as best they could and many told social workers that they had a better chance of survival on the streets as they had in the institutions where mortality was far higher than in the rest of Romanian society. Street children faced constant harassment from the public, aggression from older, more experienced children, police and the courts. Children rounded up by the police were put in institutions for juvenile offenders where they faced harsh discipline with few rights. Once released from custody, they would return to the streets where violence and mistreatment were normal.

Progress Concerning Child Protection: 1997 to the Present

Despite the legacy of the institutional crisis for children, some progress on child protection was made in the early 1990s; social work courses were taught again in the universities and became full four-year degree programmes by 1994. Prototype programmes were established to prevent further institutionalization, and to assist the reunification of children with families and the promotion of in-country substitute family care. The Romanian Orphanage Trust, a British NGO, helped to underwrite these programmes at the county council level. A government National Committee for Child Protection was founded in 1993 but was short on

---

[59] J. Ennew, 'Parentless Friends: A Cross-Cultural Examination of Networks among Street Children and Street Youth', in F. Nestman and K. Hurrelman (eds), *Social Networks and Social Support in Childhood and Adolescence* (New York: Aldine de Gruyter, 1994), 409.

[60] S.T. Flanigan and B.R. Nicholas, *Representing Romanian Children as Stakeholders in the Democratic Process: The Perspectives of Street Children and NGOs* (Bucharest: Save the Children, Romania, 2003).

detailed targets. In 1997, major child-care legislation was introduced and the Department of Child Protection (DCP) was established, requiring all sectors in Bucharest and county councils to establish social service departments for children and families.[61]

After the chaos of the unregulated international adoptions in the early to mid-1990s, in August 1997, the Romanian government issued two emergency regulations concerning adoption and child protection (numbers 25 and 26).[62] Emergency Act no. 25 (article 1) introduced the expression 'child in difficult circumstances', and stressed the right of the child to protection from community and state when his/her life within a family context was not possible. Emergency Act no. 26 gave equal rights to both Romanian and foreign couples/citizens to adopt Romanian children. The Romanian Adoption Committee was established as the official governmental body certifying valid adoptions, with specific procedures concerning the terms of approvals and certifications in order to adopt a child. New legislation was passed in 2000 in an effort to control what continued to be a lucrative business.[63]

Romania continues to make progress on child protection laws, the reintegration of children in institutions with families, integrating a new foster care system and establishing alternatives to residential care for unwanted children. New legislation was adopted in 2004 (Law no. 272/2004) regarding the protection and promotion of a child's rights. A government agency was established, the National Authority for the Protection of Child Rights – *Autoritatea națională pentru protecția drepturilor copilului* (ANPDC).[64] The new laws have extended legal protection to all children – whether they are with parents, separated or abandoned, in school or in the labour market, within the country's borders or abroad, disabled, or with behavioural problems – without any discrimination, and have acknowledged the rights enlisted in the UN Convention on the Right of the Child (*Salvați Copiii România*, 2002). These child protection laws have for the first time imposed sanctions on parents that mistreat or expose their children to at-risk situations. The law now requires social workers, medical professionals and teachers to report cases where abuse in the family is suspected. According to the National

[61] Dickens and Groza, 'Empowerment in Difficulty', 474.

[62] According to Dickens and Groza ('Empowerment in Difficulty', 474), these two legal actions were the first to establish legal precedents for children in at-risk situations. Until then, laws written in 1977 had regulated the process.

[63] According to Traynor, 'by 2000, more than 3,000 babies were sent abroad at a cost of up to £30,000 a child'. See I. Traynor, 'Romania Hails Orphanage Success Story', in *The Guardian* (3rd December 2005): https://www.theguardian.com/world/2005/dec/03/internationalcrime (accessed January 2006). Adoption laws were modified again in late 2005 to ban international adoptions.

[64] The website www.copii.ro/eindex.htm (accessed February 2006) is the official site of the ANPDC and has updates concerning child-focused legal reform in Romania – among them, the paper 'Child Care System Reform in Romania' (2004). Another acronym used in this same department is ANPCA (National Agency for the Child Protection and Adoption).

Institute of Statistics and ANPDC, in December 2015, there were 3,734,667 children (aged 0-18) in Romania of which 20,291 were under the care of residential social services and 36,988 children under the care of social services of the familial type.[65]

In Lieu of a Conclusion: The Implications for Missions

This chapter has not been easy to write and may not have been easy to read. To think critically about the pain and hardship of children is not an 'easy' task. We are aware that the human story of the participants in this drama has been somewhat shrouded in this rather cold presentation of facts. However, the research and findings from Romania clearly have a wider relevance in mission and theological work with children. I contend that FBO-church partnerships must engage in more missiological reflection, and suggest that Child Theology and Christology, in particular, provide clues to ways forward. If the self-disclosure of God in Christ is not meaningfully integrated with the physical, material and transient aspects of the humanity of children, churches may remain pietistic and concerned only with the vertical dimensions of the gospel; conversely, FBOs which tend to leave the work of salvation and conversion to the churches, whilst themselves focusing on delivering effective social services for children, run the risk of embracing a 'secular eschatology',[66] rather than a deeply and authentically *Christian* action in the world.

In working with children at risk and with all children in need of help, we do need to have realistic yet bold expectations of what it is possible to accomplish 'in Christ' on behalf of children. In 2014, after almost 24 years of intentional evangelical mission intervention in Romania and Eastern Europe, there is limited evidence that the transformation 'achieved' for children approximates to the freedom from suffering and evil promised in the Kingdom of God, as shall be revealed in 'a new heaven and new earth' (2 Pet. 3:12; Rev. 21:1). We recognize that there is more evidence of the 'not yet' presence of the Kingdom of God than the 'already finished', as many Christian organizations and churches continue to work largely in isolation from one another, and many thousands of children continue to need assistance. Christian mission and interventions with children demonstrates *in a measure* what God has already accomplished in Christ in redeeming humanity and the spiritual lives of children; this should not be trivialized. But engagement with children in crisis reveals an important theological reality: 'The already in the kingdom and in Jesus is not the

---

[65] www.copii.ro/transparenta/statistici-page (accessed 14th April 2016).

[66] Stephen Plant develops the concept of 'secular eschatology' in *Freedom as Development: Christian Mission and the Definition of Human Well-Being* (Cambridge: Henry Martyn Centre, 2002).

holistic transformation of the world or humanity… the already in Christ includes [much] pain and suffering.'[67]

Christian churches and mission organizations must continue to watch, pray and act in the knowledge that *God* establishes what is rightfully his. The Holy Spirit broods over the face of the deep and offers hope in the midst of human suffering. This is where much Christian mission has been at its best in history, struggling to bring light to the dark corners of the world. The child who lives in the midst of crisis or pain can call forth this hope for God's Kingdom. We are reminded of the many thousands of Christian churches, residential homes and care centres where the choice to serve children is a lifelong commitment, and of the caregivers who watch and pray 365 days of the year, offering their lives in Christ's service *by and in* serving children.

[67] Haddon Willmer, '*Review*: *Mission as Transformation*', 194.

BECOMING PART OF THE LANDSCAPE: CHINESE CHRISTIANS' PRESENCE IN POST-1989 HUNGARY

Dorottya Nagy

Introduction

Winston Churchill's metaphor of the 'Iron Curtain' and the image of its fall have become engrained in the collective memory of many communities worldwide. The word 'fall', however, is usually understood in the sense of something causing a sudden change, thereby giving birth to the myth that the events of 1989-1990 in Central and Eastern Europe resulted in radical transformations of the affected societies and meant a dramatic break with the past. The abrupt change paradigm fosters arguments such as 'the search for new foundations of public and private life and for new spiritual orientations came to the fore, together with a suddenly emerged cultural pluralism and religious diversity, unknown under the confines of Marxist Leninist dogma'.[1]

Interpreting the fall of the Iron Curtain from a theological-missiological point of view, the word 'fall' indicates anything but suddenness. It is rather an 'after all', 'finally', and 'at last' of a long, time-consuming spiritual engagement translated into socio-political actions which in a certain constellation of events and circumstances finally caused the fall of the Iron Curtain. The human agents of change can be identified with the various communities, including the so-called expats worldwide, on both sides of the Iron Curtain, which collectively, through well-organized networks (based on past or present migrations) and for various reasons, worked also on political changes in Central and Eastern Europe. From a theological-missiological perspective, Christian communities worldwide played a significant role in revealing that, behind the Iron Curtain, cultural pluralism and religious diversity was a historical constant. Christian communities and traditions, through their manifold manifestations and through multiple underground, legal and quasi-legal diplomatic ties, were present in Hungary already during the time of the Iron Curtain. The fall of the Iron Curtain is, then, a revealing of what had already been there as well as a further developing of networks – not an instant start of many forms of

---

* This article, with minor changes, is a reproduction of D. Nagy, 'Becoming Part of the LandScape: Chinese Christians' Presence in post-1989 Hungary', in *Acta Missiologiae,* 4 (2015), 121-48.

[1] Ina Merdjanova, 'Religious Liberty, New Religious Movements and Traditional Christian Churches in Eastern Europe', in *Religion, State & Society,* 29.4 (2001), 265.

Christianity.[2] One of the consequences of the fall of the Iron Curtain was that, through various forms of migration, it made possible even more religious diversity. Parallel to and together with diaconal support and international church relationships, Hungary, like almost all former communist countries in Central and Eastern Europe, became a destination country for missionaries, and especially Christian missionaries, from all round the world. Missionaries were among the first migrants in post-1989 Hungary. It is not sufficient to label these missionaries simply as 'Americans' or 'westerners' because, in most of the cases, the holding of a USA passport meant giving an account of one or more sets of migration histories. The existence, maintenance and broadening of a multiform Christianity in Hungary, both during communism and after 1989, cannot be interpreted and properly understood without interpreting and understanding the role of international migration (hereafter migration) in it.

The present article is an invitation for scholars engaged in Hungarian studies to reflect on the importance of migration for religious studies (studies in contemporary Christianity) and to thematise further the element of religion in migration studies by moving beyond both the so-called church-sect typology and the new religious movements framework, on the one hand, and beyond secularization theories,[3] market theories of religion[4] and methodological nationalism/ethnicity, as coined by Andreas Wimmer[5] and Nina Glick Schiller,[6] on the other. The invitation is done through an academic exercise which looks at the case of Chinese Christian migrants in Hungary (predominantly in Budapest) within the framework of Christianity in its worldwide interconnectedness (LandScape) The findings of the study are based on qualitative research (mainly participant observation and in-depth interviews) done among Chinese Christians in Budapest between May 2004 and May 2008 with follow-up studies in 2009, 2010 and 2011. This invitation to interdisciplinarity signals that missiology needs to open its doors to the academic 'other' and that inside Christian circles it is important to realize that also a theology-missiology practised within

---

[2] The presence of non-Christian religious groups and movements in Hungary might give a different picture but even their history goes back far before 1989. The Hungarian Buddhist Society, for example, was founded in 1951 and continued to operate (with restrictions) throughout the Communist time. Hindu communities were already there in the 1970s.

[3] Roy Wallis and Steve Bruce, 'Secularization: Trends, Data and Theory', in *Research in the Social Scientific Study of Religion,* 3 (1991), 1-31.

[4] Afe Adogame, 'The Quest for Space in the Global Spiritual Marketplace', in *International Review of Mission,* 1 (2000), 400-09; Paul Froese, 'Hungary for Religion: A Supply-Side Interpretation of the Hungarian Religious Revival', in *Journal for the Scientific Study of Religion,* 40.2 (2001), 251-68; Ibid., 'After Atheism: An Analysis of Religious Monopolies in the Post-Communist World', in *Sociology of Religion,* 65.1 (2004), 57-75.

[5] Andreas Wimmer and Nina Glick Schiller, 'Methodological Nationalism and Beyond: Nation-State Building, Migration and the Social Sciences', in *Global Networks,* 2.4 (2002), 301-34.

[6] Nina Glick Schiller, 'Beyond the Nation-State and Its Units of Analysis: Towards a New Research Agenda for Migration Studies. Essentials of Migration Theory', Center on Migration, Citizenship and Development: Working Papers 33.

academic settings is a valid form of theologizing. This latter observation is particularly relevant for cases in which tensions between the Christian ministry within and towards communities and the academic setting of ministerial formation is increasing.

The Migration-Religion Nexus

The relationship between migration and religion within Hungarian studies seems to be under-theorized.[7] There may be several reasons for this: during the time of communism both religious studies and migration studies had to – or chose to – operate with prescribed axioms about the weak and destructive natures of both religion and migration. Religion, certain forms (mostly linked with a homogenized Marxist Hungarianhood) of Christianity were tolerated and politically used and misused. Migration as an acceptable act was restricted to the area of exchange scholarships with other communist countries. Migrations, other than visiting other communist countries with the aim of bringing social and 'intellectual' resources back home and turning them into patriotic actions, were by definition unpatriotic acts. No academic tradition, linking migration and religion for research purposes, has ever been created.

The post-1989 renaissance of religions in Central and Eastern Europe and, together with it, the restructuring of religious studies (mainly in terms of sociology or history of religion) had rarely been linked with migration phenomena. Most of the sociologists of religion were preoccupied with proving that religion survived either in a victimized state or as being better off because of communism. By doing so, they somehow lost sight of the importance of migration for the formation and visibility of the religious transfiguration in post-1989 Hungary. Migration, as an important element of religious landscaping, escaped the attention of even such excellent scholars as István Kamarás and the late Miklós Tomka. Instead, religious studies in Hungary continue to be predominantly addressed either through outdated church-sect typology[8] or through the concept of new religious movements.[9] Identity, secularization, post-communist, market, neo-liberal

[7] This is not the case, for example, in Romanian studies or other Central and Eastern European studies which productively dialogue with researches on globalization and religion. See Dumitru Sandu, 'Emerging Transnational Migration from Romanian Villages', in *Current Sociology,* 53.4 (2005), 555-82; Ibid., 'Dynamics of Romanian Emigration after 1989: From a Macro- to a Micro-Level Approach', in *International Journal of Sociology,* 35.3 (2005), 36-56; Gertand Pickel and Kornelia Sammet (eds), *Transformations of Religiosity: Religion and Religiosity in Eastern Europe 1989-2010* (Wiesbaden, Germany: Springer, 2012).

[8] Miklós Tomka, in *Church, State and Society in Eastern Europe* (Washington, DC: The Council for Research in Values and Philosophy, 2005), addressed the problem several times but unfortunately he too worked with the church-sect typology and in some cases applied the category of 'new religious movements'.

[9] István Kamarás, 'Devotees of Krishna in Hungary', in Irena Borowik and Grzegorz Babiński (eds), *New Religious Phenomena in Central and Eastern Europe* (Kraków, Poland: Nomos, 1997); Ibid., *Kis magyar religiográfia* (Budapest: Pro Pannonia, 2003); Péter Török, 'New

and globalization theories inform religion research but these theories, at best, superficially touched upon the issue of migration and, at worst, completely avoided it. The fact that most of the migrants who arrived in Hungary in the last twenty or so years are Hungarian native speakers from neighbouring countries might explain the lack of interest in the migration element within religious studies.[10] Within the context of Hungary's underdeveloped migration policy, ad hoc intervention in apparently acute situations did not encourage research in migration and religion either. At the time that the number of Chinese migrants reached its maximum in Hungary, according to official statistics, the government introduced extremely strong immigration regulations which meant that migrants from the People's Republic of China (PRC), although to some extent still visible, were reduced to a group of people with no significant data for researching religion and with a hint of the exotic for migration studies.[11]

Migration studies in post-1989 Hungary are a novel but growing field of enquiry across various disciplines (such as anthropology, sociology, political studies and, to some extent, humanities), and they do address a broad spectrum of issues (such as refugee studies, repatriation studies, labour migration, human trafficking), yet the question of religion in relation to migration seems to be neglected. When it is addressed, it is done through various types of market theories of religion or through exercises of what Nina Glick Schiller calls methodological nationalism and/or ethnicity.[12] 'Choose an interesting gateway or global city, locate an ethnic group, add a research question and mix well' is the recipe critiqued by Nina Glick Schiller in many of her articles. Methodological nationalism assumes that 'the nation/state/society is the natural social and political form of the modern world',[13] and this assumption predicts migration management. The same assumption is clearly present in contemporary theologies which, in turn, practise methodological nationalism. The present paper fully supports the argument that focusing on transnational communities instead of the nation/state/society is not the way out of the problem. It is important to find

---

Religious Movements and Social Conflict in Hungary', in D. Hall and R. Smoczynski (eds), *New Religious Movements and Conflict in Selected Countries of Central Europe* (Warsaw: IFIS Publishing, 2010), 173-98.

[10] In the case of those migrants religion pretends to act as a settled issue. One is either Roman Catholic or Reformed or Lutheran (maybe Unitarian, or an adherent of some tolerated smaller churches) or non-religious. The Ukrainian-speaking migrants, in turn, are put again in settled religious categories. Looking at research in migration and religion in Western Europe, for example, one can observe that interest in migration and religion has increased at the time that migrants adhering to non-Christian religions have been politically envisioned as dangerous or at least problematic for society; interest in research in Christianity and migration is a rather new development.

[11] Here too the presupposition that most of the PRC migrants had no religion – or if they did, they had to be Buddhists or adherents of the so-called Chinese religion – seemed to be unquestioned.

[12] Glick Schiller, 'Beyond the Nation-State and Its Units of Analysis'.

[13] Wimmer and Glick Schiller, 'Methodological Nationalism and Beyond', 301.

units of analysis which offer the opportunity to bring both foci together as dimensions, but not necessarily as the definers of migration-constellations. This implies focus on the human dimension of the analytical unit: in this case, migrants and non-migrants.

LandScape

Spatial metaphors are commonly used both in migration and religious studies. The LandScape[14] in the title of this paper in the first instance evokes the geo-political entity called Hungary. It also evokes the geo-political entity called the People's Republic of China (PRC) and even the paradigm of an envisioned Chinese Christianity.[15] The present article however uses LandScape to refer to a theologically/missiologically defined socio-religious space and an analytic unit called world Christianity.[16] The concept by definition acknowledges the role of the socio-political context in defining identity (including ethnicity primarily played out in terms of language) but goes beyond the nation/state/society axiom and calls for a perception of worldwide Christianity in local configurations whose primary level of identification is based on a theological confession (e.g. belief in Jesus Christ) and not on patriotic affiliation of community-forming believers. 'World Christianity conceptualized affirms the integrity of all believers in the face of the gospel mandate.[17] It shifts the focus to Christianity as a lived faith and explains the ferment, varieties, renewals and plurality of voices in the movement.'[18] It immediately turns the focus onto the mobile, portable and transposable[19] nature of Christianity. Christianity in its worldwide diversity is the framework within which the

[14] I have chosen the form 'LandScape' to show that it is used with a reference to Appadurai's concepts. See Arjun Appadurai, *Modernity at Large: Cultural Dimensions of Globalization* (Minneapolis, MN: University of Minnesota Press, 1996). See below.

[15] Dorottya Nagy, 'Where Is China in World Christianity?', in *Depicting Diversities,* 12.1 (2010), 70-83.

[16] The reference 'world Christianity' could to a certain extent become functional also in the case of other religions such as Islam or Buddhism where missionization implies geographical expansion as well. World Christianity as an analytical unit counts with the danger of a Hellenizing and Aryanizing Christianity (Tomoko Masuzawa, *The Invention of World Religions* (Chicago, IL: University of Chicago Press, 2005)), especially in Central and Eastern Europe, but acknowledges that the idea behind this unit is an imaginative organic unity in diversity. From a theological point of view, a conceptual clarification between the notion of Church as the body of Christ and Christianity worldwide has to be made.

[17] The essence of the gospel mandate is that Christianity is a movement which by definition initiates relationships in order to give account of its contents.

[18] Ogbu U. Kalu, 'Globalization and Mission in the Twenty-First Century', in Ogbu U. Kalu, Peter Vethananagamony and Edmund Kee-Fook Chia (eds), *Mission after Christendom: Emergent Themes in Contemporary Mission* (Louisville, KY: Westminster John Knox Press, 2010), 36.

[19] Thomas Csordas (ed), *Transnational Transcendence: Essays on Religion and Globalization* (Berkeley, CA: University of California Press, 2009).

gospel does not necessarily need to be domesticated[20] in order to avoid the label of 'sect'. It creates the sense that imagined communities[21] and imagined worlds,[22] through agents (e.g. missionaries, migrant Christians) of global interconnectivity, become partially experienced in local visibility through physical people, through concrete Christian communities. It acknowledges that times change and that even the technical terminology of theology, religious studies, sociology or the anthropology of religion needs to be revisited. The observation that Chinese Christian communities in Budapest have a minimum or no formal contact at all with the so-called 'historic' churches and their adherents in Hungary shows that there is much hesitancy, ignorance and mistrust in dealing with Christian communities which refuse or do not see the need for denominational labelling,[23] and that it is more comfortable continuing to relate to an imagined or denominationally connected global Christianity than becoming part of local constellations of Christianity worldwide. Although the so-called Ecumenical Movement has a long history in Hungary, even there co-operation and the longing for unity are being negotiated through categories of denomination (e.g. Roman Catholic, Reformed, Lutheran, Baptist[24]). Groups of believers simply calling themselves Christians do not really fit this type of scaling global Christianity.[25] Therefore, it is worth working with a more open concept of looking at and understanding diversity within Christianity – one that is aware that academic concepts have been and continue to be the shared products of multi-levelled interactions, negotiations and struggles between powers in relations and competitions such as church and state, theology and politics. Questions of religious freedom and religion-state relationships are part of the issue as well.[26]

---

[20] Lamin Sanneh, *Whose Religion Is Christianity? The Gospel beyond the West* (Grand Rapids, MI: Eerdmans, 2003).

[21] Benedict Anderson, *Imagined Communities: Reflections on the Origin and Spread of Nationalism* (London: Verso, 1993).

[22] Appadurai, *Modernity at Large*.

[23] On the gate of the Reformed Church which lends its building to one of the Chinese communities, one finds a bilingual inscription. The Chinese text reads: Chinese Christian Church in Hungary (Hungary's Chinese language Christian Church: *Xiongyali Huayu Qitujiaohui*), while the Hungarian texts says: The worship place of the Chinese Reformed Church in Hungary (*Magyarországi Kínai Református Egyházközségistentiszteletihelye*).

[24] As long as these labels are meaningful identity markers, it is legitimate to take them as units of analysis, but it is not legitimate to use them as settled normative categories.

[25] This paper keeps a distance from the much celebrated paradigm of the 'next Christendom/global Christianity', as presented by Philip Jenkins in *The Next Christendom: The Coming of Global Christianity* (Oxford: OUP, 2002). Following the same argument, the labels 'charismatic' or 'Pentecostal movements' might become essential as well.

[26] The new law on religious communities (CCVI) in Hungary explicitly states that the state supports those religious communities which nurture the consciousness of the nation! The preamble diplomatically drops the word 'country' next to the word 'nation.' In the PRC, training and installing patriotic religious leaders is part of the policy – see Jason Kindopp and Carol Lee Hamrin (eds), *God and Caesar in China: Policy Implications of Church-State Tensions* (Washington, DC: The Brookings Institution, 2004). If there is religion (and religion is not gone) both in Hungary and in the PRC, it must serve the nation, it must be patriotic...

LandScape in terms of Christianity worldwide also recalls Arjun Appadurai's[27] ethnoscapes, mediascapes, technoscapes, financescapes and ideoscapes quintet in theorizing a set of serious 'disjunctures between economy, culture and politics' by reminding one that the shared suffix – *scape* of these terms implies that they are not objectively given relationships that look the same from every angle of vision, but rather, that they are deeply perspectival constructs, inflected by the historical, linguistic and political situatedness of different sorts of actor: nation-states, multinationals, dispersed communities, as well as sub-national groupings and movements (whether religious, political or economic), and even intimate face-to-face groups, such as villages, neighbourhoods and families. Indeed, the individual actor is the last locus of this perspectival set of landscapes, for these landscapes are eventually navigated by agents who both experience and constitute larger formations, in part from their own sense of what these landscapes offer.[28]

The LandScape by definition implies the existence and the necessity of an infinite number of landscapes: one of them for the purposes of this article could be called Chinese Christians' Presence in Hungary and could be described by a set of experienced and imagined trajectories of at least three types of actor: missionaries (called to go/sent to Hungary), people from the PRC (*women Zhongguo ren*), and Christians who identify themselves as Hungarians (*mi magyar keresztyének/keresztények*). Stories of migrations indicate that these three types of actor encounter each other in different forms in post-1989 Hungary and, by doing so, they provide glimpses of the LandScape's complexity. The very exercise of exploring dimensions of this complexity becomes a landscape construct in itself, and it is important to bear in mind that the navigator agent speaking here (the fourth type of actor) is a theologian engaged in both migration and religious studies and, by her circumstances, unavoidably engaged in Hungarian studies as well.

---

and what is in the interest of the nation, what is patriotic is in a sense already *a priori* settled. The problem is one of rivalry for loyalty; and loyalty becomes crucial when at grassroots level citizens belonging to religious communities come into conflict situations where they must choose between rival powers. As long as religious communities and state legislation go hand-in-hand, the chance of losing adherents is minimal. Post-1989 politics and religious policy in Central and Eastern Europe perfectly illustrate how the so-called historic churches became loyal agents of a so-called constitutional nationalism. Habermas's and Sternberger's (on Habermas and Sternberger, see Jan-Werner Müller, 'On the Origins of Constitutional Patriotism', *Contemporary Political Theory* 5, 2006, pp. 278-296) envisioned constitutional patriotism (*Verfassungspatriotismus*) as a solution against nationalism seems to be still distant for these contexts.

[27] Appadurai, Arjun. *Modernity at Large*.

[28] Appadurai, Arjun. *Modernity at Large*, 33.

Missionaries

Immediately after the fall of the Iron Curtain, missionaries arriving to Hungary started to (re)map the country, to check whether secondary sources and reality could be matched. In Budapest, for example, several so-called prayer walks have been done, which implied that a missionary or a small group of missionaries took a Budapest map in their hands and started to walk through the city while praying, physically passing by each and every building and walking through each and every street. While walking and observing, they mapped and scaled the city, having feelings, thoughts and visions – and taking notes.[29] These observations and experiences became crucial advisors in strategy making.[30] Missionaries arriving from multiple directions and with diverse Christian backgrounds located a large group of Chinese small traders in the city. Due to a bilateral visa agreement between China and Hungary, between the end of 1988 and April 1992 (when the agreement was cancelled) there were about fifty thousand PRC migrants in Budapest alone. In 1992 the Hungarian Chinese Association (*Xiongyali Huaren Lianhehui, Magyarországi Kínaiak Egyesülete*) was already there with its own newspaper promising to represent all PRC migrants in Hungary with an outspoken loyalty towards Beijing.[31] This was but the first one in a row to be followed by others.[32] PRC migration was more than a fever lasting for a few years. Chinese became and continue to be the largest group of migrants in Hungary after the Hungarian-speaking migrants coming from neighbouring countries.[33] News about Chinese

---

[29] 'The city of Budapest and its surroundings have a population of over two million people. It is a wonderfully beautiful city with the majestic Danube River splitting the rolling hills of Buda from the sprawling city-life of Pest. While the vast majority of residents are Hungarian, there are sizeable populations of Chinese, Vietnamese, West Europeans and Gypsies. The need for the gospel is overwhelming. Of the two million people, it is estimated that only about 1% are true, born-again believers in Christ' (prayer letter of the Bridge the Gap 2006 Team Budapest).

[30] Some of these missionaries belong to that group of Christianity that nurtures a missionary zeal to gain the whole world for Jesus Christ or to advocate Jesus Christ in the whole inhabited world, and that has a long tradition within the history of Christianity. One of its major verbalizations is linked with the Edinburgh World Missionary Conference 1910 – see Brian Stanley, *The World Missionary Conference, Edinburgh 1910* (Grand Rapids, MI: Eerdmans, 2009) – followed by numerous missionary conferences and the emergence of countless missionary organizations which operate on the principle of reaching the nations ('nations' understood in the modern sense of the concept) or ethnic groups all over the world 'in this generation'.

[31] Pál Nyíri, 'Chinese Organizations in Hungary, 1989-1996: A Case Study in PRC-Oriented Community Politics Overseas', in Frank N. Pieke and Hein Mallee (eds), *Internal and International Migration: Chinese Perspectives* (London and New York: Routledge, 1999), 251-79.

[32] Currently there are six Chinese-written monthly magazines or weekly newspapers published in Hungary. Most of them are freely distributed among PRC migrants.

[33] There are only estimates about the number of Chinese migrants (mainly PRC migrants) in Hungary. According to official statistics, in 2011 there were 3,340 PRC citizens holding immigration permits, and another 6,660 holding residence permits: www.bmbah.hu/statisztikak.php (accessed 23rd March 2012).

migrants in Budapest reached missionary headquarters in North America, the UK, Hong Kong and South Korea. Missionary organizations which were only focusing on Chinese people noted the new developments, and PRC migrants in Hungary became targets of missionary enterprise.[34]

It was in this period of mapping the territory of post-1989 Hungary that a young Methodist missionary from South Korea, Pastor K., who initially came to Hungary in order to assist the missionary outreach of the Hungarian Methodist Church, turned his full attention to PRC migrants in Budapest. A South Korean male migrant, with little knowledge of Mandarin, entered some of the open area markets in Budapest, the area where most PRC migrants in the early 1990s in Budapest spent their working life, and started to organize a Chinese Christian Fellowship. Most PRC migrants were small traders coming in larger numbers from Fujian and Zhejiang, and in smaller numbers from all parts of China: migrants looking for a better life, in the long term envisioning a better future either in China or somewhere in the West – a highly diverse group in terms of places of origin and education, men and women, most of them alone, having left their families (spouses and children) back home but sharing the same rhythm of waking up at four o'clock in the morning, entering the same social space, the open area markets, doing business in a variety of goods, some venturing with Chinese fast food restaurants, and some with aspirations of one day becoming a real business man or woman. Many of them still commute between China and Hungary and carry their goods themselves. Pastor K. started to look for Christians among the migrants. Given that Zhejiang, also called the Chinese Jerusalem, has the largest Christian population in China, it was not surprising that he was able to gather a group of people who called themselves Christians, obviously without any denominational affiliation except the one given by the PRC government (which, when translated into English, means that if you are a Christian you are either Protestant or Roman Catholic).

The first meetings of the Christian fellowship were held in a school building; later the community rented the Methodist Church in the sixth district of Budapest. The first Mandarin-speaking church in Hungary with more than one hundred members celebrated its birth on 1st December 1991 and was officially registered under the name Chinese Christian Church of Budapest (*Budapesti Kínai Keresztyén Gyülekezet*; *Budapexi Zhongguo Jitu Jiaohui*). This first PRC church in Budapest had a core group of people who were already Christians in the PRC; the church also had an increasing

[34] The so-called Chinese Christianity paradigm includes the view that Chinese people have a distinguished place in the global missionary enterprise and in Christianizing the world. After 1949, when all foreign missionaries had to leave China and when a huge number of PRC Christians left China as well, the strategy of evangelizing PRC migrants in order that they, after their return to PRC, would be able to evangelize PRC people, became one of the major ways of nurturing the importance of China within Christianity. More on celebrating Chinese Christianity and understanding the complexity which lies behind the question (see in Nagy, 'Where Is China in World Christianity?').

number of new converts. It had a clearly developed hierarchy in which the Korean missionary, in the role of Pastor, was heading the church; under him was an British-born female missionary, Mrs S., with much experience in mission work in communist settings and with a knowledge of Mandarin, who took (or was given) the position of 'helper'. And then, at a still lower level, came the PRC migrants leading the five departments of community life: mission, service, education, finance, and one without specification. Through Pastor K. there was regular interaction between the Hungarian-speaking and the Mandarin-speaking communities. The two non-PRC missionaries, the PRC migrants and the Hungarians encountered each other through various dimensions of migration (hi)stories.

Interconnectivity increased when the Korean missionary asked for support from the UK-based Chinese Overseas Christian Mission (COCM – *Jidujiao Huaqiao Budaohui*), the oldest and largest interdenominational Chinese mission organization in Europe with its motto 'Reaching the Chinese to reach Europe'.[35] In this way, PRC migrants in Hungary got into another network of missionary enterprise, establishing contacts with the Chinese Church Support ministries, with the Chinese Christian Mission, and with a Chinese Evangelical Church in Vienna which also supported the Hungarian community financially.[36] Through these connections, many Chinese ministers, famous Chinese preachers, missionaries, and short-term mission trip teams visited Hungary, and they also supported the community with Christian literature and access to Christian media.

A promising start to a new Christian community with strong international and transnational ties seemed to be there. The community was growing, and it seemed to have turned into a local community with its own socio-political and cultural setting. The name of the community indicated that the leadership wanted to form a community which was 'a light in and salt for the city' as one of the informants formulated it.[37] They wanted to be a signal for the non-Christian PRC fellow migrants and also a witnessing community in the city. The Chinese element of the community was only one-dimensional, crucial language-wise but not the primary manifestation of identification. Instead, the mega Christian narrative and being conditioned through migration informed identity development. The non-Chinese leadership and the relatively close contact with a Hungarian-

---

[35] Mrs S. most probably arrived in Hungary through COCM contacts. She heard about PRC migrants there during a lecture at the Baptist Church in York. 'Sometimes it just says "click" and you know. It was like that when I heard about the many Chinese in Hungary.' See Pauline Stableford, *Risky Business: My Adventures with Jesus in Many Languages* (Greenville, SC: Ambassador International, 2007), 131.

[36] Dorottya Nagy, *Migration and Theology: The Case of Chinese Christian Communities in Hungary and Romania in the Globalization-Context* (Zoetermeer, Netherlands: Boekencentrum, 2009).

[37] One of the reasons of the failure of the project might be the lack of knowledge of the local context on the part of the missionaries.

speaking community created a sense of celebrating multiculturality and allowed thoughts like these:

> God has talked to me through Pastor K. He is a Korean, you know, he even could not talk to me but showed me the Jesus film. I was moved. I had to come the whole way from China to Hungary, so that a Korean pastor could show me the Jesus film in my language. He also helped me with my documents. He spent hours and hours with me trying to help me. And then a Hungarian pastor baptized me. God is great! For him, it doesn't matter if you are Chinese or Korean or Hungarian, He wants you, He loves you. I pray that my family will know Him as well. (Mrs L.)

There was a sense of celebrating diversity, celebrating internationality, transdenominationality, and a sense of realized 'world Christianity'. Within the formal settings of the church, the issue of Chineseness was more a language issue and less an ethnic narrative. Their actual socio-economic situation, their migrant status, and the 'desperate longing' for a better life (which they then confessed to have found through faith in Jesus Christ) were more central than narratives of ethnic or national belonging. Through the diaconal department of the community, they started to address the question of poverty which is so visible in Budapest. They have distributed clothes among homeless people on a regular basis.

The success story, however, has been overshadowed by some tensions. The co-operation between Pastor K. and Mrs S. did not work well. This was one of the power conflicts which unintentionally influenced leadership policy among Chinese Christians for the years to come. According to Mrs S., Pastor K.'s problem was that she did not treat him in line with the Korean attitude to pastors:

> They have a very high standing in society and are very important. I made the mistake of making suggestions which, although he agreed were good, should have come from him! His problem was that he, being younger than me, needed to respect me, but I, as a non-ordained worker and a woman, had to respect him and let him make the suggestions.[38]

The issue of gender and leadership became a decisive one for the life of the community. Ultimately, Mrs S. was excommunicated and she decided to continue her work among the Chinese (which, in her words, was a task given to her by God, the highest authority in this debate). First she left the church with a group of believers and then they continued to gather in the building of one of the Baptist churches in Budapest, under the auspices of the (English-speaking) International Church.

The history of the community took an unexpected turn in 1996 when one of the most active members of the community was assassinated. From 1995 onwards, the Korean missionary had written about his and the community's fears of the 'Chinese mafia'.[39] These worries turned out not to be

---

[38] Stableford, *Risky Business*, 132.

[39] Different informants understand 'Chinese mafia' in different terms. Yet none of them wanted to enter into a detailed discussion about it.

unreasonable. The event caused much confusion and chaos in the community. It seems that the leadership of the church was not able to deal with the consequences of the event and they lost control. For a short time, Mrs S. returned to support the community. Meanwhile a Presbyterian businessman from Taiwan, Mr H., after spending some time in Hungary, understood that 'God had called him to minister among the Chinese in Hungary'. He started to work with Pastor K. but there were several misunderstandings between the two. Finally, Pastor K. left Hungary in 1997 and became a missionary in Canada. By that time, the church had split into two groups, one led by Mrs S., holding their gatherings in the Scottish Church in Budapest, and the other led by a PRC person, Mrs W., in the form of a house church. Mr H. maintained contacts with Mrs W. and became a co-worker of the group. She moved to Nyíregyháza, a town in north-east Hungary which also had a large open area market dominated by PRC small traders.

News about the situation of the Chinese community in Hungary reached the USA and troubled many missionary organizations. The following example illustrates how efficiently missionary organizations work. Having been informed about the existence of a new Chinese Christian community in a former communist country, Wang Yong Xin (the Billy Graham of the Chinese Christians), who founded the Chinese Co-ordination Center of World Evangelisation in 1976 and the Great Commission Center International (GCCI) in 1989,[40] which is also closely linked with the Back to Jerusalem Movement (BJM),[41] felt the need to visit Hungary and settle the problems among the Chinese Christians. The conflicts remained unresolved but through Wang's visit a mentoring relationship between one of the communities in Hungary and the Global Life Enrichment Center (GLEC, closely associated with GCCI) was established. This relationship developed through the arrival in 1996 of a missionary, Pastor J., who was sent to Hungary for a forty-day evangelization trip. Pastor J., however, stayed longer and left in 1998 for Spain to work among Chinese migrants there.

Mr H.'s Presbyterian background and his new status as a missionary sent out by GLEC led to contacts with the Hungarian Reformed Community of *Külsőjózsefváros*, in the VIIIth district of Budapest, close to the so-called

[40] It was also under the auspices of this organization that the 'America Return to God' movement was started. According to the project description, 'America was built by God as a Christian nation through Christian people. But America today is becoming not only non-Christian but in many areas anti-Christian!': http://gcciusa.net/English/ARTG.htm (accessed 20th February 2012). This rhetoric perfectly matches the missionary vision which operates in terms of a modern understanding of nation and nationhood. Much of this rhetoric has to do with the financial consequences for sponsoring missionary zeal and enterprise.

[41] The BJM has its roots in the 1940s in China when a number of Chinese Christian leaders envisioned the importance of Christianizing Central Asia and the Middle East. The movement, by now operating in a global setting but still using the mobilization rhetoric of God, has given the Chinese Church the vision and task that she, leading yet together with the global Christian community, should complete the imperative of the Great Commission.

Four Tiger Market,[42] which by that time had become the social area for many Chinese migrants. As a result, the Chinese community could rent the building of the Reformed Church. Through Mr H.'s Taiwanese contacts, GLEC could find the right person to mediate between the two conflicting groups. The representative of the organization visited Hungary and by efforts of mediation, she managed to bring together the two separated groups, which then on 1st September 1997 started anew together under the name *Xiongyali Hua Yu Jitu Jiaohui* (Hungary's Chinese-speaking/language Christian Church) and decided to use the building of the *Külsőjózsefvárosi* Reformed Church in *Kőris utca* for their Sunday services, and rented a room of the nearby Baptist Church for some special events. By that time, the community numbered about two hundred people (members and regular visitors). This was a new name for a new community. This may seem a small detail but it speaks to major changes in identity formation of the community and the powers behind the community influencing its identity formation. From the *Budapexi Zhongguo Jitu Jiaohui* only the identifier Christian Church remained. PRC has been replaced with *huayu* (Chinese language, implying also the myth of a single Chinese culture), and Budapest with Hungary. From then on, even by its name, it was clear that PRC migrant Christians in Budapest were seen together with the Chinese missionaries arriving from multiple directions as part of the imagined Chinese sector of Christianity. This change in name, however, did not put an end to the tensions which originated from the fact that most of the Chinese missionaries (being non-Mandarin native speakers) did not understand the (*women Zhongguo ren*, we, people from the PRC) rhetoric.

In 2000, Mr H., due to conflicts with the community, had to leave Hungary. He was replaced by another GLEC missionary couple. In 2001, however, Pastor J., who earlier was active as a GLEC missionary, returned to Hungary as an independent missionary, radically breaking with any Presbyterian contacts. Pastor J. and his wife returned to Hungary, belonging to a charismatic movement within Christianity which implied that tensions between them and the actual leaders of the community were unavoidable. It also implied further diversification among PRC Christians. In the struggle for power, Pastor J. had the advantage of a personal history with a good number of the church members (many of them converted during his earlier missionary work in Hungary). The conflicts resulted in a new split when a group of about thirty people led by Pastor J. started a new church, a charismatic one. In 2005, Pastor J. and his wife left Hungary and the community that had been led by them split into two groups. Due to unsettled power relations, the church in *Kőris utca* also split. As a result, there were three Chinese Christian communities in Budapest.

---

[42] The *Józsefvárosi piac* or Four Tiger Market was opened in 1993 and by 2000 it had become one of the tourist attractions of the city. Although called the Chinese market, it is the most multicultural place in Hungary.

It is remarkable that the community which stayed in the building of the Reformed Church temporarily had a minister who came from the PRC but who, due to immigration regulations, could not extend his stay in Hungary. This community from 2006 on managed to be church without a permanent minister but always with the hope that one day they would have a PRC-born minister. Currently they are supporting the theological studies of a PRC person, who 'has been called' to serve the PRC migrants in Hungary. Another group which left from the *Kőris utca* church, became a daughter church of one of the biggest Taiwanese missionary organizations, the Bread of Life Church (*Ling Liang Tang*), famous for their charity work, having more than three hundred communities worldwide. This group has also started mission work among Roma people in Hungary.

The history of the Chinese Christian communities in Budapest continues in the same dynamic and unpredictable manner. From time to time, advocates of unity arrive in Budapest and they work hard on unifying the communities but such attempts seem to have had only short-term results, despite the fact that of those migrants who were involved in the very first conflicts, only a few are still in Hungary. The story of the Chinese Christians' presence, from the perspective of missionaries and missionary organizations, is a story of arrivals and departures, of innumerable criss-crossing network threads which, under the conditions of contemporary globalization and nuances of Chineseness, Christian missionary zeal and global-mindedness, create unexpected patterns at the level of the local. The configurations of the patterns have a close if not inseparable link with what is called the globalization of American Christianity,[43] which is closely linked with the increase in active involvement in the international economic, political and cultural community. The roots of this global-mindedness, however – and this is rarely acknowledged in academia – must be also sought in personal and collective migration histories. The histories of modern migrations to North America (apart from melting-pot theories and the like) create a paradigm for interpreting the translation of ties modified through migration into a personal and collective global-mindedness (the notion of diaspora, the feeling of being scattered all round the world). In the present discourse, this means that behind the missionaries (who are often people with multiple migration histories themselves[44]) there are communities rooted in migration and created by migration experiences (with traumas, successes, emotions and feelings). The case of the Chinese missionary organizations beautifully illustrates the complexity of the paradigm: how identity formation is shaped by migration, and how migration addresses questions of relatedness to issues of 'ultimate concern',

[43] Robert Wuthnow, *Boundless Faith: The Global Outreach of American Churches* (Berkeley, CA: University of California Press, 2009).

[44] One of the missionaries, for example, was born in China. In 1949 he went to Taiwan and in the early 1960s he ended up in the USA where he became a prominent scholar. In his late fifties he decided to go to a Bible College and after graduation became a missionary.

and how being ultimately concerned translates into lifestyles, corporal and individual relationships, political, cultural, economic, and religious engagements. This all takes place in a continuous negotiation of fields of power from which nation-states and the nationalism nurtured by them are but one of the many.

PRC Christian Migrants

The history of the PRC migrants in Hungary – at least, its first ten to fifteen years – is well researched and well documented (first by Nyíri[45]).[46] Some aspects of religiosity in terms of missionary enterprise[47] have been touched upon and the issue of the triangulation of ethnicity, migration and Christianity has also been given attention.[48] Yet it seems that researching Chinese migration in Hungary (with few exceptions – e.g. Polonyi[49] and Irimiás[50]) seems to stagnate these days, or only focuses on broad-scale and general research projects on migration to Hungary after 1989.

The story of PRC migrants to Hungary is a story about continuous change and new constellations. PRC migrants in Hungary show a higher diversity than one which would fit categories such as small traders and entrepreneurs, human traffickers, and a ghetto mentality. Some of the major

---

[45] Pál Nyíri was the first and by many considered the only scholar who, through a high standard of research, laid the foundations for researching Chinese migration to Hungary. His findings continue to set the tone in researching different aspects of Chinese migration in Hungary but it is important, as Polonyi states, to take account of other researchers' voices as well in order to understand Chinese-related issues from other perspectives.

[46] Pál Nyíri, 'Organisation and Integration in a New Overseas Chinese Community – Hungary 1989-1997', in Endre Sík, Maryellen Fullerton and Judit Tóth (eds), *From Improvisation towards Awareness? Contemporary Migration Politics in Hungary* (Budapest: Institute for Political Sciences, Hungarian Academy of Sciences, 1997), 50-84; Ibid., 'Chinese Organizations in Hungary, 1989-1996', in Hein Mallee and Frank N. Pieke (eds), *Internal and International Migration: Chinese Perspectives* (Richmond: Curzon Press, 1999), pp. 251-273; Ibid., 'Expatriating Is Patriotic? The Discourse on "New Migrants" in the People's Republic of China and Identity Construction Among Recent Migrants from the PRC', in *Journal of Ethnic and Migration Studies,* 27.4 (2001), 635-53. Ibid., 'Global Modernisers or Local Subalterns? Parallel Perceptions of Chinese Transnationals in Hungary', in *Journal of Ethnic and Migration Studies,* 31.4 (2005), 659-74; Péter Polonyi, 'A magyarországi kínai kolónia problémáiról', in András Inotai and Otto Juhász (eds), *Kína: Realitás és esély: Tanulmányok Magyarország Kína stratégiájának megalapozásához* (Budapest: Magyar Tudományos Akadémia, Miniszterelnöki Hivatal, 2008), 328-46; Klára Mészáros, 'Kínaiak Európában. Kínai migráció az Eu-országokban', in *Korunk,* 3.8 (1998), 45-51.

[47] Pál Nyíri, 'Xenophobia in Hungary: A Regional Comparison', in *Working Paper Series* (Budapest: Central European University: Center for Policy Studies, 2003).

[48] Nagy, *Migration and Theology.*

[49] Polonyi, 'A magyarországi kínai kolónia problémáiról'.

[50] Anna Irimiás, 'Budapesten élő kínai közösség', in *Földrajzi értesítő,* LVII.1-2 (2008), 469-84. Irimiás's study introduces a new dimension of researching PRC migration into Hungary by focusing on spatially differentiated Chinese spaces in Budapest. Looking at the map of Chinese fast food restaurants presented by her, the image of PRC migrants being present as constants in the Budapest tapestry is created.

changes, especially after Hungary became a member of the European Union (2004), were as follows:

- – the appearance of (improperly so-called) second generation PRC migrants;
- – the increasing number of PRC students (partially related to the second generation) studying in Hungary;
- – the appearance of a significant group of business women and men who have few or no links with the small traders of the early 1990s;
- – a significant growth in the number of highly educated PRC people present in almost all sectors of society.

These developments are strongly linked with the flourishing financial and cultural relationships between the PRC and Hungary[51] and might be perceived in terms of professional migration generated by bilateral co-operation (migration directly generated by governmental policies). Diversification also leads to stratification. Chinese Christian communities are no exception to this. Different PRC migrants respond to different missionary enterprises. The enterprise terminology might lead to 'reductionism that goes beyond causal priority to assert that processes of religious change can be adequately described as if they were economic, in terms of "spiritual marketplace" where people "buy in" to a system of beliefs or "shop for" a religious identity'.[52] It is about how different PRC migrants (in the sense of their situatedness) are able to answer the need of what Csordas calls religion – namely, 'an inevitable, perhaps even necessary, dimension of human experience'.[53]

One way in which stratification may appear is through generation divides. For example, a Chinese missionary couple who came to Budapest from California managed to develop student ministry among young PRC adolescents. Social stratifications of the communities become visible as well. Looking at one of the communities, after a long history of tensions with missionaries who, according to the members, did not understand them,[54] they decided to support the theological training of one of their own

[51] E.g. in 2006, Hungary was the first country in Central and Eastern Europe to host a Confucian Institute. By 2012, however, most of the post-communist countries of the region had one. In 2010, the Semmelweis University, in co-operation with Heilongjiang University of Chinese Medicine, started a training programme in Traditional Chinese Medicine. In 2003, Hungary was the first Central and Eastern Europe country to open a branch of the Bank of China, and in 2004 to start a Chinese-Hungarian bilingual school with about 200 pupils (of which 60% were Chinese).

[52] Csordas, *Transnational Transcendence*, 2.

[53] Thomas Csordas, 'Asymtote of the Ineffable: Embodiment, Alterity, and the Theory of Religion', in *Current Anthropology*, 45 (2004), 163-85.

[54] Informants complained about the way they were approached by Chinese missionaries coming from North America or from Taiwan. In the case of North American missionaries, in addition to the problem that they had no PRC experience, they had an articulated perception of PRC-generated tensions, while difficulties caused by language also appeared. Some of the missionaries had Cantonese as their mother tongue and were not able to communicate fluently with Mandarin-speaking migrants.

members, a PRC-born Christian, who had the same migration history as the majority of the community. The need to train people of one's own community focusing on migration as a conditioning element of faith made Chinese Christians in Europe start theological training with the aim of serving new PRC migrants.[55] It is remarkable to see that most of the members of this community do not have higher education and most of them still work in the famous Four Tigers Chinese open area market[56] where the danger of being forced to move further has been hanging in the air for more than a decade. This is, however, still the largest community of the four Mandarin-speaking Christian communities in Budapest.

Although the Mandarin-speaking Christian communities are still dominant, PRC Christians can be found in many of the English-speaking communities in Budapest, as well as in some Hungarian (mainly non-denominational) churches. A Gordian knot would be the most fitting metaphor for capturing the complexity of the Chinese Christians' presence in Hungary (more specifically in Budapest). It is a multi-directional and multi-dimensional story, a scholarly example of local constellations within the conceptual framework of contemporary Christianity worldwide.

Being conditioned by migration, community formation and missionization constantly pose the question: 'Who am I?' The primary answer to this question in the case of PRC Christians in Budapest is never: 'I am Chinese' – the answer so much expected by scholarship consciously or unconsciously doing methodological nationalism. Gender, family status, social status, ethnicity, geographical origins and existential positioning ('I am a Christian') precede the 'Chinese' answer.[57] Identifying oneself as Christian and being acknowledged by others as Christian results in an ongoing self-reflexivity which checks if faith confessed by words corresponds with faith lived out in lifestyle, deeds and actions. There are moral standards, mainly mirroring the missionaries' Scriptural hermeneutics, set to guide the PRC Christian in Hungary. Keeping those standards and remaining – or becoming – successful entrepreneurs is not

[55] The Chinese Theological Training in Europe (*Ou Hua Shen Xue)* was opened in 2007 in Barcelona, Spain. The motto of the seminary is 'In Europe for the World'. The staff of the institute, however, is still predominantly from North America, Taiwan and Australia. This experiment, however, is not the first in recent times. In 2002, the Global Enrichment Theological Seminary (*Chuang Xin Shen Xue*), an innovative educational institution operating on the principle of 'We look on all the world as our campus' was established; their goal is 'to equip ministers and to train theological educators to serve in Chinese churches worldwide' (www.mygets.org/english/articles.php?id=4&m=20), and they started organizing theological training in Budapest. Among the students, after graduation in 2005, nine became full-time ministers and most of them gave testimony about their call to go back to the PRC to 'serve the Chinese' there.

[56] After more than a decade, in April 2012, the final decision to close the physical address of the market and relocate the entrepreneurs in other parts of the city was pronounced.

[57] Missionaries also use the tools of methodological nationalism. Typical for short-term missionaries and evangelization campaigns on the open area markets was the dialogue initiating question: '*Dui bu qi, nin Zhongguo ren ma*?' (Excuse me, are you a person coming from the PRC?).

always an ideal match. Migration continues to express the quest for a better life but PRC Christians, at the moment of joining a Christian community, will consciously deal with settling the category of good (what is good). The quest for a better life may continue to imply material prosperity but it may also inhibit economic growth. The question of migration, however, will always be linked with the quest for better, for the best life in the sense of being divinely advised in one's mobility.

Conversion narratives are scholarly examples of identity expressions and negotiations of identity. Narratives of PRC Christians in Budapest reflecting on identity verbalize three major discourses: a cosmopolitan discourse, a diaspora discourse and a settlement discourse. All three are verbalized while interpreting the personal migration story and the person's relationship with belief in Jesus Christ.

A Cosmopolitan Discourse

Cosmopolitan discourses[58] are about expressions of both social and spiritual freedom, and they properly fit the paradigm of 'lifestyle migration'.[59] It is about a group of successful business women and men who, after confirming belief in Jesus Christ as the primary force in shaping their identity, see themselves as citizens of the whole world (reducing it to urban life) who are free to move and act as their God asks them to. This might imply moving from Hungary to Canada and then back to Europe again. For these people, goods and opportunities that are enjoyed elsewhere are no longer out of reach. They fit the observation that religious organizations respond to rising but frustrating expectations by 'emphasizing moral discipline and the possibilities of divinely provided prosperity. In addition, global economic integration involves ties that combine religion with business, as in the case of business leaders serving on church boards, pastors making money from international tourism, and faith-based humanitarian organizations starting micro enterprises'.[60] These people belong to a steadily growing diverse global network, some of them having close ties with so-called 'boss Christians',[61] and some of them, as the example below shows, staying on a more individual level:

---

[58] The concept applied in the same broadness as in Steven Vertovec and Robin Cohen (eds), *Conceiving Cosmopolitanism: Theory, Context and Practice* (Oxford: OUP, 2002).

[59] Michaela Benson and Karen O'Reilly, *Lifestyle Migration: Studies in Migration and Diaspora* (Farnham, UK: Ashgate, 2009).

[60] Wuthnow, *Boundless Faith*, 92-93.

[61] This is a fast-growing Christian community in the coastal areas of the PRC that was formed by successful entrepreneurs who, through direct or indirect migration histories, accumulated significant wealth and for whom investing in church buildings, etc. is also a form of entrepreneurship; they are also agents of democracy through capitalist management practices. See Nanlai Cao, 'Boss Christians: The Business of Religion in the Wenzhou Model of Christian Revival', in *The China Journal,* 59 (January, 2008), 63-87; Cunfu Chen, 'The Emergence of a New Type of Christians in China Today', in *Review of Religious Research,* 46.2 (2004), 183-200.

> I arrived in Budapest ten years ago. Now I work in the Asia Centre. Last year I have met Pastor X. who invited me to church. I didn't want to come but I had problems in my marriage. My husband left me for another woman. I came to see this church. I came with a sister who also works in the Asia Centre. People here were very friendly and warm-hearted. I came more often. Some months ago they organized a trip to France. A famous Chinese speaker was there. I decided to go there… and there it happened. I gave my life to Jesus. I don't know how to say… I am so happy… now I read the Bible every day… I think I can manage even alone. In October there will be a trip to Israel and I am going to be baptized there… you know, in the Jordan where Jesus was also baptized… I really hope that I can be there. (Mrs W.)

The growing number of PRC students in Hungary[62] dominantly shapes the cosmopolitan discourse as well. Some of them envision their future as successful, educated people; others would like to become missionaries. Physical space is not the higher priority in making choices. It is the attitude of 'we pray about it and wait to see how God leads us' which implies openness towards migration/mobility.

> After having spent six years in a Hungarian school, two years ago I went to study at the International Christian School of Budapest.[63] This school changed my life. The teachers are Christians and are really examples for us. The atmosphere is very good. For long time I wanted to become a successful businessman but now I am thinking about going to a Bible College. I don't know. Let's pray and see what God says. Maybe I will become a missionary one day. (Mr L., a 12th grade student.)

The pattern however is the same: a continuous search for meaning which is linked with open-ended migration trajectories and a continuous engagement in the affairs of Christianity by belonging to Christian communities. The question of how Christian identity (religion) intersects with economics and politics, which are the dominant economic narratives fitting into the cosmopolitan discourse, needs to be given more attention. Neo-liberal practices and evangelical faith do not necessarily exclude one another. The Chinese dimension is there within the cosmopolitan discourses but the burden for China and the Chinese people is not bigger than the burden for North America and the people there, or the burden for any other specific area of the world. It is a discourse which conceives of Christian identity in terms of being at home on this globe and feeling responsible for the 'future of the world', and therefore actively engaged in shaping the future of Christianity in its larger context.

---

[62] Most of the PRC students study economics and have chosen to study in Hungary because of relatives living in the country, e.g. in 2008, 836 students from China started their studies in Hungarian higher education institutions, most of them in Budapest – see Balázs Danka, *Migration in Higher Education: A Research Study of Third Country Nationals Studying in Hungarian Higher Education* (Budapest: Bevándorlási és Állampolgársági Hivatal, 2010).

[63] The school was opened in 1994 with the purpose of serving the needs of the children of international missionaries'. The school prepares its students for education in North American colleges and universities: www.icsbudapest.org/#/welcome/icsb

A Diaspora Discourse

The diaspora discourse of PRC Christians in Hungary connects with at least three types of diaspora rhetoric:

1. China's diaspora rhetoric which envisions the new PRC migrants as patriots who in their scatteredness work hard and significantly contribute to increase China's international success, both in economic and cultural terms. In this case, nationalism and migration go hand-in-hand.[64]
2. The missionary enterprise which uses methodological nationalism and diaspora terminology[65] fits this rhetoric perfectly. It addresses the patriotic devotion and promises that the mix of Christianity and patriotism make to cause China to take its proper place on the international stage, both in terms of economics and culture.
3. The third type of rhetoric envisions one single Christian Chinese overseas community, one single Chinese diaspora[66] through which a Christian China and a Christian world can be envisioned. It is about migrations and the interpretations of migration stories through which it becomes clear how God uses the Chinese diaspora to 'bless China and the Chinese people'.

A major dissonance within the rhetoric, however, is the question of the place and role of China and within it the role of the Communist Party within this enterprise. In order to maintain harmony, the Christian Chinese diaspora discourse usually aspires to an apolitical attitude. This discourse is popular among PRC Christians in Hungary because it both legitimizes migration, not only in terms of patriotism but also in terms of divine guidance, and it also legitimizes a possible return to PRC even in the case of financial failure. Most of the believers, however, translate their faith in acts of patriotism for China. The aspirations of becoming a boss Christian, a missionary in China or among Chinese elsewhere on this globe, or simply being the one who evangelizes the family members left at home, a normal Christian who 'witnesses about Christ', are present in conversion narratives and expressed during prayer meetings. The love for China, the utmost patriotism, is strengthened through faith in Jesus Christ. It is the desire of these Christians to make Chinese people – compatriots – understand that Christianity is not a western religion (although, by mistake, it has been made into one) but belongs to China and is as Chinese as rice, noodles and tea.

---

[64] Nyíri, 'Expatriating Is Patriotic?'.

[65] Enoch Wan, *Diaspora Missiology: Theory, Methodology, and Practice* (Portland, OR: Western Seminary, 2011); Wonsuk Ma and S. Hun Kim, *Korean Diaspora and Christian Mission* (Eugene, OR: Regnum, 2011).

[66] Critically looked at by Laurence J. Ma and Carolyn Cartier (eds), *The Chinese Diaspora: Space, Place, Mobility and Identity* (Lanham, MD: Rowman & Littlefield, 2003); Adam McKeown, 'Conceptualizing Chinese Diasporas, 1842-1949', in *The Journal of Asian Studies*, 58 (2011), 306-37.

> God has big plans for China. Do you think it is by coincidence that there are so many Chinese all round the world? God will change the world through Chinese people. Through those who serve and love the Lord. Silently and powerfully. God loves China. We have a Chinese heart as we sing.[67] China has a future. God calls Chinese people to serve Him. (Mr L.)

The discourse grants a sense of 'being at home all over the world' – which is different from the cosmopolitan discourse that being at home is conditioned by the overall presence of Chinese Christian communities. It is this rhetoric which appeals to the middlemen mentality:

> We are here like a big family although we are not brothers and sisters in a biological sense. But we are brothers and sisters in Christ and this is very important. You may travel to Jerusalem, you will find a Chinese Church, you may go to Africa, and Chinese Christians are there.

The idea of creating the sense of one big family, one Chinese community worldwide. is a powerful rhetoric which can be used for many purposes. Diaspora theologies are always based on a collective understanding of the migration experience, and they always call for the translation of the understanding into concrete deeds for the well-being of the motherland. Sufferings of all kinds – including becoming victims of xenophobia – are interpreted within the diaspora discourse as meaningful and even unavoidable.

A Settlement Discourse

There is a small group of PRC Christians in Hungary who, after spending more than ten to fifteen (in some exceptional cases even twenty) years in the country, opt for permanent residence in Hungary. The reasons behind making such a decision are various – mixed marriages, the feeling of not being able to move further to the West or having lost the China they left behind[68] – are but some of them. Informants do acknowledge a sense of 'I love Hungary' but these statements were usually followed also by stories recalling problems and difficulties of living in Hungary. Most of the stories belonging to this discourse talk about being stuck in Hungary more than about an enthusiastic choice of the country. Here again, however, the search for meaning plays an important role. Being a PRC Christian in

[67] The speaker refers to one of the songs composed by Xiao Min, a Henan-born woman who became well-known both within and outside China by having composed more than 1,500 songs (in spite of having only a junior high level education, as stressed by informants) which link patriotism and Christian belief. Most of the songs have already been translated into English as well, and are used to address also those members of the Chinese Diaspora who no longer speak Chinese.

[68] PRC migrants who spend several years outside the PRC without spending considerable time there complain about the loss of China. 'China is changing so fast. If you are here a few years and you go back, you find a different China from the one you left behind. People change as well.' (Mrs L.)

Hungary means trying to relate to Hungarians and becoming witnesses to Jesus Christ even among people who respond with hostility:

> Well, you know I have a Hungarian lady who cleans our home and takes care of our children and I have employed two Gypsy ladies. They are doing their job quite well. Of course, I see that there are problems with the Gypsies in the city but I am a Christian. Jesus talked to Samaritans as well. The colour of your skin… is that what matters? (Mr T.)

Informants note the difficulty of creating contacts with Hungarian-speaking Christians. According to them, the major problem is that of language. To go beyond superficial contacts, one needs to be able to understand each other's language. This observation, however, is questioned in the case of those young PRC Christians who have no trouble communicating in Hungarian yet still do not have contact with Hungarian-speaking Christians. Becoming settled in Hungary as a PRC Christian means maintaining one's Christianity primarily through Mandarin-speaking communities. Efforts to mix with non-Mandarin communities are sporadic and take place mainly outside the so-called historic churches. The settlement rhetoric of PRC Christians in Hungary shows a willingness to contribute to the well-being of the country; it also expresses the inability to translate this willingness. The settlement discourse is best conceived at the level of personal life stories. Whether the settlement discourse will be displaced by the diaspora discourse or conceived under minority or diversity discourses goes beyond the scope of this study.

'Hungarians'

Identifying the Christian Hungarian actor within the Chinese Christians' LandScape in Hungary implies a set of research questions rather than research results. The Chinese Christians' presence in Hungary is rather neglected by Hungarian-speaking Christian communities and churches. Sporadic, mainly functional, contacts have been established as in the case of the above-mentioned Reformed Church in the eighth district of Budapest. Hungarian-speaking Christian communities, especially those belonging to the so-called historic churches, do not seem to be interested in relationships with non-Hungarian migrant Christians. Language problems are often a good excuse to avoid contact, but that is not a satisfactory answer to the lack of interest in establishing contacts with non-Hungarian-speaking communities. The issue is much more complex. A point of departure for further research might be the hypothesis which states that, in the case of Hungarian-speaking Christians, especially those belonging to the so-called historic churches, the ethnic element and the Christian element often go together, and this identity formation, being influenced by political forces,[69] stimulates relatedness to everything which can be labelled as Hungarian and neglects attention to anything which cannot be labelled as Hungarian. International contacts are by definition sought in trans-border ties and not within the territory of the country. Being a Christian means being a Hungarian Christian rather than being a Christian in Hungary. Relating to the framework of world Christianity talk, this implies representing the Hungarian sectors within it. The same dynamics could be observed in the case of Chinese Christians, envisioning a Chinese Christianity that calls primarily for contacts with other Chinese Christians worldwide rather than contacts with non-Chinese-speaking Christian communities of the same locality. These dynamics have much to do with the importance given to the concept of the nation-state and the nation within theology as well, and with the question of how migration and ethnic diversity are being conceived through the nation-state lens.

There is a paradox in celebrating China and China-relations both economically and culturally in terms of institutions, projects and the like while neglecting the people who, to a certain extent, embody those relationships at the larger level of society. This paradox goes even deeper when it comes to Chinese Christians. One of the reasons for this phenomenon might be the acknowledgement by the so-called historic churches of any other form of Christianity but a European one, implying Christianity negotiated in terms of denominations.

Growing post-1989 xenophobia might be the third entry to reflect on Chinese-Hungarian Christian relationships. In Hungary, 'the public debate on foreigners has been dominated by negative and stereotypical imagery, and the rhetorical deterritorialization of "the nation" has become widely accepted across the political spectrum. These factors have contributed to the development and preservation in Hungary of a more monolithically xenophobic public discourse than in other countries'.[70] Surveys show that Chinese and Arab migrants are still the least welcome in Hungary.[71] Christians and Christian organizations do not seem to raise their voices very actively against this situation.[72] The role of Chinese migrants in society is often compared with the role of the Jews at the beginning of the twentieth century: they are needed but they are not loved.[73] By the time research among Christians had started, the Reformed minister who offered his community's building for Chinese Christians pointed to a series on the

---

[69] Sabrina Ramet, *Whose Democracy? Nationalism, Religion, and the Doctrine of Collective Rights in Post-1989 Eastern Europe* (Lanham, MD: Rowman & Littlefield, 1997).
[70] Nyíri, 'Xenophobia in Hungary', 3.
[71] Anikó Bernát, *Idegenellenesség Magyarországon és a visegrádi országokban* (Budapest: TÁRKI, 2008): www.publikon.hu/application/essay/480_1.pdf
[72] In recent years, religious organizations have started to give much attention to the question of Roma people in Hungary. Here too xenophobia is a major issue.
[73] Dorottya Nagy, 'Feuerdrachen: Chinesische Gemeinschaften in Mittel- und Osteuropa', in *China Heute,* 29.4 (2010), 235-45. It would be an interesting research question to see whether xenophobia and anti-Semitism share similar psychological roots.

Chinese peril published in the weekly newspaper issued by Hungarian nationalists and freely sent to Reformed churches in Hungary.[74] The minister, who already had firsthand experience of Chinese Christians in his own church, and who talked positively about them in the sense of community, commented that the idea of the yellow peril was the other side of the same coin. In 2012, the new minister of the same community valued the community life of the Chinese Christians and said that, according to him, neither party desired co-operation – it was all about parallel lives.

A final possibility for investigating how Hungarian Christians could link with the LandScape is to see whether there was any interaction between non-historical Hungarian-speaking churches and Chinese communities. This question connects back to the role of the missionaries as migrants in shaping new constellations of Christianity in post-1989 Hungary. In a 2010 newsletter, Pastor Graham King from the Bible Speaks Church (*Magyarországi Biblia Szól Egyház*[75]) reported that one of the Chinese churches in Budapest invited him to preach in their church on a monthly basis. They also started Christian training among Chinese Christians. Lack of translators caused the ministry to cease in 2011. It seems that Hungarian Christians from the so-called non-denominational communities, due to transnational missionary networks, find it easier to establish contacts with Chinese Christians.

Art in a Part of the LandScape

The present article set the Chinese Christians' presence in Hungary in the analytical unit of Christianity worldwide. The social space Chinese Christians inhabit in Hungary is one which – paraphrasing Okólski and Grabowska-Lusińska[76] – continues to be created in the transition from a socialist to a capitalist system where excess demand for labour and over-employment are replaced by surpluses of labour and shortages of jobs, and where market forces determine the mechanisms of the selection of workers and reallocate labour across enterprises, occupations, sectors and regions. This is how new spaces and new attraction poles appeared in Hungary as well, inviting migrants (among whom are a remarkable number of PRC

---

[74] The newspaper published Imre Kőrösi's, *Sárga veszedelem, avagy a politika zsoldosai* (Budapest: Polgárok és Polgármesterek szövetsége az élhető Magyarországért Párt, 2005).

[75] The church was officially registered with a hundred Hungarian members in 1991 as a result of an 'internationally diverse team of missionaries', who arrived in Hungary in 1990 from France, Finland and the USA, and operated under the auspices of the Greater Grace World Outreach (a Baltimore, Maryland, based missionary organization having more than five hundred churches in sixty countries). The church 'does not discriminate on race, colour, gender, religion or ethnic background; we welcome every single visitor without conditions or requirements: www.bibliaszol.hu/en/about-us (accessed 12th February 2012).

[76] Marek Okólski and I. Grabowska-Lusińska, 'Introduction', in Dušan Drbohlav, Ágnes Hárs, Izabela Grabowska-Lusińska (eds), *Experiencing Immigration: Comparative Analysis of the Czech Republic, Hungary and Poland* (IDEA Working Papers: 14, 2009), 9.

migrants) to inhabit these spaces. The creation of the space, however, does not mean that religion and migration follow the same pattern and activate market theories to understand the phenomenon. The market metaphor itself might be 'seductive in the case of post-socialist Europe, where capitalism has flooded into an economic vacuum to create an emerging global market simultaneously with the florescence of religious freedom and a multitude of religious possibilities ranging from orthodox to new age'.[77] The seduction, however, should be withstood by asking questions which may lead researchers into adventures one could not enter into, either with market theory tools or with methodological nationalism.

The case of Chinese Christians' presence in Hungary, examined from the perspective of Christianity worldwide, calls researchers' attention to the fact that, behind the global-local configurations of religion – in this case, Christianity – there are human beings ultimately concerned, and also agents of change through migration. Human choices, forced or freely taken, greatly influence the artefact, the visibility of human constellations at any given time and in any part of the world. The human agent as contextual and context-making, ever so central in humanities, social sciences and theology, has been the focus of this article which has demonstrated that there are viable alternatives of analytic units which go beyond methodological nationalism, church-sect typology and the terminology of new religious movements.

By pointing to complexity and diversity, it offers a modest invitation to interdisciplinary dialogue on religion and migration also within Hungarian studies with the agenda of keeping the principles of complexity and diversity alive at the level of academic research. After all, becoming a part is always an art.

---

[77] Csordas, *Transnational Transcendence*, 2.

MILLENNIAL ESCHATOLOGY, REVIVAL AND MISSION TO THE JEWS IN THE HUNGARIAN KINGDOM

Ábrahám Kovács

Mission to the Jews has always been a challenge for the Christian church. It has become a hotly debated topic today especially after the Holocaust when most of the Christian churches failed to do their Christian duty to serve the needy, the marginalised and the persecuted. The aim of this paper is not to investigate various theological Christian arguments for or against mission to the Jews, but to show and assess how Jewish mission took place in Hungary due to Scottish Evangelicalism transplanted by the Calvinism of the Free Church of Scotland into Central Europe's largest country, the Hungarian Kingdom, during the late nineteenth and early twentieth centuries. This research paper seeks to point out how eschatology played a decisive factor in prompting the staunch Calvinist of Scotland to evangelise not only the 'lost sheep of Israel', but also the native fellow Hungarian Calvinist who were perceived by them as non-Christians. The remarkable missionary fervour of the same sending body, the Free Church of Scotland, played a key role in establishing the Evangelical Alliance, and was also anxious to fulfil the Edinburgh 1910 mandate. As Andrew F. Walls also pointed out during my personal talks with him, it is worth paying attention to their missionary endeavour which produced one of the most intriguing mission enterprises, mission to the Jews carried out not by missionary societies but originally by a national church, the Church of Scotland.

The origins of Scottish interest in mission to the Jews in some respects differed from other mission activities of the Church of Scotland. Don Chambers argues that the Scottish Mission to the Jews 'stems from a different mental world from that of the urban mission of Thomas Chalmers, the Indian mission of John Inglis, or the Gaelic mission of George Baird'.[1] He pointed out that, in contrast to other schemes of the Church of Scotland, the roots of this mission originated in a grassroots-level interest in the Jews. He is right in this assertion since many schemes of the Church of Scotland, such as the Church Extension Scheme and the Foreign Mission Scheme,

[1] Don Chambers, 'Mission and Party in the Church of Scotland, 1810-1843' (PhD dissertation, University of Cambridge, 1971), 43.

were initiated by pastors of eminence.[2] However, the Jewish scheme was different.

As early as 1810, the *Edinburgh Christian Instructor* contained regular articles on world Jewry and informed its readers on the activities of London Society.[3] The *Scottish Missionary Register* in the 1820s and the *Presbyterian Review* also published detailed articles on the work of the London Jewish Society from its inception.[4] The Jewish mission enterprise of the church began with laymen in Glasgow and was taken over by prominent Evangelical clergymen.[5] These laymen were the merchants, intellectuals and industrialists of that rapidly growing city. Consequently, the Jewish mission was to come into being as an initiative of urban rather than rural Evangelicalism. The Glaswegians, especially the bourgeoisie, viewed Britain's role in trading as God's providential gift, as well as a pressing responsibility to evangelise the world. One of them talked in this vein: 'Now let those who have any belief in *God's providence,* tell us if there is no discovery of *designing wisdom in the selection of this land as the main depository of Protestant Christianity* [italics added]'.[6] Another Glaswegian appealed to the ancient Scottish interest in the Jewish people. He directed the attention of the readers of the *Church of Scotland Magazine* to the fact that a century earlier the Scots had fasting days particularly set for the conversion of the Jewish people, and he expressed, 'We trust that the period is not far away, when the Assembly may again appoint a fast day on behalf of Israel.'[7] In addition to the long neglected 'fast-day argument', we may point to an idiosyncratic fact that it was a long historical tradition in the Church of Scotland to pray for the conversion of the Jews as a part of the regular church service.[8]

For many Evangelicals, the revival of the church and the Jewish mission were linked. One of the greatest revivalist preachers of that time, Robert M.

---

[2] *Home and Foreign Missionary Record of the Church of Scotland*, Vol. I (Edinburgh: John Johnstone, 1843), iv-v. The first volume of the *Record* knows of five schemes: Education, Propagation of the gospel in India (Foreign Mission Scheme, 1824), Church Extension Scheme (1828), Colonial Scheme (1836), while the fifth scheme was mission to the Jews.
[3] Shirley A. Fraser, *The Origins of Scottish Interest in Mission to the Jews* (Aberdeen, UK: Gilcomston South Church, 1990), 7. See also Chambers, 'Mission and Party', 46.
[4] 'Germany: London Jewish Society', in *Scottish Missionary and Philanthropic Register*, 6.2 (1825), 71. Furthermore, in the same volume, see also 3, 23, 352, 356, 359, 504, 506, 548; cf. 'Report Propagation of the Christian Gospel to the Jews', in *Presbyterian Review and Religious Journal*, 4.15 (1833), 426-33.
[5] Chambers, 'Mission and Party', 47.
[6] 'The Next Assembly', in *Church of Scotland Magazine* (hereafter *CofSM*), 5.52 (1838), 138.
[7] 'The Last General Assembly', in *Church of Scotland Magazine*, 5. 55 (1838), 245-48 (246).
[8] *A Directory for the Publique Worship of God Throughout the Three Kingdoms of England, Scotland, and Ireland. Together with an Ordinance of Parliament for the Taking Away of the Book of Common Prayer: and for Establishing and Observing of This Present Directory Throughout the Kingdom of England, and Dominion of Wales* (London: G.M. and I. F. for the Company of Stationers, 1645), 10.

M'Cheyne[9] (1813-1843) indicated that, 'the "revival" proper followed upon, rather than led to, the inauguration of Jewish Scheme'.[10] In the *Edinburgh Christian Witness* he observed: 'Is it not a remarkable fact, that in the very year in which God put it into the hearts of the church to send a mission of kind enquiry to Israel... God visited his people in Scotland by giving them bread in a way unknown since the days of Cambuslang and Moulin.'[11] The first overtures in support of a national church-initiated Jewish mission came from the industrial areas of the Clyde in 1838.[12] At the same time, the *Scottish Guardian* published several articles on the issue of Jewish mission.[13] These initiatives of laymen were taken up by several members of the Evangelical clergy, the most fervent being the Rev. John Lorimer of Glasgow[14] and the Rev. Robert Candlish of Edinburgh.[15] Lorimer brought a 'Memorial for the establishment of a mission to the Jews' to the attention of the General Assembly, written by a Glaswegian merchant, Robert Wodrow. The motion was unanimously adopted by the 1838 General Assembly.[16] This was followed by the appointment of the first Jewish Committee[17] during the 1838 General Assembly that included two sub-committees: one in Glasgow, the other in Edinburgh.[18]

The other schemes had already been in existence, and mission to the Jews was the last scheme to appear on the mission stage of the church. It was a decidedly Evangelical initiative, and the atmosphere of Evangelical

---

[9] I. Hamilton, 'M'Cheyne, Robert Murray', in Nigel M. de S. Cameron (ed), *Dictionary of Scottish Church History and Theology* (Edinburgh: T. & T. Clark, 1993), 504-05.

[10] Chambers, 'Mission and Party', 55. n. 45. Cf. Anne-Marie Kool, *God Moves in a Mysterious Way: The Hungarian Protestant Foreign Mission Movement 1756-1951* (Zoetermeer, Netherlands: Uitgeverij Boekencentrum B.V., 1993), 99.

[11] Robert M. M'Cheyne, 'Revival', in *Edinburgh Christian Witness*, 23 (May 1840), 3.

[12] National Archives of Scotland, formerly Scottish Record Office (hereafter *SRO*) *SRO*, CH 1/2/174., index. Greenock, Hamilton, Dumbarton and Glasgow Presbyteries sent separate overtures to 1838 General Assembly. Cited by Chambers, 'Mission and Party', 47. n. 20.

[13] *Scottish Guardian*, 8th February 1838, 48; 12th February 1838, 53; 2nd April 1838, 110; 30th April 1838, 142.

[14] John Gordon Lorimer (1804-1868) Minister of the Free Church of Scotland. He was the second son of Robert Lorimer, a 'Disruption divine'. James A. Wylie, *Disruption Worthies: A Memorial of 1843* (Edinburgh: Grange Publishing Works, 1881), 341.

[15] Henry Wellwood Moncrieff, 'Candlish, Robert Smith', in *Disruption Worthies*, 139-46. Robert Candlish (1806-1873) Evangelical minister of the Free Church, Edinburgh, and professor of Divinity, New College, Edinburgh.

[16] William Wingate, 'Reminiscences of Mission Work in Hungary', in *The Messenger and Missionary Report*, 3.2 (1st February 1878), 33-34 (33). See also 'Overtures relative to the Conversion of the Jews', in Supplementary Number of the *Edinburgh Christian Instructor*, containing a Digest of the Proceedings of the General Assembly, 1838, with notes and observations, in Edinburgh *Christian Instructor*, New Series 1. Supplementary Number (1838), 4-6 (4).

[17] This name sounds unfortunately misleading as it was a Committee for the Conversion of the Jews. However, by convention we are obliged to use this form of citation, 'Jewish Committee', meaning the mission board for Jewish conversion.

[18] 'Overtures Relative to the Conversion of the Jews', 4-6; See also David Brown, *Life of the late John Duncan*, 2nd rev. edn (Edinburgh: Edmonston & Douglas, 1872), 280-81. Brown is mistaken as he dated 1837 for the inception of the scheme.

excitement and the press propaganda pertaining to the Jewish Scheme alienated the Moderate leaders from immediate participation.[19] The Evangelicals' participation in the scheme was weighty. They greatly outnumbered the Moderates who had only two people on the Committee appointed by the 1838 Assembly to deal with the overtures.[20] Nonetheless, this did not mean that the Moderates were reluctant to join the Jewish mission. They also carried on the Jewish mission scheme after the Disruption in spite of the fact that most of their missionaries adhered to the Free Church of Scotland. One may wonder how mission to the Jews sprang up in Scotland where the presence of Jewish people was at a very low ebb in comparison with Hungary. Nonetheless, it is a well-known fact that modern Evangelicalism was and is the spiritual inheritor of Puritanism. It is the Free Kirk people's eschatology which was responsible for stirring interest to evangelise the Jewish people.

Since the earliest days of the Puritans, such elements as the conversion of the Jews, and the 'fullness of the Gentiles' gave rise to various millenarian ideas.[21] Allusion was made to the fact that the Scots always prayed for the Jews according to their liturgy. In the Westminster Assembly's Larger Catechism, the answer to question 191 declares: 'We pray that the kingdom of sin and Satan may be destroyed, the gospel propagated throughout the world, the Jews called, the fullness of the Gentiles brought in…'[22] The Directory for the Public Worship of God also holds a similar view, urging the ministers to pray publicly 'for the propagation of the Gospel and Kingdom of Christ to all Nations, for the conversion of the Jews, the fullnesse (sic!) of the Gentiles, the fall of the Antichrist, and the hastening of the second coming of our Lord'.[23] Stanley J. Grenz argues that the Puritans held a post-millennial view expressed by Daniel Whitby, a Puritan divine, declaring that the millennium is not the reign of the people raised from death 'but the Church flourishing gloriously for a thousand years after the conversion of the Jews and the flowing in of all nations to them thus converted to the Christian faith'.[24] Mel Scult came

---

[19] Brown, *Life of the late John Duncan*, 56.

[20] *SRO*, CH 1/1/86, 85, cited by Chambers, 55. The Committee consisted of ten ministers and eleven laymen. David Brown states in his book that a committee was appointed by the Assembly of 1837. The statement does not stand. The author has checked the materials and the date is 1838. Cf. Brown, *Life of Late John Duncan*, 280.

[21] Charles L. Chaney, *The Birth of Mission in America* (South Pasadena, CA: William Carey Library 1976), 271-74; Mel Scult, 'Millennial Expectations and Jewish Liberties', in *Studies in Judaism in Modern Times*, 2 (Leiden, Netherlands: E.J. Brill, 1978), 32-34. See also for theologies of mission, S.H. Rooy, *The Theology of Mission in Puritan Tradition* (Grand Rapids, MI: 1965).

[22] For a general discussion, see also Ian H. Murray, *The Puritan Hope* (Edinburgh: Banner of Truth, 1971).

[23] *A Directory for the Publique Worship*, 10.

[24] Daniel Whitby, *Paraphrase and Commentary on the New Testament*, cited by Stanley J. Grenz, *The Millennial Maze: Sorting Out Evangelical Options* (Downers Grove, IL: IVP Academic, 1992), 69.

to the conclusion that belief in the national conversion of the Jews between 1660 and 1750 was commonly shared by all English people including John Locke and Sir Isaac Newton.[25] This conviction, named by him as 'conversionist belief', lingered on through centuries, affecting Evangelicalism. When Joseph Frey came on the stage of Jewish mission, Evangelicalism imbued by the old Puritan agenda turned with renewed interest to the conversion of the Jews. However, Frey took a different stance on millennialism and opted for pre-millennialism that was clearly not as widespread as its counterpart.

Post-millennialists, the majority of nineteenth-century Evangelicals in Britain, expected the millennium to be attained through the preaching of the gospel.[26] They believed that transition to this stage would be smooth, and only after this period of prosperity for the church would Christ come again.[27] In opposition to this, pre-millennialists believed that the present age would climax with a period of tribulation before Christ's second coming, which is not in the distant future but can be expected imminently. The reign of Christ, who is physically present, would begin with the judgement of the Antichrist and the resurrection of the righteous followed by the millennium.[28] During the *parousia*, Satan would be bound and an era of righteousness would commence on the earth. After the millennium, Satan would be loosed to lead a brief rebellion.[29] Finally, the millennium closes with the general resurrection, the last judgement and the eternal state. Post- and pre-millennialist views gave rise to discussions; however, Evangelicals in Scotland managed to maintain a careful and peaceful balance between them.

The leading Evangelical voices involved in Jewish mission in the (Free) Church of Scotland adhered to the post-millennialism of Puritan times. John Duncan (1796-1870),[30] the first missionary to the Jews in Hungary, believed that the conversion of the Jews was dependent on the outpouring of the Holy Spirit, which was about to happen at his time as world history shifted into the final events. In a sermon preached in 1839, he articulated his belief that the future restoration of the Jews would be universal and permanent.[31] He thus believed in the 'national' conversion of the Jews as a

---

[25] Scult, 'Millennial Expectations and Jewish Liberties', 53.

[26] Roger H. Martin, *Evangelicals United: Ecumenical Stirrings in Pre-Victorian Britain 1795-1830* (Metuchen, NJ: Scarecrow, 1983), 30.

[27] Loraine Boetter, *Millennium* (Philadelphia, PA: Reformed, 1957), 4.

[28] Millar Erickson, *Contemporary Options in Eschatology: A Study of the Millennium* (Grand Rapids, MI: Baker Books, 1977), 91-92.

[29] David Brown, *Christ's Second Coming: Will it be Premillennial?* (Edinburgh: Johnstone & Hunter, 1849), 399-420.

[30] S. Isbell, 'Duncan, John', in Cameron, *Dictionary of Scottish Church History and Theology*, 262-63.

[31] J.S. Sinclair, *Rich Gleanings After the Vintage from 'Rabbi' Duncan with Biographical Sketch*, 2nd impr. edn (London: Chas. J. Thynne & Jarvis, 1925), 330.

people as the early Puritans did.[32] He thought that the Jews 'feel themselves drawn especially to British Christianity (Evangelicalism) since it was tolerant, and defended civil and religious liberty'.[33] Furthermore, he held the belief that the fullness of the Gentiles could not be completed because of the 'continuance of blindness to a part of Israel'.[34] Therefore he reasoned that it was evident that the mission to the Jews had to be a priority, a *primus inter pares*. Duncan's theological views were heirs to the Puritans in other respects as well. For him, the time he lived in was 'pregnant with mighty change'. The events of the contemporary world were linked with prophecies from the Bible; for instance, he perceived the decline of Ottoman military power and stated that the 'lune of Islam is rapidly decrescent; and all things portend that the time when the fullness of the Gentiles shall come in is nigh – even at the door'.[35] Also he believed that the 'decrepitude' of Popery, and 'idolatrous' religions of India and China, were speedily to fall and all these would hasten the national conversions of the Jews. Interestingly, Duncan never sketched a scheme of detailed prophecy like Alexander Keith[36] but dealt with the conversion of the Jewish more from 'the promise' aspect – that God would bless those who reached out to the Jews.[37]

By 1841, the Church of Scotland established a missionary post in (Buda)Pest.[38] The main object of the Scottish Mission in Hungary was to convert the Jews. Duncan was aware that Protestantism in Hungary at the time was of a kind that would impede the endeavour to proselytise Jews. He perceived Hungarian Calvinism as rationalist, and stated that political Protestantism was the major, decisive character of Hungarian religion, in marked contrast to the Scottish Evangelicalism with which Duncan was familiar. Although it was a fair observation, British Evangelicalism was

---

[32] A. Stuart Moody, *Recollections of the Late John Duncan, LL.D.* (Edinburgh: Edmonston & Douglas, 1872), 205.

[33] Brown, *Life of the Late John Duncan,* 438. It cites the speech of Duncan at the General Assembly of the Free Church of Scotland in 1862.

[34] John Duncan, 'Addresses in the Free Church Assembly on the Mission to the Jews in Hungary, and on the Christian Future of the Jewish People, 25 May, 1857', in *Proceedings of the General Assembly of the Church of Scotland Held at Edinburgh, May 1857* (Edinburgh: James Nichol, 1857), 44-48. Cf. Sinclair, *Rich Gleanings*, 360.

[35] John Duncan, 'Addresses in the Free Church Assembly on the Mission to the Jews in Hungary, and on the Christian Future of the Jewish People, 21 May 1860', in *Proceedings of the General Assembly of the Church of Scotland Held at Edinburgh May, 1860* (Edinburgh: James Nichol, 1860), 39-42.

[36] Alexander Keith, *The Land of Israel According to the Covenant with Abraham, with Isaac, and with Jacob* (Edinburgh: William Whyte, 1843). Keith was far more preoccupied by producing a voluminous book on the 'physical restoration' of Israel to their land than giving a schedule for the events. The revivalist minister went into inordinate length with his description of the 'fertile land' giving the exact latitudes of the restored Israel's territory.

[37] A. Stuart Moody, *Recollections of the Late John Duncan, LL.D.*, 205.

[38] Historically, one speaks of Budapest only from 1873. However, to provide an easy orientation for the reader we signpost it as stated above in order to enable the reader make the text more readable.

also deeply imbued with imperialism where triumphalist political and cultural nationalism played a crucial role in the public consciousness. Nonetheless, it is correct to state that Hungarian Calvinism had nothing comparable with such a wide scale of fervent piety that could be found in Scottish Evangelicalism. Realising this, Duncan suggested that, in order to achieve the goal of Jewish evangelism, the Scottish Mission should at the same time seek the Evangelical revival of the Hungarian Protestant churches, both the Reformed and the Lutheran. This led the Mission to espouse as its second goal, directly related to the first, the reshaping of the Reformed faith in Hungary in the likeness of Scottish Calvinism. In setting this goal, the Mission hoped that future members of the revived Hungarian church would continue the mission to the Jews that the Scottish Mission had initiated. No wonder that, in the course of the Mission's history, this original concept came to be revised as the Mission, particularly under the influence of the first bursars, sought the revival of the Hungarian Reformed Church as a goal in itself. The bursary scheme came into being in 1863 and the first students arrived at New College, Edinburgh, in 1865. They were exposed to the piety and praxis of Scottish Evangelicalism which had made an indelible, positive impact on the spirituality, theology and practice on the largest central European Protestant Church, the Reformed Church of Hungary. It is less researched and known, but the impact of this Mission via its Hungarian, German, Slavic and Jewish converts reached other nationalities, and contributed to the emergence of not only the revival of traditional Protestant churches in historic Hungary but also to the emergence of the Baptists, Adventist and other Protestant churches of Croatia, Serbia, Partium and Transylvania within today's Romania and Slovakia.[39]

In the eyes of Scottish Evangelicals it was, of course, essential to the understanding of revival that a revived church would be a true mission church, but this was envisaged primarily in terms of home mission as Hungary was emerging as a modern state, especially after the Compromise with the Habsburg, Austrian Empire. As regards mission to the Jews, the Scottish Mission seemed to content itself, from the 1860s, with creating small circles of revivalist Hungarian Christians who could provide a warm and welcoming community for converted Jews. In this regard, the Mission's role in creating the German Affiliated congregation (1859-1863), and supporting it as a place of evangelical renewal in relation to the Pest Reformed Church at Széna tér[40] can be considered a positive achievement, as it nurtured a place where Jewish converts could find a Christian community that took its evangelical commitment seriously in the practice

[39] This is still an unexplored area. The collected but unpublished evidence of the authors shows the remarkable interconnections of various evangelical groups coming from diverse ethnic groups.

[40] Today it is called Kálvin tér (square) but at that time it was called Széna tér.

of home mission.[41] By the end of the 1870s, the Evangelical-Pietist alliance became strong through the congregation, Bethesda Hospital and colportage, though these activities fell short of a specific mission to the Jews.[42]

In the 1880s and 1890s, there was a conscious endeavour on the Mission's part to help the emerging home mission organizations in the Hungarian-speaking part of the Reformed Church. In fact, the YMCA, the Sunday School movement, evangelizations as such, Women's Guilds like the Lórántffy Women's circle and other home mission organizations sprang from the impetus the Hungarian Reformed Church received from their Scottish brothers and sisters. Consequently, the focus of the Mission swung towards initiating the revival of the Reformed churches of Hungary. However, the Scottish Mission never lost sight of its original intention, nor did it ever give up the hope of persuading the Hungarian Reformed Church to take up Jewish evangelism itself. A significant advance in this direction was achieved when an independent Hungarian home and foreign mission emerged from the 1900s, which began to show the first signs of conscious obligation to mission to the Jews. However, mission to the Jews was and remained mainly the concern of the Scottish Mission itself for the major part of the nineteenth century. Insofar as it was able to attract local support, it was through the members of the German-speaking Reformed congregation, who included Jewish converts.

To implant an awareness of mission to the Jews into the Hungarian Reformed missionary consciousness was not an easy task for the missionaries. Initially, there were three groups of people to carry out mission to the Jews: the colporteurs, the teachers in the Mission School aided by some members of the German-speaking congregation, and the bursars. The colporteurs were Jewish converts who participated in proselytising among their own people from the very outset of the Mission and contributed to its enterprise. Other Jewish converts, for instance, Adolf Lippner who served as a medical missionary, and again others who were not employed by the mission societies, also took part in Jewish evangelization in historic Hungary and even beyond. The second group who shared in mission work among the Jews consisted of the revivalists of the German-speaking congregation. The Jewish Committee decided to support the foundation of the congregation on condition that its members would participate in Jewish mission.[43]

The motive underpinning the Scots' involvement in mission activity was their millennial understanding of the gospel. The Free Church divines, as

---

[41] Ábrahám Kovács, *The History of the German-Speaking Reformed Affiliated Church of Budapest 1858-1869* (Dr Harsányi András Alapítvány Kiadványai, 10: Debrecen, Hungary: Fábián Nyomda, 2004).

[42] 'The History of the Free Church of Scotland's Mission to the Jews in Budapest and its Impact on the Reformed Church of Hungary 1841-1914', in *Studien zur interkulturellen Geschichte des Christentums, Vol. 140* (Frankfurt, Berlin, Bern, Oxford, Wien: Peter Lang, 2006).

[43] NLS, Dep. 298.251, fol. 442.

they were often referred to, as well as German Pietists like Professor Neander, believed that mission to the Jews was a basic task of the church.[44] Rudolf Koenig, who was the head of the Scottish Mission in Pest was a native German, and had Pietist views. He cited Neander's opinion that in Christian countries there ought to be no need for separate Jewish mission organizations, since Christian ministers and their congregations 'ought to be instruments for winning the Jews to the Truth'.[45] Koenig expressed his desire that Jewish mission should indeed be a church mission. He put it in these words: 'I can perceive a realization of this theory... and I may feel persuaded that, by enlightening the congregation on the nature and importance of Jewish mission, we may gradually hope to gain workers from them.'[46]

This statement illuminates why the Committee were willing to make an agreement with the German-speaking congregation in 1863. The contract made between the Scots and that congregation indicated the expectations of the Jewish Committee: 'It is the object of the Congregation as well as the Committee to give all moral aid and support to the Mission to the Jews, the Missionaries of the Committee while acting as vicar of the Reverend Superintendent.'[47] Theodor Biberauer, the chief elder of the affiliated congregation, giving thanks for the new alliance at the annual General Assembly of the Free Church of Scotland in May 1864, emphasized how beneficial the new agreement would be for the Jewish Mission: 'The formation of this congregation proved peculiarly helpful to the work of the Jewish Mission in that place, inasmuch as many Jews do regularly attend our services (of which there are three German and one English in every week), and as soon as they become enquirers they are kindly met and taken by the hand of some of our members, but more especially when they are baptized they do not remain to themselves, but are received with Christian love to the circle of the people of God, and are protected in a great measure against the fearful assaults and enquiries to which they are exposed from their brethren according to the flesh...'[48] The formal agreement was advantageous for the Scots because the congregation was mission-minded and showed promising signs of willingness to be involved in Jewish mission.[49] As the years passed, it remained, of course, a question as to what

[44] Jacob Gartenhaus, *Famous Hebrew Christians* (Grand Rapids, MI: Baker Books, 1979), 135-41. Neander was a Jewish convert who became a well-known professor of Church History at the University of Berlin.

[45] Rudolph Koenig, 'Work among the Jews at Pesth. Letter from the Rev. Mr Koenig', *FCofSMR*, 2. 22 (2nd May 1864), 512-14.

[46] Koenig, 'Work among the Jews at Pesth'.

[47] NLS, Dep. 298.251, fol. 442. Minutes of 17th November 1863.

[48] 'Conversion of the Jews, Theodor Biberauer's Speech', in *Proceedings of the General Assembly of the Church of Scotland Held at Edinburgh May, 1864* (Edinburgh: James Nichol, 1864), 30-31 (31).

[49] It is most revealing when one notices that they preferred the foundation of a hospital to their obtaining and building a church.

extent the involvement of the congregation in the Jewish Mission lived up to the expectation of the Committee.

Although, the Scottish Evangelicals were keen on implanting mission to the Jews into the heart of Hungarian Protestantism, it must be emphasized that it took a while for even the leading voices of German-speaking Pietists to respond to the Jewish Committee's appeal emerging from Scotland. Gradually, the Pietist teachers of the Mission School, who were also the most active members of the congregation and often not ethnic Hungarians, began to become involved in Jewish evangelism. By the early 1870s, the teachers' annual reports to the Edinburgh Committee included references to their progress in winning Jews by means of the education that the Mission School provided. It is clear, also, that they were supported in this work by some members of the Affiliated Church such as Theodor Biberauer and the Jewish converts who were not involved in the running of the School itself but had other missionary tasks. However, the Affiliated Church did not undertake any corporate responsibility for Jewish mission. Only its dominating Evangelical-Pietist leadership was involved in it, but not all their members were. This might be registered as a failure on the part of the Mission to seed its priority for the conversion of the Jews in the life of the German-speaking congregation as a whole that was designed to present a model of a true missionary congregation to the Hungarian Reformed Church. However, at the very same time it has to be stated that not all Scottish Evangelicals were interested in the conversion of the Jews but had other missionary priorities even from the Mission's outset in 1838. Therefore, the picture needs to be balanced carefully. It is better to state that mission to the Jews was, and always has been, a minor topic amidst other missionary enterprises, and the emerging Hungarian case was no exception.

The Scottish Mission in Budapest and all over the country had greater success, however, with the Hungarian bursars who, especially from the 1880s, showed some signs of awareness of the importance of Jewish evangelism. The bursars' main concern was the revival of their church along the lines of the Free Church as they had experienced it in Scotland, especially its organizations for home and foreign mission. Similar to that of British Evangelicals, patriotism was a driving concern for the Hungarians, and provided the context in which they sought to create a lively and renewed national, Hungarian church. Early bursars like Ferenc Balogh, Lajos Csiky, József Szalay and Ferenc Kecskeméti, who exhibited an interest in mission, were all primarily concerned with introducing home mission to the national body of the Reformed Church, but at the same time had exhibited an exceptional openness to other developing Protestant denominations like the Baptists, Adventists and the Nazarenes.[50] It was only

---

[50] László Ötvös, *Balogh Ferenc életműve* (Debrecen, Hungary: Lux, 1997). See also on the impact of the bursars in Debrecen, Ábrahám Kovács: 'Két kálvinista centrum egymásra

later that their minds turned to the necessity of Jewish mission, once the bursars saw the fruits of their efforts to root the concept of home mission among their fellow Hungarian Protestants. Not before 1882 do we find evidence of a bursar, István Fa, expressing definite interest in mission to the Jews. This was perhaps due to the fact that he was employed by the Mission as the first bursar and as a native Hungarian, to teach in the Mission School on a regular basis.[51] Yet his initiative was not, nor could it have been at this time, independent of the Mission. One must bear in mind that, at this time, both the Jewish converts and the members of the congregation were mainly German-speaking. This impeded communication between them and the Magyar-speaking Hungarians of the Reformed Church. It was only with the growing Magyarization of Jews, and of the home mission organizations, that Hungarian interest in mission to the Jews began to emerge separately from the work of the Scottish Mission itself from 1880 onwards.[52]

It is the 1880s and 1890s, therefore, when the first home mission organizations were taking root, that we find examples of a growing awareness of Jewish mission on the part of bursars. András Hamar was the first person to appear in the missionary reports as consciously undertaking mission to the Jews on his own initiative.[53] Lajos Szabó,[54] the first bursar from Transylvania, wrote an article in the provincial periodical of his church about the importance of Jewish mission, explaining the work of various Jewish missionary societies.[55] Never short of imaginative ideas, Aladár Szabó, suggested in an article in *Új óramutató* that Jewish converts should form separate churches: 'If the Jews convert in great number, organise them into a Hungarian Jewish-Christian church.'[56] This ran counter to the Scottish Mission's approach of seeking to integrate Jews into existing churches as part of the process of reviving them evangelically, though it must be acknowledged that he later seems to have modified his idea by integrating Jews into the Reformed Church, especially through the work of Bethany Christian Endeavour.[57]

---

találása: a skóciai ösztöndíj létrehozása', in *En Christo. Tanulmányok a 85 éves Dr Bütösi János tiszteletére* szerk. GAÁL Sándor (Debrecen, Hungary: Fábián Nyomda, 2004), 177-86.

[51] Record of the Committee to the Jews (hereafter *RCJ*) of 1882, Appendix IX, 33.

[52] Viktor Karády, *Zsidóság, polgárosodás, asszimiláció* (Budapest: Cserépfalvi, 1997), 164. Here Karády says that, between 1880 and 1910, the number of Hungarian-speaking Jews doubled.

[53] Andrew Moody, 'Report on the Conversion of the Jews to the General Assembly. Pesth Appendix IX', in *Proceedings of the General Assembly of the Free Church of Scotland Held at Edinburgh May* 1890 (Edinburgh: (n.p.), 1890), 1-28 (6).

[54] Richard Hörcsik, *History of the Hungarian Scholarship at Edinburgh*, HOR I (1985), fol. 23. Szabó was a bursar during 1887-1888 from Nagyenyed.

[55] Lajos Szabó, 'Miszsziói (sic!) törekvés a zsidók között', in *Erdélyi Protestáns Közlöny*, 40-42, 43 (1887 a, b), 355-57, 363-65, 373-74, 382-83.

[56] Aladár Szabó, 'Befejezés', in Szabó (ed), *Új Óramutató* (Budapest: Hornyánszky Viktor nyomdája, 1896), 148.

[57] Aladár Szabó, 'Befejezés', in Szabó (ed), *Új Óramutató* (Budapest: Hornyánszky Viktor nyomdája, 1896), 148.

It was not until the early twentieth century, however, that these first rudimentary signs of Hungarian Reformed outreach to the Jews began to take real shape in various home mission associations. From 1903, YMCA members regularly participated in spreading the good news to Jews by way of distributing tracts.[58] Their periodical, *Ébresztő*, often published articles on mission to the Jews in other parts of Europe, such as one about Ignátz Lichtenstein's life,[59] and also discussed Jewish mission in Hungary.[60] It should not be overlooked that the leaders of the Hungarian foreign mission organization, MEKMSz,[61] also carried out mission to the Jews since Gyula Fleischer, the secretary, and Árpád Szabady, the treasurer, of the organization were both Jewish converts.[62] They organised bi-weekly prayer meetings for the conversion of the Jews.[63] They also held a charity evening in 1906 for the support of the victims of the Russian pogroms.[64] Indeed, MEKMSz's aim was to reach out to 'the heathen' abroad and the Jews in Hungary.[65] In this way, the MEKMSz combined the focus on 'foreign mission' that is included in its title with home mission to the Jews in Hungary. Mór Vai, a member of the Budapest YMCA, argued that Hungarians had a mission to the Jews as well as the Muslims throughout the Balkan region.[66] But it was mission to the Jews in Hungary that became the distinguishing feature of the *Hold utca*[67]-related people who realised that a firm base in home mission was essential to a successful initiative in mission in other parts of the world, the two aspects being justified in the Biblical vision of the gospel being shared with both the Jews and Gentiles.[68]

A further indication of the growing awareness of mission to the Jews among Hungarians is found in the initiatives taken by some ministers. Webster noted in a report of 1904: 'It was a particular joy to find in various parts of Hungary that the ministers of the Reformed Church are awakening to a *sense of their responsibility towards the Jews* (Webster's italics). In one place I found that the minister had been the means of leading quite a

---

[58] There, the following are cited. *RCJ* of 1904, Appendix VIII, 9.

[59] 'Liechtenstein, Ignácz Rabbi', in *Ébresztő*, 7. 11 (1908), 175-76.

[60] Gyula Fleischer, 'A világmisszió', in *Ébresztő*, 4.8 (1904), 119-35 (131-32).

[61] Magyar Evangélikus Külmissziói Szövetség (Hungarian Lutheran Foreign Missionary Association).

[62] James T. Webster, 'Reviving Life in Hungary', *MRUFCofS*, 4.42 (June, 1904), 246-48. As for Szabady, Webster remarked that he was 'the brother-in-law of one of our mission school teachers' (page 248). Cf. Kool, *God Moves in Mysterious Ways,* 197. n. 28. Here, Kool cites the list of officials in MEKMSz, which included Fleischer.

[63] 'Külső Misszió. A zsidókért', *Ébresztő*, 9.4 (1909), 73.

[64] ZsL. MEKMSz 12. fond. 3. box. There is a copy of an invitation for a charity evening held 27th January 1906. Cf. 'Tea estély az üldözött orosz zsidók számára', in *PEIL*, 49.6 (4th February 1906), 86-87.

[65] 'Külmisszió. A Magyar Missziói Szövetség', in *Ébresztő*, 9.3 (1909), 52. See also Gyula Forgács, *A belmisszió és cura pastolaris*, 274.

[66] Mór Vai, 'Magyar külmisszió', in *Ébresztő*, 1.5 (1900), 92-94.

[67] That is the name of the place where the German-speaking Affiliated congregation had a church and revivalists customarily referred to it as *Hold utca* (street) gatherings.

[68] ZsL, MEKMSz iratok, 12.fond/1/box. See MEKMSz Constitution paragraph 10.

number into the Church, and I know of many others elsewhere who have had a life of privilege.'[69] Reference has been made in passing to Szabó's change of mind on the question of integrating Jewish converts into the Hungarian Reformed Church through the Bethany Christian Endeavour. Csia's history of the Bethany does not include any specific reference to mission to the Jews, yet it does refer to some examples of Jewish conversions and lists the names of several Jewish converts. Amongst these the most intriguing are the conversions of two Jewish commissars of the Bolshevik dictatorship; it was atheist Jews, therefore, Sándor Szabados and Henrik Kalmár, who were converted to evangelical faith through the Bethany.[70] Csia also gives numerous references to Aladár Szabó assisting the Mission in the Christian education of Jewish converts before their baptism.[71]

In all these instances, we see signs of Hungarian Reformed Christians beginning to take their own initiatives in Jewish evangelism. If it still fell short of a fully institutional commitment on the part of the Hungarian Reformed Church, István Hamar's criticism had some force: 'If we, Hungarian Protestants (the Hungarian Reformed Church) are not carrying out either Jewish or Gentile mission, why should we not at least support the noble endeavour of the United Free Church of Scotland?'[72] But the tide was beginning to run in the right direction, at least from the point of view of the Scottish Mission. Its understanding of the imperative of Jewish evangelism continued to be featured, now in the Hungarian language, through its journal, *Élet és Munka.* Their theological premise lay on the Pauline emphasis that 'God has not rejected his own people' (Rom. 11:1), and in Jesus' commandment to go to the lost sheep of Israel (Matt. 10:6) till the fullness of the Gentiles has come (Rom. 11:25). They pointed out that, as a missionary, Paul always went first to the synagogue, showing that the priority belonged to Jewish mission.[73]

Evidence that the Scottish message was beginning to be embraced by the Hungarians is found in an important series of articles, published between 1913 and 1915, by Pál Podmaniczky, a member of Bethany and leader of

---

[69] *RCJ* of 1913, 59. It must be emphasized that there were voices within the Lutheran Church appealing for doing mission among the Jews by Hungarians. The Pietist mission-orientated reasoning is saturated with nationalism, a peculiar development of argument for the imperative of mission to the Jews. Scholtz was upset that a Jewish rabbi regarded the execution of Jesus 'legal' as he had drawn people away from monotheism. The article was published in *Egyetértés*, a Jewish paper, and an answer was written in *Evangélikus Egyházi Szemle,* on which he commented. Ödön Scholtz, 'Zsidómisszió', in *Külmisszió*, 8. 1 (March 1904), 18.

[70] ZsL (A Magyarországi Református Egyház Zsinati Levéltára), A Bethánia Egylet iratai (1903-1943), 28a. fond/ 1 folder, fol. 16. Cf. Gyurgyák, 102. Here one finds a list of Bolsheviks of Jewish origin participating in the dictatorship of Communism, and amongst the names listed we surprisingly find the aforementioned two persons.

[71] J.T. Webster, 'Budapest', in *MRUFCofS*, 13.133 (January 1912), 111.

[72] H.I. (Hamar, István), 'Az egyesült skót szabad egyház zsidómissziója', in *PEIL*, 49.41 (7th October 1906), 648-49 (649).

[73] 'Zsidó misszió', in *Élet és Munka*, 3.11 (1911. november hó), 82-84.

the MEKMSz,[74] in the Hungarian foreign mission paper, *Hajnal*.[75] His discussion of the lives of several converted Jews excited public interest.[76] He emphasised the importance of witnessing to the Jews, especially in Eastern Europe – Poland and Russia[77] – where, he observed in a note of criticism of the Hungarian Church, Finnish and Danish missionaries were already at work among Jews even though these areas bordered on Hungary and should therefore be thought of as a natural sphere of mission for the Hungarian Church: '[We] must acknowledge with shame... that we, Hungarians do not do anything for the spreading of the Gospel among the Jews.'[78] He drew attention to what had been achieved among the Jews in Hungary by the Scottish Mission in Budapest, while pointing out that this was the work of a 'foreign' Christian nation. Urging the public to respond to his call, Podmaniczky argued that the Scottish Mission had brought blessings to both the Hungarian Jews and Hungarian Christianity. He called on the Hungarian Christians to wake up to their responsibility for reaching out with the gospel to the Jews not only of Hungary, but also Galicia, which he reasoned, 'should really be our field of mission work, too'.[79] Revealing his personal passion for this mission vocation, Podmaniczky expostulated: 'Oh, if only the love of sharing Christ compelling us to work was ignited in us for the unhappy people of Israel who deserve our compassion.'[80]

Podmaniczky's call to mission to the Jews in Hungary was published in the years when Europe was becoming convulsed in World War I that was to have devastating consequences for Hungary and for Jewish-Christian relations in Hungary. Although the war and its repercussions lie beyond the scope of this paper, it is to be noted that the significant involvement of secularised Jews in the Bolshevik dictatorship, the character of which was shaped by a communism that reflected Jewish 'millennial' expectations that were pursued in rejection of the former 'Christian' rule of the Hungarian landed nobility, resulted in a fierce alienation between Hungary's Christian and Jewish populations. In this context, the Jewish mass conversion of 1919 merits careful academic scrutiny, as do the responses of the Christian home mission associations to it. I have sought to review and assess the

---

[74] Anne-Marie Kool, *God Moves in Mysterious Ways*, 197. See also on his life.

[75] See an article on Jewish Mission: 'Zsidómisszió', in *Hajnal*, 7.6-8 (1916), 1-24. This latter described the conversion of Rabinowitz, Ignácz and Károly Róbert Gottlieb, and mentioned Lichtenstein as well as Schönberger. He also exalted Delitzsch's work. The mission periodical *Hajnal* appeared, first as a supplement to the *Ébresztő* (1907-1908) and in 1909 as an independent periodical. It would not gain momentum till, in 1913, the pioneer and co-ordinator of the MÖMM, Pál Podmaniczky, became its editor. Under his leadership and vision, the *Hajnal* grew to be a mission periodical of considerable reputation.

[76] P., 'Delitzsch Ferenc', in *Hajnal*, 3.2 (1913), 11-12. The anonymous writer, Probably Podmaniczky, paid tribute to Delitzsch on the anniversary of his 100th birthday.

[77] Hall, 53. See also *RCJ* of 1912, Appendix III, 67.

[78] *Hajnal*, 6.3. (1915), 12.

[79] *Hajnal*, 6.3. (1915), 12.

[80] *Hajnal*, 7.6-8 (1916), 24.

achievement of the Scottish Mission in disseminating an understanding of and commitment to Jewish evangelism in the Hungarian Reformed Church; it can fairly be said that the seeds had been sown, and that plants were beginning to grow that would be tested in the utterly new environment of the post-war situation. An intimation of things to come can be seen in the remarkable willingness of the Bethany Christian Endeavour to embrace, as converts, two former pro-communist Jewish commissars of the Hungarian Soviet Republic, Szabados and Kalmár, in a spirit of reconciliation that witnessed the very heart of the gospel message itself.[81] Another great example of witnessing to the Jews was the life of József Pongrácz. He published an article on Samuel Schereschewsky, a Jewish convert, but he acted quietly without labelling it specifically as mission to the Jews.[82]

An objective assessment of the degree to which the Scottish Mission to the Jews in (Buda)Pest may be considered successful needs to take account of the following factors. It has been demonstrated that the commitment of the Free Church of Scotland to Jewish mission was modulated during the period of research. What began as a theologically articulate vision of the evangelization of the Jewish people (as the essential prerequisite, or at least a complement, to the revival of a national church), flourished at the time of the Disruption, when the Disruption 'divines' embraced this vision as part of the missionary revival of the church as a whole. This moment produced a commitment to Jewish mission on the part of the Free Church as a whole, and resulted in the establishment of the Scottish Mission in Pest. As the influence of the first generation of Free Church enthusiasts for Jewish evangelism declined, it fell to the Jewish Committee to sustain the initiative. This meant that not all Evangelicals of the Free Kirk gave priority to Jewish mission. It is particularly true for the second and third generations of churchgoers of the Kirk. In Pest itself the Mission was not entirely successful in implanting its millennialist ideas, either among the German-Pietist of the German-speaking Reformed Affiliated Church (except the staff, whose employer, i.e. the Mission, expected them to hold these ideas) or among the Hungarian people. Indeed, the German-speaking congregation did not embrace an institutional commitment to Jewish evangelism, despite this being a condition of the moral and financial support that was undertaken by the Edinburgh Committee. Only some of its members carried out mission to the Jews. This led to some discontent on

---

[81] József Pongrácz, 'Kína apostola, Schereschewsky Sámuel Izsák József', in *Hajnal*, 25.1 (1939), 4-7.

[82] Cf. József Éliás's letter to the memorial congress' dated 10th November 1985 published in Kövy Zsolt (ed), Pongrácz József Emlékülés Pápán, 15th November 1985, A Pápai Református Gyűjtemény évkönyve (Pápa: A Dunántúli Református Egyházkerület Nagykönyvtára, 1988), 130-31. József Éliás mentioned that once Pongrácz' wife bought him a complete set of clothes and explicitly forbade him to disclose who had helped him. Éliás, together with other people, led the Good Shepherd Committee of the Reformed Church and worked in close collaboration with Scottish Mission staff to save the Jews during World War II.

the part of the Committee, while the Mission satisfied itself with the response of individual members of the congregation, some of them Gentiles, others Jewish converts.

The case with the Hungarian Reformed Christians is somewhat different, and shows a more favourable picture in the long run. While the Hungarians were primarily concerned with the revival of the national church, once this showed promising signs of achievement, the nascent home mission organizations began to show an interest in Jewish mission. It has to be acknowledged that most regarded Jewish evangelism as simply part of the mission to the nation as a whole, but the MEKMSz where Reformed and Lutherans worked together was the first to emulate the theological model of the Scottish Free Church that made an integral link between the evangelization of Jews and Gentiles, the former leading to the latter. Though it cannot be claimed that this was given sufficient institutional expression in the period of our research, the fact that the link was made indicated that the Hungarian Reformed Church was arriving at a distinct awareness of the importance of mission to the Jews as an essential part of the whole missionary nature of the Church by the beginning of World War I. Even though the Hungarian Reformed Church's relations with the Jews was to enter a new phase in the aftermath of World War I, the fact that, by the eve of World War I, the Church was beginning to accept its responsibility for Jewish evangelism must be attributed as a success of the Mission.

Regarding the assessment as to what degree the Scottish Mission succeeded in laying the foundations of evangelical revival within the Hungarian Reformed Church, it may fairly be said that the Scottish Mission's vision of Jewish evangelism as part of the revival of the Christian Church succeeded, albeit to a lesser degree than the Disruption 'divines' would have hoped, in introducing an evangelical understanding of the Church's mission that was previously non-existent in Hungary, where Reformed theologians were captivated by a patriotic concept of mission that relied more heavily on nineteenth-century liberalism for some leaders of the church than the New Testament vision of the evangelism of Jews and Gentiles, in that order of priority. Yet there had been a new evangelical voice formed, as mentioned, through the work of Aladár Szabó. He was labelled the 'father of Hungarian Reformed Home Mission'. However, the role of Ferenc Balogh, who was the spiritual leader of the New Orthodoxy movement stemming from Debrecen also exhibits signs of Scottish Evangelicalism in all aspects, including an awareness of mission to the Jews. Finally, it must the emphasized that the political turmoil of World War I and its aftermath completely changed not only the geographical but the spiritual landscape in some aspects where further careful research is needed.

Dialogue as Mission: The Balkan Institute for Faith and Culture as a Macedonian Case Study

Kostake Milkov

Introduction

The last two decades, the world, especially the Balkans, has passed numerous turning points; through some chance, or by the logic of things – and almost simultaneously – events of monumental magnitude occurred which truly deserve the adjective 'historic'. In 1989, the Berlin Wall fell, together with Ceauşescu, announcing the unimaginable disintegration of the Soviet Union. Then the dissolution of Yugoslavia took place via bloody conflicts, beginning with Slovenia in 1991, and culminating in the bombing of Serbia in 1999 and Macedonia's civil war two years later.

The most exploited term for this series of events, particularly regarding the countries of the former Yugoslavia, is 'transition'–a term which describes the economic and cultural processes that reputedly link us with the societies of modern democracies. This terminology inevitably causes tension, though. People differ in their interpretations of what lies on the other side of this in-between period, from Messianic visions of the Heavenly Jerusalem incarnated in the European Union, to prophecies for its decadent demise as the Babylonian Harlot.

No aspect of Balkan society, moreover, remains unaffected by this transition. The sudden crumbling of the old system – almost overnight – revealed to us that we have neither the infrastructure nor the methodology necessary to incorporate the values of western democracies into our own society. We had tormented ourselves with elections that resembled tribal wars; we dressed our education without taking the time and effort to take measurements; we severed existing ties within the wider family unit without providing legal and social alternatives. But above all, we took religion and culture for granted. These two features were torn from their context while being engrafted with mythology of epic proportions.

As a result, the intellectual movements addressing religion and culture go in two directions: One side insists on the advantages of what until recently was called 'pluralism', together with the overused term 'tolerance'. The other side, conversely, advocates adamant attachment to tradition as the final defence against that same pluralism, the glorious tradition of one's faith, language, literacy and songs – in other words, one's 'pure', undefiled culture. The condition in both camps is thus that of 'ours' and 'theirs', of 'winners' and 'losers', of 'discriminated' and 'discriminators', of 'genuine' and 'falsifiers'. We are witnessing two simultaneous and contradictory movements: globalization and tribalization.

Although the heads of countries with enormous ethnic and cultural diversity recently announced the 'death of multiculturalism', this concept is still the matrix through which the ideal of the western democracies is preached. In practice, such multiculturalism leans towards decentralization of any religious and cultural affiliation whatsoever, so that none can claim some kind of primacy or exclusivity for its truthfulness. Hence the word 'tolerance', accompanied by the mantra for 'human rights', more often reduced to the 'rights of minority groups'. On the other side, those who swear by their tradition, language or existence on the basis of the established moral-social-religious-cultural premises consider this very imposition of multiculturalism and tolerance a violation of their rights. As part of the cultural majority, adherents of this view assert their right to express the values communicated to them by their ancestors.

Characteristic of both camps is the tendency to interpret their differences as reflective of an irreconcilable conflict, instead of different methodological strategies. Consequently, any sort of resolution, unless it involves unconditional acceptance of the opposite view, is considered absolutely impossible; instead of thinking of the common good of all society's participants, the opposing worldviews position themselves as mutually exclusive. The result is that the supporters of 'tolerance' apply the principle to all others except those supporting the principle of traditional values. The 'traditionalists', for their part, regard with an 'unbearable lightness' all changes to these traditional values only as deviation.

The whirlwind of this clash has left faith and culture exposed. Proponents of so-called multicultural tolerance insist on less and less space for the influence of faith in society. They hope to reduce it to the private life of the individual, while opening as wide as possible a space for culture (mainly understood as the individual expressions of the painter, writer, musician, etc.). The traditionalists, however, press for the ever-increasing influence of faith (that of the majority), pointing to it as a source of social stability and a factor in developing healthy future generations; culture, therefore, is only a wider expression of that same faith.

The turmoil of these two conflicting worldviews pervades the Balkans, especially Macedonia. This region has experienced for centuries what has plagued Europe in the second half of the twentieth century. Here in the Balkans, for nearly half a millennium, people of multiple nations lived under a single empire, speaking diverse languages and professing different faiths. History shows that most often these people managed peaceably together. However, the events of the last 100 to 150 years have rendered these differences the basis for demarcation rather than communication. The Balkans has thus been linked with nationalism and chauvinism, and has inspired the newly coined word 'genocide'.

How is this schizophrenic condition of the Balkans to be interpreted? How does one negotiate the region's almost unanimous acceptance that its future lies with a united Europe, while that region simultaneously asserts a sectarian insistence on one's tradition, especially regarding the role of faith and culture?

The Christian Legacy

One approach towards a substantial analysis and understanding of the current situation in Macedonia and its immediate Balkan context is its Eastern Orthodox legacy.

The Eastern Orthodox (hereafter EO) world claims a rich Christian legacy that, according to the official EO teaching and popular belief has not been broken ever since the times of the New Testament. This is not to say that the EO worldview does not have any sense of history. They are most certainly aware of the role of historical events that have brought dramatic changes to the position of the Church within wider society and culture.

In order to understand this self-perception of the EO, we will have to give a brief historic overview of the five periods that have defined the existence and the witness of what the EO believes to be the only true Church that has preserved the presence of the Holy Spirit in the world with its liturgy and holy mysteries (sacraments). The first period spans the time of the writing of the New Testament and the early fourth century AD. This is the time of the persecuted church that was trying to find its place in a heterogeneous empire that was lenient with a multitude of religions and was happy to exchange deities with the regions that it had incorporated within its borders. During these three centuries, according to EO theologians, we see the rise of the bishop whose role is to define the existence of the local church. This was supposedly needed in order to protect the church from false teachings on the inside and from disintegration from persecution from without. The second period is the dawn of Christendom that was announced with the acceptance of Christianity by Constantine the Great that introduced the rising religious, social, political and cultural influence of Christianity. This is also the time of the decline of the Roman Empire in the West and the increase in power of the newly-built Constantinople. By the late sixth century and the early seventh century, the breach between the East and the West is increasing, and by the mid-seventh century we can speak of a distinctive Eastern Roman Empire which has been known in the West as Byzantium. The third period in the EO's historical development is the time of the Crusades. This is the time that will enhance the final break of ties with the West that has reinvented itself as the Holy Roman Empire. The Crusades will leave a lasting imprint of mistrust in the mind of EO believers that is living even in our day. The fourth period is the time from the final fall of Constantinople in 1453 under Ottoman rule. This introduced a period of some five centuries where the EO, from a role of prominence in society, was subjected to a role of preserving Christian existence within the Ottoman Empire as a second-class religion that was tolerated, but in many ways discouraged and discriminated against. This leads us to the fifth and final period that begun in the early nineteenth century. It is a century of rapid Ottoman decline and a simultaneous national awakening of the peoples, mostly EO, who had aspired to create their own independent states usually envisioned within the boundaries of some medieval pre-Ottoman kingdom. The modern EO countries are result of this national awakening and struggle to claim as much territory as possible from the Ottomans that were withdrawing from the Balkans. Now we had a common faith (EO) but different languages and fledgling identities that are in perfect doctrinal union, but often in ecclesiastical dispute. The rise of the nation-state in the Balkans resulted with national EO churches. Thus we have the Greek Orthodox Church, the Serbian Orthodox Church, the Romanian Orthodox Church, the Macedonian Orthodox Church, etc. There is no single shared border of these countries that is not disputed.

The modern EO churches in the Balkans reflect this historical background. There is common agreement that the EO is the only true church and that the other Christian confessions (the Roman Catholics included) have fallen from communion with Christ. The ecumenical dialogue in which the EO churches are involved has not really changed this view, and it is especially strong at grassroots level.

It is not surprising, then, that one of the biggest challenge that the EO churches face is nationalism. To many EO believers, nationality is identified with a confessional belonging. Therefore, if you are Macedonian, Serbian, Bulgarian or Greek, you are an Orthodox Christian. The EO churches are well aware of this popular attitude, and they are using it to enhance people's loyalty as the traditional defender of the faith and, with that, their national identity. In the eyes of most of its clergy, the EO church which has helped the people to remain Christian during the period of Ottoman rule has the very same role in protecting its believers from other religious influences, and especially from any western form of Christianity. The number one threat to them though is Protestantism in its Evangelical form. This kind of Protestantism goes back more than one century, and in many ways, although insignificant in numbers, it can be deemed traditional. However, the number of EO converts to Protestantism has significantly increased in all the traditionally EO Balkan countries only after the fall of communism in 1989.

This increase has put the EO churches on the defensive. One has to keep in mind that the EO legacy is closely tied to the Byzantine (Eastern Roman) Empire which expected the government to be twofold: secular and ecclesiastic. The two-headed eagle on the coat of arms of the Empire is an indication that the Emperor and the Patriarch are to rule together. The Patriarch is to make sure the Empire keeps the true faith, and the Emperor is to defend that true faith. This legacy gives the EO clergy the vision of such nation-states where the one true church leads the people in the true faith and the government is to protect that particular faith.

Although all the EO Balkan countries are parliamentary democracies, and there is a constitutional separation between church and state, tacit discrimination in the religious laws is nevertheless present. Besides the constitutional discrimination, there is also the discrimination of Evangelical Christianity through state favouritism of the national EO church.

The general commitment of the common EO Christian is quite nominal. Secularism, globalization, materialism and atheism, combined with popular syncretism, are the leading worldview of the younger generations. There are revivalist movements within the EO churches that are reviving monastic spirituality and missionary work that is almost entirely focused on re-churching the nominal EO believer. The majority of these efforts are led by zealous priests that become even more defensive against any other kinds of Christianity, and because of its prominence, especially against the Evangelical denominations. There is also a minority of EO clergyman and theologians who are not hostile to the Evangelicals, but rather see in them an ally in reclaiming the countries for Christ. Such cases are very rare, but they could be – and to a certain extent already are – a stepping stone towards a fertile EO-Evangelical dialogue for better mutual understanding and appreciation rather than mere tolerance.

One of the great lessons that Evangelical Christians can learn is that a good share of the EO legacy is a common Christian legacy. The teaching about the two natures of Christ, the Trinity, the substitutionary death of Christ, the commitment to Biblical ethics, and the preservation of traditional family values, are all very prominent within the EO church. These are few of the major common themes, but one could point to numerous other less obvious ones that are common both to the EO and the Evangelical Christian.

This is not a call to Evangelicals to either stop their evangelistic work in the EO countries or to simply direct it towards making people aware of their EO faith. If we did this, we would become either autistic or schizophrenic. We would not be able to express ourselves or, whenever we spoke, we would have a split personality. I am rather trying to appeal to the common ground that could enable us to recognize the followers of Christ in the Spirit, and to prevent the all-too-common straw-man argument that leads to an outright mutual dismissal of EO vs Evangelical belief. If Evangelical Christians study the legacy of their respective Balkan countries, they could use their rich Christina legacy as an aid to their evangelism which will make them more relevant within their own culture.

Such openness is risky because it presses us Evangelicals to ask ourselves difficult questions to which the answers are not always straightforward or easy. But, most of all, it requires from us an openness and vulnerability that is possible only with spiritual maturity that goes beyond a mere declarative adherence to the right set of beliefs. It requires a tireless demonstration of Christlikeness to which we all vowed at baptism and which in theory should have initiated us into the public declaration of the good news with our personal example, and only when necessary even to use words.

For the Flourishing of Society

To illustrate this, I will outline the vision of the Balkan Institute for Faith and Culture to develop a pattern or a working method that gives up neither Biblical meaning nor ethics, and that develops not confrontation, but rather a discourse of witness in an age suspicious of systems that claim universal meaning and ethics.

My attempt will be based on the text about the Logos in John chapter one, on Gregory Nyssen's teaching on *akolouthia*, and the Old Testament's call to Abraham and the people of Israel to surrender to his will.

In the opening three verses of his Gospel, John acknowledges that the Word is Creator of the world. Nothing that has being can be outside the creative being of the Word. This reminds us of our position as contingent beings in the midst of a contingent world. John establishes the relationship between the Word and ourselves. Not only that we are his creation, but also that we are created through him indicates a more intimate intention of the relationship that the Word wants to have with us. God could have created everything by a mere fiat, commanding creation into existence. Instead he decided to create through his Word or *Logos* – something that implicates much more than an uttered sound. In this way we are not creatures whose existence indicates only God's sovereign will, but first of all his love, and his personal interest in his creation.

God desires us from the very moment of our conception in and through his Word. He has been thinking about us in love from eternity. What does this say about human beings? How we should experience ourselves? John's suggestion will be to experience ourselves as God's beloved creatures, and as, Nicholas Wolterstorff suggests, find our great worth in that belovedness. Wolterstorff goes as far as to claim that 'other creatures, if they knew about that love, would be envious'.[1]

Besides this creative intimacy, something that the Church fathers will describe as *eros*, John goes on to tell us (1:4-5), about two other exceptional concepts – Life and Light! Let us think for a moment about 'Life'. In Genesis 2:7 it says that the 'Lord breathed into his (man's) nostrils the breath of life and he become a living soul'. We discover here that the Spirit is involved in our becoming living beings. By becoming alive, we are endowed with the faculties that respond to our environment.

---

[1] Nicholas Wolterstorff, *Justice: Rights and Wrongs* (Princeton, NJ: Princeton University Press, 2008), 360.

And, in our original state, that involves experiencing creation in its full capacity. That includes our basic capacity to be amazed and awed. Amazed and awed by what? By the unity, the goodness, the beauty and the truth of the creation. The concept of life is dynamic – of living *dunamis*. Life means that we were always meant to create culture into our living space. But culture based on what Nigel Biggar calls a cosmic fulfilment that:

> ... involves the emergence and securing of beings capable of appreciating, and freely committing themselves to, what is true and good and beautiful – that is, it involves the growth and establishment of a community of virtuous human persons. This is the human good: the condition where persons flourish.[2]

The other concept helps us to grasp this further. John says that this Life is at the same time Light. In other words, the only way we can live our lives authentically is to live them in the context of Light, the first quality to enter the scene of the formless and empty earth because, as he says, the Life was Light to the people, through which John wants to remind his readers that darkness is not the last word of the world's destiny. The Light is the first and the last Word in the world's destiny. It is this Word about whom verse 14 says that it became flesh.

By taking fallen created nature upon him, the Word began work on its renewal, confirming creation's original unity, goodness, beauty and truth. By the fact that we are here, that we exist, and that we have been created in the image and likeness of the Creator, the only way we can have our wholeness, our peace, or rather our *stasis*, is to follow the example of the Word that became one of us, and lived the life of a perfect man. What Christ did is defined by Gregory of Nyssa as *akolouthia*. *Akolouthia*, in Gregory's thought, is the orderliness of the whole creation. The only way that creation can function properly is to follow the innate principles of order. Disorder is falling away from goodness and beauty. From this we see how ontology and ethics are connected, with the one inevitably following the other. 'This linking of ontology, epistemology and ethics... was a central notion in Christian patristic thought... *Akolouthia* is both 'following' intellectually and "following" as discipleship.'[3] Thus, all imperatives to live a life which is not submitted to an inner logic of createdness collapse in themselves since our trajectory is never our own but rather one of ecstasy – going outside of oneself, and thus reflecting the glory of the One whose image we carry.

In the example of the Logos of John's first chapter, the God-man Christ, humanity has been introduced to the glorious possibility of union with God. In this way, man can experience God in the depth of his being. '... By affirming that this mutual penetration without confusion occurs between

---

[2] From a manuscript by Nigel Biggar, published as *In Defence of War* (OUP, 2013).

[3] Paulos Gregorios, *Cosmic Man: The Divine Presence* (New Delhi/Kottayam: Sophia Publications, 1980), 52.

God and man, Christianity has revealed the unfathomable and indefinable mystery of the human person and his consciousness.'[4]

Since 'God is love', to experience his love is to experience the fullness of his divinity. To communicate that love to others is to communicate God himself. How can this participation be expressed? I believe John Polkinghorne's *Science and Creation* offers a scientific illustration or metaphor. Polkinghorne correlates the world of thought to the physical world and suggests that man participates in the world of thought in a manner similar to the way in which he participates in the physical world: he neither creates it nor exhausts its content by his participation in it. 'It is rather like the way in which a particular diagrammatic representation of a theorem in geometry participates in that theorem without being either its origin or its full expression.'[5] We neither create nor exhaust God. But we might participate in the divine nature without being either its origin or its full expression.[6]

The biblical view of man sees his existence and the existence of all creation as a result of God's creative sustenance. Cut from God's creative activity, a being becomes a non-being. Therefore, the decisive question about the created beings is not ontological: 'Why is this being the being it is?' The question is rather teleological: 'Why do beings exist at all?' The ontological question is asked by Greek philosophy and the answer would be that being is as it is simply because it is an eternally self-existing entity temporarily modified by matter and imperfectness. The teleological question is the pursuit of the Bible, and the biblical answer would be that the purpose of existence is to be sought in the only perfect and self-existing Being – God. From this it follows that man is not an ontologically determined entity but a being determined by the creative power of God. 'To be a finite being is to be open to the power and love of God, who, without annulling or removing anything that he has given can always, if he sees fit, give more.'[7] We are then beloved creatures of God who can participate in him without losing our individuality or humanity, and receive from him without ever exhausting him. In other words, the establishment of the Kingdom is not the end but the beginning of a communion with the inexhaustible and never fully comprehensible God.

---

[4] D. Stăniloae, *Prayer and Holiness: The Icon of Man Renewed in God* (Oxford, 1982), 14-15; A.M. Allchin, *Participation in God: A Forgotten Strand in Anglican Tradition* (Wilton, CT: Morehouse-Barlow, 1988), 73.

[5] John Polkinghorne, *Science and Creation: The Search for Understanding* (London: SPCK, 1988), 76; F.W. Norris, 'Deification: Consensual and Cogent', in *Scottish Journal of Theology*, 49. 4 (1996), 425.

[6] The Einstein-Podolsky-Rosen paradox within quantum theory indicates that when two quanta have reacted with one another, they continue to have some influence on each other no matter how far they may eventually be separated. Norris, 'Deification', 425.

[7] Eric Lionel Mascall, *The Openness of Being: Natural Theology Today, The Gifford Lectures in the University of Edinburgh, 1970-1971* (London: Darton, Longman & Todd, 1971), 247-48.

This should encourage Christians to acknowledge that the Kingdom of God is already established on earth, standing in utmost opposition to the evil kingdoms under the dominion of Satan. 'Christ is the *eschaton*, or the divinely ordained climax of crisis of history. It was as a gift of God and not on account of human effort. It was the manifest and effective assertion of the divine sovereignty in conflict with evil in the world.'[8]

When we consider the historical context of the book of Revelation, we are able to see that the mythological language of the cosmic war depicts the situation in the real world. The application of the message of Revelation has to do more with the earth than with heaven. It is the hope of heaven, the coming Kingdom of God, which gives strength to Christians to continue their fight against evil while on earth. Revelation is the message to all generations of Christians to be assured that, although it seems that each generation lives in a period of 'the eclipse of God' (Buber) and that God's existence is far from self-evident, remembering what God has done for us in the past gives us hope that he will bring the history of creation to a glorious victory over the powers of darkness, sin and evil. 'In Jesus we have exhibited the power by which God rules the world.'[9] If Jesus conquered the world (John 16:33), believers who are joined to him have done the same too.

The biblical imagery of a cosmic battle might be too abstract to appreciate its significance for our daily life. Nevertheless, the Bible never loses sight of the cosmic battle that has an impact on earth's affairs. The spiritual forces, which opposed Jesus' ministry on earth, exercised their attack through the socio-political structures in the Greco-Roman world. The Kingdom of God that Jesus inaugurated is in contrast to that of the earthly governments (Matt. 20:28 and parallels). We should identify with all victims of power as Jesus himself identified with humanity by taking on himself human flesh.

But how are Christians to achieve that? The answer of the Eastern Church Fathers points in the direction of self-denial. For example, such was Origen's desire to see the establishment of the Kingdom of God that, in one of his homilies, he writes the following:

> If I, who seem to be your right hand and am called Presbyter and seem to preach the Word of God, If I do something against the discipline of the Church and the Rule of the Gospel so that I become a scandal to you, The Church, then may the whole Church, in unanimous resolve, cut me, its right hand, off, and throw me away.[10]

Origen's deepest yearning is to be identified or named as a Christian, as someone who belongs to Christ. This is well indicated in another homily

[8] Mascall, *The Openness of Being*, 65.
[9] Gayle Gerber Koontz, 'The Liberation of Atonement', in *Mennonite Quarterly Review*, 63.2 (1989), 183.
[10] Origen, *Homilies on Jes. Nav.*; H. 7.6.

that ironically states Origen's fear of being identified as a heretic. Far from it, he states that he wants to be a man of the church, and then explains:

> I do not want to be called by the name of some founder of a heresy, but by the name of Christ, and to bear that name which is blessed on the earth. It is my desire, in deed as in spirit, both to be and to be called a Christian.[11]

What is Origen chiefly concerned with is not his personal destiny, but rather the condition of Christ's church and the establishment of God's Kingdom. It seems that the reward of the Christian life for Origen is not so much what one can get for oneself by acts of obedience to God but, paradoxically, that we are the reward that God gets for himself. From the two quotations above, it can be said that, for Origen, the pivotal importance of belonging to Christ is Christ's victory over death and sin through which he obtains believers as his reward. Salvation of the individual is significant only in the context of the redeemed people of God. An Old Testament parallel can be drawn from Isaiah 40:1-11. In verse 10 it says, 'See, the Lord GOD comes with might, and his arm rules for him; his reward is with him, and his recompense before him.' Most contemporary commentators agree that the reward and the recompense in this case refer to the people God has delivered. In Isaiah's vision of Yahweh's victorious return to his city, he is not leading captives but rather those whom he has rescued from captivity. Or, as Klaus Baltzer says, 'They are his wages, just as sheep were Jacob's wages.'[12] The people who are Yahweh's wages are the same to whom he gives the promise in Psalm 37:27 that they will dwell for ever in the promised land if they 'turn away from evil and do good'. The promise can stand on its own as it reflects the importance of obedience to God's ordinances. However, verse 28 states explicitly the motivation for this obedience. It is to be found in Yahweh's love of justice. Or, 'In other words, he shall live a moral life to please God and not at all to secure thereby a tranquil life.'[13] Tranquil life is only a corollary of this God-pleasing life.

Abraham's calling and the subsequent story is good example of this. First of all, God chooses a man who, in the context of the given culture, would have been the least likely candidate for the task. Abraham does not seem to fit. Already uprooted from his original home in Ur, he is now about to be uprooted from his closest family. In this way, Abraham is asked to leave behind the two most formative frameworks – a home country and an extended family, pertaining to one's identity and security. The verbs of promise such as 'make', 'bless', 'make great', 'be', 'bless', 'curse', 'find blessing', depend on one verb that Abraham receives as a commandment: 'Go.' It is through the going of Abraham that God will trigger into motion

[11] Origen, *Homilies on Luke*; H. 16.6.

[12] Klaus Baltzer, *Deutero-Isaiah: A Commentary on Isaiah 40-55* (trans. Margaret Kohl; Minneapolis, MN: Augsburg Fortress, 2001).

[13] Arthur Weiser, *The Psalms: A Commentary* (trans. Herbert Hartwell; Old Testament Library), (Philadelphia, PA: Westminster Press, 1962), 321.

his blessings, of which the highest one, according to Leviticus 26:11-12, is that he walks among his people. Thus, in this call to Abraham to go, we already have God's incipient promise to walk with him. This promise of walking together reminds us of God's original plan for humanity when he walked with the first people in the Garden of Eden. In other words, with Abraham, God was most distinctively reasserting his intention to continue to build people for himself to whom he offers identity, greatness, providential care and mediatorship. According to Gordon Wenham, 'what Abram is here promised was the hope of many an oriental monarch (cf. 2 Sam. 7:9; Ps 72:17)'.[14]

But the promise comes with a price. It is a call to give up all that, for Abraham, is a source of comfort. In responding to this call, he is to surrender himself to dereliction, abnegation and wandering in total surrender to God. Brueggemann's commentary on the story of the calling of Abraham observes:

> Such renunciation, of course, is exceedingly difficult to speak of in our culture which focuses on self-indulgence because 'you owe yourself this'.[15]

However, he is convinced that the same call is valid for our culture because it is not about law or discipline, but promise:

> The narrator knows that such departure from securities is the only way out of barrenness. The whole of the Abrahamic narrative is premised on this seeming contradiction: to stay in safety is to remain barren; to leave in risk is to have hope.[16]

If, with Abraham, God begins the renewal of that personal relationship with humankind represented in his walking in their midst, and Abraham is called to the life of renunciation, it seems that this renouncing act is already the reward – that is, God's full promises will be accomplished one day, but his walking has started in the here and now.

If one takes into consideration the absence of an unequivocal promise for life after death as blessing for such an obedient response by Abraham, and indeed the people of Israel, as described in the Pentateuch, the response itself and the willingness remains an inspiring reminder for what should be the motive of our surrender and submission – namely, the sheer pleasure of living a life that is pleasing to God, and which is an abundant reward.

As Oswald Sanders writes:

> True greatness, true leadership, is achieved not by reducing men to one's service but in giving oneself in selfless service to them. And this is never done without cost... The true spiritual leader is concerned infinitely more with the service he can render God and his fellow men than with the benefits

[14] Gordon J. Wenham, *Genesis 1-15* (Word Biblical Commentary, 1), (Waco, TX: Word, 1987), 275.

[15] Walter Brueggemann, *Genesis* (Interpretation: A Bible Commentary for Preaching and Teaching), (Atlanta, GA: John Knox Press, 1982), 118.

[16] Brueggemann, *Genesis*.

> and pleasures he can extract from life. He aims to put more into life than he takes out of it.[17]

The Perennial Task of the Church

But as we have seen above, contemporary culture pulls in the opposite direction – that of entitlement to rights that are usually required from society or, to be more precise, from the state that nowadays is not seen primarily to ensure everyone is fulfilling their duties for the benefit of the community, but rather to safeguard the overgrowing list of our 'inalienable' rights. This feeling is so strong that –

> Many people in the contemporary world, especially in the West, have come to believe that a flourishing human life is an experientially satisfying human life... Experiential satisfaction is what their lives are all about. It does not merely enhance flourishing; it defines it.[18]

They cannot accept that they flourish if they do not experience satisfaction, or feel happy or, in other words: no pleasure, no flourishing.

Even in the mid-1960s, this was well observed by Philip Rieff in his *The Triumph of the Therapeutic*. According to him:

> Religious man was born to be saved; psychological man is born to be pleased. The difference was established long ago, when 'I believe', the cry of the ascetic, lost precedence to 'one feels', the caveat of the therapeutic. And if the therapeutic is to win, then surely the psychotherapist will be his secular spiritual guide.[19]

One cannot deny the fact that pleasure is a most powerful drive that moves humanity. The way it makes people pursue it cannot be rivalled by other strong drives that overwhelm humanity. However, we are today faced with that situation in which pleasure has become an end in itself. In today's highly individual and personalized lives, pleasure has been isolated from what made it first a social, human experience, and as a state of the highest order of desire, it does not have any meaning beyond being simply experienced by the individual.

Going back to John chapter 1, one finds a most sobering antidote to such a fixation with one's 'experience' as the purpose of life. The statement in John 1:13 about Jesus that he 'was born, not by birth, not by blood... but by God' could be appealing to all those who think that they can reach God outside God's creation. These are the dualists – or the proto-gnostics John writes against. The verse doubtlessly sounded very appeasing to their ears: but these dualists forget that everything was created by God and through his Word. They think of God without reference to his creation. This makes

---

[17] J. Oswald Sanders, *Spiritual Leadership* (Chicago, IL: Moody, 1967), 13.

[18] Miroslav Volf, *A Public Faith: How Followers of Christ Should Serve the Common Good* (Grand Rapids, MI: Brazos Press, 2011), 57.

[19] Philip Rieff, *The Triumph of the Therapeutic: Uses of Faith After Freud* (Chicago, IL: Harper & Row, 1966).

them 'all important'. The end-result of dualism is two extremes that are two sides of the same coin. The two extremes are abstemiousness and licentiousness. Abstemiousness says that one does not want to know anything about other creatures. All one cares is that their 'gnosis' will liberate them from matter and other material creatures. Licentiousness means that the physical body is of such inconsequential importance that it is quite irrelevant how one treats it.

But the very next verse, John 1:14, exclaims that 'the Word became flesh'; this is a blow to all dualism. It was in the flesh that his glory of the only begotten was seen. Therefore, neither abstemiousness nor licentiousness can be the proper response to the challenge of being in the world, but not of the world.

A most splendid example for how to achieve this is given to us by the apostle Peter in his first epistle 2:11-12. In verse 11, he calls the followers of Christ 'sojourners' and 'exiles'. This reminds them that they cannot call any place in the world their home, and yet the wider context of the epistle emphasizes that they themselves create a home that is not a specific place or a physical building, but rather a community, a household for the homeless. In verse 12, Peter states that in spite of all the hardships and the hostility they endure, their role is not to be silent and lethargic bystanders subject to victimization. On the contrary, they are invited to enact the Kingdom of God on earth precisely because they are the people of God.

Perhaps the best commentary on this whole idea, as it applies to Christians, is a quotation from the Epistle to Diognetus, a second-century apologia for the Christian religion, written to commend the faith of the church to the emperor. The pertinent paragraph reads:

> Christians are not distinguished from the rest of mankind by locality or speech or customs... They dwell in their own countries, but only as sojourners; they take their share in everything as citizens; and they endure all hardships as strangers. Every foreign country is a fatherland to them and every fatherland is foreign... Their existence is on earth, but their citizenship is in heaven.[20]

For the mandate of the church as the people of God to be fulfilled, it is essential that all members are aware that the above are common tasks for the whole congregation, and that these tasks are not to be carried principally through the institutional church offices, but through the church as the body of Christ. This means that the whole church with the totality of its talents, gifts and skills is involved in spiritual development and the sharing of the faith in Christ.

This was truly the 'secret' of the New Testament Christians. They showed an acute sensitivity to their contemporary culture and a keen interest for the well-being of their society. Biblical wisdom demands working for the flourishing of all people – regardless of ideological

[20] *Epistle to Diognetus* 5:1, 5, 9.

affiliation. The wise life should be distinguished by the longing for deep and permanent meaning, and by habits always aware of the irrevocable dignity in the other, yearning for true reconciliation (Rom. 5:10, 18; Eph. 4:32).

It is the vision of the Balkan Institute for Faith and Culture to inspire these values within the Macedonian multi-ethnic and multi-religious environment and into the wider Balkan context.

Theological Education and the Academia: A Convictional Theological Perspective on Evangelical Learning

Parush R. Parushev

Summary

The paper addresses the challenges of the contextualization, credibility and relevance of evangelical theological education from a convictional theological perspective. The argument of the paper unfolds in the following order. It considers first the apparent dichotomy between seminary professional training for ministry and academic theological education aspiring to full recognition by the established academic standards of (non-specifically religious) university communities. A review of some of the arguments for and against competing standards of theological education is presented. Further, the challenges of the contextualization of education are reassessed to address anew the question of the mission of theological education. The main argument of the paper is that evangelical theological education has to be guided by a bifocal vision: a) in the service of strengthening the convictional identity of a faith community (through primary practices of formal and informal learning in faith communities); b) in mission to the university to educate the whole person (through secondary practices and the teleological aims of academic theological education).

The Challenge of Credibility and Relevance

In my view, theological education strives to meet two conflicting demands of relevance to the life and ministry of faith communities, and of credibility according to the established societal standards of quality education. In a widely circulated analysis,[1] Jim Plueddemann, a professor of intercultural studies at Trinity Evangelical Divinity School, Deerfield, Illinois, and the

---

[1] Jim E. Plueddemann, 'The Challenges of Excellence in Theological Education: Back to Hot Topic', SIM 2003 (circular paper presented at a series of seminars 1995-2003, in Germany for the International Council of Accrediting Agencies and in Kenya for the Nairobi Fellowship of Theological Colleges): www.sim.org. My quotations refer to the electronic copy. Originally published as J.E. Plueddemann, 'The Challenge of Excellence in Theological Education', in Robert L. Youngblood (ed), *Excellence and Renewal: Goals for Accreditation of Theological Institutions* (Carlisle, UK: Paternoster, 1989), 1-14.

former International Director for SIM,[2] addresses the challenge of practical relevance and academic excellence in theological education. His analysis, coming from a missionary perspective, is particularly relevant to the concerns of this research. In what follows, I will give a brief summary of and comment on Plueddemann's argument as I read it.

Plueddemann opens his discourse by stating that educators do have competing standards of excellence 'controlled by implicit (and different) values which are not open to dialogue'.[3] Value systems are organised along a continuum of educational philosophies between 'emphases in universals at one pole and emphases on specifics at the other pole'.[4] In other words, at the one pole are philosophies of 'top-down'[5] education, which one can associate with the Herbartian paradigm[6] of modern education, with a stress on rational values, ideas, reason, absolutes and the theoretical. At the other pole are philosophies that are having a 'bottom-up' [7] orientation by stressing the empirical, aesthetic, culturally relative and concrete specifics of the local grassroots context. One may trace the origins of these educational philosophies to the pragmatist conceptualizations of Progressive Education.[8] These two value systems are incompatible and run passing by each other as a 'rail fence'.[9] Different value systems evidence themselves in different emphases in philosophy, theology, religious styles, educational theories and standards of accreditation. The 'top-down' educational systems put the accent on the credibility of academically recognised teaching of ideas, and assume the primacy of theory over

[2] Serving with the former 'Sudan Interior Mission' in Charlotte, North Carolina, USA, Dr Plueddemann was with SIM in different capacities 1967-2003.

[3] Plueddemann, 'The Challenges of Excellence'.

[4] Plueddemann, 'The Challenges of Excellence'.

[5] The term 'top-down' has been introduced by Arthur Peacocke in his *Theology for a Scientific Age* (2nd enlarged edn), (Minneapolis, MN: Fortress Press, 1993), chap. 9.

[6] The Herbartian paradigm is named after the educational system developed by the Austrian philosopher and pedagogue Johann Friedrich Herbart (1776-1841) and his followers. For a most recent overview and critical examination of Herbart's ideas in pedagogy, see Jan Hábl, 'The Challenge of Komenský's Anthropological Teleology to Modern Czech Pedagogy', PhD dissertation, University of Wales via IBTS, Prague (ProQuest, UMI Dissertations Publishing, 2008), 24-55, 214-16. Cf. Norbert Hilgenheger, 'Johann Friedrich Herbart (1776-1841)', in *Prospects: The Quarterly Review of Comparative Education*, XXIII.3-4 (1993), 649-64: www.ibe.unesco.org/International/Publications/Thinkers/ThinkersPdf/herb arte.pdf (accessed 15th September 2013).

[7] On holism, 'top-down' and 'bottom-up' causality, see Nancey Murphy and George F.R. Ellis, *On the Moral Nature of the Universe: Theology, Cosmology, and Ethics* (Minneapolis, MN: Fortress Press, 1993), 4 and passim.

[8] It was originally proposed by the American philosopher John Dewey (1859-1952) in his *The School and Society* (first published in 1899) in reaction to Herbartianism, drawing on the thought of German idealism and European romanticism. For a critical assessment of the progressivist movement, see Hábl, 'The Challenge of Komenský's Anthropological Teleology to Modern Czech Pedagogy', 56-95, 217-20.

[9] Plueddemann, 'The Challenges of Excellence in Theological Education'. Plueddemann uses this metaphor to define the 'top-rail' rational value system and 'bottom-rail' practical value system.

practice. On the other hand, 'bottom-up' educational systems begin with a specific context and stress relevance. There is an unavoidable discrepancy between the different values and purposes of educational systems.

While in inevitable tension, these two types of educational system must not be separated, the author insists. The key to the renewal of theological education is in linking two incompatible value systems by the intentional effort of putting integrating aims which will hold the opposites together as the fence posts connect the rails of the parallel fence. So Plueddemann's solution to the challenge of competing standards of (theological) education lies in the intention of bridging the unavoidable gap that separates them.

> While theological educators debate the lack of balance between the rails, a deeper problem is that the integrating fence posts are not intentional enough, not frequent enough, and often not connected to the top or bottom rails of the fence. Fence posts in theological education are intentional and regular efforts to compel interaction between the world of ideas and the world of senses, between absolutes and specifics, between theory and practice. These efforts must intentionally be built into both the aims and methods of education.[10]

In his paper, the author also reviews the characteristic educational methods of top-down and bottom-up educational systems. He concludes that to bring intentionality to bear on educational methodology, a kind of purposeful synthesis of knowledge and experience should be achieved. 'In order to promote excellence in theological education, teaching methods must do three things: they must teach important knowledge, stimulate quality experience, and compel critical interaction between knowledge and experience.'[11]

In the last part of his paper, Plueddemann addresses briefly the accreditation of theological education and readily admits that there is never a value-neutral accreditation. He outlines the different agendas behind the accreditation of the two divergent educational systems. He agrees that the credibility of top-down systems is defined in terms of the scholarly credentials of the faculty and academic features (the library, journals, solid knowledge-based courses, etc.) of the institution. Accreditation of the bottom-up systems is defined by criteria contributing to 'the ability of the graduates to do well in ministry'.[12] The paper ends with a pessimistic assessment of the current state of theological education and with an exhortation: 'Most theological education is ineffective. Renewal requires a paradigm shift, a whole new way of thinking about knowledge and experience, about theory and practice. This is the challenge of excellence in

---

[10] Plueddemann, 'The Challenges of Excellence in Theological Education'.

[11] Plueddemann, 'The Challenges of Excellence in Theological Education'.

[12] Plueddemann, 'The Challenges of Excellence in Theological Education'. An example of differing accreditation standards is the set of educational criteria applied in many continental European countries, in which there is a clear difference of vocational and academic higher education.

theological education.'[13] The answer of how to face the challenge is left open for the readers to find.

While Plueddemann's analysis of the opposites is penetrating, his attempted synthesis is Platonic and implausible. Only forceful bolts of good intention can connect the two worlds of ideas and of practice. An organic holistic synthesis of the opposites is missing. Instead, 'bridging the gap' is left to the goodwill of the two warring educational camps. No wonder that proposals of this sort have never worked.

In the analysis of the incompatibility of the two value systems, one may see a close parallel with conservative-liberal theological divides. The emphases of the first type of value systems are similar to conservative theology's rational foundationalism based on the sole authority of the universals of Scriptures and of the factuality and precise epistemological representation of directly revealed religious truth. The emphases of the second type of value systems come very close to liberal theology's immanentism, expressivism and experiential foundationalism. The perception of meaning of any religious event cannot be separated from the performance of the event, and is embodied in contextual and specific religious experience. It is not the purpose of this paper to get into the details of the conservative-liberal theological divide as it has been done extensively elsewhere.[14] Suffice it to say that both types of foundationalism – epistemological and experiential – are reductive and do not mix and match.[15] Nor do educational systems based on similar philosophical and theological premises.

Which brings forward a number of corollary questions: who teaches who? Is theological education formative for the church's teaching? Or is the teaching of the church – the 'doctrine'[16] – the starting-point of theological reflection and, by necessity, of the theological curriculum? Where is the primary home of theological education? What is the mission of theological education for academia, or for the culture? What can church contribute to the development of the life of society, and what is the role of

---

[13] Plueddemann, 'The Challenges of Excellence in Theological Education'.

[14] Conservative vs. liberal evangelical dichotomy is unbridgeable. For an extensive argument, see Nancey Murphy, *Beyond Liberalism and Fundamentalism: How Modern and Postmodern Philosophy Set the Theological Agenda* (Rockwell Lecture Series: Valley Forge, PA: Trinity Press International, 1996), 11-82. For a summary of the argument, see her *Theology in a Postmodern Age* (The Nordenhaug Lectures 2003), (Prague: IBTS Publisher, 2003), 7-23.

[15] On the reductive nature of foundationalism, see Parush R. Parushev, 'Convictional Perspectivism: A Constructive Proposal for Theological Response to Postmodern Conditions', in John Currie and Cathy Ross (eds), *Mission in Context: Explorations Inspired by J. Andrew Kirk* (Farnham, UK: Ashgate, 2012), 111-24 (112-15).

[16] On Christian doctrine (teaching) as the primary practice of the church and on multifaceted verbal and non-verbal performances of the practice of church's teaching, see James Wm McClendon, Jr., *Systematic Theology: Volume II: Doctrine*, republished with a new introduction by Curtis W. Freeman (Waco, TX: Baylor University Press, 2012 – originally published in 1994 by Abingdon Press), 23 ff.

theological education in that? This series of questions brings me to the next point of my reflections concerning contextualization.

The Challenges of Contextualization

Before moving further into the discussion about the nature of theological education, it is important to reflect on what is theological about education. There is a complex dynamic of doctrine (teaching, education) *of the church* and doctrinal theology (teaching, education) *for the church*. The home of the practice of doctrine and the sources of theological reflections are ultimately in the holistic life of the believing community, intertwined with Bible reading. Doctrinal theology is a secondary order of reflective practice in the service of the church and its mission. While both of these practices are legitimate in their own right, they are interdependent and there is an important logical priority in the theological discourse that must not be overlooked.

James Wm McClendon argues that doctrine should not be 'manufactured by academic theologians to be marketed by churches or pastors', or teachers.[17] The church traditions existed and developed for centuries without being guided top-down by academic theologians. Rather, the practice of doctrinal theology, McClendon insists:

> … is secondary to church practice inasmuch as from a Christian point of view it need not exist, cannot Christianly exist, save in service to the other. It presupposes church practice, investigates it, seeks to assist it. Being a consultant and helper, it may not substitute itself for or guarantee the primary practice [of the church's doctrine].
>
> To put the point linguistically, the surface grammar of doctrinal theology may take various shapes: first-person confessions, historic descriptions of church teaching, axioms or theses derived from an organising principle, biblical exegesis, rhetoric ukases. Yet its deep structure is that of a grammar of persuasion seeking assent. It says, 'This is what your present convictions appear (on such and such evidence) to be; this is what (for such and such reason) they appear to mean. Would it be better (for considerations here presented) to transform these present convictions *thus*?' In such a servant's question, such a 'thus?', all theology's first-person confessions, all its axioms and principles, all its arguments find their reason for being.[18]

In other words, in the relationship of the church with its theological educational superstructure, the vector of teaching has its primary focal

---

[17] McClendon, *Systematic Theology*, 24.

[18] McClendon, *Systematic Theology*, 24 and 47. On Orthodox theological discourse, as an example of an organic theologising, see John Meyendorff, *Byzantine Theology: Historical Trends and Doctrinal Themes*, reprint from the revised second edition (New York: Fordham University Press 1983; originally published in 1974, second edition 1979), 4-7. Cf. Meyendorff's notion of 'churchly theology' in the chapter on 'The Catholicity of the Church' in his *Living Tradition: Orthodox Witness in the Contemporary World* (Crestwood, NY: St Vladimir's Seminary Press, 1978), 82.

point in the church and points to academia not the reverse. While assuming and accepting the logical priority of practising doctrine or of the primary over the secondary levels of theological discourse, it is fair to say that any church concerned with its doctrine is in urgent and never-ending need of theological service, and thus in need of theological education. At this point two important considerations must be taken into account.

First, for the service to be provided, there should be a home for the community of theological discourse, which is the theological institution. The practice of theological doctrine is hard work and requires trained practitioners and experts in the proper exercise and advancement of the practice. Turning again to McClendon's linguistic metaphor, developing the grammar of doctrinal theology presupposes using the intellectual grammar of academic, critically reflective, philosophical language of the culture. Passing the baton from one generation of theologians for the church to another is a cumulative and corporate process with its own integrity and peer supervision. This is theological education for the 'thick' community of faith,[19] shaping the identity of those belonging to it. It may be expected that the 'accreditation' of the credentials of any 'thick' educational endeavour should be done primarily in and by the community of faith and its auxiliary structures (informal educational forums, associations, consortia networks of educational institutions, peer-based accrediting associations, etc.). I will call this the 'home' mission of theological education.

Secondly, I agree with the understanding of theology as 'a science of convictions', proposed by McClendon and James M. Smith. In their view, theology is 'the discovery, examination and transformation of the conviction set of a given convictional community, carried on with a view to discovering and modifying the relation of the member convictions to one another, to other (non-convictional) beliefs held by the community, and to whatever else there is'.[20] In that understanding, the theological task cannot be compartmentalised inside the church alone. It has to take into account 'whatever else there is'. Inevitably then, theological education has another missional focus and another vector pointing beyond the church community to the world. It has the task not only to borrow and (properly) use culture's intellectual tools but also to engage the culture in a meaningful convictional discourse. To fulfil this role, theological education has to provide a

---

[19] 'Thin' community is a community excelling in virtue (or vice). It is held together by a limited range of specific interest (e.g. a community of musicians or academic theologians). 'Thick' communities are story-formed through a shared life and communal language within a particular social reality. On thick and thin communities, see Parush R. Parushev, 'Gathered, Gathering, Porous: Reflections on the Nature of Baptistic Community', in *Baptistic Theologies,* 5.1 (Spring 2013), 35-52 (37).

[20] James Wm McClendon, Jr. and James M. Smith, *Convictions: Defusing Religious Relativism* (revised and enlarged edition – Valley Forge, PN: Trinity Press International, 1994), 184 (originally published as *Understanding Religious Convictions* in 1975 by University of Notre Dame Press).

platform for participation in the 'thin' community of academic and public discourse, holding the participants in the limited interests of academic pursuits according to the rules and practices of the theological game.[21] 'University is a culture. It organizes a set of cultural practices that enables the students to experience over time what can be experienced over time...'[22] Theology has a crucially important missionary task for the university as to any other culture. In the public market of ideas, doctrinal theology has to provide for the visibility and intellectual credibility of the community of faith among other communities of faith (or of reason alone). Theology has a role to play in public universities, either by the witness of individual Christians[23] or by a conscious attempt to regain its place in the university. 'Theology had been central to the work of the university at its origin, and remains central even now.'[24] But if this is true, theological education is called to play a fair game by acquiring the best of the university's standards, including the willingness to submit to the standards of scrutiny of its academic credentials (with all the worries Plueddemann is concerned with). I will call this the 'foreign mission' of theological education.[25]

One way of assessing the diverse manifestations of theological educational institutions is to see them in their functional relevance. One may think of three symbols:

---

[21] On the differing rules of the game, see Basil Mitchel's insightful essay, 'How to Play Theological Ping-Pong', in William J. Abraham and Robert W. Prevost (eds), *How to Play Theological Ping-Pong and Other Essays on Faith and Reason* (Grand Rapids, MI: Eerdmans, 1990), 166-83. On the rules of the practice of doctrine, see McClendon's *Doctrine*, 21-62, cf. his *Systematic Theology: Volume I: Ethics*, republished from the revised edition with a new introduction by Curtis W. Freeman (Waco, TX: Baylor University Press, 2012; revised edition published 2002; originally published in 1986 by Abingdon Press), 169-82.

[22] Chris Anderson, *Teaching as Believing: Faith in the University* (Studies in Religion and Higher Education, 2), (Waco, TX: Baylor University Press, 2004), 161.

[23] See Chris Anderson's wonderfully written account of devoted Christian witness in a university, *Teaching as Believing*, passim.

[24] James Wm McClendon, Jr., *Systematic Theology: Volume III: Witness*, republished with a new introduction by Curtis W. Freeman (Waco, TX: Baylor University Press, 2012; originally published in 2000 by Abingdon Press), 398.

[25] For a detailed analysis of complex arguments for the accreditation of theological education by specifically evangelical accrediting bodies in contrast to accreditation by established or state-recognized accreditation commissions, particularly in the context of emerging evangelical educational institutions in the former Soviet bloc countries, see David Bohn, 'The Perspective on Theological Education Evident among Evangelical Church Leaders in Bulgaria, Hungary, Romania, and Russia', PhD dissertation, Trinity Evangelical Divinity School, 1997; Miriam L. Charter, 'Theological Education for New Protestant Churches of Russia: Indigenous Judgments on the Appropriateness of Educational Methods and Styles', PhD dissertation, Trinity Evangelical Divinity School, 1997; Peter Penner, *Nauchite vse narody...: Missiya bogoslovskogo obrazovaniya* (Make disciples of all nations... Mission of theological Education), (St Petersburg: 'Biblia dlya Vseh', 1999, in Russian), 157-87; a number of articles in the collection edited by Peter F. Penner, *Theological Education as Mission* (Schwartzenfeld, Germany: Neuefeld Verlag, 2005); Scott D. Edgar, 'Pastoral Training among Baptist in Ukraine: Conversation between Indigenous Voices and Theoretical Perspectives', PhD dissertation, University of Wales via IBTS, 2007.

- Growing the family (forming and affirming convictions of a particular believing community);
- Speaking to 'the village' (building a platform for denominational or intra-confessional dialogue);
- Living to tell the nations (witnessing in inter-confessional, pluralistic and public dialogue).

Another way to think about theological education is to relate the mission of education to the larger debate about the relationship of the church to the church's environs. Moving away from the stereotypical 'Christ and culture' framework of the debate set by the epigones of H. Richard Niebuhr's typology, one may see different approaches to theological education as different convictional expressions of the church's (or faith community's) attitude to culture. One may look first at the *theology of correlation* – best expressed in the works of Paul Tillich. This is an important starting-point, for Tillich, 'more than any other twentieth century theologian… is the heir… to the Protestant theology of the nineteenth century', who 'led that theology into the twentieth century'.[26] Moreover, his views and works are often considered to be the cornerstone of the theology of culture.[27] One may look next at Julian Hartt's *theology of prophetic critique.* Hart 'seeks to establish the identity of Jesus Christ and the sufficiency of his work by an analysis of Scripture's narrative'. He speaks about the door open wide for us to participate in the Kingdom of God; about love's role, which turns away from the old cultural patterns, and to the New Kingdom.[28] Finally, one may wish to visit John Howard Yoder's holistic *whole New World (new creation in Christ) theology.* The starting-point of the discussion of Yoder's theology, perhaps, will be his understanding that Jesus in his original setting, in his radical demand for justice, peacemaking and discipleship, should be the norm for Christian ethics and witness.[29] Or, for the best, one must keep in unity all perspectives outlined above:

> In transmitting the Great Story, the church must be alert to openings, hungers, hidden religious depths within the contemporary culture (thus Tillich). Even more must it become aware by the light of that long narrative of the illusions and self-deceit of the culture-world, so that its preaching enables the world rightly to see itself (thus Hartt)… [And] The church must be not only the

[26] McClendon, *Witness*, 39.

[27] See his *Theology of Culture*, edited by Robert C. Kimball (New York: Oxford University Press, 1959).

[28] McClendon, *Witness*, 43-44. See Hartt's *A Christian Critique of American Culture: An Essay in Practical Theology* (New York: Harper & Row, 1967). Cf. Jonathan R. Wilson, *Theology as Cultural Critique: The Achievement of Julian Hartt* (Studies in American Hermeneutics Series, 12), (Macon, GA: Mercer University Press, 1996).

[29] See his *The Politics of Jesus: Behold the man! Our Victorious Lamb* (2nd edn; Grand Rapids, MI: Eerdmans / Carlisle, UK: Paternoster, 1994, 1972).

preacher but also the present instance of the gospel of Jesus Christ (thus Yoder).[30]

So, what the church (and its theological institutions) needs today is a blend of these different theological perspectives, a construct that relates harmoniously their best parts with integrity. The church must be able to understand society, must be able to hear and be open to its needs and concerns. At the same time, it should not abandon its prophetic role of exposing the sins and vices of the world. The church's critique is legitimate only when the church practises what it preaches.

Education and Socialization

There is yet a third way of assessing the role of theological education in terms of socialization. Education is a primary means of socialization. It can be affirmative or subversive to one's identity. The Biblical narrative presents different contexts of socialization. In homogeneous, theocratic Hebrew society, the vehicles of socialization were the extended family, the market place, and the worshipping community gathered together in the Temple or in the synagogues. In the democracies and tyrannies of the Greco-Roman world encountered by Jewish and early Christian missionaries, these were the public baths, the coliseums, the amphitheatres and the schools of philosophical discourse in the public squares. The issues of beliefs and morals were hotly debated in the closed circles of philosophers as much as at the trading lots of the merchants.[31] It is in this cultural milieu that the Jewish diaspora and the emerging Christian communities took their roots, made themselves at home and, importantly, started developing their theological idioms.

There is an implicit sectarian syndrome hidden behind the notion of explicitly Christian (or religious) education for explicitly Christian (or religious) schools. In the world touched by the European civilization of the Enlightenment, the state school's classroom is still a place where socialization occurs and the university is still the laboratory for intellectual maturity. These are learning paths of enquiring to become the citizen of the globalised world. Having accepted multiculturalism, public universities are now facing yet another challenge – one of spirituality and the realities of life beyond reason. It is the task of a Christian and of the Christian

[30] McClendon, *Witness*, 49. For relating McClendon's analysis to the realties of post-communist Europe, see Lina Andronovienė and Parush R. Parushev, 'Church, State, and Culture: On the Complexities of Post-Soviet Evangelical Social Involvement', in *Theological Reflections: EAAA Journal of Theology*, 3 (2004), 194-212 (with translation in Russian 'Tserkov', Gosudarstvo i Obshchestvo: o slozhnosti uchastija postsovetskih evangel'skih hristian v zhizni obshchestva', in *Bogoslovskie Razmishlenija*, 174-93; and Lithuanian 'Bažnyčia, Valstibe ir Kultūra: apie evangelišku postsovietmečio bažnyčiu visuomeniškumo problematika', 213-27).

[31] St Gregory of Nazianzus complains 'about salesmen discussing the concept of "co-substantial" in the market place': see Meyendorff, *Byzantine Theology*, 5.

community in the university to help the university community accomplish its pluralistic mission of a person's holistic, teleological education.[32]

Christian education has to address this task head-on by a careful tuning of the proper ends of education, discovering the right ways of being and hermeneutically appropriating the sacred texts as well as the texts of 'whatever else there is'.

Conclusion

Christian educators are faced with the complex task of the mission of theological education at three levels. First, this is a mission for identity formation in the life of the church, which can be captured in the metaphor of filling a cup. It can be achieved by means of the primary theological level of engaging the practice of doctrine, first and foremost, in denominational Bible colleges, informal educational groups and the like. It is also a mission of clarifying and building a platform for intimate conversations. It has been my experience that national seminaries, schools of local unions and associations are becoming platforms of exchange, the clarification of opinions of diverse and yet spiritually closely-bound communities – the 'kin' of 'the like-minded'. These are places for 'passing a baton'[33] in agreed patterns of instructional teaching in ministerial formation, pastoral training and denominational identity. These are types of educational institutions for the service of larger homogeneous communities of faith or for interdenominational encounters. These undergraduate or professional graduate-level institutions have, as a primary focus of education, the church in its local and associative sense. They are called to pass or clarify convictional identity by discerning, affirming or revising convictions and conviction sets of the 'kin'. They are the places for building common ground for communal discernment for a family of faith and the embodiment of pastoral spirituality in the life of a particular family of faith. Theirs is the task of enhancing the gifts and calling for leadership

---

[32] My younger colleague, Jan Hábl, offered important insights into the usefulness of pre-modern holistic patterns of education for post-modern cultural contexts. See his doctoral dissertation, 'The Challenge of Komenský's Anthropological Teleology to Modern Czech Pedagogy', his book, *Ultimate Human Goals in Comenius and Modern Pedagogy* (Hradec Kralove, Czech Republic: Gaudeamus, 2011 – in Czech), and his paper, 'Character Formation: A Forgotten Theme of Comenius's Didactics', in *Journal of Education and Christian Belief,* 15.2 (Autumn 2011), 141-52: www.academia.edu/2008389/Character_Formation._A_ Forgotten_Theme_of._Comeniuss_Didactics (accessed 15th September 2013).

[33] My colleague, David Brown, defines the purpose of theological education in three symbolic pictures. These are the filling of the 'the empty bottle' by transmitting trivial and yet necessary information; 'passing the baton' as training a person for the role of responsibility and accountability for the ministry in a particular faith community; and 'opening the door' to wider horizons of Christian vision and inspiration. See his 'Theological Education: Filling a Bottle, Passing a Baton, Opening a Door', in *Journal of European Baptist Studies,* 1.2 (January 2001), 5-20 (7-14).

and pastoral ministry discerned by gathering communities.[34] Unless required by specific circumstances beyond the educational objectives of the faith community, secular public accreditation is irrelevant to their successful mission and may do more harm than good.

At the other end, theological education has a mission to the culture by opening the door to reach out beyond the immediate concerns of a faith community. There is a need and a place for theological institutions aiming at opening a dialogue with other religious communions or society at large. This is where upper-level research master's and doctoral programmes' place is, and this is where the accreditation and the relevance of education measured by the standards of secular academic structures is important. And this is where theological education addresses the culture on culture's own terms by building bridges and establishing alliances with the 'unlike-minded'.[35]

---

[34] Keith G. Jones, 'Spirituality and Structures', in *Journal of European Baptist Studies,* 13.2 (January 2013), 29-49 (43-47) and Parushev, 'Gathered, Gathering, Porous'.

[35] Parush R. Parushev, *Christianity in Europe: The Way We Are Now*, with a response by Vija Herefoss, in the Crowther Centre Monographs Series, Volume 9 (May 2009) (Oxford: Church Missionary Society, 2009), 4, 19.

The Challenges and Chances of Protestant Theological Education in Croatia: A Philosophical Anthropology Perspective

Julijana Mladenovska-Tešija

The Relevance of Institutions and Theological Institutions

Many of the questions central to philosophy have important implications for theology and vice versa. The plurality of their relationship has often oscillated from being a natural complement to the other's reflection to being one of mortal enemies, and is always puzzling – especially in questions of common interest where the quest for a more unified account or explanation is more likely to occur.

Being a graduate of Philosophy, with an MA in Theology, and working on my PhD in Philosophical Anthropology, it seemed natural to combine these disciplines and approaches. Bearing in mind that the topic of this article is Protestant[1] higher education and its institutions[2] in Croatia,

---

[1] The term 'Protestant' in this text will be used as a broad term to describe the higher education institutions that are related to the following denominations in Croatia: Evangelical Theological Seminary in Osijek (Evangelical Pentecostal), Theological Faculty 'Mathias Falacius Illyricus' in Zagreb (Baptist and Lutheran), Biblical Institute in Zagreb (The Church of Christ), and Adventist College in Maruševec (Seventh Day Adventists). There are two more Protestant colleges in Croatia: the Baptist Theological Academy in Krapina and the Reformed Episcopal Theological School in Tordinci. They are not part of this analysis owing to their decision to remain church-based Bible schools that do not seek state recognition and accreditation as academic institutions.

[2] Some data on Protestant education in terms of religious education for children and/or adult believers can be found in the historical analyses of S. Jambrek, *Reformation in Croatian Lands within the European Context* (Zagreb: Central Europe and the Biblical Institute, 2013); and Ibid., 'The Reformation in the Croatian Historical Lands as Spiritual and Cultural Transfer', unpublished conference paper (University of Zagreb, Faculty of Humanities and Social Sciences, 2013); J. Milić, *The History of the Reformed Church in Croatia with Special Focus on the Reformed Parish in Tordinci, 1862-1952* (Osijek, Croatia: VETU and PRCRH, 2014); and articles by D. Marinović-Jerolimov, 'Religious Changes in Transitional Conditions in Croatia: Changes in Dimensions of Religious Identification and Practice', in *Sociologija sela,* 38.1-2 (2000), 43-80; S. Zinščak, G. Črpić and S. Kušar, 'Belief and Religiosity', in *Ephemerides theologicae Zagrabienses,* 70.2 (November 2000), 233-55. The topic of higher education has been more comprehensively studied by the late D. Peterlin (1959-2011) in his socio-historical survey on 'Theological Education among Croatian Baptists to 2000: A Socio-Historical Survey', in *Baptist Quarterly,* 5 (January 2000), 239-59. In his survey, Peterlin points out that one of the first Protestant Bible schools for adults in Croatia was the Biblical school of the Pentecostal Church, founded in 1962, which continued until 1972 when it became the first Biblical Theological Institute, latterly known as the Evangelical Theological Seminary. The Protestant Theological Faculty 'Mathias Flacius Illyricus' was opened in 1976

Philosophical Anthropology, and especially German Philosophical Anthropology of the twentieth century,[3] it seemed even more appropriate for the primary interest of this text to explore the institutions of Protestant higher education in Croatia, their nature and role in contemporary Croatian society, and their relationship with the churches. To do this, the work of Arnold Gehlen (1904-1976), one of the founding fathers of Philosophical Anthropology who paid special attention to the role of institutions in human development, could not and should not be overlooked. His insights will provide the theoretical backbone for analyzing the findings of the pilot research conducted in the first three months of 2015 involving four Protestant institutions of higher education in Croatia, while the Edinburgh 2010 Pointers on theological education will serve as a platform for creating proposals and recommendations for the future of Protestant academia in Croatia.

Why the Interest for Such a Topic?

Institutions are an important part of the human social reality. They provide stability and form to our lives, are normative, regulative, as well as give scope for action; they control individual behaviour and, at the same time, provide space for the realization of human potential. But they can be 'pathological' (A. Honneth) as well as contributing to creating conditions that support social disorganization. In this sense, institutions of higher education are no exception.

Academic institutions can be focal points for 'producing new knowledge, shaping critical thinkers, problem solvers' and 'a key building block of our democratic societies'.[4] Theological institutions of higher education can play a vital role in 'the transmission of Christian tradition from one generation to the next and for integral Christian mission in today's world', bearing in mind that 'theological education is essential for the renewal and continuity of the church and its leadership', as well as 'a matter of survival for an authentic and contextual mission of the church in all contemporary contexts'.[5] At the same time, 'the gap between academic theological knowledge' and 'popular Christian perceptions' related to 'the

---

and continues to be active. The data of the Adventist Church state that the first Adventist School for Pastors was opened even earlier, in 1926, although it was active for only one year. It was reopened in 1947 and functioned until 1955, and then again in 1974 as the Adventist College, and continues to be active: http://atvu.org/povijest-adventistickog-teoloskog-fakulteta

[3] The beginnings of Philosophical Anthropology are linked with the twentieth-century German philosophers Max Scheler, Helmuth Plessner and Arnold Gehlen, but also with more contemporary thinkers such as Paul Alsberg, Frederik J.J. Buytendijk, Erich Rothacker, Adolf Portmann, Dieter Claessens, Peter Sloterdijk, etc.

[4] Report to the European Commission, *Improving the Quality of Teaching and Learning in Europe's Higher Education Institutions* (Luxembourg: Publications Office of the European Union, 2013), 13.

[5] D. Balia and K. Kim (eds), *Witnessing to Christ Today* (Regnum Edinburgh Centenary Series, 2), (Oxford: Regnum, 2010), 164.

daily realities of life', aided by 'reduced possibilities for extended theological research', can contribute to what is called 'the resurgence of religious fundamentalism and confessionalism'.[6] In the Croatian context, the relatively small size of Protestant constituencies and their sense of isolation, coupled with the ignorance and prejudice of society implying sectarianism and 'the probability of external origin',[7] inflexible legal regulations related to higher education, the lack of sufficient financial support for Protestant institutions of higher education, etc. can be factors hindering greater integration and contributing to the inner destabilization of Protestant higher education institutions within Croatian society.

The thesis of this paper is that Protestant theological institutions of higher education can contribute to the enrichment of Croatia's plural, multi-faith society and academic excellence that is in the focus of the 'Bologna Programme'. They can also be the seedbed providing education/knowledge for church and community leaders, theologians and educators, as well as for nurturing spiritual growth and *koinonia*, and teaching dialogue with the world as God's creation.

Gehlen's theory of institutions, elaborated in the first part of this text, can serve as a platform for investigating Protestant theological institutions in Croatia.[8] The second part of the text will offer a view into Protestant higher education in Croatia in the light of changes taking place in response to the European Union's Bologna Programme requirements and as part of the thorough reforming of the Croatian national higher education system. In the third part, three questions will be investigated: What is the nature and role of Protestant theological institutions in Croatia? Is their limited access to resources (human, financial, material) affected by their particular status within Croatian society and changes in the European educational setting, and how does this affect their relationship with the founding churches? And, what kind of steps are needed so they can adequately respond to these circumstances and enhance their capacity for providing both academic excellence and reflect on their fundamental relational nature to the church, to God and to the community in general?

These questions will be checked against the findings of the pilot research conducted among the four institutions of higher education in Croatia. The analysis will be presented in the final part of the paper and will serve as a basis for proposing recommendations for the future of Croatian Protestant academia in the light of the Edinburgh 2010 Pointers on theological education.

---

[6] Bal and Kim, *Witnessing to Christ Today*.

[7] J. Coakley, 'A Political Profile of Protestant Minorities in Europe', in *National Identities* 11.1 (2009), 19.

[8] The inspiration for such an approach has been found in the article of Iva Rinčić: 'Arnold Gehlen's Theory of Institutions: A Contribution to the Analysis of Bioethics Institutions', in *Filozofska istraživanja*, 30.1-2 (July 2010), 141-59.

Gehlen's Anthropological Insights on the Nature of Human Beings and the Role of Institutions

Arnold Gehlen, a German twentieth-century anthropologist, is well-known, respected and criticised for his anthropological theory of institutions based upon his investigations of the nature of the human being. His major book, *Der Mensch,* is a classic that has been reprinted in many editions and languages since it was first published in 1940. In it, Gehlen laid the foundations for his latter theory of institutions (1956). He is frequently referred to by different authors, both philosophers and theologians (J. Habermas, M. Foucault, J. Moltmann, etc. – to name just few) who 'recognise the importance of his theory' but at the same time are 'finding its implications for society unsympathetic'.[9]

Nonetheless, Gehlen's contribution to the development of Philosophical Anthropology, not as 'a philosophical sub-discipline but rather as a particular philosophical approach within twentieth-century German philosophy'[10] is beyond any doubt. Challenged by modernity, both in terms of empirical science, most notably Biology and Ethnology, as well as by the political crisis of the early twentieth century, Gehlen has succeeded in building up a systematic anthropology to respond to the key question of the time: What is a human being? To understand the nature of the human being, Gehlen searches for the totality of different functions it performs to maintain itself in the world. He was profoundly inspired by the work of the Dutch anatomist Lodewijk (Louis) Bolk (1866-1930) and his 'retardation theory' according to which humans are retarded primates, born prematurely, both ontogenetically and philogenetically, maintaining foetal characteristics throughout their whole life. The process of retardation works in two directions, according to Bolk: 'first, by an alternation of the rate of the vital processes as a whole, including morphogenesis in general', and then as 'a more particular retardation in the development of some somatic features' which, in conclusion, leads to 'nearly all typical characteristics of the human body are persisting foetal stages if compared with the development of the other primates. Somatically, man is therefore a highly foetalised form'.[11] The anti-Darwinian turn proposed by Bolk allowed Gehlen to view the human being against the impression of *scala naturae* – the peak of progress – and this connection with biology will be the basis for his new approach to anthropology. He will be interested to find the answer to the question of the unique position (*Sonderstellung*) of this particular

---

[9] D.J. Levy, 'The Anthropological Horizon: Max Scheler, Arnold Gehlen and the Idea of a Philosophical Anthropology', in *Journal of the Anthropological Society of Oxford,* 16.3 (1985), 169-87.

[10] J. Fisher, 'Exploring the Core Identity of Philosophical Anthropology through the Works of Max Scheler, Helmuth Plessner and Arnold Gehlen', in *Iris,* I.1 (April 2009), 153-70.

[11] L. Bolk, 'Origin of Racial Characteristics in Man', in *American Journal of Physical Anthropology,* 13 (1929), 1-28; J. Verhulst, 'Bolkian and Bokian Retardation in Homo Sapiens', in *Acta Biotheoretica* 47 (1999), 7-28, 8ff.

creature that can reveal and conceal itself. *Homo absconditus*, as Plessner described the human, is such that it is first and foremost characterised by its 'eccentric positionality', a formula describing human eccentricity in environmental relations and determination, and already partly anticipated by Scheler and Gehlen.[12] The human, by virtue of its nature, must of necessity be an active being, and the quintessence and sum total of that nature which is transformed into action, is culture and civilization.[13]

In his major work *Man: His Nature and Place in the World* (1940), Gehlen begins by analyzing the nature of human beings. They are insufficient, fragile, open, even problematic. Unlike others (animals, most specifically), humans cannot survive by their our own biological resources and are forced to create their own environment (culture and institutions) and consequently be, at all times, 'creatures of education' compensating by learning the defect (*Mängelwesen*) of their nature.[14] Gehlen draws his theory of institutions based upon this view of human nature as openness to the world. Humans create their life conditions, culture and institutions in order to survive, and what differentiates them from animals is their gift for action (*handelndes Wesen*) which is closely related to language and thinking.[15] Gehlen refuses to define humans only by comparing them with the world's other living creatures. His scientific mind is also philosophical and highlights the need for introspection, education and breeding. The discontinuous acts of *self-creation* or self-transformation need institutions which guarantee security, persistence and sustainability, and the development of language, culture and society.[16] We are *homo educandus* and become human by learning, discipline, breeding and self-breeding, producing our own nature according to its true capacities/features. This line of thinking in Gehlen's philosophy is certainly not new: it had been highlighted two centuries before by Immanuel Kant (1724-1804) according to whom education exhibits the most excellent and necessary way in which our efforts at self-development are to be realised.[17] Yet, Gehlen adds to it another feature: intrinsically vulnerable and exposed to the risks of insecurity, the complexity of external stimuli and internal drives,[18] we need institutions that will be 'the human, cultural substitute for the absent, behavioural guidance of instinct',[19] relieving us of the burden of constant decision-making. We need to distance from the world, thus we need

---

[12] J. Fischer, 'Exzentrische Positionalität: Plessners Grundkategorie der Philosophischen Anthropologie', in *Deutsche Zeitschrift für Philosophie*, 48 (2000), 265-88.

[13] A. Gehlen, *'Der Mensch': seine Natur und seine Stellung in der Welt* (Frankfurt am Main: Hrsg. von Karl-Siegbert Rehberg, 1993), 25.

[14] A. Gehlen, *Čovjek: Njegova narav i njegov položaj u svijetu* (Zagreb: Naklada Breza, 2005), 374ff.

[15] Gehlen, *Der Mensch*, 3, as well as in Gehlen, *Čovjek*, 30.

[16] A. Gehlen, *Čovjek i institucije* (Zagreb: Nakladni zavod Globus, 1994), 267.

[17] I. Kant, *On Education* (trans. A. Churton), (London: Thoemmess Press, 1992), 187-210 and further.

[18] Gehlen, *Čovjek*, 54 and further.

[19] Levy, 'The Anthropological Horizon', 182.

institutions to ensure the stabilization of our environment and to provide a systematic approach to, and predictability of, the decision-making process. Otherwise, we are torn between subjective motivation and improvizations, between the drive and its fulfilment.[20]

The role of institutions as a need for human survival is to unburden individuals from the need to constantly make decisions, to define the general normative patterns of behaviour (based upon habit), to provide a space for creative endeavour of individuals and engage our unburdened 'limited cognitive resources on other activities',[21] and to make space for the creation of the unique personalities of humans. 'Unlike the animal... the human being is exposed to an indefinite and immeasurable open world with plenty of unforeseen possibilities' which, due to our 'instructiveness and non-specialization – in short, because of the even physical turning of human nature to the intellect', we show a tendency towards degeneration.[22] Thus humans must unconditionally surrender to the norms valid in society and the rules of social institutions because only the socialised human being shows its capacity to become a being that 'chooses and refuses', and the area of all different possibilities for growth and creation emerges.[23] Institutions become essential, especially in times of transition from authoritarian, totalitarian forms of rule to democracy, a change which implies radical disruption, a cut from the old system towards pluralism and democratization, when they are (re)built on the rule of law. These 'shakes' produce uncertainty and disorientation in values, and are followed by improvization and an increase of the sense of fear when the individual sees him/herself by way of contrast, identification with the 'non-I (*Nicht-Ich*)' to which they can hold firm as a more or less permanent 'representantive (*Darstellung*)' of humanity.[24] Institutions become products and records of human manifestations, and this has repercussions on humans themselves: they are moulded by what they have externalized. His criticism of the modern is focused on its lack of stabilization mechanisms for the masses which is a sign of the deconstruction of institutions as well as of the deconstruction of nations. For Gehlen, institutions are necessary for the creation and preservation of the nation, although dangerous and prone for misuse at the same time, and can lead to absolutism. His criticism has a 'conservative undertone suggesting that modern institutions are decayed'[25] and yet also a prophetic one: it is not our surrender to institutions which harms our existence but, on the contrary, 'the institutional complexes of

---

[20] Gehlen, *Čovjek i institucije*, 267-68.

[21] C. Mantzavinos, 'Institutions', in I.C. Janie and J. Zamora-Bonina (eds), *The Sage Handbook of the Philosophy of Social Sciences* (London: Sage, 2011), 402.

[22] A. Gehlen, 'The Crystallization of Cultural Forms', in V. Meja, D. Misgeld and N. Stehr, *Modern German Sociology* (New York: Columbia University Press, 1987), 38.

[23] Gehlen, 'The Crystallization of Cultural Forms', 39.

[24] Gehlen, *Čovjek i institucije*, 275.

[25] Jerry Z. Muller (ed), *Conservativism: An Anthropology of Social and Political Thought from David Hume to the Present* (Princeton, NJ: Princeton University Press, 1997), 408-09.

modern society have separated themselves from cultural modernity which can now be discarded'.[26] The result is such that 'contemporary processes erode the institutions': our 'post-historical' society is not governed by cultural ideals but by purely functional forces: culture has been absorbed by institutions and has been routinised.[27] Gehlen calls this situation 'cultural crystallization' which is characterised by the lack of producing the new that was central to modernity, thus the task of politics is viewed only in completing what was essentially achieved by institutions.[28] With this argument, Gehlen criticises radicals that aspire to change by using revolutions since they fail to see that modernity is at its end, at a 'post-history' as an 'end to ideology'.[29]

Viewing institutions as human behavioural determinants that replace and compensate for our deficiencies and malfunctions by 'habitualising' our behaviour, Gehlen considers institutions as relatively stable and enduring patterns of human relationship, culturally formed to structure social behaviour and secure its survival. They represent human creation 'transcending' its human creator as archaic institutional forms whose qualities can no longer be ascribed only to its individual elements. If exposed to persistent reflection, they might cease to provide humans with necessary psychological relief. Yet, if change is avoided, institutions suffer erosion both in terms of crystallization (separating themselves from other spheres of life, and especially culture and modernization) and quasi-institutionalization (becoming too fragile and subject to constant change).

Protestant Higher Education Institutions in Croatia – Spatial Setting

There has been little systematic study of Protestant theological education in Croatia and even less on higher education, which is also the most recent one. To understand the complexity of the matter, three spatial axes should be put in place: the local (transitional and minority), the European (the Bologna Process) and global (globalization education trends).

Axis 1: Transitional and Minority Status

The 'transition paradigm' refers to the change that has occurred during the last 20-30 years of the twentieth century when many former Socialist and/or communist countries moved away from dictatorship to democratic

[26] Muller, *Conservativism*, 409.
[27] Muller, *Conservativism*.
[28] G. Delanty, *Modernity and Postmodernity: Knowledge, Power and the Self* (London: Sage, 2000), 73.
[29] A. Gehlen, *Man in the Age of Technology* (New York: Columbia University Press, 1980), 165.

regimes.[30] This change led to the Croatian declaration of independence in 1991, the Homeland War of 1991-1995,[31] political pluralization and democratization especially after 2000, followed by Croatian membership of the EU in 2014. According to the classification offered by North, Wallis and Weingast in their study on Violence and Social Order, Croatia could be characterised as a natural state in need of securing 'greater participation by citizens', 'impersonal political rights', 'transparent institutions structuring decision-making processes', 'legal support provided for a wide range of organizations including political parties and economy organizations' in order to make the transition to an open-access society.[32] Natural states, such as Croatia, often both limit access to institutions and information, as well as limiting forms of 'complexity and size' of institutions seeking to be established.[33] This is reflected especially in its relationship to minorities and their institutions. A. Marinović and D. Marinović-Jerolimov[34] use several theoretical concepts to explicate the complexity of the relationships between the Croatian state and Protestant communities: 'legal social control', 'discretion', 'discrimination', and 'third-party advocacy' referring to different forms of 'the legislative effort of the state to exert social control over minority religions' which can result in discrimination, the application of the discretion principle based on biases and personal values and prejudices, and the use of third-party advocacy,[35] either in favour of or against the interests of minority religions. Even more, Croatia has accepted a binary model of higher education where only university studies are research-oriented while college studies are profession-oriented. This means that the majority of the Protestant institutions of higher education (apart from the Protestant Theological Faculty, 'Mathias Flacius Illyricus' in Zagreb, which was accredited as a Protestant Theology Study Programme under the University of Zagreb) were allowed to accredit as private colleges, only performing 'professional studies consisting of professional programmes conducted at polytechnics or colleges of applied sciences' offering 'undergraduate professional studies, and specialist graduate professional studies'.[36] This puts additional pressures upon the Protestant

---

[30] For more, see Thomas Carothers, 'The End of Transitional Paradigm', in *Journal of Democracy*, 13 (January 2002), 5-21.

[31] The Croatian War of Independence was fought from 1991 to 1995 between Croat forces loyal to the government of Croatia – which had declared independence from the Socialist Federal Republic of Yugoslavia (SFRY) – and the Serb-controlled Yugoslav People's Army (JNA) and local Serb forces. See Ivo Goldstein, *Croatia: A History* (London: Hurst, 1999).

[32] D.C. North, J.J. Wallis and B.R. Weingast, *Violence and Social Order: A Conceptual Framework for Interpreting Recorded Human History* (New York: Cambridge University Press, 2013), 2.

[33] North, Wallis and Weingast, *Violence and Social Order*, 6.

[34] A. Marinović and D. Marinović-Jerolinov, 'What about Our Rights? The State and Minority Religious Communities in Croatia: A Case Study', in *Religion and Society in Central and Eastern Europe* 5.1 (2012), 39-53.

[35] Marinović and Marinović-Jerolinov, 'What about Our Rights?

[36] See the description of the Croatian higher education system: www.ehef.asia/croatia

academia in Croatia about how to satisfy both the quality requirements of teaching theology and providing church and community leaders, theologians and educators, nurturing the spiritual growth and *koinonia,* and the narrow and inflexible state requirements for specialization and professionalization oriented towards the global market.

Axis 2: The Bologna Programme

Protestant academia is nothing recent (the first Biblical schools for pastors can be traced as early as the 1940s[37]) and survived the turbulence of the Tito regime, Yugoslavian disintegration and the Croatian Homeland War (1991-1995). Nowadays, Protestant theological institutions are undergoing changes influenced by the European Union and the Bologna Process of Higher Education.[38] The Government of Croatia has signed the Bologna Declaration in 2001 when the process of reform of higher education in Croatia was launched. During 2008 and 2009, in line with the Act on Science and Higher Education, the process of external evaluation of higher education institution began, and the (re)accreditation procedure was carried out in accordance with this new Act. The Bologna Implementation Report from 2012 states that this 'process has transformed the face of European higher education' and 'laid the ground for higher education that is serving an increasing range of societal demands; higher education structures have been modified, quality assurance systems developed, mechanisms to facilitate mobility established, and a range of issues for the social dimension of higher education identified'.[39] These changes influenced Protestant higher education institutions in Croatia in a number of ways, the first being that they had to decide whether they would undergo the process of accreditation (which has influenced to greater or lesser degree their inner structure, vision, mission and relationships with the founding church(es)) or will remain unaccredited (considering that this step is protecting their

---

(accessed 18th March 2015). The Croatian Catholic University was established in 2006 and received its accreditation from the Ministry of Science, Education and Sports in 2008: www.zg-nadbiskupija.hr/catholic-university-of-croatia. In addition, there are three Catholic faculties of theology which are part of different state universities across the country: www.hbk.hr/?type=clanak&ID=31 (accessed 10th April 2015).

[37] See footnote 2 in the present article.

[38] The Bologna Process of Higher Education is 'a collective effort of public authorities, universities, teachers, and students, together with stakeholder associations, employers, quality assurance agencies, international organizations, and institutions, including the European Commission' to: (a) introduce the three-cycle system of higher education (bachelor/ master/ doctorate), (b) to strengthen quality assurance, and (c) to easily recognize qualifications and periods of study among the European member-states: http://ec.europa.eu/education/policy/ higher-education/bologna-process_en.htm (accessed 18th March 2015).

[39] EACEA, *The European Higher Education Area in 2012: Bologna Process Implementation Report* (Brussels: Education, Audiovisual and Culture Executive Agency, 2012), 9: www.ehea.info/Uploads/%281%29/Bologna%20Process%20Implementation%20Report.pdf (accessed 25th February 2015).

religious, academic and other freedoms). An institution, even taking the step towards accreditation, may not obtain or maintain it for several other reasons. Accreditation processes often require many years of extensive preparation and adaptation to standards set high and demanding secure financing.[40] These criteria are especially difficult to fulfil for Protestant higher education institutions, bearing in mind the overall political setting in Croatia, the relatively small constituencies supporting the colleges and faculties of Protestant background, which is reflected in limited donations and the low numbers of students enrolling and of local staff, and high state taxes related to salaries,[41] the shifting co-operation between churches and theological academia, the lack of foreign funds available for Croatian Protestant education institutions due to the post-war stabilization of the country and Croatian membership to the European Union, etc. Consequently, the situation with Protestant academia is such that there are two Bible schools operating as church-related schools, but not accredited by the Croatian Ministry of Higher Education (the Baptist Theological Academy in Krapina and the Reformed Episcopal Theological School in Tordinci); there is one Faculty or university programme of Protestant studies (the Protestant Theological Faculty, 'Mathias Flacius Illyricus' in Zagreb, which has been accredited as a Protestant Study Programme within the University of Zagreb); one college is in the process of re-accreditation of its programmes at both undergraduate and graduate level (the Evangelical Theological Seminary in Osijek, which has been accredited as an institution of higher education since 2003), while two others are in the process of initial accreditation of their programmes (the Biblical Institute in Zagreb and the Adventist Theological College in Maruševec).

Axis 3: Globalization and Higher Education

Globalization promotes international co-operation, borderless economies, the mobility of people and knowledge, international competitiveness, co-operation and interconnectedness of the global and the local, cultural diversity, the open market economy.[42] And although it creates opportunities, it also creates risks: this 'era of globalization' has been characterised above all by an uneven development. Deepak Nayyar stresses that globalization has led to prosperity 'for a few rich countries and rich

---

[40] Z. Kovacevic and B. Sisek, 'Financing of Higher Education in the Republic of Croatia', in *Poslovna izvrsnost,* I.1 (Zagreb, 2007), 139-155.

[41] A. Grdović Gnip and I. Tomić say that 'the tax wedge in Croatia is around 40.33% of total labour costs' and that 'on top of that, every city and county in Croatia may introduce personal income surtax as part of their tax revenues' which can range from 10% (for a city with fewer than 30,000 inhabitants) up to 30% (for a city like Zagreb). See A. Grdović Gnip and I. Tomić, 'How Hard Does the Tax Bite Hurt?: Croatian vs. European worker', in *Financial Theory and Practice,* 34.2 (2010), 109-42.

[42] D. Nayyar, 'Globalisation, History and Development: A Tale of Two Centuries', in *Cambridge Journal of Economics,* 30 (2006), 137-59.

people' while 'for the many poor countries and poor people, it has led to marginalization if not exclusion'.[43] For Croatia, being a developing country, the process of integration into the world economy has been slow and problematic,[44] and has not led to the much desired 'economic growth or poverty reduction'.[45] Education has been considered as 'one of the most powerful instruments for reducing poverty and inequality, and lays a foundation for sustained economic growth'.[46] It is undergoing constant challenges and changes under the effects of globalization: the whole platform of higher education is global in its scope of worldwide social and human relationships; there is a sense of connectivity between various local realities which are distanced from each other, as well as of de-territorialised interactions of individuals and cultures. The effects of globalization on higher education are multiple and bring rapid developments in technology and communications, changes within learning systems, values and knowledge, and changes in the roles of students and teachers. One of the models to respond to these changes and challenges of globalization is the European Union Bologna Programme that has become a paramount model for higher education in Croatia.

On the other hand, the Christian urge 'go into the world' shows its global, and even more, its universal orientation, both in its vision and mission. It seems that both settings, the Christian mission-oriented and world-global influence education, have the aim of integrating the local into the global and vice versa, of involving technology and at the same time protecting aspects of life from it, to care about the diversity of contexts for which students are to be prepared to work with. What separates global higher education mission from the Christian is that the latter seeks to 'develop reflective Christian identity and practice' into the changing world, 'informed and spiritually enriched access to biblical tradition' in the plural multi-faith context, 'empowering people for participating in the mission of God in this world'[47] by developing an approach to education that will meet the challenges of fast-changing systems and value-orientations and by providing content that can respond to these realities and be true to its primary vision and mission.

In the following paragraph a pilot study on Protestant institutions of higher education will be presented in order to provide insights limited in scope but valuable for further in-depth researches and analyses of the

---

[43] Nayyar, 'Globalisation, History and Development', 21.

[44] The GDP growth rate in Croatia averaged 0.38% from 2000 until 2015, reaching an all-time high of 4.20% in the first quarter of 2008 and a record low of -3.65% in the first quarter of 2009. See: IMF World Economic Outlook (WEO), April 2015: http://knoema.com/atlas/Croatia/GDP-growth (accessed 2nd July 2015).

[45] Ibid.

[46] See The World Bank: http://data.worldbank.org/topic/education?display=graph (accessed 2nd July 2015).

[47] Balia and Kim, *Witnessing to Christ Today*, 151.

relationship between theological education, globalization, culture and churches.

Protestant Institutions of Higher Education in Croatia – A Pilot Study

This insight into the Protestant higher education scene in Croatia will be provided by analyzing four higher education institutions: the Theological Faculty 'Mathias Flacius Illyricus' in Zagreb (hereafter TF MVI), the Biblical Institute in Zagreb (BIZ), the Adventist College in Maruševec (ACM) and the Evangelical Theological Seminary in Osijek (ETS) founded by different Protestant churches to be spiritually formative and practical, and to prepare for service in church and society. These institutions, some twenty years after they have been founded, seem to be facing a challenge in regard to how to secure the interests of their founding churches and how at the same time to respond properly to the changes of society

About the Research

The pilot research was used as a standard scientific tool to allow gathering preliminary data and conduct basic analysis of an area that was not studied before. It was taken during the first three months of 2015. The anonymous on-line questionnaire was used as a principal method of collecting information from individuals working at the four Protestant institutions of higher education in Croatia.

The research included the four Protestant institutions of higher education and nineteen respondents, where three were from TF MVI, four from BIZ, four from ACM and eight from ETS. The sampling was stratified ensuring that there were enough respondents included among the staff and lecturers of the four institutions, including a representative of the student body. From nineteen respondents, ten were lecturers, eight belonged to the category 'staff', and three were student representatives (independent variables). The research focused on three questions: What is the nature and role of Protestant theological institutions in Croatia, is their limited access to resources (human, financial, material) affected by their particular status within Croatian society and changes in the European educational setting, and how does this affect their relationship with the founding churches and what kind of steps are needed so that they can adequately respond to these circumstances and enhance their capacities for providing both academic excellence and reflect their fundamental relational nature to the church, to God and to the community in general (dependent variables)?

To collect the respondents' insights, an on-line questionnaire with 24 questions was designed, out of which two were open-ended and 22 close-ended. In creating the close-ended questions, the Likert scale was used. By making this choice, the intention was to measure attitudes, perceptions, values, but also knowledge, through a series of statements from which respondents might choose, in order to rate their responses.[48] Textual answers in three questions were combined with numericals to specify the intensity of respondents' feelings for a given item.[49] The questions were designed to cover the vision and mission of Protestant institutions of higher education, their relationships with founding churches, changes due to Bologna, and future prospects related to Bologna programme requirements (12 questions) and Protestant institutions of higher education's management structures/different bodies of operation and their quality of operation (12 questions).

Abbreviations used: PIHEC: Protestant institutions of higher education in Croatia; TF MVI: Theological Faculty 'Mathias Falacius Illyricus' Zagreb; BIZ: the Biblical Institute in Zagreb; ACM: the Adventist College in Maruševec; ETS: the Evangelical Theological Seminary in Osijek (ETS).

Research Findings

The findings presented are grouped around three main areas: (1) The vision and mission of Protestant institutions of higher education, and relationships with founding churches, (2) Changes occurring due to the implementation of the Bologna programme requirements, and (3) the management structures/different bodies of operation of Protestant institutions of higher education and their quality of operation.

Regarding area (1), the cross-cutting of the responses to questions 1 ('What do you think, what was the aim for establishing your institution?'), 2 ('If you were to define your institution today, what would that be?'), and 19 (the control question: 'If you were to describe your institution today, what would you say?') showed that, while the respondents were clear about their institution's vision and mission: the purpose for which it had been established (ministerial training and formation – 94.4%, academic theological education – 55.6%, promotion of Biblical values – 50%), they seemed to be more inclined to see their institutions today, first, as providing an academic theological education – 66.7%, and secondly, as institutions of theological and spiritual formation – 55.6%. This was highlighted even more by the answers provided to the control question no. 19 which showed that the majority of respondents considered PIHEC open to all who wished to study 'Protestant theology' (72.2%) and were striving for academic excellence. The dilemma over the nature of the Protestant theological academia in Croatia in terms of 'academic *versus* Biblical' is visible also in the next set of responses. Those provided to questions 16 ('Evaluate the

---

[48] P.W. Vogt, *Dictionary of Statistics and Methodology* (Thousand Oaks, CA: Sage, 1999).

[49] A. van Alphen, R. Halfens, A. Hasman and T. Imbos, 'Likert or Rasch?: Nothing Is More Applicable than Good Theory', in *Journal of Advanced Nursing,* 20 (1994), 196-201: www.researchgate.net/publication/15269359_Likert_or_Rasch_Nothing_is_more_applicable_than_good_theory (accessed 24th May 2015).

relationship of your institution with the founding churches in the last ten years'), 17 ('How important is it for your institution to continue nurturing this relationship?'), and 18 ('Does this relationship with the founding churches affects the work of your institution?'), which were multiple-choice questions, indicate that respondents considered the relationship between PIHEC and founding churches strong and important (65.9%), yet at the same time one of open co-operation with respect to differences in stances (88.9%). The importance of nurturing this relationship in the future is yet again also strong (61.1%), on almost the same footing as the tendency to maintain a degree of autonomy expressed as 'respect for differences' (50%).

About area (2), regarding changes that occurred due to the Bologna programme and the (re)accreditation procedures of the Croatian Ministry of Science, Education and Sports, the respondents' general view can be described as positive. Their answers to questions 20 ('List the changes in your institution due to the process of (re)accreditation'), 21 ('How do you value these changes?'), 22 ('What, in your opinion, should be the direction your institution should take in the future?'), 23 ('Do you see co-operation being needed between different Protestant institutions of higher education?'), and 24 ('Would some forms of co-operation help advance Protestant institutions of higher education in Croatia?') show positive steps being taken – namely that, due to changes in legislation, institutions of higher education were pushed to adopting documents, acts and specific regulations for their proper functioning (66.7%), as well as developing proper internal organization systems, setting different management bodies, employing resident lecturers and signing employment contracts (55.6%). Although state regulations demanded changes of the names of three out of the four institutions in question, this did not affect their work in a negative way, and they continued providing studies at both undergraduate and graduate levels (51%). Problems occurred, however, at the level of certificates, which for three out of four institutions were considered private (unaccredited) until the process of (re)accreditation was positively resolved. This in turn affected both the students (38.9% stated there was a decline in number of students enrolling PIHEC) and lecturers – namely, if PIHEC were to hire lecturers with a recognised level of academic competency (PhD degree with *venia docendi*, the right to teach) raising the level of PIHEC academic competency, they needed a stable income to finance this step. PIHEC usually generate their income through tuition fees and donations (only one out of the four institutions in question is having their operational costs covered by the government of Croatia). The fewer the students, the lower the income; the lower the income, the fewer the donations. This vicious circle of PIHEC's sustainability could be resolved by combining different methods, some of which were mentioned by the respondents themselves: turning to the state for funding, partnering with local universities, taking part in research projects, increasing students' mobility and taking part in 'Erasmus programmes' (http://www.erasmusprogramme.com/) of foreign student exchanges, intensifying PIHEC promotion both in Croatia and in wider Europe, intensifying academic co-operation between PIHEC, especially in terms of exchange of lecturers, and so on. Respondents also stressed the need for creating different forms of strengthened internal co-operation among the named institutions of higher education to support and promote their position in the Croatian education market, such as meetings to agree on collaborative academic programmes, joint needs assessment analysis and strategic planning, annual academic conferences, joint journal and research projects, etc.

Comparing responses about the management structures (bodies) within the PIHEC (area 3, questions 3-15), it could be said that the institutions in question have the following bodies of management: Academic Dean, Academic Board, Students' Representative, Seminary/Faculty Council, Secretary and Vice Deans. Only one institution out of four has a Board of Deans, three have no ethical and quality assurance committees. One institution has no Secretary and no Vice Dean! The quality of performance of the named functions/bodies varies. Ratings of the Deans show that only half of respondents were satisfied with the performance of their Deans (50%), while the other half graded their work only as 3-satisfactory or 2-poor. Asked in addition to state 'What are the most important functions of a Dean?' and to choose 5 out of 11 answers provided, the majority of respondents stated that the most important role of a Dean was to 'organise and lead the institution' (88.9%). This answer was followed by two equally ranked answers: 'to recommend to the Faculty/Seminary Council the curriculum and plan, strategy of development and institutions' annual budget and operation plan' and 'to represent the institution in all legal matters' (61.1%). It seems that Deans were either most successful or least effective in performing these functions.

PIHEC bodies of management such as Vice Dean(s), Secretary, Students' Representative and Academic Board, were ranked with a majority of positive 4-very good to 5-excellent grades (61% to 72.3%). Seminary/Faculty Council on the other hand, received more dispersed answers – namely, only 33.3% of respondents valued the work of this body as excellent-5 or very good-4, while 66.7% had given it grades good-3 or below (satisfactory-2 and poor-1). If we have in mind that the primary role of this body of management is to secure and supervise the proper operation of the PIHEC (66.7%), develop PIHEC capacities, financial, material, and human (61.1%), elect and dismiss the Dean and Vice Deans (50%), we ought to consider some major structural changes in its setting and functioning.

Argument and Recommendations

The main thesis of this paper is that Protestant theological institutions of higher education can contribute to the enrichment of Croatia's plural, multi-faith society and academic excellence that is the focus of the Bologna programme. Being part of Croatian society for the last 30-50 years, they have played a significant role in enriching the Croatian ecumenical and multi-faith spectrum. The new times brought forth changes that the Protestant institutions of higher education need to adapt to if they want to meet the standards of academic excellence set by the European Union market and the Bologna programme. For these changes to be effective, these institutions need adjusting to the Croatian higher education legal framework as well as having access to at least partial state funding. They also need to decide upon their nature and role in the wider community, providing education and nurturing dialogue with the world as God's creation. These changes are neither small nor quick: they demand financial, material and human resources, as well as a strong commitment on behalf of all sides involved in the process to achieve the desired results.

Studies of theological education in Central and Eastern Europe by Kool, Mark, Mojzes, Penner and others show that 'fundamental changes (in theological education in Central and Eastern Europe in general) have taken place only at the margins'; while theological academia seems keen on taking steps in term of fulfilling different accrediting requirements, less was done 'in terms of transforming its curriculum into one that is both contextually relevant and biblically and theologically grounded, in a creative tension with both context and text'.[50] The perception of a growing distance between academia and church communities is another important feature noted in Central and Eastern Europe as well as the need to find more realistic models of education that would be more suitable to the context and society in question.[51] Inasmuch as churches can help academia in their quest for identity, theological institutions can assist churches in their self-understanding of their own 'cultural trappings' that are lie between 'the culture and the Scripture'.[52]

The main findings of this research also confirm that *first*, there is a need for more dialogue between churches (as founders) and the theological academia in Croatia on the nature of their relationship, expectancies and aims; *second*, the neglect of dialogue reflects negatively on the functioning of theological academia (a lack of clearer vision and mission, a lack of

---

[50] A.-M. Kool and Penner, 'Theological Education in Eastern and Central Europe: Major Developments and Challenges since 1910', in David Esterline et al (eds), *The Handbook of Theological Education in World Christianity* (Oxford: Regnum, 2010), 13.

[51] Kool and Penner, 'Theological Education in Eastern and Central Europe', 14.

[52] J. Reed, 'New Paradigms for the Post-Modern Church', article presented at the Third Annual Conference 'Church-Based Missions: Creating a New Paradigm', 23rd October 1992: https://www.bild.org/download/paradigmPapers/2_Church%20Based% 20Missions.pdf (accessed 14th May 2015).

students, lecturers and funds); *third*, the overall political, local, European and global trends influence greatly Protestant theological studies in Croatia – academia needs to find a greater balance between its needs and wants, and be much clearer about its mandate in the world today; *fourth*, there are several models that theological academia in Croatia can follow: church-related, university-related, Christian theology study or mission-oriented, a model of co-operative compliance of academic programmes, and the like. Whatever the choice, it should be based upon an in-depth and comprehensive needs-assessment analysis to determine the needs, examine the nature and causes, and set priorities to better define the future for theological academia in Croatia; *fifth*, without setting a model of co-operation between the Protestant theological institutions of higher education in Croatia, there would be little place for building the much-needed distinctive character of 'Croatian Protestant theology', offering both academic excellence and the word of God; *sixth*, occasional tensions between the church and academia, the principles of academic learning and church/faith commitment could be viewed as a part of critical growth in thinking and lead to a better understanding of both theory and practice, resulting in mutual enrichment. In this sense, the *seventh* and last recommendation calls for a stronger push towards accepting the Bologna requirements and state accreditation demands. This may be the right way 'out' of the current standstill position: it could lead to greater professionalization of the Protestant academia, greater employee (lecturer and staff) satisfaction with the institutions, nationally and internationally recognized diplomas, an increased number of (Croatian and foreign) students, access to EU funds related to projects and researches, and greater international co-operation with institutions of a similar kind. This, in turn, need not mean that academia should necessarily forfeit either church support or church ownership. Careful management and structured dialogue between the education institutions and churches, as well as dialogue between them and the state of Croatia could produce better understanding of the changed setting in Croatia, the needs of the students, churches and academia in general, and greater flexibility on behalf of the state bearing in mind the uniqueness of the position of the Protestant community and its academia. In this sense, Bosch's call for the church is very relevant: both church and academia can become isolated in their quest for a new (paradigm) shift, or losing its critical voice through becoming related to the institutions of this world. Bosch thus strongly advocates that churches and theologians should constantly 'challenge one another's cultural, social and ideological biases'.[53] He warns against churches becoming mere institutions losing their missional connectedness which keeps their vitality – only as such can they be the much-needed 'partners' to the academia, even if they

[53] David J. Bosch, *Transforming Mission: Paradigm Shifts in Theology of Mission* (Maryknoll, NY: Orbis Books, 1991), 187.

'may be passionately convinced' that the views of their schools 'are in need of major corrections'.[54]

Protestant theological education in Croatia can learn much by accepting the affirmations and recommendations of the Edinburgh Study Group. Edinburgh 2010 as a platform can be both stimulative and inspirational for the future of Protestant academia in Croatia. Several recommendations can be drawn from all this, the *first* being that churches and theological institutions should work together to strengthen, accompany and enhance theological education. This relationship should be one of mutual respect, service, ownership and critical distance. The *second* is that this should be done by fostering dialogue between academia and the churches, but also between the four institutions analyzed, to ensure common co-operation in theological education (joint plenary meetings, (international) conferences on theological education, etc.). The *third* calls for education for cross-cultural mission and spirituality (short-term courses to lifelong learning programmes). The *fourth* stresses interdenominational networking for the mobility of both staff and students, but also academic programmes and research projects, increasing competences to avoid isolation and fragmentation in theological education, enhancing further co-operation and common responsibility. The *fifth* focuses on an understanding that both church-related theological education and university-related institutional theological education can effectively work for the Kingdom of God. Yet, to build relationship of trust and support requires mutual listening, regular contacts, and involvement in the life of institutions concerned as much as critical distance and a degree of autonomy. The *sixth* opts for 'innovative forms of theological education'[55] (one of which is the Bologna process) accompanied by distance and lifelong learning models of education which can additionally contribute to the spread of the Word of God as well as bringing about a greater sustainability of theological institutions.[56] A study of the resources available for theological education and the financial viability of theological institutions is the *seventh* and, in this context, the final recommendation of Edinburgh 2010 that is applicable for the case of Croatian Protestant institutions of higher education.

---

[54] Bosch, *Transforming Mission*, 187.

[55] Balia and Kim, *Witnessing Christ Today*, 167.

[56] In addition, there are also the models of non-formal and informal education, the UNESCO four pillars of learning model, Dr Jane Vella's dialogue model approach, and many more that can serve as a source for offering a range of educational activities to support the formal education offered. See Julijana Mladenovska-Tešija, 'Dialogue as a Method of Learning in the Theological Education: The Case of Evangelical Theological Seminary in Osijek', in *Kairos*, IX.1 (2015), 55-72; and her 'Interfaith Dialogue Is (Not) Necessary for Peace: The Four-Pillar Model of Dialogue', research supported by the Ecumenical Women's Initiative from Omiš, Croatia: www.eiz.hr/wp-content/uploads/2014/12/Julijana-Mladenovska-Tesija-ENG.pdf (accessed 2nd July 2015).

Concluding Remarks

The process of continuous and open multi-level dialogue (church-academia, church-academia-state, academia-academia, academia-society, and so on) can contribute greatly to avoid the erosion of theological institutions in Croatia, or crystallization, as Gehlen calls it. At the same time, he warns against quasi-institutionalization that occurs when institutions are too exposed to constant change which makes them fragile – and susceptible to cultural compromise, as Bosch claims.

To avoid both, a shift in focus must occur to provide renewal of Croatian theological academia based on inner redefinition of the church-academia relationship in terms of *missio Dei* as well as on 'responsive faith of service' (Bonhoeffer) between Protestant theological institutions rejecting both too great a focus on individuals, as well as too great a focus on collectives.

Only by meeting 'under the cross' (Bosch, Moltmann) will the community of exodus meet instead of the community of institutions, and only that can lead to open dialogue and co-operation in Croatia with some idea of the complementarity of educational studies and programmes. This recognition might seem pertinent today, bearing in mind the need of these institutions to survive the day, and the changes and challenges within the Croatian and European educational market.

Crossing the Drava: Interior Reflections of an Atypical American Theologian in South-Central Europe

Eric J. Titus

Introduction

When Julius Caesar crossed the shallow River Rubicon in 49 BC, he uttered the words *alea iacta est* – the die is cast. The phrase 'crossing the Rubicon' has survived for 2,000 years to indicate a point of no return, a point at which things cannot be undone.

My family and I crossed the River Drava in the summer of 2004. It forms a natural boundary with Hungary and Croatia, and meets with the Danube not far from what was to be our new home town, Osijek, Croatia. I was going to teach theology at the Evangelical Seminary, my wife to head the English Department, my children to attend the local school. I was also beginning my ThD studies at Charles University in Prague, making many trips over the Drava in the course of our tenure in Osijek. I had not thought about it during our time there, but have done so many times since – that the Drava was my Rubicon.

Rather than giving a strict narrative of my experience as a missionary-theologian, I want to consider some missiological reflections from my 'crossing the Drava' and the personal impact of serving in a post-genocidal, post-communist culture and context. To that end, I have divided this article into the following areas of consideration: exteriority and interiority, becoming versus being, the chimera of return and restoration, and a lesson for general application.

Exteriority and Interiority

New missionaries heading overseas are told in orientation that all their wide-eyed dreams about changing the world or the country to which they are going are about to run into the hard wall of reality. This is true. But I think I can say with all honesty that I did not have such notions. I was going to teach theology. It just happened to be in a country other than the one in which I was born. The truth is I did not know what to expect. I did have some idea, primarily from the works of Anthony Gittins, that I would be at the margins of the society I was in, always viewed as an outsider, at best a stranger bearing gifts.[1] Because of this tendency and the emphasis on wiping away missiological idealism and naïveté, what I missed was any bracing for expectations of what, as Michael Foucault put it, was to be the relationship between exteriority and interiority within myself, and how, continuing with Foucault, my analysis of finitude would change.[2] This understanding of the relationship of exteriority with interiority was critical.

In distilled terms, Foucault postulated that every institution constructed or presented an exterior structure, which constituted its own epistemology. All the specialized language use, customs, forms, traditions, understandings, relationships and ethical constructs within the institution form the interiority of each person within the institution. Epistemologically, an individual's truths are formed from exterior presentations. Interiority is therefore shaped by that which is outside rather than that which is inside an individual.

Foucault's thoughts are of course applicable in a broader sense. It does not require a great leap to understand that, even if one does not accept the whole of Foucault's thought, the cultures and the institutions within those cultures do in fact form to a greater extent than we realize the constitution of our interiority. Missionaries from the United States, for instance, are for the most part unaware of how much their economic preferences affect their understanding of the use of power. One of the places this is most apparent is in the American concept of freedom. The grand assumption that is made is that all people everywhere understand freedom in the same way as we do in the United States and, furthermore, they want that same sort of freedom as badly as we do. However, even a bit of biblical reading will reveal that the apostle Paul sitting in prison viewed freedom differently from most Americans. Paul's freedom was directly linked with his Christology, not his ability to go anywhere he wanted, do anything he wanted to do, or even to say everything he wanted to say. Exteriority and its impact upon the interior formation and epistemological outlook of a person cannot be emphasized enough.

This, for me, was and is especially true in the contexts in which I was teaching and studying, Croatia and the Czech Republic respectively. In Croatia, for instance, for a good portion of the last half of the twentieth century, economics had far less to do with money than it did with relationships. Power was not located in a person's bank account, but within the community and the resources which relationships provided. Like all economic systems, this one too had both its positive as well as its darker sides. Foucault's understanding of exteriority and its relationship with interiority was enlightening. It means for me – as someone who has crossed the Rubicon – that missionary engagement with other cultures should begin

---

[1] Anthony J. Gittins, *Ministry at the Margins* (Maryknoll, NY: Orbis Books, 2002); and Gittins, *Gifts and Strangers: Meeting the Challenge of Inculturation* (New York: Paulist Press, 1989).

[2] Michael Foucault, *The Order of Things* (New York: Pantheon Books, 1970).

with a rigorous examination of the institutional exteriorities one has from their native culture. This examination will perhaps become easier for future generations, whose ranks are swelling with third-culture children, such as mine, who recognize more than one culture as their native or home culture. It also means that understanding things such as economics and power need to be deeply considered in missional engagement, since these mean and hold such differing exteriorities across cultures. This means too that, with each multicultural encounter, we are dealing with individuals who, within their own culture, have an interiority formed by that culture, but also have interiorities formed by the multitude of interiorities within their own cultures.

What I was not prepared for was that the new exteriority that confronted me after I had crossed the Drava would re-order me with respect to issues of interiority, and that my analysis of finitude would also be restructured. Exterior elements like language, history, news, geographical settings, views of time, work, relationship, friends, enemies, down to the little intricacies of daily life were all, in a moment, up-ended. All expectations and realities that were in place before I had crossed the Drava were replaced with a different exteriority after I had crossed it. Issues that had high priority in the United States in my discipline also faced this challenge. Across the Drava, issues such political correctness and LGBT inclusion were hardly on the radar.

This single issue about whether or not people who are lesbian, gay, bisexual or transgender should be included without prejudice in the full life of the church has consumed vast amounts of time, energy and resource in the churches of North America. In my denomination (Reformed Church in America), it is an issue which overshadows almost any other and which threatens each year to divide the denomination right down the centre.

Quite different issues dominated the church in the countries of the former Yugoslavia in the wake of war and communist dictatorship. This was the interiority formed in the soul in the aftermath of harsh realities. To superimpose my interiority shaped by an exteriority before I crossed the Drava would be *hubris*. But what did this mean for the rest of my interior structure?

The question then became: Would the former state of my interiority stand against the confrontation of a new exteriority? That is: Would I walk out essentially unchanged with respect to my interiority, regardless of the exterior realities that surrounded me? This may seem a simple question, but in fact it is not. I saw numerous (especially American) missionaries who, while affected by the culture, showed little to no perceptible change in their theological understanding. Perhaps this was a form of self-protection of their interiority. This was not the path I went down. I had crossed the Drava; then and now I can say for good or for bad: *alea iacta est.*

Becoming versus Being

The sixth-century philosopher Heraclitus proposed that nothing was constant except becoming. While I accept this as axiomatic, I can say as a theologian and pastor of some experience that there are people so stagnant, so fixed, that one must also make room for the Eleatic School of Parmenides, who was suspicious of change and becoming because it smacked of deceitfulness.

After crossing the Drava, I sensed over time, shifts or turns within myself. Exteriority was producing within me a new interiority or, to put it in a slightly different way, my being was becoming, transforming. During the six-year period my family and I spent in Croatia, at least within the seminary and church community I served there, I sensed something happening. I was no longer ministering from the margins. I was no longer a stranger bringing gifts. I had become something other that what I had been. An example of this came when I was talking with some of my students from Romania, Croatia and Serbia. One of them began to tell a not so flattering joke about America. Another of the students stopped him and signalled him to remember that the professor was an American. His response: 'No, he's not! He's one of us.'

This would be demonstrated nowhere more strongly than our last day at the seminary in Osijek. One of our students said at a gathering: 'When we see them in the market or on the street, we do not see Americans. We see ourselves, people that belong to us and our community.' This drove home to me that a new interiority had been fostered by the narrative and exteriority of the people around me. Issues of life in the church and the theology I focused upon had been turned to the context. My being was becoming and my new reality, the one I had been told to abandon my expectations of, had expectations of me. I would teach them, yes, but they would transform me, in a sense, into the theologian they needed. I could either stand stagnantly in an eleatic interiority or become something new. To be honest, I have never been a typical American theologian, so the change for me in crossing the Drava may have been easier than for others.

The Chimera of Return and Restoration.

As certain as I was about the interior turn that had occurred within me after crossing the Drava, when circumstances dictated that my family and I had to return to the USA, I found I had fallen prey to an assumption. The assumption was that, when we crossed the Atlantic back to the USA, there would be a restoration of things we lost in crossing the Drava to begin with. This is not an altogether wild notion given readings and expectations in the Old Testament around themes of restoration.

I suppose what made my expectations more acute was that we were returning to the same county we left in New York before crossing the Drava, serving a church in the same district that we had left. It produced a chimera in my thinking that we would return to normal. At this point, my reflections above about crossing the Rubicon had not yet surfaced. I would simply return to my home country, state, church and colleagues and resume life as it had been before I left. Presumably I also thought my interiority would change too because the exteriority was to be back to 'normal'. My children would go back to school in New York, and my wife and I would pick up with old friends. We would return and be restored in all things. This is where the topsy-turviness of an international move fostered, or at least did not break, a naïveté that should have been fully expected.

After our return in 2012, I waited. We all waited. We waited for the effects of our missiological experiment to wear off. We waited for the return of 'normal'. We waited for our restoration, even our reward. This chimera, defined as a gross product of the imagination, never arrived. There was no 'normal' to which we could return, only a grossly distorted product of our imagination. We had given ourselves and our children fully and willingly over to crossing the Drava. We knew things would be different returning, but I certainly did not understand fully at the time that there was no returning. I did not understand that there was no crossing back over the Drava from whence I had come.

Missiologically and theologically, there is a point of no return, there is a reality about crossing the Rubicon. Certainly I had returned home. Certainly I was with old friends. Certainly I was in familiar surroundings. Certainly I was with many of my old colleagues. But just as certainly I was not with my old friends in the same way. My familiar surroundings turned into dissociative flashes back to Osijek or Prague. My colleagues speak the same language we spoke together before I left, but the language of my interiority is strange to them. I feel out of place, out of time, out of sorts. The rare occasions in which these things fade for me is when I am in contact with people I knew in Central Europe. The chimera of return and restoration have not completely faded, however: the exteriority of its gross imagination is gradually losing power over an interiority that is becoming again.

Related to this, I should say something about so-called 'reverse culture shock'. This was one of those things we were told to expect returning 'home'. I can say without equivocation that I no longer hold to such a phenomenon. I think this too is a chimera, a way to categorize and name something in order to gain control over it. At first I did think what I and my family were experiencing was reverse culture shock. But this phenomenon has always carried with it the idea that it will pass and that, for lack of a better terminology, 'reverse normality' would take over.

But this is precisely the point: it does not. The exteriority of Croatia and all the contexts I experienced there greatly affected my interiority. The exteriority of Croatian Christian expression and how that formed within me became for me a vital part of my spiritual becoming. The exteriority of the mission, crossing the Drava, became a part and indivisible component of the missionary. There is no reversing that. There is only an interplay now of a person whose interiority has been shaped by the exteriority of two deeply wonderful, yet diverse, understandings of Christian life. My being is that of one of God's missionary people.

A Lesson for General Application

Karl Barth provided the foundations from which arose the theology of God being a missionary God. Gittins, reflecting upon this idea, maintains that, if God is a missionary God and we are God's people, we are a missionary people. Gittins states that 'many good people still do not understand mission means me'.[3] To place this within the framework in which I have been working, it means that not just me, but each and every Christian must cross a Rubicon. But let us place another river here: the Jordan.

As Christians, we speak of crossing the Jordan as a metaphor for death. But here I want to use it in the same sense I used for crossing the Drava, something akin to Caesar's crossing the Rubicon. Missiologically, *every* Christian is under obligation and call to cross the Jordan. This crossing should be more far-reaching than me crossing the Drava or Caesar the Rubicon.

Crossing the Jordan means leaving the exteriorities of culture, history, language, context, familiarity and lifestyles that have shaped our interiorities. Because in crossing the Jordan, a new land is entered, a system contrary to our own confronts us, our priorities are up-ended; the poor are rich, the rich are poor. A new language is spoken, a language foreign to those who have not crossed the Jordan. Crossing the Jordan is not a two-week foray to dip our toes into the waters of mission, but rather an encounter with a new exteriority that will change our interiority. It is entering into the Kingdom of God. It is to stand at the foot of a new authority. It is to acknowledge that all that one has known before is wood, hay and stubble. It is to place our lives into the hands of the living God who asks us to surrender everything in faith and to follow in obedience. Crossing the Jordan means to place the totality of ourselves at God's disposal. It means encountering at the banks of this river a God who says to us, 'Pick up your cross and follow me,' and 'Whoever loses his life for my sake shall find it.'

When we cross the Jordan, we can be assured, just as I found when I tried to cross back over the Drava, that there is no going back. There is no return or restoration. There is only a warning: 'Whoever puts his hand to the plough and turns back is not fit for the Kingdom.' But whether one's hand is on the plough or one tries to turn back, there is no normal to which to return, only a waiting for a chimera – something gross and impossible in the imagination – that never materializes. Because, once one has

[3] Gittins, *Ministry at the Margins,* 11.

encountered the exteriority of the Kingdom of God, the interiority of the individual is transformed. All analysis of finitude is rewritten because the infinite Kingdom of God has overtaken it.

The great temptation is to confuse our exteriority with that of the Kingdom of God. We do this because the cost of crossing is high. We want to believe that, once we have crossed the Jordan, it will look remarkably like the place we left. We then of course do not have to deal with the transformation of interiority. We can remain stagnant, unmoved, non-reflective, stationary. The other possibility of course is that we do cross the Jordan, but we do not let its exteriority disturb us. In this case, we walk away like the rich young ruler. We remain stagnant, unmoved, stubborn. Our interiority remains unchanged because we are afraid of the process of becoming. We long for the assurance of Parmenides and remain paranoid, distrustful, xenophobic. We do not wish to become theologically or missiologically, we just want to be. The axiom of Heraclitus becomes too much to consider, but in this case we have not crossed the Jordan in any real sense. Maybe we hovered over it, but we never really entered the new land.

I end with this thought. Crossing the Drava was difficult and still to this day brings many pains and difficulties with it. So has crossing the Jordan. I am often asked if I would do it again. My response is that I cross it every day.

RE-IMAGINING THEOLOGICAL EDUCATION: A RESPONSE TO NEW HISTORICAL, SOCIAL, CULTURAL AND RELIGIOUS REALITIES – A POLISH CASE STUDY

Wojciech Szczerba

Introduction

This article focuses on the character, activity and evolution of the Evangelical School of Theology (EST), Wrocław, Poland, in the years 1990-2015. The aim is to indicate how the changing context in its broad historical, social, cultural and religious aspects has determined changes within the nature and activity of EST from its early days as the Biblical Theological Seminary (BTS). Its purpose was to offer a simple theological programme to evangelical communities in Poland. Over the last 25 years, BTS/EST has transformed into the EST Educational Center consisting of versatile programmes and projects offered to a wide-ranging Christian community in Poland and abroad.

The article has the nature of a case study, focusing on a particular institution in its dynamic context. It is written with the hope that the case of the Evangelical School of Theology may illustrate how differently the same vision and values of an institution may be applied in a changing environment. Hopefully, the case study may serve as an inspiration to other teaching institutions of a similar type in applying creative methods of theological education in their settings.

Context

It is crucial to understand the context in which the Evangelical School of Theology operates to grasp the nature of the changes introduced in its development between 1990 and 2015.[1]

---

[1] The issue of theological education in the broader context of Eastern and Central Europe is well presented in Anne-Marie Kool and Peter Penner, 'Theological Education in Eastern and Central Europe: Major Developments and Challenges since 1910', in David Esterline, Dietrich Werner, Namsoon Kang and Joshva Raja (eds), *The Handbook of Theological Education in World Christianity* (Oxford: Regnum, 2010); and Anne-Marie Kool, 'From Marginalization to Revitalization: Missiology's Contribution to the Renewal of Theological Curricula of Theological Institutions in Eastern European Contexts', in Mihai Malancea (ed), *Evangelical Mission in the Eastern Orthodox Contexts: Bulgaria, Romania, Moldova, Ukraine* (Chişinău: Universitatea Divitia Gratiae, 2013), 9-37.

Polish Catholicism

It would not be a vast exaggeration to say that Poland is one of the most Catholic countries in the world. Somewhere between 90 and 95% of the Polish population declare themselves to be Christians of Catholic persuasion.[2] Even now, in spite of the wave of secularization in recent years, about 60% of Poles regularly participate in masses, and approximately 60% of the Polish population claims to have trust in the church.[3] The number of Poles participating in sacraments is slightly lower, especially in larger cities and among the well-educated under-30s.[4] However, the numbers are still impressive, exceeding the percentage in other European countries.

There are important reasons – historically speaking – for such a high trust in the Catholic Church in Poland. First of all, it has to be noted that Christianity came to Poland via the Catholic denomination. It was officially. introduced on Polish soil in 966 with the baptism of Mieszko I, the Duke of Poland.[5] Since then, Catholicism has never left Poland or lost its leading role there. Obviously, Eastern Orthodoxy has always played an important role in the east of Poland, but due to the uneasy Polish-Russian relationship, it could never dominate Poland. For similar reasons, the Cyrillic alphabet could not be adopted for the Polish, Slavic language. In the sixteenth and seventeenth centuries, Protestantism in its Reformed form had played an important role in Poland, especially among the Polish nobility.[6] There is still extant correspondence between John Calvin and the Polish King Sigismund II Augustus as a sign of the special hopes which the Reformer had for the conversion of Poland to Protestantism.[7] Also Protestant Arianism adopted by the so-called Polish Brethren significantly influenced the Polish intelligentsia in the sixteenth and seventeenth centuries.[8] However, it was not able to permeate all the social strata of Polish society and, after banishment in 1658, Arianism[9] has never

---

[2] Irena Borowik and Tadeusz Doktór, *Pluralizm religijny i moralny w Polsce: Raport z badań* (Kraków, Poland: Nomos, 2001), 23, 127. Research of Central Statistical Office of Poland for 2015 indicates that 93% of Polish citizens consider themselves Roman Catholics: http://stat.gov.pl/obszary-tematyczne/inne-opracowania/wyznania-religijne/zycie-religij ne-w-polsce,3,1.html (accessed 16th February 2016).

[3] www.cbos.pl/SPISKOM.POL/2007/K_037_07.PDF (accessed 10th February 2015).

[4] www.cbos.pl/SPISKOM.POL/2015/K_026_15.PDF (accessed 10th April 2015).

[5] Jerzy Kłoczowski, *A History of Polish Christianity* (Cambridge: CUP, 2000), 10-13.

[6] Paul Fox, 'The Reformation in Poland', in F. Reddaway, J.H. Penson, O. Halecki and R. Dyboski (eds), *The Cambridge History of Poland: From the Origins to Sobieski (to 1696)* (Cambridge: CUP, 1950), 322-48.

[7] Jean F. Gilmont, *John Calvin and the Printed Book* (Kirksville, MO: Truman State University Press, 2005), 331.

[8] James Miller, 'The Origins of Polish Arianism', in *The Sixteenth Century Journal* 16.2 (1985), 229-56.

[9] Alan Eyre, *Brethren in Christ* (Adelaide, Australia: CSSS, 1983); Piet Visser (ed), *Bibliographia Sociniana: A Bibliographical Reference Tool for the Study of Dutch Socinianism and Antitrinitarianism* (Hilversum, Netherlands: Uitgeverij Verloren, 2004), 313.

reappeared on Polish soil in a significant form. The Counter-Reformation strengthened Catholicism in Poland and reduced the role of its adversaries.

An important moment for strengthening Polish Catholicism was the time of the partition of Poland, which lasted from the end of the eighteenth century till the beginning of the twentieth. For 123 years, the country virtually ceased to exist on the maps of Europe, being partitioned mainly between the Russian Empire and the Kingdom of Prussia.[10] It was natural then that the preservation of the nation required some kind of core Polish identity. Roman Catholicism – to put it simply – naturally came into play as a factor opposing German Lutheranism and Russian Eastern Orthodoxy. It aspired to become a haven for the Polish soul and the sphere within which Polish culture could be preserved and developed under foreign regimes.

Poland reappeared as a country in 1918, but not so long afterwards World War II began, when Poland was one of the first countries attacked by German troops on 1st September 1939, and by the Russian army on 17th September 1939. Again, the Catholic Church, in opposition to anti-Christian Nazism and communism, played an important role during WW II in the preservation of Polish culture, Polish identity and the Polish nation as such. Catholic churches became natural centres of the Polish underground movement, and many priests were involved in active opposition to the Nazis.

An analogous situation followed after the war when Poland was subjected to the communist regime for almost 45 years. The Catholic Church became over time the strongest opponent to the communists, a sphere where the opposition thrived and where the Solidarity movement was anchored. Cardinals Wyszynski, Kominek and Wojtyła played crucial roles in the preservation of Polish identity, inner freedom and dignity. What also helped in strengthening the role of the Catholic Church in Poland after World War II was, ironically, the fact of shifting Polish borders westwards according to the resolution of the Potsdam Conference in the summer of 1945.[11] This sole act of relocating the borders of Poland cut off vast eastern territories traditionally linked with Eastern Orthodoxy. Various minorities inhabiting Poland before the war shrank significantly afterwards due to the Holocaust or later migrations.[12] For example, many German citizens of western lands now inherited by Poland were forced to emigrate to Germany.[13] However dramatic these processes were, the final effect was a

[10] And partly Habsburg Austria. Norman Davies, *God's Playground: A History of Poland in Two Volumes* (Oxford: OUP, 2005), 283.

[11] John B. Allcock (ed), *Border and Territorial Disputes* (London: Longmans, 1992), 148.

[12] http://web.ceu.hu/jewishstudies/pdf/02_stola.pdf (accessed 10th February 2015). Dariusz Stola, 'Fighting against the Shadows: The Anti-Zionist Campaign of 1968' (reprint), in Robert Blobaum (ed), *Antisemitism and Its Opponents in Modern Poland* (Ithaca, NY: Cornell University Press, 2005), 284-300.

[13] Approximately 3.2 million Germans were expelled from Poland between 1945 and 1950. See Tomasz Kamusella, 'The Expulsion of the Population Categorized as "Germans" from Post 1945 Poland', in Steffen Prauser and Arfon Rees (eds), *The Expulsion of 'German'*

country ethnically almost monolithic, inhabited by Polish citizens of a predominantly Catholic identity.

Since the fall of communism in 1989, the situation has not changed much, although there had been some anticipations of the possible lessening of the role of the Catholic Church due to the disappearance of its main adversary. What stopped or slowed down the possible process of secularization in Poland, was – among other things – the leading role of Pope John Paul II and the aggressive nature of capitalism, which entered Poland after the fall of communism. One of the results of the structural changes in the beginning of the 1990s was very high unemployment, growing from less than 0% before 1989 to 16% in 1993.[14] It was natural that people, in a changing environment, were looking for some kind of support and the Catholic Church with a Polish Pope and a long tradition of serving the needy, was to hand. The strengthening of Catholicism in this context seemed inevitable and even though the end of twentieth century showed some signs of reaction to the phenomenon, paradoxically the death of the Pope in 2005 reinforced Catholicism in Polish society. Only since 2005, have there been unprecedented, clearly noticeable waves of secularism touching society at large and a process of growing scepticism towards the church and its hierarchy.[15]

To sum up the role of Catholicism in recent Polish history, it is important to pinpoint its few fundamental aspects, which have grown naturally out of the development of Polish society in the last centuries. First of all, it has to be noted that Roman Catholicism has always been linked with Poland as such. Since its introduction in 966, it has played an important role in the history and development of the nation. It has permeated all strata of society and has overcome all possible opponents. Second, Catholicism has been operating not only as a faith factor, but also as a formative force of Polish culture. Especially during the time of the partition of Poland and the regimes controlling the country in the twentieth century, Catholicism became some kind of haven within which Polish culture, character and nature could be developed and preserved. Third, the setting in which Polish Catholicism has been developing for centuries has determined its conservative character.[16] To put it simply, it has been shaped in the past centuries to preserve Polish culture and identity, and to stand against its oppressors, Germans connected in popular stereotypes with Lutheranism, Russians confessing Eastern Orthodoxy, communists opposing any kind of religion whatsoever, and now liberal capitalists

---

Communities from Eastern Europe at the End of the Second World War (HEC, 2004/1), (Florence, Italy: European University Institute, 2004), 21-33.

[14] http://stat.gov.pl/download/gfx/portalinformacyjny/pl/defaultaktualnosci/5501/13/1/13/oz_polska_1989-2014.pdf (accessed 10th April 2015).

[15] www.cbos.pl/SPISKOM.POL/2009/K_034_09.PDF (accessed 10th April 2015).

[16] 'Conservative' in the sense of striving to retain the *status quo*, reactionary attitude towards contextual changes. Iain McLean and Alistair McMillan, 'Conservatism', in *The Concise Oxford Dictionary of Politics* (3rd edn; Oxford: OUP, 2009).

infected with consumerism and globalization.[17] One of the outcomes of the situation is that, even though Polish Catholicism is quite strong as a faith or cultural factor, it has – in general – not produced any strong theological reflection. With a few exceptions, Polish theological thought has never been in the forefront of Catholicism. The pontificate of John Paul II may serve as an example of this. Fourth, since the death of Pope John Paul II, there has been a noticeable decrease of trust in the Catholic Church in Polish society. Moral issues of various kinds, financial problems, the political involvement of the church, globalization and the like, have all created a situation never seen before; the younger generations do not participate in church life as much as their older predecessors. Criticism of the church is growing, the number of vocations is steadily declining, and it seems that preserving the status of the Catholic Church may be difficult in the future.[18]

Polish Protestantism

In opposition to the Catholic Church, Polish Protestantism, after the short episode of the sixteenth and seventeenth centuries, has never dominated the Polish confessional scene. It has always been a religious minority, outnumbered by Eastern Orthodoxy, Greek Catholicism and the Jewish population.[19] Especially after World War II, with the waves of immigration, communist repression and the strengthening of Catholicism, Protestantism shrank to no more than 1% of the population.[20] According to a recent analysis, none of the churches, except for the Pentecostal denomination, has grown in recent years.[21] Most of the churches are gradually losing their members or are simply maintaining the same level of believers.

What is also important in the context of the development of the Evangelical School of Theology is the fact that none of the evangelical churches in Poland requires from their leaders any formal theological

---

[17] https://www.opendemocracy.net/globalization-vision_reflections/modernity_ 3082.jsp (accessed 10th May 2016). See Zygmunt Bauman, *Globalization* (New York: Columbia University Press 2000).

[18] www.cbos.pl/SPISKOM.POL/2015/K_026_15.PDF (accessed 16th February 2016).

[19] www.dws-xip.pl/wojna/2rp/ad3.html (accessed 3rd October 2015). Tomasz Szarota and Wojciech Materski, *Polska 1939-1945: Straty osobowe i ofiary represji pod dwiema okupacjami* (Warsaw: IPN, 2009).

[20] The largest Protestant denomination, the Lutheran Church, consists of approximately 62,000 people. Of the other mainline Protestant churches, the Reformed Church includes about 3,500 members but the Methodist community consists of no more than 4,500 people. The situation of communities traditionally included under Evangelicalism does not seem to be any better. In a country consisting of nearly 40 million people, the Pentecostal Church has no more than 23,000 people, Adventists – 9,000 members, Baptists – 4,500, and Church of God in Christ – 4,000. Other Evangelical denominations do not exceed 2,000 members each: http://stat.gov.pl/cps/rde/xbcr/gus/RS_rocznik_statystyczny_rp_ 2012.pdf (accessed 10th May 2015).

[21] http://wroclaw.stat.gov.pl/cps/rde/xbcr/wroc/ASSETS_dzial_05_w_ 13.pdf (accessed 10th July 2015).

education. It is enough to pass a so-called 'church exam' to become and serve as a pastor, leader or a worker in a given church.[22] Traditionally these churches do not value formal theological training, and some of the communities treat theology as threat to a healthy development of a community of believers.

Paradoxically, several of the Protestant churches have their own schools of higher education based on a special legal act following the Concordat agreement with the Roman Catholic Church signed in 1993.[23] The Lutheran, Baptist, Pentecostal, Methodist and Adventist churches own and operate their own theological institutions, which is an important factor considering how small the Protestant population in Poland is.

The Demography of Poland

One of the most important factors determining Polish reality after the transformation of the political system, especially in its social dimension, is demography and precisely the demographic drop experienced in Poland since 1990.[24] According to government analysis, a gradual decline of the number of births since 1990 has been observed. Whereas just after the fall of communism approximately 550,000 babies were born each year, in 2015 the expected number slightly exceeded 400,000 and it is anticipated that by 2050 the number of babies born each year will be below 300,000.[25]

What makes the situation even more complicated is the fact that, since the accession of Poland to the European Union, more than two million people have emigrated from Poland to western European countries. The vast majority, approximately 63%, of emigrants are young people leaving Poland for economic reasons. The situation does not seem to be improving, as it was expected that in 2015 about 1.29 million people would leave Poland, which would increase the total number of emigrants since 2004 to three million people.[26]

Such a situation, with the additional fact that the number of immigrants to Poland does not balance this demographical deficit, creates a very difficult context for the development of several branches of the Polish

---

[22] E.g. the Baptist church in Poland: www.baptysci.pl/akty-prawne/945-zasadnicze-prawo-wewnetrzne?start=6 (accessed 10th September 2015). The Pentecostal Church in Poland: http://kz.pl/kzw/wp-content/uploads/2009/04/Prawo-wewn%C4%99trzne-Ko%C5%9Bcio%C5%82a-Zielono%C5%9Bwi%C4%85tkowe go-w-Polsce.pdf (accessed 10th September 2015).

[23] Beata Górowska and Czesław Janik (eds), *Konkordat polski 1993: Wybór materiałów źródłowych z lat 1993-1996* (Warszawa: Instytut Nauk Politycznych Uniwersytetu Warszawskiego, 1997).

[24]: http://demografia.stat.gov.pl/bazademografia/Tables.aspx (accessed 10th September 2015).

[25] http://demografia.stat.gov.pl/bazademografia/Prognoza.aspx (accessed 10th September 2015).

[26] http://stat.gov.pl/download/gfx/portalinformacyjny/pl/defaultaktualnosci/5471/2/7/1/informacja_o_rozmiarach_i_kierunkach_emigracji_z_polski_w_latach_2004-2013.pdf (accessed 10th September 2015).

economy. One of them is tertiary education, which has been experiencing a gradual decline in the number of students. Out of more than 300 institutions of higher education existing today in Poland, about a third are expected to survive in the next five to eight years. Humanities and social sciences are suffering most in the process.[27]

Economic Changes in Poland after the Fall of Communism

Another related aspect, important in the context of analysis of the evolution of the Evangelical School of Theology, is simply the economic growth of Poland since the fall of communism. It needs to be noted that the last 25 years signify the spectacular success of the Polish economy. Since 1990, GNP has grown more than 120%; in 1989, it was $2,166 per capita, whereas in 2012 it was $12,708. The standard of living is much higher than in the past and inflation is low; the unemployment rate ranges below 10%, and salaries are gradually increasing.[28] From a devastated nation in 1989, Poland has grown to be a country catching up with western economies. The quality of life in Poland has been enormously upgraded in the last 25 years. However, this improvement is accompanied by new expectations as to further developments, different attitudes towards education, and values and the quality of life in general.[29]

The History of the Evangelical School of Theology[30]

Beginnings

The roots of the Evangelical School of Theology go back to 1990. One year after the fall of communism, Zygmunt Karel, a Baptist pastor, and Mark Young, an American missionary linked with Dallas Theological Seminary, established the Biblical Theological Seminary (BST) in Wrocław. It was a college-type school offering an undergraduate, unaccredited, programme based on evangelical models promoted in the USA at that time. The beginning of the 1990s in Poland was good for this kind of initiative. The country was poor, unemployment was growing, inflation was very high, Soviet troops were still in Poland, and the country's new-found freedom was very fragile. It was just the beginning of a transformation of the country's political and economic systems. The legal structures were not

---

[27] http://instytutsokratesa.pl/pliki/Demograficzne_Tsunami_Instytut_Sokratesa.pdf (accessed 10th July 2015).

[28] http://stat.gov.pl/download/gfx/portalinformacyjny/pl/defaultaktualnosci/5501/13/1/13/oz_polska_1989-2014.pdf (accessed 10th July 2015).

[29] http://ec.europa.eu/eurostat/statistics-explained/index.php/Quality_of_life_in_Europe_-_facts_and_views_-_overall_life_satisfaction (accessed 10th September 2015).

[30] http://en.ewst.pl/about/history (accessed 10th September 2015).

prepared for the new reality, and financial obligations towards other countries were stifling Poland. Still, there was much optimism in the country. Even though it was grey and poor, Poland was enchanted by the winds of change. Everybody was looking to the future, believing that in a few years the country would catch up with the West. The economic strategy prepared by Professor Leszek Balcerowicz and western experts predicted a few difficult years, but then created a beautiful vision for Poland and its citizens.[31] It was a prophecy which the new government and many Poles subscribed to.

Also, the spiritual atmosphere of the times was very positive. The Catholic Church, permeated by the spirit of Vatican II and guided by the Polish Pope John Paul II, was ecumenically oriented and open to various initiatives.[32] It co-operated closely on Polish soil with such Protestant movements as Campus Crusade for Christ and the International Fellowship of Evangelical Students. Many western and American Christian institutions started or strengthened their activities in Poland, sending their missionaries here, launching their programmes and supporting Polish citizens.[33] Such assistance was important for the country making its first steps in the new political and economic reality.

In such a context, BST seemed like a natural outcome of the processes going on in the country. It was relatively easy at that time to gather the required resources for a Christian educational institution. Missionaries, educated in western evangelical institutions and ready to teach in a new seminary, were to hand. Students from various churches and communities were eager to study at BST, believing that Poland was going through an awakening process, not only in the sphere of economy or politics but also in the area of spirituality. The fact that the school was essentially run by devoted, affluent westerners was an additional asset, a premonition of a dream come true for the whole country. BST was formally situated in the structures of the Polish Baptist Union, since in 1990 there was no other legal context available in Poland for such an entity.[34] Nonetheless, even though the school was interdenominational by definition, such an ecclesiastical location within the context of one of the largest Protestant communities in Poland was perceived positively. It helped as an incubator for a totally new initiative.

---

[31] www.britannica.com/topic/Balcerowicz-Plan (accessed 10th_June 2015). Andrzej K. Kozminski, 'Lessons from Recession in Central and Eastern Europe: From Survival to Continuous Improvement', in Sarah Sanderson King and Donald Cushman (eds), *Lessons from the Recession: A Management and Communication Perspective* (Albany, NY: SUNY Press, 1997), 151-78.

[32] www.kulturaswiecka.pl/node/510 (accessed 10th July 2015).

[33] Zbigniew Pasek, 'Protestantism in Poland, 1989-2000', in Irena Borowik (ed), *Religions, Churches and the Scientific Studies of Religion: Poland and Ukraine* (Kraków, Poland: Nomos, 2003), 89-105.

[34] http://isap.sejm.gov.pl/DetailsServlet?id=WDU19900650385 (accessed 10th June 2015).

Directions

It is possible to indicate several strategic decisions that were made at the beginning of the existence of BST, which had an important impact on the future character of the school. First of all, the emphasis in the curriculum centred on Biblical studies and languages, not on dogmatic theology and ecclesiastical particularities. This helped in creating a healthy ecumenical atmosphere, where the faculty and students of various ecclesiastical traditions could co-exist in one teaching environment, respecting each other. Second, theoretical studies were accompanied by the requirement of the serious practical involvement of every student. Third, all students had a tutor helping them to individualize their educational path, according to each student's gifts, personalities and, most of all, the goals set for their studies at BST. This type of attitude in education was very new in the Polish tradition of theological education and very attractive for students looking for solid, Biblical education and creative ways of serving communities in a developing Poland.

In addition, the leadership of BST realized that, if the school was to survive and develop into the future, it needed to be indigenized; it needed to be independent of any formal ecclesiastical ties and it needed to be accredited. Western missionaries and teachers were a considerable asset in the first years of the existence of the school, but it soon became obvious that BST needed to be Polish at its core if it was to serve Polish communities effectively. In a few years' time, as this strategy was followed, western teachers and the staff of BST were to a great extent replaced by a Polish team. Within twelve years of the establishment of BST, the leadership, faculty and staff were mostly Polish, prepared to serve Polish students in adequate and efficient ways for the Polish mindset. The area where, for several reasons, the idea was not applied was in the governance and the method of the school's financing. Over time, the board of directors still consisted mainly of American representatives, and even at the start of the 21st century, up to 90% of the school's budget was financed from American sources. In the early 1990s such a situation was not uncommon and, taking into account the Polish economy, promising. Ten years later there were signs that the original strategy could not be fully applied and the manner of the school's financing became a potential area of serious crisis.

The independence of the school was secured simply by moving out of the Baptist property where BST was originally located to a newly purchased building in the centre of Wrocław, and by changing the legal context of its operation to that of a self-standing educational entity. A seventeenth-century former Augustinian nunnery was purchased and renovated in a way that served the school well.[35] BST was now independent of any ecclesiastical ties, yet it served all the Protestant churches according to its innate interdenominational character. It adopted the creed of the World Evangelical Alliance and, within the scope of evangelicalism as broadly understood, it offered its theological programme for the training of pastors and church leaders for Evangelical/Protestant communities.[36]

In order to develop as an institution of higher education, serving churches in Poland by training pastors and church workers, it quickly became obvious that the school needed to be nationally accredited. This need became urgent after 1995, when several churches, following the concordat with the Catholic Church (1993), signed an agreement with the Polish government regulating their existence in Poland. The churches were given the privilege, similarly to the Catholic Church, to establish their own theological schools of higher education without the requirement of meeting the standards set by the Ministry of Education. The churches and their entities were subject to the Ministry of Internal Affairs, by-passing the regulations of the Ministry of Education. However, in the early years of its existence, BST was an interdenominational entity, not linked with any church, except by merely formal ties with the Baptists. So, there was no way of subscribing to an easy way of acquiring accreditation. BST's leadership understood that there was no option but to meet the standards of the Ministry of Education and strive for accreditation in the same way as any other secular school in Poland. They realized that the hard way, however long and costly, would actually help to secure high standards of education at BST.

There were several attempts to achieve national accreditation for BST. The final process began in 2004 with a new group of leaders directing the school. Legal representatives were engaged, a team within BST was put into place, the finances secured and the strategy prepared. It took the team three years of hard work and 15,000 pages of written documents to convince the Ministry of Education that the school met the standards and could operate as an accredited entity. It was for the first time in Polish history that a private, non-Catholic theological institution received national accreditation based on standard legal acts, and not with special agreements between a church and a government. In October 2006, the Evangelical School of Theology started their operation as a continuation of the ministry of the Biblical Theological Seminary.[37]

---

[35] www.mice.pl/opis-obiektu/ewst/p,2/Centrum-konferencyjne-Ewangelikalna-Wy%C5%BCsza-Szko%C5%82a-Teologiczna-Wroc%C5%82aw-dolno%C5%9Bl%C4%85skie-Polska (accessed 10th June 2015).

[36] http://en.ewst.pl/about/statement-of-faith (accessed 10th March 2015).

[37] www.infor.pl/akt-prawny/U16.2009.003.0000059,obwieszczenie-nr-6-ministra-nauki-i-szkolnictwa-wyzszego-w-sprawie-wykazu-uczelni-i-zwiazkow-uczelni.html (accessed 10th August 2015).

Achievements and Challenges

Gaining accreditation was a miracle, which not everybody had believed could happen. However, happen it did, or rather it was achieved. In October 2006, independent, accredited, and with a beautiful, historic building, a new leadership team and a faculty consisting of six PhDs and four Habilitations (double PhDs), with no debts, the Evangelical School of Theology began its existence. The Rubicon had been crossed; the way to Rome had been opened.[38]

However, after analysis of the context within which EST was operating, it turned out that the situation was not as ideal as it had first appeared. Sociological, ecclesiastical and financial considerations revealed several potential challenges for the school and its operation.

First of all, demography became a problem. To put it simply, it turned out that Polish society was shrinking. After the fall of communism, with all the accompanying structural and economic challenges, the birth rate plummeted. As indicated at the beginning of this chapter, the birth rate had dropped from 550,000 a year in 1990 to below 500,000 in 1995, and as low as fewer than 400,000 in 2015. In 2006, when EST began operating, the demographical drop hit primary schools in Poland and resulted in a considerable number of them closing down. It was obvious that in a few years the trend would affect high schools and schools of higher education and would cause dramatic changes in the structure of the Polish higher education system. What made the situation even more dramatic was the problem of migration. After entering the European Union and subsequently, after Poland had entered the Schengen area, hundreds and thousands of Polish citizens left the country. They were mainly young people starting their careers or dreaming of improving their living conditions. For schools of higher education in Poland it meant that the number of students would be considerably lower in a few years' time, especially in areas of study such as the humanities and, within humanities, theology.[39] What became important for students was the possibility of getting a good job after finishing their studies. It was a natural expectation in the context of growing unemployment on the one hand, and open borders in Europe and an improving Polish economy on the other. Social sciences and liberal arts did not look very promising at the beginning of the 21st century.

The ecclesiastical situation did not help the situation either. It turned out that Polish Protestantism was not developing as it had been hoped at the beginning of the 1990s. Except for the Pentecostal and charismatic denominations, most of the Protestant churches were stagnant or even losing their members. Altogether, the evangelical community did not exceed 40,000 people in a population of nearly 40 million; the total number

---

[38] http://en.ewst.pl/about/history (accessed 10th July 2015).

[39] https://www.nauka.gov.pl/en/polish-science-news/the-ministry-of-science-discussion-with-the-polish-humanities-crisis-committee,akcja,pdf.html+&cd=1&hl=pl&ct=clnk&gl=pl (accessed 10th August 2015).

of Protestants was not higher than 100-120,000. When assessing these numbers, one needs to take into consideration the simple fact that a significant number of Protestants had emigrated, so the actual number of Protestants living in Poland was lower than the statistics showed. In the analysis of the operation of the Evangelical School of Theology in its first years of existence, two additional issues called for consideration. First of all, none of the evangelical churches in Poland required higher education from their leaders, pastors or church workers. On the other hand, most of the Protestant churches had their own theological institutions, established on the basis of the agreement of a denomination with the government, where they educated their own pastors, missionaries and leaders. Thus, the obvious question arose whether educational entities like the Evangelical School of Theology were needed in a country like Poland and if so, which way it should be shaped in terms of its mission, vision and strategy to serve the Polish Christian community adequately.

Then, there was still the issue of finance and the method of supporting the institution. There was a very comfortable situation in the early 1990s with large subsidies and grants from the USA that could easily turn into a pitfall ten years later if a crisis should hit the American economy or the donors of EST should drop their support. In 2006, such a vision seemed like a fairy tale, but the situation whereby a Polish school was financed at 90% from American sources did not sound right. The potential danger was not that remote and the leadership of EST was already aware of it in 2006.

Demography, the ecclesiastical crisis, the nature of Polish Evangelicalism and the finances of EST were the major aspects detrimental to the existence of the school, demanding a resolution and the creation of good strategy for the years to come.

Resolutions – Towards an Educational Centre

After a thorough analysis of the situation in which the Evangelical School of Theology operated, its leadership made several strategic decisions concerning the future development of the institution.

First of all, the mission of the school was modified. The original mission statement, stressing the training of pastors and church workers for Evangelical churches in Poland, seemed obsolete in 2006, taking into consideration the stagnant state of the churches, the saturation of the 'ecclesiastical market' and the nature of Polish Evangelicalism. It became obvious that in time the churches would not able to absorb all the graduates of EST, simply because there were not enough vacancies in Protestant communities or because they preferred graduates of their own denominational schools. The difficulty which the large number of EST graduates were having in finding jobs in churches or Christian institutions naturally raised questions about the aims of the school's theological programme. After scrutiny of the situation, it became obvious that what the school could be doing effectively in this particular Polish context would be to strengthen Protestant/Christian culture at large rather than simply producing pastors and church workers. EST could help establish and strengthen existing faith communities in Poland, for which leaders could be subsequently trained. Thus 'equipping Christians for effective ministry to strengthen the Evangelical/Protestant movement in Poland' became the modified mission statement of EST. In other words, EST – with its accreditation and other assets – would emphasize equipping students to become responsible citizens of Polish society with theological knowledge and an understanding of Christian tradition. Such graduates could create faith communities, which would be open and willing to interact with a society undergoing fundamental and structural change. According to the mission statement, there was no longer the sole expectation that the graduates would become pastors or other types of church leaders. Rather, there was the hope that some of the graduates would continue their studies in theology or other fields to become professionals of a different sort and, by permeating society in their areas, they would strengthen Polish Christianity in an organic way.[40] The fact that EST was nationally accredited and participated in the 'Erasmus Programme', made it possible, according to the 'Bologna education process',[41] for its graduates to continue their studies at a graduate level in different fields in Poland and the whole European Union.

The next decision, which was taken by the leadership of the Evangelical School of Theology, was to close the day studies and focus on a non-residential programme and continuing education. In this way, EST focused on older and more mature students who were simultaneously studying at other schools, who were working in various places and were engaged in church or missionary ministries. The work with students took on a new dimension. The students were no longer simply high school graduates, but would come to EST already qualified as pastors, missionaries, managers and workers of Christian organizations, and already also students of various universities or professional schools. A different type of work at EST began. On the one hand, daily contact with students was lost but, on the other, more mature and determined students came to EST, already engaged in ministry and, typically, supporting themselves. The spiritual formation programme had to be modified to serve the needs of a different type of student. The content of the studies also had to focus more on the particular needs of the students already engaged in ministry, working or simultaneous studying in different fields. Determining the study curriculum was done in a more dialectic way, where Christian communities, organizations, various

---

[40] http://en.ewst.pl/welcome-to-evangelical-school-of-theology (accessed 10th August 2015).

[41] http://ec.europa.eu/education/policy/higher-education/bologna-process_en.htm (accessed 10th August 2015).

institutions, graduates and students were consulted as to the content, form and method of delivery of the courses.[42]

After closing down the full-time studies, a surplus of energy was disclosed which had to be used – namely, the school's resources, teaching hours, and the working hours of the faculty and staff. It was decided to use this energy for creating new and original programmes and initiatives that would effectively serve Protestant communities in the country, promote Protestantism in Poland, and draw EST closer to the local churches and fellowships in the area of its location, namely, Wrocław and Lower Silesia. In this way, it was believed, the mission of the school could be strengthened in a way different from the BA programme. Also, EST could answer the needs of the communities in more versatile ways, with many of the initiatives organized in close co-operation with various churches and Christian organizations. Therefore, the following were initiated:

- The Festivals of Protestant Culture, focusing on various aspects of Protestantism in Lower Silesia, in consultation with various Christian traditions;[43]
- The Days of Reformation, discussing certain aspects of the sixteenth-century Reformation and its contemporary outcomes;
- The Week of Prayer for the Unity of Christians, organized together with churches belonging to the Polish Ecumenical Board;
- The Academy of the Third Age, geared to senior citizens and offering them general programmes in the area of religious studies, various workshops, excursions, seminars, and English and German language classes;[44]
- The School of Leaders, which in time evolved into the Open Academy of Theology, where various centres of one-year theological programmes were established across Poland;[45]
- The School of Apologetics, focusing on contemporary dimensions of Christianity in Poland and the world;
- The School of Biblical Languages, offering classes of Greek, Hebrew and Latin;[46]
- The Entrepreneurship Institute, helping churches and Christian organizations to cope with the new economic reality by consultations, organizing workshops and training courses;[47]

---

[42] http://en.ewst.pl/ec-programs/theological-academy/bachelor-of-arts (accessed 10th August 2015).

[43] http://en.ewst.pl/2015/04/fifth-festival-of-protestant-culture-days-of-bonhoeffer-april-8-13-2015 (accessed 10th August 2015).

[44] http://en.ewst.pl/ec-programs/academy-of-third-age (accessed 10th August 2015).

[45] http://en.ewst.pl/ec-programs/theological-academy/open-theological-academy (accessed 10th August 2015).

[46] http://en.ewst.pl/ec-programs/theological-academy/school-of-biblical-languages (accessed 10th August 2015).

[47] http://en.ewst.pl/ec-programs/institute-of-entrepreneurship (accessed 10th August 2015).

- The *Theologica Wratislaviensia* publishing house, printing periodicals and monographs in the area of theology;[48]
- The Jonathan Edwards Center, a research centre established in co-operation with the Jonathan Edwards Center at Yale University;[49]
- Conferences, training courses, lectures, workshops, concerts, debates and consultations.

Since 2006, over twenty courses, programmes and initiatives of various kinds were organized by EST. Many of them are still in existence as an integral part of the Evangelical School of Theology as it has taken on the form of a versatile educational centre rather than one-programme type of theological institution.[50]

The economic crisis of 2008-2010 showed the structural weakness of EST as a school financed mainly by American foundations. When the crisis hit, it almost wiped EST off the map. At that time, struggling with the survival of the school, the EST leadership made a decision to sell the building purchased several years earlier. However painful it was, there was no other way to continue: the economic reality was very difficult. Many foundations, which by that time had supported EST, suddenly ceased to exist or had to considerably reduce their subsidies. EST was faced with the need to immediately find a way to finance itself or it would have gone under within a few weeks. In such a situation the building was the price for life. Fortunately, it was possible to sell it for a very good price and beyond that to negotiate staying on in the very same place for another 26 years for just the cost of utilities. The loss of the building was traumatic; however, the results were very positive. The school gained a small endowment, became self-sustaining and was able to retain its ministries.

The added value was that, in the process of selling the premises, it was realized that however important the building was for the school since it had helped to create its image and identity, the school *per se* was more than bricks and mortar. A school in terms of *paideia* is made up of interpersonal relationships, deep teaching processes, a common pilgrimage, and meetings with other human beings face-to-face and learning from them. It is mutual growth and not just the acquisition technical skills but searching in an Aristotelian way for the basic principles of reality. Selling the building was very difficult for EST, but it allowed the school to survive and reach out 'beyond its walls'. After the sale, EST naturally started realizing its projects, not only in the building but also or most of all outside, in various communities, in various districts of Wrocław, and in various cities of Poland. Places like Opole, Dzierzoniow, Kraków, Rybnik, Krapkowice and other towns in Poland became centres of various EST projects and programmes.

---

[48] http://en.ewst.pl/publications/theologica-wratislaviensia (accessed 10th August 2015). Also: http://en.ewst.pl/publications/monograph-series (accessed 10th August 2015).

[49] http://en.ewst.pl/library/jonathan-edwards-center (accessed 10th August 2015).

[50] http://en.ewst.pl/ec-programs (accessed 10th August 2015).

The EST Educational Center became a reality and a natural development of EST.[51] Its official inauguration took place in April 2014. The licentiate programme, the Open Academy of Theology, operating now as the Institute of Church Development, and the Academy of the Third Age were chosen as the core programmes of the Centre with many other projects and activities offered in various places in Wrocław, various regions of Poland and Europe. To be where theological education is needed and serve in the way which answers best the needs of communities became the main maxim of EST's Educational Center. Today the licentiate programme still serves as a kind of flagship of the Center; however, by no means does it gather the most participants or resources in the whole 'organism'. The Academy of the Third Age is almost fully subsidized by the European Union, while the Institute of Church Development receives grants from various church-oriented foundations, publications and conferences which are also supported by the 'Erasmus+ Programme'. Similarly, exchanges of faculty, staff and students with other European educational institutions take place within the Erasmus structures. In terms of numbers, the Educational Center serves approximately 1,700 participants a year, out of which only about 80 are students in the licentiate programme. Most of the participants are involved in festivals, Academies of the Third Age or Open Theology, Days of Reformation, conferences and other events. In this way, the EST Educational Center strengthens the Protestant culture in Poland in a broad manner and equips Christians for various kinds of ministry in a more focused, intensive way. Therefore, the mission of EST continues to be carried out in the dynamically changing context of Poland.

Future Challenges

The Evangelical School of Theology has evolved from a simple western-type Biblical theological seminary established in 1990 at the premises of a Baptist church in Wrocław, to the indigenized, accredited Evangelical School of Theology, to the EST Educational Center serving communities in Poland in versatile, creative ways, and being a part of European educational structures. The process took 25 years and was not very easy. Separating from a single ecclesiastical structure, purchasing a new building, obtaining national accreditation, reshaping the curriculum into an educational centre, selling the premises and so on, took much time, energy and resources. It was not easy to abandon the original vision of BST and to admit that reality would be constantly changing, especially in such a fast-developing country like Poland. Such continuous change had to be translated into EST's dynamic structure and adaptable ways of operation. The leadership, faculty and staff had to agree that nothing would be constant, or rather, that the constant core vision and values can and actually must be applied in various

[51] http://en.ewst.pl/ec-programs (accessed 10th August 2015).

ways in the Polish context. Given the systemic ongoing transformation of Poland, the drop in the birth rate, the nature and size of Polish Evangelicalism/Protestantism (and its stagnation), hard decisions had to be taken in the past and agreement as to the dynamic nature of the EST Educational Center had to be reached. Fortunately, in the process of making the changes, it was possible to shape such a team of faculty and staff which understood the contextual challenges and was open to trying new, creative ways of operation. Various tests and tribulations have strengthened the team and in the end have helped to shape it in a way which makes it possible to operate the Center in creative and versatile ways.

There is a common agreement at EST that Polish reality is constantly changing and that the school needs to continually analyze the situation to adjust its operation to the needs, challenges and questions of the communities it serves. With such a perspective, there is always a need for new and potential projects, which may replace those that are obsolete. After all the years of operation, it seems natural that, in the context of a fast-developing country with a small constituency, a typical educational project does not last longer than 3-4 years and then needs to be replaced by a new one, or needs to be reshaped according to the changed reality. *Πάντα ῥεῖ καὶ οὐδὲν μένει*, as Heraclitus[52] maintained, there is the unchanging, core *Logos* of the world, which nevertheless realizes its own existence through a constantly changing *cosmos*.

When thinking of the next steps and projects which may be applied in the EST Educational Center in the next few years, there are several ideas being worked on:

- Building closer relationships with evangelical communities, especially those of charismatic character since, in general, these are the only ones which have been growing in the Polish context for the last few years.
- Developing courses through new technologies, so that the EST Educational Center may reach Polish emigrants (approximately three million people) in other countries.
- Working with refugees, especially those from Ukraine, taking into consideration similarities between Polish and Ukrainian culture.

Closer co-operation with other European schools within the context of the 'Erasmus+ Programme'. Common didactic, research and structural projects may help in integrating theological circles in Europe. Taking into consideration the stagnant state of Protestant/Evangelical churches, at least in Central and Eastern Europe, it may be worth considering the creation of educational centres serving several countries and a common Central European theological tradition contextualized for this region of the world.

[52] As Simplikios reads the thought of Heraclites.

The Word and Its Mission: Slavic Bible Commentary – A Contextual and Relevant Commentary for Eurasia

Peter F. Penner

Introduction

Bible and mission are inseparable works of God. The interpretation of the Scriptures is an important mission activity of the church, following the model set in the Scriptures themselves and most prominently done by Jesus and his apostles. The history of the church and its involvement in mission reflects the interpretation of Scripture as conducted in the context of the interpreter and his/her community. This is why modern missions within their context of the time of colonialization have had their basis in Matthew 28:19 with the specific interpretation of 'to go'.[1]

The Bible and its interpretation were also the foundation for and the growth of the evangelical movement in Eastern Europe. In times of persecution, encouraged by the study of the Bible, the church has continued to play its witnessing role as a valid and effective kind of mission to which the suffering church felt called by the biblical texts.[2] Since the 1990s, the Eastern European church has been trying to interpret the dramatically changing context from the biblical text and Scripture from inside their context and community. Supporting this process, a one-volume Slavic Bible Commentary (SBC) was published in 2016 to respond to the history and presence of the marginalized evangelical church and its mission in the former Soviet Union.[3] As the project comes to its finish line, this article will introduce and evaluate some of the historical, contextual and missional issues underlying the creation of the commentary.

The History of International Help with Literature Production

The time before the fall of the Berlin Wall witnesses to different phases of literature production in and for Eastern Europe. An impressive group of western mission organizations has been involved with this task in Eastern

---

[1] Bernhard Ott, 'Matthew 28:16-20 and the Holistic-Mission-Debate: An Anabaptist Contribution', in *Anabaptism and Mission* (Schwarzenfeld, Germany: Neufeld Verlag, 2007), 59-84, 61, 62 and 65.

[2] Heinrich Klassen, *Mission als Zeugnis: zur missionarischen Existenz in der Sowjetunion nach dem Zweiten Weltkrieg = Mission as Witness* (Lage, Germany: Logos-Verl., 2003).

[3] http://sbc.e-aaa.info (accessed October 2015).

Europe and Central Asia. Some trace their beginnings to even before World War II, like 'Licht im Osten' (Light in the East),[4] while many more started activities later, during the time of the Cold War. In the early phase, attention was primarily given to the production of Bibles and shorter devotional books in the different languages. This changed in the early 1980s, when focus shifted to include study literature in the Bible and theology. Different western mission organizations became aware of the changes taking place in Eastern Europe and started to develop more advanced theological literature, or to offer various alternative theological education venues for the region as part of their mission to the East.

One such educational project for the training of Christians in Eastern Europe was, and still is, Biblical Education by Extension (BEE)[5] which has translated some classical western theological literature and regularly sends people to train leaders in Eastern Europe. Others, like TCM International Institute (TCM in their name stands for: "Training Christians for Ministry" and "Taking Christ to Millions"), offered some seminars in Austria especially for Central Europeans.[6] During the 1980s and 1990s, Austria was the hub of western mission organizations to the East. Some Eastern European countries, such as Romania, Hungary or the former Yugoslavia, already had a long tradition of publishing theological literature and even offering local theological education.

In the Eurasian region, defined in this chapter as the former Soviet Union (FSU), the challenge of providing Bibles and study literature in theology had already started before World War II. Several theological evangelical institutions were in operation before and shortly after World War I, but they had contributed only very little to the strengthening of the church. Walter Sawatsky writes:

> Protestant theological education in the former Soviet Union was much more severely limited than was true of Orthodoxy, and evangelicals had no earlier tradition of schools. Lutherans had relied on the theology faculty at the University of Dorpat in present-day Lithuania, or had sent students to Germany during the 19th century, but there was nothing in the 20th century except for a small institute that opened in Tallinn during the 1970s and 80s.[7]

When the Orthodox Church received more freedom for official operations, after World War II and before the Khrushchev era, it reopened seminaries in Zagorsk, Leningrad, Odessa, Minsk, Kiev, Saratov, Stavropol – and even two academies in Zagorsk and Leningrad,[8] gathering in 1955

---

[4] 'Licht Im Osten – die Geschichte': https://www.lio.org/index.php?id=geschichte-des-missionsbundes (accessed October 2015).

[5] www.beeworld.org/#/about-us/our-history (accessed October 2015).

[6] www.tcmi.edu/about-us/history (accessed October 2015).

[7] Walter Sawatsky, *Soviet Evangelicals since World War 2* (Kitchener, Ontario: Herald Press, 1981), 330ff.

[8] Ottokar Basse and Gerd Stricker, *Religionen in der UdSSR: Unbekannte Vielfalt* (Zollikon, Switzerland: G2W-Verlag, 1989), 48.

about 1,500 students in full-time and some in distance programmes.[9] By comparison, Evangelicals[10] were able to start a distance-education programme only in 1968.[11] Later, in 1986, BEE was called into existence to offer a training programme on the territory of the FSU.[12] One of the key issues then and even now was accessible quality theological literature.

When focusing on Biblical studies and particularly on Bible commentaries, there were primarily two complete collections of commentaries available at that time: (1) the Barclay New Testament Commentary, and (2) an Orthodox Commentary by Lopukhin. There was and still remains the challenge of responding to this need, either by offering translated literature or at the same time initiating the writing of literature and commentaries by national authors, or both.[13]

The Russian-language William Barclay Daily Study Bible Series has been one of the key commentaries for Russian readers for decades. In 1978, a group of leaders representing primarily western mission organizations initiated this project in Stuttgart, Germany, as a response to the cry from Evangelicals in the FSU. The initial group consisted of the following: 'Gerhard Class (then General Secretary of the European Baptist Federation, later of the Baptist World Alliance), Peter J. Dyck and Walter Sawatsky of MCC (Mennonite Central Committee), Bernd Dyck of the Licht im Osten mission, and Peter Deyneka, Jr. of the Slavic Gospel Association'.[14] This was to become one of the major projects 'between the All-Union Council of Evangelical Christians-Baptists (AUCECB), the Baptist World Alliance, and the Mennonite Central Committee', as Sawatsky comments.[15] By 1987, the New Testament set of 15-16 volumes had been translated, printed, presented and, upon official authorization of the Soviet Union, imported and handed out to Protestants and Orthodox in the country.[16] More than 12,000 sets were published and distributed, and it became one of the standard commentaries used by Russian readers.[17]

---

[9] Jane Ellis, *The Russian Orthodox Church: A Contemporary History* (Bloomington, IN: Indiana University Press, 1986), 100.

[10] The Evangelicals were at that time organized in primarily one Union. This All-Union Council of Evangelical Christians-Baptists (AUCECB) was created at the time of Stalin to combine different evangelical denominations.

[11] *Istoriya Evangeliskikh Khristian-Baptistov v SSSR* (Moscow: AUREchB, 1989), 269.

[12] Peter Penner, 'Theologische Ausbildung: Eine verpflichtende Mission' (PhD dissertation, University of South Africa, 1997), 123.

[13] Peter Penner, 'Theologische Ausbildung für Gemeinde und Mission: Ein Blick in die Gegenwart evangelikaler Christen in der GUS', in Hans Kasdorf und Heinrich Löwen, Jr. (eds), *Gemeinsam im Auftrag des Herrn. Festschrift zum 70. Geburtstag von John N. Klassen* (Bonn, Germany: PULS Verlag, 1999), 247-49.

[14] Walter Sawatsky, 'Russian Bible Commentary Finished', East-West Church & Ministry Report, Winter 1994, 11.

[15] Sawatsky, 'Russian Bible Commentary Finished'.

[16] Mary Raber, 'Remembering the Russian Bible Commentary', in *History and Mission in Europe: Continuing the Conversation* (Schwarzenfeld, Germany: Neufeld Verlag, 2011), 303.

[17] As announced by the Chairman of the Barclay Commentaries Committee and the Books and Translations Committee of the European Baptist Federation, D.S. Russell, in 'Theological

In 1994, after the collapse of the Soviet Union and at the early stage of appearance of theological institutions in the FSU, the initiators launched the production of the 18 volumes of the Old Testament, printed this time in Odessa, which completed a 15-year project.[18] Today, the Barclay commentary series is available electronically and is included in some Bible software programmes.[19] The Bible, precious in the days of persecution, had now received a commentary, and it has been treasured by many as an important asset.[20] With the opening up of the region and the fall of the Soviet Union, many have continued to use this commentary, but have also criticised it for different reasons. Some call it liberal, as Barclay's commentaries sometimes try to explain away miracles in a modernistic way.[21] Others find it unhelpful because the commentary is perceived as not supporting readers in their spirituality[22] or because it did not reflect their view of eschatology, etc. There are still not that many commentaries available on the complete Bible and, until recently, it seemed impossible to identify enough Russian-speaking Bible scholars who would be able to write a complete commentary on the Bible.[23] So Barclay's Daily Study Bible Series has continued to respond to the needs, not only of the generation of ministers in the 1980s, but also to a new generation of users in the 21st century.

With less public introductions and finances than the Barclay commentary, the commentary series written by an Orthodox author Alexander P. Lopukhin (1852-1904) and published in twelve volumes in St Petersburg from 1904 to 1913, was reprinted. The introduction informs the reader that it intends to meet the need for biblical interpretation for the Orthodox leadership and its community.[24] After Lopukhin's unexpected and

---

Literature for East European Baptists: The Barclay Commentaries in Russian', in *The Baptist Quarterly,* 32.4 (1987), 199-201, 201.

[18] Sawatsky, 'Russian Bible Commentary Finished.'

[19] For example, in Цитата из Библии (Bible Quote).

[20] Raber, 'Remembering the Russian Bible Commentary', 304-07.

[21] Russell writes already in the early stage of some such issues: 'It sometimes involved more profound theological interpretation. Not everything in Barclay was equally acceptable to the "conservative" and "pietistic" Baptist pastors who would be making use of them... of particular difficulty were some of Barclay's comments on the Virgin Birth, baptism, and his interpretation of "the last things" in the Book of Revelation". Should such "unacceptable" sections be re-written to make them more "acceptable" or should they be expurgated altogether? Internally, this raised questions of theological interpretation, and externally questions of copyright! By means of footnotes and other explanatory comments most of the difficulties were overcome and tensions resolved.' Russell, 'Theological Literature for East European Baptists: The Barclay Commentaries in Russian', 200.

[22] Raber, 'Remembering the Russian Bible Commentary', 324.

[23] As A.M. Bychkov, the General Secretary of the All-Union Council of Evangelical Christians-Baptists, writes in the main Baptist journal, *Bratskiy vestnik.* In the meeting in 1979 under 'Unfolding Minutes, Russian Bible Commentary Meeting' (1st-2nd July 1979), he commented that there were no Russian-speaking biblical scholars who could write a Russian Bible commentary (2). This has now become possible, as this article will unfold. See also Raber, 324 and 325.

[24] Толковая Библия Лопухина (Expository Bible of Lopukhin): www.Bible.by/lopuhin-Bible

untimely death, having finished only the commentary on the Pentateuch, others continued writing and completed the series just before World War I.[25] About the time of the appearance of the Barclay commentary series, the three-volume Lopukhin Reference Bible was reprinted and made available for an affordable price even before the end of the Soviet Union.[26] Its publication had offered for Protestant readers an Eastern Church perspective on the biblical text.

The Orthodox interpretation of the Lopukhin commentary had been well received in the evangelical community, even with the recognition that it had been written in an Orthodox context. The Synodal Bible translation, used by Evangelicals as their main Bible text, had the same background and worked well with Lopukhin's commentary series on the Bible. In this way, a Russian-speaking reader sometimes related better to Lopukhin's interpretation than to Barclay's modernistic twentieth-century perspective which explained mysteries rationalistically, discussed the question of historicity and what had been happening 'behind the text', and partly stripped bare some of the pietistic sentiments of Evangelicals in the FSU. Barclay, with its historical approach, stirred up questions that worried the Russian Bible reader who approached the Bible with awe and respect and with the anticipation that it spoke directly into the reader's context. These developments, as well as changes in the post-Soviet context, identified a vacuum that needed to be filled and that called for a mission in interpreting the Scriptures anew in this context.

The contemporary, theologically trained reader has a much wider choice of commentaries. Many devotional or one-volume commentaries have been translated and published in the last 25 years,[27] mostly from Anglo-American contexts, and often in the spirit of Barclay, but also those on the more conservative and sometimes fundamentalist side, debating and proving the reliability of Scripture. Different commentaries have also introduced a variety of theological positions, and this is mostly welcomed. Unfortunately, most of the translated commentaries have very little contextual relevance, as they primarily approach the Bible text with questions that are western in origin. Answering some questions, the translated commentaries also raise questions that are not asked in the Eurasian context while remaining silent on Eastern European questions.

---

[25] Introduction to the commentary of the Lopukhin Bible (О толковой Библии Лопухина) at: www.Bible.by/lopuhin-Bible (accessed October 2015). Compare also: https://commons.wikimedia.org/wiki/Толковая_Библия_под_ред._преемников_А._П._Лопухина

[26] Mark Elliott, 'Bibles East, Letters West: Religious Glasnost and the Availability of Scriptures in the Soviet Union', in *Occasional Papers on Religion in Eastern Europe,* 9.6, article 4 (1989), 27-33, 29.

[27] There is an impressive list of commentaries translated into Russian besides those already mentioned, such as Calvin's Bible Commentary, Wilhelm McDonald's Commentary, MacArthur's Bible Commentary, Craig S. Keener's Bible Background Commentary, Light in the East Commentary to the Bible, the N.T. Wright's New Testament commentary series, etc.

Still, they are appreciated as they function as an enrichment in the FSU context. But, as any commentary needs to be relevant to its context, there is a felt need in Eastern Europe for a biblical interpretation that would answer questions related to themes, such as suffering, eschatology, church praxis, etc. that are specifically contextual and that do actually receive attention in the text of the Bible. This leads to the original idea of the Slavic Bible Commentary.

The History and Focus of the Slavic Bible Commentary

Especially in the eastern context, it is important to explain how a situation or an issue developed, and history seems as important as the evaluation and recognition of the actual outcome or result. This is part of the experience if someone attempts to find out why this or that has happened in the church in Eastern Europe. Sometimes it is not simply an explanation, but also a way of demonstrating the many different processes which were involved and which led to an outcome. The previous history of commentary writing for the FSU, presented above, is part of the prehistory of the Slavic Bible Commentary and cannot be separated from it. The seeming impossibility of writing a complete Bible commentary among the Evangelicals in Eastern Europe and Central Asia is also part of the current motivation to come up with a Slavic Bible Commentary on all the books of the Bible interpreted by a local group of more than seventy authors. The number of seventy contributors caused some allusions and interpretations by drawing parallels to the famous story of the Septuagint, which this article will not develop. But the story of the commentary's production still needs to be told.

The inception of the Slavic Bible Commentary is connected with the completion of the Africa Bible Commentary, the first from a series of contextual commentaries supported by Langham Partners International.[28] Already in October 2008, the Euro-Asian Accrediting Association (EAAA) expressed its interest in the project[29] and agreed on an initial group which would develop it.30 At the International Council for Evangelical Theological Education (ICETE) gathering in Sopron, Hungary, in 2009,[31] the general editor of the Slavic Bible Commentary, Sergey Sannikov,

[28] Langham's 'investment in major regional literature projects, such as one-volume Bible commentaries, like the Africa Bible Commentary', see http://staging.langham.org/what-we-do/langham-literature (accessed October 2015), has stimulated the process of writing the Slavic Bible Commentary.

[29] EAAA has, therefore, been the initiator, owner and the structure behind the Slavic Bible Commentary in close partnership with Langham: see 'Последнее заседание Редколлегии СБК', available at: www.e-aaa.info, 22-23 (accessed October 2015).

[30] Sergey Sannikov, 'Introduction to the Slavic Bible Commentary'.

[31] See some publications on the Sopron ICETE consultation at: www.icete-edu.org/hungary (accessed October 2015).

entered into dialogue with Langham Partners,[32] who have been the major force behind the commentary. At that point, such a project for the FSU context was out of this world, an exercise in wishful thinking. The first conversations during the conference in Sopron with representatives from the EAAA enabled a list of potential commentary authors numbering a bit more than a dozen names to develop. One year later, at an Euro-Asian Accrediting Association gathering, the first attempts were made to attract additional authors from different institutions and denominations active in the region of the FSU. The vision for such a project was not picked up too enthusiastically by EAAA, as the project seemed so overwhelming and unrealistic and, in view of the crises that theological institutions faced in 2010 in Eastern Europe and Central Asia, as an impossible task. After all, in comparison with Africa, Eurasia had had at that time only about twenty years of evangelical theological education and of training people in biblical interpretation.[33] In 2011, a group of enthusiasts met near Kiev, in Irpen', trying to develop a common concept and an editorial team, a group which then became the initiators of the project.

Part of the debate from the beginning was the question of the identity of the commentary project. The term 'Slavic Bible Commentary' was suggested at first, but was also questioned as a title for such a project from its beginning. Alternative titles circulated for a while. How can a commentary claim to be Slavic if it is written in the Russian language only? Should it not include other Slavic languages, such as Ukrainian, Polish, Czech, Bulgarian, and others? Some title versions have attempted to adapt the title to the geographical region, like the Euro-Asian Commentary, or to focus on its language, calling it the Russian Bible Commentary. At some point, even the following title was discussed: 'Bible Commentary: The Modern Evangelical Perspective'.[34]

This struggle for a title was really a struggle for the commentary's identity and focus. While in the past the Russian language was a common feature of many Eastern and Central Asian countries of the former Warsaw Pact and the so-called *lingua franca* of the East, soon after the collapse of the Soviet Union and at the end of the Cold War period, it has become a symbol of Soviet dominance and oppression. With Russia's growing dominance in the early 21st century and the uneasiness of some countries nearby, expressed by a variety of actions, including the Ukrainian Maidan (2014), how can a commentary written in the Russian language be common currency for all countries in the region? Can it at least express some of the

[32] The original discussion on the Slavic Bible Commentary has its roots even earlier in the Langham Eastern European meetings, led by Chris Wright.
[33] Anne-Marie Kool and Peter Penner, 'Theological Education in Eastern and Central Europe', in Dietrich Werner (ed), *Handbook of Theological Education in World Christianity: Theological Perspectives, Regional Surveys, Ecumenical Trends* (Regnum Studies in Global Christianity), (Oxford: Regnum), 2010), 534-35.
[34] http://risu.org.ua/en/index/all_news/culture/religion_and_science/ 46949 (accessed October 2015).

common identity of Eastern European Slavs, Central Asian groups and Russian-speaking immigrants in Western Europe and North America, who have some common intersections of history, culture and religious sentiments? Maybe these groups will find themselves understood and the commentary will help in the forming of an identity in the region, with or without the Russian language of the commentary that still links the region of Eastern Europe, Central Asia and the wider diaspora who continue to use Russian. As the commentary will also be published in English, maybe it can include other Slavic Bible scholars who would contribute to the Slavic Bible commentary?[35]

As any good project, the commentary needed a proper and dignified place for its inauguration. The editorial board of the Bible Commentary met in February 2012 in Jerusalem at the AMI Center for Biblical Study and Research. However, it did not end 'a nearly two-year period of writing the Bible commentary',[36] as its writing had not really yet started at that time, except for some individual sample chapters. In Jerusalem, the editorial team was established, and experienced some adjustments over the next few years, but most of all it was a testing ground for how to organise and align the writing and formulate the hermeneutical orientation of the commentary. An important activity of the editorial team in Jerusalem consisted of reading and discussing the first attempts of commentary chapters, written by different members of the editorial team. As each member presented his preliminary chapter, reading it in front of the group, one important hermeneutical lens was being developed in praxis: the *community hermeneutic*. Another lens had already been established by the decision to write a commentary that would be *contextually relevant* for the region. A third lens was adopted which laid down that Bible texts would be read and interpreted, not only in the limits of a textual passage or even a book, but in the framework of the complete *canon*. In Jerusalem there was also identified the lens which called interpreters to follow a *missional hermeneutic*. The editorial team laid down these lenses as a common focus and communicated them by way of instructions to the growing number of commentary authors who took on the individual books of the Bible.[37]

---

[35] The introduction to the commentary, written by Sergey Sannikov, tries to explain that 'Slavic' in the concept of the commentary does not refer to the ethnic, but rather to the cultural and geopolitical context. Nevertheless, there is a limitation which is set not only by the Russian language, but also by participants who live in the geo-political region of the FSU or are part of the Russian-speaking diaspora and represent only part of the spectrum of the cultural, geo-political and ethnic context, but not all of it. Ibid.

[36] 'Slavic Bible Commentary to be published in 2015': http://risu.org.ua/en/index/all_news/culture/religion_and_science/46949 (accessed October 2015).

[37] Библейский комментарий: современная евангельская перспектива. Пояснительная записка для авторов к написанию библейского комментария и богословских статей Версия 7.4 (Bible Commentary: modern evangelical perspective. Explanatory notes for authors on the writing of the commentary and theological articles, Version 7.4), 25.02.2012, 5.

This way, the Jerusalem meeting can be perceived as the real start of the Slavic Bible Commentary. The final point can be identified in the October 2015 meeting in Kiev-Irpen'. Kiev also carries symbolic meaning as the original location, not only for the forming of the editorial team in 2011, but as a place where the Kiev Rus[sia] had become a Christian nation. It is a place from where many evangelicals have sent missionaries into different parts of the world, even before the fall of communism.

After the Jerusalem gathering in March 2012, a competition was announced for national authors to submit writing samples, thus qualifying for participation in the production of the commentary. Some 100 prospective authors responded by presenting short commentaries on a Bible book of their expertise to the editorial team. Most of them are now involved in the actual interpretation of one or more books of the Bible commentary while other participants wrote various shorter articles as part of the commentary, oriented specifically along eastern Slavic contextual issues.[38] Contributors of articles and commentators come from different Protestant-Evangelical backgrounds and denominations. The following section presents some of the key components which mark the commentary as a Slavic Bible Commentary.

The Hermeneutical Approach of the Bible Commentary

In the presentation addressed to potential contributors to the commentary and the invitation to participate in the competition, the editorial team offers an orientation for the contributors as follows:

> The commentary is written by Evangelical ministers in Eastern Europe
>
> ... for pastors, preachers, teachers, leaders of small groups and anyone involved in different types of ministry in the local church;
>
> ... offers a contextual evangelical perspective that should help interpreting and applying biblical truths to the various aspects of church life;
>
> ... reflects the traditional way of reading the biblical text, by local evangelical churches in Eastern Europe;
>
> ... contains about one hundred relevant articles on important issues of spiritual and practical Christian living of the church in society'.[39]

This orientation follows the hermeneutical principles proposed and approved by the editorial team. It intended to help prospective authors of the commentary to catch the vision and, later, offer future readers a concise statement of purpose. This way, working with clearly formulated guidelines for the SBC, it seemed more likely to achieve some unity in diversity, to produce one commentary, but one written by many authors. Right into the

---

[38] This way more than seventy contributors have been involved in the commentary's writing, as Sergey Sannikov explains in the 'Introduction to the commentary'.

[39] 'Обращение к авторам (Call to authors)', unpublished document, March 2012.

early discussions on the principles of commentary writing came a *Festschrift* in honour of Grant R. Osborne, with relevant articles for the not yet experienced commentary writers.[40] The exegesis part of this book has been extremely helpful in the discussion: the article by Darrel L. Bock on the 'Commentaries of the Synoptic Gospels: Traditional issues of introduction'[41] especially helping with the creation of the New Testament part of the commentary. These and other helpful resources resulted in clear definitions of how to work with the biblical text, encouraging concentration on the text itself rather than spending time with raising classical introductory questions and attempting to reconstruct a possible scenario behind the text, the original context and its recipients.[42] The following statement became a key phrase: 'Aware of these limitations (of interpreting, especially the Gospels, through reconstructing the historical contextual scene) and trying to avoid speculations about historical and cultural events, we consider it expedient to choose a more conservative approach and identify the meaning of the text, based on the text itself, instead of constructing sometimes speculative reconstructions "behind the text"'.[43] Other articles, like Craig Blomberg's article on the 'Genre in Recent New Testament Commentaries',[44] helped craft introductory articles in the SBC related to that genre.

As mentioned before, one of the lenses, proposed by the editorial team for the commentary, was Brevard Childs' canonical reading of the text of the Bible, called by Dale A. Brueggemann a 'paradigm-shifting method'.[45] It was hoped that authors would not lose themselves in a discussion of reconstructing the text, date and context of individual Bible books, but would read the different passages and the entire Bible text within the framework of the final, given canon. The guidelines promote this idea by emphasizing that 'the voice of a book should be understood as one of the voices of the whole biblical orchestra, which plays a special role, and at the

---

[40] Stanley E. Porter, Eckhard J. Schnabel, and Grant R. Osborne (eds), *On the Writing of New Testament Commentaries: Festschrift for Grant R. Osborne on the Occasion of his 70th Birthday* (Texts and Editions for New Testament Study), (Leiden, Netherlands: E.J. Brill, 2013).

[41] Porter, Schnabel and Osborne, *On the Writing of New Testament Commentaries,* 339-64.

[42] Another guiding document called 'Герменевтические рамки при написании Библейского комментария (В помощь авторам)' (Hermeneutical framework for writing the Bible Commentary – Instructions for authors), March 2012, which offers principles for exegetical work for SBC writers on page 2.

[43] 'Осознавая данные ограничения и пытаясь избежать слишком многих спекуляций по поводу историко-культурных событий, считаем целесообразным выбрать более консервативный подход и попытаться выявить значение текста, исходя из него самого, вместо сконструированных и иногда даже спекулятивных реконструкций «за текстом', Ibid., 2.

[44] Porter, Schnabel and Osborne, *On the Writing of New Testament Commentaries*, 73-90.

[45] Dale A. Brueggemann, 'Brevard Childs' Canon Criticism: An Example of Post-Critical Naïveté', in *JETS,* 32.3 (September 1989), 311-26.

same time leads to a better understanding of the entire canon and of its narrative unity'.[46]

A canonical reading of the biblical text, of the different books and even each of the passages, leads to a common centre of the biblical text in its biblical theology, as set by Christ in Luke 24:44-47, which identifies Scripture interpretation as messianic and missional. 'In determining the biblical theology of the book or of the author, the interpreter should consider the whole of the Old and New Testaments, as well as biblical and theological studies encompassing the "centre" of the Bible.'[47] As a basis for missional hermeneutics, books published by Christopher J.H. Wright and others[48] offered help in defining the missional lens. It focuses on 'the *missio Dei*, which is evident throughout the canon', focuses on the involvement of individuals, Israel's and the church's participation in the mission of God, and tries to engage the individual reader or the present church through the text to also 'participate in God's mission'.[49]

It is also the missional reading of the Bible that leads to the contextually relevant reading of the Bible, and this was a clear focus when writing the commentary. One of the limitations of translated commentaries is that they are created primarily in a western context, with a western worldview, and usually answering the questions of western individuals or churches. The mission of the SBC includes helping Christians who live in a post-Soviet context, which has now been additionally shaped by the national independence of each of the countries, in their search for identity, including the search for their religious identity. The post-Soviet context reveals a new religiosity in addition to the previous influence of traditional pre-Soviet religiosity and spirituality, such as, respectively, Orthodox, Catholic, Islamic, Buddhist, etc. But the context of the evangelical reader is also determined by their relationship with society, and their past and present place was usually at the margins and not in the centre. Finding themselves in this place and reflecting on their respective identity, readers look to the commentary for relevant and contextual missional comments, derived from the biblical text.[50] Part of the commentary therefore is also to offer help to

---

[46] Герменевтические рамки (Hermeneutical framework), Ibid., 4.

[47] Ibid., 4 and 5.

[48] Christopher J.H. Wright, *The Mission of God: Unlocking the Bible's Grand Narrative* (Nottingham: IVP, 2006), 29-188, and Peter F. Penner, *Missionale Hermeneutik: biblische Texte kontextuell und relevant lesen* (Schwarzenfeld, Germany: Neufeld Verlag, 2012), 209-49.

[49] Герменевтические рамки (Hermeneutical framework), Ibid., 5.

[50] Taras Dyatlyk, director of the Euro-Asian Accrediting Association, told Religious Information Service of Ukraine (RISU) of the practical, contextual and missional role of the commentary: 'The Bible Commentary is a Russian single-volume commentary on all canonical books of the Old and New Testaments, which is designed for pastors, preachers, teachers, leaders of small groups and anyone involved in various kinds of service in local churches. The main goal of the Bible Commentary is to foster better understanding of the Bible and the better use of the biblical text in different areas of church ministry, to encourage

the reader in how the biblical text may be applied and become relevant to the readers' context.[51]

One key approach to the writing of the commentary was an emphasis on the use of community hermeneutics, as it is discussed particularly in Anabaptist contexts.[52] John Yoder may be one of the prominent proponents of this approach who believes that commentary authors often 'reject the hermeneutic problem as not a real problem because of their assumption that what constitutes the proper literal reading of the text is unchallengeable. If you do not read the text the way they do, you don't believe'.[53] The SBC had set the goal of going beyond an individualized authorship of a commentary and involving different people in the hermeneutical task. The editorial team had basically become a hermeneutical community for the author of the commentary on a particular Bible book, reflecting and critiquing, challenging and expanding the individual's interpretation. Quite often, the editorial team also invited others, especially persons from a different denominational background from the author's, to respond, widen or present an alternative reading of a particular passage.[54] Presented in this way, with sometimes differing views on the interpretation, the reader is invited to participate in the hermeneutical community. The question that the commentary then poses to the reader is, 'Do you also see what this commentary offers as the interpretation of the Biblical text?', thereby creating a dialogue and a community between text, author, reader and other readers.[55]

---

the development of the cultural study of the Bible, and to improve the quality of preaching the Gospel in local communities.'

[51] Bible Commentary, Ibid., 11.

[52] Stuart Murray, *Biblical Interpretation in the Anabaptist Tradition*, Vol. III (Studies in the Believers' Church Tradition), (Kitchener, Ontario: Pandora, 2000). Stuart speaks into the actual practice of how biblical interpretation is done in the evangelical (Mennonites, Baptists, Pentecostals and other) churches in Eastern Europe when he writes, 'When someone comes to the church and constantly hears only one person speaking and all the listeners are silent, neither speaking nor prophesying, who can or will regard or confess the same to be a spiritual congregation?' 160. It is this praxis that traditional evangelical churches also use when, at Sunday morning worship service, participants listen to three sermons. This praxis has been picked up from 1 Corinthians 14:29 where Pauls writes, 'Let two or three prophets speak, and let the others weigh what is said.'

[53] John Yoder, *Preface to Theology: Christology and Theological Method* (Grand Rapids, MI: Baker Books, 2002), 273.

[54] Following the warning of Hart – 'But we should never take the fatal step of identifying our interpretations (however careful they may be) with the text itself, or with "the meaning of the text itself". To do so is to bestow upon them a finality, a sufficiency, which lifts them above the text and out of the reach of criticism' (138) – the editorial team emphasized the creation of a hermeneutics community. See Trevor A. Hart, *Faith Thinking: The Dynamics of Christian Theology* (Eugene, OR: Wipf & Stock, 2005).

[55] The danger of this approach can be, as is sometimes observed in the practice of the priesthood of all believers in evangelical churches, that the comparison of different interpretations may depend on the 'weight' and role of the interpreter in relation to others, and therefore that the interpretations in the SBC will also be determined by whoever has the influence for a final reading of the text.

Concluding Remarks

The commentary has received much recognition, and many in the context of the Russian-speaking evangelical world look forward to its publication with anticipation. In many ways, the commentary will fill and bridge some of the gaps, which other translated commentaries could not do. This is part of the mission of this commentary. It will also be more easily understood by the eastern Slavic evangelicals, as all contributors and authors come from its midst and are actively involved in the mission of that community. But as the evangelical community in the FSU is far from being homogeneous and has, since 1990, experienced various and quite different influences by global, and especially western, biblical interpretation and theology, it will also cause some controversial discussion, disagreement and maybe even rejection. This is part of a legitimate process of a contextual commentary, and these responses may help trigger a wave of more commentary writing targeted at different readers and at different levels of interpretation. This will also be a good contribution which the Slavic Bible Commentary can offer to the missional context of post-Soviet evangelical communities.

Eastern European Churches Engaging Roma People: Historical and Missiological Perspectives

Anne-Marie Kool

Introduction

Quoting a government report of the 1970s, Ian Hancock reminds us that Marxist ideology described the 'Gypsy problem' as the Roma's unwillingness to accept Marxist principles, because they had inherited pre-communist notions of capitalism and, with one or two exceptions, were still 'beggars, thieves, violent and a scourge in the countryside'.[1] Since the fall of the Berlin Wall in 1989, conditions for Europe's Gypsies have worsened dramatically. Before the wall fell down, although not all Gypsies and not all over Central and Eastern Europe, still many had a job with a guaranteed minimum salary.[2] When you were unemployed for more than three months, you were seen as a 'parasite and work evader'. Therefore, when the Wall came down, and many lost their jobs, they were once again perceived by society as criminals, as before World War II.[3]

For the Eastern European churches, the fall of the Berlin Wall opened up many new doors for mission work. Many felt ill prepared. Some did remember 'the good old days' of foreign mission, when they were supporting their missionaries to China or Africa. Many churches did not have a clue of how to be 'missionaries' to their own nominal church members. How to 'translate' the gospel to those for whom Christianity was for 'old ladies with scarves'?

Against the background of this context, the present chapter explores how the Eastern European churches have responded to the Roma people since the fall of the Berlin Wall. It first introduces the current responses of Eastern European churches from a bird's-eye view, especially with respect to the Conference of European Churches, the European Baptist Federation, Gypsy Pentecostalism, and the Roman Catholic Church. The chapter then gives a critical analysis of the underlying 'models' or paradigms and related images, seeking to uncover the motivation behind these responses. Finally,

---

[1] Ian Hancock, 'The Roma Today: Issues and Identity', in Hristo Kyuchukov and Ian Hancock (eds), *Roma Identity* (Prague: NGO Slovo 21, 2010), 15: www.slovo21.cz/nove/images/dokumenty_integrace/fin_cd_roma_identity_part%201.pdf

[2] Lucia Abellan and Miquel Mora, 'The Specter of Racism in Europe', in *El Pais* (2013): http://elpais.com/m/elpais/2013/12/30/inenglish/1388408298_024800. html?rel=rosEP

[3] Abellan and Mora, 'The Specter of Racism in Europe'.

a way forward is pointed out to overcome the limitations of these paradigms, ending with some practical suggestions. It will be argued that a key question for the Eastern European 'majority' churches is how they could facilitate moving from 'mission to the Roma' to 'Roma churches' or to a 'Church for all'! The final purpose of this chapter is to initiate a process of reflection from a missiological perspective, to draw lessons from how churches and mission organizations are responding to the Roma people and why, as well as to stimulate further research at grassroots level, in which theological perspectives are taken into consideration.

A Missiological Point of Departure

In taking a missiological perspective as our point of departure, three key words are used: incarnation, translation and transformation, significant for the mission historian and theologian Andrew F. Walls.[4] He focuses on the 'expansion of Christian faith by its interaction with different cultures and even languages',[5] emphasizing the development of the church across cultures to be linked with the incarnation. It started with a 'historical event leading to a historical process'.[6] After the resurrection of Jesus Christ, a small group of disciples set out to do what he had commanded them to do: 'As the Father has sent me, I am sending you'. (John 20:21). They followed in his footsteps, with the same mindset of Jesus, the Son of God, to 'live the gospel... with incarnational love and sacrificial service', as 'God's life-transforming power at work in the world'. 'It is the power of God for the salvation of everyone who believes.'[7] The essence of the gospel is the incarnation of Jesus Christ: He came down to take us up, to reconcile us with God. Christ's incarnation is about Christ's coming in a specific culture, and ultimately, being spread among cultures and traditions. Thus for Walls 'the expansion of Christianity as a cross-cultural story'.[8]

The second key word of translation refers to the process started with the disciples to translate the message of reconciliation with God through Jesus Christ in other cultures. Their purpose was to make it understandable to those to whom this message was foreign, so that it would make sense. It was a complicated task. There were no recipes. This process of translation

---

[4] For an excellent introduction to Andrew Walls' missiological thinking, see: William R. Burrows, Mark R. Gornik and Janice A. McLean, *Understanding World Christianity: The Vision and Work of Andrew F. Walls* (Maryknoll, NY: Orbis Books, 2011).

[5] Andrew F. Walls, *The Cross-Cultural Process in Christian History: Studies in the Transmission and Appropriation of Faith* (Maryknoll, NY: Orbis Books / Edinburgh: T. & T. Clark, 2002), 9-10.

[6] Mark Gornik, 'Profiles: Andrew Walls and the Transformation of Christianity', in *Catalyst. Contemporary Perspectives for United Methodist Seminarians* (2005): www.catalystresources.org/andrew-walls-and-the-transformation-of-christianity. See also Burrows, Gornik and McLean, *Understanding World Christianity*.

[7] *The Cape Town Commitment* (South Hamilton, IA: The Lausanne Movement, 2010).

[8] Gornik, 'Profiles'.

is closely related to another key concept in Walls' thought: conversion. It is a process of applying the authority and Kingship of Christ into thought, life, culture and mind. Therefore, says Walls: 'New life in Christ is not about cultural uniformity… but always about fresh appropriations or translations of the Christian faith.'[9] Converts should therefore be distinguished from proselytes.[10] The proselyte is 'simply and wrongly… forced to repeat a foreign cultural form of belief and practice'.[11] This carries much importance for the practice of cross-cultural ministry. Conversion leads to the 'embodiment of faith in diverse cultures' by way of translation. 'Theologically, God is a translator, centrally as Christ took on human form. Translation is linguistic and cultural, and is always taking place.'[12] This notion of the translation of the gospel into other cultures never occurs without a critique of culture.

Major discussions have taken place what to reject and what to accept (Acts 15). In this process, culture is transformed, Christianized. So incarnation initiates a process of translation leading to the third key word, that of transformation. In our societies, churches and personal lives, there is a need for transformation. Social transformation and spiritual transformation are frequently used notions. They are inseparably connected, and have their roots in God. He is the initiator of transformation, as stated in the Cape Town Commitment: 'The whole Bible reveals the mission of God to bring all things in heaven and earth into unity under Christ, reconciling them through the blood of his cross. In fulfilling his mission, God will transform the creation broken by sin and evil into the new creation in which there is no more sin or curse… God will destroy the reign of death, corruption and violence when Christ returns to establish his eternal reign of life, justice and peace…'[13]

These three concepts – incarnation, translation and transformation – define a missiological perspective. Spreading the gospel starts with incarnation, the message that Jesus Christ, the Son of God, who became flesh to reconcile us with God. It continues with translation of the gospel into other cultures, and transformation, the impact of the conversion to Jesus Christ on our personal lives, churches, societies and cultures. These three key words are used as tools to reflect on the Eastern European churches' responses to Roma people, not with the aim of judging, but rather of analyzing, comparing and evaluating what is going on!

Knowledge about these responses and about what is going on in Roma (Christian) communities is still very limited, and often dominated by stereotyped images. Therefore, safe spaces are needed in which processes

---

[9] Gornik, 'Profiles'.

[10] See Walls' excellent article: Andrew F. Walls, 'Converts or Proselytes? The Crisis over Conversion in the Early Church', in *International Bulletin of Missionary Research,* 28 (2004).

[11] Gornik, 'Profiles'.

[12] Gornik, 'Profiles'.

[13] *The Cape Town Commitment*, I.10.

of listening, asking questions for clarification and learning, could be initiated, in an open and humble attitude. Such conversations should include expressing mutual fear and asking for forgiveness for what has been done wrong or what is left undone.

A Historical Point of Departure

In understanding the Eastern European Churches' responses to the Roma from a historical perspective, Klaus-Michael Bogdal's much-discussed study *Europa Erfindet Die Zigeuner* (Europe Invents Gypsies) serves to find a historical point of departure.[14] He tells the compelling story of how, during the 600 years Roma have been in Europe, they have been perceived as 'threatening'. Based on a thorough and careful analysis of literature from the Middle Ages till our own day, it provides an insightful historical overview of the reality of the Roma over the ages.[15] His conclusion is that the history of Roma people is a history of stereotypes, images, and behavioural patterns and legends – a history of 'inventions', not of realities, in which 'repeatedly exterminatory fantasies turned into exterminatory practices'.[16] Throughout history, the mere existence of the Roma was considered as an omnipresent threat. The fear is fed by the image that these incomprehensible strangers form a deadly threat.[17] Experience with individuals does not play any part. This threat requires a distance, exclusion. But this is not a solution; it only increases the distance. This image needed to be reinforced and repeated continuously, with refined variations and adaptations. That has happened – according to Bogdal – during the past six centuries.

This created image reinforces the certainty that is contrary to any experience, that co-existence with the Roma is totally impossible and is always linked with incalculable risks and disadvantages for the majority population. Whereas the first conclusion is related to a highly emotional threat, this second one is supported by seemingly rational considerations, related to the completely different lifestyle of the Roma. These thoughts seem to show that the attitude of distancing and exclusion is right. Because these reflections are untruthful and misleading, no trust can be built between the Roma and the majority population.

---

[14] Marcus End, 'Antigypsyism in the German Public Sphere: Strategies and Mechanisms of Media Communication (Heidelberg, Germany: Dokumentations und Kulturzentrum. Deutscher Sinti und Roma, 2015), 33: www.sintiundroma.de/fileadmin/ dokumente/publikationen/extern/2015KurzfassungStudieMarkusEndAntiziganismusEnglisch.pdf (accessed 29th February 2016.

[15] Klaus-Michael Bogdal, *Europa Erfindet Die Zigeuner: Eine Geschichte Von Faszination Und Verachtung* (1. Aufl. ed.; Berlin: Suhrkamp, 2011). See also 'Europe Invents the Gypsies: The Dark Side of Modernity', in *Eurozine,* 24 (February 2012): www.eurozine.com/ articles/2012-02-24-bogdal-en.html.

[16] Bogdal, *Europa Erfindet Die Zigeuner.* Ibid., 'Europe Invents the Gypsies', 2.

[17] Bogdal, *Europa Erfindet Die Zigeuner*, 480.

The development of European civilization can be measured in literature by the way it views the Roma people. The 'worth' accounted to the Roma decreases, because they do not keep pace with this development in European civilization.[18] Therefore the 'gypsies' are not really perceived as part of the European peoples. Rather, the greatest differences are emphasized and not the common features, not even the smallest common denominator. Unfortunately, these existing stereotypes of the Roma are not corrected, but live on till today. Europe still 'invents' gypsies! The Roma continue to be considered as scapegoats.[19]

Bogdal points to the 'interpretative power of science' as the root of Europe 'inventing' gypsies. For the philanthropic reformers in the eighteenth century, the Roma (Gypsies) 'did not pass the test of civilization', as they were seen as 'incapable of development' and placed 'at the bottom of their ethnic hierarchy'.[20] Bogdal comes to the stunning conclusion that 'not "knowledge" about the Gypsies made the Holocaust seem necessary but, the fact that after 1933 there was a power capable of imposing a particular "knowledge" on all areas of life'.[21] He believes that the history of the Roma in Central and Eastern Europe in the twentieth century can be summarized as one of terrible suffering. Bogdal's shocking conclusion: 'In historical reality, these imaginary representations culminated in genocide'.[22]

It is against this background of perpetuating 'fantasy' exclusion that we need to interpret the responses of the Eastern European churches to the Roma. Europe 'invents' the Roma, and thus sees them, not in reality, but as a stereotyped image created and repeated over the centuries. This created image still defines an attitude of exclusion held by millions of Europeans.

---

[18] Bogdal, *Europa Erfindet Die Zigeuner*, 481-82.

[19] Bogdal, *Europa Erfindet Die Zigeuner*, 482.

[20] In the nineteenth century, trivial Gypsy romanticism, emphasizing the images of the 'Hungarian fiddler and the Andalusian flamenco dancer', continued to give a 'distorted reflection of reality'. European Ethnology in the nineteenth century changed the Roma from a 'people' to a 'tribe', 'a pre-civilizational people… incapable of development'. In order to maintain the self-image of Europe as the heart of civilization, the Roma continued to be measured by 'one's own, supposedly more valuable, degree of civilisation'. Bogdal observes that it was ethnology that 'created' the Gypsies as a 'marginal people on the peripheries of European high culture'. He concludes that both Enlightenment anthropology and European Ethnology led to the de-Europeanization of the Roma. 'It presented the body, thought and behaviour of the Roma in such a way that their otherness again acquired threatening contours. There was no space within Europe for them. Ethnic cleansing always begins on paper.' In the first half of the twentieth century, the image of the Gypsies of a 'criminal band of swindlers, thieves and infant abductors', that had been established over nearly six hundred years, was not dispelled by racial theories, but rather redefined and intensified. This happened especially in Germany. As an entire ethnic group, they were characterized as 'antisocial', 'socially deviant' and 'work-shy'. These views were used to justify the mass murder of the Roma in World War II.

[21] Bogdal, 'Europe Invents the Gypsies', 8.

[22] Bogdal, 'Europe Invents the Gypsies', 8.

The Limitations of Paper

Mapping the Eastern European churches' responses to Roma people is an impossible task. This is, first, because the 'Eastern European churches' are a mixture of 'traditional' churches that have existed for ages, with many 'new' churches planted after 1989. Secondly, because 'off the radar' and also on the periphery, many local, often independent, initiatives are taking place, with the sacrificial commitment of many a lonely worker. Not much has been published about these initiatives. The complexity of mapping the Eastern European churches' responses to the Roma people is increased by language barriers.

Numerous studies have been published on the Roma (Gypsies) from an anthropological, sociological, ethnological, human rights and human development perspective.[23] The Roman Catholic Romologist Gernot Haupt observed in 2009 that few studies dealt with the Roma people from a religious perspective, as this element has been completely left out of the planning and implementation of charity programmes. At the same time, according to Haupt, it is this religious element that has had a decisive influence on the effectiveness and success of the projects.[24] More and more studies also now focus on the churches as a 'religious phenomenon' and their impact on Roma communities.[25] Still, a theological, missiological perspective is missing. Only recently (2009), a ground-breaking study was published on the Gypsy Pentecostal movement in Bulgaria by Miroslav Atanasov.[26]

---

[23] Some of the more recent ones: David Thurfjell and Adrian Marsh, *Romani Pentecostalism: Gypsies and Charismatic Christianity* (Frankfurt, Germany: Peter Lang, 2014); Katharine Quarmby, 'Romani Pilgrims: Europe's New Moral Force', Newsweek Limited: www.myilibrary.com?id=662195; David Thurfjell, *Faith and Revivalism in a Nordic Romani Community: Pentecostalism Amongst the Kaale Roma of Sweden and Finland* (Library of Modern Religion: London / New York: I.B. Tauris, 2013); Morton Kjaerum, 'Ending Roma Discrimination in Europe: Yearning to Breath Free', in *The European Magazine* (2012): http://theeuropean-magazine.com/529-kjaerum-morten/530-ending-roma-discrimination-in-europe; Michael Stewart and Márton Rövid, *Multi-Disciplinary Approaches to Romany Studies* (Budapest / New York: Central European University Press, 2011); Tatiana Podolinská and Tomáš Hrustič, *Religion as a Path to Change: The Possibility of Social Inclusion of the Roma in Slovakia* (Bratislava: Institute of Ethnology, 2011): www.uet.sav.sk/files/religion_as_a_path_to_ change.pdf; Laszlo Foszto, *Ritual Revitalisation after Socialism: Community, Personhood, and Conversion among Roma in a Transylvanian Village* (Halle Studies in the Anthropology of Eurasia), (Münster, Germany / Piscataway, NJ: Transaction Publishers, 2009); Peter Vermeersch, *The Romani Movement: Minority Politics and Ethnic Mobilization in Contemporary Central Europe* (Studies in Ethnopolitics), (New York: Berghahn Books, 2006).

[24] Gernot Haupt, *Antiziganismus und Religion: Elemente Einer Theologie der Roma-Befreiung* (Vienna: Lit Verlag, 2009), 30.

[25] E.g. Bogdal, *Europa Erfindet Die Zigeuner*; Foszto, *Ritual Revitalisation after Socialism*; Thurfjell and Marsh, *Romani Pentecostalism*; Thurfjell, *Faith and Revivalism in a Nordic Romani Community*.

[26] Miroslav A. Atanasov, 'Gypsy Pentecostals: The Growth of the Pentecostal Movement among the Roma in Bulgaria and Its Revitalization of Their Communities' (PhD dissertation, Asbury Theological Seminary, 2008); Ibid., *Gypsy Pentecostals: The Growth of the*

Four Responses of Eastern European Churches

In the following part, I will deal with four responses of (Eastern) European churches with a bird's-eye view. Following an analysis of common/ecumenical documents of churches that belong to the Conference of European Churches (CEC), I will deal with some single cases of the Baptist and the Pentecostal Churches, and fourthly with the response of the Roman Catholic Church. The response of the Orthodox Church is included in the first category as they belong to the CEC. At this stage in research, it is not possible to give a more in-depth insight in and overview of how, at a local level, churches of the various Christian traditions are engaging with the Roma communities.

Miroslav Atanasov reminds us that the historical relationship between the Roma and Christianity is remarkable. Although the Roma have lived among Christians for centuries, they have always been marginalized and overlooked by them.[27] It is striking that the Roma 'issue' was only recently put on the agenda of the EU. In preparation for EU enlargement in 2004, many in the western part of Europe feared a massive East-West migration of poor Eastern Europeans, considered as a dangerous wildfire in Europe's back garden. Many (Eastern) European churches too have started to address the so-called 'Roma question'.

The Conference of European Churches (CEC)

The CEC, a major church body in Europe of which many Eastern European churches are members, organized a major conference on Roma in 2001 entitled *Living in Community, Equal Opportunities and Overcoming Discrimination.* With regard to making *Living in Community* possible, churches are reminded that they have been part of the history of the Roma, as the Roma have had to face neglect, harassment, persecution and murder. For true dialogue to be possible, European peoples, including the churches and councils of churches, 'need to recognize what they/we did to wrong the Roma in the past... and express their repentance for wrongs in the past'.[28] In many countries, churches have excluded Roma from their church services, refused them sacraments, marriage and burial services/rituals. It is also recommended that the churches become actively involved in the empowerment of Roma.[29] Therefore, churches are encouraged to call upon

---

Pentecostal Movement among the Roma in Bulgaria and Its Revitalization of Their Communities (The Study of World Christian Revitalization Movements in Pentecostal/Charismatic Studies), (Lexington, KY: Emeth Press, 2010).

[27] Atanasov, 'Gypsy Pentecostals', 98.

[28] The Churches' Commission for Migrants in Europe, Conference of European Churches, 'Recommendations for Churches' Contributions to Living in Community, Equal Opportunities and Overcoming Discrimination' (paper presented at Living in Community – Towards Equal Opportunities and Overcoming Discrimination. The Situation of Roma in Central and Eastern Europe, Bratislava, 2nd-6th May 2001), 1-2.

[29] The Churches' Commission for Migrants in Europe, 1-2.

governments and authorities who have the obligation to protect their national minorities. They are especially reminded of the importance of diaconal work, to improve social conditions. The role of the churches is seen rather as lobbying authorities to provide resources and to request the European Commission to do more to overcome prejudice, but their activities should not replace the obligation of national and local government.[30] The churches do express a general commitment to building a human community 'based on justice, equal human rights and equal opportunities'. They envisage a community free from fear and racism.[31] Whether the churches have a specific task apart from lobbying the EU, is not clear. So far, this has been the response of the CEC in 2001.

One decade later, the Roma issue is again on the agenda of the CEC. The European churches draft a proposal for an 'ecumenical contribution of European churches' to the EU framework of national Roma integration.[32] The official document of the EU summarizing the EU strategy till 2020 focuses on anti-discrimination.[33] The reason seems to be mainly economic. It would require a change of mindsets of both communities, of the majority society as well as of members of the Roma communities.[34] European churches and diaconal organizations commit themselves to contribute to the successful implementation of the EU framework, both at a national and at a European level. They are willing to act as 'relevant actors in advocacy and grassroots work with Roma communities',[35] based on the 'Christian conviction that every person is created in the image of God and shares equal rights and dignity as a human being'.[36]

The churches and Eurodiaconia[37] recommend participation of the Roma, and are ready to co-operate with all those that consider the needs of people 'in a holistic manner'.[38] It is not clearly defined what this 'holistic manner'

---

[30] The Churches' Commission for Migrants in Europe, 1-2.

[31] The Churches' Commission for Migrants in Europe, 5.

[32] Eurodiaconia, 'An Ecumenical Contribution of European Churches and Diaconal Organisations to the EU Framework for National Roma Integration Strategies' (paper presented at the EU Framework for National Roma Integration Strategies Consultation – MRE (Reformed Church in Hungary) Synod Office, 2011).

[33] 'Member States are responsible that Roma are not discriminated against, but treated like any other EU citizens, with equal access to all fundamental rights as enshrined in the EU Charter of Fundamental Rights'. Quoted from European Commission, 'Communication from the Commission to the European Parliament, the Council, the European Economic and Social Committee and the Committee of the Regions. An EU Framework for the National Roma Integration Strategies up to 2020' (Brussels: EU, 2012).

[34] An EU Framework for the National Roma Integration Strategies up to 2020', 1. The first version read: 'Integrating the Roma people will not only bring social benefits, but will also economically benefit both Roma people as well as the communities they are part of.'

[35] Eurodiaconia, 'An Ecumenical Contribution of European Churches and Diaconal Organisations to the EU Framework for National Roma Integration Strategies' (paper presented at the EU Framework for National Roma Integration Strategies Consultation – Mre Synod Office), 1.

[36] Eurodiaconia, 'An Ecumenical Contribution', 1.

[37] See online at: <https://www.eurodiaconia.org/hu/>, accessed on: 3 February 2017.

[38] Eurodiaconia, 'An Ecumenical Contribution', 1.

entails, neither what the specific input of the churches is.[39] Thus, in general, it seems that the EU is considered as the major agency responsible for implementing Roma integration strategies and the churches assist it in doing so.

As we focus our attention on Hungary as a case study, it is remarkable that Hungarian strategy for social inclusion 2011-2020, issued by the Hungarian authorities, is much more specific on the role of the churches.[40] The contribution of 'pastoral and missionary activities' is emphasized, because the 'intensive motivation' of the members of the Christian communities does have a unique impact on members of the Roma communities.[41] Also it is stressed that churches and other communities reach members of Roma communities with their missionary activities.[42] The importance of close co-operation with the Roma community and the churches is emphasized, as it may contribute to a change in the attitude and mindset of the majority society.[43] The remarkable fact is that it is the *government* which expects churches to assist them in dealing with the Roma issues according to their particular way of dealing with the matter. Hungarian churches focus especially on implementing diaconal aid, as well as on education in providing student housing and related community living to Roma high school and university students. They established a Christian network for student housing (*Keresztyén Roma szakkollégiumi hálózat*), consisting of five student houses.[44] In 2013, the Reformed Church of Hungary issued a strategic document on Roma mission called 'Reconciliation, Health and Hope'.[45] So the Hungarian government explicitly emphasizes the unique role of the churches. It seems they almost exceeded the primary economic objective of the framework. A very promising recent development is an initiative of the Baptist, Lutheran, Methodist, Pentecostal and Reformed leaders of ministries among the

---

[39] It is stated, in general, that church-related organizations and local congregations can play an important role in 'bridging communities and providing for such discussions and community dialogue'. Eurodiaconia, 'An Ecumenical Contribution', 1.

[40] 'National Social Inclusion Strategy – Extreme Poverty, Child Poverty, the Roma (2011-2020)', ed. Ministry of Public Administration and Justice State Secretariat for Social Inclusion (Budapest, 2011).

[41] 'National Social Inclusion Strategy'.

[42] 'National Social Inclusion Strategy'.

[43] The churches could in particular play a mediator's role, which would result in increased inclusion from the side of the majority society. In this strategy document, it is also stated that Christian communities not only serve with their unique 'religious motivation', but also that church projects could help at grassroots level in social, educational and employment initiatives.

[44] 'Keresztyén Roma Szakkollégiumi Hálózat': http://krszh.hu

[45] Reformed Church in Hungary, 'Reconciliation – Health – Hope: Concept of the Reformed Church in Hungary's Ministry among Roma. Working Paper' (2011): www.reformatus.hu/data/documents/2013/10/25/Concept_of_Roma_Ministry_of_RCH_full_text_working_paper_fin.pdf. An elaborate vision is stated of what should happen; however, the particular targets are rather broad and at this stage still lack a specific action plan of how to accomplish these targets.

Roma to strengthen co-operation, because of their common faith and similar thinking. Their common mission statement closes with the words: 'We believe that salvation based on faith in Christ is the solution also in the life of the Roma.'[46] However, the question remains as to how the Hungarian churches will use this unique opportunity as they also face the huge challenge of reaching out to the large nominal fringe of their church membership, like many Eastern European churches.

The European Baptist Federation

The second Eastern European church 'family' is the European Baptist Federation. Local Baptist churches all over Eastern Europe are responding to the Roma people, sometimes co-ordinated at a national level. The EBF's purpose is 'to seek in all its endeavours to fulfil the will of Jesus Christ, Lord and Saviour'.[47] In their mission and evangelism work, the focus is on evangelism and church planting.[48]

A unique project of the European Baptist Federation is the Anti-Trafficking Network, established ten years ago. Human trafficking is defined as the illegal trade of human beings, mainly for the purposes of forced labour and sex trafficking. Unfortunately, Roma have been portrayed as perpetrators of trafficking, but more often as victims. Many people are trafficked from Eastern Europe with a Roma background.[49]

The Ruth School in Bucharest is a remarkable educational initiative with related ministries. It was established in 1992, when an American missionary challenged the local Baptist pastor, Pastor Oti, about what was going on among Roma children on the streets of Bucharest. It started as a Sunday School, and was extended into a day centre. Soon it evolved into a literary class as it was realized that most children could neither read nor write and had never gone to school. As they were close to teenage age, there was no other opportunity in a regular school programme for them to enrol into. The local educational system did not recognize that there was an illiteracy problem. In the meantime, the Ruth School also started to offer a

---

[46] 'Közös Küldetésnyilatkozat', in *Tükör* 2014. 'Do nothing out of selfish ambition of vain conceit. Rather, in humility, value others above yourselves, not looking to your own interests but each of you to the interests of others. In your relationships with one another, have the same mind set as Christ Jesus… (Phil. 2:3-5). In following the example of Christ, co-workers in Roma Mission of Baptist, Lutheran, Methodist, Pentecostal and Reformed churches turn in humility to the Roma people, and encourage all our fellow human people to do so. On the basis of our conviction, stemming from our faith and our experience, we would like to share with them the life-changing gospel message that proclaims to all nations equally the deliverance of a sinful, lost lifestyle. We believe that salvation based on faith in Christ is the solution also in the life of the Roma.'

[47] http://ebf.org/about-ebf (accessed 27th September 2014).

[48] http://ebf.org/about-ebf (accessed 27th September 2014).

[49] European Roma Rights Center, *Breaking the Silence: Trafficking in Roma Communities* (Budapest: European Roma Rights Center and People in Need, 2011): www.errc.org/cms/upload/file/breaking-the-silence-19-march-2011.pdf

hot meal at school, along with basic medical care as well as hygiene programmes.

The Ruth School is committed 'to giving education to the marginalized and disadvantaged, particularly those coming from Roma (Gypsy) families in order to help them reach their highest potential. Through education, the Ruth School seeks to assist in the inclusion of Roma in society as well as their future educational endeavours (high school, vocational schools, etc.)'.[50] Since its establishment, 2,000 students have been educated and taken care of. The Naomi Center, linked with the Project, now offers professional counselling to mainly Roma women, designed to help them better their lives in a way which will affect their entire families.

Project Ruth also provides leadership and biblical training for leaders of Gypsy (Roma) churches through the Gypsy Smith School, or GSS, as it is known for short. Since its initial start in 1997, over 120 Gypsy pastors, missionaries and community leaders have been trained and continue to serve in their churches and communities. The GSS offers week-long courses four times a year, at a level suitable to their needs and relevant to their culture and environment.[51]

Gypsy Pentecostalism

The third Eastern European churches' response is that of the Pentecostal churches.[52] A book was recently published on *Romani Pentecostalism* by David Thurfjell and Adrian R. Marsh from the perspective of a study of religions.[53] The authors seek to give more insight into the 'multi-faceted and complex phenomenon that Romani Pentecostalism has become and is today', and to inspire further academic interest and research.[54] This study serves as an important starting-point for future theological and missiological research! Pentecostal revivals are mentioned in a number of missionaries' blogs and newsletters. Although we know that such newsletters tend to emphasize the 'successes' and not the downfalls, it should be our priority to map and study how God's Spirit is moving among the Roma.[55]

---

[50] http://projectruth.ro/uk/ruth_school.htm (accessed 23rd September 2014).

[51] http://projectruth.ro/uk/other_programs.htm (accessed 23rd September 2014).

[52] As far as I know, there is no common statement of the Pentecostal European Fellowship, a 'network of 55 Pentecostal movements across Europe working together, with a vision to reach Europe with the Good News of the Gospel, through mutual prayer and co-operation'. Many Pentecostal mission organizations are working among the Roma. It is impossible to deal with each one of them in this presentation.

[53] Thurfjell and Marsh, *Romani Pentecostalism*, 7.

[54] Thurfjell and Marsh, *Romani Pentecostalism*, 7.

[55] We read of a revival in the eastern part of Slovakia: Jim Sabelle, AGWM area director for Central Southeast Europe shares: 'But suddenly, in the midst of this misery, the Spirit of God has swept into the Roma community of eastern Slovakia. An awakening – unprecedented and unabated – is sweeping from village to village, gaining momentum as it goes… I have never, ever seen anything like it. No one can take credit for starting it,' he says emphatically. 'Christ

One example is offered by Miroslav A. Atanasov in his dissertation. He engages in such a mapping of Gypsy Pentecostal churches in Bulgaria by 'building the case for Roma revitalization as a result of the Christian faith'.[56] Initially, the complex indigenous Roma Pentecostal movement was started under the guidance and support of ethnic Bulgarian evangelical leaders, but the main responsibility has now largely been transferred to the Roma.[57] The more the church is led by Roma, the more indigenous it becomes.[58] Atanasov deals with specific examples of community revitalization,[59] like the impact on Roma family life. Roma traditions were revitalized according to biblical standards in a process of discernment: 'Being mostly younger believers, the Roma have needed and relied on that *gajo* guidance and leadership. As they mature in the faith, however, the Roma are developing their own processes of internal dialogue to decide on what to do with these practices. Some of them are rejected, some accepted, and others modified. While Roma Christians mostly agree on the handling of certain practices, there is also some variation and disagreement among them in regard to others. Fortune-telling, stealing and trickery, for example, are unanimously rejected as pagan and unacceptable'.[60] This response is 'the work and vision of the Roma pastors who feel the inspiration of the Holy Spirit to bring about community transformation through reconstitutive discourse'.[61]

Whereas the Bulgarian Gypsy Pentecostal movement is indigenous in nature, many other Gypsy Pentecostal communities in Eastern Europe have their roots in the Pentecostal revival among Roma that started in 1950s in France[62] through the ministry of Clément Le Cossec.[63] The scope of this chapter does not allow for an extensive treatment of this remarkable revival movement that also influenced Eastern Europe. Le Cossec established

---

the King has gone into the highways and byways, inviting whosoever will to come to his table. And the Roma are coming in droves.' Krisztel Ortiz, 'Gypsy Awakening', in *Pentecostal Evangel,* 2013. See also Thurfjell, *Faith and Revivalism in a Nordic Romani Community.*

[56] Atanasov, 'Gypsy Pentecostals', 232.

[57] Atanasov, 'Gypsy Pentecostals', 220.

[58] Atanasov, 'Gypsy Pentecostals', 230.

[59] Atanasov, 'Gypsy Pentecostals', 234-56.

[60] Atanasov, 'Gypsy Pentecostals', 257.

[61] Atanasov, 'Gypsy Pentecostals', 273.

[62] In September 2010, the Christian Science Monitor had the headline: 'In France, an evangelical Gypsy group shakes up the immigration debate.' At the same time as the collective expulsions of Roma out of France back to Romania in August, 26,000 evangelical Gypsies gathered in the heart of France to sing, give testimonies and read the Bible. 'The Gypsy stereotypes are no longer valid.' According to recent statistics, out of the 425,000 French Gypsies, 145,000 joined the evangelical movement. Robert Marquand, 'Gypsies Leave France amid Crackdown on Illegals', in *Christian Science Monitor,* 2010. Other sources mention 200,000 out of the 500,000. Trevor Persaud, 'Christianity Thrives among "Gypsies" despite Prejudice. Roma Revival: Missionary Efforts Continue to Succeed', in *Christianity Today,* 54.11 (2010).

[63] The periodical *Lumière du monde* (1947-1960), *Vie et Lumière* (1961-1995), reports on the ministry of this movement all over the world, including Eastern Europe.

several organizations, of which the most important is *Vie et Lumière*, to which about 200 Roma churches belong. Since 1994, this organization has operated a Roma Bible School in Gyönk, Hungary, \also in Moscow and even one in Bangalore, India.[64] Le Cossec also established the *Centre Missionaire Evangélique de Rom International* (CMERI). Marie Bidet,[65] a French Romologist, characterizes these Gypsies in her doctoral thesis thus: 'They are serious, respectable: they vote, they don't want to burn cars, they want everyone living in peace. That's the opposite from their traditional image… it can be emphasized that they succeed in their approach.'[66] A sub-organization is GATIEF, Gypsies and Travellers International Evangelical Fellowship, led by René Zanellato, working in more than forty countries.[67] The movement can be characterized with three main objectives: 1. Evangelism, 2. Training of co-workers and 3. Establishing churches.[68] In the middle of the 1990s, Le Cossec counted 6,000 Gypsy preachers all over Europe. The evangelical Gypsy movement spread out of France over the whole world. Currently, more than two million believers in 44 countries belong to this movement. Marc Bordigone, an anthropologist of Provence University, describes the work of Le Cossec: 'Le Cossec's approach paradoxically enabled Gypsies to keep their identity through a faith, Christianity, that asserts what he calls a universal character.'[69]

Le Cossec describes his ministry as: 'Not for a minute was it a question of lecturing them with morals, telling them they should not drink, lie, steal or 'soothsay' any more. I knew that, by receiving the message of Christ, everything in their lives would change.'[70] Thomas Acton emphasizes that the movement does not teach its converts to be 'ashamed of being Romani; on the contrary, it tells them that they can be better Gypsies for being Christian – and better Christians for being Gypsies – for, unlike the poor non-Gypsies who are tied down to one place by their houses, the Gypsy can carry on his witness for Christ wherever he wanders.'[71]

Le Cossec is clear about the holistic scope of the 'Gypsy evangelical Mission':

> We first have to preach Christ, according to the apostle's formula. It has always been a priority for me… We do not lose sight of the fact that our first goal is to speak of Christ, the living bread come down from heaven. We have to understand that there is no possible salvation for man apart from Jesus

---

[64] www.nyest.hu/hirek/elet-es-feny-a-tolnai-hegyhaton-teritok-a-cigany-apostol-nyomaban

[65] See also Frank Dawson, 'Christian Outreach to Romany in Central Europe and Russia', in *East-West Church Ministry Report,* 10.3 (2002): www.eastwest report.org/issues/articles-1993-2005/93-vol-10-no-3-summer-2002. See also Atanasov, 'Gypsy Pentecostals'.

[66] Marquand, 'Gypsies Leave France amid Crackdown on Illegals', 2.

[67] www.romanomissio.fi/zanelatto.htm (accessed 27th September 2014).

[68] *Vie et Lumière Inde,* 148.3 (1995).

[69] Marquand, 'Gypsies Leave France amid Crackdown on Illegals', 2.

[70] Farid Djilani-Sergy, 'Clément Le Cossec: Un Serviteur de Dieu qui a Marqué Son Siècle', (1996) www.paroles.ch (Radio Réveil).

[71] Thomas Acton, 'The Gypsy Evangelical Church', in *The Ecumenical Review,* 31.3 (1979), 291, cited in Atanasov, 'Gypsy Pentecostals', 220.

> Christ. He has come to earth, he has lived as a poor man, he has brought the good news of salvation by grace… If we do not ourselves have the experience of conversion, how could we communicate to others the spiritual realities the gospel supports and the testimony which goes with it? It is essential to assure the doctrinal bases to a true life of faith.[72]

The Roman Catholic Church

In 1965, a group of about 2,000 Gypsies arrived from all over Europe on a pilgrimage to Rome. Their goal was to ask the Pope for official protection of their nomadic way of life. Gernot Haupt reminds us[73] that there is one sentence that has been quoted in every document since: 'You are not at the margins of the church, you are – in a certain sense – in the centre; you are at the heart of the church.' A few years later, Pope Paul VI established the *Pontificia Commissio de Spirituali Migratorum atque Itinerantium Cura* (Pontifical Council for the Pastoral Care of Migrants and Itinerant People). The purpose of the Council was to study 'people on the move', evangelize them, and provide them with appropriate spiritual shepherding. Under the auspices of this Council was the Department of Pastoral Care for Gypsies, which organized several world congresses.[74] A first Pastoral Letter for Nomadic people in 1999 warns of the dangers of sects that push them to abandon the church and lose their faith. Therefore, religious education is needed.[75] The document calls our attention to the positive characteristics of the Gypsy world, 'such as fraternal and generous hospitality, a deep sense

---

[72] Djilani-Sergy, 'Clément Le Cossec'. Le Cossec established a separate organization to deal with the social dimension.

[73] Haupt is very critical about this document. Gernot Haupt, 'Discrimination of Roma People', in *Reflection Group of Roma People* (Brussels: COMECE and CCEE, 2011): www.ifsoz.org/content/download/pdf/110301Brussels.pdf, 8-9. It is a quotation taken out of context. The full greeting reads: 'Best greetings to you, eternal pilgrims; to you, voluntary fugitives; to you, who are always on the run… Best greetings to you, who have chosen your little tribe, your caravan, as your separated and secret world; to you, who look at the world with distrust and are looked at with distrust from all; to you who wanted to be foreigners everywhere and for ever… ' According to Haupt, this is the original Italian text.

[74] The Fifth World Congress of the Pastoral Care of Gypsies took place in Budapest in 2003. It is noteworthy that for the first time a considerable group of Gypsies took place: priests, nuns and lay people. Clear theological principles are stated how true communion among people is realized: 'i.) when every human creature is respected as the child and image of God; ii.) if differences between persons are accepted as gifts for all; iii.) when the life of relationships is lived, humbly, along with others, in recognition of the fact that we are all strangers and pilgrims on this Earth; and iv.) if we can offer authentic hospitality to each and every one.' The Pontifical Council for the Pastoral Care of Migrants and Itinerant People, 'Final Document' (paper presented at the Fifth World Congress of the Pastoral Care for Gypsies, Budapest, Hungary), 30th June-7th July 2003). Practical advice is shared as to the shape of the Pastorate. The Congress recommends that 'ecumenical and inter-religious dialogue be extended to the Gypsy world as well, but deplored the sectarian approach harking back to Pentecostalism' adopted by certain groups, 'professing to be Christian', and 'exhorts Catholic pastoral operators to be aware of this danger'.

[75] Anthony Chirayath, 'Pastoral Care of Nomadic People: The Church's Response', in *People on the Move,* 81 (1999), 4-5.

of solidarity, strong attachment to the faith, and the religious traditions of their ancestors'.[76] A few years later, an important document is issued after many years of preparation. The 'Guidelines for the Pastoral Care of Gypsies' deals, among others, with the issue of how to overcome suspicion, referring to what happened in the past.[77] This document was announced in the German press under the headline of 'Pope asks Sinti and Roma for forgiveness'.[78]

In June 2014, Pope Francis called attention to the Gypsies in a meeting on 'The Church and Gypsies: To Announce the Gospel in the Peripheries', where he emphasized that Gypsies are one of the groups most vulnerable to new forms of slavery.[79] Following the example of Jesus Christ, he called for closeness and solidarity with the Roma.

Five Different Paradigms and Their Underlying Images

As we analyze and compare the Eastern European churches' responses among the Roma people, with what is by some perceived as the 'Gypsy problem', we find a variety of models or paradigms. A paradigm is a model or way of doing something that can be copied. Paradigms may exist parallel

---

[76] It also emphasizes that the participation of the Gypsies in society should be strengthened: 'It will be necessary to set up structures to guarantee the continuity of the process of furthering Gypsies' participation in society, and of their acceptance characterized by encounter, understanding and respect for their identity, by friendly dialogue and reciprocal help, also material'.

[77] 'Guidelines for the Pastoral Care of Gypsies', in *People on the Move,* 100 (April 2006): www.vatican.va/roman_curia/pontifical_councils/migrants/pom2006_100-suppl/rc_pc_migrants_pom100-suppl_orientamenti-en.html

[78] Jan Opiela expresses his disappointment as 'Guidelines' were finally published offering a pastoral theological foundation for the pastoral care of Gypsies. With regard to dealing with the past, Opiela considers it of much more importance, that at the Day of Forgiveness in 2000, the Public Intercession prayer was ministered in the presence of Pope John Paul II by Stephen Fumino Karinal Hamao from Japan, President of the Pontifical Council for the Pastoral Care for Migrants and Itinerant People: 'Let Christians look up to Jesus, who is our Lord and our peace. Give, that they can regret, what they have done wrong in word and deed. Often they have let themselves be led by pride and hatred, by the will to dominate others, by hostility to the adherents of other religions and to those groups in society that are weaker than they, like the migrants and the Gypsies.' The Pope responded in his prayer of forgiveness: 'They have violated the rights of tribes and people, and scorned their cultures and religious traditions: Extend us your patience and your mercy! Forgive us! Therefore, we pray you, through Christ our Lord.' According to Opiela, it is remarkable that such a prayer is prayed for the sisters and brothers in the faith, since a large percentage of the Roma and Sinti have affinity with Christianity or are baptized into the Catholic Church. It took the Church almost 500 years to express such a confession of guilt, but what is 500 years in view of a history of 2,000 years? Jan Opiela (ed), *Zur Seelsorge Für Sinti Und Roma. 'Orientierungen Für Eine Pastoral Der Zigeuner'*, Die Stellung Der Kirchen Zu Den Deutschen Sinti Und Roma (Marburg, Germany: I-Verb.de, 2008), 91-92. Solms expresses his hope that the German Catholic Church will one day join this confession of guilt. Ibid., 105.

[79] Pope Francis, 'Address', in Meeting of the Pontifical Council for the Pastoral Care of Migrants and Itinerant People: The Church and Gypsies: To Announce the Gospel in the Peripheries (Clementile Hall: Vatican News, 2014).

with each other, and they also can overlap. Paradigms help us to understand what we are doing and why. Paradigms are based on images. Various images result in various paradigms, in various formats. Bogdal's conclusion, that most of the images of the Roma are not based on reality but are inventions, should motivate us to search for that which is real. Stereotypes and negative labels have considerable impact on the way we relate to each other and are closely related with our responses. We respond in a certain way on the basis of how we view someone, what image we have. There are also multiple images of how the Roma identify themselves. The following paradigms and underlying images can be identified:

The Human Development Paradigm

The first paradigm is the human development paradigm. It has its roots in a document issued in 2001 by the United Nations Development Programme.[80] It is peculiar that this study, focusing on all Central and Eastern Europe was considered to be a 'representative study', whilst being based on just over 5,000 questionnaires for the whole region. This study became the basis for the policy of the EU in years to come. As we have seen in the case of CEC (and Eurodiaconia), this paradigm has been also adapted for 'strategy building' by numerous churches. It is no surprise that they accepted this human development paradigm, since that has long been a dominant paradigm of the European churches in their mission work in Africa.[81]

Characteristic of this paradigm is the image of the 'gypsy' that combines a way of life with low socio-economic and social status (the marginalized one) and is always on the move. The analysis of Klaus-Michael Bogdal revealed that these are created images of the Roma which have been dominant in European society for six centuries.

Although criticized, the image of Roma as nomads and travellers[82] still dominates the Roman Catholic Church's response, as its ministry among the Roma is located in the 'Pontifical Council for the Pastoral Care of Migrants and Itinerant People', although those who are settled now

---

[80] A. Ivanov, *The Roma in Central and Eastern Europe: Avoiding the Dependency Trap: A Regional Human Development Report* (Bratislava: United Nations Development Programme, 2002): www.ircwash.org/resources/roma-central-and-eastern-europe-avoiding-dependency-trap-regional-human-development-report. It is based on 5,034 questionnaires from all over Central and Eastern Europe, and allegedly considered to be 'representative', 1.

[81] A well-known African missiologist described the nineteenth and twentieth-century missionary enterprise of the European churches in Africa as being part of a benevolent western movement to elevate the condition of African peoples, according to which Christianity was spread with a western cultural package. The aim was to help the poor Africans become more civilized, to develop a lifestyle similar to the western way of life, since that was considered the best. Like many African people, they viewed the Roma as poor, deprived, and thus in need of 'development', in need of 'western civilization'. The question, of course, is whether the western way of living is indeed the best.

[82] The term 'traveller' is used in the UK to refer to the Roma (Gypsy).

comprise 90% of all Roma.[83] This image is theologically related to the self-image of the Catholic Church as pilgrims. Therefore, the Roma serve the Church as an eternal *homo viator*: 'They live in such a special way, as in fact the whole Church should live.'[84]

Gernot Haupt states that exclusion has led to a situation that the history of the Roma is characterized by a 'constant being on the road. When the Christian majority society in Europe had shown hospitality to the Roma and had taken them up, in their midst and in their heart... then this permanent flight would not have been necessary'.[85] British Romologist David Mayall concludes that the images of this category are almost always negative, 'creating a sense of conflict, mistrust and antagonism'.[86] Roma scholar Thomas Acton severely criticizes this human development approach as it is based on an incorrect image of the Roma, exclusively focusing on the social image of poverty and not addressing the key issue of exclusion.[87]

So this approach is reductionist in that it focuses on alleviating one aspect of the 'problem', poverty, but does not deal with its roots: the walls of exclusion. It does not address the majority society's attitude of anti-gypsyism.

From a missiological perspective, it is also reductionist. When we evaluate this paradigm from our missiological point of departure, it seeks to bring about transformation, but there is no translation of the gospel, while the incarnational aspect is missing altogether.

Chris Wright's focus on integral mission, emphasizing that, in God's mission, compassion and justice are closely related,[88] could help to overcome these reductions. The Old Testament perspective to care for the poor and the marginalized saturates the mind of Jesus.[89] As in the Sermon on the Mount, Jesus commands his disciples to 'Let your light shine before others, that they may see your good deeds and glorify your Father in heaven'. (Matt. 5:14-16), He emphasizes 'see your good deeds', and speaks of lives that are attractive by being filled with goodness, mercy, love,

---

[83] Therefore, there is a shift of focus from special pastoral care to pastoral care in the parishes! A holistic approach is defined as evangelism and social action hand-in-hand. Wilhelm Solms, *Konzept Der Katholischen Zigeunerseelsorge in Deutschland* (ed), Udo Engbring-Romang and Gesellschaft für Antiziganismusforschung, Die Stellung Der Kirchen Zu Den Deutschen Sinti Und Roma (Marburg, Germany: I-Verb.de, 2008). Ibid., 106.

[84] Haupt, *Antiziganismus und Religion*, 174.

[85] Haupt, *Antiziganismus und Religion*, 174.

[86] David Mayall, *Gypsy Identities, 1500-2000: From Egipcyans and Moon-Men to the Ethnic Romany* (London / New York: Routledge, 2004), 5-8.

[87] Thomas Acton, 'Romani Politics, Scholarship, and the Discourse of Nation-Building', in Adrian Marsh and Elin Strand (eds), *Gypsies and the Problem of Identities: Contextual, Contructed and Contested* (Transactions of the Swedish Research Institute in Istanbul: Istanbul: 2006).

[88] Chris Wright, 'Integral Mission and the Great Commission: "The Five Marks of Mission"', in *Public Lecture* (2013): www.loimission.net/wp-content/uploads/ 2014/03/Chris-Wright-IntegralMissionandtheGreatCommission.pdf, 11-15.

[89] Wright, 'Integral Mission and the Great Commission', 12.

compassion and justice. After a decade of human development approach, a general consensus occurs that money used to 'solve poverty' is not a solution to this 'problem', as it also has an adverse effect. The projects aimed at the Roma community created new walls of division (and jealousy) with the majority society, rather than serving the purpose of bringing the Roma up to an economic standard of living to prevent them moving *en masse* to Western Europe.[90]

The Human Rights Paradigm

The second paradigm, the human rights paradigm, emphasizes the importance of equal rights and equal opportunities for the Roma. The Eastern European mainline churches rightly emphasize the importance of equal opportunities, as they adopt EU strategy. However, this paradigm operates on a legal framework of thought, and not within a theological framework. The EU framework for Roma inclusion as adopted in 2011 includes this approach. The image behind this paradigm is similar to that which is behind the human development paradigm, that of the impoverished gypsy, without rights.

Evaluating the human rights paradigm from a missiological perspective, we observe the same reduction as with the human development paradigm: it seeks to bring about transformation, but the translation and incarnational element is missing altogether. As in the human development paradigm, it is important to note that focusing on compassion and social justice is part of God's mission in serving society, but it cannot be separated from evangelism as the central element of God's mission. Evangelism flows from the message of the incarnation of Christ, and is part of the process of translating the gospel and embodying Christ in other cultures.

Neither can the human development paradigm nor the human rights paradigm ever be the only focus, as they often focus only on the Roma and do not deal with their massive exclusion in the majority society.

The Anti-Gypsyism or Discrimination Paradigm

The third paradigm is the anti-gypsyism or discrimination paradigm. In the thorough literature analysis of Klaus-Michael Bogdal of the general 'atmosphere' in Europe – including Eastern Europe – regarding the Roma people over the centuries, it is clear that anti-gypsyism has been and is clearly still is present in Europe. This paradigm is openly referred to in the mainline churches and Eurodiaconia network documents. There is almost unanimous agreement that discriminating attitudes prevent the Roma from having access to education, employment, housing, etc.

---

[90] Cf. Larry Beman (17th July 2013), *The Roma of Europe* (Kindle location 845-851), (United Methodist Women – Kindle edition).

The images behind this paradigm, related to racism, are negative images of the Roma, and focus only on the attitude of the majority society. In many churches, it is still taboo to speak openly about exclusion. It is a huge theological and missiological challenge to deal theologically with this 'apartheid system'!

From a missiological perspective, transformation is possible only as it is rooted in the incarnation. Overcoming exclusion by the transformation of deep-seated prejudices towards the Roma can flow only out of a clear focus on the message of the incarnation translated into the specific context of reconciliation with God in Christ, and on the implications in everyday life for social reconciliation. Only the Holy Spirit can work out such profound changes. This is possible only when evangelization of both the Roma and the majority society is given its central place in mission.

From a Roman Catholic perspective, Haupt suggests an approach which focuses on mission in Christ's way, by following the healing Christ, and which helps people to get on their feet. Only then do they have the possibility of starting to follow this Saviour voluntarily, and to turn themselves into healing people. So in Haupt's proposal, our three missiological concepts of incarnation, translation and transformation are closely related. Haupt therefore rejects the evangelization method of the Evangelical and Pentecostal churches, because the identity of a Christian or a convert replaces the pure ethnic Roma identity fully – no translation of the gospel takes place – even although it seems from outside that this approach is very successful.[91] He uses the gospel story of the healing of the leper (Mark 1:40-45), in which the leper is touched by Jesus although, in doing so, he is acting contrary to the law of Leviticus 13. A sensible pastoral concept should start by overcoming the anti-gypsy exclusion. Only then do they have the possibility of starting to follow this Saviour voluntarily and of turning themselves into a healing people. Just as the Roma in the Pentecostal churches are being touched by the Holy Spirit, according to Haupt, in the same way they should feel the touch by other Christians in the Spirit of Jesus, whether those Christians are ordained or not. Haupt emphasizes that, in overcoming discrimination, we need to focus on both the Roma themselves and the majority society, the *Gadje*. Haupt emphasizes the importance of the creative and a variety of strategies of inclusion, in which empowerment is a basic principle. The Roma should themselves be put in the position of changing their fate; they should turn into subjects of change, of evangelization, and should not be objects of pastoral care.

From a missiological perspective, we could say that they themselves should be involved in the process of translating the gospel in the Roma culture, as is emphasized by Atanasov: 'The leading human factor in the

---

[91] Gernot Haupt, 'Der Antiziganismus und Eine Theologie der Roma-Befreiung', in *Jahrestagung des 'Comité Catholique International pour les Tsiganes': Friedensstifter in einer romafeindlichen Umwelt'* (Trogir, Croatia: 2008), 198.

revitalization process is the work and vision of the Roma pastors who feel the inspiration of the Holy Spirit in bringing about community transformation through reconstitutive discourse.'[92] Priority should be given to the stimulation of self-organization. Only in this way will the Roma experience that God has seen their distress, and that he turns to them. This turning includes and communicates a spiritual energy and strength, without which any external help provided will remain superficial and without effect. This motivating and healing turning of God can only be experienced through people. Therefore Haupt considers 'the involvement of people in Roma projects much more important than material resources and the pouring out of money'. We should as Christians 'dare to come near'.[93]

Haupt considers the second target group to be the majority society. This element, according to Haupt, is often forgotten. He states that those involved in Roma ministry should spend at least as much time and energy in missionizing their own congregations and other church-related institutions as on the Roma themselves. Not only is the liberation of the Roma from their misery and exclusion at stake, but also our own liberation from a position of paternalism to an attitude of partnership and brotherhood.[94]

From a Pentecostal perspective, in addressing the future of Pentecostalism in Europe, Raymond Pfister calls for a 'spirituality of reconciliation' to face the challenges of the 'damaging effects of cultural and religious clashes'. With Kirsteen Kim, he emphasizes the work of the Holy Spirit in reconciliation as the reconciling Spirit that enables a reconciling community. He thus defines the ministry of the Spirit as a ministry of reconciliation. Pfister observes that not enough attention is given to the fact that God's reconciling initiative in Christ is not limited to individual reconciliation, but that it extends to social reconciliation.[95]

Pfister's proposal may offer a relevant new perspective also to the Eastern European churches as they struggle to overcome exclusion in their societies and churches. In his proposal, incarnation, translation and transformation are closely connected.

---

[92] Atanasov, 'Gypsy Pentecostals', 273.

[93] Haupt, *Antiziganismus und Religion*, 200. Haupt emphasizes the importance of the creative and a variety of strategies of inclusion, in which empowerment is a basic principle. Roma should themselves be put in a position to change their fate; they should turn into subjects of change, and should not be objects of pastoral care. Only in this way will the Roma experience, that God has seen their distress, and that he turns to them.

[94] Haupt, *Antiziganismus und Religion*, 202.

[95] Raymond Pfister, 'The Future(s) of Pentecostalism in Europe', in William K. Kay and Anne E. Dyer (eds), *European Pentecostalism* (Global Pentecostal and Charismatic Studies), (Boston: Brill, 2011).

The Evangelism Paradigm

A fourth paradigm is the evangelism paradigm. Missiologist David Bosch considers evangelism as one of the crucial elements of mission. Bosch mentions eighteen points as elements of a constructive understanding of evangelism. One of these is of great relevance to the context of Roma mission: 'Evangelism is only possible when the community that evangelizes – the church – is a radiant manifestation of the Christian faith and exhibits an attractive lifestyle'.[96]

Behind this paradigm is the image of seeing people through the eyes of Jesus, with their deepest needs being reconciled with God through Jesus Christ. This paradigm considers the Roma as an ethnic and cultural minority, an image that is now also behind the new EU strategy, and following the EU behind that of many (Eastern) European churches. This paradigm is more prominently present in the responses of the Baptist and Pentecostal churches and is hardly mentioned in the mainline churches' responses.

This fact is probably related to the fact of Europe being a mission continent. In the course of its history, the church has used different ways of spreading the gospel to the ends of earth. Sometimes evangelism was done 'the McDonald's way'.[97] The three missiological principles of Andrew F. Walls are not materialized. The gospel message of the incarnation of Jesus Christ was communicated faithfully, but with no consideration for its translation into other cultures. In these cases, the gospel message was often considered as irrelevant. No transformation took place. At other times, the church almost forgot about its gospel message, and turned more into a human enterprise or business as it fully accommodated itself to the surrounding culture. It resulted in no incarnation, 'over-translation' and no transformation. In the evangelism paradigm, we face two challenges as it comes to the translation of the gospel. Into what culture should it be translated – the local Roma culture or the majority culture in which they live? And who takes the decisions in this process?

Evangelism linked with social action is often referred to as 'holistic mission'. Chris Wright reminds us of the 'centrality of evangelism' in holistic mission, as a hub is central to a wheel.[98] Often evangelism is excluded or considered as one option among many, which turns mission into a business, into an anthropocentric enterprise. Evangelism is closely linked with the translation of the gospel into other cultures, but also with transformation. He emphasizes that evangelism leads to 'obedience to Christ, incorporation into his Church and responsible service in the

[96] David J. Bosch, *Transforming Mission: Paradigm Shifts in the Theology of Mission* (American Society of Missiology Series, 16), (Maryknoll, NY: Orbis Books, 1991), 414.
[97] John Drane, 'Resisting Mcdonaldization', in Viggo Mortenson and Andreas Osterlund Nielsen (eds), *Walk Humbly with the Lord: Church and Mission Engaging Plurality* (Grand Rapids, MI: Eerdmans, 2010).
[98] Wright, 'Integral Mission and the Great Commission', 7-8.

world... The salvation we proclaim should be transforming us in the totality of our personal and social responsibilities. Faith without works is dead'.[99]

Chris Wright also emphasizes the close relationship between evangelism and teaching, in building the church. Teaching, in all its forms, is an intrinsic part of mission, including theological education. It is not an extra.[100] Atanasov also emphasizes teaching. He states that 'while Roma churches have been strong on evangelism... their discipleship has been less effective'.[101] It is effective discipleship that will strengthen the faith of the Roma, but it will also inevitably move them towards social transformation.[102] Teaching is also important for the majority society churches, to include themes relevant for ministry among the Roma in the curricula of theological education and to focus on the missionary education of local congregations and the importance of social reconciliation.[103] This brings us to the fifth and last paradigm: the paternalistic paradigm.

The Paternalistic Paradigm

The fifth paradigm is the paternalistic paradigm. This paradigm can best be characterized as a 'we' versus 'them' paradigm, instead of an 'us' paradigm, or even a 'them' versus 'us' paradigm. What can we learn from the Roma people? Fear plays an important role in this paradigm. It is similar to the deep-seated fear in European society towards the Roma that Bogdal observes, based on widespread 'invented' images and the lack of knowledge of their daily reality. Bogdal describes how European society has tried for centuries to bring the Roma up to the same level as the 'civilized' majority society, to assimilate to Eastern European culture. Power and control are used to overcome fear of the perceived threat of the Roma, but the Roma resisted and still resist. They cling to their own ethnicity, and stick to their own cultural expressions, or what is left of it. The problems remain or even grow worse as 'we' take responsibility for 'their' behaviour and attitudes.

In the Eastern European 'majority' churches' responses, a similar spirit of hanging on to power and trying to keep control can be detected. At best, there is an attitude of not knowing how to involve them, and how to release responsibility. Often this is clothed in a different form. It could be

[99] Wright, 'Integral Mission and the Great Commission', 7-8.
[100] Wright, 'Integral Mission and the Great Commission', 10.
[101] Atanasov, 'Gypsy Pentecostals', 30, 300-04.
[102] Atanasov, 'Gypsy Pentecostals', 30, 303.
[103] Anne-Marie Kool, 'Missiological Issues That Need to Be Kept in Mind in Designing Ministry with Roma' (paper presented at the Roma Ministry Exploration Trip sponsored by PC USA, Refomed Guest House of Hungarian Bible Society, Budapest, 2001): https://www.academia.edu/9267182/Missiological_issues_that_need_to_be_kept _in_mind_in_designing_ministry_with_Roma (accessed 16th February 2016).

expressed as making them good Christians, good 'Baptists' or good 'Reformed'.

In the terms of our missiological point of departure, there is a focus on the incarnation, but the process of translating the gospel into the Roma culture is controlled by the majority society, leading to a forced, *Gadje*-ized transformation. It is striking to see what is happening in churches with an emerging Roma leadership, with 'majority' churches rather playing a facilitating role, and not a paternalistic one! In such a setting, the process of translating the gospel is put into the hands of Roma pastors. So a key question for the Eastern European 'majority' churches is how they could facilitate moving from 'mission to the Roma' – in which they 'control' the process of translating the gospel – to 'Roma churches' – in which Roma pastors are involved in the process of translating the gospel, or to a 'church for all'! In this latter case, both the Roma community and the majority church community are involved in the translation process, in each other's context and culture, preventing an over-contextualization. It is necessary to keep on asking questions of each other, how it is perceived that certain practices are related to the gospel. It is a similar process to what has been going on in Africa, with the European mission's churches changing into African churches.

The importance of 'taking ownership' is also the outcome of a study of Tatiana Podolinska and Tomas Hrustic. They ask whether churches have an impact on Roma communities in Slovakia. Among the recommendations made to local churches is that ministry works best when it involves Roma in leadership and decision-making,[104] and when it expects Roma to contribute financially, where possible, to the ministries taking place. People feel more included and are more willing to take ownership in the congregation when they contribute to it.

Conclusion

A massive exclusion is still going on in Europe, and also in Eastern Europe. It is an experienced reality. Many negative, 'invented' images exist. The Eastern European churches seek in various ways to respond to the Roma people. They are all in a learning process, together with the numerous mission organizations for 'Roma mission'.

The key words of missiology – incarnation, translation and transformation – work out differently with different paradigms. Some emphasize only incarnation, others only transformation. In many outward places, off the beaten track, many small 'embraces in Christ's name' are taking place. There are signs of revival among the Roma, hardly noticed on the official EU radar, because they operate with another, secular, worldview, unable to link with the incarnation in Christ. At most, they view

[104] Podolinská and Hrustič, *Religion as a Path to Change*.

religion as an interesting 'phenomenon', and churches as a reliable partner in implementing EU strategy. They do not view the gospel, as 'the power of God that brings salvation to everyone who believes' (Rom. 1:16). They have no antennae for the *dunamis* of the gospel that is able to bring transformation to the nominal churches of Eastern Europe as well as to Roma communities suffering from exclusion and distress by deep poverty.

Collaborative, relevant research is needed to find key local Roma figures that have played, and still play, a role in the growth of Roma Christianity. Their life story needs to be written. They are virtually absent from the standard scholarly reference works, just as was the case with many African peoples.

We know little about revivals taking place, little about the Roma Christian communities themselves or their Roma pastors. There are no dictionaries, encyclopaedias or handbooks with descriptions of the Roma church fathers and mothers, just as there weren't of the African churches until recently. African church history was written exclusively from the perspective of missionaries and their supporting churches, without paying attention to the role of the Africans themselves in bringing the gospel to their people.

Giving the Roma Christianity a face, taking steps towards getting to know Roma church history, will not only be beneficial in teaching the Roma churches, but also in helping the majority society to move from image to reality. In this process, a key notion should be: Nothing about us without us.

We celebrated that 25 years ago when the Berlin Wall came down. On that wall was written: 'Many small people, who in many small places, do many small things, can alter the face of the earth.' The Eastern European churches are called, together with the Roma communities, to be his instruments in bringing light to their communities. Roma communities and churches face challenges. Many of the Eastern European churches are struggling with a large nominal fringe in their membership. The common challenge is to seek ways to work together in God's mission in Europe! Many first may be the last and many lasts may be the first.

Roma Christianity in Central and Eastern Europe: Challenges, Opportunities for Mission, Modes of Appropriation and Social Significance

Melody Wachsmuth

Introduction

In the twentieth century, Central and Eastern European (CEE) state socialist policies towards the Roma varied, including attempted assimilation and forced sedentarization; but generally, the policies led to an increased socio-economic stability for the Roma. The collapse of these regimes, however, for the most part led to a worsened socio-economic state and in some contexts, to a continued deterioration of relationships between the Roma and the majority culture.[1] In the last twenty years, although increased international attention, policy changes and money has been focused on Romani communities, the expected results have not materialized.[2] Juxtaposed to these realities is the continued growth of Roma Christianity, particularly in Pentecostal and charismatic forms.

Research in Roma Christianity has been much better documented in Western Europe – with the beginning of the Gypsy revivals in France in the 1950s that rapidly spread to Spain and beyond, leading to mission efforts into Eastern Europe and Russia. Serious research of Roma Christianity in CEE exists only in certain contexts, most notably in Hungary, Slovakia, the Czech Republic and Bulgaria. Despite these limitations, it is possible to see snapshots of the developing picture of Roma Christianity in CEE – from the large-scale revivals such as found in Toflea, Romania, to the work of the long-established churches in Bulgaria, to the young Pentecostal and Evangelical churches recently appearing in South-eastern Europe. Roma Christianity reflects the diverse mosaic of Roma culture and languages:

[1] Zoltan D. Barany, *The East European Gypsies: Regime Change, Marginality, and Ethno-Politics* (Cambridge / New York: Cambridge University Press, 2002), 117-25, 201.

[2] For example, the Decade of Roma Inclusion (2005-2015) was twelve-country commitment to close the gaps between Roma and non-Roma in education, housing, employment and health: www.romadecade.org/index. One report, highlighting ten CEE countries, states that, although small gains are visible, 'summarizing data across the Decade region suggests a worsening of the situation of Roma and a widening of the gap with the total population in regard to poverty, particularly the risk of poverty'. 'Roma Inclusion Index 2015' (Budapest: Decade of Roma Inclusion Secretariat Foundation, 2015), 19: www.romadecade.org/cms/upload/file/9810_file1_roma-inclusion-index-2015-s.pdf

growth has been both explosive and slow, varied and multi-textured, and developing in spite of and in response to the numerous challenges, including social isolation, severe poverty and frequent disenfranchisement with majority culture churches. With this background, I suggest two things in this chapter: the Roma church has a unique role to play in both the transformation of Roma communities and as a catalyst for reconciliation with the larger society; and by placing Roma Christianity in its place within the larger mosaic of the global church, Roma Christians have a uniquely important part in the church's participation in the *missio Dei.*

This chapter, although broad both in subject matter and geography, aims to provide a general introduction to Roma Christianity, specifically focusing on South-eastern Europe, Romania and Bulgaria. First, it places the topic in historical context, highlighting state and church attitudes towards the Roma. Next, it highlights selected themes from Roma churches emerging from numerous survey trips conducted over the last four years, from about fifty Roma communities in the region. Finally, it will extrapolate themes and implications from the churches across diverse contexts with the hope of raising further questions, showcasing the challenges, and pointing to further areas of needed research.

The research methodology was primarily field notes elicited from informal conversations, observations in churches and within Romani homes (both leaders and lay people), and semi-structured interviews. Secondary literature has been used to balance the primary research, although secondary literature pertaining to this topic in these particular countries is limited. The lack of secondary literature, the vastness of the topic, and the lack of in-depth research in specific contexts certainly prevents firm conclusions being drawn – and indeed should serve as a precaution regarding applying the themes unreservedly to every Roma church in the CEE context. Certainly, there are hundreds of Roma churches, particularly in Romania, that have not been surveyed.

Who Are the Romani? Indicators of Identity

The Romani are thought to number 10-12 million in Europe, with the majority living in CEE. The general public often thinks of them as a monolithic group, either romanticized as exotic and mysterious or demonized as sub-human and parasitic on society. These images create a picture of the Roma as being on a static plane through history and into the present, somehow outside the ongoing dynamic interchange that is inherent in cultures and societies.

Who are the people we talk about when we use the term 'Roma'? Roma groups can actually be quite diverse in terms of language and culture, so are we applying the label as a social or as an ethnic term, particularly if a group may not self-identify as Roma? Questions of identity drive much discussion among policy makers, Roma groups, NGOs, academics and ordinary citizens. Consequently, there are many ideas, images, emotions and implications that can be attached to the words Romani, Roma or Gypsy. Confusingly for a *Gadje,* or non-Roma, Roma communities will sometimes self-identity differently from the label designated by the cultures around them. Sometimes communities self-identify as Gypsy, in other communities this is considered a slur, and in still other Roma communities, Roma themselves use the term 'gypsy' (in more of an adjectival sense) to pejoratively depict those who are dirty, extremely poor, engaged in crime and generally living undesirable lives.

To describe identity amidst the diversity, some sociologists and political scientists classify Roma communities on the basis of certain indicators such as language, borders of endogamy, professional specializations, tribal affiliation, religion, settlement period in their respective countries, etc.[3] In addition, there may also be a sense of belonging with the country in which they have lived for an extended amount of time. There are some Roma who speak of their 'Roma nation' while others differentiate between Roma clans to exclude certain groups. Because of this complexity, it is the whole picture that needs to be taken into account: the sociological indicators, the communities' self-identification, and the relationship between the Roma communities and the majority cultures. With this in mind, this chapter will use the term 'Romani' and 'Roma' in a broad sense, depicting a diverse collection of groups, who self-identify as Roma, Romani or Gypsy, and who may have a general conception of shared experience/history, some characteristics of similar culture, and consciousness of the associated dialects making up the Romani language.[4] However, since the term 'Roma' did not become the primary term of public discourse until after 1989, Gypsy will be used when it is contextually and historically appropriate.

It goes beyond the scope of this chapter to discuss the debates surrounding the origins and migration patterns of the Roma, although linguistic evidence ties them to north-west India. Migrating through Persia, Armenia and Byzantium, there is evidence of significant settlement of Gypsies in the Balkans between the eleventh and thirteenth centuries, sources acknowledging their presence in Serbia, Bulgaria, Wallachia and Moldavia. It was in the fourteenth and fifteenth centuries that sources cite their appearance and gradual spread to other European countries. By the

---

[3] Elena Marushiakova and Veselin Popov, 'Historical and Ethnographic Background: Gypsies, Roma and Sinti', in Will Guy (ed), *Between Past and Future: The Roma of Central and Eastern Europe* (Hatfield, UK: University of Hertfordshire Press, 2001), 36-41; Barany, *The East European Gypsies*, 12.

[4] Adrian Marsh and David Thurfjell, 'Introduction', in David Thurfjell and Adrian Marsh (eds), *Romani Pentecostalism: Gypsies and Charismatic Christianity* (Frankfurt, Germany: Peter Lang, 2014), 8. I include groups such as the Bajash, who although speaking old Romanian rather than Romani, often refer to themselves as Gypsy or Roma. There are other groups such as Ashkali/Egyptians, found in Kosovo, Montenegro and Albania who claim different origins and do not regard themselves as Roma.

sixteenth and seventeenth centuries, large populations existed in CEE as part of the socio-political environment.[5]

Historical Context

The discussion of Roma Christianity cannot be divorced from the past relationship between the Roma and society – it is important in order to understand the present realities and the church's unique role in a given community. In fact, the Romani relationship with societies has varied over the centuries. There are many accounts of societies taking advantage of the variety of skills and abilities offered by these peoples. However, societies under the differing policies of the Ottoman Empire, Austro-Hungarian Empire, Fascism and the socialist states more frequently responded to the so-called 'Gypsy problem' – that is, making such people fit into the constraints of mainstream society – in ways that created marginalization through the mechanisms of forced assimilation, socio-economic marginalization, enslavement, death, and genocide.[6, 7]

The Roma During State-Socialism[8]

After the often-harsh exclusionary policies of former regimes and the disastrous consequences of World War II for the Roma,[9] communism and state socialism ushered in a new perspective towards the Roma. State socialism viewed the Roma primarily through a social lens, as a social problem to be solved, as well as offering a large labour force for their

---

[5] Some scholars argue for a ninth-century appearance. Marushiakova and Popov, 'Historical and Ethnographic Background', 35; Barany, *The East European Gypsies*, 9-12.

[6] Many excellent sources have examined this history. See, for example, Angus M. Fraser, *The Gypsies* (Oxford, UK / Cambridge, USA: Blackwell, 1995); David Crowe, *A History of the Gypsies of Eastern Europe and Russia* (New York: Palgrave Macmillan, 2007); Viorel Achim, *The Roma in Romanian History* (Budapest: Central European University Press, 2004).

[7] Elena Marushiakova and Veselin Popov have identified two primary patterns of relationship between Roma and non-Roma in CEE: the traditional pattern and the national pattern. In the former, largely in the pre-industrial age, the Gypsies were seen as alien, although having a symbiotic relationship with society. In the latter, which coincided with the Enlightenment, attitudes were fostered by the ethno-national states; as they began to see them as sub-human, attempts were made to assimilate, control, or even destroy them. Marushiakova and Popov, 'Historical and Ethnographic Background', 45.

[8] Of course, this is a general summary and each state varied in its policies and enforcement towards the Roma under Communism. In addition, state policy changed over the course of regimes. For more in-depth discussion of Roma under Communism, see Will Guy (ed), *Between Past and Future: The Roma of Central and Eastern Europe* (Hatfield, UK: University of Hertfordshire Press, 2001); Barany, *The East European Gypsies*.

[9] For a brief summary on the Holocaust and the Roma, see Ian Hancock, *We Are the Romani People = Ame sam e Rromane džene* (Hatfield, UK: Centre de recherches tsiganes / University of Hertfordshire Press, 2002). For a more in-depth study, see Donald Kenrick (ed), *The Gypsies During the Second World War: In the Shadow of the Swastika* (2 vols), (Hatfield, UK: Gypsy Research Centre and University of Hertfordshire Press, 1999).

agendas.[10] Therefore, communist policy included them in education, employment and housing, and downplayed their language and culture.[11] Generally, this afforded them greater social and economic security. Will Guy notes: 'Instead of subsisting as pariahs, eking a precarious living as a dispensable pool of casual labour, they were now full citizens, at least formally, with the potential of entering the mainstream labour force at equal wages to their non-Roma fellow workers.'[12]

However, despite some of the positive economic and social outcomes, the long-term effects did not show sustainable socio-economic change. On the one hand, because of the assimilation policies and forced sedentarization, Roma joined the working class, but most remained at the bottom of the socio-economic scale and separated in ever-growing mahalas. Because most of the jobs were based on unskilled labour, when the regimes changed, there was no longer the need for such vast amounts of labour. Mandatory educational methods, while improving educational levels, also led in some cases to educational segregation and the creation of special schools that added to the creation of an unskilled or semi-skilled workforce.[13] Finally, assimilation eroded some of the Gypsy traditions – culture, kinship networks and language – as well as losing the momentum of political capital gained during the inter-war period.[14]

Roma Communities after State Socialism

Losing the security of jobs and state-sponsored housing after the collapse of communism and beginning of the free market economies, the general socio-economic condition of the Roma deteriorated. As unemployment rose to higher levels than the rest of the general population, an increase in begging, crime and homelessness during the 1990s increased feelings of hostility from the larger society and contributed to ethnically rooted scapegoating and violence against Roma individuals and communities.[15]

[10] Will Guy, 'Romani Identity and Post-Communist Policy', in Will Guy (ed), *Between Past and Future: The Roma of Central and Eastern Europe* (Hatfield, UK: University of Hertfordshire Press, 2001), 9.

[11] Marushiakova and Popov, 'Historical and Ethnographic Background', 47.

[12] Guy, 'Romani Identity', 9

[13] Andrzej Mirga and Nicolae Gheorghe, 'The Roma in the Twenty-First Century: A Policy Project on Ethnic Relations' (1997), 48, 60: www.per-usa.org/1997-2007/21st_c.htm

[14] Barany, *The East European Gypsies*, 151-52. Because the Roma were viewed through a social lens and did not meet Stalin's criteria for a national minority, some states did not qualify them for the laws pertaining to special educational and cultural minority rights. In many state censuses and documents, they appeared under the heading of 'other'. Yugoslavia, however, was the most tolerant, their 1974 constitution recognizing the equality of all nationalities, and by 1981 the federal state recognized their nationality status and allowed the Roma to display their own symbols. Zoltan D. Barany, 'Politics and the Roma in State-Socialist Eastern Europe', *Communist and Post-Communist Studies* 33.4 (December 2000), 423.

[15] Mirga and Gheorghe, 'The Roma in the Twenty-First Century'.

Although sociologists and Roma leaders argue that most criminals came from the most deprived segment of the population, 'their criminality, in turn, is largely responsible for the way ordinary people view the entire Romani community'.[16]

Today, despite vast international attention and allocated financial resources from governments, EU institutions, NGOs and religious entities as well as Romani politicians, intellectuals and grassroots organizations, steps and policies to minimize Romani social isolation continue to make only small, ineffective, or retro-active progress in CEE.[17] For the most part, Romani communities often have higher rates of illiteracy, unemployment, crime and deeper levels of poverty, and bear an uneasy relationship with the majority community, locked in mutual images of 'the other' which solidifies their social isolation. As Barany puts it: 'Most ordinary people are not inclined to reflect on the multifarious causes of the Gypsies' predicament, particularly because long-entrenched biases and prejudices – often confirmed by personal experience – have already shaped their view of the Roma.'[18]

Responses of the Roma

To speak merely about socialist policies and post-socialism's effect on the Roma is to classify them as passive subjects or hapless victims – but of course the Roma have been active at many levels of society. Roma political activism has been present since the late nineteenth and early twentieth centuries.[19] Although political mobilization was stalled during communism, other Roma scholars and activists have argued that the integration of Roma into state and party hierarchies became the 'unintentional training ground' for later Roma activists. The declining influence of traditional Roma leaders coincided with a growing Romani intelligentsia, estimated to be about 2-3,000 people in 1989, consisting of sociologists, writers, poets, teachers and musicians.[20] In some countries, such as Poland and Yugoslavia, Roma formed cultural associations. Leadership from CEE activists in Western Europe encouraged the development of organizations such as the Gypsy Council in Britain. All of this led to the first world Romani conference in 1971, attended by individuals from fourteen countries.[21] Today, there are numerous Romani organizations, NGOs,

---

[16] Barany, *The East European Gypsies*, 180-81.

[17] See, for example, initiatives such as the Decade of the Roma (2005-2015) and the European Commission's 'An EU Framework for National Roma Integration Strategies up to 2020': http://ec.europa.eu/justice/policies/discrimination/docs/com_2011_173_en.pdf

[18] Barany, *The East European Gypsies*, 189.

[19] For example, Roma conferences aimed at mobilizing activism for Romani rights took place in Hungary (1879), Bulgaria (1906) and Romania (1934). Reported by Acton (1974) and Hancock (1991) in Guy, 'Romani Identity', 19.

[20] Barany, *The East European Gypsies*, 152, 144.

[21] Guy, 'Romani Identity', 19.

political and social activists and academics, actively working on behalf of their people. However, criticism has been levelled on several fronts: for example, the so-called 'Gypsy Industry'[22] and the immense gap existing between the intelligentsia and the reality of Roma communities. Alongside these other Roma activists and voices, Roma pastors have sometimes become a voice of mediation, earning respect from the non-Roma and also trusted by their own communities.[23]

The Roma and the Church

The Roma are Catholic, Greek Catholic, Orthodox, Muslim, Protestant and Neo-Protestant – typically adhering, at least by name, to the dominant religion of the country in which they are living. Often, however, although they are clear on their religious identity, they are not an active part of the institutional church.[24] In European history, the church's response has often been no different from that of mainstream society in regard to its attitudes, images and exclusionary practices.[25] For example, between 1497 and 1774, the Holy Roman Empire released 146 decrees opposed to the Gypsies.[26] In Eastern Europe, in the principalities of Wallachia, Moldova and Transylvania, the church profited from the labour of monastery Gypsy slaves from the fourteenth century until the twenty-year emancipation process finally eradicated slavery from Romanian principalities in 1855-1856. There were, however, a few priests that cared for the spiritual needs of the Gypsies in the late eighteenth century, and eventually a few voices that spoke out, denouncing slavery in the early nineteenth century.[27]

Thomas Acton argues that the eighteenth-century assertion that the Gypsies were 'insincere' in their attachment to all religions and had no

---

[22] The Gypsy Industry refers to organizations made up of non-Romani who hire a 'token Gypsy', regardless of his/her qualifications, with the sole purpose of financial or political gain, or those who falsely claim Romani heritage in order to have a career within academia or political activism. See, for example, D. Le Bas and T. Acton (eds), *All Change! Romani Studies Through Romani Eyes* (Hatfield, UK: University of Hertfordshire Press, 2010); A. Ryder, S. Cemlyn, and T. Acton (eds), *Hearing the Voices of Gypsy: Roma and Traveller Communities* (Bristol, UK: Policy Press, 2014).

[23] See, for example, Miroslav Atanasov's findings on pastors in Bulgaria, 'Gypsy Pentecostals: The Growth of the Pentecostal Movement among the Roma in Bulgaria and Its Revitalization of Their Communities' (PhD dissertation, Asbury Theological Seminary, 2008); or the church's role as advocate and mediator in Leskovac, Serbia, in Melody J. Wachsmuth, 'Separated Peoples: The Roma as Prophetic Pilgrims in Eastern Europe', in *International Bulletin of Missionary Research,* 37.3 (July 2013), 145-50.

[24] Elin Strand, '"One Scattered Race Like Stars in the Sight of God": The International Gypsy Evangelical Church', in David Thurfjell and Adrian Marsh (eds), *Romani Pentecostalism: Gypsies and Charismatic Christianity* (Frankfurt, Germany: Peter Lang, 2014), 111.

[25] Strand, '"One Scattered Race"', 111.

[26] Margalit (1999), quoted in Miroslav A. Atanasov, 'Gypsy Pentecostals', 99.

[27] Viorel Achim, *The Roma in Romanian History*, 94-96.

morality actually masked an exclusionary racism.[28] Indeed, Roma were denied church-sanctioned marriages, refused admission to the church and participation in the Mass.[29] This exclusion was not just about spiritual access – although churches played a key role in education during the Ottoman and Hapsburg periods, they were not worried about including Roma children until the late eighteenth and early nineteenth centuries.[30]

In the past two to three decades, many churches have officially changed their orientation towards the Roma or become more cognizant of their exclusionary attitudes. The Roman Catholic Church began to turn its attention to Roma communities after witnessing the rapid growth of Romani Pentecostalism in France and Spain in the 1950s and 1960s, resulting in a historic meeting between Pope John IV and 2,000 Gypsies.[31] In 1970, the Pontifical Council for the Pastoral Care of Migrants and Itinerant People was established, having a special division for the pastoral care of Gypsies. Since then, they have held several world congresses and have produced important documents recognizing Romani marginalization through history and the church's complicity, as well as outlining approaches to holistic mission. In 2007, the report of the Roman Catholic Church's first world meeting of Gypsy priests, deacons and religious people opened with Archbishop Marchetto acknowledging: 'The Church discovers in her children that she is still too stifled by stereotypes and prejudices with regard to the Gypsies, but wishes to renew the dialogue and give a cordial welcome'. It concludes by calling for a mutuality of learning and love between Roma and *Gadje* and mutual collaboration.[32]

The Churches' Commission for Migrants in Europe (CCME), founded in 1964, also began to interact proactively with churches regarding their relationship with Roma communities. In 2001, they co-sponsored a conference entitled 'Living in Community – towards equal opportunities and overcoming discrimination: The situation of Roma in Central and Eastern Europe'. In 2013, CCME, together with the Lutheran World Federation, hosted a conference in Frankfurt for diaconal workers across Europe to continue 'building alliances with other churches, non-governmental organizations and Roma advocacy groups', encourage

---

[28] Thomas A. Acton, 'New Religious Movements among Roma, Gypsies and Travellers: Placing Romani Pentecostalism in an Historical and Social Context', in David Thurfjell and Adrian Marsh (eds), *Romani Pentecostalism: Gypsies and Charismatic Christianity* (Frankfurt, Germany: Peter Lang, 2014), 28.

[29] Atanasov, 'Gypsy Pentecostals', 99-101.

[30] Barany, *The East European Gypsies*, 88.

[31] Atanasov, 'Gypsy Pentecostals', 102-03.

[32] This council report indicates that there were at this time 100 consecrated Roma, Sinti, Kales, Manousche, Bhill and Jajabor living in sixteen countries (Europe, Americas, Asia). Pontifical Council for the Pastoral Care of Migrants and Itinerant People, 'The First World Meeting of the Consecrated Gypsies', in *People on the Move*, N. 105 (December 2007).

churches in Europe to protest against anti-gypsyism, and create spaces for 'face-to-face' encounters between Roma and non-Roma.[33]

Neo-Protestant churches[34] also have focused some missionary efforts on the Roma. The Evangelical Baptist Mission to the Gypsies in Bulgaria under the auspices of the Baptist Union has been active among Roma from the 1930s.[35] More recently, a Baptist church in Bucharest began an initiative called Project Ruth in the early 1990s which works to 'transform Roma communities' by providing education and literacy training, vocational programmes, health programmes, etc. Under the umbrella of the Croatian Pentecostal Church, the first Roma church in Croatia was started in October 2012. The *Borongajci*, a Croatian charismatic indigenous movement, planted another one or two churches. International mission organizations have also become active in their efforts to work in Roma communities, their activities ranging from evangelism and discipleship, community development, education, and literacy and translation efforts.[36]

Despite shifting attitudes at official levels, the many individuals and groups active in serving Roma communities, and Roma testimonies directly related to the love and care they have been shown in a local church,[37] the fact remains that exclusion and marginalization are still ongoing realities.[38] Sometimes there can be a latent posture of superiority undergirding the missional approach to a community.[39] Sometimes non-Roma individuals are working without support from their church body because of the perception they are wasting their time on 'those gypsies', or are put off by a fear that too many Roma coming into one church could 'split the church'.[40] This is symptomatic in every Christian tradition in Eastern Europe from Bulgaria

---

[33] Lutheran World Federfation (LWF), 'Call for Justice-Orientated Engagement with Roma people: Diaconal Workers Develop Recommendations for Continuing Ministry' (Lutheran World Federation, 2013).

[34] Protestant religious communities forming after the Reformation but with roots in the Reformation.

[35] Atanasov, 'Gypsy Pentecostals', 122-27.

[36] For example, some American denominational mission organizations such as the Southern Baptist's International Mission Board (IMB) and the Methodist Church have specific Roma ministries in CEE. Larger para-church organizations such as Operation Mobilization, SIL International, YWAM, World Vision, and SEND International also have missionaries and/or projects in CEE. Fida International is the development and mission arm of the Finnish Pentecostal Church, and they work in partnership with various churches to encourage holistic mission.

[37] Interviews by the author with Biljana Nikolić (Vukovar, Croatia, 2012, 2013), Zvanko Pavić (Varaždin, Croatia, 2011), and Mariana Tănasie (Sadova, Romania, 2013).

[38] See, for example, G. Haupt, 'Discrimination of Roma People', in *Reflection Group of Roma People* (Brussels: COMECE & CCEE, 2011): www.ifsoz.org/content/download/pdf/110301Brussels.pdf

[39] This observation comes from comments to the author from various non-Roma leaders regarding the inability of Roma to lead their own churches without oversight. See section below: *Why Won't You Be Like Us?*

[40] Field notes depicting conversations with missionaries in Bulgaria (2015), Macedonia (2015) and Croatia (2013).

to Croatia, but the sentiment was well articulated by Bishop Leo Cornelio in his address at the 2003 World Congress of the Pastoral Care for Gypsies:

> Gypsies are not at ease in our churches and in Christian gatherings. It is also not rare to meet priests, women religious and lay people at the service of Gypsies who declare their loneliness and the lack of recognition their commitments receive from the communities or from other priests and religious. Their efforts to create a team for reflection in touch with Gypsies do not often receive great support from other ministers and religious. These observations and experiences highlight for us the distance that exists between Gypsies and the Catholic Church.[41]

Snapshots of Roma Christianity in CEE

The spread of Christianity among the Roma, particularly in its Pentecostal forms, have begun to challenge some of these attitudes in church and society. A commonly expressed sentiment from Roma leaders is that 'this is the time for the Roma': that there is a general openness to Christian faith in Roma communities.[42] Looking at this from a mission history point of view, this essay hypothesizes that God's *praeparatio evangelica*, that is, his divine initiation and preparation which precedes any kind of human action, has been brought in the fullness of time to Roma communities in CEE.[43] Not only that, considering the estimated numbers of the Roma's population in CEE, widespread conversion and transformation could have a significant impact on wider society.

Indeed, the long-term transformative effects of the gospel in Roma communities are astonishing. A limited number of studies[44] in specific geographical contexts have shown that the impact of Christianity on Roma communities is twofold: it is linked to with social change, including a rise of education levels, literacy, a decrease in crime, and better relationships with the majority culture, while studies of Pentecostalism, in particular, have shown it to be instrumental in the fostering of a 'trans-national' identity and the revitalization of their respective Roma identities.

If, however, we see God the Father as the initiator of mission and 'Lord of the Harvest', the counterpart of Luke 10:2 is also painfully accurate in this context: the workers are too few. Particularly in South-eastern Europe, one of the most commonly uttered needs by Roma leaders is the lack of

---

[41] 'Pastoral Care of Gypsies for a "Spirituality of Communion"', Fifth World Congress of the Pastoral Care for Gypsies, Budapest, 2003.

[42] A sentiment articulated by Roma leaders and some non-Roma working in Roma communities throughout CEE. For example, Roma pastors Aleksandar Subotin and Miki Kamberović in Serbia (interviews in 2011 and 2015), and a non-Roma pastor (S.N.) of a Roma church at a Roma conference in Budapest, 2014.

[43] Timothy Tennent, *Invitation to World Missions: A Trinitarian Missiology for the Twenty-first Century* (Grand Rapids, MI: Kregel Academic, 2010), 71.

[44] See, for example, Johannes Ries, 'The Cultural Dynamics of Romani/Gypsy Ethnicity and Pentecostal Christianity', in David Thurfjell and Adrian Marsh (eds), *Romani Pentecostalism: Gypsies and Charismatic Christianity* (Frankfurt, Germany: Peter Lang, 2014).

trained, mature workers to bring these seeds to growth and fruition.[45] Most leaders bear tremendous burdens due to the multi-faceted needs in impoverished Roma communities. These needs are partly the reasons for the other reality: although the 'field is ripe for harvest', discipleship is slow and laborious.

In many cases, although many are open and willing to hear about Jesus and profess an acceptance of faith, quite a few Roma pastors explain the circular nature of discipleship – falling away, coming back, and repeating the cycle. The reasons for this are undoubtedly complex, but one can point to a few contributing factors. In impoverished communities, survival can be the all-consuming focus for each day, making it difficult to participate in church activities. In some churches, illiteracy among adults is still a primary factor and audio tools have had few successes. Some communities are quite deeply broken with high rates of domestic violence, alcoholism, abuse, witchcraft and violence between neighbours. Because many communities are tightly enmeshed and intensely social, new Christians face daily challenges to act out their new faith.[46]

Still, the few studies that have been done point to the trend that, while many programmes have proved to be ineffective in Roma communities, Christianity is making major inroads and spreading, largely in Pentecostal or Charismatic forms, through Roma Christians themselves. Why the success of Pentecostalism over other forms? Some scholars have suggested it is the ecclesiological structure of Pentecostalism that allows freedom, dignity and a renewed identity by the anointing of the Holy Spirit. Elin Strand's work synergistically links Pentecostal theology and Romani culture, applying the work of Toulis who claims that 'Pentecostalism as an important arena for constructing new identities while challenging racist representations'. Strand suggests that the Romani Pentecostal church links social change by introducing a new morality in communities in which God is the 'omnipresent agent of social change'.[47] The following summaries of various studies will help provide snapshots of Roma Christianity in various countries.

[45] This is particularly, although not exclusively, the case in places like Croatia, Macedonia, Albania and Bosnia, where the churches are small and fairly new. It is also characteristic with pastors working in more than one church. Often the church members are so young in the faith that there has not been suitable time for the Roma pastor to mentor leadership to share the burdens. In one interview, for example, the pastor explained that teams want to come and do short-term projects, but that these had little lasting value. What he hoped for was long-term help to invest in the people. Interview with T.M. by the author (Macedonia, January 2015).

[46] Wachsmuth, 'Separated Peoples: The Roma as Prophetic Pilgrims in Eastern Europe'.

[47] N.R. Toulis, *Believing Identity – Pentecostalism and the Mediation of Jamaican Ethnicity and Gender in England* (Oxford: Berg, 1997), quoted in Strand, '"One Scattered Race"', 117.

Bulgaria[48]

Christianity among the Roma began through the Baptists in the early twentieth century – but the beginning and growth of Roma Pentecostalism began about the same time as it was taking place in France in the 1950s. However, the quickest growth took place in the 1990s, after communism fell. Roma Christians now constitute the majority of total evangelical numbers in Bulgaria, most of them Pentecostal, and the number of their churches today is estimated at 700-800.[49] Miroslav Atanasov's important study of Romani Pentecostalism in Bulgaria concludes that Pentecostalism has revitalized communities and that Roma leaders believe it will change their social and political standing: 'The degree of revitalization might vary from one Roma community to another, but Pentecostalism has clearly provided new ways for this *ethnos* to cope with the constant stress caused by their poverty, oppression and marginal social status.'[50] Interestingly, similar to other contexts, he points out the importance of the Roma pastor who is concerned with a range of aspects of social change including assisting their members in obtaining legal documentation and jobs, and elevating educational levels among his people. His conclusions highlight the changes in attitudes towards women, increasing education, changing ethics and morality in communities, a decrease in crime, improved relationships with the majority culture, challenging certain aspects of Roma culture, renewed identity and integration.

Romania

In terms of Roma Christianity, Romania is one of the most complex and under-researched places in CEE; and yet it has the largest population of Roma as well as quite possibly the largest number of Roma Christians. One can see big movements of Roma Christianity, some of which are under the Romanian Pentecostal or Baptist Unions, and others that are independent, such as the Christian Union of Roma Pentecostals in Romania (reportedly having 200 churches in Romania). One can see extremes of poverty and wealth: wealthy churches and communities of mansions contrasted with other communities of poorly constructed shacks built on garbage. Apart from the bigger movements, there are numerous and uncounted small, independent churches begun by Roma dotting the many villages and towns.

---

[48] For other research from Bulgaria, see Velislav Altanov and Milena Benovska-Sabkova 'The Protestant Conversion Among Roma in Bulgaria: Between Global and Local', in *Българска етнология*, 1-2 (2010), 32-50; Magdalena Slavkova, 'Evangelical Gypsies in Bulgaria: Way of Life and Performance of Identity', in *Romani Studies*, 17.2 (2007), 205-46; Veselin Popov and Elena Marushiakova, 'The Relations of Ethnic and Confessional Consciousness of Gypsies in Bulgaria', in *FACTA UNIVERSITATIS – Series Philosophy, Sociology, Psychology and History*, 06 (1999), 81-89.

[49] Atanasov, *Gypsy Pentecostals*, 171-73.

[50] Atanasov, *Gypsy Pentecostals*, 223.

Some of these churches and movements focus primarily on their own clan, while others look beyond to other clans or ethnicities.

Perhaps one of the best-known movements under the Romanian Pentecostal Union is the 'Rugul Aprins' (Burning Bush) movement that began in Toflea in the early 1990s, born out of the evangelism and prayer of three women and one man (both Romanian and Romani). Toflea was a town well-known for violence, gangs and alcoholism, and therefore the small group of 'Repenters', consisting primarily of women, underwent persecution from the rest of the village for years. The number of Christians began to grow, influenced by factors such as the obviously transformed lives of the Repenters. For example, one man leading a drug-running gang was converted in Germany and returned to Toflea, shocking everyone with his transformation, since previously they had been afraid of his violent behaviour.

One distinctive way that change was seen in the community was attitudes towards women. Soon after Christianity began spreading, women were illiterate, stayed at home, and 'their spirits were bitter since they felt like servants'.[51] However, when the women started becoming Christians, 'all the women wanted to know the word of God'.[52] One day the pastor had a revelation from Luke 8:1-3. If women were supporting and providing for Jesus' ministry, should not the women in his community see themselves as part of ministry? After this, the church began teaching the women alongside the men, doing family camps, and teaching men to honour their wives instead of treating them like servants.

Toflea became known internationally for their large baptisms, the largest one taking place in 2003 with over 500 people. The church has a strong emphasis on piety and holiness, and has become known in Romania and beyond for its music. Now the church reports 80-90% of the village being converted, and 4,000 members of their church spread over ten churches in Romania, five in the UK, one in Spain, and one in Germany.[53]

South-Eastern Europe

Compared with the growth of Roma Christianity in Romania and Bulgaria, growth has only more recently begun in South-eastern Europe. Except for Serbia, the churches are much fewer and, in general, younger in Macedonia, Bosnia, Croatia, Montenegro and Albania. Some of these countries have the additional challenge of many Roma identifying as

---

[51] Interview with Vasile Căpitanu by the author (Toflea, Romania).

[52] Interview with Anuşa Căpitanu by the author (Toflea, Romania).

[53] Information accumulated through interviews by the author with Anuşa Căpitanu (Toflea, Romania, July 2015), Ilia Bolmandăr (Bucharest, Romania, July 2015), and Ioan Caba (Oradea, Romania, July 2015).

Muslim. Even if they are not practising Muslims, there can still be serious opposition to evangelism and conversion in certain contexts.[54]

Serbia

Among all the countries of South-eastern Europe, Serbia is the exception – it has a thriving Roma Pentecostal movement, with many of the churches influenced or begun in Leskovac, a city in southern Serbia that has a population of 8-10,000 Roma. Although Serbian pastor Mio Stanković began to minister to Roma in the mid-1970s after an encounter with a Roma women, rapid growth did not begin until the 1990s after word spread regarding healings and miracles.[55] In the late 1990s, the church promoted a church-planting project in partnership with an organization from the UK and planted seven churches throughout Serbia. The church split in 2005 but there are an estimated 1,000 believers between the two churches. Not all the church plants survived, but there are still numerous house groups and church plants originating from this movement: an estimated eight smaller house groups of 20-40 people and eight bigger churches.[56] Most of the churches also have other house groups in the Roma communities surrounding their town or city. In addition, the church in Leskovac has been active in evangelism efforts in Croatia.

As the church has been deeply rooted in Leskovac, change over the last couple of decades has been remarkable with the same kind of revitalization noted by Atanasov – a decrease in crime, increasing education, less domestic violence and less violence in the community, and a better relationship with the Serbian community. Serif Bakić, a pastor of one of the churches, notes: 'Serbians could see the change in the Roma… Before Christ, the police could come seven times because of all the fighting… The government in Leskovac loves us because we have such a positive influence.'[57]

Selected Qualities of Roma Christianity

As already noted, just as there is much diversity between Roma communities in CEE, so also one cannot speak monolithically about Roma Christianity – as if the qualities, emphases, expressions, theology, and

---

[54] For example, J.S., now the pastor of a small Roma church in Bosnia, converted to Christianity from Islam when he was 19. Although his father was initially supportive, he threatened to disown him when he wanted to marry in a church. The conflict eventually progressed to his father renouncing him on television and privately threatening to kill him until eventually undergoing a change of heart towards his son. Interview with J.S. by the author (Bosnia, 2012).

[55] Interview with Selim Alijević by the author (Leskovac, Serbia, 2012).

[56] Estimates coming from Miki Kamborović (Jagodina, Serbia, 2015) and Goran Saitovic (Leskovac, Serbia, 2013).

[57] Interview with Šerif Bakić by the author (Leskovac, Serbia, 2012).

missional intent were all the same in each context. However, from observation and interviews, is possible to trace various themes emerging from multiple communities and countries. These themes are important when considering the opportunities, challenges and areas of further research into the Roma church and its contribution to the global church. This is by no means an exhaustive list, but similar to the 'snapshots', and several themes have been chosen.

The Vulnerable Church

Because of Romani history, Roma churches and Christians often operate in a position of 'vulnerability' shaped by their poverty and relationship with the outside community. Countless stories emerging from Roma communities tell of unspeakable suffering caused by poverty, abuse, violence, alcoholism, rejection and discrimination. Of particular note is the suffering of Roma women who bear the double stigma of having low value in their own culture as well as the mainstream culture. The suffering is not just physical, but also in terms of identity and self-worth. One Roma pastor described how, before God's love had transformed his own self-worth, his identity had been marred by the constant ill treatment by teachers throughout his schooling: 'It is hurting and damaging your life. It makes you feel insecure... it is one thing to be discriminated against but it is another to accept that you are lower than others... I couldn't imagine sitting down in the company of white (Serbian) people.'[58]

Most pastors have a strong sense of burden for serving their own people, desiring not just repentance but also to help uplift their situation. Bakić notes: 'We are thinking that someone must save the Roma people. And who will besides the Roma people?'[59] Part of this is because of a history of neglect by the church; the other part lies in the ability of Roma leaders to understand incarnationally the suffering of their people from their own experiences. A Roma leader in Croatia testifies, for example, that her difficult childhood and trials as a young teenage bride helps her empathize and identify with the people she now serves.[60] Many church leaders are quite poor themselves, because of limited education or job opportunities. Therefore, when they exhort their people to trust in the Lord's provision, their own situation testifies to this reality.[61]

This vulnerability often acts as a pathway to the presence of a God who suffers along with the weak and oppressed. One can see the nearness of

---

[58] Interview with Miki Kamberović by the author (Jagodina, Serbia, January 2015). Other interviewees in Romania talked about seeing their parents or grandparents automatically defer to a non-Roma or being instructed to 'keep your head down' (2015).

[59] Bakić, 2012.

[60] Nikolić, 2013.

[61] Of course, there are exceptions. Particularly in Romania, the author interviewed a few Roma pastors who were quite wealthy and had thriving businesses.

God to the vulnerable in the many signs, visions and healings that are part and parcel of Roma testimonies throughout CEE. One man talked about his relationship to the story of Jesus weeping in John chapter 11, how he 'cries in his inner man' when he reads it to know that when you are suffering, Jesus is crying with you.[62] A vulnerable church also acts as a powerful sign to the world and points the global church to mission in the way of Christ: Jesus' self-emptying of privilege and status in order to identify with humanity and eventually conquer the power of death through his death and resurrection.

A Church of the Supernatural

In many communities, magic, curses, a belief in spirits and a holistic spiritual worldview are part of the invisible landscape – this may be another reason for the abundance of supernatural encounters and signs. Visions, dreams, healings, or healing testimonies often play a role in conversion, discipleship and leadership. For example, in a small church in Croatia, at least half the adults are functionally illiterate, and yet some of the new Christians testify to a dream or vision of Jesus who provided reassurance of love and encouragement, exhortation or instruction.[63] Leaders also attest to being supernaturally guided by the direct leading of the Holy Spirit. One Roma pastor in Lom, Bulgaria, was illiterate at the fall of communism, but taught himself to read, using the Bible. He spoke of several instances in his leadership where he felt the Holy Spirit telling him the next step in his ministry. For example, his own vision for building a new church was a small house to reflect the number currently converted, but he told how the Holy Spirit communicated the exact measurements of a new, large church that would accommodate the hundreds who would eventually join.[64]

Of course, because of an openness to dreams and visions, there can also be the problem of discerning the spirits. One German missionary in Bosnia noted the difficulty they had in discerning certain visions of Christ in their community. A Roma pastor who planted a church in Apatin, Serbia, reported that his village had a 'spirit of witchcraft' so they often had to weed out false prophets.[65]

A Church for all Peoples

Although exclusion has been the dominant theme in regard to non-Roma churches' relationship to Roma, many Roma pastors in South-eastern

[62] Interview with Florian Tănasie by the author (Sadova, Romania, January 2013.)
[63] This information comes from ongoing observation and participation by the author in the church.
[64] Interview with Ilia Georgiev by the author (Lom, Bulgaria, January 2015).
[65] Interview with Zvezdan Bakić by the author (Apatin, Serbia, May 2012).

Europe have a theological problem with the idea of a 'Roma church'.[66] Ironically, in contrast to many non-Roma church leaders who argue that it is better for the Roma to have their own church, Roma leaders interviewed in Croatia, Serbia and Macedonia specifically articulated their vision of having integrated churches, a 'church for all peoples'. One pastor in Serbia initially put up a church sign advertising it as a Roma church. After realizing that, if a Serbian walked by, he or she would never be inclined to enter, he took the sign down.[67]

However, with the reality that many would still not enter a Roma church, pastors argue that the Roma church must first demonstrate change, and that this will attract non-Roma to their doors. Bakić notes:

> We also think of the Serbian people, not just the Roma people. The Orthodox believers just go once or twice to church for Christmas and Easter… But what about their souls? We are using [ways] just as Paul did when he did mission. He first went to the synagogue and witnessed first to the Jews and then went to the non-Jews. The Roma can forgive and work with all people. But the Serbians are not going to receive you… you must first be an example. To see Jesus in us.

Serving the greater community is another strategy employed to witness to the non-Roma. Pastors in Serbia related the change in community attitudes when they served the entire community by bringing sheets and blankets to a no-frills hospital or painting a local school. Such service challenges the societal stereotypes of Roma being dependent or parasitic on society.

A Church in Movement

Most Roma in CEE are sedentary; however, migration, emigration and immigration have been a reality throughout Romani history, 'both as the outcome of dynamic change in order to adapt to new circumstances and as a response to historical opportunities'.[68] For example, after the abolition of Romani slavery, a mass exodus of Vlach Roma at the end of the nineteenth and early twentieth centuries have about four million descendants spread round Europe and the Americas.[69] Since the fall of communism, many Roma (family units, multiple families from a community, or individuals) have migrated to other EU states or countries in search of economic

---

[66] Preliminary research indicates that this attitude is not as prevalent in Romania where the tribal lines between Roma groups appear much less porous. However, more research would need to be done to say anything conclusive.

[67] Conversations with Miki Kamberović by the author (Budapest, Hungary, June 2015).

[68] Reyniers, quoted in Yaron Matras, 'Romani Migrations in the Post-Communist Era: Their Historical and Political Significance', in *Cambridge Review of International Affairs,* 13:2 (2000), 34.

[69] Matras, 'Romani Migrations', 34.

opportunities or in response to racism and/or hostility.[70] Placing this in the larger context of historical exclusion, Yaron Matras explains this movement as 'non-identification and non-confidence' in the systems of the larger societies whereby they 'seek individual alternatives rather than aim at participating in collective processes of change' in their home societies.[71] In other words, they do not trust a government system to take them into account, so they look for their own solutions and possibilities.

In this context, migration is not always or even usually permanent – many retain their home in their countries of origin and return periodically. Due to lack of research, it is difficult to ascertain accurate statistics, particularly in terms of Roma migrant churches that pop up where parts of clan groups have moved. Sometimes there is a circular path of movement where one or more family members of a given household are in Western Europe for a period of time looking for work before returning. Since 1990, the main countries of origin for migration (whether temporary, semi-permanent or permanent) have been found to be Bosnia-Herzegovina, Macedonia and Romania, and – since 1995 – Poland, the Czech Republic and Slovakia. The main destination countries have been Germany, Italy, France, Austria and, more recently, the UK, Canada, Belgium and Finland.[72]

This movement and migration is both fraught with challenge and possibilities for Roma churches in Eastern Europe. Pastors in Serbia, Romania and Bulgaria all relate to the difficulties of establishing regular discipleship, the development of leadership teams, and the growth of the church when their members are migrating or constantly in movement for economic purposes. Often it is not just one family from a church that leaves, but several. This can leave the pastor, particularly if it is a small church, struggling to bear the leadership load on his own and having difficulty bringing the people to mature discipleship.[73]

On the other hand, because most Roma groups are collective in nature, they will migrate or move as a family, several families, or as a group from their clan.[74] If they are coming from a particular church, the pastor may appoint a deacon so that their small migrant church may be seen as an extension of the primary church back in their country of origin. In this way, Roma churches based in Eastern Europe have extensions all over Western

[70] European Union Agency for Fundamental Rights (FRA), 'The Situation of Roma EU citizens moving to and settling in other EU Member States', Conference Report, November 2009. This report focused on the destination countries of France, Spain, Italy, the UK and Finland.

[71] Matras, 'Romani Migrations', 36.

[72] Matras, 'Romani Migrations', 35.

[73] For example, interviews by the author with the leadership of Râmnicu Sârat (Romania, July 2015), Ilia Georgiev (Lom, Bulgaria, January 2105), Đeno Nikolić (Darda, Croatia, 2014), and conducted over Skype with Sokrat Apostolovski (Macedonia, December 2015).

[74] Matras, 'Romani Migrations', 36-37.

Europe. For example, the above-mentioned church in Toflea, Romania, reports that only 1,200 members out of 4,000 now live in Toflea.[75]

Although it might be easy to assume that these pathways of migration and movement naturally host mission, more study and research would need to be done to see how much these satellite churches look missionally beyond their own Roma community or tribe to another Roma group or beyond to the host culture. Like many who migrate, they face the challenges of language and adaptation (although they may indeed find another Roma group which speaks the same dialect of Romani), but they might also encounter the additional challenge of a host country's preconceived negative images of the Roma. However, Roma churches have the unique possibility of placing their ongoing movement in the context of God's mission – to train those who are leaving for work to think of themselves as missionaries to whoever crosses their paths.

Challenges, Themes, and Significance

The Myth of Separate but Equal

The concept of Roma churches raises a question that is quite common in multicultural settings: Is it better for Roma churches to remain Roma churches as opposed to having multi-ethnic churches? This question is multi-faceted and can easily be whitewashed to argue for separation based on cultural preference, when it may only be a smokescreen to mask an exclusionary racism that does not want to deal with the problems that would certainly surface.

However, the issues of prejudice are not just on the non-Roma side; the Roma can also be ethnocentric in regard to other Roma groups and the *Gadje*. Some Roma may not be willing to receive or listen to the message or instruction from the non-Roma.[76] One Roma pastor related how he grew up in a village that, although having pleasant 'surface' relationships between Romanians and Roma, could never move deeper because of a 'boundary, a wall between the two. They don't want to pass. They like each other because they live in the same village. But somewhere the relationship stops'.[77] In Sorin Gog's study on Roma in Romania, his informants saw the church as a place for the ethnic majority, even if the priest and pastor was active in wanting to include them, and therefore chose not to attend or be a part.[78]

---

[75] Interview with Vasile Căpitanu by the author (Toflea, Romania, July 2015).
[76] Bakić, 2012.
[77] Interview with Marius Constantin by the author (Timişoara, Romania, 2013).
[78] Sorin Gog, 'Post-Socialist Religious Pluralism: How Do Religious Conversions of Roma Fit into the Wider Landscape? From Global to Local Perspectives', in A. Boscoboinik and F. Ruegg (eds), *Transitions: Nouvelles identités rom en Europe centrale et orientale* (Université Libre de Bruxelles, 2009), 100-04.

Although there are always stories that contrast with this, interviews with individuals from Croatia, Serbia, Macedonia, Montenegro and Bulgaria echo this theme. There are centuries of exclusion from the majority culture, but there are also centuries of Roma becoming accustomed to exclusion and assuming it exists when in fact it may not. When Mariana Tănasie was a teenager, she assumed a Romanian church would despise her, perceiving her to be 'a gypsy of no value'. She was shocked, however, when a Romanian church adopted her very poor family while they were working nearby as brickmakers, inviting them into their homes: 'When it is the first time in your life that a Romanian family would take you in and sit you at the table and give you a glass and silverware, to eat at the table. I felt I was a king...' When the church came and visited their camp of improvised tents, the Romanians took turns cooking for them, and brought them beds and a table. This love changed Mariana's life: 'They did not make any distinction between the gypsy or Romanian... it was then that I understood there was a God and he could create such love.'[79]

For both the Roma and the *Gadje*, these perceptions, assumptions, constructed images, and certainly racism, erect complex, mutually reinforcing barriers of isolation and separation that present a serious challenge to the church's participation in God's mission in CEE. If Paul admonishes the Thessalonians not to 'quench the spirit' in the context of Christian conduct towards each other, then certainly such barriers in Christian mission would have the potential to quench the Spirit's work (1 Thess. 5:19). One Roma pastor in Macedonia spoke of this phenomenon in Eastern Europe as a 'curse', calling it the 'chains of nationalism'. His vision is to have all nationalities – Albanians, Roma and Macedonians, whom he claims are all racist in their own right – to be a part of his church.[80]

Reconciliation and Love – The Linchpin of Mission in CEE?

Given the serious nature of these issues, the theological and missiological justifications for pursing reconciliation and unity cannot be ignored. With the view that mission is understood through *missio Dei,* it is God's Triune being that is the very foundation of mission. God the Father initiates mission, the sent Son incarnates mission in the world, and the Spirit empowers mission.[81] Critical to this is the relationality of the Trinity as part of its very essence – a network of relationality that can neither be separated from God's ongoing redemption in human history nor from the church's role in God's mission. As Timothy Tennent points out: 'The church has been ordained by God to reflect the Trinity through redemptive actions in

[79] Tănasie, 2013.

[80] Interview with Tefik Musoski by the author (Bitola, Macedonia, January 2015).

[81] Tennent, *Invitation to World Missions,* 75.

the world.'[82] As we enter into relationship with God, we step into God's family as sons and daughters, and into the community of God, which should reflect the Trinity in love and mutual self-giving.

Given this foundation and the historic relationship between Roma and *Gadje*, it can be argued that reconciliation and love between the two groups bears witness to the Kingdom's holistic redemption, and has the possibility of transforming culture.[83] In this intersection of living transformed relationships in the midst of societal and cultural tensions, the church's prophetic voice will sound like a ringing bell. Because of deeply rooted images, concrete and intentional initiatives need to be thoughtfully promoted by the church, offering repentance, forgiveness and a chance to develop relationships to see 'the other' as a human being. For example, in 2015, the Reformed Church in Hungary's Roma mission organized a conference for reconciliation for peoples of different ethnic groups, among them Roma. During the conference, the participants listened to each other's stories, repented and admitted their own feelings of hatred, superiority, exclusion and scapegoating, and then received forgiveness from 'the other'.[84]

Why Won't You Be Like Us? The Need for Kenotic Mission

After centuries of policies trying to fit the Roma into society, there has been a shift in attitudes captured by the phrase 'nothing for us without us'. Like many other historical mission endeavours, mission to the Roma has often been clothed with the values and requirements of the surrounding culture – associating Roma lifestyle with being 'non-Christian' and thus requiring an adoption of the lifestyle of the predominant civilization of the time. In other contexts, this paternalistic attitude has been flushed out and brought to justice in the literature and mission praxis. However, it all too frequently persists in attitudes towards the Roma today, seen in both subtle and also overt ways. Sometimes it appears as 'benevolent god-playing' – that is, using the poor to exert and promote a reputation or superior technology while keeping a relational distance. At other times, it appears as more overt paternalistic control, an expressed frustration of 'they just won't behave as they should'.[85] There is often a subject-object dynamic when it comes to Roma communities – are the Roma mere objects to be saved or also subjects in God's mission? Do only their souls matter, or do their bodies also matter?

---

[82] Tennent, *Invitation to World Missions,* 56.

[83] Daryl Balia and Kirsteen Kim (eds), *Edinburgh 2010 Witnessing to Christ Today* (two volumes; Oxford: Regnum, 2010), 208-09.

[84] 'Roma and Non-Roma People apologized to each other in Balatonszárszó', Reformed Church in Hungary, 2015: http://reformatus.hu/mutat/10635

[85] Andy Crouch, *Playing God: Redeeming the Gift of Power* (Downers Grove, IL: IVP, 2013), 73.

Clearly, there is often a power differentiation – based on money, status, access to resources and relational power – when an outsider enters a Roma community. Jayakumar Christian's concept of 'marred identity' is part and parcel of entrenched poverty: no longer knowing who you are or believing you have a vocation of value.[86] When the assumption of power collides with this, mission can and will be skewed. On the one hand, there is an identity that assumes they have the answers, and on the other, an identity that bows to status of power and money.

Further, paternalistic ideas can unintentionally enter a community with good motives. For example, there is a danger of merely adopting a western neo-liberal idea of development as part of an adequate missiological approach without taking seriously the nature of transformational development within the Roma culture (as it varies from community to community). One Roma leader from Bulgaria, after years of seeing discouraged missionaries and failed projects, urges mission efforts to take into consideration the 'epistemology' of the Roma people, arguing that development must make sense within the Roma understanding or it will not be effective.[87]

And therein lies the two-pronged challenge – there is an increasing awareness of the Roma, and with this awareness comes the danger of mission groups flooding communities with project ideas and money. Are non-Roma Christians willing to consider seriously what human flourishing means in a Roma context, and as defined by the Roma? What does transformation look like in the Roma context when it cannot be separated from the vice-like grip of the nation-state and socio-economic viability? These are serious questions that Roma leaders must grapple with and communicate to non-Roma mission practitioners and church leaders. Aleksandar Subotin, who has started multiple churches and house groups in north-western Serbia, says: 'Why do white (non-Roma) people think it is not really that important to learn the culture? Is it because they think the culture is just stealing, lazy, and poor and uneducated, and that is all the people are made up of?'[88]

Thus, outsiders who set aside their positions of social, political and economic power demonstrate Christ's own incarnational and self-emptying model of mission. Entering into a community in a learning posture, accepting Roma hospitality to enter homes and eat together, fostering trust through relationships, begins to build a community of solidarity. This process must entail mutual giving and receiving, and together walking towards transformation.[89]

---

[86] Bryant L. Myers, *Walking with the Poor: Principles and Practices of Transformational Development* (Maryknoll, New York: Orbis Books, 2006), 77.

[87] Interview with Radko Kratsov by author (2014).

[88] Interview by the author (Kucura, Serbia, March 2012).

[89] Balia and Kim (eds), *Edinburgh*, 124.

This mutuality enables missionaries to have their own cultural assumptions and forms of Christianity challenged. By being with the Roma in their spaces and listening, there is the opportunity to deepen one's own knowledge of God and his mission. As Lamin Sanneh expressed, if the missionary assumes that God has preceded her into a given culture, '"... to discover His [God's] true identity, the missionary would have to delve deep into the local culture" to discover "the hidden reality of this divine presence"'.[90]

However, this setting aside of power must take into consideration the structures and systems of injustice that enable poverty. A 'liberative action in solidarity' can balance mutuality and a conscious use of social and political power to work towards reconciliation, justice and peace between Roma communities and the larger societies.

Theological Education

Theological education, it has been argued, is key to an ongoing renewal of the church, commitment to unity, and for 'dialogue between church and society'.[91] In many Roma communities, theological education or Bible training is an expressed need. Sometimes this is due to church multiplication and church growth, although it is hard to determine what kind of growth it is. For example, a Roma pastor in Romania related that at least some of the growth comes from troubling causes: 'A man with a lot of power, if he repents, he opens the church and everyone has to listen to him. He doesn't know anything, he can't read or write, but he wants to be the boss... not just the pastor, but the boss.' He goes on to say that a big problem is a lack of understanding of the Scriptures and low levels of literacy and schooling.[92]

There are many challenges regarding theological education for church leaders. A high percentage of lower educational levels in Roma communities continue to be the reality in many places in Eastern Europe, although in some contexts there have been some substantial changes. However, if high school has not been completed, they cannot be accepted at most theological colleges.[93] Another challenge is the often seasonal nature of the work schedule for families in rural settings. Finally, theological education needs to take into account the particular cultural, socio-economic

---

[90] Tennent, *Invitation to World Missions*, 70.
[91] Balia and Kim (eds), *Edinburgh*, 157.
[92] Constantin, 2013.
[93] Of course, there are exceptions to this. One young Roma from Albania received special permission to attend a Bible school in Tirana, even without finishing high school. He successfully graduated, but related how difficult the first year had been since he did not have the proper study skills, and only by 'the grace of God' and encouragement from his fellow students did he keep going. Interview with Andrea Avdiu by the author (Moravë, Albania, April 2015).

and spiritual issues in Roma communities, as well as those involving the history of Roma Christianity within the larger story of global Christianity.

Theological education that addresses these challenges would facilitate theology and missiology from a Romani perspective. Although almost certainly 'oral theologizing' happens all the time, greater written reflection would continue to strengthen, mature and orient Roma churches to their part in God's mission. In addition, the global church would benefit from the particular perspectives of Romani theologians and missiologists.

Conclusion

This chapter does not claim to be a comprehensive picture of Roma Christianity but rather, it offers snapshots and general themes in the context of the larger socio-political position of the Roma in CEE. The intersection between the general failure of public policy and EU initiatives to 'change' Roma communities and the growth of Roma Christianity has important implications for mission in CEE. Amidst enormous social, political and economic challenges, the Roma church is a vulnerable yet missionally active church, with an eye to transformation as the missional bridge to the non-Roma, and emphasizes the role of the Holy Spirit as both present in suffering and bringing healing and deliverance. In this, Roma churches bear witness to the power of the gospel to the larger society. Their sense of mission to the non-Roma, despite ongoing discrimination, serves as a reminder to the global church – where all too often barriers stand between Christians – of the generous and reconciling love of Christ.

However, missional challenges are formidable: how to understand holistic transformation in a way that honours Roma culture and yet can integrate with wider society? How to challenge the stereotypes and preconceived images held by both Roma and non-Roma? How can Roma and non-Roma Christians lay aside power and exclusivism to be shaped and changed by each other? How can Roma leaders join with non-Roma leaders to offer contextually appropriate theological training? Given these challenges, it is crucial that mission be approached holistically, rooted deeply in the foundations of a Triune God actively at work to reconcile and transform individuals, Roma communities, and wider society.

In order for Roma Christianity to be better known within the mosaic of global Christianity, further research needs to be done – particularly in Romania, where the largest number of Roma live and the growth of charismatic and Pentecostal forms of Christianity have exploded in recent years. Also, more research needs to be done in regard to church plants in Western Europe as a result of economic migration. How missional are these churches? What kind of influence do they have? Next, as previously noted, many barriers continue to exist between Roma and non-Roma churches. How can a model of mission as reconciliation affect the landscape of CEE? Finally, more research needs to be done regarding the theologies of the

Roma church. How does theology emerging from these contexts challenge and enrich the global church?

If 'this is the time for the Roma', then this is the time to listen, learn and join in with what God is already initiating in Roma communities. As David Smith points out, Christians in the West cannot predict or control the form of Christianity emerging from the global South.[94] Likewise, non-Roma Christians in Europe cannot predict or control the shape and texture of Roma Christianity – the questions it asks and the issues it faces in contexts of poverty and oppression could serve to unsettle and reshape the forms of non-Roma Christianity that surround it.

---

[94] David Smith, *Against the Stream: Christianity and Mission in an Age of Globalization* (Nottingham, UK: IVP, 2003), 63.

Reading and Writing as *Imitatio Dei*: A Theological Evaluation of the Use of Education as a Mission Strategy of the Evangelical Church Saraj

Aleksandar Apostolovski

The Man Who Would Be Mayor

The year is 2009.[1] Municipal elections are due in the only Roma municipality in the world. Elvis Bajram, the son of a Member of Parliament, controversial businessman and mosque-builder, is regarded as the favourite to become the next mayor of Šuto Orizari. In the midst of his campaign, he makes a remarkable promise. Cognizant of the fact that, should he be elected to his post, he would be the least educated incumbent of a high office in the history of Macedonian democracy, he vows to earn a high school diploma.[2]

As remarkable as this story may be, it is a case in point with regard to demonstrating the actual level of education among the Roma in Macedonia. Many Christians would also perceive it as an opportunity to effect radical cultural transformation. Surely investing in a young Roma's education would put them in line for positions of influence.

This study will illustrate some of the negative consequences which the inadequate education of its Roma members has had on the ministry and mission of the Evangelical Church Saraj, located on the western outskirts of Skopje. Also, two strategies, implemented by the church leadership over a period of twelve years, will be described. These include an after-school programme, intended for school-going children aged six to eighteen, and a literacy class, intended for illiterate women and girls.

In the final analysis, it will emerge that the missionary activities of Sokrat and Lena Apostolovski, the leaders of the said congregation, could be judged as a partial success. Contrary to their opinions, greater success was not denied them by the lack of suitable partnering organizations, the scarcity of helping hands or the paltry conditions in which their efforts were conducted. While there is no doubt that resolving any one of these

---

[1] Many of the ideas discussed in this study were first broached in conversations with Miss Kristina Apostolovska. Therefore, the following pages are dedicated to her.

[2] For more on this story, see V. Tanurovski, 'Ќе се Запишам во Средна Школа' (I Will Enrol into High School), *Vest,* 7 (2009): www.vest.mk/default.asp?ItemID=28E79E25275E9748BABA50068A36887B

shortcomings would make a long-term difference, this study will suggest that their expectations were based on a somewhat inadequate model for Christian mission with regard to education. Their failure to question their faith in the power of reading and writing as agents of transformation would be identified as the chief source of dissatisfaction and frustration with regard to their efforts. Both this and the application of an inadequate yardstick against which to measure it have denied them appreciation of the success which has been achieved.

There are no published records of the activities of any Roma church in Macedonia. Consequently, this study will have to rely on other sources. The most important of these are the newsletters which the Apostolovskis sent to their friends and supporters between the winter of 2003 and the summer of 2015.[3] They will be supplemented by insights gleaned from various project proposals submitted for the benefit of the congregation[4] and a reflection about the early days of the ministry which Mr Apostolovski wrote in 2013. Finally, the stories of Kenan Osman and Mirveta Ismaili, whose experiences typify the after-school programme and literacy classes, and official statistics from the Macedonian Statistics Agency will be used in the process of assessment.

A Walk to Remember

Saraj is the name of both a small rural municipality and the village in which the municipal seat is located. The inhabitants are predominantly ethnic Albanians (over 93% out of a total population of 35,408 according to the census of 2002).[5] The Roma make up a tiny minority of its population (only 273 in 2002).[6] Most of them live in a single village.

The municipality contains many natural resources and sporting facilities. It is amenable to those who enjoy hill walking, kayaking or just strolling by the banks of the River Vardar. But this is not the case in the area where the Roma village is located. There the banks are bare, rocky and full of refuse.

---

[3] This study had access to 31 of these documents. The Apostolovskis' strategy in recent years has been to aim to produce a newsletter every quarter. Although they are not available in published form, access to them can be gained by writing to Mr Sokrat Apostolovski at apotolfamilija@gmail.com. The same applies to the project proposals, the reflection on the early days given below and the two stories used in this study.

[4] Three particular project proposals deserve special mention. There has been an attempt to raise funds in order to purchase an appropriate building for the after-school programme. At the time of writing, it had not yet met with success. Calls to assist young Roma children to attend a variety of Christian events away from home are usually sent every spring. Positive responses usually follow. Finally, the Apostolovskis wished to repair an old building in order to turn it into an appropriate study area for the benefit of illiterate women and girls. No positive response has been received to date.

[5] See *2002 Census of Population, Households and Dwellings in the Republic of Macedonia* (Republic of Macedonia State Statistics Office, 2005), 20.

[6] *2002 Census*, 34.

Yet, in late 2003, not knowing why, the Apostolovskis decided to take a stroll in this direction.[7]

As they walked upstream, they saw a small village in the distance. They decided to visit it, still not knowing why. As they descended a tiny dusty road, they found themselves in an area made of makeshift habitations built of metal, cardboard and, rarely, brick. Suddenly they were surrounded by a large group of Roma children. There were puzzled expressions on the faces of the local inhabitants. They seemed to be wondering what these two non-Roma people were after. A short informal encounter, which was attended both by some children and some parents, followed. Yet, the same question kept on being asked: 'What are you doing here?' The Apostolovskis had no answer to give.

With this question ringing in their ears, the Apostolovskis left the village. On the way home, a prayerful conversation ensued. They sought the reason for what, in every respect, seemed to be a random visit to a group of extremely poor, disadvantaged and marginalized members of society.

A decision to treat the visit as a call to action followed. Aware of the fact that these people had been treated in such a way as to limit their human dignity to a minimum, the Apostolovskis contemplated doing something which might contribute towards transforming the predicament of the Roma villagers. Since the Christmas season was at hand, they decided to offer the children Christmas boxes delivered by Samaritan's Purse. In doing so, they hoped that such an act might also serve as a springboard for the sharing of the gospel message.

When the boxes arrived, they were distributed to every child in the village. Although they were initially received with a dose of curiosity and mild apprehension, the children's faces soon told another story. The Apostolovskis were later informed by the villagers, that both children and parents were astonished to realize that, after all, there was someone who did care for them. Since the vast majority of Roma in Macedonia declare themselves to be Muslims, none of them had ever received a Christmas present. On the contrary, popular imagination always tended to ascribe a variety of petty crimes and superstitions to them. Hence, they found it gratifying to receive different treatment.

The Apostolovskis are very fond of the 'walk to remember', as they put it. They believe that this random act of kindness was of crucial importance when it came to gaining the villagers' trust. Although the Christmas season was followed by a few months of intensive observation on the part of the Roma, an initial relationship was established. During this period, frequent visits were exchanged. At the end of it, an oral invitation to commence a house church in the villagers' homes was extended and accepted. This was the beginning of the Evangelical Church Saraj, whose missionary activities

[7] The following account is based on a brief reflection which Sokrat Apostolovski wrote in 2013.

pertaining to education will be described and assessed in the following pages.

Another Nation on our Doorstep

But the issues faced by the villagers went deeper than not having had an opportunity in the past to receive a Christmas present. Neither the initial encounter nor the months of observation provided a very clear insight into their nature. For, in the beginning, the shoe was on the other foot. Sustained relationships with the Roma put Sokrat and Lena in line for a culture shock. They had Roma friends, neighbours and colleagues. Lena spent two years teaching at a Christian kindergarten for Roma children. Yet neither one of them realized that they were dealing with another people group. Divine providence, it would appear, had arranged things in such a manner that they were able to speak of themselves as missionaries without having to travel to another country.

Slowly but surely, the problems emerged. Some of them lacked either a clear solution or the means to implement one. There was an extremely high unemployment rate among the villagers. The only work available was labour-intensive and of short duration. Nevertheless, unloading trucks, digging canals, picking fruit and vegetables, or collecting scrap iron and plastic bottles for recycling could scarcely provide sufficient funds to sustain families of five or more members.

The problem of having decent living quarters was scarcely less serious. Although the villagers live in them permanently, their homes have the appearance of being temporary dwellings. For the most part, they are built of scrap metal and/or cardboard. There is no permanent supply of running water in them. The sewage system is improvised. Electricity is provided by illegal means. A large rubbish dump is located a stone's throw from their thresholds. Finally, these habitations are built on property which does not belong to the villagers. Thus eviction, though never carried out or even threatened, hangs over their heads like the sword of Damocles.

The above serves an incentive for the villagers to seek their fortunes elsewhere. Macedonian citizens have been granted open access to the countries of the Schengen Zone since 2009. The vast majority of the villagers sought to take advantage of the social welfare systems of other countries. Previous experience had taught them to favour Italy, France, Belgium and, especially, Germany.[8] The asylum-seekers left in stages. Often, they remained abroad only as long as it took for the local authorities to reject their applications for economic asylum.[9] Others were deported home because they had overstayed their welcome.

---

[8] Conversations with the middle-aged villagers revealed that many of them had the opportunity to spend short periods of their lives abroad during the Kosovo Crisis of 1998-2000.

[9] According to the villagers, in Germany this process could last between twelve and eighteen months.

The constant coming and going created a peculiar problem for the church leadership. When a decision to relocate was made, it included all members of the family. And no time could be lost because relocation would take the children out of school for an indefinite period of time. Although information about departures was diligently kept from the Apostolovskis until it was too late, this did not soften the blow or avoid the negative consequences of the move.

A further form of turnover affected young females. The Roma are among the very few ethnic groups in Europe who still prefer to conclude marriage agreements when both the future bride and the future groom are relatively young. This usually takes place in early adolescence in order to maintain the sexual purity of the bride. It also involves a suitable financial transaction between the parents of the newly-weds. This, in turn, has motivated even churchgoers to disregard the religious preferences of their daughters in favour of monetary compensation.

This custom has provoked a very rare outburst of anger and frustration on the part of the Apostolovskis. Although their newsletters are usually written in a moderate and thankful tone, one of them, sent after several young girls were married in this way, opens by drawing the reader's attention to the diabolic nature of this practice. It expresses a view which equates this act with Satan's attempts to steal sheep from the flock of the Good Shepherd (John 10).[10] This custom remains an ongoing problem.

Asylum-seeking and premature marriages are seen as two peculiar examples of a lack of willingness to effect a decisive break with a lifestyle which preceded the villagers' decisions to follow Christ. It seems to occur in other Roma congregations too. Sokrat and Lena have often characterized this lack of transformation as evidence of the parents' short-sightedness concerning their children's future. Both of these actions have the effect of removing young children from the system of education and ensuring that they will encounter further difficulties.

One such problem is the inability to read the Bible for oneself. This was true of many of the villagers. The reasons for this were complex. Yet, illiteracy and a lack of education were at the core of the problem. Since evangelical Christianity regards intimacy with the Word of God as an absolute necessity with regard to living the Christian life, the leadership of the Evangelical Church Saraj took an early decision to promote education and literacy among its younger members. It was believed that this would contribute towards personal transformation. It could enhance the Roma's prospects in life. The Apostolovskis also hoped that it might affect future employability, departures to Western Europe and the marriage situation. In short, education was perceived as a means to practise a form of mission which would be both holistic and transformational.

---

[10] This occurs in a newsletter written in April of 2008.

Life of Kenan: A Story of Partial Success

The earliest newsletter available for this study, written after Christmas 2003, clearly notes the low level of education among the villagers as a challenge which was facing the Apostolovskis. Indeed, with regard to the municipality of Saraj, it was an issue noted by the national census of 2002. According to it, 1,252 citizens, aged fifteen and above, were registered as lacking any formal education.[11] In addition to this, another 2,319 had dropped out of primary school (a basic eight-year training in literacy, mathematics and the sciences), and 17,139 citizens had never gone beyond the basics.[12]

And as for the villagers, there was no high school graduate among them. The only student who was enrolled in secondary education was on the brink of dropping out. Even though Gjulferina was one of the best students in her class, her parents were convinced that she would do much better if she learned a trade and started working at the age of sixteen!

Thus, it is not to be wondered at that stimulating education was met with strong opposition on the part of the parents. There were various objections put forward by them. According to some, education was not a worthwhile investment as it was not a guaranteed means of securing a better job. And, in any case, it was too expensive.[13] Others objected that going to school would hardly prepare young Roma girls for imminent marriage and the family responsibilities which it entailed. One parent even went so far as to claim that his daughter, who was present in the room at the time of the utterance, was 'too stupid' for education. A final objection came from the existence of schools for children with special needs. It was not uncommon for parents to enrol their children into such institutions. The procurement of documents which would allegedly confirm infirmity or mental impairment was not difficult. The parents believed that the possession of a medical diagnosis might qualify them for social aid and the children for work.

The Apostolovskis possessed no effective means of countering these objections. They only marvelled at what they considered to be a clear case of wrong priorities in life. Nevertheless, they persisted with their encouragement. They also sought to provide some financial means by calling on their friends for help.

Despite their misgivings, the parents permitted some of their children to return to school or to enrol into high school. This, no doubt, was yet another attempt to test the waters akin to a time of intense observation. The

---

[11] *2002 Census*, 36.

[12] *2002 Census*, 36. By comparison, the predominantly Roma municipality of Šuto Orizari, whose total population in 2002 was 22,017, had 1,869 uneducated citizens, 2,635 early dropouts and 8,092 high school graduates (*2002 Census*, 20, 36).

[13] According to the winter 2004 newsletter, the annual cost for a high school student at the time was 250 Euros per year. This sum would be sufficient to cover a student's textbooks, other school necessities and a bus ticket. Subsequent changes in the legislative system have seen a major reduction of this sum owing to the fact that an attempt has been made to ensure that high school education is free for all citizens.

summer of 2004 saw three young people, two boys (Elvis and Atiljan) and a girl (Afrodita), enrolled at the local textiles high school. Gjulferina's parents relaxed some of their pressure and allowed her to continue her education. Four years later, to the astonishment of the villagers in general and their parents in particular, three of the students graduated from high school.[14] One of them, Gjulferina, had results which were near the top of her class.[15] This success motivated other children, notably Elvis' younger brother Remzi, to attempt further education.

Yet, this success did not come overnight. When the school year started, it emerged that they lacked adequate study areas. Their small and overcrowded homes were less than adequate. Also, younger children, who only spoke the Roma language, found it difficult to follow classes delivered in Macedonian. Finally, there were those who needed help with homework assignments. The consequence of this was that school results were not as good as they could have been.

Although not a teacher by profession, Lena had taught in two Christian kindergartens. One of them, located in Šuto Orizari, was designed to provide Roma children with both a Christian environment and an effective way of preparing them for primary education. Lena learned the Roma language. She also had firsthand experience with solving the types of difficulties encountered by young Roma.

Drawing upon her experience, Lena was convinced that her knowledge could be used to address the issues which young villagers faced. Consequently, she suggested a day-care programme. It was based on the Montessori curriculum which she had used in the kindergarten. The day was structured round periods for study, a light meal, games and Bible study. The ministry was meant to improve the children's performance at school and to allow them opportunities to show ambition, leadership and care for others.

The ministry commenced in 2005. Between then and the time of writing, more than fifty children have benefited from it in one way or another. The performance of the majority of them steadily improved, as evidenced by improved grades at the end of successive school years. Also, as students matured, they were given opportunities to tutor and assist younger children. The aid rendered included, but was not limited to, assistance in mastering difficult concepts, writing homework assignments, translation from Roma to Macedonian and vice versa, etc. These activities offered a rare example

[14] A memorable story, recounted in the November 2007 newsletter, illustrates the parents' reactions to an extent. In their opinion, the custom of eating cake is reserved for weddings. Therefore, they were surprised when the Apostolovskis brought two large ones in June of 2007. Apparently, a rumour was circulated that one of the Apostolovskis' children was getting married. Yet, the intention was to celebrate the achievements of the Roma children who had completed yet another year of their education.

[15] Having to take care of a demented mother and a blind father proved to be too much for Atiljan. He failed to complete his second year and dropped out of school altogether.

of a case in which Roma were helping other Roma with regard to education. Kenan Osman was the outstanding performer in the programme.

Kenan came from the village.[16] His family, consisting of his parents, twin brother and younger sister, lived in severe poverty. By his own admission, food could sometimes be scarce. He was unable to do much to alter that. He was diagnosed with a heart problem at a very young age. This meant that he could not perform the labour-intensive tasks which were the main source of income for the villagers. Only education offered any prospects for him. Yet, even that required funds which were not available to his family. Moreover, his parents feared for his health and safety. Nevertheless, heeding the advice and with the encouragement of the Apostolovskis, he enrolled into high school.

It was at this time that three major developments took place. First, word was spread that the government intended to make secondary education both free and compulsory. This meant that all students would be provided with free transport and essential learning materials. Other school supplies, such as food and clothing, remained the responsibility of the parents. Secondly, the Apostolovskis' calls for help came to fruition as some of their friends and partners, notably Macedonian Outreach, expressed their desire to support various children on their way to completing their education. Finally, Lena started having sessions with the children as part of the after-school programme. Kenan could both rely on assistance when he needed it and render it when others asked him for it.

The effect of these developments was that Kenan could attend to his studies without being concerned about finance. During his four years at school he consistently achieved respectable results. His care for his classmates was also evidenced by his assumption of the role of class representative for two years. At the end of this period, he graduated and joined Afrodita, Elvis and Gjulferina, who had done the same a year before.

But unlike his fellow villagers, all of whom decided to form families after completing this stage of their education, Kenan chose to go a step further. Shortly after his graduation, he expressed his desire to attend a Bible School. Yet again, timely aid was rendered and financial means became available for him to enrol in a two-year programme at a Bible School in Belgrade, Serbia.[17] His course permitted him to devote himself to studying the contents of the Bible. Also, he had ample opportunity to put some of the skills he had mastered in the after-school programme to good use. These included ministering in a variety of church contexts, prayer, evangelistic activities and various forms of social involvement.

The Apostolovskis saw him on rare occasions. Yet, even then, he would be eager to spend time with his fellow villagers, seeking to impart some of

---

[16] The following story is based on a testimony which Mr Osman wrote in the summer of 2010. The Apostolovskis also reproduced it in their next newsletter.

[17] The absence of an Evangelical theological seminary, or even a Bible School, remains a sad fact of Macedonian church life at the time of writing.

his newly-found knowledge into their lives. The Apostolovskis could have been forgiven for thinking that, here, at long last, was the fruit of their labours coming to full maturity.

But this was not to be. Kenan's heart problems returned. It was discovered that he might be able to find healing in a hospital in Germany. What followed was a repeat of the asylum-seeker's adventure described above. Although it brought Kenan some much-needed relief, it was deeply frustrating to the Apostolovskis. On the spur of the moment, they regarded the whole affair as yet another failure.

Yet, critical distance and hindsight are able to shed a different perspective both on the still ongoing after-school programme and on the life of Kenan, which encapsulates it. A verdict of partial success is more appropriate. After all, a significant number of children were given opportunities which they would not have had otherwise. One might argue that the results of their education could only be fully perceived once their stories have come to a conclusion. Further, Kenan has settled, got married and plays an active part in the life of a church in Austria. There is no doubt that his life's story, so far as it has unfolded, is one of undoubted success, albeit partial.

If You Can Read This, Thank a Teacher

Illiteracy is another problem which was detected at an early stage. It often became apparent when villagers were asked to read a Bible passage. It was by no means restricted to an age group or a gender, although it was prevalent among women. Somewhat surprisingly, it occurred also among those who were considered to be literate by the census commission. There are two components to the definition of literacy. If one lacked any formal education, one needed to demonstrate an ability to read and write by composing or reading a letter. On the other hand, the completion of grade three of primary school (usually achieved at the age of nine or ten) automatically qualified a person as literate for the purposes of the census.[18]

Unfortunately, working with the villagers made it clear that this was not the case even if many of them fulfilled the second of the two conditions for literacy. Many reasons contributed towards such an outcome. Many Roma communities still retain characteristics of oral nomadic or semi-nomadic groups. Within this context, it is regrettable to observe that there exists a strong tendency to prioritize male over female children. Therefore, it would make little sense to invest in the literacy of females who are destined to join another household in the near future. A decision not to send them to school would then appear as a logical one. If there was to be a solution for these women, it would have to come from outside the usual channels of education.

---

[18] *2002 Census*, 17.

Inspired by the after-school programme, Lena thought that organizing classes for illiterate women and girls would go some way towards overcoming their inability to read the Bible for themselves. This was the beginning of the literacy programme, an informal class session which took place once a week in the homes of the participants.

Two different realities became apparent from the beginning. These young women and girls were accustomed to the rigours of everyday life in a tough environment. Yet, they found writing to be significantly more difficult than cooking, cleaning or washing clothes. Even holding the pencil was pain to them. The completion of writing tasks was often accompanied by audible groans. Nevertheless, most of them persisted in their endeavour.

A second reality was also apparent. Success in accomplishing even the simplest of the assignments brought enormous satisfaction to them. They were much gratified to discover that they were capable of success. Lena made sure that this lesson was properly taught. She was well aware that issues of self-confidence were being addressed in an adequate way.

On paper, Mirveta Ismaili did not exist.[19] Having to share her living quarters with three brothers, two of whom had families of their own, and a sister made life difficult. Still worse, her mother suffers from schizophrenia. Having been born in the village itself, Mirveta did not possess any documents which would prove that she was not a non-entity. And even if she did, she would be unable to read them.

Although the village can scarcely be described as a literate environment, admitting one's inability to read and write still carries a certain stigma accompanied by shame. Therefore, only a brave woman could do what Mirveta did next. Although she would be the youngest of the participants in the literacy class, she asked Lena for permission to enrol. Enduring the taunts and jeers of her peers, she applied herself to learning the alphabet. Through tears and hardships, she completed a full year's training.

One Wednesday afternoon, Mirveta's father was seen approaching the house-cum-school. This was a rarity. It could foreshadow anything from a violent confrontation to an announcement that a marriage agreement had been concluded on her behalf. Everyone, Mirveta included, awaited the outcome as he strode the last few yards of the muddy track.

But there was no need for alarm. He had indeed come to make an announcement. Yet what he said was met with a round of applause. Earlier that day, he and his daughter were watching the villagers' favourite television programme – a soap opera. To his lasting pleasure, he had realized that his daughter was able to read the subtitles from off the screen for him. Regardless of what the census commission might say, his daughter had met his standards for literacy!

Her experience with the literacy class shaped Mirveta in significant ways. She is now able to read her Bible for herself. In fact, she is one of a

[19] The following story is based on Lena's recollections.

handful of people in the village actually to do so. Although she has never been to a regular school, her sincerest wish is to become a teacher. Being able to assist Lena in working with some of the younger children goes some way towards the realization of her desire.

Yet again, Mirveta's story speaks of partial success. There is little doubt that her experience is remarkable. It may indeed serve as an inspiration to many. Nevertheless, it falls short of the Apostolovskis' expectations with regard to the effects of education and literacy. Mirveta's ability to read and write has not caused a radical break with the old ways of living. Neither has it made her more employable. Her marriage situation is yet to be resolved. All of this, along with the entire literacy programme which Mirveta typifies, is a source of frustration, rather than inspiration, to the Apostolovskis.

Reading and Writing as *Imitatio Dei*: A Theological Evaluation

In the final analysis, both the after-school programme and the literacy classes have produced notable success. Both the children and their parents have been shown that they can cope with the demands of the system. Kenan's story demonstrates that there are possibilities of going further. Mirveta's story illustrates the transformative power of literacy and the crucial influence a teacher can play in one's life. Both Kenan and Mirveta attained a level of education which permitted them to instruct other Roma.

Nevertheless, neither the after-school programme nor the literacy classes have succeeded in remedying certain chronic conditions. Some of the high school graduates were employed by the municipality. Nevertheless, their level of education has not brought them vast improvements in their living standards. While there is no doubt that such an outcome mirrors the problem of unemployment in Macedonia, it stands to reason that the treatment of the relationship between education and future employability as one of cause-and-effect is not justified by the evidence presented above.

Likewise, education has brought neither a massive increase to the conversion rate nor a dramatic transformation in the lifestyles of the Roma churchgoers. A lack of clear manifestation of the fruit of the Spirit is, admittedly, a cause of frustration among workers with Roma throughout the region. As this study has amply demonstrated, the Apostolovskis have not been immune from it. Yet, the cases considered in the previous two sections of this study call for a re-evaluation of one's expectations. Unfortunately, the combined power of the Word of God and education does not necessarily produce a religious revival.

The same, to a lesser extent, applies to combating under-age marriages. Here, at least, it seems as though enrolment into secondary education contributes somewhat to delaying such realities. The sources available for this study are unable to pinpoint the precise reason(s) which may contribute to this outcome. Yet, the mitigating nature of the effects of education ought not to be overlooked. Hence, the Apostolovskis have been spared the need for further outbursts of the kind described above.

The Apostolovskis are fully cognizant of these shortcomings. Nevertheless, they remain convinced that greater application of themselves to the task at hand, improvements in the infrastructure, or joint efforts with relevant partnering organizations might yet bring the desired outcomes. While there is little doubt that a permanent solution to these problems will contribute towards the effectiveness of their work, it could be the case that the pressures, which they undoubtedly feel, have been generated by the result-driven paradigms of Christian mission. Alternatively, their attitude may reflect the aftermath of failed expectations. Finally, it seems as though an altogether inappropriate yardstick, i.e. John Stuart Mill's faith in the power of education, has unwittingly been used to measure success and failure. In what follows, this study will demonstrate that all three hypotheses postulated above are relevant to the present predicament of the Apostolovskis' missionary undertakings. An attempt will also be made to provide suitable alternatives which are more thoroughly grounded in biblical perceptions of Christian mission and its use of education for the realization of its goals.

The result-driven model is typified by mission as means of spreading civilization. Thus, education is intended to discard the residue of irrational beliefs and practices. The adoption of such an approach is proof of ongoing culture shock. It also presupposes superiority on the part of the missionary as more civilized or, in its Christian equivalent, more spiritual. The missionary, perceived as Christ incarnate, is the chief agent of transformation. The transformation expected is all-encompassing and it requires an instantaneous conversion, as opposed to the realization of a gradual call. Its hero is the apostle Paul, while the other disciples, notably Peter, are somehow to be regarded as his poor relations. Thus, no time is given for the unfolding of processes which, normally, require time. This model brings massive cultural baggage with it. It is a true child of the Enlightenment. All too often, it is implemented through the double agency of *Bible and Sword*, as Barbara W. Tuchman has astutely observed with regard to the Middle East.[20] Its trust in literacy as an agent of cultural transformation has been shown to cause ruination to the societies which it allegedly attempts to civilize.[21]

Contrary to this model's perception of the mission field as a Promised Land which needs to be conquered, the alternative proposed here is closer

[20] Barbara W. Tuchman, *Bible and Sword: England and Palestine from the Bronze Age to Balfour* (New York: New York University Press, 1956).

[21] Kevin B. Maxwell, *Bemba Myth and Ritual: The Impact of Literacy on an Oral Culture* (New York: Peter Lang, 1983). Maxwell's warnings should be heeded. One of them is the establishment of a corollary between literacy, brought to the Bemba by Christian missionaries, and oppression. Nevertheless, any analogous claims with regard to the potential ruination of traditional Roma social norms by stimulating education fail to find support in the evidence presented above.

to the Roma themselves. As many of them find part-time jobs related to either building or planting, it is suggested that perceiving the mission field as a temple in need of restoration (1 Cor. 3:5-17; Rev. 21:1-10; cf. Gen. 1:1-2:24) may be more appropriate. The gradual nature of the images employed allows for latitude along both the spatial and the temporal axes. God, who 'causes' the crops 'to grow' (1 Cor. 3:6) is the chief agent of transformation. His 'co-workers' (3:9) are not expected to do everything on their own (3:6). Neither are they necessarily expected to accomplish the grand tasks of gardening and temple-building (3:6, 10-15, cf. v. 16) within their lifetime (cf. Jer. 29:10-14). As in the cases of Abraham (Gen. 15:1-19; 21:1-7; 23:1-20; cf. 12:1-3) and the entire Pentateuch (Ex. 1:1-7; 19:1-24:10; Num. 21:21-36; 27:1-11), partial fulfilment is more than acceptable.[22] In the final analysis, it will contribute to 'the renewal of all things' (Matt. 19:28; cf. 1 Cor. 3:16; 15:58; Rev. 21:22-26). Thus, this deeply counter-intuitive vision of a temple in the course of its restoration may truly be liberating to the Apostolovskis. They may also be beneficial to others involved in ministering to the Roma.[23]

The Apostolovskis' response to failure appears to be highly reminiscent of the effects of cognitive dissonance described in the work of Festinger.[24] According to him, failure of expectations is usually followed by reinterpretation. This typically takes three forms. One can pretend that the time for the realization of one's expectations has not yet dawned. Alternatively, one can turn to oneself and find fault with one's performance. Finally, a reinterpretation of the experience(s) or the text(s) which have generated the expectations may ensue. This study has clearly demonstrated the Apostolovskis' willingness to apply the second of Festinger's mechanisms of coping with failure. Their early decision to prioritize the younger generations of villagers may have overtones of claims that the signs of the times have been misread. Finally, although not highlighted above, their ongoing reassessment of priorities may be seen as evidence of re-evaluation being at work. Thus, the cumulative effect of failing to question their faith in education as an agent of transformation has been the chief source of the Apostolovskis' frustrations with their apparent failure.

Finally, although neither of them is familiar with the work of John Stuart Mill, the Apostolovskis seem to have shared this atheist philosopher's faith in education. Contemplating his father's perceptions of its potency over people's intellect, Mill writes: 'Whenever it [reason transmitted through

[22] For the crucial role which the notion of partial fulfilment has for the unity of the Pentateuch, see David J.A. Clines, *The Theme of the Pentateuch* (JSOT Supp. 10), (Sheffield, UK: JSOT Press, 1978).

[23] Many of these ideas are developed further in Gregory K. Beale, *The Temple and the Church's Mission: A Biblical Theology of the Dwelling Place of God* (Grand Rapids, MI: Zondervan, 2004).

[24] See Leon Festinger, Henry W. Riecken and Stanley Schachter, *When Prophecy Fails* (Minneapolis, MN: University of Minnesota Press, 1956).

education] is allowed to reach them... *all would be gained* if the whole population were taught to read, if all sorts of opinions were allowed to be addressed to them by word and in writing...'[25] The reasons for this correspondence in thought are difficult to fathom. Nevertheless, it suffices to observe the unfortunate fact that such a collaboration has little in common with biblical thought-processes.

Yet, the worldview of the Bible offers a viable alternative. The prophetic books of the Old Testament contain at least two passages (Jer. 36:1-26; Zech. 5:1-5) in which scrolls, i.e. books, are clearly depicted as agents of God.[26] Further, both the books of Deuteronomy (5:22; cf. 9:10; 10:4) and Jeremiah (31:31-34) clearly depict God as a writer. Moreover, both books are clear that human writing, or even human teaching, are direct outcomes of God's assumption of these tasks (cf. Deut. 6:4-9; 11:18-21; Jer. 23:30; 31:34).[27] Hence, recent scholarship has rightly suggested that the concept of *imitatio Dei* may be applicable to the analysis of the theology of writing in the Old Testament.[28] By analogy, a similar conclusion could be drawn about the theological function of reading and writing within the context of Christian mission.

The implication of this is that the efforts of the Apostolovskis are not to be evaluated by the number of conversions reported in newsletters or other forms of communication. They have value in themselves as acts by means of which one may enjoy communion with God inasmuch as literacy is a means of discovering and obeying his will.[29] Hence, when young Roma were taught to read and write, be that within the system of education or outside it, they were granted a means of drawing near to their God and Saviour. This, in turn, was the original intention of the Apostolovskis.

The case studies presented above may have at least two implications for global mission as envisaged by the delegates at the Edinburgh 2010 conference. First, although due attention has been paid to theological education, Wendy Strachan is very much in the minority when she explores

---

[25] John J. Coss (ed), *Autobiography of John Stuart Mill* (New York: 1924), 74, emphasis added.

[26] This idea is broached in my 'Children out of Stones, Servants out of Books: Scrolls as Yahweh's Agents in Some Prophetic Books', in Marcel V. Măcelaru and Corneliu Constantineanu (eds), *Theological Pilgrimages: Collected Faculty Papers, 2007-2009* (Osijek, Croatia: Evanđeoski teološki fakultet, 2009), 49-60.

[27] For a treatment of the relationship between divine and human writing in Deuteronomy, see Jean-Pierre Sonnet, *The Book within the Book: Writing in Deuteronomy* (Biblical Interpretation Series, 14), (Leiden, Netherlands: E.J. Brill, 1997), 41-71. For a treatment of the same subject in Jeremiah, albeit with significant differences, see R.P. Carroll, 'Inscribing the Covenant: Writing and the Written in Jeremiah', in A. Graeme Auld (ed), *Understanding Poets and Prophets: Essays in Honor of George Wishart Anderson* (JSOT Supp. 152: Sheffield, UK: Sheffield Academic Press, 1993), 61-76.

[28] See Joachim Schaper, 'Theology of Writing: The Oral and the Written, God as Scribe, and the Book of Deuteronomy', in Louise J. Lawrence and Mario L. Aguilar (eds), *Anthropology and Biblical Studies: Avenues of Approach* (Leiden, Netherlands: Deo Publishers, 2004), 113.

[29] Schaper, 'Theology of Writing, 114.

the role of children as producers of theology.[30] The concept of reading and writing as *imitatio Dei,* proposed above, should be seen as complementary to her work. Further, it supplements her observations that children should be granted greater attention and allotted greater funds. Yet, rather than doing so on account of their numbers and openness towards the gospel message alone, mission through education could be conducted as a reflection of God's scribal activity.

Secondly, the twentieth century has witnessed raging debates between proponents of the so-called 'social gospel' and those who would insist on preaching the gospel message as an utmost priority. The Edinburgh 2010 delegates were correct to stress the need for practising holistic mission.[31] This study has demonstrated that education on its own is unable to be a catalyst of transformation. It also cautions against expectations of instantaneous cultural transformation as a consequence of encountering the gospel message. The stories of partial success narrated above demonstrate attempts to come to terms with tensions inherent in holistic approaches to mission.

Elvis Bajram did become the new mayor of Šuto Orizari. In so doing, he imitated his father by launching a political career. In time, he kept his promise to earn a high school diploma. Yet, his level of education was not the deciding factor with regard to the opportunities which he was granted. On the other hand, by 2015, the after-school programme of the Evangelical Church Saraj had assisted nine young Roma on their way to completing their secondary education. Moreover, six women and girls mastered the skills of reading and writing. Although education had not granted the young Roma villagers opportunities to assume high administrative posts, it allowed them to practise *imitatio Dei.*

[30] Wendy Strachan, 'Welcoming Children: Reinstating Children in our Theological Reflections on Mission': www.edinburgh2010.org/en/resources/papersdocuments577d.pdf ?no_cache=1&cid=33883&did=22130&sechash=df5c3e49

[31] See 'Edinburgh 2010: Common Call': www.edinburgh2010.org/en/resources/papers documentscc36.pdf?no_cache=1&cid=33104&did=21646&sechash=f043be23

Part Three

ECUMENICAL DIALOGUE IN A NEW EUROPE: STEPS TOWARDS A PURIFICATION OF HISTORICAL MEMORIES IN THE BALKANS

Bogdan Dolenc

Introduction

'Europe has a very special responsibility with regard to ecumenism. It is in Europe that the major divisions between East and West have arisen. However, it is also in Europe that serious efforts directed towards Christian reconciliation and the search for full visible unity have taken place.'[1] These words by the late Pope John Paul II, addressed to the participants of the Second European Ecumenical Assembly in Graz, Austria (1997), should introduce my reflection on ecumenical dialogue in a new Europe. I write from a Roman Catholic perspective and refer often to the texts of the magisterium. Since I live in a country which borders on the Western Balkans, I give special attention to Central and Eastern Europe, which has experienced profound changes in recent decades.

How can Europe realize its responsibility with regard to ecumenism? It is a continent with unquestionable Christian roots and soul, and a place of numerous ecumenical initiatives, but it reveals its profound ambiguity by having originated many divisions and evils. Among challenges and opportunities of future ecumenical work, I single out especially *purification of the memory* and *reconciliation*. These two elements are important elements of the commemoration of the anniversary of the Reformation (2017), to emphasize its ecumenical character.

Progress in ecumenical dialogue, which has its deepest source in the same Word of God, represents a sign of hope for the church of today: the growth of unity among Christians is, in fact, mutually enriching for all. This positive attitude was prevailing at the two Synods of Bishops for Europe (1991 and 1999) and found its expression in the words: 'This is one of the great gifts of the Holy Spirit for a continent like Europe which gave rise to tragic divisions between Christians during the second millennium and which still suffers from their consequences.'[2]

---

[1] 'Message of H.H. Pope John Paul II', in *Reconciliation: Gift of God and Source of New Life: Documents from the Second European Ecumenical Assembly* (Graz / Wien / Köln: Styria, 1998), 165.

[2] John Paul II, *Post-synodal Apostolic Exhortation Ecclesia in Europa*, No. 17: http://w2.vatican.va/content/john-paul-ii/en/apost_exhortations/documents/hf_jp-ii_exh_20030628_ecclesia-in-europa.html (accessed 8th April 2016).

Although Europe's history has been decisive for the rest of the world through centuries, the times of *Eurocentrism* are definitely over. Europe transmitted to other parts of the world numerous cultural and technical goods, which belong to the heritage of world civilization. European history, though, has also many dark sides, such as the imperialism and oppression of many nations together with unjust exploitation of their riches. Today we can recognize many harmful consequences of such a *Eurocentrism*. Therefore, it must be entirely rejected.

European Christianity must admit that other continents have taken the lead. Let me cite the words of the World Council of Churches (WCC) general secretary, the Rev. Samuel Kobia, as he presented new visions and challenges to ecumenism in the 21st century:

> The ecclesial landscape is changing still. European Protestantism was a main pillar of the 20th century ecumenical movement in general and WCC in particular. By the end of the 20th century, European Protestantism had begun to decline and this will have consequences for ecumenism in the 21st century. On the other hand, Christianity is witnessing a high growth in Africa, Asia and Latin America/Caribbean. The centre of gravity of Christianity is shifting to the global South. This trend will also have a big impact on ecumenism in the 21st century... While this reference has been primarily to Protestant churches, I would like to note that similar changes are underway in the Roman Catholic Church, especially in countries of the North. Orthodox churches are also undergoing changes. For churches in formerly Eastern Europe, the demise of communism has led to new opportunities for Orthodox church growth, to changing relationships with their governments, and to increased 'competition' from Western missionaries. While institutional or mainline Protestantism may be in the decline in North America and Europe, Christianity is thriving in the countries of the South. New churches are springing up in all regions.[3]

We became aware of the fact that Europe is more than the European Union. As Christians we share the responsibility for shaping Europe as a continent of peace, solidarity, participation and sustainability. 'If somebody is doubtful whether European Union makes sense or not, he should visit military cemeteries across the continent. Millions of fallen soldiers lie there. European Union is the greatest peace project in modern times.'[4] Indeed, Europe was initially a political project to secure peace and it now needs to become a Europe of the peoples, more than an economic area.[5] It needs to become a Europe of dialogue at all levels.

---

[3] Rev. Dr Samuel Kobia, *New Visions and Challenges to Ecumenism in the 21st Century*: www.oikoumene.org/en/resources/documents/general-secretary/speeches/17-11-06-new-visions-and-challenges-to-ecumenism-in-the-21st-century.html (accessed 8th April 2016).

[4] Words spoken by a politician in a TV discussion (cited from memory).

[5] EEA3 Sibiu, *Final Message*: www.eea3.org/documenti/final/FinalmessageEN.pdf (accessed 8th April 2016).

A History of Europe with Its Shades and Burdens...

The present decreasing importance of Europe as to the share of Christians, however, does not disclaim the fact that Europe was for long centuries a decisive factor in historical developments on other continents. Its history evidences many bright and praiseworthy aspects, but it is also a history of manifold evil which affected the whole world.

Is it, therefore, right to speak of the Christian roots of Europe? This question engaged the participants of two Synods of Bishops for Europe.[6] Certainly, it is insufficient to simply appeal in a nostalgic or romantic way to Europe's great heritage, to its Christian roots and Christian soul.[7] The *working document* or *Instrumentum laboris*, taking into account the responses of the bishops to the initial document, shows that only a few responses maintained that today's Europe has a Christian soul.

> Indeed, such an affirmation raises serious questions considering European history in this century with its dramatic events, conflicts, human oppression and accompanying ideologies, and the diverse cultural phenomena – negative and exceedingly problematic – which now exist in Europe. Perhaps, it would be more acceptable to maintain that... though greatly deteriorated because of the process of secularisation, these roots are not completely decayed... No one wishes to propose that Europe and Christianity are one and the same thing. This was never the case and is even less likely today.[8]

The Christian roots of Europe, if rediscovered and revitalised, are able to instil a living hope and a new dynamic force in everyone, a force which will help all overcome the difficulties of the present moment and ensure a future of increasing spiritual and human progress.

---

[6] The first Synod for Europe took place in 1991 and the second in 1999. I had the opportunity of participating at the former as an *adiutor* (theological expert).

[7] 'We need a heart and a soul. The door is open for whoever can offer a heart and a soul.' According to Laurens Hogebrink, this is how on 5th November 1990 Jacques Delors, President of the European Commission, formulated his well-known 'heart and soul' appeal to the churches. He writes: 'On 5th November 1990, a delegation of Protestant and Anglican Church leaders met with a delegation of the European Commission, including its President Jacques Delors, two other Commissioners and several high-ranking civil servants. The full day meeting concluded with a session with Delors in which he appealed to the churches to contribute to 'the heart and soul of Europe'. In his Foreword to the named book, the Rev. Dr Guy Liagre, General Secretary of the Conference of European Churches (CEC), thus explains the sense of this historic appeal: 'The challenge still stands: "We need a heart and a soul." It is not only about markets; it is also about values and culture. Delors underlined that, in the hierarchy of values, the cultural ones range above the economic ones, and that if the economy is a necessity for our lives, culture is really what makes our life worth living. However, as General Secretary of the Conference or European Churches, I am afraid that today's reality looks quite different. To the outside world – and to its own citizens – Europe continues to present itself first of all as an economic power, insisting on using political and financial arguments over cultural and social ones at any given time.' Laurens Hogebrink, *Europe's Heart and Soul: Jacques Delors' Appeal to the Churches* (Geneva: Globethics.net, 2015): www.globethics.net/documents/4289936/17575651/GE_CEC_2_web.pdf (accessed 8th April 2016), 13, 10.

[8] *Instrumentum laboris. Synod of Europe II*: https://www.ewtn.com/new_evangelization/europe/synod/instrument.htm (accessed 8th April 2016).

The final text of the *Postsynodal apostolic exhortation Ecclesia in Europa*[9] does not hesitate to speak openly of Europe as of 'a unity, rooted in a common Christian inspiration' (No. 4), of 'its religious heritage, and in particular, its profound Christian soul' (No. 7). At the same time, the *Exhortation* underlines 'the urgency of not squandering this precious patrimony and of… revitalizing her original Christian roots' (No. 25). The text ends with an imploring appeal: 'Europe, as you stand at the beginning of the third millennium, "Open the doors to Christ! Be yourself. Rediscover your origins. Relive your roots"' (No. 120).

Today's Christians in Europe are fully aware of the tragedies that were part of European history, especially in the twentieth century. Nobody can ignore the fact that both World Wars originated here and that the *Shoah* took place in the middle of *Christian* Europe. In 2014, Protestant churches all over Europe commemorated the beginning of World War I a hundred years ago with numerous services and events and a one-minute silence. The four years of military conflict cost the lives of 17 million people. The paper adopted by the CPCE Council[10] recalls the victims of this *seminal catastrophe*. The war profoundly changed the political map of Europe. Its consequences are still visible in the Balkans and Ukraine. The CPCE paper also deals critically with the role of Protestant churches and theologians in 1914. God and war were placed in a positive relationship, it notes. The churches were profoundly nationalistic and most of them welcomed the outbreak of war. Moreover, they were concerned to find theological grounds for their own countries' involvement in terms of a *just war*. The voices calling for peace were shouted down in 1914.[11]

H.-G. Stobbe thus sums up his views on conflicts in Central and Eastern Europe and their overcoming:

> Historical events of the 20th Century – the two World Wars with all their far-reaching and traumatic consequences, the rise of communist regimes and their decline, the first steps towards a democratic society – all this helps us to understand the complexity of the ethnic, national, and religious situation in Central and Eastern Europe today. In the wake of all these changes, strong tensions of an ethnic and nationalist character were engendered not only on the Balkan Peninsula, in the area of Yugoslavia, but the nationalities of the disintegrating Soviet Union also came into severe conflicts with one another. It has become clear that there can be no peaceful solutions without a high degree of willingness to compromise, and without devoting attention to the concerns of the ethnic and religious groups between which the conflict

---

[9] John Paul II, *Post-synodal Apostolic Exhortation Ecclesia in Europa*: http://w2.vatican.va/content/john-paul-ii/en/apost_exhortations/documents/hf_jp-ii_exh_20030628_ecclesia-in-europa.html (accessed 8th April 2016).

[10] Community of Protestant Churches in Europe (CPCE), *The Community of Protestant Churches in Europe commemorates the outbreak of the First World War*: www.leuenberg.net/sites/default/files/special-causes/cpce_-_commemoration_wwi.pdf (accessed 8th April 2016).

[11] *Churches for minute's silence to commemorate World War*: www.ekd.de/english/4250-5091.html (accessed 8th April 2016).

> existed or still exists. All parties to the conflict must learn to see themselves and the other side through God's eyes. This is precisely the business of ecumenical dialogue. Our Christian faith obliges us all to be ecumenical.[12]

I cannot ignore the current discussion on protecting *Christian Europe* against the *invasion* of Muslim migrants. Are they really threatening our Christian traditions? European politicians differ profoundly in their views on this dilemma. But Christian leaders seem to be unanimous in appealing to Christ's warning words: 'I was a stranger, but you did not welcome me' (Matt. 25:43). Pope Francis, giving a speech to an audience of French Christians, reflected on Europe's history of migration and the positive impact it has had on its culture today. He described the migrant crisis as 'a social fact' before explaining the change will help Europe in the future by making it more multicultural. He referred to an 'Arab invasion' when he was recalling the moments of mass migration to Europe in history. He went on to explain that the arrival of migrants, predominantly from Syria and Iraq, should be seen from a wider perspective in time and impact. He insisted Europe will 'go forward and find itself enhanced by the exchange among cultures'.[13]

... and with Its Sources of Inspiration

Cardinal Walter Kasper said on different occasions that the ecumenical movement represents one of the brightest points of the twentieth century. 'Ecumenism is a response to the signs of the times. In one of the darkest and most bloodstained centuries, marked by two World Wars which took a toll of millions of lives... Christians have decided to overcome their ancient divisions, showing it is possible to be reconciled despite the faults committed in the past by all.'[14] European history, therefore, is not just a source of conflicts and resentments. An unbiased look at it can discern traces of God's Providence, which prepared the era of Ecumenism. Let me single out some events and facts which can be seen as principal sources of inspiration for future ecumenical work in Central and Eastern Europe:

- Seven *Velehrad Congresses*[15] (also called *Unionist Conventions*) (1907-1936), which paved the way for the Catholic-Orthodox

---

[12] Heinz-Günther Stobbe, 'Religious Implications of Conflicts in Central and Eastern Europe', in *Steps towards Reconciliation* (Budapest: Ecumenical Study Center in Hungary, 1996), 108. The author was Professor of Systematic Theology and Theological Peace Studies at the University of Siegen, Germany, before his retirement.

[13] Jean-Pierre Denis, *Il Papa e i pesci rosa*: www. osservatoreromano.va/it/news/il-papa-e-i-pesci-rosa (accessed 8th April 2016).

[14] Cardinal Walter Kasper, *Charting the Road of the Ecumenical Movement*: www.vatican.va/roman_curia/pontifical_councils/chrstuni/card-kasper-docs/rc_pc_chrstuni_doc_20080117_kasper-ecumenismo_en.html (accessed 8th April 2016).

[15] Velehrad in the Czech Republic is the ancient heart of the Great Moravian Empire. It is the place from where Saints Cyril and Methodius, brothers from Thessaloniki, launched their apostolic mission among the Slavs.

dialogue; the Velehrad Academy organized international meetings of theologians which were preparing the basis for the development of contemporary ecumenism;[16]

- The experience of inter-Church contacts during the *first* (1919-1941) and the *second Yugoslavia* (1945-1991), a place where the western tradition meets the eastern and both live in close neighbourhood with Islam;
- The ecumenical springtime in the Roman Catholic Church after the Second Vatican Council (1962-1965) with its innumerable initiatives;
- The fruits of bilateral and multilateral doctrinal dialogues within the framework of International Theological Commissions;
- The personality, work and ideas of Pope John Paul II; his pastoral visits to the Catholic communities of these countries included ecumenical prayer meetings; ecumenically significant are his Encyclical *Ut unum sint* (1995) and the Apostolic Letter *Lumen Orientale* (1995);
- The excellent ecumenical work of the Vienna foundation *Pro Oriente*, founded by Cardinal Franz König in 1964;
- The three European Ecumenical Assemblies (Basel 1989, Graz 1997, Sibiu 2007) with their broad echo and their inspiring Declarations;
- Two Special Assemblies of the Synod of Bishops for Europe (1991 and 1999) and their respective Post-synodal Apostolic Letters;
- Charta Oecumenica (2001).

I will return to some of these items as I continue.

Challenges and Opportunities of Future Ecumenical Work in Central and Eastern Europe

L. Hogebrink perceives today's European Union 'in deep internal crisis rather than one faced with promising new challenges… Dialogue is more necessary than ever. And in our contested world of growing instability, we as churches must keep reminding the European Union of its original raison d'être of solidarity, peace and reconciliation.'[17] I will attempt to draw attention to some challenges and opportunities which must be on the agenda of churches and peoples in Central and Eastern Europe.

[16] Exhaustive reports on all Velehrad Congresses are available on the homepage of The Tablet: The International Catholic News Weekly (Archive) – e.g.: http://archive.thetablet.co.uk/article/25th-july-1936/26/a-congress-for-reunion (accessed 8th April 2016).

[17] L. Hogebrink, *Europe's Heart and Soul*.

Accomplishing the Purification of the Memory

John Paul II was presumably the first pope who referred to the need of *the purification of the memory*. In his encyclical *Ut unum sint*, he describes the essence and the personal presuppositions of dialogue. It serves as an examination of conscience and is a kind of dialogue of conscience permeated by the spirit of conversion. Dialogue involves purification of memories and prayer for forgiveness of sins; not only personal sins but also social sins and the sinful structures that have contributed and continue to contribute to division and to the reinforcement of division. On several occasions, especially at the liturgy of repentance on the first Sunday of Lent 2000, Pope John Paul II has provided a worthy and moving example of this purification of memories with an attitude of honesty, humility, conversion and prayer for forgiveness of sins. Let me quote the respective passage from his encyclical *Ut unum sint*:

> Nevertheless, besides the doctrinal differences needing to be resolved, Christians cannot underestimate the burden of long-standing misgivings inherited from the past, and of mutual misunderstandings and prejudices. Complacency, indifference and insufficient knowledge of one another often make this situation worse. Consequently, the commitment to ecumenism must be based upon the conversion of hearts and upon prayer, which will also lead to the necessary purification of past memories. With the grace of the Holy Spirit, the Lord's disciples, inspired by love, by the power of the truth and by a sincere desire for mutual forgiveness and reconciliation, are called to re-examine together their painful past and the hurt which that past regrettably continues to provoke even today. All together, they are invited by the ever-fresh power of the Gospel to acknowledge with sincere and total objectivity the mistakes made and the contingent factors at work at the origins of their deplorable divisions (No. 2).

An eminent example of this process found its historical expression in the ecclesial act whereby 'there was removed from memory and from the midst of the Church' the remembrance of the excommunications which nine hundred years before, in 1054, had become the symbol of the schism between Rome and Constantinople. 'That ecclesial event, so filled with ecumenical commitment, took place during the last days of the Council, on 7th December 1965. The Council thus ended with a solemn act which was at once a healing of historical memories, a mutual forgiveness, and a firm commitment to strive for communion' (No. 52).

John Paul II knew very well that the ministry of the Bishop of Rome constitutes a difficulty for most other Christians, 'whose memory is marked by certain painful recollections', and he readily joined his Predecessor Paul VI in asking forgiveness 'to the extent that we are responsible for these' (No. 88).

Pope Benedict XVI, too, often referred to the necessary *purification of the memory* and saw *inner conversion* as the indispensable premise for progress on the ecumenical journey. Among the ideas brainstormed by him and his ex-students at the meeting in 2012, there was also the one of a reciprocal *mea culpa* with Lutheran Churches. The Pope – one of the participants explained – 'always had in mind that there was the need for a purification of memory'.[18]

This idea became a *leitmotiv* in the ecumenical strivings of Cardinal Walter Kasper during his presidency of the Pontifical Council for Promoting Christian Unity. Among the elements of the ecumenical *ethos* he names 'renunciation of all kinds of open or hidden proselytism… healing the wounds left by history (purification of memories), and wider reception of the ecumenical dialogues and agreements already achieved'.[19]

The anniversary of the Reformation (2017) would be such an opportunity to accomplish such a *purification of historical memory* of European churches. On such an occasion, deplorable events and facts such as acts of violence on any side during the Counter-Reformation and in the wars of religion should be ascertained and named. Christians must give to the world an authentic example of reconciliation, showing that we are able to forgive and receive forgiveness.

The necessity of purification of memories is still one of the greatest challenges in Central and Eastern Europe, especially in the area of the Balkans. In the 1990s, all the great changes of the regimes took place. Tensions of an ethnic and nationalist character were engendered on the Balkan Peninsula. The nationalities of the disintegrating Soviet Union also came into severe conflicts with one another. It could be felt that the churches in Central and Eastern Europe were more and more exposed to the spirit of nationalism which, fostered by historical traditions, might, after decades of stifled national sentiments, be burdened with very great dangers to bring the Christian testimony into discredit.[20]

I remember the sense of disappointment among our population during hostile activities of the Yugoslav army from 1991 onwards, since the European institutions were so hesitant to identify and to stop the aggressor. It is quite comforting, therefore, to read confessions such as this: 'Those of us who come from western European countries have a special concern to say explicitly that during those times many of us turned away from the suffering of Christians who had to live in countries under communist rule. We are not talking about forgetting. There is more at stake than just respect for our memories. We see reconciliation among us as constantly trying

[18] *Benedict XVI and the Challenge of Ecumenism*: www.mondayvatican.com/ecumenism-2/benedict-xvi-and-the-challenge-of-ecumenism (accessed 8th April 2016).

[19] Cardinal Walter Kasper, *Present Situation and Future of the Ecumenical Movement*: www.vatican.va/roman_curia/pontifical_councils/chrstuni/card-kasper-docs/rc_pc_chrstuni_doc_20011117_kasper-prolusio_en.html (accessed 8th April 2016).

[20] Stobbe, 'Religious Implications', 193.

anew to take the bitterness and repression out of our memories and in this way to allow them to be healed.'[21]

Theologians in Central and Eastern Europe have made many efforts to support this *healing of memories*, which were so terribly wounded during the wars. In the area of the former Yugoslavia, they initiated a fruitful ecumenical process after Vatican II. Three theological faculties – in Ljubljana (Slovenia), in Zagreb (Croatia) and in Belgrade (Serbia) – organized nine Ecumenical Symposia in the period 1972-1990. This series of ecumenical meetings resumed within a new, much broader frame of participants in 2014 with the interreligious and ecumenical symposium in Maribor (Slovenia). Many other faculties from the region participated. Collaboration with the neighbouring Faculty of Catholic Theology at Graz University (Austria) and the *Graz Process*[22] has been initiated. Contacts between the named faculties have since been renewed, and in many cases mutual agreements on co-operation have been signed.

Reconciliation

Closely linked with *purification of memory* appears the great theme of reconciliation. *Reconciliation: Gift of God and Source of New Life* – this was the theme which gathered European Christians at the Second European Ecumenical Assembly (EEA2) in Graz, Austria, 23rd-29th June 1997. Its *Final Message* puts it thus: 'As Christians in churches which are still divided, we experience fears, tensions, problems and barriers as fellow Europeans, indeed, as do all human beings. But in our hearts there was the strong hope of taking steps on the road towards reconciliation.'[23]

The documents reflect the political situation in Europe, joy for the deep changes in Europe, and fears for an uncertain future:

> What can *reconciliation* mean to us in Europe, when we recall that many among us still suffer from the consequences of two terrible world wars, when we grieve for hundreds of thousands of victims of armed conflicts which have wounded our continent since the fall of the Berlin Wall?... In central and eastern Europe, the social and economic conditions of much of the population have undergone radical changes. In a number of former socialist countries, problems have arisen from the fact that the legal tradition and institutions have been unready to undergo renewal and slow to develop.[24]

---

[21] 'Basic text', in *Reconciliation'*, 41-42.

[22] The *Graz Process* is an instrument to establish a network between European theological faculties of different Christian confessions in the areas of research and theology as well as theological education. It is a platform for the academic exchange of issues concerning theological studies and is based on the understanding of Europe as defined in the *Charta Oecumenica*: https://static.uni-graz.at/fileadmin/kath/Formulare/Grazer_Prozess/folder_2013_2_englisch.pdf (accessed 8th April 2016).

[23] 'Final Message', in *Reconciliation*, 31.

[24] 'Basic text', in *Reconciliation*, 35.

Let me emphasize some leading ideas that were discussed at the Assembly. Reconciliation is a gift of God's mercy. According to Paul 'in Christ, God was reconciling the world to himself... and entrusting the message of reconciliation to us' (2 Cor. 5:19). But we Christians have repeatedly been unworthy messengers of reconciliation. God's Spirit is at work among us as the power of reconciliation. As we come before God, we become mindful of our common brokenness and sinfulness before God. We recognize both our individual and our corporate sin. The reconciliation which comes from God leads us through the narrow gate of repentance into the wide valley of reconciled life.

EEA2 adopted a *Final Message*, a *Basic Text* which described the main statements on the Assembly theme, and developed ethical directions for thinking. This rich and programmatic text addresses the dimensions of evil that are deeply ingrained in our memories as Christian communities in Europe: divisions among the churches; a long history of guilt with regard to the Jewish people; an unworthy attitude to women in our churches and our societies; a rupture between the generations; European superiority and domination over the peoples of the earth; abuse of creation.

Finally, some fundamental dimensions of reconciliation are named, which have not ceased to be opportunities for future ecumenical work: the realm of politics as an important arena for reconciliation; reconciliation in the household of life (or: reconciliation with Nature); reconciliation and the worldwide redistribution of wealth; reconciliation as accepting that we are finite.

Besides the *Basic Text*, EEA2 adopted a set of *Recommendations for Action*, inviting all churches in Europe to 'develop a common study document containing basic ecumenical duties and rights. From this, a series of ecumenical guidelines, rules and criteria could be developed'. This recommendation was the starting-point for the *Charta Oecumenica* process, which can be considered as the most important follow-up action of EEA2. After a comprehensive process of studying and discussing it as a draft, the *Charta Oecumenica* was signed at the Strasbourg Encounter (22nd April 2001) and since then has become the ecumenical document which has been the most widely distributed and discussed in Europe so far.

Enabling Europe to Breathe with Both Lungs

'The Church must breathe with her two lungs!' These words were often pronounced by Pope John Paul II during the first decade of his ministry. The idea of European Christianity, breathing *with both lungs*, has a prophetic significance for the future of Europe: the West needs the East, and vice versa.

Europe is looking back to great personalities of its history, from whom it can draw ecumenical inspiration for its present and its future. Besides St Benedict (sixth century) and the Benedictine monks, his *spiritual sons*, who evangelized predominantly Western Europe, nations in Central and Eastern Europe are used to contemplating with high esteem, the two brothers Saints Cyril and Methodius (ninth century), missionaries of the yet undivided church and fathers of their culture. Their message is more relevant than ever, because it is based on the encounter, dialogue and discovery of 'the other', and contributes to a modern Europe capable of expressing simultaneously all the riches of both Eastern and Western traditions. Their legacy of linking together both traditions and their inculturation efforts among the Slavs are a perpetual source of inspiration for Europe. They oblige us to engage in ecumenical dialogue and the search for unity.

As the newly elected pope, Karol Wojtyła appeared on the balcony of St Peter's (16th October 1978) and delivered a brief speech in Italian, saying that the 'cardinals have called a new bishop of Rome. They called him from a faraway country… far, but always near in the communion of faith and the Christian tradition'. These words can be taken as an anticipation of his later endeavours to bring the East of Europe closer to its West. As a son of a Slav nation, he wanted to sharpen an awareness that Europe means much more than just Western Europe. Indeed, Europe reaches 'from the Atlantic to the Urals, from the North Cape to the Mediterranean', as the *Charta Oecumenica* puts it.[25]

The named pope felt as his sacred duty to pay homage to the two brothers Cyril and Methodius by writing his fourth Encyclical *Slavorum Apostoli* (1985).[26] Methodius ended his days at Velehrad in Greater Moravia one thousand years earlier (885). The Pope introduced his Encyclical by saying: 'Considering the grateful veneration enjoyed for centuries by the holy Brothers from Salonika, especially among the Slav nations, and mindful of their incalculable contribution to the work of proclaiming the gospel among those peoples; mindful too of the cause of reconciliation, friendly co-existence, human development and respect for the intrinsic dignity of every nation… I proclaimed Saints Cyril and Methodius Co-Patrons of Europe' (No. 1).

Reminding the church and the world of the apostolic merits of both the brothers, he continues: 'Cyril and Methodius are, as it were, the connecting links or spiritual bridge between the Eastern and Western traditions, which both come together in the one great Tradition of the universal Church. For us they are the champions and also the patrons of the ecumenical endeavor of the sister Churches of East and West… Cyril and Methodius, in their personality and their work, are figures that awaken in all Christians a great "longing for union" and for unity between the two sister Churches of East and West' (No. 27).

---

[25] *Charta Oecumenica: Guidelines for the Growing Cooperation among the Churches in Europe*: www.ceceurope.org/current-issues/charta-oecumenica (accessed 8th April 2016).

[26] John Paul II, *Slavorum Apostoli*: http://w2.vatican.va/content/john-paul-ii/en/encyclicals/documents/hf_jp-ii_enc_19850602_slavorum-apostoli.html (accessed 8th April 2016).

In his Encyclical *Ut unum sint*, the Pope explains further the metaphor of the two lungs: 'In the first millennium of the history of Christianity, this expression refers primarily to the relationship between Byzantium and Rome. From the time of the Baptism of Rus (988) it comes to have an even wider application: evangelization spread to a much vaster area, so that it now includes the entire Church. If we then consider that the salvific event which took place on the banks of the Dnieper goes back to a time when the Church in the East and the Church in the West were not divided, we understand clearly that the vision of the full communion to be sought is that of unity in legitimate diversity' (No. 54).[27]

What practical aspects can we identify lest this profound metaphor remain just an abstract idea? The Synod of Bishops for Europe is suggesting that '*dialogue*... should be carried on under different aspects (doctrinal, spiritual and practical), following the logic of the exchange of gifts which the Spirit awakens in every Church'.[28] Cardinal W. Kasper puts it thus: 'Dialogue has not only a horizontal but also a vertical dimension; it cannot take place merely on a horizontal level, consisting of meetings, exchanges of points of view or even sharing of gifts, but it has a primarily vertical thrust directed towards the One who is himself our reconciliation.'[29]

Professor Grigorios Larentzakis, director of the Eastern Orthodox theology department at the University of Graz in Austria, appeals for a stronger presence of Orthodox theology at western universities. Graz gives a good example – from the early 1970s, Orthodox theology has been an integral part of teaching and research programmes at its university. According to Larentzakis, courses of Orthodox theology at western faculties would help to rectify traditional prejudiced notions formed during the period of mutual estrangement and ignorance. Students should be

---

[27] The 2014 crisis in the Ukraine strengthens the argument of the need to build bridges between East and West. Henry A. Kissinger wrote: 'Far too often the Ukrainian issue is posed as a showdown: whether Ukraine joins the East or the West. But if Ukraine is to survive and thrive, it must not be either side's outpost against the other – it should function as a bridge between them... The west is largely Catholic; the east largely Russian Orthodox. The west speaks Ukrainian; the east speaks mostly Russian. Any attempt by one wing of Ukraine to dominate the other – as has been the pattern – would lead eventually to civil war or break-up. To treat Ukraine as part of an East-West confrontation would scuttle for decades any prospect to bring Russia and the West – especially Russia and Europe – into a co-operative international system'. Henry A. Kissinger, 'To settle the Ukraine crisis, start at the end', in *Washington Post* (5th March 2014): https://www.washingtonpost.com /opinions/henry-kissinger-to-settle-the-ukraine-crisis-start-at-the-end/2014/03/05/46dad868-a496-11e3-8466-d34c451760b9_story.html (accessed 8th April 2016).

[28] John Paul II, *Post-synodal Apostolic Exhortation Ecclesia in Europa*, No. 31: http://w2.vatican.va/content/john-paul-ii/en/apost_exhortations/documents/hf_jpii_exh_20030628_ecclesia-in-europa.html (accessed 8th April 2016).

[29] Cardinal Walter Kasper, *Nature and Purpose of Ecumenical Dialogue*: www.vatican.va/roman_curia/pontifical_councils/chrstuni/card-kasper-docs/rc_pc_chrstuni_doc_20030227_ecumenical-dialogue_en.html (accessed 8th April 2016).

informed of the outcomes of theological dialogues between churches. This would promote the process of their reception and realization.[30]

Charta Oecumenica, too, obliges the churches 'to promote ecumenical openness and co-operation in Christian education, and in theological training, continuing education and research' (No. 3).

Apostolic Letter *Orientale Lumen*[31] is supporting the same idea as it writes that 'meeting one another regularly is very important... It is important to acknowledge the spiritual riches of the different Christian traditions, to learn from one another and so to receive these gifts... Another form of meeting consists in welcoming Orthodox professors and students to the Pontifical Universities and other Catholic academic institutions. We will continue to do all we can to extend this welcome on a wider scale' (No. 25).

I am not going to enlarge upon the official theological dialogues, which certainly represent a major challenge and opportunity for ecumenical work. In this context, let me state that dialogue with its twofold dimension (*dialogue of truth* and *dialogue of love*) means more than just an exchange of thoughts and insights. It takes the form of an *exchange of gifts*, giving churches and communities the opportunity to share between them their own richnesses.

Anniversary of the Reformation: Occasion of Joy and Sorrow

In 2017 Protestants commemorated the 500th anniversary of Martin Luther's publicizing his Ninety-Five Theses about conditions prevalent in the church at the time, at the Castle Church in Wittenberg. With this act of protest, Luther (1483-1546) is regarded as having triggered the worldwide Reformation. Lutherans did not want to keep this commemoration just among themselves, but also to celebrate it together with Catholics. This invitation evoked many questions and dilemmas as to the form of possible participation.

I am turning some attention to this theme since the presence of Protestant churches is quite considerable in Central and Eastern Europe.

Pope Benedict XVI, addressing the delegation from the United Evangelical Lutheran Church in Germany on 24th January 2011 at a private audience, emphasised that on this occasion Lutherans and Catholics would have an opportunity 'to celebrate throughout the world a common ecumenical commemoration, to grapple at the world level with fundamental issues', and to do this not 'in the form of a triumphant celebration, but as a

---

[30] Grigorios Larentzakis, 'Orthodoxe Theologie an westlichen Universitäten', *G2W – Glaube in der 2. Welt* 7/8 (2003), 18-21.

[31] John Paul II, *Apostolic Letter Orientale Lumen*: http://w2.vatican.va/content/john-paul-ii/en/apost_letters/1995/documents/hf_jp-ii_apl_02051995_orientale-lumen.html (accessed 8th April 2016).

common profession of faith in the One Triune God, in common obedience to Our Lord and to his Word'.[32]

Cardinal Kurt Koch, President of the Pontifical Council for Promoting Christian Unity, presented the official stand of the Catholic Church on the possible common commemoration of the Reformation (Geneva, 17th June 2013). Here I quote some of his statements, where the idea of *purification of memories* appears again:

> In accepting the invitation, the Pope at the same time expressed three specific expectations, which we want to consider together. For him it is first of all important that in this celebration an important place is given to 'common prayer and to heartfelt entreaties addressed to our Lord Jesus Christ for the forgiveness of mutual wrongs and for the faults related to those divisions'. But also, for Pope Benedict, part of this purification of memories and of conscience is the 'reciprocal exchange on how we should appraise the 1,500 years that preceded the Reformation, and which are therefore common to us both'. And thirdly, Pope Benedict emphasised that it is particularly important to 'pray together assiduously for the help of God and the assistance of the Holy Spirit' in order to 'take further steps towards the unity that we long for, and not to be satisfied with what has been achieved so far'.

Cardinal Koch then refers to the ambivalent character of this anniversary:

> One of the first priorities in relation to common commemoration of the Reformation is also the need to listen to one another, to hear what this commemoration really means for both sides. It is understandable that, for you as Lutherans, what is paramount is joy over the rediscovery by the Reformation above all of the gospel message of justification through grace alone. We Catholics share this joy with you: but at the same time we ask for your understanding that this Reformation commemoration is associated with deep sorrow, because it led to the division of the Church and many negative consequences.[33]

According to Cardinal Koch, the commemoration of the Reformation has to be perceived as an ecumenical opportunity:

> A common Reformation commemoration in 2017 will be a good opportunity if that year is not the conclusion but a new beginning of the ecumenical struggle for full communion between the churches and ecclesial communities that emerged from the Reformation and the Catholic Church, in particular in the triad of repentance, gratitude and hope – from which no part can be omitted if it is to be perceived as a symphonic triad chord… It remains to be hoped that, 500 years later, the Reformation commemoration of the year 2017

[32] Cardinal Kurt Koch, *From Conflict to Communion: Principles and Possibilities for the Ongoing Ecumenical Process*: www.vatican.va/roman_curia/pontifical_councils/chrstuni/lutheran-fed-docs/rc_pc_chrstuni_doc_20130617_presentation-card-koch_en.html (accessed 8th April 2016).

[33] Koch, *From Conflict to Communion.*

> can provide further clarification on the nature of the Church, and will thus serve the growing ecclesial communion between Lutherans and Catholics.[34]

I was happy to hear that Pope Francis plans to visit Sweden in October 2016 to participate in an ecumenical service and the beginning of a year of activities to mark the anniversary. Leaders from the Catholic Church and the Lutheran World Federation will meet on 31st October for the ecumenical celebration in Lund, Sweden, where the LWF was founded in 1947. The event will highlight ecumenical developments between Catholics and Lutherans over the past fifty years. The announcement came on 25th January, the feast of the conversion of St Paul, the last day of the Week of Prayer for Christian Unity.[35]

Conclusion

I have tried to open some windows upon the vast panorama of ecumenism and delineate some prospects for its future. The list is far from complete. Many further areas and aspects would deserve our attention. One of them is *spiritual ecumenism*, which should be regarded as the soul or the heart of the whole ecumenical movement and which includes change of heart, holiness of life and prayer. At the core of Christian unity is prayer because, when we pray, we pray to God in Jesus Christ, and the closer we come to Jesus Christ, the closer we are to each other.

An atmosphere of prayer and repentance characterized the conference on Christian Faith and Human Enmity in 1995 (held at Kecskemet, Hungary), which I took part in. At the time, armed conflicts and war crimes were still ravaging the Balkans. The concluding *Letter to Christians and Churches of Central, Eastern and South-eastern Europe* insists upon the need for prayer and *metanoia*:

> We met in worship, Bible study and prayer, lectures, discussion groups… We are very aware of and saddened by the brokenness and suffering of our world, especially in the Southeastern and Eastern parts of Europe… In our study of the Biblical story of Jesus and the disciples in the boat during a storm (Matt. 8:23) we gained the insight that Jesus continues to be with us in the current storms of life. We receive the assurance that Jesus can transform our enmities and fears into faith and hope. Our certainty is that history is ultimately in God's hands… God will, indeed, bring reconciliation and justice… We do not wish to indulge in allocating blame but have joined in intense awareness of our common shortcomings and sins of omission and commission. With a

---

[34] Cardinal Kurt Koch, *The Commemoration of the Reformation as an Ecumenical Opportunity Towards a Joint Declaration on Church, Ministry and Eucharist*: www.ekumenia.fi/data/liitteet/2015_helsinki-commemoration_of_reformation.pdf (accessed 8th April 2016).

[35] Carol Glatz, 'Pope plans to visit Sweden to commemorate Reformation anniversary', *Catholic News Service* (25th January 2016): www.catholicnews.com/services/englishnews/2016/pope-visit-sweden-commemorate-reformation-anniversary.cfm (accessed 8th April 2016).

> contrite heart, we admit our individual and collective failure to live up to the image intended for us by God... Instead of living as sisters and brothers, we have become aliens and even enemies who inflict unspeakable suffering upon each other, such as massacres, forcible migrations, hostile propaganda, and denial of basic human rights. We repent for whatever we may have done or failed to do that has contributed to the pain of our fellow human beings.[36]

The three European Ecumenical Assemblies (EEA1 – Basel 1989, EEA2 – Graz 1997, EEA3 – Sibiu 2007) deserve closer attention because two of them took place in the area of Central or Eastern Europe. They have proved to be an excellent instrument of encounter between churches, nations, pastors and the faithful; their messages (peace, justice, ecology, reconciliation, centrality of Christ), resumed and applied in the *Charta Oecumenica*, need actualization and continuation. The *Final Message* of the Sibiu Assembly made a step in this direction, adding ten *Recommendations* to the text.[37]

Charta Oecumenica is definitely a stimulating guideline for our ecumenical journey in Europe.[38] It describes fundamental ecumenical responsibilities, from which follow a number of guidelines and commitments. It is designed to promote an ecumenical culture of dialogue and co-operation at all levels of church life, and to provide agreed criteria for this. Its fourth chapter affirms that at the 'European level it is necessary to strengthen co-operation between CEC and CCEE, and to hold further European Ecumenical Assemblies'. Following this recommendation, the Assembly in Sibiu was prepared.

The profound changes in Europe in the last ten years and the accompanying tensions would suggest the need of another Assembly. I had the opportunity to participate in two of them (Graz and Sibiu) and experienced them as moments of grace. Every participant would agree with Cardinal W. Kasper who wrote: 'In the ultimate analysis, ecumenism is an adventure of the Spirit.'

I want to conclude by quoting a beautiful, hopeful text from the oft-mentioned encyclical *Ut unum sint*:

> To believe in Christ means to desire unity... The Church... asks the Spirit for the grace to strengthen her own unity and to make it grow towards full communion with other Christians... And should we ask if all this is possible, the answer will always be yes. It is the same answer which Mary of Nazareth heard: with God nothing is impossible (No. 9; 102).

---

[36] 'The Kecskemet Ecumenical Conference Letter', in *Steps towards Reconciliation* (Budapest: Ecumenical Study Center in Hungary,1996), 188-89.
[37] *The light of Christ shines upon all! Assembly Message*: www.eea3.org/documenti/final/FinalmessageEN.pdf (accessed 8th April 2016).
[38] *Charta Oecumenica.*

MISSION IN THE CZECH REPUBLIC: A SEARCH FOR A RELEVANT MISSION THEOLOGY IN A POST-SECULAR ENVIRONMENT

Pavel Černý

Introduction

The present paper explores the missionary practice of the gospel in the context of post-communist Czech Republic. It first introduces the context of historical and political changes that have definitely altered the mindset of the Czech people and affected the life and work of Christian churches. The paper than gives a critical overview of sociological and cultural context and the specific features of the Czech environment. The contemporary mission in multi-faith situation is then developed with a focus on the question of secularism. Finally, contemporary trends in mission in the context of European situation and theology are discussed and some possibilities of church work proposed.

Changing Context

Historical and Political Changes

Many theories have been developed about why Czechs are so indifferent to religion, especially to Christian churches and organized religion. Some historians speak about the long-term influence of the horrible events of the Thirty Years' War (1618-1648). This war was followed by 150 years of severe counter-reformation which almost destroyed the Protestant Christianity majority. Many negative attitudes of contemporary Czech citizens towards the church correspond with the forcible re-Catholicization of the predominantly Protestant nation. The Habsburgs are linked with three centuries of violent religious, political and nationalistic pressure.

After the break-up of the Austro-Hungarian state in 1918, the leaders of free Czechoslovakia interpreted the meaning of Czech history. The past history of the Hussite movement and the tradition of the Old Unity of Czech Brethren were highlighted. This interpretation of history was definitely anti-clerical. The First Czechoslovak Republic put a lot of stress on non-Catholic forms of church. Many people (about three million) left the Roman Catholic Church after 1918. This was the movement 'away from Rome'. Some of them just left, some established the new denomination called the Czechoslovak Hussite Church and some joined other Protestant denominations. What began as a political ambition to 'break from Vienna' continued as a movement 'away from Rome,' because the Austro-Hungarian Empire was politically connected with the Roman Catholic ideology and religious oppression. Unfortunately, many of these changes were motivated by nationalism and politics and not for spiritual reasons.

During World War II and after it, the alienation between the church and a large part of the Czech nation increased. There was a strong shift of many Czech intellectuals towards leftist ideology. Some of them became communists while others inclined to a more moderate form of left-wing philosophy. The working class considered the Czech churches to be more linked with factory owners, i.e. not being interested in unfavourable working conditions. The working class movement often accepted hostile attitudes towards the church. The communist ideology of Marx-Leninism provided a substitute religion for its adherents. But still in the 1950s more than 90% of Czech citizens had some sort of religious affiliation.

The Christian churches in the Czech Republic survived more than forty years of permanent persecution and harassment from the communist regime. In the Czech Republic, all church social projects were interrupted, church educational and social organizations forbidden and their buildings confiscated. This happened in 1949 through the implementation of the new religious laws. Church mission strategy was mainly transformed into so-called 'centripetal mission'.[1] Churches were allowed to conduct their limited and controlled activities inside their buildings under the control of the government officials and the secret police. In spite of that situation, centripetal mission brought some fruit and churches developed new strategies of rather closed but solid fellowships. There was always some segment of underground mission activities present. Churches strived to continue mission activities in small house groups, camps, sport clubs, etc. This work was constantly under attack from the totalitarian regime and often penetrated from the inside by those who collaborated with political power. In spite of various missional endeavours, many churches were diverted from mission into closed ghettos, focusing on their own needs.

Political changes and the so-called 'Velvet Revolution' in 1989 in the former Czechoslovakia brought many new challenges. Almost overnight, churches were given full political and religious freedom. Immediately, new possibilities opened up to serve society. Churches were allowed to use public media (radio, TV and publishing) to establish educational

[1] Centripetal mission, evangelism, or churches are 'centre-seeking'. They push towards the centre, revolve around the middle, and are rather passive. This type of mission was predominant in the Old Testament where Jerusalem, the tabernacle, and the temple all gathered people in. The message was, 'Come to the blessing!' Centripetal and centrifugal types of mission – these terms first used in: Johannes Blauw, *The Missionary Nature of the Church: A Survey of the Biblical Theology of Mission* (New York: McGraw-Hill, 1962).

institutions, to renew social ministry and to develop chaplaincies in the army, in prisons and medical institutions. There have been many things to renew and transform. Unfortunately, not many Christians had been trained for these new situations. In many churches, a centripetal mission mentality persisted.

After the 1989 'Velvet Revolution', Christian churches were viewed in a positive light because of their certain opposition to communist ideology and because of the suffering of many pastors, priests and other Christians. In 1991,[2] 44% of the population professed some form of religious affiliation. However, this rate of popularity for the church did not last long. Apparently, the hopes that had been placed in the church were not realized and the traditional distrust of religious institutions quickly followed. The Czechs have a deeply-rooted distrust of all institutions and also the church.

> A typical assumption of a large part of Czech society is the suspicion that institutions do not pursue the interests of the citizens they are supposed to serve, but in reality just serve themselves and only pursue their own interests in the form of power and money. The Czech distrust of religious institutions is a specific example of this general phenomenon.[3]

Czech society does not want a rich and powerful church. People expect the church to be humble and ready to serve. The church should be modest and self-sacrificing. Then, the church lost additional popularity due to prolonged negotiations with the state regarding property confiscated by the communist regime. It took 22 years to solve that problem, the Czech Republic being the last one to do so out of all the post-communist countries. Czech society would like to see churches caring for old, sick and dying people and taking care of historical sites.[4] Long-term political disputes over the restitution of church property severely damaged the reputation and credibility of the Czech churches. Today, most Czechs don't believe in God and have negative attitudes towards churches, but on the other hand, they have very high inclination to various forms of religiosity.[5]

The Social and Cultural Context

Speaking from the perspective of mission within the Czech Republic, I have to mention our usual prerogative. Our country is considered to be one

---

[2] Government census: https://www.czso.cz

[3] Pavel Hošek, 'Discerning the Signs of the Times in Post-communist Czech Republic: A Historical, Sociological and Missiological Analysis of Contemporary Czech Culture', in Tomáš Halík and Pavel Hošek (eds), *A Czech Perspective on Faith in a Secular Age* (Washington, DC: The Council for Research in Values and Philosophy, 2015), 23.

[4] Zdeněk Nešpor, *Příliš slábi ve víře: Česká (ne)religiozita v evropském kontextu* (*Too Weak in Faith: Czech (Non)-Religiosity in European Context*) (Prague: Kalich, 2010), 99.

[5] Dana Hamplová, *Náboženství v české společnosti na prahu 3. století* (*Religion on the Threshold of the Third Millennium*) (Prague: Charles University, 2013), 136.

of the most secular and atheistic countries in the world.[6] The index of Christianity is also very low, and according to the statistics, we hold the last position within the European Union, even lower than Sweden, Denmark and Belgium.[7] Only a very small proportion of people profess faith in God, just 21% of Czech citizens. Czech atheism is considered to be unique. According to sociological research as well as practical church experience, there are not many convinced atheists in the Czech Republic. Still, according to the statistics, the Czech Republic holds the fourth position in the EU in their use of superstition (magic, astrology, attempting to foretell the future by means of horoscopes, faith in various transcendental powers, etc.). However, these statistics as well as a recent census in 2011 are not convincing regarding atheism because almost half of the population did not answer the questions regarding religion and Christian churches.[8] I agree with religionist Pavel Hošek who says:

> It is interesting to note that Czech atheists do not seem to be particularly orthodox in their atheism either. According to a number of surveys, those citizens of the Czech Republic who either profess themselves to be atheists or say that they are without religious affiliation (which does not have to be the same thing), admit the existence of supernatural phenomena and take an interest in them.[9]

Censuses in 2001 and in 2011 showed a dramatic decrease in membership of the three largest church denominations. On the other hand, there was definite growth in some of the smaller protestant church denominations, with some of them experiencing considerable growth. It is true that churches with more formal membership dropped, but their church attendance has not declined dramatically in the last few years. It seems that so-called 'Volkskirche' is slowly dying in comparison with certain growth of professing forms of church ecclesiological models independent of confession.

	1950	**1991**	**2001**	**2011**
Roman Catholic Church	76.3 %	39 %	26.8%	10.3%
Czech Brethren Evangelical	4.5 %	2.0 %	1.1 %	0.5 %
Czechoslovak Hussite Church	10.6 %	1.7 %	1.0 %	0.4 %
Other churches	2.4 %	1.0 %	3.2 %	2.8 %
Believers without church affiliation	-	-	-	6.7 %
Without religion	5.8 %	39.9 %	59.0 %	34.2 %
Not answered	0.3 %	16.2 %	8.8 %	45.1 %

---

[6] www.osacr.cz/2012/05/16/potvrzeno-cesi-jsou-nejateistictejsi-stat-na-svete (accessed 1st May 2015).

[7] Hamplová, *Náboženství v české společnosti na prahu 3. století*, 74.

[8] https://www.czso.cz/documents/10180/29508960/1702201402.pdf/35 de35a0-fb2d-4921-9416-7d01fb0c8e05?version=1.0 (27th February 2014), (accessed 15th May 2015).

[9] Hošek, 'Discerning the Signs of the Times in the Post-Communist Czech Republic', 26.

Secularization or the Return of Religion?

Friedrich Nietzsche foretold the death of God and many after him monotonously repeated, 'God is dead.' But it seems that the phrases 'God is back' or 'gods are back' would fit the current situation better. Everything points towards the fact that the global trend of secularization has stopped. In 1990, 67% of people professed one of the four world's largest religions (Christianity, Islam, Buddhism and Hinduism). In 2005, it was up to 73%. According to estimates, it will be 80% of the world's population by 2025.

In the 1960s and 1970s, many theological documents considered secularization irreversible. European academic theology in particular has been strongly affected by the concept of secularization as church membership declined year after year and as Christianity gradually became a minority religion.[10] Unquestionably, certain waves of secularization have taken place. On the other hand, it is also true that on a global scale the process of secularization has not been as successful. Be it the effect of population migrations or the spreading of post-modern paradigm of spirituality and its desire for transcendence, we can now speak about the 'return of gods' in Europe and in the Czech Republic as well.

Zdeněk R. Nešpor offers a thorough sociological analysis of secularization trends and their opposites in his recently published book, *Too Weak in Faith: Czech (Non)-religiosity in European Context.*[11] He strongly challenges Europe's understanding of secularization. The publication gathers material which strongly shakes the stereotypes of our understanding of secularization. For a long time, many have thought that the whole world would develop according to the western secularization model. However, the idea of science and technology replacing and destroying the religious realm, supported by Marx-Leninist propaganda, faded away. Nešpor does not hesitate to talk about the 'secularist ideology', which represented a fundamental misunderstanding of religion and its function.[12] In the current Czech situation, it is essential to push secularist

---

[10] A lot of inspiration to overestimate secularization comes out of the late writings of Dietrich Bonhoeffer. It is well documented in David F. Wells, *The Search for Salvation* (Leicester, UK: IVP, 1978). Also, e.g. Charles Van Engen, *Mission on the Way: Issues in Mission Theology* (Grand Rapids, MI: Baker Books, 1996), 148-49. Ján Liguš approves that those exponents, welcoming all kinds of secularization trends, saw in Bonhoeffer's fragments from the Nazi prison more than the author wanted to say. Ján Liguš, *Christus Praesens: Ekleziologie Dietricha Bonhoeffera se zřetelem k reformačnímu odkazu Martina Luthera* (ThD thesis, Komenského evangelická teologická fakulta, Prague, 1981). Overestimation of secularization is seen also in documents, e.g. World Council of Churches, *Minutes of the Second Meeting of the Commission on World Mission and Evangelism, Mexico City, 8 December 1963* (Geneva: WCC, 1963), 121. Johannes C. Hoekendijk, *The Church Inside Out* (Philadelphia, PA: Westminster, 1966). World Council of Churches, *The Church for Others and the Church for the World: A Quest for Structures for Missionary Congregations* (Geneva: WCC, 1967), 17-18.

[11] Zdeněk Nešpor, *Příliš slábi ve víře: Česká (ne)religiozita v evropském kontextu* (2010).

[12] Nešpor, *Příliš slábi ve víře*, 34-35.

ideology out of our society, which relied on the wrong presuppositions of a decline in religiosity.

Nešpor concludes: 'Contemporary Czech society is still not as atheistic as it might like to "proudly" think and claim for itself. It is rather anti-clerical. Generally speaking, Czechs refuse the Christian God, but they do not cease to believe in something, identifying it occasionally with the structures of the fragmentary Christian memory tucked in [their] social consciousness.'[13] He adds: 'Czechs have chosen the path of progressive de-religionization, which they have not managed to pursue properly yet, and the effects of their ambiguous relation to religion have been apparent until today.'[14]

In bookstores, it is possible to see a large number of books dedicated to religion and various spiritual-philosophical paths. Many people buy and read books about an immaterial explanation of life and reality. This tendency reveals itself in many alternative lifestyles, medicinal approaches and diets, physical fitness programmes and ecological living modes that seek to be in harmony with nature and cosmic forces. According to the 2011 census, there are 750,000 people in the Czech Republic who consider themselves believers but who refuse for various reasons to associate with any church.[15] This makes them the second largest religious group in the country.

Commercialized spirituality is simply a market economy issue. It offers what the people are asking for. The production and distribution of such religious and pseudo-religious goods is more cost-efficient than for goods with a material value.

What are the Current Needs in the Czech Context?

A Missional Situation

The current missional situation is actually much closer to that of the first century AD than to that of four or five decades ago. Today we also encounter polytheism, a myriad of mystery cults and various forms of old and new religions. It is quite obvious that communist totalitarian ideology also had its religious content and character. From this point of view, it is quite surprising that an emphasis on the rational aspects of Christian faith still prevails over religious experience in many Protestant churches. The gospel is very often presented as a system of beliefs which must be accepted by human reason. On the other hand, the contemporary situation

---

[13] Nešpor, *Příliš slábi ve víře*, 188.
[14] Nešpor, *Příliš slábi ve víře*, 190.
[15] Believers with any association with churches: https://www.czso.cz/documents/10180/29508960/1702201402.pdf/35de35a0-fb2d-4921-9416-7d01fb0c8e05?version=1.0 (27th February 2014), (accessed 15th May 2015).

shows a human hunger for religious experiences. Pietistic, Charismatic, Pentecostal and even Roman Catholic emphases on religious experience seem to be the complement to traditional Protestant emphases on rational aspects of our Christianity.

The gospel of Christ, which crosses all human boundaries, connects, unifies and overcomes differences, contradictions and disputes. How can the gospel of Christ influence the Christian church's mission and its practice of the gospel in the secular environment of the Czech Republic?

The Specific Czech Environment

According to sociological research, Czech people are not so much against religion in various forms but against *organized* religion. Evangelical theologian Pavel Hošek suggests moving 'from a traditional *believers – non-believers* paradigm to the more illuminating and adequate *seekers – dwellers* paradigm'.[16] The Czech situation completely differs from all the neighbouring countries (Austria, Germany, Slovakia, Poland). All those countries have a much higher number of people with positive attitudes towards faith and membership of a church. In the Czech Republic, the so-called 'grey zone' between traditional believers and convinced atheists continues to increase.

Roman Catholic theologian and sociologist Tomáš Halík emphasises that our churches must focus their outreach on this 'grey zone' of seekers. It is obvious, given Czech historical and cultural development, that the faith of seekers tends to be wary of religion. Czech seekers are very shy about their faith. In this specific Czech situation, Halík and Hošek argue for a kenotic hermeneutics of contemporary culture, guided by the biblical metaphor of 'discerning the signs of the times' (Matt. 16:2-3).[17] Their missional suggestions for the churches 'includes listening attentively to and trying to understand the actual questions people are asking, as they are articulated in one way or another in art, in philosophy, in the climate of society, in changes of public opinion in media and so on'.[18]

Summary

Surprisingly, Czech atheists are not particularly orthodox in their atheism. It means that suggested concepts about continuing secularization are not confirmed. There is a larger segment of the population that admits the

---

[16] Pavel Hošek, 'Towards a Kenotic Hermeneutics of Contemporary Czech Culture', in Tomáš Halík and Pavel Hošek (eds), *A Czech Perspective on Faith in a Secular Age* (Washington, DC: The Council for Research in Values and Philosophy, 2015), 2ff. Charles Taylor has offered this distinction in *A Secular Age* (Cambridge, MA: Harvard University Press, 2007).

[17] Halík and Hošek, *A Czech Perspective on Faith in a Secular Age*, 5.

[18] Halík and Hošek, *A Czech Perspective on Faith in a Secular Age*, 5.

existence of supernatural phenomena and takes an interest in them. These findings must be taken into account in developing missional approach.

The 'Seekers – dwellers' paradigm seems to respond well to the missional situation and mindset of the general Czech population. Kenotic hermeneutics can be a key concept for the contemporary mission of Christian churches. This approach and missional dialogue with people seems to be important in the post-communist situation, where people have been exposed to various kinds of indoctrination for a long time.

Figuratively, we can in these days speak about the 'return of gods' in Europe and in the Czech Republic as well. The Czech population is not so much atheistic but rather anti-clerical and against organized religion. Many people seek a mystical explanation of life and reality and very often they are open to various spiritual experiences. The post-modern mindset values spiritual experience very much.

Changing Responses

Traditional paradigm: CENTRIPETAL

Changing the Paradigm of Mission

Due to the fact that it has been often misused by various ideologies and distorted by incorrect historical interpretations, the term 'mission' in the Czech context has evolved merely into a swear-word or at least into a word with pejorative connotations in many churches. Just to speak about mission under the oppressive communist regime was politically incorrect and could lead to the loss of professional jobs or of the possibility of studying. The neglect of mission may be the result of the 41 years the Czech churches experienced in the totalitarian era, when very limited and restricted religious freedoms were preserved, with a focus mainly on the performance of liturgical acts inside churches, chapels and prayer rooms. The churches were not allowed to appear in public life. Thus churches and congregations, little by little, became used to caring more for themselves than for missionary work and evangelization outside their communities.

Despite all these distortions, the term 'mission' is still in use to indicate the call of the contemporary church in the world. The term still appears in the language of Czech ecumenical dialogue, and today it is a permanent issue in academic theological research. No wonder – as *missio Dei,* it represents the key concept of contemporary biblical hermeneutics and has never ceased to be an inspiring model of church service to society. The mission of the church is again more closely related to the practice of the gospel in the secular environment of the Czech Republic; through its new understanding, which springs from re-reading Bible in a missionary perspective and a radical contextualization of the gospel of Christ, it inspires ecumenical dialogue, helps churches in their orientation, and leads to their co-operation in the field of improvement of the current practice of the gospel.

Repeatedly, articles, publications and dialogues reveal the accent on the gospel of Christ, which crosses various borders between people, and connects, unifies and overcomes differences, contradictions and disputes. I try to respond on the basis of the biblical theology of mission, which deals both with evangelization and social action, i.e. the church in service to the world.

Even now, some Christians react antagonistically upon even hearing the terms 'mission' or 'evangelization', considering them to be anachronisms or relics of the past.[19] Surprisingly, such an attitude cannot be found in the world church ecumenical organizations – be it the World Council of Churches, which has produced a vast number of missiological documents, or the Community of Protestant Churches in Europe – the Leuenberg Church Fellowship[20] or the Conference of European Churches. *Charta Oecumenica*, a document signed by a majority of churches in the Czech Republic, says: 'The most important role of churches in Europe is the collective preaching of the gospel in words and acts for salvation of all people.'[21] Important conferences of the world ecumenical movement never miss out on the issue of mission and evangelization. The same can be said about the Roman Catholic Church, which often mentions the issue in its encyclicals and other important documents.

If we consider the wider ecumenical context, we can observe that it has been the three recent popes who heavily influenced the discussion on mission and evangelization by their encyclicals and exhortations. I have in mind especially *Evangelii nuntiandi* by Paul VI[22] and *Redemptoris missio* (about the permanent validity for missionary work) by John Paul II[23] and *Evangelii Gaudium* by Francis.[24] These emphases on mission and evangelism proclaimed from outside the country, acclaimed officially by some Christians, stated clearly and plainly that Europe needs a new evangelization. Our understanding of mission has been helped recently by

---

[19] Exceptions to this trend are the following publications and articles: Josef Smolík, *Současné pokusy o interpretaci evangelia* (*Contemporary Attempts to Interpret the Gospel*) (Prague: KEBF, 1968); Ibid., 'Evangelizace: Ekumenická diskuse', *Křesťanská revue,* 48.1 (1981), 5-10; Pavel Filipi, 'Chudým evangelium se zvěstuje', *Křesťanská revue,* 50 (1983), 123. Articles by Miroslav Heryán and Cyril Horák are also worth mentioning.

[20] A document named: 'Evangelizing: Protestant perspectives for the Churches in Europe. 2002-2004', issued in 2006: www.leuenberg.net/sites/default/files/publications/evangelising.pdf (accessed 30th July 2015).

[21] *Charta Oecumenica*, Art. 2: www.ceceurope.org/introduction/charta-oecumenica (accessed 30th July 2015).

[22] Paul VI, *Evangelii nuntiandi* (Prague: Zvon, 1990).

[23] John Paul II, *Redemptoris missio* (Prague: Zvon, 1994).

[24] Francis, *Evangelii Gaudium* (Czech edition; Prague: Paulínky, 2014).

the WCC mission document *Together Towards Life*,[25] and *The Cape Town Commitment* of the Lausanne Movement.[26] All these documents strongly support the importance of church-based mission and evangelism in these days.

The study of mission and evangelization in the Czech environment is evolving very slowly, and is still not adequately reflected at an academic level.[27] Nevertheless, it is worth mentioning that interest in the issue is slowly increasing and a historic first study day, organized by the Ecumenical Council of Churches in the Czech Republic, focused on the understanding of mission in its particular ecclesial structures.[28]

In the Czech environment, theology professor Pavel Filipi often treats mission and related issues in his publications in connection with ecclesiology. He emphasizes that the church, mirroring the inner relations within the Trinity, must have a purpose other than itself: it is here for the world. The place of the church in the divine plan of salvation is defined by its sending out into the world. In a certain perspective, the church does not perform mission, but rather the church as such is God's mission to the world. This is exactly where Filipi seeks its *raison d'être* and the norm for its ecclesiological structures. The unity of church also has its missionary dimension and is a clear testimony of faith to the world. Besides the passive testimony of the church, i.e. when the church makes its teaching public and offers its 'goods' to people, there is also the active model: mission work and evangelization, marching across the market places of the world with a prophetic appeal, a kind of a 'home delivery'.[29] According to Matthew 28:19, the Great Commission, i.e. entrusting the disciples of Jesus with a missionary quest, is today more understood as approaching people in their environment and conditions, seeking a common language, not respecting any borders or lines of division. Filipi concludes: 'From the eschatological perspective, the world is more important than the church. A Noah's Ark mentality, the high self-confidence of an isolated island of a few rescued

---

[25] 'Together Towards Life: Mission and Evangelism in Changing Landscapes' (A New WCC Affirmation on Mission and Evangelism, 2012, Presented to the 10th General Assembly of WCC, Busan, Korea 2013).

[26] The Third Lausanne Congress on World Evangelization, 2010. (Printed in Czech: Závazek z Kapského Města, *Theologia vitae*, Vol. 2014, No. 2, 149-204.)

[27] *Do we need missiology? And if so, why do we not teach it and develop it systematically?* (Conference proceedings from the first conference of the Central European Centre for Mission Studies ECMS issued in the Czech-Slovak and English version by the CECMS, Prague, 2007).

[28] The first study day of the Czech Ecumenical Council of Churches took place in Prague on 24th May 2004. Various perspectives on mission and missionary work were presented there: the Roman-Catholic (Bishop František Radkovský), the Eastern Orthodox (Josef Hauzar), the mainline Protestant (Ladislav Beneš), and the evangelical (Pavel Černý).

[29] Pavel Filipi, *Církev a církve: Kapitoly z ekumenické eklesiologie* (Brno, Czech Republic: CDK, 2000), 34-35.

from the global flood, does not have a place in the universal vision of the Kingdom of God.'[30]

However, application and development of the active model of the church based on mission and evangelization is rather problematic in the Czech environment. After all, it means approaching people, searching for a comprehensible language, ignoring any limitations and disturbing the self-confidence of 'an isolated island of a few rescued'. This is exactly the point where we have to deal with serious questions of our understanding of the missionary work of the church. I believe that a new paradigm of mission is slowly evolving, putting more stress on centrifugal mission. A new paradigm of mission directs instead from the centre to the margins, following more closely a New Testament pattern.

TOWARDS A CULTURE-SENSITIVE AND CONTEXTUALIZED MISSION PARADIGM

Missiologist and theologian Jonathan J. Bonk has written, 'Theology can be liberated from cultural bounds only through mission.'[31] This understanding is hardly new. We can verify its validity on the pages of Scripture itself, depicted in the development of the early church. An archetypical bearer of this missionary task is the apostle Paul, who in preaching the gospel links Jewish and Greek thought. His theology is shaped by his mission, which entails a spiritual struggle to contextualize the gospel in a foreign cultural environment.

Another problem is that the missionary work of congregations, parishes and churches is often still affected by secularizing trends. Today, we encounter modern polytheism and new religious movements and cults offering their spiritualities and mystical experiences. The emphasis on the rational aspect of the divine revelation is not expressing the gospel of God's love and grace. Emphases on relational aspects of God's love are slowly gaining attention in various churches. The Triune God of the Scriptures is a relational being offering his unique presence in Christ Jesus through the fellowship of the Holy Spirit. The Trinitarian aspect of the Christian faith leads people more into closer personal relationship with God and among themselves, and is usually accompanied by various religious experiences.

It remains questionable whether Barthian dialectic theology and neo-orthodoxy popular in Protestant academic circles did not somehow contribute to the communication barrier of current church mission. In contrast, narrative theology and symbolic language seemed to be rising in popularity and proving to be very vital mediators in modern preaching. The subjective experience of faith, which has been overlooked and neglected in

---

[30] Filipi, *Církev a církve*, 35.

[31] Jonathan J. Bonk, 'Missions and the Liberation of Theology', in *International Bulletin of Missionary Research*, 34.4 (2010), 194.

European Protestant theology for a long time, is also experiencing a massive revival. American sociologist Peter L. Berger notes: '... hope that the explosive pluralism of our times can lead to the rebirth of a new theological synthesis does not seem in any way exaggerated.'[32]

We have to interpret secular culture as a challenge for new evangelization. Since modernity stood on two pillars – the development of science and the new self-understanding of an individual – the post-modern era brings religion back onto the stage, even though it has the shape of a wide pluralism. Irish Jesuit Gallagher is right in describing post-modernity as 'cultural hopelessness and inconsolability', but on the other hand it also means a 'new openness to faith'.[33] He reminds us also of Cardinal Newman's wise opinion that 'departure from Christianity is not a matter of the intellect, but of the heart'.[34] Thus, Christianity is not a 'theorem' to which evangelization should bring a proof. Rather, it is an experience, which a Christian must go through authentically and then testify to it and share it with others. These approaches seem to be important in the contemporary Czech post-modern environment.

The hermeneutics of mission seems to be one of the most important prerequisites for a proper understanding and application of the biblical text. Missiological emphases very often shine through the writings of the New Testament and the Old Testament authors. Christopher Wright presents a very helpful hermeneutical approach in his book *The Mission of God*, which develops an important hermeneutical approach and application of the biblical missiological foundations.[35] To approach the biblical text without any knowledge of the missionary quest of Israel and that of the early church means giving too much leeway to modern culture, which may result in a lack of authentic contextual understanding and consequently in 'missing the target' in interpretation.[36]

A New Paradigm: CENTRIFUGAL

Mission in the Multi-Faith World

The peaceful co-existence of world religions is very important, and inter-religious dialogue is deeply rooted in the ground of the theology of mission. Nevertheless, it is important to discern what exactly we expect

---

[32] Peter L. Berger, *Vzdálená sláva: Hledání víry ve věku lehkověrnosti* (*A Far Glory, The Quest for Faith in the Age of Credulity*, Doubleday, New York 1993, and Prague: Barrister & Principal, 1997, 69).

[33] Jan Regner, Evangelizace v sekularizovaném světě, *Universum*, XXI, No. 4. 2011, 30-31.

[34] Regner, 'Evangelizace v sekularizovaném světě', 2011, 31.

[35] Christopher J.H. Wright, *The Mission of God* (Unlocking the Bible's grand narrative), (Nottingham, UK: IVP, 2006).

[36] Pavel Černý, The Relationship between Theology and Missiology: The Missiological Hermeneutics, in *European Journal of Theology*, Vol. 19.2. (2010), 104-09.

from this dialogue. It seems that proselytizing has nearly been eliminated in the Czech churches. They mutually respect their annunciations of the Saviour's grace and the diversity of gifts of the Spirit. Is it possible, however, to adopt such a stance also towards other religions? Is it not the case that we should rather proselytize among members of those religions and give them the same opportunities? Is it not, rather, important to grasp anew the theological reflection on what the Christian churches worship and serve, and what other religions do? Theological research should help us make a clear decision about whether we want partnership or religious association with other religions, or whether we should try to proselytize among them – on the assumption that the other religions will do the same. There is no doubt that we have much to learn from other religions and that inter-religious dialogue is an important part of our mission. The Scripture testifies that the Lord as God is in dialogue with his people. God incarnated in Jesus Christ remains in the dialogue. The early church is a living example of leading dialogue with the Jewish synagogue and Hellenistic society.

There is no doubt we have to respect other religions and treat them with dignity, but it does not mean that our testimony of Jesus Christ should be concealed as an esoteric teaching. In an inter-religious dialogue, it is the very integrity of our faith which is tested. A dialogue with a partner who hides the most precious thing he has soon ceases to be interesting. Members of other religions very often express disdain and mockery for those unable or unwilling to confess their faith.

Filipi also warns about a danger of confessional vagueness in our environment. False tolerance, which defends itself with such vagueness, is not a positive value.[37] Inter-religious dialogue should not be taken as a 'warehouse' of diverse beliefs. Friendly relations among people of different religions should not be an obstacle to confessional straightforwardness in the context of universalism of the Christian understanding of salvation.

New Ecclesiological Forms – Fresh Expressions of Church

According to sociological research, the influence of sects and cults has reached its peak. Various sects flourished, mostly in the 1990s, filling a spiritual vacuum after the communist period. In these days, people are more open to eastern religions, the New Age movement and various spiritualities connected with yoga, transcendental meditation and a healthy lifestyle. It means that many seekers are open to connecting with Christians from non-formal and non-traditional churches.

In the Czech situation, traditional churches can address some 'seekers' by preaching, liturgy and evangelistic outreach. Other seekers show such a deep antagonism towards organized religion that new ecclesiological forms

---

[37] Filipi, *Církev a církve*, 21.

are needed. Due to our situation, we support the importance of new missional expressions within the church. Fresh Expressions of Church in some places grow up and in their networks allow development of deeper and supportive relationships among people.[38] Some evangelical churches, which committed themselves to church-planting programmes, have been able to approach Czech seekers in a different way. Some of them experienced positive developments in mission work, which resulted in conversions and church growth.[39] The Gospel, brought in fresh and non-formal ways, can speak to Czech anti-clerical attitudes and shy seekers.

This approach is nothing else than a missional strategy of the Apostle Paul to be a Jew to the Jews, to win the Jews, to those under the law to become like one under the law, to win those under the law, for the weak to become weak, to win the weak (1 Cor. 9:20-22).

I can say that church-planting seems to be one of the most effective ways of evangelism. It is because new churches are usually flexible in developing various new ecclesiological forms. New church plants create fresh expressions of the church that are able to make bridges into society in a different way. We can see young churches attracting school children, university students and families with children, various generation and cultural groups. These new churches put a lot of stress on relationships among people. They respond to the need of contemporary citizens and their lack of family life, trusting friendships and deeper fellowship. Worship style in these new churches is often less structured, more flexible and non-formal.

The Holistic Dimension of the Church. Kenotic Christology shapes and fosters Christian mission. People appreciate an incarnational approach in sharing their needs. In the Czech Republic, more than every second marriage ends in divorce. It means that many people and their children live in broken relationships and suffer because of severe loneliness. There is also a very high number of people affected by alcoholism, drug abuse and gambling. Many people fall into debt because of poor stewardship of money. Those are just some examples of the need for kenotic Christology. Christians have to enter into these difficult situations in humble way to share in the pains and problems of others.

Churches must not divide evangelism and social ministry. Evangelism and social action belong together. This is also one important lesson the Czech church is again given. Even new church buildings should not be used just for our worship, but need to incorporate some clubrooms, schoolrooms,

---

[38] Michael Moynagh and Philip Harrold, *Church for Every Context: An Introduction to Theology and Practice* (London: SCM, 2012): https://www.freshexpressions.org.uk

[39] We can see such growth and more young people involved, especially in some evangelical and charismatic churches: Církev bratrská (Church of the Brethren – Evangelical Reformed), Apoštolská církev (Pentecostal Church), Bratrská jednota baptistů (Baptist Union), Křesťanská společenství (Christian Fellowship – charismatic) and Adventisté sedmého dne (Adventists of Seventh Day). According to Hamplová, *Náboženství v české společnosti na prahu 3. století,* 41-44, 86.

dining halls, units for the needy, etc. Sanctuaries have to be open for concerts, public meetings and other secular encounters. The Czech church is being taught to function as a social entity within society.

There are also various minorities of sick and disabled people who need the help and ministry of the church. Compassion and justice is an important part of mission. The church has to serve also as model of Christian ethics. It is very interesting how most people know how Christians should behave. There is an expectation of Christians observing a Christian lifestyle. The church is compelled to meet and to care for marginalized people on the edge of society, many of whom show an interest in religion and church-related affairs. But they, like Zacchaeus (Luke 19:1-10), need to be encouraged to meet with Jesus in their houses.

Dialogues and Co-operation. The Czech Republic still does not have as many immigrants as Western Europe. However, Korean, Russian, Ukrainian, Vietnamese, Japanese and multinational congregations have emerged on Czech soil. Some of these churches belong to traditional denominations while some of them are independent. It brings great opportunities for theological dialogue and mutual enrichment in the field of mission.

At a time when the European concept of multiculturalism is in decay or even obsolete, Christian churches should be able to express their ability to overcome ethnocentrism and cultural differences. New churches are beginning to evangelize among Czech citizens and are spreading their faith in a country which to them is foreign. Will Czech Christians be able to create a favourable environment for newly contextualized missionary church models? Will they be open to dialogue that can positively influence the missionary work of existing churches? This still remains an open question.

Conclusion

Current missionary conditions in the Czech Republic lead us to re-evaluate many well-trodden tracks of church paradigms. We have to learn more from the global church. For many years, we Europeans used to play a leading role at theological conferences; now it is our turn to show humility and accept that newly contextualized missionary types of non-European churches are being established in our country. It is not easy to learn from those whose Christianity still has a short history. We should pay attention to the cultural study of the epoch we live in. Culture determines an individual much more than we are willing to admit.

The Czech churches have to learn how to be a minority community of faith without falling into sectarianism or escapism, and so abandoning open evangelism in which the gospel is offered to all. To live a free life in a free and democratic society is not easy. People in churches will have to learn how to be Christians in a new, freer way that is not backward-looking or nostalgic. They will need to accommodate and contextualize Christian tradition in a quite different way. Communism has helped to privatize and hide Christian faith. Today, we need to encourage a professing and active Christianity, engaged in society and involved in serving others. In the past, Christians faced the pressure of materialistic ideology. Today, they face materialism in reality. Christians have to be aware of that danger and have to put the emphasis on simple Christian lifestyle which frees them for ministry. New Age or post-modern spirituality flourishes in our country, precisely because it seems to be rooted in feeling without direction, in the relationships of persons in the present, who are agnostic and unworried about where history might be going.

The goal of contemporary churches is, of course, not a renewal of the former church-state relationship before communism. Nor do the churches want to accept the American model of a complete separation between church and state. In our situation, we must work to develop the model of co-operation. There are areas where separation and full freedom is needed, but there are areas like social work where co-operation is useful for both sides. For example, churches run the majority of hospices and the state is happy to pay for operational costs. Similar co-operation is developed in chaplaincies within the army, in prison ministry, in the health services, and also in some co-operation with the police in the area of pastoral care.

Theological schools should make a sort of a missionary 'audit' of their curriculum and ethos to improve their service to the missionary quest of churches and answer the challenges of today.[40] A theological synthesis, which does not take account of the missionary quest of the church, is endangered by 'escapism' from current ecumenical research and the struggles of Christian churches. It can lose its relevance and miss its quest to serve as a helper and guardian to the current process of evangelization and social mission of the church. The materially saturated Czech Republic has been displaying spiritual hunger in recent years. Just try to 'Google' the words 'religion, 'spirituality' or 'new religious movements'. Many thousands of links will appear. Despite the fact that many of them are linked with occultism or paranormal phenomena, we can recognize in this phenomenon a certain sign of our epoch – people in the Czech Republic are experiencing the feeling that there might be something more than material life. People seek answers to their difficult questions. They are craving for spiritual experience and search for the meaning of life. What will be the answer of the mission theology of the Czech churches in the light of these spiritual and material needs?

---

[40] Pavel Černý, 'The Relationship between Theology and Missiology: The Missiological Hermeneutics', in *Do We Need Missiology? And if so, Why Do We Not Teach It and Develop It Systematically?* Conference proceedings from the first international conference of the Central European Centre for Mission Studies (Prague: Issued in the Czech-Slovak and English version by the CECMS, 2007).

MARKETING IN RELIGIOUS ORGANIZATIONS IN THE DIGITAL AGE

Branimir Dukić

Introduction

In the history of humankind, two major technological leaps have occurred. The first one was about six thousand years ago when humankind started to engage in agriculture and the first civilization was established. A settled form of living and agriculture brought about new technologies such as metal processing, as well as innovations such as the calendar, the alphabet, cartography and the first great religions. The second leap occurred after World War II, over seventy years ago, with new materials such as polymers and the development of new technologies such as space technology and computers, as well as information and communication technology (ICT). In the future, space technology is expected to enable humankind to colonize space, and resolve problems caused by overpopulation of the Earth. Initially, people used ICT to increase the efficiency of manual administrative processes. Over time, ICT has become a global technology used in all areas of human activity connected with data processing, information and knowledge. Today, it has created a parallel 'virtual' world which provides a platform for social activities, as well as a new form of business, i.e. e-Business. Moreover, ICT has created a new type of product – digital products whose share in the market has been rapidly increasing. This has radically changed human society, which has entered a new era – the digital age.

The digital age is primarily characterised by the globalization, individualization and virtualization of human society. Consequently, marketing orientation and informational superiority has become fundamental for the survival of business organizations. The concern for survival is felt not only by businesses, but also by religious organizations. The amount and quality of information in modern society has increased immensely, causing organizations to have to organize an optimal system of communicating with their consumers. The operation of religious organizations is essentially based on information and knowledge transfer. For example, the primary mission of Christian organizations is spreading the gospel, which has been conducted using marketing principles. Also, in *The Common Call* of the World Missionary Conference of Edinburgh 2010, all the items highlight the need to engage in marketing activities with reference to their main tasks:[1]

1. ... we are called to incarnate and proclaim the good news of salvation, of the forgiveness of sin, of life in abundance, and of liberation for all poor and oppressed.
2. ... we are called to authentic dialogue, respectful engagement and humble witness among people of other faiths – and no faith.
3. ... we are called to become communities of compassion and healing, where young people are actively participating in mission.
5. ... continual calling of children and young people to further the gospel.
6. ... also fostering the participation of children.
7. Hearing the call of Jesus to make disciples of all people... we are called as communities of faith to mission from everywhere to everywhere.
8. ... and recognise our need for mutuality, partnership, collaboration and networking in mission.
9. ... and we invite all to join with us as we participate in God's transforming and reconciling mission of love to the whole creation.

Thus, for religious organizations the question is not: Should we do it? The right question is: How shall we do it? However, modern times require a new approach, so religious organizations have had to adopt new marketing principles to keep their position when interacting with their customers – i.e. believers, as well as potential customers. Thus, the focus of this research was to answer the following research questions: What is marketing? What are evolution trends in marketing? How can marketing be used by religious organizations? What is the digital age? How does the digital age affect marketing? How does marketing change the relationship between religious organizations and the faithful?

The goal of this research is a conceptual marketing model of religious organizations for the digital age. Taking into account the research questions and the goal, the focus of the research is not on the question 'Why', but rather on 'How to do it in the digital age', putting the technological approach to the forefront. ICT is the foundation of World Globalisation and Transparency, and universally accepted by young people who were in the focus of the World Missionary Conference of Edinburgh 2010. Finally, ICT is widespread in Central and Eastern Europe, which is especially important for this research. This paper will try to argue for the implementation of a marketing philosophy in achieving the mission of religious organizations in Central and Eastern Europe.

[1] Kirsteen Kim and Andrew Anderson (eds), *Edinburg 2010 – Mission Today and Tomorrow* (Oxford: Regnum, 2010), 1-2.

Marketing Definition, Evolution and Interaction with Religious Organizations

Although a number of definitions have been used in modern science to describe marketing, most of them concur with the definition provided by the American Marketing Association. The definition has changed over time to become what it is today: 'Marketing is the activity, set of institutions, and processes for creating, communicating, delivering and exchanging offerings that have value for customers, clients, marketers and society at large.'[2] The preferred definition of marketing in business practice is the one provided by the Chartered Institute of Marketing which reads as follows: 'The management process responsible for identifying, anticipating and satisfying customer requirements profitably.'[3] It is important to note that in the 1980s marketing was considered to be a business function. Today, marketing is recognized as a management philosophy that enables the survival of business organizations by satisfying customer needs.

Given the trends resulting from the evolution of ICT, it is necessary to look at marketing from a different standpoint. Marketing can be defined as an information process whose primary task is to:

- provide information to business organizations about customer needs, and
- provide information to customers about products which can satisfy their needs.

Marketing as an information process involves communication in two directions: from a customer to a business organization, and vice versa. A business organization is at its centre, using the marketing research process to collect data about the market, customer needs and requirements, as well as customer behaviour. The data collected is processed by business organization information systems, and the information and knowledge extracted are used for decision-making in business. The information and knowledge are the basis for market segmentation and customer profiling, as well as the development and implementation of marketing plans. A marketing plan contains, as a minimum, the following information about the marketing mix: the product production plan, the product price, the methods of product distribution, and the product's promotion. Product promotion is an extension of the information process which involves the dissemination of information about products to customers.

Outside the framework of the marketing theory, marketing is usually perceived as and equated with the product promotion process and understood as a selling concept. On the contrary, however, marketing is

[2] Gregory T. Gundlach and William L. Wilkie, *The American Marketing Association's New Definition of Marketing: Perspective and Commentary on the 2007 Revision*, 262: http://business.nd.edu/faculty/pdf/2009mktgdefinationgundlachandwilkiejppm.pdf (accessed 25th January 2016).

[3] *Marketing and the 7Ps: A Brief Summary of Marketing and How It Works*: www.cim.co.uk/files/7ps.pdf (accessed 9th December 2015).

focused on marketing research, especially on customer needs identification. Fundamental marketing concepts claim that it is not necessary to promote a product that completely satisfies customer needs. Therefore, marketing is a philosophy according to which a customer pulls a product from a business organization, while in a selling concept a business organization pushes a product to the customers, regardless of whether they need it or not. Thus, in the marketing concept, collecting information about customer needs is a primary process, while in the selling concept the main process is the dissemination of information through aggressive promotion. It follows that marketing is a 'win-win' concept, while the selling concept is a 'win' concept, because in the latter only merchandisers' needs have to be satisfied. Hence, one can argue that: 'The simplest way is to consider marketing as a business philosophy that should be primarily used by management, and whose task is to satisfy consumers' needs. To achieve this, marketing focuses on consumers. Whereas the selling concept is focused on the buyer and finding ways to persuade him/her to buy a product, the marketing concept explores consumers' needs and tends to satisfy these needs through identification of a suitable product, its price, distribution method and method of presenting the product and providing information about it. Consequently, the selling concept is aggressive in its approach, whereas the marketing concept tends to communicate with buyers and receive from them information about their needs, and provide information about the product.'[4] Figure 1 shows the development phases in the business philosophy.

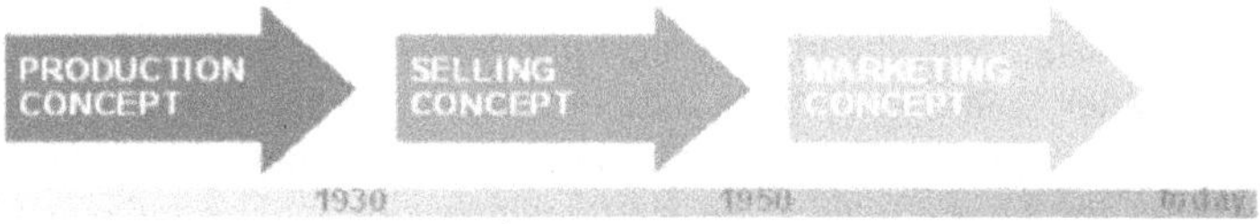

Fig 1. Evolutionary processes that resulted in marketing:[5]

Marketing is not a homogeneous business philosophy. It has evolved through several phases. Meler, who analyzed the evolution of marketing through the decades, identified the following phases in its evolution:[6]

- 1950-1960 – mass marketing
- 1970s – market segmentation
- 1980s – niche marketing
- 1990s – micro-marketing

[4] Branimir Dukić, Ivan Ružić and Stojanka Dukić, 'A Comparative Analysis of Traditional and e-Marketing Potentials in the Baking Industry' (paper presented at the *International Congress FLOUR- BREAD '13*, Opatija, 2013).

[5] Source: M. Meler, *Osnove marketinga* (Ekonomski fakultet u Osijeku), (Osijek, Croatia: 2005), 12.

[6] Marcel Meler and Branimir Dukić, *Upravljanje odnosima – od potrošača do klijenta (CRM)* (Ekonomski fakultet u Osijeku), (Osijek, Croatia: 2007), 34.

Meler used the level of market segmentation as the basis for delineating different phases in the evolution of marketing. The last phase, i.e. micro-marketing, has evolved from one-to-one marketing to relationship marketing. While all the phases prior to relationship marketing support asynchronous one-way communication between a business entity and a customer, relationship marketing involves synchronous bi-directional communication. Asynchronous one-way communication means that the stage during which information about customers' needs is received is clearly separated from the stage at which information about products is conveyed through promotional activities. Synchronous bi-directional communication means that there is a continuous parallel transfer of information about customers' needs and products (continuous marketing research and promotion). Modern ICTs enable synchronous bi-directional communication which is the reason why relationship marketing and its application concept, i.e. Customer Relationship Management (CRM), emerged in the 1990s.

Steven White recognized the five phases in the marketing evolution (see Figure 2), but argued that there were two more: relationship marketing which emerged in the 1990s, and Social/Mobile marketing which developed within the Web 2.0 concept – social web concept.

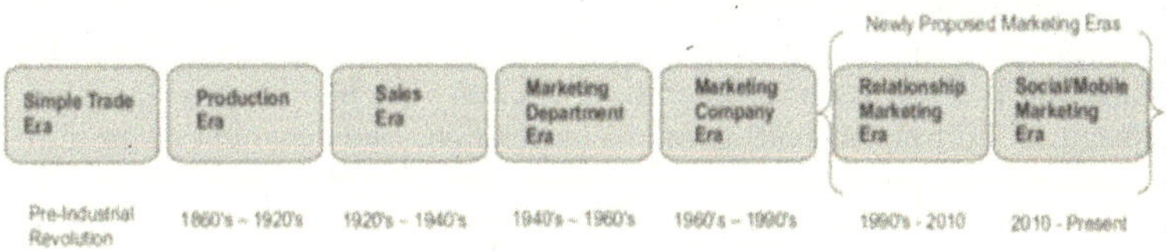

Fig 2. Evolutionary processes in marketing:[7]

In addition to distinguishing marketing by time dimension, it can also be distinguished by the area of application. Essentially, the fundamental motive of the existence of business organizations is their survival. Dukić has identified three derivative goals as a function of survival:[8]

- Growth
- Efficiency / Effectiveness
- Flexibility

Explaining the difference between efficiency and effectiveness, Dukić wrote:

> Efficiency is defined as a relationship between inputs and outputs which implies that a profitable business entity has the preconditions for survival. Effectiveness can be viewed as an alternative to efficiency. These two notions

[7] Source: Steven White, *The Evolution of Marketing*: http://dstevenwhite.com/2010/06/18/ the-evolution-of-marketing (accessed 4th February 2015).

[8] Stojanka Dukić, 'E-Marketing humanitarnih i vjerskih organizacija' (PhD thesis, Ekonomski fakultet u Osijeku, 2012), 114.

comprise different sets of success criteria. It is possible for non-efficient organizations to have the preconditions for survival. In such a case, the efficient part of the community is willing to forgo part of its profits and thus help the non-efficient organization to survive, provided this organization generates socially beneficial effects and thus meets certain social needs.[9]

Daft classified business organizations in two segments:[10]

- Profit organizations: managers direct their activities towards earning money for the company.
- Non-profit organizations: managers direct their efforts towards generating some kind of social impact.

According to the motivation of a business organization for participation in a business activity of any kind, marketing can be divided into:

- Profit marketing
- Non-profit marketing.

Given that religious organizations are non-profit organizations, the focus of this study was non-profit marketing:

> We define nonprofit marketing as the use of marketing tactics to further the goals and objectives of nonprofit organizations. Although advertising, public relations, and fund-raising are examples of nonprofit marketing tactics, nonprofit marketing also includes a broad array of other activities. Gathering and processing information for decision making are considered components of nonprofit marketing. Relations with governments, board members, donors, and volunteers are part of nonprofit marketing. In a broader view, nonprofit marketing is a management orientation that helps the nonprofit organization expand its horizon beyond its internal operations and programmes to also encompass the external world that affects the organization. A nonprofit organization that has a marketing orientation is able to focus its various activities and external communications to project a consistent image of itself and influence the way the external world perceives it.[11]

Conservative theological authors[12] reject the idea that the religious organization's mission and the business company's mission have anything in common. In principle, they do not observe church functioning as the business process. The fact is that all business is driven by a mission, which is comparable with religious organizations. On the other hand, religious organizations are on the market, although they never change their 'product' primarily for the sake of money. Their mission is to satisfy human needs, which is essentially a marketing philosophy. If we accept this, all the

---

[9] Dukić, 'E-Marketing'.

[10] Richard L. Daft, *Organization Theory and Design*: http://www.proz-x.com/stephanlangdon/Library/CESACORE/N_Daft_Organization.pdf (accessed 9th December 2015).

[11] Walter Wymer, Patricia A. Knowles and Roger Gomes, *Nonprofit Marketing: Marketing Management for Charitable and Nongovernmental Organizations* (Thousand Oaks, CA: Sage, 2006), 4.

[12] William D. Taylor (ed), *Global Missiology for the 21st Century*, 109-12: www.worldevangelicals.org/resources/rfiles/res3_161_link_129244293 9.pdf (accessed 26th January 2015).

functioning principles that are valid for business organizations are valid for religious organizations as well. Religious organizations are not above human society or the laws of human society. Therefore, marketing in religious organizations is a neutral tool which can help to satisfy human needs through transmitting and interpreting God's messages on which religious organizations are founded. Marketing philosophy is the same philosophy for profit and non-profit organizations, and the problem is that people who do not understand marketing philosophy view marketing as propaganda or some type of selling. This approach is frequently observed with theological authors whose marketing approach was focused on promotional activities alone.

Berger, referenced in Martens,[13] defines religious organizations as follows:

> We define the following institutional setting as an Organized Religion: it is a group composed of individuals who partake in a costly and observable activity. When an organized religion exists in equilibrium, the strategy of an agent may depend on whether his opponent is associated with the religious organization or not. Given these strategies, agents choose whether to join the religion or not.[14]

A distinction can be drawn between the following categories of religious organizations:[15]

- Cults
- Sects
- Denominations
- Ecclesiae (Churches)

Table 1 below shows the ideal types of religious organizations.

[13] Kerstin Martens. 'Mission Impossible? Defining Nongovernmental Organizations', in *Voluntas: International Journal of Voluntary and Nonprofit Organizations,* 13.3 (2002), 271-85.

[14] Julia Berger, *Religious Non-Governmental Organizations: An Exploratory Analysis*, 1: www.global.ucsb.edu/orfaleacenter/luce/luce08/documents/Harvard%20Summary%20paper.pdf (accessed 18th December 2015).

[15] *World Religions*: http://cnx.org/contents/en08KoUm@3/World-Religions (accessed 28th January 2016).

characteristic	CULT ➧	SECT ➧	DENOMINATION	CHURCH or ECCLESIA
Relation to state and/or secular powers	Avoiding	Uneasy, tenuous	On good terms, sometimes influential	Conflates citizen with member
Relation to other religious groups	Rejection, separation, isolation, withdrawal	Avoiding	Tolerant, friendly, accepting pluralism	Claims universality, attempts to eliminate competition
Source of new membership	Voluntary conversion, "kidnapping"	Voluntary, often evangelical	Birth, conversion, some evangelical	Birth, socialization, conversion, conquest, missionized salvation
Relation to doctrinal change	New revelations, insights, discoveries	Return to original sources	Modestly changing, adaptive doctrine	Rigidly interpreted theologies, highly intellectualized
Doctrinal focus	Highly spiritual	Otherworldly	Practical	Both otherworldly and practical; politically sensitive
Form of ritual or worship	Esoteric, highly symbolic	Often informal, spontaneous	Ritualized, routine, less spontaneous	Highly ritualized, elaborate
Type of leadership	Charismatic, individual	Charismatic, lay leadership	Professional, trained, licensed clergy	Professional, trained, licensed clergy
Form or Degree of Organization	Very loose, even democratic	Informal	Somewhat hierarchical, often congregational	Hierarchical, structured, authoritarian
Degree of member involvement	Exclusive, Intense, emotional	Exclusive	Non-exclusive, integrated	Lifelong, extensive, non-exclusive (altho see conflation)
Potential or desired size	Small	Small, but growing	Large, growing (in decline)	Large, expansive, comprehensive, all-inclusive
Relation to social class	Disenfranchised, marginal, alienated	Lower SES	Upper and Middle SES	All classes, tho differentially

Table 1. Ideal types of religious organization:[16]

All religious organizations function as mediators between God and humans. Dukić claims:

> To put it simply, Christian marketing organizations behave like marketing agencies that 'promote' a product that will be 'consumed' at the end of the earthly Life. This product is resurrection and/or eternal life. From the moral aspect, it is questionable whether it is appropriate to compare Christian churches or any other religious organizations with marketing agencies, particularly in the light of the fact that in the broader population, due to lack of understanding of the marketing concept, marketing agencies are seen as something negative, exhausting, and therefore immoral. However, the fact is that there are no significant differences in the principles of operation of religious organizations and marketing agencies. An additional reason to avoid putting religious organizations, particularly Christian ones, in a negative context, lies within the fact that the basic teaching of these organizations is the foundation on which moral, cultural, social and other pillars of modern western society are built.[17]

The primary mission of religious organizations is to transmit and interpret God's messages to people. 'Mission is not the ultimate goal of the church. Worship is. Missions exist because worship doesn't. Worship is ultimate, not missions, because God is ultimate, not man. When this age is over, and the countless millions of the redeemed fall on their faces before

[16] http://web.pdx.edu/~tothm/religion/Religious%20Organizations.pdf (accessed 9th December 2015).

[17] Dukić, 'E-Marketing', 224.

the throne of God, missions will be no more. It is a temporary necessity. But worship abides for ever.'[18] Ferguson, Packer and Wright claim that the mission of the church has considerably more tasks than evangelization itself, and they list the following mission tasks accordingly:[19]

1. The church has to be involved in responsible and ethical management of material resources of everything that was created,
2. The church has to compassionately serve and help with alms to human beings in all their common and uncommon needs, regardless of their mutual differences,
3. The church shall continuously spread evangelism and be a credible witness of the truth to Jesus (Eph. 4:21),
4. The church shall stand up for achieving God's justice and righteousness, peace, reconciliation and forgiveness in all aspects of the society,
5. The responsibility of the church is to use its own model of functioning to show a reconciled and liberated society in the middle of the fallen, anxious and desperate world. The church should be both a law and a model of God's creation of a new social and natural order where His peace and justice will rule.

Regarding the mission of religious organizations and marketing Dukić claims:

> Related to the mission which is focused on satisfying the spiritual needs of the population, Christian churches as well as other religious organizations are actually organizations acting on the principles of marketing philosophy which they apply wittingly and in an organized manner or unwittingly (in a less formal way). For religious organizations as well as for other organizations, the mission is the starting-point for defining strategic goals, whether formally or informally. Formalization of strategic goals and their formation through time and space dimension results in the marketing strategy. Marketing strategy is used to define target markets and consumer segments, and to adapt the marketing mix accordingly. As evangelization, i.e. spreading of faith is at the core of any mission activities of religious organizations, these organizations, in addition to their operation in the market of their own consumers – believers, also operate in the market of potential consumers.[20]

Religious organizations can operate on the principles of the selling philosophy and push their products, or on marketing principles which is more advisable as this concept seeks to satisfy a need – the human need for God's word. 'Marketing is a tool to carry out a mission, ministry and management of the organization more effectively. Its role is not to substitute spirituality or religious leaders; it gives an opportunity to the governing board to be efficient and effective. Spirituality develops from

---

[18] John Piper, *Let the Nations Be Glad!: The Supremacy of God in Missions* (Grand Rapids, MI: Baker Books, 1993), 11.

[19] Sinclair B. Ferguson, J.I. Packer and David F. Wright (eds), *New Dictionary of Theology* (Downers Grove, IL: IVP, 1988), 434.

[20] Dukić, 'E-Marketing', 223.

one's relationship with God and a desire to surrender to God's will. Marketing increases organizations' awareness and responsiveness to various groups whose needs are to be satisfied. Marketing is analyzing, planning, organizing, leading, implementing and controlling carefully formulated programmes that target specific groups to accomplish the organizations' mission.'[21]

Is religious organization marketing a completely new concept? 'We're familiar with Jesus' "Great Commission" mandate found in Matthew 28:19-20: "Therefore go and make disciples of all nations, baptizing them in the name of the Father and of the Son and of the Holy Sprit, and teaching them to obey everything I have commanded you." This first-century command still applies. God wants us to actively live and speak His truth today – in ways that communicate to our 21st-century culture. [Do you] think church marketing is just a modern invention? Take a look at the story of Pentecost, an amazing picture of God using what we now identify as strategic marketing and communication principles to grow His church.'[22]

Beaver points out the five myths about church marketing:[23]

1. Marketing is a misguided attempt at evangelism.
2. Marketing is manipulative and deceptive.
3. Marketing is forcing things with human effort instead of surrendering to God's leadership.
4. Marketing puts churches in competition with each other.
5. Marketing is a luxury that we should only consider when all the other needs are met.

The myths noted by Beaver are a result of inadequate knowledge about marketing in theological circles. This problem, however, is not limited to this particular group: the term 'marketing' has been misused since the beginning of marketing philosophy. Non-experts usually equate it with the philosophy of selling.

> Remember: marketing is simple communication that prompts a targeted audience to action. Whether direct mail, advertising, radio, television or just the traditional church marquee, God is using marketing strategies today in much the same way He used them in biblical times. And while the methods can and should be tailored to reach people in a changing cultural landscape, the life-changing message of salvation is still the same.[24]

---

[21] Mehmed Elezovic, *The Role of Leadership in Marketing Religious Organizations*: www.asrec.org/wp-content/uploads/2015/10/Elezovic-Leadership-in-Marketing-Organization-ASREC09.pdf (accessed 7th February 2016).

[22] Andrea B. Willits, *Is Church Marketing Biblical?*: www.churchleaders.com/outreach-missions/outreach-missions-articles/139683-is-church-marketing-biblical.html (accessed 2nd February 2016).

[23] Jerry Beaver, *Biblically Marketing a Church*: http://jerrybeaver.net/upload/1274401997.biblically_marketing_a_church.pdf (accessed 2nd February 2016).

[24] Willits, *Is Church Marketing Biblical?*

The Digital Age and Its Influence on Modern Marketing

ICT is one of the fastest-growing technologies in the world. It is also a driving force in global social transformations, pushing the world into a new post-industrial era, often referred to as the 'information age', 'knowledge age', 'electronic age' or 'digital age'. Information and knowledge have become the most important resources, whereas the terms 'electronic age' and 'digital age' are characteristic of the type of technology used in data processing. Figure 3 shows the relationship between data, information, knowledge and wisdom.

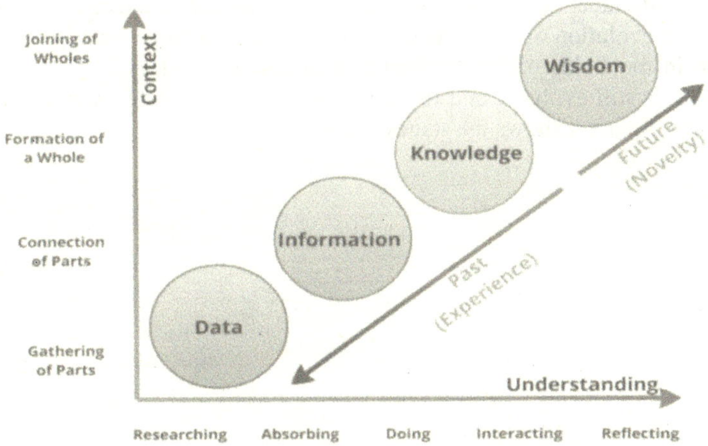

Fig 3. Relationship between data, information, knowledge and wisdom[25]

In fact, the digital age is a fairly recent term. It was used extensively in the Digital Agenda 2010: 'The Digital Agenda presented by the European Commission forms one of the seven pillars of the Europe 2020 Strategy which sets objectives for the growth of the European Union by 2020. The Digital Agenda proposes to better exploit the potential of Information and Communication Technologies (ICTs) in order to foster innovation, economic growth and progress.'[26] Some of the key features of the Digital Agenda 2010 are:

- The ICT evolution (Internet and Virtual Society)
- Global transparency (Global economy)
- The Knowledge Society (Knowledge economy)
- Changes in lifestyle
- The Evolution of human needs

[25] www.easterbrook.ca/steve/2012/09/what-is-climate-informatics (accessed 1st October 2015).

[26] http://eur-lex.europa.eu/legal-content/EN/TXT/?uri=URISERV%3Asi0016 (accessed 14th February 2016).

- The Evolution of the Consumer
- The Personalization and individualization of production
- Marketing time (Marketing Concept vs. Production Concept) – CRM time

According to changes in human society, it can be said that the following characteristics are general characteristics of the digital age:

- Industrial goods: Potentials greater than human needs
- Customer-centric society
- Business survival: Marketing Orientation + Information Superiority
- Knowledge Management
- Individualized needs: Customer Relationship Management (CRM).

In the evolution of ICT over the past ten years, the greatest progress was made in the fields of the Internet and mobile technology evolution. The Internet is still evolving and thereby continually providing users with new features. Figure 4 shows the stages of the Web evolution.

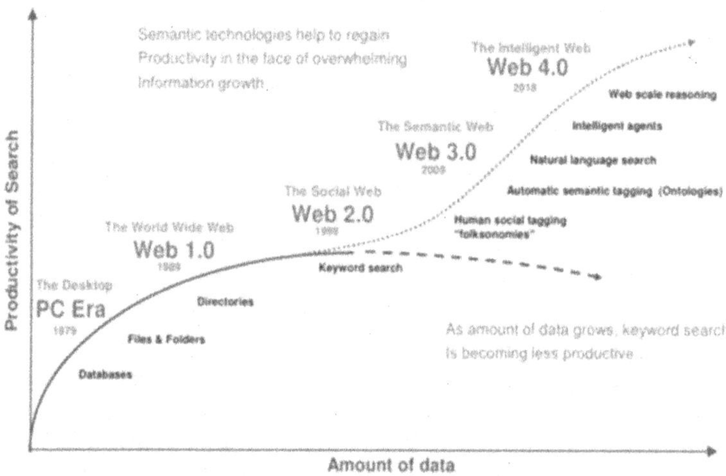

Fig 4. The stages of the Web evolution:[27]

Today, the most interesting Web technology for marketing is Web 2.0. Table 2 shows a brief overview of Web 2.0 technologies.

Web 2.0 technologies	Description	Category of technology
Wiki, commenting, shared workspaces	Facilitates co-creation of content/applications across large, distributed set of participants	Broad collaboration
Blogs, podcasts, videocasts,	Offers individuals a way to	Broad

[27] Nova Spivack, *Web Evolution*: www.slideshare.net/novaspivack/web-evolution-nova-spivack-twine (accessed 20th January 2013).

peer-to-peer	communicate/share information with broad set of other individuals	communication
Prediction markets, information markets, polling	Harnesses the collective power of the community and generates a collectively derived answer	Collective estimation
Tagging, social bookmarking/filtering, user tracking, ratings, RSS (Really Simple Syndication)	Adds additional information to primary content to prioritize information or make it more valuable	Metadata creation
Social networking, network mapping	Leverages connections between people to offer new applications	Social graphing

Table 2. Brief overview of Web 2.0 technologies:[28]

Owing to the convergence that has taken place in today's information technology and owing to network infrastructure, mobile phones now offer possibilities otherwise offered by PCs. Mobility implies virtual market interaction, not only at any time, but also at any place. Figure 5 shows the ICT evolution and the convergence of technologies that are taking place now.

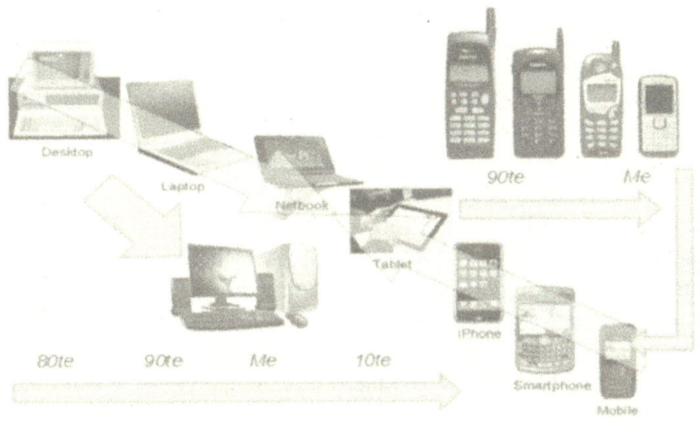

Fig 5. The ICT evolution – technology convergence:[29]

One of the key factors of competitiveness in modern conditions of doing business is so-called 'informational superiority'. It refers to the better competitive position of an operator who is able to offer more and better information on his product than the competition, i.e. the superiority of a business entity having better information on its consumers. Informational superiority in modern business circumstances is provided by ICT, especially its mobile component, because it provides the opportunity to

[28] www.rachelcolic.com/documents/6%20Ways%20to%20Make%20Web%202.0%20 Work.pdf (accessed 7th June 2012).

[29] http://brel54.blogspot.com/2010_11_01_archive.html (accessed 15th September 2011).

permanently provide good information to consumers, on the one hand, and gather information on consumer needs, on the other. As for religious organizations, this would mean striving to learn about their members' needs. Although the faithful have the same basic needs defined in their organization's mission, there are also individual needs to consider, from existential to social needs. Modern man is increasingly aware of his needs and requires these needs to be met at an individual level. The time when needs were satisfied *en masse* is in the past. To find out about their members' needs – which means to achieve informational superiority – and to satisfy those needs and thus retain their members, religious organizations have to communicate continuously with them, which is almost impossible without ICT. It might be equally important to recognize and satisfy the needs of the non-faithful. When religious organizations fail to recognize and meet the needs of people, the consequence is often that such people are disappointed; they tend to waver in their beliefs and change their religious organization.

Accordingly, there are two ways of deriving informational superiority:

- By transmitting information (through marketing communication) to consumers
- By receiving information (through decision-making = data → decision model → decision = feedback) about consumer needs

Two approaches to informational superiority should be distinguished:

- Yesterday – interaction with a group
- Today – individual, personalized (bi-directional) communication through relationship marketing

A derivative of relationship marketing is customer relationship management (CRM). CRM enables individual, personalized communication with consumers. As it can be seen in Figure 6, in its development, marketing has evolved from a mass concept that reduced all consumers to an average, to an individual approach to consumers; this approach was enabled by the advances in ICT, which grew from individual expensive data processing into cheap systems for mass data processing.

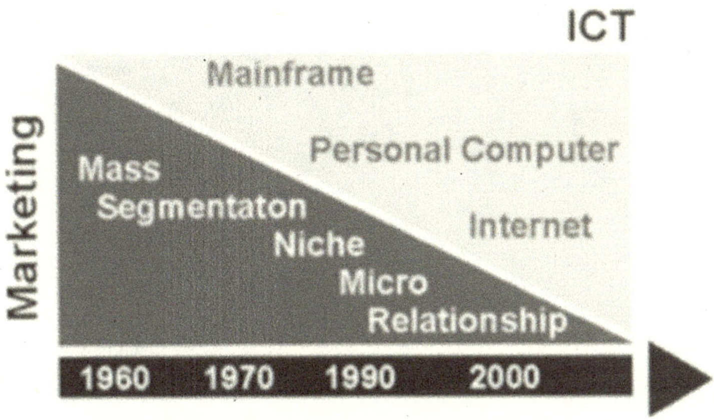

Fig 6. The relationship between the development of marketing and ICT

As a derivate of marketing, CRM evolved at the end of the 1990s, and it has gained in significance with the growth of e-Business and e-Marketing. E-Marketing or digital marketing belongs to the digital era. Figure 7 shows the most important elements of digital marketing.

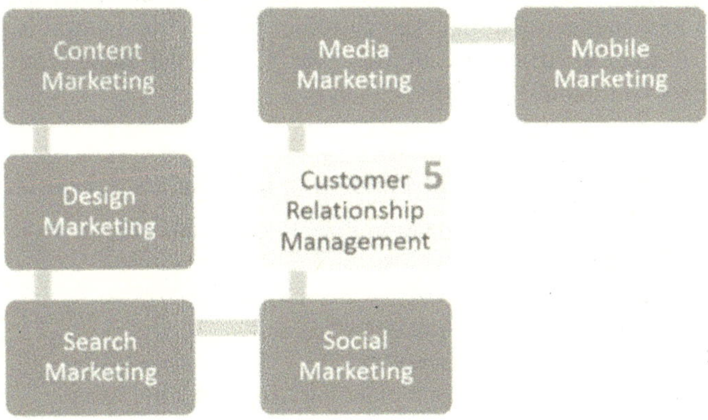

Fig 7. The most important elements of digital marketing:[30]

Most of the components shown in Figure 5 are part of the Web 2.0 concept. Social marketing includes some of the most popular social networks:[31]

1. Facebook

---

[30] Dave Lloyd, *Social Enablement Strategy*: http://blogs.adobe.com/digitalmarketing/ digital-marketing/social-enablement-strategy (accessed 9th January 2016).

[31] eBizMBA Guide, *Top 15 Most Popular Social Networking Sites*: www.ebizmba.com/ articles/social-networking-websites (accessed 10th January 2016).

2.	Twitter
3.	LinkedIn
4.	Pinterest
5.	Google Plus+
6.	Tumblr
7.	Instagram
8.	VK
9.	Flickr
10.	MySpace
11.	Tagged
12.	Ask.fm
13.	Meetup
14.	MeetMe
15.	ClassMates

The origins of CRM can be traced back to the concept of relationship marketing. CRM includes the following three concepts:

- Marketing
- Management, and
- ICT

CRM is a business philosophy, business concept, business strategy and software. CRM 2.0 version is especially interesting to religious organizations because it enables them to personalise customer experience using social media platforms. The customer in the virtual world is referred to as a 'hybrid customer'. In the near future, the number of virtual customers will rapidly increase.

The Application of Digital Marketing in Religious Organizations

Marketing in religious organization goes through the general stages of the marketing process:[32]

1. Market research
2. Defining marketing goals
3. Defining marketing strategy
4. Marketing performance planning (the marketing mix)
5. Marketing control

Important differences between the marketing of profit-oriented organizations and the marketing of non-profit religious organizations include primarily:[33]

- Definition of e-Marketing goals,
- Definition of e-Marketing mix, and

[32] Aleksandar Bazala, *Istraživanje tržišta – metode i područja istraživanja* (Zagreb: Velebit – Velegraf, 1991), 16.

[33] Branimir Dukić, Stojanka Dukić and Ivan Ružić, 'Model for Implementing Marketing in Religious Organisation in a Virtual Environment', in *Responsibility and Sustainability – Socio-economic, Political and Legal Issues,* 2-3 (2014), 38.

- Definition of e-Marketing control (defined quantity and quality criteria).

The first step in planning and preparing for marketing research is choosing the market, and the market segment. Balog presents the following global market segmentation that primarily refers to Christian religious organizations, particularly churches, but it can be also applied to other religious organizations:[34]

Market A. Towards persons categorised as potential believers, which have not become believers yet;

Market B. Towards believers who actively practise Christian religion and belong to the Christian community by their birth;

Market C. Towards potential donors and sponsors of the Christian religious community;

Market D. Towards various subjects from a narrow or broad social environment of the Christian religious community in order to achieve various political, social, economic and other goals.

The marketing mix of religious organizations includes:[35]

- Production mix of religious organizations:
  - **Liturgy – religious messages**
  - **The pastoral care of believers and families**
  - **Human resources**
  - **Church institutions and church communities**
  - **The results of scientific and professional work as products of church colleges**
  - **Material, financial and non-material resources of religious communities**
  - **Service for the common good**
- Prices:
  - **Transparent,**
  - **Non-transparent,**
  - **Imaginary, and**
  - **Transcendental (without amount and currency unit)**

The main 'products' of the Christian community are resurrection and 'eternal life'. Balog has analyzed and defined the product mix, as well as identifying a number of other elements of the marketing mix:[36]

1. Worship, i.e. Gospel messages as the main product (from the standpoint of the church and believers):

A. Gospel message about the Good News, i.e. Gospel sermon
B. Ceremonies or sacraments
C. Large religious gatherings
D. Pilgrimages to holy places

2. The Pastoral care of believers and families

[34] Antal Balog, 'Marketing Kršćanskih vjerskih zajednica u funkciji evangelizacije' (PhD thesis, Ekonomski fakultet u Osijeku, 2012), 33.
[35] Dukić, Dukić and Ružić, 'Model for Implementing Marketing'.
[36] Balog, 'Marketing Kršćanskih vjerskih zajednica u funkciji evangelizacije', 243.

A. Individual, family, parish, diocesan, church
B. Religious education – catechism

3. Human resources as products of the Christian religious community (from the standpoint of society):

A. Believers and believer groups in general
B. Priest services: priests, missionaries, spiritual guides, clergymen
C. Co-operating services: catechists, Christian instructors in catechism, theology teachers and professors, scientists and researchers in the field of Christian theology
D. Other services: managers of church institutions and other church organizations

4. Church, i.e. ecclesial communities and institutions and the general church community

A. Parish and diocesan communities and the general church community
B. Educational institutions in the field of theology (secondary schools – seminaries, theological seminaries, i.e. Faculty of Theology, scientific institutes)
C. Museum and archive institutions
D. Press and publishing institutions
E. Church institutions in the field of social services

5. Results of the scientific and professional work in the scientific field of theology as products of the church faculties (results from the standpoint of academic community and scientific public):

A. Scientific and professional (individual and/or group) projects
B. Scientific and professional books
C. Scientific and professional magazines
D. Scientific and professional seminars and congresses
E. Internet publications, interest groups, information exchange.

6. Material, financial and non-material resources of the Christian religious community as products (from the standpoint of the user of internal or external environment)

A. Material resources of the Christian religious community: church (sacral) buildings and other facilities, land (agricultural land, forests), church equipment and installations, libraries, museums and archives with existing funds, works of art
B. Financial resources of the religious community: money, shares, bonds, fund shares, receivables
C. Non-material resources of the religious community: rights (author rights and other rights), organizational culture, image of religious communities and their general reputation in the society

7. Serving the public good (from the standpoint of the user of internal or external environment)

A. The permanent influence of its own point of view and system of values on a broader environment (other religious communities, educational and scientific institutions, non-profit sector, public and private means of mass communication, political and state system, non-formal groups, public opinion, family)
B. Participation in public discussions about laws pertaining to the field of morale, human rights, freedom, tolerance, civil society, etc.

C. Social services of the Christian religious community.

The main types of distribution channels of the Christian religious community and their mutual combinations are as follows:[37]

1. Direct distribution channels. There is one distribution place where religious gathering occurs for the purpose of worship. This is the most frequent model among Christian religious organizations, not only due to general efficiency, but also because of the theological imperative of the regular gathering of all believers belonging to a group or a parish. This is the zero level of distribution channel, because the service is held at the same place where consumers are.
2. Network distribution channels. In addition to the main distribution site, there is also a network of regional centres in owned or rented spaces. For example, if the goal is to promote some religious teaching programmes, then networks of primary and secondary schools can be used as channels of distribution. Some Christian religious organizations organise religious teaching of adults in a way that they organise a network of small home-based prayer groups with up to ten members. Such a network is evenly distributed among particular parts of a town or the villages within a region.
3. Diffused distribution channels. Conveying Christian messages without the presence of the recipient in sacral spaces. For example, publications (books, magazines, course books, scripts, manuscripts, audio and video recordings) are targeted at believers, i.e. the target market. For example, the Christian message can be distributed through electronic means of public communication (radio, television).
4. The Internet distribution channel. In the near future, this channel of distribution for messages of Christian religious organizations is going to decrease the significance of simple and network distribution. The possibility of watching the liturgy via the Internet, participation in on-line gatherings and use of religious texts as well as access to watching religious meetings that have already been held on demand will significantly improve the availability for anyone interested in such content. This level of distribution initiated the thorough change of the current paradigm of Christian religious organizations in general.

Today, marketing application and control largely depend on the application of modern ICT and the further development of new service concepts such as:[38]

1. Further development of social networks (Web 2.0), and micro segmentation of the society through social networks, the development of social applications on the Web, as well as creation

[37] Balog, 'Marketing'.

[38] Dukić, Dukić and Ružić, 'Model for Implementing Marketing', 35.

and evolution of the semantic (Web 3.0) and intelligent Web (Web 4.0),

2. Further development of geolocation systems and contextual geolocation as well as the development of ambiental intelligence,
3. Significant development of biometric systems (connected with geolocation systems) as well as development of supervisory systems based on both biometric methods and social data mining (analyzing data from social networks),
4. Development of increasingly complex, smart, interactive and interoperable Web software applications adapted to all technological requirements (computers, advanced phones, tablets),
5. Processing spoken languages and development of applications that can use them, implying the changed importance of input sub-system (from writing to speaking to a machine),
6. Universal data platforms (the ability to read everything on everything), development of universal development tools, broad interconnectivity and freedom of virtual moving and acting,
7. Creation of virtual 'avatar' communities within the concept of virtual reality.

Marketing based on the use of ICTs (marketing in the digital age) is referred to as electronic marketing or e-Marketing. A structural model of e-Marketing of religious organizations can be symbolically represented as follows:[39]

$$eM_{Vo} = eIT_{Vo} + eMmix_{Vo} + eMp_{Vo} + eMk_{Vo}$$

where:

eM – e-Marketing

Vo – religious organizations

eIT – Market research in virtual environment

eMmix – e-Marketing mix

eMp – Implementation (application) of e-Marketing

eMk – e-Marketing control

Important success factors for the application of ICT and e-Marketing in the next 5-10 years are as follows:[40]

- The two-way nature of communication that accepts the fact that in modern circumstances every individual wants to create the content in virtual space is an important element,
- The important element is content (blogs chats, video chats, social networks, location intelligence services – ambient intelligence…),

---

[39] Dukić, Dukić and Ružić, 'Model for Implementing Marketing', 39.

[40] Branimir Dukić, Ivan Ružić and Stojanka Dukić, 'Technology-driven e-Marketing Model of Croatian Tourism Product with an Emphasis on Web 2.0 Potentials', in Bruno Gr et al (eds), *Marketing Insights from a Changing Environment* (London: Pearson Education Limited, 2015), 48.

- The important element is constant generation of new multimedia content providing continuous attention,
- The important element is the impact of an individual on a group (social character), i.e. engagement of highly motivated people who have a high index of social influence – the so-called opinion makers,
- The important element is to have exclusivity of both content and content creator (creating its own content and fighting for opinion-makers),
- The important element is to have information on processes in the social environment (constantly measuring indices of social presence and social influence).

Opposite these important tasks there are key problems:[41]

- Large scope (a large number of social networks),
- The loss of exclusivity – everybody sees everything, everybody has information on everyone,
- Everyone can reach everyone, everyone can comment on anything,
- Constant presence (24/7) – negative trigger should not be allowed,
- Growth of communication speed,
- Maintaining user interest and
- Continuous adjustments.

The technological structural model for implementation of e-Marketing of religious organizations that will be used in the next 5-10 years can be symbolically presented as follows:[42]

$$eMp(thl) = mobile(transf(min(Web1.0) \rightarrow Web\ 3.0) + max(Web2.0) + HRvi + Wmetrix + BIsu + CRM2.0 + SEO + GEO)$$

Where:

mobile – Everything needs to have mobile functionality

transf(min(Web1.0)→ Web 3.0) – Transformation of Web 1.0 into Web 3.0, with minimising the content created by the religious organization

max(Web2.0) – Increase the presence on social networks

Wmetrix – Using the services (such as Cloud) that measure the users' influence on the community (social index or index of social influence of a person – showing how much a particular person publishes, how much he/she follows, and how much this person is followed in all services)

HRvi – Using persons with high social index (for example, a community manager)

BIsu – Using own business intelligence tools to measure social index of both individuals on the web and the entire organization

---

[41] Dukić, Ružić and Dukić, 'Technology-driven e-Marketing Model'.
[42] Dukić, Ružić and Dukić, 'Technology-driven e-Marketing Model', 39.

SEO – Search Engine Optimization – managing search engine positioning (also available in Web 3.0)

GEO – Using ambiental intelligence (for example, FourSquare).

In addition to ICT, optimal implementation of e-Marketing in religious organization requires an optimal set of e-Marketing techniques. The preferred e-Marketing techniques of religious organizations include:[43]

- Viral marketing – The potential of opinion leaders should be used, i.e. of persons with high social index to encourage chain reaction
- Affiliate marketing – Assistance of significant popular websites that allow putting banners of religious organizations as well as links to their sites
- Referral marketing – Combination of the first two, with significant success through social networks, i.e. Web 1.0 links to social networks ('tell a friend')
- One-to-One marketing – An integral part of the Web 2.0 concept, but also of CRM – allows for adaptation of a product to consumer, and monitoring consumers' behaviour in pre-sale, sale and post-sale activities.
- Real-time marketing – 'In the right place at the right time' – just-in-time
- Content marketing – A technique of creating and distributing relevant content to attract, gain and involve the most important users of the transfer of religious organizations (The Paretto Principle 80:20).

Final Recommendations for the Implementation of Marketing in Religious Organizations in the Digital Age in Central and Eastern Europe

Marketing implementation in religious organizations in Central and Eastern Europe in the digital age is very similar to such activities anywhere else in the world. The technological model presented above includes ICT platforms that will remain usable until the technological framework is changed to such an extent as to require a new platform. It is envisaged that the present model is sustainable for the next 5-10 years. Such a model calls for particular e-Marketing techniques, also presented above. Although Central and Eastern Europe, like most transitional regions, lags behind developed countries with regard to ICT infrastructure, this is not as significant as to bring into question whether the concept can be realized. In such conditions, it is better to concentrate on practical ideas that can help in establishing and improving the e-Marketing activities of religious

[43] Dukić, Ružić and Dukić, 'Technology-driven e-Marketing Model'.

organizations. In that sense, Perry suggests some ideas for improving the implementation of church marketing:[44]

1. Give away a free e-book or mp3 podcast on your website/blogsite in exchange for their email so you can keep in touch with them. Use an autoresponder too. We use 'aweber'.
2. Create a specially-themed blog and update it at least once a week (configure it to broadcast out to your Facebook page and Twitter account) and start a blog-talk show.
3. Design exciting church bulletins with 'spiritual nuggets' written by yourself. Make it a keeper and motivational tool to be shared with non-church members.
4. Brand your sermon series with CD covers, banners/postcards throughout the church and create a 'Facebook cover' so members can promote it on their Facebook pages too.
5. Start an email newsletter or E-zine. Repurpose the articles in article directories like ezinearicles.com.
6. Create cool, glossy postcards for members to give out to invite people to church.
7. Give a community award – pick a worthy policeman or fire-fighter from your community and honour them with a nice award. Make it a big deal. Send out a press release. Videotape the event and put on YouTube.
8. Attend a church marketing conference and engage in social media like Facebook and Twitter.
9. Invest in a quality graphics/branding. Create a custom Twitter background and Facebook cover and page.
10. Order a standard podium cover to match your corporate ID for special meetings in venues like hotels where their name is displayed. Brand your logo and name. Make sure your website URL is on it too.
11. Canvas the neighbourhood of the church with door hangers. Many neighbours are just waiting for a formal invitation to visit your church. Be creative – give a gift that matches your church's brand.
12. Do something different and 'outside the box' – change up your routine, do not just do the standard stuff you and every other church does each year. Find a different way to do the same thing from a different perspective. Be playful and fun – and attract the youth.
13. Read one good book on ministry marketing.
14. Plan out your marketing efforts – yes, make a plan! Consult with a marketing consultant to help you lay out a strategy within your budget.
15. Allow members to 'check in' when they enter the church using Foursquare on their mobile phones. Make sure your Foursquare

[44] www.pamperrypr.com/15-church-marketing-idea-market-your-ministry-with-excellence (accessed 29th January 2016).

profile is complete and includes the website URL. This is a great way to spread the gospel easily and effortlessly. This is word-of-mouth on steroids.

Morgan focuses on several marketing mistakes churches often make that should be *avoided* as one strives to reach people:[45]

1. Promoting your church instead of generating a response. No one really cares that you are First Church Such-and-Such. And, no one really cares what your building looks like. Promote a message series over the church. Promote a conversation over the church. But don't promote the church or a specific ministry. Others will do that for you if it is worth promoting.
2. Making a promise you can't keep. The world already thinks churches are filled with hypocrites, so make sure you exceed expectations on everything you say you'll do. The easiest place to begin is with the guest experience. Are you delivering a welcoming, friendly environment? When someone takes a step to connect with your ministry, make sure your team is ready to follow through.
3. Trying to be all things to all people. Yes, we want the world to know Jesus, but who has God put into *your* world? That's who you need to reach. And, more specifically, what person within your world are you most likely to reach? Design your ministry to connect with him or her. That means some people may not like your church. That's OK. God uses different ministries to reach different people.
4. Thinking other churches are your competition. We are competing with today's culture. Other churches are on *our* team. It doesn't help if you distinguish yourself from another church. You need to distinguish your message from the world people live in. Clearly communicate why someone should connect with your church instead of spending their time doing a million other things.
5. Publicizing programmes that compete with one another. More choices create more confusion. You may have lots of great programmes, but the more options you provide, the less likely people will be to take a step. I know – it is counter-intuitive. But you don't want a situation where your men's ministry is competing with your discipleship classes that are competing with your home groups that are competing with volunteer opportunities. Work out what you do well and what God is using to reach people for Jesus – and do that.

Taking into account the theses arising from *The Common Call* of the World Missionary Conference of Edinburgh 2010 listed in the introduction, the features to be included in marketing and in future research include the question of how to reach young people and involve them in activities

[45] Tony Morgan, *Top 5 Church Marketing Mistakes*: www.churchleaders.com/outreach-missions/outreach-missions-articles/139202-5-marketing-mistakes-churches-make.html (accessed 12th February 2016).

within religious organizations. Furthermore, it should be considered how the media can be used to reach the poor and the oppressed. As always, most attention should be given to recognizing the needs, but also to the shaping of leaders. When Jesus called us to spread the good word, he meant to everybody and at every occasion. Even as missionaries, people have a need for mutuality, partnership, collaboration and networking. When we invite others to join us, we are engaging in a marketing activity.

Business as Mission: A Christian Perspective

Eugen Jugaru

Major Transformations in Central and Eastern Europe Towards the End of the Twentieth Century

From the beginning, I want to reveal that the economy in former communist countries was poor because of a lack of real competition and a lack of private initiative. The economy under the communist regime was a centralized economy where the orders and direction of economic development did not start from the existing needs of the population, but from the centralization of political leadership. Wayne Grudem presents several arguments against a centralized economy in communist countries and against egalitarianism, which hinders economic progress. According to his perspective, a uniform or nearly equal payment for all workers is unfair because people have varied interests, ambitions and abilities, but also because equality of payment would lead to the good habits of those who work hard being penalized and bad habits being rewarded, or it would lead to profligate wastefulness. On the other hand, a free market is desirable because the Bible supports this position. The Bible sanctions private property, sustains the liberty of those who desire to work and spend time as they wish, and finally shows that history often demonstrates that a free market brings better results than a government-controlled economy.[1]

Unfortunately, a capitalist economy was heavily exposed to communist criticism – as being a spent force while the communists proudly proclaimed that the economies of communist countries registered record rates of production in both agriculture and industry. Towards the end of 1980, Ceausescu, the Romanian president and dictator, paid all the external economic debts of the country but at a heavy price, by starving the population, by the isolation and limitation of the contacts of Romanian people with the rest of Europe behind the Iron Curtain, and by the development of a kind of Stalinist primitivism.[2] The result was all kinds of riots, strikes and finally a revolution to remove a system that had shown its limits. These historical events have proved the truth that without a stable

---

[1] Wayne Grudem, *Politics According to the Bible* (Grand Rapids, MI: Zondervan, 2010), 275-76, 282.

[2] Daniel Chirot, *Originile înapoierii în Europa de Est* (Bucharest: Corint, 2004), 6.

and relatively dynamic economic system, grounded on principles accepted among the people, the result would be chaos and social instability.[3]

The historical reality of the years since the fall of communism regarding the economic and social transformation of Central and Eastern Europe leads us to admit that R.H. Tawney was right when he says that 'Societies, like individuals, have their moral crises and their spiritual revolutions.'[4]

The fall of communism brought two new elements in former communist countries: freedom and a kind of vacuum in human life. Freedom was the desire of everyone but once it had been won, due to a lack of experience and the fact that freedom was something altogether novel, many people did not know what freedom really meant. The lack of a clear understanding of the rule of law, and the lack of political authority and coherence led to pronounced instability in these countries – an instability fuelled by the scourge of corruption. This lack of understanding can be explained by the anti-theistic propaganda of the doctrine of a dialectical materialist scientific worldview. As a political system that always tried to limit the influence of the churches, it permitted the holding of religious services but prevented the churches from being publicly visible.[5]

Challenges and Opportunities for Christians in Central and Eastern Europe

The challenges for the citizens of Central and Eastern Europe after the fall of communism were many, such as: how to use freedom fairly without offending other people, how to protect and develop democracy, how to correct the wrong mindset brought about by communism, how to increase confidence and private initiative for economic development, how to win the battle against poverty and corruption, how to promote voluntary initiatives, with an emphasis on developing human dignity and human value – the list of these *how*-s is endless. Christian business people have sought to answer these challenges in a practical way. It is interesting to note that, despite major pressure exerted by the political leadership, making the life of Christians very difficult during the communist period, the number of evangelical Christians has not decreased but rather the opposite. In Romania, during 1992, the first census after the fall of communism showed that there were 324,462 Pentecostals, 126,639 Baptists and 22,827 Brethren. Because the number of evangelical believers is quite large, they could bring about a beneficial transformation in society.

---

[3] Max L. Stackhouse, 'What Then Shall We Do? On Using Scripture in Economic Ethics', in Max L. Stackhouse, Dennis McCann, Shirley J. Roels (eds), *On Moral Business* (Grand Rapids, MI: Eerdmans, 1995), 112.

[4] Richard H. Tawney, *Religion and the Rise of Capitalism* (New Brunswick / London: Transaction Publishers, 2005), 277.

[5] Charles C. West, 'Marxism and Christianity', in Stackhouse et al (eds), *On Moral Business*, 284.

Two possibilities could be seen regarding the Christian presence in life (economic, political or cultural) beyond the churches: one was the church's passivity or a withdrawal from this sphere, based on the philosophy that the church must be kept separate from politics, business and culture; or, another was the idea that the church must be actively engaged in all spheres of life to redeem them by bringing the new influence of the Christian ethic into a secular system. The first was strongly rooted in the mentality of many Christians after the fall of communism, causing a kind of stagnation. For example, if we refer to economics, the concept of business had an aura of unfairness or dishonesty in the Romanian understanding during the 1990s.

Over the years, however, this 'monastic perspective' of withdrawing from the public arena was gradually replaced by a more accommodating one, so that the number of evangelical Christians who understood that there was a personal duty to be involved in transforming society increased considerably. Steve Brinn encouraged Christians to follow the example of Christ being involved in social life. He imagined that if Jesus Christ were a businessman he would get his hands dirty and learn the basics. Then he would get involved and take his faith to the place where the action was.[6] John Stott noticed that business has a practical side since it sets different goals to be followed and fulfilled. Finally, a business is profitable because one can measure a company's profits, such profit being the fuel for future development.[7] Grudem's perspective regarding the glorification of God through worship, evangelism, giving, moral living, faith, and also through business, is embraced by evangelical Christians too. Things such as profit, money, competition and the owning possessions is not evil in itself; these are all fundamentally good things but they carry all kinds of temptation.[8] Also, regarding the purpose of economics from a Christian perspective, Emil Brunner emphasized that 'the primary purpose of economics willed by God is to minister to human needs, service to life. This implies that economic order is a means and not an end'.[9]

The need for Christian involvement in the economic sphere was required because the economy of the former communist countries remained far behind the economies of countries in Western Europe and poverty had reached its peak. Romania, for example, despite its abundant natural resources, remained very weak economically.[10] According to Grudem, we

---

[6] Steve Brinn, 'Tough Business: In Deep, Swift Waters', in Scott B. Rae and Kenman L. Wong (eds), *Beyond Integrity* (Grand Rapids, MI: Zondervan, 2004), 67.
[7] John Stott, *Issues Facing Christians Today* (4th edn; Grand Rapids, MI: Zondervan, 2006), 242-43.
[8] Wayne Grudem, *Business for the Glory of God* (Wheaton, IL: Crossway Books, 2003), 12-16.
[9] Emil Brunner, *The Divine Imperative* (Philadelphia, PA: Westminster Press, 1947), 402.
[10] Daniel Chirot, *Schimbarea într-o societate periferică* (Bucharest: Corint, 2002), 6.

notice the profound truth that 'Communism enslaves people and destroys human freedom of choice'.[11]

After the fall of communism, almost everyone in Central and Eastern Europe longed for a prosperous economic life based on the western model, and as a consequence, when they had the chance, they emigrated to Western Europe. This phenomenon of migration became possible when the borders were opened and people discovered that Western businesses were looking for cheap labour and offering higher salaries. Today the number of Romanian workers who work in western countries is about 2½ million. Today, many people in Romania are still poor and in great material need. In his book, *Money, Possessions and Eternity,* Randy Alcorn gives ten reasons for personal poverty: 'Insufficient natural resources; adverse climate; lack of knowledge or skill; lack of needed technology; catastrophes, such as earthquakes or floods; exploitation and oppression; personal laziness; wasteful self-indulgence; religion or worldview; and personal choices by some to identify with and serve the poor.'[12]

A New Framework: Business as Mission and Mission as Business

Business can be understood as mission only when the business people are born-again Christians and their ability to develop economic activity is understood as a means of proclaiming the Kingdom of God. That Kingdom of God has been inaugurated when Jesus Christ died for humanity on the cross, and this Kingdom brings responsibilities for Christians 'to model that transformation, however imperfectly, as a foretaste of the perfect redemption that must ultimately await the age to come'.[13]

For genuinely Christian business people, economic activity has to be orientated towards people and their needs, and not towards the economy itself.[14]

Business is important because it can be a vehicle for the transformation of society, for bringing hope and encouragement towards the development of the Kingdom of God on earth, to imitate the creativity of God and glorify him.[15]

As I said above, the number of Christians in Central and Eastern Europe engaged in business greatly increased after the fall of communism. Their contribution and expertise is very important for economic development because of their experience of spiritual regeneration through the renewal of their minds. They bring Christian ethics into the business sphere: fairness,

[11] Grudem, *Politics According to the Bible*, 262.

[12] Randy Alcorn, *Money, Possessions and Eternity* (Carol Stream, IL: Tyndale House Publishing, 2007), 232.

[13] Craig L. Blomberg, *Neither Poverty nor Riches* (Leicester, UK: Apollos, 2005), 247.

[14] Arthur Rich, *Business and Economic Ethics* (Leuven / Paris / Dudley, MA: Peeters, 2006), 277.

[15] Grudem, *Business for the Glory of God*, 27.

productivity, a healthy self-esteem, resistance to temptation, and a respect for business partners and for truth. John Stott noticed the lack of commitment of many pastors to preach about economic or work issues: this was not a cause of boasting for pastors.[16]

The Christian business person understands that business is a mission from the Lord and he is the one before all others to whom they will be held accountable for their behaviour. According to Paul's teaching, they should behave justly towards their employees because the real Master of all is in heaven (Eph. 5:9; Col. 4:1).

Furthermore, a large number of Christian business people understand that their ability to do business is not an end in itself but a means of promoting fairness in business, providing jobs for people and, not least, proclaiming the practical reality of God's Kingdom among people. Max Weber says that capitalism does not mean the accumulation of wealth and the generalization of greed, because this instinct is found in all societies, not only in the capitalist world, but on the contrary, 'capitalism is identical to the pursuit of profit, the profit constantly renewed through continuous enterprise, continual rational, capitalist'.[17] At the same time, Christians have to be aware of the trap of materialism because materialism 'fosters amnesia concerning God's provision, eroding our ability to think straight and fostering a spirit of disobedience'.[18]

I think that an important document regarding ethical principles for Christian business development is the *Oxford Declaration on Christian Faith and Economics.*[19] The *Oxford Declaration* highlights mankind being constantly faced by two opposite challenges regarding economics: either a selfish individualism that neglects the needs of the community, or a rigid collectivism that suspends human freedom (art. 4), both affecting human dignity negatively. The production of certain items is important not only to make life easier or more comfortable, but also to express creativity and ingenuity.

Regarding the activity and process of work, *The Oxford Declaration* put forward that this was one of the major purposes for which man was created by God, and by fulfilling this mandate, man glorifies God. According to Miroslav Volf, a noted theologian, knowing the dynamism of contemporary economic life, the new emphasis is no longer on the conventional

---

[16] Stott, *Issues Facing Christians Today*, 230.

[17] Max Weber, *Etica Protestantă* (*Die protestantische Ethik und der Geist des Kapitalismus*, trans. A. Diaconovici), (Bucharest: Incitatus, 2003), 16.

[18] Neil Hood, *God's Wealth* (Carlisle, UK: Authentic Lifestyle, 2004), 38.

[19] *The Oxford Declaration,* issued in January 1990 by over one hundred theologians and economists, church leaders, ethicists and managers, represents an evangelical perspective on freedom and economic justice. *The Oxford Declaration* contains four major chapters: (I) Creation and management; (II) Work and recreation; (III) Poverty and justice; (IV) Freedom, governance and economy. *The Oxford Declaration* was intended to show which biblical principles promote business, and which are the most appropriate ways of developing vocation in accordance with Christian teaching and tradition.

Protestant reflection concept of *vocatio*, but on the new concept of *charisma*, the gifts of the Holy Spirit. Within an agrarian society, the concept of vocation, which has a narrow sense, was properly understood during the last centuries, but today, the concept of charisma seems more appropriate for a dynamic society because it encompasses a broader perspective.[20]

The purpose of work as emphasized in *The Oxford Declaration,* is directed in several different directions: first, towards God for his glorification; second, for the personal satisfaction and fulfilment of the worker; third, towards the company, since it accounts for the workers' contribution to the common good of society; and finally, for needy people to help them live a decent life (art.16-19).

The conclusion of *The Oxford Declaration*, remarks that too often Christians have allowed companies to shape their vision and failed to apply the teaching of the Scriptures in economic life. Knowing this reality, Christians are encouraged to promote Christian values in the economic field by structural and institutional changes that will help them to implement these values in the communities they belong to. The document ends with an eschatological perspective that turns eyes towards the *parousia,* the event awaited by Christian believers who are looking for Jesus Christ, whose return will take place when 'justice and peace will embrace [one another]'.[21]

A New Model and a New Outcome for Business

Referring to a new model of doing business, I do not mean a certain kind of scientific or technical aspect of business but a model that seeks to promote Christian business ethics in the business field. In this regard, the social involvement of Christians goes beyond business dictated only by the profit motive but includes social involvement, for the transformation of society and not least for the spiritual salvation of those who have not yet had the experience of a genuine conversion. As is stipulated in the Lausanne document, *Business as Mission*, business is important because it restores dignity and empowers people, provides the context for discipleship, promotes environmental stewardship, and is able to reinforce peace and strengthen the church.[22] The business people I contacted agreed with Lausanne Document and understood their task for this generation. Linked with Christian influence in society, I noticed Robert Sirico's interesting perspective about this important topic. He says that Christ is present everywhere by virtue of his omnipresence but he must be found in all

---

[20] Miroslav Volf, 'Works and the Gifts of the Spirit', in H. Schlossber, V. Samuel and R.J. Sider (eds), *Christianity and Economics in the Post-Cold War Era: The Oxford Declaration and Beyond* (Grand Rapids, MI: Eerdmans, 1994), 35.

[21] 'The Oxford Declaration', in *Transformation,* 7.2 (April-June 1990), art. 65.

[22] https://www.lausanne.org/networks/issues/business-as-mission

spheres of life, including business; in this way the Christian businessman's task is not the 'Christianizing' of society or the field of business but the task of 'Christo-finalize'[23] – something more than simply influence, rather the transformation of society is the task to be accomplished.

The new business model does not take into account the possibility of earning a lot of money in a short time, but of developing a kind of impatience which leads some business people to seek all kinds of 'shortcuts' or poor interpretations of economic law for their personal benefit.

The principle of 'profit at any cost' is not a Christian one, since it relegates the Christian ethic to second place; it may be sustainable, but echoes a lack of scruples and the abandonment of ethics, and promotes selfishness and indifference to people and business partners. Tawney said very clearly that there is a clear dichotomy between greed and Christian conduct: 'Compromise is as impossible between the Church of Christ and the idolatry of wealth, which is the practical religion of capitalist societies, as it was between the church and state idolatry of the Roman Empire'.[24]

A Christian businessman knows that he must work hard to promote consistent ethical conduct, but at the same time he recognizes that God is the source of any kind of blessing. This perspective shows that the financial income is not the most important item. Looking enviously towards business people from Western Europe, many Eastern European business people make the profit motive a modern idol to be worshipped, whilst neglecting their families seeing the happiness they had hoped for vanishing.

A recent issue that has to do with the spiritual and moral formation of business people was highlighted by specific conferences for Christians in business. These conferences emphasized the importance of business for the development of society, with responsibility in work seen as a duty to God, and the role that Christian business people can play in promoting the Christian faith and hope in a disappointed society. In some large churches, more experienced business people sometimes share out of their experience and expertise with beginners in business.

There are also Christian business people who see their business mainly as a way to proclaim their faith in God, to promote the Kingdom of God between people on earth, to use the business as an efficient tool for Christian ethical and social transformation.

Out of many that I have interviewed, few Christian business people in Romania have much understanding regarding this issue.

I.N.[25] is a Romanian businessman who started his business in 1999. His business is property development: he builds houses and all kinds of buildings, large and small, working together with his team of twelve

---

[23] Robert Sirico, 'The Entrepreneurial Vocation', in Scott B. Rae and Kenman L. Wong (eds), *Beyond Integrity* (Grand Rapids, MI: Zondervan, 2004), 65.

[24] Tawney, *Religion and the Rise of Capitalism*, 286.

[25] I.N., interview with the author, 10th June 2015, Vulcan, Braşov, Romania.

employees. The economic crisis of 2008 has affected his business, and as a result he was forced to reduce the number of his employees. He is aware that being a Christian businessman involves paying a price, that it means being an example of Christian behaviour and right attitudes for all his employees. For I.N., surprisingly, the most important consideration is not financial gain, although it is an important element in the business, but instead he is interested in the well-being of his employees and their families; in other words, he puts people's interests above the interests of his company.

I.N. graduated from a theological seminary while he continued his business, and is currently an elder in the local church. He combines constant care for his employees with his spiritual ministry and his duty as a businessman. For example, he helped one of the employees, who had four children, to extend his small house, to build more rooms needed for the family. He developed, in partnership with a group of English people, a programme to feed about one hundred poor Roma children with a daily meal. Besides this, he is interested in the health of his employees.

During the winter, when it is very cold in Romania, he is working together with his employees indoors. He is very careful to ensure that all his employees have good working conditions in order to stay healthy. One aspect that his employees appreciate, is that I.N. is a very good craftsman, a skilled builder, and one who is able to study construction plans in the smallest detail and gives clear direction to the work. As a Christian businessman, he prays for his workers and encourages them to give up bad habits that could put their health at risk.

For instance, he advises a worker who smokes too many cigarettes to renounce this bad habit, explaining to him that he would save the money that he normally spends each day on cigarettes, and in one month he would raise an amount sufficient to buy a nice gift for his wife or some useful items for the house. The result was that the worker agreed with this suggestion, gave up smoking and in turn he advised his wife to do the same. I.N. understood that, while he considered the material welfare of the workers, he should also pursue their spiritual welfare. He also thoughtfully invites his workers to attend worship services in the church, especially at Easter and Christmas.

F.C.[26] is another businessman who uses his business as a tool for the Kingdom of God. His field of activity is building and repairing roofs. Although he is young, in his thirties, he began to be engaged in business very early, when he was 18 years old. He is a specialist in his work and has contracts with both private companies and individuals. F.C. is very fair in paying salaries for his employees and sometimes, when there are some funds available, he rewards his workers above their normal salary. He is aware that business ethics for Christian business people is mandatory. He

[26] F.C., interview with the author, 12th June 2015, Codlea, Brașov, Romania.

works together with his employees to put a great emphasis on the quality of work so that customers are very satisfied. F.C. engages in various activities to help the needy, sponsoring some social programmes and giving material and spiritual assistance to people.

A.S.[27] is a prosperous Christian businessman who believes that business gives opportunities to help people, providing a place of work, and developing services for an open market. As a Christian, A.S. aims to share the gospel and to proclaim the Kingdom of God in a very practical way. He is involved in many social projects helping poor and needy people, whether they are evangelical Christians or not. For example, in partnership with a group of Christians from Ireland, he built a house for a poor family with eight children. A.S. understands the importance of material support for building churches as a place of worship. Accordingly, with this perspective, he has built two churches in his area. Regarding his ecumenical openness, although he is a Pentecostal, A.S. has contributed financially for the construction of a monastery belonging to the Orthodox Church. He is also one of the main sponsors who modernized student dormitories at the Pentecostal Theological Institute in Bucharest.

The businessman A.B.[28] has a family business and sells various parts and machinery for work in the agricultural field. Although his efforts in keeping the company prosperous are great, he understands his business is one way by which he can promote the Christian faith. He puts the importance of family life and fairness in business above the profit motive. A.B. is involved in major projects for help to needy people since he understands that it is his responsibility to bless others since God has blessed him. A.B. is very active in helping Roma children by popularizing the need that this ethnicity has, and by seeking volunteers to work with children through an after-school programme.

M.P.[29] is a well-known Christian businessman from the west of Romania. Through his business he searches for new ways to promote his faith and beliefs. M.P. has over 250 employees and over 50% of his company's products are sold on the Western European market. He considers that through his attitudes, by fairness in business, by honest discussions with business partners and workers, by pursuing customer and workers' satisfaction, he fulfils the task of proclaiming in a practical way the Kingdom of God. Although M.P. is involved in many social projects helping a lot of poor people, he does not want to talk about this, considering that this issue is something private, and that it is a Christian's responsibility towards his fellow people.

The last business person which I mention here is B.O.[30] He is a wealthy businessman who believes that the first responsibility of his, or of any

[27] A.S., interview with the author, 15th June 2015, Târgovişte, Argeş, Romania.
[28] A.B., interview with the author, 16th June 2015, Braşov, Romania.
[29] M.P., interview with the author, 19th June 2015, Oradea, Bihor, Romania.
[30] B.O., interview with the author, 3rd June 2015, Timişoara, Romania.

Christian business person, is to promote the gospel and to find ways for the transformation of society through diligent work. Out of all B.O.'s employees, 60% are non-Christians, and B.O. thinks that it is his duty as a Christian businessman to be an example to them of fairness, kindness and honesty. He is involved in many social projects aiming to promote the Kingdom of God, while he also helps the needy regardless of their beliefs. Every year, when children start school, B.O. buys school supplies for them, especially for those whose parents cannot afford them.

During late 2014, B.O. donated school supplies for about fifty poor families from a former mining town which is now in a state of economic collapse. Through this charity project, B.O. does not discriminate between children by religion or ethnicity, but tries to help them, promoting the Kingdom of God anywhere and everywhere there is a real need.

Just now in Romania there is the project 'Schools for Christ', which aims to send packages with Christian literature and CDs for teachers and professors at 24,000 schools, secondary schools and kindergartens. B.O. is actively involved in this, ensuring from his own resources the transport of these materials to schools everywhere in Romania. B.O. has a major passion for this project, and believes that in developing it, the Kingdom of God will be proclaimed and Romanian society will experience a real transformation.

Conclusion

Most of the Christian business people from former communist countries today offer an ethical way of doing business. They understand, as I stated above in my dialogue with some of them, that their activity is not only a way of making money, but a mission from God for society. After more than 25 years of political change in Eastern Europe, there are still challenges in the field of corruption, dishonesty, a lack of trust and bureaucracy. I notice also that some business people started small businesses, especially family businesses, which later became very prosperous. Most of them did not lose their confidence and faith in God, or had their church life interrupted, and they discovered a proper way to combine their faith with their business successfully.

More than that, Christian business people realize that God has given them the great opportunity to do business not only for making money or for the sake of activity, but to present a Christian profile in society, a model of fairness, and an example to be followed. Many of them find proper ways of combining business with belief, of bringing together the spiritual and material sides of life. The major goal for these people is not merely a prosperous earthly life, but finding new ways to bring the Kingdom of God through the vehicle of business between people, to save them not only from their poverty, but also from the slavery of sin, and to encourage them to make a new start in a better life. Many of them did it successfully and, in my opinion, the number of those who will imitate them will increase in the near future.

RE-IMAGINING THE SEMINARY: A CONFERENCE REPORT

Corneliu Constantineanu and Marcel V. Măcelaru

Introduction

This paper reports on the *Re-Imagining the Seminary* conference held at the Institutul Teologic Penticostal in Bucharest, Romania, 11th-14th September 2013 – an event we consider theologically and missiologically relevant, as it addressed issues related to seminary leadership models, educational strategies and theological methodology, all of these in full awareness of the specifics of the contexts of ministry in Central and Eastern Europe, while also having the nature and values of the Kingdom of God, as expressed by Jesus' symbolic gesture of placing a child in the midst of a theological argument on leadership in the Kingdom in Matthew 18, as a central theological motif and motivator.

The *Re-Imagining the Seminary* conference was initiated in order to offer a platform for reflection and discussion among and between theological educators and Christian leaders. To that end, Institutul Teologic Penticostal from Bucharest, Romania, and Evanđeoski Teološki Fakultet from Osijek, Croatia, in partnership with the Child Theology Movement, took the initiative of bringing together some sixty participants – theologians, seminary deans and presidents, pastors and practising theologians representing various theological institutions and Christian ministries from Central and Eastern Europe, and Russia – for a consultation on the scope, task and practices of theological seminaries in the region, in the light of the new social, political, economic and ecclesial realities brought about by the fall of communism. The following pages are the result of the discussions that ensued at that meeting.

The authors of this report are thankful to the people who participated and contributed to the conference with their experience and thoughts. Also, a special note should be made here of the Conference Reporting Team, whose written assessments of the conference are the basis of much of the following.

Conference Background and Rationale

Contemporary Christian communities are facing unique circumstances. The increased secularization of society, the relativization of truth claims, and the multiplication of religious options are concerns facing the church globally. In addition to these, the context of post-communist Central and Eastern Europe is marked by deeply rooted injustices, unresolved historical conflicts, the remnants of sweeping ideologies, social unrest, moral decline, political opportunism and economic instability. These external factors, accompanied by the 'idols' of fame, success, immorality and power, are painful realities affecting the life and ministry of the churches today.

These unprecedented challenges provide the background against which theological educators in Central and Eastern Europe are called to engage in deep theological reflection and undertake serious theological research in order to provide responses and enable the church to carry out her mission in the world – to proclaim and embody the gospel in meaningful and truthful ways for the contemporary generation. This call comes out of the conviction that Seminaries exist to serve the church in her mission. As such, 're-imagining seminaries' is a task that begins with thinking theologically about what 'church' and 'mission' mean. To that extent, it seemed suitable to the organizers of the conference to take Jesus' action of placing a child in the midst of a theological argument about leadership in the Kingdom of God as the central call of the gospel to rethink our believing and doing.

Jesus' action as recorded in Matthew 18 shows the gospel to be a disturbing message. Admittedly, this is a message that puts the gospel in danger of looking ridiculous, because it talks in terms of transcendent 'impossible possibilities'. But it is also a message that sets the church under the radical call of the Kingdom of God, which makes no working compromise with this world. 'Turn,' says Jesus – 'and the Kingdom of God lies on the other side of the turning.' For until we turn, we cannot imagine the Kingdom of God nor can we enter it. Only when we begin to see its truth, at least in partial glimpse, can we re-imagine church and seminary in an adequate way.

The Kingdom of God, when witnessed to in direct simplicity, as with Jesus, leaves us mystified. Jesus confronts us with the nearness of the Kingdom of God, and that calls for efforts to help the disciples cope with bemusement. For, if we have to deal with the Kingdom of God with what we have available in our own imagination, we see it as something like the organizations we know in the world, and start thinking of careers and greatness. However, Jesus did not merely proclaim the Kingdom of God, and did not merely go to the outcasts to bring them in; he also worked with his poor disciples, who were doing their best to keep themselves out of the Kingdom, in the most pious way. Jesus explained the practice of the Kingdom of God by his own life of love, self-giving, self-denial, in the way of the cross.

So, to help us understand such a Kingdom, Jesus deliberately adds another outlier, one that is in several respects standing on the opposite side of the institutional core – the child. The child is visible, personal, specific; the child is lowly, not a temptation to greatness. The child is small, local, immediate. A child, in whom God is present, inviting our reception, gives us the message: 'Do not ask what the Kingdom can do for you; ask what you can do for the King, incognito.'

Conference Objectives

As stated above, Jesus' action of placing a child in the midst of the disciples, who were engaged in a theological argument about leadership in the Kingdom, prompts us all to rethink our believing and doing. Particularly, it calls for a reconsideration of our motivation and praxis of theological education. Having these in mind, the objectives of the conference were to:

- Reflect on, discuss and imagine, new ways of following and embodying the values of the Kingdom of God while living in the kingdoms of this world.
- Rethink the nature of Christian leadership from the perspective of the Kingdom of God as opposed to models following paradigms available in the contemporary predominant culture.
- Evaluate and reshape the content of our teaching.
- Re-examine the way we teach, serve and relate to students, colleagues and communities so that our praxis reflects the model of Jesus.

In terms of concrete outcomes, it was hoped that the conference would result in:

- Further opportunities for theologians, educators, church leaders and children/youth workers from Eastern and Central Europe to reflect together on the issues addressed throughout the event.
- Biblically and theologically sound understandings of the place and role of children and youth in the life and mission of churches in this region.
- Further exploration of the meaning of the statement 'theology needs to get practical and ministry needs to get theological foundations'.
- Publications of the presentations and findings of the conference, as well as responses to, and reflections on, these, to be made available as a resource to schools and Christian communities in Eastern and Central Europe.

Conference Structure

The conference was held at Institutul Teologic Penticostal, in Bucharest, Romania, and lasted for three days, beginning on Wednesday afternoon, 11th September, through to lunch on Saturday, 14th September 2013. The event was structured round five plenary presentations, prefaced by a one-hour Bible reflection each day. Also, in order to make the most of the participants' experiences and ideas, there was plenty of time allocated for discussion (both in smaller groups and all together as participants shared in the aftermath of the plenary sessions); these were times in which everyone had the chance to offer their ideas, and they also included some planned presentations of documented case studies from about a third of the participants. As some of the participants commented afterwards, these discussions 'made the event' for them, since through them one could discover that there had already been some re-imagining going on.

Such sharing and interaction made this conference an active process that gave the participants the chance to learn from each other in the hope of boosting everyone's confidence in adopting and developing in their own contexts strategies and tactics used for theological education in other contexts, including the adoption of programming and evaluative practice that would result in transformative development.

The presentations and the ensuing discussions were recorded by the Conference Reporting Team, which was tasked with providing report summaries each day in order to track the direction of the discussions.

Conference Contributions

The following pages offer summary remarks in regard with what had been discussed and achieved during the conference. The purpose here is not to draw final conclusions or to reiterate for the reader new models of, and methods for, theological education. Rather, these are intended as initial steps on a journey towards re-imagining the seminary to which all theological educators are invited. To that end, we will here highlight the themes that dominated the discussions during the conference, posing questions that were raised, and will note the tentative answers that were offered. It is hoped that, in reading these conference highlights, the reader will be prompted to engage in a process of reflection on two foundational topics debated during the conference:

- Jesus placed the child in the midst as a sign of the Kingdom of God. What are the implications of this for your seminary?
- What contribution does welcoming the child in the name of Jesus make to re-imagining your seminary?

Highlights from Plenary Presentations and the Ensuing Discussions

The conference revolved round two distinct primary motifs: 'The Kingdom of God' and 'Theological Imagination'. Regarding the first, the motif of the Kingdom of God is a strong theme (perhaps *the* theme) in Jesus' ministry and was so within the consultation. The Kingdom appeared and reappeared throughout the conference; it helped to challenge and shape the presentations and the discussions. Some of the motifs that arose were:

- The challenge of humility as the way into the Kingdom – what does this humility look like today?

- The Kingdom is not static – it grows and changes.
- How is caring for our own children a sign of the Kingdom?
- Kingdom is about being not achieving – how does this relate to seminaries and a culture of top-down teaching?
- There are tensions between values of different kingdoms – the Kingdom of God clashes with the kingdoms of this world. This clash can be subtle or violent. We can be seduced by the kingdoms of the world, or persecuted. Daily we need to pray 'Thy Kingdom come…', knowing that we live in tension between the visible and the invisible.
- What are the signs of the Kingdom in our times?
- What powers shape our reflections about the Kingdom?
- How can we (or our seminaries) be signs of the Kingdom without giving in to the desire for greatness and 'success'?

The second motif, that of Theological Imagination, received central attention as in one of the introductory exercises the participants, divided in smaller working groups, were asked to sketch an image or images that reflected how they did theology – how they envisioned the practice of theology in their lives. Broadly speaking, there were three main styles of pictures:

- Boxes – a type of compartmentalizing of the different aspects of one's life, such as doing theology in the classroom or in church or in the family.
- A road – an attempt at finding a unifying theme, such as ethics, prayer or evangelism.
- A flow diagram – attempting to spell out the connection between the various spheres of one's life.

Within the pictures, there were two main ways in which theological education was re-imagined. Either it was suggested that theology is done within particular contexts, such as family, the local church, the community, the classroom, within denominational structures, the world. Or, theology was described as a practice, such as prayer, breaking bread, worship, social engagement, hospitality. The point was made, however, that whether within contexts or practices, it is of the utmost importance that theologians continue to ask: Where is Jesus in the picture? And even more, Which Jesus is in the picture? That is, are we, in the process of re-imagining, taking the gospel narratives seriously? Is the Jesus we teach in our institutions the Jesus who puts the child in the midst and who challenges the disciples to become humble in order to enter the Kingdom?

A further question that emerged during and out of the discussions concerns the relationship between being signs of the Kingdom and the work of theological education, whether in churches, seminaries or small groups of pastors. How do these different parts relate to one another? For example, how does raising children in the Kingdom of God relate to how one teaches someone else's child at the seminary? How is the work of training pastors to serve churches and communities a sign of the Kingdom? And how can these trainees become such signs? Underlying this discussion was the reminder of the call to repentance – the need to recognize how quickly we are like the disciples, striving towards greatness, missing the point of Jesus' life and his demand upon our lives. We are called by our Lord to repent and become like the child. Only in this way can we enter the Kingdom.

Re-Imagining the Seminary

The issues related to the seminary have appeared in various ways throughout the discussions, sometimes more explicitly in plenary or small groups, at other times in stories or questions. We have drawn these together in this section, beginning with themes that refer to the role of the seminary, both current and some imagined roles. We continued by looking at some of the systemic problems that can limit our re-imagination of the seminary. Finally, this section closes with the key questions emerging from the plenary sessions and small group discussions. Some of these also have tentative answers, glimpses of our joint re-imagining, which we have also included here.

WHAT IS THE ROLE OF THE SEMINARY?

- to form pastors
- to educate
- to be a place for theological reflection
- to prepare students
- to be a research centre
- to be a prophetic voice
- to help churches prioritize their ministry
- to be an influence on other academic institutions/universities
- to meet the needs of the church
- to build up an evangelical culture
- to help churches 'live the gospel'

WHAT ARE SOME OF THE SYSTEMIC PROBLEMS?

Of course, there are significant structural issues that face seminaries and may impose limits on any change or re-imagining. Such issues include economics, but perhaps we are too focused on the financial aspect and forget other issues that can be more dangerous, such as:

- Tensions between seminaries and churches, especially when a seminary is part of a denominational structure
- Changing societal contexts

- The systemic problems of making pastors in the image of the seminary

To bring a change to a seminary may require organizational restructuring. Perhaps applying some of the principles of organization theory could help us in this task.

WHAT ARE SOME OF THE EMERGING QUESTIONS?

- Why re-imagine the seminary?
  Some answers:
  - Because change is necessary for the Christian as we are being transformed into the likeness of Jesus
  - Because of the separation between the seminary and fast-changing society
  - Because the seminary could make a stronger contribution to mission and society than it currently does
- How to re-imagine the seminary?
  Some answers:
  - By re-imagining our theological method that must be both ecclesial and relational
  - By strengthening educational leadership
  - By reminding ourselves of our educational values based on the Kingdom of God
    - People matter more than institutions
    - Including, not excluding
    - The logic of the Kingdom of God
    - The value of relationships
    - The value of hospitality – indeed, its very necessity
    - Faithfulness to Jesus

Highlights of Ongoing Re-Imagining – Snapshots from Participants

In this section, a summary of stories that have shaped this conference are presented – stories of seminaries that have faced different challenges and found ways to overcome, to re-imagine themselves in the service of the church and the society in which they find themselves; stories of seminaries that are in crisis, where the pressures of a fast-changing world have been too heavy, or where the leadership or faculty are more shaped by an academic drive towards greatness than by service in the Kingdom of God; stories of informal education, of discipleship groups and mentoring. As is always the case with any story, it can be told in different ways, from different perspectives. Thus, in this spirit, we hope we can all learn from the narratives and the imagination of our sisters and brothers.

POLAND

The Evangelical School of Theology in Wrocław has undergone significant changes in response to an interplay of historical, cultural and ecumenical factors. In the light of 95% Catholicism in Poland, and a community of 0.01% Protestantism, EST has taken fluid and flexible shape to serve evangelical currents wherever they may flow within the ecumenical faith expressions, both Protestant and Catholic. EST has taken a bold and evidently visionary move away from a core business of pastor production, cancelling day classes, and re-orientating the focus of the college to serving a broader cross-section of the ecumenical faith community in theological engagement. Demographic sectors that had previously been marginally represented in the 'seminary' culture have become a significant constituency for the college: senior believers and business professionals, psychologists, lawyers, medics and teachers have been a fruitful source of growth.

A further component in the emancipation of theological education from the grip of 'pastor-manufacture' ethos is decentralization. Theological resources are dispersed, and made accessible in local venues, as well as through the ubiquitous cyber venues of on-line delivery. While most colleges at least dabble in on-line and 'extension' courses to some degree, EST has 'crossed the Rubicon', so to speak, taking the concrete step of selling their substantial property while remaining tenants of the building. In a business-savvy manoeuvre, this has not only released financial resources to implement the decentralization of delivery, but also established in operative terms the intentional strategy of mobility. EST initiatives provoke further theological reflection on the ways in which such models potentially align with doctrinal distinctives, such as the priesthood of all believers, as well as missiological currents of incarnational and contextual theologies. Where the context of theological engagement is liberated from the 'sermon-as-end-point' imperatives of ordination and training, a plethora of alternative assessment expressions become apparent, available and compelling.

BULGARIA

A Seminary was started in 1991 by the Pentecostal Union of Bulgaria. In about 2007, for financial reasons, the decision to close the residential programme was made to allow greater freedom for doing other work elsewhere; the students who came to the seminary were very young and with little experience, and therefore saw little purpose in what they were learning. The seminary found that older people, who had been working and involved in ministry informally for 10-15 years, were much more interested in learning and studying theology for ministry. So they closed the residential programme and started an educational extension programme in various locations. The teachers travel to the place once a month and run intensive courses. They help those who are already doing ministry, equipping them to do it better. Practically none of these extension students will become full-time pastors. Sometimes they get 15-20 people from one church who come to learn, and who take that learning with them back into their work contexts and into the church. It helps the pastor and takes better account of the context and the realities of where they are.

The programme is interdenominational and has helped build relationships between people from different churches. They find through this that they are not so different one from another and that they often share the same challenges, the same struggles within their communities. This programme currently runs in three locations. They have also started a one-year programme for lay people. The curriculum includes Bible and theology, helping students to make the connection between what they are studying and the particularity of their contexts (e.g. Christians living in a Muslim-majority village). These events are open to all and students have been drawn from universities, etc. This programme also trains teachers. There is a recognition that this programme is always changing, and that it might look very different in 3-5 years. This flexibility allows them to be more contextual, even if it doesn't allow for one-to-one training in a residential setting. The seminary also offers a camp for young people, bringing local pastors and major leaders to the event to link these young people with the work of the churches and alternative theological education formats. The idea is that, out of this event, new leaders will emerge and so help in the future with the transition in leadership between one generation and the next.

The Romanian Diaspora

The Ekklesia Bible College started in 2003, offering education for Pentecostal Romanian pastors in the USA and Canada. However, the programme has mostly people who are not training to be pastors. The initial idea was to have a central place to which students could travel, but this did not work, so it became an extension programme, beginning in ten locations across the USA and Canada. The expectation was of some 100 students, but in fact there was a starting group was of over eighty participants in just one location. The curriculum is a four-year BA programme run with about 25 teaching staff from Romania and the Romanian diaspora community. The final project requires a paper of about 20-30 pages. Most of the students are not in the programme in order to seek ordination. They are lay people interested in studying theology and trying to relate their theological studies with their work, such as engineering, the academy, etc.

MOSCOW, RUSSIA

In the aftermath of the revival that took place in the 1990s, a Seminary was started in Moscow in order to prepare ministers to serve the rapidly growing evangelical Christianity in Russia. It is a denominational school (Church of God), but is open to students from all churches. The curriculum was at first largely based on the Church of God training programme in the USA. This was good training for the students, but it did not help them connect with their churches and they were often at odds with the communities from which they had originally come. This led to a decline in students that coincided with a generation gap that the entire country was facing. The seminary also had an identity crisis – who are we? We are Russians, but we are not Orthodox. So for the context in Russia it was necessary to go back to the Reformation as a starting-point and to root the history of the seminary in something that was neither Orthodox nor American. One example was teaching the 'doctrine of the priesthood of all believers', and the realization that this was not something that was actually practised in the churches today. How do we practise this afresh today and how does it change how the seminary views itself? – and if we believe in the priesthood of all believers, how can a seminary be a place that trains only pastors? One way to address this question has been to open the doors of the seminary for university students who are studying other degrees but are living on the campus. In the evenings they are given theological courses that aim to help them link their Christian convictions with their secular work.

MACEDONIA

The Evangelical Church is wondering if it is time for it to have its own training institution. But evangelicals are a very small minority so why have a school? Yet, the church feels that the seminaries in neighbouring countries are not really offering training in the Macedonian context. The denomination constructed a building that is too big for a church but could possibly be a place for educational training. But since the economic crisis of 2007-2010, plans for its re-ordering were put on hold. One main question has been: how many people do we need to go through this programme to make it viable? So it was felt that maybe they should start with a simpler training programme and then, 3-6 years later, see where they had got and then look into issues of accreditation. The church in Macedonia, as elsewhere, is less in need of pastors and more in need of people who can assist with evangelism, church planting, etc. A second question is: what do we do about another generation that can envision the challenges that will come?

ZAGREB, CROATIA

Croatia is 95% Catholic. There are four evangelical theological schools, serving some 10,000 evangelicals in the country. The Biblical Institute in Zagreb has about 30-40 students and offers 2, 3 and 4-year programmes. Only the one-year programme is the school's 'own'. For the other programmes, the school partners with the Evangelical Theological Seminary in Osijek. Throughout this partnership, the school leadership has questioned whether it would just be a small denominational school or grow bigger, and about what it means to be a seminary between heaven and earth. They asked what God wanted of them as a school. This has led them to open their doors to students from other traditions, even to those whose traditions are very closed to others. They have made an deliberate decision not to compete with other schools. They are also in partnership with other universities, such as with the University of Zagreb. There is some questioning by the churches regarding the problems they are facing and the school tries to work together with them to find solutions; the same was done in the creation of a journal for publishing the work of Croatian theologians. This journal has been put into English so that Christians in the West can have access to theological reflection from Croatia. Finally, the school has also established partnerships with public libraries for lectures and is offering its library space to students from disciplines other than theology to come to study and do research.

OMSK AND NOVOSIBIRSK, RUSSIA

This is a region that was developed through economic incentives before the 1917 October Revolution. A Seminary was started in Novosibirsk, Russia in 1999, located in the heart of the academic and research area. It is a Baptist seminary that serves the whole region and receives new students every two years. At the moment there are about sixty, most supported by their local churches. For four days they study and for three days they work in the churches. The students who want to go on academically can also do a Master's in Christian ministry.

These reports suggest four key words that could be used to describe what has been going on in this region of the globe with regard to theological education:

1. Survival – due to contextual challenges (economic, socio-cultural, demographic, etc.) all the schools in the region are facing questions relating to their very survival. As such, creative ways of re-imagining have emerged.
2. Faithfulness – each case presented is a testimony to the faithfulness of the educators who continue to serve and minister despite significant challenges.
3. Provision – each story is also a testimony to God's provision, for although significant re-imagining has had to occur in most cases, the

ministry of these seminaries remains relevant and a real presence in church and society.

4. Creativity – it was impressive to see how much re-imagining has already been going on in this part of the world, where economic, social, demographic and other factors have caused traditional models to fail.

Conclusions, Lessons, Recommendations

Challenges Faced and Lessons Learned

A number of challenges were faced, and lessons learned, in the course of organizing and overseeing the conference. These included:

1. The planning process was not easy. The steering committee included people from different cultures, who once again had to accept that we had different ways of going about things. We did not altogether overcome the difficulties arising from this. Meeting on Skype, although a great way of saving time and money, has had its limitations, which impeded our work. More preparation, including written plans working out details and providing a basis on which to debate the issues arising, would be advisable.
2. It was adventurous to mix Child Theology with re-imagining the seminary. We did not work out in advance how the two related to each other, or what the balance was between them.
3. There was not enough information on what was involved in re-imagining the seminary in Eastern Europe. As it turned out, several seminaries in this region had already done some creative re-imagining.
4. For most people, this was the first time they'd come across Child Theology and Child Theology insights. Although this is a great positive, better preparation in terms of process would have probably enhanced the experience by providing specific questions for discussion and more opportunities for the audience to interact.
5. Initially, it was planned that the presenters should meet together a month before the conference and evaluate what was to be said. Not holding that meeting due to financial limitations meant that the conference lacked a common link between the various contributions given.

Key Findings

The participants in the conference felt that the event was beneficial to them as it provided an opportunity to:

- Reflect on, discuss and imagine new ways of following and embodying the values of the Kingdom of God while living in the kingdoms of this world.
- Rethink the nature of Christian leadership from the perspective of the Kingdom of God – as opposed to models following paradigms available in the contemporary predominant culture.
- Take stock of how Christian seminaries in Eastern Europe have developed since 1990 in relation to church and mission in society.
- Ask what seminaries are called to become and what they are to make of themselves.
- Re-imagine the seminary by reconsidering the content and methods of teaching and learning.

Recommendations

The conference was concluded with a meeting in which the participants were asked to reflect on the things discussed and offer their thoughts/recommendations. Out of this discussion, as well as out of a follow-up Skype meeting of the Steering Committee, the following recommendations to the participants, the organizers and theological educators in the region, are made:

1. Create and maintain channels of dialogue between seminaries, other Christian institutions and ministries, and the churches they serve.
2. Create and maintain channels of communication between participating institutions for the purpose of raising awareness of achievements and dilemmas, and for sharing experiences and promoting co-operation.
3. Find ways to promote role models and good practice in theological education informed by motifs explored throughout the conference: kingdoms and repentance; leadership and humility; hope and faithfulness.
4. Devise strategies to aid the continuation of the dialogue and reflection initiated during the conference. These should include a self-evaluation template to help assessment of seminaries and of individual practice, and a follow-up after six months to discover directions of reflection and changes that were the direct consequences of participating at the conference.

Disseminate the ideas discussed and the findings of the conference for a wider audience. In particular, besides this initial report, the contributions given in the conference and responses to, and reflections on, these contributions should be collected and published in a volume to be made available to seminaries and theological educators worldwide.

BUILDING A NATION: THE MISSION OF THE CHURCH IN CONTEMPORARY SOCIETY

Mihai Himcinschi

Preliminaries

Democracy as a socio-political way of life was actively noted in the international arena since the nineteenth century and it proves to be the perfect model regarding the relationship between people and their elected leaders. Church life and doctrine, taking a stance regarding the social issues faced by believers in their everyday life, has always supported this social target without promoting a political theology or a religious policy, as the church was always aware that the Kingdom and the way of life it preaches is not of this world (John 18:36). Why do we need in the context of mission to debate the God-Trinity in relation to society? Would not be easier to deduce the Christians' behaviour in the content of the Holy Scriptures, from the church's sacred teachings, or from the Church Fathers' doctrine?

People and Trinitarian Communion

Thinking socially, ever since its historical beginnings, the church has recognized and supported the principle of self-determination in the political life of countries around the world. The principle is based on recognizing the values within the political units that promote, or should primarily promote, the quality of life: intellectual and cultural progress, human relationships based on dialogue and openness to dialogue, equal treatment without discrimination.

These are the proper precepts of missionary evangelism (Luke 19:10; Rom. 1:14). These principles are promoted by the third millennium church, which is aware that 'the affirmation of democratic form was not the fruit of a more or less triumphant starting-point that emanated from primitive forms of political cohabitation, un-adapted to its economic and cultural level, but was, and still is, the expression of a hard-won moral and intellectual life choice'.[1]

Why then argue that Christian Trinitarian monotheism is, or can be, the best model for social and political relationships? Firstly, because of the structure of interpersonal communion model displayed by the Trinity, an interpersonal communion based on love and unity. The divine model can serve as a premise for expressions of unity among dynamic beings

[1] Michele Nicoletti, *Homo politicus. I dilemmi della democrazia* (Rome: Gregoriana Libreria Editrice, 1998), 9-10.

(humans) who are in an open communion of love. This is the base for dialogue and social peace. Secondly, because the Christological nature of the mission of the Church on earth, which, simply put, is: 'on earth as it is in heaven' (Matt. 6:10).

There is no doubt that, during the two thousand years of Christianity, true Christians have strayed from these sources of eternal life. However, God and the world remain two indisputable facts: one purely transcendent as a being, the other purely immanent.

> It is widely accepted that ideology goes through a period of crisis. In this regard, it was argued that the reforms undertaken define indeed the end of the ideology epoch through the fall of the ideological system of socialism. Such an interpretation may be wrong of course, if based only on the fall of walls or socialist regimes as the social formation and acceptance of the principles of various ideological systems preceded their association with such regimes or with raising the walls. Indeed, ideology's co-existence with state power was, as we know, a strange and contradictory historical comity that, although it provisionally offered each dimension the possibility to pursue its own interests, it contained the seeds of resistance and the prospect of breakdown. Indeed, state power absorbed from ideology its generalization of authority, and ideology indulged this association in order to impose their broader principles, with all its reserved or negative position towards the state and state authority. It is therefore easy to understand that breaking this association does not mark the ideology's end, nor releases it of liability, leading it to a period of internal crisis and to an inevitable reformulation and modernization of its principles.[2]

Thirdly, while for a Unitarian monotheist it would be illogical to support total obedience to an individual or a socio-political system, a Trinitarian personalist faith is aware that it should not accept such a system as an undeniable socio-political model. Such a Unitarian model will have to struggle for an inter-personalist Trinitarian foundation that cannot be replaced by any political theory. It will have to run after a divine command concerned about the socio-political environment, or after a perfect social model that can only be found in the Trinitarian Christian revelation par excellence.

It is clear that many Trinitarian Christians in the past have seen –a triple-hypostatic power considered divine. Such development of social-ecclesial thinking was indeed expected initially, given that monotheism first replaced polytheism as the state religion, at a time when autocracy was well established. Kings lacking divine prestige were compensated by the parallelism of the only heavenly God with a single leader on earth. Actually, in terms of the Trinity doctrine, this position was not illegitimate. It was not legitimate when it claimed to be directly validated by the Christian understanding of God-Trinity.

---

[2] Damaschinos Papandreou, *Biserică, societate, lume* (Iaşi, Romania: Trinitas, 1999), 73-74.

Democracy belongs exclusively to human history, to any society wishing for a free way of being and without any trace of totalitarianism. The democratic form of a political community's social organization is not the natural and definitive source of history,[3] but the result of a voluntary and constantly renewed choice. This choice is restricted to freedom in defending the complex cultural, economic, social and spiritual interests, all practical principles underlying the natural co-existence between all members of a group, community and nation. As Christians, freely consenting, choose an evangelical, Christological and Trinitarian lifestyle, they also choose, as citizens, a civil cohabitation based on freedom, with rules and institutions supporting the ordee of the human spirit. Like soteriology, democracy also has anthropological roots, worthy of reflection.

Regarding the anthropological plane, a further dilemma of democracy can be avoided – a dilemma of contemporary origins consisting of a trend of egalitarian dynamics that is present in today's democratic regimes, based on alignment and the absorption of the human individual by the community. This tendency may cause that the development of such democracy will destroy a people's social, cultural and spiritual bases; that is, the destruction of inherited foundations that caused a people's birth, consisting of the sense of freedom whereby a person claims its own autonomy, and that establishes the foundations for an internationally constructive affirmation.

The possibility of a free and loving communion with the Trinity finds its base on the internal relationship of the three Persons within Godhead and in the fact that the Trinity acts oikonomically in relation with the created world, The implication of *oikonomia* in this context is that the triune God, as a unitary, yet multi-personal divine being, relates as such to any area of human life. God would not have revealed himself as Trinity if it was not necessary for our life, and this revelation – once accepted and understood – should be considered as the basis of the social life of humans created in the image of God.

In light of the western essentialist model, distortions of the above understanding of Trinity are also advanced. In such view, the dimension of communion' is downplayed and the Trinitarian God is interpreted as three divine persons characterised solely by a common nature. I argue that such distortion of God's revelation, however, leads to undesirable consequences in regard with the social thought of the church: individualism, secularization, economic crisis, globalization, etc.

> Throughout Scripture we see the divine ancestry holily praised as *monada* and *enada*, for the simplicity and unity undivided beyond nature, of which, as from a unifying power, we and our divided differences also unite, focusing above the world, we gather into a divinely monad and in a unit that imitates God, but we see it also as Trinity, for the threefold hypostatic manifestation

---

[3] Ralph Dahrendorf, *Quadrare il cerchio. Bebessere economico, coesione sociale e libertà politica* (Roma-Bari: Laterza, 1995), 42.

of fertility above the being through which it exists and through which all fatherhood in heaven and on earth is called.[4]

Christology and Democracy

Democracy and theology claim a common ground: truth. In theology, Truth was made Man, a divine-human person, a subject with two natures: Jesus Christ. In politics, although also promoting "truth", this is truth turned ideology, or even party ideologies, which, paradoxically end up in permanent conflict. This is ethical relativism, the kind of thinking that leads to extreme consequences: the theory that the existence of Truth as being is not only a problem, but also a risk to the democratic society (Matt. 10:34-35). As sociology argues, Truth as being enters in conflict with policies that aim to tidy conflicts in order to achieve a reasonable *modus vivendi*, and does so by coercing and parenthesising man's great existential questions.[5] In terms of theology, Truth admits no different tones, no compromises – a position which, in social terms, would inevitably divide the social group. Because of this, ethical relativism concludes, logically, that it is better to completely abandon the issue of Truth issue, or to at least exclude it from the political sphere.

In the early twentieth century, German philosopher Hans Kelsen,[6] argued that democracy would not last over time if based on an absolutist conception of truth, for such a conception is a characteristic of the religious / metaphysical perspective and would endanger the democratic basis of genuine respect for the opinion of citizens and for the majority principle. In this perspective, he believes that there is only one critical-relativistic view of truth, compatible with democracy, even if such a view cannot provide a foundation of democracy, but it offers only a conditional justification. In the Kelsenian picture, the choice for democracy does not appear completely rationally founded, but – like any other valuable choice – remains entrusted to individuals' responsibility. The one who does not believe in absolutes chooses democracy; it does not take refuge in secure ideologies, but lives the experience of constantly changing political movements assuming leadership and accepts the risk of confrontation. Kelsen thus refuses any possibility of democracy's religious foundation, with explicit reference to the attempts led by Emil Brunner, Reinhold Niebuhr, and Jacques Maritain. To tragically symbolize a possible conflict between truth and democracy, several times, he cites the Gospel story of Pilate asking the people to find out whether he should release Christ or Barabbas: and the people vote against Jesus.[7]

---

[4] Saint Dionysius the Areopagite, *Opere complete* (Bucharest: Paideia, 1996), 136.

[5] Giorgio Campanini, 'La democrazia fra ideologie e valori', in *Homo politicus. I dilemmi della democrazia* (Rome: Gregoriana Libreria Editrice, 1998), 24.

[6] Hans Kelsen, *Essenza e valore della democrazia* (Bologna, Italy: Il Mulino, 1984), 143.

[7] Michele Nicoletti, *Homo politicus*, 12.

In the Christian's relationship with society, Orthodox spirituality is deeply marked by the Godhead's triune and personalist nature, making possible its knowledge of grace. Knowing God means loving him as a merciful and lawgiver God, and in direct relationship with the world. Current syncretistic ideologies, although conceiving of God as an omnipotent and omniscient creator, most often see such a God's relationship with the world based on a number of purely speculative arguments and draw erroneous conclusions about his existence in relation to social environment, thus making Revelation devoid of meaning. 'Creation is not entirely put out of Trinity. However, it is put from the beginning, and it remains in the Spirit, not intermingling with Him, thus with the Trinity (pantheism). There is something paradoxical in the creation's way of being. On the one hand, it is not part of the Trinity, or is beyond It, on the other hand is not entirely beyond It (deism)'.[8]

The church in mission sees revelation as the central point of divine love expressed in the act of sacrifice – a revelation of two great acts of power: the act of God in relation to creation, and the act of the future action by which God pushes human history to an end. Nothing that happens in society is a necessity; this leads to the conclusion that everything within history is at least desired by God, who will also bring it to an end according to the purpose for which it was created.

At first glance, a Trinitarian Christian should perceive this assessment as idolatry. God is Trinity, and he has revealed himself, and will for ever determine our whole vision of divinity as creative person, as he is knowable by his revelation and not due to abstract philosophical considerations on speculations about God's involvement or lack of involvement in the public life. This perspective is fundamental to us in understanding both the nature of God's power and the human history in terms of the Holy Trinity's oikonomical involvement. The common ground between our human conception of power as exercised in the public area and the concept of God's power, is that the latter allows us know him as the Monad and Triad God also in the social plan, given the charismatic power working in the world to fulfil all positive ideals, including the social ones. The autonomous human concept can add to this main idea a halo of idolatry – creating social self-affirmation, or a distorted mystical fascination with oneself. Would the creator of everything end his creative process, he would tend to express a singular egoist's self-sufficiency. However, in God, the barrier of individual selfishness is overcome by the intrinsic communal life of theology and *oikonomia*.

Determining God's power in the world, which is reflected in his very revelation, requires careful consideration, because exercising the divine power within the social area, is also a review of this revelation. The authority of his power comes from a constant state of self-abnegation,

[8] Dumitru Stăniloae, *Note 64*: Saint Athanasius the Great, *Epistola I către Serapion* (P.S.B. 16: Bucharest: Editura Institutului Biblic şi de Misiune al B.O.R., 1988), 58.

modelled after his incarnate son, who willingly accepted all the sufferings (Isa. 53:4).

The synergy between the human concept of power, especially socio-political power, and the eternal power of God is best illustrated by the icons of where he wears a royal crown and high priest robes. At first glance, the picture seems to proclaim a union of religious and political authority. In fact, the gospel view on Christ's leadership is open at both ends, one proclaiming that 'My kingdom is not of this world' (John 18:36), and the other, 'Take eat, this is my body' (Matt. 26:26). God's power is exercised until the end of the ages, and his greatness in the social space, through the church, becomes apparent not in self-affirmation, but in self-abnegation.

In the light of Trinitarian revelation, society should be seen not only as the ultimate expression of divine omnipotence, but also as a deliberate and personal restriction of omnipotence, designed to lead the world towards the ultimate goal.

'We believe in one God, in one principle, without beginning, uncreated, unborn, imperishable and immortal, eternal, infinite, uncircumcised, infinitely powerful, simple, un-compounded, incorporeal, incorruptible, impassible, immutable, candid, unseen, the fountain of goodness and justice, spiritual light, inaccessible; power that cannot be known by any measure, but being measured only by its own will. For it cans everything it wants',[9] both in the logical sense that all was done in history, cannot be undone, and in the purpose of world's perfecting through grace, an unforced, free and conscious completeness. Creation's autonomy that underlies all natural laws is not only an expression of God's creative power or just an expression of his creative love, but the expression itself of our free response as social beings.

Secularization and Ecclesial Solidarity

The secular phenomenon emphasizes this limitation and self-blur of God in his creation, and it claims to provide the basis for a well-known accusation that God accepts temporary social distress and the eternal hell suffering. This sad but real situation of the world, always divided by the consequences of sin, inevitably leads to our contemporaries' question: How is it possible for a society to exist and to last as a stable and just society, having free and equal citizens, while deeply divided by incompatible, though rational, religious, philosophical and moral doctrines?

God answered this charge, not by an act of power in the sense of human understanding, but by an act of solidarity with the man, with whose burden of suffering was burdened his son. Simultaneously, God has revealed himself as loving communion of Three Persons, with which people can

[9] John Bordley Rawls, *Political Liberalism: The John Dewey Essays* (Philosophy, 4: New York: Columbia University Press, 1993), 6-7.

have a personal relationship, starting a real experience, an experience different from that of a world that operates under the necessity of conclusive natural laws. The Trinity promises a new social life, in and through the church, in freedom and love, an ideal to be fully accomplished by its end. This is true eschatology. The truth in Christian revelation, in terms of the glory of God, is that this glory is complete in heaven, and it will soon be complete on earth. Secondly, that the glory remains the glory of the God-Trinity, who voluntarily came in human social suffering. Thirdly, that the human will deliberations of the public area are of crucial importance, no matter how far off their completion date, although in God's terms it is very close (John 14:3, 18, 28).

It is, however, little of what we know about the nature of such days, or about its stages of expression. In particular, there is no reason to assume that a final exercise of the divine destructive power will be included, because it would be the opposite of love deduced from the self-revelation of God-Trinity by his own revelation (1 John 4:8). However, there is a natural tendency for the socially persecuted to see in the exercise of God's eschatological power, at least in part, a revenge following the ruthless exercise of divine power (Matt. 25:41) on the second *Parousia*, and now advanced on earth by the suffering of so many innocent people.

Once the distinction between the human way of understanding God's power and God's way of exercising his power is understood, we can be freed from the illusion that the central political currents of history must also include God's work. Surely, God can, but certainly acts in history. On the one hand, his action is subjective due to human freedom that he does not want restricted in any way, and on the other hand, he guaranteed his creation charismatic freedom where man is both the crown and its priest.

> Today, the conflict between individual and collective interests is still the main problem that every state hopes to solve and to survive. While law and the legal mentality that can result from it, have been associated with state control, almost all religions never tried such a human behaviour control. Combining religion with law and rationalism can lead to behaviour contrary to society's interests, but it has no cures for people's inner suffering (passions) that leads to this antisocial behaviour. In other words, such a solution is not enough. Even the Holy Fathers recognized that the Decalogue (the Ten Commandments) only succeeded to try a fundamental regulation of human society. However, even the lawmakers of the most secular states will try to keep the crowds traditional values under the guise of morality and therefore the Church must continually watch over political life. This life does not need moralising, but an offering of sacrificial love that is sensitive to the needs of every citizen.[10]

[10] Andrew Sopko, *Pentru o cultură a iubirii jertfelnice: Teo-antropologia Arhiepiscopului Lazăr Puhalo* (Cluj-Napoca, Romania: Eikon, 2004), 96-97.

Conclusions

The social life of believers cannot ignore the anthropological foundations of democracy. Contemporary reflection on this reality highlights the profound ambivalence of the relationship between the church and society, between theology and culture, between reason and faith.

In terms of ecclesia, human complexity is always optimistic, but cannot ignore the socio-political perspective, which it sees as complementary, not antagonistic, to the extent that it leaves an open door to the multi-personalist transcendental spirituality, namely, to the eternal Trinitarian nature.

PUBLIC THEOLOGY: CHRISTIAN FAITH AND THE PUBLIC SPHERE IN CENTRAL AND EASTERN EUROPE

Corneliu Constantineanu

Introduction

The historical context of Central and Eastern Europe is a complex one and has witnessed significant transformations in the last hundred years, i.e. from the first to the second Edinburgh World Mission Conference. Communism has dominated the entire region for some fifty years through a regime of fear, violence and terror. As far as religion was concerned, there was no doubt: Marxists did not like religion! One of the most distinguishable Marxist 'prophecies' was that religion would soon disappear from human consciousness and would no longer play any role in society. And they worked hard to eradicate it and thought they could! Contrary to that, and somewhat unexpectedly, what we have witnessed at the end of the 20th and beginning of the 21st century, was a surprising and spectacular return of the religious phenomenon as an important and influential factor in the social arena. However, what the communists did manage to do was to discredit religion and to push it into the private sector of life, totally detached from any aspect of real life. In their struggle to survive, churches either withdrew from society or collaborated with the communist authorities conceding to their imposed limitations on the churches. Unfortunately, the ultimate consequence of this tragic reality was that churches accepted this state of affairs and took their faith as something purely spiritual, between the believer and God, a faith that had nothing to do with the wider cultural, social, and political world! When freedom came, we thought that everything would change for the better, and that we would experience an abundance of milk and honey of the promised land of democracy. However, we soon realised that our new-found freedom and democracy did not automatically bring with them a transformation of life as we had imagined, least of all a grand spiritual renewal. The transition to democracy meant that churches needed to think afresh as to what their witness should be in the new situation.

It is in this context that it became evident that one of the most important and urgent missiological tasks of the church was to become an authentic witness in the public realm. The constant challenge before us is to fight against a simplistic and narrow definition of mission and try to develop afresh a holistic, comprehensive public theology of *missio Dei* for our day, and articulate clearly the co-ordinates on which the gospel is to be channelled for addressing the social, economic, political and religious issues facing society in our context today. This should be a theology which emphasizes the mission of God to redeem the entire creation, which points to the lordship of Christ over entire reality, a theology which articulates clearly the contribution the gospel can bring for the common good and human flourishing. This may be, indeed, one of the most important missiological concerns for Christians of this generation, in this context: to proclaim and embody the gospel as public truth, i.e. concerned with and addressing the *entire reality* of the life of society. This is, in my opinion, an urgent missiological preoccupation for Christians in this part of the world: to search for and articulate a solid public theology of culture, work, power, social justice and reconciliation, a public theology of the common good and human flourishing.

In this paper I would like to offer a brief reflection on public theology as a missiological endeavour of the church in this post-totalitarian, ever-in-transition context. Learning from, and in interaction with, those who have reflected on these issues before us, I would like to point out several significant features of public theology and highlight some of the most relevant issues of public engagement in the context of Central and Eastern Europe. I begin with a closer look at the Romanian context and the contradictory reality this illustrates regarding religion and public life. Then I will touch briefly on the danger and potential of religion in the public sphere. The larger part of the chapter is devoted to a discussion of public theology and a presentation of several significant issues of public theology relevant to our context. I will end the chapter with a few concluding remarks.

Faith and Life in Romania: A Contradictory Reality

In religious adherence, Romania ranks among the highest in Europe, with over 99% of the population indicating they belong to a religious group, with only 0.11% atheists and 0.10% indicating no religious affiliation.[1] However, the implications of this high religiosity for the everyday life of people and its effect on the concrete social, cultural, political and economic realities of the country reveal a disturbing and contradictory reality. Romania, the country with the highest ranking of religiosity in Europe, is also among the leading countries in terms of corruption, poverty, abortions, lack of trust.[2] For such a state of affairs, the causes are many – as for the

[1] According to the National Census conducted in 2011: www.insse.ro/cms/files/publicatii/pliante%20statistice/08-ecensamintele%20despre%20religie_n.pdf (accessed 28th October 2015).

[2] Silviu Rogobete, 'Between Fundamentalism and Secularization: The Place and the Role of Religion in Post-Communist Orthodox Romania', in S. Devetak, O. Sîrbu and S. Rogobete (eds), *Religion and Democracy in Moldova* (Maribor, Slovenia / Chişinău: ISCOMET/ASER, 2005), 105-10. See also Tom Gallagher's impressive and detailed analysis of the complex causes and factors which undermined the development of a stable, independent and

discrepancy between such religiosity and the way people actually live. This discrepancy does not invalidate the thesis that religion has a potential for being a positive factor for social, economic and political change. It shows, however, at least two things: first, that the religious 'potential' is not automatically translatable into social realities; and, second, that it is not just any kind of religiosity that could contribute effectively to human flourishing and well-being. For an effective and beneficial practice of faith, and in order for its potential to bring about hope, compassion, reconciliation and social healing, we must find resources within our own religious texts and traditions, and explicate them in ways that are relevant to the concrete social and political realities of communities.[3]

For far too long the church has divorced faith from the other aspects of reality and reduced it to a purely spiritual dimension with terrible consequences for the embodiment of the gospel. We have reduced faith to church attendance and to a private life of prayer and spirituality, a faith for Sundays and primarily within the walls of the church. Consequently, we did not gain the theology or the practical skills to embody the Christian faith in our families, at our work, in society at large, from Monday to Saturday. The biblical usage of the term 'the gospel' testifies to its public nature, as the Greek term used, *euangelion*, meant *good news* which was announced in the public square, for all to hear, concerning the life of the people and affecting everyone. The Christian gospel was never intended to be a hidden thing, a 'private' matter, because its proclamation about God in Jesus Christ as *gospel*, 'entails an over-arching claim to public truth'.[4] The gospel is thus not simply a dialogue 'partner' in the public sphere but has the capacity to contribute to public life, to model it in a specific way. This understanding of the gospel as public truth is essential for the development of a public theology for the common good. Just before we turn our attention to look closer to a public theology for this context, a brief word is in order about the danger and potential of religion in public sphere.

---

autonomous democracy in Romania, *Theft of a Nation: Romania Since Communism* (London: C. Hearst & Co, 2004).

[3] Two specific studies in the Romanian context illustrate the positive role that religion could have for a healthy political culture: Violeta Barbu, 'Bisericile în Europa – un partner social?' (Churches in Europe – A Social Partner?) in Radu Carp (ed), *Un suflet pentru Europa: Dimensiunea religioasă a unui proiect politic* (Bucharest: Anastasia, 2005); and Alina Mungiu-Pippidi, 'Biserica şi politica: religia ca determinant al culturii politice' (Church and Politics: Religion as a Determinant of Political Culture) in Mungiu-Pippidi, *Politica după comunism* (Bucharest: Humanitas, 2002). See also my study on the biblical foundations for the social dimension of the gospel, and its application to the Romanian context: *The Social Significance of Reconciliation in Paul's Theology: Narrative Readings in Romans* (London / New York: T. & T. Clark, Continuum, 2010).

[4] Gavin Drew, 'The Gospel as Public Truth in a Pluralistic World: A Reflection on Lesslie Newbigin's Thought', in *Evangel*, 24.2 (Summer 2006), 53.

Faith in the Public Sphere: Its Danger and Potential

People are afraid to bring religion into public life. And this fear is not necessarily because of religion *per se* but rather fear of an imposed religious totalitarianism. This fear of the imposition of a single religion in the public arena, determines, in turn, a refuge in another extreme, namely, that of the complete elimination of religion from public life. But, as Miroslav Volf correctly points out, none of these options are viable or desirable.[5] There is, on the other hand, the real possibility of a positive contribution of faith to public life, but for that to happen we need at least two things: to understand well the public dynamic of political pluralism – which means that no religious person should grab all the attention and no religion should be imposed by constraint; similarly, faith should neither be understood as simply 'private', dealing only with the intimate life of the soul, nor should it be an aggressive faith. If these two conditions are met, contends Volf, there is a proper place for faith in public life. The purpose of the public engagement of faith is not to impose a single viable alternative for the social arena. On the contrary, the ultimate goal of faith is contributing to human flourishing, which is also the essence of Christian faith. But human flourishing could only be attained when people find their proper place in the order created by God: a stance which has to be in harmony with the creator, with self, with fellow human beings, with nature. From a Christian perspective living a good life means loving God and loving your neighbour. The concern for human flourishing and for the common good belongs to the essence of biblical faith and Christian identity. We are very much aware that we live no longer under Christendom when Christianity occupied the central place in the market place, but in a context in which Christianity is only one of the players in the public arena. In such a context, any form of manipulation and/or constraint must disappear, and all the resources and the wisdom of faith must encourage a holistic, integrative understanding of faith within the whole of life and must be used for the common good. This can only be done by an authentic practice of forgiveness and love, by maintaining and developing the greatest respect for the freedom and integrity of every human being.

Thus, for a proper and beneficial contribution of faith to public life, we must acknowledge the great diversity of religious views in our contemporary societies, and have a proper understanding of the way in which religion functions in the context of liberal democracies – in which everyone is free to live according to their own perceptions and interpretation of life. It is vital that this freedom is guaranteed for everyone. Again, from a Christian perspective, one of the greatest commandments from God is to love our neighbour – and this includes respecting his or her

---

[5] For this argument and for a more complex and comprehensive analysis of the public dimension of faith, see Miroslav Volf, *A Public Faith: How Followers of Christ Should Serve the Common Good* (Grand Rapids, MI: Brazos Press, 2011).

religious conscience. There is no right we could or should demand for ourselves which we are not ready to grant to our neighbours. To learn to speak and behave properly in the public sphere is key for the integration of faith in public life – and this means learning to hear, understand and respect other voices and allowing co-operation and partnership of all factors and actors involved in public life towards the common good.

Public Theology: Definition, Characteristics, Approaches, Tasks

Even though in our part of the world this field of study is relatively new or even unknown, it is probably true to say that public theology is quite a flourishing discipline in Christian theology nowadays. As we will see, there are many approaches and proposals regarding the public significance of theology and, even though it is not the room here to go into much detail, we will look briefly at some of the most relevant definitions and categories that public theology operates with.

When we talk about *public* theology, we have in mind a public activity, done in the public domain and in search for public truth, just as William Storrar and Andrew Morton correctly show: 'Public theology has to do with the public relevance of a theology which has at the core of its Christian identity a concern for the coming of God's Kingdom in the public world of human history.'[6] Duncan Forrester, a pioneer and significant figure in public theology, gives a more detailed description of it:

> Public theology is... talk about God, which claims to point to publicly accessible truth, to contribute to the public discussion by witnessing to a truth that is relevant to what is going on in the world and to the pressing issues which are facing people and societies today... It takes the public square and what goes on there seriously, but it tries to articulate in the public square its convictions about truth and goodness... Public theology is confessional and evangelical. It has a gospel to share, good news to proclaim. Public theology attends to the Bible and the tradition of faith at the same time as it attempts to discern the signs of the times and understand what is going on in the light of the gospel.[7]

Public theology does not affect only private life and it is not just a function of individual subjectivity. It is regularly assumed, and people usually work on the assumption, that the private and public dimensions of life are clearly demarcated and even totally separated. But reality shows that this is not the case at all. Even though these are distinguishable

---

[6] William F. Storrar and Andrew R. Morton, 'Introduction', in William F. Storrar and Andrew R. Morton (eds), *Public Theology for the 21st Century* (London, T. & T. Clark Continuum, 2004), 1. In similar fashion, Moltmann states: 'Its subject alone makes Christian Theology a *theologia publica,* a public theology. It gets involved in the public affairs of society. It thinks about what is of general concern in the light of hope in Christ for the Kingdom of God'. See Jurgen Moltmann, *God for a Secular Society* (London: SCM, 1999), 1.

[7] Duncan B. Forester, *Truthful Action: Explorations in Practical Theology* (Edinburgh: T. & T. Clark, 2000), 127-28.

dimensions of our life, they are inseparable: the personal and institutional, the private and public, are permanently interacting with each other. Who we are and what we do in private life affects and determines to a great extent who we are and what we do in public life. And vice versa. That is why we have to resist the tendency and temptation to make a sharp distinction between the private and the public and, especially, to confine faith and theology to the private sector. The *gospel* makes public claims about the way things are – about God, about human beings, about the world, about society, about life – and therefore it is *public* truth, concerned with and addressing the entire reality, private *and* public. And as a result, theology, whose subject matter is the gospel/good news of God the creator, sustainer and redeemer of the entire creation, must be an activity concerned with and engaging the whole of reality.[8]

Theology is done in public, in the public forum and so involves two major components: the proclamation of the good news to individual people and to society for the common good; and also dialogue with other interlocutors from the public domain – which implies a careful listening and receptiveness to the other. It is clear then that public theology is not simply a communication exercise but it is in the actual conversation with the other actors of public life that theology is produced. Or, in the words of Andrew Morton, 'such conversation involves throughout both the persuasive eloquence of advocacy and the attentive silence of receptivity'.[9]

As we become interested in theological engagement in the public realm, we need to have a correct understanding of both the possibilities and limitations of the contribution of theology to public life, and so we should be aware of two temptations: to overestimate the contribution that theology can realistically make or, on the other hand, to underestimate the significance of theology for public life.[10] Given the reality that theology has lost the privileged status it once had, many do question whether theology has any public significance at all. But as De Gruchy rightly observes, 'We should not confuse the one-time public status of theology with the real contribution it can make when rightly pursued within public life.'[11] Theology can thus make a real contribution to the public realm but it needs to be pursed rightly and be aware of its own limitations and specifics.

In order to have a better understanding of public theology, a few words about the term 'public' are in order. What is the 'public domain'? Is there only one or can we talk of several? If we understand 'public' as a place or places where dialogue takes place, where difference exists and is accepted and therefore a particular distance is allowed, where people are free to

---

[8] Andrew R. Morton, 'Duncan Forrester: A Public Theologian', in Storrar and Morton, *Public Theology for the 21st Century*, 25-26.

[9] Morton, 'Duncan Forrester: A Public Theologian', 28.

[10] John W. De Gruchy, 'From Political to Public Theologies: The Role of Theology in Public Life in South Africa', in Storrar and Morton, *Public Theology for the 21st Century*, 45.

[11] De Gruchy, 'From Political to Public Theologies', 45.

disagree, then we can think first of society as a whole, the public domain as being such a space – a place where the social, the cultural, the economic, the political and the religious sectors of life all meet. And this will probably be the main 'public domain'. Others define this as being formed from various entities, individual or organized in various associations, which mediate between the state and society.[12] For Charles Taylor, the public sphere is a 'common space in which the members of society are deemed to meet through a variety of media: print, electronic, and also face-to-face encounters; to discuss matters of common interest; and thus to be able to form a common mind about these'.[13] Duncan adds two further categories, 'church' and 'academy', which meet the criteria for public entities referred to above. What it is important to remember is that these are all related to each other and we have to consider this reality very carefully when we reflect on public theology.

A few words are in order about the different approaches to public theology. Duncan Forrester speaks about two broad ways of doing public theology: one more 'top-down', the *magisterial* mode, in which the church/theology teaches the truth (which is believed to be *public* truth) authoritatively to the powers-that-be; and the other, more 'bottom-up', the *liberationist* mode, which springs out of from the everyday realities and experiences of life, closest to the least powerful in society.[14] The first position is a bit pretentious and authoritative as it presupposes the church or Christianity to be in a position of neutrality, without interests of its own or promoting any particular agenda, attempting to offer a strong theology with which to set and control the public agenda from above, from the high place of power. The second position seeks to allow the voice, the experience, the emotions of those at the margins to be heard and then attempts to relate them to the gospel story. While this approach is somewhat closer to the experienced reality of many, it tends to lack solid theological questions about the fundamental issues involved. And so both of these approaches are important for a realistic public theology as it needs to relate to both centres of power and, eventually, hold the tension between them. Max Stackhouse, one of the most productive proponents of public theology, proposes a fourfold pattern, or four pillars on which to build a public theology: creation and liberation; vocation and covenant; moral law, sin and freedom; ecclesiology and Trinity.[15]

---

[12] Radu Carp, *Dumnezeu la Bruxelles: religia în spaţiul public european* (God in Brussels: Religion in the European Public Space),, (Theologia Socialis: Cluj-Napoca: EIKON, 2009), 11-12.

[13] Charles Taylor, *Modern Social Imaginaries* (Durham, NC: Duke University Press, 2004), 82.

[14] Duncan B. Forrester, *Truthful Action: Explorations in Practical Theology* (Edinburgh, T. & T. Clark, 2000), 118-25.

[15] Max L. Stackhouse, *Public Theology and Political Economy: Christian Stewardship in Modern Society* (Grand Rapids, MI: Eerdmans, 1987), 33. Chris Green, in *A Higher Throne: Evangelicals and Public Theology* (Nottingham, UK: IVP, 2008), takes a more evangelical

Raymond Plant reminds all of us of the truth that public policies are closely related to questions of value. All the difficult issues and concerns related to a meaningful life together in society – freedom, equality, punishment, retribution, rehabilitation, restitution, distributive justice, human rights, social solidarity, welfare, etc. –are important moral issues, vital for our humanity, and it is our responsibility to consider them carefully in our engagement with public life.[16] And it is exactly here that public theology finds the first element of its difficult task: 'to formulate a theologically coherent account of the moral issues facing public policy in a complex society', together with the second '*meta-task* to do with arguing for a role for theology amongst the voices in society brought to bear upon these question'.[17] Thus, public theology is attempting 'to articulate a Christian social vision, which can be brought to bear upon the problems of civil and political life and arguing for a very strong case for the seriousness of that voice to be heard and respected within the conversation of modern society'.[18]

Many affirm today an obvious truth, namely, that we live in a 'glocal' context, which is simultaneously global and local, with dynamic, pluralistic, multicultural societies, with numerous and increasing links and interconnections, especially with regard to our economy and technology. This new reality requires that we reflect afresh theologically and respond appropriately to the new situation. It is in response to exactly this challenging new context that Max Stackhouse considers four areas of public theological explorations, which are, in his opinion, much neglected in contemporary thought: 1) a perspectival shift from 'orders of creation' to dynamic *spheres* of relative sovereignty; 2) a theological analysis of the global *powers* – principalities, authorities, thrones and dominions; 3) a comparative investigation of how *religion shapes civilizations*; 4) a recovery of covenantal thought as a mode of *public theology* for global civil society.[19]

Public theology is a theology which seeks the welfare of the city and would consider itself an instrument in the service of the common good and human flourishing. Miroslav Volf is right in arguing that a vision of human

---

approach by emphasizing the core biblical doctrines of creation, fall, redemption and revelation around which he builds his public theology. For a similar approach, see George Hunsberger, 'The Mission of Public Theology: An Exploration', in *Swedish Missiological Themes,* 93.3 (2005), 315-24. At the other end of the spectrum, we find Kathryn Tanner, who believes in a common basis of both religion and public square, and argues that the universal values and principles (equality, liberty, justice, mutual regard and the pursuit of happiness) should be the starting-point of a public theology, in 'Public Theology and the Character of Public Debate', in *Annual of the Society of Christian Ethics* (1996), 79-101.

[16] Raymond Plant, 'Forward', in Storrar and Morton, *Public Theology for the 21st Century*, ix-x.

[17] Plant, 'Forward', x.

[18] Plant, 'Forward', xi.

[19] Max L. Stackhouse, 'Public Theology and Political Economy in a Globalizing Era', in Storrar and Morton, *Public Theology for the 21st Century*, 181-91.

flourishing is the most important contribution Christian faith brings to the common good, especially as this is not done 'by imposing on others their vision of human flourishing and the common good but by bearing witness to Christ, who embodies the good life'.[20] And if Jesus placed at the centre of his ministry love of God and love of one's neighbour, so should Christians, as both God and neighbour are fundamental to human flourishing.[21]

Issues in Public Theology for Central and Eastern Europe

For those living in this part of the world, it is obvious that the legacy of the totalitarian regime is still visible today in several areas of life. One such issue, to begin with, is the atrophy of the capacity for dreaming, for envisioning a better world, the capacity for imagination and hope. Most people living through the difficult period of a long transition, with such a high rate of corruption and poverty, have lost any hope of solid, substantial social change. There are no solid institutions and structures in these young democracies, and people are really struggling enormously to live a normal life. Similarly, other crucial dimensions of life – such as work, family, society, justice, to name just a few – have been downplayed and so need to be recovered. Not least important is the lack of trust and of various networks of partnerships and co-operation. A public theology for Central and Eastern Europe would need to address such issues, among others, and it is exactly to these that we will now turn.

A Vision of a Better World

One significant task of public theology which Forrester highlights is *vision.*[22] Starting from the familiar but truthful wisdom saying, according to

---

[20] Volf, *A Public Faith*, xi.

[21] For a solid argument on human flourishing, see two very recent books: Miroslav Volf, *Flourishing: Why We Need Religion in a Globalized World* (New Haven, CT: Yale University Press, 2015); Miroslav Volf and Justin Crisp (eds), *Joy and Human Flourishing: Essays on Theology, Culture, and the Good Life* (Minneapolis, MN: Fortress Press, 2015). I am very glad to see that theologians from our part of the world are beginning to pay attention to the concept of human flourishing. See, for example, Marcel Măcelaru, who argues that 'human flourishing describes a state of being, a mode of existence that is markedly Christian – its definition needs a Christian mindset and its full experience is available only to the believer': Marcel V. Măcelaru, 'Human Flourishing – A Theological Perspective', in Geogeta Rață and Patricia Runcan, *Happiness Through Education* (Bucharest: Editura Didactică şi Pedagogică, 2014), 233. Similarly, my younger colleague, Beniamin Mocan, concludes his discussion on public theology by stating that 'a thorough public theology will always aim to seek the welfare of the city. It will always work towards human flourishing, and it will always do it with respect to the plurality and diversity existing within the public': Beniamin Mocan, 'Social Imagination and the Possibility of a Pentecostal Public Theology' (MTh thesis, Evangelical Theological Seminary, Osijek, Croatia, 2014), 40.

[22] See Forrester, *Truthful Action*, 143-57. The other two significant tasks he elaborates on are *prophecy* and *theological fragments.*

which 'where there is no vision the people perish' (Prov. 29:18), he elaborates on the crucial role that *vision* has for life in society, and for the particular contribution that a Christian vision brings to the discussion. Without vision, people perish because 'they are locked in their past and present, and incapable of imagining a future that will be better, because they have lost hope. For vision is what generates purpose for a society. Without vision, public life becomes a battle of interests, unconstrained by a larger horizon of meaning'.[23] In a Christian understanding of the social vision, 'the imagination is shaped and resourced by the symbols, narratives and imagery of the Christian and biblical tradition. An imaginative vision, which encompasses the purpose and sweep of history, is open to the future and hence not at ease in the present; is also shaped by a descriptive yet critical vision of the present; and it is not afraid to name oppression and injustice and ugliness and lies – all that distinguishes the present from the Reign of God'.[24] Theology's task is thus not only to pose theoretical, abstract, academic questions or to address particular problems and moral issues. It is also preoccupied with visions that provide a horizon of meaning for life in society. And if we really want to offer a contribution in the social arena, we need to rediscover the religious language, the symbols and narratives of the Bible which can serve as the vehicles for a renewed vision of society, one which will offer an alternative future which will enable people to live meaningfully with one another. As for the nature of that vision, there is no doubt:

> Ultimately, for Christians, true vision is the vision of God and of fellowship in and with the Triune God. The Church is called to be a kind of preliminary manifestation, or earnest, of that vision. That does not mean that the Church or theology generates or devises the Christian vision. But they have a responsibility to discern, explore, manifest and proclaim it. In the New Testament, the visions were not visions of the glorious future of the Church, but of a new heaven and a new earth, the renewal of the whole world, a New Jerusalem in which there will be no church or temple, but God will be all in all. Thus we are constantly reminded that judgement begins with the household of faith, the community that nurtures and commends the Christian vision. For we are stewards, not possessors, of the Christian vision.[25]

Our culture of fear and anxiety has almost annihilated our capacity for dreaming, for imagining and envisioning a possible new future. It is in this context that the biblical prophetic tradition comes as an important resource for a public theology of engagement. From their authentic spirituality of resistance and lament we learn the importance of analysis, critique and condemnation, but also the crucial aspect of imagining and envisioning alternatives, a new future which they proclaim from God, a new dream to follow.

---

[23] Forrester, *Truthful Action*, 143-44.
[24] Forrester, *Truthful Action*, 144-45.
[25] Forrester, *Truthful Action*, 150.

If our part of the world experiences a great spiritual crisis of morality and values, an important part of the answer is to be found in recovering an authentic spirituality for life. Mary Grey proposes that a Christian theology of the Spirit may bring a significant contribution to the public sphere, 'a conviction that it is the power of the Spirit to reconnect personal life with public, and reawaken a people become apathetic and disillusioned with public life and church life alike'.[26] And if we speak of the need to recover the dreaming, the imagination and the vision for an alternative world, for human flourishing and the common good, for an alternative way of being in the world and for the world, nothing is more important than the Spirit of God – which is the Spirit of prophetic hope, of truth, of justice, of love, of peace and reconciliation, of solidarity, of boundary-crossing, of integration, the Spirit of life. It is therefore mandatory that we explore in more depth and from fresh perspectives the biblical evidences for the active and powerful role of the Spirit in enabling us to re-imagine, to re-envision, the transformation of the world through the communities of those who have experienced healing and reconciliation, and thus rekindle hope for a better future, for a better world.

A public theology of engagement will make its first priority the inspiration of a new generation of believers to pursue with all intellectual seriousness a holistic vision of Christian faith and mission, a vision in which faith determines a particular way of being *in* and *for* the world. A holistic understanding of Christian life and mission will lead to an appropriate involvement of the church in the world as an agent of change and social transformation. If there is any truth in the affirmation that our conduct is shaped by the condition of our vision, it follows that, in order to transform this world, we need a particular vision of life. Not just any vision but a vision of righteousness, reconciliation and hope for this world; a vision for a culture of love and acceptance, of forgiveness and grace, of justice and mercy, a vision of the new creation in Christ.

Christianity and Nation-Building

There is no question that one of the crucial issues in mission for countries emerging from a totalitarian context is the need for a theology of nation-building. And one does not need to be an expert in politics or economics in order to realize the great struggle of a nation to recover and rebuild after almost half a century of totalitarianism. Probably it is not too much to say that nation-building is one of the most important and urgent tasks that we, as Christians, should be concerned with and contribute to at this time. After over twenty-five years of freedom and the young democracies in this part of the world are still recovering from a potent totalitarian legacy: mistrust,

[26] Mary C. Grey, 'Living Without Dreams: Is There a Spirituality for Justice in a Globalized World?' in Storrar and Morton, *Public Theology for the 21st Century*, 241.

corruption, poverty, watered-down democracies, the denial of fundamental human rights and freedoms, social injustice, etc. In such circumstances, it is vital that we struggle to find the way in which the Christian message addresses these crucial questions and the way it contributes to a better social justice and democracy, in strengthening civil society, political stability and peace.

To be sure, nation-building is a slow and complex process which involves, among other things, increasing the capacity of a nation for solid communities and economic development; building strong institutions that are able to respond to the challenges of today's world; a sustained effort to (re)build robust societies that work; raising the standard of living; building democracy; preserving nations' distinct and unique identities, etc. In sum, as Professor Jeremi Suri puts it, nation-building is 'an effort to build institutions and practices that allow a people to govern themselves in peaceful and prosperous ways'.[27] It is not the church's task or her call to respond to such challenges. Rather, her job is more limited and refers more specifically to a possible Christian contribution to the development of specific values and behaviours, strengthening the capacity of cultural, social, economic and political institutions that are able to sustain and enhance the development of a particular nation which should have as its ultimate goal the flourishing of human beings. Particularly, it should concentrate on such issues as mindset and mentality change, the alleviation of poverty, moral reformation, processes of reconciliation and social integration, and a vision of freedom and democracy which enhances life and is conducive to human flourishing.

An important step towards reflecting on, and equipping for, nation-building is the need for a fresh reading of our biblical resources in such a way as to rediscover the social and political dimensions of the gospel. In research into the social dimension of reconciliation in Paul's theology, I have shown that, contrary to common perception, the apostle Paul was very much aware of the social, political, cultural and religious contexts in which he lived, and that he encouraged a positive interaction with these realities. Anchored in a strong creational theology, with a perception of God's sovereignty over history, and with the conviction that the historical reality was irreversibly affected by God's intervention in Christ, Paul had a positive view of the world and of the structures of society. For him and all first-century Christians, there was one realm of reality in which body and soul, religion and politics, private and public, individual and social aspects of reality were intermingled in a complex unified vision of life. The gospel Paul proclaimed was not in any way detached from everyday reality, and it also had a political message at its heart. Further still, I have shown that the

---

[27] Jeremi Suri, 'Five Principles Critical to Successful Nation-Building': www.utexas.edu/news/2011/09/26/nation-building (accessed 12th January 2016). See also his book, *Liberty's Surest Guardian: American Nation-Building from the Founders to Obama* (New York: Simon & Schuster, 2011).

political dimension of the gospel was not secondary or incidental to Paul's writings, but rather an integral and fundamental element of it. The gospel of the crucified and resurrected Christ, it is claimed, not only has a few social and political implications, but rather it is political to its core.[28] It is these aspects and dimensions of faith that we need to rediscover for a proper public theology of nation-building.

Faith and Work

Work takes the major part of people's active life; it encompasses and determines the lives of men and women. It is thus appropriate that 'work', one of the central components of daily living, has becomes a major concern for society at large, from many angles and for many considerations: in terms of providing the possibility and access for everyone to work, for improving the conditions of work, for limiting exploitation at work, for the transformation of the meaning of work. What is even more revealing is the fact that, after an over-long neglect of the subject in Christian quarters, there is an increased theological and ecclesiastical interest in the question of work. There is a greater sense of the significance and urgency of theological reflection on the subject of work from a biblical perspective.

Work is enormously important for the life of human beings in society. Its significance consists first of all in the fact that, through it, people provide for their subsistence. In order to live, one has to work. It is not a surprise to anyone that the apostle Paul understood it very well when he admonishes the Thessalonians: 'If anyone will not work, neither let him eat' (2 Thess. 3:10). But work also provides a sense of individual and social identity as our daily work shapes and determines, to a certain extent, what we are. Thus, work is indispensable for people's continued existence, well-being and identity. Being such a vital area of our lives, it has to be a substantial issue for theological reflection.

The second reason for serious theological consideration of work is given by what can be called 'the crisis of work', which is experienced in various degrees throughout the world. Whether we think of child labour, unemployment and discrimination, or exploitation and dehumanization, at work, these are serious challenges that many people face in the contemporary world. This is not the place to go into any details about these sobering problems or even to begin to unpack the various personal, structural or technological causes of this crisis. Their very existence forces us to think responsibly and creatively in order to find possible and realistic solutions. Unfortunately, throughout the history of Christianity, the subject of work has been of little concern to the church. As a consequence, many Christians have inadequate, defective and even negative attitudes towards

[28] See Corneliu Constantineanu, *The Social Significance of Reconciliation in Paul's Theology: Narrative Readings in Romans* (Library of New Testament Studies 421; Edinburgh: T & T Clark, 2010).

work. This is yet another reason for the urgent need for biblical and theological reflection on work.

A public theology for our context, if it wants to be as comprehensive as possible, cannot avoid this crucial subject. On the contrary, it should strive to find the larger biblical story about the ultimate significance and meaning of human life within which to integrate the topic of work. We should, therefore, look for stories, for theological and biblical principles that serve as guidelines for the practical decisions we have to make in order to relate our beliefs to the world of work. The contours of a biblical theology of work, however, could only be properly understood and interpreted within the larger story of God's good creation, of the fall with its devastating consequences for humankind and the entire creation and, especially, in the light of the great story of God's redemption that culminated with the death and resurrection of Christ and the beginning of the new creation 'in Christ'. Further still, a proper public theology of work will be integrated into the larger context of God's work, of human creation in the image of God, of God's command for people to work as part of his provision for human life and of human co-operation with God in work. It will show that it is the Spirit of God who inspires and endows people with gifts and skills for various work and activities (Ex. 31:2-5; Jgs 3:10; 1 Sam. 16:13), that work has both an intrinsic and instrumental value, that our work matters to God, that work as co-operation with God has fundamental meaning and ultimate significance in the context of the eschatological transformation of the world. Such a theology of work, understood as service, will bring dignity to labour and see work as involving social benefit and a contribution to the common good of society.

Faith and Society

The last aspect I would like to mention in a public theology for the common good in this context is the dynamic relationship of Christians to society at large. If one's faith is primarily lived out 'in the world', then one has to find appropriate resources for authentic Christian living in the world, for a proper relationship to the life of contemporary culture and society. Given the lordship of Christ over entire reality, Christians should be concerned to make sense of their faith as it interacts with all aspects of life in society. A public theology dealing with this issue would strive to reunite different compartments of human existence into one realm of reality in which body and soul, religion and politics, private and public, individual and social aspects of reality are intermingled in a complex, unified vision of life. To be sure, it will have to take into consideration the ambivalence and the dialectical relationship of Christians to the world as they experience the tension of being *in* the world yet not *of* the world. Paul's language of 'belonging' and 'separation' offers a view into the way in which the identity of those who 'belong to Christ' was maintained and positioned vis-à-vis the outside world. On the one hand, the 'insider/outsider' terminology implies a negative perception of society and the 'qualitative difference' between outsiders and insiders. On the other hand, however, Christians are not to withdraw from society. Paul encouraged his congregations not only to continue to participate, as good citizens, in the life of the city, but also to behave in a manner that would bring approval from outsiders. Thus, for example, the strong work ethic of the believers in Thessalonica was intended to 'earn the respect of outsiders' (1 Thess. 4:12), while the exercise of the spiritual gifts in the Corinthian congregation was to be amended to avoid giving the wrong impression to the outsiders (1 Cor. 14:23).

The attitude and relationship of early Christians to the outside world was complex and it should be given careful consideration. The tension should not be removed: the world is God's good creation and yet is now in a present state of corruption and the 'god of this world' is active in it; Christians were 'resident aliens' in this world and had their 'citizenship in heaven' (Phil. 3:20), and yet they were encouraged neither to withdraw from the world (1 Cor. 5:10) nor to totally deny or reject its realities and values. In fact, it was precisely because of their new identity and status that they were able to work towards the transformation of this world. 1 Thessalonians, one of Paul's earliest letters, is an excellent example of how Paul was, from the very beginning of his ministry, concerned with both the internal cohesion and growth of Christian communities, but also with the Thessalonians' social conduct and positive attitude and behaviour towards outsiders. It was of the greatest importance for Paul that Christians should not 'repay evil for evil but always seek to do good to one another and *to all*' (1 Thess. 5:15); that they should 'increase and abound in love for one another and *for all*' (1 Thess. 3:12); that they should 'aspire to live quietly, to mind [their] own affairs, and to work with [their] hands... so that [they] *may behave properly towards outsiders*' (1 Thess. 4:11-12).

One important aspect when dealing with faith and society, therefore, is to encourage an active and positive, even though at times critical, involvement of the Christian in the world, advocating practices that are conducive to a meaningful and peaceful life in the larger society. In the new context of the re-emergence of religion as a major factor in the public domain, there is an important and urgent task of public theology to rethink afresh the relationship between faith and society, between church and public domain, between moral leadership and cultural values, between religion and political economy, between the Christian faith and the everyday life of society. And the more so, since within contemporary biblical studies there is a growing understanding that the fundamental theological concepts of the New Testament, such as those regarding the Kingdom of God, redemption, salvation, peace and justice, forgiveness and reconciliation, are understood to have significance far beyond the individual and private spheres of life, and as involving the change and transformation of life in its totality. It is true, in order to function properly and authentically, such public theology needs to be self-critical, sensitive to the historical context, concrete in its attempt to bring insight into the debate, and to speak the truth clearly and unequivocally to the powers-that-be. Thus, a public theology does not seek to maintain the status quo of society but rather to contribute to its transformation and redemption. It points to sources beyond individual self-interest, to the renewing power of the Spirit of God who 'gives creatures the energy to act in the world according to the distinctions that the Creator has made, and to struggle with the powers that are reduced to chaos. The Spirit is a renewing power that, not for the first time, inspires us to restore a lost order, but that creates order time and again'.[29] The story of the Spirit at work in human history to renew and redeem represents a great source of inspiration for Christians to engage with society in a responsible way and with hope, and to work towards its transformation.

In this discussion I have offered only a few remarks on some of the relevant issues which need to be addressed. To be sure, a public theology for Central and Eastern Europe should address further important and urgent issues such as corruption, education, migration, public policy, justice, Roma communities, human rights and social inequality, to name only some of the most significant.

Platforms for Public Theology

As we look to the future, the specific and complex political, cultural, social, economic and religious context of Central and Eastern Europe makes urgent the creation of adequate platforms for advanced, interdisciplinary, integrative reflection and research in public theology which will promote a transformative public engagement for the common good. While academic endeavours among Evangelicals in Romania, for example, started almost a hundred years ago, due to the isolation and specific circumstances under which the church lived during the communist era, theological efforts have been local and provisional. After 1989, in the newly experienced freedom, some specific phenomena took place. The Evangelical community grew in number at a fast pace, and the number of Evangelicals studying theology increased exponentially in order to meet the ministerial and educational needs of each Evangelical denomination. Although these developments are certainly necessary and useful for the different churches, little effort has gone into systematic and co-ordinated research in the various missiological aspects of the theology, mission and life of Evangelical communities. Consequently, there is a need for meaningful reflection and reliable research into the theology, history, life and ministry of the evangelical

---

[29] Kees J. Klop, 'Equal Respect and the Holy Spirit: The Liberal Demand for Moral Neutrality in the Political Sphere and Christian Respect for Creation', in Storrar and Morton, *Public Theology for the 21st Century*, 97.

churches as well as into the directions for theological and missiological development in connection with the contemporary needs and challenges of society. The need is still there for the creation of an appropriate framework within which these needs will be addressed by providing a platform for promoting and sustaining research efforts, and by networking theologians and scholars for fruitful academic dialogue. Such platforms will be able to carry out and co-ordinate various research projects on the religious life and various trends in contemporary society in general. They will also represent centres for documentation and research, with a significant collection of theological resources made easily available by means of a centralized database. Further, they will stimulate and develop reliable integrative interdisciplinary academic research within and for the Christian communities in this context. Lastly, at least some of these platforms will be learning institutions which will be offering specific educational research programmes at graduate and postgraduate levels. There are already several excellent endeavours in this regard which gives great reason for hope in future efforts towards a constructive public theology in Central and Eastern Europe – and I would like to mention some of these: the *Centre for Faith and Culture* within the University of Bucharest, Romania; the *Balkan Institute for Faith and Culture*, Skopje, Macedonia; the *Areopagus Centre for Christian Studies and Contemporary Culture*, Timişoara, Romania; the *Osijek Institute for Mission Studies*, within the Evangelical Theological Seminary in Osijek, Croatia; the *Institute for Faith and Human Flourishing*, Timişoara, Romania; the *Evangelical Theological Centre*, Wrocław, Poland; *Teologia Socialis*, Cluj-Napoca, Romania.

Conclusion

I conclude that building on the biblical understanding of the gospel as public truth for the common good and human flourishing, churches can make a contribution to the social reality in a post-totalitarian context by offering and maintaining a sense of fundamental values for human life in the world; by discerning, unmasking and resisting any form of totalitarianism and absolutism; by offering a framework of hope and a vision of life that will enable people not simply to cope with 'otherness' and 'difference', but also to promote a culture of peace and justice, of freedom and love, a culture of life and human flourishing.

As Bible teachers, educators, theologians and missiologists, we do take it as our task to inspire a new generation of believers, and especially Christian professionals, to pursue with all intellectual seriousness a holistic vision of Christian life and mission. We should make it our goal to equip all Christians with a holistic understanding of reality, to prepare them to engage deeply with God's world, with all aspects of cultures and societies. The gospel is not a matter of private interest but a public truth, a statement about the whole of reality – about God, about the world, about meaning, about life. In our search for an authentic public theology, we should revive God in the public consciousness, and not a God limited by an individualistic, selfish perception, nor a God interested in a spirituality which emphasizes only the unseen dimension of human beings. But rather a God of the whole reality, the Creator of all things – and therefore, the God of all peoples. It is only this God, Christ incarnated, who lived among us, died for all, was raised from the dead, who offers hope for future. Only he can help us, through the power of the Spirit and through his Word, to recapture the joy, fulfilment and innocence of a humanity created in God's image. Confronting the world with the Word of God and promoting what is good and right, what enriches us in art, science, culture, and society, we will urge our communities towards a new understanding of what is true, worthy of praise, pure, just, worthy to be loved. This is what it means that live out the reality of the gospel as public truth in the service of the common good and human flourishing.

A MISSIOLOGIST'S LOOK AT THE FUTURE: A MISSIOLOGICAL MANIFESTO FOR THE 21ST CENTURY

Anne-Marie Kool

Introduction

In many European contexts, the existence of the academic discipline of missiology, including that of ecumenism and evangelism is, according to Dietrich Werner,

> fragile and precarious. Missiological institutes get closed or reduced because allegedly they are not in accordance with the core mandates of university bureaucracies or some church policies, the number of chairs for mission and evangelism has been reduced, missiology is pushed out of public universities and driven to private institutes, if at all. On the whole, the existence of the few chairs and institutes of missiology still left is still fragile and not automatically guaranteed for long-term perspectives. The voice of European missiological institutes and European solid and academic training for evangelism becomes weaker and weaker in the international concert, despite the fact that Europe would have to give and to share a lot of its historical expertise on issues of mission and evangelism. Europe does not have any major high-level research institute on World Christianity, evangelism and contemporary world mission which could compete with other centers and hubs of international research in this direction. Therefore, the voice, visibility and international connectedness of Europe at this stage are also endangered at present.[1]

This missiological manifesto for the decade seeks to contribute to the ongoing conversation on the future of the church in mission in Europe with a special focus on Central and Eastern Europe in the light of Werner's assessment. It is based on my personal experience of three decades living and working as a missionary and missiologist in the eastern part of Europe, but still keeping in touch with developments in my country of birth, the Netherlands, and elsewhere in Europe, and in North America. The result is a missiological manifesto for Europe, with a Central and Eastern European bias. What I offer is a statement of vision and values, reflecting on future perspectives and challenges in six key areas.

My aim is to present food for thought for continuing the conversation within global Christianity on issues important for mission in Europe and to better understand our own biases. My hope is that this process will result in

---

[1] Dietrich Werner, 'Evangelism in Theological Education in Europe – 12 Considerations from ETE/WCC', in *WCC Consultation on Evangelism in Theological Education and Missional Formation in Europe, 28-31 October 2012* (Bossey, Switzerland: WCC, 2012).

'acquiring the posture of a missional church'[2] in our own European contexts, and in a true shift from western to global Christianity by taking away western philosophy-induced hindrances for the advance of the gospel. The term 'missiological' is chosen bearing in mind that a missiological approach is all about a critical interaction between mission practice and mission theory, which should always aim at revitalizing the church to grow in missional posture, in which biblical and theological perspectives are dominant.

In this missiological manifesto, I deal with a number of issues to help stimulate critical and constructive discussion about the future of church and mission in Europe, divided along six different themes. These themes originate from an analysis of the images of Europe used in the *Atlas of Global Christianity*.[3] Each theme encompasses a number of statements or quotes with brief comments.

The Impact of Secular Values on Church and Mission

'Business-ization' of Mission Organizations and Churches

Mission organizations and churches in Europe operate increasingly 'on the basis of secular business principles instead of theological principles, focusing more on output and results instead of fruits growing in a hidden way, on value for money instead of free grace, on success stories instead of sacrifice and commitment, on quantity instead of quality, on superficial quick results instead of long-term transformation and incarnation, characterized by hanging on to power instead of commitment to offering humble service'.[4]

The 'secularized Europe' image does not apply only to European society but also to the European mainline churches. Secularization has impacted the church by embracing secular values or value systems that have 'affected the church, obscured her mission, and have eroded her credibility in the

---

[2] George R. Hunsberger, 'Acquiring the Posture of a Missionary Church', in George R. Hunsberger and Craig Van Gelder (eds), *The Church between Gospel and Culture: The Emerging Mission in North America* (Grand Rapids, MI: Eerdmans, 1996).

[3] This chapter is based on the last part of: Anne-Marie Kool, 'Re-Visiting Mission in Europe through Contemporary Image-Formation: A Missiological Manifesto for the 21st Century', in *Fuller Theological Seminary: 50th Anniversary Celebration and 2015 Missiology Lectures* (Pasadena, CA: 2015). The first part of that presentation is published in Anne-Marie Kool, 'Revisiting Mission in, to and from Europe through Contemporary Image Formation', in Charles E. van Engen (ed), *The State of Missiology Today: Global Innovations in Christian Witness (Missiological Engagements)* (Downers Grove, IL: IVP Academic, 2016).

[4] Anne-Marie Kool, 'Spiritual Transformation: A Reponse', in Mark Oxbrow and Tim Grass (eds), *The Mission of God: Studies in Orthodox and Evangelical Mission* (Oxford: Regnum, 2015). See also John Drane, 'Resisting Mcdonaldization', in Viggo Mortenson and Andreas Osterlund Nielsen (eds), *Walk Humbly with the Lord: Church and Mission Engaging Plurality* (Grand Rapids, MI: Eerdmans, 2010).

world', as they are opposed to Christian values.[5] Secular philosophy has intimidated the church to conform the gospel to a system of 'humanism', therefore a call to confess a lack of discernment and discipline, as well as for an erosion of moral and social standards, with hypocrisy and dishonesty within the church, is addressed. Also the leadership is called to repent as it has more conformed to the world than acted like the disciples of Christ, in bringing in 'the ways of the world and its systems' rather than 'changing the church'.[6] This theme was taken up in the Lausanne movement, first in 1980 and later in 2010.

The Challenge of New Religiosity and Paganism

Lesslie Newbigin stated in his autobiography: 'I have been forced to recognize that the most difficult missionary frontier in the contemporary world is the one of which the churches have been – on the whole – so little conscious, the frontier that divides the world of biblical faith from the world whose values and beliefs are ceaselessly fed into every home on the television screen. Like others, I had been accustomed, especially in the 1960s, to speak of England as a secular society. I have now come to realize that I was the easy victim of an illusion from which my reading of the gospels should have saved me. No room remains empty for long. If God is driven out, the gods come trooping in. England is a pagan society and the development of a truly missionary encounter with this very tough form of paganism is the greatest intellectual and practical task facing the Church.'[7]

Willem A. Visser 't Hooft, the first General Secretary of the WCC, in a very insightful paper on Evangelism among Europe's Neo-Pagans, written in 1977, concluded with the following words: '... evangelization of Europe's neo-pagans is so urgent, so difficult that it ought to have the highest priority among the tasks of the church. How many of our theologians are working in this field? How many pastors? Far too few. What courses concerning neo-paganism are given in our theological faculties and in our lay training institutes?'[8]

The question is: Do we live in a 'Christian', a secularized or a neo-pagan context? Among nationalistic, extreme-right ideologies, pagan practices reappear. A few years ago, a special pastoral letter was sent out within the Roman Catholic Church in Hungary to warn against these practices.[9] Students tell stories of occult practices taking place among their peers, how

---

[5] LCWE, *The Thailand Report on Secularists: Christian Witness to Secularized People*, Lausanne Occasional Paper No. 8 (Lausanne Committee for World Evangelization, 1980).
[6] LCWE, *The Thailand Report*.
[7] J.E. Lesslie Newbigin, *Unfinished Agenda: An Updated Autobiography* (Edinburgh: St Andrew Press, 1993), 236.
[8] Willem A. Visser 't Hooft, 'Evangelism among Neo-Pagans', in *International Review of Mission*, 66.254 (1977).
[9] See online at: <http://www.katolikus-honlap.hu/0610/neopog.htm>, accessed on 3 February 2017.

they are attracted to worshipping the 'Hungarian god', because it is Hungarian. It is a form of over-contextualizing the gospel. On the other hand, the way the gospel is presented in many churches is not conceived of as relevant. It may be faithful to the gospel, but unrelated to the context. We do not get any further by following the advice of one of the bishops: 'We should not deal with this nonsense.' There is thus a huge missiological challenge in our mission and evangelism in relating the gospel to culture.

Looking Afresh at Our 'Chart and Compass'

Lesslie Newbigin emphasized, back in 1962, that our missionary methods have been too much conformed to the world in which we live.[10] We need to look afresh 'to our chart and compass and to ask how we now use the new winds and the new tides to carry out our sailing orders'.[11] It contains the 'costly, but exciting task... of fundamental theological thinking, of Bible study, and of discerning the signs of the times'.[12]

This is what Searle and Cherendov[13] envision as they recommend the creation of an international learning community and professional theological society as a cross-pollution and meeting-point between post-Soviet evangelical Protestantism, western Protestantism and Russian Orthodoxy, to undertake relevant research and to provide the churches with fundamental documents on current issues related to mission and missiology, etc. to reflect together on the theology of national evangelical authors of the 'global North' and the 'global South', as well as to intensify publishing activities and construct a multi-tiered system of formal, non-formal and informal education. It is the task of fundamental theological reflection combined with discerning the signs of the times.

Issues of Otherness and the Reconciling Role of Churches

From Exclusion to Embrace

One of the burning issues all over Europe is undoubtedly that of 'otherness' and exclusion, especially in Eastern Europe with regard to the 10-12 million Roma (Gypsies), but also with regard to e.g. migrants. The

---

[10] J.E. Lesslie Newbigin, 'Bringing Our Missionary Methods Under the Word of God', in *Occasional Bulletin from the Missionary Research Library,* XIII.11 (1962), 2.

[11] Newbigin, 'Bringing Our Missionary Methods Under the Word of God', 2.

[12] J.E. Lesslie Newbigin, *One Body, One Gospel, One World: The Christian Mission Today* (London and New York: International Missionary Council, 1958), 11; cf. Anne-Marie Kool, 'Changing Images in the Formation for Mission: Commission V in Light of Current Challenges – A Western Perspective', in Kenneth Ross (ed), *Edinburgh 1910: Mission Then and Now* (Oxford: Regnum / Pasadena, CA: William Carey / Bangalore: SATHRI, 2009).

[13] Joshua T. Searle and Mykhailo N. Cherenkov, *A Future and a Hope: Mission, Theological Education, and the Transformation of Post-Soviet Society* (Eugene, OR: Wipf & Stock, 2014).

changing landscape in Europe and European Christianity will probably give rise to more exclusion. Overcoming exclusion by the transformation of the deep-seated prejudices towards e.g. the Roma can only flow out of a clear focus on the message of incarnation, of reconciliation with God in Christ, and the implications in everyday life for social reconciliation. Only the Holy Spirit can work out such profound changes in our lives.

When dealing with exclusion, difference becomes the ground for considering 'the other' to be inferior, rather than understanding difference as something to celebrate, that reveals yet something else of the mystery of God present in the world.[14] According to a recent study, the stereotyped image of the impoverished gypsies that was created and repeated over the centuries defines the attitude of exclusion of millions of Europeans.[15] Miroslav Volf has dealt extensively with the concept of 'otherness' and ethnicity, dealing specifically with his own, Croatian, roots. He states that otherness should be placed at the centre of theological reflection. 'The future of the whole world depends on how we deal with ethnic, religious and gender otherness.'[16] His response to otherness is a 'theology of embrace'.[17]

The Emergence of Reconciling Communities Needed

The role of pastors is to empower their local congregations to grow into open, welcoming, reconciling and missional communities that embody and radiate the love of Christ to 'indigenous' and 'strangers' alike. To enable such communities to emerge, an emphasis should be placed on the fact that we are all created in God's image, on the unconditional love of God in Christ who died on the cross for our sins to reconcile us with God, and on the work of the Holy Spirit.

Focusing on the future(s) of Pentecostalism in Europe, Raymond Pfister calls for a 'spirituality of reconciliation' to face the challenges brought about by the 'damaging effects of cultural and religious clashes'. The work of the Holy Spirit in reconciliation as the reconciling Spirit enables such a reconciling community to come into existence, defining the ministry of the Spirit as a ministry of reconciliation. In a similar way as Volf, Pfister observes that God's reconciling initiative in Christ is not limited to individual reconciliation, but extends to social reconciliation.[18]

---

[14] See also Anne-Marie Kool, 'The Church in Hungary and Central and Eastern Europe: Trends and Challenges', in *Princeton Theological Seminary Bulletin,* 28.2 (2007).

[15] Klaus-Michael Bogdal, 'Europe Invents the Gypsies: The Dark Side of Modernity', in *Eurozine,* 24 (February 2012): www.eurozine.com /articles/2012-02-24-bogdal-en.html (accessed 23rd September 2014).

[16] Miroslav Volf, *Exclusion and Embrace: A Theological Exploration of Identity, Otherness, and Reconciliation* (Nashville, TN: Abingdon Press, 1996), 5.

[17] Volf, *Exclusion and Embrace.*

[18] Raymond Pfister, 'The Future(s) of Pentecostalism in Europe', in William K. Kay and Anne E. Dyer (ed), *European Pentecostalism* (Global Pentecostal and Charismatic Studies), (Leiden,

Ecclesiology and Mission: Missional Church, Church Planting, Emerging Churches, Fresh Expressions

From Preoccupation with Power and Control to an Attitude of Humility

In western culture, the starting-point for mission and missiology is most often the reality of a widespread Christendom ecclesiology, characterized by a preoccupation with power, which is heightened in modern culture by a confidence of being in control of our environment, our life, and even our destiny.[19] In Christendom, the church has lived for 1,500 years in a position of power. Her calling is now to let go of power and control,[20] accepting a minority position, and to recover the redemptive power of the gospel message as defined by the cross. Nothing less than a *metanoia* of the church is needed, a re-formation,[21] with an attitude of waiting on God in deep humility.

A widespread search for new, contextually relevant, missional ecclesiologies is taking place in Europe.[22] The reality of institutional erosion within the European churches gives rise to probably the greatest challenge of letting go of the high statistics, often with related financial benefits from the state, to accept a minority position. The question is whether the Christian churches in Europe are willing to surrender their resistance to and fear of change, agreeing instead to be transformed as a missional church to affect their own culture as well as serving the rest of the world. In this, non-western churches have much to teach us.[23]

At a slightly broader level, letting go of power and control is closely linked with a process of de-westernizing Christianity. The global North is trying to hold on to power and control also in terms of methodology, while the global South seeks to communicate: 'We do not want your methods based on western philosophy as it is detrimental to the evangelistic and missionary zeal and a hindrance for others in becoming Christian. We do not want to buy the western cultural package that is often linked with your

---

Netherlands: E.J. Brill, 2011).

[19] Wilbert R. Shenk, 'Training Missiologists for Western Culture', in *Changing Frontiers of Mission* (American Society of Missiology Series, 28), (Maryknoll, NY: Orbis Books, 1999), 136-37.

[20] Drane, 'Resisting Mcdonaldization', 164-65.

[21] Darrell L. Guder, *The Continuing Conversion of the Church* (The Gospel and Our Culture Series: Grand Rapids, MI: Eerdmans, 2000).

[22] Henning Wrogemann, *Den Glanz Widerspiegeln: Vom Sinn Der Christlichen Mission, Ihren Kraftquellen Und Ausdruckgestalten: Interkulturelle Impulse Für Deutsche Kontexte* (Frankfurt am Main: Verlag Otto Lembeck, 2009); Harald Hegstad, *The Real Church: An Ecclesiology of the Visible* (Church of Sweden Research Series, 7: Eugene, OR: Wipf & Stock, 2013); Michael Moynagh and Philip Harrold, *Church for Every Context: An Introduction to Theology and Practice* (London: SCM, 2012); Michael Herbst, *Kirche Mit Mission: Beitraege Zur Fragen Des Gemeindeaufbaus* (Neukirchen-Vluyn: Neukirchener Verlaggesellschaft mbH, 2013).

[23] Kool, 'Changing Images in the Formation for Mission', 174.

strategies.' This would imply a new take on partnerships between 'South' and 'North', not just on paper but in reality, with a focus on mutual learning to 'Walk humbly with the Lord'[24] and with the 'North' to be ready to fulfil – only – the role of facilitator, enabler, in truly equal partnerships, ready to learn from the South, or from churches in post-communist Europe, on their terms! That would give birth to a framework for a real global Christianity.

On a practical level, issues like creating safe spaces, and an open learning environment, where North and South could mutually ask each other honest and probing questions without any fear of financial repercussions, should be given priority. It would require an attitude of admitting one's weaknesses and strengths, and being ready to give and receive from each other and letting go of triumphalism and self-importance – in short, ultimately, to accept the shift from being in the centre of western Christianity to the periphery of global Christianity.

Fresh Expressions and Mixed Economy Churches

The second statement related to ecclesiology and mission is 'Fresh Expressions of Church', based on a 'serving-first journey' rather than on a 'worship-first journey'. It is a process that starts with listening to God and to the community one feels called to serve, an act of love in itself. Out of the listening emerges service. *Being* the Good News precedes *sharing* the Good News, showing genuine concern for others. The community begins to build loving relationships and to engage in a variety of acts of service, as Jesus did, and a climate is created for sharing the gospel. This is the start of 'incarnational mission', allowing people to explore becoming disciples of Christ. The last step to decide on is the nature of the worship service. 'Fresh expressions are not about planting a congregation which worships the way the planters prefer and then hoping that other people like it! Listening come first, decisions about worship styles last.'[25]

In 2003, the Church of England published a report called 'Mission-Shaped Church',[26] out of which the 'Fresh Expressions of Church' movement emerged. It is spreading from the UK to Germany, the Netherlands and Switzerland, because of its solid theological and missiological rationale, and a clear contextual focus. Another factor that makes it attractive is that the movement is open to keeping the old and the new together in a 'mixed economy' church[27] – referring to a double strategy of making financial investments both in established churches and in the so-

---

[24] Viggo Mortenson and Andreas Osterlund Nielsen, *Walk Humbly with the Lord: Church and Mission Engaging Plurality* (Grand Rapids, MI: Eerdmans, 2010).
[25] Moynagh and Harrold, *Church for Every Context*, 206-10.
[26] Rowan Williams, *Mission-Shaped Church* (London: Church House Publishing, 2003).
[27] Moynagh and Harrold, *Church for Every Context*, 433-34.

called 'fresh expressions of Church'. The movement is also an exploration into a 'de-McDonaldized' church.[28]

Apart from the 'Fresh Expressions of Church' initiative, the Gospel and our Culture Network with its focus on the missional church conversation had a significant impact on the search for new missional ecclesiologies, especially in Denmark.[29] Tim Keller's Redeemer Presbyterian Church has also gained significant influence in Europe through the Redeemer City to City network, because of their openness in taking the European context seriously. Recently, a European edition of Keller's Center Church was published,[30] with several contributions from Central and Eastern Europe, as well as a Dutch edition.[31] Still some responded: 'Keller is very American.' From Anabaptist perspectives, a wide range of post-Christendom ecclesiologies have been published.[32] They contribute to a greater religious plurality in European Christianity, albeit mainly within the 'indigenous' European churches, under whose auspices they operate.

The Myth and Reality of Migrants as 'Outsiders' Reaching Out to 'Insiders' in 'Reverse Mission'

Migration experiences in Central and Eastern Europe differ significantly from those in Western Europe. 'The opening of the political borders after the "changes" in 1989-1990 did generate migration from Central and Eastern Europe to mainly Western Europe and North America, while migration to Central and Eastern Europe through people such as missionaries, international investors, tourists, small entrepreneurs, work migrants, students and professionals had a significant impact on community formation. Typical of these migrations was that they included people from all over the world, from west and north and east and south. Since most of the post-communist countries did not have well-developed migration policies, Central and Eastern Europe became an intensely diverse field where people of all sorts with a variety of aspirations arrived and left. The

---

[28] Drane, 'Resisting Mcdonaldization', 156ff.

[29] Jeppe Bach Nikolajsen, 'Missional Folk Church: A Discussion of Hans Raun Iversen's Understanding of the Danish Folk Church as a Missional Church', in *Swedisch Missiological Themes,* 100.1 (2012), 30; Mogens Mogensen, 'A Missiology of Listening for a Folk Church in a Postmodern Context', in Emma Wild-Wood and Peniel Rajkumar (eds), *Foundations for Mission* (Oxford: Regnum, 2013).

[30] Timothy J. Keller and Stefan Paas, *Center Church Europe: Doing Balanced, Gospel-Centered Ministry in Your City* (Franeker, Netherlands: Uitgeverij Van Wijnen, 2014).

[31] Timothy Keller, Stefan Paas and Zwany Kamerman-Bos, *Centrum-Kerk: Het Evangelie Midden in Je Stad* (Franeker, Netherlands: Uitgeverij Van Wijnen, 2014).

[32] Wilbert R. Shenk, 'New Wineskins for New Wine: Toward a Post-Christendom Ecclesiology', in *International Bulletin of Missionary Research,* 29.2 (2005); Douglas John Hall, 'Theology of the Cross: Challenge and Opportunity for the Post-Christendom Church', in Marit Trelstad (ed), *Cross Examinations: Readings on the Meaning of the Cross Today* (Minneapolis, MN: Fortress Press, 2006), 252-58; Douglas John Hall, *The End of Christendom and the Future of Christianity* (Eugene, OR: Wipf & Stock, 2002).

"Yugoslav Wars" challenged some of the Balkan countries to experiment with asylum-seeking and refugee services.'[33]

The image of migrants as 'outsiders' reaching out to 'insiders' in 'reverse mission' and fulfilling a factor in the revitalization of European Christianity could in many respects be considered a myth. Most often, the so-called ethnic 'migrant churches' are serving as diaspora churches for their own people.[34] A remarkable new development is the Chinese churches' interest in reaching out to the Roma of Eastern Europe. The second 'mission' they fulfil is among their own ethnic people. Many charismatic/Pentecostal churches from African and Brazilian background are focused on evangelizing the Germans, as they[35] consider the 'unbelievers' in Germany, sometimes even the German Protestant churches, as a mission field, while still only a very few migrant churches in Germany have German members. For many countries in the Central and Eastern part of Europe, the influx of migrants is a rather new phenomenon, causing similar distancing attitudes based on negative stereotyped images regarding the 'others', the Roma, with whom they have co-existed for centuries. These attitudes are often fuelled by a lack of adequate information and as well as by historical factors.

Promoting Mutual Learning

Speaking on the dynamics between the local and the 'migrant churches', Dawit Olinka Terfassa, of the Ethiopian Evangelical Church Mekane Yesus in Sweden, emphasized: 'In our multicultural context in Europe today, we need to promote mutual learning between local and "migrant churches", contextualizing evangelistic approaches to the needs of our communities.'[36]

The challenge of promoting mutual learning starts with deconstructing the stereotyped images of migrants. Efforts to give them a face by creating informal safe spaces for story-telling, could serve as a first step. The role of theological education in teaching (future) pastors to develop innovative non-formal and informal training programmes and to create places for

---

[33] Call for papers for the Central and Eastern European Association for Mission Studies (CEEAMS): 'Green pastures? Human Mobility and Christian Communities in Central and Eastern Europe', Osijek, Croatia, 10th-13th May 2016.

[34] In her inaugural lecture, Dorottya Nagy critically addresses the term 'migrant churches': Dorottya Nagy, 'Theologie-Missiologie in Beweging: Liefhebben En De Ander, Terug Naar Af', in *Inaugural Lecture at the Protestant Theological University, Amsterdam* (Amsterdam: Free University, 2016).

[35] Bianca Dümling, 'Migrationskirchen in Deutschland', in *Die Zukunft der Kirche in Europa* (Greifswald, Germany: Alfried Krupp Wissenschaftskolleg Greifswald, 2015).

[36] Kyriaki Avtzki et al, 'Report, WCC Consultation on Evangelism in Theological Education and Missional Formation in Europe', in *WCC Consultation on Evangelism in Theological Education and Missional Formation in Europe, 28-31 October 2012* (Bossey, Switzerland: WCC, 2012).

drinking 'three cups of tea'.[37] in their congregations in which both migrants and 'indigenous' people participate, is crucial and can help in overcoming the widespread fear of these 'unknown others' that are 'invading' us, 'threatening our level of civilization' and endangering the future of our 'Christian continent', as the majority belong to a religion, Islam, we know of only through extreme Islamic movements.

Towards Inclusive Communities and Creative Local Partnerships

Bianca Dümling emphasized that the formation of such creative local partnerships contains many challenges, as the horse-and-cart images below show us.

'A farmer wants to bring his hay into the barn before the rain. For this purpose, a horse and cart stand at his disposal. The horse stands for the living elements, the people, their relationships and their vitality. The cart stands for the infrastructure, organizational structures, knowledge of culture and society, the level of education and access to resources.

'Ideally, this is how it looks. The horse is healthy and the cart is intact. The farmer can bring his hay to the barn without difficulty. But the reality is often removed from this ideal case:

'The situation of migrant churches is similar to this picture:

[37] Greg Mortenson emphasized the importance of a relationship-focused approach over and against a project-focused approach. Greg Mortenson and David Oliver Relin, *Three Cups of Tea: One Man's Mission to Fight Terrorism and Build Nations – One School at a Time* (New York: Viking, 2006).

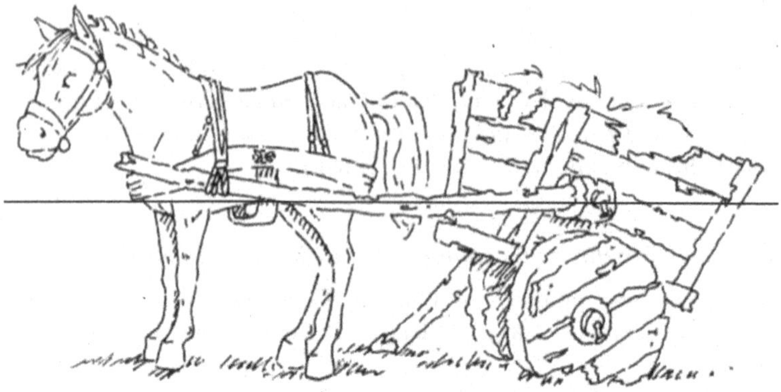

'The horse is often strong, there are vital communities, and committed people. But the carriage has more or less broken down. Some migration churches have their own accommodation, while others rent it. Other migration churches often hold their worship services as guests in state or free churches, but even then they can barely afford the rent. Add to this the fact that few congregations can pay their pastor as migrants' qualifications are often not recognized, as only low-paid jobs are available to them.

Now here is the image that rather describes the situation of the German Protestant churches:

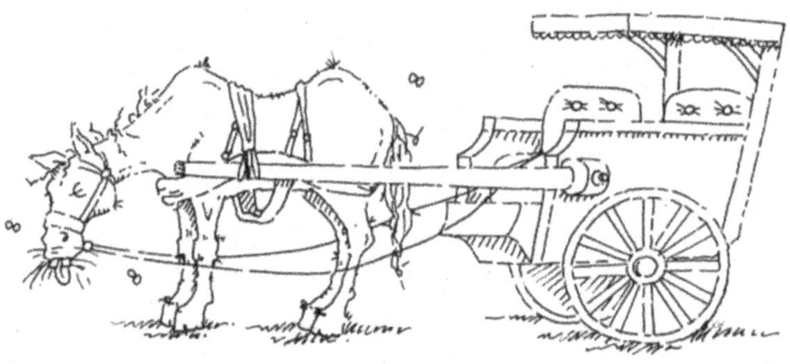

Some German Protestant churches do face challenges. However, unlike the migrant churches, they have a well-functioning carriage: strong organizational structures and access to a variety of resources. Here it is rather the horse needs the support. The reality of the German Protestant churches is that there is only a small number of active members in the communities and their overall number decreases steadily.'[38]

[38] Bianca Dümling, *Migrationskirchen in Deutschland: Orte Der Integration* (Lembeck, Germany: 2011).

Both indigenous and migrant communities face the quest of becoming inclusive communities, reaching out to each other and joining hands in shaping the missional work of the church.[39] The migrant communities are often strong, vital communities, with committed people, but they face challenges related to finding affordable facilities to hold their worship services and paying their pastor as the qualifications of migrants are often not recognized, so only the low-paying jobs are available to them. Also 'indigenous' communities do face challenges. However, unlike the migrant churches they have strong organizational structures and access to a variety of resources. The reality is that there is only a small number of active members in the communities and their overall number decreases steadily.[40]

How could migrant churches be strengthened in their needs and the indigenous churches be cared for? To strengthen the other does not mean to know everything better, to patronize him or her or to forget about oneself. The question is how then can a local partnership be lived out, in mutually strengthening each other, learning from each other? What theological clarification processes are important in such a local partnership? Which prejudices need to be overcome? Where are repentance and reconciliation needed?

The Roma at Europe's Periphery: An Unknown 'Revival'?

The religious landscape of Europe is changing significantly, also with a surprising growth of independent churches. Many of Europe's 'outcasts', the Roma, belong to the Charismatic-Pentecostal tradition. Only recently has the sociology of religious studies taken an interest in Gypsy Pentecostalism.[41] Missiological and theological perspectives are still completely lacking. It is time to confess and to take steps to fill this gap.[42]

Periphery Reviving the Centre?

The Hungarian theologian Ferenc Szucs stated more than a decade ago that involvement in reaching out to the Roma may have a renewal effect on the church, because it compels the church to reflect on issues of Gospel and

[39] Avtzki et al, 'Report, WCC Consultation on Evangelism in Theological Education and Missional Formation in Europe'.
[40] Cf. Dümling, *Migrationskirchen in Deutschland.*
[41] See e.g. David Thurfjell and Adrian Marsh (eds), *Romani Pentecostalism: Gypsies and Charismatic Christianity* (Pieterlen, Switzerland: Peter Lang, 2014); Miroslav A. Atanasov, 'Gypsy Pentecostals: The Growth of the Pentecostal Movement among the Roma in Bulgaria and the Revitalization of Their Communities' (PhD dissertation, Asbury Theological Seminary, 2008).
[42] See also Anne-Marie Kool, 'Eastern European Churches Engaging Roma People: Historical and Missiological Perspectives', in Corneliu Constantineanu et al (eds), *Mission in Central and Eastern Europe: Realities, Perspectives, Trends* (Regnum Edinburgh Centenary Series, 34), (Oxford: Regnum, 2016).

Culture. It requires them to reflect on how to translate the gospel in the mindset of the Roma, whose culture is so far removed from that of the Reformed Church. He anticipates that this would at least 'stir up the dead waters of our *Volkskirche*' (people's church), because it is the greatest mission challenge we face. If the churches do not involve themselves, this social bomb is going to go off right in our midst, and the consequences are unforeseeable.[43]

Relevant Research Needed

Collaborative, relevant research is needed to find key local Roma figures that have played and play a role in the growth of Roma Christianity. We need to get to know them, writing up their life story, and honour their lives. They are virtually absent from the standard scholarly reference works.

We know little about the revivals going on in France and Spain, but also in Slovakia, Romania, Serbia, Bulgaria, Finland and Russia. There is little written material about the Roma Christian communities themselves, and their Roma pastors. There are no dictionaries, encyclopaedias or handbooks with descriptions of the Roma church fathers and mothers, just as till recently there was little on African church history, apart from what had been written exclusively from the perspective of missionaries and their supporting churches, which gave little or no attention to the role of the Africans themselves, in bringing the gospel to their people.

Giving Roma Christianity a face, taking steps towards getting to know Roma church history, will not only be beneficial in teaching the Roma churches, but will also help the majority society to move from image to reality. In this process, a key notion should be: Nothing about us without us.

The Role of Missiological Education in Revitalizing and Transforming European Churches and Societies

Although the academic discipline of missiology was born in the context of Europe, the paradox is that the discipline is 'currently... in a fragile state of existence... [while] application of basic missiological principles for our own... context, is still a great need and only very partially fulfilled and realized within the European context'.[44]

The churches of Europe are in great need of leaders who are willing to incarnate a Christlike, serving attitude rather than clinging to power, and who are able to articulate a Christian worldview and live accordingly. Agents of transformation and innovation are needed, well-equipped to deal

---

[44] Werner, 'Evangelism in Theological Education in Europe – 12 Considerations from ETE/WCC'.

with the burning issues of their contexts, like the churches' response to otherness and exclusion, nationalism and ethnicity, while the revitalization of the churches into missional communities – which communicate the gospel in a relevant way to the de-churched (nominal) and un-churched people and radiate reconciliation in church and society – is needed no less. Jason Ferenczi's vision for theological education in the former Soviet Union is relevant to the whole of Europe, to 'develop leaders who can articulate a Christian worldview in the context of extremely pluralistic societies in a way that answers the deep spiritual questions of a highly educated population'.[45]

The question is: what curriculum for missiological education is needed to play a role in the process of revitalizing and transforming European churches and societies, and why – focusing on the importance of relevant research of the context as a basis for developing a truly contextually relevant dimension of missiology that can address the issues at stake in Europe and European Christianity. Innovative, multi-tiered programmes and teaching methods could stimulate and facilitate critical, missiological reflection on mission praxis as well as missional learning and formation. The challenge is to investigate what kind of innovative structures could offer a safe space for acquiring knowledge and for facilitating learning processes to take place.

A Missiological Curriculum to Face European Realities

A missiological curriculum to face current European realities should be contextually relevant, theologically solid and spiritually sound, reflecting a multi-directional focus to prevent it from becoming either overly provincial or overly global. In addition, priority should be given to dealing with migration issues and ethnic minorities – like the Roma in Hungary and Central Europe whom many consider to be a 'time bomb' within our societies – as well as Islam in Europe.[46]

The learning process should start with a 'missiology of listening', 'a missional mindset to listen to the context, to find ways to love and serve in a holistic and incarnational way'. It should be followed by a thorough contextual analysis of particular issues, e.g. issues related to the local European reality and modern culture, and the changing religious landscape or the institutional erosion of European churches. Finally, it should then move on to exploring what biblical/theological themes address this issue.

---

[45] Jason E. Ferenczi, 'Theological Education in the Former Soviet Union: Some Recent Developments', in *Religion in Eastern Europe*, XXI.6 (2001), 1.

[46] Cf. Kool, 'Changing Images in the Formation for Mission', 173; and Anne-Marie Kool, 'From Marginalization to Revitalization: Missiology's Contribution to the Renewal of Theological Curricula of Theological Institutions in Eastern European Contexts', in Mihai Malancea (ed), *Evangelical Mission in the Eastern Orthodox Contexts: Bulgaria, Romania, Moldova, Ukraine* (Chişinău: Universitatea Divitia Gratiae, 2013).

An important challenge for a missiology for Europe is developing a contextual theology of evangelism.[47] Rather than putting our trust fully in 'horses and carriages', in management principles and new strategies, the focus should be on exercising great humility in using strategic planning and looking to the future with much hope, 'trusting the ability of the gospel to be incarnated in the midst of much chaos'.[48] Priority should be given to strategic thinking, rather than strategic planning, which means first of all 'theologizing' to undergird mere activity.

The curriculum should also give attention to practising and strengthening personal and corporate spiritual disciplines like prayer and Bible reading. Furthermore, it should teach pastors and Christian leaders to empower the laity. Apart from formation for mission aimed at the local church and its leadership, it should focus on reminding the local congregation that it is part of a worldwide community.

Stimulate Relevant Research in Mission and Evangelism-Related Issues

Co-ordinated efforts to strengthen relevant research and develop joint European research projects on issues of mission and evangelism, with initiatives to assist young scholars and pastors to write up their research for publication in so-called writing weeks should be explored and implemented.[49]

In Europe we need to embark on painstaking contextual approaches that are not easily measurable, or developing contextual educational programmes, while keeping a clear theological and biblical focus. Relevant research is needed to make this happen. However, the pragmatic bias and dominance of quantitative factors in church and mission do not favour the slow and often costly production of contextual textbooks on mission and evangelism-related topics and the financing of the research needed for it. Translating a book from English is often considered more efficient. That is true in the global South,[50] but also in Central and Eastern Europe. It is much easier to raise funds for short-term projects that are easily quantifiable, for emergency aid or for church-planting projects, with a more or less clear output. The result is that relatively little is known about dynamic and innovative initiatives in mission and evangelism taking place in the eastern part of Europe. Those who have the experience, skills and qualifications to

[47] Avtzki et al, 'Report, WCC Consultation on Evangelism in Theological Education and Missional Formation in Europe'.

[48] Birger Nygaard, 'Strategic Reflections Coming out of the Present Predicament for Christian Mission', in Viggo Mortenson and Andreas Osterlund Nielsen (eds), *Walk Humbly with the Lord: Church and Mission Engaging Plurality* (Grand Rapids, MI: Eerdmans, 2010), 44-45.

[49] Cf. Avtzki et al, 'Report, WCC Consultation on Evangelism in Theological Education and Missional Formation in Europe'.

[50] J. Samuel Escobar, 'Evangelical Missiology: Peering into the Future at the Turn of the Century', in William D. Taylor (ed), *Global Missiology for the 21st Century: The Iguassu Dialogue* (Globalization of Mission Series), (Grand Rapids, MI: Baker Books, 2000), 111.

research and write up these mission practices in order to draw out the lessons for their own context, correct the existing images of European Christianity and enrich European and global Christianity, are overloaded in their ministries, and do not have the quality time or access to the relevant e-resources, that are so easily available in the university libraries of the West.

Innovative Teaching Methodologies

Innovative teaching methodologies are important as we try to relate to the Millennial Generation or Generation Y. This teaching methodology is all about teaching students first to ask questions and to listen, leading to understanding the (world) view of someone else instead of formulating quick judgements.

This teaching methodology helps them to realize that there is more than one (often stereotyped) image to capture reality, and that there are multiple images that can each have validity. Learning is more than just gathering information; it starts with reflecting on the teaching material and being changed by it. In this way, students turn into agents of transformation for their churches and societies.

Develop International and Interdenominational Learning Communities

Developing international and interdenominational learning communities, places for missiological education and missional formation for people from different backgrounds, including migrants, where integrity in the way theology is done and lived out through spirituality, is key – and in which the art of honouring each other by asking questions is practised. It is important that different cultural and theological perspectives are brought together for both the student body and faculty. Innovative structures are needed to provide a safe space for this process of acquiring knowledge and facilitating learning processes to take place.

A recent consultation on evangelism in theological education and missional formation in Europe addressed an urgent call to church leaders and leaders of theological institutions to give missiology and the teaching of evangelism a substantial place in the curriculum.[51] The paradox is that the current academic and church climate in Europe does not favour responding to this call, despite the current challenges of Europe and European Christianity. The time has come to establish innovative structures that resemble a 'starfish' rather than a 'spider':[52] network organizations that maximize on flexibility, co-operation and the sharing of resources.

---

[51] Avtzki et al, 'Report, WCC Consultation on Evangelism in Theological Education and Missional Formation in Europe'.

[52] Ori Brafman and Rod A. Beckstrom, *The Starfish and the Spider: The Unstoppable Power of Leaderless Organizations* (London: Portfolio, 2007).

Provision should be made for the establishing of a fund that could offer stable, long-term teaching and research positions in missiology and evangelism, with the partners actively participating in the accountability structures.

Such network organizations should closely co-operate with established theological institutions as they are the place where the formation of missional leadership for the church takes or should take place, although they are often geared at achieving individual academic 'success'. Alternatively, there should be a focus on the training of pastors, helping them to lead their church community and its members to live 'worthily of the gospel', to expose the idols of modern culture, to bridge differences, to reflect critically on the culture, and to be examples of the love and grace of Jesus Christ in their families and in the market place.

At the same time, it is important expose to the colourful worldwide body of Christ, the vital models of missional churches on other continents, with the persistent question in mind of how these experiences can cross-fertilize their own European context.

Conclusion

In this missiological manifesto for the decade, my aim was to contribute to the ongoing conversation on the future of the church in mission in Europe with a special focus on Central and Eastern Europe. I have offered a statement of vision and values, reflecting on what I consider to be the important future perspectives and challenges in six key areas: the impact of secular values on the church, issues of otherness and reconciliation, ecclesiology and mission, the myth and reality of migrants as 'outsiders' reaching out to 'insiders', the Roma at Europe's periphery constituting a 'revival', and the role of missiological education in revitalizing and transforming European churches and societies.

My hope is that a practice of drinking 'three cups of coffee' in one of the many coffee places round Central and Eastern Europe, whilst asking questions in relation to the themes offered in this missiological manifesto, will stir up a process that will result in 'acquiring the posture of a missional church'[53] in our own European contexts, and in a true shift from western to global Christianity by taking away western philosophy-induced hindrances for the advance of the gospel. In this missiological manifesto I have dealt with a number of issues to help stimulate such critical and constructive discussion about the future of church and mission in Central and Eastern Europe that may also spill over to other parts of Europe.

---

[53] Hunsberger, 'Acquiring the Posture of a Missionary Church'.

LIST OF CONTRIBUTORS

Aleksandar Apostolovski (Macedonia) is a doctoral student at the University of Aberdeen, Scotland.

Pavol Bargár, ThD (Slovakia/Czech Republic) is a post-doctoral researcher at the Protestant Theological Faculty, Charles University in Prague, Czech Republic. He also serves as secretary of the Central and Eastern European Association for Mission Studies and is a member of the Executive Board of the International Council of Christians and Jews.

Dana Bates, PhD (USA/Romania) is the principle architect of the IMPACT service learning model, initially launched in Romania, and subsequently expanded to include over 150 clubs in fourteen different countries. He is also Adjunct Professor at Northwestern College, Orange City, IO, and at Gordon College, Massachusetts, USA.

Gelu Călina, PhD (Romania) is Chair of Mission Studies and Ecumenism at the Faculty of Theology and Professor in the Doctoral School of Theology, University of Craiova, Romania. He is also an Archdeacon in the Romanian Orthodox Church.

Corneliu Constantineanu, PhD (Romania) is Professor of Biblical Theology at the Faculty of Humanities and Social Sciences, 'Aurel Vlaicu' University of Arad, Romania, and Director of Research at the Institute for Faith and Human Flourishing in Timişoara, Romania. He is also an ordained pastor with the Pentecostal Church of Romania.

Bogdan Dolenc, PhD (Slovenia) is Assistant Professor of fundamental theology, ecclesiology and ecumenism at the Catholic Faculty of Theology, Ljubljana, Slovenia, and a Catholic priest in the Diocese of Ljubljana.

Ovidiu Dorin Druhora, PhD (USA/Romania) is the founding dean of Ekklesia Bible College, an international practiced-based seminary, with campuses in Europe, India, Africa and USA. He is also Adjunct Faculty at the Global University in Springfield, Missouri, USA.

Branimir Dukiæ, PhD (Croatia) is a lecturer of information and communication sciences, and economics, at the Faculty of Economics, 'J.J. Strossmayer' University of Osijek, Croatia.

Pavel Èerný, ThD (Czech Republic) is lecturer at the Evangelical Theological Seminary in Prague, Czech Republic, an institution which he helped establish. He is also an ordained pastor and served 1993-2009 as President of his evangelical denomination and President of the Czech Ecumenical Council of Churches.

Jan Górski, PhD (Poland) is Professor of Missiology and Theology of Religions at the Silesian University in Katowice, Poland. He is also the President of the Association of Polish Musicologists, consulter of the Congregation for the Evangelization of Peoples in Rome, and a member of International Association for Mission Studies and International Association of Catholic Missiologists. Professor Górski also serves as a Catholic priest.

Mihai Himcinschi, PhD (Romania) is a tenured Professor of Orthodox Missiology at the Orthodox Faculty of Theology, '1 Decembrie' University of Alba Iulia, Romania. He also serves as a priest in the Romanian Orthodox Church.

Eugen Jugaru, PhD (Romania) is Assistant Professor of Systematic Theology at the Theological Pentecostal Institute in Bucharest, Romania. He is an ordained pastor with the Pentecostal Church of Romania and also serves in the regional leadership structures of his denomination.

Zuzana Jurechová, PhD (Slovakia/Czech Republic) currently serves as a Lutheran pastor in Prague, Czech Republic. She formerly served as project director for the Central European Centre for Mission studies in Prague.

Anne-Marie Kool, PhD (Hungary/Croatia/The Netherlands) is Professor of Missiology at the Evangelical Theological Seminary in Osijek, Croatia, and vice-President of the Central and Eastern European Association for Mission Studies. She also serves as Associate Professor of Missiology at the Baptist Theological Academy in Budapest, Hungary, and Adjunct Faculty and Regent of the Bakke Graduate University, Dallas, USA.

Ábrahám Kovács, PhD (Hungary) is Associate Professor of Dogmatic and Historical Theology at Debrecen Reformed University, Hungary and the General Secretary of the Hungarian Association for the Academic Study of Religion.

Zorica Kuburiæ, PhD (Serbia) is Professor of Sociology of Religion and Sociology of Education at the Faculty of Philosophy, University of Novi Sad, Serbia, and President of the Centre for the Empirical Research of Religion (www.ceir.co.rs). She is founder and chief editor of the *Journal of Religion and Tolerance* (2002-2016). She is also a lecturer at the Centre for Women's Studies in Novi Sad, and guest lecturer at several theological institutions in the region.

Peter Kuzmič, ThD (Croatia/USA) is the Eva B. and Paul E. Toms Distinguished Professor of World Missions and European Studies at Gordon-Conwell Theological Seminary, Boston, USA, and the founding President of Evanđeoski Teološki Fakultet in Osijek, Croatia.

Jaroslaw M. Lipniak, PhD (Poland) is Head of the Department of Intercultural Dialogue and Ecumenism of the Pontifical Faculty of Theology in Wrocław, Poland, and a professor within the same institution. He is also a Catholic priest.

Ligia M. Măcelaru (Romania) is the founding Director of ACAS (the Association for Capacitating Special Abilities), based in Timişoara, Romania, a volunteer-based ministry assisting people with disabilities in the Western part of Romania. She formerly served as Co-ordinator of the Counselling Programme, Lecturer in Counselling Studies, and Student Dean at Evanđeoski Teološki Fakultet in Osijek, Croatia (2009-2012).

Marcel V. Măcelaru, DPhil (Oxford) (Romania/Croatia) is Associate Professor of Old Testament at the Faculty of Theology within the Theological Pentecostal Institute in Bucharest, Romania, and founding President of the Institute for Faith and Human Flourishing in Timişoara, Romania. He formerly served as Vice-President/Dean of Evanđeoski Teološki Fakultet in Osijek, Croatia.

Dănuţ Mănăstireanu, PhD (Romania) served as Director for Faith and Development for the Middle East and the Eastern Europe Region of World Vision International, and taught Theology and Spirituality at Eastern University in St Davids, Pennsylvania, USA, at 'Emanuel' University in Oradea, Romania, at the Evangelical Theological Seminary in Osijek, Croatia, and at the International Baptist Theological Seminary in Prague, Czech Republic.

Vasile Marchiş, PhD (UK/Romania) is a researcher on Romanian Pentecostalism, with a focus on missiology and practical theology. He works for an organization that helps some of the most disadvantaged and marginalized individuals within the community.

Kostake Milkov, DPhil (Oxford) (Macedonia) is the founding President of the Balkan Institute for Faith and Culture in Skopje, Macedonia, and a visiting lecturer in Systematic Theology at the Evangelical Theological Seminary in Osijek, Croatia.

Julijana Mladenovska-Tešija (Macedonia/Croatia) is completing a doctorate in Anthropology and Culture at 'J.J. Strossmayer' University of Osijek, Croatia, and serves as a lecturer in Philosophy at the Evangelical

Theological Seminary, Osijek, Croatia. She is also a PR specialist, research evaluator, and EU project writer for 'Slagalica' – the Foundation for Local Community Development in Osijek, Croatia.

Dorottya Nagy, PhD (Hungary/Romania/The Netherlands) is Professor of Missiology at the Protestant Theological University in Amsterdam, the Netherlands, and a member of the Executive Committee of the Central and Eastern European Association for Mission Studies.

Parush R. Parushev, PhD (Bulgaria/The Netherlands) is Rector of the St Trivelius Higher Theological Institute in Sofia, Bulgaria; Senior Research Fellow, Senior Lecturer in Theology and the Director of the Institute for Systematic Studies of Contextual Theologies at the International Baptist Theological Study Centre in Amsterdam, the Netherlands; and the Director/Rector of the International Baptist Theological Seminary, of the European Baptist Federation, in Prague, Czech Republic. He is also a senior faculty member at the Faculty of Theology, Free University of Amsterdam.

Peter Penner, PhD (Austria) served as pastor and theological educator in different places while being involved in the leadership of St Petersburg Christian University (Russia), International Baptist Theological Seminary (Czech Republic), TCM International Institute (Austria) and the Euro-Asiatic Accrediting Association (Eurasia).

Bill Prevette, PhD (USA/UK) is the Admissions and Practitioner Research Tutor at the Oxford Centre for Mission Studies, UK, a board member for the Child Theology Movement in the UK, and an appointed missionary to Europe with the Assemblies of God World Mission, USA.

Gheorghe Petraru, PhD (Romania) is Professor of Orthodox Missiology at the 'Dumitru Stăniloae' Faculty of Orthodox Theology, at 'Al. I. Cuza' University of Iaşi, Romania, and serves as Vice-President of the Central and Eastern European Association for Mission Studies.

Gheorghe Riţişan (Romania) is the President of the Romanian Pentecostal Agency for Foreign Missions since 2008. He is also an ordained minister with the Romanian Pentecostal Church, and formerly served as Pastor and Church Planter in the Constanţa County, an area in South-East Romania (1992-2008).

Anton Rus, PhD (Romania) is Assistant Professor of Spirituality and Patristics at the Faculty of Greek-Catholic Theology, 'Babeş-Bolyai' University of Cluj-Napoca, Romania, and a priest in the Blaj eparchy of the Greek-Catholic Church of Romania.

Viktória Šoltésová, PhD (Slovakia) is a lecturer in the Department of Theology and Christian Education at Matej Bel University in Banska Bystrica, Slovakia. She lectured at the South African Theological Seminary (2008), Tanzania, accredited by the University of Johannesburg; and within the International Symposium on Culture and Translation organised by the Nida School for Translation Studies, Italy.

Wojciech Szczerba, PhD (Poland) is Rector/President of the Evangelical School of Theology, Wrocław, Poland, and Editor-in-Chief of the journal *Theologica Wratislaviensia.*

Ciprian Flavius Terinte, PhD (Romania) is Assistant Professor of New Testament and Homiletics, and the Director of the Master's Programme at the Faculty of Theology within the Theological Pentecostal Institute in Bucharest, Romania, and formerly served as Academic Dean at the same institution. He also serves as pastor with the Romanian Pentecostal Church.

Eric J. Titus, ThD (USA) is Senior Pastor of St John's Reformed Church in Red Hook, New York, USA. He formerly served as Senior Lecturer in Theology at the Evangelical Theological Seminary in Osijek, Croatia (2004-2011).

Alexandru Vlasin, PhD (Romania) is the Mission Director of the Romanian Baptist Union and Assistant Professor of Missiology at the Baptist Faculty of Theology, University of Bucharest, Romania. He also serves as a member in the Executive Board of the European Evangelical Mission Association.

Melody J. Wachsmuth (USA/Croatia) is a PhD student at the Oxford Centre for Mission Studies, UK, studying Romani identity and Pentecostalism in Croatia and Serbia.

Mato Zovkić, PhD (Bosnia and Herzegovina) has been Professor Emeritus of University of Sarajevo since 2015. He formerly served as Professor of New Testament Exegesis at the Catholic Theological Faculty in Sarajevo, and was a member of the Interreligious Council of Bosnia and Herzegovina. A Catholic priest of the Sarajevo Archdiocese, he was appointed by Cardinal Vinko Puljic as Vicar of the Sarajevo Archdiocese for relations with other faith communities, a position he held until 2012.